The Consumer Credit and Sales
Legal Practice Series

CREDIT DISCRIMINATION

Sixth Edition

Jeremiah Battle, Jr.

Keyword Search Entire Book

Go to
www.nclc.org/books

See *page ix* for details.

Contributing Authors: Sandra Mitchell Wilmore, Alys I. Cohen, Chi Chi Wu,
Charles Delbaum, Arielle Cohen, Emily Green Caplan, Geoff Walsh

National Consumer Law Center®
7 Winthrop Square, 4th Floor   Boston, MA 02110   www.nclc.org

About NCLC®

The National Consumer Law Center®, a nonprofit corporation founded in 1969, assists consumers, advocates, and public policy makers nationwide who use the powerful and complex tools of consumer law to ensure justice and fair treatment for all, particularly those whose poverty renders them powerless to demand accountability from the economic marketplace. For more information, go to www.nclc.org.

Ordering NCLC Publications

Order securely online at www.nclc.org, or contact Publications Department, National Consumer Law Center, 7 Winthrop Square, 4th Floor, Boston, MA 02110, (617) 542-9595, FAX: (617) 542-8028, e-mail: publications@nclc.org.

Training and Conferences

NCLC participates in numerous national, regional, and local consumer law trainings. Its annual fall conference is a forum for consumer rights attorneys from legal services programs, private practice, government, and nonprofit organizations to share insights into common problems and explore novel and tested approaches that promote consumer justice in the marketplace. Contact NCLC for more information or see our website.

Case Consulting

Case analysis, consulting and co-counseling for lawyers representing vulnerable consumers are among NCLC's important activities. Administration on Aging funds allow us to provide free consulting to legal services advocates representing elderly consumers on many types of cases. Massachusetts Legal Assistance Corporation funds permit case assistance to advocates representing low-income Massachusetts consumers. Other funding may allow NCLC to provide very brief consultations to other advocates without charge. More comprehensive case analysis and research is available for a reasonable fee. See our website for more information at www.nclc.org.

Charitable Donations and Cy Pres Awards

NCLC's work depends in part on the support of private donors. Tax-deductible donations should be made payable to National Consumer Law Center, Inc. For more information, contact Gerald Tuckman of NCLC's Development Office at (617) 542-8010 or gtuckman@nclc.org. NCLC has also received generous court-approved *cy pres* awards arising from consumer class actions to advance the interests of class members. For more information, contact Robert Hobbs (rhobbs@nclc.org) or Rich Dubois (rdubois@nclc.org) at (617) 542-8010.

Comments and Corrections

Write to the above address to the attention of the Editorial Department or e-mail consumerlaw@nclc.org.

About This Volume

This is the Sixth Edition of *Credit Discrimination*. Discard prior editions and supplements. This book includes a companion website. Continuing developments can be found in periodic supplements to and revised editions of this volume, on the companion website, and in NCLC eReports.

Cite This Volume As

National Consumer Law Center, Credit Discrimination (6th ed. 2013).

Attention

> *This publication is designed to provide authoritative information concerning the subject matter covered. Always use the most current edition and supplement, and use other sources for more recent developments or for special rules for individual jurisdictions. This publication cannot substitute for the independent judgment and skills of an attorney or other professional. Non-attorneys are cautioned against using these materials to conduct a lawsuit without advice from an attorney and are cautioned against engaging in the unauthorized practice of law.*

ISBN: 978-1-60248-127-5 (this volume)
ISBN: 978-0-943116-10-5 (Series)

Library of Congress Control Number: 2013943148

About the Authors

Jeremiah Battle, Jr. is an NCLC staff attorney and a contributing author to several NCLC publications, including *Consumer Credit Regulation, Unfair and Deceptive Acts and Practices*, and *Repossessions*. He also works on NCLC's *Working Cars for Working Families* initiative. Previously, he was a staff attorney with Northeast New Jersey Legal Services and a managing attorney with what is now Disability Rights New Jersey.

Sandra Mitchell Wilmore is an attorney with the firm of Relman, Dane & Colfax, P.L.L.C., in Washington, D.C., where she works primarily on fair lending and consumer credit matters. She is a contributing author to the prior edition of this title. Previously, she was a senior attorney in the Federal Trade Commission's Bureau of Consumer Protection, Division of Financial Practices, where her work involved credit discrimination, predatory lending, and other consumer credit practices.

Alys I. Cohen is a staff attorney at NCLC's Washington office, where she focuses on predatory mortgage lending, mortgage servicing, and foreclosure prevention issues. She is a co-author of *Stop Predatory Lending*, and a contributing author to *Truth in Lending, Mortgage Lending* and *Consumer Credit Regulation*. Formerly, she was an attorney in the Federal Trade Commission's Bureau of Consumer Protection, Division of Financial Practices, where she was involved in credit discrimination and predatory lending matters.

Charles Delbaum is a senior litigator at NCLC, focusing on class actions. He is co-author of *Consumer Class Actions* and a contributor to several other NCLC treatises. Immediately prior to joining NCLC, he was the director of litigation and advocacy at New Orleans Legal Assistance. He has also been a United States District Court law clerk, a staff attorney specializing in nursing home patient rights in the law reform division of the Cleveland Legal Aid Society, and a private practitioner in Cleveland, Ohio with the plaintiffs' firm of Stege, Delbaum and Hickman.

Geoff Walsh worked as a legal services attorney for over twenty-five years. A co-author of *Foreclosures* and a contributing author to *Consumer Bankruptcy Law and Practice* and *Student Loan Law*, he was a staff attorney with Vermont Legal Aid and with the housing and consumer units of Community Legal Services in Philadelphia. He is currently a staff attorney with NCLC in its Boston office. His practice has focused upon housing and bankruptcy issues.

Chi Chi Wu is an NCLC staff attorney working on consumer credit, credit reporting, and medical debt issues. She is a co-author of *Fair Credit Reporting* and *Collection Actions* and a contributing author to *Truth in Lending* and *Consumer Credit Regulation*. She was formerly an assistant attorney general with the Massachusetts attorney general's office and an attorney with Greater Boston Legal Services.

Arielle Cohen is an NCLC staff attorney focusing on class action litigation and other advocacy. She is co-author of *Consumer Class Actions* and a contributing author to *Consumer Credit Regulation*. Prior to joining NCLC, she was a Skadden Fellow at the New Jersey Institute for Social Justice, where she engaged in state legislative advocacy, litigation, organizing, and program development related to mortgage foreclosure prevention and preservation of affordable and racially and economically integrated rental housing.

Emily Green Caplan has worked in both the public and private sectors as an attorney focusing on discrimination matters. She has been an author and researcher for the Massachusetts Commission Against Discrimination for over fifteen years and is a contributing author to *Foreclosures*. Previously, she worked in the labor and employment practice of McCutchen, Doyle, Brown and Enersen in San Francisco.

Acknowledgments

Thanks to Jon Sheldon, Michael Allen, Lucy Colby, Kurt Terwilliger, Mary Kingsley, Allen Agnitti and Lucy Colby for legal research and writing. We are especially grateful to Dorothy Tan for editorial supervision; Kim Calvi for editorial assistance; Shirlron Williams for assistance with cite checking; Shannon Halbrook and Microsearch for designing and implementing the companion website; Mary McLean for indexing; and Xylutions for typesetting services.

What Your Library Should Contain

The Consumer Credit and Sales Legal Practice Series contains 20 titles, updated annually, arranged into four libraries, and designed to be an attorney's primary practice guide and legal resource in all 50 states. Titles are available individually or as part of the complete 20-volume series. Each title includes free access to a companion website containing sample pleadings, primary sources, and other practice aids, allowing pinpoint searches and the pasting of text into a word processor. Access remains free as long as purchasers keep their titles current.

Debtor Rights Library

2012 Tenth Edition (Two Volumes) and Companion Website

Consumer Bankruptcy Law and Practice: the definitive personal bankruptcy manual, from the initial interview to final discharge, including consumer rights when a company files for bankruptcy. This practice package contains the leading expert analysis of individual bankruptcy law and such practice aids as over 150 pleadings and forms, a client questionnaire and handout, the latest Bankruptcy Code, Rules, and fee schedules, a date calculator, and means test data.

2011 Seventh Edition (Two Volumes), 2013 Supplement, and Companion Website

Fair Debt Collection: the basic reference covering the Fair Debt Collection Practices Act and common law, state statutory and other federal debt collection protections. Thousands of unique case summaries cover reported and unreported FDCPA cases by category. The companion website contains sample pleadings and discovery, the FTC Commentary, an index to and the full text of *all* FTC staff opinion letters, and other practice aids.

2012 Fourth Edition, 2013 Supplement, and Companion Website

Foreclosures: examines RESPA and other federal and state requirements placed on mortgage loan servicers, including the new CFPB regulations, and details on loan modification and mediation programs implemented by federal and state governments. The volume features standing and substantive and procedural defenses to foreclosure and tactics after the foreclosure sale. Special chapters cover tax liens, land installment sales contracts, manufactured home and condominium foreclosures, and other topics.

2010 Seventh Edition, 2012 Supplement, and Companion Website

Repossessions: a unique guide to motor vehicle and mobile home repossessions, threatened seizures of household goods, statutory liens, and automobile lease and rent-to-own default remedies. The volume examines UCC Article 9 and hundreds of other federal and state statutes regulating repossessions.

2010 Fourth Edition, 2012 Supplement and Companion Website

Student Loan Law: collection harassment; closed school, disability, and other discharges; tax intercepts, wage garnishment, and offset of social security benefits; and repayment plans, consolidation loans, deferments, private student loans, and non-payment of loan based on school fraud.

2011 Fifth Edition and Companion Website

Access to Utility Service: consumer rights as to regulated and unregulated utilities, including telecommunications, terminations, billing errors, low-income payment plans, utility allowances in subsidized housing, LIHEAP, and weatherization.

Credit and Banking Library

2012 Eighth Edition (Two Volumes) and Companion Website

Truth in Lending: detailed analysis of *all* aspects of TILA, the Consumer Leasing Act, the Fair Credit Billing Act, the Home Ownership and Equity Protection Act (HOEPA), and the Credit CARD Act, including the major 2010 amendments. Appendices and the website contain the Acts, Reg. Z, Reg. M, and their official staff commentaries, numerous sample pleadings, rescission notices, two programs to compute APRs, TIL legislative history, and a unique compilation of *all Federal Register* notices and supplementary information on Regulation Z since 1969. The text references to both FRB and CFPB versions of Regulation Z.

2010 Seventh Edition, 2012 Supplement, and Companion Website

Fair Credit Reporting: the key resource for handling any type of credit reporting issue, from cleaning up blemished credit records to suing reporting agencies and creditors for inaccurate reports. Covers the new FACTA changes, identity theft, creditor liability for failing to properly reinvestigate disputed information, credit scoring, privacy issues, the Credit Repair Organizations Act, state credit reporting and repair statutes, and common law claims.

Superseded

The Cost of Credit is replaced by two new titles, *Mortgage Lending* and *Consumer Credit Regulation*. Responding to major changes in the nature and regulation of mortgage lending and other consumer credit, these two new titles expand upon, update, and re-organize *The Cost of Credit* material.

2012 First Edition, 2013 Supplement, and Companion Website, replacing The Cost of Credit

Mortgage Lending: covers federal and state regulation (and federal preemption) of the origination and the terms of mortgage loans, including ability to pay, steering, churning, flipping, appraisals, loan broker compensation, insurance, adjustable rates, negative amortization, interest rate limitations, late fees, reverse mortgages, holder-in-due course, mortgage litigation, and claims against failed banks.

2012 First Edition, 2013 Supplement, and Companion Website, replacing The Cost of Credit

Consumer Credit Regulation: examines federal and state regulation (and federal preemption of state regulation) concerning credit cards, payday loans, automobile finance and installment sales, auto title pawns, rent-to-own, refund anticipation loans, "sale" of the consumer's future income stream and other non-mortgage lending. Special chapters on credit math, what is interest, and credit insurance.

2013 Fifth Edition and Companion Website

Consumer Banking and Payments Law: covers checks, telechecks, electronic fund transfers, electronic check conversions, money orders, and debit, payroll, unemployment, and other prepaid cards. The title also covers new federal regulations on remittances, banker's right of setoff, electronic transfers of federal and state benefit payments, and a special chapter on electronic records and signatures.

2013 Sixth Edition and Companion Website

Credit Discrimination: analysis of the Equal Credit Opportunity Act, Fair Housing Act, Civil Rights Acts, and state credit discrimination statutes, including reprints of all relevant federal interpretations, government enforcement actions, and numerous sample pleadings.

Consumer Litigation Library

2011 Second Edition, 2013 Supplement, and Companion Website

Collection Actions: a complete guide to consumer defenses and counterclaims to collection lawsuits filed in court or in arbitration, with extensive discussion of setting aside default judgments and limitations on a collector's post-judgment remedies. Special chapters include the rights of active duty military, and unique issues involving medical debt, government collections, collector's attorney fees, and bad check laws.

2011 Sixth Edition, 2012 Supplement, and Companion Website

Consumer Arbitration Agreements: successful approaches to challenge arbitration agreements' enforceability and waivers of class arbitration, the interrelation of the Federal Arbitration Act and state law, class actions and punitive damages in arbitration, implications of NAF's withdrawal from consumer arbitrations, the right to discovery, import of recent Supreme Court rulings, and other topics.

2013 Eighth Edition and Companion Website

Consumer Class Actions: makes class litigation manageable even for small offices, including numerous sample pleadings, class certification memoranda, discovery, class notices, settlement materials, and much more on the companion website. Includes a detailed analysis of the Class Action Fairness Act, state class action rules and case law, and other topics.

Website and 2012 Index Guide: ALL pleadings from ALL NCLC treatises, including Consumer Law Pleadings Numbers One through Eighteen

Consumer Law Pleadings: over *2000* notable pleadings from all types of consumer cases, including predatory lending, foreclosures, automobile fraud, lemon laws, debt collection, fair credit reporting, home improvement fraud, student loans, and lender liability. Finding aids pinpoint desired pleading in seconds, ready to paste into a word processor.

Deception and Warranties Library

2012 Eighth Edition and Companion Website

Unfair and Deceptive Acts and Practices: the only practice manual covering all aspects of a deceptive practices case in every state. Citations to tens of thousands of state UDAP and FTC cases. Special sections on automobile sales, unfair insurance practices, unfair and deceptive credit practices, third party liability, attorney fees, and many other topics.

2011 Fourth Edition, 2013 Supplement, and Companion Website

Automobile Fraud: examination of title law, "yo-yo" sales, odometer tampering, lemon laundering, sale of salvage and wrecked cars, undisclosed prior use, and prior damage to new cars. The website contains numerous sample pleadings and title search techniques.

2010 Fourth Edition, 2013 Supplement, and Companion Website

Consumer Warranty Law: comprehensive treatment of new and used car lemon laws, the Magnuson-Moss Warranty Act, UCC Articles 2 and 2A, mobile home, new home, and assistive device warranty laws, FTC Used Car Rule, tort theories, car repair and home improvement statutes, service contract and lease laws, with numerous sample pleadings.

2012 First Edition and Companion Website

Federal Deception Law: new treatise covering FTC and CFPB rulemaking, special chapters on the FTC Holder and Telemarketing Sales Rules, federal restrictions on unwanted calls and texts, junk faxes and spam, federal and state RICO, the federal False Claims Act, federal and state regulation of debt relief services, and more.

NCLC's Companion Websites

Every NCLC manual includes a companion website, allowing rapid access to appendices, pleadings, primary sources, and other practice aids. Search for documents by category or with a table of contents or various keyword search options. All documents can be downloaded, printed, and copy-pasted into a word processing document. Pleadings are also available in Word format. Web access is free with each title ordered and remains free as long as a title is kept current.

Website continually subject to update

Consumer Law on the Web: combines *everything* from the 20 other NCLC companion websites. Using *Consumer Law on the Web*, instead of multiple individual companion websites, is often the fastest and most convenient way to pinpoint and retrieve key documents among the thousands available on our individual companion websites.

Other NCLC Publications for Lawyers

Over 100 articles a year

NCLC eReports: a web-based newsletter (currently free to those on automatic subscription to updates to NCLC treatises) containing over 100 articles a year, with the latest consumer law developments, novel ideas, innovative tactics, and key insights from NCLC's experienced consumer law attorneys. Articles can be copy-pasted into a word processor, web links are live, and past articles are easily searchable. Optional free e-mail alerts announce new articles and list the latest new regulations, statutes, and key court decisions.

2013 Second Edition and Companion Website

Bankruptcy Basics: A Step-by-Step Guide for Pro Bono Attorneys, General Practitioners, and Legal Services Offices: provides everything attorneys new to bankruptcy need to file their first case, with a companion website that contains software, sample pleadings, and other practice aids that greatly simplify handling a bankruptcy case.

2013 Second Edition

Instant Evidence: A Quick Guide to Federal Evidence and Objections: facilitates objection by rule number and includes common objections and motions at every stage of a case—all in 21 pages! Spiral-bound to lay flat, all pages are laminated, allowing new notations for each trial with a dry-erase pen.

Second Edition with CD-Rom

The Practice of Consumer Law: Seeking Economic Justice: contains an essential overview to consumer law and explains how to get started in a private or legal services consumer practice. Packed with invaluable sample pleadings and practice pointers for even experienced consumer attorneys.

National Consumer Law Center Guide Series are books designed for consumers, counselors, and attorneys new to consumer law:

2013 Edition

NCLC Guide to Surviving Debt: a great overview of consumer law. Everything a paralegal, new attorney, or client needs to know about home foreclosures and mortgage modifications, debt collectors, managing credit card debt, whether to refinance, credit card problems, evictions, repossessions, credit reporting, utility terminations, student loans, budgeting, and bankruptcy.

First Edition

NCLC Guide to the Rights of Utility Consumers: explains consumer rights concerning electric, gas, and other utility services: shut off protections, rights to restore terminated service, bill payment options, weatherization tips, rights to government assistance, and much more.

First Edition

NCLC Guide to Consumer Rights for Domestic Violence Survivors: provides practical advice to help survivors get back on their feet financially and safely establish their economic independence.

Visit **www.nclc.org/books** to order securely online or for more information on all NCLC publications and companion websites, including the full tables of contents, indices, and **web-based searches of the publications' full text**.

About the Companion Website and Other Online Resources

> Visit **www.nclc.org/books** for links to all the book-related online resources listed below, including the treatises' companion websites, *NCLC eReports*, a search engine to search the full text of all treatises, the Quick Reference, and our online bookstore.

The Companion Websites: www.nclc.org/webaccess

Purchase of any title in NCLC's consumer law practice series includes free access to its companion website. Access remains free if you subscribe or continue to purchase updates to that title. Frequently updated, NCLC companion websites offer the treatises' appendices plus hundreds of additional documents in PDF and Microsoft Word formats—pleadings, forms, statutes, regulations, agency interpretations, legislative and regulatory history, and much more—all easily located with flexible, powerful search tools. The sites can be easily viewed on a smartphone or tablet, and documents can be electronically searched, printed, downloaded, and copy-pasted into a word processor.

The companion website to *Credit Discrimination* contains federal statutes, regulations, commentary, supplemental information, and regulatory history relating to the Equal Credit Opportunity Act, Fair Housing Act, Civil Rights Acts, HMDA and Community Reinvestment. Pleadings include complaints, interrogatories, document requests, class pleadings, summary judgment motions, expert reports, and jury instructions. The website also includes instructive government enforcement actions, reports, and consumer handouts.

We highly recommend reading the Help page on the website, found at the top of the left toolbar once you are logged in.

Registering for the Companion Website

One-time registration is required to access the companion website. Once registered, a user subsequently logging in will be granted immediate access to all the companion websites he or she is authorized to use.

To register for the first time, go to **www.nclc.org/webaccess** and click "Register as a New User." Enter the Companion Website Registration Number[1] found on the packing statement or invoice accompanying this book. Then enter the requested information to create your account. An e-mail address may be used for the username, or a different username may be chosen.

Users do *not* need to register more than once.[2] If you subsequently purchase additional NCLC titles, you will automatically be given access to the corresponding companion websites. Registering a second time with the same registration number overrides a prior username and password.

Once registered, go to www.nclc.org/webaccess, enter your username and password, and click the Login button. Then select a companion website from the list.

An alternative log-in method may be particularly useful for libraries, legal aid offices, or law firms that subscribe to the entire set of NCLC treatises. Simply send an e-mail to publications@nclc.org with a list or range of static IP addresses for which access should be permitted. Users from those addresses can then go to **www.nclc.org/ipaccess** to be granted access *without* entering a username and password.

Once logged in, users can click the Preferences link located on the top toolbar to change their account information.

Locating Documents on the Companion Website

The companion website provides three ways to locate documents:

1. The search page (the home page) uses keyword searches to find documents—full text searches of all documents on the website or searches of just the documents' titles. Enter text in the appropriate field and click the Search button.

- Narrow the search to documents of a certain type (for example, federal regulations or pleadings) by making a selection from the "Document Type" menu, and then perform a full text or document title search.
- To locate a specific appendix section, select the appendix section number (for example, A.2.3) or a partial identifier (for example, A) in the search page's "Appendix" drop-down fields.

---

1 If you cannot locate this number, contact NCLC Publications at (617) 542-9595 or publications@nclc.org.

2 If you have not updated *any* of your NCLC treatises for some time, your account may be deleted; if this happens, you must re-register if you subsequently purchase a book.

- When searching documents' full text, each entry in your search results will include excerpts of the document, showing your search terms highlighted in context.
- Click on the "Search Hints" link for a quick reference to special search operators, wildcards, shortcuts, and complex searches. Read this information closely, as syntax and search operators may be slightly different from those used by other search engines.

2. The contents page (click the "Contents" tab at the top of the page) is a traditional nested table of contents. Click a branch to expand it into a list of sub-branches or documents. Each document appears once in this contents tree.

3. The pleading finder page (click the "Pleading Finder" link at the top of the search page, if available) allows pleadings to be located using one or more menus, such as "Type of Pleading" or "Subject." **Select more than one item from a menu, or deselect items, by holding the Ctrl key while clicking.** For example, make one selection from "Type of Pleading–General," one from "Subject," and three from "Legal Claims" to locate all pleadings of that type and subject that contain one or more of the three legal claims selected. If this search produces insufficient results, simply broaden the search by deselecting "Subject" and/or "Legal Claims" to find pleadings of that type in any subject area or based upon any legal claim. This page also includes optional fields to specify terms to be found in the documents' text or titles, to further narrow search results.

Over 2000 pleadings are also available at NCLC's *Consumer Law Pleadings* website using the same search techniques discussed above. Pleadings can also be located using *Consumer Law Pleadings*' index guide, which lists pleadings organized by type, subject area, legal claim, title, and other categories identical to those on the website.

How to Use the Documents, Find Microsoft Word Versions, and Locate Additional Features

Click a document title in your search results or on the contents page to view the document in your web browser. Text may be copy-pasted directly from the page or the full document may be downloaded as a PDF file for easier printing. (You will need a PDF reader to open PDF documents; the free Adobe Reader is available at www.adobe.com.) Additionally, pleadings and certain other documents can be downloaded in Microsoft Word format, enabling the opening of entire documents in a word processor. Icons to download PDF and Word versions are found at the top of the page.

Links on the left-hand toolbar bring you to credit math software, search tips, other websites, tables of contents and indices of all NCLC treatises, and other practice aids. Links to especially important new developments will be placed toward the bottom of the "Search" page.

Search the Full Text of NCLC's Treatises: www.nclc.org/keyword

> Keyword Search Entire Book Q

NCLC offers a handy online utility to search the full text of our publications. This **free** search utility is found at **www.nclc.org/keyword** and requires no registration or log-in. While the chapters' text is not available online, this web-based search engine will find a word or phrase, which can then easily be located in this printed treatise. Select this book, enter a search term or combination of search terms—such as a case name, a regulation citation, or other keywords—and the page numbers containing those terms will be listed. Search results are shown in context, enabling selection of the most relevant pages.

The search utility can also be used to search other NCLC publications. Simply perform the search as described above and select the publication to be searched.

NCLC eReports*: www.nclc.org/ereports*

NCLC eReports, found alongside the treatises' companion websites at **www.nclc.org/webaccess** or **www.nclc.org/ereports**, is a collection of short articles by NCLC's experts discussing recent consumer law developments. About ten new articles are published each month, with older articles available in a searchable archive. Treatise subscribers have free access to *NCLC eReports*, while others may purchase a one-year subscription. Current summaries and sample articles can be found on the NCLC online bookstore at www.nclc.org/shop. NCLC sends occasional eAlerts to inform our readers about new *eReports* articles and other news items; visit **www.nclc.org/ealerts** to sign up.

NCLC's Online Bookstore: www.nclc.org/shop

Our online bookstore at **www.nclc.org/shop** provides information about all twenty NCLC treatises and our other titles, including current tables of contents, indices, sample pages, and more. Click the "For Lawyers" link and scroll down to the book you are interested in. The PDF-format documents found there can be quickly searched for a word or phrase.

Quick Reference, a Series-Wide Index: www.nclc.org/qr

The Quick Reference, found at **www.nclc.org/qr**, is an alphabetical index spanning all twenty NCLC treatises. It lists over 1000 subjects and indicates the book(s) and section(s) where each subject is discussed.

Summary Contents

Contents

Chapter 2   Scope

Chapter 3   Prohibited Bases for Discrimination

Chapter 4

Proving Credit Discrimination

Chapter 5   Discrimination in Pre-Application and Application Procedures

Chapter 6   Discrimination in Credit Evaluation

Chapter 7

Redlining

Chapter 8   Discrimination Law Challenges to Predatory Lending and Unfair Pricing

Chapter 9   Discrimination Subsequent to the Granting of Credit

Contents

Chapter 12   Government Enforcement

Chapter 1

Introduction and First Considerations

1.1 Credit Discrimination Laws—A Powerful Answer to a Pervasive Problem

1.1.1 Credit Discrimination Is a Widespread Problem

Credit discrimination permeates American society. Minorities and other protected groups face difficulties obtaining market-rate first and second mortgages. Many banks do not maintain branches in minority neighborhoods. The disparity in mortgage approval rates between whites and non-whites, as well as disparities in the terms on which mortgage credit is offered, are evidence that discrimination in the marketplace persists.[1]

Credit discrimination is not limited to home mortgages. Car dealers, finance companies, and credit card companies have all engaged in credit discrimination. The practice is not limited to racial discrimination. Creditors may discriminate on the basis of an applicant's national origin, sex, marital status, familial status, sexual orientation, disability, age, religion, or the fact that an applicant receives public assistance.

Creditors may discriminate at every stage of the credit transaction, including which customers they solicit for business, to whom they grant credit, the terms and conditions on which credit is extended, and how customers are treated in subsequent stages of the credit transaction, such as loan servicing and debt collection.

One direct consequence of credit discrimination is lost opportunity—lost opportunity for home ownership, lost opportunity for a college education, and denial of access to medical care and other essential services. Another consequence of credit discrimination is the emergence of predatory lending in communities underserved by traditional lenders.

Predatory lending is a direct and measurable cost of credit discrimination. Subprime, high-interest-rate first and second mortgage lenders target the very groups discriminated against by traditional lenders. These lenders often offer loans with high interest rates, outrageous fees, and onerous terms. This type of predatory lending, targeting minority or other protected groups, itself constitutes a form of credit discrimination.[2]

Credit discrimination starts many families into a downward spiral. Deprived of market-rate unsecured credit, the family may turn to a high-interest finance company which may flip the loan continuously until a small, unsecured loan becomes a large, unaffordable obligation secured by the family home, leading to foreclosure. Another consequence for consumers of being forced to borrow from high-rate creditors is that these creditors are quicker to call in loans when the borrower is delinquent and more likely to engage in aggressive collection tactics and seizure of property.

Those discriminated against and others in their communities often resort to fringe lenders as their only alternative. These consumers end up paying interest rates of several hundred percent for payday loans, rent-to-own goods, tax refund anticipation loans and, in some states, auto title pawns.[3] Pawnbrokers, loan brokers charging unconscionable commissions, and car dealers selling overpriced used cars on credit with astronomical interest rates, flourish where market-rate lenders refuse to tread.

The adverse impact of credit discrimination on individuals, families, and entire communities cannot be overstated. Advo-

---

1 For example, in 2007 African-American applicants were 3.2 times more likely than white applicants to receive a high-cost conventional loan and 2.6 times more likely to be denied a loan. Robert B. Avery, Kenneth P. Brevoort, & Glenn B. Canner, Div. of Research & Statistics, Fed. Reserve Bd., *The 2007 HMDA Data*, 94 Fed. Reserve Bull. A107 (Dec. 2008).

   Hispanic applicants were 2.6 times more likely to receive a high-cost conventional loan and 2.3 times more likely to be denied a loan. *Id.*; *see also* Andrew Jakabovics & Jeff Chapman, Ctr. for American Progress, Unequal Opportunity Lenders? Analyzing Racial Disparities in Big Banks' Higher Priced Lending (Sept. 2009), *available at* www.americanprogress.org/issues/2009/09/tarp_lending.html; Ass'n of Cmty. Orgs. for Reform Now (ACORN), The Great Divide: Home Purchase Mortgage Lending Nationally and in 120 Metropolitan Areas 1 (Oct. 2004), *available at* www.acorn.org; Calvin Bradford, Ctr. for Cmty. Change, Risk or Race: Racial Disparities and the Subprime Refinance Market (May 2002); Daniel Immergluck & Marti Wiles, Woodstock Institute, Two Steps Back: The Dual Mortgage Market, Predatory Lending, and the Undoing of Community Development (1999), *available at* www.woodstockinst.org; Nat'l Cmty. Reinvestment Coalition, The Broken Credit System: Discrimination and Unequal Access to Affordable Loans by Race and Age (2003); Office of Pol'y Dev. & Research, United States Dep't of Hous. & Urban Dev., All Other Things Being Equal: A Paired Testing Study of Mortgage Lending Institutions, Final Report (Apr. 2002).

2 *See* ch. 8, *infra* (discussing this form of credit discrimination, called reverse redlining).

3 For more information about non-mortgage predatory lending, see National Consumer Law Center, Consumer Credit Regulation (2012); Lynn Drysdale & Kathleen Keest, *The Two-Tiered Consumer Financial Services Marketplace: The Fringe Banking System and Its Challenge to Current Thinking About the Role of Usury Laws in Today's Society*, 51 S.C. L. Rev. 589 (2000).

cates who fight against such discriminatory practices play an important role in ensuring equal credit opportunities for all.

1.1.2 Laws Against Credit Discrimination Provide Far-Reaching Remedies

A series of federal and state statutes provides significant remedies to victims of credit discrimination. Violations of the Equal Credit Opportunity Act (ECOA), the Fair Housing Act, and 42 U.S.C. §§ 1981 and 1982 (hereinafter referred to as the federal Civil Rights Acts) can result not only in recovery of out-of-pocket damages but in recovery for such intangible injuries as humiliation, deprivation of rights, and damage to credit rating. These statutes also provide for punitive damages, equitable relief, and attorney fees.

Certain state credit discrimination statutes also provide for minimum statutory damages; state unfair or deceptive acts and practices statutes sometimes provide for treble damages or minimum statutory damages. The Fair Housing Act and certain state discrimination laws provide consumers with relief pursuant to an administrative proceeding in which the consumer need not pay attorney fees, filing fees, or investigational costs. As a result, victims of credit discrimination have an impressive array of remedies available to them.

These statutes prohibit credit discrimination when a creditor treats individuals differently because of certain specified factors that are referred to as "prohibited bases." While the prohibited bases for discrimination vary by statute, one or more of the credit discrimination statutes prohibit discrimination on the basis of race, color, religion, national origin, sex, marital status, familial status, age, disability, public assistance status, and exercise of rights under federal consumer credit statutes. Other bases for discrimination, such as sexual orientation or location of a residence, are also actionable under certain state discrimination statutes and can sometimes be actionable under the federal statutes.

When discrimination is based directly on a prohibited basis this practice constitutes illegal disparate treatment. Illegal discrimination may also occur when a practice not discriminatory in and of itself has a disproportionate impact or effect on a protected class, such as minorities, women, the disabled, public assistance recipients, or older consumers. Such a practice may not be illegal if a creditor has a legitimate business purpose for its action and that purpose may not be achieved by less discriminatory means. When a creditor claims such a legitimate business purpose the person claiming discrimination must establish either that the purpose is not legitimate or that there are less discriminatory means of achieving the purpose.

In order to challenge a discriminatory practice the person bringing the action need not necessarily be a member of the group discriminated against, as long as the discrimination affects that person.[4] For example, a white woman who was refused credit because she lived in an African-American neigh-

borhood has an action under the credit discrimination statutes. Under the Fair Housing Act and federal Civil Rights Acts, the plaintiff need not even have sought credit but could be a housing organization, neighbor, or other person affected by the discrimination against a credit applicant.

The credit discrimination statutes prohibit discrimination at all stages of a credit transaction, including differential treatment pre-application and during the application process, or concerning credit evaluation, credit terms, co-signer requirements, the price of related goods and insurance, loan servicing, and debt collection. Credit discrimination statutes reach more than just transactions with stated interest charges and may apply to leases, utility service, certain medical treatment, and other transactions in which the consumer's obligation to pay is deferred until after receipt of the goods or services.[5] Credit discrimination laws may even apply to differences in the cash price of the goods or services related to the credit transaction.

1.1.3 Growth in the Utilization of Credit Discrimination Laws

Despite the far-reaching remedies available, credit discrimination laws were not utilized significantly until the 1990s and may not yet be fully utilized. Throughout the 1980s only a small number of ECOA cases were brought each year. The Fair Housing Act, the federal Civil Rights Acts, and state antidiscrimination statutes were rarely applied to credit discrimination.

In the 1990s more credit discrimination cases were brought, particularly after 1988 when Congress eliminated weaknesses in the Fair Housing Act.[6] In addition, several restrictive Supreme Court decisions in the employment discrimination area (which affected the interpretation of the credit discrimination laws) were overturned by the passage of the Civil Rights Act of 1991.[7]

Federal agencies began to take a leadership role in the 1990s by bringing a series of credit discrimination cases. The Department of Justice, as well as the Federal Trade Commission and the Department of Housing and Urban Development, settled major cases against lenders' discriminatory credit practices. The Federal Reserve Bank of Boston issued a seminal report defining for the first time the exact nature of banks' racial discrimination in mortgage lending.[8] Enforcement agencies, including the Office of the Comptroller of the Currency, began using paired testers to investigate possible discriminatory practices.

In the last decade the pace of federal enforcement actions slowed but did not disappear and began to pick up near the end

---

4 Havens Realty Corp. v. Coleman, 455 U.S. 363, 373–75, 102 S. Ct. 1114, 71 L. Ed. 2d 214 (1982).

5 *See* Reg. B, 12 C.F.R. § 1002.3 [§ 202.3].

6 *See* Pub. L. No. 100-430, 102 Stat. 1636 (1988).

7 Pub. L. No. 102-166, 105 Stat. 1071 (1991).

8 Lynn Z. Browne, James McEneaney, Alicia Munnell, & Geoffrey M.B. Tootell, *Mortgage Lending in Boston: Interpreting HMDA Data*, 86 Am. Econ. Rev. 25 (1996), *also available at* www.bos.frb.org/economic/wp/wp1992/wp92_7.pdf; *see* ch. 12, *infra* (discussion of government enforcement authority to address credit discrimination).

of the decade. Meanwhile, private litigants successfully used credit discrimination laws to challenge the scourges of predatory mortgage lending and reverse redlining.[9]

Public awareness also increased in the 1990s and 2000s concerning the existence of widespread credit discrimination and the consequences of that discrimination. More housing and other non-profit community organizations began to challenge credit discrimination.

Perhaps most importantly, consumer attorneys started to understand that credit discrimination statutes provide a promising avenue of attack in many different types of credit cases. Particularly attractive are the significant opportunities to recover large damages for intangible injuries, punitive damages, and attorney fees, as well as the option to bring cases in federal or state court and as individual or class actions. Consumer attorneys began utilizing credit discrimination statutes to challenge a multitude of abusive credit practices, including predatory lending and hidden broker kickbacks disproportionately charged to minority customers.

1.1.4 Effective Uses of Credit Discrimination Statutes

Listed below are some practices that may be attacked through the use of credit discrimination statutes. These statutes may be used to attack common discriminatory practices and to challenge many different types of creditor practices. They may be used by individuals, groups, or in class actions. Some of the statutes also include procedural requirements that apply even when discrimination cannot be established. When discrimination laws are violated practitioners should carefully evaluate whether to proceed with a case seeking equitable relief, actual out-of-pocket damages, actual damages for intangible losses (such as humiliation, affront, deprivation of rights, damage to credit rating), punitive damages (potentially available even when the violation is procedural only, such as a defect in a required notice), attorney fees, or some combination of the above.

- *Discrimination against a wide variety of groups.* Credit discrimination laws prohibit discrimination on a number of bases in addition to race, national origin, sex, and religion. Creditors violate credit discrimination statutes if they discriminate:
  - against single parents, divorced women, pregnant women, or those taking in foster children;
  - on the basis of disability, including AIDS/HIV status;
  - on the basis of sexual orientation, but only in a few states or under certain limited circumstances; or
  - on the basis of age.
- *Discrimination based on source of income.* Credit discrimination statutes protect applicants whose income is derived from:
  - public assistance;
  - part-time employment;
  - alimony or child support; or
  - retirement benefits.
- *Denying or restricting credit to residents of certain geographic areas, known as redlining.* The practice of redlining is one of the most common and devastating forms of credit discrimination. Redlining can be challenged under the ECOA and the Fair Housing Act if the residents of the area are predominately minorities or of another protected class. A few state credit discrimination laws explicitly prohibit geographic redlining.
- *Banks discouraging minority applications.* It is illegal for a bank to avoid having branches in minority communities that are otherwise part of its service area, to target marketing to non-minorities, and to otherwise discourage minority applications.
- *Preferential treatment or coaching for non-minorities in the application process.* Discrimination in the lending process often does not consist of blatant racism or hostility against protected class members but rather exists in subtle forms of preference given to white applicants. Paired testers may be able to uncover creditors who treat individuals differently in the application process by helping only certain applicants overcome blemishes in their credit record. Seemingly identical applicants will consequently have very different looking files that the creditor (and the secondary market) will use to determine creditworthiness.
- *Differential treatment of Native Americans living on reservations.* Redlining can specifically affect Native Americans when creditors refuse credit to those living on reservations. Even if a creditor has a legitimate business reason for such conduct, which has a disparate impact on Native Americans, the conduct may be illegal if the same business consideration may be addressed using another factor that has a less disparate impact.
- *Reverse redlining.* Credit discrimination statutes may not only cover creditors denying credit but also high-interest rate lenders preying on minorities or other protected groups. It is clearly illegal for a lender to offer low-interest loans to whites and high-interest loans to similarly qualified African Americans; it may also be illegal for a lender only offering predatory terms to seek out primarily African-American or other minority borrowers.
- *Car dealers, brokers, or others steering minorities to different creditors or charging them higher prices and fees.* Arrangers of credit are covered by the credit discrimination statutes, and it is illegal for them to steer minorities and non-minorities to different creditors or credit programs or to charge minorities more for credit and services.
- *Discrimination by all kinds of creditors.* Too often practitioners think only of discrimination in bank credit, credit cards, or similar market-rate credit. All creditors are subject to credit discrimination statutes, and actions can be brought against finance companies, loan brokers, car dealers, pawnbrokers, and others. Insurance companies are

---

9 *See* ch. 8, *infra.*

liable under the Fair Housing Act for discriminating in the provision of insurance for homes.

- *Discrimination by appraisers*. Appraisers may not use different standards or measures to appraise property if those standards or measures are derived from a prohibited basis.
- *Discrimination by eventual loan purchaser*. It is a violation of the credit discrimination laws for an institution that will purchase a loan to discriminate on a prohibited basis in the way it pre-approves or otherwise participates in the credit determinations of an originating lender.
- *Discrimination by utilities*. A utility transaction is subject to the ECOA, so there cannot be differences in deposit requirements or disconnection procedures based on race, public assistance status, or other prohibited bases.
- *Differing standards as to when a merchant requires cash up front*. Many sellers require cash up front or even before payment, while others will bill the consumer and expect one lump sum payment (without any finance charges) within approximately thirty days. The ECOA prohibits sellers from requiring cash up front from minorities, public assistance recipients, single mothers, or other protected groups if the same seller allows deferral of payment for others.
- *Discrimination in leases*. Credit discrimination laws apply to certain types of leases.[10]
- *Different requirements as to collateral, co-signers, down payments, guarantors*. A creditor may seek whatever reasonable protection it wants against a consumer's potential default, but it may not discriminate in the type of protection it seeks if the reason for this difference is the applicant's race, or some other prohibited basis.
- *Requiring a spouse as co-signer*. The ECOA has detailed rules as to when a creditor may and may not seek a spouse's co-signature. A successful ECOA challenge to a creditor's violation of these rules may void the spouse's improperly induced signature and provide the spouse with an action for damages equal to the full extent of any obligation resulting from the improper signature.
- *Organizations concerned with home mortgage discrimination can bring actions in their own name*. Although the ECOA requires the plaintiff to be an applicant or someone obligated to pay a loan, the Fair Housing Act allows housing organizations and others to institute suit as long as they are in any way aggrieved.
- *Defects in notice of reasons for credit denial*. The ECOA requires that creditors provide a specific notice to applicants when taking an adverse action. The creditor may be liable for actual damages, punitive damages, and attorney fees if it fails to provide this notice, if the reason stated for the adverse action is not specific enough or is not the creditor's real reason, or if the notice is otherwise defective.

- *Home improvement contractor reneging on promised credit or changing credit terms*. Home improvement contractors may promise favorable credit terms but then renege after the work has been done, often saying that the application has not been approved. This behavior is an ECOA violation if the contractor does not notify the applicant of the adverse action within thirty days of the credit application.
- *Termination or denial of credit because of a Truth In Lending (TIL) or other consumer credit claim*. Creditors may not discriminate against an applicant because the applicant has in good faith exercised his or her rights under various federal consumer protection laws. Thus, even though a consumer has sued a creditor under such a law, the creditor and other creditors may not use the suit as the basis for denying credit or terminating existing credit.
- *Reporting credit history inaccurately because of a TIL or other federal consumer credit claim*. It is an ECOA violation for a creditor to report inaccurate information about a customer to a consumer reporting agency because that individual is pursuing a consumer credit claim against the creditor.

1.2 How to Use This Treatise

1.2.1 Abbreviations

This treatise commonly uses the following abbreviations and shorthand:

- CFPB for Consumer Financial Protection Bureau;
- ECOA for the Equal Credit Opportunity Act;
- FRB for the Federal Reserve Board;
- HUD for the United States Department of Housing and Urban Development;
- DOJ for the United States Department of Justice;
- Federal Civil Rights Acts for 42 U.S.C. §§ 1981 and 1982;
- UDAP for general state statutes that prohibit unfair and deceptive acts and practices;
- HMDA for the Home Mortgage Disclosure Act;
- ADA for the Americans with Disabilities Act.

1.2.2 Overview of the Chapters

The first three chapters of this book cover preliminary issues in credit discrimination cases. This chapter introduces the reader to the issue of credit discrimination and to the various statutes that can be used to address it. It contains an overview and history of the ECOA and the Fair Housing Act, as well as descriptions of other statutes that are useful in challenging credit discrimination. Chapter 2, *infra*, details the scope and coverage of the credit discrimination statutes, including who is covered and what types of actions are covered. It discusses the definitions of credit, applicant, and creditor for purposes of the ECOA. Chapter 2 should always be consulted if the practitioner is considering filing an action under the ECOA or the Fair Housing Act, to ensure that the statute covers the transaction at

---

10 *See* § 2.2.2.2, *infra*.

issue. The chapter includes a useful list comparing causes of action under the ECOA versus the Fair Housing Act.

Chapter 3, *infra*, contains an in-depth description of the prohibited bases under both the ECOA and the Fair Housing Act, the ECOA alone, the Fair Housing Act alone, the federal Civil Rights Acts, and the ADA. It also notes additional prohibited bases that appear solely in state credit discrimination statutes. A practice cannot be found discriminatory unless it discriminates on one of these prohibited bases. Chapter 4, *infra*, examines the two major forms of credit discrimination, disparate treatment and disparate impact. It also discusses the elements necessary to prove each form of discrimination.

Chapters 5 and 6, *infra*, enumerate specific types of discrimination at different stages of a credit transaction. Chapter 5 focuses on discrimination prior to and during the credit application process, including prohibited requests for information and co-signatures. Chapter 6 focuses on discrimination during the credit evaluation process. It includes sections on the topics of credit scoring and discrimination based upon source of income.

Chapters 7 and 8, *infra*, discuss the practices of redlining and reverse redlining. Chapter 7 examines redlining, the practice of separating out certain neighborhoods for disparate treatment in the granting of credit. Historically, redlining explicitly targeted communities of color for worse treatment. While no longer explicit for the most part, redlining still disproportionately affects neighborhoods of color. Chapter 7 includes a separate section on insurance redlining. Chapter 8 examines "reverse redlining," a form of predatory lending targeting communities of color. In reverse redlining, lenders predominantly offer high-cost, subprime loans to such communities in contrast to the better loan products and terms offered in white communities. Chapter 8 explains why reverse redlining is a form of credit discrimination.

Chapter 9, *infra*, focuses on discrimination during the latter stages of the credit transaction, after credit has been granted. This includes discrimination in loan servicing, debt collection after default, adverse actions taken on existing accounts, and credit reporting.

Chapter 10, *infra*, focuses on the ECOA's procedural requirements, including its notice and record retention requirements. The ECOA's notification requirements are very specific and apply whether or not discrimination can be established. Chapter 10 gives examples of how practitioners have used the ECOA's notification requirements to challenge abusive credit practices.

Finally, Chapters 11 and 12, *infra*, cover private and governmental actions against credit discrimination. Chapter 11 discusses the issues involved in litigating a credit discrimination case, including standing, deciding whom to sue, forum selection, private remedies, and creditor defenses. Chapter 12 focuses on the enforcement authority of various government agencies to challenge credit discrimination.

1.2.3 Violation of the General Prohibition Against Discrimination Versus Violation of Specific ECOA Rules

A useful way to approach this treatise and a credit discrimination case in general is to determine if a case involves the general prohibition against discrimination or whether it involves a specific ECOA requirement. Each type of case will require practitioners to focus on different chapters of this treatise. In both types of cases, however, practitioners are advised always to consult Chapter 2, *infra* (scope) and Chapter 11, *infra* (private remedies and litigation strategies).

A case involving the general prohibition against discrimination will require practitioners to prove their case under either a disparate treatment or a disparate impact theory. The practitioner will need to focus on Chapter 3, *infra* (prohibited bases) and Chapter 4, *infra* (disparate treatment and disparate impact). Chapter 7, *infra* (redlining) and Chapter 8, *infra* (reverse redlining) may also need to be consulted if a particular community or geographic neighborhood is excluded or targeted.

The ECOA has a number of specific rules concerning a variety of topics, such as requests for information on a prohibited basis, co-signer requirements, and notification requirements. The chapters which describe these requirements are Chapters 5, 6, and 9, *infra* (discrimination at various stages of a credit transaction) and Chapter 10, *infra* (notification requirements).

1.2.4 This Treatise Analyzes Several Different Statutes

This treatise analyzes a number of different credit discrimination statutes. The ECOA is the primary statute discussed, in part because it has the broadest application and the most detailed standards. The Fair Housing Act is also given extensive consideration because it includes several prohibited bases not found in the ECOA (familial and handicap status), any aggrieved party (even a tester, a neighbor, or housing organization) can bring an action, punitive damages are not limited, and the Fair Housing Act more directly prohibits discrimination in residential leases and in the sale of residences. Although the Fair Housing Act only applies to credit relating to a dwelling, it applies to first and second mortgages and to unsecured loans used to improve or maintain a dwelling. The Fair Housing Act also provides critical remedies in predatory lending cases.

42 U.S.C. §§ 1981 and 1982, the federal Civil Rights Acts, are also analyzed but in less detail. These statutes, like the Fair Housing Act, are broader in some respects than the ECOA. Under these statutes any aggrieved party (not just an applicant) may bring an action; they clearly apply to all types of leases and even to sales not involving credit; and they are not limited in the amount of punitive damages available. These advantages make these statutes important in certain situations, particularly when the Fair Housing Act does not apply. The federal Civil Rights Acts may also be useful when the two-year ECOA and

Fair Housing Act limitations period has run because the federal Civil Rights Acts limitations period will be either four years or based on the analogous state law limitations period, which may be greater than two years. However, relief under these Acts may be limited to claims of race or nation origin discrimination.

The Americans with Disabilities Act[11] (ADA) is also briefly discussed in this treatise. Title III of the ADA,[12] prohibits discrimination by places of public accommodation—which includes banks, retailers, and other service establishments—on the basis of disability.[13] The ADA may be especially useful in non-housing financing cases because the ECOA does not include disability as a prohibited basis. However, the ADA's remedies are not as comprehensive as those under the ECOA, Fair Housing Act or federal Civil Rights Acts as the ADA does not provide a monetary damages remedy in its private right of action.

The treatise also briefly covers state credit discrimination laws, particularly pointing out when using such laws may be helpful. The state laws themselves are summarized in Appendix F, *infra*. These statutes are particularly important when the plaintiff wants to stay in state court or when the state statute contains a prohibited basis not covered by the federal laws—such as sexual orientation. State discrimination laws also sometimes provide minimum statutory damages that are not found in the federal statutes.

A final category of laws mentioned in this treatise are state UDAP statutes, that is, state statutes of general applicability prohibiting unfair and deceptive acts and practices. These statutes are treated in detail in another NCLC treatise[14] and are only referred to in this treatise when they are uniquely helpful in a credit discrimination case. They may offer longer limitations periods or better remedies (multiple damages or minimum statutory damages) and they may prohibit unfair discrimination even if the discriminatory basis is not covered by the credit discrimination statutes.

The recently enacted Dodd-Frank Wall Street Reform and Consumer Protection Act ("Dodd-Frank Act") includes a provision creating a federal standard for unfair, deceptive. and abusive acts and practices. It will also be referred to as appropriate.

Actions may generally be brought under multiple theories of liability; however, there are certain exceptions. An action to recover money damages for credit discrimination may be brought under either the ECOA or a state law but recovery may not be had under both. If an action is brought under the ECOA and certain provisions of the Fair Housing Act, recovery may only be had under one or the other statute. But, in all other cases, multiple theories may be used in the same suit though equitable considerations may limit recovery.

If a practitioner is uncertain which statute to utilize, the discussion in each chapter will explain the relative merits of the various statutes. Once the relevant statutes are selected, the treatise clearly indicates which sections of each chapter are relevant to those statutes.

1.2.5 Source Materials Found in This Treatise

This treatise contains the basic source materials for a credit discrimination case. Appendix A, *infra*, contains the relevant federal statutes. Appendix B, *infra*, contains the Consumer Financial Protection Bureau's (formerly the Federal Reserve Board's) Regulation B, which implements the ECOA and has the force of law. Appendix C, *infra*, contains the CFPB's (formerly the FRB's) official interpretations of Regulation B.

Appendix D, *infra*, contains important excerpts from HUD's fair housing regulations. Appendix E, *infra*, contains selected provisions of the Home Mortgage Disclosure Act (HMDA), the CFPB's (formerly the FRB's) Regulation C, which implements the Act, and the CFPB's (formerly the FRB's) official interpretations of Regulation C. Appendix F, *infra*, summarizes state discrimination laws; practitioners should supplement their use of this appendix by consulting their own state statutes to find any recent amendments and in order to make a careful study of the law.

Other appendices include sample complaints (Appendix G, *infra*), discovery materials (Appendix H, *infra*), client handouts about credit discrimination laws (Appendix I, *infra*), a bibliography of social science research on credit discrimination issues (Appendix J, *infra*), a list of useful credit discrimination weblinks (Appendix K, *infra*). This treatise is accompanied by a companion website that includes additional sample pleadings, consent judgments from credit discrimination cases brought by government agencies, and selected sections of other relevant federal statutes and accompanying regulations (the Community Reinvestment Act and the Americans with Disabilities Act). Appendix L, *infra*, provides instructions on how to find pleadings and primary sources on the companion website.

Many unreported cases and certain other documents are cited in this treatise using a "Clearinghouse" number. These documents are available through the Sargent Shriver National Center on Poverty Law (formerly the National Clearinghouse for Legal Services). They may be ordered from the National Center on Poverty Law by mail at 50 East Washington Street, Suite 500, Chicago, Illinois 60602, by telephone at (800) 621-3256 or (312) 263-3830, by facsimile at (312) 263-3846, or by e-mail at admin@povertylaw.org. Many documents are also available on their website: www.povertylaw.org. If a document is available only in hard copy, it can be ordered for $10 plus actual shipping costs.

This treatise should be used in conjunction with its most current cumulative supplement: NCLC typically releases annual cumulative supplements. NCLC REPORTS *Consumer Credit and Usury Edition* provides even more current credit

---

11   42 U.S.C. §§ 12101–12213.

12   42 U.S.C. § 12182(a).

13   42 U.S.C. § 12181(7)(F).

14   National Consumer Law Center, Unfair and Deceptive Acts and Practices (8th ed. 2012).

discrimination developments six times a year.[15] Contact the National Consumer Law Center's Publications Department by mail at 7 Winthrop Square, 4th Floor, Boston, Massachusetts 02110, by telephone at (617) 542-9595, by facsimile at (617) 542-8028, or by e-mail at publications@nclc.org for more information.

1.3 The ECOA

1.3.1 Overview

The Equal Credit Opportunity Act (ECOA) has two important features. First, it sets out a general rule that creditors cannot discriminate in any way against any applicant in any stage of a credit transaction on any of the following bases:

- Race;
- Color;
- Religion;
- National origin;
- Sex;
- Marital status;
- Age (provided the applicant is old enough to contract);
- Receipt of public assistance income; and
- Exercise of rights under the Consumer Credit Protection Act.[16]

Second, the ECOA's Regulation B sets out various procedural requirements that creditors must follow.[17] These procedural requirements are intended to implement the Act's prohibitions against discrimination.[18] Restrictions include factors that may not be considered in determining creditworthiness, when an existing account may be closed, and ways in which information concerning spouses may be reported to credit reporting agencies. They limit what information can be sought in the application process, and they place restrictions on when a spouse can be required to co-sign an application. They provide for a required notice when action is taken on an application and a required notice as to an applicant's right to a copy of any appraisal of the value of the applicant's home.

Both the general rule against discrimination and the procedural requirements have a broad scope (with certain itemized exceptions).[19] Any individual applying for credit or obligated to pay on a loan may bring an action against any creditor. Creditor is defined broadly to include those arranging and participating in loans. The ECOA applies not only to transactions involving multiple installments and to those involving a finance charge but to some simple deferrals of payment. The ECOA also applies not just to consumer credit but to business credit as well. Exceptions narrow the procedural requirements that apply to incidental consumer credit, utility credit, business credit, and securities credit.

ECOA remedies are actual damages, punitive damages (up to a maximum of $10,000 in an individual action), equitable relief, and attorney fees.[20] Actions may be brought in federal or state court and may be brought on an individual or class basis.[21] Creditor defenses are limited.[22] Various federal agencies also have enforcement authority over ECOA violations.[23]

1.3.2 History

1.3.2.1 1974 ECOA Version Targeted Sex and Marital Status Discrimination

An important impetus for the ECOA's passage were hearings held by the National Commission on Consumer Finance[24] in 1972 documenting the difficulties women face in obtaining consumer credit:

- Single women found it more difficult to obtain credit than did single men in the same financial circumstances, especially in the area of mortgage credit;
- Married women often could not obtain credit in their own names;
- Women frequently were asked to reapply for credit in their husbands' names when they married;
- Creditors refused to consider part or all of the wife's income when a married couple applied for credit, even if she provided the primary or only source of income;
- Married women often were required to offer assurances that they employed birth control or, in extreme circumstances, to provide medical certification that they were no longer capable of bearing children; and
- Divorced or widowed women found it extremely difficult to obtain credit because credit previously obtained in their husbands' names was not taken into consideration when they attempted to apply for credit in their own names.

Responding to these concerns, in 1973 the United States Senate passed S. 2101 by a vote of ninety to zero.[25] The bill died in the House. The Senate Report accompanying S. 2101 is instructive in that it contains examples of the types of discriminatory practices on the basis of sex and marital status that the bill was designed to eliminate.[26]

The ECOA was not enacted until 1974, when a House-Senate Conference Committee reconciled two later bills, S.

---

15 Available from the National Consumer Law Center's Publications Department. The other three editions of NCLC REPORTS are titled *Deceptive Practices & Warranties, Bankruptcy & Foreclosures,* and *Debt Collection & Repossession.*

16 42 U.S.C. § 1691; *see also* Reg. B, 12 C.F.R. §§ 1002.2(z), 1002.4 [§§ 202.2(z), 202.4].

17 *See generally* chs. 5, 6, 9, 10, *infra.*

18 *See, e.g.,* Citgo Petroleum Corp. v. Bulk Petroleum Corp., 2010 WL 3931496, at *4 (N.D. Okla. Oct. 5, 2010).

19 *See* § 2.2, *infra.*

20 *See* § 11.8, *infra.*

21 *See* § 11.5, *infra.*

22 *See* § 11.9, *infra.*

23 *See* ch. 12, *infra.*

24 *See* Nat'l Comm'n on Consumer Finance, Report on Consumer Credit in the United States (1972).

25 S. 2101, 93d Cong. (1973).

26 S. Rep. No. 93-278, at 3 (1973).

3492 and H.R. 14856.[27] The House conferees acceded to the Senate in limiting coverage of the final ECOA only to sex and marital status discrimination (and not to race, color, religion, national origin, or age as covered by the House bill), but the enacted version of the ECOA included several other provisions from H.R. 14856.[28]

This first version of the ECOA[29] was enacted on October 28, 1974, and became effective on October 28, 1975. The ECOA amended the Consumer Credit Protection Act[30] by adding a new Title VII, making it unlawful for any creditor to discriminate on the basis of sex or marital status with respect to any aspect of a credit transaction.[31]

1.3.2.2 1976 Amendments Broaden ECOA's Scope

A 1975 hearing before the House Committee on Banking, Currency, and Housing gave special attention to age discrimination, finding that creditors often established arbitrary age limits (usually around sixty-five years of age), after which credit would not be granted and existing credit would be revoked. Empirical data supplied to the Committee proved that senior citizens were often better than average credit risks.[32] In response, the Committee reported out H.R. 6516, prohibiting discrimination on the basis of race, color, religion, national origin, and age.

Senate hearings in the same year before the Consumer Affairs Subcommittee[33] reached the same conclusion on age discrimination and also focused on discrimination against racial minorities; for example, studies indicated a strong probability of race discrimination in mortgage credit.[34] The Department of Justice urged inclusion of race, color, religion, and national origin as prohibited bases to parallel other civil rights legislation.[35]

The Senate hearings led to a revised bill which was eventually enacted by the Senate on February 2, 1976. The bill added the following prohibited bases for discrimination to the ECOA: age, race, color, religion, national origin, receipt of public assistance benefits, and the exercise of rights under the Consumer Credit Protection Act. The bill also added the ECOA's present remedial scheme, supplementing and expanding on that found in the 1974 statute.[36]

On March 9, 1976, the House and Senate approved the Conference Report. President Ford signed the Equal Credit Opportunity Act Amendments into law on March 23, 1976, effective one year from that date.[37]

In January 1977 the Federal Reserve Board (FRB), pursuant to its statutory responsibility to implement regulations effectuating the ECOA's purposes,[38] adopted a new version of the implementing regulation called Regulation B.[39] This regulation interpreted both the 1974 statute and the 1976 amendments.

1.3.2.3 1985 Revision of Regulation B and Issuance of FRB Commentary

In 1985, the Federal Reserve Board issued an overall revision of Regulation B.[40] At the same time, the FRB issued an official staff commentary to Regulation B which supersedes all previous FRB Board and staff interpretations and letters.[41] This commentary is sometimes referred to as "Supplement 1 to Regulation B" or as "ECO-1." The 1985 revision of Regulation B included (as appendices B and C) model application and notification forms which replaced all previous model forms released by the FRB.[42]

1.3.2.4 Women's Business Ownership Act of 1988

The Women's Business Ownership Act of 1988[43] contained amendments to the ECOA chiefly relating to the Federal Reserve Board's treatment of business credit but also applying to other FRB-created exclusions from the ECOA. The legislative history in the House Report expresses concern about the continued discrimination against women in business credit transactions.[44] Of particular interest is the House Report's criticism of the exemption allowed by the FRB under the ECOA for certain aspects of business and commercial credit that led to an erroneous perception that the ECOA was not intended to apply to business credit.[45]

The ECOA was amended to clarify that it applied to business and commercial loans and to preclude the FRB from making regulatory exceptions to the Act's coverage unless it expressly finds that applying the ECOA to the type of transaction exempted would not substantially affect the ECOA's purposes. As a result of the Women's Business Ownership Act, the FRB

---

27 The ECOA was actually offered as an amendment to H.R. 11221 in the Senate.

28 S. Rep. No. 93-902, at 4 (1974), *reprinted in* 1974 U.S.C.C.A.N. 6152.

29 15 U.S.C. §§ 1691–1691f (1974).

30 15 U.S.C. §§ 1601–1681t (1970).

31 15 U.S.C. § 1691(a) (1974).

32 H.R. Rep. No. 94-210, at 3–4 (1975) (accompanying H.R. 6516).

33 *Equal Credit Opportunity Act Amendments and Consumer Leasing Act—1975: Hearings on S. 483, S. 1900, S. 1927, S. 1961 and H.R. 6516 Before the Subcomm. on Consumer Affairs of the Senate Comm. on Banking, Hous. & Urban Affairs,* 94th Cong. (1975).

34 *Id.* at 39.

35 *Id.* at 317–319.

36 *See* S. Rep. No. 94-589, at 1 (1976), *reprinted in* 1976 U.S.C.C.A.N. 403.

The text of the revised Senate bill was substituted for H.R. 6516.

37 Pub. L. No. 94-239, 90 Stat. 251 (1976) (amending 15 U.S.C. §§ 1691–1691f).

38 15 U.S.C. § 1691(b) (1976).

39 42 Fed. Reg. 1242 (1977).
    Regulation B is codified at 12 C.F.R. part 202 [pt. 1002].

40 50 Fed. Reg. 48,018 (Nov. 20, 1985).

41 *Id.*

42 Reg. B, 12 C.F.R. pt. 202 [pt. 1002], app. B (model application forms), app. C (sample notification forms).

43 Pub. L. No. 100-533, 102 Stat. 2689, 2692–2693 (1988).

44 H.R. Rep. No. 100-955, at 7 (1988), *reprinted in* 1988 U.S.C.C.A.N. 3535.

45 H.R. Rep. No. 100-955, at 15 (1988), *reprinted in* 1988 U.S.C.C.A.N. 3535; *see also id.* at 26.

issued revisions to Regulation B in 1989[46] and to the official staff commentary in 1990.[47]

1.3.2.5 1991 Amendments

In 1991, the ECOA was amended as part of the Federal Deposit Insurance Corporation Improvement Act of 1991.[48] The most significant change for consumers was the amendment to section 1691, which mandated that the creditor provide, upon the applicant's request, a copy of its appraisal report on residential real property offered as security for a loan. The amendments also broaden public agencies' enforcement powers in relation to branches of foreign banks, create additional requirements that federal enforcement agencies refer cases to the Department of Justice for prosecution, create additional requirements that federal enforcement agencies refer Fair Housing Act violations to the Department of Housing and Urban Development (HUD), and clarify the Department of Justice's ability to seek monetary damages.

1.3.2.6 1996 Amendments

In 1996, the ECOA was amended as part of the Omnibus Consolidated Appropriations Act of 1996.[49] Incentives for self-testing and self-correcting were added, providing that reports or results of self-tests are privileged information under specified conditions. The FRB (in consultation with HUD) promulgated regulations dealing with these issues effective January 1998.[50]

1.3.2.7 2003 Revision of Regulation B and Official Staff Commentary

In 1999, the FRB issued an extensive set of proposed revisions to Regulation B and the official staff commentary.[51] The FRB issued its final rule and revisions to the official staff commentary almost four years later, in March 2003.[52] The changes made by the final rule were significantly more limited in scope than the proposed rule.

1.3.2.8 CFPB Now Issues Regulation B and Its Official Interpretations

The Consumer Financial Protection Bureau (CFPB) now has authority to issue Regulation B.[53] On December 21, 2011, the CFPB issued its version of Regulation B and its official interpretations.[54] The Federal Reserve Board (FRB) has not with-

drawn its Regulation B, certain kinds of credit are not within the CFPB's enforcement authority, and the FRB regulation thus may remain relevant.

At the moment, the major change is that 12 C.F.R. part 202 citations are replaced by citations to 12 C.F.R. part 1002. Other changes are stylistic and not substantive. Appendices C and D (supplement), *infra*, contain redline versions indicating how the CFPB's Regulation B and its official interpretations have changed from the FRB version of Regulation B and its commentary.

The FRB version of the regulation and commentary, the redlined versions, and the CFPB's versions (with supplemental information) are all found on the companion website to this treatise.

1.3.3 Sources of ECOA Precedent and Authority

1.3.3.1 The Statute, Regulation, and Official Interpretations

Any ECOA analysis begins with the statute, Regulation B, and its official interpretations. The statute is found at 15 U.S.C. §§ 1691 to 1691f and is reprinted in Appendix A.1, *infra*. The ECOA requires the federal regulatory agency to issue regulations to carry out the statute's purposes,[55] and the FRB did that through enactment of Regulation B, 12 C.F.R. part 202. This responsibility has been passed on to the CFPB. A redline version showing the changes between the CFPB and FRB versions of Regulation B can be found at Appendix B, *infra*.

The ECOA specifically states that any reference to a requirement under the statute includes the requirements of Regulation B.[56] Thus, a cause of action is available under the ECOA for a violation of a requirement that appears only in Regulation B.

In 1985 the Federal Reserve Board replaced all of its existing Board and staff interpretations and staff letters with an FRB official staff commentary.[57] The FRB planned to incorporate all future Regulation B interpretations into this commentary rather than continuing to release individual interpretations.[58] The CFPB is expected to do the same. A redline version showing the changes between the CFPB's official interpretations and the FRB's commentary can be found at Appendix C, *infra*.

1.3.3.2 Legislative History

Both the 1974 and 1976 versions of the ECOA were accompanied by extensive hearings and congressional reports. The ECOA's legislative history is discussed in § 1.3.2, *supra*. In summary (and in chronological order), the legislative history is found in the following sources:

---

46 54 Fed. Reg. 50,482 (Dec. 7, 1989).

47 55 Fed. Reg. 12,471 (Apr. 4, 1990).

48 Pub. L. No. 102-242, 105 Stat. 2300 (1991).

49 Pub. L. No. 104-208, 110 Stat. 3009 (1996).

50 Final regulations were published in 62 Fed. Reg. 66,412 (Dec. 18, 1997).

51 64 Fed. Reg. 44,581 (Aug. 16, 1999).

52 68 Fed. Reg. 13,144 (Mar. 18, 2003).

53 *See* 15 U.S.C. § 1691b, *as amended by* Pub. L. No. 111-203, tit. X, §§ 1085(3), 1100H, 124 Stat. 2083, 2113 (July 21, 2010).

54 *See* 76 Fed. Reg. 79445 (Dec. 21, 2011).

---

55 15 U.S.C. § 1691b(a)(1).

56 15 U.S.C. § 1691a(g).

57 *See* Official Staff Commentary [Official Interpretations] to Reg. B, 12 C.F.R. pt. 202 [pt. 1002], Supp. I, Introduction-3.

58 Reg. B, 12 C.F.R. pt. 202 [pt. 1002], app. D(1).

- S. Rep. No. 93-278 (1973) (to accompany S. 2101).
- *Credit Discrimination: Hearings on H.R. 14856 and H.R. 14908 Before the Subcomm. on Consumer Affairs of the House Comm. on Banking & Currency*, 93d Cong. (1974).
- S. Rep. No. 93-902 (1974), *reprinted in* 1974 U.S.C.C.A.N. 6119, 6152–53.
- H.R. Rep. No. 94-210 (1975).
- *To Amend the Equal Credit Opportunity Act of 1974: Hearings on H.R. 3386 Before the Subcomm. on Consumer Affairs of the House Comm. on Banking, Currency & Housing*, 94th Cong. (1975).
- *Equal Credit Opportunity Act Amendments and Consumer Leasing Act—1975: Hearings on S. 483, S. 1900, S. 1927, S. 1961, and H.R. 6516 Before the Subcomm. on Consumer Affairs of the Senate Comm. on Banking, Hous. & Urban Affairs*, 94th Cong. (1975).
- S. Rep. No. 94-589 (1976), *reprinted in* 1976 U.S.C.C.A.N. 403.
- *Credit Card Redlining: Hearings on S. 15 Before the Subcomm. on Consumer Affairs of the Senate Comm. on Banking, Hous. & Urban Affairs*, 96th Cong. (1979).[59]
- H.R. Rep. No. 100-955 (1988), *reprinted in* 1988 U.S.C.C.A.N. 3535.
- H.R. Rep. No. 102-330 (1991), *reprinted in* 1991 U.S.C.C.A.N. 1901.

1.3.3.3 Other Sources of Authority

Historically, several federal agencies, including the Federal Trade Commission, the Office of the Comptroller of the Currency, the Office of Thrift Supervision, the Federal Deposit Insurance Corporation, and the National Credit Union Administration had enforcement power under the ECOA.[60] However, the Dodd-Frank Act makes the CFPB the agency currently responsible for regulation and enforcement of the ECOA. The Department of Justice retains its authority to enforce the ECOA.

Prior Federal Trade Commission and Justice Department proceedings have often been reported in the Consumer Credit Guide (CCH). Reports of agency actions may also be found on the websites of the respective agencies. The agencies with ECOA enforcement powers occasionally issued "informal" correspondence addressing specific credit situations under their jurisdiction.

In addition, some state attorneys general have issued advisory opinions concerning the ECOA's relationship to state law. Law review articles are another useful source of information about the ECOA. ECOA cases are sometimes brought in state court, so state or regional reporters should be searched as well for pertinent cases.

1.3.3.4 The ECOA Should Be Liberally Construed

The Equal Credit Opportunity Act (ECOA) must be liberally construed to achieve its central goal of eradicating credit discrimination in the American marketplace.[61] The ECOA is designed to remedy what Congressional hearings revealed to be widespread credit discrimination based on gender, age, race, marital status, and other factors. As with other remedial statutes, the ECOA must be liberally construed in favor of consumers to effectuate the underlying Congressional purpose.[62] Moreover, Congress believed that strong enforcement of the ECOA was essential to accomplish its goal.[63] Courts have considered the broad language and underlying anti-discriminatory purpose of the ECOA in rejecting unduly restrictive interpretations of the Act or regulations.[64]

Courts have also considered the fact that the ECOA is part of a comprehensive umbrella statute, the Consumer Credit Protection Act (CCPA), designed to protect the interest of consumers.[65] In interpreting the other titles of the CCPA, most notably the Truth in Lending Act, courts have considered the overarching purpose and the remedial nature of these statutes and held that they must be liberally construed in favor of consumers.[66]

---

59 No legislation was enacted in response to these hearings.

60 *See* Reg. B, 12 C.F.R. pt. 202 [pt. 1002], app. A (federal enforcement agencies). A redline version of Regulation B showing changes between the CFPB's and FRB's versions can be found at Appendix B, *infra*.

61 *See* Brothers v. First Leasing, 724 F.2d 789, 793–94 (9th Cir. 1984); Williams v. AT & T Wireless Servs., Inc., 5 F. Supp. 2d 1142, 1147 (W.D. Wash. 1998).

62 *See, e.g.*, Silverman v. Eastrich Multiple Investor Fund, Ltd. P'ship, 51 F.3d 28, 33 (3d Cir. 1995) (noting the broad remedial provisions in the ECOA); *see also* Peyton v. Rowe, 391 U.S. 54, 64–65, 88 S. Ct. 1549, 20 L. Ed. 2d 426 (1968) (this approach to the statute is consistent with the canon of construction that remedial statutes should be liberally construed); Tcherepnin v. Knight, 389 U.S. 332, 336, 88 S. Ct. 548, 19 L. Ed. 2d 564 (1967) (remedial legislation should be construed broadly to effectuate its purposes).

63 United States v. Landmark Financial Servs. Inc., 612 F. Supp. 623, 628 (D. Md. 1985) (quoting S. Rep. No. 94-589 (1976)).

64 *See, e.g.*, United States v. ITT Consumer Fin. Corp., 816 F.2d 487, 489 (9th Cir. 1986); Thompson v. Galles Chevrolet Co., 807 F.2d 163, 168 (10th Cir. 1986); Brothers v. First Leasing, 724 F.2d 789, 793–94 (9th Cir. 1984) (the ECOA should be liberally construed in light of the clear, strong purpose evidenced by the Act); Miller v. American Express Co., 688 F.2d 1235, 1239 (9th Cir. 1982) (a restrictive interpretation of the regulations is not warranted in light of ECOA's purpose to protect women against the arbitrary denial or termination of credit); Williams v. AT & T Wireless Servs., Inc., 5 F. Supp. 2d 1142, 1147 (W.D. Wash. 1998) (ECOA should be interpreted broadly).

65 *See, e.g.*, Silverman v. Eastrich Multiple Investor Fund, Ltd. P'ship, 51 F.3d 28, 33 (3d Cir. 1995); Brothers v. First Leasing, 724 F.2d 789, 793 (9th Cir. 1984).

66 *See, e.g.*, Begala v. PNC Bank, 163 F.3d 948, 950 (6th Cir. 1998) (TILA is a remedial statute and therefore should be given a broad, liberal construction in favor of the consumer); Smith v. Fidelity Consumer Discount Co., 898 F.2d 896, 898 (3d Cir. 1988); Bizier v. Globe Financial Servs., Inc., 654 F.2d 1, 2 (1st Cir. 1981) (the Truth in Lending Act is intended to balance scales thought to be weighted in favor of lenders and should be liberally construed in favor of borrowers). *See generally* National Consumer Law Center, Truth in Lending § 1.5.2.3 (8th ed. 2012).

1.4 The Fair Housing Act

1.4.1 Overview

The Fair Housing Act (FHA) contains two different provisions primarily applicable to credit discrimination. Section 3605 of the FHA prohibits discrimination in residential real-estate-related transactions.[67] The other provision, section 3604, prohibits discrimination in the terms or conditions of the sale or rental of a dwelling.[68]

As noted above, section 3605 of the FHA bars discrimination in residential real-estate-related transactions. This includes not only loans to purchase a dwelling but also loans in which a dwelling is taken as collateral or when the proceeds will go to improve or maintain residential property.[69] This section will generally be useful in a credit discrimination case involving housing financing, especially home equity lending.

Section 3604 of the FHA bars discrimination in the terms or conditions of a sale or lease of any dwelling, the services or privileges associated with such a sale or rental, or the advertising of any dwelling, as well as discrimination making housing otherwise unavailable. Section 3604 also forbids the misrepresentation of the availability of any dwelling based on a discriminatory category and mandates that reasonable modifications for the disabled must be allowed.[70] Section 3604 covers a broader range of actors than section 3605; however, many courts have not applied it to home equity lending cases unless a purchase is involved. Other courts have clearly stated that section 3604's prohibition of practices that "otherwise make unavailable or deny" housing on a discriminatory basis applies to discrimination in the availability of mortgage financing.[71] The two sections are not mutually exclusive.[72]

There are two other provisions in the FHA that may be useful in a credit discrimination action. Section 3606 bars real estate brokers from discriminating in the provision of their services. Additionally, section 3617 provides that it is unlawful to coerce, intimidate, threaten, or interfere with the exercise or enjoyment of various rights granted or protected by the Fair Housing Act, including the rights set forth in sections 3603, 3604, 3605, and 3606.[73]

Both section 3604 and section 3605 prohibit discrimination on the basis of race, color, religion, national origin, sex, familial status, and handicap. Thus there is considerable overlap with the ECOA; however, only the Fair Housing Act prohibits familial status and handicap discrimination, while only the ECOA prohibits discrimination based on age, marital status, public assistance status, and exercise of rights under the Consumer Credit Protection Act. The FHA also does not impose any specific procedural requirements such as those found throughout the ECOA.

Remedies under the FHA include actual damages, punitive damages (unlike the ECOA, there is no limit on the size of punitive damages awards), equitable relief, and attorney fees. The Fair Housing Act provides for both administrative and judicial proceedings for redress of violations. Plaintiffs can pursue either approach or both simultaneously (up until the time one or the other goes to actual trial).

Any party aggrieved by discrimination can bring an action, and the Act generally applies to most entities that might be involved in credit discrimination. There are few explicit exemptions from the Act's requirements.

1.4.2 History

The Fair Housing Act was originally passed in 1968 as Title VIII of the Civil Rights Act of 1964.[74] The Civil Rights Act was enacted pursuant to the Thirteenth Amendment's grant of power to Congress to implement laws eliminating the badges and incidents of slavery[75] and declares that "it is the policy of the United States to provide, within constitutional limitations, for fair housing throughout the United States."[76]

The Fair Housing Amendments of 1988 significantly amended the Act.[77] While the Fair Housing Act has always included a prohibition against discrimination in the financing of housing, the 1988 amendments significantly extended the reach of the statute in this area. The amendments also expanded the Act to cover discrimination based on disability and familial status and not merely on race, color, religion, national origin, and sex. The limit on the amount of punitive damages was also removed, meaning Fair Housing Act claims—whether brought on an individual or class basis—have no statutory cap as to the amount of punitive damages that may be awarded.

In addition to the above changes to the prior law, the amendments also provide for liberal recovery of attorney fees, an expansive definition of an "aggrieved" party, and a two-year statute of limitations for private actions. Taken together, these amendments make the Fair Housing Act a powerful tool in

---

67 42 U.S.C. § 3605.

68 42 U.S.C. § 3604.

69 *See* § 2.3.2, *infra*.

70 Section 3605 does not include a similar "reasonable accommodation" requirement for disabled consumers.

71 *See* Nat'l Cmty. Reinvestment Coal. v. Accredited Home Lenders Holding Co., 573 F. Supp. 2d 70, 76–77 (D.D.C. 2008); Nat'l Cmty. Reinvestment Coal. v. NovaStar Financial, Inc., 2008 WL 977351 (D.D.C. Mar. 31, 2008).

72 *See* § 2.3.3, *infra* (analyzing use of section 3605 versus section 3604, or both, in predatory mortgage lending cases).

73 *See* United States v. American Institute of Real Estate Appraisers, 442 F. Supp. 1072, 1079 (N.D. Ill. 1977) (the promulgation of standards which cause real estate appraisers and lenders to treat race and national origin as negative factors in determining the value of dwellings and in evaluating the soundness of home loans may "interfere" with persons in the exercise and enjoyment of rights guaranteed by the Fair Housing Act in contravention of section

3617); Laufman v. Oakley Bldg. & Loan Co., 408 F. Supp. 489, 498 (S.D. Ohio 1976) (mortgage redlining "interferes" with the exercise of one's right to voluntary interracial association in contravention of section 3617).

74 42 U.S.C. §§ 3601–3619.

75 Williams v. Matthews Co., 499 F.2d 819, 825 (8th Cir. 1974); United States v. Hunter, 459 F.2d 205, 214 (4th Cir. 1972).

76 42 U.S.C. § 3601.

77 Pub. L. No. 100-430, 102 Stat. 1636.

credit discrimination cases as a companion, or an alternative, to the ECOA.[78]

In January, 1989, the Department of Housing and Urban Development (HUD) issued regulations interpreting the Act, as amended by the 1988 amendments.[79] Accompanying those regulations as initially proposed was an important preamble, indicating the conduct made unlawful by the Act with examples based on then-existing case law.[80] However, the preamble was subsequently withdrawn.[81]

On September 30, 1996, the FHA was amended as part of the Omnibus Consolidated Appropriations Act of 1996.[82] Incentives for self-testing and self-correcting were added, providing that reports or results of self-tests are privileged information under specified conditions. HUD (in cooperation with the Federal Reserve Board) promulgated regulations dealing with these issues effective January 1998.[83]

HUD issued regulations, effective March 18, 2013, regarding the implementation of the Fair Housing Act's discriminatory effects standard.[84] The rule explains the applicability of the FHA to practices with an unjustified discriminatory effect, regardless of whether there was an intent to discriminate.

1.5 The Federal Civil Rights Acts: Sections 1981 and 1982

This treatise also briefly treats two other federal statutes with some importance to credit discrimination. These two statutes, 42 U.S.C. §§ 1981 and 1982, are referred to throughout this treatise as the federal Civil Rights Acts. These are recodifications of statutes enacted after the Civil War.

Section 1981, among other things, guarantees to all persons within the jurisdiction of the United States the same right as white citizens to make and enforce contracts. Section 1982 provides all citizens with the same right as is enjoyed by white citizens to purchase, lease, sell, hold, and convey real and personal property.

These statutes clearly apply to many aspects of credit transactions[85] and also apply to many transactions beyond the scope of the ECOA and the Fair Housing Act. They are particularly useful in challenging discrimination in the leasing and sale of personal property.

The federal Civil Rights Acts generally apply only to racial discrimination, but the Supreme Court has expanded the scope of the Acts to include certain types of ethnic discrimination.[86] In addition, section 1981 should reach discrimination against non-citizens.[87] On the other hand, section 1982 does not provide rights to non-citizens.[88]

The federal Civil Rights Acts provide for actual and punitive damages, equitable relief and attorney fees. Like the Fair Housing Act, and unlike the ECOA, there is no statutory cap on the size of punitive damages awards. Unlike both the Fair Housing Act and the ECOA, the federal Civil Rights Acts only apply to cases of intentional discrimination and do not apply to cases of disparate impact—that is, the "effects test" is not available to prove violations of the federal Civil Rights Acts.[89]

The Civil Rights Act of 1991 amended section 1981 significantly. It added two new subsections, (b) and (c), and redesignated the prior text as subsection (a).[90] Subsection (b) added a definition of the phrase "make and enforce contracts," stating that it extends to both the "making, performance, modification, and termination of contracts" and the "enjoyment of all benefits, privileges, terms, and conditions of the contractual relationship."[91] This definition makes clear that section 1981 applies to discrimination in a contractual relationship that occurs after the formation of the contract. Subsection (c) added a provision making clear that section 1981 prohibits discrimination by both private and governmental entities.[92]

The limitations period for the federal Civil Rights Acts is somewhat complicated. The limitations period for a cause of action that could be brought under provisions of the Act that existed prior to the 1991 amendments is determined by state law, so the period may be longer or shorter than the Fair Housing Act's and the ECOA's two-year limitations periods. To

---

78 For a detailed discussion of the amendments, see Joseph G. Cook & John L. Sobieski, 3 Civil Rights Actions ch. 19 (1992); James A. Kushner, Fair Housing: Discrimination in Real Estate, Community Development, and Revitalization § 1.05 (2d ed. 1995 and Supp.).

79 24 C.F.R. pt. 100.

80 53 Fed. Reg. 44,992 (Nov. 7, 1988).

81 54 Fed. Reg. 3232 (Jan. 23, 1989).

82 Pub. L. No. 104-208, 110 Stat. 3009 (1996).

83 62 Fed. Reg. 66,423 (Dec. 18, 1997).

84 24 C.F.R pt. 100.

85 *See, e.g.*, Jackson v. NovaStar Mortgage, Inc., 2007 WL 4568976 (W.D. Tenn. Dec. 20, 2007) (motion to dismiss claim that defendants violated sections 1981 and 1982 by racial targeting and by offering credit on less favorable terms on the basis of race denied); Johnson v. Equicredit Corp., 2002 U.S. Dist. LEXIS 4817 (N.D. Ill. Mar. 22, 2002) (predatory lending/reverse redlining case brought pursuant to section 1981); Hargraves v. Capital City Mortgage Corp., 140 F. Supp. 2d 7 (D.D.C. 2000) (predatory lending/reverse redlining case brought under both sections 1981 and 1982), *recon-*

sideration granted in part, denied in part, 147 F. Supp. 2d 1 (D.D.C. 2001) (section 1981 claim dismissed for lack of standing, but not section 1982 claim); Doane v. Nat'l Westminster Bank, 938 F. Supp. 149 (E.D.N.Y. 1996) (mortgage redlining case brought under sections 1981 and 1982); Fairman v. Schaumberg Toyota, Inc., 1996 U.S. Dist. LEXIS 9669 (N.D. Ill. July 10, 1996) (section 1981 suit over allegedly predatory credit scheme targeting African Americans and Hispanics); Steptoe v. Sav. of America, 800 F. Supp. 1542 (N.D. Ohio 1992) (mortgage redlining case brought under sections 1981 and 1982 and the Fair Housing Act); Evans v. First Fed. Sav. Bank of Ind., 669 F. Supp. 915 (N.D. Ind. 1987) (section 1982 can be used in mortgage lending discrimination case); Associates Home Equity Serv. v. Troup, 778 A.2d 529 (N.J. 2001) (predatory lending/reverse redlining case brought pursuant to section 1981).

86 *See* § 3.6.1, *infra.*

87 *See* § 3.6.2, *infra.*

88 Davis v. Strata Corp., 242 F. Supp. 2d 643 (D.N.D. 2003) (credit discrimination case brought under section 1981; no liability without proof of intentional or purposeful discrimination).

89 *See* § 4.3, *infra* (discussing the "effects" test).

90 Pub. L. No. 102-166, 105 Stat. 1071 (1991).

91 42 U.S.C. § 1981(b).

92 42 U.S.C. § 1981(c).

the extent, however, that a cause of action is made possible by the provisions added by the 1991 amendments, they are subject to the four-year "catch-all" federal statute of limitations found in 28 U.S.C. § 1658(a).[93]

1.6 The Americans with Disabilities Act

Another potentially useful tool for addressing credit discrimination is the Americans with Disabilities Act (ADA). The purpose of the ADA includes the "elimination of discrimination against individuals with disabilities" and the regulation of "commerce in order to address the major areas of discrimination faced day to day by people with disabilities."[94] The ADA may be especially useful in non-housing financing cases because the ECOA does not include disability as a prohibited basis.

Title III of the ADA[95] prohibits discrimination on the basis of disability by places of public accommodations.[96] Public accommodation is defined to include banks, retailers, and other service establishments.[97] One significant and explicit prohibition under Title III of the ADA is the imposition or application of eligibility criteria that screen out or tend to screen out individuals with disabilities or any class of individuals with disabilities from fully and equally enjoying any goods, services, facilities, privileges, advantages, or accommodations, unless such criteria can be shown to be necessary for the provision of the goods, services, facilities, privileges, advantages, or accommodations being offered.[98] However, courts have generally held that while the ADA "operates to afford equal *access* to goods, services, facilities, privileges, advantages and accommodations, [it] does not regulate the *content* of such goods, services, facilities, privileges and advantages."[99] Therefore, while a lender "may not refuse to provide equal access to its mortgage policies on the basis of the disabilities of potential mortgagors, it [is] not required to alter the otherwise universally applicable terms or conditions of its mortgage policies to accommodate the disabilities of borrowers."[100] Thus, while a mortgage lender's office would have to be accessible to persons with disabilities,

for example, the lender would not have to alter its loan terms to accommodate a disability.

The limitations period for the ADA will be determined by state law.[101] The remedies under the ADA may not be as comprehensive as those found in the other discrimination statutes because it does not provide for monetary damages in its private right of action.

1.7 State Credit Discrimination Laws

State laws dealing with credit discrimination are of several different types. State equal credit laws are generally patterned after the ECOA. State fair housing laws are generally patterned after the Fair Housing Act.[102] In the wake of the 1988 amendments to the Fair Housing Act, many states amended their fair housing statutes to add familial status and disability to the list of protected classes, to increase the statute of limitations from one to two years, and to eliminate the ceilings for punitive damages awards. States occasionally amend their credit discrimination laws, often to add protected classes. Consequently, the analysis of state housing laws found in Appendix F, *infra*, should be updated with the most current state amendments.

Sometimes recent amendments to the state fair housing acts offer broader protections than are found in the federal statutes. For example, several states explicitly prohibit discrimination based upon sexual orientation, political affiliation, or geographic boundaries.

1.8 State UDAP Statutes

Every state has a general statute prohibiting deceptive and unfair marketplace conduct. This treatise adopts the typical term commonly used to refer to these statutes: UDAP (an acronym for Unfair and Deceptive Acts and Practices). UDAP statutes are treated in detail in another NCLC treatise, *Unfair and Deceptive Acts and Practices*.[103]

UDAP statutes are important in that they provide excellent remedies and because they apply to any kind of deceptive and unfair conduct. Thus, violations of a credit discrimination statute can also violate a state UDAP statute, providing treble damages and/or minimum statutory damages and a relatively long limitations periods in some states. However, when a consumer alleged credit discrimination on the basis of race as a violation of a state UDAP statute, but not as a violation of the ECOA or Fair Housing Act, the claim was dismissed without prejudice.[104] Credit discrimination on a basis not prohibited by

---

93 Jones v. Donnelley, 541 U.S. 369, 124 S. Ct. 1836, 158 L. Ed. 2d 645 (2004); *see* § 11.9.2.1.2, *infra* (more on the limitations period for federal Civil Rights Act cases); *see also* Johnson v. Lucent Techs. Inc., 653 F.3d 1000, 1005–06 (9th Cir. 2011).

94 42 U.S.C. § 12101(b)(1), (b)(4).

95 42 U.S.C. §§ 12181–12189.

96 42 U.S.C. § 12182(a). *But see* Peoples v. Discover Financial Servs., Inc., 387 Fed. Appx. 179, 183–84 (3d Cir. 2010) (credit card transaction conducted at a private residence does not involve a place of public accommodation with regard to the credit card issuer).

97 42 U.S.C. § 12181(7)(F); *see, e.g.,* Webster Bank v. Oakley, 830 A.2d 139, 160 (Conn. 2003) ("[M]ortgage servicing and enforcement are 'services' provided by [a place of public accommodation] under 42 U.S.C. § 12182(a), and that Title III of the ADA, therefore, applies to the provision of such services.").

98 42 U.S.C. § 12182(b)(2)(A)(i).

99 Webster Bank v. Oakley, 830 A.2d 139, 161 (Conn. 2003) (emphasis in the original).

100 *Id.*

---

101 Gaona v. Town & Country Credit, 324 F.3d 1050 (8th Cir. 2003).

102 *See, e.g.,* Ojo v. Farmers Group, Inc., 565 F.3d 1175, 1185 (9th Cir. 2009) (in enacting the Texas Fair Housing Act, the Texas legislature sought to "provide rights and remedies substantially equivalent to those granted under federal law" (citations omitted)), *reh'g granted,* 586 F.3d 1108 (9th Cir. 2009).

103 (7th ed. 2008).

104 *See* Mayoral v. WMC Mortgage, L.L.C., 2009 WL 3272697 (N.D. Ill. Oct. 6, 2009).

a credit discrimination statute could still be an unfair practice under a state UDAP statute.

The Dodd-Frank Act prohibits deceptive, unfair, and abusive acts or practices, creating a federal UDAP statute.[105]

1.9 The Community Reinvestment Act (CRA)

The Community Reinvestment Act (CRA) requires federal bank supervisors to monitor and evaluate how banks serve the credit needs of the entire communities from which they receive deposits, including both low-income and moderate-income neighborhoods.[106] It is distinct from the Fair Housing Act and the Equal Credit Opportunity Act (ECOA) in that it addresses inequalities in the distribution of credit among geographic areas rather than discrimination against particular protected groups.

However, commentators have noted that, for a number of reasons, CRA issues often become inescapably intertwined with addressing racial disparities in lending.[107] The CRA regulations state that federal regulators will consider evidence of lending discrimination in assigning a CRA rating.[108]

The CRA applies to all institutions whose deposits are covered by federal deposit insurance. The basic premise of the CRA is that banks and savings institutions, although privately capitalized, have an underlying obligation to serve their local communities. This obligation is generally considered to have been assumed in exchange for government backing, for example, federal deposit insurance that banks need to survive. One limitation of the CRA is that most mortgage loans, and many other types of lending, are now originated by non-bank lenders[109] which do not receive deposits.

The CRA requires regulatory agencies to publicly disclose certain findings and conclusions regarding lending institutions, including whether an institution is meeting community needs.[110] In addition, regulators are permitted to impose sanctions on lenders with weak records.[111]

In general, the CRA has not been aggressively enforced by regulatory agencies.[112] However, banks have a strong incentive to maintain a positive CRA rating because federal bank regulatory agencies may deny merger or expansion applications from institutions with low ratings. Advocates have the ability to formally comment and intervene during a lender expansion application proceedings.[113] Thus, some advocates have been able to use it effectively to address unfair and discriminatory lending practices.[114]

However, advocates and community groups lack standing to sue to enjoin bank or thrift expansions on CRA grounds.[115] In general, there is no private right of action under the CRA.[116] Thus, the Act may not be directly relevant to individual litigation.[117] However, as part of an overall advocacy plan, it can be an effective tool for change.

1.10 Other Sources of Precedent

1.10.1 Housing Law in the Non-Credit Discrimination Context

There is an extensive body of cases brought under the Fair Housing Act in the rental, zoning, and other non-credit contexts. Much of this case law is used by courts as a source of precedent in credit discrimination cases brought under both the Fair Housing Act and the ECOA, even in non-housing finance cases.[118] Some of these cases are discussed in this treatise when relevant. However, for a more extensive discussion of fair housing case law, advocates are advised to consult available fair housing treatises and other resources.[119]

---

105 12 U.S.C. § 5531.

106 12 U.S.C. § 2903.

107 Patricia A. McCoy, Banking Law Manual §§ 8.03[1][a], 8.04[3] (2d ed. 2001); Keith N. Hylton & Vincent D. Rougeau, *Lending Discrimination: Economic Theory, Econometric Evidence, and the Community Reinvestment Act*, 85 Geo. L.J. 237 (1996).

108 12 C.F.R. § 228.28.

109 Susan R. Jones, *Planting Money Where It's Needed Most*, ABA Bus. Law Today, Nov./Dec. 2003, at 47.
    Banks have criticized the CRA on this basis; however, it would seem that a more effective solution would not be to abolish the CRA but to broaden it to other lenders.

110 12 U.S.C. § 2906(b)(2).

111 12 U.S.C. § 2903.

112 For example, a review of CRA examinations found that only eleven banks out of 1500 received a failing grade on the service test portion. Kelly Cochran, Robert Faris, & Michael Stegman, Brookings Institution, Policy Brief No. 96, Creating a Scorecard for the CRA Service Test (Mar. 2002).

113 *See generally* Allen Fishbein, *The Community Reinvestment Act After Fifteen Years: It Works, But Strengthened Federal Enforcement Is Needed*, 20 Fordham Urb. L.J. 293 (1993).

114 *See generally* Michael S. Barr, *Credit Where It Counts: The Community Reinvestment Act and Its Critics*, 80 N.Y.U. L. Rev. 513 (2005); Frank Lopez, *Using the Fair Housing Act to Combat Predatory Lending*, 6 Geo. J. on Poverty L. & Pol'y 73 (1999); Allen Fishbein, *The Community Reinvestment Act After Fifteen Years: It Works, But Strengthened Federal Enforcement Is Needed*, 20 Fordham Urb. L.J. 293 (1993) (it is not the lack of laws but rather the lackluster enforcement of the CRA that has contributed to the continuance of neighborhood disinvestments and lending discrimination).

115 Inner City Press v. Bd. of Governors, 130 F.3d 1088 (D.C. Cir. 1997); Lee v. Bd. of Governors, 118 F.3d 905 (2d Cir. 1997).

116 Powell v. American Gen. Finance, 310 F. Supp. 2d 481 (N.D.N.Y. 2004).

117 One credit discrimination litigant was unsuccessful in his attempt to use negative CRA findings in his individual lawsuit. Stuart v. First Sec. Bank, 15 P.3d 1198 (Mont. 2000) (a negative CRA report by the FRB and subsequent "Notice of Adverse Action Taken" were not sufficient to create a genuine issue of material fact whether the real reason for a loan denial was racial bias).

118 *See, e.g.*, Coleman v. Gen. Motors Acceptance Corp., 196 F.R.D. 315, 325 n.21 (M.D. Tenn. 2000) (applying Fair Housing Act case law in a non-housing finance ECOA case), *vacated on other grounds*, 296 F.3d 443 (6th Cir. 2002).

119 *See, e.g.*, Robert G. Schwemm, Housing Discrimination: Law and Litigation (2008 ed.); John P. Relman, Housing Discrimination Practice Manual (2007 Supp.); James A. Kushner, Fair Housing: Discrimination in Real Estate, Community Development, and Revitalization (2d ed. 1995 and Supp.).

1.10.2 Employment Discrimination Law

In addition to housing discrimination cases, many courts have relied on the extensive body of law in the employment discrimination area as a source of precedent in credit discrimination cases.[120] For example, courts often turn to employment discrimination law when analyzing disparate impact claims in credit discrimination cases.[121] In addition, most federal courts in credit discrimination cases have used a modified version of the three-part, burden-shifting analysis developed by the Supreme Court for employment law cases in the *McDonnell-Douglas* case.[122] Advocates might consider using employment discrimination law theories to develop novel legal theories in credit discrimination cases. For example, one commentator has suggested tackling the problem of discrimination in the offering of pre-screened credit by using the analysis developed in cases challenging discrimination in employment recruitment.[123]

However, there are some differences between the two areas of law. For example, creditors are prohibited by the ECOA from favoring married couples over unmarried couples by only allowing the former to open joint accounts.[124] In contrast, several courts have held that state employment laws which forbid marital status discrimination do not prohibit employers from discriminating against unmarried couples.[125]

---

120 The Equal Employment Opportunity Commission's website, www.eeoc.gov, is a good resource on federal employment anti-discrimination law and includes relevant statutes, regulations, and the EEOC's enforcement guidance, which is its interpretation of current issues in the law. Other employment anti-discrimination law resources include Paul Grossman & Barbara Lindemann, Employment Discrimination Law (3d ed. 1996 and Supp.).

121 *See, e.g.*, Bhandari v. First Nat'l Bank of Commerce, 808 F.2d 1082, 1101 (5th Cir. 1987), *rev'd in part on other grounds*, 829 F.2d 1343 (5th Cir. 1987) (en banc), *vacated and remanded*, 492 U.S. 901, *reinstated*, 887 F.2d 609 (5th Cir. 1989); Coleman v. Gen. Motors Acceptance Corp., 196 F.R.D. 315, 325–26 (M.D. Tenn. 2000), *vacated on other grounds*, 296 F.3d 443 (6th Cir. 2002); Buycks-Roberson v. Citibank, 162 F.R.D. 332 (N.D. Ill. 1995); Gross v. United States Small Bus. Admin., 669 F. Supp. 50 (N.D.N.Y. 1987), *aff'd*, 867 F.2d 1423 (2d Cir. 1988); Williams v. First Fed. Sav. & Loan Ass'n, 554 F. Supp. 447 (N.D.N.Y. 1981), *aff'd*, 697 F.2d 302 (2d Cir. 1982); Cherry v. Amoco Oil Co., 490 F. Supp. 1026 (N.D. Ga. 1980).

122 *See* § 4.2.3.2, *infra* (describing the *McDonnell-Douglas* test and the split among federal courts as to whether it should be applied in credit discrimination cases).

123 Timothy J. Lambert, *Fair Marketing: Challenging Pre-Application Lending Practices*, 87 Geo. L.J. 2181 (1999).

124 Markham v. Colonial Mortgage Serv. Co., 605 F.2d 566 (D.C. Cir. 1979); Diaz v. Virginia Hous. Dev. Auth., 101 F. Supp. 2d 415, 419–20 (E.D. Va. 2000), *subsequent proceeding at* 117 F. Supp. 2d 500 (E.D. Va. 2000); Official Interpretations of Reg. B [Official Staff Commentary on Reg. B], 12 C.F.R. pt. 1002 [pt. 202], Supp. I, § 1002.6(b)(1)-1 [§ 202.6(b)(1)-1].

125 *See* Parker-Bigback v. St. Labre Sch., 7 P.3d 361 (Mont. 2000); Waggoner v. Ace Hardware Corp., 953 P.2d 88 (Wash. 1998); John C. Beattie, *Prohibiting Marital Status Discrimination: A Proposal for the Protection of Unmarried Couples*, 42 Hastings L.J. 1415 (1991).

Note that Title VII of the federal Civil Rights Act, which is the federal anti-discrimination employment law, does not prohibit marital status discrimination. 42 U.S.C. § 2000e-2(a)(1).

Chapter 2   Scope

2.1 Introduction

Credit discrimination statutes apply broadly to a wide range of credit-related activities. In addition, the statutes cover a wide range of credit actors, including lenders, brokers, assignees, and even secondary market purchasers.

This chapter deals specifically with who is covered and what types of actions are covered. Subsequent chapters address the various stages of the credit process at which discrimination might occur and when this discrimination might be illegal. As requirements are different under the different statutes, each statute is treated separately in this chapter.

2.2 Scope of the ECOA

2.2.1 Introduction

Before bringing an ECOA action, an advocate must consider three preliminary questions:

- Has there been an extension of "credit" or an application for an extension of credit covered by the ECOA? If so, is the transaction fully subject to the requirements of the ECOA or has the transaction been exempted from certain requirements under the Act or Regulation B?
- Is the client an "applicant" who can invoke the statute's protection and recover under its remedy provisions?
- Is the party being sued a "creditor" under the ECOA definition and therefore subject to the statute's requirements and liable for damages?

All three of these initial issues must be affirmatively resolved before the advocate can begin to consider specific ECOA violations that may have been committed in the client's transaction.[1]

2.2.2 The ECOA Applies to "Credit" Transactions

2.2.2.1 Definition of Credit

2.2.2.1.1 General

The ECOA generally only applies to credit transactions.[2] For ECOA purposes, the definition of credit is quite broad. Credit is the right granted by a creditor to:

- Defer payment of a debt;
- Incur debt and defer its payment; or
- Purchase property or services and defer payment.[3]

The ECOA's definition is intentionally broader than that found under the federal Truth in Lending Act (TILA).[4] TILA's definition of credit includes only the first two prongs of the ECOA definition.[5] Furthermore, TILA requires that a transaction involve either a finance charge, at least five installment payments, or a credit card.[6] In addition, the ECOA's coverage (unlike TILA's) includes not only consumer but also commercial credit, such as credit for business, agricultural, or investment purposes.[7]

The ECOA explicitly applies to any purchase in which payment is deferred.[8] This obligation can arise by contract, by oral agreement, or by conduct.[9] Common examples are medical

---

[1] *See, e.g.,* Smalls v. Mortgage Electronic Registration System, Inc. v. Countrywide Home Loans, 2010 WL 3719314, at *10 (E.D. Cal. Sept. 16, 2010) (ECOA action dismissed for failure to state a claim because plaintiffs failed to allege, *inter alia,* that they applied for credit with defendants).

[2] *See* Reg. B, 12 C.F.R. § 1002.4 [§ 202.4] (general rule prohibiting discrimination).

[3] 15 U.S.C. § 1691a(d); Reg. B, 12 C.F.R. § 1002.2(j) [§ 202.2(j)].

[4] Official Interpretation of Reg. B. [Official Staff Commentary on Reg. B], 12 C.F.R. pt. 1002 [pt. 202], Supp. I, § 1002.1(a)-1 [§ 202.1(a)-1].

[5] 15 U.S.C. § 1602(e); *see* National Consumer Law Center, Truth in Lending § 2.2.4 (8th ed. 2012).

[6] *See also* Official Interpretation of Reg. B. [Official Staff Commentary on Reg. B], 12 C.F.R. pt. 1002 [pt. 202], Supp. I, § 1002.2(j)-1 [§ 202.2(j)-1]; National Consumer Law Center, Truth in Lending § 2.3.4 (8th ed. 2012). *Compare* 15 U.S.C. § 1691a(e) (ECOA), *with* 15 U.S.C. § 1602(f) (TILA).

[7] Official Interpretation of Reg. B. [Official Staff Commentary on Reg. B], 12 C.F.R. pt. 1002 [pt. 202], Supp. I, § 1002.1(a)-1 [§ 202.1(a)-1]; *see also id.* § 202.2(j)-1.

[8] *See* Official Staff Commentary to Reg. B, 12 C.F.R. pt. 1002 [pt. 202], Supp. I, § 1002.2(j)-1 [§ 202.2(j)-1] ("Regulation B covers a wider range of credit transactions than Regulation Z. . . . [A] transaction is credit if there is a right to defer payment of a debt. . . .").

[9] *See, e.g.,* Mick v. Level Propane Gases, Inc., 183 F. Supp. 2d 1014 (S.D. Ohio 2000) (stating, in finding propane supplier to be creditor, that it is the nature of the service transaction, not the creditor's characterization, that is most important).

bills, bills from repair people and other workers, and even a tab that a customer runs up at the local store.

Although the ECOA's definition of credit is broader than TILA's, not all financial transactions are covered.[10] The ECOA only applies to transactions that involve deferred payments. Not all transactions meet this broad definition. For example, courts have held that the ECOA does not cover applications for automatic teller machine (ATM) cards and savings accounts because they did not qualify as deferred payment arrangements.[11] In addition, the mere charging of interest without other indications that the transaction involves a deferral of payment has been held insufficient to meet the definition of credit.[12] Allegations of discriminatory valuations of property in a government lease/buyback program were also held not to involve a "credit transaction."[13] The ECOA also excludes certain types of credit transactions, including "incidental credit," from many of its procedural requirements.[14]

2.2.2.1.2 Is "debt" required to meet the ECOA definition of credit?

All three elements of the ECOA definition of credit require deferment of payment. However, the third category, the right granted by a creditor to "purchase property or services and defer payment," is distinguishable from the first two in that it does not refer specifically to debt. Some courts have held that this distinction means the existence of debt is not a prerequisite to an ECOA credit transaction.[15]

For example, a credit transaction was found when a propane gas delivery company gave a twenty-day deferred payment option to its customers.[16] The customers did not owe the company anything during the twenty days and therefore were not in debt. However, because there was a deferral of payment,

there was a credit transaction under the third category of the ECOA definition of credit.[17]

The definition of credit in Regulation B lends further support to this interpretation. Regulation B replaces the term "debtor" used in the statutory definition of credit in section 1691a(d), with the term "applicant."[18] At least one court noted that Regulation B's definition makes it clear that applicants who have yet to be granted credit and who therefore may not be debtors are nonetheless covered by the ECOA.[19]

The critical issue, therefore, is whether a deferred payment arrangement exists or is contemplated. However, even if such an arrangement exists, the creditor may still be exempted from complying with some of the procedural requirements of the ECOA if the transaction is considered to be "incidental credit."[20] Examples may include deferment of payment by doctors, lawyers, hospitals, and some small retailers.[21]

2.2.2.2 Do Leases Involve Credit?

2.2.2.2.1 Overview

There are four primary types of consumer leases: (1) leases involving residences (such as apartments and manufactured home park space), (2) automobile and other durable-goods leases covered by the federal Consumer Leasing Act,[22] (3) credit sales disguised as leases, and (4) rent-to-own leases (terminable at will subject to forfeiture of any built-up equity) of electronic entertainment equipment, appliances, furniture, and other consumer items. The arguments to support the application of the ECOA to leases differ depending on the type of lease involved.

2.2.2.2.2 Disguised credit sales

If a lease is really a disguised credit sale, it should certainly fall within the ECOA's definition of credit. Statutes utilize various standards to determine if a transaction is a disguised credit sale. Under the Truth in Lending Act, a lease is "credit" if the customer contracts to pay a sum substantially equivalent to, or in excess of, the value of the property or services involved and will become the owner at no extra cost, or for a nominal consideration, upon full compliance with the lease's terms.[23]

---

10 *See, e.g.*, Liberty Mutual Ins. Co. v. Marine Electric Co., 2012 WL 5207537, at *3 (W.D. Ky. Oct. 22, 2012) (the execution of an indemnity agreement is not an extension of credit).

11 *See, e.g.*, Butler v. Capitol Fed. Sav., 904 F. Supp. 1230, 1234 (D. Kan. 1993) (plaintiff's application to open a savings account is not a credit transaction because it is not a right to defer payment of a debt); Dunn v. American Express Co., 529 F. Supp. 633, 634 (D. Colo. 1982) (application for an automatic teller machine (ATM) card did not involve a credit transaction because no evidence that application gave plaintiff right to defer the payment of any debt).

12 Riethman v. Berry, 287 F.3d 274 (3d Cir. 2002) (the imposition of an interest charge on any outstanding balance does not constitute the extension of credit under ECOA because it does not grant the debtor the right to defer payment of debt; also characterizing charges by attorneys on clients' unpaid balances as a penalty rather than interest).

13 Robinson v. Veneman, 124 Fed. Appx. 893 (5th Cir. 2005).

14 *See* § 2.2.6, *infra*.
   The exclusions for "incidental credit" are similar to the Truth in Lending Act exclusions.

15 *See, e.g.*, Barney v. Holzer Clinic, Ltd., 110 F.3d 1207 (6th Cir. 1997); Mick v. Level Propane Gases, Inc., 183 F. Supp. 2d 1014 (S.D. Ohio 2000).

16 Mick v. Level Propane Gases, Inc., 183 F. Supp. 2d 1014 (S.D. Ohio 2000).

17 *Id.*

18 Reg. B, 12 C.F.R. § 1002.2(j) [§ 202.2(j)].

19 Barney v. Holzer Clinic, Ltd., 110 F.3d 1207, 1209 (6th Cir. 1997) (applicants who have yet to be granted credit and who therefore may not be debtors are nonetheless covered by the ECOA; however, holding that the Medicaid-recipient plaintiffs did not meet the definition of applicant under the ECOA and therefore were not covered by the ECOA).

20 *See* Williams v. AT & T Wireless Servs., Inc., 5 F. Supp. 3d 1142 (W.D. Wash. 1998) (application for cellular phone service held to be credit, but creditor exempted from notice requirements because considered to be incidental credit). *See generally* § 2.2.6.3, *infra*.

21 *See* § 2.2.6.3, *infra*.

22 15 U.S.C. § 1667.

23 Reg. Z, 12 C.F.R. § 226.2(a)(16), uses this definition of credit sale. *See, e.g.*, Waldron v. Best T.V. & Stereo Rentals, 485 F. Supp. 718

Section 1-201(37) of the Uniform Commercial Code provides a more detailed standard as to whether a transaction is a lease or whether it involves a security interest (and thus should be treated as a credit sale).[24]

2.2.2.2.3 Personal property leases covered by the Consumer Leasing Act

The leading case, *Brothers v. First Leasing*,[25] a Ninth Circuit opinion, holds that the ECOA applies to personal-property leases covered by the Consumer Leasing Act (CLA). While the decision details numerous reasons for this result, there are two major grounds for the holding. First, in the lease at issue (and most other leases covered by the CLA), the consumer is obligated to make a total payment over the lease term and payment is deferred through monthly installment payments. This deferred-payment arrangement meets the ECOA's definition of credit.[26]

The second ground for the Ninth Circuit holding stems from the fact that the ECOA and the CLA are both part of the federal Consumer Credit Protection Act (CCPA). A review of the CCPA's structure indicates that Congress intended the ECOA to apply to all transactions regulated by the CCPA. Congress also did not intend that lessors engage in otherwise illegal discrimination.[27]

Not all courts have followed *Brothers*. For example, one court concluded that the lessee of equipment had not necessarily incurred a debt for which payment was deferred, because a mitigation clause in the agreement provided that the lessee's financial obligation would be extinguished upon surrender of possession of the equipment.[28] The court's reasoning is dubious, as the lessee would not be released from its obligations under the lease unless the lessor succeeded in mitigating its damages. It is always true that one party's obligation under a contract *could* be extinguished if the other party were to mitigate its damages. This contingency is not, however, a sound basis for concluding that no obligation existed in the first place.

Some courts have also found it significant that in 1985 the Federal Reserve Board responded to the *Brothers* case by stating in supplemental information to Regulation B that the ECOA should not be construed to cover leases.[29] These courts appear to overstate the significance of the 1985 interpretation. Since the interpretation, no conforming changes have been made to Regulation B or to the official staff commentary. On the contrary, since 1985 the broad definition of credit has been reasserted.[30]

2.2.2.2.4 Residential leases

The *Brothers* holding is explicitly limited to personal property leases covered by the Consumer Leasing Act (CLA). Apartment leases, leases of manufactured home park space, and other real-estate-related leases are not covered by the CLA and thus do not fall under the precise *Brothers* court's holding. Moreover, the *Brothers* reasoning concerning the CLA and ECOA being part of the same statute is inapplicable to residential leases.

Whether or not the ECOA applies to residential leases is particularly important when a landlord denies a rental application because of problems with the prospective tenant's credit report. Under the Fair Credit Reporting Act, a landlord rejecting a prospective tenant's application based on a credit report is only required to inform the applicant that the application was denied based on the report and provide information on how to obtain a copy of the report.[31] These limited requirements may allow landlords to use applicants' credit reports to hide discriminatory decisions based on prohibited grounds. Application of the ECOA to residential leases would force landlords to

---

(D. Md. 1979); Johnson v. McNamara, 1979 U.S. Dist. LEXIS 13081 (D. Conn. Apr. 12, 1979).

24 *See* National Consumer Law Center, Truth in Lending § 13.2.3 (8th ed. 2012); National Consumer Law Center, Repossessions §§ 14.1.2.1–14.1.2.3.3 (7th ed. 2010 and Supp.).

   Note that the U.C.C. § 1-201(37) definition of security interest was significantly amended in conjunction with the enactment of Article 2A on leases in 1987 and 1990. Subsequently, most jurisdictions have adopted the new version of section 1-201(37).

25 724 F.2d 789 (9th Cir. 1984); *see also* Bo Foods, Inc. v. Bojangles of America, Inc., 1987 U.S. Dist. LEXIS 531 (N.D. Ill. Jan. 23, 1987). *Contra* Liberty Leasing Co. v. Machamer, 6 F. Supp. 2d 714 (S.D. Ohio 1998) (relevant to the inquiry to determine whether a lease is considered credit under ECOA is whether the incremental payments constitute a contemporaneous exchange of consideration for the possession of the leased goods; in finding car lease not to be credit under the ECOA, explicitly rejecting *Brothers'* holding that a lease obligation is credit under ECOA as a matter of law).

26 Brothers v. First Leasing, 724 F.2d 789, 792 (9th Cir. 1984); *see also* Gallegos v. Rizza Chevrolet, Inc., 2003 WL 22326523 (N.D. Ill. Oct. 9, 2003) (automobile lease was a "credit transaction"); Williams v. AT & T Wireless Servs., Inc., 5 F. Supp. 2d 1142 (W.D. Wash. 1998) (application for a cell phone service agreement involved an application for credit); Ferguson v. Park City Mobile Homes, 1989 WL 111916 (N.D. Ill. Sept. 18, 1989) (the language of the ECOA is certainly broad enough to cover the lease of a manufactured home lot).

27 *See* Brothers v. First Leasing, 724 F.2d 789, 794 (9th Cir. 1984).

28 Liberty Leasing Co. v. Machamer, 6 F. Supp. 2d 714 (S.D. Ohio 1998).

29 50 Fed. Reg. 48,018, 48,019–48,020 (Nov. 20, 1985); *see* Laramore v. Richie Realty Mgmt. Co., 2003 WL 22227148 (N.D. Ill. Sept. 25, 2003), *aff'd*, 397 F.3d 544 (7th Cir. 2005); Head v. North Pier Apartment Tower, 2003 WL 22127885 (N.D. Ill. Sept. 12, 2003); Liberty Leasing Co. v. Machamer, 6 F. Supp. 2d 714 (S.D. Ohio 1998).

30 Federal Reserve Board staff interpretations were accorded less weight than the FRB's official staff commentary. The FRB in fact noted that the official staff commentary replaced all previous FRB interpretations of the ECOA. Notably, the commentary did not adopt the 1985 interpretation regarding leasing. *See* Reg. B, 12 C.F.R. pt. 202 [pt. 1002], app. D. *See generally* Brian S. Prestes, *Application of the Equal Credit Opportunity Act to Housing Leases*, 67 U. Chi. L. Rev. 865 (2000).

   The commentary is the means by which the official interpretations of Regulation B are issued. The CFPB now has authority to issue its own commentary, renamed as the "official interpretations of Regulation B," and it too does not adopt the 1985 interpretations regarding leasing.

31 15 U.S.C. § 1681m(a). *See generally* National Consumer Law Center, Fair Credit Reporting ch. 8 (7th ed. 2010 and Supp.).

provide prospective tenants with the specific reasons why their credit reports were inadequate, presumably providing some additional protection from illegal discrimination.[32] The issue is important in the federally subsidized housing context, as well, within which landlords are increasingly using credit scores and other tools to evaluate prospective tenants' applications for housing. If these transactions were covered by the ECOA, landlords would be required to provide notices of credit decisions to rental applicants in addition to complying with the ECOA anti-discrimination provisions.[33]

In 2005, the Seventh Circuit became the first circuit court to specifically address the issue of ECOA coverage of residential leases. The court held that the rental lease at issue was not a "credit transaction" pursuant to the ECOA.[34] The court reasoned that a typical residential lease involves a contemporaneous exchange of consideration—the tenant pays rent to the landlord on the first of each month for the right to continue occupying the premises. The responsibility to pay the total amount of rent does not arise when the lease is signed, according to the court, and so there is no deferment of a debt.[35] Prior to the Seventh Circuit decision, the Illinois federal district courts had sent some mixed signals on this issue.[36]

There is still hope for renters or prospective renters seeking to bring claims under the ECOA. First, only the Seventh Circuit has ruled to date and there is no nationwide rule or Supreme Court ruling. In addition, the Seventh Circuit was explicit that its holding in *Laramore* did not conflict with *Brothers* which

dealt with consumer leases.[37] The court also recognized that the parties to a residential lease could conceivably craft an agreement that would come under the ECOA. The holding in *Laramore* was limited to leases that provide for leasing of residential premises for a term and roughly equal rental payments due at the beginning of each month.[38]

According to at least one commentator writing before the Seventh Circuit decision, the determination of whether a lease is covered by the ECOA depends on a close reading of the terms of the lease and of landlord-tenant law in the particular jurisdiction.[39] The key issue is whether relevant laws permit or require the lease to take on the characteristic of deferred payment. For example, from the landlord's perspective, a lease is not an extension of credit so long as the landlord can terminate the lease immediately upon nonpayment by the tenant. In contrast, if the landlord cannot force the tenant to surrender possession upon nonpayment, the lease more closely resembles credit because the tenant can continue in possession beyond the period for which she has paid.

In cases involving discrimination on the basis of race, national origin, religion, or sex, it may not matter whether the ECOA applies to residential leases, because the Fair Housing Act clearly applies.[40] Nevertheless, ECOA coverage is important if rental discrimination is based on the tenant's age, marital status, receipt of public assistance, or exercise of Consumer Credit Protection Act rights, as these bases are not covered by the Fair Housing Act.[41]

2.2.2.2.5 *Rent-to-own and other terminable leases*

Rent-to-own transactions (such as those involving televisions, electronic equipment, and appliances) are structured so that the consumer can terminate the lease at any time. Termination of the lease results in the forfeiting of any built-up equity from past lease payments, but the consumer owes no other early termination penalty. Typically, payments are made weekly or monthly, and the consumer has the option to keep the property after a stipulated number of payments.

Because they are terminable at will without penalty, rent-to-own transactions are not covered by the Consumer Leasing Act.[42] Consequently, the holding in *Brothers* does not explicitly apply, and the coverage under the ECOA is unclear. Moreover, rent-to-own companies may claim that there is no deferral of payment, because each payment is due in advance. They will claim that, in effect, the transaction is a series of weekly or monthly transactions, each paid in cash in advance, thus involving no credit.

32　*See* § 10.5.4.2, *infra*. *See generally* Brian S. Prestes, *Application of the Equal Credit Opportunity Act to Housing Leases*, 67 U. Chi. L. Rev. 865 (2000).

33　*See generally* ch. 10, *infra* (ECOA procedural provisions).

34　Laramore v. Richie Realty Mgmt. Co., 397 F.3d 544 (7th Cir. 2005).
　　For a circuit court decision in a commercial real estate case, see Mick's at Pennsylvania Ave., Inc. v. BOD, Inc., 389 F.3d 1284 (D.C. Cir. 2004) (restaurant sublease was not an ECOA "credit transaction"). *See also* Portis v. River House Assocs., 498 F. Supp. 2d 746 (M.D. Pa. 2007) (applying *Laramore* to find that "typical residential lease" is not covered by the ECOA). However, the *Laramore* case was distinguished in Murray v. New Cingular Wireless Servs., Inc., 432 F. Supp. 2d 788, 791–92 (N.D. Ill. 2006) (contract for wireless telephone service found to be credit).

35　Laramore v. Richie Realty Mgmt. Co., 397 F.3d 544 (7th Cir. 2005).

36　The key case holding that a real property lease constitutes deferred payment and therefore credit is Ferguson v. Park City Mobile Homes, 1989 WL 111916 (N.D. Ill. Sept. 15, 1989) (while not following the reasoning of *Brothers*, denying nevertheless creditor's motion to dismiss claim that the ECOA applies to lease of manufactured home lot).
　　The *Ferguson* court stated that any lease to be paid in installments is a credit transaction, because the willingness of the lessor to defer payments over the life of the lease depends upon the perceived creditworthiness of the lessee. The broad ruling in *Ferguson* would allow nearly all leases to be considered credit transactions, as most leases require periodic payments throughout the lease term. *See also* Gallegos v. Rizza Chevrolet, Inc., 2003 WL 22326523 (N.D. Ill. Oct. 9, 2003) (an automobile lease, as a consumer lease transaction, may constitute a credit transaction). *But see* Head v. North Pier Apartment Tower, 2003 WL 22127885 (N.D. Ill. Oct. 9, 2003) (distinguishing the facts in *Brothers* and finding that plaintiff tenant did not enter into any form of credit transaction).

37　Laramore v. Richie Realty Mgmt. Co., 397 F.3d 544, 546 n.1 (7th Cir. 2005).

38　*Id.* at 547 n.2.

39　*See generally* Brian S. Prestes, *Application of the Equal Credit Opportunity Act to Housing Leases*, 67 U. Chi. L. Rev. 865 (2000).

40　*See* § 2.3, *infra*.

41　*See* § 3.4, *infra*.

42　National Consumer Law Center, *Truth in Lending* § 13.2.1 (8th ed. 2012).

There are several arguments why a rent-to-own transaction is covered by the ECOA. If the transaction is viewed as a disguised credit sale (and this is the result that a significant number of cases produce), the ECOA clearly applies.[43] Nevertheless, to determine if a rent-to-own transaction is a disguised credit sale requires a careful reading of any special state statute dealing with rent-to-own leases, the state's retail installment sales act, and that state's version of the Uniform Commercial Code, particularly its version of UCC § 1-201(37).[44] Many states now have special rent-to-own statutes that explicitly state that these transactions are not credit sales.[45]

Alternatively, the rent-to-own transaction may still involve a deferral of payment. This may turn on whether the first payment is viewed as a refundable security deposit and whether payments are always made before the weekly or monthly rental period and never a few days late.

If rent-to-own transactions are covered by the ECOA, preliminary data exists which suggests a pattern of differential treatment of customers that may be attributable to race. A legal services attorney in Minneapolis examined court replevin filings by Rent-A-Center, the nation's largest rent-to-own company.[46] Survey results showed that, of the sixty-eight customers subject to replevin in Minnesota in the period covered, 60% were African American and 12% were white. (African Americans made up about 35% of Rent-A-Center's customer base, while whites made up 57%; both groups had similar income levels.) In addition, court records revealed that, on average, African Americans and other consumers of color were in default for a shorter period of time before repossession than whites, even though whites tended to be further along in the contract than the other minority groups—a factor which is not inconsistent with being provided a longer default period prior to repossession.

2.2.2.3 Utility Service

There is no question that utility service involves credit for the purposes of the ECOA. The official interpretation states that a utility company is a creditor when it supplies utility service and bills the user after the service has been provided.[47] Virtually all utility service is provided in this manner. Service is received, a monthly bill is sent, and some time after that payment is expected.

Regulation B exempts most forms of government-regulated utility service from a few procedural ECOA provisions but the ECOA generally applies to utility service, and no utility service is exempt from the general rule against discrimination.[48]

2.2.2.4 Check-Cashing and ATM Cards

Denial of an automated teller machine (ATM) card that merely accesses a savings account, without providing any accompanying overdraft privileges, has been found not to involve the right to defer payment of a debt and therefore not to involve "credit."[49] Another court also found a store's check-cashing service to be a customer accommodation rather than an extension of credit.[50] Accepting payment by check, rather than cash, does not involve credit.[51]

2.2.2.5 "Pay as You Go" Is Not Credit

For credit to be involved, there must be a deferral of payment of money owed. Thus a court has found no credit involved when a home improvement contract's schedule of payments substantially coincided with completion of the work, and there was no right given by the creditor to defer payment of the obligation.[52] Similarly, when payment is made immediately upon the service being provided, there is no extension of credit.[53]

The line between "pay as you go" and a deferred-payment transaction is not always clear. For example, a cellular telephone service company argued that it was not covered by the ECOA because it billed customers on a monthly basis and payment was due each month. Customers could not defer payment of amounts owed.[54] The court disagreed with this argument, focusing on the fact that the transaction involved was an application for cellular services in which the customer sought to use the service and pay for it later.[55]

---

43 Fogie v. Thorn Americas, Inc., 95 F.3d 645 (8th Cir. 1996), *aff'd*, 190 F.3d 889 (8th Cir. 1999); Miller v. Colortyme, Inc., 518 N.W.2d 544 (Minn. 1994); Green v. Cont'l Rentals, 678 A.2d 759 (N.J. Super. Ct. Law Div. 1994); *see also* National Consumer Law Center, Unfair and Deceptive Acts and Practices § 8.8 (8th ed. 2012).

44 National Consumer Law Center, Repossessions § 14.3 (7th ed. 2010 and Supp.).

45 *See* National Consumer Law Center, The Cost of Credit: Regulation, Preemption, and Industry Abuses § 7.5.3.5 (4th ed. 2009 and Supp.).

46 *Hearing Before the Senate Banking Comm.*, 103d Cong. (May 13, 1994) (statement of David Ramp, Legal Aid Society of Minneapolis) (available as Clearinghouse No. 49,965).

47 Official Interpretations of Reg. B [Official Staff Commentary on Reg. B], 12 C.F.R. pt. 1002 [pt. 202], Supp. I, § 1002.3(a)-2 [§ 202.3(a)-2].

48 Official Interpretations of Reg. B [Official Staff Commentary on Reg. B], 12 C.F.R. pt. 1002 [pt. 202], Supp. I, § 1002.3-1 [§ 202.3-1]; *see* § 2.2.6.2, *infra*.

49 *See* Butler v. Capitol Fed. Sav., 904 F. Supp. 1230 (D. Kan. 1995) (opening a savings account is not a credit transaction because it is not a right to defer payment of a debt); Dunn v. American Express Co., 529 F. Supp. 633 (D. Colo. 1982).

50 Bailey v. Jewel Cos., Inc., 1979 U.S. Dist. LEXIS 9193 (N.D. Ill. Oct. 12, 1979).

51 Roberts v. Walmart Stores, Inc., 736 F. Supp. 1527 (E.D. Mo. 1990).

52 Shaumyan v. Sidetex Co., 900 F.2d 16 (2d Cir. 1990).

53 Universal Bonding Ins. Co. v. Esko & Young, Inc., 1991 U.S. Dist. LEXIS 2359 (N.D. Ill. Feb. 28, 1991).

54 *See* Williams v. AT & T Wireless Servs., Inc., 5 F. Supp. 2d 1142 (W.D. Wash. 1998).

55 *Id.* (distinguishing *Shaumyan* because plaintiffs in that case prepaid a substantial portion of the amount due).

2.2.2.6 Medical Treatment

Medical care is another area in which denial of credit is almost equivalent to denial of service. Although some routine services may be offered only on a cash basis, more typically medical care involves deferred payment, to which the ECOA applies.

The fact that the medical provider does not assess a finance charge and requires eventual payment in one installment does not exclude this transaction from ECOA coverage.[56] Instead, the transaction becomes one involving incidental consumer credit, to which several ECOA procedural requirements do not apply but to which the general rule against discrimination does apply.[57]

In fact, the official interpretation specifically refers to one area of potential discrimination involving medical providers. Medicare and Medicaid payments are defined as public assistance benefits for purposes of considering the actions of doctors, hospitals, or any other entity to whom such benefits are payable.[58] Thus, medical providers, nursing homes, and others who receive Medicare or Medicaid benefits may not discriminate between patients on Medicare or Medicaid and those with private insurance. Of course, under various federal and state laws including the ECOA, medical providers also may not treat patients differently based on the other prohibited bases: race, religion, national origin, sex, and marital status.

At least one court has held, however, that Medicaid patients were not applicants for credit within the meaning of the ECOA and were therefore not protected by the ECOA.[59] The court ruled that Medicaid recipients under Ohio's Medicaid payment scheme were merely third-party beneficiaries of a reimbursement agreement between state and medical care givers and, as such, had neither the right to "purchase" services nor the right to defer payment for services. The court also observed that the Medicaid system "allows states to pay either the provider or, in some circumstances, the patient"[60] but did not discuss whether a patient who directly received Medicaid payments would meet the definition of applicant for credit under the ECOA.

The exception for incidental consumer credit, however, may exclude medical service providers from certain procedural ECOA requirements, including the record retention requirements, which may be essential to prove discrimination.[61] State and federal laws, such as those that prohibit discrimination by nursing homes or require provision of emergency medical service, may provide an alternative remedy.[62]

2.2.2.7 ECOA Coverage by Agreement of the Parties

A transaction may also be subject to the ECOA when it is so designated by the creditor, even if it would not otherwise fall within the statutory definition. A creditor may contract to subject itself to a consumer protection law.[63]

2.2.3 The ECOA Applies to All Stages of a Credit Transaction

Once a transaction involves credit, then all stages of that transaction—from the initial request for credit through the final payment or collection action—are covered by the ECOA's general prohibition against discrimination. The ECOA makes it unlawful for a creditor to discriminate in "any aspect of a credit transaction."[64] Regulation B defines credit transaction as including "[e]very aspect of an applicant's dealings with a creditor regarding an application for credit, or an existing extension of credit (including, but not limited to, information requirements; investigation procedures; standards of creditworthiness; terms of credit; furnishing of credit information; revocation, alteration, or termination of credit; and collection procedures)."[65] Thus, discriminatory actions that occur after credit is initially extended may be covered by the ECOA, including borrowers' efforts to alter or terminate credit arrangements.[66] Subsequent chapters detail the various stages of a credit transaction to which the ECOA applies.

2.2.4 The ECOA Prohibits Discrimination Against "Applicants"

2.2.4.1 Definition of Applicant

Only applicants are protected under most ECOA provisions.[67] The statute defines an "applicant" as "any person who

---

56 *See* § 2.2.2.1, *supra* (definition of credit).

57 Official Interpretations of Reg. B [Official Staff Commentary on Reg. B], 12 C.F.R. pt. 1002 [pt. 202], Supp. I, § 1002.3-1 [§ 202.3-1].

58 *Id.* § 1002.2(z)-3 [§ 202.2(z)-3].

59 Barney v. Holzer Clinic, Ltd., 110 F.3d 1207 (6th Cir. 1997).

60 *Id.* at 1210.

61 *See* § 2.2.6.3, *infra*.

62 *E.g.*, Conn. Gen. Stat. § 19a-533 (prohibiting nursing homes from discriminating on the basis of indigence).

63 Mack Financial Corp. v. Crossley, 550 A.2d 303 (1988); Tim O'Neill Chevrolet v. Forristall, 551 N.W.2d 611 (Iowa 1996) (when promissory note provided "this loan is subject to the provisions of the Iowa Consumer Credit Code applying to consumer loans" and "this is a consumer credit transaction," transaction was subject to Iowa consumer credit code even though not subject to the code by force of statute alone); First Northwestern Nat'l Bank v. Crouch, 287 N.W.2d 151 (Iowa 1980); Farmers State Bank v. Haflich, 699 P.2d 553, 557 (Kan. 1985); *see* U.C.C. §§ 1-102(3), 1-105(2).

64 15 U.S.C. § 1691(a); Reg. B, 12 C.F.R. § 1002.2(m) [§ 202.2(m)]; *see, e.g.*, Chiang v. Schafer, 2008 WL 3925260 (D. V.I. Aug. 20, 2008).

65 Reg. B, 12 C.F.R. § 1002.2(m) [§ 202.2(m)]; *see, e.g.*, Ramirez v. Greenpoint Mortgage Funding, Inc., 268 F.R.D. 627, 631 (N.D. Cal. 2010) (discrimination in pricing of mortgage loans based on race/ national origin may violate ECOA).

66 *See, e.g.*, Hamilton v. O'Connor Chevrolet, Inc., 2004 WL 1403711 (N.D. Ill. June 23, 2004) (summary judgment for creditor denied because ECOA applied to discriminatory statements made to borrower when she was seeking to alter or terminate credit arrangements).

67 15 U.S.C. § 1691(a),(d),(e); Reg. B, 12 C.F.R. §§ 1002.4 [202.4],

applies to a creditor directly for an extension, renewal, or continuation of credit or applies to a creditor indirectly by use of an existing credit plan for an amount exceeding a previously established credit limit."[68]

Regulation B defines an applicant as including "any person who requests or who has received an extension of credit from a creditor," including "any person who is or may become contractually liable regarding an extension of credit."[69] An applicant includes a corporation.[70] In addition, Regulation B states that, for purposes of section 1002.7(d) [section 202.7(d)], "applicant" includes guarantors, sureties, endorsers, and similar parties.[71] The regulatory definition is broader than the statutory definition.[72]

Regulation B defines "contractually liable" as being expressly obligated to repay all debts on an account, pursuant to an agreement.[73] Regulation B defines "extension of credit" as the granting of credit in any form, including but not limited to credit granted in addition to existing credit, open-end credit, refinancings, renewals, and consolidations, or the continuation of existing credit.[74]

Thus, a co-signer is an applicant, but an authorized user on someone else's credit account may not be an applicant unless the user is obligated to repay all debts on the account.[75] A

spouse whose signature is improperly required is an applicant. Someone who does not sign the promissory note itself but who is required to sign a mortgage securing that note is contractually liable, because the note can be satisfied from that property.[76]

There are limits to who might be contractually liable and therefore a credit applicant under the Act. For example, individual members of a church were not considered applicants for a loan request made on behalf of the nonprofit church corporation.[77] In addition, the sole shareholder and officer of a corporation was held not to be an applicant when a loan was sought on behalf of his corporation.[78]

2.2.4.2 Guarantors, Sureties, and Similar Parties

Regulation B states that guarantors, sureties, endorsers, and similar parties are applicants "for purposes of § 1002.7(d) [dealing with spouses' signatures]."[79] One interpretation of this

---

1002.5 [202.5] (also applies to prospective applicants), 1002.6 [202.6], 1002.7 [202.7] (includes guarantors, sureties, endorsers, and similar parties), 1002.9 [202.9].

68 15 U.S.C. § 1691a(b).

69 *Id. But see* Estate of Davis v. Wells Fargo Bank, 633 F.3d 529 (7th Cir. 2011) (finding that successor mortgagor's offer to modify a loan is an "extension of credit" under ECOA and mortgagee is therefore an "applicant" and could bring discrimination claim; finding no evidence of discrimination); Lawrence v. Lenders for Cmty. Dev., 2010 WL 4922662, at *6 (N.D. Cal. Nov. 29, 2010) (plaintiff failed to provide information required to complete application, so not an applicant entitled to relief); Farmer v. Ill. Power Co., 2010 WL 1521342, at *2–3 (S.D. Ill. Apr. 14, 2010) (utility added plaintiff's name to spouse's account, but plaintiff lacked standing to claim discrimination in violation of ECOA because not an applicant on the account). For further discussion of these issues, see § 5.6, *infra*.

70 *See, e.g.,* Torgerson v. Wells Fargo Bank S.D., 2009 WL 255995, at *7 (D.S.D. Feb. 3, 2009).

71 Reg. B, 12 C.F.R. § 1002.2(e) [§ 202.2(e)].
    Section 1002.7(d) [section 202.7(d)] of Regulation B deals with rules concerning signatures of spouses and others. *See* §§ 2.2.4.2 (discussing whether guarantors and others are required to comply only with the section 1002.7(d) [section 202.7(d)] provisions); 5.6 (discussing spousal signature requirements), *infra*.

72 Carter v. Buckeye Rural Electric Coop., 2001 WL 1681104 (S.D. Ohio Sept. 7, 2001) (if plaintiff satisfies the definition of applicant in the regulations, she is entitled to the protection of the ECOA).

73 Reg. B, 12 C.F.R. § 1002.2(i) [§ 202.2(i)].

74 Reg. B, 12 C.F.R. § 1002.2(q) [§ 202.2(q)].
    However, opening a savings account is not an aspect of a credit transaction, and a person seeking to open a savings account is not an applicant. Chizh v. Polish & Slavic Fed. Credit Union, 2011 WL 2680495, at *4 (E.D.N.Y. July 8, 2011).

75 Reg. B, 12 C.F.R. § 1002.7(c) [§ 202.7(c)]; *see also* Official Interpretations of Reg. B [Official Staff Commentary on Reg. B], 12 C.F.R. pt. 1002 [pt. 202], Supp. I, § 1002.7(c)(1)-1, (c)(2)-1 [§ 202.7(c)(1)-1, (c)(2)-1]. *Cf.* Miller v. American Express Co., 688 F.2d 1235 (9th Cir. 1982) (in challenging American Express's

policy of automatically canceling a supplementary cardholder's account upon the death of the principal cardholder, plaintiff was found to be more than a mere user of her husband's account; the ECOA applied because plaintiff was personally liable under the contract creating the supplementary account for all debts charged on her card by any person).
    Note that, under the ECOA, a creditor may require that a user become contractually liable on the account in order to be designated an authorized user, as long as the condition is not imposed on a discriminatory basis. Official Interpretations of Reg. B [Official Staff Commentary on Reg. B], 12 C.F.R. pt. 1002 [pt. 202], Supp. I, § 1002.7(a)-1 [§ 202.7(a)-1].

76 Carter v. Buckeye Rural Electric Coop., 2001 WL 1681104 (S.D. Ohio Sept. 7, 2001) (plaintiff could be "contractually liable" and thus was an "applicant" when electric cooperative added her name to husband's account without her consent); Ford v. Citizens & Southern Nat'l Bank, 700 F. Supp. 1121 (N.D. Ga. 1988) (husband required to put up a mortgage to secure note signed by his wife was contractually liable and therefore was aggrieved party with standing to sue), *aff'd on other grounds*, 928 F.2d 1118 (11th Cir. 1991).

77 Hargraves v. Capital City Mortgage Corp., 147 F. Supp. 2d 1 (D.D.C. 2001) (claims of individual plaintiffs, who did not receive or apply for credit as individuals but rather were involved in obtaining the loan for their church, dismissed; the ECOA provides a cause of action for the church, but individuals cannot assert the church's legal interest; section 1981 claims also dismissed because the church, not the individual plaintiffs, was party to the loan contract); Church of Zion Christian Ctr., Inc. v. Southtrust Bank, 1997 U.S. Dist. LEXIS 12425 (S.D. Ala. July 30, 1997) (individual plaintiffs held not to have standing to bring an ECOA action when loan application was made on behalf of a corporation and plaintiffs never entered into any oral or written agreement with defendants).

78 Bentley v. Glickman, 234 B.R. 12 (N.D.N.Y. 1999).

79 *See* Reg. B, 12 C.F.R. § 1002.2(e) [§ 202.2(e)]; *see, e.g.,* Citgo Petroleum Corp. v. Bulk Petroleum Corp., 2010 WL 3931496, at *7–9 (N.D. Okla. Oct. 5, 2010) (spousal guarantor protected as applicant under ECOA); Suntrust Bank v. Hamway, 2010 WL 146858, at *5–7 (S.D. Fla. Jan. 11, 2010) (creditor may not require the signature of spouse as guarantor if applicant is individually qualified). *But see* LOL Finance Co. v. F.J. Faison, Jr. Revocable Trust, 2010 WL 3118630, at *8–10 (D. Minn. July 13, 2010), *report and recommendation adopted by* LOL Finance Co. v. F.J. Faison, Jr. Revocable Trust, No. Civ. 09-0741 JFT/RLE, 2010 WL 3118583 (D. Minn. Aug. 4, 2010) (plaintiffs claiming that defendants discriminated against them by requiring spouses as guarantors failed to

phrase is that guarantors and similar parties are *not* otherwise applicants.[80] In fact, until 1985, Regulation B explicitly excluded guarantors, sureties, and similar parties from the definition of applicant.[81]

On the other hand, guarantors, sureties, and similar parties would seem to fall within the definition of those "who may become contractually liable" on the obligation. The pre-1985 version limited applicants to those who may *be* contractually liable, while the 1985 amendment changed that phrasing to those who may *become* contractually liable. The implication is that guarantors (who are not initially liable but who may become liable) are applicants.[82] Actual liability or an admission of liability should not be required.[83]

Regulation B does specify that guarantors are applicants for purposes of section 1002.7(d) [section 202.7(d)], but this could arguably be viewed as an effort to unambiguously overrule some earlier cases to the contrary and not as an attempt to modify the ability of guarantors more generally to qualify as applicants.[84] Regulation B does not state that guarantors are applicants *only* for purposes of section 1002.7(d) [section 202.7(d)].

The Fourth Circuit in 2002 became the first federal appellate court to address whether the ECOA and its state analogues apply to surety bonds.[85] Although there appears to be little practical difference, the court focused on whether a surety bond is a covered transaction rather than on whether a surety is a covered actor under the ECOA. The court concluded that surety bonds do not constitute a credit transaction as defined by the ECOA because there is nothing in the surety bond transaction or the indemnity agreement entitling anyone to defer payment of any debt or other obligation.[86]

Whatever the outcome as to the coverage of those secondarily liable, such as guarantors and sureties, co-signers are applicants. That is, if an individual is immediately liable on an obligation before another party defaults, that party should be considered an applicant.

2.2.4.3 Applicant Need Not Make a Complete Application

To be an applicant, one need not submit a full application to a creditor.[87] Application is a defined term under the ECOA, and certain ECOA provisions apply only if there is an "application." But the definition of applicant does not require or even mention an application.

Regulation B defines an application as "an oral or written request for an extension of credit that is made in accordance with procedures established by the creditor for the type of credit request."[88] This definition gives creditors flexibility to establish the type of process they wish to use. The official interpretation, however, encourages creditors to provide consumers with the information needed to shop for credit.

For example, in one case, the plaintiff's telephone request for credit did not meet the creditor's usual standards for an application. Nevertheless, the court found that the plaintiff came within the definition of applicant.[89] At least one court found that the ECOA may even cover a preemptive denial of credit,[90] such as a company's refusal to extend credit to anyone living or doing business within the boundaries of a Chippewa Indian reservation.[91]

It is not always clear when a consumer is merely making an inquiry about credit and when the consumer is applying for

---

establish that they qualified for credit absent use of jointly owned property as security).

80 *See, e.g.*, Durdin v. Cheyenne Mountain Bank, 98 P. 3d 899 (Colo. App. 2004); Douglas Cnty. Nat'l Bank v. Pfeiff, 809 P. 2d 1100 (Colo. App. 1991) (quoting 50 Fed. Reg. 48,020 (Nov. 20, 1985), that the principal effect of the 1985 change was to give guarantors and similar parties standing to seek legal remedies when a violation occurred under section 202.7(d)).

81 Reg. B, 12 C.F.R. § 202.2(e) [§ 1002.2(e)] (as amended in 1978 and 1979, but not as amended in 1985); *see also* Bank of America Nat'l Trust & Sav. Ass'n v. Hotel Rittenhouse Assocs., 595 F. Supp. 800 (E.D. Pa. 1984); Morse v. Mut. Fed. Sav. & Loan Ass'n, 536 F. Supp. 1271 (D. Mass. 1982); Quigley v. Nash, 1981 U.S. Dist. LEXIS 18177 (D.D.C. Nov. 13, 1981); Delta Diversified, Inc. v. Citizens & Southern Nat'l Bank, 320 S.E.2d 767 (Ga. Ct. App. 1984).

82 *But see* Champion Bank v. Reg'l Dev., L.L.C., 2009 WL 1351122, at *2–3 (E.D. Mo. May 13, 2009) (guarantors do not fall within definition of applicant).

83 *See, e.g.*, Carter v. Buckeye Rural Electric Coop., 2001 WL 1681104 (S.D. Ohio Sept. 7, 2001) (plaintiff who was disputing liability on a debt was not required to admit liability in order to be considered an "applicant" for ECOA purposes).

84 *See* Silverman v. Eastrich Multiple Investor Fund, Ltd. P'ship, 857 F. Supp. 447 (E.D. Pa. 1994), *rev'd on other grounds*, 51 F.3d 28 (3d Cir. 1995); Gen. Electric Capital Corp. v. Pulsifer, Clearinghouse No. 46,778 (D. Me. Oct. 28, 1991); Douglas Cnty. Nat'l Bank v. Pfeiff, 809 P.2d 1100 (Colo. App. 1991). *But see* Jordan v. Delon Olds Co., 887 F.2d 1089 (9th Cir. 1989) (table) (text available at 1989 WL 123647) (guarantors or others requested as additional signatories found not to be applicants protected by ECOA); Bo Foods, Inc. v. Bojangles of America, Inc., 1987 U.S. Dist. LEXIS 531 (N.D. Ill. Jan. 23, 1987).

85 Capitol Indem. Corp. v. Aulakh, 313 F.3d 200 (4th Cir. 2002).

86 *Id.*; *see* § 2.2.2.1.1, *supra* (credit transactions covered by the ECOA); *see also* Ulico Cas. Co. v. Superior Mgmt. Serv., Inc., 89 Fed. Appx. 278 (D.C. Cir. 2004); Universal Bonding Ins. Co. v. Esko & Young, Inc., 1991 WL 30049 (N.D. Ill. Feb. 28, 1991) (rejecting a claim that ECOA applied to suretyship promise).

87 *See, e.g.*, Cragin v. First Fed. Sav. & Loan Ass'n, 498 F. Supp. 379 (D. Nev. 1980) (although plaintiff held to be an applicant for credit, court found that plaintiff failed to prove a prima facie case of discrimination); *see also* Gallegos v. Rizza Chevrolet, Inc., 2003 WL 22326523 (N.D. Ill. Oct. 9, 2003) (plaintiff's allegation that a car dealer employee referred him to the dealer's finance person in order to complete the financing for purchase of a vehicle was sufficient allegation to show plaintiff's qualification as an "applicant").

88 Reg. B, 12 C.F.R. § 1002.2(f) [§ 202.2(f)].

89 Cragin v. First Fed. Sav. & Loan Ass'n, 498 F. Supp. 379 (D. Nev. 1980).

90 Davis v. Strata Corp., 242 F. Supp. 2d 643 (D.N.D. 2003) (finding sufficient evidence to support a prima facie case of discrimination, although noting factual disputes as to whether plaintiff was an "applicant" within the scope of the ECOA).

91 Davis v. Strata Corp., 242 F. Supp. 2d 643 (D.N.D. 2003).

credit. Prior to the issuance of the 1999 proposed revisions to Regulation B, comments were solicited on whether this distinction should be further clarified.[92] This solicitation for comments was motivated by the growth of new delivery channels for loan product information, such as the Internet, and the growth in credit counseling and pre-qualification programs, which resulted in consumers asking for information about credit products and seeking an evaluation of their creditworthiness before ever submitting a formal application.[93]

Based on the various responses, it was proposed that the definition include requests for pre-approval under certain procedures.[94] However, the proposed language on pre-approvals was ultimately not adopted.[95] The changes were, however, added to the official staff commentary.[96] The commentary (renamed "official interpretations" by the Consumer Financial Protection Bureau) now distinguishes between inquiries and pre-qualification requests on the one hand and certain pre-approval requests, on the other, for purposes of determining whether an application exists. The commentary (official interpretations) clarifies that pre-qualification requests are subject to the same test applicable to inquiries.[97]

In general, a request or inquiry will become an application for purposes of the ECOA if the creditor responds not only by providing information but also by evaluating information about the consumer. The term "applicant" was changed to "consumers" in the official interpretations to emphasize that an application may exist for purposes of the ECOA even if the consumer has not actually submitted a formal application.[98] It was explained that using the term "applicant" presumes that an application exists, while the point of the comment is that, in the case of an inquiry or pre-qualification request, an application may or may not exist depending upon the circumstances.[99]

Concerns were also noted that creditors could discriminate in the use of direct-marketing prescreened solicitations. These solicitations often include discounted introductory rates and other favorable credit terms. Despite the raising of these concerns, the 1999 proposed revisions to Regulation B did not extend the ECOA to cover prescreened credit offers.[100] However, new provisions were ultimately adopted requiring record retention of certain information used in these solicitations.[101]

2.2.4.4 Applicant Need Not Be Seeking New Credit

Applicants are not just persons attempting to open a new account. The statutory definition includes a person applying for an "extension, renewal or continuation of credit" and someone who "applies to a creditor indirectly by use of an existing credit plan for an amount exceeding a previously established credit limit."[102] The regulations clarify that the term also includes any person who has requested or received an extension of credit.[103]

An applicant then could be a person who inquires about credit, a person who requests credit, a person who submits a formal application, a person whose application is approved and who opens an account, a person whose application is approved but who decides not to accept the credit offered, a person who requests an increase of an existing credit limit, or a person who has existing credit with a creditor. The official interpretations explicitly state that a home buyer is an applicant when that buyer seeks to assume the seller's mortgage loan unless the creditor's policy is not to permit assumptions.[104] The ECOA can apply even to *potential* applicants, so creditors whose practices discourage applications on a prohibited basis are liable.[105]

2.2.5 *Creditors and Related Parties Subject to the ECOA*

2.2.5.1 General

The ECOA identifies three types of creditors who are subject to its requirements:

- Any person who regularly extends, renews, or continues credit;
- Any person who regularly arranges for the extension, renewal, or continuation of credit; or
- Any assignee of an original creditor who participates in the decision to extend, renew, or continue credit.[106]

---

92 63 Fed. Reg. 12,326 (Mar. 12, 1998).

93 64 Fed. Reg. 44,582, 44,589 (Aug. 16, 1999).

94 *Id.* (proposing to amend 12 C.F.R. § 202.2(f)).

95 68 Fed. Reg. 13,144, 13,145, 13,154–13,155 (Mar. 18, 2003).

96 *Id.* (amending Official Staff Commentary to Reg. B, 12 C.F.R. pt. 202, Supp. I, § 202.2(f)-5).

97 Official Staff Commentary on Reg. B [Official Interpretations of Reg. B], 12 C.F.R. pt. 202 [pt. 1002], Supp. I, § 202.2(f)-3 [§ 1002.2(f)-3].

98 68 Fed. Reg. 13,144, 13,145, 13,154–13,155 (Mar. 18, 2003).

99 *Id.*

100 64 Fed. Reg. 44,582 (Aug. 16, 1999); *see* § 5.3.2.6, *infra*.

101 68 Fed. Reg. 13,144 (Mar. 18, 2003); *see* § 10.12.1, *infra* (record retention).

102 15 U.S.C. § 1691a(b).

103 Reg. B, 12 C.F.R. § 1002.2(e) [§ 202.2(e)]; *see, e.g.*, Powell v. Pentagon Fed. Credit Union, 2010 WL 3732195, at *5 (N.D. Ill. Sept. 17. 2010) (plaintiff with existing VISA card account is applicant because of having received an extension of credit).

104 Official Interpretations of Reg. B [Official Staff Commentary on Reg. B], 12 C.F.R. pt. 1002 [pt. 202], Supp. I, § 1002.2(e)-1 [§ 202.2(e)-1].

105 *See* § 5.3.2.1, *infra*.

106 15 U.S.C. § 1691a(e); *see, e.g.*, *In re* First Franklin Financial Corp. Litig., 2009 WL 1260178, at *2–3 (N.D. Cal. May 6, 2009) (plaintiff permitted to amend complaint to add additional creditors); Miller v. Countrywide Bank, 571 F. Supp. 2d 251, 260 (D. Mass. 2008) (bank's liability for discriminatory mortgage pricing decisions made by retail lenders flowed from bank's participation in the transaction as the creditor who set the price markup policy). *But see* Omoregie v. Boardwalk Auto Ctr., Inc., 2008 WL 3823697 (N.D. Cal. Aug. 13, 2008) (plaintiff lessee failed to allege the nature of any beneficial interest assigned as required to support the conclusion that defendant assignees were creditors).

Regulation B defines "creditor" as a person who, in the ordinary course of business, regularly participates in a credit decision, including setting the terms of the credit.[107] Previously, Regulation B defined creditors as those persons who regularly participate in the decision of whether or not to extend credit. The new language was intended to clarify that the definition includes entities that make the credit decisions as well as those that negotiate and set the terms of the credit.[108]

Understanding these definitions is crucial to selecting appropriate defendants in an ECOA action. Often it is possible to select as defendants not only the creditor originally extending the loan but also those who arrange the loan, assignees who participate in the credit determination, and even secondary market purchasers.

2.2.5.2 "Regularly" Extends, Renews, or Continues Credit

The ECOA applies to any person that "regularly" extends, renews, or continues credit.[109] Regulation B interprets this definition to require participation in a credit decision, including setting the terms of credit.[110] Contentious issues in this category generally involve entities such as automobile dealers arguing that they only arrange credit for consumers and do not participate in credit decisions.[111]

In addition, some creditors will argue that they only infrequently extend credit or infrequently participate in credit decisions.[112] Neither Regulation B and its official interpretations nor existing ECOA case law define "regularly." The best precedent is that found under the old Truth in Lending Act and Regulation Z. Regulation Z's pre-simplification (that is, pre-1983) definition of creditor also required that such a person "regularly" extend credit in the ordinary course of business.[113] It seems clear that the federal regulatory agency had this

Regulation Z language in mind when it promulgated the Regulation B requirement that a creditor regularly extend credit. Under cases interpreting old Regulation Z, if a transaction represents more than an "isolated," "incidental" occurrence, then the creditor regularly extends credit.[114]

2.2.5.3 Arrangers of Credit

The ECOA's definition of creditor includes persons who regularly arrange for the extension, renewal, or continuation of credit.[115] Arrangers include entities that may not provide credit but whose discrimination may prevent applicants from receiving credit.

Regulation B further defines this category and also limits liability for "arrangers." Regulation B indicates that a creditor includes someone who, in the ordinary course of business, regularly refers applicants or prospective applicants to creditors or who selects or offers to select creditors to whom requests for credit may be made.[116] The official interpretation clarifies that this category may include certain persons such as real estate brokers, automobile dealers, home builders, and home improvement contractors.[117]

For example, some car dealers do not provide credit directly but may have arrangements with one or more creditors to provide car loans to their customers. The car dealer would violate the ECOA if it disproportionately directed purchasers from protected classes to high-cost creditors.[118]

---

107 Reg. B, 12 C.F.R. § 1002.2(*l*) [§ 202.2(*l*)]; *see, e.g.*, Diamond Ventures v. Baruah, 699 F. Supp. 2d 57, 60 (D.D.C. 2010) (Small Business Administration's role as creditor under ECOA included licensing of Small Business Investment Companies when the SBA guarantees payment in event of default by the SBIC, which then becomes indebted to the SBA for repayment).

108 *See* 64 Fed. Reg. 44,582, 44,594 (Aug. 16, 1999); 68 Fed. Reg. 13,144, 13,145 (Mar. 18, 2003).

Some parties involved in the transaction, however, may not meet the definition of a creditor. *See* Jones v. Countrywide Home Loans, Inc., 2010 WL 551418, at *7 (N.D. Ill. Feb. 11, 2010) (title insurance company that conducted loan closing is not a creditor under the ECOA).

109 15 U.S.C. § 1691a(e).

110 Reg. B, 12 C.F.R. § 1002.2(*l*) [§ 202.2(*l*)].

111 *See* §§ 2.2.5.3, 2.2.5.4, *infra*.

112 *See, e.g.*, Riethman v. Berry, 113 F. Supp. 2d 765 (E.D. Pa. 2000) (attorneys not considered creditors under ECOA because they did not regularly extend credit to their clients), *aff'd*, 287 F.3d 274 (3d Cir. 2002); *see also* Mick's at Pennsylvania Ave., Inc. v. Bod, Inc., 389 F.3d 1284 (D.C. Cir. 2004); Bayard v. Behlmann Automotive Servs., Inc., 292 F. Supp. 2d 1181 (E.D. Mo. 2003) (dealer unsuccessfully attempted to argue that it did not regularly extend credit).

113 Reg. Z, 12 C.F.R. § 226.2(s) (1973) (this section was deleted in the 1983 revisions).

114 *See, e.g.*, Eby v. Reb Realty, Inc., 495 F.2d 646 (9th Cir. 1974) (extension of credit in three out of seven land sales in a nineteen-month period made real estate broker a creditor); James v. Ragin, 432 F. Supp. 887 (W.D.N.C. 1977).

Currently, Regulation Z defines "regularly" to mean twenty-five credit extensions per year or five times per year for transactions secured by a dwelling. Reg. Z, 12 C.F.R. § 226.2(a)(17), n.3.

115 15 U.S.C. § 1691a(e).

116 Reg. B, 12 C.F.R. § 1002.2(*l*) [§ 202.2(*l*)]; *see also* Official Interpretations of Reg. B [Official Staff Commentary on Reg. B], 12 C.F.R. pt. 1002 [§ 202], Supp. I, § 1002.2(*l*)-2 [§ 202.2(*l*)-2].

Other than the Regulation B standard, the best source of precedent defining when a person is an arranger of credit can be found in old Truth in Lending (TILA) cases on arrangers. After TILA was "simplified" in 1982, credit arrangers were no longer covered. But before 1982 the Federal Reserve Board defined an arranger as a person who either received a fee or similar consideration for services or who had knowledge of the credit terms and participated in preparation of the contract documents. Reg. Z, 12 C.F.R. § 226.2(h) (1973) (this section was deleted by the 1983 revisions); *see also* Price v. Franklin Inv. Co., 574 F.2d 594 (D.C. Cir. 1978); Hinkle v. Rock Springs Nat'l Bank, 538 F.2d 295 (10th Cir. 1976).

117 Official Interpretations of Reg. B [Official Staff Commentary on Reg. B], 12 C.F.R. pt. 1002 [pt. 202], Supp. I, § 1002.2(*l*)-2 [§ 202.2(*l*)-2].

Prior to the 2003 regulatory amendments, the FRB's official staff commentary mentioned only real estate brokers in this category. 68 Fed. Reg. 13,144, 13,188 (Mar. 18, 2003).

118 *See, e.g.*, Treadway v. Gateway Chevrolet, Oldsmobile, Inc., 362 F.3d 971 (7th Cir. 2004); Aikens v. Northwestern Dodge, Inc., 2004 WL 2967549 (N.D. Ill. Dec. 1, 2004); Bayard v. Behlmann Automotive Servs., Inc., 292 F. Supp. 2d 1181 (E.D. Mo. 2003) (dealer's activities placed it at a point on the continuum where it participated

There are important differences that result from categorizing an auto dealer or other entity as a credit "arranger" as opposed to a "creditor." Creditors are subject to liability for violations of all provisions of the ECOA and Regulation B whereas arrangers are liable only for violations of sections 1002.4(a) [section 202.4(a)] (general rule prohibiting discrimination) and 1002.4(b) [section 202.4(b)] (general rule against discouraging applications) of Regulation B.[119] This limitation means that arrangers are not responsible for ECOA procedural violations even if they actively participate in, or are the actual cause of, the violation. The most important practical difference is that arrangers are not required to comply with the ECOA notice and record-keeping requirements.[120]

Amendments to Regulation B provide some guidance to clarify the distinction between arrangers and creditors. It was explained that an automobile dealer may accept and refer applications for credit or it may accept applications, perform underwriting, and make decisions regarding the extension of credit. When the dealer only accepts applications for credit and refers those applications to a creditor who makes the credit decisions, the dealer is an arranger subject only to the anti-discrimination provisions of the ECOA.[121] A dealer that participates in setting the terms of credit and making credit decisions is subject to all ECOA provisions.[122]

Courts have begun to recognize that there is a continuum of participation in a credit decision from no involvement, to referring applications to the decision maker, to involvement in the final decision-making.[123] At some point along that continuum, a party becomes a creditor for purposes of the notification and other procedural requirements of the ECOA.[124]

Dealers and similar entities should not be able to escape ECOA liability by arguing that they do not make credit decisions or do not participate in making credit decisions when they, in fact, do. The key in these cases is convincing the judge that a dealer can fit within both the arranger *and* creditor definitions and that the categories are not mutually exclusive. Many dealers, for example, will argue that, if their activities do not precisely fit within the definition of arranger found in the regulation and official interpretations, they cannot be a creditor. This is clearly incorrect. In practice, most dealers, home improvement contractors, and real estate brokers are sufficiently involved in the credit decision-making process to be considered creditors. For example, the dealer may have written the legally binding credit contract executed by the applicant but may still argue either that it is not a creditor or that it is merely an arranger.

Careful pleading and discovery is essential in these cases. Courts will not find dealers to be creditors unless the supporting facts are carefully developed.[125] The Seventh Circuit *Treadway* decision is extremely helpful in laying out the types of activities the court found persuasive in ruling that the auto dealer was a "creditor."[126] The court noted that, in addition to deciding whether to pass on credit applications, the dealer frequently

---

in the decision of whether or not to extend credit and was thus subject to ECOA notice provisions); Gallegos v. Rizza Chevrolet, Inc., 2003 WL 22326523 (N.D. Ill. Oct. 9, 2003); Cannon v. Metro Ford, Inc., 242 F. Supp. 2d 1322 (S.D. Fla. 2002) (dealers that regularly refer applicants to creditors may be subject to the ECOA); Mungia v. Tony Rizza Oldsmobile, Inc., 2002 WL 554504 (N.D. Ill. Apr. 15, 2002); Johnson v. Equicredit Corp. of America, 2002 U.S. Dist. LEXIS 4817 (N.D. Ill. Mar. 21, 2002) (plaintiff presented sufficient evidence to state a claim against a mortgage origination company; company could be considered an arranger of credit); Burns v. Elmhurst Auto Mall, Inc., 45 U.C.C. Rep Serv. 2d 247 (N.D. Ill. 2001).

119 Reg. B, 12 C.F.R. § 1002.2(*l*) [§ 202.2(*l*)]; *see, e.g.*, Chastain v. N.S.S. Acquisition Corp., 2009 WL 1971621, at *6–7 (S.D. Fla. July 8, 2009), *aff'd*, 378 Fed. Appx. 983 (11th Cir. 2010).

120 *See, e.g.*, Salvagne v. Fairfield Ford, Inc., 2010 WL, 2010 WL 3292967, at *10 (S.D. Ohio Aug. 19, 2010), *motion to certify appeal granted*, Salvagne v. Fairfield Ford, Inc., MO. 1:09-CV-00324, 2010 WL 5087993 (S.D. Ohio Dec. 7, 2010) (when a dealership only refers applications to lenders, dealership is a creditor only with respect to anti-discrimination and anti-discouragement provisions of ECOA and is not required to comply with adverse action requirements). *See generally* ch. 10, *infra*.

121 68 Fed. Reg. 13,144, 13,155 (Mar. 18, 2003).

122 *Id.*

123 *See, e.g.*, Whitley v. Taylor Bean & Whitacker Mortgage Corp., 607 F. Supp. 2d 885, 895–96 (N.D. Ill. 2009) (loan broker that used creditor's credit granting policies, rate sheets, product sheets, loan pricing software, and training materials to process creditor's loans was more involved than simply bringing borrower and lender together; facts were sufficient to create inference of agency relationship).

124 Treadway v. Gateway Chevrolet Oldsmobile, Inc., 362 F.3d 971 (7th Cir. 2004) (citing Bayard v. Behlman Auto Servs., Inc., 292 F. Supp. 2d 1181 (E.D. Mo. 2003)); Drewry v. Starr Motors, Inc., 2008 WL 2035607 (E.D. Va. May 12, 2008); *see also* Aikens v. Northwestern Dodge, Inc., 2004 WL 2967549 (N.D. Ill. Dec. 1, 2004); Gallegos v. Rizza Chevrolet, Inc., 2003 WL 22326523 (N.D. Ill. Oct. 9, 2003); Cannon v. Metro Ford, Inc., 242 F. Supp. 2d 1322 (S.D. Fla. 2002) (dealers that regularly refer applicants to creditors may be subject to the ECOA); Mungia v. Tony Rizza Oldsmobile, Inc., 2002 WL 554504 (N.D. Ill. Apr. 15, 2002); Burns v. Elmhurst Auto Mall, Inc., 45 U.C.C. Rep. Serv. 2d 247 (N.D. Ill. 2001); *cf.* McWhorter v. Elsea, 2007 WL 1101249 (S.D. Ohio Apr. 11, 2007) (citing *Treadway* but finding that, when more unfavorable package was not related to dealer receiving a portion of the increased interest rate and was related to creditor checking with assignee regarding acceptable rates for purchase, dealer did not take adverse action).

125 *See, e.g.*, Flowers v. S.W. Motor Sales, Inc., 2008 WL 4614307 (N.D. Ill. Oct. 14, 2008) (plaintiff failed to allege that defendant was a creditor for the purpose of the notice requirement); Hunter v. Bev Smith Ford, 2008 WL 1925265 (S.D. Fla. Apr. 29, 2008) (contract stated that dealer did not provide financing, therefore dealer not a creditor and not required to provide adverse action notice); Conte v. Sonic-Plymouth Cadillac, 2008 WL 783632 (E.D. Mich. Mar. 20, 2008) (finding dealer not to be a creditor and therefore not required to provide adverse action notice, but subject to anti-discrimination provision of ECOA); Logsdon v. Dennison Corp., 2007 WL 1655239 (C.D. Ill. June 7, 2007) (granting summary judgment for dealer on ECOA claim after applying *Treadway*; finding that "record is devoid of evidence" indicating that the dealer participated in the credit decision although borrower alleged that dealer regularly referred applicants to lenders and because it reviewed credit reports and decided which assignees should receive retail installment contracts).

126 Treadway v. Gateway Chevrolet, Oldsmobile, Inc., 362 F.3d 971 (7th Cir. 2004).

participated in credit decisions by restructuring the terms of the sale in order to meet creditor concerns. For example, the dealer might insist that the consumer put more money down or request that the consumer find a co-signer.[127] Additionally, the dealer regularly set the APR associated with car sales and could increase the APR in order to induce the lender to agree to extend credit.[128] If the dealer had just taken the application and decided not to pass it on, the court speculated that this action alone would probably be insufficient to meet the ECOA creditor category.[129]

However, if the dealer's decision not to pass the application on to the creditor was based on the dealer's knowledge that the application did not meet the creditor's standard for approval, one could argue for a different result. In another case, a mortgage broker that participated in setting the terms of the credit arrangements and determined the loan type, loan terms, and interest rate, as well as actively solicited consumers to refinance their property, was held to be a creditor under the ECOA.[130] Because this analysis is fact-specific, guidelines have developed to support this determination including: whether

the dealer sets the terms of the credit; whether the dealer negotiates with the customers as to the payment terms; whether the dealer receives proceeds from a portion of the interest rate charged to the applicant; and whether the dealer conducts an initial assessment of the customer's credit application to screen out those that it determines not to send to a lender.[131]

Unfortunately, some courts are misapplying *Treadway*. For example, in *Fultz v. Lasco Ford*,[132] the court concluded that because the dealer had forwarded the applications to several lenders that made the credit decisions, the dealer did not engage in any adverse action and therefore could not be a creditor for purposes of the statute's adverse action notice requirement. The court did not examine, as required under *Treadway*, whether the dealers participated in setting terms, down payment amounts, interest rates or other conditions that may have affected the decisions of the lenders. The *Fultz* court instead focused just on whether or not the dealer forwarded the credit applications; because it did, the court ended its inquiry.

Another strategy to get around the problem of who is considered to be the creditor under the ECOA is to sue both the dealer and the assignee in the same lawsuit. The assignee will generally argue that the dealer, not the assignee, was the creditor. Although both the assignee and the dealer may be considered ECOA creditors, the assignee's finger-pointing can help draw out the dealer's crucial role in extending credit.[133]

In "spot delivery" or "yo-yo sales" cases, assignees will often argue that they did not participate in the credit decision because the sale was allegedly consummated when the contract was initially signed, before credit information was transmitted to or approved by the assignee.[134] Courts have concluded, to the contrary, that the "true purchase of the car" takes place when financing has been secured, terms have been set, and the final contract has been signed.[135] The assignee in these circumstances should be liable as a "creditor" regardless of whether it initially extended the credit.[136] The dealer or other entity that initially handled the conditional, unfunded finance contract should also be a "creditor" and not just an "arranger" if it was

---

127 *Id.*; *see also* Payne v. Ken Diepholz Ford Lincoln Mercury, Inc., 2004 WL 40631 (N.D. Ill. Jan. 5, 2004) (dealer that attempts to help customers obtain financing on a regular basis, selects lenders to which it will submit customers' credit applications, negotiates the terms of financing for its customers, and has the discretion to set a higher interest rate than the lender requires is a creditor as defined by the ECOA).

128 Treadway v. Gateway Chevrolet, Oldsmobile, Inc., 362 F.3d 971 (7th Cir. 2004).

The court was referring to the common practice of automobile dealers splitting the APR mark-up with creditors. This issue has been the subject of numerous discrimination lawsuits. *See* §§ 8.6.2, 8.6.3, *infra*.

129 Treadway v. Gateway Chevrolet, Oldsmobile, Inc., 362 F.3d 971 n.8 (7th Cir. 2004); *see also* Cochran v. Northeast Mortgage, 2007 WL 2412299 (D. Conn. Aug. 21, 2007) (following *Treadway* and holding that mortgage broker who did not submit plaintiff's loan application to any lenders participated in a credit decision and was a creditor under the ECOA).

The *Treadway* court cited the FRB's official staff commentary to support its conclusion that entities which only select or offer to select creditors to whom requests can be made are merely arrangers and not regular creditors. Official Staff Commentary on Reg. B [Official Interpretations of Reg. B], 12 C.F.R. pt. 202 [pt. 1002], Supp. I, § 202.2(*l*)-2 [§ 1002.2(*l*)-2].

Presumably in response to this potential "loophole," at least some dealers are now requiring prospective buyers to sign a document that, among other provisions, states that the dealer is not the decision maker as to whether credit will be approved. *See* Imtiazuddin v. North Ave. Auto, Inc., 2004 WL 2418295 (N.D. Ill. Oct. 27, 2004) (denying buyer's attempt to exclude a document signed by buyer affirming that dealer is not a creditor).

This debate will presumably continue until dealers finally concede or the courts definitively establish that they are arrangers and creditors unless they sell a car for cash. *See* Cathy Brennan, Dealers ALWAYS Extend Credit, Spot Delivery (Dec. 2004), www.counselorlibrary.com.

In addition, as the *Treadway* court pointed out, the ECOA notice requirement is not particularly arduous. *See* Treadway v. Gateway Chevrolet, Oldsmobile, Inc., 362 F.3d 971 n.2 (7th Cir. 2004).

130 Kivel v. Wealthspring Mortgage Corp., 398 F. Supp. 2d 1049 (D. Minn. 2005).

131 Barnette v. Brook Road Inc., 457 F. Supp. 2d 647 (E.D. Va. 2006); *see also* Stegvilas v. Evergreen Motors, 2007 WL 1438372 (N.D. Ill. May 11, 2007).

132 Fultz v. Lasco Ford, 2007 WL 3379684 (E.D. Mich. Nov. 13, 2007); *see also* Henry v. Westchester Foreign Autos, Inc., 522 F. Supp. 2d 610 (S.D.N.Y. 2007) (omitting any *Treadway*-type analysis and holding that the question of whether the auto dealer sets the terms of the credit is inapplicable because the claim is for adverse action and not discrimination; finding that it is a factual question whether dealer regularly arranges or participates in credit decisions in the ordinary course of its business and thus is not appropriate for summary judgment).

133 *See* § 2.2.5.4, *infra*.

134 *See, e.g.*, Aikens v. Northwestern Dodge, Inc., 2004 WL 2967549 (N.D. Ill. Dec. 1, 2004); *see also* § 10.4.2, *infra*.

135 Aikens v. Northwestern Dodge, Inc., 2004 WL 2967549 (N.D. Ill. Dec. 1, 2004) (citing Coleman v. Gen. Motors Acceptance Corp., 220 F.R.D. 64 (M.D. Tenn. 2004)).

136 *Id.* (finance company is in the business of providing financing for auto purchasers and was a "creditor" even though it did not provide financing in this case).

sufficiently involved, as discussed above, in the credit transaction. This result should apply regardless of whether financing is ultimately obtained for the consumer.[137] Many entities or individuals will fit into more than one ECOA definitional category.

2.2.5.4 Participants in the Credit Decision, Including Assignees

The Regulation B definition of creditor includes any person who in the ordinary course of business regularly participates in a credit decision, including setting the terms of the credit.[138] The ECOA statute also specifically includes in the definition of creditor any *assignee* of an original creditor who participates in the decision to extend, renew, or continue credit.[139] Regulation B further clarifies that this category includes persons such as a creditor's assignee, transferee, or subrogee.[140] The official interpretation elaborates that "creditor" includes all persons participating in the credit decision and may include an assignee or a potential purchaser of the obligation who influences the credit decision by indicating whether it will purchase the obligation if the transaction is consummated.[141]

Many assignees and other secondary creditors will fit into this definition because they participate in the credit decision in some way.[142] If the creditor is held not to have participated in the credit decision, the assignee can still be held liable, but the plaintiff will have to prove that the secondary creditor had knowledge or reasonable notice of the violation.[143]

There are limits to this broad standard. FBI agents forwarding inaccurate credit information about an applicant to a bank were found not to have participated in the credit decision and were not considered "creditors."[144] While an appraiser might be a creditor, depending on its role in the credit transaction, in one instance an appraiser that inflated the appraisal for the transaction in question was not considered a creditor because plaintiff did not allege that the appraiser participated in the decision to extend credit.[145] A company was found not to be a creditor when it merely received the mortgage application and acted as a conduit to the actual financier.[146] In addition, the ECOA's coverage is not as broad as the extended liability provisions in the Home Ownership Equity Protection Act (HOEPA).[147]

A mortgage holder who forwarded a credit report to a second lender was, however, considered a creditor for purposes of ECOA liability.[148] A Department of Housing and Urban Development (HUD) mortgagee letter concluded that both HUD and mortgagee banks were creditors on applications for HUD-insured mortgage financing.[149] At least one court has held that the president and sole owner of a lending institution who directed and controlled the institution's actions could be held liable as a creditor under the ECOA.[150] If parent companies are involved in setting policies and procedures for a subsidiary

---

137 *See, e.g.*, Treadway v. Gateway Chevrolet, Oldsmobile, Inc., 362 F.3d 971 (7th Cir. 2004) (although the dealer failed to get credit for plaintiff, it was still a regular arranger of credit; dealer also far enough along continuum of credit participation to be considered a creditor).

138 Reg. B, 12 C.F.R. § 1002.2(*l*) [§ 202.2(*l*)].

139 15 U.S.C. § 1691a(e).

140 Reg. B, 12 C.F.R. § 1002.2(*l*) [§ 202.2(*l*)].

141 Official Interpretations of Reg. B [Official Staff Commentary on Reg. B], 12 C.F.R. pt. 1002 [pt. 202], Supp. I, § 1002.2(*l*)-1 [§ 202.2(*l*)-1]; *see* Hunter v. Ford Motor Co., 2010 WL 3385225, at *9–10 (D. Minn. July 28, 2010), *report and recommendation adopted*, Hunter v. Ford Motor Co., No. 08-CV-4980 PJS/JSM, 2010 WL 3385228 (D. Minn. Aug. 23, 2010) (granting summary judgment for defendants as plaintiff failed to show that defendant Ford was involved in transaction or that alleged dealer pricing markup was result of discrimination in violation of ECOA); Zivanic v. Washington Mut. Bank, F.A., 2010 WL 2354199, *7–8 (N.D. Cal. June 9, 2010) (ECOA claim dismissed for failure to show defendant's participation in decision to extend, renew, or continue credit).

142 *See* § 2.2.5.5, *infra*.

143 Reg. B, 12 C.F.R. § 1002.2(*l*) [§ 202.2(*l*)]; *see* Levey v. CitiMortgage, Inc., 2009 WL 2475222, at *2–4 (N.D. Ill. Aug. 10, 2009) (dismissing complaint against assignee creditor when plaintiff failed to allege or insufficiently alleged that assignee knew or should have known of violations by originating lender); § 2.2.5.5, *infra*.

144 Ricci v. Bancshares, 768 F.2d 456 (1st Cir. 1985).

145 Morilus v. Countrywide Home Loans, 2007 WL 1810676 (E.D. Pa. June 20, 2007).

 This case may be distinguishable from other fact patterns in which it can be alleged that the appraiser in fact was participating in the credit decision.

146 Markham v. Colonial Mortgage Serv. Co., 605 F.2d 566 (D.C. Cir. 1979). *Contra* Kimberton Chase Realty Corp. v. Main Line Bank, 1997 U.S. Dist. LEXIS 17966 (E.D. Pa. Nov. 3, 1997) (individual who asked for clarification and updated financials, gave loan package to lenders, and provided guidance to credit applicant could be "creditor"; claim survives motion to dismiss).

147 15 U.S.C. § 1641(d); *see In re* Barber, 266 B.R. 309 (Bankr. E.D. Pa. 2001) (when HOEPA and ECOA claims are raised in the same case, the assignee liability provisions of HOEPA do not trump the more limited provisions under the ECOA; in order to bring an ECOA claim against the assignee, plaintiff had to show that assignee participated in original credit decision or had knowledge of the act that constituted the ECOA violation). *See generally* National Consumer Law Center, Truth in Lending § 13.7 (8th ed. 2012).

148 Luby v. Fid. Bond & Mortgage Co., 662 F. Supp. 256 (E.D. Pa. 1985).

 The court reached this conclusion on the grounds that, although the mortgage holder was not the party who denied the plaintiff's mortgage application, it met the ECOA's definition of creditor and allegedly engaged in discriminatory acts that led to the denial of credit, including furnishing a credit report to the institution that denied the plaintiff's mortgage application.

149 Dep't of Hous. & Urban Dev., HUD Mortgagee Letter No. 77-17, Consumer Cred. Guide (CCH) ¶ 98,192 (Apr. 22, 1977).

150 Fed. Trade Comm'n v. Capital City Mortgage Corp., 1998 U.S. Dist. LEXIS 22115 (D.D.C. July 13, 1998); *see also* Kimberton Chase Realty Corp. v. Main Line Bank, 1997 U.S. Dist. LEXIS 17966 (E.D. Pa. Nov. 3, 1997) (chief executive officer and 97% stockholder of lending institution could be creditor even if no actual participation).

 A 2003 United States Supreme Court decision addressed the issue of vicarious liability under the Fair Housing Act. *See* Meyer v. Holley, 537 U.S. 280, 123 S. Ct. 824, 154 L. Ed. 2d 753 (2003). Implications of this decision for holding individuals and corporations liable in credit discrimination cases are discussed in § 11.3, *infra*.

theycan be held liable because they control or participate in credit decisions.[151]

2.2.5.5 Exclusions and Partial Exclusions from Definition of Creditor

There are two exclusions or partial exclusions from the definition of creditor. A person whose only participation in a credit transaction involves honoring a credit card is not a creditor.[152] In addition, Regulation B states that a person is not a creditor regarding any violation of the act or regulation *committed by another creditor* unless the person knew or had reasonable notice of the act, policy, or practice that constituted the violation before becoming involved in the credit transaction.[153] This limitation can make it much more difficult to pursue liability against assignees and other secondary creditors for ECOA violations.[154]

For example, a car dealer may make a preliminary credit determination and require the signature of a spouse before submitting the proposed transaction to a finance company. If this practice violates the ECOA, the finance company might then claim ignorance of the dealer's action and claim that it is not liable for the dealer's ECOA violations. This argument is only viable if the finance company is not directly liable as a creditor under the ECOA, as it would be, for example, if the finance company were responsible for the policy.

The first part of the definition of "creditor" in Regulation B defines creditors as those who in the ordinary course of business regularly participate in the credit decision, including setting the terms of credit.[155] Immediately following this definition is an explanation that this category includes a creditor's

assignee, transferee, or subrogee who regularly participates in the credit decision.[156] Therefore, assignees who regularly participate in common secondary market practices, such as setting terms regarding the loans they will buy, should be directly liable for ECOA violations even if the credit was actually extended by the dealer or another creditor.[157] Knowledge or reasonable notice of the violation is required only for assignees and other secondary creditors who do not participate in the credit decision in this way.

This distinction is critical as it allows plaintiffs to pursue claims against assignees, secondary market purchasers, and others who create financing policies and set the offered terms of credit without having to prove that these creditors had specific knowledge or notice of the ECOA violations committed by dealers and other creditor partners. This issue has been a key point of contention in cases against General Motors Acceptance Corp. (GMAC) and Nissan Motor Acceptance Corp. (NMAC) alleging that their subjective mark-up pricing schemes result in significantly higher interest rates for African-American buyers than for white buyers with similar credit profiles.[158]

GMAC and NMAC, as assignees of the loans in question, argued that they did not fit into the ECOA definition of direct creditors. As a result, they argued, the plaintiffs had to prove that they had knowledge of any discriminatory actions taken by the car dealers. The companies further alleged that they had no notice or knowledge of these violations, characterizing themselves as "mere paper buyers." In denying defendants' motions for summary judgment, the court agreed that the defendants could be held directly liable as participating creditors under the ECOA.[159]

---

151 Zamudio v. HSBC North America Holdings Inc., 2008 WL 517138 (N.D. Ill. Feb. 20, 2008).

152 Reg. B, 12 C.F.R. § 1002.2(*l*) [§ 202.2(*l*)].

153 *Id.*; *see, e.g.*, Beard v. Dominion Homes Financial Servs., 2007 WL 2137944 (S.D. Ohio July 23, 2007) (denying defendant's motion to dismiss when defendant's representatives were present when alleged discriminatory conduct occurred); Sovereign Bank v. Catterton, 2004 WL 834721 (E.D. Pa. Apr. 15, 2004) (bank held not to have knowledge of possible ECOA violation committed by its predecessor even though the two banks were in the process of merging at the time of the alleged violation).

154 The Federal Reserve Board considered, but rejected, changes to this knowledge/reasonable notice requirement. 64 Fed. Reg. 44,582, 44,590 (Aug. 16, 1999).

In its *Advanced Notice of Proposed Rulemaking*, the FRB solicited comments on whether it should modify the knowledge/reasonable notice standard. 63 Fed. Reg. 12,326 (Mar. 12, 1998).

The FRB chose to retain the present standard, however, stating "that it is not possible to specify with particularity the circumstances under which a creditor may or may not be liable for a violation committed by another creditor." 64 Fed. Reg. at 44,590.

On the other hand, the FRB stated that under some circumstances the reasonable notice standard may carry with it the need for a creditor to exercise some degree of diligence with respect to third parties' involvement in credit decisions. *Id.*

The Consumer Financial Protection Bureau (CFPB) now has authority to issue Regulation B. *See* § 1.3.2.8, *supra.*

155 Reg. B, 12 C.F.R. § 1002.2(*l*) [§ 202.2(*l*)].

156 *Id.*; *see* § 2.2.5.4, *supra.*

157 For a government enforcement action alleging liability of a lender at least in part for the actions of its brokers, see Settlement Agreement and Order, United States v. Long Beach Mortgage Co., No. CV 96-6159 (C.D. Cal. Sept. 5, 1996), *available on the companion website to this treatise.*

158 Fourth Amended Complaint, Coleman v. Gen. Motors Acceptance Corp., No. 3-98-0211 (M.D. Tenn. Aug. 9, 2000), *available on the companion website to this treatise*; Fourth Amended Complaint, Cason v. Nissan Motor Acceptance Corp., No. 3-98-0223 (M.D. Tenn. June 9, 2000), *available on the companion website to this treatise*; *see* § 8.6, *infra.*

The GMAC and NMAC litigation paved the way for similar cases against auto financers. *See* § 8.6.2, *infra.*

159 Coleman v. Gen. Motors Acceptance Corp., 196 F.R.D. 315 (M.D. Tenn. 2000), *class certification vacated and remanded on unrelated grounds by* 296 F.3d 443 (6th Cir. 2002), *on remand,* Coleman v. Gen. Motors Acceptance Corp., 220 F.R.D. 64 (M.D. Tenn. 2004); *see also* Smith v. Chrysler Financial Co., 2003 WL 328719 (D.N.J. Jan. 15, 2003); Osborne v. Bank of America, 234 F. Supp. 2d 804 (M.D. Tenn. 2002); Wide *ex rel* Estate of Wilson v. Union Acceptance Corp., 2002 WL 31730920 (S.D. Ind. Nov. 19, 2002) (allowing plaintiffs to maintain action against lender directly as a creditor); Jones v. Ford Motor Credit Co., 2002 WL 1334812 (S.D.N.Y. June 17, 2002), *vacated,* 358 F.3d 205 (2d Cir. N.Y. 2004) (vacating district court judgment that dismissed car company's counterclaims and remanding to district court to rule on class certification and on supplemental jurisdiction over counterclaims), *on remand,* 2004 WL 1586412 (S.D.N.Y. July 15, 2004).

However, a creditor who purchased a mortgage at a trustee's sale and was not alleged to have been involved in the transaction at the time of the application was found not to be a creditor regarding violations that may have occurred at the time of the application.[160]

2.2.5.6 The Government As Creditor

Transactions in which credit is extended *by* a government or a governmental subdivision, agency, or instrumentality are subject to the provisions of the ECOA and Regulation B,[161] except that no action can be brought against a governmental creditor for the recovery of punitive damages.[162] However, if a government agency is operating a special purpose credit program, it is exempted from provisions of the ECOA and Regulation B that relate specifically to the program's special purpose.[163]

When a governmental agency, such as the Federal Deposit Insurance Corp. (FDIC) or the Resolution Trust Corp. (RTC), takes over a bank, the ECOA still applies. Under the doctrine of *D'Oench Duhme & Co. v. Federal Deposit Insurance Corp.*,[164] as partially codified in 12 U.S.C. § 1823(e), defenses based on unrecorded side agreements are not available. However, an ECOA violation may be apparent on the face of the bank's records (for example, requirement of a spouse's signature when the credit application shows the applicant is creditworthy). Thus, courts agree that an ECOA violation may be raised against the RTC or the FDIC either as a special defense of illegality or as a counterclaim for damages.[165]

Some government agencies extend credit directly to consumer or business applicants, and the ECOA applies to those transactions.[166] In 1999, a consent decree was approved and entered against the United States Department of Agriculture (USDA) in a class action case alleging systemic discrimination against African-American farmers who sought or obtained farm loans from the USDA.[167] The initial lawsuit was barred under the two-year statute of limitations under the ECOA, but Congress passed special legislation to waive the limit.[168] The extension of time applied to African-American farmers who had filed a discrimination complaint unrelated to employment against the USDA between 1981 and 1997.[169] Persons to whom

---

160 *See* Permpoon v. Wells Fargo Bank, 2009 WL 3214321 (S.D. Cal. Sept. 29, 2009).

161 Moore v. United States Dep't of Agric., 55 F.3d 991, 994 (5th Cir. 1995) (ECOA contains a waiver of United States sovereign immunity); *see also* Sanders v. Vilsack, 2009 WL 1370919, at *5 (M.D. Ga. May 14, 2009). *But see* The Cowtown Found., Inc. v. Beshear, 2010 WL 3340831, at *2–3 (W.D. Ky. Aug. 20, 2010) (ECOA does not abrogate state sovereign immunity to permit suit against a state creditor for ECOA violations).

162 15 U.S.C. § 1691e(b).

163 *See* § 3.8, *infra*; *see also* Moore v. United States Dep't of Agric., 55 F.3d 991, 995 (5th Cir. 1995).

164 315 U.S. 447, 62 S. Ct. 676, 86 L. Ed. 956 (1942).

165 CMF Va. Land, Ltd. P'ship v. Brinson, 806 F. Supp. 90 (E.D. Va. 1992); Diamond v. Union Bank & Trust, 776 F. Supp. 542 (N.D. Okla. 1991); Fed. Deposit Ins. Corp. v. Allen, 1988 U.S. Dist. LEXIS 17565 (W.D. Okla. Nov. 3, 1988).

166 *See, e.g.*, Robinson v. Schafer, 305 Fed. Appx. 629 (11th Cir. 2008) (the ECOA applies to the federal government through the definition of creditor); Chiang v. Schafer, 2008 WL 3925260 (D. V.I. Aug. 20, 2008) (United States Department of Agriculture is a creditor under the ECOA); *see also* Ivy v. United States Dep't of Agric., 2010 WL 2559885, at *2–4 (N.D. Miss. June 23, 2010) (United States district court has subject matter jurisdiction over claims against Department of Agriculture, but complaint fails to state a claim of discrimination in violation of ECOA).

---

167 Pigford v. Glickman, 185 F.R.D. 82 (D.D.C. 1999) (consent decree), *aff'd*, 206 F.3d 1212 (D.C. Cir. 2000).

The decree did not contain any provisions to prevent future discrimination. *See generally* Monica M. Clark, *So Near, Yet So Far: The Past, Present, and Future of the Complaints Process Within the USDA*, 32 S.U. L. Rev. 139 (2005).

This settlement was challenged by non-African-American farmers in Green v. Veneman, 159 F. Supp. 2d 360 (S.D. Miss. 2001), *aff'd in part*, 46 Fed. Appx. 731 (5th Cir. 2002).

The court in *Green* upheld the *Pigford* settlement on the basis that the non-African-American farmers were not similarly situated to the *Pigford* class members. The consent decree in *Pigford* allowed class members to choose between two claims procedures. Track A awarded $50,000 to farmers able to meet only minimal burdens of proof of discriminatory treatment or damages. Track B imposed no cap on damages but, after limited discovery, required farmers to prove claims by a preponderance of evidence in one-day mini-trials before an arbitrator. The strict time frames for filing Track B hearings have been challenged due to problems with the class counsel appointed to represent clients in the decree implementation phase. *See* Pigford v. Veneman, 292 F.3d 918 (D.C. Cir. 2002); Haynie v. Veneman, 272 F. Supp. 2d 10 (D.D.C. 2003) (loan applicant entitled to amend complaint in action against the USDA alleging racial discrimination against her and her husband and discrimination in retaliation to their participation in civil rights activities); *see also* Pigford v. Veneman, 416 F.3d 12 (D.C. Cir. 2005).

Similar cases alleging discrimination in the USDA farm lending program have also been filed on behalf of Latino farmers: Garcia v. Veneman, 211 F.R.D. 15 (D.D.C. 2002); female and other farmers, Love v. Veneman, No. 00-2502 (D.D.C. filed Oct. 19, 2000); Native-American farmers, *In re* Veneman, 309 F.3d 789 (D.C. Cir. 2002) (petition for review of District Court's decision to grant class certification for equitable relief only denied), Keepseagle v. Veneman, No. 99-3119 (D.D.C. 2001); and older farmers, Jones v. Glickman, 42 Fed. Appx. 292 (10th Cir. 2002) (an individual claim against the USDA based on alleged age discrimination was found to be untimely); *see also* Chiang v. Veneman, 213 F.R.D. 256 (D. V.I 2003), *aff'd in part, vacated in part*, 385 F.3d 256 (3d Cir. 2004) (class certification granted in case alleging race, gender, and national origin discrimination in the Rural Housing Service's administration of programs in the United States Virgin Islands). *But see* Chiang v. Schafer, 2008 WL 3925260 (D. V.I. Jan. 28, 2008) (case filed outside of two-year statute of limitations under ECOA, and section 741 exception did not apply; plaintiffs failed to establish a prima facie case of a pattern or practice of national origin discrimination).

168 *See* Agricultural, Rural Dev., Food and Drug Administration, and Related Agencies Appropriation Act, Pub. L. No. 105-277, § 741, 112 Stat. 2681 (1999) (interim rule codified at 7 U.S.C. § 2297).

169 *See, e.g.*, Stovall v. Veneman, 394 F. Supp. 2d 21 (D.D.C. 2005) (rejecting plaintiff African-American farmer's claim to extend ECOA statute of limitations because he did not file complaint until 2004 and his claims were based on events that occurred between 1999 and 2001); *see also* Bell v. Schafer, 2009 WL 2182170, at *2 (E.D. Mo. July 22, 2009) (rejecting African-American farmer's claim to

the waiver applied were given the option to proceed directly in federal court[170] or, alternatively, to seek an administrative determination of the merits of their complaints by the USDA and then to obtain judicial review in federal court if their claims were denied administratively. Persons who chose to proceed administratively were required to exhaust administrative remedies before going to federal court.[171]

The class included approximately 20,000 members. Among other charges, the class alleged that the Farm Service Agency, an agency within the USDA, routinely discouraged applications from some farmers, delayed processing their applications, or denied applications for credit and benefits on a discriminatory basis.[172] In a March 2003 decision, the district court for the District of Columbia affirmed that those individuals who did not opt out of the *Pigford* class and who pursued their claims under the *Pigford* consent decree could not later raise claims that they raised or could have raised in *Pigford*.[173] However, *Pigford* class members were free to file new cases based on later acts of discrimination.[174] Several *Pigford* plaintiffs have filed subsequent actions to interpret and enforce the terms of the consent decree.[175]

Plaintiffs who chose to proceed in federal court could not sue under the Administrative Procedure Act for the USDA's past failure to process their claims as the ECOA provided them an adequate remedy.[176] Plaintiffs who chose to file administratively, and had the administrative law judge's finding of ECOA violations overturned by the USDA's Assistant Secretary for Civil Rights, could not obtain relief in federal court as the court was required to give substantial deference to the agency's interpretation of its own regulations.[177] In 2010 the USDA agreed to pay $1.25 billion to resolve outstanding claims.[178]

---

extend statute of limitations because he did not file complaint until 2008 and alleged discrimination occurred between 1970 and 1994).

170 Cases were to be brought in the district court for the District of Columbia. Allen v. Schafer, 2009 WL 2245220, at *3 (N.D. Miss. July 27, 2009).

171 Benoit v. United States Dep't of Agric., 577 F. Supp. 2d 12, 23 (D.D.C. 2008), *aff'd*, 608 F.3d 17, 23–24 (D.C. Cir. 2010).

172 *See generally* Stephen Carpenter, *Discrimination in Agricultural Lending*, 33 Clearinghouse Rev. 166 (1999).

173 Wise v. Glickman, 257 F. Supp. 2d 123 (D.D.C. 2003).

174 *Id.* at 130; *see* Young v. U.S. Dep't of Agric., 2011 WL 864977, at *3 (W.D. Ky. Mar. 11, 2011) (denying motion to dismiss based on claim preclusion when case brought on bases independent of *Pigford*).

175 *See, e.g.*, Pigford v. Schafer, 536 F. Supp. 2d 1 (D.D.C. 2008); Pigford v. Conner, 2007 WL 4545851 (D.D.C. Dec. 21, 2007).

176 *See* Garcia v. Vilsack, 563 F.3d 519, 523–24 (D.C. Cir. 2009), *cert. denied*, 78 U.S.L.W. 3131 (U.S. 2010).

177 *See* Wilkinson v. Vilsack, 666 F. Supp. 2d 118, 121–22 (D.D.C. 2009).

178 Press Release, United States Dep't of Agric., USDA and Department of Justice Announce Historic Settlement in Lawsuit by Black Farmers Claiming Discrimination by USDA (Feb. 18, 2010), *available at* www.usda.gov/wps/portal/usda/usdahome?contentidonly= true&contentid=2010/02/0072.xml.

2.2.6 Transactions Partially Exempted from the ECOA

2.2.6.1 General

Regulation B creates *partial* exemptions from ECOA coverage for five classes of credit: public utility credit, incidental consumer credit, business credit, securities credit, and credit extended to the government. It is important to realize that these are *partial* exemptions applicable to procedural ECOA requirements and that these partially exempt creditors must still comply with *all* other ECOA requirements. In every case, the general rule prohibiting discrimination against applicants on a prohibited basis applies to these five special forms of credit.[179]

Broader exemptions in effect at one time have since been repealed[180] and replaced by the current, partial exemptions.[181]

---

179 Official Interpretations of Reg. B [Official Staff Commentary on Reg. B], 12 C.F.R. pt. 1002 [pt. 202], Supp. I, § 1002.3-1 [§ 202.3-1].

180 There was considerable controversy over whether the Federal Reserve Board had the authority to exempt certain transactions from the ECOA, particularly with respect to public utility and incidental credit. The Women's Business Ownership Act of 1988 changed the standards as to when and how the Board could create exemptions. Pub. L. No. 100-533, § 301, 102 Stat. 2689, 2692 (1988).

181 The Federal Reserve Board (FRB) then reissued its regulations creating these exemptions under this new authority, essentially rendering moot the issue as to whether the FRB had the authority to issue the regulations *pre-1988*. There were two reasons that the old exemptions were controversial. First, there was an issue as to whether the ECOA allowed the FRB to make exemptions relating to consumer transactions, specifically its exemptions for incidental consumer credit and public utility credit. Read literally, the language of the statute precluded any regulatory authority to carve out exemptions in the consumer area. "[S]uch regulations may exempt from one or more provisions of [ECOA] any class of transactions *not primarily for personal, family, or household purposes. . . .*" 15 U.S.C. § 1691b(a) (1976) (emphasis added).

Transactions primarily for personal, family, or household purposes are consumer credit. *See* Reg. B, 12 C.F.R. § 202.3(g) (1975) (12 C.F.R. § 1002.2(h) under the CFPB); *see also* Truth in Lending Act, 15 U.S.C. § 1602.

Secondly, it is also arguable that none of the exemptions were promulgated in a manner that complied with the statutory directives as to the proper procedure and standards to be used in creating them. In passing the Women's Business Ownership Act of 1988, Congress severely criticized the FRB for failure to comply with the statute when it created the then-existing business credit exemptions. The House Report accompanying the amendments notes that, contrary to the specific requirements of the Act, "[the FRB never made the required] 'express finding' that application of the Act's provisions would not further the goals and purposes of the Act. No such findings have ever been made, nor evidence presented to support the special treatment accorded by Regulation 'B' to business credit transactions." H.R. Rep. No. 100-955, at 15–16, *reprinted in* 1988 U.S.C.C.A.N. 3535, 3544.

As the same procedure and standards were used to create all the original exemptions, then by this report's standards none of them were created in compliance with the statute.

2.2.6.2 Public Utility Credit

Regulation B contains a very limited exemption for public utility credit. While public utilities must comply with most ECOA provisions, they need not comply with the following provisions of Regulation B:

- Section 1002.5(d)(1) [section 202.5(d)(1)], which forbids requests by creditors for information on marital status except in defined situations; and
- Section 1002.12(b) [section 202.12(b)], which requires creditors to retain records of credit applications for a prescribed period of time.[182]

All other provisions of the ECOA and Regulation B apply, including other provisions related to discrimination based on marital status.[183]

Prior to the 2003 amendments, there was an additional exemption from section 202.10 (section 1002.10 under the CFPB), which concerned reporting of credit information in the names of both spouses.[184] In response to concerns of commentators about eliminating this exemption, it was clarified that the reporting requirement applies only to creditors that furnish information to reporting agencies. In these circumstances, utilities are now required to furnish information that reflects the participation of both spouses.[185]

The exemption from complying with sections 1002.5(d)(1) [section 202.5(d)(1)] and 1002.12(b) [section 202.12(b)] apply *only* to the provision of service by a public utility and thus do not apply to certain other utilities and other utility practices. The exemption applies only to utilities whose charges are filed with or regulated by a governmental unit.[186] Thus the exemption does not apply to rural electric cooperatives or other unregulated utilities.[187] Municipal utilities are generally unregu-

lated and should be outside the exclusion unless the government ownership of the utility is deemed sufficient to find that charges are filed with a government unit. The exemption also does not apply to a telephone company that is not regulated by a government unit and that does not file its charges for service, delayed payment, or discount for prompt payment with a government unit.[188]

The utility exemption applies only to credit related to utility service. If even a regulated utility grants credit for purposes other than utility service, such as for financing the purchase of a gas dryer, telephone equipment, or other durable goods or for insulation or other home improvements, then the ECOA is fully operative.[189] However, if the utility exemption does not apply, the transaction may still be exempt under the incidental consumer credit exemption.[190]

2.2.6.3 Incidental Consumer Credit

2.2.6.3.1 Definition of incidental consumer credit

Regulation B provides a limited exemption for "incidental consumer credit." Incidental consumer credit is defined as:[191]

- Primarily for personal, family, or household purposes;
- Not made pursuant to the terms of a credit card account;
- Not subject to any finance charge; and
- Not payable by agreement in more than four installments.[192]

In addition, the incidental credit category explicitly does not include public utilities or securities credit,[193] which are separately exempted from certain provisions of the ECOA.[194]

This definition in part mimics the scope of the federal Truth in Lending Act (TILA), which only applies to transactions involving a finance charge, more than four installments, or a credit card. While the ECOA is substantially broader in scope than the TILA, the scope of *certain* ECOA provisions has in

---

182 Reg. B, 12 C.F.R. § 1002.3(a)(2)(ii) [§ 202.3(a)(2)(ii)].

   The public utility exemption was republished for review without proposed change as a result of the 1988 Women's Business Ownership Act amendments. 54 Fed. Reg. 29,734 (July 14, 1989).

   It was subsequently readopted. 54 Fed. Reg. 50,482 (Dec. 7, 1989).

183 *See, e.g.*, McGee v. East Ohio Gas Co., 111 F. Supp. 2d 979 (S.D. Ohio 2000) (defendant utility's summary judgment motion denied when plaintiff alleged marital status discrimination based on utility's conditioning of wife's account on payment of arrearages owed by her husband only on a previous account), *later op. at* 200 F.R.D. 382 (S.D. Ohio 2001) (granting class certification under Fed. R. Civ. P. 23(b)(2)).

184 68 Fed. Reg. 13,144, 13,145–46 (Mar. 18, 2003).

185 *Id.*; *see* § 9.4, *infra*.

186 Reg. B, 12 C.F.R. § 1002.3(a)(1) [§ 202.3(a)(1)]; *see, e.g.*, Mays v. Buckeye Rural Electric Coop., Inc., 277 F.3d 873 (6th Cir. 2002) (finding no public utilities credit when rural electric cooperative was not required to file rates with any government entity; however, transaction was considered incidental credit and therefore exempt from certain ECOA provisions).

187 As deregulation/restructuring of the electric industry unfolds around the country, it is likely that these exemptions will no longer apply to electric utilities or that only part of a utility's services will be exempted. However, resolution of the exemption's application will depend largely on what, if anything, still has to be filed with or

regulated by a government unit or even what it means to be "filed." In any event, these are issues that vary from state to state and should be examined on a case-by-case basis. *See* National Consumer Law Center, Access to Utility Service § 5.2.2 (5th ed. 2011 and Supp.); National Consumer Law Center, Truth in Lending § 2.4.6 (8th ed. 2012).

188 Official Interpretations of Reg. B [Official Staff Commentary on Reg. B], 12 C.F.R. pt. 1002 [pt. 202], Supp. I, [§ 1002.3(a)-3 [§ 202.3(a)-3].

189 *Id.* § 1002.3(a)-1 [§ 202.3(a)-1].

190 *See, e.g.*, Mays v. Buckeye Rural Electric Coop., Inc., 277 F.3d 873 (6th Cir. 2002) (finding no public utilities credit when rural electric cooperative was not required to file rates with any government entity; however, transaction was considered incidental credit and therefore exempt from certain ECOA provisions); *see also* § 2.2.6.3, *infra*.

191 Reg. B, 12 C.F.R. § 1002.3(c) [§ 202.3(c)]; *see also* Reg. B, 12 C.F.R. § 1002.2(b) [§ 202.2(b)]; Official Interpretations of Reg. B [Official Staff Commentary on Reg. B], 12 C.F.R. pt. 1002 [pt. 202], Supp. I, § 1002.3(c)-1 [§ 202.3(c)-1].

192 Reg. B, 12 C.F.R. § 1002.3(c)(1) [§ 202.3(c)(1)].

193 *Id.*

194 *See* § 2.2.6.2, *supra*; § 2.2.6.5, *infra*.

effect been limited through regulation to the scope of the TILA.[195]

Typical examples of incidental consumer credit may include (depending on whether there is a finance charge or more than four installments) deferment of payment by doctors, home heating oil companies, lawyers, hospitals, and some small retailers.[196]

2.2.6.3.2 Exemptions applicable to incidental credit

The following requirements of Regulation B do not apply to incidental consumer credit:[197]

- Section 1002.5(c) [section 202.5(c)], which limits inquiries about the applicant's spouse or former spouse;
- Section 1002.5(d)(1) [section 202.5(d)(1)], which forbids requests by creditors for information on marital status except in defined situations;
- Section 1002.5(d)(2) [section 202.5(d)(2)], which limits inquiries about income derived from alimony, child support, and separate maintenance payments;
- Section 1002.5(d)(3) [section 202.5(d)(3)], which forbids inquiries about the applicant's sex;[198]
- Section 1002.7(d) [section 202.7(d)], which restricts the circumstances in which creditors may request the signature of a co-signer;
- Section 1002.9 [section 202.9], which requires notification of adverse action, reasons for the action, and ECOA rights;
- Section 1002.10 [section 202.10], which concerns reporting of credit information in the names of both spouses; and
- Section 1002.12(b) [section 202.12(b)], which requires creditors to retain records of credit applications for a prescribed period of time.

All other ECOA provisions apply to incidental consumer credit, including the general prohibition against discrimination.[199]

The Regulation B exclusions for incidental consumer credit (and TILA's similar exclusion) has led some not-so-incidental creditors to restructure their business so as to avoid many ECOA procedural requirements (and TILA entirely).

For example, there are "ninety-day same as cash" transactions in which the seller may hide the finance charge in a higher selling price. As this arrangement is incidental consumer credit, the creditor can avoid the ECOA's general prohibition against requiring a spouse to co-sign such a purchase agreement. A great many such contracts are assigned to finance companies which then, at the end of ninety days, "flip" that contract (which has the signatures of both spouses) into a loan with a finance charge, thereby ushering the non-applicant spouse into a credit obligation through the back door.

2.2.6.4 Business Credit

The ECOA applies to business credit. Partial exemptions had been granted to credit extended primarily for business and commercial purposes,[200] but the Women's Business Ownership Act of 1988[201] amended the ECOA to limit the Federal Reserve Board's ability to make such exemptions. The FRB, in response, deleted or altered each of those exemptions to ensure that small business owners were given procedural rights more in line with those available to consumer borrowers.[202]

As it now stands, business credit is subject to different procedural standards in areas such as notice and recordkeeping,[203] and the requirement that the reporting of credit information be in the names of both spouses applies only to consumer credit and not to business credit.[204] In deciding whether an application is for business or consumer credit, the primary purpose controls.[205] For example, if a consumer purchases a

---

195 The numerous Truth in Lending cases that discuss finance charges and the four-installment rule are useful in ECOA cases involving this issue. *See* National Consumer Law Center, Truth in Lending § 2.3.4 (8th ed. 2012).

196 *See* Official Interpretations of Reg. B [Official Staff Commentary on Reg. B], 12 C.F.R. pt. 1002 [pt. 202], Supp. I, § 1002.3(c)-1 [§ 202.3(c)-1]; *see also* Mays v. Buckeye Rural Electric Coop., Inc., 277 F.3d 873 (6th Cir. 2002); Williams v. AT & T Wireless Servs., Inc., 5 F. Supp. 2d 1142 (W.D. Wash. 1998) (application for cellular telephone service is a credit transaction but qualifies for the incidental credit exception to the ECOA notice requirement).

197 Reg. B, 12 C.F.R. § 1002.3(c)(a) [§ 202.3(c)(a)].

   The incidental consumer credit exemption was republished for review without proposed change as a result of the 1988 Women's Business Ownership Act amendments. 54 Fed. Reg. 29,734 (July 14, 1989).

   It was subsequently readopted. 54 Fed. Reg. 50,482 (Dec. 7, 1989).

198 This exemption applies only to the extent that the information is necessary for medical records or similar purposes.

199 Official Interpretations of Reg. B [Official Staff Commentary on Reg. B], 12 C.F.R. pt. 1002 [pt. 202], Supp. I, § 1002.3-1 [§ 202.3-1].

200 Reg. B, 12 C.F.R. § 202.3(d) (1985) (this section was deleted in the 1989 revisions); Official Staff Commentary to Reg. B, 12 C.F.R. pt. 202, Supp. I, § 202.3(d)-1 (this section was deleted in the 1990 revisions).

201 Pub. L. No. 100-533, § 301, 102 Stat. 2689, 2692 (1988).

202 *See* Supplementary Information, 54 Fed. Reg. 50,482 (Dec. 7, 1989); *see also* Cherry v. D.B. Swirn Special Opportunities Fund, 2010 WL 41313, at *5 (M.D. Fla. Jan. 27, 2010) (finding application for business credit to be within the two-year statute of limitations for continuing violations under the ECOA, but dismissing case on other grounds), *aff'd*, 433 Fed. Appx. 870 (11th Cir. 2011).

   The Federal Reserve Board proposed extending the incidental credit exception to incidental business credit as well. 64 Fed. Reg. 44,582, 44,595 (Aug. 16, 1999) (proposing to amend 12 C.F.R. § 202.3(c)(1)].

   In final rules announced in 2003, the Board decided not to adopt this proposal. 68 Fed. Reg. 13,144, 13,146 (Mar. 18, 2003). In explaining its decision, the Board cited concerns about possible discrimination against minority-owned businesses.

203 *See* § 10.9.2, *infra* (notification of adverse action).

204 Official Interpretations of Reg. B [Official Staff Commentary on Reg. B], 12 C.F.R. pt. 1002 [pt. 202], Supp. I, § 1002.10-1 [§ 202.10-1].

205 Official Interpretations of Reg. B [Official Staff Commentary on Reg. B], 12 C.F.R. pt. 1002 [pt. 202], Supp. I, § 1002.2(g)-1 [§ 202.2(g)-1].

   Truth in Lending also uses the primary purpose test, and cases interpreting that provision may provide useful guidance. *E.g.*, Gallegos v. Stokes, 593 F.2d 372 (10th Cir. 1979); Redhouse v. Quality Ford Sales, Inc., 523 F.2d 1 (10th Cir. 1975) (en banc) (per curiam)

pick-up truck primarily for consumer use but also for occasional business use, the transaction involves consumer credit.

2.2.6.5 Securities Credit

A partial exemption from Regulation B is provided for extensions of credit subject to regulation by the Securities Exchange Act of 1934 or offered by a broker or dealer under that Act.[206] The following specific provisions of Regulation B are not applicable to securities credit transactions:[207]

- Section 1002.5(c) [section 202.5(c)], which limits inquiries about the applicant's spouse or former spouse;
- Section 1002.5(d)(1) [section 202.5(d)(1)], which forbids requests by creditors for information on marital status except in defined situations;
- Section 1002.5(d)(3) [section 202.5(d)(3)], which forbids inquiries about the applicant's sex;
- Section 1002.7(b) [section 202.7(b)], which requires creditors to allow applicants to open or maintain accounts in various combinations of first names and surnames;[208]
- Section 1002.7(c) [section 202.7(c)], which limits the circumstances under which creditors may require reapplication, change terms, or terminate an existing open-end credit account;[209]
- Section 1002.7(d) [section 202.7(d)], which restricts the circumstances in which creditors may request the signature of a co-signer;
- Section 1002.10 [section 202.10], which concerns reporting of credit information in the names of both spouses; and
- Section 1002.12(b) [section 202.12(b)], which requires creditors to retain records of credit applications for a prescribed period of time.

All other provisions of the ECOA and Regulation B apply.[210]

2.2.6.6 Credit Extended to the Government

Regulation B has exempted from ECOA procedural requirements transactions in which credit is extended *to* governments or governmental subdivisions, agencies, or instrumentalities. The only provision of the ECOA and Regulation B applicable to such transactions is the general rule forbidding discrimination against credit applicants on a prohibited basis.[211]

It is important to note that this exemption is only for credit extended *to* a government agency, which is not the same as credit extended *by* a housing agency or some other government agency to a consumer or business.[212] The application of the ECOA to the government as a creditor is discussed in § 2.2.5.6, *supra*.

2.3 Scope of the Fair Housing Act

2.3.1 Overview

Three different provisions of the Fair Housing Act may apply to credit discrimination. The first Fair Housing Act provision covering credit discrimination (42 U.S.C. § 3605) applies to "residential real estate-related transactions." A second Fair Housing Act provision (42 U.S.C. § 3604) covering credit discrimination applies to the sale, rental, or advertising of dwellings. The third relevant provision (42 U.S.C. § 3617) provides that it is unlawful to coerce, intimidate, threaten, or interfere with the exercise or enjoyment of various rights granted or protected by the Fair Housing Act, including the rights set forth in sections 3604 and 3605.

The discussion that follows analyzes the differing scope of each of these provisions. Because section 3605 most clearly applies to housing-related lending, it is discussed first. The next subsection reviews the provisions of section 3604, focusing on whether the various provisions of this section are likely to apply to housing-related lending. The implications of a court's limiting housing-related lending claims to section 3605 are also covered in this subsection. The final subsection includes information about section 3617 of the Act.

2.3.2 Residential Real Estate-Related Transactions: Scope of Section 3605

2.3.2.1 General

Section 3605 of the Fair Housing Act prohibits discrimination in "residential real estate-related transactions."[213] Residential real estate-related transactions are defined to include the making or purchasing of loans or the provision of other financial assistance:

- For purchasing, constructing, improving, repairing or maintaining a dwelling,[214] or
- Secured by residential real estate.[215]

(superseding 511 F.2d 230 (10th Cir. 1975)); Smith v. Chapman, 436 F. Supp. 58 (W.D. Tex. 1977). *See generally* National Consumer Law Center, Truth in Lending § 2.4.2.1 (8th ed. 2012).

206 Reg. B, 12 C.F.R. § 1002.3(b) [§ 202.3(b)].
    The securities exemption was republished for review without proposed change as a result of the 1988 Women's Business Ownership Act amendments. 54 Fed. Reg. 29,734 (July 14, 1989).

207 Reg. B, 12 C.F.R. § 1002.3(b)(2) [§ 202.3(b)(2)].

208 This exemption is effective only to the extent necessary to prevent the violation of rules concerning accounts in which a broker or dealer has an interest or necessitating the aggregation of spouse's accounts.

209 This exemption is effective only to the extent that such action is taken following a change in the account holder's name or marital status.

210 Official Interpretations of Reg. B [Official Staff Commentary on Reg. B], 12 C.F.R. pt. 1002 [pt. 202], Supp. I, § 1002.3-1 [§ 202.3-1].

211 Reg. B, 12 C.F.R. § 1002.3(d) [§ 202.3(d)].

212 Official Interpretations of Reg. B [Official Staff Commentary on Reg. B], 12 C.F.R. pt. 1002 [pt. 202], Supp. I, § 1002.3(d)-1 [§ 202.3(d)-1].

213 42 U.S.C. § 3605.

214 42 U.S.C. § 3605(b)(1)(A).

215 42 U.S.C. § 3605(b)(1)(B).

Residential real estate-related transactions also include the selling, brokering, or appraising of residential real property.[216]

2.3.2.2 Transactions Covered by Section 3605

2.3.2.2.1 *Loans and other financial assistance used to buy, improve, repair, or maintain a dwelling*

Section 3605 applies to any loan or other financial assistance used to purchase, build, improve, repair, or maintain a dwelling.[217] The loan does not have to come from the entity doing the selling, building, or improving. The loan does not have to be secured by the dwelling.

For example, the Fair Housing Act (FHA) applies to a mortgage to purchase a home, a loan to purchase building materials, a loan to finance a home improvement contract, or a loan to pay for plumbers, roofers, carpenters, electricians, and even carpet cleaners or window washers. The Act should apply if a home owner obtains a $500 unsecured loan from a finance company to buy some paint, wood, and other items that the home owner intends to use to spruce up his or her home. Arguably, the Act would apply even to loans to purchase refrigerators, sinks, stoves, or other appliances necessary to improve or maintain a dwelling.

The loan must be used to purchase, improve, or maintain a dwelling. The term "dwelling" is broadly construed. A dwelling is defined as any structure or portion of a structure that is occupied or intended to be occupied as a *residence* by one or more families and any vacant land offered for sale or lease for the construction or location of such a structure.[218]

The term "residence" is not defined in the Act. Courts have generally found that residence means either a temporary or permanent dwelling place to which one intends to return.[219]

Although this category generally does not include transient dwelling places, the line is not always clear. Places such as homeless shelters and halfway houses have been held to be "residences" for purposes of the Act.[220] With respect to housing for seniors, the Act has been held to cover (1) all types of "independent living" units, including condominiums, cooperatives, manufactured home parks and various other age-restrictive residences;[221] (2) all types of "assisted living" units, including those in age-restricted communities;[222] and (3) all types of residential units in age-restricted retirement communities, including cottages, townhouses, and apartments.[223] The issue is less clear with respect to nursing homes, although a number of courts have applied the Act to these facilities.[224]

As the Act does not specify who must live or intend to live in a building for it to be considered a dwelling, a plaintiff does not have to live in a building in order to bring a claim under the Act.[225] Therefore, a dwelling may include a residence the

---

216 42 U.S.C. § 3605(b)(2); *see also* Frederick v. Select Portfolio Servicing, Inc., 2009 WL 230597, at *5 (N.D. Ill. Jan. 30, 2009) (defendant's sale of plaintiff's home at sheriff's sale constitutes residential real estate-related transaction).

217 42 U.S.C. § 3605(b)(1); *see* 24 C.F.R. § 100.115(a).

218 42 U.S.C. § 3602(b); 24 C.F.R. § 100.20.
 The definition of "dwelling" applies to other sections of the FHA as well. *See also* Schwarz v. City of Treasure Island, 544 F.3d 1201, 1213 (11th Cir. 2008) (halfway houses qualify as dwellings under the FHA); Lakeside Resort Enters., Ltd. P'ship v. Bd. of Supervisors of Palmyra Twp., 455 F.3d 154, 158 (3d Cir. 2006) (describing factors that determine whether a facility is a dwelling for purposes of the FHA). *But see* JAT, Inc. v. Nat'l City Bank of Midwest, 460 F. Supp. 2d 812, 819 (E.D. Mich. 2006) (dismissing FHA claim when loan transaction did not involve a dwelling).

219 *See, e.g.,* United States v. Columbus Country Club, 915 F.2d 877, 881 (3d Cir. 1990) (seasonal bungalows used by annual members who returned each year for five months at a time fell within the meaning of the statute); Lauer v. Waushara Cnty. Bd. of Adjustment, 986 F. Supp. 544 (E.D. Wis. 1997) (migrant worker housing); The Tara Circle, Inc. v. Bifano, 1997 U.S. Dist. LEXIS 10153 (S.D.N.Y. July 15, 1997) (citing Hovsons, Inc. v. Township of Brick, 89 F.3d 1096, 1102 (3d. Cir. 1996)); Woods v. Foster, 884 F. Supp. 1169, 1173 (N.D. Ill. 1995) (homeless shelter determined to be a "residence"); United States v. Hughes Mem'l Home, 396 F. Supp. 544 (W.D. Va. 1975) (home for needy children, although not

intended as a permanent home, was a residence within the meaning of the Act).

220 *See* Schwarz v. City of Treasure Island, 544 F.3d 1201, 1213 (11th Cir. 2008) (halfway houses qualify as dwellings under the FHA); Woods v. Foster, 884 F. Supp. 1169, 1173 (N.D. Ill. 1995).

221 *See, e.g.,* Elderhaven, Inc. v. Lubbock, 98 F.3d 175 (5th Cir. 1996) (applying the FHA to shared living residence for older disabled persons). *See generally* Robert G. Schwemm & Michael Allen, *For the Rest of Their Lives: Seniors and the Fair Housing Act*, 90 Iowa L. Rev. 121 (2004).

222 *See, e.g.,* Lapid-Laurel, L.L.C. v. Zoning Bd. Of Adjustment, 284 F.3d 442 (3d Cir. 2002) (parties agreed that ninety-five-bed care facility for older persons is a "dwelling" under the FHA); Smith & Lee Assocs., Inc. v. Taylor, Mich., 102 F.3d 781 (6th Cir. 1996); Town & Country Adult Living, Inc. v. Mount Kisco, 2003 WL 21219794 (S.D.N.Y. May 21, 2003) (assuming the FHA applies to assisted-living residence for disabled older citizens); United States v. Lorantffy Care Ctr., 999 F. Supp. 1037 (N.D. Ohio 1998).

223 *See, e.g.,* Fair Hous. in Huntington v. Huntington, 316 F.3d 357 (2d Cir. 2003); Eastern Paralyzed Veterans v. Lazarus-Burman Assocs., 133 F. Supp. 2d 203 (E.D.N.Y. 2001); United States v. Hillhaven Corp., 960 F. Supp. 259 (D. Utah 1997); United States v. Forest Dale, Inc., 818 F. Supp. 954 (N.D. Tex. 1993). *See generally* Michael Allen & Robert G. Schwemm, *For the Rest of Their Lives: Seniors and the Fair Housing Act*, 90 Iowa L. Rev. 121 (2004) (noting that, even though it would seem to be clear that all assisted-living and retirement communities are covered by the FHA, there is a good deal of evidence that providers of such housing often behave as if they are exempt).

224 *See, e.g.,* Lapid-Laurel L.L.C. v. Zoning Bd. Of Adjustment, 284 F.3d 442 (3d Cir. 2002) (parties agreed that a nursing home for older individuals was a "dwelling"); Hovsons, Inc. v. Township of Brick, 89 F.3d 1096 (3d Cir. 1996); Caron v. Pawtucket, 307 F. Supp. 2d 364 (D.R.I. 2004); United States v. Puerto Rico, 764 F. Supp. 220 (D. P.R. 1991). *See generally* Michael Allen & Robert G. Schwemm, *For the Rest of Their Lives: Seniors and the Fair Housing Act*, 90 Iowa L. Rev. 121 (2004).

225 *See, e.g.,* Hovsons, Inc. v. Township of Brick, 89 F.3d 1096 (3d Cir. 1996) (Act covered those living in a nursing facility as well as one plaintiff who did not); *see also* Brief of the United States As Amicus Curiae in Support of Plaintiffs' Opposition to Defendants' Motion for Judgment on the Pleadings or, in the Alternative, for Summary Judgment, Hargraves v. Capital City Mortgage Corp., 140 F. Supp. 2d 7 (D.D.C. 2000), *available on the companion website to this treatise*.

consumer has recently vacated or intends to move into or even one that the consumer does not plan to live in but intends to use as rental property, or even leave vacant, at a particular point in time. However, in a case in which a plaintiff owned residential property as a commercial venture, a court would not allow plaintiffs to assert an FHA claim unless they were residing in the dwelling or would have resided there absent the unlawful discrimination.[226]

2.3.2.2.2 Home equity and other loans taking home as collateral

Section 3605 of the Fair Housing Act also applies to other types of loans as long as the loan is secured by residential real estate.[227] The loan proceeds do not have to be used in any way related to the dwelling provided the residential real estate is taken as collateral for the loan.

This definition applies to home equity loans, in which the consumer establishes a credit line using residential real estate as collateral. In addition, homes and other real estate are frequently used as collateral on many finance company refinancings and even some car loans, credit card obligations, and other types of credit transactions. Because many subprime and predatory lenders take a security interest in a borrower's home to finance home improvements and other work, section 3605 can be a powerful tool to challenge the actions of predatory lenders.[228]

The Act applies to any loan that takes "residential real estate" as collateral. Unlike "dwelling," this term is not defined. Residential real estate should include any piece of realty used for residential purposes, whether or not the owner is the resident. It should apply to any form of realty used for that purpose but may not apply to personalty. Thus, there is an issue under this test as to whether a manufactured home is residential real estate if the security is taken only in the structure and not in the land on which the home is situated. Land used as the site of a manufactured home likely would be considered residential real estate.

2.3.2.3 Credit Actors Covered by Section 3605

2.3.2.3.1 General

Residential real estate-related transactions include transactions involving lenders and those providing other financial assistance related to the making of the loans.[229] Thus the Fair Housing Act applies to loan brokers, financial consultants, or anyone else providing financial assistance related to a loan covered by the Act.

A residential real estate-related transaction would be excluded from the Act's coverage only if the lender or other party's business does not include engaging in such transactions.[230] Real estate transactions need not be the person's exclusive or even primary business. However, in order for a person to be covered by section 3605, residential real estate transactions must be part of its overall business functioning.[231] As discussed above, "residential real estate transactions" are defined broadly, including not only the making or purchasing of loans but also providing other financial assistance related to real estate.[232] The category explicitly includes the selling, brokering, or appraising of residential real estate.[233]

The various credit actors that may be covered under section 3605 are discussed in the following subsections.

2.3.2.3.2 "Makers" of loans

Section 3605 applies to a wide range of actors involved in *making* loans or providing other financial assistance for a dwelling or financial assistance secured by a dwelling. The regulations implementing the Act identify some of the prohibited practices in this category.[234]

Prohibited practices under this section include, but are not limited to, failing or refusing to provide to any person, in connection with a residential real estate-related transaction, information regarding the availability of loans or other financial assistance, application requirements, procedures or standards for the review and approval of loans or financial assistance, or providing information that is inaccurate or different from that provided others because of a prohibited basis.[235]

---

226 Home Quest Mortgage L.L.C. v. American Family Mut. Ins. Co., 340 F. Supp. 2d 1177 (D. Kan. 2004); *see also* Miller v. Bank of America, 2005 WL 1902945 (D.D.C. July 13, 2005), *aff'd*, 222 Fed. Appx. 1 (D.C. Cir. 2007).

227 42 U.S.C. § 3605(b)(1)(B); *see, e.g.*, Willingham v. Novastar Mortgage, Inc., 2006 WL 6676801, at *20–21 (W.D. Tenn. Feb. 7, 2006). *But see In Re* Wells Fargo Residential Mortgage Lending Discrimination Litig., 2010 WL 4791687, at *2 (N.D. Cal. Nov. 18, 2010) (property purchased for investment purposes, so plaintiff lacked standing under Fair Housing Act).

228 *See* § 8.2, *infra*.

229 42 U.S.C. § 3605(a); 24 C.F.R. § 100.115(a).

230 *See, e.g.*, Beard v. Worldwide Mortgage Corp., 354 F. Supp. 2d 789 (W.D. Tenn. 2005) (section 3605 claim dismissed when plaintiff failed to allege that settlement agent and notary were engaged in the business of residential real estate); Steptoe v. Beverly Area Planning Ass'n, 674 F. Supp. 1313 (N.D. Ill. 1987) (section 3605 did not apply to nonprofit corporation accused of racial steering because plaintiffs failed to allege facts showing that the nonprofit made commercial real estate loans or had any connection with the financing of real estate).

231 *See* Eva v. Midwest Nat'l Mortgage Bank, Inc., 143 F. Supp. 2d 862 (N.D. Ohio 2001).

232 42 U.S.C. § 3605(b)(1).

233 42 U.S.C. § 3605(b)(2); *see* § 2.3.2.1, *supra*.

234 24 C.F.R. § 100.120.

235 *See, e.g.*, Honorable v. The Easy Life Real Estate System, 100 F. Supp. 2d 885 (N.D. Ill. 2000) (plaintiffs alleged that defendant real estate company took advantage of a segregated housing market by, among other actions, falsely telling plaintiff borrowers that their company's financing program was the only program available to plaintiffs); *see also* Davis v. Wells Fargo Bank, 685 F. Supp. 2d 838, 844–46 (N.D. Ill. 2010), *motion for relief from judgment denied*, Davis v. Wells Fargo, 2010 WL 1257789 (N.D. Ill. Mar. 26, 2010), *aff'd*, Estate of Davis v. Wells Fargo Bank, 633 F.3d 529 (7th Cir. 2011) (servicer and investor not liable under section 3605 because they did not lend money to plaintiff); Johnson v. Equity Title & Escrow Co. of Memphis, L.L.C., 476 F. Supp. 2d 873 (W.D. Tenn.

Those making loans or providing other financial assistance that is related to the purchase, construction, improvement, repair, or maintenance of a dwelling or secured by residential real estate are also prohibited from discriminating in the *terms and conditions* for making those loans available.[236]

Prohibited conduct under this section includes, but is not limited to, using different policies, practices, or procedures in evaluating or determining the creditworthiness of any person in connection with the provision of any loan or other financial assistance for a dwelling or for any loan or other financial assistance which is secured by residential real estate because of a prohibited basis. This section also prohibits financial actors from determining the type of loan or other financial assistance to be provided or fixing the amount, interest rate, duration, or other terms for a loan because of a prohibited basis.

2.3.2.3.3 Purchasers of loans

The Fair Housing Act also applies to the activities of one who purchases loans[237]—that is, to the activities of those who buy mortgages and other loan paper from the originating lender—as long as the loans themselves are covered by the Act. This provision means that lenders who participate in the original loan decision are covered, and lenders who do not participate before the fact but whose decision as to which loans to purchase involves discrimination on a prohibited basis are also covered.[238] The pooling and sale of not only loans but also loan servicing rights are included.

The regulations implementing the Act present a non-exhaustive list of unlawful practices, including the purchasing of housing-related loans or other debts or securities on a discriminatory basis.[239] This regulation applies to traditional "redlining" practices.[240] It prohibits redlining practices not only in connection with the purchasing of loans but also in connection with the pooling or packaging of loans or other debts.[241]

The Fair Housing Act, therefore, may be used to extend liability to secondary market purchasers. The ECOA also may apply to secondary market actors. Loan purchasers that create financing policies and set credit terms should be held directly liable as creditors for any ECOA violations committed by the primary lenders or others.[242] When a secondary market purchaser is not sufficiently involved in the transaction to fall within the definition of creditor, the ECOA requires that these actors have knowledge or reasonable notice of the discriminatory actions of the primary lenders before they can be held

liable.[243] There is no similar requirement in the Fair Housing Act. However, the regulation does specify that it is not meant to preclude loan purchasers from considering factors justified by business necessity.[244]

2.3.2.3.4 Sellers, brokers, and appraisers

The Fair Housing Act applies to persons or businesses engaging in the selling, brokering, or appraising of residential real property.[245] The Act's regulations define broker or agent to include any person authorized to act on behalf of another person regarding any matter related to the sale or rental of a dwelling.[246] Brokers should also be covered under the provisions prohibiting discrimination in the terms and conditions for making loans or other financial assistance available.[247]

Appraisal practices that are unlawful include, but are not limited to, using an appraisal of residential real property when the person knows or reasonably should know that the appraisal improperly takes into consideration race, color, or other characteristics protected by the Act.[248]

While brokers, appraisers, and others may be liable for violations of the Fair Housing Act, creditors have no right to contribution or indemnity from such parties for their own liability under the Act.[249]

2007) (title company); Carr v. Home Tech Co., 476 F. Supp. 2d 859, 866–67 (W.D. Tenn. 2007) (loan arranger and title company could be liable for violation of the FHA under section 3605).

236 24 C.F.R. § 100.130.
237 24 C.F.R. § 100.125(a).
238 *But cf.* Levey v. CitiMortgage, Inc., 2009 WL 2475222, at *2 (N.D. Ill. Aug. 10, 2009) (complaint dismissed against assignee creditor when plaintiff failed to plead any facts related to purchase of loan).
239 24 C.F.R. § 100.125.
240 *See generally* ch. 7, *infra* (redlining).
241 24 C.F.R. § 100.125(b)(2).
242 *See* § 2.2.5.5, *supra.*
243 *See* § 2.2.5.5, *supra.*
244 24 C.F.R. § 100.125(c).
    A 2003 United States Supreme Court decision addressed the issue of vicarious liability under the FHA. *See* Meyer v. Holley, 537 U.S. 280, 123 S. Ct. 824, 154 L. Ed. 2d 753 (2003). Implications of this decision for holding individuals and corporations liable in credit discrimination cases are discussed in § 11.3, *infra.*
245 42 U.S.C. § 3605(b)(2); 24 C.F.R. § 100.135; *see, e.g.,* Sanchez v. Thompson, 252 F.R.D. 136 (E.D.N.Y. 2008) (seller's refusal to sell home to plaintiffs because they were from Puerto Rico stated a claim of national origin discrimination under FHA).
246 24 C.F.R. § 100.20. *But see* Jones v. Countrywide Home Loans, Inc., 2010 WL 551418, at *7 (N.D. Ill. Feb. 11, 2010) (title insurance company that conducted closing did not engage in practice covered by Fair Housing Act).
247 *See* § 2.3.2.3.2, *supra.*
    For a government enforcement case involving loan brokers, see Settlement Agreement and Order, United States v. Long Beach Mortgage Co., No. CV-96-6159 (C.D. Cal. Sept. 5, 1996), *available on the companion website to this treatise.*
248 Cases involving appraisal practices include: Hood v. Midwest Sav. Bank, 95 Fed. Appx. 768 (6th Cir. 2004) (affirming that FHA applies to appraisal practices, but no violation in this case as defendant could not complete the appraisal because of unavailability of comparable sales); Brown v. Interbay Funding, L.L.C., 2004 WL 2579596 (D. Del. Nov. 8, 2004); Latimore v. Citibank, 979 F. Supp. 662 (N.D. Ill. 1997) (finding that plaintiff did not bring a prima facie case of discrimination; registering displeasure with plaintiff's joining of the appraiser as a defendant—even though appraisers can be covered by the FHA and ECOA, finding no evidence of racial motives here), *aff'd,* 151 F.3d 712 (7th Cir. 1998); Steptoe v. Savings of America, 800 F. Supp. 1542 (N.D. Ohio 1992); Old West End Ass'n v. Buckeye Fed. Sav. & Loan, 675 F. Supp. 1100 (N.D. Ohio 1987).
249 *See* Mathis v. United Homes, L.L.C., 607 F. Supp. 2d 411, 421–23 (E.D.N.Y. 2009).

2.3.3 Scope of Section 3604

2.3.3.1 Transactions Covered Under Section 3604

2.3.3.1.1 General

Section 3604 is titled "Discrimination in the Sale or Rental of Housing and Other Prohibited Practices." Of most relevance to consumer credit, the first two subsections make it unlawful:

> (a) To refuse to sell or rent after the making of a bona fide offer, or to refuse to negotiate for the sale or rental of, or otherwise make unavailable or deny, a dwelling to any person because of race, color, religion, sex, familial status, or national origin.
>
> (b) To discriminate against any person in the terms, conditions, or privileges of sale or rental of a dwelling, or in the provision of services or facilities in connection therewith, because of race, color, religion, sex, familial status, or national origin.[250]

Unlike section 3605, sections (a) and (b) of section 3604 do not specify "handicap" as a protected basis. A separate provision, section 3604(f), applies to handicapped renters or buyers. Section 3604(f) prohibits discrimination in the sale or rental of, or otherwise making unavailable or denying, a dwelling to any buyer or renter because of a handicap of the buyer or renter, to a person residing in or intending to reside in that dwelling after it is sold, rented, or made available, or to any person associated with that buyer or renter.[251] This section also prohibits discrimination against any person in the terms or conditions or privileges of sale or rental of a dwelling because of a handicap.[252]

The regulations implementing the Act describe a broad range of prohibited conduct including prohibited real estate practices;[253] unlawful refusal to sell, rent, or negotiate for the sale or rental on a prohibited basis;[254] discrimination in terms, conditions and privileges and in services and facilities;[255] other prohibited sale and rental conduct;[256] discriminatory represen-

tations on the availability of dwellings;[257] blockbusting;[258] and discrimination in the provision of brokerage services.[259]

In addition, section 3604(c) provides that it is unlawful to make, print, or publish or cause to be made, printed, or published any notice, statement, or advertisement with respect to the sale or rental of a dwelling that indicates any preference, limitations, or discrimination based on race, color, religion, sex, handicap, familial status, or national origin or indicates an intention to make any such preference, limitation or discrimination.[260] This section can be useful in bringing claims against brokers, lenders, and other entities that redline particular communities by not marketing to those communities or by discriminating in advertising.[261]

The broad scope of the term dwelling is detailed above—it includes homes, apartments, manufactured homes, manufactured home parks and trailer courts, house boats, and about any other structure within which an individual could reside.[262]

2.3.3.1.2 Does section 3604 apply to home equity loans?

Most courts to date have agreed that sections 3604 and 3605 are not mutually exclusive.[263] Thus a claim in a home equity lending case may be brought under section 3604 or section 3605 alone or under both.

There is precedent for the position that the language of section 3604 applies to lending. In one case, the court described "mortgage financing" as an "essential service" within the coverage of section 3604.[264] In other cases, the courts have held that section 3604 applied to reverse redlining in lending.[265]

The majority of courts have held that section 3604 does not require a literal sale or rental of a dwelling.[266] The clearest

---

250 42 U.S.C. § 3604(a), (b); *see, e.g.*, Greater New Orleans Fair Hous. Action Ctr. v. United States Dep't of Hous. & Urban Dev., 723 F. Supp. 2d 14, 2010 WL 3488250, at *5 (D.D.C. Sept. 7, 2010) (refusing to dismiss Fair Housing Act claim that formula used by HUD to distribute block grants was discriminatory in violation of section 3604(a), to "otherwise make unavailable or deny, a dwelling. . . .").

251 42 U.S.C. § 3604(f)(1).

252 42 U.S.C. § 3604(f)(2).

253 24 C.F.R. § 100.50.
 This includes steering prospective buyers away from particular properties on a prohibited basis. *See, e.g.*, Gladstone Realtors v. Vill. of Bellwood, 441 U.S. 91, 99 S. Ct. 1601, 60 L. Ed. 2d 66 (1979); Tillery v. The Darby-Rogers Co., 2006 WL 27134 (M.D. Fla. Jan. 5, 2006).

254 24 C.F.R. § 100.60.

255 24 C.F.R. § 100.65.

256 24 C.F.R. § 100.70. *But see* Woodworth v. Bank of America, Nat'l Ass'n, 2011 WL 1540358 (D. Or. Mar. 23, 2011) *report and recommendation adopted sub nom.* Woodworth v. Bank of America, 2011 WL 1542514 (D. Or. Apr. 21, 2011) (section 3604 applies only to sale or rental transactions, not to refinancing of previously owned

property); Coe v. CMH Homes, 2006 WL 1932664, at *2 (M.D.N.C. July 11, 2006) (dismissing FHA claim; ruling that section 3604 did not provide a claim based on the moving and installation of a manufactured home that the plaintiff already owned).

257 24 C.F.R. § 100.80.

258 24 C.F.R. § 100.85.

259 24 C.F.R. § 100.90.

260 42 U.S.C. § 3604(c); 24 C.F.R. § 100.75.

261 *See, e.g.*, Saunders v. Gen. Serv. Corp., 659 F. Supp. 1042 (E.D. Va. 1987). *See generally* Andrene N. Plummer, Comment, *A Few New Solutions to a Very Old Problem: How the Fair Housing Act Can Be Improved to Deter Discriminatory Conduct by Real Estate Brokers*, 47 How. L.J. 163 (2003).

262 *See* § 2.3.2.2, *supra*.

263 *See, e.g.*, Nationwide Mut. Ins. Co. v. Cisneros, 52 F.3d 1351 (6th Cir. 1995) (sections 3604 and 3605 overlap and are not mutually exclusive); Eva v. Midwest Nat'l Mortgage Bank, Inc., 143 F. Supp. 2d 862 (N.D. Ohio 2001) (agreeing that sections 3604 and 3605 are not mutually exclusive although finding that section 3604 did not apply to refinancing loans).

264 Clifton Terrace Assocs., Ltd. v. United Techs. Corp., 929 F.2d 714, 719–20 (D.C. Cir. 1991).

265 Hargraves v. Capital City Mortgage Corp., 140 F. Supp. 2d 7 (D.D.C. 2000); *see also* Laufman v. Oakley Bldg. & Loan Co., 408 F. Supp. 289 (S.D. Ohio 1976).

266 *See, e.g.*, Michigan Prot. & Advocacy Serv., Inc. v. Babin, 18 F.3d 337 (6th Cir. 1994) (Congress intended section 3604 to reach a broad range of activities that have the effect of denying housing opportunities to a member of a protected class); United States v.

application outside of the sale or rental context has been to property insurance.[267] Some courts have allowed section 3604 lending claims to go forward only when the lending directly involved a sale.[268] However, other courts have clearly stated that section 3604's prohibition of practices that "otherwise make unavailable or deny" housing on a discriminatory basis applies to discrimination in the availability of mortgage financing.[269]

The Department of Justice (DOJ) made an extensive analysis of this issue in an amicus brief filed in 2000 in *Hargraves v. Capital City Mortgage*.[270] The DOJ argued successfully that section 3604(a) covers "discrimination that adversely affects the availability of housing."[271] Discrimination in housing-related financing, particularly predatory lending, can have this effect. Under the broad language of the Act, a direct refusal to rent or sell housing is not required for either section 3604(a) or section 3604(b) to apply.

In another case the plaintiff succinctly, but unsuccessfully, set forth the arguments why both sections (a) and (b) of section 3604 should apply in predatory lending cases.[272] Under section 3604(a) the plaintiffs argued that extending loans designed to fail and easily result in loss of homes makes housing unavailable.[273] With respect to section 3604(b) the plaintiffs argued that the defendant's conduct unreasonably interfered with the use and enjoyment of their property.[274] The court, while agreeing that section 3604 should be construed broadly, did not extend it to the facts in that case.[275]

This is still an open issue without a settled result. Some courts have found that section 3604 does not apply to mortgage financing cases when the borrower already acquired the dwelling at issue.[276] For example, the Supreme Court of Connecticut cited the Department of Housing and Urban Development's Fair Housing Act regulations to support its conclusion that enforcement of mortgage loan agreements is governed solely by section 3605.[277] However other courts have been willing to extend the reach of section 3604 more broadly in the lending context.[278]

Yonkers Bd. of Education, 837 F.2d 1181 (2d Cir. 1987) (applying section 3604 to exclusionary zoning); Hanson v. Veterans Admin., 800 F.2d 1381 (5th Cir. 1986) (applying section 3604 to discriminatory appraisals); Munoz v. Int'l Home Capital Corp., 2004 WL 3086907 (N.D. Cal. May 4, 2004); Whisby-Myers v. Kiekenapp, 293 F. Supp. 2d 845 (N.D. Ill. 2003) (section 3604 applied when African-American family sued neighbors for shouting racial epithets and other harassment); Matthews v. New Century Mortgage, 185 F. Supp. 2d 874 (S.D. Ohio 2002) (section 3604 should be read liberally to go beyond the literal scope of selling or renting housing, although it did not reach the transactions in this case); Eva v. Midwest Nat'l Mortgage Banc, 143 F. Supp. 2d 862 (N.D. Ohio 2001) (section 3604 does not require a literal sale or rental of a dwelling, although court did not apply it to mortgage refinance); United States v. Pospisil, 127 F. Supp. 2d 1059, 1064 (W.D. Mo. 2000) (plaintiffs stated a claim under section 3604 by alleging that defendants firebombed the front porch of plaintiffs' home); Woods v. Foster, 884 F. Supp. 1169, 1174–75 (N.D. Ill. 1995) (sexual harassment can make a homeless shelter unavailable under section 3604); Dunn v. Midwestern Indem., Mid-American Fire & Cas., 472 F. Supp. 1106 (D.C. Ohio 1979); Laufman v. Oakley Bldg. & Loan Co., 408 F. Supp. 489 (S.D. Ohio 1976) (agreeing with plaintiffs that section 3604(a) not only prohibits conduct constituting a refusal to sell or rent but also conduct that otherwise makes dwellings unavailable; applied in this case to mortgage redlining); *see also* Brief of the United States As Amicus Curiae in Support of Plaintiffs' Opposition to Defendants' Motion for Judgment on the Pleadings or, in the Alternative, for Summary Judgment, Hargraves v. Capital City Mortgage Corp., 140 F. Supp. 2d 7 (D.D.C. 2000), *available on the companion website to this treatise*.

267 *See, e.g.*, NAACP v. American Family Mut. Ins. Co., 978 F.2d 287 (7th Cir. 1992); Nat'l Fair Hous. Alliance, Inc. v. Prudential Ins. Co. of America, 208 F. Supp. 2d 46, 56 (D.D.C. 2002) (section 3604 applies to insurance redlining); Wai v. Allstate Ins. Co., 75 F. Supp. 2d 1, 6 (D.D.C. 1999) (same); § 7.3.4.2.1, *infra*; *see also* Nationwide Mut. Ins. Co. v. Cisneros, 52 F.3d 1351, 1357 (6th Cir. 1995). *But see* Saunders v. Farmers Ins. Exch., 537 F.3d 961, 967–68 (8th Cir. 2008) (McCarran-Ferguson Act preempts claim of unlawful insurance price discrimination under FHA).

268 *See, e.g.*, Munoz v. Int'l Home Capital Corp., 2004 WL 3086907 (N.D. Cal. May 4, 2004); Laufman v. Oakley Bldg. & Loan Co., 408 F. Supp. 489 (S.D. Ohio 1976).

269 *See* Nat'l Cmty. Reinvestment Coal. v. Accredited Home Lenders Holding Co., 573 F. Supp. 2d 70, 76–77 (D.D.C. 2008); Nat'l Cmty. Reinvestment Coal. v. NovaStar Financial, Inc., 2008 WL 977351 (D.D.C. Mar. 31, 2008).

270 *See* Brief of the United States as Amicus Curiae in Support of Plaintiffs' Opposition to Defendants' Motion for Judgment on the Pleadings or, in the Alternative, for Summary Judgment, Hargraves v. Capital City Mortgage Corp., 140 F. Supp. 2d 7 (D.D.C. 2000), *available on the companion website to this treatise*.

271 Brief of the United States as Amicus Curiae in Support of Plaintiffs' Opposition to Defendants' Motion for Judgment on the Pleadings or, in the Alternative, for Summary Judgment 21, Hargraves v. Capital City Mortgage Corp., 140 F. Supp. 2d 7 (D.D.C. 2000), *available on the companion website to this treatise* (citing Clifton Terrace Assocs. v. United Tech. Corp. 929 F.2d 714, 719 (D.C. Cir. 1991)).

272 *See* Eva v. Midwest Nat'l Mortgage Bank, Inc., 143 F. Supp. 2d 862, 886 (N.D. Ohio 2001).

273 *See id.*

274 *See id.*

275 *See id. But see* Willingham v. Novastar Mortgage, Inc., 2006 WL 6676801, at *18–20 (W.D. Tenn. Feb. 7, 2006).

276 *See, e.g.*, Gibson v. Household Int'l, Inc., 151 Fed. Appx. 529 (9th Cir. 2005) (plaintiff failed to provide any authority that section 3604 applies to claims involving non-purchase money loans); Matthews v. New Century Mortgage, 185 F. Supp. 2d 874 (S.D. Ohio 2002); Eva v. Midwest Nat'l Mortgage Bank, Inc., 143 F. Supp. 2d 862, 886 (N.D. Ohio 2001) (section 3604 relates to acquiring a home, while section 3605 applies to the making or purchasing of loans or providing other financial assistance for maintaining a dwelling previously acquired); Thomas v. First Fed. Sav. Bank of Ind., 653 F. Supp. 1330 (N.D. Ind. 1987) (redlining cases that affect the availability of housing are actionable under section 3604, but cases affecting the financing of housing are more properly brought under section 3605); Webster Bank v. Oakley, 830 A.2d 139 (Conn. 2003) (section 3605, not section 3604, applied to alleged discrimination in foreclosure process).

277 Webster Bank v. Oakley, 830 A.2d 139 (Conn. 2003).

278 *See, e.g.*, Beard v. Worldwide Mortgage Corp., 354 F. Supp. 2d 789 (W.D. Tenn. 2005) (predatory lending targeted at African-American communities states claim under sections 3605 and 3604(b)); *see also* Neals v. Mortgage Guar. Ins. Corp., 2011 WL 1897442, at *3 (W.D. Pa. Apr. 6, 2011) (section 3604 reaches post-acquisition

2.3.3.1.3 Implications of the section 3604 versus section 3605 debate

In many cases it will not matter whether a section 3604 claim is available because section 3605, discussed above, will clearly apply. However, some potentially discriminatory practices do not fit within the parameters of section 3605 but may fit within a broad reading of section 3604.

The provision of section 3604(a) prohibiting any practice that has the effect of making housing unavailable is probably the main advantage of adding a section 3604 claim in a home financing case, particularly in a predatory lending case. A wide range of predatory loans and predatory lending creditors may be covered by the Act because predatory lending is a practice, according to the DOJ, of making loans that are designed to fail.[279] Housing is made unavailable if borrowers lose their homes because they cannot repay predatory loans. In addition, the denial of reasonably priced financing to protected groups, often resulting in foreclosure, makes housing unavailable.[280]

In addition, section 3605 is applicable only to those entities that are in the business of making real estate-related financing. Section 3604 applies to any person or entity selling or renting property.[281]

Another implication is that the ECOA prohibition against bringing claims under both the ECOA and the Fair Housing Act applies only to section 3605.[282] Thus, plaintiffs should be able to bring claims under both the ECOA and the Fair Housing Act if the basis of the Fair Housing Act claim is anything other than section 3605.

2.3.3.2 Credit Actors Covered by Section 3604

Section 3604 applies to any person selling or renting property, with the following exceptions. The Fair Housing Act (except for the discriminatory advertising section) does not apply to the sale or rental of a single-family house by an owner as long as the owner has an interest only in three or fewer homes and as long as the owner does not use an agent or broker or other person in the business of selling or renting dwellings.[283] The Act also does not apply to the rental of units in an owner-occupied four-family or smaller home.[284]

2.3.4 Interference, Coercion, Intimidation, or Threats: Scope of Section 3617

Section 3617 of the Fair Housing Act makes it unlawful to coerce, intimidate, threaten, or interfere with any person in the exercise or enjoyment of, or his or her having exercised or enjoyed, or his or her having aided or encouraged any other person in the exercise or enjoyment of, the rights granted or protected by sections 3603, 3604, 3605, or 3606 of the Act.[285] Thus, if defendants have violated one of the four enumerated sections, they have also violated section 3617.[286] It is also possible to bring an action under section 3617 even if there is no claim of a violation of one of the enumerated sections.[287] As discussed above, however, credit discrimination suits brought under the Act generally involve violations of sections 3604 or 3605.[288]

Plaintiffs have brought suit under section 3617 in cases involving mortgage redlining,[289] insurance redlining,[290] and other practices,[291] on the theory that such discrimination "interferes" with the exercise and enjoyment of Fair Housing Act rights. Although many cases alleging violations of section 3617 involve violent conduct, violence or physical coercion is not a prerequisite to a section 3617 claim.[292] The regulations imple-

---

discrimination), *adopted by* 2011 WL 1897452 (W.D. Pa. May 18, 2011).

279 Brief of the United States As Amicus Curiae in Support of Plaintiffs' Opposition to Defendants' Motion for Judgment on the Pleadings or, in the Alternative, for Summary Judgment 21–23, Hargraves v. Capital City Mortgage Corp., 140 F. Supp. 2d 7 (D.D.C. 2000), *available on the companion website to this treatise.*

280 *Id.* at 21–22.

281 *See* § 2.3.2.3.1, *supra.*

282 *See* 15 U.S.C. § 1691e(i); § 11.6.2, *infra.*

283 24 C.F.R. § 100.10(c)(1); *see also* 24 C.F.R. § 100.20 (definitions of dwelling, broker or agent, and person in the business of selling or renting dwellings).

284 24 C.F.R. § 100.10(c)(2).

285 42 U.S.C. § 3617.

286 Whisby-Myers v. Kiekenapp, 293 F. Supp. 2d 845 (N.D. Ill. 2003) (section 3617 applied when African-American family sued neighbors for shouting racial epithets and other harassment); Halprin v. The Prairie Single Family Homes of Dearborn Park Ass'n, 208 F. Supp. 2d 896, 903–04 (N.D. Ill. 2002), *aff'd in part, rev'd in part,* 388 F.3d 327 (7th Cir. 2004); Bryant v. Polston, 2000 U.S. Dist. LEXIS 16368 (S.D. Ind. Nov. 2, 2000) (plaintiffs stated a claim under section 3617 when Caucasian home owners sued neighbors for intimidating and harassing them because of their association with African Americans); Dunn v. Midwestern Indem., Mid-American Fire & Cas. Co., 472 F. Supp. 1106, 1111 (S.D. Ohio 1979).

287 *See* Williams v. Deerfield, 2005 WL 3455867 (N.D. Ill. Dec. 13, 2005); Nevels v. Western World Ins. Co., 359 F. Supp. 2d 1110 (W.D. Wash. 2004); Stackhouse v. DeSitter, 620 F. Supp. 208 (N.D. Ill. 1985) (firebombing case).

288 *See* §§ 2.3.2 (section 3605), 2.3.3 (section 3604), *supra.*

289 Laufman v. Oakley Bldg. & Loan Co., 408 F. Supp. 489, 498 (S.D. Ohio 1976).

290 Dunn v. Midwestern Indem., Mid-American Fire & Cas. Co., 472 F. Supp. 1106 (S.D. Ohio 1979).

291 *See, e.g.,* United States v. American Institute of Real Estate Appraisers, 442 F. Supp. 1072 (N.D. Ill. 1977) (the promulgation of standards that cause real estate appraisers and lenders to treat race and national origin as negative factors in determining the value of dwellings and in evaluating the soundness of home loans violates section 3617).

292 *See, e.g.,* Halprin v. Prairie Single Family Homes of Dearborn Park Ass'n, 388 F.3d 327 (7th Cir. 2004); Michigan Prot. & Advocacy Serv., Inc. v. Babin, 18 F.3d 337, 347 (6th Cir. 1994); King v. Metcalf 56 Homes Ass'n, Inc., 385 F. Supp. 2d 1137 (D. Kan. 2005); Nevels v. Western World Ins. Co., 359 F. Supp. 2d 1110 (W.D. Wash. 2004); Fowler v. Borough of Westville, 97 F. Supp. 2d 602 (D.N.J. 2000); People Helpers, Inc. v. City of Richmond, 789 F. Supp. 725 (E.D. Va. 1992).

menting the Act set out the types of conduct considered to be unlawful under section 3617.[293]

Interference under section 3617 has been broadly applied, reaching all practices that have the effect of interfering with the exercise of rights under federal fair housing laws.[294]

2.3.5 Aggrieved Persons May Bring Actions

The Fair Housing Act prohibits certain types of discrimination and specifies that these prohibitions protect "any person."[295] The only limit as to who can bring a case under the Act is that the individual be "aggrieved."[296] "Aggrieved person" is defined in the regulations implementing the Act as any person who claims to be injured by a discriminatory housing practice or believes he or she will be injured by a discriminatory housing practice that is about to occur.[297] This requirement under the Act that the plaintiff be aggrieved is to be generously construed to foster "truly integrated and balanced living patterns."[298]

The Supreme Court has held that Congress intended standing under the Fair Housing Act to "extend to the full limits of Article III," thereby eliminating the prudential barriers to standing.[299] There are limits to this broad standard. In particular, federal statutes may not abrogate the minimum requirement of Article III that a plaintiff demonstrate (1) an injury in fact, (2) a causal connection between the injury and the conduct complained of, and (3) the likelihood, as opposed to mere speculation, that the injury will be redressed by a favorable decision.[300] Thus members of unprotected classes may bring claims as well if they are alleging discrimination based on their association with members of protected classes.[301]

Moreover, a series of Supreme Court cases makes clear that testers, nonprofit housing organizations, and municipalities have standing to bring Fair Housing Act claims. Municipalities can be affected by racial discrimination in housing patterns in various ways, including their tax base, and such injury is sufficient for a municipality to bring a claim under the Act concerning discrimination as to its residents.[302] Courts have also held that state agencies have standing to enforce the Act.[303] However, it is possible that they are preempted from doing so with respect to national banks and their subsidiaries.[304]

The definition of aggrieved person under the Fair Housing Act is broader than the analogous term under the ECOA, which requires that an individual be an "applicant." An individual not seeking credit—such as those who would benefit if credit were granted—can bring a Fair Housing Act action. For example, tenants of a two-family house could bring a Fair Housing Act claim if their landlord was unfairly deprived of a home improvement loan to fix up the tenant's apartment.

2.4 Scope of Federal Civil Rights Acts

The federal Civil Rights Acts apply only to discrimination based on race, certain ethnic origins, and citizenship status.[305] Within these parameters, however, they are generally broad in scope.

Section 1981 provides to all persons within the United States the same rights to make contracts as is enjoyed by white citizens. This statute applies to all types of contracts, all types of borrowers or related individuals, and any type of creditor or other type of merchant. For example, non-citizens are persons within the scope of the statute, so they may bring section 1981 actions.[306]

The Civil Rights Act of 1991 added an express provision to the statute making it applicable to all aspects of the contractual relationship, including "making, performance, modification,

---

293   24 C.F.R. § 100.400.

294   *See, e.g.*, Michigan Prot. & Advocacy Serv. v. Babin, 18 F.3d 337 (6th Cir. 1994). *But see* Hood v. Midwest Sav. Bank, 95 Fed. Appx. 768 (6th Cir. 2004) (a bank does not interfere with a person's rights under section 3617 every time it declines to grant a loan on terms favorable to the borrower).

295   42 U.S.C. §§ 3604, 3605, 3617; *see* Jordan v. Khan, 969 F. Supp. 29 (N.D. Ill. 1997).

296   42 U.S.C. § 3613.

297   24 C.F.R. § 100.20.

298   Trafficante v. Metro. Life Ins. Co., 409 U.S. 205, 211, 93 S. Ct. 364, 34 L. Ed. 2d 415 (1972).

299   Havens Realty Corp. v. Coleman, 455 U.S. 363, 373–75, 102 S. Ct. 1114, 71 L. Ed. 2d 214 (1982); Gladstone Realtors v. Vill. of Bellwood, 441 U.S. 91, 103, 99 S. Ct. 1601, 60 L. Ed. 2d 66 (1979); Trafficante v. Metro. Life Ins. Co., 409 U.S. 205, 211, 93 S. Ct. 364, 34 L. Ed. 2d 415 (1972); Toll Bros., Inc. v. Twp. of Readington, 555 F.3d 131, 143–44 (3d Cir. 2009) (real estate developer with option to purchase parcel of land found to have standing under the Fair Housing Act to challenge zoning restrictions that would have prevented planned development of the land); *see also* Inclusive Cmtys. Project, Inc. v. Texas Dep't of Hous. & Cmty. Affairs, 749 F. Supp. 2d 486, 2010 WL 3766714, at *4–6 (N.D. Tex. Sept. 28, 2010) (nonprofit affordable housing organization had standing to bring Fair Housing Act claim); *see* § 11.2, *infra*.

300   Lujan v. Defenders of Wildlife, 504 U.S. 555, 560–61, 112 S. Ct. 2130, 119 L. Ed. 2d 351 (1992).

301   *See, e.g.*, Bryant v. Polston, 2000 U.S. Dist. LEXIS 16368 (S.D. Ind. Nov. 2, 2000) (FHA claim brought by white home owners

against neighbors, alleging discrimination based on plaintiffs' association with African Americans).

302   Gladstone Realtors v. Vill. of Bellwood, 441 U.S. 91, 99 S. Ct. 1601, 60 L. Ed. 2d 66 (1979); Vill. of Bellwood v. Dwivedi, 895 F.2d 1521 (7th Cir. 1990); *see* § 11.2.2, *infra*.

303   *See* Kaw Hous. Auth. v. City of Ponca City, 952 F.2d 1183, 1195 (10th Cir. 1991) (Indian housing authority); Support Ministries for Persons with IDS, Inc. v. Vill. of Waterford, 799 F. Supp. 272, 279 (N.D.N.Y. 1992) (State of New York); *see also* Clearing House Ass'n v. Cuomo, 510 F.3d 105 (2d Cir. 2007) (declining to decide whether the State of New York has standing to enforce the FHA but noting the "extraordinarily permissive" standing under the Act), *aff'd in part, rev'd in part on other grounds*, 129 S. Ct. 2710 (2009) (not addressing FHA issue, but finding that states are not preempted from enforcing their own state laws against national banks).

304   *See* Clearing House Ass'n v. Cuomo, 510 F.3d 105 (2d Cir. 2007) (declining to address issue), *aff'd in part, rev'd in part on other grounds*, 129 S. Ct. 2710 (U.S. 2009) (not addressing FHA issue, but finding that states are not preempted from enforcing their own state laws against national banks).

305   *See* § 3.6, *infra*.

306   *See* Graham v. Richardson, 403 U.S. 365, 91 S. Ct. 1848, 29 L. Ed. 2d 534 (1971); § 3.6, *infra*.

and termination [of the contract], and the enjoyment of all benefits, privileges, terms, and conditions of the contractual relationship."[307] The amendments also make it clear that section 1981 bars both public and private discrimination.[308] Section 1982, like the ECOA, does not require that a credit application be denied and may apply if the application was approved but on discriminatory terms or was withdrawn due to discrimination.[309] However, section 1981 only protects persons who have (or sought) rights under a contractual relationship that has been impaired, including parties to the contract and, potentially, third-party beneficiaries of the contract.[310] Unless the person has or would have had some rights under that contract, section 1981 does not provide a remedy, even if the person is the target of discrimination and loses benefits as a result of the contract impairment. Section 1981 plaintiffs must identify injuries flowing from a racially motivated breach of their own—and not of someone else's—contractual relationship.[311]

Section 1982 grants all citizens the same rights as are enjoyed by white citizens to inherit, purchase, lease, sell, hold, and convey real and personal property. This statute does not apply to discrimination against non-citizens. Nevertheless, it applies to any form of sale or rental practice by any individual or entity that discriminates against a citizen on the basis of race or ethnic origin.

Section 1982 applies to a loan in any way used to purchase or rent property.[312] However, it is not limited to real estate lending. Some courts have interpreted the section quite broadly, allowing claims that do not relate specifically to real estate transactions. For example, plaintiffs alleging harassment and intimidating conduct by their neighbors have been found to state a claim under the provision requiring equality in the right to hold real and personal property.[313] The statute bars discrimination by both state and private actors.[314] Section 1983 provides a cause of action for damages that constitutes the exclusive federal remedy for violations by state governmental units of the rights guaranteed in section 1981.[315]

While it is widely accepted that proof of discriminatory impact or effect can establish a violation of the credit discrimination provisions of the Fair Housing Act and the ECOA, courts have found that proof of discriminatory impact is not sufficient in federal Civil Rights Acts claims brought under sections 1981 and 1982.[316] Thus, proof of intentional discrimination, whether by direct or circumstantial evidence, is required in these cases.[317]

While various parties to a credit transaction may be liable for violations of the federal Civil Rights Acts, there is no federal right to contribution or indemnity among such parties under the Acts.[318]

---

307 42 U.S.C. § 1981(b).

308 42 U.S.C. § 1981(c).

Since the 1991 amendments to section 1981, courts have clarified that section 1981 provides a claim against private discrimination on the basis of alienage. *See* Anderson v. Conboy, 156 F.3d 167 (2d Cir. 1998); Angela M. Ford, Comment, *Private Alienage Discrimination and the Reconstruction Amendments: The Constitutionality of 42 U.S.C. § 1981*, 49 U. Kan. L. Rev. 457 (2001); § 3.6.2, *infra*.

Under the 1991 amendments, section 1981 also bars retaliation against those who advocate for rights protected under that provision of law. CBOCS West, Inc. v. Humphries, 128 S. Ct. 1951, 170 L. Ed. 2d 864 (2008).

309 *See* JAT, Inc. v. Nat'l City Bank of the Midwest, 460 F. Supp. 2d 812 (E.D. Mich. 2006).

310 *See* Domino's Pizza, Inc. v. McDonald, 546 U.S. 470, 126 S. Ct. 1246, 1249 n.3, 163 L. Ed. 2d 1069 (2006) (declining to affirm or exclude the possibility that third-party intended beneficiaries of a contract have rights under section 1981); *see also* Withers v. Dick's Sporting Goods, Inc., 636 F.3d 958, 965–66 (8th Cir. 2011) (discriminatory surveillance of African-American shoppers, possibly rude treatment, and inappropriate assistance did not involve formation of contract); Gregory v. Dillard's, Inc., 565 F.3d 464, 475 (8th Cir. 2009) (discriminatory surveillance of African-American shoppers did not involve formation of contract); Barfield v. Commerce Bank, 484 F.3d 1276 (10th Cir. 2007) (individuals who asked bank to make change for large bills made a contract offer within section 1981, notwithstanding that bank would not have received remuneration for service; state law determines contours of a contract for purpose of civil rights claim under section 1981). *But see* Cherry v. D.B. Zwirn Special Opportunities Fund, 2010 WL 415313, at *5–6 (M.D. Fla. Jan. 27, 2010) (stockholders do not have standing under section 1983 to bring a derivative claim on behalf of corporation under sections 1981 and 1982), *aff'd*, 433 Fed. Appx. 870 (11th Cir. 2011).

311 *See* Domino's Pizza, Inc. v. McDonald, 546 U.S. 470, 126 S. Ct. 1246, 163 L. Ed. 2d 1069 (2006).

312 *See* Evans v. First Fed. Sav. Bank, 669 F. Supp. 915 (N.D. Ind. 1987) (section 1982 count allowed to stand when borrower alleged redlining in the denial of a home equity loan to be used to purchase a car and pay college tuition).

313 *See, e.g.,* Egan v. Schmock, 93 F. Supp. 2d 1090 (N.D. Cal. 2000) (applying same analysis to section 1982 claim as to Fair Housing Act claim and holding that both statutes prohibit discriminatory conduct intended to drive individual out of her home); Bryant v. Polston, 2000 U.S. Dist. LEXIS 16368 (S.D. Ind. Nov. 2, 2000); Bryd v. Brandeburg, 922 F. Supp. 60 (N.D. Ohio 1996) (allegations of racially motivated firebombing stated claim under section 1982). *But see* Spahn v. Colonial Vill., Inc., 899 F.2d 24, 35 (D.C. Cir. 1990) (in finding that section 1982 did not prohibit real estate advertising that indicated discriminatory preferences, court stated that sections 1981 and 1982 are not meant to be all-purpose anti-discrimination statutes or comprehensive open housing laws).

314 Jones v. Alfred H. Mayer Co., 392 U.S. 409, 88 S. Ct. 2186, 20 L. Ed. 2d 1189 (1968).

315 McGovern v. City of Phila., 554 F.3d 114, 120–21 (3d Cir. 2009) (race discrimination in employment claim brought against city only under section 1981 dismissed).

316 *See* § 4.3, *infra*.

317 *See, e.g.,* Gen. Bldg. Contractors Ass'n v. Pennsylvania, 458 U.S. 375, 102 S. Ct. 3141, 73 L. Ed. 2d 835 (1982); Duran v. Cmty. First Bankshares, Inc., 92 Fed. Appx. 756 (10th Cir. 2004); Guides, Ltd. v. Yarmouth Group Prop. Mgmt., Inc., 295 F.3d 1065 (10th Cir. 2002); Barkley v. Olympia Mortgage Co., 2007 WL 2437810 (E.D.N.Y. Aug. 22, 2007) (evidence of intentional targeting of minorities supported an inference of intentional discrimination under sections 1981, 1982, and 1985(3)); Jiang v. Allstate Ins. Co., 199 F.R.D. 267 (N.D. Ill. 2001) (discrimination cases may not be proven based on disparate impact under sections 1981 and 1982); *see also* Wiltshire v. Dhanraj, 421 F. Supp. 2d 544 (E.D.N.Y. 2005). *See generally* § 4.2, *infra*.

318 *See* Mathis v. United Homes, L.L.C., 607 F. Supp. 2d 411, 423–26 (E.D.N.Y. 2009).

2.5 Scope of State Credit Discrimination Statutes

By and large, the scope of state credit discrimination statutes follows the scope of the federal statute they are modeled after. Nevertheless, sometimes the scope of a state statute will be broader than the scope of the analogous federal statute, and it may prove particularly valuable in those situations. The state laws should be preempted only if they are inconsistent with the ECOA and Regulation B and then only to the extent of the inconsistency.[319] The Fair Housing Act and federal civil rights laws should also not preempt state laws that offer similar or greater rights.[320]

Because of significant state variations, readers are referred to Appendix F, *infra*, for a summary of the scope of various state credit discrimination statutes. Particularly because states continue to make changes to bring their state statutes more in line with the current version of the federal Fair Housing Act and other federal statutes, it is important to examine the most recent version of the state statute.

2.6 Scope of State UDAP Statutes

Occasionally, a state statute generally prohibiting unfair or deceptive acts or practices (a UDAP statute) may be used to challenge credit discrimination not prohibited by any other statute, or a UDAP claim may be useful if a discrimination statute does not provide a sufficient remedy.[321] Nevertheless, various scope issues may limit the applicability of a state UDAP statute to credit discrimination.

State UDAP statutes vary significantly, and this variation is most pronounced concerning scope issues. A thorough analysis of UDAP scope issues is found in NCLC's *Unfair and Deceptive Acts and Practices*.[322] This section will only briefly list some of the possible scope problems found in *some* state UDAP statutes.

Some UDAP statutes apply only to the sale of goods and services, and there will be an issue as to whether credit (related or unrelated to a sale) involves the sale of goods and services.[323] In other states, the statute applies to trade or commerce, and credit should clearly fall within the statute's coverage.[324]

Certain state UDAP statutes do not apply to banks or other creditors regulated by federal or state agencies.[325] NCLC's *Unfair and Deceptive Acts and Practices* treatise contains a state-by-state survey of coverage of credit transactions and creditors under state UDAP statutes.[326] There may also be an issue as to whether a UDAP statute applies to debt collection practices (which may be the subject of a credit discrimination action)[327] or offers protections to loan guarantors[328] or businesses.[329]

It is important to note that each of these issues applies only to certain UDAP statutes and not to most state UDAP statutes. Nevertheless, it is always important before bringing any UDAP claim to review carefully the scope of the particular state statute.

The Dodd-Frank Wall Street Reform and Consumer Protection Act ("Dodd-Frank Act") prohibits deceptive, unfair, and abusive acts or practices, creating a federal UDAP statute with broader applicability than many state statutes.[330]

2.7 Summary of Key ECOA and FHA Provisions

An advocate will often have to choose whether to bring claims under the ECOA or the Fair Housing Act (FHA). Claims under both laws are not viable in some cases because of a provision in the ECOA that no person aggrieved by an ECOA violation and, in the same transaction, by a violation of the FHA's prohibitions concerning residential real estate-related discrimination can recover under both the ECOA and the FHA.[331]

---

319 15 U.S.C. § 1691d(f); Reg. B, 12 C.F.R. § 1002.11(a) [§ 202.11(a)]; *see, e.g.,* Ojo v. Farmers Group, Inc., 600 F.3d 1201 (9th Cir. 2010) (referring to Texas Supreme Court for interpretation of whether challenged credit scoring practice for property insurance, which had disparate impact on minorities, violated Texas anti-discrimination statute). *But see* Office of the Comptroller of the Currency v. Spitzer, 396 F. Supp. 2d 383 (S.D.N.Y. 2005) (although national banks must comply with state fair housing laws insofar as those laws do not prevent or significantly interfere with the bank's exercise of its powers, attorney general of New York cannot enforce these laws through judicial actions against national banks or their subsidiaries), *aff'd in part, rev'd in part sub nom.* Cuomo v. Clearing House Ass'n, L.L.C., 129 S. Ct. 2710, 2712–14 (2009) (OCC's preemption regulation was reasonable to extent that it referred to OCC's own supervisory powers, but unreasonable to extent that it prohibited state attorney general from bringing action against national bank to enforce state law); *see also* § 12.4.3, *infra*. *See generally* §§ 11.6.1.3, 12.4 (state and local enforcement), *infra*.

320 *See* § 11.6.1.3, *infra*.

321 *See, e.g.,* Diaz v. Bank of America Home Loan Servicing, 2010 WL 5313417 (C.D. Cal. Dec. 16, 2010) (California UDAP law applies to borrowers' rescission claims against broker alleged to have misrepresented credit terms to Spanish-speaking applicants).

322 (8th ed. 2012).

323 *See, e.g.,* M & T Mortgage Corp. v. White, 736 F. Supp. 2d 538 (E.D.N.Y. 2010) (purchase of home mortgage is "consumer-oriented" transaction covered by New York General Business Law and may be basis for reverse redlining claim); *see* National Consumer Law Center, Unfair and Deceptive Acts and Practices § 2.2.1.2 (8th ed. 2012).

324 *See id.* § 2.2.1.1.

325 *See id.* § 2.2.1.5; § 2.3.3 (discussing relationships between UDAP statutes and state regulatory schemes covering similar activities); § 2.5 (discussing federal preemption of state UDAP statutes); *see also* § 12.4.3, *infra* (discussing recent Supreme Court rulings on federal preemption of state laws).

326 *See id.* § 2.2.1.7.

327 *See id.* § 2.2.2 (includes state-by-state survey of coverage of debt collection by state UDAP statutes).

328 *See id.* § 2.4.3.

329 *See id.* § 2.4.5.

330 12 U.S.C. § 5531.

331 15 U.S.C. § 1691e(i); *see* § 11.6.2, *infra*.

Key advantages and disadvantages of each law are discussed below:

1. *Scope.* ECOA coverage extends to all types of credit transactions. The FHA applies only to housing. Advocates challenging discrimination in car financing, for example, do not have the option of proceeding under the FHA.

2. *Protected Classes.* Race and color, religion, national origin, and sex or gender are prohibited bases of discrimination under both laws. The ECOA prohibits discrimination based on marital status while the FHA prohibits discrimination based on familial status. The ECOA has three additional protected classes that are not covered by the FHA. These are age, public assistance status, and good faith exercise of legal rights under the Consumer Credit Protection Act. The FHA, but not the ECOA, includes disability or handicap as a prohibited basis for discrimination. (Chapter 3, *infra*).

3. *Standing.* The FHA has broader standing provisions, including standing for testers and organizational plaintiffs. The ECOA limits causes of action to "applicants." (Section 11.2, *infra*).

4. *Extended Liability.* Provisions for extended liability vary somewhat. The FHA explicitly applies to loan purchasers. Thus lenders who participate in the original loan decision are covered, as are lenders who do not participate before the fact but whose decision as to which loans to purchase involves discrimination on a prohibited basis. The ECOA applies to any creditor, with creditor being broadly defined. Loan purchasers that create financing policies and set credit terms, or otherwise participate in the credit transaction should be held liable as creditors for any ECOA violations committed by the primary lenders or others. (Sections 2.2.5, 2.3, *supra,* § 11.3, *infra*). A loan purchaser that does not meet the ECOA definition of a creditor may be liable for a creditor's conduct if that loan purchaser had knowledge or reasonable notice of the discriminatory actions of the creditor.

5. *Relief.* Relief under both laws is similar, with one major difference. Only the ECOA places a cap on punitive damages. Class actions are available under both statutes but, again, the ECOA places a cap on punitive damages in both class and individual cases. Punitive damages are not awarded for FHA administrative claims. (Chapter 11, *infra*).

6. The FHA gives plaintiffs a choice of an administrative or judicial forum. (Section 11.5.2, *infra*).

7. Disparate impact should be available as a theory under either law. (Section 4.3, *infra*).

8. Both laws until recently had two-year statutes of limitations for affirmative claims and both allow defensive actions (recoupment) in certain circumstances. Extending the statute of limitations through the "continuing violation theory" is more established in FHA case law, but this theory should arguably apply to the ECOA as well. The Dodd-Frank Act extended the statute of limitations under the ECOA to five years. (Section 11.9.2, *infra*).

9. The ECOA explicitly lists certain creditor defenses. (Section 11.9, *infra*).

10. Only the ECOA requires creditors to meet certain procedural requirements such as providing notices of adverse actions and retaining certain records. Violations of these provisions can be raised even in cases in which discrimination is not alleged. (Chapter 10, *infra*).

Chapter 3   Prohibited Bases for Discrimination

3.1 Introduction

Federal and state credit discrimination laws do not prohibit all forms of discrimination. They do not prevent creditors from making reasonable distinctions between applicants, denying credit, or offering less advantageous terms to higher-risk borrowers. The credit discrimination laws generally do not even require that creditors act reasonably in making a determination as to which applicants are high risk.

Instead, credit discrimination laws prohibit creditors from utilizing certain factors, such as race, national origin, or sex, as the *basis* for the credit determination. A credit determination is prohibited if it is based upon a prohibited distinction. This chapter lists the various types of prohibited bases for credit discrimination found in the ECOA, the federal Fair Housing Act, the federal Civil Rights Acts, the Americans with Disabilities Act, and state credit discrimination laws.

The chapter also details the one major ECOA exception to this prohibition: under a special-purpose credit program, creditors can act on a prohibited basis to grant credit.[1] That is, under specified conditions (usually when a group traditionally discriminated against is provided special-purpose credit opportunities), creditors may restrict a credit program only to those who share one common characteristic, even if that characteristic is race, national origin, sex, or some other prohibited basis.

A final credit discrimination principle detailed in this chapter is that a credit applicant can challenge discrimination even when the applicant is not part of the group discriminated against on a prohibited basis.[2] The applicant need only be affected by the discrimination and have dealings with, or be related to, the group discriminated against on a prohibited basis. For example, white credit applicants have a claim if their mortgage application is denied because they live in a predominantly African-American neighborhood.

3.2 When Is Discrimination Made on a Prohibited Basis?

Creditors are in the business of distinguishing between good and bad credit risks; creditors discriminate against bad risks all the time. Credit discrimination laws do not generally prevent creditors from denying credit or providing less favorable terms to bad credit risks. In fact, such laws do not generally prevent creditors from making bad judgments and denying credit to good credit risks. What credit discrimination laws do is outlaw the practice of treating individuals differently *because* of their race, religion, national origin, sex, or some other prohibited basis.

At the same time, credit discrimination statutes are not violated merely because an applicant is adversely treated and the applicant is a member of a protected group.[3] Discrimination is prohibited if there is a link between the discrimination and the prohibited basis, such that the creditor's decision-making process results in individuals being treated differently because of a prohibited basis. This type of discrimination is called "disparate treatment." Chapter 4, *infra*, discusses the fundamentals of disparate treatment in credit discrimination cases.

Another important credit discrimination principle is that a practice can involve illegal discrimination even when the creditor does not intend to discriminate on a prohibited basis. A practice can be illegal if it has the *effect* of discriminating on a prohibited basis.[4] This "effects test" provides an alternative approach when it is impossible to prove that the creditor intended to treat applicants differently. The effects test is discussed fully in Chapter 4, *infra*.

---

1 *See* § 3.8, *infra*.

2 *See* § 3.9, *infra*.

    The issue of associational discrimination is closely related to the issue of standing in a credit discrimination case. The topic of standing is discussed in § 11.2, *infra*.

3 *See* O'Dowd v. South Cent. Bell, 729 F.2d 347 (5th Cir. 1984) (rejecting white couple's claim that telephone company discriminated in requiring a deposit because of their exchange's racial composition when couple had history of late payments and deposits were required of all such customers); Cooley v. Sterling Bank, 280 F. Supp. 2d 1331 (M.D. Ala. 2003) (bank's denial of unsecured line of credit to African-American applicant on basis of high debt-to-income ratio was not discriminatory), *aff'd*, 116 Fed. Appx. 242 (11th Cir. 2004); Gross v. United States Small Bus. Admin., 669 F. Supp. 50 (N.D.N.Y. 1987) (no ECOA violation based on sex or marital status discrimination because applicant was rejected due to past delinquent loan with same agency), *aff'd*, 867 F.2d 1423 (2d Cir. 1988); Sayers v. Gen. Motors Acceptance Corp., 522 F. Supp. 835 (W.D. Mo. 1981) (married African-American woman did not establish discrimination on the basis of race, sex, or marital status, as creditor's disparate treatment in approving twenty-five male applicants with similar credit histories was due to "extenuating circumstances," that is, prior dealings with creditor or larger equity in property purchased).

4 *See* § 4.3, *infra*.

3.3 Prohibited Bases Under Both the ECOA and the FHA

3.3.1 Race and Color

Race and color are prohibited bases under both the ECOA[5] and the Fair Housing Act.[6] They are also prohibited bases under the federal Civil Rights Acts[7] and virtually all state credit discrimination legislation.[8] Native Americans are a protected race.[9] For example, one settled lawsuit alleged that a lender violated the FHA by discriminating against Native Americans by prohibiting loans secured by properties located on Indian reservations.[10] Discrimination against whites is also actionable under the ECOA.[11]

Racial discrimination may include discrimination not only against individuals of color but against those living in neighborhoods whose residents are predominantly individuals of color.[12] Such determinations can constitute disparate treatment if the creditor is taking an action because of the racial composition of a community.

Such actions may also constitute discrimination based on disparate impact if the creditor does not know the racial composition of a particular community and only discriminates against areas because of average income levels, payment histories, or similar characteristics. This geographic discrimination may still have a disproportionate impact on certain races. Redlining and reverse redlining are discussed in full in Chapters 7 and 8, *infra*.

3.3.2 Religion, Creed, and Political Affiliation

Religion is a prohibited basis for discrimination under the ECOA,[13] the federal Fair Housing Act,[14] and most state credit discrimination statutes.[15] The only exception under the ECOA is that creditors may favor applicants of a particular religion when offering a special-purpose credit program meeting the standards set out in Regulation B.[16]

Creed might be a broader standard than religion because a creed may comprise a set of fundamental beliefs that are not necessarily religious in nature. Federal discrimination laws do not list creed as a prohibited basis, but a number of state credit discrimination statutes do.[17] At least one state statute lists political affiliation as a prohibited basis.[18]

3.3.3 National Origin

3.3.3.1 General

National origin is a prohibited basis under the ECOA,[19] the federal Fair Housing Act,[20] and most state credit discrimination statutes.[21]

3.3.3.2 Ancestry or Country of Birth

National origin is not defined in United States Department of Housing and Urban Development (HUD) regulations but has been the subject of some interpretation under the ECOA. It seems clear that national origin is included as a prohibited basis to prevent discrimination based on an individual's ancestry. Examples of such discrimination include discrimination against individuals with Hispanic or Asian surnames or against individuals of Italian origin because of stereotypes involving organized crime.[22] It also includes discrimination against Native

---

5 15 U.S.C. § 1691(a)(1); Reg. B, 12 C.F.R. § 1002.2(z) [§ 202.2(z)]; Reg. B, 12 C.F.R. § 1002.6(b)(9) [§ 202.6(b)(9)] (emphasizing that, except as otherwise permitted or required by law, a creditor may not consider race, color, religion, national origin, or sex (or an applicant's decision not to provide such information) in any aspect of a credit transaction).

6 42 U.S.C. §§ 3604, 3605; *see* 24 C.F.R. § 100.110(b).

7 42 U.S.C. §§ 1981, 1982; *see* § 3.6.1, *infra*.

8 *See* appx. F, *infra* (summaries of state credit discrimination statutes).

9 Davis v. Strata Corp., 242 F. Supp. 2d 643 (D.N.D. 2003).

10 Settlement Agreement, Nat'l Cmty. Reinvestment Coal. v. NovaStar Financial, No. 1:07-cv-00861 (D.D.C. Oct. 27, 2009).

11 Moore v. United States Dep't of Agric., *ex rel.* Farmer's Home Admin., 993 F.2d 1222 (5th Cir. 1993) (district court incorrectly dismissed action for race discrimination under the ECOA for lack of standing by white plaintiffs who were denied the opportunity to participate in sale of inventory farmland held by Farmer's Home Administration solely because they were white).

12 Cherry v. Amoco Oil Co., 481 F. Supp. 727 (N.D. Ga. 1979); Official Interpretations of Reg. B [Official Staff Commentary on Reg. B], 12 C.F.R. pt. 1002 [pt. 202], Supp. I, § 1002.2(z)-1 [§ 202.2(z)-1]; *see also* § 3.9, *infra*.

13 15 U.S.C. § 1691(a)(1); *see* Reg. B, 12 C.F.R. §§ 1002.2(z), 1002.6(b)(9) [§§ 202.2(z), 202.6(b)(9)].

14 42 U.S.C. §§ 3604, 3605; *see* 24 C.F.R. § 100.110(b); *cf.* Tien Tao

v. Kingsbridge Park Cmty. Ass'n, 953 S.W.2d 525, 532 (Tex. App. 1997) (enforcement of residential deed restrictions by neighborhood association did not violate federal or state fair housing acts even though enforcement may impact manner that home owners observed their religion).

15 *See* appx. F, *infra* (summarizing state credit discrimination statutes).

16 *See* § 3.8, *infra*.

17 *See, e.g.*, Colo. Rev. Stat. § 5-1-109 (Colorado Consumer Credit Code); Colo. Rev. Stat. § 24-34-502 (housing financing); Del. Code Ann. tit. 6, § 4604 (fair housing); Iowa Code § 537.3311 (Iowa Consumer Credit Code); Iowa Code § 216.8A (housing financing); Iowa Code § 216.10 (civil rights); La. Rev. Stat. Ann. § 51:2254 (real estate financing); La. Rev. Stat. Ann. § 51:2255; Md. Code Ann., Com. Law §§ 12-305, 12-113 (West); Md. Ann. Code art. 49B, § 22 (housing financing); Minn. Stat. § 363A.16; Minn. Stat. § 363A.09(3) (housing financing); Mont. Code Ann. § 49-2-305(7) (housing financing); Mont. Code Ann. § 49-2-306; N.J. Stat. Ann. § 10:5-12(i) (West); N.Y. Exec. Law § 296-a (McKinney); 43 Pa. Cons. Stat. § 955(h) (housing financing); S.D. Codified Laws § 20-13-21 (housing financing); Tenn. Code Ann. § 4-21-606 (housing financing); Vt. Stat. Ann. tit. 9, § 4503(a)(6); Wash. Rev. Code §§ 49.60.030(1)(d), 49.60.175, 49.60.176; Wash. Rev. Code § 49.60.222(j) (housing financing).

18 *See, e.g.*, Iowa Code § 537.3311 (Iowa Consumer Credit Code); P.R. Laws Ann. tit. 1, § 13(e) (housing financing).

19 15 U.S.C. § 1691(a)(1); *see* Reg. B, 12 C.F.R. §§ 1002.2(z), 1002.6(b)(9) [§§ 202.2(z), 202.6(b)(9)].

20 42 U.S.C. §§ 3604, 3605; *see* 24 C.F.R. § 100.110(b).

21 *See* appx. F, *infra* (summarizing state credit discrimination statutes).

22 *See* Ricci v. Key Bancshares, 662 F. Supp. 1132 (D. Me. 1987).

Americans.[23]

It is equally clear that national origin is included as a prohibited basis to prevent discrimination based on an individual's country of birth.[24] Similarly, creditors should not discriminate against anyone simply because they were born outside of the United States.

3.3.3.3 English Language Ability

Any discrimination based on an individual's inability to speak or read English should be considered a form of discrimination based on national origin. For example, regulations set out by the Office of Thrift Supervision[25] indicate that requiring fluency in the English language as a prerequisite for obtaining a loan may be discrimination based on national origin.[26]

Granting credit on less preferable terms on the basis of language ability may also constitute discrimination or "reverse redlining" on the basis of national origin.[27] Creditors who exploit the vulnerability of limited-English speakers, targeting them for abusive credit terms, may be liable for claims of discrimination as well as claims for unfair or deceptive trade practices.[28]

Several states have enacted statutes which require that loan documents be provided in translation or that written consent from the consumer be obtained before a lender may act as translator in negotiating the transaction.[29] A lender's failure to comply with one of these state laws when preparing loan documents that impose onerous terms on a non-English speaker will certainly strengthen all of the consumer's legal claims against the lender.[30]

3.3.3.4 Immigration Status

3.3.3.4.1 Discrimination against immigrants

Credit discrimination against immigrants occurs frequently and often overtly, especially in mortgage lending.[31] Noncitizens who are not lawful permanent residents generally may be subject to heightened requirements to obtain mortgage loans, such as higher down payments and additional documentation requirements.[32] They may be unable to obtain loans that con-

---

23 Davis v. Strata Corp., 242 F. Supp. 2d 643 (D.N.D. 2003).

24 Official Interpretations of Reg. B [Official Staff Commentary on Reg. B], 12 C.F.R. pt. 1002 [pt. 202], Supp. I, § 1002.2(z)-2 [§ 202.2(z)-2].

25 The Dodd-Frank Wall Street Reform and Consumer Protection Act, Pub. L. No. 111-203, 124 Stat. 1376, transferred all OTS rulemaking authority to the Office of the Comptroller of the Currency and republished the OTS regulations, effective on July 21, 2010.

26 12 C.F.R. § 128.9(c)(2) (former Office of Thrift Supervision regulation, 12 C.F.R. § 528.9(c)(2)).

   Note that Equal Employment Opportunity Commission (EEOC) guidelines also state that a blanket English-only workplace rule may constitute national origin discrimination. 29 C.F.R. § 1606.7; *see also* Pacheco v. N.Y. Presbyterian Hosp., 593 F. Supp. 2d 599 (S.D.N.Y. 2009) (reviewing recent decisions on enforcement of "English only" workplace rules).

   However, the EEOC guideline has provoked mixed reactions from the federal courts. *Compare* Equal Emp't Opportunity Comm'n v. Premier Operator Serv., 113 F. Supp. 2d 1066 (N.D. Tex. 2000) (upholding EEOC guideline), *with* Garcia v. Spun Steak Co., 998 F.2d 1480 (9th Cir. 1993) (rejecting EEOC guidelines and holding that an English-only rule does not create an adverse impact prohibited by Title VII).

   HUD has also issued regulations setting standards for limited English proficiency services applicable to all entities that receive federal financial assistance directly or indirectly from HUD. 72 Fed. Reg. 2731–2754 (Jan. 22, 2007).

27 *See generally* ch. 8, *infra* (discussing reverse redlining).

28 Diaz v. Bank of America Home Loan Servicing, 2010 WL 5313417 (C.D. Cal. Dec. 16, 2010) (refusing to dismiss FHA claim alleging intentional targeting of Spanish-speaking borrowers for subprime loans through agents who spoke Spanish but used loan documents printed only in English); Gonzalez v. Ameriquest Mortgage Co., 2004 WL 2472249 (N.D. Cal. Mar. 1, 2004) (plaintiff permitted to proceed with ECOA claim alleging that lender targeted Hispanics for predatory mortgages; plaintiff alleged, *inter alia*, that lender took advantage of her limited English abilities); Gallegos v. Rizza Chevrolet, 2003 WL 22326523 (N.D. Ill. Oct. 9, 2003) (denying motion to dismiss Hispanic consumer's allegation of ECOA viola-

tion by auto dealer who took advantage of consumer's limited English abilities by intentionally deceiving him into signing a lease agreement instead of a retail installment contract); Hua Bai v. Bob Wondries Assoc., No. BC286661 (Cal. Super. Ct. complaint filed Dec. 10, 2002) (monolingual Chinese speakers targeted for predatory auto loans; complaint alleges violation of California consumer protection and discrimination laws), *available on the companion website to this treatise*.

29 *See, e.g.,* Ariz. Rev. Stat. Ann. § 6-631 (requiring notice in Spanish of right to get loan disclosure in Spanish); Cal. Civ. Code § 1632 (West); 815 Ill. Comp. Stat. § 505/2N; Tex. Fin. Code Ann. § 341.502(a) (West); *see also* Jo Carillo, *In Translation for the Latino Market Today: Acknowledging the Right of Consumers in a Multilingual Housing Market*, 11 Harv. Latino L. Rev. 1 (2008) (discussing California statute requiring lenders to provide unexecuted translations of loan documents and proposed amendments to statute). *See generally* Hernandez v. Sutter West Capital, 2010 WL 539133 (N.D. Cal. Feb. 8, 2010) (Cal. Civ. Code § 1632, requiring translation of mortgage documents, applies to mortgage broker, not just lender); Lorna M. Neill, *Mi Casa Es Su Casa? Spanish Speaking Home Mortgage Borrowers Need to Understand Their Loans*, 60 Consumer Fin. L.Q. Rep. 510 (2006); National Consumer Law Center, Unfair and Deceptive Acts and Practices § 5.6.1 (8th ed. 2012).

30 *See, e.g.,* Martinez v. Freedom Mortgage Team, Inc., 527 F. Supp. 2d 827 (N.D. Ill. 2007) (borrower may proceed with Fair Housing Act, ECOA, and state law claims challenging lender's disparate treatment of Hispanic customers through imposition of higher yield spread premiums; provision was included in loan documents that lender translated for borrower without written consent for lender to translate, as required by Illinois statute).

31 *See generally* Charu A. Chandrasekhar, *Can New Americans Achieve the American Dream? Promoting Homeownership in Immigrant Communities*, 39 Harv. C.R.-C.L. L. Rev. 169 (2004).

32 *See, e.g.,* Howe v. Bank of America, N.A., 102 Cal. Rptr. 3d 506 (Cal. Ct. App. 2009) (interpreting California anti-discrimination law and holding that lender's application requirement for Social Security numbers of citizens was not discrimination on basis of national origin); Jennifer S. Cowley, *More Paperwork, Higher Interest: Nonpermanent Residents Face Stricter Mortgage Requirements*, Tierra Grande, Oct. 2000, *available at* http://recenter.tamu.edu/pdf/1430.pdf (describing examples of mortgage requirements for non-permanent resident immigrants).

form to secondary market requirements and may be required to pay higher interest rates.[33]

Addressing credit discrimination against immigrants under the ECOA and FHA is complicated. A more promising alternative may be an action under the federal Civil Rights Acts.[34]

3.3.3.4.2 The ECOA standard

A denial of credit on the basis that the applicant is a non-citizen of the United States is not per se discrimination and actionable under the ECOA. The ECOA allows some latitude for credit distinctions based on immigration status.[35] Creditors may inquire about and consider an applicant's permanent residence status and immigration status.[36] A creditor may consider this information and other information necessary to determine the creditor's rights and remedies in case of default.[37]

For example, a creditor may differentiate between a non-citizen who is a long-time resident with permanent residence status and a non-citizen who is temporarily in this country on a student visa.[38] Nevertheless, the creditor may not discriminate against non-citizens of a specific national origin but only make distinctions between applicants who are permanent residents and those with a temporary immigration status. Each application must be judged on its individual merits.

A creditor also may refuse to grant credit because a law, regulation, or executive order imposes limitations on dealings with citizens or governments of certain other countries.[39] A prime example would be a creditor's refusal to extend credit to an applicant who wishes to conduct business with an officially embargoed nation.

An interesting issue is whether discrimination based on immigration status, even if not per se prohibited, may be seen as having the effect of discriminating based on national origin. For example, any policy that discriminates against non-citizens may have a disparate impact upon individuals whose national origins are in Latin America or Asia. It is best to establish statistical or other evidence of this disparate impact on such individuals and not to rely solely on the theoretical argument that discrimination based on alienage is effectively discrimination against persons of certain national origins.[40] Additionally, discrimination that involves immigration status may be a pretext for disparate treatment on the basis of national origin discrimination, if it is only directed at one group.

3.3.3.4.3 The Fair Housing Act standard

The Fair Housing Act is not clear as to whether its prohibition on discrimination based on national origin would apply to discrimination based on immigration status.[41] Unlike the ECOA, there is no explicit exception allowing distinctions based on immigration status. Thus a discrimination action based on immigration status could conceivably be available under the Act. At the very least, discrimination based on alienage would violate the Fair Housing Act if it had the effect of discriminating against individuals of a particular national origin.[42]

---

33 Jennifer S. Cowley, *More Paperwork, Higher Interest: Nonpermanent Residents Face Stricter Mortgage Requirements*, Tierra Grande, Oct. 2000, *available at* http://recenter.tamu.edu/pdf/1430.pdf.

34 *See* § 3.6.3, *infra*.

35 12 C.F.R. 1002.6(7) (a creditor may consider the applicant's immigration status or status as a permanent resident of the United States and any additional information that may be necessary to ascertain the creditor's rights and remedies regarding repayment.); Official Interpretations of Reg. B [Official Staff Commentary on Reg. B], 12 C.F.R. pt. 1002 [pt. 202], Supp. I, § 1002.6(b)(7)-2 [§ 202.6(b)(7)-2]; *see also* Bhandari v. First Nat'l Bank of Commerce, 808 F.2d 1082 (5th Cir. 1987) (denial of credit to all aliens not an ECOA violation), *rev'd in part on other grounds*, 829 F.2d 1343 (5th Cir. 1987) (en banc), *vacated*, 492 U.S. 901, *reinstated*, 887 F.2d 609 (5th Cir. 1989).

On the other hand, the Comptroller of the Currency has stated that national bank creditors under its jurisdiction may not maintain a blanket policy of refusing to grant credit to non-citizens; instead, such applications must be considered on their individual merits. William B. Glidden, Office of the Comptroller of the Currency, Interpretive Staff Letter, Fed. Banking L. Rep. (CCH) ¶ 85,026 (Sept. 9, 1977) (also available at 1977 OCC Ltr. LEXIS 64).

36 National bank creditors are permitted to inquire about and to consider an applicant's permanent residence and immigration status and may maintain a policy of requiring foreign student credit applicants to possess an alien registration card. William B. Glidden, Office of the Comptroller of the Currency, Interpretive Staff Letter, Fed. Banking L. Rep. (CCH) ¶ 85,026 (Sept. 9, 1977) (also available at 1977 OCC Ltr. LEXIS 64); Thomas W. Taylor, Office of the Comptroller of the Currency, Interpretive Staff Letter, Fed. Banking L. Rep. (CCH) ¶ 85,023 (Sept. 6, 1977) (also available at 1977 OCC Ltr. LEXIS 68).

37 Reg. B, 12 C.F.R. § 1002.6(b)(7) [§ 202.6(b)(7)]; *see also* Bhandari v. First Nat'l Bank of Commerce, 808 F.2d 1082 (5th Cir. 1987), *rev'd in part on other grounds*, 829 F.2d 1343 (5th Cir. 1987) (en banc); Nguyen v. Montgomery Ward & Co., 513 F. Supp. 1039 (N.D. Tex. 1981) (credit refusal based on lack of United States citizenship does not constitute discrimination on the basis of national origin; no ECOA violation because no evidence that alien was denied credit given to other aliens); Hanna v. Security Pac. Bus. Credit, 281 Cal. Rptr. 857 (Cal. Ct. App. 1991) (credit refusal based on lack of citizenship is not national origin discrimination); Abuzant v. Shelter Ins. Co., 977 S.W.2d 259 (Ky. Ct. App. 1998) (denial of insurance policy on basis of non-citizenship does not necessarily constitute discrimination on basis of national origin under Kentucky civil rights statute).

38 Official Interpretations of Reg. B [Official Staff Commentary on Reg. B], 12 C.F.R. pt. 1002 [pt. 202], Supp. I, § 1002.6(b)(7)-1 [§ 202.6(b)(7)-1].

39 *Id.* § 1002.2(z)-2 [§ 202.2(z)-2].

40 *See* Bhandari v. First Nat'l Bank of Commerce, 808 F.2d 1082 (5th Cir. 1987), *rev'd in part on other grounds*, 829 F.2d 1343 (5th Cir. 1987) (en banc); Abuzant v. Shelter Ins. Co., 977 S.W.2d 259 (Ky. Ct. App. 1998) (denial of insurance policy on basis of non-citizenship does not necessarily constitute discrimination on basis of national origin under Kentucky civil rights statute).

41 *But see* Martinez v. Partch, 2008 WL 113907, at *1–2 (D. Colo. Jan. 9, 2008) (granting defendant's motion to dismiss Fair Housing Act claim based on alienage discrimination); *cf.* Espinoza v. Farah Mfg. Co., 414 U.S. 86, 94 S. Ct. 334, 38 L. Ed. 2d 287 (1973) (Equal Employment Opportunity Act's prohibition of discrimination based on national origin does not prohibit discrimination on basis of alienage).

42 Espinoza v. Hillwood Square Mut. Ass'n, 522 F. Supp. 559 (E.D. Va. 1981) (housing cooperative's policy of excluding aliens could

3.3.4 Sex and Sexual Orientation

3.3.4.1 General

An applicant's sex is a prohibited basis for credit discrimination under the ECOA,[43] the federal Fair Housing Act,[44] and many state credit discrimination statutes.[45] Sex discrimination is often related to discrimination based on marital status, discussed *infra*.[46] It is thus important to consider both bases in any case involving one or the other.

The prohibitions against sex discrimination should also extend to discrimination based on gender-related stereotyping. For example, the ECOA should prohibit discrimination by automobile dealers who routinely mark up financing higher for female customers than male customers based on the belief that "women tend not to be as aggressive in negotiations as men."

3.3.4.2 Special ECOA Protections

The ECOA provides women with specific protections against creditor inquiries or credit decisions based on a woman's childbearing or childrearing intentions, including plans for maternity leave.[47] For example, a civil penalty has been assessed against a credit union which denied loans to female members who anticipated taking maternity leave.[48] Similarly, the Fair Housing Act prohibits discrimination on the basis of familial status, which includes discrimination against women who are pregnant.[49]

Sex discrimination may also be prohibited based on how creditors treat income sources traditionally associated with women. Regulation B sets out detailed standards as to whether creditors may discriminate against applicants whose incomes are based on part-time employment or consist of alimony, child support, separate maintenance, or public assistance.[50]

Sex discrimination may also take the form of discrimination based on gender-defined occupations. For example, the Federal Trade Commission has successfully challenged a credit scoring system that evaluated applications by giving waitresses no points for their occupation while giving waiters a positive number of points.[51]

Because of historical differences as to how husbands and wives have been treated, factors that appear neutral can have a disparate impact on women, and discrimination based on these may be prohibited. For example, credit accounts traditionally were kept in only the husband's name, with the consequence that many women today do not have independent credit histories. The ECOA sets out special rules by which to judge the credit history of women whose accounts have been subsumed under the name of their husbands.[52]

Similarly, because telephone listings traditionally were often listed in only the husband's name, the ECOA prohibits creditors from considering whether a telephone is listed in the applicant's name. Instead, creditors may only consider whether there is a telephone at the applicant's residence.[53]

3.3.4.3 Sexual Orientation

Neither the ECOA nor the Fair Housing Act specifically includes sexual orientation as a protected class. Sex discrimination, however, may take the form of discrimination against applicants who do not conform to gender-specific stereotypes or behave in gender-specific ways. For example, a sex discrimination claim under the ECOA was allowed to proceed against a bank that refused to allow a man who dressed in "feminine" clothing to apply for credit.[54] Thus, the prohibition against sex discrimination may also cover discrimination based on sexual orientation or transgender identity if the animus is based upon the applicant's failing to appear or act "like a man/woman."[55] Several states include sexual orientation as a prohibited basis.[56]

In some cases, discrimination based on sexual orientation may be challenged as discrimination based on marital or familial status.[57] Regulation B prohibits creditors from favoring married couples over unmarried couples in evaluating applicants for joint credit, which should protect same-sex joint applications.[58] In states that permit same-sex marriage, there

---

violate the Fair Housing Act if it had the effect of discriminating on the basis of national origin). *See generally* Rigel C. Oliveri, *Between a Rock and a Hard Place: Landlords, Latinos, Anti-Illegal Immigrant Ordinances and Housing Discrimination*, 62 Vand. L. Rev. 55 (2009) (discussing Fair Housing Act claims pertaining to municipal efforts to curtail housing opportunities based on alienage).

43 15 U.S.C. § 1691(a)(1); *see* Reg. B, 12 C.F.R. §§ 1002.2(z), 1002.4, 1002.6(b)(9) [§§ 202.2(z), 202.4, 202.6(b)(9)].

44 42 U.S.C. §§ 3604, 3605.

45 *See* appx. F, *infra* (summarizing state credit discrimination statutes).

46 *See* § 3.4.1, *infra*.

47 *See* § 5.5.2.2.3, *infra*.

48 United States v. Georgia Telco Credit Union, Clearinghouse No. 31,075 (N.D. Ga. July 25, 1980); *see also* Williams v. Countrywide Home Loans, 2002 WL 31270283 (Ohio Ct. App. Oct. 11, 2002) (granting class certification in lawsuit alleging lender violated state anti-discrimination law by refusing to consider income of female borrowers whom lender believed would be on maternity leave when loan closed).

49 *See* § 3.5.1, *infra*.

50 These requirements are analyzed in § 6.5.2, *infra*.

51 *In re* Alden's, Inc., 92 F.T.C. 901 (Fed. Trade Comm'n 1978).

52 *See* § 6.5.3, *infra*.

53 *See* § 6.5.4, *infra*.

54 Rosa v. Park West Bank & Trust, 214 F.3d 213, 216 (1st Cir. 2000) (stereotyped remarks about dressing in a more feminine or masculine manner can be evidence of gender bias).

55 *See* Centola v. Potter, 183 F. Supp. 2d 403 (D. Mass. 2002); Enriquez v. West Jersey Health Systems, 777 A.2d 365 (N.J. Super. Ct. App. Div. 2001). *See generally* Laura Eckert, *Inclusion of Sexual Orientation Discrimination in the Equal Credit Opportunity Act*, 103 Com. L.J. 311 (1998); Taylor Flynn, *Transforming the Debate: Why We Need to Include Transgender Rights in the Struggles for Sex and Sexual Orientation Equality*, 101 Colum. L. Rev. 392 (2001).

56 *See* § 3.7, *infra*.

57 *But see* Levin v. Yeshiva Univ., 754 N.E.2d 1099 (N.Y. 2001) (university's housing policy giving preferential treatment to married couples over unmarried couples, including same-sex partners, did not violate New York fair housing law prohibition against marital status discrimination).

58 *See* § 3.4.1, *infra*.

could be a potential argument that discrimination against same-sex couples is gender discrimination. If a creditor will grant a loan to a married couple consisting of a man and a woman but not a couple consisting of a man and a man, then the creditor is denying the loan because one of the applicants is not a woman.

Significantly, several state credit discrimination and housing financing statutes specifically list sexual orientation as a prohibited basis.[59] A few states also prohibit discrimination based upon an applicant's gender identity, which should protect transgender applicants.[60] New Jersey lists domestic partnership status as a prohibited basis.[61]

3.4 Prohibited Bases Under the ECOA But Not the FHA

3.4.1 Marital Status

Marital status is a prohibited basis under the ECOA[62] and many state credit discrimination and fair housing statutes.[63] Generally, marital status as a prohibited basis includes any discrimination against an individual because that individual is single, divorced, separated, married, or widowed. Creditors are required to treat married and unmarried applicants using the same standards unless otherwise permitted or required by law.[64]

Some of the exceptions permitted by law are discussed at the end of this chapter.

It is an ECOA violation not only to discriminate between married and unmarried applicants but also to discriminate between single and divorced applicants. The Federal Trade Commission (FTC) has successfully challenged the practices of a major creditor who divided credit applicants into divorced and single categories by circling or otherwise emphasizing information contained in credit reports run on the applicants.[65]

The prohibition against marital status discrimination prevents creditors from favoring married couples over unmarried couples in evaluating applicants for joint credit.[66] However, a government-authorized special-purpose credit program is permitted to favor married couples over unmarried couples.[67]

A creditor who would not aggregate the incomes of an unmarried man and woman applying jointly for a mortgage has been found to have discriminated based on marital status.[68] However, it would not be a violation of the ECOA for a creditor to refuse to combine the incomes of two parties when one is a co-signer or guarantor and not a joint applicant.[69] The Seventh Circuit, however, has rejected an ECOA claim made by a spouse who acted as a guarantor in a large commercial transaction. The court expressed great doubt about the federal regulatory agency's view that a guarantor is an "applicant" protected by the ECOA.[70]

---

59 *See, e.g.,* Cal. Gov't Code § 12955 (West); Colo. Rev. Stat. § 24-34-501(3) (housing transactions); Conn. Gen. Stat. §§ 46a-81f, 46a-98; D.C. Code § 1-2515 (human rights); Haw. Rev. Stat §§ 515-1 to 515-20 (housing); 775 Ill. Comp. Stat. §§ 5/1-102(A), 5/1-103; Iowa Code § 216.10 (credit transactions); Me. Rev. Stat. tit. 5, §§ 4595–4598 (credit transactions); Me. Rev. Stat. tit. 5, §§ 4451–4632, 4581–4583 (housing transactions); Md. Code Ann, State Gov't §§ 20-705 (West) (discriminatory housing practices), 20-707 (real estate related discrimination), 20-1103 (interference with housing activities); Mass. Gen. Laws ch. 151B, § 4(3B), (14) (excluding persons whose sexual orientation involves minor children as sex object); Minn. Stat. §§ 363A.09(3) (housing financing), 363A.16; N.H. Rev. Stat. Ann. § 354-A:10; N.J. Stat. Ann. § 10:5-12(i) (West); N.M. Stat. Ann. § 28-1-7 (human rights); N.Y. Exec. Law § 296-a (McKinney) (credit transactions); N.Y. Exec. Law § 296(5)(a)–(c) (McKinney) (housing transactions); R.I. Gen. Laws §§ 34-37-4(b), 34-37-4.3, 34-37-5.4; Vt. Stat. Ann. tit. 8, §§ 1211, 1302, 10403; Vt. Stat. Ann. tit. 9, §§ 2362, 2410, 4503(a)(6); Wash. Rev. Code § 49.60.175 (financial transactions); Wis. Stat. §§ 106.04, 224.77(1)(o).

There are also a number of municipalities that include sexual orientation in their credit discrimination ordinances. The Lambda Legal Defense and Education Fund has a list of these municipalities on its website at www.lambdalegal.org.

60 775 Ill. Comp. Stat. § 5/1-103(O-1) (definition of "sexual orientation" includes gender-related identity); Iowa Code § 216.10 (credit discrimination); N.M. Stat. Ann. § 28-1-7 (human rights); N.J. Stat. Ann. § 10:5-12(g) (West); R.I. Gen. Laws §§ 34-37-4(b) (housing financing), 34-37-4.3; Vt. Stat. Ann. tit. 8, § 10403 (financial institutions).

61 N.J. Stat. Ann. § 10:5-12(i) (West).

62 15 U.S.C. § 1691(a)(1); *see* Reg. B, 12 C.F.R. § 1002.2(z) [§ 202.2(z)].

63 *See* appx. F, *infra* (summarizing state credit discrimination statutes).

64 12 C.F.R. § 1002.6(b)(8) [§ 202.6(b)(8)].

65 *In re* Westinghouse Credit Corp., 94 F.T.C. 1280 (Fed. Trade Comm'n 1979); *see also* Shuman v. Standard Oil, 453 F. Supp. 1150 (N.D. Cal. 1978) (divorced woman alleged that the creditor discriminated against her on the basis of her marital status, as revealed in a credit report).

66 Reg. B, 12 C.F.R. § 1002.6(b)(8) [§ 202.6(b)(8)].

In contrast to Regulation B, courts interpreting state laws that prohibit marital status discrimination are split as to whether these provisions prohibit discrimination against unmarried couples. Levin v. Yeshiva Univ., 754 N.E.2d 1099 (N.Y. 2001); Hoy v. Mercado, 266 A.D.2d 803 (N.Y. App. Div. 1999). *See generally* Jason C. Long, *Housing Discrimination and the Status of Unmarried Cohabitants—Living with McCready v. Hoffus*, 76 U. Det. Mercy L. Rev. 99 (1998).

New Mexico's credit discrimination law has substituted "spousal affiliation" for "marital status" as a prohibited basis. N.M. Stat. Ann. § 28-1-1.

67 Diaz v. Va. Hous. Dev. Auth., 101 F. Supp. 2d 415, *subsequent proceeding at* 117 F. Supp. 2d 500 (E.D. Va. 2000); *see* § 3.9.3, *infra* (discussion of special purpose credit programs).

68 Markham v. Colonial Mortgage Serv. Co., 605 F.2d 566 (D.C. Cir. 1979).

However, on remand, the district court decided that the applicants had been denied credit because their combined income was insufficient and not because of their marital status. Markham v. Colonial Mortgage Serv. Co., Consumer Cred. Guide (CCH) ¶ 97,403 (D.D.C. 1980).

69 *See* Official Interpretations of Reg. B [Official Staff Commentary on Reg. B], 12 C.F.R. pt. 1002 [pt. 202], Supp. I, § 1002.6(b)(1)-1 [§ 202.6(b)(1)-1 (explained at 60 Fed. Reg. 29,965, 29,967 (June 7, 1995)].

70 Moran Foods, Inc. v. Mid-Atlantic Mkt. Dev. Co., L.L.C., 476 F.3d 436 (7th Cir. 2007); *see also* Champion Bank v. Reg'l Dev., L.L.C., 2009 WL 1351122 (E.D. Mo. May 13, 2009) (spouse who was required to sign as guarantor for husband's business loan not an

Marital status as a prohibited basis does not directly address sexual orientation. However, the prohibition against favoring married couples over unmarried joint applicants should protect same-sex joint applicants. At least one state explicitly prohibits discrimination in a credit transaction based on domestic partnership status.[71]

While the ECOA does not prohibit discrimination based on familial status, some forms of familial status discrimination may be challenged under the ECOA as discrimination based on sex or marital status. For example, discrimination based on an applicant being pregnant should be challenged under the ECOA as sex discrimination.[72] If there is discrimination based on whether a family has children, it is unclear if this constitutes marital status discrimination. Children are more likely to be correlated with married couples than with single individuals, particularly those who have never married.

On the other hand, this correlation is not particularly uniform or accurate. Many divorced, separated, and unmarried individuals have children and many married couples do not. Thus, one court has rejected a challenge to a credit scoring system that gave positive consideration to applicants with children because there was no evidence that the end result of the credit scoring system was to differentiate based on marital status.[73]

Regulation B includes a number of detailed rules concerning marital status discrimination that are discussed in later chapters, including:

- A creditor's ability to require that spouses join in credit applications if joint property is involved;[74]
- A creditor's ability to consider an applicant's marital status if it implicates the creditor's rights and remedies upon default;[75]
- The right of a creditor such as a utility to refuse to grant credit to one spouse on the basis of a delinquency owed by the other spouse to the same creditor;[76] and
- The manner in which a creditor must treat income that is associated with divorced or separated applicants, such as alimony, child support, and separate maintenance payments.[77]

3.4.2 Age

The ECOA[78] and a number of state credit discrimination laws[79] list age as a prohibited basis. In practice, however, the ECOA mainly prohibits discrimination against older consumers. That is, the central purpose and chief effect of the ECOA provision is to protect older persons, who historically have been subjected to arbitrary denial or revocation of credit when they reached a certain age, regardless of their actual credit histories or income levels.[80]

Regulation B defines the term "elderly" to include all persons aged sixty-two or older.[81] As a result, the ECOA offers special protections to those age sixty-two or older but offers significantly less protection against discrimination to, for example, a sixty-year-old.[82] Similarly, less protection is offered to a twenty-two-year-old who is discriminated against because of a brief work or credit history.[83]

There are a number of special ECOA rules that permit certain types of age discrimination.[84] These include the following circumstances:

- A creditor may consider the applicant's age to determine if the applicant is too young under state law to enter into a binding contract.[85]
- A creditor may consider the age of an applicant sixty-two years old or older in order to provide favorable treatment or more favorable credit terms to that applicant.[86]
- A creditor may consider the age of an applicant sixty-two years old or older in order to evaluate a pertinent element of creditworthiness for a reverse mortgage.[87]
- Under certain circumstances, a creditor may also take age into account as a factor in a credit scoring system, as long as those aged sixty-two and over receive the highest possible score for that factor.[88]

"applicant" with standing to bring ECOA claim; follows *Moran Foods*). *But see In re* Westbrooks, 440 B.R. 677 (Bankr. M.D.N.C. 2010) (guarantor of business loan had standing to challenge requirement for his wife to sign guarantee of note and deed of trust without independent evaluation of creditworthiness of business and potential guarantors); Citgo Petroleum Corp. v. Bulk Petroleum Corp., 2010 WL 3931496 (N.D. Ohio Oct. 5, 2010) (follows Regulation B on coverage of guarantors); Bank of the West v. Kline, 782 N.W.2d 453 (Iowa 2010) (adhering to view under Regulation B that "applicant" specifically includes guarantors, sureties, endorsers, and similar parties).

71 N.J. Stat. Ann. § 10:5-12(i) (West).
72 *See* §§ 3.3.4.1–3.3.4.3, *supra*.
73 Carroll v. Exxon Co., 434 F. Supp. 557 (E.D. La. 1977).
74 *See* § 5.6, *infra*.
75 *See* § 6.6.4, *infra*.
76 *See* § 5.5.2.4, *infra*.
77 *See* § 6.5.2.6, *infra*.

---

78 15 U.S.C. § 1691(a)(1); *see* Reg. B, 12 C.F.R. §§ 1002.2(z), 1002.4 [§§ 202.2(z), 202.4].
79 *See* appx. F, *infra* (summarizing state credit discrimination statutes).
80 *See* H.R. Rep. No. 94-210, at 3–4 (1975) (legislative history of the ECOA provisions addressing age discrimination).
81 Reg. B, 12 C.F.R. § 1002.2(o) [§ 202.2(o)].
82 Government enforcement of the age discrimination prohibition has also focused on older citizens. United States v. Money Tree, Inc., No. 6:97-CV-7 (M.D. Ga. Feb. 4, 1997), *available on the companion website of this treatise* (settlement between the Department of Justice (DOJ) and The Money Tree, Inc., over allegations of discrimination against older applicants and applicants who received public assistance), *available at* www.ftc.gov.
83 The only official attention to the problems of young credit applicants is contained in the official interpretations to Regulation B (12 C.F.R. pt. 1002 [pt. 202], Supp. I, § 1002.6(b) [§ 202.6(b)]), under which a creditor may consider an applicant's age when, for example, assessing the significance of the applicant's length of employment or residence.
84 These rules are discussed in detail in § 6.6.2, *infra*.
85 *See* § 6.6.2.2, *infra*.
86 *See* § 6.6.2.2, *infra*.
87 *See* § 6.6.2.2, *infra*.
88 *See* § 6.6.2.4, *infra*.

There are also special ECOA rules concerning the treatment of income associated with older consumers. These essentially prevent creditors from automatically excluding or considering only a portion of income derived from part-time employment, annuities, pensions, or other retirement benefits.[89] These rules are discussed in full in Chapter 6, *infra*.

3.4.3 Public Assistance Status

The ECOA lists as a prohibited basis for discrimination that "all or part of the applicant's income derives from any public assistance program."[90] This is an important category of prohibited discrimination for low-income consumers. It is not found in the federal Fair Housing Act. It is sometimes found in state fair housing laws and infrequently found as a prohibited basis in state credit discrimination laws.[91]

The Federal Trade Commission has brought two cases involving discrimination against public assistance recipients.[92] In 2012 the Department of Justice (DOJ) obtained a consent order against a lender for, among other things, requiring disabled applicants who received public assistance income to provide a doctors letter verifying that their public benefits income would continue for a certain length of time.[93]

Under Regulation B, a protected public assistance program is "[a]ny federal, state, or local governmental assistance program that provides a continuing, periodic income supplement, whether premised on entitlement or need."[94] According to the official interpretations of Regulation B, examples of such programs

include, but are not limited to, Temporary Assistance to Needy Families, food stamps, rent and mortgage supplement or assistance programs, Social Security and Supplemental Security Income, and unemployment compensation.[95] Other programs within this definition should include veterans' benefits, emergency relief programs, and federal fuel assistance.

Medicare and Medicaid payments are public assistance benefits only for the purposes of doctors, hospitals, or others to whom such benefits are payable.[96] Many doctors and hospitals are creditors[97] who extend credit.[98] Thus the ECOA could be used against medical providers who, for example, treat Medicare recipients less favorably than private insurance patients during any phase of the credit transaction.[99]

Although public assistance status is generally a prohibited basis for discrimination under the ECOA, there are some exceptions. There is an absolute prohibition against using the fact that income derives from public assistance in a credit scoring system.[100] However, creditors using systems other than credit scoring for evaluating creditworthiness may consider the source of such income to the extent it has a demonstrable relationship to determining creditworthiness.[101] The official interpretation gives several examples of such relationships, including how long the applicant will remain eligible for such income or whether the income may be garnished. These exceptions to the general rule against discrimination based on public assistance status are described in Chapter 6, *infra*.[102]

3.4.4 Good Faith Exercise of Consumer Credit Protection Act or Other Legal Rights

3.4.4.1 General

A prohibited basis unique to the ECOA is the applicant's good faith exercise of federal Consumer Credit Protection Act (CCPA) rights.[103] Only a few states have an analogous provision listing exercise of rights under state credit legislation as a prohibited basis.[104] Also, the Fair Housing Act prohibits retaliating against any person because that person has made a complaint, testified, assisted, or participated in any manner in a proceeding under the Fair Housing Act.[105]

Under the ECOA, a creditor may not discriminate against an applicant because that person has exercised, in good faith, any

---

89 *See* § 6.5.2.5, *infra*.

90 15 U.S.C. § 1691(a)(2); *see* Reg. B, 12 C.F.R. § 1002.2(z) [§ 202.2(z)].

91 *See, e.g.*, Conn. Gen Stat. § 46a-64c (housing finance; source of income); D.C. Code § 1-2515 (human rights; source of income); 815 Ill. Comp. Stat. § 120/3 (Fairness in Lending Act); Iowa Code § 537.3311 (Iowa Consumer Credit Code); Mass. Gen. Laws ch. 151B, § 4(10); Minn. Stat. § 363A.16 (public assistance, including medical or rental assistance); Minn. Stat. § 363A.09(3) (housing financing); N.J. Stat. Ann. § 10:5-4 (West) (source of income); N.C. Gen. Stat. § 41A-4 (housing assistance); N.D. Cent. Code § 14-02.4-17 (housing financing); Okla. Stat. tit. 25, § 1452(A)(7)–(9) (housing financing; public assistance, as specified); Or. Rev. Stat. § 659A.421 (source of income); Tex. Fin. Code Ann. § 341.401 (West) (Social Security and Supplemental Security Income only); Utah Code Ann. § 57-21-5 (West) (source of income); Vt. Stat. Ann. tit. 9, § 4503(a)(6) (housing financing); Wis. Stat. § 106.50 (housing finance; source of income), § 224.77 (certain housing finance; source of income).

92 United States v. Franklin Acceptance Corp., No. 99-CV-2435 (E.D. Pa. 1999), *available at* www.ftc.gov; United States v. Money Tree, Inc., No. 6:97-CV-7 (M.D. Ga. Feb. 4, 1997), *available at* www.ftc.gov *and on the companion website to this treatise.*

    Franklin Acceptance Corp. resulted in an $800,000 settlement, the largest civil penalty settlement obtained up to that time for alleged violations of the ECOA.

93 Complaint and Consent Decree, United States v. Bank of America, No. 3:12-cv-00605 (W.D.N.C. filed Sept. 13, 2012), *available at* www.usdoj.gov *and on the companion website to this treatise.*

94 Official Interpretations of Reg. B [Official Staff Commentary on Reg. B], 12 C.F.R. pt. 1002 [pt. 202], Supp. I, § 1002.2(z)-3 [§ 202.2(z)-3].

95 *Id.*

96 *Id.*

97 *See* § 2.2.2.6, *supra*.

98 *See* § 2.2.2.6, *supra*.

99 *See* § 2.2.2.6, *supra*.

100 12 C.F.R. §§ 1002.2(t), (y) [202.2(t), (y)] (definitions); 1002.6(b) (2)(i), (ii), (iii) [202.6(b)(2)(i), (b)(2)(ii), (b)(2)(iii)] (prohibition).

101 12 C.F.R. §§ 1002.2(t) [202.2(t)] (definition); 1002.6(b)(2)(iii) [202.6(b)(2)(iii)].

102 *See* § 6.6.3.2, *infra*.

103 15 U.S.C. § 1691(a)(3); *see* Reg. B, 12 C.F.R. § 1002.2(z) [§ 202.2(z)].

104 *See, e.g.*, Iowa Code § 537.3311 (Iowa Consumer Credit Code); Mo. Rev. Stat. § 408.550.

105 42 U.S.C. § 3617; *see* 24 C.F.R. § 100.400(c)(5).

right under the CCPA[106] or any state statute substituted for it, in whole or in part, with the federal regulatory agency's approval.[107] This protection does not extend to rights exercised by persons other than the applicant.[108] The intent of this provision is to prevent "retaliatory credit denials or terminations"[109] of credit accounts when applicants exercise their legal rights. Similarly, a creditor may not condition granting new credit on an applicant's release of existing CCPA claims.[110]

The protection of this section is contingent on showing three separate elements:

- Rights were exercised under the federal Consumer Credit Protection Act or a substituted state statute;
- The rights were exercised in good faith; and
- The rights were exercised by the applicant.

A federal court of appeals case discussing this section has characterized it as prohibiting "retaliation" and utilized a framework that has been used in retaliation-based Title VII employment discrimination cases. In order to make out a prima facie case, the court held that a consumer must allege facts sufficient to show that he or she engaged in a statutorily protected activity and suffered an adverse credit action and that there is a causal connection between the two (a retaliatory motive).[111] Another court of appeals characterized the prima facie test as requiring plaintiffs to show that they (1) exercised in good faith (2) a right under the Consumer Credit Protection Act and (3) as a result, the creditor discriminated against them with respect to the credit transaction.[112]

3.4.4.2 Exercise of Rights Under the Federal Consumer Credit Protection Act or a Substituted State Statute

The federal Consumer Credit Protection Act (CCPA)[113] is an umbrella act comprised of a number of separately enacted statutes focusing on various credit issues. Exercise of rights under any of the following statutes triggers the protection of the ECOA for credit applicants:

- Truth in Lending Act;[114]
- Fair Credit Billing Act;[115]
- Consumer Leasing Act;[116]
- Federal Garnishment Act;[117]
- Federal Credit Repair Organization Act;[118]
- Fair Credit Reporting Act;[119]
- Fair Debt Collection Practices Act;[120]
- Electronic Fund Transfer Act;[121] and
- Equal Credit Opportunity Act.[122]

When a state has obtained an exemption from one of these acts because it has enacted its own equivalent or more protective statute,[123] exercise of rights under the state statute would also invoke the protection of the ECOA.

The exercise of CCPA rights is not limited merely to litigation under the CCPA or substituted state statutes. Exercise of rights also includes use of procedures such as the billing statement dispute mechanisms of the Fair Credit Billing Act[124] and exercise of rescission rights under the Truth in Lending Act.[125] Furthermore, if the creditor denies credit because the applicant does not wish to buy credit insurance, which is supposedly optional under the creditor's Truth in Lending disclosure form, the applicant may have an ECOA claim for discrimination on the basis of good faith exercise of rights under the CCPA.[126]

3.4.4.3 "Good Faith" Exercise of Rights

The applicant is protected only when an exercise of rights under the CCPA was done in "good faith."[127] The legislative history of 1976 ECOA amendments explains: "The 'good faith' qualification recognizes that some applicants may engage in frivolous or nuisance disputes which do reflect on their willingness to honor their obligations."[128]

106 15 U.S.C. §§ 1601–1693r.

107 15 U.S.C. § 1691(a)(3); *see* Reg. B, 12 C.F.R. § 1002.4 [§ 202.4], § 1002.2(z) [§ 202.2(z)].

108 *See* Official Interpretations of Reg. B [Official Staff Commentary on Reg. B], 12 C.F.R. pt. 1002 [pt. 202], Supp. I, § 1002.2(z)-1 [§ 202.2(z)-1].

109 S. Rep. No. 94-589, at 5 (1976), *reprinted in* 1976 U.S.C.C.A.N. 403, 407.

110 Owens v. Magee Finance Serv., 476 F. Supp. 758 (E.D. La. 1979).

111 Lewis v. ACB Bus. Serv., Inc., 135 F.3d 389 (6th Cir. 1998) (plaintiff failed to show a causal connection between the creditor's collection action and the plaintiff's earlier lawsuit against the creditor and therefore failed to claim an adverse credit action, as the creditor was just collecting its debt); Prince v. U.S. Bank, 2009 WL 2998141 (S.D. Ala. Sept. 14, 2009) (mortgagee's commencement of foreclosure action after receipt of borrower's TILA rescission notice did not state claim for discrimination under 15 U.S.C. § 1691(a)(3)).

112 Bowen v. First Family Financial Servs., Inc., 233 F.3d 1331 (11th Cir. 2000); *see also* Kivel v. Wealthspring Mortgage Corp., 398 F. Supp. 2d 1049 (D. Minn. 2005) (rejecting plaintiff's claim of discrimination based on exercise of right to receive ECOA adverse action notice because plaintiffs failed to establish that they were entitled to the notice).

113 15 U.S.C. §§ 1601–1693r.

114 15 U.S.C. §§ 1601–1667f.

115 15 U.S.C. §§ 1666–1666j.

116 15 U.S.C. §§ 1667–1667f.

117 15 U.S.C. §§ 1671–1677.

118 15 U.S.C. §§ 1679–1679j.

119 15 U.S.C. §§ 1681–1681u.

120 15 U.S.C. §§ 1692–1692o.

121 15 U.S.C. §§ 1693–1693r.

122 15 U.S.C. §§ 1691–1691f.

123 For example, several states have been granted an exemption from the federal Truth in Lending Act, pursuant to 15 U.S.C. § 1633. *See, e.g.*, Conn. Gen. Stat. §§ 36-393 to 36-417j.

124 15 U.S.C. § 1666(a).

125 15 U.S.C. § 1635; Reg. Z, 12 C.F.R. § 226.9.

126 Bryson v. Bank of N.Y., 584 F. Supp. 1306 (S.D.N.Y. 1984).

127 15 U.S.C. § 1691(a)(3); Reg. B, 12 C.F.R. § 1002.2(z) [§ 202.2(z)].

128 S. Rep. No. 94-589, at 5 (1976), *reprinted in* 1976 U.S.C.C.A.N. 403, 407.

    An example of such an action would be the initiation of a Fair Credit Billing Act inquiry solely to delay payment of an outstanding credit card balance. Compare the legislative history of the Fair Debt

Decisions under the ECOA have not developed the definition of "good faith." One reported case dealing with discrimination based on an applicant's exercise of CCPA rights concluded as a matter of law that the applicant had previously exercised her Truth in Lending rights in good faith, in the absence of any creditor claim to the contrary.[129]

Several of the statutes that comprise the CCPA create good faith or bona fide error defenses for creditors.[130] However, cases interpreting these provisions are not likely to provide useful guidance in interpreting the ECOA's standard of good faith exercise of CCPA rights. The context is very different, and these statutory defenses include specific elements that the creditor must establish—such as the maintenance of reasonable procedures to prevent errors—that are irrelevant to the question of whether a consumer asserted CCPA rights in good faith.

A more relevant source of precedent on the meaning of good faith in the ECOA context are the standards for an award of attorney fees to a defendant when a plaintiff has brought an action in bad faith under the CCPA or similar statutes. For instance, the Fair Debt Collection Practices Act (FDCPA) provides that a court may award attorney fees to a defendant when a plaintiff brings an action under the Act "in bad faith and for the purposes of harassment."[131] A reasonable standard for good faith in the ECOA context would be any exercise of rights that would not expose the consumer to an award of defendant's fees under that part of the CCPA. Another source of standards would be Rule 11 and common law standards for the award of defendant's fees for bad faith litigation.[132]

Under these standards, the creditor claiming that a CCPA suit was not brought in good faith bears a heavy burden of proof. The creditor must prove that the consumer acted out of malice or with an intent to harass in instituting the action. Good faith should be proven automatically if the consumer's action was successful.

After an unsuccessful CCPA action, the creditor trying to argue for the consumer's lack of good faith would have to show not only that the consumer had no basis for believing that the CCPA had been violated but also that the consumer in fact did not believe that such violations had occurred. Furthermore, the creditor must show that the purpose of the suit was harassment.

3.4.4.4 "Applicant" Must Exercise the Rights

The applicant must have exercised the CCPA rights. Applicant is a defined term under Regulation B and includes a credit applicant, one who has been extended credit, and a co-signer or other party who is contractually obligated on the loan.[133] If any of these individuals had previously exercised CCPA rights, the creditor may not use that as a basis for discrimination.

3.5 Prohibited Bases Under the FHA, but Not the ECOA

3.5.1 Familial Status

The federal Fair Housing Act (FHA) lists familial status as a prohibited basis for credit discrimination,[134] as do most state credit discrimination and housing financing statutes.[135] Generally, this prohibition forbids creditors from discriminating on the basis that applicants have children (or do not have children), are pregnant, or are legal custodians of children.

The regulations implementing the Act define familial status as a parent, legal custodian, or designee of such person having one or more children under the age of eighteen domiciled with them.[136] Thus there is discrimination on the basis of familial status when an apartment complex has a policy of refusing to rent apartments to families with more than a certain number of family members (that is, total of adults and children) when it would rent the same unit to the same number of individuals if all the tenants were adults.[137]

In one case, the court found a prima facie violation on the basis of familial status when the condominium association published rules prohibiting children under twelve and neither removed those restrictions prior to the tenancy nor communicated their unenforceability to the tenant, even though the

---

Collection Practices Act, a subtitle of the Consumer Credit Protection Act, which recognizes that "the number of persons who willfully refuse to pay just debts is minuscule [sic]." S. Rep. No. 95-382 (1977), *reprinted in* 1977 U.S.C.C.A.N. 1695, 1697.

129 Owens v. Magee Finance Serv., 476 F. Supp. 758 (E.D. La. 1979).

130 *See, e.g.*, Truth in Lending Act, 15 U.S.C. § 1640(c) (bona fide error defense), (f) (good faith compliance with rule, regulation, or interpretation); Fair Debt Collection Practices Act, 15 U.S.C. § 1692k(c) (bona fide error defense). *See generally* National Consumer Law Center, Truth in Lending §§ 12.4.2, 12.4.4 (8th ed. 2012); National Consumer Law Center, Fair Debt Collection § 7.2 (7th ed. 2011 and Supp.).

131 15 U.S.C. § 1692k(a)(3).

132 Fed. R. Civ. P. 11; Alyeska Pipeline Serv. v. Wilderness Soc'y, 421 U.S. 240, 258–59, 95 S. Ct. 1612, 44 L. Ed. 2d 141 (1975) (noting common law rule allowing fee award when losing party has "acted in bad faith, vexatiously, wantonly, or for oppressive reasons"); *cf.* Christiansburg Garment Co. v. Equal Emp't Opportunity Comm'n, 434 U.S. 412, 98 S. Ct. 694, 54 L. Ed. 2d 648 (1978) (interpreting prevailing party fee award provision of Equal Employment Opportunity Act to allow award to defendant only if suit is frivolous, meritless, or vexatious).

133 *See* § 2.2.4, *supra*.

134 42 U.S.C. §§ 3604, 3605; *see* 24 C.F.R. § 100.110(b).

135 *See* appx. F, *infra* (summarizing state credit discrimination and housing financing statutes).

136 24 C.F.R. § 100.20.

137 Glover v. Crestwood Lake Section 1 Holding Corp., 746 F. Supp. 301 (S.D.N.Y. 1990).

Note that the Fair Housing Act contains an exemption which states that occupancy limits per se do not violate the Act. 42 U.S.C. § 3607(b)(1); *see also* Ortega v. Brownsville Hous. Auth., 572 F. Supp. 2d 829 (S.D. Tex. 2008) (familial status discrimination exists under FHA when housing authority requires adult to be legal guardian of child in household rather than be simply a "designee" with valid authority from child's parents allowing child to reside in household).

However, this exemption is to be narrowly construed, and occupancy limits cannot be based upon the familial relationships (or lack thereof) of the occupants. City of Edmonds v. Oxford House, 514 U.S. 725, 115 S. Ct. 1776, 131 L. Ed. 2d 801 (1995).

association took no action to enforce the rules and the tenancy was terminated for failure to pay rent.[138]

Familial status also includes being pregnant or in the process of gaining legal custody of a child under eighteen years of age.[139] Thus, discrimination against a family that takes in foster children should be discrimination under the Fair Housing Act.[140]

A lender may consider the *costs* of caring for children in determining creditworthiness but cannot have a policy of treating those with children less favorably than those without.[141] Creditors also should not be able to discriminate on the basis of the number of children.[142]

In addition, the prohibition on familial status discrimination does not apply to certain housing for older consumers,[143] allowing housing developments for older persons to restrict children. This exclusion should have little application to credit discrimination.

3.5.2 Disability or Handicap

3.5.2.1 General

The Fair Housing Act and many state credit discrimination statutes[144] directly prohibit credit discrimination based on an applicant's status as handicapped or disabled.[145] The Americans with Disabilities Act (ADA)[146] also prohibits discrimination by creditors on the basis of disability. On the other hand, the ECOA does not provide for an individual's disability as a protected basis.

3.5.2.2 Definition of Handicap or Disability

Handicap or disability is defined in the FHA and in the ADA as a physical or mental impairment which substantially limits one or more major life activity, having a record of such impairment, or being considered as having such an impairment.[147] It is not enough to have an impairment. The disability also must substantially limit one or more major life activity, such as caring for oneself, performing manual tasks, walking, seeing, hearing, speaking, breathing, learning, or working.[148]

On the other hand, the individual need not presently have such a physical or mental impairment. It is sufficient if a record exists of the individual having, or having been classified (or even misclassified) as having, a history of mental or physical impairment. Also, it is enough if the individual is considered to have such an impairment, meaning that the impairment does not substantially limit a major life activity but others view and treat the individual as having an impairment which constitutes such a limitation.[149]

It always makes sense to compare the definition of disability under the Fair Housing Act and the ADA with definitions found in any relevant state credit discrimination law to determine if one or the other is more applicable in a specific case. For example, several state credit discrimination and housing financing laws[150] consider persons with HIV or AIDS to be disabled or handicapped (as does the ADA).[151]

3.5.2.3 Application of the Americans with Disabilities Act to Credit Transactions

The ADA can combat credit discrimination involving applicants with disabilities, especially for non-housing financing cases.[152] Title III of the ADA prohibits discrimination by places of public accommodation on the basis of disability.[153] Public accommodation is defined to include banks, retailers, and other

---

138 Martin v. Palm Beach Atl. Ass'n, 696 So. 2d 919 (Fla. Dist. Ct. App. 1997).

139 24 C.F.R. § 100.20.

140 *See* Gorski v. Troy, 929 F.2d 1183 (7th Cir. 1991).

   However, familial status does not include a group home consisting solely of children unless the caretakers of the children actually live with them in the home. Keys Youth Serv. v. City of Olathe, 248 F.3d 1267 (10th Cir. 2001).

141 H.R. Rep. No. 100-711 (1988), *reprinted in* 1988 U.S.C.C.A.N. 2173, 2191–92.

142 For example, occupancy limits based upon the number of children are prohibited. Indiana Civil Rights Comm'n v. County Line Park, 738 N.E.2d 1044 (Ind. 2000); *see also* Kelly v. United States Dep't of Hous. & Urban Dev., 3 F.3d 951, 952 (6th Cir. 1993).

143 *See* 24 C.F.R. § 100.300; Covey v. Hollydale Mobilehome Estates, 116 F.3d 830 (9th Cir. 1997); Massaro v. Mainlands Section 1 & 2 Civic Ass'n, 3 F.3d 1472 (11th Cir. 1993).

144 42 U.S.C. §§ 3604, 3605; *see, e.g.*, Idaho Code Ann. §§ 67-5901 to 67-5912; *see also* appx. F, *infra* (summaries of state credit discrimination statutes).

   Some state statutes use the term "disability" rather than "handicapped." *See, e.g.*, Me. Rev. Stat. tit. 5, § 4582 (housing financing); N.D. Cent. Code §§ 14-02.4-13 (housing financing), 14-02.4-17; Wis. Stat. § 106.04.

145 United States v. Space Hunters, Inc., 429 F.3d 416 (2d Cir. 2005); Michigan Prot. & Advocacy Serv., Inc. v. Babin, 18 F.3d 337 (6th Cir. 1994); Nevels v. Western World Ins. Co., 359 F. Supp. 2d 1110 (W.D. Wash. 2004).

146 42 U.S.C. § 12101.

147 42 U.S.C. § 3602(h) (Fair Housing Act); 42 U.S.C. § 12102(2)(A), (B), (C) (Americans with Disabilities Act); 24 C.F.R. § 100.201.

   Handicap for purposes of the Fair Housing Act's credit discrimination provision is actually defined in 24 C.F.R. § 100.20, but this provision merely refers to the definition found in 24 C.F.R. § 100.201.

148 Toyota Mfg. v. Williams, 534 U.S. 184, 122 S. Ct. 681, 151 L. Ed. 2d 615 (2002) (in this employment discrimination case, a unanimous Supreme Court ruled that, "to be substantially limited in performing manual tasks, an individual must have an impairment that prevents or severely restricts the individual from doing activities that are of central importance to most people's daily lives, and the impairment must be permanent or long-term").

149 *Id.*

150 *See* Fla. Stat. § 760.25; N.J. Stat. Ann. § 10:5-12(i) (West).

151 *See* Bragdon v. Abbott, 524 U.S. 624, 118 S. Ct. 2196, 141 L. Ed. 2d 540 (1998).

152 *See* § 1.6, *supra* (briefly describing the ADA).

153 42 U.S.C. § 12182(a) ("No individual shall be discriminated against on the basis of disability in the full and equal enjoyment of the goods, services, facilities, privileges, advantages, or accommodations of any place of public accommodation by any person who owns, leases (or leases to), or operates a place of public accommodation.").

service establishments.[154] Thus many creditors should be covered by the ADA because they constitute places of public accommodation.

Furthermore, credit transactions should be covered under the scope of Title III of the ADA. Title III prohibits discrimination on the basis of disability in the full enjoyment of "goods, services, facilities, or privileges."[155] Credit is considered a "service" under this provision.[156]

Most of the courts that have considered whether the ADA applies to credit transactions have held that it does.[157] In addition, a number of courts have held that the ADA applies to insurance products.[158] In doing so, these courts have noted that the ADA regulates not just physical access to a place of public accommodation but also applies to the products sold therein.[159]

The ADA's legislative history also provides support for the application of the ADA to credit transactions. The House Report explains that a store may not ask on a credit application if a person has epilepsy, has ever been hospitalized for mental illness, or has any other disability.[160]

There are several specific ADA provisions that should be useful in credit discrimination cases. One such provision prohibits the imposition or application of eligibility criteria that screen out or tend to screen out individuals with disabilities and prevent them from fully and equally enjoying any goods, services, facilities, or privileges, unless such criteria can be shown to be necessary for the provision of the goods, services, facilities, or privileges being offered.[161] Another provision is the requirement for places of public accommodation to provide auxiliary devices to ensure effective communication with the public.[162] The ADA also prohibits unnecessary inquiries about disabilities.[163]

In an example of the ADA's applicability to credit transactions, the New York attorney general's office settled a claim of discrimination against HSBC Card Services, Inc., when the creditor agreed to improve access to the company's customer service operations for its customers with vision and hearing impairments.[164] The state's investigation began when a customer complained that HSBC had repeatedly told her that she could not dispute a charge on her statement unless she completed a written form. The customer could not read the form due to her vision impairment. As part of its agreement with the state HSBC agreed to overhaul its website so that it could be used by customers with hearing and vision loss; offer forms in formats accessible for the visually impaired; make reader services available through a special assistance line; train its staff to work with customers with hearing and speech impairments; and track reasonable accommodation requests in the future. In addition to the ADA, the New York attorney general relied upon the similar New York state laws requiring service providers to make reasonable accommodations for customers with disabilities.

A limitation in the use of the ADA to address credit discrimination is that, while United States attorneys can seek monetary relief as well as injunctive relief and civil penalties for the victims of discrimination,[165] the remedies for private plaintiffs under the ADA are limited to injunctive relief and attorney fees. Compensatory damages are not available under the Act.[166] However, an ADA violation in some states may be treated as a per se violation of a state unfair and deceptive acts and practices statute, which will provide a private damages remedy.[167]

3.5.2.4 Reasonable Accommodation

In addition to prohibiting discrimination on the basis of disability, both the ADA[168] and the Fair Housing Act[169] provide that a refusal to make a reasonable accommodation for a disabled person is a form of discrimination. However, the Fair Housing Act's requirement of reasonable accommodation applies only to claims under section 3604 (discrimination in the sale or rental of housing), not section 3605 (discrimination in residential real estate transactions, including loans).[170] The judicial trend is to find that section 3604 does not apply to

---

154   42 U.S.C. § 12181(7)(F).

155   42 U.S.C. § 12182(a).

156   Webster Bank v. Oakley, 830 A.2d 139 (Conn. 2003).

157   Gaona v. Town & Country Credit, 324 F.3d 1050 (8th Cir. 2003); Webster Bank v. Oakley, 830 A.2d 139 (Conn. 2003).

      The only case to date which has held that the ADA does not apply to credit transactions is Kloth v. Citibank, 33 F. Supp. 2d 115 (D. Conn. 1998). In that case, which was brought by a *pro se* plaintiff, the court dismissed the public accommodations claim by rather oddly citing only the ADA section concerning discrimination in employment, while ignoring Title III.

158   Pallozzi v. Allstate Life Ins. Co., 198 F.3d 28, *as amended*, 204 F.3d 392 (2d Cir. 2000); Doe v. Mut. of Omaha Ins. Co., 179 F.3d 557 (7th Cir. 1999); Wai v. Allstate Ins. Co., 75 F. Supp. 2d 1 (D.D.C. 1999) (home owners insurance case; also involved FHA claim).

159   Pallozzi v. Allstate Life Ins. Co., 198 F.3d 28, *as amended*, 204 F.3d 392 (2d Cir. 2000); Wai v. Allstate Ins. Co., 75 F. Supp. 2d 1 (D.D.C. 1999).

160   *See* H.R. Rep. No. 101-485II, at 105 (1990), *reprinted in* 1990 U.S.C.C.A.N. 267, 388.

161   42 U.S.C. § 12182(b)(2)(A)(i).

162   *See* U.S. Dep't of Justice, ADA Title III Technical Assistance Manual, *available* at ww.usdoj.gov/crt/ada/taman3.html.

163   *Id.*

164   Settlement Agreement Between State of New York and HSBC Card Services, Inc. (Sept. 1, 2009), *available on the companion website to this treatise.*

165   42 U.S.C. § 12188(b)(2).

166   42 U.S.C. § 12188(a); A.R. v. Kogan, 964 F. Supp. 269, 271 (N.D. Ill. 1997).

167   *See generally* National Consumer Law Center, Unfair and Deceptive Acts and Practices §§ 3.2.7, 4.3.9 (8th ed. 2012).

168   42 U.S.C. § 12182(b)(2)(A)(ii).

169   42 U.S.C. § 3604(f)(3).

170   42 U.S.C. § 3604(f)(3) (limiting the scope of the reasonable accommodation requirement to "this subsection"); Gaona v. Town & Country Credit, 324 F.3d 1050 (8th Cir. 2003) (creditor was not required to provide sign language interpreter to deaf consumers as reasonable accommodation under section 3605 of the Fair Housing Act); Fletcher v. Homecomings Financial, L.L.C., 2010 WL 1665265 (M.D.N.C. Apr. 2, 2010) (section 3605 of FHA applies to practices involving modification of existing mortgage loans but does not require reasonable accommodations); Webster Bank v. Oakley, 830 A.2d 139 (Conn. 2003) (relying on *Gaona*).

home-secured loans when the borrower has already acquired the dwelling.[171] Thus a creditor may be required to make reasonable accommodation under the Fair Housing Act for disabled applicants with regard to purchase money mortgages and rentals, but not for non-purchase money mortgage loans such as home equity credit. The ADA, on the other hand, requires reasonable accommodation for all forms of credit.

Reasonable accommodation can involve either physical access modifications or accommodations in rules, policies, practices, or services.[172] Thus, a lender could be required to make an exception to its rules or policies in order to reasonably accommodate a disabled applicant.

The ADA provides that any modifications must be reasonable and must not fundamentally alter the nature of the services provided.[173] The critical issue then is the kind of rules and policies that a lender could be required to modify to accommodate a disabled applicant. For example, should a lender be required to modify its underwriting criteria or loan requirements?

In *Scherer v. Mission Bank*,[174] the Tenth Circuit held that the ADA did not require a lender to make an exception to its underwriting inquiry for a disabled applicant to satisfy the requirement of reasonable accommodation. *Scherer* involved a *pro se* plaintiff who, according to the Tenth Circuit, failed to specify what exception the lender should have made to accommodate his disability, instead making a general assertion that the ADA required the lender to modify its policies.[175] The court held that the plaintiff failed to make out a prima facie claim under the Fair Housing Act because he was not qualified for the loan.

The court used an analysis similar to the one established by the Supreme Court in *McDonnell-Douglas v. Green*.[176] However, the use of a *McDonnell-Douglas* analysis in a disability discrimination case may not always be appropriate. Requiring the applicant to show that he was initially qualified for the loan would foreclose any argument that the reasonable accommodation itself is one that requires making an exception to the lender's underwriting standards. A *McDonnell-Douglas* analysis would also beg the question of whether the lending criteria themselves discriminate by tending to screen out disabled applicants in violation of the ADA.

In *Webster v. Oakley*,[177] the Connecticut Supreme Court held that a mortgage lender was not required to make an exception to its foreclosure policies to accommodate a recently disabled borrower. The court in *Webster* distinguished equal access to a service, such as applying for and receiving a mortgage, from the content of that service (which presumably includes foreclosure policies), stating that the ADA ensures the former but does not regulate the latter.[178] The court believed that changing the content or terms of loan policies would "fundamentally alter the nature" of the loan and noted that the ADA specifically states that entities are not required to make modifications to such an extent.[179]

The analysis in *Webster* distinguishing *access* to a service versus *content* of that service might arguably provide a basis for requiring a lender to modify certain underwriting policies to accommodate disabled applicants because such criteria control access to the services at issue, that is, the credit transaction. Modification of underwriting policies would most appropriately be required if these policies were somewhat related to the applicant's disability. Such a conclusion would also be supported by the ADA provision prohibiting places of public accommodation from imposing eligibility criteria that screen out or tend to screen out individuals with disabilities.[180]

Indeed, the United States Department of Justice (DOJ) has on two occasions required creditors to modify their policies because these policies screened out disabled consumers in violation of the ADA. The DOJ took enforcement action against a department store that allegedly discriminated against disabled customers by granting check payment privileges only to customers with driver's licenses (which certain disabled individuals cannot obtain).[181] The DOJ also issued an informal opinion letter stating that, under the ADA, a bank must modify its signature policies to accommodate a quadriplegic who was unable to sign his name because of his disability.[182]

The Ninth Circuit's interpretation in *Giebeler* of the Fair Housing Act's reasonable accommodation requirement in the context of a rental housing application should support similar arguments for modification of credit application standards to accommodate the disabled.[183] Mr. Giebeler applied to rent an apartment which he could clearly not afford based on his Supplemental Security Income (SSI). The apartment managers had a policy of refusing to allow co-signers on leases. Because her son could not afford the apartment, Giebeler's mother offered to rent the apartment in her name, with the understanding her son would live in the unit and she would help with the rent. It was not disputed that Giebeler's mother qualified under all financial requirements for renting the apartment. Nevertheless, the apartment managers still rejected the application based on their "no co-signers" policy.

---

171 *See* §§ 2.3.2 and 2.3.3, *supra* (discussing scope of section 3604 versus section 3605).

172 42 U.S.C. § 3604(f)(3)(A), (B); 42 U.S.C. § 12182(b)(2)(A)(ii). *See generally* Joint Statement, United States Dep't of Hous. & Urban Dev. & United States Dep't of Justice, Reasonable Accommodations Under the Fair Housing Act (May 17, 2004), *available at* www.hud.gov/offices/fheo/disabilities/index.cfm.

173 42 U.S.C. § 12182(b)(2)(A)(ii).

174 34 Fed. Appx. 656 (10th Cir. 2002).

175 34 Fed. Appx. 656 (10th Cir. 2002).

176 411 U.S. 792, 93 S. Ct. 1817, 36 L. Ed. 2d 668 (1973); *see* § 4.2.3.1, *infra* (analyzing *McDonnell-Douglas*).

177 830 A.2d 139 (Conn. 2003).

178 *Id.*

179 *Id.*

180 42 U.S.C. § 12182(b)(2)(A)(i).

181 Disability Rights Section, United States Dep't of Justice, Enforcing the ADA: Looking Back on a Decade of Progress § C.1 (2000), *available* at www.usdoj.gov.

182 United States Dep't of Justice, Informal Opinion Letter (Dec. 29, 1994), *available at* www.usdoj.gov/crt/foia/cltr149.txt.

183 Giebeler v. M & B Assocs., 343 F.3d 1143 (9th Cir. 2003).

Giebeler then brought an action under the Fair Housing Act against the apartment managers, alleging that they had refused to make a reasonable accommodation in their rules based on his disability. He lost in the district court, but prevailed on appeal. The court of appeals held that Giebeler had requested precisely the type of simple modification of standards that the Act contemplated. The Fair Housing Act required the managers to make an assessment of Giebeler's risk factors independent of the standards they used for non-disabled applicants. His request for a modification was reasonable and should have been implemented.[184]

3.6 Prohibited Bases Under the Federal Civil Rights Acts

3.6.1 Race and Ethnicity

Race is the sole prohibited basis under the federal Civil Rights Acts.[185] One important issue in the definition of race under the federal Civil Rights Acts is whether racial discrimination includes discrimination against ethnic or Caucasian groups—such as Arabs, Jews, and Hispanics.

A unanimous Supreme Court in 1987 interpreted racial discrimination under the federal Civil Rights Acts to be based on the nineteenth century notions of race (when the first civil rights acts were enacted). The Court concluded that the statutes protected "identifiable classes of persons who are subjected to intentional discrimination solely because of their ancestry or ethnic characteristics."[186]

In that case, the Court found the Civil Rights Acts applied to discrimination against Arabs. In another 1987 case, the Court held that the federal Civil Rights Acts apply to discrimination against Jews because, in the nineteenth century, Jews were also considered a separate race.[187]

Other courts have held that Hispanics,[188] Native Americans,[189]

Italians,[190] and Filipinos[191] are considered racial minorities for purposes of the federal Civil Rights Acts. The federal Civil Rights Acts do not prohibit discrimination on the basis of religion, and the key to coverage is to define a group (such as Jews) not as a religious group but as a "race" according to Nineteenth Century notions of race.[192]

3.6.2 Citizenship Status

Only citizens are given the right to utilize section 1982, since the statutes state explicitly that "all citizens of the United State shall have the same right. . . ." On the other hand, section 1981 states that "all persons within the jurisdiction of the United States shall have the same right to make and enforce contracts . . . as is enjoyed by white citizens."[193] Thus, a noncitizen can bring actions under that statute when that noncitizen does not have the same rights as "white citizens."[194]

Thus section 1981 prohibits not only discrimination based on race but also on citizenship status, sometimes called alienage. The Supreme Court has clearly interpreted the statute in this manner.[195] Prior to the enactment of 1991 amendments to section 1981, courts were split as to whether section 1981 applied to private alienage discrimination.[196]

The 1991 amendments clarified that the rights enumerated in section 1981 are protected from private as well as governmental discrimination.[197] Prior decisions that required state action for a finding of alienage discrimination have therefore been legislatively superseded.[198] Thus, a section 1981 claim should be

---

184   *Id.* at 1159; *see also* Bell v. Tower Mgmt. Servs., L.P., 2010 WL 2346651 (N.J. Super. June 11, 2010) (applying New Jersey anti-discrimination law, landlord must make reasonable accommodation to its policy of refusing to rent to any applicant earning less than $28,000 annually when disabled applicant with income under threshold was eligible for government subsidy that paid full rent). *But see* Sutton v. Piper, 344 Fed. Appx. 101 (6th Cir. 2009) (rejecting Fair Housing Act reasonable accommodation challenge by rejected tenant who failed to present evidence of co-signer's creditworthiness).

185   42 U.S.C. §§ 1981, 1982.

186   Saint Francis College v. Al-Khazraji, 481 U.S. 604, 107 S. Ct. 2022, 95 L. Ed. 582 (1987).

187   Shaare Tefila Congregation v. Cobb, 481 U.S. 615, 107 S. Ct. 2019, 95 L. Ed. 2d 594 (1987).

188   Rodriguez v. Beechmont Bus Serv., 173 F. Supp. 2d 139 (S.D.N.Y. 2001) (Hispanic employee allowed to bring racial discrimination claim, but not national origin discrimination claim, under section 1981); Cantu v. Nocona Hills Owners Ass'n, 2001 U.S. Dist. LEXIS 11010 (N.D. Tex. July 30, 2001) (Mexican American plaintiff permitted to bring section 1981 claim as a racial minority).

189   Davis v. Strata Corp., 242 F. Supp. 2d 643 (D.N.D. 2003). *But see* Torgerson v. City of Rochester, 643 F.3d 1031 (8th Cir. 2011) (a

---

race claim based upon Native American status must be stated as a race claim).

190   *See, e.g.,* Bisciglia v. Kenosha Unified School Dist. No. 1, 45 F.3d 223 (7th Cir. 1995) .

191   *See, e.g.,* Sonaire v. NME Hosp., Inc., 27 F.3d 507 (11th Cir. 1994), *aff'd,* 182 F.3d 903 (3d Cir. 1999) (table).

192   *See* King v. Twp. of E. Lampeter, 17 F. Supp. 2d 394 (E.D. Pa. 1998) (Amish are not a protected group under section 1981, as they are a religious and not an ethnic group).

193   *See* Graham v. Richardson, 403 U.S. 365, 91 S. Ct. 1848, 29 L. Ed. 2d 534 (1971); Anderson v. Conboy, 156 F.3d 167 (2d Cir. 1998).

194   *See, e.g.,* Lozano v. City of Hazelton, 496 F. Supp. 2d 477 (M.D. Pa. 2007) (striking down municipal ordinance that attempted to bar undocumented aliens from entering into leases, holding that an undocumented alien is a "person" under section 1981), *aff'd in part and vacated in part on other grounds,* 620 F.3d 170 (3d Cir. 2010), *cert. granted, judgment vacated,* 131 S. Ct. 2958 (2011).

195   Takahashi v. Fish & Game Comm'n, 334 U.S. 410, 68 S. Ct. 1138, 92 L. Ed. 1478 (1948).

196   *Compare* Bhandari v. First Nat'l Bank of Commerce, 829 F.2d 1343 (5th Cir. 1987), *vacated,* 492 U.S. 901, *reinstated,* 887 F.2d 609 (5th Cir. 1989) (section 1981 prohibits only state action discriminating against aliens, not private discrimination), *with* Duane v. Geico, 37 F.3d 1036 (4th Cir. 1994) (the pre-1991 version of section 1981 prohibited private as well as state alienage discrimination).

197   42 U.S.C. § 1981(c), *as added by* Pub. L. No. 102-166, § 101, 105 Stat. 1071 (1991).

198   *See* Anderson v. Conboy, 156 F.3d 167 (2d Cir. 1998); Nagy v. Baltimore Life Ins. Co, 49 F. Supp. 2d 822 (D. Md. 1999), *vacated in part on other grounds,* 2000 U.S. App. LEXIS 12307 (4th Cir. June 5, 2000); Chacko v. Texas A & M Univ., 960 F. Supp. 1180 (S.D. Tex. 1997) (following *Cheung*); Cheung v. Merrill, Lynch,

available to challenge credit discrimination against non-citizens, even when such discrimination would not be actionable under other fair lending laws such as the ECOA or the Fair Housing Act.

3.7 Other Prohibited Bases

3.7.1 General

If discrimination does not involve one of these listed prohibited bases under the ECOA, the federal Fair Housing Act, the federal Civil Rights Acts, or a state's general anti-discrimination statute, the consumer has three strategies to show such discrimination to be actionable. First, does the basis for credit discrimination have a disparate impact on a protected class? For example, if credit is based on the income level associated with an applicant's zip code, does this have a disparate impact on individuals of color even though the income level associated with the zip code is not itself a prohibited basis?[199] If so, there can be a violation of the ECOA or the Fair Housing Act.[200]

Second, there are specialized state or federal statutes that may prohibit discrimination on bases not enumerated under the general federal and state discrimination statutes. The United States Bankruptcy Code, for example, places certain limitations on creditors' ability to seek reaffirmation of a debt as a precondition to a new loan and may limit government entities' right to deny loans based on an applicant's prior bankruptcy.[201] Federal regulations prohibit federal savings associations from discriminating based on the location or age of the dwelling.[202] Instead, the creditor should consider the dwelling's market value and any factors that can be documented that would directly result in a change in that market value.[203]

In addition, both the Fair Housing Act and the ECOA contain specific provisions stating that these federal statutes do not preempt state laws that require consistent or greater protections than those granted by the federal statutes.[204] And a number of state statutes do provide protections not found in these federal statutes.

Two states prohibit discrimination based on genetic information.[205] The District of Columbia's statute extends to domestic violence victims protections from discrimination.[206] Wisconsin has added a similar protection to its statute.[207] New York prohibits discrimination on the basis of military status,[208] and Washington's statute protects veterans and honorably discharged servicemembers.[209] Illinois prohibits discrimination based on an applicant's unfavorable discharge from the military.[210]

A New Jersey statute prohibiting geographic redlining in the granting of home mortgages is not preempted by the ECOA.[211] Several other state statutes also prohibit discrimination based on the geographic area of residence.[212]

To the extent that these state or federal statutes prohibit specific forms of discrimination but do not provide adequate private remedies for violation of such statutes, there is a good argument that a violation of these statutes is also a violation of the state's general statute prohibiting deceptive marketplace behavior (UDAP statute).[213] The argument is particularly strong if the UDAP statute prohibits not only deceptive but also unfair or unconscionable conduct.[214]

An unfair practice is defined as a practice which causes substantial consumer injury that consumers cannot reasonably avoid and that is not outweighed by the countervailing benefits to competition.[215] Thus credit discrimination on a particular basis can be unfair because it injures less-favored applicants. The remaining issues are whether consumers may avoid the discrimination and whether the benefits of the discrimination to competition outweigh the injury. The UDAP approach is therefore strongest when the consumer has limited alternative sources of credit (a utility transaction would be a classic example) and the discrimination is not based on a sound business justification but instead is based on creditor prejudice or an overly broad classification.[216]

Pierce, Fenner & Smith, Inc., 913 F. Supp. 248 (S.D.N.Y. 1996) (1991 amendments mooted previous arguments over whether Congress meant to prohibit private citizenship discrimination; in agreement with *Anderson* decision). *See generally* Angela M. Ford, Comment, *Private Alienage Discrimination and the Reconstruction Amendments: The Constitutionality of 42 U.S.C. § 1981*, 49 U. Kan. L. Rev. 457 (2001).

199 *See* 12 C.F.R. § 128.9(c)(6) (Office of the Comptroller of Currency guidelines relating to non-discrimination in lending, formerly Office of Thrift Supervision regulation 12 C.F.R. § 528.9(c)(6)).

200 *See* § 4.3, *infra*.

201 *See* National Consumer Law Center, Consumer Bankruptcy Law and Practice ch. 15 (10th ed. 2012).

202 12 C.F.R. §§ 128.2(a), 128.3(a) and 128.11(a) (formerly Office of Thrift Supervision regulation 12 C.F.R. §§ 528.2(a), 528.3(a)); *see* ch. 7, *infra* (discussing redlining generally).

203 12 C.F.R. § 128.9(c)(7) (formerly Office of Thrift Supervision regulation 12 C.F.R. § 528.9(c)(7)).

204 15 U.S.C. § 1691d(f) (ECOA); 42 U.S.C. § 3615 (Fair Housing Act).

205 Mass. Gen. Laws ch. 151B, § 4(3B); N.J. Stat. Ann. §§ 10:5-1 to 10:5-42 (West).

206 D.C. Code §§ 2-1401.02, 2-1402.21.

207 Wis. Stat. § 224.77 (housing financing).

208 N.Y. Exec. Law § 296-a (McKinney) (credit transactions); N.Y. Exec. Law § 296(5)(a)–(c) (McKinney) (housing transactions).

209 Wash. Rev. Code § 49.60.176.

210 775 Ill. Comp. Stat. §§ 5/3-101, 5/4-101; 815 Ill. Comp. Stat. § 140/1a.

211 Nat'l State Bank v. Long, 630 F.2d 981 (3d Cir. 1980).

212 815 Ill. Comp. Stat. §§ 120/1 to 120/6; Iowa Code §§ 535A.1 to 535A.9; Md. Code Ann., Com. Law § 12-603 (West); Mich. Comp. Laws §§ 445.1601 to 445.1614; Minn. Stat. § 363A.09(3)(c); N.Y. Banking Law § 9-f (McKinney); Wash. Rev. Code §§ 30.04.500 to 30.04.515; *see* ch. 7, *infra* (discussing redlining generally).

213 *See id.* §§ 3.2.7, 4.3.9.

214 *See* Colvard v. Francis, 416 S.E.2d 579 (N.C. Ct. App. 1992) ("acts designed to unfairly deny credit are unlawful"); *see also* National Consumer Law Center, Unfair and Deceptive Acts and Practices § 4.3 (8th ed. 2012).

215 National Consumer Law Center, Unfair and Deceptive Acts and Practices § 4.3.2 (8th ed. 2012).

216 *See, e.g.,* § 8.6, *infra* (discussing credit mark-up practices).

3.7.2 Discrimination and the Digital Divide

A growing practice that is likely to have a disparate impact on protected classes is the offering of preferential or exclusive credit terms to consumers who apply on-line.[217] Studies indicate lower access and use of the internet by various protected groups, such as African Americans, Hispanics, older citizens, the disabled, and those on public assistance.[218] Therefore, a creditor who offers "Internet-only" deals, or special discounts for applying on-line, is likely disproportionately excluding racial and ethnic minorities, older consumers, the disabled, and public assistance recipients.[219]

The Office of Comptroller of Currency warned one bank that the use of a different credit scoring system for loans made over the Internet might treat similarly situated borrowers differently, and it raises a question of whether the differential treatment violates Regulation B.[220] A Federal Reserve Bank senior examiner has warned that financial institutions offering certain products or services only through Internet sites may be vulnerable to claims of "weblining."[221]

Weblining may be challenged under Regulation B's prohibition against advertising that discourages prospective applicants on a prohibited basis.[222] In cases involving housing finance, such practices may also be challenged under the Fair Housing Act.[223] In particular, given the Act's requirement of reasonable accommodation for disabled individuals, the Fair Housing Act may be used to challenge housing finance programs on the Internet that exclude the disabled.[224] For example, an Internet-only mortgage program might effectively exclude all prospective visually impaired applicants.[225]

A related issue is the possibility that Internet-based businesses will engage in old-fashioned redlining based on zip code or other geographic boundaries.[226] These concerns are exacerbated by the ease with which information—including information on race, ethnicity, gender, religion, and age—can be collected about users of the Internet.[227] Such demographic information can also be easily "mined" by companies other than the business to whom the consumer originally provided the information.[228] The ease of information-gathering in electronic transactions may also exacerbate issues around customer profiling and whether such practices result in discrimination against protected groups.[229]

---

217 Gary A. Hernandez et al., *Symposium on Insurance and Technology: Insurance Weblining and Unfair Discrimination in Cyberspace*, 54 SMU L. Rev. 1953 (2001); Cheryl R. Lee, *Cyberbanking: A New Frontier for Discrimination?*, 26 Rutgers Computer & Tech. L.J. 277 (2000).

218 U.S. Dep't of Commerce, Econ. & Statistics Admin. & Nat'l Telecomm. & Info. Admin., Exploring the Digital Nation: Computer and Internet Use at Home (Nov. 2011), *available at* www.ntia.doc.gov.

219 A related issue in electronic transactions is whether a creditor has met the consumer consent requirements of the Electronic Signatures in Global and National Commerce Act. 15 U.S.C. §§ 7001–7031; *see* National Consumer Law Center, Consumer Banking and Payments Law ch. 11 (4th ed. 2009 and Supp.) (discussing these requirements in detail); *see also* § 10.6.2.2, *infra* (discussion of Regulation B's requirements when ECOA notices are provided electronically).

220 Elizabeth H. Corey, Office of the Comptroller of the Currency, Interpretive Staff Letter No. 759 (May 1, 1996).

221 *Internet-Only Products, Services, May Spark Claims of "Weblining,"* 71 U.S.L.W. 2390 (Dec. 17, 2002).

222 Reg. B, 12 C.F.R. § 1002.5 [§ 202.5]. *See generally* § 5.3.2, *infra* (discussing ways to challenge marketing discrimination in lending).

223 In one Internet-related advertising case, a lender was sued for operating a webpage that steered potential homebuyers to areas in which the buyer's race predominated. The district court initially permitted the plaintiffs to bring a claim under the Fair Housing Act. Isaac v. Norwest Mortgage, 153 F. Supp. 2d 900 (N.D. Tex. 2001).

However, the court ultimately held that the plaintiffs lacked standing because they failed to show that their communities had actually been injured by the lender's practices. Isaac v. Norwest Mortgage, 2002 WL 1119854 (N.D. Tex. May 23, 2002), *aff'd*, 58 Fed. Appx. 595 (5th Cir. 2003).

A Federal Reserve Bank senior examiner has warned lenders that website content can heighten liability because any discriminatory material on a website instantly becomes a "pattern or practice" of such conduct. *Internet-Only Products, Services, May Spark Claims of "Weblining,"* 71 U.S.L.W. 2390 (Dec. 17, 2002).

224 42 U.S.C. § 3604(f)(3).
Recall that the ECOA does not include a prohibition against discrimination on the basis of disability.

225 In the case of non-mortgage lending, such discrimination might violate the public accommodations section of the Americans with Disabilities Act. 42 U.S.C. § 12182(a).
For general discussions of the ADA's applicability to web-based commerce, see Joshua Newton, *Virtually Enabled: How Title III of the Americans with Disabilities Act Might be Applied to Online Virtual Worlds*, 62 Fed. Comm. L.J. 183 (Jan. 2010); Ryan Campbell Richards, *Reconciling the Americans with Disabilities Act and Commercial Websites: A Feasible Solution?* 7 Rutgers J. of L. & Pub. Policy (Spring 2010).

226 For example, a lawsuit was filed against an Internet-based delivery company for allegedly excluding predominately African-American neighborhoods from its delivery areas. Clive Thompson, *Redlining Online: The Door-to-Door Digital Divide*, N.Y. Newsday, Apr. 30, 2000, at B15; *see* ch. 7, *infra* (general discussion on redlining).

227 Gary A. Hernandez et al., *Symposium on Insurance and Technology: Insurance Weblining and Unfair Discrimination in Cyberspace*, 54 SMU L. Rev. 1953, 1970–71 (2001).

228 *Id.*; *Weblining: Companies Are Using Your Personal Data to Limit Your Choices and Force You to Pay More for Products*, BusinessWeek Online, Apr. 3, 2000, www.businessweek.com (describing an information broker company that offers the "InfoBase Ethnicity System," a database which allows businesses to sort households by race and ethnicity).

229 Gary A. Hernandez et al., *Symposium on Insurance and Technology: Insurance Weblining and Unfair Discrimination in Cyberspace*, 54 SMU L. Rev. 1953, 1970–71 (2001); Chet Dembeck, *Report: Online Privacy Crisis Yet to Come*, E-Commerce Times, June 7, 2000, www.ecommercetimes.com (quoting research firm Forrester predicting that "a consumer profiled as an inner-city minority, for example, would get offered the worst prices for on-line goods (because he's unlikely to be an affluent high-valued customer) and dumbed-down content (because his demographic isn't seen as sophisticated)"); *Weblining: Companies Are Using Your Personal Data to Limit Your Choices and Force You to Pay More for Products*, BusinessWeek Online, Apr. 3, 2000, www.businessweek.com.

3.8 ECOA Prohibited Bases Do Not Apply to Special Purpose Credit Programs

3.8.1 General

The ECOA and Regulation B set out a clearly delineated and limited exception to the general rule prohibiting discrimination on a prohibited basis, called special purpose credit programs.[230] These programs may require that program participants share a common characteristic, such as race, national origin, or sex.[231] For example, a special purpose credit program may be set up to assist individuals of color, women, or young applicants.[232] The Congressional intent for the special purpose credit exception is to increase access to the credit market by persons previously foreclosed from the market.[233] The official interpretations of Regulation B clarify this purpose to mean that programs may be designed to benefit a class of persons who not only would otherwise be denied credit but who would also receive credit on less favorable terms.[234]

This ECOA exception does not apply to a Fair Housing Act or a federal Civil Rights Act claim. There is no case law as to how such special purpose credit programs would fare under these other laws.

State credit discrimination laws cannot be utilized to challenge the practices of a special purpose credit program if the ECOA and Regulation B authorize such practices. Regulation B specifically preempts state statutes that prohibit inquiries necessary to establish or administer a special purpose credit program.[235] The federal regulatory agency views such laws as inconsistent with Regulation B because they are less protective of credit applicants.[236]

3.8.2 Qualifying As a Special Purpose Credit Program

A creditor does not violate the ECOA by denying credit solely because the applicant fails to qualify under the requirements of a special purpose credit program, provided that the program was not established for the purpose of evading the ECOA and it fits into one of the following categories:[237]

- *Government-established*: A credit assistance program offered pursuant to federal, state, or local statute, regulation or ordinance, or by judicial or administrative order to benefit an economically disadvantaged class.[238] The federal Small Business Administration (SBA) loan program, which makes a special effort to extend credit to minority and female applicants, is such a program. A remedial program set up by a consent order to benefit past victims of discrimination is another example.[239]
- *Nonprofit*: A credit assistance program administered by a not-for-profit organization (as defined by I.R.S. Code § 501(c)) for its members or for an economically disadvantaged class.[240]
- *For-profit*: A special purpose credit program offered by a for-profit organization to meet "special social needs." Regulation B requires that this type of program be established and administered under a written plan which identifies the class or classes to be benefited and which sets forth the procedures and standards for extending credit.[241]

---

230 15 U.S.C. § 1691(c); Reg. B, 12 C.F.R. § 1002.8 [§ 202.8].
231 Reg. B, 12 C.F.R. § 1002.8 [§ 202.8].
   In 1999, the Federal Reserve Board proposed deleting the phrase "to meet special social needs" from the requirements of qualifying special purpose credit programs listed in 12 C.F.R. § 202.8. 64 Fed. Reg. 44,582, 44,598 (Aug. 16, 1999).
   The FRB did not adopt this proposal out of concern that, by removing the phrase, a creditor might not understand that a program must meet special social needs and because the ECOA itself uses the phrase. 68 Fed. Reg. 13,144, 13,151 (Mar. 18, 2003).
232 *See, e.g.*, Moore v. United States Dep't of Agric., 55 F.3d 991 (5th Cir. 1995) (status of program to benefit socially disadvantaged applicants—who consisted of "Women, Blacks, American Indians, Alaskan Natives, Hispanics, Asians, and Pacific Islanders"—not resolved).
233 *See* S. Rep. No. 94-589, at 7 (1976), *reprinted in* 1976 U.S.C.C.A.N. 403, 409; H.R. Rep. No. 94-873, at 8 (1976), *reprinted in* 1976 U.S.C.C.A.N. 403, 428.
234 Official Interpretations of Reg. B [Official Staff Commentary on Reg. B], 12 C.F.R. pt. 1002 [pt. 202], Supp. I, § 1002.8(a)-5 [§ 202.8(a)-5].
235 Reg. B, 12 C.F.R. § 1002.11(b)(1)(v) [§ 202.11(b)(1)(v)].
   Special purpose credit programs address the credit needs of economically disadvantaged groups and may request and consider information on race, sex, and other protected categories in ways forbidden to other forms of credit. The federal regulatory agency ruled that two New York statutes were preempted by the ECOA to the extent that they barred creditors from taking a prohibited basis into account (national origin) when establishing eligibility for cer-

tain special purpose programs based on national origin and barred them from requesting and considering information regarding characteristics required for eligibility for such programs. Official Interpretations of Reg. B [Official Staff Commentary to Reg. B], 12 C.F.R. pt. 1002 [pt. 202], Supp. I, § 1002.11(a)-1 [§ 202.11(a)-1]; *see also* 54 Fed. Reg. 9416 (Mar. 7, 1989); 53 Fed. Reg. 45,756 (Nov. 11, 1988).
236 15 U.S.C. § 1691d(f); Reg. B, 12 C.F.R. § 1002.11(a) [§ 202.11(a)].
237 15 U.S.C. § 1691(c); Reg. B, 12 C.F.R. § 1002.8(b)(2) [§ 202.8(b)(2)]; *see also* Official Interpretations of Reg. B [Official Staff Commentary on Reg. B], 12 C.F.R. pt. 1002 [pt. 202], Supp. I, § 1002.8 [§ 202.8] (which gives numerous examples of allowable programs and credit-granting procedures).
238 *See* Official Interpretations of Reg. B [Official Staff Commentary on Reg. B], 12 C.F.R. pt. 1002 [pt. 202], Supp. I, § 1002.8(a)-3 [§ 202.8(a)-3].
239 *E.g.*, Green v. Veneman, 159 F. Supp. 2d 360 (S.D. Miss. 2001) (consent decree providing for special program for African-American farmers who filed credit discrimination lawsuit, Pigford v. Glickman, 185 F.R.D. 82 (D.D.C. 1999), did not violate the ECOA), *aff'd in part*, 2002 WL 1973156 (5th Cir. July 29, 2002).
   Interestingly, the court in this case did not rely on the special purpose credit exception to the ECOA; instead, the court held that there was no discrimination because the plaintiff non-African-American farmers could not show discrimination, as they were not similarly situated to the African-American farmers.
240 Reg. B, 12 C.F.R. § 1002.8(a)(2) [§ 202.8(a)(2)].
241 Reg. B, 12 C.F.R. § 1002.8(a)(3)(i) [§ 202.8(a)(3)(i)].

The failure to have a written plan should be enough to disqualify a for-profit organization's program.[242]

Regulation B also requires that a for-profit organization's special purpose credit program extend credit to a class of persons who, under the organization's usual creditworthiness standards, probably would not receive such credit or would receive it on less favorable terms than are ordinarily available.[243] In determining that a class of persons would receive less favorable terms or be denied credit, the organization can use its own research or external data, such as Home Mortgage Disclosure Act (HMDA) data.[244]

An example of such a program run by a for-profit organization is a bank home mortgage program that extends credit on homes in a defined economically depressed neighborhood and gives favored treatment to neighborhood residents. The special purpose credit program need not give this class of applicants its most favorable terms, only terms more favorable than it would offer absent the existence of the special purpose program.[245] Recognizing that special purpose credit programs are designed to fulfill a particular need, the written plan must contain information that supports the designated need and must also state a specific duration for the program or set a date when the program will be reevaluated to determine if there is a continuing need for it.[246]

The federal regulatory agency does not determine for an organization whether a program qualifies as a special purpose credit program. The organization must make its own determination at its own risk.[247] If the organization is mistaken, it is subject to an ECOA action. But a creditor does not violate the ECOA when it complies in good faith with a regulation promulgated by a government agency implementing a special purpose credit program expressly authorized by federal or state law to benefit an economically disadvantaged class.[248]

3.8.3 Special Purpose Credit Programs Must Still Comply with Most ECOA Requirements

A special purpose credit program is exempt only to the extent necessary to carry out the program.[249] For example, a program to promote minority business ownership would still have to comply with the ECOA regarding provision of notices of adverse action taken on an application.[250]

For special purpose credit programs that are not government-established, a creditor may only require applicants to share those factors inextricably tied to the need being addressed.[251] However, a government-established special purpose credit program has more flexibility to establish eligibility requirements.[252]

Perhaps the most important limitation for non-government-established programs is that, once the program is set up to benefit one particular group, it must not discriminate on a prohibited basis within that group.[253] For example, if a program is set up to assist young applicants, it may not then provide its most favorable terms to young white unmarried female applicants.[254] In another example, "[a] creditor might establish a credit program for impoverished American Indians. If the program met the requirements of section 202.8(a) [section 1002.8(a)], the creditor could refuse credit to non-Indians, but could not discriminate among Indian applicants on the basis of sex or marital status."[255]

Note that this limitation does not apply to special purpose credit programs that are government-established. These special purpose credit programs may discriminate on a prohibited basis within the group of potential beneficiaries.[256] Also, there is no violation when a bank establishes a loan program available only to active members of the military and refuses credit to the male spouse of an active member of the military.[257]

3.9 Injury Flowing from Discrimination Against Those Associated with Credit Applicant

3.9.1 The General Rule Under the ECOA

Prohibited credit discrimination under the ECOA may be based not only on the characteristics of the applicant but on the

---

242 United States v. American Future Sys., Inc., 743 F.2d 169 (3d Cir. 1984).

243 Reg. B, 12 C.F.R. § 1002.8(a)(3)(ii) [§ 202.8(a)(3)(ii)].

244 *See* Official Interpretations of Reg. B [Official Staff Commentary on Reg. B], 12 C.F.R. pt. 1002 [pt. 202], Supp. I, § 1002.8(a)-5 [§ 202.8(a)-5] (revised by 68 Fed. Reg. 13,144, 13,156 (Mar. 18, 2003)).

    The official interpretation specifically notes that a creditor can design products to reach consumers who lack sufficient credit history to meet traditional standards of creditworthiness. *Id.*

245 United States v. American Future Sys., Inc., 743 F.2d 169 (3d Cir. 1984).

246 *See* Official Interpretations of Reg. B [Official Staff Commentary on Reg. B], 12 C.F.R. pt. 1002 [pt. 202], Supp. I, § 1002.8(a)-6 [§ 202.8(a)-6].

247 *Id.* § 1002.8(a)-1 [§ 202.8(a)-1].

248 *Id.* § 1002.8(a)-2 [§ 202.8(a)-2].

249 Reg. B, 12 C.F.R. § 1002.8(b)(1) [§ 202.8(b)(1)].

250 Official Interpretations of Reg. B [Official Staff Commentary on Reg. B], 12 C.F.R. pt. 1002 [pt. 202], Supp. I, § 1002.8(b)-1 [§ 202.8(b)-1]; *see* ch. 10, *infra* (ECOA's notice requirements).

251 United States v. American Future Sys., 743 F.2d 169 (3d Cir. 1984).

252 Diaz v. Virginia Hous. Dev. Auth., 101 F. Supp. 2d 415, *subsequent proceeding at* 117 F. Supp. 2d 500 (E.D. Va. 2000).

253 *See* Reg. B, 12 C.F.R. § 1002.8(b)(2) [§ 202.8(b)(2)]; United States v. American Future Sys., 743 F.2d 169 (3d Cir. 1984).

254 United States v. American Future Sys., Inc., 743 F.2d 169 (3d Cir. 1984).

255 42 Fed. Reg. 1248 (Jan. 6, 1977).

256 Diaz v. Virginia Hous. Dev. Auth., 101 F. Supp. 2d at 419, 420.

257 Williams v. Amity Bank, 703 F. Supp. 223 (D. Conn. 1988).

characteristics of the applicant's business partners, its officers (in the case of a corporate applicant), and the individuals with whom the applicant affiliates or associates.[258] Thus, the ECOA prevents discrimination in the offering of credit based on the race, religion, sex, or other characteristics of those with whom the applicant deals or of those who will benefit if the applicant obtains the credit.

For example, a creditor is prohibited under the ECOA from discriminating against an applicant because of the applicant's business dealings with members of a certain religion.[259] Similarly, a creditor may not deny financing for an apartment complex because of the national origin of the complex's tenants.[260] A loan applicant planning to build an apartment building for older citizens is afforded the statute's protection, as is an applicant seeking a mortgage on property located in a neighborhood chiefly populated by older persons. Nor can a mortgage be denied because of the race of other residents in the neighborhood.[261]

The ECOA's applicability to discrimination based on the characteristics of those affiliated with or related to the applicant, however, has certain limits. The ECOA does not provide a basis for a plaintiff associated with the applicant to challenge the discrimination suffered by the applicant but not by the plaintiff.[262] The ECOA generally only provides remedies to those who *apply* for credit, not those affiliated with those who apply. For example, the ECOA would only provide a remedy for the landlord and not for the African-American tenants when the landlord was denied a loan to fix up the apartment because of the tenants' race.

3.9.2 Application of ECOA Rule to Public Assistance and to the Exercise of CCPA Rights

The general ECOA rule that a creditor may not discriminate against an applicant because of individuals the applicant associates with is at least true when the discrimination is based on the race, color, religion, national origin, sex, marital status, or age of those with whom the applicant deals.[263] This "associational" protection should also extend to the remaining two protected ECOA categories—receipt of public assistance and good faith exercise of rights under the Consumer Credit Protection Act.

Prior to 1985, these two bases were specifically excluded from this broader protection by a footnote to Regulation B.[264] However, that exclusion disappeared from the Regulation in the 1985 revisions and, unlike the contents of other pre-1985 Regulation B footnotes, this one did not explicitly reappear in the official staff commentary.[265] Instead, the commentary specifically provided for associational protection generally—discrimination should not be based on the characteristics of individuals the applicant associates with. In listing examples of such characteristics, the commentary did not include receipt of public assistance and good faith exercise of rights, but that list was only explanatory and not definitional.[266] And, of course, there is no statutory basis for treating these two bases differently.

In addition, it is difficult to think of a valid reason why these two characteristics should be excluded from the general rule favoring associational protection. For example, a lender may not discriminate against a builder wishing to build an apartment complex in neighborhoods of color. There is no rational distinction between this situation and that of a lender discriminating against a builder who wishes to build low-income housing units (many of whose tenants might be recipients of public assistance) or a nursing home (many of whose residents might receive Social Security, SSI, Medicare, or Medicaid benefits). Similarly, some consumer lawyers who regularly bring Truth in Lending Act or other Consumer Credit Protection Act suits may be *persona non grata* to local creditors, who should not be allowed to discriminate against such lawyers or their other clients because of the advocates' association with persons who exercise their rights under the Consumer Credit Protection Act.

---

258 Official Interpretations of Reg. B [Official Staff Commentary on Reg. B], 12 C.F.R. pt. 1002 [pt. 202], Supp. I, § 1002.2(z)-1 [§ 202.2(z)-1].

    The issue of associational discrimination is related to the issue of standing in a credit discrimination case. The topic of standing is covered in § 11.2, *infra*.

259 *See* Official Interpretations of Reg. B [Official Staff Commentary on Reg. B], 12 C.F.R. pt. 1002 [pt. 202], Supp. I, § 1002.2(z)-1 [§ 202.2(z)-1].

260 *Id.* § 1002.2(z)-1 [§ 202.2(z)-1].

261 *Id.* § 1002.2(z)-1 [§ 202.2(z)-1]; Cherry v. Amoco Oil Co., 481 F. Supp. 727 (N.D. Ga. 1979) (a white woman living in a predominantly African-American area of Atlanta had been directly affected by the creditor's alleged racial discrimination because the creditor's scoring system penalized all applicants residing within her zip code).

    Ms. Cherry's case ultimately failed on the merits because she did not produce sufficient evidence that the creditor's practice actually treated otherwise qualified African-American and white applicants in a significantly different manner. *See* 490 F. Supp. 1026 (N.D. Ga. 1980).

262 *See* Evans v. First Fed. Sav. Bank, 669 F. Supp. 915 (N.D. Ind. 1987) (nonprofit organization lacked standing to bring ECOA action on behalf of individuals challenging mortgage redlining); Marine American State Bank v. Lincoln, 433 N.W.2d 709 (Iowa 1988).

263 Official Interpretations of Reg. B [Official Staff Commentary on Reg. B], 12 C.F.R. pt. 1002 [pt. 202], Supp. I, § 1002.2(z)-1 [§ 202.2(z)-1].

264 Under then-existing Regulation B, 12 C.F.R. § 202.2(z) n.3 (1985).

265 *See* 50 Fed. Reg. 10,890 (Mar. 18, 1985) (proposed revisions); 50 Fed. Reg. 48,018 (Nov. 20, 1985) (final revisions).

    The explanatory materials to the revisions, without referring specifically to the contents of pre-1985 note 3, generally indicate that no substantive changes were intended. This comment would support the proposition that these two exceptions remain in force.

266 Official Staff Commentary on Reg. B [Official Interpretations of Reg. B], 12 C.F.R. pt. 202, Supp. I, § 202.2(z)-1.

3.9.3 *The Associational Rule Under the Fair Housing and Civil Rights Acts*

The ECOA rule allowing an applicant to bring an action for discrimination against those associated with the applicant applies in Fair Housing Act and federal Civil Rights Acts cases. The plaintiff need not be a member of a protected class as long as consideration of a prohibited basis injured the plaintiff.[267] Standing has been granted to a white house seller suing his potential African-American buyers' lender,[268] whites married to African Americans,[269] whites associated with African Americans,[270] whites buying[271] or selling[272] homes in African-American neighborhoods, a white landlord seeking financing to convert his building in a minority neighborhood into cooperative housing that would likely have been minority owned,[273] a white landlord challenging discrimination against non-white tenants,[274] and whites indirectly injured by discrimination against African-American applicants.[275]

In fact, the Fair Housing Act's scope is broader than the ECOA's, and anyone in any way aggrieved by discriminatory credit practices can bring an action.[276] The plaintiff need not even be a credit applicant. Less clear is the rule under the federal Civil Rights Acts.[277]

---

267 Harrison v. Otto G. Heinzeroth Mortgage Co., 430 F. Supp. 893 (N.D. Ohio 1977); *see, e.g.*, Jimenez v. Servicios Agricolas Mex., Inc., 742 F. Supp. 2d 1078(D. Ariz. 2010) (section 1981 protections apply to non-aliens denied jobs because employer hired only aliens); *see also* § 11.2, *infra* (general discussion of standing in credit discrimination cases).

268 Doane v. Nat'l Westminster Bank, 938 F. Supp. 149 (E.D.N.Y. 1996); *see also* Torgerson v. Wells Fargo Bank S.D, 2009 WL 62441 (D.S.D. Jan. 9, 2009) (seller of business may pursue claim under Civil Rights Acts related to discrimination against buyer, an Indian tribe that applied for credit to finance purchase of the business).

269 Stewart v. Furton, 774 F.2d 706 (6th Cir. 1985).

270 Woods-Drake v. Lundy, 667 F.2d 1198 (5th Cir. 1982) (whites entertaining African-American guests); Lane v. Cole, 88 F. Supp. 2d 402 (E.D. Pa. 2000).

271 Harrison v. Otto G. Heinzeroth Mortgage Co., 414 F. Supp. 66 (N.D. Ohio 1976).

272 Doane v. Nat'l Westminster Bank, 938 F. Supp. 149 (E.D.N.Y. 1996); Old West End Ass'n v. Buckeye Fed. Sav. & Loan, 675 F. Supp. 1100 (N.D. Ohio 1987).

273 Simms v. First Gibraltar Bank, 83 F.3d 1546 (5th Cir. 1996).

While a white landlord has standing to challenge discrimination against minority tenants under the Fair Housing Act, one case has held that a protected class landlord cannot bring an action under the Act for discrimination against the landlord herself because the landlord would not be using the property as a "dwelling." Home Quest Mortgage L.L.C. v. American Family Mut. Ins. Co., 340 F. Supp. 2d 1177 (D. Kan. 2004).

274 Raab Family P'ship v. Borough of Magnolia, 2009 WL 361135 (D.N.J. Feb. 13, 2009) (white landlord may bring FHA challenge to ordinance enacted to deter non-white tenants from moving into municipality).

One case has held that a protected class landlord cannot bring an action under the Act for discrimination against the landlord herself because the landlord would not be using the property as a "dwelling." Home Quest Mortgage L.L.C. v. American Family Mut. Ins. Co., 340 F. Supp. 2d 1177 (D. Kan. 2004).

275 Sec'y, United States Dep't of Hous. & Urban Dev., *ex rel.* Herron v. Blackwell, 908 F.2d 864 (11th Cir. 1990); Inclusive Cmtys. Project, Inc. v. Texas Dep't of Hous., 749 F. Supp. 2d 486 (N.D. Tex. 2010) (challenge to housing agency's policy of giving out tax credit housing subsidy grants primarily in minority neighbors and not making subsidies available in white neighborhoods stated claim for violation of FHA and the Civil Rights Acts). *See generally* Kennedy v. City of Zanesville, 505 F. Supp. 2d 456, 495 (S.D. Ohio 2007) (collecting cases on standing under Fair Housing Act of non-minorities who have been negatively affected by hostile conduct toward protected class members).

276 *See* Hargraves v. Capital City Mortgage Corp., 147 F. Supp. 2d 1 (D.D.C. 2001) (church pastor and financial secretary did not have standing to bring ECOA redlining claims on behalf of church but could bring Fair Housing Act and section 1982 claims); § 2.3.5, *supra*.

277 *See* Domino's Pizza, Inc. v. McDonald, 546 U.S. 470, 126 S. Ct. 1246, 163 L. Ed. 2d 1069 (2006) (after corporation, which was party to broken contract, released its own claims in bankruptcy, African-American plaintiff who was sole shareholder and president of corporation could not assert his own claims under 42 U.S.C. § 1982).

Chapter 4 — Proving Credit Discrimination

4.1 Introduction

4.1.1 Overview

Credit discrimination can be proved in either of two instances: when a creditor utilizes a prohibited factor in making a credit decision or, alternatively, when a creditor uses factors that are not necessarily prohibited or improper but nevertheless have a disparate impact upon a protected group.[1] At the same time, credit discrimination statutes are not violated merely because an applicant is adversely treated and the applicant is a member of a protected group. Adverse treatment is prohibited only if there is a linkage, or nexus, between the treatment and a prohibited basis.

Disparate treatment on a prohibited basis is one method for proving credit discrimination discussed in this chapter. In practice it is often difficult to prove that a decision was made on a prohibited basis and not based on some other permissible factor. The creditor will almost always present a legitimate business justification for its actions. The disparate treatment case will then center on whether the stated reason for the creditor's adverse action was the real reason or whether it was a mere pretext for unlawful discrimination. The plaintiff is not required to prove that the creditor used a prohibited basis knowingly, but only that the prohibited basis was a factor in the creditor's conduct. Disparate treatment can be proven either through direct evidence or through indirect or circumstantial evidence.[2]

If a creditor does not engage in disparate treatment, the creditor's conduct can still be challenged under the ECOA and the Fair Housing Act for its disparate impact. If the stated business justification for a practice is, in fact, the real basis for the creditor's conduct, the creditor's conduct may still be illegal if the business justification has a disparate impact on protected groups. This disparate impact theory, or "effects test," is a critical tool for plaintiffs. It is available in addition to or as an alternative to disparate treatment analysis.

This chapter covers both the disparate treatment and disparate impact methods of proving credit discrimination. The section on legal requirements is followed by a discussion of sources of information that can be useful in proving credit discrimination.

This chapter focuses on proving discrimination as opposed to specific ECOA procedural violations such as failure to provide an applicant with a notice of adverse action. Procedural violations are discussed in Chapter 10, *infra*.

4.1.2 Pleading Requirements

Care should be taken in pleading credit discrimination claims, as courts following the United States Supreme Court's decision in *Ashcroft v. Iqbal*,[3] have sometimes found conclusory allegations insufficient. Lower federal courts have been applying *Iqbal* in credit discrimination cases and dismissing claims of discrimination under the Fair Housing Act, ECOA, and Civil Rights Acts, at least in individual cases in which statistical evidence of disparate impact is too expensive to procure and broad allegations of disparate treatment are made against multiple defendants who played arguably different roles in loan origination and servicing.[4] *Pro se* litigants may face

---

1 The various prohibited bases are discussed in Chapter 3, *supra*. Creditors may take prohibited bases into account in limited circumstances when considering applicants for "special purpose credit programs." *See* § 3.8, *supra*.

2 *See* § 4.2, *infra*.

3 129 S. Ct. 1937, 173 L. Ed. 2d 868 (2009).

4 *See, e.g.*, Hilliard v. Vilsack, 2011 WL 474588 (E.D.N.C. Feb. 4, 2011); Grant v. Vilsack, 2011 WL 308418 (E.D.N.C. Jan. 27, 2011); Davenport v. Litton Loan Servicing, 725 F. Supp. 2d 862 (N.D. Cal. 2010); Ng v. HSBC Mortgage Corp., 2010 WL 889256 (E.D.N.Y. Mar. 10, 2010); Hafiz v. Greenpoint Mortgage Funding, Inc., 652 F. Supp. 2d 1039 (N.D. Cal. 2009) (dismissing with leave to seek to amend); Singh v. Wells Fargo Bank, 2009 WL 2365881, at *4 (N.D. Cal. July 30, 2009) (dismissing with leave to seek to amend); Williams v. 2000 Homes Inc., 2009 WL 2252528, at *5 (E.D.N.Y. July 29, 2009); Joseph v. Northwood Group, L.L.C., 2009 WL 2252336 (S.D.N.Y. July 23, 2009); Akhavein v. Argent Mortgage Co., 2009 WL 2157522 (N.D. Cal. July 18, 2009); *see also* Mayor of Baltimore v. Wells Fargo Bank, 677 F. Supp. 2d 847 (D. Md. 2010) (applying *Twombly/Iqbal* standard to city's allegations of standing and finding them insufficient); Rodriguez v. Bear Stearns Cos., 2009 WL 995865 (D. Conn. Apr. 14, 2009) (dismissing claims of intentional discrimination after some discovery and two amendments to the pleadings). *But see* Lax v. 29 Woodmere Blvd. Owners, Inc., 812 F. Supp. 2d 228 (E.D.N.Y. 2011) (citing *Twombly* and *Iqbal* but denying motion to dismiss FHA discrimination claim); Mejia v. EMC Mortgage Corp., 2011 WL 2470060 (C.D. Cal. June 16, 2011) (citing *Twombly* and *Iqbal* but noting that standard for pleading ECOA discrimination claim is no higher than the fair notice required by Fed. R. Civ. Pro. 8(a) and denying motion to dismiss); Floyd-Keith v. Homecomings Financial, 2010 WL 231575 (M.D. Ala. Jan. 14, 2010) (denying motion to dismiss *pro se* plaintiff's claims of discrimination under the FHA and ECOA); NAACP v. Ameriquest Mortgage Co., 635 F. Supp. 2d 1096, 1104 (C.D. Cal. 2009) (applying Bell Atl. Corp. v. Twombly, 550 U.S.

particular difficulties in satisfying the heightened pleading standards.

In *Iqbal* the Court reiterated the "plausibility" requirement it established in *Bell Atlantic Corp. v. Twombly*,[5] and affirmed its application to all cases, not just securities litigation. *Iqbal* established a two-step process for evaluating complaints. First, the court must identify allegations in the complaint "that are not entitled to the assumption of truth" normally accorded to pleadings at the dismissal stage because they are "bare assertions" amounting to "nothing more than a formulaic recitation of the elements" of the claim.[6] The remaining allegations, which must be accepted as true, are then evaluated to see if they "plausibly suggest an entitlement to relief."[7] In *Iqbal* the Court disregarded as conclusory allegations relating to the knowledge and intent of certain parties accused of discrimination.

Legislation was introduced to restore pre-*Twombly*/*Iqbal* pleading standards but did not pass.[8] It is likely that judges in Fair Housing Act and ECOA cases will look to developments in employment discrimination law on this issue, as they do regarding other aspects of credit discrimination cases.[9]

This chapter discusses the elements of establishing a prima facie case of discrimination under the treatment or effects tests.[10] Although pleadings must meet the *Twombly*/*Iqbal* standard, most courts have found that the prima facie test is a procedural device designed to establish an order of proof and production and thus is an evidentiary standard rather than a pleading requirement.[11] Therefore plaintiffs should not have to

allege the elements of a prima facie case to survive a motion to dismiss.

4.2 Proving Disparate Treatment

4.2.1 Introduction

Discrimination is prohibited if there is a linkage between the discrimination and a prohibited basis such that the creditor's decision-making process results in individuals being treated differently because of a prohibited basis.

It is relatively easy to show that a creditor treated an individual differently than other applicants. For example, the creditor may have refused to offer credit to that applicant but extended credit to many other applicants. The difficult part of a disparate treatment case is to show that the creditor acted on a prohibited basis in treating applicants differently.[12]

It is not enough to show that the applicant denied credit was African American, a woman, or had some other characteristic protected by credit discrimination legislation.[13] The plaintiff

---

544 (2007); plaintiff's allegations were sufficient, especially considering that discovery is only way for plaintiff to obtain more information); Miller v. Countrywide Bank, 571 F. Supp. 2d 251, 255 (D. Mass. 2008) (same); Zamudio v. HSBC North America Holdings Inc., 2008 WL 517138, at *2 (N.D. Ill. Feb. 20, 2008) (same).

An example of a complaint which should withstand a motion to dismiss under *Iqbal* may be found in Appendix G.2, *infra*.

5   Bell Atl. Corp. v. Twombly, 550 U.S. 544, 127 S. Ct. 1955, 167 L. Ed. 2d 929 (2007).

6   Ashcroft v. Iqbal, 129 S. Ct. 1937, 1951, 173 L. Ed. 2d 868 (2009).

7   *Id.*

8   Notice Pleading Restoration Act of 2009, S. 1504, 111th Cong. (2009).

9   *See* §§ 4.2, 4.3, *infra*.

10 *See* §§ 4.2.2, 4.2.3, 4.3.2, *infra*.

11 *See, e.g.*, Swierkiewicz v. Sorema Nat'l Ass'n, 534 U.S. 506, 122 S. Ct. 992, 152 L. Ed. 2d 1 (2002) (plaintiff asserting disparate treatment claims under Title VII and ADEA need not allege specific facts establishing a prima facie case of discrimination under *McDonnell Douglas* in order to survive a motion to dismiss); St. Mary's Honor Ctr. v. Hicks, 509 U.S. 502, 113 S. Ct. 2742, 125 L. Ed. 2d 407 (1993); Lindsay v. Yates, 498 F.3d 434 (6th Cir. 2007); Sparrow v. United Air Lines, Inc., 216 F.3d 1111 (D.C. Cir. 2000) (employment discrimination case); Gilligan v. Jamco Dev. Corp., 108 F.3d 246 (9th Cir. 1997); Ring v. First Interstate Mortgage, Inc., 984 F.2d 924 (8th Cir. 1993) (fair housing context); Lax v. 29 Woodmere Blvd. Owners, Inc., 812 F. Supp. 2d 228 (E.D.N.Y. 2011) (following *Swierkiewicz*); Mejia v. EMC Mortgage Corp., 2011 WL 2470060 (C.D. Cal. June 16, 2011) (reciting four elements but noting that standard for pleading ECOA discrimination claim is no higher than the fair notice required by Fed. R. Civ. Pro. 8(a); denying motion to dismiss); Gonzalez v. Ameriquest Mortgage Co., 2004 WL 2472249 (N.D. Cal. Mar. 1, 2004) (the *McDonnell Douglas* standard does not dictate the required

elements of a claim for discrimination in the Ninth Circuit); Jiang v. Allstate Ins. Co., 199 F.R.D. 267 (N.D. Ill. 2001). *But see* Johnson v. Levy, 812 F. Supp. 2d 167 (E.D.N.Y. 2011) (granting motion to dismiss because plaintiff failed to prove he met qualifications for rental unit); Hilliard v. Vilsack, 2011 WL 474588 (E.D.N.C. Feb. 4, 2011) (granting motion to dismiss because plaintiff failed to plead facts establishing third or fourth elements, despite an allegation that no white, male farmers in the area "have been forced to sell" as plaintiff allegedly was as a result of loan delays and denials); Grant v. Vilsack, 2011 WL 308418 (E.D.N.C. Jan. 27, 2011) (granting motion to dismiss because plaintiff failed to plead facts establishing fourth element of prima facie ECOA disparate treatment claim); Lea v. U.S. Dep't of Agric., 2011 WL 182698 (W.D. Ky. Jan. 19, 2011) (granting motion to dismiss because plaintiffs failed to advance facts showing fourth element); Errico v. Pac. Capital Bank, 753 F. Supp. 2d 1034 (N.D. Cal. 2010) (requiring plaintiffs to allege elements of a prima facie claim in order to survive a motion to dismiss).

12 *See, e.g.*, Lynn v. Vill. of Pomona, 212 Fed. Appx. 38 (2d Cir. 2007) (affirming summary judgment for defendant on Fair Housing Act claim on the grounds that plaintiff had failed to show disparate treatment).

13 *See, e.g.*, Matthiesen v. Banc One Mortgage Corp., 173 F.3d 1242 (10th Cir. 1999) (finding no prima facie case of gender discrimination because plaintiff did not prove that she was qualified for the loan); O'Dowd v. South Cent. Bell, 729 F.2d 347 (5th Cir. 1984) (rejecting white couple's claim that telephone company discriminated in requiring a deposit because of their exchange's racial composition, when couple had history of late payments and deposits were required of all such customers); Omoregie v. Boardwalk Auto Ctr., Inc., 2008 WL 4891019 (N.D. Cal. Nov. 12, 2008) (no evidence that plaintiff was treated less favorably than others on the basis of race); Sallion v. SunTrust Bank, Atlanta, 87 F. Supp. 2d 1323 (N.D. Ga. 2000) (plaintiff failed to show prima facie case of race and marital status discrimination because she was not qualified for the loan); Gross v. Small Bus. Admin., 669 F. Supp. 50 (N.D.N.Y. 1987) (no ECOA violation based on sex or marital status discrimination because applicant was rejected due to past delinquent loan with same agency), *aff'd*, 867 F.2d 1423 (2d Cir. 1988) (table); Thomas v. First Fed. Sav. Bank, 653 F. Supp. 1330 (N.D. Ind. 1987) (no evidence of differing treatment of black second-mortgage applicants or of "impermissible adverse impact").

must show that the credit decision was at least in part based on this characteristic. The creditor will typically claim that the credit denial was not based on such a protected characteristic but on objective standards of creditworthiness or other legitimate factors.[14]

As most applicants have some kind of blemish on their credit record, employment history, or income potential, it is relatively easy for a creditor to point to a specific legitimate reason for denying credit to an applicant. The plaintiff will have to show that this legitimate reason was not the real reason for the creditor's action but that the real reason was the applicant's race, sex, or some other protected characteristic.

If the creditor's business justification is a mere pretext for the real reason, which is a prohibited basis, then it is irrelevant how good a business justification the creditor has presented. Even if the justification is an absolute business necessity, if the real reason for its actions was a prohibited basis, then there is disparate treatment.

Conversely, if the business justification is the real reason, it is irrelevant that the justification is not a good one or that there are other ways of accomplishing the same business goal with a narrower impact on a prohibited basis.[15] Instead, such a case should be brought for its disparate impact, not because of disparate treatment.

It is important to look for disparate treatment not only in the granting of credit but also earlier during the application process. For example, there is disparate treatment if whites are encouraged to apply and African Americans are discouraged, even if a creditor treats all those who do apply equally.[16] There is also disparate treatment if whites are coached more in filling out their applications, even if all written applications are then treated equally.[17]

4.2.2 Direct Evidence of Disparate Treatment

There are two ways to prove that the creditor used a prohibited basis in making a credit decision: through direct evidence or through circumstantial evidence. Direct evidence of disparate treatment on a prohibited basis will clearly constitute a prima facie violation of a credit discrimination statute.[18] If the plaintiff can show through direct evidence that the credit decision was based upon an impermissible factor, the creditor must then respond by proving by a preponderance of the evidence that it would have made the same decision even if it had not taken the impermissible factor into account.[19]

Although courts generally agree that it is rare for plaintiffs to provide sufficient direct evidence of discrimination, there are

---

did not discriminate against public assistance recipient by requiring proof of employment to reinstate defaulted auto loan, because there was no evidence that recipient took an action to reinstate the contract).

The court's reasoning in *Brooks* is unusual, requiring that an applicant seek the more favorable term and be denied in order to show discrimination. However, the ECOA has no such requirement to prove discrimination. In this case the plaintiff alleged that, because the company's notice stated that pay stubs or proof of employment was required in order to reinstate a contract, she assumed that she could not qualify and did not apply.

18 *See, e.g.,* Moore v. United States Dep't of Agric., 55 F.3d 991 (5th Cir. 1995); Pinchback v. Armistead Homes Corp., 907 F.2d 1447, 1452–53 (4th Cir. 1990) (in sections 1981 and 1982 case, plaintiff produced sufficient evidence of direct discrimination, and thus *McDonnell Douglas* method of proof was not relevant); Whitley v. Taylor Bean & Whitacker Mortgage Corp., 607 F. Supp. 2d 885, 900–901 (N.D. Ill. 2009) (denying motion to dismiss FHA, ECOA, and section 1981 intentional discrimination claims against mortgage broker and lender when plaintiffs alleged defendants had "fraudulently misrepresented their income, property value and loan terms, and also imposed higher YSP's because Plaintiffs are African-American"); Tribett v. BNC Mortgage, Inc., 2008 WL 162755 (N.D. Ill. Jan. 17, 2008) (although stating that vague allegations of discrimination will not suffice to state a Fair Housing Act claim, permitting the plaintiffs to amend their complaint to allege that either the defendant or its brokers disproportionately targeted African-American and Hispanic communities for loans and that the defendant continued to pay yield spread premiums despite knowing of price disparities in subprime loans that were due to race); Hu v. Cantwell, 2007 WL 1030468, at *2 (N.D. Ill. Mar. 29, 2007) (conclusory allegations of racial discrimination sufficed for purpose of surviving a motion to dismiss a Fair Housing Act claim). *But see* Campbell v. Robb, 162 Fed. Appx. 460 (6th Cir. 2006) (to make a prima facie case under section 1981, unlike Title VII plaintiff must show that she was qualified to rent apartment even if plaintiff has direct evidence of discrimination); Johnson v. Levy, 812 F. Supp. 2d 167 (E.D.N.Y. 2011) (incorrectly analyzing plaintiff's claims under circumstantial evidence standard, despite property manager's statement that he was denying application because plaintiff had AIDS); *cf.* Hallmark Developers, Inc. v. Fulton Cnty., 466 F.3d 1276, 1284 (11th Cir. 2006) (ruling that plaintiff had failed to make a prima facie case under the Fair Housing Act of disparate treatment by zoning authority).

19 *See, e.g.,* Saldana v. Citibank, 1996 U.S. Dist. LEXIS 8327 (N.D. Ill. June 13, 1996) (defendant's account executive made remarks about plaintiff's neighborhood, including that it was not the same as it had been when he grew up there; finding that these remarks did not constitute direct evidence of discrimination).

---

14 *See, e.g.,* Thompson v. Marine Midland Bank, 198 F.3d 235 (2d Cir. 1999) (table) (text available at 1999 U.S. App. LEXIS 22960) (although a member of a protected class, plaintiff failed to prove discrimination because defendant presented a legitimate reason for denying application; defendant argued that the history of large financial losses at the auto dealer together with the incomplete nature of plaintiff's submissions made full review of plaintiff's application impossible); Cartwright v. American Sav. & Loan Ass'n, 880 F.2d 912, 923 (7th Cir. 1989); Anderson v. Frye, 2007 WL 912290, at *7–8 (S.D. Ohio Mar. 22, 2007) (affirming summary judgment against the plaintiff on FHA claim when she could not demonstrate that she was qualified for the loan and failed to rebut evidence of the defendants' nondiscriminatory actions in denying her loan); Powell v. American Gen. Fin. Inc., 310 F. Supp. 2d 481 (N.D.N.Y. 2004) (plaintiff failed to allege sufficient facts to show that she actually had a sufficient credit history, sufficient collateral, or a necessary co-signer); Sassower v. Field, 752 F. Supp. 1182, 1188 (S.D.N.Y. 1990), *aff'd in part, vacated in part,* 973 F.2d 75 (2d Cir. 1992).

15 *See* Tex. Dep't of Cmty. Affairs v. Burdine, 450 U.S. 248, 101 S. Ct. 1089, 67 L. Ed. 2d 207 (1981) (employment case); McDonnell Douglas Corp. v. Green, 411 U.S. 792, 93 S. Ct. 1817, 36 L. Ed. 2d 668 (1973) (employment discrimination case).

16 For more information on pre-application and marketing discrimination, see § 5.3, *infra.*

17 *See* §§ 5.3.3.1, 5.3.3.2, *infra. But see* Brooks v. O'Connor Chevrolet, 2003 WL 22427795 (N.D. Ill. Oct. 23, 2003) (finance company

cases in which this evidence might be available. Sometimes a creditor will actually admit that a credit decision was based on public assistance status—"we do not handle Medicare or Medicaid patients" or "we do not rent to those on public assistance"—or that it was based on familial or marital status or age. It is less likely that a creditor will admit to acting based on an individual's race, religion, or national origin. However, use of a racial slur by a lending agent may provide direct evidence of discrimination.[20] Courts will require that there be a sufficient nexus between the remarks in question and the adverse action taken.[21]

Direct evidence can sometimes be obtained from former employees of the creditor, from those with whom the creditor communicated, or from notations in the creditor's records. Any statements that the creditor made to the applicant should be scrutinized to see if they constitute admissions as to the reason for the creditor's action.

Plaintiffs should carefully decide what specific disparate treatment to attempt to prove. For instance, it may be difficult to show that an applicant's race was the basis for a denial of credit but not difficult to show that the application *process* was different for whites than for non-whites.[22]

4.2.3 Circumstantial Evidence

4.2.3.1 The *McDonnell Douglas* Burden Shifting Analysis

If the plaintiff does not have direct evidence of disparate treatment, a prima facie case may be established through circumstantial evidence.[23] To prove disparate treatment using circumstantial evidence, most courts will require that a plaintiff first establish a prima facie case by showing: (1) membership in a protected class; (2) application for credit for which the plaintiff was qualified; (3) rejection despite qualification; and (4) that defendant continued to approve credit for similarly qualified applicants.[24]

---

20 Cases in the employment area: *see, e.g.,* Jones v. Robinson Prop. Group, Ltd. P'ship, 427 F.3d 987 (5th Cir. 2005) (race-based comments indicating that African Americans would not be hired absent extenuating circumstances constituted direct evidence relating directly to failure to hire); Chuang v. Univ. of Cal. Davis Bd. of Trustees, 225 F.3d 1115 (9th Cir. 2000) (finding direct evidence of discriminatory animus when decision-making body stated that "two Chinks were more than enough"); Cordova v. State Farm Ins. Co., 124 F.3d 1145, 1149 (9th Cir. 1997) (employer's reference to a new hire as a "dumb Mexican" was sufficient evidence to create an inference of discrimination); *cf.* Walker v. Todd Vill., L.L.C., 419 F. Supp. 2d 743 (D. Md. 2006) (seller's declared racial animus to tester in Fair Housing Act case constituted direct evidence of discriminatory motive). *But see* Jones v. Overnite Transportation Co., 212 Fed. Appx. 268 (5th Cir. 2006) (finding race-based comments not to be direct evidence because they lacked specificity and causation); Jones v. Bessemer Carraway Medical Ctr., 151 F.3d 1321, 1323 (11th Cir. 1998) (racial statements made by supervisor did not constitute direct evidence, and it could not be inferred that it was more likely than not plaintiff's termination was based on racial criteria in light of events preceding her discharge); McCarthy v. Kemper Life Ins. Co., 924 F.2d 683 (7th Cir. 1991) (racial slurs by fellow employees insufficient to provide direct evidence and prove prima facie case of discriminatory discharge); Mancuso v. Douglas Elliman, L.L.C., 808 F. Supp. 2d. 606 (S.D.N.Y. 2011) (owner's concern, expressed through rental agent, about wheelchair and service animal scratching floors of apartment did not clearly convey a discriminatory preference); Anderson v. Wachovia Mortgage Corp., 609 F. Supp. 2d 360, 368 (D. Del. 2009) (loan officer's statement that "you people" do not understand the process was ambiguous inasmuch as there were three African-American couples who were all seeking loans on their adjacent residential properties; summary judgment granted to defendant), *aff'd*, 621 F.3d 261 (3d Cir. 2010).

21 *See, e.g.,* Anderson v. Wachovia Mortgage Corp., 609 F. Supp. 2d 360, 368 (D. Del. 2009) (even if loan officer's use of the term "you people" was direct evidence of racial discrimination, this would not establish Wachovia's liability as he lacked decision making authority on the loan); Steinhauser v. City of St. Paul, 595 F. Supp. 2d 987, *aff'd in part, rev'd in part on other grounds, sub nom.* Gallagher v. Magner, 619 F.3d 823 (8th Cir. 2010) (affirming dismissal of disparate treatment claim but reversing dismissal of disparate impact claim due to fact issue); Faulkner v. Glickman, 172 F. Supp. 2d 732 (D. Md. 2001) (to constitute direct proof of discriminatory intent statements in question must be more than stray or isolated remarks) (citing O'Connor v. Consol. Coin Caterers Corp., 56 F.3d 542, 549 (4th Cir. 1995), *rev'd on other grounds*, 517 U.S. 308 (1996)); MBG Industries, Inc. v. WestAmerica Bank, 2007 WL 867124 (Cal. Ct. App. Mar. 23, 2007) (use of term "widow" in denying loan application insufficient to establish discriminatory animus in ECOA case); *see also* Leach v. Baylor College of Medicine, 2009 WL 385450 (S.D. Tex. Feb. 17, 2009) (employ-

ment case; comment that area hospitals would be unlikely to offer "black boys" endowed chair without "Michael Jackson type transformation" held not to be direct evidence of discrimination because comment was not "sufficiently specific or unambiguous" to allow trier of fact to conclude race was reason plaintiff's contract was not renewed without inference or presumption of nexus).

22 *See generally* ch. 5, *infra* (discussing discrimination in the application process).

23 If the plaintiff *does* have direct evidence of discriminatory intent, the court need not consider the four elements that follow—these elements are "never intended to be rigid, mechanized, or ritualistic." *See* Ring v. First Interstate Mortgage, Inc., 984 F.2d 924, 927 (8th Cir. 1993).

24 *See, e.g.,* Boykin v. KeyCorp, 521 F.3d 202 (2d Cir. 2008) (*pro se* complaint sufficiently pleaded elements of Fair Housing Act claim alleging discrimination on bases of race, gender, and racial makeup of neighborhood in which property was located; no need to allege discriminatory animus for disparate treatment claim to be properly pleaded); Ring v. First Interstate Mortgage, Inc., 984 F.2d 924 (8th Cir. 1993); Shiplet v. Veneman, 620 F. Supp. 2d 1203 (D. Mont. 2009) (applicant for U.S. Department of Agriculture loan failed to demonstrate she was qualified for it and also failed to show that similarly situated borrowers who were not members of the group allegedly discriminated against had received more favorable treatment), *aff'd*, 383 Fed. Appx. 667 (9th Cir. 2010) (African-American loan applicants stated claim for race discrimination under FHA against lender, appraiser, and appraiser's employee); Nicholson v. Johanns, 2007 WL 3407045 (S.D. Ala. Nov. 13, 2007), *aff'd sub nom.* Nicholson v. United States Dep't of Agric., 275 Fed. Appx. 878 (11th Cir. 2008) (per curiam); *see also* Martinez v. Freedom Mortgage Team, Inc., 2007 WL 4415247, at *2–3 (N.D. Ill. Dec. 19, 2007) (refusing to dismiss Fair Housing Act claim based on allegations that the defendants put more pressure on applicants of Hispanic origin to accept higher rates than on white applicants,

This is a modification of the standard established by the Supreme Court in an employment discrimination case, *McDonnell Douglas Corp. v. Green*.[25] With certain exceptions discussed below, most courts use this test for claims brought under the ECOA, the FHA, and the federal Civil Rights Acts.[26] Most courts correctly recognize that discrimination laws reach discriminatory credit terms, not just credit denials, and modify this test accordingly, but a few have erroneously insisted that plaintiffs demonstrate that they were denied credit in order to establish a prima facie case.[27] The test must also be modified for cases alleging reverse-redlining or targeting, because defendants may not make more favorable loans to another group.[28]

If the plaintiff can establish a prima facie case, the burden then shifts to the creditor to articulate a legitimate nondiscriminatory basis for the adverse action.[29] If the defendant does so, the plaintiff must show that the "legitimate" reasons were merely a pretext for discrimination.[30] The plaintiff may satisfy this burden either directly, by persuading the court that a discriminatory motive more likely motivated the employer or creditor, or indirectly, by showing that the proffered explanation is unworthy of belief.[31] To rebut the defendant, the plaintiff

must create a genuine issue of material fact as to the veracity of the defendant's nondiscriminatory reason. This may include evidence presented as part of the prima facie case. However, proving that the defendant's reasons are a pretext for discrimination requires a more substantial showing than the prima facie case.[32]

4.2.3.2 Is the *McDonnell Douglas* Test Applicable in Credit Discrimination Cases?

With the notable exception of the Seventh Circuit, most circuit courts that have addressed the issue have found that the *McDonnell Douglas* standard is appropriate for use in credit discrimination cases.[33] However, not all circuits have addressed

---

rejecting the defendants' argument that the plaintiff must show that he was denied credit to state a claim); Sallion v. SunTrust Bank, Atlanta, 87 F. Supp. 2d 1323 (N.D. Ga. 2000).

25 McDonnell Douglas Corp. v. Green, 411 U.S. 792, 93 S. Ct. 1817, 36 L. Ed. 2d 668 (1973).

Note that, in mixed motive cases, when a plaintiff alleges that an impermissible reason was one of several reasons for a defendant's actions, some of which may be legitimate and nondiscriminatory, a plaintiff need only show that a prohibited basis was a "motivating factor" for the disputed action. 42 U.S.C. § 2000e-2(m); Price Waterhouse v. Hopkins, 490 U.S. 228, 109 S. Ct. 1775, 104 L. Ed. 2d 268 (1989).

In order to avoid liability, a defendant must then demonstrate that it would have taken the same action in the absence of the impermissible motivating factor. 42 U.S.C. § 2000e-5(g)(2)(B).

26 *See, e.g.*, Lindsay v. Yates, 498 F.3d 434 (6th Cir. 2007), *rev'd on other grounds*, 578 F.3d 407 (6th Cir. 2009).

27 *See* § 8.3, *infra*.

28 *See* § 4.2.3.3, *supra*.

29 *See, e.g.*, Dismuke v. Connor, 2007 WL 4463567 (W.D. Ark. Dec. 14, 2007) (retaliation claim; defendant in farm loan case showed legitimate nondiscriminatory reasons for delay of loan decision when loan application was incomplete, borrower requested an increase in loan amount after initial application, and outside agency was hired to complete title work and do appraisal; plaintiff did not contend these arguments were pretextual); Sallion v. SunTrust Bank, Atlanta, 87 F. Supp. 2d 1323 (N.D. Ga. 2000); *cf.* Metoyer v. Chassman, 504 F.3d 919 (9th Cir. 2007) (employer cannot raise a mixed-motive defense to liability for discrimination claims brought under section 1981, but can in defending retaliation claim); Mancuso v. Douglas Elliman, L.L.C., 808 F. Supp. 2d 606 (S.D.N.Y. 2011) (unclean hands defense not applicable in FHA discrimination case).

30 *See, e.g.*, Simms v. First Gibralter Bank, 83 F.3d 1546 (5th Cir. 1996) (must show similar applicants were treated differently); Saldana v. Citibank, 1996 U.S. Dist. LEXIS 8327 (N.D. Ill. June 13, 1996); Farris v. Jefferson Bank, 194 B.R. 931 (Bankr. E.D. Pa. 1996).

31 *See, e.g.*, Owens v. Nationwide Mut. Ins. Co., 2005 WL 1837959 (N.D. Tex. Aug. 2, 2005) (defendant insurance company success-

fully argued that credit is a predictor of insurance loss and that this was a legitimate business reason for using credit history to make insurance decisions; plaintiff failed to rebut defendant's rationale); Cooley v. Sterling Bank, 280 F. Supp. 2d 1331 (M.D. Ala. 2003) (claims brought under section 1981, ECOA, and Fair Housing Act), *aff'd*, 116 Fed. Appx. 242 (11th Cir. 2004).

32 *See, e.g.*, Williams v. Vilsack, 620 F. Supp. 2d 40 (D.D.C. 2009) (plaintiffs failed to show that the U.S. Department of Agriculture's asserted nondiscriminatory reasons were not the actual reasons for the denial of their loan applications and that race was the real reason); Anderson v. Wachovia Mortgage Corp., 609 F. Supp. 2d 360, 370–371 (D. Del. 2009) (mortgagee's preconditions to granting loans, such as requiring repairs to obtain a satisfactory appraisal, were not pretext for race discrimination); Owens v. Nationwide Mut. Ins. Co., 2005 WL 1837959 (N.D. Tex. Aug. 2, 2005) (plaintiff failed to rebut defendant's nondiscriminatory reason in insurance discrimination case); *see also* Brady v. Office of Sergeant at Arms, 520 F.3d 490, 492–493 (D.C. Cir. 2008) (on summary judgment, whether plaintiff could make out a prima facie case becomes irrelevant when employer asserts a legitimate nondiscriminatory reason for its challenged conduct).

33 In the Seventh Circuit, see Greer v. Bank One, 2002 WL 203221 (7th Cir. Feb. 6, 2002) (Fair Housing Act (FHA) claim) and Latimore v. Citibank Fed. Sav. Bank, 151 F.3d 712 (7th Cir. 1998) (the *McDonnell Douglas* standard is inappropriate in the ECOA and FHA context). Unlike the Seventh Circuit, other Circuits have applied the *McDonnell Douglas* standard to cases brought under either the FHA, ECOA or both:

First Circuit: Rosa v. Park West Bank & Trust Co., 214 F.3d 213 (1st Cir. 2000) (ECOA and state claims); Mercado-Garcia v. Ponce Fed. Bank, 979 F.2d 890 (1st Cir. 1992) (ECOA and other federal claims).

Second Circuit: Gross v. United States Small Bus. Admin., 669 F. Supp. 50, 52–53 (N.D.N.Y. 1987), *aff'd*, 867 F.2d 1423 (2d Cir. 1988) (ECOA).

Third Circuit: Anderson v. Wachovia Mortgage Corp., 621 F.3d 261 (3d Cir. 2010) (discriminatory lending claims under section 1981); *see also* Chauhan v. M. Alfieri Co., 897 F.2d 123 (3d Cir. 1990) (housing discrimination claims under section 1981 and the New Jersey Law Against Discrimination).

Fourth Circuit: Crestar Bank v. Driggs, 995 F.2d 1062 (4th Cir. 1993) (ECOA).

Fifth Circuit: Simms v. First Gibralter Bank, 83 F.3d 1546 (5th Cir. 1996) (FHA).

Sixth Circuit: Hood v. Midwest Sav. Bank, 95 Fed. Appx. 768 (6th Cir. 2004) (FHA and ECOA); Michigan Prot. & Advocacy Ser., Inc. v. Babin, 18 F.3d 337 (6th Cir. 1994) (FHA).

Eighth Circuit: Ring v. First Interstate Mortgage, 984 F.2d 924 (8th Cir. 1993) (FHA).

the issue.[34]

Although there is no nationwide rule on this issue and the Supreme Court has yet to grant review, the split can be characterized to date as mainly the Seventh Circuit against the other circuits. The Seventh Circuit in *Latimore v. Citibank Federal Savings Bank* reasoned that the *McDonnell Douglas* test is more appropriate in an employment situation because members of protected classes compete directly with others for jobs. The court found it important that, by contrast, a person in a credit situation applying for credit is not in direct competition with other credit applicants and is not literally competing for the same loans.[35] It is the competitive situation, according to the *Latimore* court, "the black facing off as it were against the white—that creates the (minimal) suspicion, and there is no comparable competitive situation in the usual allegation of credit discrimination. Latimore was not competing with a white person for a $51,000 loan. A bank does not announce, 'We are making a $51,000 real estate loan today; please submit your applications, and we'll choose the application that we like best and give that applicant the loan.' "[36]

In continuing to utilize the *McDonnell Douglas* test, other courts have tended to bypass the concerns expressed by the *Latimore* court. Some courts have simply altered the *McDonnell Douglas* employment-based test to better suit the credit discrimination context. These courts have noted that the prima facie case under *McDonnell Douglas* may vary depending on the facts of the particular case.[37] Courts have also modified the

test in cases brought under the federal Civil Rights Acts.[38] In other cases, courts have noted the Seventh Circuit's concerns but have applied the *McDonnell Douglas* test anyway.[39]

Almost all of these courts do not interpret the fourth prong of the *McDonnell Douglas* standard literally. The fourth prong can be particularly problematic, as it requires plaintiffs to provide evidence that similarly qualified borrowers were able to get credit. If interpreted literally, this could mean that the loan the plaintiff applied for would have to remain available and offered to a similarly situated consumer that is not in a protected class. Courts, however, have not required plaintiffs to show an exact match between their loan applications and the applicants outside of the protected class that received loans.[40] Although an exact match is not required, courts do reject cases in which comparators are insufficiently similar to the plaintiff.[41] At least a few courts have used a modified version of the *McDonnell Douglas* test that does not include this fourth element.[42]

Eleventh Circuit: Boykin v. Bank of America Corp., 2005 WL 3479878 (11th Cir. Dec. 21, 2005); Cooley v. Sterling Bank, 280 F. Supp. 2d 1331, 1337 (M.D. Ala. 2003) (FHA, ECOA, and section 1981), *aff'd*, 116 Fed. Appx. 242 (11th Cir. 2004) (table).

34 *See, e.g.*, Duran v. Cmty. First Bankshares, Inc., 92 Fed. Appx. 756 (10th Cir. 2004) (noting, but not reaching, the open question of whether the *McDonnell Douglas* standard applies to ECOA cases); Crawford v. Signet Bank, 179 F.3d 926 (D.C. Cir. 1999) (plaintiff failed to meet *McDonnell Douglas* burden, and therefore no need to reach issue of whether the test is appropriate in credit discrimination cases); Matthiesen v. Banc One Mortgage Corp., 173 F.3d 1242 (10th Cir. 1999) (finding it unnecessary to reach the question of whether *McDonnell Douglas* standard should be applied, because plaintiff did not demonstrate that he was a qualified borrower).

35 Latimore v. Citibank Fed. Sav. Bank, 151 F.3d 712, 714 (7th Cir. 1998); *see also* Swanson v. Citibank, 614 F.3d 400 (7th Cir. 2010) (following *Latimore* but reversing district court's dismissal of FHA claims and finding that, at motion to dismiss stage, plaintiffs' stated a claim in their allegation that they were discriminated against when appraisal placed a much lower value on the home than another appraisal; court made clear that plaintiffs would need much more evidence to prove such a claim). *See generally* Mane Hajdin, *The McDonnell Douglas Standard in Lending-Discrimination Cases: A Circuit Split?*, 33 McGeorge L. Rev. 1 (2001).

36 Latimore v. Citibank Fed. Sav. Bank, 151 F.3d 712, 714 (7th Cir. 1998).

37 *See, e.g.*, Anderson v. Wachovia Mortgage Corp., 609 F. Supp. 2d 360, 369–370 (D. Del. 2009) (adopting a modified *McDonnell Douglas* test but granting summary judgment for defendant as plaintiffs submitted no evidence of how Caucasians were treated); Jiang v. Allstate Ins. Co., 199 F.R.D. 267 (N.D. Ill. 2001); *see also* Visconti v. Veneman, 2005 WL 2290295 (D.N.J. Sept. 20, 2005) (finding traditional *McDonnell Douglas* framework inappropriate

when claim was based not on application for and denial of credit but on the government's collection efforts regarding credit already extended; applying modified version of *McDonnell Douglas* analysis); *cf.* Chiang v. Schafer, 2008 WL 3925260 (D. V.I. Aug. 20, 2008) (finding it appropriate to import Title VII analysis in analyzing ECOA claim and utilizing employment discrimination case law "as it may be appropriate in the context of credit transaction discrimination").

38 *See, e.g.*, Duran v. Cmty. First Bankshares, Inc., 92 Fed. Appx. 756 (10th Cir. 2004) (to establish a prima facie case under section 1981, plaintiff must show that: (1) he is a member of a protected class; (2) the defendant had the intent to discriminate on the basis of race; and (3) the discrimination interfered with a protected activity as defined in section 1981); *see also* JAT, Inc. v. Nat'l City Bank of the Midwest, 2008 WL 2397657 (E.D. Mich. June 10, 2008).

39 Anderson v. Wachovia Mortgage Corp., 621 F.3d 261, 268 (3d Cir. 2010) ("[W]e do not agree that *McDonnell Douglas* is limited to cases where a plaintiff can produce evidence of a defendant's treatment of directly comparable individuals."); *see* Jiang v. Allstate Ins. Co., 199 F.R.D. 267 (N.D. Ill. 2001); *see also* Cooley v. Sterling Bank, 280 F. Supp. 2d 1331 (M.D. Ala. 2003) (noting that, although Seventh Circuit's approach in *Latimore* is "interesting," traditional Title VII method of analysis governs in Eleventh Circuit).

40 *See, e.g.*, Sallion v. SunTrust, Atlanta, Bank 87 F. Supp. 2d 1323 (N.D. Ga. 2000). *See generally* Mane Hajdin, *The McDonnell Douglas Standard in Lending-Discrimination Cases: A Circuit Split?*, 33 McGeorge L. Rev. 1 (2001).

41 *See, e.g.*, Boykin v. Bank of America Corp., 2005 WL 3479878 (11th Cir. Dec. 21, 2005) (plaintiff failed to establish a prima facie case because she did not demonstrate that similarly situated applicants were treated differently); Floyd-Keith v. Homecomings Financial, 2010 WL 231575 (M.D. Ala. Jan. 14, 2010).

42 *See, e.g.*, Anderson v. Wachovia Mortgage Corp., 621 F.3d 261, 272–73 (3d Cir. 2010) (holding that "comparative, or competitive, evidence is not a necessary component of a discrimination plaintiff's prima facie case," and noting that *McDonnell Douglas* itself called for the test to be tailored depending on the fact situation); Mays v. Buckeye Rural Electric Corp., 277 F.3d 873 (6th Cir. 2002) (modifying the *McDonnell Douglas* test to require plaintiff to show that: (1) plaintiff was a member of a protected class; (2) plaintiff applied for credit from defendants; (3) plaintiff was qualified for the credit; and (4) despite plaintiff's qualification, defendants denied her credit application); Fair Hous. of the Dakotas, Inc. v. Goldmark Prop. Mgmt., Inc., 778 F. Supp. 2d 1028, 1037 (D.N.D. 2011) (noting that

It is unclear what the consequences would be even if other courts directly addressed the concerns raised in *Latimore*. On one hand, the Seventh Circuit's rejection of the standard could hurt plaintiffs, as it means that courts will not immediately shift the burden of proof to the defendant upon a prima facie showing of discrimination.[43] That failure would, for example, require plaintiffs to provide more evidence of discrimination to defeat a motion for summary judgment. The problem for plaintiffs is that direct evidence is rarely available at this stage of the case.[44] However, a court's rejection of the *McDonnell Douglas* burden-shifting analysis may in some circumstances give the plaintiff greater flexibility in presenting a prima facie case of discrimination.[45]

4.2.3.3 The *McDonnell Douglas* Standard in Predatory Lending/Reverse Redlining Cases

In reverse redlining cases, it is critical to ensure that the court uses a modified test for determining whether a prima facie case

exists. The key difference in predatory lending cases is that lenders generally grant credit, but on predatory terms. Thus, the traditional third prong of the *McDonnell Douglas* analysis requiring that the applicant be denied credit will not be met. Borrowers may also argue in some cases that they were given a loan that they did not have the ability to repay. Using the traditional *McDonnell Douglas* analysis, these borrowers would not meet the second requirement that they applied for credit for which they were qualified.[46]

The plaintiff should not have to prove that he or she could afford to repay a particular loan in question. Instead, the prima facie case in a reverse redlining claim should require the plaintiff to show that the plaintiff could have afforded to repay a loan offered to him or her on favorable terms.[47]

In order to address these concerns in reverse redlining cases, courts have required a plaintiff to show (1) that she is a member of a protected class, (2) that she applied for and was qualified for a loan, (3) that the loan was given on grossly unfavorable terms, and (4) that the lender continues to provide loans to other applicants with similar qualifications but on significantly more favorable terms.[48] Alternatively, the fourth prong may be met

---

"[t]he elements of a prima facie case of discrimination vary from case to case, depending on the allegations and the circumstances"). *But see* Hood v. Midwest Sav. Bank, 95 Fed. Appx. 768 (6th Cir. 2004); Hilliard v. Vilsack, 2011 WL 474588 (E.D.N.C. Feb. 4, 2011) (same as *Grant v. Vilsack*); Grant v. Vilsack, 2011 WL 308418 (E.D.N.C. Jan. 27, 2011) (granting motion to dismiss because plaintiff failed to plead facts establishing that "others of similar credit stature were extended credit or were given more favorable treatment"); Lea v. U.S. Dep't of Agric., 2011 WL 182698 (W.D. Ky. Jan. 19, 2011) (following *Hood* and granting motion to dismiss because plaintiffs have "failed to advance any facts indicating disparate treatment"); Errico v. Pac. Capital Bank, 753 F. Supp. 2d 1034 (N.D. Cal. 2010) (granting motion to dismiss in part because plaintiffs did not allege that similarly situated applicants were treated more favorably).

The *Hood* court rejected the analysis in *Mays* and found that the plaintiff met all elements of the prima facie test except for the fourth. The court speculated that the exact statement of the elements of the prima facie case was likely not critical in the *Mays* case and that the *Mays* court simply overlooked the existing Sixth Circuit formulation. Hood v. Midwest Sav. Bank, 95 Fed. Appx. 768, 778 n.7 (6th Cir. 2004); *see also* JAT, Inc. v. Nat'l City Bank of the Midwest, 2008 WL 2397657 (E.D. Mich. June 10, 2008) (articulating prima facie case including all four elements; affirming motion for summary judgment and holding that plaintiffs failed to create genuine issue of material fact as to fourth element).

43 The court of appeals in *Latimore*, for example, required the plaintiff to present evidence of actual discrimination on some prohibited ground, such as race, in order to state a claim. Latimore v. Citibank Fed. Sav. Bank, 151 F.3d 712 (7th Cir. 1998).

44 *See, e.g.*, Williams v. Vilsack, 620 F. Supp. 2d 40 (D.D.C. 2009) (husband and wife plaintiffs presented no evidence from which racial discrimination in denial of Farm Service Agency loan could reasonably be inferred).

45 *See, e.g.*, Ring v. First Interstate Mortgage, Inc., 984 F.2d 924, 927 (8th Cir. 1993) (noting that four factors were "never intended to be rigid, mechanized, or ritualistic"); Simpson v. Flagstar Bank, 2003 WL 22244789 (S.D. Ind. Aug. 11, 2003) (it is open to plaintiff to show in a conventional way, without relying on any specific doctrine of burden shifting, that there is enough evidence to create a triable issue; plaintiff not required to identify a similarly situated person of a different race who was afforded more favorable treatment).

46 *See, e.g.*, Woodworth v. Bank of America, Nat'l Ass'n, 2011 WL 1540358, at *19 (D. Or. Mar. 23, 2011), *report and recommendation adopted sub nom.*, 2011 WL 1542514 (D. Or. Apr. 21, 2011) (granting motion to dismiss reverse-redlining claim with leave to amend because plaintiffs failed to plead that they were "qualified for any loan other than the one they received"); Equicredit Corp. of N.Y. v. Turcios, 752 N.Y.S.2d 684 (N.Y. App. Div. 2002) (in defending a foreclosure action, mortgagors brought counterclaim arguing that they were given high rate loans that they could not repay; finding, in these circumstances, that mortgagors could not have established a prima facie case for violation of the ECOA or Fair Housing Act because their claims are based on the contention that they did not qualify for the loans).

47 Woodworth v. Bank of America, Nat'l Ass'n, 2011 WL 1540358, at *19 (D. Or. Mar. 23, 2011), *report and recommendation adopted sub nom.*, 2011 WL 1542514 (D. Or. Apr. 21, 2011) (using reverse-redlining formulation of test but granting motion to dismiss because plaintiffs failed to plead that they were "qualified for any loan other than the one they received"); *see, e.g.*, Barkley v. Olympia Mortgage Co., 2007 WL 2437810 (E.D.N.Y. Aug. 22, 2007); Matthews v. New Century Mortgage Corp., 185 F. Supp. 2d 874 (S.D. Ohio 2002); *see also* § 8.3, *infra*.

48 *See, e.g.*, Mejia v. EMC Mortgage Corp., 2011 WL 2470060 (C.D. Cal. June 16, 2011) (noting other circuits' use of four-part reverse-redlining test and denying motions to dismiss FHA and ECOA claim even though loan was approved); Barkley v. Olympia Mortgage Co., 2007 WL 2437810, at *13–15 (E.D.N.Y. Aug. 22, 2007) (to state a prima facie case for a Fair Housing Act violation, plaintiffs may meet the second element by showing that they applied for and were qualified for a fairly priced loan, rather than the precise predatory loan offered and may establish the fourth element with evidence of intentional targeting; Munoz v. Int'l Home Capital Corp., 2004 WL 3086907 (N.D. Cal. May 4, 2004); Gonzalez v. Ameriquest Mortgage Co., 2004 WL 2472249 (N.D. Cal. Mar. 1, 2004); Matthews v. New Century Mortgage Corp., 185 F. Supp. 2d 874 (S.D. Ohio 2002); *see also* Newman v. Apex Financial Group, Inc., 2008 WL 130924, at *4 (N.D. Ill. Jan. 11, 2008) (denying defendant's motion to dismiss FHA claim, rejecting argument that the plaintiff's FHA complaint failed to comport with the standard of Bell Atl. Corp. v. Twombly, 550 U.S. 544, 127 S. Ct. 1955, 167 L.

by evidence of intentional targeting of minorities, without evidence of disparities compared to other groups; to hold otherwise would allow predatory lending schemes to continue as long as they are exclusively perpetrated upon one racial group.[49] Courts also may not require the second prong—proof that the plaintiff was qualified for a favorable loan. For example, one court found that an African-American plaintiff who could not afford her mortgage stated a claim of race discrimination under section 1981 by alleging that she had successfully obtained mortgages from defendants for houses in minority neighborhoods; that when she applied for a mortgage for a house in a white neighborhood, she was required to meet different appraisal, home improvement, and financial requirements, which ultimately proved too burdensome; and that the conditions were contrary to defendants' policies and procedures and to the requirements imposed on similarly situated whites.[50]

4.3 Proving Disparate Impact

4.3.1 Introduction

An alternative under the Fair Housing Act and the ECOA to proving disparate treatment is proving disparate impact. Under a disparate impact theory, the creditor may not be treating applicants differently on a prohibited basis, but there still may be illegal discrimination if the *effect* of the creditor's practices is to adversely impact a particular protected class.

It is widely accepted that proof of discriminatory impact or effect can constitute a violation of the discrimination provisions of the Fair Housing Act.

The legislative history of the ECOA demonstrates that Congress intended that an effects test should be used in actions brought under the statute. The relevant Senate committee report states:

> In determining the existence of discrimination . . . courts or agencies are free to look at the effects of a creditor's practices as well as the creditor's motives or conduct in individual transactions.[51]

The official interpretations of Regulation B affirm that Congress intended that the "effects test" doctrine should apply in the credit area.[52] The case law follows the same trend.[53]

All of the federal circuit courts that have considered the issue have held that the Fair Housing Act (FHA) also encompasses claims based upon the disparate impact theory.[54] Many of these

---

Ed. 2d 929 (2007)). *But see* Equicredit Corp. of N.Y. v. Turcios, 752 N.Y.S.2d 684 (N.Y. App. Div. 2002) (in defending a foreclosure action, mortgagors brought counterclaim arguing that they were given high rate loans that they could not repay; in these circumstances, court found mortgagors could not have established a prima facie case for violation of the ECOA or FHA). *See generally* Raymond Brescia, *Subprime Communities: Reverse Redlining, The Fair Housing Act and Emerging Issues in Litigation Regarding the Subprime Mortgage Crisis*, 2 Alb. Gov't L. Rev. 164 (2009).

49 *See, e.g.*, M & T Mortgage Corp. v. White, 736 F. Supp. 2d 538 (E.D.N.Y. 2010); Barkley v. Olympia Mortgage Co., 2007 WL 2437810 (E.D.N.Y. Aug. 22, 2007); Wiltshire v. Dhanraj, 421 F. Supp. 2d 544 (E.D.N.Y. 2005) (plaintiffs have alternative to fourth prong if they present direct evidence that the lender intentionally targeted them for unfair loans on a protected basis); Contract Buyers League v. F & F Inv., 300 F. Supp. 210 (N.D. Ill. 1969).

In Hargraves v. Capital City Mortgage Corp., 140 F. Supp. 2d (D.D.C. 2000), the court also noted that plaintiffs in reverse-redlining cases do not need to show that defendants made loans on more favorable terms to anyone other than the targeted class as long as they show that the terms of the loans are unfair and predatory. However, the *Hargraves* court was not explicitly examining the revised *McDonnell Douglas* test.

50 Anderson v. Wachovia Mortgage Corp., 497 F. Supp. 2d 572 (D. Del. 2007).

51 S. Rep. No. 94-589, at 4 (1976), *reprinted in* 1976 U.S.C.C.A.N. 403, 406; *see also* Coleman v. Gen. Motors Acceptance Corp., 196 F.R.D. 315, 325 (M.D. Tenn. 2000) ("[T]he legislative history of the ECOA indicates that the Congress intended an 'effects test' concept, as outlined in the employment field in the Supreme Court in the cases of *Griggs v. Duke Power Co.*, 401 U.S. 424 (1971) and *Albemarle Paper Co. v. Moody*, 422 U.S. 405 (1975).") (citing 12 C.F.R. § 202.6(a) n.2).

52 Official Interpretations of Reg. B [Official Staff Commentary on Reg. B], 12 C.F.R. pt. 1002 [pt. 202], Supp. I, § 1002.6(a)-2 [§ 202.6(a)-2].

53 *See, e.g.*, Haynes v. Bank of Wedowee, 634 F.2d 266 (5th Cir. 1981) (noting use of disparate impact standard in ECOA case); Palmer v. Homecomings Financial, L.L.C., 977 F. Supp. 2d. 233 (D.D.C. 2010); Rodriguez v. SLM Corp., 2009 WL 598252, at *3 (D. Conn. Mar. 6, 2009) (refusing to dismiss disparate impact claim under ECOA when lender allegedly charged minority borrowers higher interest rates and fees than similarly situated Caucasians on private student loans); Zamudio v. HSBC N. America Holdings Inc., 2008 WL 517138 (N.D. Ill. Feb. 20, 2008) (it is well established that there is a disparate impact claim under the ECOA and FHA; case involves claim that racially discriminatory assumptions are embedded in statistical formulas used to analyze credit information and underwrite loans); Powell v. American Gen. Finance, Inc., 310 F. Supp. 2d 481 (N.D.N.Y. 2004) (ECOA provides for a private cause of action based on disparate impact or disparate treatment); Osborne v. Bank of America, 234 F. Supp. 2d 804 (M.D. Tenn. 2002); Wilson v. Union Acceptance Corp., 2002 WL 31730920 (S.D. Ind. Nov. 19, 2002) (unlike statutes like Title VI of the Civil Rights Act and the ADEA, in creating the ECOA Congress clearly intended to prohibit conduct that has the effect of discrimination); A.B. & S. Auto Serv., Inc. v. South Shore Bank of Chi., 962 F. Supp. 1056 (N.D. Ill. 1997); Sayers v. Gen. Motors Acceptance Corp., 522 F. Supp. 835, 839 (W.D. Mo. 1981)), *vacated and remanded on unrelated grounds*, 296 F.3d 443 (6th Cir. 2002).

54 *See, e.g.*, Graoch Assocs. #33, Ltd. P'ship v. Louisville/Jefferson Cnty. Metro Human Relations Comm'n, 508 F.3d 366 (6th Cir. 2007) (discussing *Arthur* and setting forth the burden-shifting framework for analyzing disparate impact claims against private defendants under FHA); Cox v. City of Dallas, 430 F.3d 734, 746 (5th Cir. 2005); Langlois v. Abington Hous. Auth., 207 F.3d 43 (1st Cir. 2000), *aff'g in part* 1998 WL 1029207 (D. Mass. Dec. 30, 1998); Simms v. First Gibraltar Bank, 83 F.3d 1546, 1555 (5th Cir. 1996); Mountain Side Mobile Estates P'ship v. Sec'y of Hous. & Urban Dev., 56 F.3d 1243 (10th Cir. 1995); Jackson v. Okaloosa Cnty., 21 F.3d 1531, 1543 (11th Cir. 1994); United States v. Badgett, 976 F.2d 1176, 1179 (8th Cir. 1992); Keith v. Volpe, 858 F.2d 467, 484 (9th Cir. 1988); Huntington Branch NAACP v. Town of Huntington, 844 F.2d 926 (2d Cir. 1988), *aff'd*, 488 U.S. 15 (1988); Arthur v. City of Toledo, 782 F.2d 565, 575 (6th Cir. 1986); Smith v. Town of Clarkton, 682 F.2d 1055, 1065 (4th Cir. 1982); Resident Advisory Bd. v. Rizzo, 564 F.2d 126, 147–48 (3d Cir. 1977); Metro. Hous. Dev. Corp. v. Vill. of Arlington Heights (*Arlington Heights II*), 558

opinions were issued before Congress significantly amended the Act in 1988, lending support to the view that Congress accepted and intended such an interpretation of the FHA.[55] The statutory language provides additional support: section 3605(c) explicitly allows appraisers to take into account non-prohibited factors, and section 3607(b)(1) explicitly allows zoning restrictions on the number of occupants in a building. These sections would be superfluous if the FHA applied only to intentional discrimination. The Department of Housing and Urban Development (HUD), which has authority to administer and implement the FHA, has interpreted the Act to include discriminatory effects liability in policy statements,[56] formal adjudications,[57] and most recently in a final rule clarifying the burden of proof required for such claims.[58]

Although four decades of case law has consistently held that disparate impact claims are cognizable under the FHA, defendants continue to raise challenges to the doctrine. For example, a 2001 Supreme Court decision, *Alexander v. Sandoval*,[59] eliminated an individual's ability to enforce the Title IV disparate impact regulations through an implied private right of action. Creditor defendants have referenced *Sandoval* and related cases in arguing that the disparate impact theory is not available under the ECOA. However, several courts have rejected this argument,[60] and other cases have found that *Sandoval* does not prohibit disparate impact claims under either the FHA or the ECOA.[61]

Defendants have also argued that an effects test is not available under the ECOA based on *Smith v. City of Jackson*,[62] a case interpreting the Age Discrimination in Employment Act (ADEA). In *Jackson*, the Supreme Court held that the ADEA provides a cause of action for disparate impact, noting that the ADEA, like Title VII, contains express language prohibiting conditions that "adversely affect" employment status on account of age. The ECOA and FHA do not contain the same language. However, numerous courts have rejected the argument that *Smith v. City of Jackson* implies that the ECOA and the FHA do not permit disparate impact claims.[63] Furthermore,

---

F.2d 1283, 1289 (7th Cir. 1977); *see also* Greater New Orleans Fair Hous. Action Ctr. v. St. Bernard Parish, 641 F. Supp. 2d 563, 577 (E.D. La. 2009).

   Although the D.C. Circuit has not addressed the issue, at least three D.C. district court judges have recognized the disparate impact theory in FHA cases. *See* Nat'l Cmty. Reinvestment Coal. v. Accredited Home Lenders Holding Co., 573 F. Supp. 2d 70 (D.D.C. 2008) (finding specifically that disparate impact claims pursuant to the FHA are not precluded by Smith v. City of Jackson, 544 U.S. 228, 125 S. Ct. 1536, 161 L. Ed. 2d 410 (2005)); Samaritan Inns v. Dist. of Columbia, 1995 U.S. Dist. LEXIS 9294 (D.D.C. June 30, 1995) (the D.C. government's suspension of plaintiff's permit to rehabilitate home for disabled violated the FHA under theories of intentional discrimination and disparate impact), *aff'd in part, rev'd in part*, 114 F.3d 1227 (D.C. Cir. 1997); Brown v. Artery Org., Inc., 654 F. Supp. 1106, 1115 (D.D.C. 1987); *cf.* Hargraves v. Capital City Mortgage Corp., 140 F. Supp. 2d 7 (D.D.C. 2000) (prima facie case of reverse redlining under FHA or ECOA requires showing that loan practices and terms were unfair and predatory and that either defendants intentionally targeted on the basis of race or there is a disparate impact on the basis of race).

55 *See, e.g.*, H.R. Rep. No. 100-711, at 2182 (1988) (citing courts of appeals decisions in discussing a policy that could have a "discriminatory effect" on minority households "[b]ecause minority households tend to be larger"); *Fair Housing Amendments Act of 1987: Hearings Before the Subcomm. on the Constitution of the S. Comm. on the Judiciary*, 100th Cong., 1st Sess. 529-557 (1987) (testimony of Professor Robert Schwemm, University of Kentucky Law School) (discussing "strong consensus" in federal courts of appeals that the Fair Housing Act prohibited disparate impact discrimination); 134 Cong. Rec. 23711-12 (1988) (statement of Sen. Kennedy) (noting unanimity of courts of appeals as to the disparate impact test).

56 Policy Statement on Discrimination in Lending, 59 Fed. Reg. 18,266, 18,269 (Apr. 15, 1994).

57 *See, e.g.*, Sec'y, U.S. Dep't of Hous. & Urban Dev. v. Pfaff, 1994 WL 592199, at *8 (Dep't of Hous. & Urban Dev. A.L.J. Oct. 27, 1994), *rev'd on other grounds*, 88 F.3d 739 (9th Cir. 1996); Sec'y, U.S. Dep't of Hous. & Urban Dev. v. Mountain Side Mobile Estates P'ship, 1993 WL 367102, at *6 (Dep't of Hous. & Urban Dev. A.L.J. Sept. 20, 1993); Sec'y, U.S. Dep't of Hous. & Urban Dev. v. Carter, 1992 WL 406520, at *6 (Dep't of Hous. & Urban Dev. A.L.J. May 1, 1992); Sec'y, U.S. Dep't of Hous. & Urban Dev. v. Twinbrook Vill. Apts., No. 02-00025600-0256-8, 2001 WL 1632533, at *17 (Dep't of Hous. & Urban Dev. A.L.J. Nov. 9, 2001).

58 Final Rule, Dep't of Hous. & Urban Dev., Implementation of the Fair Housing Act's Discriminatory Effects Standard, 78 Fed. Reg. 11,460 (Feb. 15, 2013).

   The supplementary information accompanying the proposed and final rules is a useful source for case law and other support for the availability of disparate impact claims and the particular formulation of the burden-shifting test formalized in the rule. *See* Proposed Rules, Dep't of Hous. & Urban Dev., Implementation of the Fair Housing Act's Discriminatory Effects Standard, 76 Fed. Reg. 70,921-01 (Nov. 16, 2011).

   The three step burden-shifting test is discussed in detail in § 4.3.2, *infra*.

59 532 U.S. 275, 121 S. Ct. 1511, 149 L. Ed. 2d 517 (2001). *See generally* Jane Perkins & Sarah Jane Somers, *Sandoval's Retrenchment on Civil Rights Enforcement: The Ultimate Sorcerer's Magic*, 35 J. of Poverty L. & Pol'y 433 (2001).

60 *See, e.g.*, Smith v. Chrysler Financial, Co., 2003 WL 328719 (D.N.J. Jan. 15, 2003); Osborne v. Bank of America, 234 F. Supp. 2d 804 (M.D. Tenn. 2002) ("Properly construed then, *Sandoval* holds only that regulations may not create private rights of action where no such right was intended by Congress. But that is not the case with the ECOA.").

61 *See, e.g.*, Beaulialice v. Fed. Home Loan Mortgage Corp., 2007 WL 744646 (M.D. Fla. Mar. 6, 2007); *see also* Greater New Orleans Fair Hous. Action Ctr. v. St. Bernard Parish, 641 F. Supp. 2d 563 (E.D. La. 2009) (applying disparate impact test to claim under the FHA based on parish's enactment of a moratorium on construction of multifamily housing).

62 544 U.S. 228, 125 S. Ct. 1536, 161 L. Ed. 2d 410 (2005).

63 *See, e.g.*, The Comm. Concerning Cmty. Improvement v. City of Modesto, 583 F.3d 690, 711 (9th Cir. 2009); Barrett v. H & R Block, Inc., 652 F. Supp. 2d 104 (D. Mass. 2009); NAACP v. Ameriquest Mortgage Co., 635 F. Supp. 2d 1096, 1104–1105 (C.D. Cal. 2009); Nat'l Cmty. Reinvestment Coal. v. Accredited Home Lenders Holding Co., 597 F. Supp. 2d 120 (D.D.C. 2009) (denying certification to appeal the issue as there was no substantial ground for a difference of opinion); Rodriguez v. SLM Corp., 2009 WL 598252, at *3 (D. Conn. Mar. 6, 2009); Guerra v. GMAC L.L.C., 2009 WL 449153, at *3 (E.D. Pa. Feb. 20, 2009); *see also* Ramirez v. GreenPoint Mortgage Funding, Inc., 633 F. Supp. 2d 922 (N.D. Cal. 2008) (denying motion to dismiss; "GreenPoint reads Smith too

in *Jackson*, the majority and Justice Scalia's concurrence gave weight to the EEOC's interpretation of the statute to permit disparate impact claims. As discussed above, the regulatory agencies with authority over the ECOA and FHA have interpreted the statutes to permit disparate impact claims.

In 2011, the Supreme Court granted certiorari in *Magner v. Gallagher*[64] to consider the viability of disparate impact claims under the FHA and whether a burden-shifting framework is the correct test, but the petitioners withdrew their request for judicial review.[65] More recently, a petition for certiorari raising very similar issues was filed in *Township of Mount Holly v. Mt. Holly Gardens Citizens in Action, Inc.*[66] Although the Supreme Court has not indicated whether it will grant the petition, it has invited the solicitor general to file a brief in the case expressing the views of the United States.[67] Of course, the Supreme Court's decision in *Mount Holly* could have enormous impact on practitioners' ability to bring disparate impact claims under the FHA and on the burdens of proof required.

In contrast to the ECOA and FHA, courts have found that evidence of discriminatory purpose or intent is necessary for claims brought under the federal Civil Rights Acts[68] or the Equal Protection Clause.[69] Thus, proof of intentional discrimination, whether by direct or circumstantial evidence, is required in federal Civil Rights Acts cases.

The disparate impact approach gives the plaintiff another avenue to pursue whenever disparate treatment cannot be proven. Even though the business justification is the real reason for the creditor's actions, the creditor's actions may still be illegal if they have a disparate impact on a protected class and use of some other factor would satisfy the creditor's legitimate business needs with less of a disparate impact. The plaintiff does not need to show intent to discriminate but instead must show that a facially neutral policy has a discriminatory effect.

For instance, a creditor might refuse to grant credit to applicants from all zip code areas in which its computer indicates that default losses in the past have been greater than a stated frequency. It might be impossible to prove that this system is a mere pretext for illegal discrimination, particularly if the creditor claims not to even know the racial composition of various zip code areas. But it might be possible to prove that the affected zip code areas were predominantly non-white and that this credit factor could be replaced by some other factor, such as the applicant's own credit history, that would have less of a disparate impact.

The disparate impact test also significantly broadens the reach of the prohibited bases listed in the ECOA and the Fair Housing Act and, in effect, creates many new prohibited bases. When the factors that creditors utilize in differentiating credit applications have a disparate impact on a prohibited basis, these other seemingly non-prohibited factors can become prohibited bases.

For example, a creditor's practice may have a disparate effect on a protected category if the creditor denies credit to anyone who relies on child support payments as income. As this practice would affect divorced and separated women almost exclusively, it would have a disproportionately negative impact on the basis of sex and marital status and thus, in effect, becomes a prohibited basis.[70]

---

broadly, and no court has applied *Smith* to find that disparate impact claims are not cognizable under the FHA or ECOA"); Amended Order Granting in Part and Denying in Part Defendants' Motion to Dismiss, Garcia v. Countrywide, No. CV 07-cv-1161 (C.D. Cal. Jan. 17, 2008) (noting that the Court in *Smith v. City of Jackson* relied in its decision on not only textual analysis but also the legislative history and purpose of the ADEA). *See generally* Michael Aleo & Pablo Svirsky, *Foreclosure Fallout: The Banking Industry's Attack on Disparate Impact Race Discrimination Claims Under the Fair Housing Act and the Equal Credit Opportunity Act*, 18 B.U. Pub. Int. L.J. 1 (2008) (arguing that, despite lenders' arguments to the contrary, *Smith v. City of Jackson* does not prohibit disparate impact claims under other statutes that do not contain "effects" language).

64 619 F.3d 823 (8th Cir. 2010), *cert. granted*, 132 S. Ct. 548 (2011).

65 The plaintiffs were owners of residential property rented to low-income, disproportionately minority tenants who asserted disparate treatment and disparate impact discrimination based on the way the city of St. Paul enforced its housing code. The district court granted summary judgment to the city (Steinhauser v. City of St. Paul, 595 F. Supp. 2d 987 (D. Minn. 2008)), but the Eighth Circuit reversed as to the disparate impact claims, finding that the owners had established a prima facie case (Gallagher v. Magner, 619 F.3d 823 (8th Cir. 2010)).

A number of amicus briefs were submitted to the Supreme Court expressing a range of positions. Notably, the United States (specifically HUD and the Department of Justice) submitted an amicus brief defending the availability of disparate impact claims under the FHA and the use of a burden-shifting analysis but arguing that the Eighth Circuit applied it incorrectly in this case. Brief for the United States as Amicus Curiae in Support of Neither Party, *available on the companion website to this treatise*; *see also* Brief Amici Curiae of the American Civil Liberties Union, The National Community Reinvestment Coalition, Futures Without Violence, and the National Network to End Domestic Violence, in Support of Respondents, *available on the companion website to this treatise*.

66 Mt. Holly Gardens Citizens in Action, Inc. v. Twp. of Mount Holly, 658 F.3d 375 (3d Cir. 2011) (petition for certiorari filed June 11, 2012).

67 Twp. of Mount Holly, N.J. v. Mt. Holly Gardens Citizens in Action, Inc., 133 S. Ct. 569, 184 L. Ed. 2d 336 (2012).

68 *See, e.g.*, Gen. Bldg. Contractors Ass'n v. Pennsylvania, 458 U.S. 375, 102 S. Ct. 3141, 73 L. Ed. 2d 835 (1982); Duran v. Cmty. First Bankshares, Inc., 92 Fed. Appx. 756 (10th Cir. 2004); Guides, Ltd. v. Yarmouth Group Prop. Mgmt., Inc., 295 F.3d 1065 (10th Cir. 2002); Roy v. Bd. of Cnty. Comm'rs, 607 F. Supp. 2d 1297, 1308–09 (N.D. Fla. 2009); Jiang v. Allstate Ins. Co., 199 F.R.D. 267 (N.D. Ill. 2001) (a case for disparate impact discrimination under sections 1981 and 1982 will not lie). *But see* NAACP v. Ameriquest Mortgage Co., 635 F. Supp. 2d 1096, 1104 (C.D. Cal. 2009) (refusing to dismiss disparate impact claim under section 1982 in reverse redlining case; relying on Phiffer v. Proud Parrot Motor Hotel, Inc., 648 F.2d 548, 551 (9th Cir. 1980), which was not a disparate impact case).

69 *See, e.g.*, Vill. of Arlington Heights v. Metro. Hous. Dev. Corp., 429 U.S. 252, 265 (1977).

70 The drafters of Regulation B, recognizing this potential problem, specifically prohibited such a practice. *See* Reg. B, 12 C.F.R. § 1002.6(b)(5) [§ 202.6(b)(5)].

4.3.2 Burdens of Proof

4.3.2.1 General

There is limited case law on the disparate impact theory of liability in credit discrimination cases. As a result, both FHA and ECOA cases rely heavily on the much more developed body of law in the employment discrimination area.[71] Thus it is important for practitioners to keep track of the continuing evolution of the disparate impact theory in the area of employment.

In general, disparate impact cases are analyzed under a three-step burden-shifting framework. In the first step, the plaintiff establishes a prima facie showing of disparate impact.[72] In step two, the burden shifts to the defendant to demonstrate a "business necessity" or other justification for the practice.[73] In step three, the plaintiff has the opportunity to show that there is a less discriminatory alternative practice or action that would provide a comparably effective means of meeting the defendant's goal.[74] Each of these steps is addressed in detail in the following sections.

While it is generally well settled that no showing of discriminatory intent is necessary in a disparate impact case,[75] a few courts have allowed an intent-based standard to "infect" the analysis.[76]

---

71 *See, e.g.*, Chiang v. Schafer, 2008 WL 3925260, at *30 (D. V.I. Aug. 20, 2008) ("[I]t is appropriate to import the analysis from Title VII cases in analyzing a claim of discrimination brought under ECOA and . . . utilize Title VII employment discrimination case law as it may be appropriate in the context of credit transaction discrimination.").

72 *See* § 4.3.2.4, *infra*.

73 *See* § 4.3.2.5, *infra*.

74 *See* § 4.3.2.6, *infra*.

75 Huntington Branch, N.A.A.C.P. v. Town of Huntington, 844 F.2d 926, 935 (2d Cir. 1988) ("The lower court's [analysis] vividly demonstrates the extent to which an intent-based standard can infect an analysis and draw it away from its proper focus. Accordingly, we will not require proof of discriminatory intent to establish a prima facie disparate impact case under Title VIII."), *aff'd in part sub nom.* Town of Huntington, N.Y. v. Huntington Branch, N.A.A.C.P., 488 U.S. 15 (1988); Metro. Hous. Dev. Corp. v. Vill. of Arlington Heights, 558 F.2d 1283, 1290 (7th Cir. 1977) ("we agree that a showing of discriminatory intent is not required under section 3604(a)"); Nikolich v. Vill. of Arlington Heights, Ill., 870 F. Supp. 2d 556, 563 (N.D. Ill. 2012) ("Disparate impact, unlike disparate treatment, does not require that an individual be treated less favorably because of a protected characteristic.").

76 *See generally* Peter E. Mahoney, *The End(s) of Disparate Impact: Doctrinal Reconstruction, Fair Housing and Lending Law, and the Antidiscrimination Principle*, 47 Emory L.J. 409 (1998) (describing conflict between the precedent set by Griggs v. Duke Power Co., 401 U.S. 424, 91 S. Ct. 849, 28 L. Ed. 2d 158 (1971), in which liability was found in employment discrimination upon disparate impact alone, versus the line of cases flowing from Washington v. Davis, 426 U.S. 229, 96 S. Ct. 2040, 48 L. Ed. 2d 597 (1976), finding that, in order to sustain a constitutional challenge under the Equal Protection Clause, the plaintiff must prove that the conduct in question was motivated by a discriminatory purpose).

4.3.2.2 ECOA Burden of Proof

The burden of proof in disparate impact cases is somewhat clearer for ECOA claims than for FHA claims. Unlike the FHA, the legislative history of the ECOA expressly instructs the courts to use employment discrimination cases in construing the ECOA "effects test."[77]

In addition, the official interpretations of Regulation B state:

> The Act and regulation may prohibit a creditor practice that is discriminatory in effect because it has a disproportionately negative impact on a prohibited basis, even though the creditor has no intent to discriminate and the practice appears neutral on its face, unless the creditor practice meets a legitimate business need that cannot reasonably be achieved as well by means that are less disparate in their impact.[78]

Four standards are implicit in this statement:

- A practice that does not appear to discriminate on a prohibited basis can still be prohibited if the practice has a disparate impact on a prohibited basis.
- To be actionable, the impact must be "disproportionately negative" (by using this term, the official interpretation suggests some balancing of the negative impact with the business justification).
- If the practice has such an impact, it is prohibited unless the practice meets a legitimate business need that cannot reasonably be achieved by a practice that has a less disparate impact.
- The creditor's lack of intent to discriminate is irrelevant.

The official interpretations also indicate that the ECOA standard as to disparate impact is based on two Supreme Court employment discrimination decisions, *Griggs v. Duke Power Co.*[79] and *Albermarle Paper Co. v. Moody*.[80]

4.3.2.3 FHA Burden of Proof

Historically, courts have taken two approaches to analyzing FHA disparate impact cases.[81] The first approach is a balancing

---

77 *See* S. Rep. No. 94-589 (1976) ("Thus, judicial construction of antidiscrimination legislation in the employment field, in cases such as *Griggs v. Duke Power Co.* 401 U.S. 424 (1971) and *Albemarle Paper Co. v. Moody* are intended to serve as guides in the application of this Act, especially with respect to the allocations of burden of proof.").

78 Official Interpretations of Reg. B [Official Staff Commentary on Reg. B], 12 C.F.R. pt. 1002 [pt. 202], Supp. I, § 1002.6(a)-2 [§ 202.6(a)-2].

79 401 U.S. 424, 91 S. Ct. 849, 28 L. Ed. 2d 158 (1971) (establishing that discriminatory impact violates Title VII, which prohibits employment discrimination). *See generally* Elaine W. Shoben, *Disparate Impact Theory in Employment Discrimination: What's Griggs Still Good For? What Not?*, 42 Brandeis L.J. 597 (2004).

80 422 U.S. 405, 95 S. Ct. 2362, 45 L. Ed. 2d 280 (1975) (setting out disparate impact analysis for prima facie employment discrimination case by plaintiff, defendant's burden of proving business necessity, and plaintiff's opportunity to show less discriminatory means).

81 *See, e.g.*, Cent. Alabama Fair Hous. Ctr. v. Magee, 835 F. Supp. 2d

test articulated by the Seventh Circuit in *Metropolitan Housing Development Co. v. Village of Arlington Heights*, ("*Arlington Heights II*").[82] The second is a burden-shifting framework akin to the one used in employment discrimination and ECOA cases and first articulated by the Second Circuit in *Huntington Branch NAACP v. Town of Huntington*.[83]

In general, in cases involving government defendants, courts have utilized some variant of the Seventh Circuit's *Arlington Heights II* test.[84] The Sixth Circuit, for example, adopted a modified disparate impact analysis by eliminating the "some evidence of discriminatory intent" requirement of the *Arlington Heights II* test.[85] However, in cases involving private defendants, results have been mixed. Some courts have applied the Seventh Circuit standard without reference to a distinction between government and private defendants.[86] Other courts have turned more to employment law precedent, either because

the case also involved an ECOA claim[87] or because that circuit court has specifically rejected the *Arlington Heights II* standard.[88] Still others have applied a hybrid.[89] The Supreme Court has not yet ruled directly on this issue.[90]

In its final rule implementing the Fair Housing Act's discriminatory effects standard,[91] the Department of Housing and Urban Development (HUD) endorses a three-step burden-shifting test identical to the one used in ECOA cases for cases against both governmental and private defendants.[92] If the Supreme Court grants certiorari in *Mount Holly*,[93] one question will be the extent of deference due to HUD's interpretation of the statute.

4.3.2.4 Prima Facie Case for ECOA and FHA Claims

4.3.2.4.1 Introduction

Despite the confusion in FHA cases, most courts in credit discrimination cases will follow the employment law standards, asking whether a policy, procedure, or practice specifically identified by the plaintiff has a significantly greater discriminatory impact on members of a protected class.[94] HUD's regulation clarifying the standard for disparate impact claims under

---

1165, 1195 (M.D. Ala. 2011) ("There are two possible paths: courts either apply a burden-shifting approach similar to that used in workplace-discrimination cases under Title VII of the Civil Act of 1964, as amended, 42 U.S.C. §§ 1981a, 2000e through 2000e–17, or a balancing test designed to uncover the appropriateness of the defendants' behavior.").

82 558 F.2d 1283 (7th Cir. 1977).

83 Huntington Branch, N.A.A.C.P. v. Town of Huntington, 844 F.2d 926, 934 (2d Cir. 1988), aff'd, 488 U.S. 15 (1988) (quoting United States v. City of Black Jack, 508 F.2d 1179, 1184–85 (8th Cir. 1974)); *see also* Tsombanidis v. West Haven Fire Dep't, 352 F.3d 565, 574–75 (2d Cir. 2003).

84 The court articulated a test that asks four questions: (1) How strong is the plaintiff's showing of discriminatory effect? (2) Is there some evidence of discriminatory intent, though not enough to satisfy the constitutional standard of *Washington v. Davis*? (3) What is the defendant's interest in taking the action complained of? (4) Does the plaintiff seek to compel the defendant affirmatively to provide housing for a protected class or merely to remove obstacles to private provision of such housing? Metro. Hous. Dev. Co. v. Vill. of Arlington Heights, 558 F.2d 1283 (7th Cir. 1977); *see also* Betsey v. Turtle Creek Assocs., 736 F.2d 983, 989 n.5 (4th Cir. 1984) (noting that balancing test was only appropriate when defendant is a public body; in cases against private defendants, the three-step burden-shifting framework should be used).

85 Arthur v. City of Toledo, 782 F.2d 565 (6th Cir. 1986); *see also* Graoch Assocs. #33, Ltd. P'ship v. Louisville/Jefferson Cnty. Metro Human Relations Comm'n, 508 F.3d 366 (6th Cir. 2007) (discussing *Arthur* and setting forth the burden-shifting framework for analyzing disparate impact claims against private defendants under FHA). *See generally* David M. Bonelli, *If You Build It "They" Will Come: Intentional Discrimination and Disparate Impact Theory in Buckeye Community Hope Found. v. City of Cuyahoga Falls— Does a Municipality's Use of Referendum to Block an Approved Housing Project Violate Equal Protection and Title VIII?*, 26 Hamline L. Rev. 631 (2003).

86 *See, e.g.*, United States v. Badgett, 976 F.2d 1176 (8th Cir. 1992) (applying *Arlington Heights II* test to private defendant); Old West End Ass'n v. Buckeye Fed. Sav. & Loan, 675 F. Supp. 1100, 1105 (N.D. Ohio 1987) (in dismissing motion for summary judgment, court applied the *Arlington Heights II* standard to a claim of redlining). *See generally* Peter E. Mahoney, *The End(s) of Disparate Impact: Doctrinal Reconstruction, Fair Housing and Lending Law, and the Antidiscrimination Principle*, 47 Emory L.J. 409 (1998).

87 *See, e.g.*, A.B. & S. Auto Serv. Inc. v. South Shore Bank of Chi., 962 F. Supp. 1056 (N.D. Ill. 1997); Thomas v. First Fed. Sav. Bank, 653 F. Supp. 1330 (N.D. Ind. 1987); Cherry v. Amoco Oil Co., 490 F. Supp. 1026, 1031 (N.D. Ga. 1980).

88 *See, e.g.*, Bronson v. Crestwood Lake Section 1 Holding Corp., 724 F. Supp. 148 (S.D.N.Y. 1989).

89 *See, e.g.*, Graoch Assocs. #33, Ltd. P'ship v. Louisville/Jefferson Cnty. Metro Human Relations Comm'n, 508 F.3d 366, 373 (6th Cir. 2007) (balancing test incorporated as elements of proof after second step of burden-shifting framework); Mountain Side Mobile Estates v. Sec'y of Hous. & Urban Dev., 56 F.3d 1243, 1252, 1254 (10th Cir. 1995) (incorporating a three-factor balancing test into the burden-shifting framework to weigh defendant's justification).

90 In 1988, in Town of Huntington v. Huntington Branch, N.A.A.C.P., 488 U.S. 15, 109 S. Ct. 276, 102 L. Ed. 2d 180 (1988), the Court declined to "endorse" the "precise analysis" used by the Second Circuit, while affirming the result. The Court was poised to address this issue in 2003 in a case coming up from the Sixth Circuit, Buckeye Cmty. Hope Found. v. City of Cuyahoga Falls, 263 F.3d 627 (6th Cir. 2001). However, the plaintiffs abandoned their FHA claims. See City of Cuyahoga Falls v. Buckeye Cmty. Hope Found., 538 U.S. 188, 123 S. Ct. 1389, 155 L. Ed. 2d 349 (2003); *see also* Greater New Orleans Fair Hous. Action Ctr. v. U.S. Dep't. of Hous. & Urban Dev., 639 F.3d 1078 (D.C. Cir. 2011) (declining to reach the question of whether *Arlington Heights* or *Huntington Branch* test should apply, because both required proof of disparate impact that plaintiffs were unable to provide).

91 Final Rule, Dep't of Hous. & Urban Dev., Implementation of the Fair Housing Act's Discriminatory Effects Standard, 78 Fed. Reg. 11,460 (Feb. 15, 2013).

92 78 Fed. Reg. 11,460, 11,462 (Feb. 15, 2013).

93 Mt. Holly Gardens Citizens in Action, Inc. v. Twp. of Mount Holly, 658 F.3d 375 (3d Cir. 2011) (petition for certiorari filed June 11, 2012); *see* § 4.3.1, *supra*.

94 *See, e.g.*, Simms v. First Gibraltar Bank, 83 F.3d 1546 (5th Cir. 1996); NAACP v. Ameriquest Mortgage Co., 635 F. Supp. 2d 1096, 1103 (C.D. Cal. 2009).

the FHA defines discriminatory effect (and what the plaintiff must demonstrate in order to establish a prima facie case) as:

> Discriminatory effect: A practice has a discriminatory effect where it actually or predictably results in a disparate impact on a group of persons or creates, increases, reinforces, or perpetuates segregated housing patterns because of race, color, religion, sex, handicap, familial status, or national origin.[95]

Many courts have required the plaintiff to demonstrate three elements to establish a prima facie showing of discrimination: *identification* of a specific policy, disparate *impact* of the policy on a protected group, and *causation* (a causal link between the policy and the disparate impact). Each is discussed in detail in the sections below.

The following sections summarize existing case law; it remains to be seen how courts will interpret and apply HUD's formulation of the burden of proof in the coming years.

4.3.2.4.2 Identification of a specific policy

The plaintiff first must show that a specific policy caused a significant disparate effect on a protected group. Although the policy being challenged is often not in question, there are instances when the defendant will challenge whether the plaintiff has in fact identified a specific policy.[96]

Defendants may also challenge whether the particularity requirement is met when the plaintiff is challenging subjective discriminatory practices that occur under a facially neutral policy, as opposed to challenging objective or standardized tests. For example, in a case challenging auto finance mark-up policies, defendants argued that the finance company's policy that permitted subjective treatment by the car dealers was not subject to disparate impact analysis.[97] The policy in question

was a mark-up pricing scheme in which dealers, based on creditor instructions, were given discretion to mark up interest rates above the creditor's minimum buy rate.[98] The court disagreed with defendants, finding no discernible reason not to use disparate impact analysis in these circumstances.[99]

The Supreme Court addressed and resolved this issue in the employment discrimination context in *Watson v. Fort Worth Bank and Trust*.[100] Previously, there was a split among the circuits as to whether employees could challenge employers' use of subjectivity in decision making. In the *Watson* case, the defendant bank relied on the subjective judgment of its supervisors to evaluate job candidates. A unanimous Supreme Court held that disparate impact could be applied to this type of discretionary or subjective decision making.[101] According to the *Watson* court, "disparate impact analysis in principle is no less applicable to subjective employment criteria than to objective or standardized tests, since, in either case, a facially neutral practice, adopted without discriminatory intent, may have effects that are indistinguishable from intentionally discriminatory practices."[102] Despite this clear direction from the Supreme Court, some lower courts have continued to construe allegations of disparate impact based on subjectivity in decision making as individual disparate treatment claims.[103]

A principal's delegation of authority to make subjective decisions can also be challenged. The Supreme Court noted in *Watson* that delegating employment decisions to those employees who are most familiar with the jobs to be filled and with the candidates for those jobs could constitute an employment prac-

---

95　Final Rule, Dep't of Hous. & Urban Dev., Implementation of the Fair Housing Act's Discriminatory Effects Standard, 78 Fed. Reg. 11,460, 11,482 (Feb. 15, 2013) (*codified at* 24 C.F.R. § 100.500(a)).

96　*See, e.g.*, Simms v. First Gibraltar Bank, 83 F.3d 1546 (5th Cir. 1996) (plaintiff failed to specifically identify a policy, procedure, or practice of the defendant that had a disparate impact); Rodriguez v. Bear Stearns Cos., Inc., 2009 WL 5184702 (D. Conn. Dec. 22, 2009) (finding that plaintiffs failed to identify a facially neutral practice, when allegations were essentially that defendant's overall servicing of non-prime loans differed from its servicing of prime loans); Roy v. Bd. of Cnty. Comm'rs, 607 F. Supp. 2d 1297, 1308 (N.D. Fla. 2009) (plaintiffs landowners failed to identify any facially neutral policy to support their FHA disparate impact claim regarding their development rights); Powell v. American Gen. Finance, Inc., 310 F. Supp. 2d 481 (N.D.N.Y. 2004) (plaintiff failed to allege a specific policy to support disparate impact claim; *see also* Smith v. City of Jackson, 544 U.S. 228, 125 S. Ct. 1536, 161 L. Ed. 2d 410 (2005) (it is not enough in ADEA case to simply allege that there is a disparate impact on workers or point to a generalized policy that leads to such an impact; plaintiffs here failed to identify a specific practice responsible for the alleged statistical disparities).

97　Coleman v. Gen. Motors Acceptance Corp., 196 F.R.D. 315, 325 (M.D. Tenn. 2000), *vacated and remanded on unrelated grounds*, 296 F.3d 443 (6th Cir. 2002).

98　*See id. See generally* § 8.6.1, *infra*.

99　*Id.*; *see* Buycks-Roberson v. Citibank Fed. Sav. Bank, 162 F.R.D. 322, 331 (N.D. Ill. 1995) (the subjective application of neutral underwriting criteria is standardized conduct because the loan originators have the opportunity to use their discretion with respect to each loan application and the standardized conduct can be readily identified for purposes of assessing evidence of disparate impact); *see also* Watson v. Forth Worth Bank & Trust, 487 U.S. 977, 990, 108 S. Ct. 2777, 101 L. Ed. 2d 827 (1988) (Title VII employment case; disparate impact analysis is no less applicable to subjective employment criteria than to objective or standardized tests).

100　487 U.S. 977, 108 S. Ct. 2777, 101 L. Ed. 2d 827 (1988).

101　487 U.S. 977, 108 S. Ct. 2777, 101 L. Ed. 2d 827 (1988).

102　*Id.*; *see also* Barrett v. H & R Block, Inc., 652 F. Supp. 2d 104 (D. Mass. 2009) (challenge to defendants' discretionary pricing policy in mortgage lending; following *Watson*); Guerra v. GMAC L.L.C., 2009 WL 449153, at *4 n.5 (E.D. Pa. Feb. 20, 2009) (same); Ramirez v. GreenPoint Mortgage Funding, Inc., 633 F. Supp. 2d 922 (N.D. Cal. 2008) (plaintiffs adequately identified specific policy in "Discretionary Pricing Policy" that relied upon both subjective and objective criteria); Miller v. Countrywide Bank, 571 F. Supp. 2d 251, 255 (D. Mass. 2008) (same).

103　*See, e.g.*, Wright v. Circuit City Stores, 201 F.R.D. 526 (N.D. Ala. 2001); Lott v. Westinghouse Savannah River Co., 200 F.R.D. 539 (D.S.C. 2000); Zachery v. Texaco, 185 F.R.D. 230 (W.D. Tex. 1999); Abram v. Kelsey-Seybold Medical Group Inc., 178 F.R.D. 116 (S.D. Tex. 1997). *But see* Dukes v. Wal-Mart Stores, Inc., 603 F.3d 571, 612 (9th Cir. 2010), *cert. granted in part*, 131 S. Ct. 795 (2010) (recognizing subjective decision making processes as "ready mechanism[s]" for discrimination and affirming certification of a class of female employees).

tice that can be challenged using disparate impact theory.[104] Delegation, just like subjectivity, is not per se unlawful, but it can be challenged as having a discriminatory impact.[105]

The Supreme Court's opinion in *Wal-Mart Stores, Inc. v. Dukes*,[106] while not overruling *Watson*, does arguably make it more difficult to bring a disparate impact claim based on subjectivity in decision making. In *Wal-Mart*, the Court noted that, even in *Watson*, "merely proving that the discretionary system has produced a racial or sexual disparity *is not enough*" and that "the plaintiff must begin by identifying the specific employment practice that is challenged."[107] The *Wal-Mart* plaintiffs sought to certify a nationwide class of all female employees in Wal-Mart stores, alleging that Wal-Mart's policy of giving local supervisors discretion over pay and promotion decisions produced a disparate impact. The Supreme Court found that the proposed class did not satisfy the commonality requirement of Federal Rule of Civil Procedure 23 because plaintiffs could not identify a particular policy or "a common mode of exercising discretion that pervades the entire company."[108] The practices complained of in *Wal-Mart* included both pay and promotion decisions that were made based on a number of objective and subjective criteria.[109] Cases challenging discretionary credit mark-ups[110] should be distinguished from *Wal-Mart*, because all the transactions in a credit mark-up case are of the same type and the factors relevant to each borrower's creditworthiness are objective, measurable, and were in fact used to set the base price before the discretionary mark-up was applied.[111] Nevertheless, a number of district courts have seized on *Wal-Mart* to deny or revoke class certification in cases alleging disparate impact as a result of policies that allow discretionary markups in credit decisions.[112]

Sometimes it is difficult to pinpoint exactly which business practice has a particular disparate impact, but it is clear that a combination of factors has a disparate effect.[113] While some Supreme Court employment discrimination cases indicated that the plaintiff must specify what particular business practice had what particular disparate impact,[114] with the passage of the Civil Rights Act of 1991, Congress declared unequivocally that the specific discriminatory practices need not be separately proven, but a combination of policies may be shown to have a disparate impact.[115] As summarized by one court, the 1991 Act "encodes the Court's requirement that employment practices be identified with specificity, while also allowing for broad-based challenges where such specificity is not possible."[116] Courts have relied on this Title VII statutory language to allow plaintiffs to challenge practices when specific identification of the policy or practice in question was not possible.[117]

The HUD final rule implementing the FHA discriminatory effects standard endorses this view:

> In HUD's experience, identifying the specific practice that caused the alleged discriminatory effect will depend on the facts of a particular situation and therefore must be determined on a case-by-case basis. Moreover, as recognized in the employment context under Title VII, the elements of a decision-making process may not be capable of separation for analysis, in which case it may be appropriate to challenge the decision-making process as a whole. For example, in

---

104   Watson v. Forth Worth Bank & Trust, 487 U.S. 977, 990, 108 S. Ct. 2777, 101 L. Ed. 2d 827 (1988); *cf.* Miller v. Countrywide Bank, 571 F. Supp. 2d 251, 256 (D. Mass. 2008) ("*Watson's* focus on subjective decisionmaking has particular resonance . . . where the fundamental question under the ECOA and the FHA is creditworthiness"); Commonwealth of Mass. v. H & R Block, No. 08-2474-BLS1 (Mass. Super. Ct. Nov. 10, 2008) (finding that plaintiffs identified a sufficiently specific policy), *available at* www.nclc.org/unreported.

105   Watson v. Fort Worth Bank & Trust, 487 U.S. 977, 990, 108 S. Ct. 2777, 101 L. Ed. 2d 827 (1988); *see also* Equal Emp't Opportunity Comm'n v. Joe's Stone Crab Inn, 296 F.3d 1265 (11th Cir. 2002) (focusing, in employment discrimination case, on the fact that the restaurant owners never conveyed concern to the managers with hiring authority about compliance with civil rights laws); Smith v. Chrysler Financial Co., 2003 WL 328719 (D.N.J. Jan. 15, 2003); Buycks-Roberson v. Citibank, 162 F.R.D. 322 (N.D. Ill. 1995) (the alleged policy or practice at issue is the bank's subjective application of underwriting criteria, not the particular types of criteria alone; the standardized conduct is the granting of subjectivity because the loan originators have the opportunity to use their discretion with respect to each applicant); § 8.6.4, *infra*.

106   131 S. Ct. 2541 (2011).

107   Wal-Mart Stores, Inc. v. Dukes, 131 S. Ct. 2541, 2555 (2011) (citing Watson v. Fort Worth Bank & Trust, 487 U.S. 977, 994 (1988) (emphasis in original).

108   Wal-Mart Stores, Inc. v. Dukes, 131 S. Ct. 2541, 2554–55 (2011).

109   131 S. Ct. 2541, 2547 (2011).

110   *See* § 8.6, *infra* (discussing issue).

111   *See, e.g.*, Barrett v. H & R Block, Inc., No. 08-10157-RWZ, 2011 WL 1100105 (D. Mass. Mar. 21, 2011) (plaintiffs asserted that discretionary pricing strategy they challenged was executed uni-

formly, and its adverse effects were felt in the same way by plaintiffs and all class members). This decision was issued before *Wal-Mart* but discusses commonality in a way that arguably anticipates and meets the *Wal-Mart* standard. The defendant's motion to decertify the class in light of *Wal-Mart* was pending at the time of this printing.

112   Rodriguez v. Nat'l City Bank, 277 F.R.D. 148 (E.D. Pa. 2011); *In re* Countrywide Financial Mortgage Lending Practices Litig., No. 08-MD-1974, 2011 WL 4862174 (W.D. Ky. Oct. 13, 2011); *In re* Wells Fargo Residential Mortgage Lending Discrimination Litig., 2011 WL 3903117 (N.D. Cal. Sept. 6, 2011).

113   *See* United States v. Inc. Vill. of Island Park, 888 F. Supp. 419 (E.D.N.Y. 1995).

114   *See* Wards Cove Packing Co. v. Atonio, 490 U.S. 642, 109 S. Ct. 2115, 104 L. Ed. 2d 733 (1989) (employment discrimination case).
      The legislative history of the Civil Rights Act of 1991 specifically discusses overruling *Wards Cove*. 1991 U.S.C.C.A.N. 561.

115   42 U.S.C. § 2000e-2(k)(1)(B)(i).

116   McClain v. Lufkin Industries, Inc., 187 F.R.D. 267, 272 (E.D. Tex. 1999), *aff'd in relevant part*, 519 F.3d 264 (5th Cir. 2008); *see also* Stender v. Lucky Stores, Inc., 803 F. Supp. 259 (N.D. Cal. 1992).

117   *See, e.g.*, Howard v. Gutierrez, 571 F. Supp. 2d 145, 160 n.5 (D.D.C. 2008); O'Neal v. Wackenhut Servs., Inc., 2006 WL 1469348, at *16 (E.D. Tenn. May 25, 2006); Butler v. Home Depot Inc., 1997 WL 605754 (N.D. Cal. Aug. 29, 1997); Stender v. Lucky Stores, 803 F. Supp. 259 (N.D. Cal. 1992).
      In the credit discrimination context, see Buycks-Roberson v. Citibank, 162 F.R.D. 322, 331–33 (N.D. Ill. 1995) (the fact that the policy is defined broadly does not mean that plaintiffs have failed to adequately identify a policy or practice).

a reverse redlining case, there may be multiple acts or policies which together result in a discriminatory effect.[118]

4.3.2.4.3 Disparate impact on a protected group

Second, the plaintiff must identify or demonstrate the adverse impact of the policy on a specific class of persons protected by the discrimination law. This element is further divided into two categories: in the first, the plaintiff must show the adverse impact on protected persons; in the second, the plaintiff must then show that the unfavorable consequences are felt disproportionately by the members of the protected class in comparison to nonmembers who are similarly situated.[119] Expert testimony will be necessary to make both of these showings.

Care must be taken in determining exactly what data is to be compared. Statistics which merely show that a higher percentage of African Americans are turned down for credit than whites are unlikely to be persuasive to a court. Courts will look instead to see if a higher percentage of *qualified* African Americans are turned down than whites.[120] For example, if a creditor denies credit to those with active delinquencies, a court may not find that this shows a disparate impact on African Americans when the only evidence produced is that African Americans are more likely to be delinquent than whites, not that otherwise creditworthy African Americans are more likely

to be delinquent than otherwise creditworthy whites. On the other hand, courts will likely find a disparate impact if a plaintiff can show that a creditor's insistence on a credit history from a bank, and not just a finance company, is more likely to impact creditworthy African Americans than creditworthy whites.

It is often difficult for plaintiffs to show that they used a proper pool for comparison purposes. The Supreme Court's general guidance in the employment area is that, "while a statistical showing of disproportionate impact [need not] always be based on an analysis of the characteristics of actual applicants,"[121] "statistics based on an applicant pool containing individuals lacking minimal qualifications for the job would be of little probative value,"[122] and " 'evidence showing that the figures for the general population might not accurately reflect the pool of qualified job applicants' undermines the significance of such figures."[123] In a case involving a city's policy of denying water service to tenants if a landlord owed the city for a prior tenant's unpaid water bills, the Sixth Circuit found that the plaintiffs failed to state a claim under the ECOA because of flaws in the statistical comparisons.[124] Specifically, the court rejected the plaintiff's reliance on a statistical comparison between all renters in the relevant geographical area and all home owners. The court found that the category of all renters was over-inclusive because it included many renters without individual water meters. The group of all home owners, the court found, was under-inclusive because it excluded a group of residents who were eligible to apply for water service without having to obtain approval from another (those who live with owners of residences with water meters).[125] The court did, however, allow plaintiffs to proceed with an equal protection argument.

Many cases rely on the "applicant pool" method set out in *Wards Cove Packing Co. v. Atonio.*[126] In that case, the Court held that, in using the applicant pool method, the proper comparison was between the racial composition of those hold-

---

118 Final Rule, Dep't of Hous. & Urban Dev., Implementation of the Fair Housing Act's Discriminatory Effects Standard, 78 Fed. Reg. 11,460, 11,469 (Feb. 15, 2013).

119 Donnelly v. Rhode Island. Bd. of Governors for Higher Education, 929 F. Supp. 583, 590 (D.R.I. 1996), *aff'd*, 110 F.3d 2 (1st Cir. 1997) (citing Equal Emp't Opportunity Comm'n v. Steamship Clerks Union Local 1066, 48 F.3d 594, 601 (1st Cir. 1995)); *see also* Mt. Holly Gardens Citizens in Action, Inc. v. Twp. of Mount Holly, 658 F.3d 375 (3d Cir. 2011) (rejecting defendant's argument that, because 100% of minorities and 100% of non-minorities in a neighborhood slated for redevelopment would be treated the same way, there was no prima facie evidence of disparate impact and instead instructing district court to consider statistics that 22.54% of African-American and 32.31% of Hispanic households in township would be affected by demolition compared to only 2.73% of white households); Reinhart v. Lincoln Cnty., 482 F.3d 1225, 1231 (10th Cir. 2007) (affirming summary judgment for the defendant on FHA claim when the plaintiffs were unable to demonstrate the specific impact on protected groups of the defendant's change in regulations); Rodriguez v. Bear Stearns Cos., Inc., 2009 WL 5184702, at *10 (D. Conn. Dec. 22, 2009) (finding that proper analysis for testing plaintiffs allegations of differential loan servicing would be to compare impact of defendant's loan servicing policies on minority and non-minority borrowers, not to compare the percentage of minorities in defendant's prime and non-prime loan pools).

   For purposes of surviving a motion to dismiss in a class action alleging racially discriminatory mortgage lending, however, reliance on general lending studies and reports may be sufficient. *See, e.g.*, Guerra v. GMAC L.L.C., 2009 WL 449153, at *5 (E.D. Pa. Feb. 20, 2009).

120 *See* Albemarle Paper Co. v. Moody, 422 U.S. 405, 95 S. Ct. 2362, 45 L. Ed. 2d 280 (1975) (employment discrimination case); Saldana v. Citibank, 1996 U.S. Dist. LEXIS 8327 (N.D. Ill. June 13, 1996) (mortgage redlining case).

121 Dothard v. Rawlinson, 433 U.S. 321, 330, 97 S. Ct. 2720, 53 L. Ed. 2d 786 (1977).

122 Watson v. Fort Worth Bank & Trust, 487 U.S. 977, 997, 108 S. Ct. 2777, 101 L. Ed. 2d 827 (1988).

123 New York City Transit Auth. v. Beazer, 440 U.S. 568, 587 n.29, 99 S. Ct. 1355, 59 L. Ed. 2d 587 (1979) (quoting Int'l Brotherhood of Teamsters v. United States, 431 U.S. 324, 340 n.20, 97 S. Ct. 1843, 52 L. Ed. 2d 396 (1977)).

124 Golden v. City of Columbus, 404 F.3d 950 (6th Cir. 2005); *see also* Greater New Orleans Fair Hous. Action Ctr. v. U.S. Dep't of Hous. & Urban Dev., 639 F.3d 1078 (D.C. Cir. 2011) (rejecting plaintiffs' disparate impact claims related to a post-Katrina grant program because the analysis 'cherry-picked' certain aspects of the grant formula and certain parishes rather than considering impact of grant program as a whole).

125 *Id.*; *see also* Roy v. Bd. of Cnty. Comm'rs, 607 F. Supp. 2d 1297, 1308–1309 (N.D. Fla. 2009) (granting summary judgment to defendants as landowners' statistical proof of worse treatment of African Americans in regards to development rights failed on numerous grounds).

126 Wards Cove Packing Co. v. Atonio, 490 U.S. 642, 650, 109 S. Ct. 2115, 104 L. Ed. 2d 733 (1989).

ing the more desirable (non-cannery) jobs and the racial composition of the qualified population in the relevant labor market.[127]

The test is slightly different in a reverse redlining case.[128] In a typical reverse redlining case, a plaintiff using the applicant pool approach collects applicant data from all of the lenders' branches. The plaintiff would then show that, under the lenders' lending criteria, the percentage of qualified white applicants receiving terms at the favorable rate significantly exceeds the percentage of qualified non-whites receiving such rates.[129] This data can be supplemented with census data, for example, to show the racial composition of particular neighborhoods and to show that predatory lenders target those areas for the highest-price credit products.[130]

A problem with this approach is that many non-whites may be deterred from applying for loans at the pre-application stage.[131] This discrimination will not show up in an analysis based on applicants only. As an alternative, plaintiffs could use general population statistics and compare, for example, the percentage of non-whites holding the more desirable jobs versus the percentage of non-whites in the general population for the targeted area. However, such a comparison pool is vulnerable to challenge for over-inclusiveness. For example, in a mortgage lending case, defendants will likely argue that comparisons with the general population fail to differentiate between those who are creditworthy and those who would not qualify for credit.

4.3.2.4.4 Causation

Finally, plaintiffs must show causation. Establishing a prima facie case requires more than a mere showing of statistical disparities. The suspect practices must be identified and causally linked with the statistically demonstrated adverse impact.[132] Again, credit discrimination cases borrow from the employment area in determining what is required to show this element.

In employment cases, the Supreme Court decisions have generally required plaintiffs to show that the particular practice or policy has a disparate impact upon the identified pool of protected persons that is significant or substantial enough to raise an inference of causation.[133] In employment cases, plaintiffs typically make this showing by using statistical analyses.[134] However, the Court has not adopted a particular statistical standard that could show "significance" in every case, relying instead on a case-by-case approach.[135]

In home mortgage lending cases, in particular, the causation element is critical to balance "mere" findings from HMDA data (or other sources) of statistical disparities in approval and rejection rates. This element requires that the plaintiff show that the specific policy in question caused the disparate effect.[136]

---

127 *Id.; see also* Diamond Ventures, L.L.C. v. Baruah, 699 F. Supp. 2d 57, 63 (D.D.C. 2010) (finding that plaintiff made a sufficient showing of disparate impact to avoid summary judgment when defendant did not keep data on the race of applicants turned down for loans and plaintiff's expert used an "applicant pool" method).

128 *See generally* § 8.5.2, *infra*.

129 *See also* City of Memphis v. Wells Fargo Bank, N.A., 2011 WL 1706756 (W.D. Tenn. May 4, 2011). *See generally* Frank Lopez, *Using the Fair Housing Act to Combat Predatory Lending*, 6 Geo. J. on Poverty L. & Pol'y 73 (1999).

130 *See, e.g.*, Hargraves v. Capital City Mortgage Corp., 140 F. Supp. 2d 7 (D.D.C. 2000).

131 *See generally* § 5.3, *infra* (discussion of pre-application discrimination).

132 *See* A.B. & S. Auto Serv., Inc. v. South Shore Bank of Chi., 962 F. Supp. 1056 (N.D. Ill. 1997); Saldana v. Citibank, 1996 U.S. Dist. LEXIS 8327 (N.D. Ill. June 13, 1996); United States v. Inc. Vill. of Island Park, 888 F. Supp. 419, 446 (E.D.N.Y. 1995) (the fact that no African Americans received any of the forty-four homes constructed under a government-subsidized housing plan was combined with evidence of a facially neutral process which did not allow for selection of applications from African Americans); *see also* Anderson v. Frye, 2007 WL 912290, at *7 (S.D. Ohio Mar. 22, 2007) (granting summary judgment to bank on FHA claim on

grounds that plaintiff had failed to show that she was qualified for the mortgage).

133 *See* Watson v. Fort Worth Bank & Trust, 487 U.S. 977, 995, 108 S. Ct. 2777, 101 L. Ed. 2d 827 (1988) (plaintiffs in Title VII cases must show that the "test in question select applicants for hire or promotion in a racial pattern significantly different from that of the pool of applicants"); *see also* Meacham v. Knolls Atomic Power Lab., 128 S. Ct. 2395 n.13, 171 L. Ed. 2d 283 (2008) (citing *Watson* for requirement that "statistical disparities must be sufficiently substantial that they raise . . . an inference of causation"); Smith v. City of Jackson, 544 U.S. 228, 125 S. Ct. 1536, 161 L. Ed. 2d 410 (2005) (it is not enough in ADEA case to simply allege that there is a disparate impact on workers or point to a generalized policy that leads to such an impact; plaintiffs here failed to identify a specific practice responsible for the alleged statistical disparities); Connecticut v. Teal, 457 U.S. 440, 446, 102 S. Ct. 2525, 73 L. Ed .2d 130 (1982); New York City Transit Auth. v. Beazer, 440 U.S. 568, 584, 99 S. Ct. 1355, 59 L. Ed. 2d 587 (1979); Dothard v. Rawlinson, 433 U.S. 321, 329, 97 S. Ct. 2720, 53 L. Ed. 2d 786 (1977); Washington v. Davis, 426 U.S. 229, 246–47, 96 S. Ct. 2040, 48 L. Ed. 2d 597 (1976).

134 *See, e.g.*, Watson v. Fort Worth Bank & Trust, 487 U.S. 977, 994, 108 S. Ct. 2777, 101 L. Ed. 2d 827 (1988).

135 Watson v. Fort Worth Bank & Trust, 487 U.S. 977, 996 n.3, 108 S. Ct. 2777, 101 L. Ed. 2d 827 (1988).

136 *See, e.g.*, City of Memphis v. Wells Fargo Bank, N.A., 2011 WL 1706756 (W.D. Tenn. May 4, 2011); Guerra v. GMAC L.L.C., 2009 WL 449153, at *6 (E.D. Pa. Feb. 20, 2009) (denying motion to dismiss when plaintiffs alleged that defendants' discretionary pricing policy accounted for a significant portion of the alleged statistical disparities in rates, fees, and terms between similarly situated minority and non-minority borrowers); Hoffman v. Option One Mortgage Corp., 589 F. Supp. 2d 1009, 1010–12 (N.D. Ill. 2008) (FHA and ECOA plaintiffs must identify specific practice or policy responsible for disparate impact) (citing Smith v. City of Jackson, 544 U.S. 228, 125 S. Ct. 1536, 161 L. Ed. 2d 410 (2005)); Taylor v. Accredited Home Lenders, Inc., 580 F. Supp. 2d 1062, 1068–69 (S.D. Cal. 2008); Miller v. Countrywide Bank, 571 F. Supp. 2d 251 (D. Mass. 2008); Commonwealth of Mass. v. H & R Block, No. 08-2474-BLS1 (Mass. Super. Ct. Nov. 10, 2008), *available at* www.nclc.org/unreported.

The question of whether statistics alone can be used to prove discriminatory bias is the subject of much academic debate. *See generally* Joseph T. Lynyak, *Developments in Fair Lending Affecting the Residential Mortgage Industry*, 61 Consumer Fin. L.Q. Rep. 775 (2007); Peter E. Mahoney, *The End(s) of Disparate Impact:*

Here again, expert testimony is essential. Even when in an individual case some racially hostile comments have been made, such comments on their own may not demonstrate discrimination if causation cannot be shown and the business justification analysis is met.[137]

4.3.2.5 Business Justification

If the plaintiff meets the prima facie burden described above, then the burden of proof shifts to the creditor to show a legitimate and necessary business justification.[138] That the plaintiff need only initially show the discriminatory impact and that the burden of showing the business justification then shifts to the creditor is buttressed by Congressional action in the employment area. Supreme Court employment discrimination cases had been increasingly placing a greater burden on the plaintiff concerning the business justification.[139] In response, Congress enacted the Civil Rights Act of 1991, which unequivocally declares that the defendant retains the burden of proving that a

---

Doctrinal Reconstruction, Fair Housing and Lending Law, and the Antidiscrimination Principle, 47 Emory L.J. 409 (1998); Peter P. Swire, *The Persistent Problem of Lending Discrimination: A Law and Economics Analysis*, 73 Tex. L. Rev. 787 (1995); Stephen M. Dane, *Eliminating the Labyrinth: A Proposal to Simplify Federal Mortgage Lending Discrimination Laws*, 26 U. Mich. J.L. Reform 527, 530 (1993).

137 *See* Takele v. Mayo Clinic, 576 F.3d 834 (8th Cir. 2009) (in employment case under Title VII, hostile comments by employer relating to plaintiff's race and national origin did not on their own constitute pretext for, or inference of, discrimination, even when comments compared Ethiopian employee's work to "a thousand monkeys getting together to write the Bible" and references to "foreigners and someone Ethiopian" were made).

138 *See, e.g.*, Huntington Branch NAACP v. Town of Huntington, 844 F.2d 926 (2d Cir. 1988), *aff'd*, 488 U.S. 15, 18 (1988) (not reaching the question of appropriateness of the pure effects test because the defendant had not challenged its application, but commenting that it was "satisfied on this record that disparate impact was shown, and that the sole justification proffered to rebut the prima facie case was inadequate"); Betsey v. Turtle Creek Assocs., 736 F.2d 983 (4th Cir. 1984); United States v. Parma, 661 F.2d 562 (6th Cir. 1981); Resident Advisory Bd. v. Rizzo, 564 F.2d 126 (3d Cir. 1977); United States v. City of Black Jack, 508 F.2d 1179 (8th Cir. 1974); Dismuke v. Connor, 2007 WL 4463567 (W.D. Ark. Dec. 14, 2007) (defendant in farm loan case showed legitimate nondiscriminatory reasons for delay of loan decision when loan application was incomplete, borrower requested an increase in loan amount after initial application, and outside agency was hired to complete title work and do appraisal; plaintiff did not contend these arguments were pretextual); Curley v. JP Morgan Chase Bank, 2007 WL 1343793 (W.D. La. May 7, 2007), *aff'd*, 261 Fed. Appx. 781 (5th Cir. 2008); Williams v. 5300 Columbia Pike Corp., 891 F. Supp. 1169 (E.D. Va. 1995) (because plaintiffs presented a valid prima facie claim under Fair Housing Act, burden shifted to defendants to assert a legitimate business purpose or purposes for the challenged practice); Interagency Policy Statement on Discrimination in Lending, 59 Fed. Reg. 18,266 (Apr. 15, 1994) (discussed in § 12.2.6, *infra*).

139 *See* Wards Cove Packing Co. v. Atonio, 490 U.S. 642, 109 S. Ct. 2115, 104 L. Ed. 2d 733 (1989) (employment discrimination case), which the legislative history of the Civil Rights Act of 1991 specifically discusses overruling. 1991 U.S.C.C.A.N. 561.

challenged practice constitutes a business necessity.[140] Congress' purpose in passing the 1991 Act was to return to the principles of *Griggs v. Duke Power Co.*[141] and *Albemarle Paper Co. v. Moody*,[142] which contained more generous standards for the plaintiff[143] and were the cases upon which the ECOA standard of disparate impact was based.[144]

Although the 1991 Act clarified the burden of proof, it did not establish a clear standard of what constitutes a "business necessity." As a result, courts have articulated a number of different tests and definitions, including "compelling need,"[145] "manifest relationship,"[146] "legitimate, nondiscriminatory rationale,"[147] and "demonstrably necessary."[148] The legitimate nondiscriminatory rationale and manifest relationship tests are the most commonly used.

The HUD final rule implementing the FHA discriminatory effects standard does not use the phrase "business necessity," because that language may not be easily understood in the context of government or nonprofit defendants.[149] Instead, the regulation refers to "a legally sufficient justification" that exists when a challenged practice "is necessary to achieve one or more substantial, legitimate, nondiscriminatory interests."[150]

According to HUD, the "substantial, legitimate, nondiscriminatory interest" standard "is equivalent to the 'business necessity' standard" and "is not to be interpreted as a more lenient standard."[151]

The regulation specifies that a legally sufficient justification "must be supported by evidence and may not be hypothetical or speculative."[152] Defendants bear the burden of proving that the

---

140 42 U.S.C. § 2000e-2(k)(1)(A).

141 401 U.S. 424, 91 S. Ct. 849, 28 L. Ed. 2d 158 (1971) (establishing that discriminatory impact violates Title VII's prohibition of employment discrimination).

142 422 U.S. 405, 95 S. Ct. 2362, 45 L. Ed. 2d 280 (1975) (setting out disparate impact analysis for prima facie case by plaintiff, defendant's burden of proving business necessity, and plaintiff's opportunity to show less discriminatory means).

143 *See* 1991 U.S.C.C.A.N. 561.

144 *See* § 4.3.2.2, *supra*.

   The official interpretations affirm that Congress intended the Title VII effects test to apply to credit discrimination. Official Interpretations of Reg. B [Official Staff Commentary on Reg. B], 12 C.F.R. pt. 1002 [pt. 202], Supp. I, § 1002.6(a)-2 [§ 202.6(a)-2].

145 *See, e.g.*, Bradley v. Pizzaco of Neb., Inc., 7 F.3d 795, 797 (8th Cir. 1993).

146 *See, e.g.*, Smith v. City of Des Moines, 99 F.3d 1466, 1271 (8th Cir. 1996); Mountain Side Mobile Estates P'ship v. Sec'y of Hous. & Urban Dev., 56 F.3d 1243 (10th Cir. 1995).

147 *See, e.g.*, Equal Emp't Opportunity Comm'n v. Steamship Clerks Union Local 1066, 48 F.3d 594, 602 (1st Cir. 1995).

148 Fitzpatrick v. City of Atlanta, 2 F.3d 1112, 1119 (11th Cir. 1993).

149 Final Rule, Dep't of Hous. & Urban Dev., Implementation of the Fair Housing Act's Discriminatory Effects Standard, 78 Fed. Reg. 11,460, 11,470–71 (Feb. 15, 2013) ("HUD chooses not to use the phrase 'business necessity' in the rule because the phrase may not be easily understood to cover the full scope of practices covered by the Fair Housing Act, which applies to individuals, businesses, nonprofit organizations, and public entities.").

150 *Id.* at 11,482 (codified at 24 C.F.R. § 100.500(b)).

151 *Id.* at 11,470.

152 *Id.* at 11,482 (codified at 24 C.F.R. § 100.500(b)(2)).

practice is necessary to achieving a substantial, legitimate, and nondiscriminatory interest.[153] HUD's approach comports with existing case law on the burden of proof for the business justification.

In a disparate impact case, the creditor carries the burden of proving not only that its business justification is the reason it acted but that its business justification is a legitimate and necessary basis to evaluate credit risks.[154] If the business justification is the real reason for the creditor's actions, but the justification is not relevant to creditworthiness, then the plaintiff's prima facie case of disparate impact will be sufficient for the plaintiff to prevail.[155] However, there is no particular type of evidence the defendant must present in order to carry this burden.[156]

With respect to claims under the ECOA, no guidance is given in Regulation B as to what might constitute a legitimate business necessity in credit discrimination cases. However, the official interpretation does give this example:

> For example, requiring that applicants have incomes in excess of a certain amount to qualify for an overdraft line of credit could mean that women and minority applicants will be rejected at a higher rate than men and non-minority applicants. If there is a demonstrable relationship between the income requirement and creditworthiness for the level of credit involved, however, use of the income standard *would likely* be permissible.[157]

Plaintiffs should argue that the business necessity defense requires proof of two complementary elements, both of which must be met in order for a defendant creditor to successfully justify a disparate impact. First, the policy in question must be related to creditworthiness and, second, the policy must be consistent with business necessity. The analogous test in Title VII requires employers to show that a policy is "job related for the position in question and consistent with business neces-

sity."[158] Just as the business necessity defense in employment cases requires the defendant to show "job relatedness," an ECOA or FHA impact case requires a demonstrable relationship between a creditor's practice and a consumer's creditworthiness.

Creditworthiness is the core concept in fair lending. As articulated by Representative Annunzio in 1975:

> The essential concept of nondiscrimination in the extension of credit is that each individual has a right when he applies for credit, to be evaluated as an individual: to be evaluated on his individual creditworthiness, rather than based on some generalization or stereotype about people who are similar to him in race, color, national origin, religion, age, sex or marital status. Bias is not creditworthiness. Impression is not creditworthiness. An individual's ability and willingness to repay an extension of credit is creditworthiness.[159]

It is particularly critical to emphasize that all defenses must be tied to creditworthiness. For example, a creditor's policy allowing dealers to subjectively mark up interest rates should not be justifiable on the grounds that this is how business is done in the industry or because it generates maximum profits. By requiring a relationship to job performance in the employment discrimination area, the Supreme Court set a standard which rejects broad general justifications such as "competition."[160] Creditors, however, may argue that the standards in credit discrimination cases should be more lenient than in employment cases.[161]

Thus, only attributes related to a decision maker's expected marginal cost, including a reasonable profit, provide a valid business justification, and regression testing for unjustified

---

153 *Id.* at 11,482 (codified at 24 C.F.R. § 100.500(c)(2)).

154 Congress in 1991 codified this standard for employment discrimination cases. *See* 42 U.S.C. § 2000e-2(e)(1)(A).

155 *See* Wards Cove Packing Co. v. Atonio, 490 U.S. 642, 109 S. Ct. 2115, 104 L. Ed. 2d 733 (1989) (employment discrimination case); Watson v. Fort Worth Bank & Trust, 487 U.S. 977, 108 S. Ct. 2777, 101 L. Ed. 2d 827 (1988) (employment discrimination case); *see also* Town of Huntington v. Huntington Branch NAACP, 488 U.S. 15, 16, 109 S. Ct. 276, 102 L. Ed. 2d 180 (1988) (sole justification offered to rebut the prima facie housing discrimination case was inadequate); Mountain Side Mobile Estates P'ship v. Sec'y of Hous. & Urban Dev., 56 F.3d 1254 (10th Cir. 1995) (mere insubstantial justification of manifest relationship is insufficient, because such a low standard would permit discrimination to be practiced through the use of spurious seemingly neutral practices); *see also* Diamond Ventures, L.L.C. v. Baruah, 699 F. Supp. 2d 57, 64 (D.D.C. 2010) (finding that defendant had not proffered "any empirical evidence" linking its specific application requirements with success of businesses receiving loans).

156 Watson v. Fort Worth Bank & Trust, 487 U.S. 977, 998, 108 S. Ct. 2777, 101 L. Ed. 2d 827 (1988).

157 Official Interpretations of Reg. B [Official Staff Commentary on Reg. B], 12 C.F.R. pt. 1002 [pt. 202], Supp. I, § 1002.6(a)-2 [§ 202.6(a)-2] (emphasis added).

158 42 U.S.C. § 2000e-2(k)(1)(A)(i).
    Title VII codified the standard set by the Supreme Court in Griggs v. Duke Power Co., 401 U.S. 424, 91 S. Ct. 849, 28 L. Ed. 2d 158 (1971), and Albermarle Paper Co. v. Moody, 422 U.S. 405, 95 S. Ct. 2362, 45 L. Ed. 2d 280 (1975), which required both business necessity and job-relatedness. Congress intended that Title VII disparate impact doctrine and analysis apply to credit discrimination. *See* Official Interpretations of Reg. B [Official Staff Commentary on Reg. B], 12 C.F.R. pt. 1002 [pt. 202], Supp. I, § 1002.6(a)-2 [§ 202.6(a)-2]. *See generally* Susan S. Grover, *The Business Necessity Defense in Disparate Impact Discrimination Cases*, 30 Ga. L. Rev. 387 (1996).

159 121 Cong. Rec. 16, 740 (1975) (statement of Rep. Annunzio).
    Furthermore, creditworthiness is quantifiable and easily susceptible to comparison. *See* Coleman v. Gen. Motors Acceptance Corp., 220 F.R.D. 64 (M.D. Tenn. 2004) (granting plaintiffs motion for national class certification); CEIBA, Inc. v. Ford Motor Credit Co., 2003 WL 22204560 (E.D. Pa. Sept. 22, 2003).

160 Griggs v. Duke Power Co., 401 U.S. 424, 91 S. Ct. 849, 28 L. Ed. 2d 158 (1971). *But see* Owens v. Nationwide Mut. Ins. Co., 2005 WL 1837959 (N.D. Tex. Aug. 2, 2005) (defendant successfully showed that use of credit histories in making insurance decisions is correlated with defendant's competitiveness in the industry, and plaintiff failed to show a less discriminatory alternative).

161 *See, e.g.*, Robert Detlefsen, Wash. Legal Found., Disparate Impact Theory Provides No Support for Banning Credit Scoring in Insurance (Apr. 8, 2005).

disparate impacts should include (and control for) only those variables that would provide a valid business justification. Conversely, attributes related solely to the potential for supra-competitive revenues that might be extracted from different classes of consumers merely because the creditor or other entity has the power to do so do not constitute a valid business justification.

4.3.2.6 Are There Alternative Practices with Less Disparate Impact?

Once the creditor carries its burden of establishing a legitimate and significant business justification, then the remaining issue is whether the legitimate business concern can be met in some other fashion with less of a disparate impact. If the creditor demonstrates a significant business justification, the plaintiff can still prove discrimination if another practice meeting the creditor's legitimate concerns would have less of a discriminatory impact.[162]

In the credit discrimination realm, courts and regulatory agencies have sent mixed messages as to whether the plaintiff or defendant must carry the burden of showing that a less discriminatory alternative exists.[163] In 1995, both the Department of Justice and the Department of Housing and Urban Development endorsed the Title VII (employment discrimination law) burden of proof standards as the appropriate standards in FHA cases.[164] The HUD final rule implementing the FHA

discriminatory effects standard discusses the allocation of the burden of proof for this step of the analysis and concludes that it should be placed on the plaintiff:

> [T]his framework makes the most sense because it does not require either party to prove a negative. Moreover, this approach will ensure consistency in applying the discriminatory effects standard while creating the least disruption because . . . most federal courts using a burden-shifting framework allocate the burdens of proof in this way.[165]

HUD also notes that this allocation is consistent with the approach in Title VII and ECOA cases.[166] The text of the regulation provides that, if the defendant satisfies its burden of showing that the challenged practice is necessary to achieve a "substantial, legitimate, nondiscriminatory interest,"[167] the plaintiff "may still prevail upon proving that the substantial, legitimate, nondiscriminatory interests supporting the challenged practice could be served by another practice that has a less discriminatory effect."[168]

Regulatory language also has been adopted indicating that the burdens of proof under the ECOA are to follow the employment law standards codified in the Civil Rights Act of 1991.[169]

Although it is now well established in employment law that the plaintiff has the burden of showing that an alternative practice exists with less of a discriminatory impact, the standards for showing this alternative are not clear.[170] Some courts in employment law cases have required the plaintiff to show that the alternative practice can be statistically proven to be equally effective in achieving the business objectives underlying the challenged practice and to have a less disproportionate effect.[171]

---

162 Albemarle Paper Co. v. Moody, 422 U.S. 405, 425 (1975) (once defendant shows that an employment requirement has "manifest relationship" to a legitimate employer goal, burden shifts back to plaintiff to show existence of a less discriminatory alternative in order to prove that defendant's showing of job-relatedness was pretext for discrimination); Gallagher v. Magner, 619 F.3d 823 (8th Cir. 2010) (reversing district court's dismissal of FHA disparate impact claim because it is a fact issue whether the city had viable alternative means to achieve its legitimate housing code policy objective without discriminatory effects and thus summary judgment precluded); Resident Advisory Bd. v. Rizzo, 564 F.2d 126, 149 (3d Cir. 1977) (FHA case); Official Interpretations of Reg. B [Official Staff Commentary on Reg. B], 12 C.F.R. pt. 1002 [pt. 202], Supp. I, § 1002.6(a)-2 [§ 202.6(a)-2]; Final Rule, Dep't of Hous. & Urban Dev., Implementation of the Fair Housing Act's Discriminatory Effects Standard, 78 Fed. Reg. 11,460, 11,482 (Feb. 15, 2013) (codified at 24 C.F.R. § 100.500).

163 *See, e.g.*, Mt. Holly Gardens Citizens in Action, Inc. v. Twp. of Mount Holly, 658 F.3d 375, 385 (3d Cir. 2011) (defendant must show that there is no less discriminatory alternative, but then burden shifts to plaintiff to provide evidence of such alternative); Gallagher v. Magner, 619 F.3d 823, 834 (8th Cir. 2010) (burden of showing a less discriminatory alternative exists is on plaintiff); Huntington Branch, N.A.A.C.P. v. Town of Huntington, 844 F.2d 926, 939 (2d Cir. 1988) (placing burden of proving no less discriminatory alternative on defendant and reversing order of consideration for "analytical ease"); Inclusive Communities Project, Inc. v. Tex. Dep't of Hous. & Cmty. Affairs, 860 F. Supp. 2d 312, 326 (N.D. Tex. 2012) (placing burden on defendant to show that no other less discriminatory alternatives could be adopted).

164 *See* Mountain Side Mobile Estates P'ship v. Sec'y of Hous. & Urban Dev., 56 F.3d 1243 (10th Cir. 1995) (Department of Justice petition for en banc rehearing of the Tenth Circuit's decision).

165 Final Rule, Dep't of Hous. & Urban Dev., Implementation of the Fair Housing Act's Discriminatory Effects Standard, 78 Fed. Reg. 11,460, 11,474 (Feb. 15, 2013).
   Earlier, HUD had implied that it believed the burden of proof on less discriminatory alternatives should be placed on defendants. *See, e.g.*, Unified Agenda of Fed. Regulations, Dep't of Hous. & Urban Dev., Proposed Rules, Disparate Impact Rule, 59 Fed. Reg. 57,087, 57,102 (Nov. 14, 1994). HUD later withdrew the rule from its list of regulatory priorities.

166 Final Rule, Dep't of Hous. & Urban Dev., Implementation of the Fair Housing Act's Discriminatory Effects Standard, 78 Fed. Reg. 11,460, 11,474 (Feb. 15, 2013).

167 *See* § 4.3.2.5, *supra*.

168 Final Rule, Dep't of Hous. & Urban Dev., Implementation of the Fair Housing Act's Discriminatory Effects Standard, 78 Fed. Reg. 11,460, 11,482 (Feb. 15, 2013) (codified at 24 C.F.R. § 100.500(c)(3)).

169 Official Interpretations of Reg. B [Official Staff Commentary on Reg. B], 12 C.F.R. pt. 1002 [pt. 202], Supp. I, § 1002.6(a)-2 [§ 202.6(a)-2].

170 *See generally* Peter E. Mahoney, *The End(s) of Disparate Impact: Doctrinal Reconstruction, Fair Housing and Lending Law, and the Antidiscrimination Principle*, 47 Emory L.J. 409 (1998).

171 *See, e.g.*, York v. AT & T, 95 F.3d 948 (10th Cir. 1996); MacPherson v. Univ. of Montevallo, 922 F.2d 766, 771 (11th Cir. 1991); Dusek v. City of Moorhead, 2007 WL 4321823, at *5 (D. Minn. Dec. 6,

As in employment law, in credit discrimination cases there is little guidance regarding the showing required to meet the burden of proving that a less discriminatory alternative exists. However, assuming that courts in credit discrimination cases will follow the employment standards, a plaintiff will need to show that a less discriminatory alternative would be "equally effective" in meeting the defendant's legitimate business objective.[172]

4.4 Sources of Evidence

4.4.1 The Consumer's Own Records

The plaintiff should possess certain information useful for a credit discrimination case. The first item to check for is whether the plaintiff received a notice of action taken by the creditor and whether this notice is in the proper format.[173] The ECOA requires that creditors provide notice of an adverse action, generally in writing.[174] The notice must either state the reason for the action taken or give the applicant the right to request the reason. In the latter case, the applicant must request the reason within sixty days of the notice of adverse action.[175] If notice was not sent, there may be an ECOA violation triggering a cause of action for actual and punitive damages as well as attorney fees.[176]

While every effort should be made to request the reasons for the adverse action within the sixty-day deadline, if the sixty-day deadline has passed, the information should still be requested. If the creditor refuses, the information should be sought through a formal request for production of documents. The ECOA in most cases requires the creditor to retain such information for twenty-five months.[177]

The Fair Credit Reporting Act requires the creditor to advise the consumer if an adverse action was taken due to information contained in a credit report from a reporting agency.[178] The creditor must advise the consumer of the name and address of the agency making the report, and the consumer may then obtain a copy of the credit report from the agency at no charge as long as the request is made within sixty days. Otherwise, there may be a charge for the report.[179]

A consumer who applied for a mortgage or home equity loan may have another useful piece of information: an appraisal report on the applicant's home. The ECOA requires that creditors provide applicants with notice of their right to receive a copy of any appraisal, specifying the address to which the applicant should send their written request.[180] The applicant's request must be received by the creditor within ninety days of the creditor's action on the application, or the creditor need not provide a copy of the report.[181] The report may also be obtained later through discovery. In many cases, to avoid the extra step of sending applicants the notice of a right to an appraisal report, the creditor has sent the report to the applicant unsolicited.

4.4.2 The Creditor's Own Files

The creditor's files are critical in any credit discrimination case. The ECOA sets out specific records that creditors must retain for twenty-five months following the date the creditor notifies an applicant of the action taken on an application (that is, the records are supposed to be retained until the statute of limitations usually has expired on possible ECOA actions).[182]

The creditor must retain the following documents:

- Any application form that the creditor receives;
- Information obtained for monitoring purposes;
- Any other written or recorded information used in evaluating the application and not returned to the applicant upon request;
- Written notification to the applicant of the action taken on the application, or notes concerning oral notification;
- Written notification to the applicant of the specific reasons for adverse action, or notes concerning oral notification; and
- Any written statement submitted by the applicant alleging a violation of the ECOA or Regulation B.[183]

When adverse action has been taken on a credit transaction outside of the application process, such as when the creditor has terminated or changed terms on an existing account, the creditor also must preserve the following records for twenty-five months after notification to the applicant of the adverse action:[184]

- Any written or recorded information concerning the adverse action; and
- Any written statement submitted by the applicant alleging a violation of the ECOA or Regulation B.[185]

When an offer of credit is made to potential customers, the creditor must retain:

- The text of any prescreened solicitations;
- The list of criteria the creditor used to select potential

2007) (plaintiff must demonstrate "that a comparably effective alternative practice would produce a significantly smaller adverse impact on the protected class").

172 *See* Graoch Assocs. #33, Ltd. P'ship v. Louisville/Jefferson Cnty. Metro Human Relations Comm'n, 508 F.3d 366 (6th Cir. 2007) (FHA case); Wilson v. Glenwood Intermountain Properties, 876 F. Supp. 1231, 1242 (D. Utah 1995) (FHA case); Villas West II of Willowridge Homeowners Ass'n v. McGlothin, 885 N.E.2d 1274 (Ind. 2008) (FHA case; adopting "prevailing" test).

173 *See* § 10.2, *infra*.

174 *See* § 10.5, *infra*.

175 *See* § 10.5.4.2, *infra*.

176 *See generally* ch. 11, *infra* (private remedies for ECOA violations).

177 *See* § 10.12.1, *infra*.

178 15 U.S.C. § 1681m(a); *see also* National Consumer Law Center, Fair Credit Reporting (7th ed. 2010 and Supp.).

179 *See* § 4.4.3, *infra*.

180 *See* § 10.11, *infra*.

181 *Id.*

182 *See* § 10.12.1, *infra*.

183 Reg. B, 12 C.F.R. § 1002.12(b)(1) [§ 202.12(b)(1)].

184 Reg. B, 12 C.F.R. § 1002.12(b)(2) [§ 202.12(b)(2)].

185 Chapter 10, *infra*, provides more details on ECOA record-retention requirements, particularly concerning exemptions from these requirements and the inadvertent error defense. *See* § 10.12, *infra*.

recipients of the solicitation; and

- Any correspondence related to complaints (formal or informal) about the solicitation.[186]

In transactions involving more than one creditor, even those creditors not required to comply with the notification provisions of Regulation B must retain all written or recorded information they possess concerning the applicant for a period as long as that required of the notifying creditor.[187] This information must include any notations concerning adverse actions.

In addition, once a creditor receives actual notice that a civil action has been filed or that the creditor is under investigation or is subject to an enforcement proceeding for an ECOA violation, the creditor must retain all required records until there is a final disposition of the matter, unless an earlier time is allowed by the agency or court.[188]

Certain creditors, including public utilities, creditors dealing in securities credit, and incidental consumer creditors, are exempt from some of the record retention requirements.[189]

Creditors must also retain certain information obtained for monitoring purposes. This information can be very helpful for credit discrimination claims, because it consists of information concerning the race, sex, and other characteristics of mortgage applicants.[190]

Written copies need not be retained by creditors using a computerized system, provided that the information can be regenerated in a timely manner.[191]

4.4.3 Credit Reporting Agency Files

Information collected on an applicant by a credit reporting agency is useful for several reasons. If information from a credit reporting agency is given by the creditor as the grounds for denial of credit, it is useful to check to see if the creditor in fact contacted the agency before denying credit and what the applicant's record indicates. In any case, as it is likely that the creditor will bring up that record as a defense,[192] it will be important for the applicant to know what the record contains.

If information from a reporting agency is the grounds for denial of credit, the creditor must disclose this fact, along with the name of the reporting agency utilized. The applicant may obtain a copy of the record for no charge if a request is made to the reporting agency within sixty days.[193]

A credit applicant who does not receive a notice of credit denial or fails to request a copy of the report within sixty days can still order a report directly from the main credit reporting agencies. Reports can be ordered from the three main agencies—Equifax, Experian, and Trans Union—by mail or phone or via the Internet.[194]

Consumers are entitled to a free report if, as noted above, they were denied credit because of information in the file within the past sixty days. In addition, consumers can obtain free reports in a number of circumstances:

- All consumers are able to get one free credit report from each of the three major credit reporting bureaus in any twelve-month period.[195]
- A consumer who is unemployed and planning to apply for a job within sixty days has the right to one free credit report in any twelve-month period.[196]
- A consumer who is receiving public welfare assistance has the right to one free credit report in any twelve-month period.[197]
- A consumer who reasonably believes the credit file contains errors due to fraud has the right to a free credit report.[198]
- Some states provide additional rights, such as one free report each year (arguably in addition to the free annual credit report allowed by federal law).[199]

A consumer who is not entitled to a free report for one of these reasons will have to pay for it, but fees are limited by federal law and in some cases by state law.[200]

4.4.4 Testers

Testers are an important source of information about a creditor's practices. Testers are most frequently used by fair housing organizations, other non-profit organizations and, in some cases, the government. Typically, paired testers are used

---

186 Reg. B, 12 C.F.R. § 1002.12(b)(7) [§ 202.12(b)(7)]. These records need to be retained for only twelve months for business credit.

187 Reg. B, 12 C.F.R. § 1002.12(b)(3) [§ 202.12(b)(3)]; *see* § 10.12.1, *infra*.

188 12 C.F.R. § 1002.12(b)(4) [§ 202.12(b)(4)]; *see* § 10.12.2, *infra*.

189 *See* § 10.12.4, *infra*.

190 This information is described in more detail in § 4.4.5, *infra*.

191 Official Interpretations of Reg. B [Official Staff Commentary on Reg. B], 12 C.F.R. pt. 1002 [pt. 202], Supp. I, § 1002.12(b)-1 [§ 202.12(b)-1].

192 Though lenders often rely on credit scores to rebut claims of discrimination, credit scores themselves vary among demographic groups and have come under attack for that reason. *See* § 6.4, *infra*.

193 15 U.S.C. § 1681m(b).

194 The websites, as of March 2009, are Equifax: www.equifax.com; Experian: www.experian.com; Trans Union: www.transunion.com. However, consumers should make use of their free annual credit report, available from www.annualcreditreport.com, before ordering one directly from a credit reporting agency. A consumer who orders a credit report from a credit reporting agency should also be very cautious to avoid inadvertently ordering other products and services, such as fee-based credit monitoring services. *See generally* National Consumer Law Center, Fair Credit Reporting §§ 3.3.6, 3.3.7, and 3.4 (7th ed. 2010 and Supp.).

195 15 U.S.C. § 1681j(a).
   Consumers should go to www.annualcreditreport.com to exercise this right. *See* National Consumer Law Center, Fair Credit Reporting § 3.4.2 (7th ed. 2010 and Supp.).

196 15 U.S.C. § 1681j(c).

197 *Id.*

198 15 U.S.C. §§ 1681c-1, 1681j(d); *see* National Consumer Law Center, Fair Credit Reporting § 3.3.5 (7th ed. 2010 and Supp.).

199 For a list of these states and additional information, see National Consumer Law Center, Fair Credit Reporting § 3.3.9 (7th ed. 2010 and Supp.).

200 *See generally* National Consumer Law Center, Fair Credit Reporting Ch. 3 (7th ed. 2010 and Supp.).

who have been similarly trained and who are instructed to act in an identical manner and provide identical information. The only difference is the tester's race, sex, or other characteristic that would suggest discrimination on a prohibited basis.

Courts have approved the use of testers in the context of fair housing litigation, agreeing that it would be difficult to prove discrimination in housing without this means of gathering evidence and that the evidence from testing is frequently valuable, if not indispensable.[201] Testers can even bring actions in their own name for Fair Housing Act violations, although a tester must be a legitimate "applicant" to bring an ECOA action.[202]

Testers are perhaps the best approach to use to determine if potential applicants are being turned away *before* they can submit an application. This is because Home Mortgage Disclosure Act (HMDA) data and other statistics on the racial or other composition of loan denials do not measure pre-application discrimination. Testers can discover, for example, if the white tester's application is taken at the local branch office while the African-American tester is sent across town to a different office.[203] Evidence of discrimination prior to application should on its own be sufficient to show violation of the credit discrimination laws, even without specific evidence of subsequent discrimination in the application process.[204]

As testing evidence is factual evidence, it can be admitted into evidence independently from any expert testimony.[205] Testing evidence should be admissible as long as it is relevant and otherwise admissible under the Federal Rules of Evidence. However, when experts are involved in the testing or in reviewing the results of it, courts have subjected their testimony to the analysis established by the Supreme Court in *Daubert v. Merrell Dow Pharmaceuticals, Inc.*[206]

Fair housing and other advocates have begun developing ways to use testing to demonstrate the discriminatory impact of predatory lending practices. There are a number of additional hurdles involved in testing for lending discrimination compared to testing for discrimination in the rental housing market. For example, the cost of filling out a loan application is prohibitive for most testing organizations.[207] It is also difficult for testers to provide the level of personal information required to submit a loan application. For these reasons, most testing of discrimination in lending has focused on showing discrimination prior to the submission of loan applications.

Pre-application testing can be effective in revealing some forms of discrimination. For example, in one case, pre-application testing evidence was presented to show that prospective applicants of different races were directed to different neighborhoods to look for housing and to different real estate agents.[208] Testers may also find that lenders discriminate in the way they provide information regarding the availability of loans or in giving out information about application requirements.[209]

Some of the variables to examine in pre-application testing include: consistency in the lender's requests for information from each tester; the lender's community image as presented through brochures or instructional literature; any discriminatory emphasis on qualification standards; differences in interest rates or loan terms; general attitude of the lender toward the tester; response of the lender to past credit problems of testers; and differences in information on the variety of mortgage programs.[210]

Several years ago, the Department of Housing and Urban Development (HUD) contracted with the Urban Institute to more rigorously assess the effectiveness of paired testing for determining whether minority homebuyers receive the same treatment and information as prospective white homebuyers at

---

201 *See, e.g.*, Havens Realty Corp. v. Coleman, 455 U.S. 363, 102 S. Ct. 1114, 71 L. Ed. 2d 214 (1982); Richardson v. Howard, 712 F.2d 319 (7th Cir. 1983); Hamilton v. Miller, 477 F.2d 908, 910 n.1 (10th Cir. 1973); Zuch v. Hussey, 394 F. Supp. 1028 (E.D. Mich. 1975).

202 *See* §§ 11.2.2, 11.2.3, *infra.*

203 *See* § 5.3, *infra.*

204 *See, e.g.*, United States v. Lorantffy Care Ctr., 999 F. Supp. 1037 (N.D. Ohio 1998) (evidence of discrimination in treatment of testers acting as "walk-ins" requesting information about assisted living facility may show FHA violation even though facility did not admit residents on the basis of walk-in visits, as decision-makers can discriminate against applicants long before they reach the point of deciding whether to accept an application).

205 In fair housing litigation, fact finders routinely hear testing evidence without the assistance of any expert testimony analyzing that evidence. *See, e.g.*, Gresham v. Windrush Partners, Ltd., 730 F.2d 1417, 1420–21 (11th Cir. 1984); Walker v. Todd Vill., L.L.C., 419 F. Supp. 2d 743 (D. Md. 2006); Pollitt v. Bramel, 669 F. Supp. 172, 174 (S.D. Ohio 1987); Davis v. Mansards, 597 F. Supp. 334, 338–42 (N.D. Ind. 1984); Hobson v. George Humphreys, Inc., 563 F. Supp. 344, 348–50 (W.D. Tenn. 1982).

　　Likewise, the United States has introduced testing evidence without analysis by an expert. *See, e.g.*, United States v. Space Hunters, Inc., 429 F.3d 416 (2d Cir. 2005); United States v. Balistrieri, 981 F.2d 916, 928–30 (7th Cir. 1992); United States v. Youritan Constr. Co., 370 F. Supp. 643, 647, 656 (N.D. Cal. 1973), *aff'd as modified*, 509 F.2d 623 (9th Cir. 1975).

206 509 U.S. 579, 113 S. Ct. 2786, 125 L. Ed. 2d 469 (1993). *See, e.g.*,

Mitchell v. DCX, Inc., 274 F. Supp. 2d 33 (D.D.C. 2003) (testing case); Metro St. Louis Equal Hous. Opportunity Council v. Gordon A. Gundaker Real Estate Co., 130 F. Supp. 2d 1074 (E.D. Mo. 2001) (testing case). *See generally* National Consumer Law Center, The Practice of Consumer Law (2d ed. 2006).

207 *See, e.g.*, Paschal v. Flagstar Bank, 295 F.3d 565 (6th Cir. 2002) (director of Fair Housing Center testified that testers did not fill out loan applications because of the high cost and because the Center found they could get a lot of information about how people are treated by loan officers before getting to the point of filling out an application).

208 Paschal v. Flagstar Bank, 295 F.3d 565 (6th Cir. 2002).

209 *See Rooting Out Discrimination in Mortgage Lending: Using HMDA As a Tool for Fair Lending Enforcement, Hearing Before the Subcomm. on Oversight & Investigations of the House Comm. on Fin. Servs.* (July 25, 2007) (testimony of John Taylor and Saul Solorzano), *available at* www.house.gov (discussing use of testing in finding mortgage discrimination).

210 *See* Stella J. Adams, Testing and Investigating for Fair Housing Violations: Designing an Appropriate Test in Lending and Predatory Practices Cases (Apr. 12, 2002), prepared for the John Marshall Law School seminar, Testing and Investigating for Fair Housing Violations, Apr. 12–13, 2002. The document is available from the John Marshall Law School.

the pre-application phase of the mortgage lending process.[211] The testers in the study consisted of one white and one minority individual, posing as homebuyers to inquire about the availability and terms for home mortgage loans. The two members of the tester team presented themselves as equally qualified borrowers in every respect except their race or ethnicity. The HUD study consisted of a pre-test and a pilot stage. The agency focused on collecting data from mortgage lenders but indicated that future studies should explore other information sources, particularly mortgage brokers and real estate agents.

HUD's pre-test study found that one of the most serious forms of discrimination that can be discerned by paired testing at the pre-application stage is in the differential estimates of home price and total loan amount.[212] According to the report, these estimates can be critical in determining where people search for housing and whether they decide they can afford to become homebuyers. The agencies noted the complexity of this type of testing, demanding more from both testers and testing organizations than routine rental testing. They concluded that not all fair housing organizations necessarily have the capacity to effectively conduct these tests.

The agencies also conducted pilot tests, finding that, in both Los Angeles and Chicago, African-American and Hispanic homebuyers face a significant risk of receiving less favorable treatment than their white counterparts when visiting mortgage lending institutions to inquire about financing options.[213] The unequal treatment took different forms. In Los Angeles, African Americans were offered less coaching than comparable white homebuyers and were more likely to be encouraged to consider an FHA loan. Hispanics were denied basic information about loan amount and house prices, informed about fewer products, and received less follow-up compared to white homebuyers. In Chicago, African Americans were denied basic information about loan amount and house prices, informed about fewer products, offered less coaching, and received less follow-up. Hispanics were quoted lower loan amounts or house prices, informed about fewer products, and offered less coaching.[214]

In addition, HUD has found that Asian and Pacific Islander homebuyers experience consistent adverse treatment 20.4% of the time, with systematic discrimination occurring in housing availability, inspections, financing assistance, and agent encouragement.[215] This level of discrimination is comparable to the level experienced by African-American homebuyers in similar HUD studies and significantly higher than the level of discrimination against Hispanics.

4.4.5 Home Mortgage Disclosure Act (HMDA) Data

4.4.5.1 General

The Home Mortgage Disclosure Act (HMDA)[216] and the implementing regulations ("Regulation C"[217]) require that lenders collect certain data on loan applicants and that the Federal Financial Institutions Examination Council (FFIEC) prepare disclosure statements and produce various reports on the practices of these individual lenders. In addition to disclosures for each lender, the Council produces aggregate reports for all lenders within each metropolitan statistical area, broken down by census tract.[218] Plaintiffs can then compare a particular lender's experience with that of the aggregate lenders for the same geographic area.

The Federal Reserve Board initially had authority to issue implementing regulations for HMDA.[219] Pursuant to the Dodd-Frank Act Wall Street Reform and Consumer Protection Act ("Dodd-Frank Act"), the Consumer Financial Protection Bureau (CFPB) now has the authority.[220] On December 19, 2011, the CFPB issued its version of Regulation C and the regulation's official interpretations.[221] The Federal Reserve Board (FRB) has not withdrawn its version of Regulation C. Certain kinds of credit are not within the CFPB's enforcement authority, and the FRB regulation thus may remain relevant.

At the moment, the major difference is that 12 C.F.R. part 203 citations are replaced by citations to 12 C.F.R. part 1003. Other changes are stylistic and not substantive. Appendix E, *infra*, contains the CFPB's Regulation C and its official interpretations. The FRB version of the regulation and commentary and the CFPB's version (with supplemental information) can be found on the companion website to this treatise.

HMDA is designed: (1) to help determine whether financial institutions are serving the housing needs of their communities; (2) to assist public officials in distributing public sector investment so as to attract private investment to areas where it is needed; and (3) to assist in identifying possible discriminatory lending patterns and enforcing antidiscrimination statutes.[222]

Strong statistical evidence is particularly critical in proving disparate impact claims, and HMDA data is one of the most effective and accessible sources of data. However, there are a number of limits to HMDA data discussed below. Still, advocates bringing reverse redlining claims and credit discrimination cases will almost always want to examine HMDA data

---

211 Office of Policy Dev. & Research, United States Dep't of Hous. & Urban Dev., All Other Things Being Equal: A Paired Testing Study of Mortgage Lending Institutions, Final Report (Apr. 2002).

212 *Id.*

213 *Id.*

214 *Id.*

215 *See* Office of Policy Dev. & Research, United States Dep't of Hous. & Urban Dev., Discrimination in Metropolitan Housing Markets: Phase 2—Asians and Pacific Islanders (Mar. 2003).

216 12 U.S.C. §§ 2801–2810.

217 12 C.F.R. pts. 1003.1–1003.6 [pts. 203.1–203.6].

218 12 U.S.C. § 2809.

219 12 C.F.R. §§ 203.1–203.6.

220 *See* 12 U.S.C. § 2804, *as amended by* Dodd-Frank Wall Street Reform and Consumer Protection Act, Pub. L. No. 111-203, § 1094, 124 Stat. 1376 (July 21, 2010)).

221 *See* 76 Fed. Reg. 78,468 (Dec. 19, 2011) (codified at 12 C.F.R. pts. 1003.1–1003.6).

222 12 C.F.R. § 1003.1(b) [§ 203.1(b)].

and, in many situations, use it to support their cases.[223]

HMDA data has been the focus of a number of reports and government enforcement actions.[224] In addition, the Department of Justice has used HMDA data in suits against banks for alleged discriminatory lending practices. One case, for example, was based on an alleged disparity in rejection rates between African-American and white credit applicants.[225]

The HMDA collection requirements have changed over time. In January 2002, the Federal Reserve Board (FRB) announced changes in Regulation C intended to provide more consistent and comprehensive information about mortgage lending activity and to aid in fair lending enforcement.[226] According to the FRB, these changes were intended to improve the accuracy and usefulness of data reported pursuant to the HMDA.[227] Additional revisions to HMDA requirements were included in the Dodd-Frank Act.[228] Changes under the Dodd-Frank Act expanded the required information to include the borrower's age[229] and credit score[230] as well as the origination channel.[231] These changes have not yet been implemented in Regulation C.

4.4.5.2 Scope of HMDA

4.4.5.2.1 Covered lenders

The HMDA reporting requirements apply to federally insured or regulated lenders or to loans that are insured by a federal agency or that the lender intends to sell to Fannie Mae or Freddie Mac.[232] These institutions must also have a home or branch office in a metropolitan statistical area (MSA) or Metropolitan Division, originate at least one home purchase loan or refinancing loan secured by a first lien on a one-family to four-family dwelling, and have total assets above a threshold set annually by the CFPB.[233] Adjustments to the total asset threshold are published in the official interpretations.[234] State chartered or state licensed financial institutions are exempted from HMDA if the CFPB determines that the institution is subject to state disclosure laws that are substantially similar to HMDA.[235]

In addition, certain for-profit mortgage lending institutions (other than banks, saving institutions, or credit unions) are covered by HMDA requirements. In order to be covered, these institutions must have originated home purchase loans (including refinancings) that equaled at least 10% of the institution's loan-origination volume or home purchase loans (including refinancing) that equaled at least $25 million, have a home or branch office in an MSA, and either have total assets of more than $10 million or have originated at least 100 home purchase loans, including refinancings.[236]

Institutions not subject to the HMDA requirements must still keep information for monitoring purposes pursuant to the ECOA.[237] The range of information required to be reported under HMDA, however, is broader in scope than that required by the ECOA.[238]

4.4.5.2.2 Required data collection

Covered lenders must collect data regarding applications for, and originations and purchases of, home purchase loans, home improvement loans, and refinancings for each calendar year.[239] Home purchase loans are defined as loans secured by and made for the purpose of purchasing a dwelling.[240] A home improvement loan is defined as a loan secured by a lien on a dwelling or a non-dwelling-secured loan that is for the purpose, in whole or in part, of repairing, rehabilitating, remodeling, or improving a dwelling or the real property on which it is located and that is classified by the financial institution as a home improvement loan.[241] Lenders have discretion whether to report information

---

223 *See, e.g.*, Paschal v. Flagstar Bank, 295 F.3d 565 (6th Cir. 2002) (HMDA data, along with tester results and testimony, considered sufficient evidence to support jury's finding of racial discrimination).

224 *See* §§ 4.4.5.5–4.4.5.6, 8.5.2, *infra*.

225 Complaint, United States v. Decatur Fed. Sav. & Loan Ass'n (N.D. Ga. 1992), *available on the companion website to this treatise.*

   The complaint resulted in a far-reaching consent decree. *See* Consent Decree, United States v. Decatur Fed. Sav. & Loan Ass'n (N.D. Ga. 1992), *available on the companion website to this treatise.*

226 67 Fed. Reg. 7222 (Feb. 15, 2002).

227 73 Fed. Reg. 63,329-01 (Oct. 24, 2008).

228 12 U.S.C. §§ 2801–2809, *as amended by* Dodd-Frank Wall Street Reform and Consumer Protection Act, Pub. L. No. 111-203, § 1094, 124 Stat. 1376 (July 21, 2010).

229 12 U.S.C. § 2803(b)(4), *as amended by* Pub. L. No. 111-203, § 1094, 124 Stat. 1376 (July 21, 2010).

230 12 U.S.C. § 2803(b)(6), *as amended by* Pub. L. No. 111-203, § 1094, 124 Stat. 1376 (July 21, 2010).

231 *Id.*

232 12 C.F.R. § 1003.2(e)(iv) [§ 203.2(e)(iv)].

233 12 C.F.R. § 1003.2(e)(1) [§ 203.2(e)(1)].

234 12 C.F.R. pt. 1003 [pt. 203], Supp. I. The initial threshold was $34 million. 69 Fed. Reg. 77,139 (Dec. 27, 2004). The threshold was: $35 million for data collection in 2006, 70 Fed. Reg. 75,718 (Dec.

21, 2005); $36 million for 2007, 71 Fed. Reg. 77,247 (Dec. 26, 2006); $37 million for 2008, 72 Fed. Reg. 72,234 (Dec. 20, 2007); and $39 million for 2009, 73 Fed. Reg. 78,616 (Dec. 23, 2008).

235 12 C.F.R. § 1003.3 [§ 203.3].

236 12 C.F.R. § 1003.2 [§ 203.2(e)(2)].

   Prior to the 2002 amendments, for-profit lenders were exempt unless they had assets over $10 million, originated more than one hundred home purchase or refinance loans in the preceding year, and their lending activity constituted 10% or more of their total loan volume measured in dollars. This requirement was changed in response to concerns that a number of large consumer finance companies that are active mortgage lenders apparently were not required to report HMDA data because they did not reach the 10% volume level. Rather than eliminating the 10% requirement, a requirement was added that non-depository lenders whose mortgage-lending activity amounted to $25 million in the previous calendar year must report HMDA data, even if this lending constituted less than 10% of the institutions' total loan volume. 67 Fed. Reg. 7222 (Feb. 15, 2002).

237 *See* § 4.4.7, *infra*.

238 *See* § 4.4.5.2.2, *infra*.

239 12 C.F.R. § 1003.4(a) [§ 203.4(a)].

240 12 C.F.R. § 1003.2(h) [§ 203.2(h)].

241 12 C.F.R. § 1003.2(g) [§ 203.2(g)].

   In the 2002 final rules, the definition of a home improvement loan was changed to include any loan secured by a dwelling that is made

about "home equity lines of credit."[242]

A refinancing is defined as any dwelling-secured loan that replaces another dwelling-secured loan to the same borrower. A reportable refinancing therefore is a new obligation that satisfies and replaces an existing loan with the same borrower, when both the current obligation and the one replacing it are secured by a lien on the dwelling.[243]

Covered lenders must keep the following data for each covered loan:

(1) An identifying number for the loan or loan application and the date the application was received;

(2) The type of loan or application;

(3) The purpose of the loan or application;

(4) Whether the application is a request for pre-approval and whether it resulted in a denial or in an origination;[244]

(5) The property type to which the loan or application relates;[245]

(6) The owner-occupancy status of the property to which the loan or application relates;

(7) The amount of the loan or the amount applied for;

(8) The type of action taken and the date;

(9) The location of the property to which the loan or application relates, by MSA or by metropolitan division, by state, by county, and by census tract, if the institution has a home or branch office in that MSA or metropolitan division;

(10) The ethnicity, race, and sex of the applicant or borrower and the gross annual income relied on in processing the application;[246]

(11) The type of entity purchasing a loan that the institution originates or purchases and then sells within the same calendar year;

(12) For originated loans subject to Regulation Z, 12 C.F.R. § 1026 (Truth in Lending), the difference between the loan's annual percentage rate (APR) and the yield on Treasury securities having comparable periods of maturity, if that difference is equal to or greater than 1.5 percentage points for loans secured by a first lien on a dwelling or equal to or greater than 3.5 percentage points for loans secured by a subordinate lien on a dwelling;

(13) Whether the loan is subject to the Home Ownership and Equity Protection Act of 1994; and

(14) The lien status of the loan or application.[247]

Creditors are required to ask the applicant for information about ethnicity, race, and sex but cannot require that the applicant provide it.[248] Creditors must also inform the applicant that the federal government requests this information in order to monitor compliance with federal statutes that prohibit lenders from discriminating against applicants on these bases. When the application is taken in person, creditors must inform applicants that, if the information is not provided, the creditor is required to note the data on the basis of visual observation. Creditors must also note on the data collection form for applications taken in person if an applicant chooses not to provide the information. If the application is taken via phone, mail, or Internet and the applicant declines to answer the questions, the creditor does not need to provide the data but must indicate that the application was received via these means if it is not otherwise evident.[249]

A number of these requirements were added in 2002 (effective January 1, 2004) and were mainly intended to improve data collection about subprime loans.

The provisions added in 2002 include a requirement that lenders designate on their HMDA reports which of the loans they originate are high-cost loans, subject to the provisions of the Home Ownership Equity Protection Act (HOEPA).[250] This

---

in whole or in part for home improvement purposes. Previously, lenders had discretion whether to classify a loan as a home improvement loan. This discretion will remain only for home improvement loans that are not secured by a dwelling. The exception to this new reporting requirement is "home equity lines of credit," which lenders currently have the option to report or not. This discretion remains unchanged. 67 Fed. Reg. 7222 (Feb. 15, 2002).

242 12 C.F.R. § 1003.4(c) [§ 203.4(c)].

243 12 C.F.R. § 1003.2(k) [§ 203.2(k)].

The 2002 final rules also changed the definition of a refinancing loan that must be reported under the HMDA. The new definition covers loans that pay off and replace an existing loan when both loans are secured by a lien on the dwelling. Previously, lenders could choose from among four scenarios in deciding which refinancing loans to report, leading to inconsistent data.

244 Pre-approval programs are defined as programs under which, after a comprehensive analysis of the creditworthiness of the applicant, the lender issues a written commitment to lend borrowers up to a specific amount for a specific period of time, subject only to limited conditions, such as finding a suitable property. 12 C.F.R. § 1003.2(b)(2) [§ 203.2(b)(2)].

245 In the 2002 final rules, it was decided that lenders should be required to specify when loans involve manufactured housing. 67 Fed. Reg. 7222 (Feb. 15, 2003).

The definition of "manufactured housing" found in HUD regulations was adopted. 12 C.F.R. Pt. 1003.2(i) [§ 203.2(i)] (citing the HUD regulation at 24 C.F.R. § 3280.2).

The Federal Reserve Board's (FRB) initial analysis of the newly available HMDA data provides interesting information about manufactured home lending. Among other findings, the FRB concluded that it is a relatively concentrated business. The ten lenders that extended the largest number of manufactured home loans in 2004 accounted for one-third of all such loans that year and the top twenty accounted for 42%. In addition, only about 18% of manufactured-home purchasers were members of a racial or ethnic minority group, whereas about 30% of purchasers of site-built homes were. Robert B. Avery, Glenn B. Canner, & Robert E. Cook, *New Information Reported Under HMDA and Its Application in Fair Lending Enforcement*, Fed. Reserve Bull. 344–94 (Summer 2005).

246 In 2002, rules were published that changed the way that race and ethnicity are reported to allow borrowers to designate more than one race or ethnicity. This change is in conformance with other government standards. 67 Fed. Reg. 7222 (Feb. 15, 2002).

247 12 C.F.R. § 1003.4(a) [§ 203.4(a)].

248 12 C.F.R. pt. 1003 [pt. 203], app. B.

249 *Id.*

250 67 Fed. Reg. 7222, 7230 (Feb. 15, 2002) (amending 12 C.F.R.

change should expand the information available on HOEPA loans but does not capture the large numbers of loans that lenders fail, intentionally or not, to categorize as high-rate HOEPA loans.

A second predatory-lending-related change requires additional reporting on loan pricing. In 2002, a proposal to require reporting of APRs was rejected; instead, a scheme was adopted based on the difference between the APR on the loan and the yield on a comparable security issued by the U.S. Treasury.[251] For first-lien loans, if that spread is more than one-and-one-half (1.5) percentage points, lenders must report how big the spread is. For junior lien loans, lenders must report the spread if it is more than three-and-one-half (3.5) percentage points.[252]

It was clarified that data collection about pricing is limited to originations of home purchase loans, secured home improvement loans, and refinancings.[253] The following are excluded from the reporting requirements: (1) applications that are incomplete, withdrawn, denied, or approved but not accepted; (2) purchased loans; and (3) unsecured home improvement loans.[254]

A third change that relates to subprime lending is the requirement that lenders distinguish which loans are unsecured or secured by first liens or subordinate liens. Lenders are required to report lien status on applications and originations but not for loans that they purchase.[255] A comment to the official interpretations was added clarifying that this change does not mean that lenders will have to do title searches. They are merely required to report the best information readily available to them at the time final action is taken on a loan application.[256]

4.4.5.3 Access to HMDA Data

The HMDA disclosure statements, aggregate data, and other reports are available to the public at central data depositories in each metropolitan area.[257] They are also available electronically.[258] Depository institutions are to make every effort to have disclosure statements available before July 1 of the following year.[259] The aggregate data should be produced a few months later.[260]

The FFIEC releases HMDA data on-line.[261] Data obtained in this way is designed to allow users to look up one lender at a time. To do more in-depth analysis, users will need to import the data into statistical software or a database manager.[262]

The disclosure statement is also available to the public at the lender's own home office (certain data will also be available at branch offices) for five years after it has been completed.[263] In addition, the public has access to the bank's complete loan application register (that is, the original data before it is aggregated for statistical purposes) after the bank makes certain modifications to protect the individual applicants' privacy.[264] Requests for the previous calendar year's register received March 1 or before must be fulfilled by March 31. After March 31, requests must be fulfilled within thirty days.[265] Unlike the disclosure statement, the loan application register need only be retained for three years.[266] The lender must make the disclosure statement and the register available for copying and inspection during normal business hours, and it may impose a reasonable photocopying charge.[267]

4.4.5.4 Limitations of HMDA Data

Great care must be taken in using HMDA and other monitoring data. Data showing higher rejection rates for members of protected groups may not prove illegal discrimination. It may be that these applicants have lower incomes, have different housing collateral, have different credit histories, or some other variable. Further refinement of data is needed to present a persuasive case.

While raw HMDA data can be indicative of discrimination, it can be made more persuasive by further analysis. The Federal Reserve Bank of Boston did the first study that actually took into account the missing variables—information related to legitimate indicators of creditworthiness not contained in HMDA data.[268]

The results of the Boston study go a long way toward explaining the difficulties of proving credit discrimination. The study found that, for over 80% of borrowers of whatever race, there is a legitimate creditworthiness reason to deny credit. The minority of people who are truly creditworthy, irrespective of race, almost always will be offered credit.

However, the Boston study found that, for the remaining 80% of applicants, while nondiscriminatory factors account for

---

§ 203.4(a)(13)). *See generally* National Consumer Law Center, Truth in Lending ch. 9 (7th ed. 2012) (HOEPA).

251 67 Fed. Reg. 7222 (Feb. 15, 2002).

252 12 C.F.R. § 1003.4(a)12) [§ 203.4(a)(12)]. Prior to 2008, the spreads were three and five percentage points for first and junior lien loans, respectively.

253 67 Fed. Reg. 7222, 7228 (Feb. 15, 2002).

254 *Id.*

255 67 Fed. Reg. 43,218, 43,219 (June 27, 2002).
     Conforming changes have been made to the HMDA/LAR and the HMDA/LAR Code Sheet in HMDA's appendix A.

256 *Id.*

257 12 U.S.C. § 2803(f).

258 *See* www.ffiec.gov/hmda.

259 12 U.S.C. § 2803(*l*).

260 12 U.S.C. § 2803(*l*).

261 To obtain more information by phone, call (202) 452-2016 (HMDA Assistance Line); on-line, visit www.ffiec.gov/hmda.

262 *See generally* Jo Craven McGinty, Home Mortgage Lending: How to Detect Disparities (Investigative Reporters & Editors, Inc. 2000). A number of websites have information about analyzing and obtaining access to HMDA data, including the Center for Community Change (www.communitychange.org), the Inner City Press (www.innercity press.org), and the National Fair Housing Advocate (www.fair housing.com).

263 12 C.F.R. § 1003.5(b), (d) [§ 203.5(b), (d)].

264 12 C.F.R. § 1003.5(c) [§ 203.5(c)].

265 12 C.F.R. § 1003.5(c) [§ 203.5(c)].

266 12 C.F.R. § 1003.5(d) [§ 203.5(d)].

267 12 C.F.R. § 1003.5(c) [§ 203.5(d)].

268 Lynn Z. Browne, James McEneaney, Alicia Munnell, & Geoffrey M.B. Tootell, *Mortgage Lending in Boston: Interpreting HMDA Data*, 86 Am. Econ. Rev. 25 (1996), *also available at* www.bos.frb.org/economic/wp/wp1992/wp92_7.pdf.

a large portion of the discrepancy in denial rates, race remains a significant factor.[269] In Boston, the raw HMDA data showed that the African-American denial rate was 170% higher than the white denial rate. However, the researchers found that some of this difference was not based on race but on the fact that African Americans were more likely to have higher loan-to-value ratios, had weaker credit histories, and were more likely to seek loans on multifamily instead of single-family homes.

This expanded HMDA study looked at thirty-eight additional variables, identified from extensive discussions with lenders as to what they consider in making a credit decision. While the raw HMDA data showed that the African-American denial rate was 170% higher than the white denial rate, the expanded Boston HMDA study, after controlling for all of the relevant characteristics, showed that the rate was still 56% higher. In other words, much of the difference could be explained by legitimate factors that more heavily impact African Americans, but a significant part of the difference could only be explained by race.[270]

A major problem with HMDA or related data is that it tends to miss subtle forms of discrimination that prevent individuals from even applying to a lender, thus keeping these individuals out of the HMDA data completely. One way to discover if this sort of discrimination is happening is to use paired testers.[271] In addition, the location of the lender's branches, racial composition of its staff, advertising practices, and other conduct may indicate whether there is discrimination on a prohibited basis as to the way consumers are encouraged or discouraged to apply.[272]

A second problem with HMDA data is that the legacy of discrimination affects standards of creditworthiness such as accumulated wealth, income, and property values in non-white neighborhoods. There is a debate as to whether a difference in, for example, the granting of credit to non-whites today is primarily due to these factors of creditworthiness which vary by race or ethnicity or to ongoing discrimination. In any case, the HMDA data does not illuminate this debate because the data set does not question the premises of what it means to be creditworthy or the extent to which the traditional standards are inherently biased due to past discrimination.[273]

Despite these limitations, HMDA data is a reliable and accessible source of data to show discrimination. Particularly when combined with other evidence of discrimination such as testing and/or witness and expert testimony, HMDA data can be very effective in proving discrimination.[274]

4.4.5.5 HMDA Analysis

The Federal Reserve Board has released an overview of each year's HMDA data since 2004.[275] These FRB overviews focus on many different aspects of mortgage market activity but over the years have consistently found substantial differences in the incidence of higher-priced lending and in application denial rates across racial and ethnic lines.[276] These differences cannot be fully explained by factors included in the HMDA data.[277]

In contrast to the results of analyses based on race or ethnicity, the FRB reports have tended not to find disparities in the data related to the sex of the borrower.[278] Other research has

---

269 *Id.*

270 *Id.*

271 *See* § 4.4.4, *supra.*

272 *See* § 5.3, *infra; see also* Urban Institute, Mortgage Lending Discrimination: A Review of Existing Evidence ch. 1 (Margery Austin Turner & Felicity Skidmore, eds., 1999) (a summary of possible discrimination in all phases of a credit transaction, including a summary of evidence from advertising and outreach, pre-application inquiries, loan approval or denial, and loan administration).

273 Urban Institute, Mortgage Lending Discrimination: A Review of Existing Evidence ch. 1 (Margery Austin Turner & Felicity Skidmore, eds., 1999).

274 *See, e.g.,* Paschal v. Flagstar Bank, 295 F.3d 565 (6th Cir. 2002) (HMDA data along with tester studies and testimony is sufficient

evidence to support jury finding of racial discrimination even though econometrics expert omitted certain variables in his analysis and aggregated data across different loan programs with different underwriting standards); *see also* § 4.4.5.5, *infra* (discussion of recent studies combining HMDA data with other data on creditworthiness).

275 Robert B. Avery, Neil Bhutta, Kenneth P. Brevoort, & Glenn B. Canner, Fed. Reserve Bd., *The Mortgage Market in 2011: Highlights from the Data Reported under the Home Mortgage Disclosure Act,* 98 Fed. Reserve Bull. No. 6 (Dec. 2012), *available at* www.federalreserve.gov/pubs/bulletin/2012/articles/HMDA/default.htm; Robert B. Avery, Neil Bhutta, Kenneth P. Brevoort, & Glenn B. Canner, Fed. Reserve Bd., *The Mortgage Market in 2010: Highlights from the Data Reported under the Home Mortgage Disclosure Act,* 97 Fed. Reserve Bull. Vol. No. 6 (Dec. 2011), *available at* www.federalreserve.gov/pubs/bulletin/2011/articles/HMDA/default.htm; Robert B. Avery, Neil Bhutta, Kenneth P. Brevoort, & Glenn B. Canner, Fed. Reserve Bd., *The 2009 HMDA Data: The Mortgage Market in a Time of Low Interest Rates and Economic Distress,* Fed. Reserve Bull. A39 (Dec. 2010), *available at* www.federalreserve.gov/pubs/bulletin/2010/articles/2009HMDA/default.htm; Robert B. Avery, Neil Bhutta, Kenneth P. Brevoort, Glenn B. Canner, & Christa N. Gibbs, Fed. Reserve Bd., *The 2008 HMDA Data: The Mortgage Market During a Turbulent Year,* Fed. Reserve Bull. A169 (Apr. 2010), *available at* www.federalreserve.gov/Pubs/Bulletin/2010/pdf/hmda08final.pdf; Robert B. Avery, Kenneth P. Brevoort, & Glenn B. Canner, Fed. Reserve Bd., *The 2007 HMDA Data,* Fed. Reserve Bull. A107 (Dec. 2008), *available at* www.federalreserve.gov/pubs/bulletin/2008/pdf/hmda07final.pdf; Robert Avery, Kenneth P. Brevoort, & Glenn B. Canner, Fed. Reserve Bd., *The 2006 HMDA Data,* Fed. Reserve Bull. A73 (Dec. 2007), *available at* www.federalreserve.gov/pubs/bulletin/2007/pdf/hmda06final.pdf; Robert B. Avery, Kenneth P. Brevoort, & Glenn B. Canner, Fed. Reserve Bd., *Higher-Priced Home Lending and the 2005 HMDA Data,* 2006 Fed. Reserve Bull. A123 (Sept. 8, 2006), *available at* www.federalreserve.gov/pubs/bulletin/2006/hmda/bull06hmda.pdf; Robert B. Avery, Glenn B. Canner, & Robert E. Cook, New Information Reported Under HMDA and Its Application in Fair Lending Enforcement, Fed. Reserve Bull. 344–94 (Summer 2005) (reviewing data from 2004), *available at* www.federalreserve.gov/pubs/bulletin/2005/summer05_hmda.pdf; *see also* Keith Ernst & Deborah Goldstein, Ctr. for Responsible Lending, Comment on Federal Reserve Analysis of Home Mortgage Disclosure Act Data (Sept. 14, 2005), *available at* www.responsiblelending.org.

276 Robert B. Avery et al., Fed. Reserve Bd., *The Mortgage Market in 2011: Highlights from the Data Reported under the Home Mortgage Disclosure Act,* 98 Fed. Reserve Bull. No. 6, at 32 (Dec. 2012).

277 *Id.*

278 *See, e.g.,* Robert B. Avery et al., Fed. Reserve Bd., *The Mortgage Market in 2011: Highlights from the Data Reported under the Home Mortgage Disclosure Act,* 98 Fed. Reserve Bull. No. 6 at 34 (Dec.

sometimes found sex disparities, however.[279]

All findings based on HMDA data must be considered with caution. Disparities in the incidence of high-priced loans are not per se evidence of discrimination; it is necessary to examine the factors that contributed to pricing decisions as well, and HMDA does not include all of the necessary data fields.[280]

Other studies have combined HMDA data with other data sources to attempt to tease out how much of observed disparities can be explained by factors related to creditworthiness and how much is the result of apparent discrimination on the basis of race, sex, or geography (that is, residence in a neighborhood with a high percentage of a particular racial or ethnic group). The following is a (necessarily incomplete) list of national and regional research finding persistent lending disparities:

- Several studies have found that observed disparities on the basis of race or gender *increase* as income levels increase.[281]

- Many studies have found that African-American and Hispanic borrowers were more likely to receive subprime loans.[282]

- A Consumer Federation of America (CFA) study, based on a proprietary database and not on HMDA data, found that African-American and Hispanic borrowers were more likely to receive interest-only and payment option mortgages than non-minority borrowers.[283]

- Which lending channel—prime or subprime—that a borrower enters can have a large impact on the price paid for a home loan. For example, a study by a coalition of groups found that 75.9% of the loans of Washington Mutual (WaMu) to African Americans were made through its subprime subsidiary, Long Beach Mortgage Company, and that, regardless of race, 90% of Long Beach borrowers received higher-cost home purchase loans. By contrast, WaMu's prime lender, Washington Mutual Bank, accounted for more than 80% of all WaMu's home purchase loans to whites, and less than 1% of the bank's loans were at higher cost.[284]

- A number of studies have shown connections between lending disparities, subprime lending, and foreclosure rates.[285]

2012); Robert B. Avery, Kenneth P. Brevoort, & Glenn B. Canner, Fed. Reserve Bd., *The 2007 HMDA Data*, Fed. Reserve Bull. A107, A140 (Dec. 2008).

279 A Consumer Federation of America study based on the 2005 HMDA data found that, controlling for income, women are more likely than men to receive higher-cost mortgages. Unlike the Federal Reserve Board's analysis, the CFA study looked not only at loans with a single female borrower but also at those with a male co-applicant when the female was listed as the primary borrower. In the CFA study, the disparities increased as income rose. Allen J. Fishbein & Patrick Woodall, Consumer Fed'n of America, Women Are Prime Targets for Subprime Lending: Women Are Disproportionately Represented in High-Cost Mortgage Market (Dec. 2006), *available at* www.consumerfed.org/pdfs/WomenPrimeTargets Study120606.pdf.

280 *See, e.g.*, Joseph M. Kolar & Jonathan D. Jerison, *The Home Mortgage Disclosure Act: Its History, Evolution, and Limitations*, 59 Consumer Fin. L.Q. Rep. 189 (2005).

281 *See, e.g.*, ACORN Hous. Corp., Foreclosure Exposure: A Study of Racial and Income Disparities in Home Mortgage Lending in 172 American Cities (Sept. 5, 2007), *available at* www.acorn.org/fileadmin/HMDA/2007/HMDAreport2007.pdf; Nat'l Cmty. Reinvestment Coal., Income Is No Shield Against Racial Differences in Lending: A Comparison of High-Cost Lending in America's Metropolitan Areas (July 2007), *available at* www.ncrc.org.; Allen J. Fishbein & Patrick Woodall, Consumer Fed'n of America, Women Are Prime Targets for Subprime Lending: Women Are Disproportionately Represented in High-Cost Mortgage Market (Dec. 2006), *available at* www.consumerfed.org/pdfs/WomenPrimeTargets Study120606.pdf; Nat'l Cmty. Reinvestment Coal., Homeownership and Wealth Building Impeded (Apr. 2006), *available at* www.ncrc.org/policy/analysis/policy/2006/2006-04-20_NCRC-OA-PRRACReport.pdf.

282 ACORN Hous. Corp., Foreclosure Exposure: A Study of Racial and Income Disparities in Home Mortgage Lending in 172 American Cities (Sept. 5, 2007), *available at* www.acorn.org/fileadmin/HMDA/2007/HMDAreport2007.pdf (geographic concentration of subprime lending, particularly in communities along the Texas/Mexico border, suggests language barriers may play a role); Allen J. Fishbein & Patrick Woodall, Consumer Fed'n of America, Subprime Locations: Patterns of Geographic Disparity in Subprime Lending (Sept.

5, 2006), *available at* www.consumerfed.org/pdfs/Subprime LocationsStudy090506.pdf; Debbie Gruenstein Bocian, Keith S. Ernst, & Wei Li, Ctr. for Responsible Lending, Unfair Lending: The Effect of Race and Ethnicity on the Price of Subprime Mortgages (May 31, 2006), *available at* www.responsiblelending.org/issues/mortgage/reports/page.jsp?itemID=29371010 (combining HMDA with a proprietary dataset and finding disparities even after controlling for credit scores, loan-to-value ratios, and other underwriting factors); Allen Fishbein & Patrick Woodall, Consumer Fed'n of America, Subprime Cities: Patterns of Geographic Disparity in Subprime Lending (Sept. 8, 2005); Nat'l Cmty. Reinvestment Coal., Preapprovals and Pricing Disparities in the Mortgage Marketplace (June 2005); Woodstock Institute, Reinvestment Alert No. 28 (May 2005), *available at* www.woodstockinst.org/publications/reinvestment_alerts (analyzing patterns in the Chicago region).

283 Allen Fishbein & Patrick Woodall, Consumer Fed'n of America, Exotic or Toxic? An Examination of the Non-Traditional Mortgage Market for Consumers and Lenders (May 24, 2006), *available at* www.consumerfed.org/pdfs/Exotic_Toxic_Mortgage_Report0506.pdf.

284 Cal. Reinvestment Coal., Cmty. Reinvestment Ass'n of N.C., Empire Justice Ctr., Mass. Affordable Housing Alliance, Neighborhood Economic Dev. Advocacy Project, & Woodstock Institute, Paying More for the American Dream: A Multi-State Analysis of Higher Cost Home Purchase Lending (Mar. 2007), *available at* www.nedap.org.

285 Debbie Gruenstein Bocian et al., Ctr. for Responsible Lending, Lost Ground, 2011: Disparities in Mortgage Lending and Foreclosures (2011), *available at* www.responsiblelending.org/mortgage-lending/research-analysis/Lost-Ground-2011.pdf (reporting that approximately one in four of African American or Latino homeowners have lost their homes to foreclosure while fewer than one in eight white homeowners have lost their homes); Cal. Reinvestment Coal., Cmty. Reinvestment Ass'n of N.C., Empire Justice Ctr., Mass. Affordable Hous. Alliance, Neighborhood Economic Dev. Advocacy Project, Ohio Fair Lending Coal., & Woodstock Institute, Paying More for the American Dream: The Subprime Shakeout and Its Impact on Lower-Income and Minority Communities (Mar. 2008), *available at* www.woodstockinst.org/publications/download/paying-more-for-the-american-dream-%11-the-subprime-shakeout-and-its-impact-on-lower%11income-and-minority-communities; Allen J. Fishbein, Consumer Fed'n of America, Piggyback Loans at the Trough: California Subprime Home Purchase and Refinance Lending in

• Changes in the lending market after the peak of the fore-closure crisis also appear to have a disparate impact on minority borrowers.[286]

In addition to the studies above, the HMDA data has enabled other groups to examine the racial and ethnic disparities in higher-priced lending in particular communities and by particular lenders.[287]

4.4.5.6 Policy Responses to HMDA Data

Commentary from several advocacy groups and public officials based on the 2006 HMDA data can be found in the testimony presented at a hearing before the U.S. House of Representatives.[288] The Office of the Comptroller of the Currency (OCC) has reportedly told lenders that, if the new data shows high concentrations of high-cost loans in minority neighborhoods, lenders will bear the burden of showing that this result was the product of nondiscriminatory lending decisions.[289] According to one report, although only 2% of the lenders who report HMDA data have lender-product combinations that show statistical problems, those lenders were responsible for 40% to 50% of all lending activity.[290]

State enforcement officials have also used the data to crack down on predatory lenders.[291] In July 2008, the Office of the Attorney General of New York reached a fair lending agreement with GreenPoint Mortgage resulting in the issuance of approximately one million dollars in restitution to African-American and Latino customers who were charged more for loans between 2004 and 2006 than similarly situated white customers. This agreement stemmed from an inquiry into Green-Point's lending practices and the commissioning of expert statistical analyses prompted by the initial review of HMDA data indicating a disparity with respect to customers receiving high-priced loans in New York.[292] Still, state enforcement officials may run into preemption problems if they are aiming at national banks, even at the investigatory stage. For example, the New York attorney general sent letters to several banks requesting their 2004 HMDA data and other information. The Office of the Comptroller of the Currency, joined by several of the banks, sued to enjoin the investigative and enforcement efforts. The Second Circuit upheld the OCC's position that any effort by the attorney general to investigate or enforce provisions of the ECOA or state credit discrimination laws against national banks or their operating subsidiaries was an unlawful exercise of visitorial powers preempted by the National Bank Act. The court declined to decide whether state enforcement of the federal Fair Housing Act using the HMDA data is similarly preempted. That issue was not ripe for adjudication as New York had not yet filed suit under the FHA and the FHA does not contain a pre-enforcement mechanism similar to the broad investigative power under state law.[293] Note that in June 2009 the United States Supreme Court reversed in part and affirmed in part the rulings of the Second Circuit and the New York district court in the *Clearing House* litigation.[294] The Supreme Court vacated the district court's injunction that had prohibited the New York attorney general from initiating court actions to enforce non-preempted state credit discrimination laws against

---

2006 (Jan. 2008), *available at* www.consumerfed.org (the rate of piggyback loans was particularly high in California, placing many of those borrowers at risk of foreclosure); Kristopher Geradi et al., Subprime Outcomes: Risky Mortgages, Homeownership Experiences, and Foreclosures (Fed. Reserve Bank of Boston, Working Paper 07-15, Dec. 3, 2007), *available at* www.bos.frb.org (correlation between subprime lending and foreclosures, not based on HMDA data).

286 U.S. Dep't of Hous. & Urban Dev., Policy Development and Research, A Second Look at FHA's Evolving Market Shares by Race and Ethnicity (Aug. 2012), www.huduser.org/portal/pdredge/pdr_edge_featd_article_080312.html (finding that African Americans and Hispanics continue to be more affected by the post-housing-crisis tightening of conventional underwriting than whites); Furman Ctr. for Real Estate & Urban Policy, Mortgage Lending During the Great Recession: HMDA 2009 (Nov. 2010), http://furmancenter.org/files/publications/HMDA_2009_databrief.pdf (showing disproportionate drop in conventional lending to black and Hispanic New Yorkers, partially replaced by larger share of FHA/VA lending).

287 *See, e.g.*, Nat'l Cmty. Reinvestment Coal., Fair Lending Helps Community Prosperity: An Analysis of Fair Lending Disparities in the New Orleans Metro Area (June 2007), *available at* www.ncrc.org; Jim Campen, Borrowing Trouble VII: Higher-Cost Mortgage Lending in Boston, Greater Boston and Massachusetts, 2005 (Jan. 2007), *available at* http://mahahome.org/issues (census data and HUD income data); Kevin Stein, Cal. Reinvestment Coal., Who Really Gets Higher-Cost Home Loans? Home Loan Disparities by Income, Race and Ethnicity of Borrowers and Neighborhoods in 14 California Communities in 2005 (Dec. 2006), *available at* www.calreinvest.org.

288 *See Mortgage Lending Disparities: Hearing Before the House Comm. on Financial Servs.*, 110th Cong. (Oct. 15, 2007), *available at* www.house.gov.

289 *See OCC Vows Early Activist Stance on HMDA*, 83 Banking Rep. (BNA) No. 12, at 501 (Oct. 4, 2004).

290 *See Though Few Lenders Under HMDA Review, They Account for Large Share of Total Loans*, 86 Banking Rep. (BNA) No. 7, at 316 (Feb. 13, 2006).

291 *See, e.g.*, Commonwealth v. Fremont Inv. & Loan, 897 N.E.2d 548 (Mass. 2008) (affirming grant of preliminary injunction regarding foreclosure on loans possessing specific combination of loan characteristics); *see also* Stipulated Final Judgment and Order, Fed. Trade Comm'n v. Gateway Funding Diversified Mortgage Servs., Ltd. P'ship, No. 08-5805 (E.D. Pa. 2008) (policy of allowing loan officers to charge "discretionary overages" resulted in African Americans and Hispanics paying higher prices, and Gateway failed to monitor whether minority borrowers were paying more than white borrowers), *available at* www.ftc.gov/os/caselist/0623063/081216gatewaystiporder.pdf.

292 *See* Press Release, N.Y. State Office of the Att'y Gen., Attorney General Cuomo Obtains Approximately $1 Million for Victims of GreenPoint's Discriminatory Lending Practices (July 16, 2008), *available at* www.ag.ny.gov/press-release/attorney-general-cuomo-obtains-approximately-1-million-victims-greenpoints.

293 *See* Clearing House Ass'n, L.L.C. v. Cuomo, 510 F.3d 105 (2d Cir. 2007), *cert. granted*, 129 S. Ct. 987 (2009). *See generally* § 11.6.1.3, *infra*; National Consumer Law Center, National Consumer Law Center, The Cost of Credit: Regulation, Preemption, and Industry Abuses Ch. 3 (4th ed. 2009 and Supp.).

294 Cuomo v. Clearing House Ass'n, L.L.C., 129 S. Ct. 2710, 174 L. Ed. 2d 464 (2009); *see* § 12.4.3.3.2, *infra* (in-depth discussion of case).

national banks. At the same time the Supreme Court affirmed the district court and Second Circuit's rulings barring New York state officials from conducting administrative investigations into national banks' lending practices. The Supreme Court ruling left intact the district court order prohibiting the state officials from issuing administrative subpoenas for national banks' records.

Cities have also used HMDA data to bolster their reverse redlining claims against lenders. For example, in 2008 the City of Baltimore filed suit against Wells Fargo Bank, alleging that the bank violated the Fair Housing Act by targeting underserved and vulnerable minority neighborhoods for subprime loans, which in turn lead to a disproportionately high foreclosure rate in African-American neighborhoods. The complaint used HMDA data to argue that the bank's high-cost loans are disproportionately located in those neighborhoods.[295]

4.4.6 Other Sources of Mortgage Data

4.4.6.1 General

There are some supplementary data sources that can be useful in analyzing HMDA data. Census data, for example, provides detailed information for each census tract and can be obtained from the Bureau of the Census.[296] The Department of Housing and Urban Development (HUD) publishes an annual list of manufactured home lenders and subprime lenders (using its own definition of that term).[297] Information about the location of lenders' offices is available from the Federal Deposit Insurance Corp.[298] The Federal Reserve also has some useful information available on its website.[299]

Community Reinvestment Act ratings may also be helpful. These are available only from lenders who are required to provide the information.[300] Advocates should also consider contacting government enforcement agencies for information about public investigations and complaints.

4.4.6.2 Government-Sponsored Enterprise (Freddie Mac and Fannie Mae) Data

Federal law requires HUD to make available to the public data submitted to HUD by the Federal National Mortgage Association (Fannie Mae) and the Federal Home Loan Mortgage Corp. (Freddie Mac) relating to those entities' mortgage purchases.[301] However, the statute allows HUD to withhold "proprietary information" from release.[302] HUD's regulations define "proprietary information" as data submitted by Fannie Mae and Freddie Mac that contains "trade secrets or privileged or confidential, commercial, or financial information that, if released, would be likely to cause substantial competitive harm."[303] HUD's regulations also prohibit the release of mortgage data that would constitute an invasion of personal privacy.[304]

Prior to 2005 HUD, by its own admission, had taken a conservative approach in making determinations about information that is "proprietary."[305] In 2005, HUD amended its regulations to allow the release of more data. Specifically, the regulation now provides that HUD may reclassify data from proprietary to non-proprietary status and then release both past and future data.[306] Second, HUD may allow release of aggregated data that is derived from proprietary loan-level data.[307] Third, HUD may make a determination that data that was previously considered proprietary loses that status after five years and can be released.[308]

4.4.7 Monitoring Data Required by the ECOA

In addition to the HMDA requirements, the ECOA also requires creditors to retain certain information for monitoring purposes. This requirement is significant for two reasons. First, certain smaller institutions, institutions that do not do business within a metropolitan area, and lenders with no federal connection are not required to comply with the HMDA requirements.[309] The ECOA requirements, in contrast, apply to all creditors that receive an application for credit for the purchase or refinancing of a dwelling and for which the credit will be secured by the dwelling.[310]

Second, the ECOA requirement includes some information not required by the HMDA (although much of the HMDA data is not required by the ECOA). In addition to certain information also required by the HMDA (the applicant's race or national

---

295 Mayor & City Council of Balt. v. Wells Fargo Bank, No. L08CV062 (D. Md. Jan. 8, 2008), *available on the companion website to this treatise. See generally* Raymond Brescia, *Subprime Communities: Reverse Redlining, The Fair Housing Act and Emerging Issues in Litigation Regarding the Subprime Mortgage Crisis*, 2 Alb. Gov't L. Rev. 164 (2009).

296 Census data is available on-line at www.census.gov.

297 *See* United States Dep't of Hous. & Urban Dev., HUD Subprime & Manufactured Home Lender List, *available at* www.huduser.org/datasets/manu.html.

298 This information is available on-line at www.fdic.gov, by calling (877) ASK-FDIC (275-3342), or by mail from the Federal Deposit Insurance Corp., Office of the Ombudsman, 550 17th St., N.W., Washington, D.C. 20429-9990.

299 See the Federal Financial Institution Examination Council's website at www.ffiec.gov/NIC/default.htm.

300 *See* § 1.9, *supra.*

301 12 U.S.C. § 4543.

302 12 U.S.C. § 4546.

303 24 C.F.R. § 81.2.

304 24 C.F.R. § 81.72(b)(3).

305 *See* 65 Fed. Reg. 12,632 (Mar. 9, 2000).

306 24 C.F.R. § 81.75(b)(1), (b)(2).

307 24 C.F.R. § 81.75(c).

308 24 C.F.R. § 81.75(b)(3).

309 *See* § 4.4.5.2.1, *supra.*

310 *See* Reg. B, 12 C.F.R. § 1002.13(a) [§ 202.13(a)].

origin and sex), the ECOA requires information on marital status (married, unmarried, or separated) and age.[311]

The ECOA data is not routinely compiled into reports like the HMDA data and the data is not generally open for inspection. Nevertheless, the relevant enforcement agency may have requested the data and may have compiled it in some fashion. The enforcement agency may also require the lender to provide additional or different information.[312]

The monitoring information required by the ECOA should also be available through discovery from the creditor itself, although the creditor need not have compiled the information. The original records must be retained by the creditor for at least twenty-five months and cannot be disposed of once an investigation or civil action is instituted.[313]

4.4.8 Non-Mortgage Data

Except for HMDA and ECOA mortgage data, a creditor legally should not have statistics as to the racial, sexual, or other characteristics of those denied or approved for credit. However, there are other possible sources of data. For example, in cases challenging the mark-up policies of car financing creditors, plaintiffs based their statistical proof of discrimination on race-coded driver's licenses.[314]

Other studies have examined the concentration of high-rate lenders, such as payday lenders, in particular census tracts. For example, a study by the Center for Responsible Lending analyzed the total number of payday lending stores in North Carolina divided by the total population in tracts statewide. Comparing census tracts by concentration of African Americans, the Center found that the concentration of payday storefronts in North Carolina was substantially greater in neighborhoods with higher proportions of African Americans.[315]

Many types of government data can be combined with other data sources to explore patterns of lending discrimination.[316]

Useful data sources include census data, the Federal Reserve Board's *Survey of Consumer Finances*, and the Department of Housing and Urban Development's estimate of median family income by metropolitan area, among other HUD data sets.[317]

Private data sources, when they are available, can also be useful. For example, the Federal Reserve Board shed further light on the 2006 HMDA data by combining it with two proprietary databases from a credit reporting agency, TransUnion: one that measures loan performance at the geographic level and another containing summary statistics about the mean credit scores of individuals by census tract.[318] Of course, credit scores themselves vary by race and ethnicity, though whether the differences reflect discrimination is a matter of dispute.[319]

4.4.9 Non-Mortgage Creditors' Self-Testing Data

In 1999, the Federal Reserve Board proposed removing the prohibition on seeking information about an applicant's race, color, religion, national origin, and sex for non-mortgage credit products.[320] This proposal was made in response to comments from the Department of Justice and the federal financial enforcement agencies that the enhanced ability to obtain data on race and ethnicity would aid fair lending enforcement, particularly with respect to small business lending.[321] The proposal would have removed the prohibition on collecting such data but would not have required creditors to gather this information.

Finally, in 2003, the FRB decided not to remove the prohibition,[322] explaining that retaining the prohibition was, in its view, the best way to reduce discrimination.[323] An express concern was that lifting the prohibition would create some risk that the data would be used for discriminatory purposes such as selective inquiry or notation.[324] In June 2008, in response to a request from Congress, the General Accounting Office issued a report.[325]

---

311 Reg. B, 12 C.F.R. § 1002.13(a) [§ 202.13(a)].

312 Reg. B, 12 C.F.R. § 1002.13(d) [§ 202.13(d)]; Official Interpretations of Reg. B [Official Staff Commentary on Reg. B], 12 C.F.R. pt. 1002 [pt. 202], Supp. I, § 1002.13(d)-1 [§ 202.13(d)-1].

313 *See* § 10.12, *infra*.

314 Select expert reports in these cases are reproduced on the companion website to this treatise and are also available on NCLC's website, www.nclc.org. *See* § 8.6.5, *infra*.

315 Neighborhood Economic Dev. Advocacy Project, Predatory Tax-Time Loans Strip $324 Million from New York City's Poorest Communities: An Analysis of Tax Refund Anticipation Lending in NYC 2002–2005 (Jan. 2007), *available at* www.nedap.org; Keith Ernst, Delvin Davis, Uriah King, & Wei Li, Ctr. for Responsible Lending, Race Matters: The Concentration of Payday Lenders in African-American Neighborhoods in North Carolina (Mar. 22, 2005).

316 *See, e.g.,* Christian Weller, Ctr. for American Progress, Access Denied: Low Income and Minority Families Face More Credit Constraints and Higher Borrowing Costs (Aug. 2007) (analyzing survey of consumer finances), *available at* www.american progress.org; Jim Campen, Borrowing Trouble VII: Higher-Cost Mortgage Lending in Boston, Greater Boston and Massachusetts, 2005 (Jan. 2007), *available at* http://mahahome.org/issues (com-

bining HMDA data with census data and HUD's median family income data).

317 HUD's data sets are described at www.huduser.org/datasets/pdrdatas.html.

318 *See* Robert Avery, Kenneth P. Brevoort, & Glenn B. Canner, Fed. Reserve Bd., *The 2006 HMDA Data*, Fed. Reserve Bull. A73 (Dec. 2007), *available at* www.federalreserve.gov.

319 *See* § 6.4, *infra*.

320 64 Fed. Reg. 44,582, 44,586 (Aug. 16, 1999) (amending 12 C.F.R. § 202.5). The FRB had first floated the possibility of removing this prohibition in 1995.

321 64 Fed. Reg. 44,582, 44,586 (Aug. 16, 1999).

322 68 Fed. Reg. 13,144, 13,147–13,150 (Mar. 18, 2003).

323 *Id.* at 13,148.

324 *Id.*

325 Gen. Accounting Office, Fair Lending: Race and Gender Data are Limited for Nonmortgage Lending (June 2008), *available at* www.gao.gov/new.items/d081023t.pdf.

The report found that, while the testimony presented by researchers and others did not completely comport with the FRB's 2003 stated rationale for keeping the ban on the voluntary collection of data, there was nevertheless a general acknowledgment that voluntarily collected data would have only limited efficacy. This acknowl-

Instead of lifting the ban in 2003, a new exception was created for collection of this information for the purpose of conducting a self-test under section 202.15 (section 1002.15 under the CFPB).[326] The self-test exception allows creditors that wish to monitor and ensure compliance with the ECOA to inquire and note information about non-mortgage credit applicants' personal characteristics. Creditors that collect this information must disclose at the time the information is requested that the applicant will not be required to provide the information, that the creditor is requesting the information to monitor its compliance with the federal Equal Credit Opportunity Act, that federal law prohibits the creditor from discriminating on the basis of this information or on the basis of an applicant's decision not to furnish the information and if applicable, that certain information will be collected based on visual observation or surname if not provided by the applicant or other person.[327]

In order to avail itself of the self-test exception, a creditor must meet the requirements for conducting a self-test under Regulation B, 12 C.F.R. § 1002.15 [§ 202.15]. The creditor must have a program, practice, or study that (1) is designed and used specifically to determine the extent or effectiveness of the creditor's compliance with the ECOA and (2) creates data or factual information that is not available and could not be derived from loan or application or other records related to credit transactions.[328]

This information is privileged only if the creditor takes appropriate corrective action when the creditor determines that it is more likely than not that a violation has occurred.[329] Assuming corrective action is taken when warranted, the results of the self-test cannot be obtained by a government agency in an examination or investigation or by any agency or any applicant in any proceeding or lawsuit alleging a violation of the ECOA or Regulation B.[330]

The supplemental information to the March 2003 final rule contains additional requirements regarding the self-test exception. Any information about an applicant's personal characteristics collected as part of a self-test must be kept separate from the loan file, application file, or other records related to credit transactions.[331] This information should be analyzed in a timely fashion as part of the self-test. Creditors are expected to develop a written plan when conducting a self-test that includes the specific purposes of the self-test, the methodology, the geographic area covered, the types of credit transactions involved, the entity that will analyze the data, and the time frame.[332] Creditors are generally required to retain records of the self-test for twenty-five months after completion.[333]

---

edgment was based not only on the conclusion that any data gathered voluntarily would be collected on an inconsistent basis but also on an apprehension that few lenders would ultimately participate in such voluntary collection due to concern that such participation would invite enhanced regulatory scrutiny of their lending practices and the potential for litigation. The report also found that, while requiring lenders to collect and report data could help deal with the data limitations that interfere with the complete assessment of possible discrimination, such a requirement would necessarily create additional costs for lenders that would likely end up getting passed on to consumers. The FRB did not take a position on the report's analysis.

326 Gen. Accounting Office, Fair Lending: Race and Gender Data are Limited for Nonmortgage Lending (June 2008), *available at* www.gao.gov/new.items/d081023t.pdf. The new exception was codified at 12 C.F.R. § 202.5(b)(1) [§ 1002.5(b)(1) under the CFPB].

327 12 C.F.R. § 1002.5(b)(1) [§ 202.5(b)(1)].

---

328 Reg. B, 12 C.F.R. § 1002.15(b)(1) [§ 202.15(b)(1)].

329 Reg. B, 12 C.F.R. § 1002.15(a)(2), (c) [§ 202.15(a)(2), (c)].

330 Reg. B, 12 C.F.R. § 1002.15(d) [§ 202.15(d)].

331 68 Fed. Reg. 13,144, 13,149 (Mar. 18, 2003). It was stated that the additional guidance would be incorporated into the official staff commentary at a later date, as appropriate.

332 *Id.*

333 Reg. B, 12 C.F.R. § 1002.12(b)(6) [§ 202.12(b)(6)].

Chapter 5

Discrimination in Pre-Application and Application Procedures

5.1 Introduction

5.1.1 The Special ECOA Requirements

As a fundamental principle, the Equal Credit Opportunity Act (ECOA), the Fair Housing Act (FHA), and other credit discrimination statutes set forth a general rule against discrimination in every aspect of a credit transaction. In addition, the ECOA has specific prohibitions and procedural requirements that creditors must follow in the various stages of a credit transaction. The Fair Housing Act and federal Civil Rights Acts do not contain equivalent specific prohibitions and requirements but nevertheless apply broadly to all stages of a credit transaction.

For purposes of the specific ECOA prohibitions and requirements, there are five major stages in a credit transaction:

- The application for credit and other initial procedures;
- The creditor's evaluation of that application;
- The decision to grant credit and on what terms credit is granted;
- Notification to the applicant of the creditor's decision; and
- The various procedures after credit is granted.

It is important to remember that the specific ECOA prohibitions and requirements are in addition to, and do not in any way limit, the general rule against discrimination in the ECOA, the FHA, and the federal Civil Rights Acts.[1]

5.1.2 Discussion of the Stages of a Credit Transaction in This Treatise

The next few chapters of this treatise will follow the four major stages in a credit transaction. Each chapter will discuss both general discriminatory practices and the special ECOA requirements specific to that stage of the credit process.

This chapter focuses on discrimination in the pre-application and application stages of a credit transaction. It will discuss general discrimination at these stages, including discriminatory marketing of credit and disparities in the application process for protected groups. This chapter also discusses the relevant special ECOA requirements, including what information creditors can request in an application and who can be required to co-sign a credit obligation.

Chapter 6, *infra*, analyzes general discrimination and special ECOA requirements concerning the evaluation of an application. Chapter 7, *infra*, discusses discrimination in the granting of credit, focusing on the issue of redlining. Chapter 8, *infra*, discusses discrimination regarding the terms of credit, focusing on the critical issue of predatory lending as a form of such discrimination. Chapter 9, *infra*, discusses discrimination following the granting of credit. Chapter 10, *infra*, discusses the special ECOA requirements for notification of action taken on an application for credit.

5.2 General Rule Against Discrimination

5.2.1 Introduction

Before discussing discrimination specific to each stage of the credit transaction, it is helpful to understand some principles about the general rule against discrimination embodied in the ECOA, the FHA, the Civil Rights Acts, and other credit discrimination statutes.

5.2.2 What Is "Discrimination" Under the General Rule?

To "discriminate" is defined by Regulation B as treating an applicant less favorably than other applicants.[2] Consequently, the ECOA prohibits treating an applicant less favorably than other applicants on a prohibited basis at any stage of the credit transaction, ranging from application procedures to terms of the transaction to subsequent handling of defaults. This broad standard can be applied aggressively and innovatively to many types of creditor conduct that treat one debtor less favorably than others.

The Fair Housing Act also uses the term "to discriminate" but, unlike the ECOA and its implementing regulation, does not define the term. Most likely, it will be considered as having the same meaning as articulated under the ECOA. Similarly, the

---

1 *See* Official Interpretations of Reg. B [Official Staff Commentary on Reg. B], 12 C.F.R. pt. 1002 [pt. 202], § 1002.4(a)-1 [§ 202.4(a)-1] ("Thus, whether or not specifically prohibited elsewhere in the regulation, a credit practice that treats applicants differently on a prohibited basis violates the law because it violates the general rule.").

2 Reg. B, 12 C.F.R. § 1002.2(n) [§ 202.2(n)].

federal Civil Rights Acts require that individuals be treated the "same" as white citizens, indicating a similar standard to that of the ECOA.

Even though unfavorable treatment constitutes discrimination, it is not necessarily *illegal* discrimination. Discrimination in credit transactions is generally legal unless the discrimination is on a prohibited basis. An earlier chapter of this treatise discusses when discrimination is on a prohibited basis and therefore illegal.[3]

5.2.3 The General Rule Applies to All Aspects of a Credit Transaction

The general rule against discrimination applies during every stage of the credit transaction. This is true for the ECOA, the FHA, and the federal Civil Rights Acts.

The ECOA prohibits any creditor from discriminating against any applicant on a prohibited basis with respect to *any* aspect of a credit transaction.[4] The official interpretations of Regulation B (hereafter "official interpretations") elaborate that this rule "covers all dealings, without exception, between an applicant and a creditor, whether or not addressed by other provisions of the regulation."[5]

The Fair Housing Act also offers a broad standard as to prohibited conduct. The two different sections that provide the main avenues for relief in credit discrimination cases are both broadly worded. The provision dealing with housing-related financing prohibits discrimination "in making available such a transaction, or in the terms or conditions of such a transaction."[6] The other regulatory provision, dealing with the sale or lease of realty, generally prohibits discrimination: in any conduct that would make unavailable the sale or rental of dwellings; in the terms, conditions, or privileges of a sale or rental; or in statements or advertisements offering dwellings for sale or rent.[7] Thus the Fair Housing Act would seem to apply to virtually every stage of a transaction involving the sale or rental of a dwelling or the financing related to a dwelling.[8]

The federal Civil Rights Acts apply even more clearly to all aspects of a transaction. Section 1981, which ensures the right to "make and enforce contracts," explicitly defines the phrase to include "the making, performance, modification, and termination of contracts, and the enjoyment of all benefits, privileges, terms, and conditions of the contractual relationship."[9] Section 1982 refers to the right of all citizens to "inherit, purchase, lease, sell, hold, and convey real and personal property" and would seem to apply to every aspect of a transaction relating to purchasing or holding real or personal property, including every aspect of a credit transaction.

5.3 Discrimination in the Pre-Application Stage of a Credit Transaction

5.3.1 Overview

The first stage of a credit transaction in which discrimination may take place occurs prior to the actual application—when the creditor takes various actions to encourage or discourage persons from seeking credit from that creditor. While most of the ECOA applies only to "applicants,"[10] Regulation B does include a pre-application prohibition forbidding creditors from discouraging prospective applicants on a prohibited basis.[11] The Fair Housing Act contains a similar prohibition.[12]

Attacking pre-application discrimination is critical because creditors who want to discriminate illegally have a strong incentive to keep people of color, public assistance recipients, or others from applying. If an individual never applies, it will be difficult for that individual to complain about being denied credit. Similarly, the federal Home Mortgage Disclosure Act requires creditors to report racial and other characteristics of mortgage applicants.[13] If individuals never apply, the lender need not report the individual as being denied credit.

---

3 *See* ch. 3, *supra.*

4 15 U.S.C. § 1691(a); *see* Reg. B, 12 C.F.R. § 1002.4(a) [§ 202.4(a)]; *see also* Reg. B, 12 C.F.R. § 1002.6(b)(9) [§ 202.6(b)(9)] (emphasizing that, except as otherwise permitted or required by law, a creditor may not consider race, color, religion, national origin, or sex in any aspect of a credit transaction). *See also* Narayan v. Ind. Bank Corp., 2012 WL 3229156 (S.D. Ind. Aug. 6, 2012) (finding that the ECOA does not necessarily require denial of a loan application for claim to be actionable, since section 1691(a) applies to "any aspect of a credit transaction"; thus, if plaintiff alleged that its loan was made on less favorable terms and conditions than others because of national origin, then it would state a claim under the ECOA but did not do so here).

5 Official Interpretations of Reg. B [Official Staff Commentary on Reg. B], 12 C.F.R. pt. 1002 [pt. 202], Supp. I, § 1002.4(a)-1 [§ 202.4(a)-1].

6 42 U.S.C. § 3605(a); *see* 24 C.F.R. § 100.110(b).

7 42 U.S.C. § 3604(a), (b); 24 C.F.R. § 100.50.

8 *See* Hirschfeld v. Metlife Bank, N.A., 2012 WL 3240669, at *6 (E.D.N.Y. July 31, 2012) ("In light of the breadth that courts have been instructed to give to provisions of the FHA, it is clearly

appropriate to treat mortgage lending as a service that may 'otherwise make unavailable or deny' dwellings to interested purchasers. Defendants offer no compelling arguments in support of adopting the narrow construction they ask to have imposed. Accordingly, the court holds that § 3604(a) of the FHA encompasses the discriminatory denial of mortgage financing.").

9 42 U.S.C. § 1981; *see also* Gregory v. Dillard's, Inc., 494 F.3d 694 (8th Cir. 2007) (fact that store patrons left in frustration after allegedly being denied service or being harassed did not preclude finding of "protected activity" element of patrons' section 1981 action against store owner, that is, it did not preclude contractual interest), *judgment vacated*, (8th Cir. Sept. 20, 2007); JAT, Inc. v. Nat'l City Bank of the Midwest, 460 F. Supp. 2d 812 (E.D. Mich. 2006) (plaintiffs who withdrew loan application due to delay, and who were granted loans on allegedly more restrictive terms, could state claim under section 1981).

10 Official Interpretations of Reg. B [Official Staff Commentary on Reg. B], 12 C.F.R. pt. 1002 [pt. 202], Supp. I, § 1002.4(b)-1 [§ 202.4(b)-1]; *see* § 2.2.4, *supra* (discussing scope of "applicant").

11 Reg. B, 12 C.F.R. § 1002.4(b) [§ 202.4(b)]; *see* § 5.3.2.1, *infra.*

12 42 U.S.C. § 3604(a), (b); *see* § 5.3.2.2, *infra.*

13 12 U.S.C. § 2801; *see* § 4.4.5, *supra*; § 5.5.3, *infra.*

In addition, pre-application discrimination has become important because of the growth in predatory lending targeted at communities that are predominantly African American and Hispanic, known as reverse redlining, discussed in Chapter 8, *infra*. One potential factor supporting this growth is discriminatory marketing by lenders, resulting in white applicants being steered to prime products while applicants of color are steered to subprime products.

5.3.2 Marketing Discrimination

5.3.2.1 The ECOA Standard

Regulation B specifically prohibits any oral or written statement to prospective applicants in advertising or otherwise that would discourage, on a prohibited basis, a reasonable person from pursuing an application.[14] Similarly, the ECOA's general rule against discrimination prohibits advertising and other marketing that discriminates on a prohibited basis as to who is encouraged to apply.[15]

The Regulation B prohibition covers oral or written statements by the creditor in advertising or otherwise.[16] A reasonable person test is used to determine whether the applicant "should have been" discouraged by the creditor's actions.[17]

The official interpretations give examples of prohibited discouragement, which include:[18]

- A statement that the applicant should not bother to apply after the applicant states that he is retired;
- Use of words, symbols, models or other communication in advertising that even implies or suggests a discriminatory preference; and
- Use of interview scripts that discourage applicants on a prohibited basis.

However, prohibited discouragement is not limited to these examples.[19]

Other creditor actions that discourage applications include creditor practices at its place of business such as sending people of color to different locations to apply, encouraging prospective applicants to apply at other banks, and indicating that it would take a long time to have an application processed.[20] Another means of discouraging such applicants is through the hiring of an all-white workforce by the creditor or using solely white actors in advertisements.[21] Unreasonably delaying the processing of applications from members of protected groups may also be discriminatory.[22] But one court has ruled that creditors need not provide prospective credit applicants with pamphlets or other informational literature explaining their rights under the ECOA, concluding that failure to provide such literature was irrelevant to whether the creditor was discouraging credit applications.[23]

The prohibition against acts to discourage applicants in no way prevents creditors from encouraging applications from protected groups. The official interpretation specifically states: "A creditor may affirmatively solicit or encourage members of traditionally disadvantaged groups to apply for credit, especially groups that might not normally seek credit from that creditor."[24]

---

14 Reg. B, 12 C.F.R. § 1002.4(b) [§ 202.4(b)].

15 *See* § 5.2.2, *supra*.

16 Reg. B, 12 C.F.R. § 1002.4(b) [§ 202.4(b)].

17 *Id.* No guidance is given as to what constitutes a reasonable person under this provision. Arguably, reference should be to a reasonable person belonging to the protected category. Clearly, the test should not be whether a reasonable middle-class white male applicant who has never encountered discrimination based on race or sex would have been discouraged by the creditor's actions.

18 Official Interpretations of Reg. B [Official Staff Commentary on Reg. B], 12 C.F.R. pt. 1002 [pt. 202], Supp. I, § 1002.4(b)-1 [§ 202.4(b)-1].

   As part of the March 2003 revisions to Regulation B, references were changed from "potential" applicants to "prospective" applicants in this commentary section with no substantive change intended. 68 Fed. Reg. 13,144, 13,155 (Mar. 18, 2003).

19 Examples of discriminatory marketing practices are discussed in § 5.3.2.4, *infra*. Some commentators have argued that marketing discrimination is not actionable under the ECOA and the FHA because there is no individual applicant who has been discriminated against. *See* Richard L. Jacobs & Michael B. Mierzewski, *What Hath Justice Department Wrought*, Banking Pol'y Rep., Feb. 6, 1995, at 8; John Spina, *U.S. v. Albank, FSB: Is 'Justice' Served in*

the *Enforcement of Fair Lending Laws*, 2 N.C. Banking Inst. 207 (1998).

   These commentators fail to fully consider Regulation B's prohibition against discouraging prospective applicants on a prohibited basis, 12 C.F.R. § 1002.4(b) [§ 202.4(b)].

20 *See* §§ 5.3.3.1, 5.3.3.2, *infra*.

21 *See, e.g.*, Ragin v. Harry Macklowe Real Estate, Co., 6 F.3d 898 (2d Cir. 1993); Saunders v. Gen. Servs. Corp., 659 F. Supp. 1042 (E.D. Va. 1987); *cf.* Lawrence v. Lenders for Cmty. Dev., 2010 WL 4922662 (N.D. Cal. Nov. 29, 2010) (allegations under federal civil rights acts and ECOA that defendant's website replaced images of African-American clients with images of immigrant clients provided "paltry support" that plaintiff was denied a loan because of his race; distinguishing plaintiff's "weak and conclusory" allegations that shift in advertising correlated with a policy of reducing loans to African-American small businesses and "regular" provision of loans to "white applicants, immigrants, and Hispanics" by comparing the instant case to U.S. v. Hazelwood School Dist., 534 F.2d 805 (8th Cir. 1976), which makes reference to explicit advertisement for "white only" teachers). *But see* Powell v. American Gen. Finance, 310 F. Supp. 2d 481 (N.D.N.Y. 2004) (the fact that lender's loan officers were all white did not support inference of disparate treatment).

22 *See* Thompson v. Marine Midland Bank, 1999 U.S. App. LEXIS 22960 (2d Cir. Sept. 16, 1999) (finding that, although plaintiffs' allegations of delay in processing of applications may have constituted disparate treatment, defendant provided a legitimate, nondiscriminatory reason for the delay; therefore, a prima facie case of discrimination was not established); *cf.* Chiang v. Schafer, 2008 WL 3925260 (D. V.I. Aug. 20, 2008) (practice of keeping waiting list of names of individuals interested in loan applications rather than physically distributing applications did not constitute national origin discrimination or improper denial of access to rural housing program administered by defendant; no direct evidence of discrimination or statistical evidence from which discrimination could be inferred).

23 Vander Missen v. Kellogg-Citizens Nat'l Bank, 481 F. Supp. 742 (E.D. Wis. 1979).

24 Official Interpretations of Reg. B [Official Staff Commentary on

For example, the Federal Reserve Board (FRB) gave approval to a California statute that requires creditors to provide Spanish-speaking applicants with the opportunity to obtain an unexecuted Spanish language contract.[25] The FRB reasoned that the statute made contract terms more understandable to applicants of one national origin without interfering with the interests of any other group and therefore did not frustrate the intent of the ECOA.[26]

5.3.2.2 The Fair Housing Act Standard

The Fair Housing Act (FHA) explicitly prohibits discrimination in advertising with respect to the sale or rental of a dwelling.[27] This prohibition applies to all written and oral notices or statements[28] and thus should apply to marketing discrimination. The FHA regulations give examples of discriminatory advertising, including selecting media or locations for advertising that deny housing information to prospective buyers on a prohibited basis.[29] There are also nonbinding HUD guidelines on nondiscriminatory advertising that are referenced in the FHA regulations.[30]

The FHA's advertising prohibitions are contained in section 3604 and apply specifically to the sale or rental of a dwelling.

The judicial trend is to find that section 3604 does not apply to home-secured loans when the borrower has already acquired the dwelling.[31] Thus these FHA advertising prohibitions will clearly cover discriminatory marketing of purchase money mortgages and rentals but will probably not apply to discriminatory marketing of home equity refinancings. However, these prohibitions and the examples of discriminatory advertising found in the FHA regulations and nonbinding HUD guidelines could serve as examples in making out a case of marketing discrimination under section 3605, which does apply to home equity refinancings.

Furthermore, the FHA regulations contain a separate set of prohibitions against discrimination in the marketing of loans in connection with residential real estate-related transactions. These regulations, which should apply to marketing of both purchase money mortgages and home equity refinancings, prohibit creditors from failing to provide information regarding the availability of loans because of a prohibited basis.[32] They also prohibit providing information that is different from that provided to others because of a prohibited basis.[33] These regulations are not limited to applicants but apply to a creditor's provision of information to any "persons."[34] Thus, they could be used to challenge certain types of advertising and marketing discrimination in the provision of housing-related credit.[35]

5.3.2.3 Other Guidance

An examination procedures guide from the Federal Financial Institutions Examination Council (FFIEC) describes the following scenarios as potential indicators of disparate treatment in marketing:[36]

- Advertising only in media serving non-minority areas of the lender's market;
- Marketing through brokers or other agents that the lender knows (or has reason to know) would serve only one racial or ethnic group in the market;
- Use of marketing programs or procedures for residential loan products that exclude one or more regions or geographies within the lender's assessment or marketing area

---

Reg. B], 12 C.F.R. pt. 1002 [pt. 202], Supp. I, § 1002.4(b)-2 [§ 202.4(b)-2].

25 Cal. Civ. Code § 1632 (West).

In 2003, this act was amended to extend its provisions to the languages of Chinese, Tagalog, Vietnamese, and Korean, as well as Spanish. The amendment became effective July 1, 2004. *See also* Cal. Civ. Code § 1632.5 (West).

Regulation B permits creditors to provide ECOA notices in a language other than English as long as it is available in English upon request. Reg. B, 12 C.F.R. § 1002.4(e) [§ 202.4(e)].

This provision was added as part of an interim final rule, issued March 30, 2001, concerning electronic disclosures. 66 Fed. Reg. 17,779 (Apr. 4, 2001); *see* § 10.6.2.1, *infra*.

26 Fed. Reserve Bd., Official Board Interpretation § 202.1102, 42 Fed. Reg. 22,861 (May 5, 1977).

This interpretation was not included in the 1985 official staff commentary to Regulation B. However, the Federal Reserve Board chose not to include in the official commentary any interpretation which did not preempt state law and so, presumably, the California statute remains acceptable. Moreover, section 202.1102 is an official board interpretation, not a staff interpretation, and should therefore not be superseded by staff commentary.

27 42 U.S.C. § 3604(c).

28 24 C.F.R. § 100.75(b).

29 24 C.F.R. § 100.75(c)(3).

30 These guidelines were formerly codified at 24 C.F.R. pt. 109, and the FHA regulations still cite them as such. 24 C.F.R. § 100.75(d).

However, the guidelines were removed from the *Code of Federal Regulations* as part of a regulatory streamlining in 1996. 61 Fed. Reg. 14,378 (Apr. 1, 1996).

The guidelines are available at 54 Fed. Reg. 3232, 3308–10 (Jan. 23, 1989). The guidelines provided further guidance and examples of potentially discriminatory advertising, including:

- Selective use of only certain media outlets, such as exclusively using English language media or non-minority media;
- Advertising only in certain geographic areas; and
- Selective use of human models in advertising.

54 Fed. Reg. at 3309–10.

31 *See* §§ 2.3.2, 2.3.3, *supra* (discussing scope of sections 3604 and 3605 of the FHA).

32 24 C.F.R. § 100.120(b).

33 *Id.*

34 *Id.*

35 *See, e.g.*, Jackson v. Novastar Mortgage, Inc., 2007 WL 4568976, at *8–9 (W.D. Tenn. Dec. 20, 2007) (refusing to dismiss the plaintiff's FHA section 3605 claim).

36 Fed. Financial Institutions Examination Council, Interagency Fair Lending Examination Procedures Guide 21 (1999), *available at* www.ffiec.gov/PDF/fairlend.pdf.

The FFIEC is a formal interagency body that prescribes uniform standards for the examination of financial institutions by the Federal Reserve Board, the Federal Deposit Insurance Corp., the National Credit Union Administration, the Office of the Comptroller of the Currency, and the Consumer Financial Protection Bureau. The FFIEC is also responsible for reporting HMDA data. *See* § 4.4.5.3, *supra*; § 12.2.5, *infra*.

that have significantly higher percentages of minority residents; and

- The proportion of applicants from protected class is significantly lower than that group's representation in the total population of the market area.

The FFEIC guidance also considers it an indication of disparate treatment if a lender has most of its branches in predominantly white neighborhoods, while the lender's subprime mortgage subsidiary has branches that are located primarily in predominantly minority neighborhoods.[37]

A self-assessment guide from the Federal Deposit Insurance Corp. (FDIC) on fair lending practices cautions lenders about the following marketing practices that may discourage applicants on a prohibited basis:

- Marketing strategies that fail to include contact with minority realtors and other realtors serving predominantly minority areas (the FDIC guide notes that, in those instances, there is almost always a low level of minority applicants); and
- Failing to advertise in media directed to minority areas or in media known to appeal to minorities, which can limit the ability of the institution to attract minority applicants.[38]

5.3.2.4 Marketing Discrimination As a Force in Predatory Lending

Many studies have shown that, from 1999 to 2009, subprime lenders provided the greater share of lending in non-white neighborhoods.[39] This pattern appeared to hold true even in middle-class and higher-income areas, indicating that the segmentation of the market into prime and subprime was correlated more strongly with race than with income.[40]

If the prime and subprime markets were segmented more by race than income, it means that many individuals who received subprime loans were actually qualified for prime loans.[41] This phenomenon raises questions as to why the prime and subprime markets were so strongly segmented by race and why such an inordinate number of applicants of color who potentially qualified for prime loans ended up with subprime loans.

One reason for this troubling dual market was the use of disparate and even discriminatory marketing practices by lenders. On the one hand, prime lenders focused their marketing efforts almost exclusively in white neighborhoods. These lenders located their branches in predominately white neighborhoods, making it convenient for white applicants to apply and obtain prime loans. They advertised only in mainstream media.

Their loan officers, who were mostly white, marketed loans almost exclusively to realtors serving white neighborhoods. Additionally, these lenders may have also offered better deals on the Internet, which has its own racial divide.[42]

On the other hand, subprime lenders focused their marketing efforts on communities of color.[43] These lenders placed their advertisements in media outlets that traditionally targeted African Americans and Hispanics, and they solicited business from mortgage brokers who served communities of color. They located their offices in these communities and often represented the sole option for borrowers, given the lack of bank branches in these neighborhoods.

In some instances, the subprime lender was actually a subsidiary of, or otherwise related to, a prime lender. For example, Bank of America, a prime lender, owned Equicredit, a subprime lender. A credit discrimination lawsuit brought in Chicago alleged that Equicredit made loans almost exclusively in "minority areas" while Bank of America made loans in predominately white areas.[44] Another major financial institution with subprime subsidiaries was Citigroup, which acquired subprime lender Associates National Bank in November 2000. Community groups objected to the acquisition for a number of reasons, including the fact that Citigroup's prime lending unit primarily made loans in white neighborhoods, while Associates' subprime and often predatory loans were made in neighborhoods of color.[45]

The official interpretations implicitly recognize that targeting "minority applicants" for subprime loans while marketing prime products to white applicants may be discrimination in violation of the ECOA.[46] Targeted marketing to protected

---

37 Fed. Financial Institutions Examination Council, Interagency Fair Lending Examination Procedures Guide 21 (1999), *available at* www.ffiec.gov/PDF/fairlend.pdf *and on the companion website to this treatise.*

38 Fed. Deposit Ins. Corp., Side-by-Side, A Guide to Fair Lending 28 (June 1996), *available at* www.fdic.gov/regulations/resources/side.

39 *See* § 8.4, *infra* (and studies cited therein).

40 *Id.*

41 *See Id.*

42 *See* § 3.7.2, *supra* (discussing credit discrimination and the digital divide).

43 For an interesting analysis of why individuals of color are targeted for predatory loans, see Cecil J. Hunt, *In the Racial Cross-Hairs: Reconsidering Racially Targeted Predatory Lending Under a New Theory of Economic Hate Crime*, 35 U. Tol. L. Rev. 211 (2003) (positing that people of color, and especially African Americans, are targeted on the basis of race as a proxy for market weakness and exploitability, which the author terms "economic racial profiling"). *See also* Creola Johnson, *The Magic of Group Identity: How Predatory Lenders Use Minorities to Target Communities of Color*, 17 Geo. J. on Poverty L. & Pol'y 165 (Spring 2009).

44 Johnson v. Equicredit Corp., 2002 U.S. Dist. LEXIS 4817 (N.D. Ill. Mar. 22, 2002).

45 *See, e.g.*, Letter from Malcolm Bush, President, Woodstock Institute, to the Office of the Comptroller of Currency (Oct. 2, 2000) (regarding Citigroup/Associates Merger), *available at* www.woodstockinst.org; *Hearing Before the New York Banking Comm'n* (Nov. 10, 2000) (statement of Alan Fisher, California Reinvestment Coalition), *available at* www.calreinvest.org; *see also* Lew Sichelman, *Community Groups Claim CitiFinancial Still Predatory*, Am. Banker, Jan. 2002, at 25 (noting that prime loans are still only available through Citibank, while CitiFinancial subsidiary—formerly Associates—offers only subprime loans).

46 Official Interpretations of Reg. B [Official Staff Commentary on Reg. B], 12 C.F.R. pt. 1002 [pt. 202], Supp. I, § 1002.5(a)-2(1)(A) [§ 202.5(a)-2(1)(A)] (disparate treatment includes "provid[ing] information only on 'subprime' and similar products to minority applicants who request information about the creditor's credit mortgage products, but provid[ing] information on a wider variety of mortgage products to similarly situated non-minority applicants";

classes may not only be discriminatory but may also violate unfair and deceptive practices and other consumer protection laws. For example, in 2005, the Illinois Attorney General sued two Florida-based credit card companies for deceptively marketing credit cards to Hispanic consumers in Illinois.[47] The companies ran advertisements claiming that they wanted to help fellow Hispanics. According to the complaint, contrary to representations, the companies actually charged consumers a high fee up front to obtain the card, and the cards could only be used to purchase merchandise from the company's catalogs and websites. The Federal Trade Commission (FTC) also filed a suit against these companies in 2004. A final judgment and order in the FTC case was entered in October 2005.[48]

5.3.2.5 How Discrimination in Marketing Happens

A good example of how the dual market for credit develops can be found by contrasting the cases of two lenders in the Washington, D.C., area: Chevy Chase Federal Savings Bank and Capital City Mortgage Corp. Chevy Chase, a metropolitan District of Columbia bank, and its subsidiary, B.F. Saul Mortgage, Co., were sued by the United States Department of Justice (DOJ) for engaging in a pattern of encouraging white and discouraging African-American mortgage applicants.[49] According to the DOJ, Chevy Chase located nearly 95% of its bank branches and mortgage offices in white neighborhoods, excluding the vast majority of the predominately African-American population in the D.C. area. Nearly 98% of the loan officers/originators hired by the mortgage company were not African American, despite the fact that over 65% of the city's population is African American. These loan officers actively solicited real estate brokers serving white neighborhoods but rarely solicited brokers serving African-American neighborhoods. Chevy Chase also did not advertise in African-American media outlets.[50]

As a result of the bank's practices, about 95% of its mortgage applicants in 1993 came from white neighborhoods and only 5% came from African-American neighborhoods. Of the mortgages granted by the bank and its mortgage subsidiary, 95% were secured by properties located in majority white neighborhoods while only 5% were secured by property located in predominantly African-American neighborhoods.[51]

Contrast Chevy Chase's marketing practices with those of Capital City Mortgage Corp. Capital City is a subprime lender also located in the metropolitan Washington, D.C., area that was sued by both the FTC[52] and private parties for engaging in reverse redlining.[53]

Unlike Chevy Chase Bank, Capital City made every effort to reach out to African Americans in the District of Columbia. It located its offices in African-American neighborhoods.[54] It distributed flyers and advertisements to the African-American community.[55] Capital City courted and solicited brokers who worked predominately in the African-American community.[56] Capital City's office even prominently displayed a portrait of its president standing next to the Reverend Jesse Jackson and former mayor of Washington, D.C., Marion Barry.[57]

As a result of Capital City's practices, about 95% of the mortgages it made in the District of Columbia were secured by properties located in African-American neighborhoods, as were

---

however, the example is limited to applicants who have actively requested information about mortgage products and does not cover marketing discrimination).

47 *See* Press Release, Office of the Illinois Att'y Gen. (Jan. 13, 2005).

48 Fed. Trade Comm'n v. Call Ctr. Express Corp., No. 04-22289 (S.D. Fla.), *available at* www.ftc.gov/os/caselist/0423117/051025final 0423117.pdf.

49 *See* Consent Decree, United States v. Chevy Chase Fed. Sav. Bank, No. 94-1824-J6 (D.D.C. 1994), *available on the companion website to this treatise.*

Some commentators have been critical of the DOJ's actions against Chevy Chase and other banks allegedly engaged in marketing discrimination. In the view of these commentators, marketing discrimination is not actionable under the ECOA and Fair Housing Act because there is no individual applicant who has been discriminated against. *See* John Spina, *U.S. v. Albank, FSB: Is 'Justice' Served in the Enforcement of Fair Lending Laws,* 2 N.C. Banking Inst. 207 (1998); Michael B. Mierzewski & Richard L. Jacobs, *What Hath Justice Department Wrought* 8, Banking Pol'y Rep. (Feb. 6, 1995).

50 Consent Decree, United States v. Chevy Chase Fed. Sav. Bank, No. 94-1824-J6 (D.D.C. 1994), *available on the companion website to this treatise.*

51 *Id.*

A few years earlier, the Department of Justice had alleged that the Decatur Savings Federal Savings and Loan Association engaged in similar conduct that had the effect of discouraging applications from African Americans in the Atlanta, Georgia, area. The case resulted in a consent decree providing for broad affirmative relief that included opening more branches in African-American neighborhoods, establishing greater safeguards with respect to the treatment of applications from African Americans and close monitoring of compliance with the plan. Decatur also agreed to place $1,000,000 in a fund for those aggrieved by its prior actions. *See* Consent Decree, United States v. Decatur Fed. Sav. & Loan Ass'n (N.D. Ga. 1992), *available on the companion website to this treatise.*

The DOJ has brought similar cases more recently against Old Kent Financial Corp. and Mid America Bank. *See* United States v. Old Kent Financial Corp., 2004 WL 1157779 (E.D. Mich. May 29, 2004); Complaint and Consent Order, United States v. Mid America Bank, No. 02C 9458 (N.D. Ill. complaint and consent order filed Dec. 20, 2002), *available at* www.usdoj.gov *and on the companion website to this treatise.*

52 Fed. Trade Comm'n v. Capital City Mortgage Corp., 1998 U.S. Dist. LEXIS 22115 (D.D.C. July 13, 1998).

53 Hargraves v. Capital City Mortgage Corp., 140 F. Supp. 2d 7 (D.D.C. 2000).

The Department of Justice filed an amicus brief in this case supporting the private plaintiffs. Brief of the United States as Amicus Curiae in Support of Plaintiffs' Opposition to Defendants' Motion for Judgment on the Pleadings, or, In the Alternative, For Summary Judgment, Hargraves v. Capital City Mortgage Corp., No. 98-1021, 140 F. Supp. 2d 7 (D.D.C. 2000), *available on the companion website to this treatise.*

54 Hargraves v. Capital City Mortgage Corp., 140 F. Supp. 2d 21 (D.D.C. 2000).

55 *Id.*

56 *Id.*

57 *Id.*

74% of its mortgages in Prince George's County.[58] In another "reverse redlining" case, a court denied the defendants' motion to dismiss, finding that the plaintiffs sufficiently alleged specific conduct which, if proven, could support an inference of intentional discrimination based on race. The case involved, *inter alia*, allegations that defendants, as part of a carefully orchestrated subprime mortgage and property sales scheme, used advertising featuring minority consumers, placed advertisements in community newspapers that served the West Indian immigrant community but did not advertise in that same newspaper chain's publications that served primarily white neighborhoods, and used "race-conscious outreach strategies," such as pairing individuals with an African-American salesperson who assured plaintiffs that he "takes care of his own."[59]

5.3.2.6 Market Segmentation and Pre-Screened Marketing

Another form of potential marketing discrimination occurs when lenders use direct marketing to send solicitations, including pre-approved credit offers, to potential applicants. Lenders, like many other businesses, will pre-screen potential applicants using sophisticated computer technology.[60] Often, the technology consists of enormous databases of computer information that is easily and cheaply analyzed and sorted, allowing lenders to "segment" their target population into ever smaller subsets of consumers.[61] Lenders have the added advantage of using the plethora of information available from credit reporting agencies to conduct this pre-screening.[62]

This pre-screening often segments the target audience by factors such as geography, demographics (including age and sex), and income—the very factors that are either prohibited bases or proxies for prohibited bases.[63] Despite these concerns and the mounting evidence discussed above that lenders regularly engage in marketing discrimination, the 1999 proposed revisions to Regulation B did not extend the ECOA to cover pre-screened credit offers.[64] However, changes were adopted requiring creditors to retain records for certain pre-screened credit solicitations.[65]

The Federal Financial Institutions Examination Council (FFIEC) takes the position that discrimination in pre-screened solicitations does not violate ECOA but does violate the Fair Housing Act.[66] It provides the following practices as examples of discrimination in pre-screening:[67]

- Explicitly excluding groups of prospective borrowers on a prohibited basis; and
- Excluding geographies (for example, census tracts, zip codes, and so forth) within the institution's marketing area that have significantly higher percentages of minority group residents than does the remainder of the marketing area.

---

58 Brief of the United States as Amicus Curiae in Support of Plaintiffs' Opposition to Defendants' Motion for Judgment on the Pleadings, or, In the Alternative, For Summary Judgment, Hargraves v. Capital City Mortgage Corp., No. 98-1021, 140 F. Supp. 2d 7 (D.D.C. 2000), *available on the companion website to this treatise.*

59 Barkley v. Olympia Mortgage Co., 2007 WL 2437810 (E.D.N.Y. Aug. 22, 2007). *But see* M&T Mortgage Corp. v. White, 736 F. Supp. 2d 538 (E.D.N.Y 2010) (employing African-American agents whose stated "personal mission" was to help minorities achieve the dream of home ownership could show some degree of intentional targeting, but selling real estate primarily to minorities does not indicate as a matter of law that plaintiffs were intentionally targeted due to their race; denying summary judgment on FHA and ECOA claims, as issues of targeting and discrimination were for a factfinder to determine); Steed v. EverHome Mortgage Co., 308 Fed. Appx. 364 (11th Cir. 2009) (agreeing with Hargraves court's approach to analyzing reverse redlining cases, but finding no prima facie case when plaintiff failed to provide evidence of where defendant advertised or whether defendant had made an unusual number of loans in minority areas or targeted debtors for foreclosure); Grimes v. Fremont Gen. Corp., 785 F. Supp. 2d 269, 292 (S.D.N.Y. 2011) (no reverse redlining claim when plaintiffs asserted that lender targeted African Americans yet provided no facts indicating how such targeting was conducted "in contrast to properly-pled reverse redlining claims, where the complaint contained detailed allegations of targeting by advertising and minority-focused outreach" (citing Barkley v. Olympia Mortgage Co., 2007 WL 2437810, at *12 (E.D.N.Y. Aug. 22, 2007)); plaintiffs' allegations of disparate treatment were also "very generalized, as they fail to plead that any specific similarly-situated non-African-American applicant received a better loan"); Williams v. 2000 Homes, Inc., 2009 WL 2252528 (E.D.N.Y. July 29, 2008) (no reverse redlining when plaintiff failed to make claim that he was treated differently from similarly situated individuals and allegations were conclusory).

60 *See generally* Timothy C. Lambert, *Fair Marketing: Challenging Pre-Application Lending Practices*, 87 Geo. L.J. 2181 (1999).

61 Timothy C. Lambert, *Fair Marketing: Challenging Pre-Application Lending Practices*, 87 Geo. L.J. 2181 (1999)*; see also* Benjamin Howell, Comment, *Exploiting Race and Space: Concentrated Subprime Lending As Housing Discrimination,* 94 Cal. L. Rev. 101 (2006).

62 *See* National Consumer Law Center, Fair Credit Reporting (7th ed. 2010 and Supp.).

63 *See generally* Timothy C. Lambert, *Fair Marketing: Challenging Pre-Application Lending Practices*, 87 Geo. L.J. 2181 (1999).

Such segmentation is made possible in part by information brokers who offer databases that allow businesses to sort households by race and ethnicity. *Weblining: Companies Are Using Your Personal Data to Limit Your Choices and Force You to Pay More for Products*, BusinessWeek Online, Apr. 3, 2000, www.businessweek.com (describing an information broker company that offers the "InfoBase Ethnicity System").

64 64 Fed. Reg. 44,582, 44,584–44,585 (Aug. 16, 1999).

65 Reg. B, 12 C.F.R. § 1002.12(b)(7) [§ 202.12(b)(7)].

Creditors are required to retain the text of solicitations, the selection criteria for recipients, and any consumer complaints concerning those pre-screened solicitations defined as "firm offers of credit" under the Fair Credit Reporting Act, 15 U.S.C. § 1681a(1). *See* § 10.12.1, *infra.*

66 Fed. Financial Institutions Examination Council, Interagency Fair Lending Examination Procedures Guide 21 (1999), *available at* www.ffiec.gov/PDF/fairlend.pdf *and on the companion website to this treatise.*

67 *Id.*

5.3.3 Discrimination in Treatment of Prospective Applicants

5.3.3.1 Steering

Even if an applicant from a protected group can get past the marketing discrimination and through the creditor's door, pre-application discrimination may still take place in the creditor's office. One means of discouraging applicants on a prohibited basis is a practice called "steering." Steering occurs when a loan officer refers prospective applicants away from one type of product or market (for example, a prime product) to another (for example, a subprime product).[68]

The official interpretation prohibits one form of steering: a creditor engages in unlawful disparate treatment if it provides information only on subprime mortgage products to minority applicants but provides information on a wider variety of mortgage products to similarly situated non-minority applicants.[69] An FFIEC guidance document suggests that steering on a prohibited basis violates Regulation B and that indicators of discriminatory steering include the following scenarios:[70]

- If a lender has a subprime mortgage subsidiary, any significant differences, by loan product, in the percentage of applicants from a protected group for the lender versus the subprime subsidiary;
- Lack of clear objective standards for (1) referring applicants to subsidiaries or affiliates, (2) classifying applicants as "prime" or "subprime" borrowers, or (3) deciding what kinds of alternative loan products should be offered or recommended to applicants;
- For a lender that makes both prime and subprime loans for

the same purpose, difference in the percentage of applicants from a protected group in each of the alternative loan product categories; or
- A lender with a subprime subsidiary integrates its loan application processing for both entities, such that steering between the prime and subprime products can occur almost seamlessly (that is, a single loan processor could simultaneously attempt to qualify any applicant to the bank or the mortgage company under either the bank's prime criteria or the mortgage company's subprime criteria).

Steering sometimes occurs when lenders offer government-backed mortgages as well as conventional mortgages. The FFIEC guidance addresses steering of minorities to government-backed mortgages, as indicated by the following scenarios:[71]

- For a lender that makes both conventional and FHA mortgages, any significant differences in the percentages of prohibited-basis-group applicants in each of these two loan products, particularly with respect to loan amounts of $100,000 or more;
- Loan officers having broad discretion regarding whether to promote conventional or FHA loans or both to applicants, and the lender has not issued guidelines regarding the exercise of this discretion.

5.3.3.2 Testing

Sometimes, differential encouragement at the pre-application stage can be very subtle and may be discovered only through the use of paired testers. Some of the variables to examine in pre-application testing include: consistency in the lender's requests for information from each tester; the lender's community image as presented through brochures or instructional literature; any discriminatory emphasis on qualification standards; differences in interest rates or loan terms; general attitude of the lender toward the tester; response of the lender to past credit problems of testers; and differences in information on the variety of mortgage programs.[72]

A number of studies involving paired testers have shown subtle and not so subtle discrimination by loan officers and employees of mortgage lenders.[73] The Department of Housing and Urban Development (HUD) contracted with the Urban Institute to more rigorously assess the effectiveness of paired testing for determining whether African-American and Hispanic homebuyers receive the same treatment and information as prospective white homebuyers at the pre-application phase

---

68   *Id.*; *see, e.g.*, Johnson v. Equicredit Corp., 2002 U.S. Dist. LEXIS 4817 (N.D. Ill. Mar. 22, 2002) (allegations of steering against Bank of America, a prime lender, which owns Equicredit, a subprime lender); *In re* Wells Fargo & Co. and Wells Fargo Financial, Nos. 11-094-BHC1, 11-094-I-HC1, 11-094-B-HC2, 11-094-I-HC2, *available at* www.federalreserve.gov/newsevents/press/enforcement/2011enforcement.htm (Federal Reserve Board issues consent cease and desist order and $85 million dollar penalty against Wells Fargo & Company and its subsidiary, Wells Fargo Financial, to resolve allegations of steering). *But see* Cabrera v. Countrywide Financial, 2012 WL 5372116 (N.D. Cal. Oct. 30, 2012) (no ECOA claim when plaintiffs argued that a similarly situated white borrower would have received a more favorable loan than plaintiffs did because they were Hispanic; statistical evidence showing that Hispanics were given worse loans than white borrowers with the same borrower risk, and that Hispanic borrowers, otherwise qualified for prime loans, were steered into subprime loans at rates between 2.6 and 3.5 times higher than similarly situated white borrowers, was insufficient to support claim when plaintiffs failed to allege that they themselves were qualified for a prime loan or better loan terms than the ones they received).

69   Official Interpretations of Reg. B [Official Staff Commentary on Reg. B], 12 C.F.R. pt. 1002 [pt. 202], Supp. I, § 1002.4(a)-2(i)(A) [§ 202.4(a)-2(i)(A)].

70   Fed. Financial Institutions Examination Council, Interagency Fair Lending Examination Procedures Guide 21 (1999), *available at* www.ffiec.gov/PDF/fairlend/pdf *and on the companion website to this treatise.*

71   *Id.*

72   *See* Stella J. Adams, John Marshall Law School, Testing and Investigating for Fair Housing Violations: Designing an Appropriate Test in Lending and Predatory Practices Cases (Apr. 12, 2002) (available from the John Marshall Law School); *see also* P. Rivka Schochet, *A Case Study of Paired Testing: Documenting Differences Contributes to a $725,000 Consent Decree*, 41 Urb. Law. 293 (2009) (discussing paired testing practices in FHA case involving discrimination in the rental of apartments).

73   *See* § 4.4.4, *supra.*

of the mortgage lending process.[74] The testers in the study consisted of one white and one non-white individual posing as homebuyers to inquire about the availability and terms for home mortgage loans. The two members of the tester team presented themselves as equally qualified borrowers in every respect except their race or ethnicity. The HUD study consisted of a pre-test and a pilot stage. The agency focused on collecting data from mortgage lenders but indicated that future studies should explore other information sources, particularly mortgage brokers and real estate agents.

HUD's pre-test study found that one of the most serious forms of discrimination to be discerned by paired testing at the pre-application stage is in the differing estimates of home price and total loan amount.[75] According to the report, these estimates can be critical in determining where people search for housing and whether they decide they can afford to become homebuyers. The agencies noted the complexity of this type of testing, demanding more from both testers and testing organizations than routine rental testing. They concluded that not all fair housing organizations necessarily have the capacity to effectively conduct these tests.

The agencies also conducted pilot tests, finding that, in both Los Angeles and Chicago, African-American and Hispanic homebuyers face a significant risk of receiving less favorable treatment than their white counterparts when visiting mortgage lending institutions to inquire about financing options.[76] The unequal treatment took different forms. In Los Angeles, African Americans were offered less coaching than comparable white homebuyers and were more likely to be encouraged to consider an FHA loan. Hispanics were denied basic information about loan amount and house prices, informed about fewer products, and given less follow-up compared to white homebuyers. In Chicago, African Americans were denied basic information about loan amount and house prices, informed about fewer products, offered less coaching, and given less follow-up. Hispanics were quoted lower loan amounts or house prices, informed about fewer products, and offered less coaching.[77]

In addition, HUD has found that Asian and Pacific Islander homebuyers experience consistent adverse treatment 20.4% of the time, with systematic discrimination occurring in housing availability, inspections, financing assistance, and agent encouragement.[78] This level of discrimination is comparable to the level experienced by African-American homebuyers in similar HUD studies and significantly higher than the level of discrimination against Hispanics.

A series of studies conducted by the National Fair Housing Alliance also used paired testers to show significant differences in treatment at the pre-application stage.[79] These studies matched white and minority testers, giving them similar debt-to-income ratios.[80] The testers posed as prospective mortgage applicants seeking information about the types and terms of mortgage loans for which they might qualify. The studies found that:

- Minority testers were more likely to be denied the opportunity to speak with a loan officer at the pre-application stage;
- Even when they were able to meet with a loan officer, minority testers were more likely to be denied basic information, such as what types of loans they would qualify for;
- Lenders spent longer amounts of time with white testers than with their minority counterparts;
- Lenders provided more information to white testers, including a greater number of quotes on loan products; and
- Minority testers were more likely to be quoted a higher interest rate than their white counterparts.

An earlier study by the same organization found that lender employees actively discouraged African-American testers who walked into their office.[81] Employees told African-American testers that the lender did not accept applications at that office and that they needed to go across town to the bank's mortgage lending division, while white applicants were told they were in the right place. African-American applicants were often told that the loan process was long and complicated and that all the paperwork must first be completed, while white borrowers were quickly told that they were likely to qualify even though a full application was not provided.

Another series of studies conducted by the Fort Worth Human Relations Commission uncovered evidence of pre-application discrimination with respect to pre-qualification or pre-approval quotes given by lenders.[82] African Americans and Hispanics who had similar financial profiles to their white counterparts received significantly lower quotes for pre-approval or pre-qualification. In one case, a white tester was qualified for a $70,000 loan on the same day that an African-American tester, who had more favorable finances, was quali-

---

74 Office of Policy Dev. & Research, United States Dep't of Hous. & Urban Dev., All Other Things Being Equal: A Paired Testing Study of Mortgage Lending Institutions, Final Report (Apr. 2002).

75 *Id.*

76 *Id.*

77 *Id.*

78 *See* Office of Policy Dev. & Research, United States Dep't of Hous. & Urban Dev., Discrimination in Metropolitan Housing Markets: Phase 2—Asians and Pacific Islanders (Mar. 2003).

79 Michelle DeLair & Robin Smith, *New Evidence from Lender Testing: Discrimination at the Pre-Application Stage, in* Urban Institute, Mortgage Lending Discrimination: A Review of Existing Evidence 23–41 (1999).

The Urban Institute report constitutes a re-analysis of raw data provided by the National Fair Housing Alliance.

80 *Id.* at 24.

81 Cathy Cloud & George Galster, *What Do We Know About Racial Discrimination in Mortgage Markets*, 22 Rev. of Black Pol. Econ. 101 (1993) (available as Clearinghouse No. 47,964).

82 *See* Michael Janofsky, *Texas Lenders Pledge $1.4 Billion in Housing Case*, The N.Y. Times, Mar. 10, 1998; *Fort Worth Human Relations Commission Study Leads to $1.375 Billion Fair Lending Settlement*, Nat'l Fair Hous. Advocate, Apr. 1998, at 1; *HUD Settles with Texas Mortgage Lender Charged with Fair Housing Act Violations*, 70 Banking Rep. (BNA) 688 (Apr. 27, 1998).

These studies prompted the Department of Housing and Urban Development to take action against five lenders, resulting in settlements providing $3.5 billion in loan commitments for African-American and Hispanic borrowers.

fied for only $55,000.[83] At another bank, a white tester was told he would qualify for a loan of $158,000 while an African-American tester was told that he would qualify for a loan of only $100,000, even though the latter had a slightly higher income, a higher down payment, more savings, and less debt.[84]

5.4 Application Procedures

5.4.1 General

The next stage of the credit transaction involves the procedures for application for credit.[85] In general, under the ECOA, there can be no differences in the application procedures if those differences are on a prohibited basis.[86] The Fair Housing Act's general rule against discrimination also prohibits such discrimination in housing financing.

Discrimination in the application process may involve requesting more or different types of information from or about protected class applicants, providing disparate levels of assistance, or using different investigation methods. This section also focuses on issues concerning oral applications.

The next few sections discuss special ECOA rules concerning the application process, including prohibited requests for information about protected class characteristics, whether spouses or others must act as co-signers to a loan, and under what name the consumer may request a credit account.

5.4.2 Oral Applications for Credit

5.4.2.1 General

A caveat exists regarding the application process in that Regulation B permits creditors to take either oral or written applications for credit. However, applications must be in writing when credit is used to purchase or refinance the applicant's principal residence and when the residence is taken as security for the loan.[87] Thus, except for home mortgage applications, creditors may base their credit decisions on information taken orally from applicants and on notations of conversations.

This provision is both a help and a hindrance to applicants. On the one hand, it brings a great deal of creditor activity within the scope of the statute. For example, the protective provisions can be triggered by a mere conversation between a prospective applicant and a creditor's employee if credit is extended or denied on the basis of that conversation. On the other hand, the lack of a written application requirement increases the risk of arbitrary and evasive action by creditors and makes an ECOA plaintiff's burden of proof more difficult. Often the only written record of the transaction is the employee's own memorandum documenting the conversation. However, when a creditor conducts the application process orally, it must still maintain written records of the process and its reasons for taking a particular action on the application.[88]

5.4.2.2 The Home Mortgage Exception

Applications must be in writing when credit is used to purchase or refinance the applicant's principal residence and when the residence is taken as security for the loan.[89] This requirement assists federal supervisory agencies in their enforcement of the ECOA and the Fair Housing Act.[90]

The creditor need not use a preprinted form, and it is sufficient for the creditor just to write down the information that it normally considers in making a credit decision. The creditor may complete the application for the applicant and need not ask for a signature from the applicant.[91] This process can even be done over the telephone.[92] The written application requirement is also satisfied if the information is entered directly into and retained by a computerized system.[93]

5.4.3 Providing Disparate Levels of Assistance in the Application Process

Most credit discrimination appears to occur in the context of applicants who are marginally qualified. That is, applicants who are clearly qualified or clearly unqualified are treated in the same manner no matter what their race or other characteristics. But a majority of applicants—one study estimates perhaps as many as 80%—have some blemish on their application, and the question is whether creditors differentiate on the basis of race or some other prohibited characteristic among this group.[94] If an individual is denied credit, the creditor can point to the blemish as the basis for the denial. Similarly, it may be difficult to establish a case of discriminatory discouragement when an applicant is known to be experiencing financial difficulties.[95]

83 Michael Janofsky, *Texas Lenders Pledge $1.4 Billion in Housing Case*, The N.Y. Times, Mar. 10, 1998.

84 *HUD Settles With Texas Mortgage Lender Charged With Fair Housing Act Violations*, 70 Banking Rep. (BNA) 688 (Apr. 27, 1998).

85 *See* § 2.2.4.3, *supra* (discussing what constitutes an "application" for credit).

86 Official Interpretations of Reg. B [Official Staff Commentary on Reg. B], 12 C.F.R. pt. 1002 [pt. 202], Supp. I, § 1002.4-1 [§ 202.4-1].

87 Reg. B, 12 C.F.R. § 1002.4(c) [§ 202.4(c)].
Information entered directly into and retained by a computerized system qualifies as a written application. Official Interpretations of Reg. B [Official Staff Commentary on Reg. B], 12 C.F.R. pt. 1002 [pt. 202], Supp. I, § 1002.4(c)-3 [§ 202.4(c)-3]; *see* §§ 5.4.2.2, 10.5, *infra*.

88 Reg. B, 12 C.F.R. § 1002.12(b) [§ 202.12(b)]; *see* § 10.12, *infra* (discussing record retention requirements).

89 Reg. B, 12 C.F.R. § 1002.4(c) [§ 202.4(c)].

90 Official Interpretations of Reg. B [Official Staff Commentary on Reg. B], 12 C.F.R. pt. 1002 [pt. 202], Supp. I, § 1002.4(c)-1 [§ 202.4(c)-1].

91 *Id.*

92 *Id.* § 1002.4(c)-2 [§ 202.4(c)-2].

93 *Id.* § 1002.4(c)-3 [§ 202.4(c)-3].

94 Lynn Z. Browne, James McEneaney, Alicia Munnell, & Geoffrey M.B. Tootell, *Mortgage Lending in Boston: Interpreting HMDA Data*, 86 Am. Econ. Rev. 25 (1996), *also available at* www.bos.frb.org/economic/wp/wp1992/wp92_7.pdf.

95 De Jesus-Serrano v. Sana Inv. Mortgage Bankers, Inc., 552 F. Supp. 2d 196 (D. P.R. 2007) (no ECOA claim when alleged "derogatory

Nevertheless, even if applicants have credit blemishes, illegal discrimination occurs if, for example, creditors work more with white applicants with credit blemishes to qualify them for a loan than they do with similarly situated African-American applicants. It is discriminatory to facilitate the application process for certain applicants but to place roadblocks before other applicants when the difference in treatment is based on the applicant's race or some other prohibited basis. For example, a marginal white applicant might be coached on how to make the grade, while an applicant of color—though treated quite nicely—may not receive such coaching.

One study using paired testers found subtle distinctions between how marginally qualified white and African-American applicants were treated.[96] White applicants were more likely to be provided helpful hints and secrets that are often critical to the success of marginally qualified applicants. African Americans might be told the rules but not the exceptions.

For example, both white and African-American applicants were told that a 10% down payment would require the applicant to keep six monthly payments in escrow. But only whites might be told that, if an 11% down payment was made, the escrow would be reduced to only two months' payments. Similarly, only white applicants might be told that they could improve their chances by obtaining gift letters from relatives or by applying on payday, when they would have the most money in the bank.

Related conduct has sometimes been described as the "fat file" phenomenon. White applicants are provided the opportunity to explain credit blemishes and document the applicant's suitability while loan officers do not provide African-American applicants with the same opportunity. Studies have found that many applicants fail to meet minimum loan underwriting standards—such as those addressing loan amount to income or total outstanding debt to income—and still obtain credit. The issue is not whether an applicant meets the creditor's stated minimum standards but what additional information is placed in the file that allows for an exception. It should be illegal not to assist African Americans (or another protected class) to the same extent that the creditor assists white applicants in building the case for an exception to normal underwriting standards.

Raising the issue of disparate levels of assistance received by applicants of color is especially important given the predominant legal test, based on the Supreme Court's decision in *McDonnell Douglas Corp. v. Green*, for proving disparate treatment.[97] This test requires the plaintiff to show that the plaintiff was qualified for the credit for which he or she applied.[98] If in 80% of the cases the creditor can point to a blemish to argue that an applicant was not qualified for the credit, it is important to show that the disparate treatment lies in the preferential assistance received by Caucasian applicants with similarly blemished files.[99]

5.4.4 Requesting More Information About Applicants from Protected Groups

One type of discrimination in the application process involves how much and what types of information a creditor requires from an applicant. Requiring too much personal or hard to obtain information may discourage applicants from completing their applications. For instance, it may constitute discrimination when a lender delays the loan process by requesting additional financial information after the loan has already been initially approved for closing.[100] However, a stray question regarding the origin of an applicant's name falls short of evincing direct evidence of discrimination.[101] Regulation B specifically prohibits discrimination on a prohibited basis as to "information requirements."[102] Thus it would be discriminatory to require more information from public assistance recipients than from other applicants.[103] For example, the DOJ sued

---

96 Cathy Cloud & George Galster, *What Do We Know About Racial Discrimination in Mortgage Markets*, 22 Rev. of Black Political Econ. 101 (1993) (available as Clearinghouse No. 47,964).

97 411 U.S. 792, 93 S. Ct. 1817, 36 L. Ed. 2d 668 (1973).

98 *See* § 4.2.3.1, *supra*.

99 *See, e.g.*, Cooley v. Sterling Bank, 280 F. Supp. 2d 1331 (M.D. Ala. 2003) (bank's denial of unsecured line of credit to African-American applicant held not discriminatory because applicant had a high debt-to-income ratio; finding no discrimination despite the fact that bank had granted unsecured lines of credit to twenty white applicants and had not bothered to calculate debt-to-income ratios for nineteen of these applicants); *see also* Wise v. Vilsack, 2012 WL 5359504 (4th Cir. Nov. 1, 2012) (unpublished) (affirming lower court's decision finding no ECOA violation in case alleging that plaintiffs were "intentionally and unlawfully discouraged, delayed and denied" in their attempts to obtain a loan, since complaint revealed no colorable allegations supporting "similarly situated" prong of an ECOA claim).

100 Torgerson v. Wells Fargo Bank S.D., 2009 WL 255995 (D.S.D. Feb. 3, 2009) (genuine issue of material fact as to whether defendant improperly discriminated against Native American female with respect to race and gender when it requested additional financial information from her after indicating the loan was ready for closing).

101 *See* Four A's Inv. Co., L.L.C. v. Bank of America Corp., 2010 WL 2720713 (W.D. Mo. July 6, 2010) (only remark complained of was "stray" inquiry about name origin; summary judgment granted to defendant).

102 Regulation B, 12 C.F.R. § 1002.2(m) [§ 202.2(m)], defines information requirements as part of a credit transaction, and Regulation B, 12 C.F.R. § 1002.4(a) [§ 202.4(a)], prohibits discrimination concerning any aspect of a credit transaction.

103 *But see* Cartwright v. American Sav. & Loan Ass'n, 880 F.2d 912 (7th Cir. 1989) (mortgage lender did not violate ECOA by placing an application on indefinite hold after applicant agreed to lender's request that she provide information on comparable housing prices (which she referenced during a conversation with lender's vice

---

comment" that plaintiffs sell their properties and buy a "shack" was insufficient to demonstrate that they were discouraged from applying for a loan based on age discrimination, especially when plaintiffs had received five loans in previous years and were currently experiencing financial difficulties). *See also* Swanson v. Citi, 706 F. Supp. 2d 854 (N.D. Ill. 2009) (loan representative's statements that defendant's loan requirements were more stringent that those of other bank (which had previously denied plaintiffs a loan) did not demonstrate actionable discouragement), *rev'd in part on other grounds*, 614 F.3d 400 (7th Cir. 2010) (allowing FHA claims for discrimination regarding value of appraisal).

a mortgage lender under the FHA for allegedly demanding information from a disabled applicant about the details of her disability and her children's disabilities. The lender repeatedly demanded personal and intimate information that was allegedly unnecessary for the application process.[104]

However, suggesting that both a husband and wife be present during the loan application process, when both spouses were intended applicants, did not necessarily constitute discriminatory discouragement under the ECOA, especially when one spouse was ultimately permitted to proceed with the application process without the other.[105] And it is not necessarily discriminatory to require an applicant to submit additional pay stubs and other proof of employment when inconsistencies exist as to net pay between paychecks and a lender harbors a reasonable concern that the applicant's income will not be sufficient to satisfy loan payments.[106]

Regulation B also prohibits engaging in different investigatory procedures on a prohibited basis. The regulation specifically prohibits discrimination on a prohibited basis as to "investigation procedures."[107] Thus creditors may not order credit reports exclusively on the spouses of married women who apply for individual accounts while simultaneously refraining from ordering such reports on the spouses of married male applicants for individual accounts,[108] as this practice impermissibly takes into account sex and marital status in a method of evaluating credit applications.

Similarly, creditors may not discriminate as to the information they actually review. When a couple applies for a joint account, it would be discriminatory to solely or primarily consider the husband's credit report without considering the wife's credit record.[109]

5.5 Prohibited Requests for Information

5.5.1 General Considerations

5.5.1.1 Introduction

There are a number of special ECOA requirements and prohibitions concerning requests for information, especially information relevant to the prohibited bases. These requirements specify that various types of information may not be requested or may be requested only in certain situations.

Aside from the specified ECOA requirements and prohibitions, the ECOA states that "a creditor may request any information in connection with a credit transaction."[110] Yet, even if a request for information is not specifically covered by the ECOA or Regulation B, advocates should analyze whether it discourages applicants on a prohibited basis. Furthermore, such a request may be prohibited by some other federal or state law regarding privacy, privileged information, credit reporting limitations, or similar restrictions.[111]

5.5.1.2 ECOA Restricts Creditor from "Requesting" Information About an "Applicant"

An important aspect of the general rule regarding prohibited requests for information is the definition of the term "applicant" because the prohibitions only cover those information requests made about "applicants."[112] Regulation B defines an applicant as including "any person who requests or who has received an extension of credit" and "any person who is or may become contractually liable regarding an extension of credit."[113] Regulation B defines "contractually liable" as being expressly obligated to repay all debts on an account pursuant to an agreement.[114]

One issue is whether guarantors, sureties, and others who are secondarily liable on an obligation are applicants and thus covered by this prohibition.[115] Regulation B includes guarantors, sureties, endorsers and similar parties as applicants "for purposes of section 202.7(d) 03 [dealing with spouses' signatures]."[116] One interpretation of this phrase is that guarantors and similar parties are *not* otherwise applicants.[117] Indeed, the case of *Moran Foods, Inc. v. Mid-Atlantic Market Development Co.*[118] has called into question the definition of "applicant" in

---

president) in a largely minority neighborhood—a burden generally borne by lenders).

104 Complaint and Consent Degree, United States v. Bank United (W.D.N.Y. 1999), *available at* www.usdoj.gov *and on the companion website to this treatise.*

105 Swanson v. Citi, 706 F. Supp. 2d 854 (N.D. Ill. 2009) (loan representative's statements that both wife and her husband should be present for application process did not demonstrate actionable discrimination), *rev'd in part on other grounds*, 614 F.3d 400 (7th Cir. 2010) (reversing dismissal of FHA race discrimination claim based upon bank's refusal to follow through with its announced plan to use federal money to make more loans and the loan representative's statements that he had a mixed-race family; allowing FHA claims for discrimination regarding value of appraisal).

106 Floyd-Keith v. Homecomings Financial, L.L.C., 2010 WL 3927596 (M.D. Ala. Sept. 17, 2010), *adopted by* 2010 WL 3943646 (M.D. Ala. Oct. 7, 2010).

107 Regulation B, 12 C.F.R. § 1002.2(m) [§ 202.2(m)], defines investigation procedures as part of a credit transaction, and Regulation B, 12 C.F.R. § 1002.4(a) [§ 202.4(a)], prohibits discrimination concerning any aspect of a credit transaction.

108 *In re* Alden's, Inc., 92 F.T.C. 901 (Fed. Trade Comm'n 1978); *see also* Shuman v. Standard Oil Co., 453 F. Supp. 1150 (N.D. Cal. 1978) (divorced woman's suit withstood a motion for partial summary judgment when she alleged that creditor had discriminated on basis of sex or marital status as revealed in a credit report).

109 Consent Order, United States v. John Wanamaker, Phila., Clearinghouse No. 44,328 (E.D. Pa. Apr. 14, 1989).

110 *See* Reg. B, 12 C.F.R. § 1002.5(a)(1) [§ 202.5(a)(1)].

111 Reg. B, 12 C.F.R. § 1002.5(a)(1) n.1 [§ 202.5(a)(1) n.1].

112 The term "applicant" is analyzed in detail in § 2.2.4, *supra*.

113 Reg. B, 12 C.F.R. § 1002.2(e) [§ 202.2(e)]; *see* § 2.2.4, *supra*.

114 Reg. B, 12 C.F.R. § 1002.2(i) [§ 202.2(i)].

115 *See* § 2.2.4.2, *supra* (and cases cited therein; analyzing issue of whether those secondarily liable are "applicants").

116 *See* Reg. B, 12 C.F.R. § 1002.2(e) [§ 202.2(e)].

117 In fact, until 1985, Regulation B explicitly excluded guarantors, sureties, and similar parties from the definition of applicant. Thus, the 1985 change can be seen as expanding the scope of the term applicant in this area solely for the purposes of section 202.7(d) [section 202.7(d)]. *See* § 2.2.4.2, *supra* (and cases cited therein).

118 476 F.3d 436 (7th Cir. 2007); *see also* Champion Bank v. Reg'l

Regulation B as including a guarantor, stating that embracing this definition "opens vistas of liability that the Congress that enacted the Act would have been unlikely to accept."[119] However, in the case of *Citgo Petroleum Corp. v. Bulk Petroleum Corp.,*[120] the court declined to follow *Moran Foods*, stating instead that it "adheres to Regulation B, such that guarantors who are required to sign a guaranty in connection with an extension of credit covered by the ECOA will continue to receive protection."[121]

On the other hand, guarantors, sureties, and similar parties would seem to fall within the definition of those "who may become contractually liable" on the obligation. It seems equally repugnant to the purposes of the ECOA to request racial, ethnic, religious, or similar information from a guarantor as from the applicant. Regardless of whether guarantors and sureties are covered by this prohibition, it seems clear that co-signers are applicants.

To be an applicant, one need not submit a full application to a creditor. Only a request for credit needs to be made, even if the request does not constitute an application according to the creditor's usual standards.[122] An "application" is a defined term under the ECOA, and certain ECOA provisions apply only if there is an application. But the definition of applicant does not require or even mention an application.[123]

5.5.1.3 Information Legally Obtained Sometimes May Not Be Utilized by Creditor

Regulation B's specific prohibitions on seeking information are constrained to "requests" for information or "inquiries" about an applicant.[124] Thus, the regulation only prohibits active steps by the creditor to obtain prohibited information about the applicant. The creditor may still *receive* information from the applicant, a reporting agency, or other source, as long as the creditor did not seek out the information.[125] If the creditor receives information concerning a prohibited basis, however, it still cannot use that information to discriminate against the applicant on a prohibited basis.[126] Thus, even if a creditor is permitted to obtain certain information, there may still be restrictions as to how that information may be used. Chapter 6, *infra*, details such restrictions.

5.5.1.4 Should Regulation B Permit or Require Creditors to Request Information About Prohibited Bases?

In 1999, the Federal Reserve Board proposed removing the prohibition on seeking information about an applicant's race, color, religion, national origin, and sex for non-mortgage credit products.[127] This change was made in response to comments from the Department of Justice and other federal financial enforcement agencies that the enhanced ability to obtain data on race and ethnicity would aid fair lending enforcement, particularly with respect to small business lending.[128]

The proposal to allow voluntary data collection was particularly controversial. According to the Federal Reserve Board, most banking organizations were against the change, arguing that it would increase their regulatory burden and would be an invasion of their customers' privacy. On the other side, most regulators, including the Departments of Justice and Housing and Urban Development, as well as consumer and small business advocates, supported the change. Many of these groups, however, argued that voluntary data collection should only be a temporary step and that, ultimately, this data collection must be mandatory in order to be effective.

It was ultimately decided not to remove the prohibition against seeking information about prohibited bases;[129] instead, a new exception was created for collection of this information for the purpose of conducting a self-test under section 1002.15 [section 202.15].[130] The stated rationale was that, because the existing prohibition restricted creditors' access to information about applicants' personal characteristics, retaining the prohibition was the best way to reduce or avoid discrimination.[131]

The rationale for prohibiting collection of information regarding prohibited bases seems limited in its utility, especially

---

Dev., L.L.C., 2009 WL 1351122 (E.D. Mo. May 13, 2009) (finding reasoning of *Moran Foods* to be persuasive and holding that spouse cannot show discrimination because she chose to guarantee her husband's business loan).

119 Moran Foods, Inc. v. Mid-Atlantic Mkt. Dev. Co., 476 F.3d 436 (7th Cir. 2007).

120 2010 WL 3931496 (N.D. Okla. Oct. 5, 2010); *see also* LOL Finance Co. v. F.J. Faison, Jr. Revocable Trust, 2010 WL 3118630 (D. Minn. July 13, 2010) (stating that the court was "wary of categorically discounting the Federal Reserve Board's regulations"), *adopted by* 2010 WL 3118583 (D. Minn. Aug. 4, 2010).

121 2010 WL 3931496, at *9. The *Citgo* court also went so far as to say that the holding in *Moran Foods* "eliminated entire aspects of the Federal Reserve Board's implementation scheme" and that the court would continue to extend the ECOA's protections "to guarantors such as [the wife-signator]" unless and until the Tenth Circuit mandated that the definitions and scheme in Regulation B ran contrary to Congressional intent. *Id.*

122 Cragin v. First Fed. Sav. & Loan Ass'n, 498 F. Supp. 379 (D. Nev. 1980). *But see* Chizh v. Polish & Slavic Fed. Credit Union, 2011 WL 2680495 (E.D.N.Y. July 8, 2011) (plaintiff, who submitted an application for membership in a credit union that provided the right to open a deposit account, was not an "applicant" for "credit"; application does not constitute an "aspect of a credit transaction" under the ECOA).

123 *See* § 2.2.4, *supra*.

124 Reg. B, 12 C.F.R. §§ 1002.5, 1002.12(a) [§§ 202.5, 202.12(a)].

---

125 Reg. B, 12 C.F.R. § 1002.12(a) [§ 202.12(a)]; Official Interpretations of Reg. B [Official Staff Commentary on Reg. B], 12 C.F.R. pt. 1002 [pt. 202], Supp. I, § 1002.12(a)-1 [§ 202.12(a)-1].

126 Reg. B, 12 C.F.R. § 1002.6(a) [§ 202.6(a)]; *see also* 15 U.S.C. § 1691(a)(1); Reg. B, 12 C.F.R. §§ 1002.4(a), 1002.6(b)(9) [§§ 202.4(a), 202.6(b)(9)].

127 64 Fed. Reg. 44,582, 44,596 (Aug. 16, 1999) (amending 12 C.F.R. § 202.5 [§ 1002.5]).

128 64 Fed. Reg. 44,582, 44,586 (Aug. 16, 1999).

129 68 Fed. Reg. 13,144, 13,147 (Mar. 18, 2003).

130 *Id.* The new exception is codified at section 1002.5(b)(1) [section 202.5(b)(1)] and is discussed in further detail in § 5.5.3.5, *infra*.

131 68 Fed. Reg. 13,144, 13,148 (Mar. 18, 2003).

for race, national origin, and gender.[132] For example, this prohibition would not in many instances protect against discrimination when applicants apply for credit in person or even sometimes over the telephone, because the creditor often will be able to discern race or national origin.[133] The prohibition will also be limited in its effectiveness in preventing gender discrimination and in protecting applicants with names that indicate race or national origin.[134]

Another concern expressed by the Federal Reserve Board was that lifting the prohibition would create some risk that the data gathering itself would be discriminatory, in that creditors would selectively inquire or note information about protected class characteristics for certain applicants.[135] In general, it was felt that the reliability of voluntarily collected data was questionable.[136] Indeed many creditors, in commenting on the proposed lifting of the prohibition against requesting information on prohibited bases, stated that they would not collect this information.[137] What this problem indicates is the need for mandatory collection of data to document non-mortgage credit discrimination.

In 2010, section 1071 of the Dodd-Frank Wall Street Reform and Consumer Protection Act[138] ("Dodd-Frank Act") amended the ECOA and instituted requirements for lenders to collect certain data at the time an application is submitted if the applicant is a small business or a minority-owned or women-owned business.[139] These amendments mandate that such data—which includes the type and purpose of loan applied for, the amount of credit applied for and approved, the type of action taken with respect to each application, the census tract of the principal place of business, the business' gross annual revenue, and the race, sex, and ethnicity of the principal owners for the business—must be collected, maintained, and reported to the Consumer Financial Protection Bureau on an annual basis.[140] The stated purpose of the amendments regarding small business loan data is "to facilitate enforcement of fair lending laws and enable communities, governmental entities, and creditors to identify business and community development needs and opportunities of women-owned, minority-owned, and small businesses."[141] Section 704B of the ECOA, the section that was amended by the Dodd-Frank Act, became effective on the date that general rulemaking authority for the ECOA was transferred to the Consumer Financial Protection Bureau, or July 21, 2011.

5.5.2 Types of Information That Creditors Cannot Seek

5.5.2.1 Race, Color, Religion, and National Origin

With certain special exceptions set out later in § 5.5.3, *infra*, the current Regulation B prohibits creditors from requesting the race, color, religion, or national origin of the applicant or any other person in connection with a credit transaction.[142] For example, if the director of a day care center serving African-American families applies for a bank loan to defray some of the center's debts until payments are received, the bank may not ask the race of the center's director or students.

However, a creditor may inquire about an applicant's permanent residence and immigration status.[143] Creditors are also permitted to inquire about the immigration status of any other person in connection with a credit transaction.[144] The Comptroller of the Currency has authorized national banks to maintain a policy of requiring foreign student credit applicants to possess an alien registration card.[145]

The general restriction on requests for information on an applicant's national origin should not prevent a creditor from determining the language spoken by the applicant in order to provide that applicant with information in the appropriate language. In fact, Regulation B specifically permits creditors to provide ECOA notices in a language other than English, as long as it is available in English upon request.[146] Also, the Federal

---

132 *See generally* Winnie Taylor, *Proving Racial Discrimination and Monitoring Fair Lending Compliance: The Missing Data Problem in Nonmortgage Credit*, 31 Rev. Banking & Fin. L. 199 (2011) (examining question of whether expansion of mandatory data collection to cover nonmortgage lenders is appropriate and, if so, to what extent).

133 Studies and fair housing testing have documented the phenomenon of linguistic profiling, in which a person can discern a telephone caller's race or ethnicity by their speech. *See* Patricia Rice, *Linguistic Profiling: The Sound of Your Voice May Determine If You Get That Apartment or Not*, Wash. Univ. in St. Louis News & Information, Feb. 2, 2006, http://news-info.wustl.edu/tips/page/normal/6500.html (describing research by John Baugh showing that some companies do not return answering machine messages of those whose voices seem to identify them as African American or Latino, and that some companies instruct their telephone clerks to avoid face-to-face meetings based on the sound of a caller's voice); *see also* Jeffrey D. Dillman, *New Strategies for Old Problems: The Fair Housing Act at 40*, 57 Clev. St. L. Rev. 197, 202 n.128 (2009) ("Rather than explicitly stating that s/he will not rent to African Americans, for example, a discriminating landlord is more likely to use linguistic profiling to screen tenants, and then either not return their phone calls or engage in other types of discrimination, such as misrepresenting availability of units, quoting different terms or conditions (such as higher rents, lesser amenities, or not offering rebates or specials), etc.").

134 For example, one study has documented that the mere use of an "African-American sounding" name resulted in one-third fewer responses from employers. *What's in a Name*, MIT News, Jan. 24, 2003, http://web.mit.edu/newsoffice/nr/2003/resumes.html.

135 68 Fed. Reg. 13,144, 13,148 (Mar. 18, 2003).

136 *Id.*

137 *Id.*

138 Pub. L. No. 111-203, 124 Stat. 1376 (July 21, 2010).

139 15 U.S.C. § 1691c-2.

140 15 U.S.C. § 1691c-2(e).

141 15 U.S.C. § 1691c-2(a).

142 Reg. B, 12 C.F.R. § 1002.5(b) [§ 202.5(b)].

143 Reg. B, 12 C.F.R. § 1002.5(e) [§ 202.5(e)]; *see also* William B. Glidden, Office of the Comptroller of Currency, Interpretive Staff Letter, Fed. Banking L. Rep. (CCH) ¶ 85,026 (Sept. 9, 1977) (also available at 1977 OCC Ltr. LEXIS 64) (similar rule for national banks).

144 Reg. B, 12 C.F.R. § 1002.5(e) [§ 202.5(e)].

145 Thomas W. Taylor, Office of the Comptroller of Currency, Interpretive Staff Letter, Fed. Banking L. Rep. (CCH) ¶ 85,023 (Sept. 6, 1977) (also available at 1977 OCC Ltr. LEXIS 68).

146 Reg. B, 12 C.F.R. § 1002.4(e) [§ 202.4(e)].

Reserve Board has given approval to a California statute which requires creditors to provide Spanish-speaking applicants with the opportunity to obtain an unexecuted Spanish-language contract.[147] The Board reasoned that the statute made contract terms more understandable to applicants of one national origin without interfering with the interests of any other group and therefore did not frustrate the intent of the ECOA.[148]

5.5.2.2 Sex; Optional Use of Courtesy Titles

5.5.2.2.1 Inquiries about applicant's gender

A creditor generally may not request the sex of the applicant as required information.[149] There are five exceptions. A creditor may inquire into the applicant's gender: (1) when securities credit is involved;[150] (2) when incidental consumer credit is involved, but only to the extent necessary for medical records or similar purposes;[151] (3) to determine eligibility and premium rates for insurance;[152] (4) when a residential real estate-related loan is involved;[153] and (5) when a special purpose credit program is involved.[154]

Unless the creditor employs mail-in applications and the applicant uses only initials, or the creditor's employee who takes the application is not the person making the credit decision, the prohibition concerning requesting the applicant's sex is of limited practical effect. The creditor will usually be able to determine for itself whether the applicant is a man or woman.

5.5.2.2.2 Courtesy titles

The applicant may be asked, but not required, to designate a courtesy title for the account (Ms., Miss, Mrs., or Mr.),[155] and the application form must "appropriately" indicate that selection of such a designation is optional.[156] All other terms used on the application must be gender-neutral.[157]

5.5.2.2.3 Birth control, childbearing, or childrearing

A creditor may not request any information about the applicant's birth control practices, intention or capacity to bear children, or intention to rear children.[158] A creditor, however, may request information about the applicant's present dependents (such as the number of dependents and their ages) and related financial obligations for these present dependents, as long as this information is not solely requested from a group protected by the statute.[159] For example, a creditor would violate the ECOA if it requested information on child care expenses only from female applicants or only from recipients of public assistance.

5.5.2.3 Marital Status

5.5.2.3.1 When marital status information may be requested

Whether a creditor may ask about an applicant's marital status will depend on the type of credit account being sought. If an account is joint between husband and wife, or the credit account is secured by property, the creditor may seek information about the applicant's marital status.[160]

But a creditor must allow a married applicant to apply for an individual account if the applicant so desires.[161] If the applicant seeks an individual, unsecured account, a creditor is severely restricted as to when it can seek marital status information. The creditor in that situation may *not* ask the applicant's marital status unless:

- The applicant resides in a community property state or is relying on any property located in such a state to establish creditworthiness;[162]
- The credit involves a regulated utility company, incidental consumer credit, or securities credit;[163]

---

147 Cal. Civ. Code § 1632 (West).

In 2003, this act was amended to extend its provisions to the languages of Chinese, Tagalog, Vietnamese, and Korean, as well as Spanish. The amendment became effective July 1, 2004. *See also* Cal. Civ. Code § 1632.5 (West).

148 Fed. Reserve Bd., Official Board Interpretation § 202.1102, 42 Fed. Reg. 22,861 (May 5, 1977).

This interpretation was not included in the 1985 official staff commentary to Regulation B. However, the Federal Reserve Board chose not to include in the commentary any interpretation, such as section 202.1102, which did *not* preempt a state law and so, presumably, the California statute remains acceptable. Moreover, section 202.1102 is an official board interpretation, not a staff interpretation, and thus should not be superseded by staff commentary.

149 Reg. B, 12 C.F.R. § 1002.5(b) [§ 202.5(b)].

150 *See* § 2.2.6.5, *supra.*

151 Reg. B, 12 C.F.R. § 1002.3(c)(2)(i) [§ 202.3(c)(2)(i)].

152 This information may not be sought for purposes of making the credit decision. *See* Official Interpretations of Reg. B [Official Staff Commentary on Reg. B], 12 C.F.R. pt. 1002 [pt. 202], Supp. I, § 1002.7(e)-2 [§ 202.7(e)-2].

153 *See* § 5.5.3.1, *infra.*

154 *See* § 5.5.3.4, *infra.*

155 Reg. B, 12 C.F.R. § 1002.5(b)(2) [§ 202.5(b)(2)].

156 *Id.*

157 *Id.*

158 Reg. B, 12 C.F.R. § 1002.5(d)(3) [§ 202.5(d)(3)]. *See generally* Maureen R. St. Cyr, *Gender, Maternity Leave, and Home-Financing: A Critical Analysis of Mortgage Lending Discrimination Against Pregnant Women,* 15 U. Pa. J. L. & Soc'y Change 109 (2011) (arguing "that discrimination against women and families based on pregnancy or familial status is sex discrimination, and should be understood as such—and not as prudent underwriting, justified by economic realities"); *see also* Tara Siegel Bernard, *Need a Mortgage? Don't Get Pregnant,* N.Y. Times, July 19, 2010, www.nytimes.com/2010/07/20/your-money/mortgages/20mortgage.html.

159 Reg. B, 12 C.F.R. § 1002.5(d)(3) [§ 202.5(d)(3)].

160 Reg. B, 12 C.F.R. § 1002.5(d)(1) [§ 202.5(d)(1)].

161 15 U.S.C. § 1691d(c); Reg. B, 12 C.F.R. § 1002.7(a) [§ 202.7(a)].

The statute explicitly overrides any state laws prohibiting the separate extension of consumer credit to spouses.

162 Reg. B, 12 C.F.R. § 1002.5(d)(1) [§ 202.5(d)(1)]; *In re* Alden's, Inc., 92 F.T.C. 901 (Fed. Trade Comm'n 1978) (creditor was ordered to stop asking about applicants' marital status when an individual unsecured account was requested in a non-community property state).

163 *See* §§ 2.2.6.2, 2.2.6.5, *supra.*

- The creditor seeks the information solely to determine eligibility and premium rates for insurance;[164]
- A residential real estate-related loan is involved;[165] or
- The creditor seeks the information solely to determine eligibility for a special purpose credit program.[166]

Unless the transaction involves only incidental consumer credit,[167] the creditor also must make an "appropriate" disclosure to the applicant that income from alimony, child support, or separate maintenance payments need not be revealed unless the applicant wants it to be considered in evaluating the application.[168] Regulation B does not define the term "appropriate," although a good standard to measure appropriateness may be found on the regulation's model credit application forms. These model forms indicate in bold letters that "[a]limony, child support, or separate maintenance income need not be revealed if you do not wish to have it considered as a basis for repaying this obligation."[169]

This disclosure must *precede* any general request for income information so that it can be seen before the applicant answers the question.[170] On the other hand, the disclosure need not be made at all if the creditor seeks only specific income information that would not include alimony, support payments, or the like—for example, if the creditor asks for salary, wages, and investment income.[171]

If the applicant does not want alimony, child support, or separate maintenance income to be considered, then the creditor is prohibited from making any inquiries about these sources of income.[172] The creditor must instead evaluate the application based on the applicant's other income sources.

At least one court has held that a creditor who asked a female applicant if she anticipated getting married did not violate the ECOA, as the question was posed in the context of a discussion of the applicant's financial troubles and her need for a guarantor.[173]

5.5.2.3.2 Types of marital status information which may be requested

In situations in which creditors may request an applicant's marital status, creditors may categorize the applicant only as unmarried (which includes single, divorced, and widowed persons), married, or separated.[174] These terms are to be defined by applicable state law.[175] The creditor may explain that the category "unmarried" includes single, divorced, and widowed persons but is not required to do so.[176]

5.5.2.3.3 Creditors may also seek information that indirectly discloses marital status

Creditors also may ask for certain information that indirectly discloses the applicant's marital status. Examples of such permissible indirect inquiries include:[177]

- Whether the applicant is responsible for paying alimony, child support, or separate maintenance payments;
- The source of income that is to be used as a basis for the repayment of the credit requested (which may disclose that it is a spouse's income);
- Whether any obligation disclosed by the applicant has a co-obligor (which may disclose that the co-obligor is a spouse or former spouse); or
- The form of ownership of assets that are being relied on in extending credit (which may disclose the interest of a spouse).

A creditor may also ask the applicant to list any other account for which the applicant is liable and to provide the name and address in which the account is held.[178] The creditor also may ask the applicant to list the names under which the applicant has previously received credit.[179] This provision serves chiefly as a means of obtaining credit reports on women who have changed names through marriage or divorce and to track experience with prior business loans.

5.5.2.4 Information About Spouse or Former Spouse

With enumerated exceptions, a creditor may not make any inquiry about an applicant's spouse or former spouse.[180] This prohibition applies not only to inquiries directed to the applicant but also to inquiries directed to a credit reporting agency, other creditors, or other sources.

---

164 This information may not be sought for purposes of making the credit decision. *See* Official Interpretations of Reg. B [Official Staff Commentary on Reg. B], 12 C.F.R. pt. 1002 [pt. 202], Supp. I, § 1002.7(e)-2 [§ 202.7(e)-2].

165 *See* § 5.5.3.1, *infra.*

166 *See* § 5.5.3.4, *infra.*

167 *See* § 2.2.6.3, *supra.*

168 Reg. B, 12 C.F.R. § 1002.5(d)(2) [§ 202.5(d)(2)]; *see* § 6.5.2.6, *infra.*

Disclosures under section 1002.5(d)(2) [section 202.5(d)(2)] need not be made in writing but, if the creditor chooses to make them in writing, they must be clear and conspicuous. These disclosures are exempt from the requirement that they be made in a form the applicant can retain. 12 C.F.R. § 1002.4(d) [§ 202.4(d)].

169 12 C.F.R. pt. 1002 [pt. 202], app. B (model form for credit application), *reprinted at* appx. B, *infra.*

170 Official Interpretations of Reg. B [Official Staff Commentary on Reg. B], 12 C.F.R. pt. 1002 [pt. 202], Supp. I, § 1002.5(d)(2)-2 [§ 202.5(d)(2)-2].

171 *Id.* § 1002.5(d)(2)-3 [§ 202.5(d)(2)-3].

172 Reg. B, 12 C.F.R. § 1002.5(d)(2) [§ 202.5(d)(2)].

173 *Para v. United Carolina Bank*, 1998 U.S. Dist. LEXIS 16843 (E.D.N.C. Aug. 25, 1998).

174 Reg. B, 12 C.F.R. §§ 1002.2(u), 1002.5(d)(1) [§§ 202.2(u), 202.5(d)(1)].

175 Reg. B, 12 C.F.R. § 1002.2(u) [§ 202.2(u)].

176 Reg. B, 12 C.F.R. § 1002.5(d)(1) [§ 202.5(d)(1)].

177 Official Interpretations of Reg. B [Official Staff Commentary on Reg. B], 12 C.F.R. pt. 1002 [pt. 202], Supp. I, § 1002.5(d)(1)-1 [§ 202.5(d)(1)-1].

178 Reg. B, 12 C.F.R. § 1002.5(c)(3) [§ 202.5(c)(3)].

179 *Id.*

180 Reg. B, 12 C.F.R. § 1002.5(c)(1) [§ 202.5(c)(1)].

The prohibition on inquiring about a spouse or former spouse does not prohibit a creditor from reviewing information about the spouse if it is already included in a credit report on the applicant. However, several cases have prohibited the denial of credit based on information that the creditor received on the applicant's spouse or former spouse.[181] In particular, these creditors violated the ECOA because they refused to grant individual credit to one spouse on the basis of a delinquency owed by the other spouse to the same creditor.

A creditor may request information about the applicant's spouse or former spouse *only* if:[182]

• The spouse will be permitted to use the account;[183]
• The spouse will be contractually liable on the account;[184]
• The applicant is relying on the spouse's income for repayment of the credit;[185]
• The applicant resides in a community property state or is

relying on property which is located in such a state for repayment;[186]
• The applicant is relying on alimony, child support, or separate maintenance payments from a spouse or former spouse for repayment of the credit;[187] or
• The transaction involves incidental consumer or securities credit.[188]

In the above situations, the creditor may request any information about the spouse or former spouse that may be requested about the applicant.[189] It may prove difficult for divorced applicants to comply with creditor requests for information about their ex-spouses because the applicant may not have easy access to current financial information concerning an ex-spouse.

The Federal Trade Commission (FTC) has issued an interpretation of the Fair Credit Reporting Act concerning when a credit reporting agency is permitted to provide creditors with the credit history of the credit applicant's spouse. Under this interpretation, a creditor can seek a spouse's credit history whenever:

• The spouse will be permitted to use the account;
• The spouse will be contractually liable on the account;
• The applicant is relying on the spouse's income for repayment of the credit;
• The state law doctrine of necessaries applies to the transaction;[190]
• The applicant resides in a community property state or the property, upon which the applicant is relying to establish creditworthiness, is located in a community property state; or
• The applicant is acting as the agent of the non-applicant spouse.[191]

Other than in these situations, the creditor does not have a permissible purpose to request a credit report on a non-applicant spouse, and the Fair Credit Reporting Act prohibits reporting agencies from furnishing such reports.[192] However, the FTC's staff commentary on the FCRA allows creditors to access a spouse's credit history in two situations not provided for in Regulation B: when a state necessaries doctrine applies and when the applicant is acting as the spouse's agent. There could conceivably be some situations in which the FTC staff commentary comes into conflict with Regulation B. However, the FTC staff commentary also states that there is never a permissible purpose for seeking a credit report when Regulation B prohibits a creditor from seeking such information or

---

181 *See* McGee v. East Ohio Gas Co., 111 F. Supp. 2d 979 (S.D. Ohio 2000) (ECOA prohibits utility from refusing credit to one spouse on the basis of a delinquency owed by the other spouse to the same utility), *class cert. granted*, 200 F.R.D. 382 (S.D. Ohio 2001); *In re* Brazil, 21 B.R. 333 (Bankr. N.D. Ohio 1982) (a public utility company discriminated against a bankruptcy petitioner on the basis of marital status by refusing to accept her application for service while her husband was still residing in their home and there was an outstanding bill in his name); *see also* § 2.2.2.3, *supra* (a more extensive discussion of prohibited forms of credit discrimination by utilities). *But see* Haynes v. Bank of Wedowee, 634 F.2d 266 (5th Cir. 1981) (no discrimination on basis of marital status shown when bank accelerated wife's loan due to husband's bankruptcy filing and bank had relied on existence of a joint account in original credit extension); Haynsworth v. South Carolina Electric & Gas Co., 488 F. Supp. 565 (D.S.C. 1979) (no unlawful discrimination when a utility company refused to open an account in a woman's name because of an outstanding bill at the same residence in the name of her separated husband); Vander Missen v. Kellogg-Citizens Nat'l Bank, 481 F. Supp. 742 (E.D. Wis. 1979); Cherry v. Hughes Supply Co., 539 S.E.2d 536 (Ga. Ct. App. 2000) (a creditor does not violate the ECOA by requiring applicant to pay spouse's delinquency to that same creditor before granting new credit when creditor justifiably believes that applicant is liable for spouse's delinquency).

182 Reg. B, 12 C.F.R. § 1002.5(c)(1), (c)(2) [§ 202.5(c)(1), (c)(2)].

183 Reg. B, 12 C.F.R. § 1002.5(c)(2)(i) [§ 202.5(c)(2)(i)].
    The term "use" refers only to open-end credit accounts. *See* Reg. B, 12 C.F.R. § 1002.2(a), (w) [§ 202.2(a), (w)].

184 Reg. B, 12 C.F.R. § 1002.5(c)(2)(ii) [§ 202.5(c)(2)(ii)].
    A person is contractually liable when he or she is expressly obligated (for example, by written agreement) to repay all debts arising on an account. *See* Reg. B, 12 C.F.R. § 1002.2(i) [§ 202.2(i)].

185 Reg. B, 12 C.F.R. § 1002.5(c)(2)(iii) [§ 202.5(c)(2)(iii)].
    A creditor may not presume that, because the spouse's income is listed, the applicant is relying on that income to establish creditworthiness. "Whether an applicant is relying on the future earnings of a non-applicant spouse is for the creditor to determine. Because section 202.5(c)(2)(iv) permits a creditor routinely to request information about a non-applicant spouse, the mere fact that the non-applicant spouse's income is listed on an application form is insufficient to show that the applicant is relying on the spouse's income." 50 Fed. Reg. 11,044, 11,045 (Apr. 5, 1988) (explanatory material for revision of Official Staff Commentary on Reg. B [Official Interpretations of Reg. B], 12 C.F.R. § 202.7(d)(5)-2 [§ 1002.7(d)(5)-2)].

186 Reg. B, 12 C.F.R. § 1002.5(c)(2)(iv) [§ 202.5(c)(2)(iv)].

187 Reg. B, 12 C.F.R. § 1002.5(c)(2)(v) [§ 202.5(c)(2)(v)].

188 *See* § 2.2.6.3, *supra*.

189 Reg. B, 12 C.F.R. § 1002.5(c)(2) [§ 202.5(c)(2)].

190 *See* § 9.3, *infra* (impact of the ECOA on necessaries doctrines and family expense statutes).

191 Fed. Trade Comm'n, Official Staff Commentary on the Fair Credit Reporting Act § 604(3)(A) item 5A (interpreting 15 U.S.C. § 1681(b)).

192 *Id.* § 604(3)(A) item 5B.

when the non-applicant spouse is divorced, separated, or has expressed an intent to legally disassociate from the marriage.[193]

5.5.2.5 Public Assistance Status

With the exceptions of home mortgages and special purpose credit programs,[194] a creditor is likely to be limited in the information it may seek about an applicant's public assistance status. Whether a creditor may ask about the applicant's public assistance status depends on what kind of credit evaluation system it uses. If the creditor utilizes a credit scoring system it, may not consider—and therefore presumably may not ask about—public assistance status.[195]

If a creditor uses a judgmental system, it may ask whether an applicant's income derives from public assistance payments in order to determine the amount and probable continuance of the payments, the applicant's credit history, and other "pertinent elements of creditworthiness."[196] A creditor may be able to ask, for example, how long the applicant has been receiving public assistance, whether the applicant intends to remain in a state that provides income from a state-funded program not offered in adjoining states, or the age of the applicant's dependents in order to ascertain how long present benefits will continue. If the creditor's inquiries become demeaning, Regulation B can arguably be invoked to prohibit statements which would discourage a reasonable person from making or pursuing a credit application.[197]

5.5.3 Exceptions to Restrictions on Requested Information

5.5.3.1 The Home Mortgage Monitoring Requirements

The major exception to the ECOA's prohibitions on prohibited inquiries is in the area of home mortgages. Both Regulation B and the Home Mortgage Disclosure Act (HMDA)[198] require lenders to collect certain information regarding the residential real estate-related loans that they make. The HMDA requires lenders to collect information including the race, sex, and income of each applicant for a home mortgage.[199] Regulation B requires lenders to collect information including race, national origin, sex, marital status, and age so that creditor compliance with the ECOA and other statutes can be monitored.[200]

Although the creditor is required to seek this information, the applicant is not required to provide it. Under both Regulation B and HMDA, if the applicant does not provide the required information or any part of it, the creditor must note that fact on its form(s) and, to the extent possible, also note the applicant's race or national origin and sex on the basis of visual observation or surname.[201] This information may be used only for monitoring; it may not be used to discriminate against the applicant.[202]

The impact of the HMDA in requiring collection of information on race, gender, and income has been very positive for protected groups. HMDA data has been used quite effectively to reveal startling racial disparities in the area of home mortgages, including disparities in approval rates and rates of subprime versus prime loans based on racial composition of neighborhoods.[203] HMDA data is also useful in litigation to prove credit discrimination.[204] These studies and lawsuits in turn have attracted more attention and activism toward efforts to increase lending to protected groups.[205] In fact, the success of the HMDA may have provided an impetus to the ultimately unsuccessful effort to revise Regulation B to allow requests for information on prohibited bases in non-mortgage credit.

---

193 *Id.*

   In another interpretation of the Fair Credit Reporting Act, the Federal Trade Commission set out requirements for credit reporting agencies which allow the applicant to request that favorable reports be considered. The agencies were asked to adopt procedures to ensure that "undesignated information" in the file of married persons—that is, information reported in only one spouse's name, information on joint accounts, or information on individual accounts on which the other spouse was an authorized user of the account—could be "accessed" in the name of either spouse who wishes to rely on it. *See* Fed. Trade Comm'n, Official Staff Commentary on the Fair Credit Reporting Act § 607(3)(A).

194 *See* § 5.5.3, *infra.*

195 Reg. B, 12 C.F.R. § 1002.6(b)(2) [§ 202.6(b)(2)]; *see* § 6.3, *infra* (an explanation of the different types of credit evaluation systems).

196 Reg. B, 12 C.F.R. § 1002.2(y) [§ 202.2(y)].

   The use of public assistance status in credit evaluation is discussed in further detail in § 6.6.3, *infra.*

197 Reg. B, 12 C.F.R. § 1002.4(b) [§ 202.4(b)].

198 12 U.S.C. §§ 2801–2810; *see* § 4.4.5, *supra* (more on HDMA and its implementing regulation, Regulation C).

199 12 C.F.R. § 203.4(a).

   HMDA requires lenders to collect other information in addition to protected class information. *See* § 4.4.5.2.2, *supra.*

200 Reg. B, 12 C.F.R. § 1002.13 [§ 202.13].

201 Reg. B, 12 C.F.R. § 1002.13(c) [§ 202.13(c)]; 12 C.F.R. pt. 1003 [pt. 203], app. B.

   Regulation B, 12 C.F.R. § 1002.13(c) [§ 202.13(c)], provides that the creditor must inform the applicant that the information is being requested for the purpose of monitoring compliance with federal anti-discrimination statutes and that, if the applicant chooses not to provide the information, the creditor is required to note the race or national origin and sex on the basis of visual observation or surname. The disclosures under section 1002.13(c) [section 202.13(c)] need not be made in writing but, if the creditor chooses to make them in writing, they must be clear and conspicuous. 12 C.F.R. § 1002.4(d) [§ 202.4(d)]. Also, creditors are exempt from the requirement that the disclosures be made in a form the applicant can retain. 12 C.F.R. § 1002.4(d) [§ 202.4(d)].

202 Reg. B, 12 C.F.R. § 1002.6(a) [§ 202.6(a)].

203 Many of the studies are discussed in § 8.4, *infra.*

204 *See* § 4.4.5, *supra* (using HDMA to prove credit discrimination).

205 Richard D. Marsico, *Shedding Some Light on Lending: The Effect of Expanded Disclosure Laws on Home Mortgage Marketing, Lending and Discrimination in the New York Metropolitan Area,* 27 Fordham Urb. L.J. 481 (1999); *see* §§ 4.4.5, *supra,* 8.4, *infra* (additional studies analyzing HMDA data).

5.5.3.2 Scope of the Home Mortgage Monitoring Requirements

HMDA requires "covered lenders" to collect certain information regarding applications for home purchase loans, home improvement loans, and refinancings for each calendar year.[206] Lenders have discretion whether to report information about home equity lines of credit.[207] A detailed analysis of HMDA's requirements and coverage is discussed in § 4.4.5.2.2, *supra*. For loans covered by HMDA, the information that lenders are required to obtain includes information on race, national origin, and gender.[208]

Regulation B similarly requires home mortgage lenders to seek out information on race, national origin, and gender.[209] In addition, it requires these lenders to request information about marital status and age.[210] The ECOA requirements apply to all creditors that receive an application for credit for the purchase or refinancing of a dwelling when the credit will be secured by the dwelling.[211] This includes lenders not subject to the HMDA requirements.[212] The scope of the information required by HMDA, however, is broader than under Regulation B.[213] Also, information collected pursuant to Regulation B is not required to be compiled into reports, unlike the HMDA data, thus limiting its utility.[214]

5.5.3.3 Information Required by Any Other Federal or State Statute or by Court Order for Monitoring Purposes

In addition to the home mortgage exception, creditors are permitted to make requests for information otherwise prohibited by Regulation B when any other federal or state statute or regulation requires collection of the information.[215]

Perhaps the biggest exception, then, to the prohibition on requesting information on prohibited bases is the Treasury Department's customer identification regulation issued pursuant to the USA Patriot Act.[216] The Patriot Act regulation requires financial institutions to verify the identity of all customers[217] and, in particular, suggests the use of government-issued identification containing a photograph or similar safeguard.[218] Yet a creditor that requests applicants to provide photographic identification also indirectly seeks the applicants' race and gender.

While the request for photographic identification pursuant to the Patriot Act regulation qualifies for the exception allowing information requests required by "other" federal and state laws, *retention* of the identification will not qualify. The Patriot Act regulation does not require creditors to *retain* a copy of identification documents—a description of the document will suffice.[219] Ironically, the Treasury Department had originally proposed a retention requirement; however, this requirement was modified in part due to concerns by creditors that "requiring banks to keep copies of documents that have pictures, such as driver's licenses, could expose the bank to allegations of unlawful discrimination, even if the retention of this information were not prohibited under ECOA."[220]

Apart from the photo identification issue, the Treasury Department specifically noted that the collection and retention of a customer's date of birth, which is required by the regulation, does not relieve the creditor of its obligations to comply with laws prohibiting age discrimination such as the ECOA.[221]

Creditors may also make otherwise forbidden inquiries if required to by an order or agreement issued by, or entered into with, a court or an enforcement agency.[222] The most common example of such an order would be one issued in an ECOA or Fair Housing lawsuit in which a creditor's future performance is to be monitored by a government enforcement agency.

5.5.3.4 Special Purpose Credit Programs

Regulation B creates special rules for special purpose credit programs, which are programs that address the credit needs of economically disadvantaged groups.[223] If participants in such a program are required to possess one or more common characteristics (such as race, national origin, or sex), a creditor may request information regarding those common characteristics.[224] For example, if an energy conservation program is created to assist older consumers, the creditor may ask the applicant's age. A creditor may also inquire about the applicant's minority status when offering credit under a Minority Enterprise Small Business Investment Corp. program.[225]

If financial need is one of the criteria for the special purpose credit program, the creditor may also request information about marital status, alimony, child support, separate maintenance income, and the spouse's or parents' financial resources.[226]

---

206 12 C.F.R. § 1003.4(a) [§ 203.4(a)]; *see* § 4.4.5, *supra* (discussing in detail HMDA's requirements).

207 12 C.F.R. § 1003.4(c) [§ 203.4(c)].

208 It includes numerous other items of information as well, including data on certain high-cost loans. *See* § 4.4.5.2.2, *supra*.

209 *See* Reg. B, 12 C.F.R. § 1002.13(a) [§ 202.13(a)].

210 Reg. B, 12 C.F.R. § 1002.13(a) [§ 202.13(a)].

211 *Id.*

212 *See* § 4.4.7, *supra*.

213 *See* § 4.4.5.2.2, *supra*.

214 *See* § 4.4.7, *infra*.

215 Reg. B, 12 C.F.R. § 1002.5(a)(2) [§ 202.5(a)(2)].

216 31 C.F.R. § 103.121.

217 31 C.F.R. § 103.121(b)(2).

218 31 C.F.R. § 103.121(b)(2)(ii)(A)(1).

219 31 C.F.R. § 103.121(b)(3)(i)(B).
   The creditor must retain the identification information required under the customer identification regulation for five years after the account is closed or, for credit cards, when the account becomes dormant or is closed. 31 C.F.R. § 103.121(b)(3)(ii).

220 68 Fed. Reg. 25,090, 25,102 (May 9, 2003).

221 68 Fed. Reg. 25,090, 25,097 (May 9, 2003).

222 Reg. B, 12 C.F.R. § 1002.5(a)(2) [§ 202.5(a)(2)].

223 Reg. B, 12 C.F.R. § 1002.8 [§ 202.8]; *see* § 3.9.2, *supra* (describing requirements for a special purpose credit program).

224 Reg. B, 12 C.F.R. § 1002.8(c) [§ 202.8(c)].

225 Official Interpretations of Reg. B [Official Staff Commentary on Reg. B], 12 C.F.R. pt. 1002 [pt. 202], Supp. I, § 1002.8(c)-2 [§ 202.8(c)-2].

226 Reg. B, 12 C.F.R. § 1002.8(d) [§ 202.8(d)].

Examples of such programs are subsidized housing programs for low to moderate income households and student loan programs based on the family's financial need.[227]

5.5.3.5 Self-Test Exception

As part of revisions to Regulation B in March 2003, a new exception was created permitting a creditor to request information about an applicant's race, color, religion, national origin, and sex for the purpose of conducting a self-test under section 1002.15 [section 202.15].[228]

In order to avail itself of the self-test exception, a creditor must meet the requirements for conducting a self-test under Regulation B.[229] The creditor must have a program, practice, or study that (1) is designed and used specifically to determine the extent or effectiveness of the creditor's compliance with the ECOA and (2) creates data or factual information that is not available and could not be derived from loan or application or other records related to credit transactions.[230] The creditor must take appropriate corrective action if the self-test shows that a violation is more likely than not to have occurred.[231]

Assuming corrective action is taken when warranted, the results of the self-test cannot be obtained by a government agency in an examination or investigation or by any agency or any applicant in any proceeding or lawsuit alleging a violation of the ECOA or Regulation B.[232] The latter point appears to address creditors' concerns about the risk of litigation if the ban had been lifted as proposed.[233] Even if the creditor subsequently waives or loses the self-test privilege, the exception to the ban on inquiring about prohibited bases still applies.[234]

The supplemental information to the March 2003 final rule contains additional requirements regarding the self-test exception and collection of information about prohibited bases. Any information about an applicant's personal characteristics collected as part of a self-test must be kept separate from the loan file, application file, or other records related to credit transactions.[235] This information should be analyzed in a timely fashion as part of the self-test.[236] Creditors are expected to develop a written plan when conducting a self-test that includes the specific purposes of the self-test, the methodology of the self-test, the geographic area covered, the types of credit transactions involved, the entity that will analyze the data, and the

timeframe of the self-test.[237] Creditors are generally required to retain records of the self-test for twenty-five months after completion.[238]

If the creditor seeks information about an applicant's race, color, religion, national origin, or sex as part of the self-test exception, the creditor must make certain disclosures either orally or in writing.[239] The creditor must disclose that the applicant is not required to provide this information, that the creditor is requesting the information to monitor compliance with the ECOA and is prohibited from considering this information or the applicant's decision not to furnish this information in making the credit decision, and, when applicable, that this information will be collected based on visual observation or surname if not provided.[240]

5.6 Co-Signature of Spouse or Other Person

5.6.1 General

The general rule against discrimination prevents a creditor from seeking a spouse or other person to co-sign or guarantee a loan on a prohibited basis.[241] Thus creditors may not ask husbands to co-sign loans while not requiring wives to do so or require only applicants on public assistance to provide co-signers.

The ECOA also sets other limitations as to when a creditor may seek a guarantor or co-signer that apply particularly to creditor requirements that spouses co-sign loans. The rules vary depending on whether an applicant's creditworthiness depends on property that is jointly owned, whether a community property state is involved, and whether the application is for joint credit. The rest of this chapter details these differing rules.

---

227 Reg. B, 12 C.F.R. § 1002.15 [§ 202.15]; *see* Official Interpretations of Reg. B [Official Staff Commentary on Reg. B], 12 C.F.R. pt. 1002 [pt. 202], Supp. I, § 1002.8(d)-2 [§ 202.8(d)-2].

228 Reg. B, 12 C.F.R. § 1002.05(b)(1) [§ 202.05(b)(1)].

229 *Id.*

230 *Id.*

231 Reg. B, 12 C.F.R. § 1002.15(c)(1) [§ 202.15(c)(1)].

232 Reg. B, 12 C.F.R. § 1002.15(d)(1) [§ 202.15(d)(1)].

233 68 Fed. Reg. 13,144, 13,148 (Mar. 18, 2003).

234 68 Fed. Reg. 13,144, 13,149 (Mar. 18, 2003).

235 *Id.*

It was stated that the additional guidance set forth in the supplemental information will be incorporated into the official staff commentary at a later date, as appropriate. *Id.*

236 68 Fed. Reg. 13,144, 13,149 (Mar. 18, 2003).

237 68 Fed. Reg. 13,144, 13,149 (Mar. 18, 2003).

238 Reg. B, 12 C.F.R. § 1002.12(b)(6) [§ 202.12(b)(6)].

239 Reg. B, 12 C.F.R. § 1002.5(b)(1) [§ 202.5(b)(1)].

If the creditor chooses to make these disclosures in writing, they must be clear and conspicuous. Reg. B, 12 C.F.R. § 1002.4(d) [§ 202.4(d)].

However, these disclosures are exempt from the requirement that they be made in a form the applicant can retain. Reg. B, 12 C.F.R. § 1002.4(d) [§ 202.4(d)].

240 Reg. B, 12 C.F.R. § 1002.5(b)(1)(i)–(iv) [§ 202.5(b)(1)(i)–(iv)].

241 *See* Fed. Deposit Ins. Corp. v. Medmark, Inc., 897 F. Supp. 511 (D. Kan. 1995) (granting summary judgment in favor of wife-guarantor because lender failed to set forth any facts to controvert assertion that wife's guaranty violated ECOA because husband was independently creditworthy); *see also* Citgo Petroleum Corp. v. Bulk Petroleum Corp., 2010 WL 3931496 (N.D. Okla. Oct. 5, 2010) (affirming general principles but ultimately declining to grant summary judgment to wife-signator because she did not establish as a matter of law that creditor "required" her to sign); Frontenac Bank v. T.R. Hughes, Inc., 2012 WL 4486312, at *13 (Mo. Ct. App. Sept. 25, 2012) (evidence demonstrated that bank routinely required personal guarantees from wives on loans of certain size because "the bank would otherwise question why they were not willing to 'step up' if they wanted the money lent").

Before addressing specific rules, certain rules that are generally applicable should be mentioned. Regulation B specifically indicates that, when a creditor violates the rules governing when co-signers and sureties can be required, not only the applicant but also guarantors, sureties, endorsers, and similar parties have the right to bring ECOA actions for damages.[242] However, these rights are still limited to aggrieved parties—persons for whom accommodation signers were required and the accommodation signers themselves. Mere involvement in a transaction in which the ECOA may have been violated does not give one standing to sue under the ECOA.[243]

In addition to bringing an affirmative ECOA action, an aggrieved party whose signature was obtained illegally may be able to challenge the ECOA violations defensively through recoupment.[244] In fact, if the creditor has already filed an action in state court to collect on the loan or foreclose property securing the loan, the aggrieved party may not be able to bring an affirmative ECOA action in federal court for injunctive or declaratory relief due to the prohibitions of the Anti-Injunction Act.[245] Another advantage of recoupment is that it can be asserted as a defense after the statute of limitations has run.[246]

Even when the ECOA would otherwise limit a creditor's ability to seek an additional signatory, a creditor may require such an additional signature pursuant to a special purpose credit program.[247] For example, a creditor may obtain a parent's signature as guarantor on a guaranteed student loan when required to do so by federal or state law or agency regulations.[248] In addition, the rules concerning co-signers do not apply to securities credit or incidental consumer credit.[249] Courts are also reluctant to apply these rules in a business context—for example, when a businessperson is signing a guaranty for a corporation as opposed to a spouse being asked to co-sign a consumer loan—as none of the ECOA's purposes appear to be relevant.[250]

State laws addressing credit discrimination are preempted to the extent that they are inconsistent with the ECOA and Regulation B.[251] Regulation B specifies that state laws prohibiting the individual extension of consumer credit to both parties to a marriage if each spouse individually and voluntarily applies for such credit are inconsistent with the ECOA and therefore are preempted by it.[252]

5.6.2 Individual Credit When No Joint Property Is Involved

A creditor may not require the signature of a spouse or any other additional person on a credit instrument if the applicant has requested an individual account, no jointly held or community property is involved, and the applicant individually meets the creditor's standards for creditworthiness for the amount and terms of credit requested.[253] For example, a credi-

---

242 Reg. B, 12 C.F.R. § 1002.2(e) [§ 202.2(e)]; *see* Sovereign Bank v. Catterton, 2004 WL 834721 (E.D. Pa. Apr. 15, 2004); Silverman v. Eastrich Multiple Investor Fund, Ltd. P'ship, 857 F. Supp. 447 (E.D. Pa. 1994), *rev'd on other grounds*, 51 F.3d 28 (3d Cir. 1995); Gen. Electric Capital Corp. v. Pulsifer, Clearinghouse No. 46,778 (D. Me. Oct. 28, 1991); Douglas Cnty. Nat'l Bank v. Pfeiff, 809 P.2d 1100 (Colo. App. 1991).

This right did not always exist, at least with regard to guarantors and sureties. *See* Reg. B, 12 C.F.R. § 202.2(e) (as amended in 1978 and 1979 but not as amended in 1985); *see also* Bank of America Nat'l Trust & Sav. Ass'n v. Hotel Rittenhouse Associates, 595 F. Supp. 800 (E.D. Pa. 1984); Morse v. Mut. Fed. Sav. & Loan Ass'n, 536 F. Supp. 1271 (D. Mass. 1982); Quigley v. Nash, Consumer Cred. Guide (CCH) ¶ 97,051 (D.D.C. Nov. 13, 1981) (also available at 1981 U.S. Dist. LEXIS 18177); Delta Diversified, Inc. v. Citizens & Southern Nat'l Bank, 320 S.E.2d 767 (Ga. Ct. App. 1984).

243 Riggs Nat'l Bank v. Linch, 36 F.3d 370 (4th Cir. 1994) (party whose independent creditworthiness was established and whose spouse was not required to cosign guaranty has no standing to sue under the ECOA because creditor required signature of a co-guarantor's spouse); *see also* Integra Bank/Pittsburgh v. Freeman, 839 F. Supp. 326 (E.D. Pa. 1993) (guarantor of loans could not invoke lender's alleged ECOA violation in requiring another guarantor's wife to sign guaranty agreements either as defense to liability or by way of recoupment) (discussed in §§ 11.8.5.3, 11.9.2.2, *infra*); *cf.* Farmer v. Ill. Power Co., 2010 WL 1521342 (S.D. Ill. Apr. 14, 2010) (no ECOA standing for husband whose name was later placed on wife's utility company account, since husband did not apply for account and was not required to sign any documents relating to account).

244 §§ 11.8.5.3, 11.9.2.2, *infra* (discussing this issue in more detail).

245 28 U.S.C. § 2283; *see* Borkon v. First Union Nat'l Bank, 2001 WL 1042854 (E.D. Pa. Sept. 7, 2001), *aff'd*, 47 Fed. Appx. 177 (3d Cir. 2002); Bledsoe v. Fulton Bank, 940 F. Supp. 804 (E.D. Pa. 1996).

246 *See, e.g.*, Sovereign Bank v. Catterton, 2004 WL 834721 (E.D. Pa. Apr. 15, 2004).

247 Official Interpretations of Reg. B [Official Staff Commentary on Reg. B], 12 C.F.R. pt. 1002 [pt. 202], Supp. I, § 1002.8(d)-1 [§ 202.8(d)-1]; *see* § 3.9.2, *supra* (discussing when credit qualifies for the special credit program exception and the scope of this exception).

248 Official Interpretations of Reg. B [Official Staff Commentary on Reg. B], 12 C.F.R. pt. 1002 [pt. 202], Supp. I, § 1002.8(d)-3 [§ 202.8(d)-3].

249 *See* Reg. B, 12 C.F.R. § 1002.3(b)(2)(vi), (c)(2)(v) [§ 203.3(b)(2) (vi), (c)(2)(v)]; §§ 2.2.6.3, 2.2.6.5, *supra*.

250 *See* Mick's at Pennsylvania Ave., Inc. v. BOD, Inc., 389 F.3d 1284 (D.C. Cir. 2004) (no violation of ECOA for lessor to require personal guaranty of husband of restaurant owner when husband signed lease as a principal, officer, and shareholder of restaurant corporation); First Fid. Bank v. Best Petroleum, Inc., 757 F. Supp. 293 (S.D.N.Y. 1991) (co-signer for corporation had no ECOA standing in absence of allegation that he was subjected to discrimination on improper basis). *But see* Boyd v. U.S. Bank, 2007 WL 2822518 (D. Kan. Sept. 26, 2007) (creditor required signature of borrower's spouse for small business loan; finding genuine issue of material fact regarding whether creditor actually determined that borrower was not creditworthy before requiring his wife's guaranty and whether wife's guaranty violated the rules under 12 C.F.R. § 202.7(d) [§ 1002.7(d)]).

251 15 U.S.C. § 1691d(f); Reg. B, 12 C.F.R. § 1002.11(a) [§ 202.11(a)]; *see* § 11.6.1.3, *infra. But see* Abbett v. Bank of America, 2006 WL 581193 (M.D. Ala. Mar. 8, 2006) (no preemption of state law by ECOA; noting that Regulation B's outline and prior determinations are inapplicable).

252 Reg. B, 12 C.F.R. § 1002.11(b)(1)(ii) [§ 202.11(b)(1)(ii)].

253 Reg. B, 12 C.F.R. § 1002.7(d)(1) [§ 202.7(d)(1)]; *see also* Suntrust Bank v. Dowdy, 2010 WL 3834573 (E.D.N.C. Sept. 30, 2010) (allegations that lender routinely demanded guaranty agreements to

tor may not automatically require that applications by married women for individual credit be signed by their husbands or that unmarried female applicants obtain co-signers for loans, because many of these applicants have sufficient individual assets to qualify for credit.[254]

This provision of Regulation B prohibits the creditor from requiring the signature, not only of the applicant's spouse *but of any other person* if the applicant seeks individual credit and is creditworthy.[255] In fact, a creditor may not require an applicant who is individually creditworthy to provide a co-signer even if the creditor applies the requirement without regard to sex, marital status, or any other prohibited basis.[256]

Creditors may determine that an individual does not meet its standards of creditworthiness and condition credit on the applicant obtaining a co-signer.[257] In making its determination of creditworthiness, a creditor is permitted to apply its own criteria, as long as they are valid, reasonable, and nondiscriminatory.[258] In order to prove a violation of the ECOA, the plaintiff must show that the credit denial constitutes marital status discrimination.[259]

If the creditor requires a co-signer, it may not require that the spouse be this person, nor may the creditor impose any requirements on the additional person that may not be imposed on the applicant.[260] If the applicant's income alone will not support the credit, creditors may not tell such applicant that his or her spouse will have to co-sign. Instead, the creditor should state that a co-signer is necessary without specifying the spouse.[261]

The creditor may place certain restrictions on who the co-signer is. For example, the creditor could insist that the additional signatory live in the creditor's market area.[262] But the creditor may not discriminate on the basis of sex, marital status, or any other prohibited basis. For example, creditors may not discriminate on a prohibited basis by giving greater credibility to male as opposed to female co-signers.[263]

Similarly, if an applicant is relying on another's income in making the credit application, the creditor may require the signature of that person so that the income will be available to pay the debt.[264] A creditor may likewise require the signature of the owner of a spouse's property used in an applicant's disclosure of net worth.[265] The same is true in a community property

---

be executed by spouses stated a plausible claim for relief); Bolduc v. Beal Bank, 994 F. Supp. 82 (D.N.H. 1998) (ECOA violation when wife was required to co-sign credit instrument despite husband being independently creditworthy), *vacating preliminary injunction*, 167 F.3d 667 (1st Cir. 1999); Marine American State Bank v. Lincoln, 433 N.W.2d 709 (Iowa 1988) (bank violated ECOA by requiring spouse's signature when applicant was qualified individually); Frontenac Bank v. T.R. Hughes, Inc., 2012 WL 4486312 (Mo. Ct. App. Sept. 25, 2012) (in "exceeding the limits set forth in Regulation B's exception to the rule against requiring an applicant's spouse to sign a credit instrument if the applicant qualifies alone under the creditor's standards of creditworthiness," the bank clearly violated the ECOA). *But see* Citgo Petroleum Corp. v. Bulk Petroleum Corp., 2010 WL 3931496 (N.D. Okla. Oct. 5, 2010) (denying summary judgment to wife-guarantor on ECOA defense; finding there was no evidence to demonstrate that creditor "required" wife to sign guaranty or that she was not a "willing guarantor," and that wife was not entitled to have inferences drawn in her favor that she signed because the creditor required her to do so); First Fid. Bank v. Best Petroleum, Inc., 757 F. Supp. 293 (S.D.N.Y. 1991) (bank could ask owner to co-sign for corporation even if corporation was creditworthy; owner did not claim to be member of protected class).

254　However, one court has held that a blanket policy of requiring spousal signatures regardless of creditworthiness of the applicant did not violate the ECOA because the applicant and spouse presented themselves as joint applicants. Southwestern Pa. Reg'l Council v. Gentile, 776 A.2d 276 (Pa. Super. Ct. 2001).

255　Reg. B, 12 C.F.R. § 1002.7(d)(1) [§ 202.7(d)(1)].

256　*See also* Official Interpretations of Reg. B [Official Staff Commentary on Reg. B], 12 C.F.R. pt. 1002 [pt. 202], Supp. I, § 1002.7(d)(1)-1 [§ 202.7(d)(1)-1].

257　*See, e.g.,* Miller v. Elegant Junk, 616 F. Supp. 551 (S.D. W. Va. 1985) (co-signature requirement based on applicant's lack of creditworthiness); Paulson v. Centier Bank, 704 N.E.2d 482 (Ind. Ct. App. 1998) (requiring wife's signature did not violate the ECOA because bank could have reasonably concluded husband was not independently creditworthy); Spears v. Voss Chevrolet, Inc., 1986 Ohio App. LEXIS 9412 (Ohio Ct. App. Dec. 16, 1986) (no ECOA violation when woman wished to apply individually for a loan but creditor took information on both her and her husband and approved financing contingent on his co-signature in the absence of evidence that the woman was qualified individually); Roper Bros. Lumber Co. v. Westover Homes, Inc., 44 Va. Cir. 448 (Va. Cir. Ct. 998) (no ECOA violation when wife's co-signature was required after creditor determined husband was not independently creditworthy).

258　Riggs Nat'l Bank v. Linch, 36 F.3d 370 (4th Cir. 1994); Boyd v. U.S. Bank, 2007 WL 2822518 (D. Kan. Sept. 26, 2007).

259　Haynes v. Bank of Wedowee, 634 F.2d 266, 270 (5th Cir. 1981) (no discrimination under ECOA when bank considered bankruptcy of plaintiff's husband in deciding whether to accelerate plaintiff's loan); Cherry v. Hughes Supply Co., 539 S.E.2d 536 (Ga. Ct. App. 2000) (no evidence that denial was a pretext for marital status discrimination).

　　A key issue is whether this claim may be raised as an affirmative defense or only as a counterclaim. *See* §§ 11.8.5.3, 11.9.2.2, *infra*.

260　Reg. B, 12 C.F.R. § 1002.7(d)(5), (d)(6) [§ 202.7(d)(5), (d)(6)]; *see also* Thames v. City Nat'l Bank of Baton Rouge, 370 So. 2d 892 (La. Ct. App. 1978); Nat'l Auto Dealers Exch., L.P. v. Sauber, 2011 WL 4529928 (N.J. Super. Ct. App. Div. Oct. 3, 2011) (reversing and remanding for further proceedings lower court's purportedly "common sense ruling" that lender could demand wife's signature even though she had no personal involvement with husband's business and her income was "meager at best").

261　*See* Reg. B, 12 C.F.R. § 1002.7(d)(5) [§ 202.7(d)(5)].

　　When a spouse's income is being relied upon to support the ability to repay, the spouse may be required to sign to the extent necessary to make that income available to pay the debt. *See* Official Interpretations of Reg. B [Official Staff Commentary on Reg. B], 12 C.F.R. pt. 1002 [pt. 202], Supp. I, § 1002.7(d)(5)-2 [§ 202.7(d)(5)-2].

262　Official Interpretations of Reg. B [Official Staff Commentary on Reg. B], 12 C.F.R. pt. 1002 [pt. 202], Supp. I, § 1002.7(d)(5)-1 [§ 202.7(d)(5)-1].

263　United States v. Citizens Bank & Trust Co., Clearinghouse No. 31,077 (E.D. Ky. 1979).

264　Official Interpretations of Reg. B [Official Staff Commentary on Reg. B], 12 C.F.R. pt. 1002 [pt. 202], Supp. I, § 1002.7(d)(5)-2 [§ 202.7(d)(5)-2]; *see also* Riggs Nat'l Bank v. Webster, 832 F. Supp. 147, 151 (D. Md. 1993).

265　Riggs Nat'l Bank v. Webster, 832 F. Supp. 147, 151 (D. Md. 1993).

state if the applicant is relying on the spouse's separate income or future earnings that cannot be characterized as community property until earned.[266]

5.6.3 Reliance on Jointly Owned Property to Establish Creditworthiness

If an applicant requests individual unsecured credit and relies on jointly owned property to establish creditworthiness, the creditor may require the signature of a spouse or other person on an instrument necessary to make the property available to the creditor in case of death or default.[267] For example, if a house is held in tenancy by the entirety under state law and cannot be transferred by only one spouse, the creditor may request the wife's signature if the husband applies for credit and relies on the house to establish creditworthiness. In the context of loans for small businesses, the spouse is often listed as a partner or principal in the business, and the creditor may in those instances require the spouse's signature.[268]

This exception is a sweeping one. Many married applicants jointly own a house or car and rely upon them as assets in an application for credit, even if that property does not secure the loan. Therefore, creditors can frequently obtain a spouse's signature legitimately, even for unsecured credit accounts.

The first issue, however, is whether the individual is relying on the jointly owned property to establish creditworthiness. Simply because a creditor's application asks an applicant to list property should not be taken to indicate that the applicant is relying on such property to establish creditworthiness.[269] How-

ever, even if the applicant does not intend or need to rely on jointly owned property to establish creditworthiness, some courts may construe the mere fact that the applicant listed the property to imply that the spouse voluntarily signed.[270]

Furthermore, if the applicant is relying on jointly held property to establish creditworthiness and, under state law, can individually transfer enough of that property to meet the creditor's creditworthiness standards, no additional signature may be required.[271] In determining the value of the applicant's interest in jointly owned property, a creditor may consider factors such as the form of ownership and the property's susceptibility to attachment, execution, severance, or partition, and the cost of such action.[272] However, the value of an applicant's interest prior to or at consummation (without factoring in the possibility of subsequent changes resulting from marriage or divorce, for example) is the relevant issue in making a credit decision.[273]

If the applicant's interest in the property is not sufficient to protect the creditor, the creditor may give the applicant another option of providing additional support for the extension of credit, such as finding another party (that is, not the spouse) to act as a co-signer, converting the application to one for secured credit, or asking for the signature of the co-owner of the property on an instrument that ensures access to the property but does not impose personal liability unless necessary under state law.[274]

Finally, if the creditor requires a signature from the co-owner of the property, the signature is required only on instruments necessary (or reasonably believed to be necessary) under state law to make the property available in the event of death or default.[275] That is, the co-owner may not have to sign the note

---

266 Official Interpretations of Reg. B [Official Staff Commentary on Reg. B], 12 C.F.R. pt. 1002 [pt. 202], Supp. I, § 1002.7(d)(5)-2 [§ 202.7(d)(5)-2]; *see also* Resolution Trust Corp. v. Forest Grove, Inc., 1993 U.S. Dist. LEXIS 12575 (E.D. Pa. Sept. 7, 1993), *rev'd in part on other grounds*, 33 F.3d 284 (3d Cir. 1994).

267 Reg. B, 12 C.F.R. § 1002.7(d)(2) [§ 202.7(d)(2)]; Official Interpretations of Reg. B [Official Staff Commentary on Reg. B], 12 C.F.R. § 1002.7(d)(2)-1, (d)(4)-3 [§ 202.7(d)(2)-1, (d)(4)-3].

268 Mick's at Pennsylvania Ave., Inc. v. BOD, Inc., 389 F.3d 1284 (D.C. Cir. 2004) (no violation of ECOA for lessor to require personal guaranty of husband of restaurant owner when husband signed lease as a principal, officer, and shareholder of restaurant corporation); Taylor v. Albina Cmty. Bank, 2001 U.S. Dist. LEXIS 21519 (D. Or. Nov. 23, 2001); Cherry v. Hughes Supply Co., 539 S.E.2d 536 (Ga. Ct. App. 2000); Zollman v. Geneva Leasing Assocs., 780 N.E.2d 387 (Ind. Ct. App. 2002).

269 *See* Reg. B, 12 C.F.R. § 1002.7(d)(1) [§ 202.7(d)(1)] (prohibiting creditors from treating the submission of joint financial information or other evidence of joint assets as an application for joint credit); *see also* Frontenac Bank v. T.R. Hughes, Inc., 2012 WL 4486312 (Mo. Ct. App. Sept. 25, 2012) (evidence established that, rather than conducting an analysis of the makers of the promissory note, the bank improperly deemed the joint financial statement of one of the makers to be an offer by that maker's spouse to provide her guarantee as well). *But see* Riggs Nat'l Bank v. Linch, 36 F.3d 370 (4th Cir. 1994) (lender did not violate ECOA by requiring wife to sign as co-guarantor in loan to husband's business after lender discovered that many of the assets listed on husband's personal financial statement were jointly owned by husband and wife and that husband was not independently creditworthy for loan amount requested).

270 *See, e.g.*, Southwestern Pa. Reg'l Council v. Gentile, 776 A.2d 276 (Pa. Super. Ct. 2001). *But see* LOL Finance Co. v. F.J. Faison, Jr., Revocable Trust, 2010 WL 3118630 (D. Minn. July 13, 2010) (no genuine issue of material fact with respect to creditor's reason for requiring wives' signatures when husbands submitted financial statements that listed assets and liabilities under heading containing wives' names, were signed by both spouses, and contained no information that property was listed as anything but jointly held), *adopted by* 2010 WL 3118583 (D. Minn. Aug. 4, 2010).

271 Reg. B, 12 C.F.R. § 1002.7(d)(1) [§ 202.7(d)(1)]; *see also* Roberta W. Boylan, Office of the Comptroller of the Currency, Interpretive Staff Letter, Fed. Banking L. Rep. (CCH) ¶ 85,042 (Oct. 27, 1977) (also available at 1977 OCC Ltr. LEXIS 28); Roberta W. Boylan, Office of the Comptroller of the Currency, Interpretive Staff Letter, Fed. Banking L. Rep. (CCH) ¶ 85,043 (Oct. 27, 1977) (also available at 1977 OCC Ltr. LEXIS 29).

272 Official Interpretations of Reg. B [Official Staff Commentary on Reg. B], 12 C.F.R. pt. 1002 [pt. 202], Supp. I, § 1002.7(d)(2)-1(i) [§ 202.7(d)(2)-1(i)].

273 *Id.* § 1002.7(d)(2)-1(i) [§ 202.7(d)(2)-1(i)].

274 *Id.* § 1002.7(d)(2)-1(ii) [§ 202.7(d)(2)-1(ii)].

275 Reg. B, 12 C.F.R. § 1002.7(d)(2) [§ 202.7(d)(2)]; *see In re* McMullan, 196 B.R. 818 (Bankr. W.D. Ark. 1996), *aff'd*, 162 F.3d 1164 (8th Cir. 1998) (Arkansas and Louisiana state law required wife's signature on note to obtain valid lien on personal and real property); *see also* Anderson v. United Finance Co., 666 F.2d 1274 (9th Cir. 1982) (discrimination shown when finance company insisted that loan applicant obtain her husband's signature on note, when applicant specifically desired to establish individual credit, husband was

evidencing the obligation to pay but only a document protecting the creditor's access to the property in the case of default.

The creditor will not be held liable if it can show it "reasonably believed" that the spouse's signature was necessary. Reasonable belief can be shown if the creditor came to this conclusion based on a "thorough review" of applicable statutes and case law.[276]

5.6.4 Reliance on Community Property to Establish Creditworthiness

If a married applicant requests individual unsecured credit in a community property state or relies on property located in such a state, the creditor may request the spouse's signature on instruments necessary to make community property available in case of death or default.[277] Similarly, in a community property state, if an applicant for individual credit relies on the future earnings or income of another person, the creditor may require the signature of that individual[278] (the official interpre-

tations allow creditors to assume that anyone applying for credit in a community property state is a resident of that state).[279] But the request for the spouse's signature may be made only if the applicant does not have enough separate property to be considered individually creditworthy and state law denies the applicant control over sufficient community property to be considered individually creditworthy.[280]

A creditor may not presume that, because income or assets are listed, the applicant is relying on them to establish creditworthiness.[281] Moreover, the creditor may request the spouse's signature only on the documents that would make the property available in case of default; there is no reason to make the spouse jointly liable on the note if a signature on some other document would suffice.[282]

5.6.5 Individual Credit When Jointly Owned Property Is Taken As Security

If an applicant requests individual *secured* credit, the creditor may require the signature of the spouse or other person jointly holding property offered as security but only on instruments necessary under state law to ensure its availability in case of default.[283] Examples of such documents include instruments to

disabled and receiving public benefits, and creditor did not show that a valid lien on joint property could not be created without husband's signature on note); Roberta W. Boylan, Office of the Comptroller of the Currency, Interpretive Staff Letter, Fed. Banking L. Rep. (CCH) ¶ 85,042 (Oct. 27, 1977) (also available at 1977 OCC Ltr. LEXIS 28); Roberta W. Boylan, Office of the Comptroller of the Currency, Interpretive Staff Letter, Fed. Banking L. Rep. (CCH) ¶ 85,043 (Oct. 27, 1977) (also available at 1977 OCC Ltr. LEXIS 29); *cf.* Evans v. Centralfed Mortgage Co., 815 F.2d 348 (5th Cir. 1987) (necessity of husband's signature on deed based on "commercially reasonable belief").

276 Farris v. Jefferson Bank, 194 B.R. 931 (Bankr. E.D. Pa. 1996); *see also* Citgo Petroleum Corp. v. Bulk Petroleum Corp., 2010 WL 3931496 (N.D. Okla. Oct. 5, 2010) (creditor was not entitled to summary judgment on issue of community property exception in absence of evidence to support how it formed a "reasonable belief" that wife's signature was required on guaranty or whether it considered the state's property laws); Boyd v. U.S. Bank Nat'l Ass'n, 2007 WL 2822518 (D. Kan. Sept. 26, 2007).

277 Reg. B, 12 C.F.R. § 1002.7(d)(3) [§ 202.7(d)(3)]; *see also* McKenzie v. U.S. Home Corp., 704 F.2d 778 (5th Cir. 1983) (no violation of ECOA when a mortgage company told an applicant she could not obtain a loan unless her divorce was finalized or her husband signed the deed of trust, because the company was acting lawfully to ensure a valid lien on the mortgaged property in a community property state); United States v. ITT Consumer Financial Corp., Clearinghouse No. 38,924 (N.D. Cal. 1985), *aff'd*, 816 F.2d 487 (9th Cir. 1987) (no ECOA violation for requiring husbands to co-sign loans on applications by creditworthy women in equal management community property states); Fed. Trade Comm'n, Informal Staff Opinion, Clearinghouse No. 37,097 (Jan. 7, 1985) (creditor in a community property state may obtain a non-applicant spouse's signature on a security agreement, but not a promissory note, when the other spouse has applied for individual secured credit and is qualified). *But see* Citgo Petroleum Corp. v. Bulk Petroleum Corp., 2010 WL 3931496 (N.D. Okla. Oct. 5, 2010) (residence in a community property state and reliance upon property in that state is not enough to trigger community property exception; creditor must provide evidence of community property relied upon and that creditor actually considered it at the time the guarantor's signature was obtained).

278 Official Interpretations of Reg. B [Official Staff Commentary on Reg. B], 12 C.F.R. pt. 1002 [pt. 202], Supp. I, § 1002.7(d)(5)-2

[§ 202.7(d)(5)-2]; *see also* United States v. ITT Consumer Financial Corp., 816 F.2d 487 (9th Cir. 1987) (as future earnings cannot be characterized prospectively as community property, it was not an ECOA violation to require the signature of an applicant's spouse when the applicant was relying on a spouse's future earnings to qualify for a loan).

279 Official Interpretations of Reg. B [Official Staff Commentary on Reg. B], 12 C.F.R. pt. 1002 [pt. 202], Supp. I, § 1002.7(d)(3)-1 [§ 202.7(d)(3)-1].

280 Reg. B, 12 C.F.R. § 1002.7(d)(3) [§ 202.7(d)(3)]; *see also* Clark v. Avco Financial Servs. of Maricopa, Inc., Clearinghouse No. 33,885 (D. Ariz. June 24, 1981) (creditor violated ECOA by requiring an applicant's spouse to sign an application for an unsecured loan when the applicant had authority under state law to bind enough community property to make her individually creditworthy).

281 *See* Reg. B, 12 C.F.R. § 1002.7(d)(1) [§ 202.7(d)(1)] (prohibiting creditors from treating the submission of joint financial information or other evidence of joint assets as an application for joint credit).

In addition, the explanatory material for the revision of the official interpretations of Regulation B [official staff commentary on Regulation B], 12 C.F.R. pt. 1002 [pt. 202], Supp. I, § 1002.7(d)(5)-2 [§ 202.7(d)(5)-2], states that "[w]hether an applicant is relying on the future earnings of a non-applicant spouse is for the creditor to determine. Because § 202.5(c)(2)(iv) [§ 1002.5(c)(2)(iv)] permits a creditor routinely to request information about a non-applicant spouse, the mere fact that the non-applicant spouse's income is listed on an application form is insufficient to show that the applicant is relying on the spouse's income." 50 Fed. Reg. 11,044, 11,045 (Apr. 5, 1988).

282 Reg. B, 12 C.F.R. § 1002.7(d)(3) [§ 202.7(d)(3)]; *see* Fed. Trade Comm'n, Informal Staff Opinion, Clearinghouse No. 37,097 (Jan. 7, 1985). *But cf.* Evans v. Centralfed Mortgage Co., 815 F.2d 348 (5th Cir. 1987) (necessity of husband's signature on deed based on "commercially reasonable belief").

283 12 C.F.R. § 1002.7(d)(4) [§ 202.7(d)(4)]; *see also* Evans v. Centralfed Mortgage Co., 815 F.2d 348 (5th Cir. 1987) (no ECOA violation when creditor required all married borrowers to obtain their spouse's signatures on the warranty deed and deed of trust for the property

create a valid lien, pass clear title, waive inchoate rights, or assign earnings.[284]

Generally, a signature to make secured property available will be needed only on a security agreement.[285] According to the official interpretation, before a creditor requests the other party's signature on the note itself, the creditor must thoroughly review statutory and decisional law or an opinion of the state attorney general.[286]

It is particularly important for advocates representing borrowers to scrutinize transactions in which the creditor uses integrated documents. These are documents in which the note, security agreement and, sometimes, the Truth in Lending disclosure statement are combined. If the non-applicant spouse's signature is needed only on the security agreement, the creditor may not require the non-applicant spouse to sign an integrated document unless the document makes clear that the signature is only for the purpose of granting a security interest and that no personal liability is imposed.[287]

5.6.6 When Do Applicants Voluntarily Enter into a Joint Account?

When a joint, rather than an individual, application for credit is made, the creditor clearly has the right to ask for the signature of both persons involved.[288] However, in order for an account to be truly joint and thus avoid ECOA co-signer limitations, the co-signer must have voluntarily entered into the loan. The official interpretation states that a joint applicant "refers to someone who applies contemporaneously with the applicant for shared or joint credit. It does not refer to someone whose signature is required by the creditor as a condition for granting the credit requested."[289]

Determining whether applicants voluntarily entered into a joint account, or were required or convinced to do so by the creditor, can be complicated. The distinction hinges on the intent of the applicants at the time of the application[290] and is

---

purchased but not on the note); Wilson v. JPMorgan Chase Bank, N.A., 2010 WL 2574032 (E.D. Cal. June 25, 2010) (no ECOA violation when wife's signature was required to create a valid lien on jointly-owned property); Siffel v. NFM, Inc., 2009 WL 3049716 (E.D. Pa. Sept. 23, 2009) (no ECOA violation; wife's signature was appropriate because it allowed lender to establish security interest in couple's home), *aff'd*, 386 Fed. Appx. 169 (3d Cir. 2010); Bolduc v. Beal Bank, 994 F. Supp. 82 (D.N.H. 1998) (creditor is permitted to require spouse's signature on documents necessary to create an undisputed interest in jointly held property offered as security), *vacating preliminary injunction*, 167 F.3d 667 (1st Cir. 1999); Tease v. First Union Home Equity Bank, 974 F. Supp. 1408 (D. Kan. 1997) (creditor may escape ECOA liability by showing it has policy of requiring all individuals with actual or potential interest in pledged property to sign loan documents); *In re* Huston, 2010 WL 4607823 (Bankr. E.D. Tenn. Nov. 5, 2010) (no ECOA violation; when Florida property was held as a tenancy in the entirety and state law required both spouses' consent to render an encumbrance upon the property effective, creditor needed wife's signature in order to obtain a limited guaranty and make property available in case of default); Transnation Title Ins. Co. v. Livingston, 2004 WL 203075 (Mich. Ct. App. Feb. 3, 2004) (no ECOA violation in requiring spouse to sign mortgage and note when Michigan law required spouse's signature to convey interest in jointly held property that secured loan); Liberty Sav. Bank v. Sortman, 1998 Ohio App. LEXIS 1667 (Ohio Ct. App. Apr. 17, 1998) (no ECOA violation because spouse's signature was required to create a valid lien against jointly held property). *But see* Frontenac Bank v. T.R. Hughes, Inc., 2012 WL 4486312, at *14–15 (Mo. Ct. App. Sept. 25, 2012) (finding the "*unlimited* personal guaranty" that bank required from wife in this case "is more than a financial instrument necessary to make property being offered as security available to satisfy a debt upon default, as the exception in Regulation B describes"; stating that neither *In re Huston* nor the regulation "provide[s] for such a broad relinquishment of rights from a spouse or other joint owner in order to make the property available to satisfy a debt").

284 Reg. B, 12 C.F.R. § 1002.7(d)(4) [§ 202.7(d)(4)]; *see* Gonzalez v. NAFH Nat'l Bank, 93 So. 3d 1054, 1058 (Fla. Dist. Ct. App. 2012) (finding that it was not discriminatory for creditor to require wife's signature on mortgage when property being offered as security to satisfy debt at issue was jointly owned by husband and wife).

285 United States v. Security Pac. Financial Systems, Clearinghouse No. 37,095 (S.D. Cal. 1983) (creditor may not generally require non-applicant spouse to assume liability on note or on integrated note and security agreement). *But see* Riggs Nat'l Bank v. Webster, 832 F. Supp. 147, 151 (D. Md. 1993) (when bank could have required applicant's spouse to sign lien documents on her solely owned property, it causes no injury to require her to sign the promissory note instead).

The *Webster* court failed to consider the personal liability which attached upon signing the promissory note that does not attach upon signing lien documents alone. If the house burned down, she would be injured by having personal liability on the note when none should have attached.

286 Official Interpretations of Reg. B [Official Staff Commentary on Reg. B], 12 C.F.R. pt. 1002 [pt. 202], Supp. I, § 1002.7(d)(4)-2

[§ 202.7(d)(4)-2]; *cf.* Rooms with a View v. Private Nat'l Mortgage Ass'n, 7 S.W.3d 840 (Tex. App. 1999) (state constitutional amendment requiring both spouses' signatures on a home improvement contract in order to create a valid mechanic's lien against the homestead does not violate the ECOA).

287 *See* Official Interpretations of Reg. B [Official Staff Commentary on Reg. B], 12 C.F.R. pt. 1002 [pt. 202], Supp. I, § 1002.7(d)(4)-3 [§ 202.7(d)(4)-3].

288 Reg. B, 12 C.F.R. § 1002.7(d)(1) [§ 202.7(d)(1)]; *see also* Midlantic Nat'l Bank v. Hansen, 48 F.3d 693 (3d Cir. 1995); Bank of America Nat'l Trust & Sav. Ass'n v. Hotel Rittenhouse Assocs., 595 F. Supp. 800 (E.D. Pa. 1984).

289 Official Interpretations of Reg. B [Official Staff Commentary on Reg. B], 12 C.F.R. pt. 1002 [pt. 202], Supp. I, § 1002.7(d)(1)-2 [§ 202.7(d)(1)-2]; *cf.* United States v. Meadors, 753 F.2d 590 (7th Cir. 1985) (signature voluntary when creditor did not provide signature block for applicant's spouse and creditor was not present when applicant's spouse added signature); BayBank v. Bornhofft, 694 N.E.2d 854 (Mass. 1998) (combination of contemporaneous application for credit and shared ownership interest in the collateral makes the defendant a joint applicant). *But see* Southwestern Pa. Reg'l Council v. Gentile, 776 A.2d 276 (Pa. Super. Ct. 2001) (not a violation of ECOA for lender to require spouse's signature under a blanket policy of requiring spousal guarantees regardless of creditworthiness if the applicant and spouse presented themselves as joint applicants).

290 Official Interpretations of Reg. B [Official Staff Commentary on Reg. B], 12 C.F.R. pt. 1002 [pt. 202], Supp. I, § 1002.7(d)(1)-3 [§ 202.7(d)(1)-3] ("A person's intent to be a joint applicant must be evidenced at the time of application."); *cf.* Morris v. Trans Union, 420 F. Supp. 2d 733 (S.D. Tex. 2006) (ECOA does not authorize a creditor to report a person as a joint account holder without some

often a question of fact.[291] Typical debtors do not know that spousal signatures often are not required, and the creditor is under no obligation to disclose the debtor's ECOA rights. Thus it is usually not difficult for a creditor to procure both spouses' signatures, especially if both are physically present when one spouse is applying for credit, but this does not make the signature voluntary.

Advocates should ascertain whether the creditor encouraged both spouses to be physically present or indicated that both spouses' signatures were required on the promissory note for a secured debt (even though the second signature on the security agreement alone might be adequate under state law to protect the creditor's security interest in such collateral).[292]

The fact that two people have signed a promissory note does not make it a joint account—otherwise, any co-signature procured illegally by a creditor would become legal because the account would have been turned into a joint one.[293] For the same reason, the fact that two people signed an application should also not necessarily mean that they intended to apply for a joint account. However, the official interpretation states that "signatures or initials on a credit application affirming the applicants' intent to apply for joint credit may be used to establish intent to apply for joint credit."[294] In addition, the model application forms in Regulation B's appendix B include a specific line where applicants can sign or initial to indicate that they intended to apply for joint credit.[295] When a bank uses a "Notice of Intent to Apply for Joint Credit" form that is compatible with the model sanctioned by the federal regulatory agency, signatures on such a form will suffice to demonstrate voluntary intent to apply for joint credit.[296]

Submission of joint financial information or other evidence of jointly held assets cannot be used to demonstrate that the applicants voluntarily entered into a joint account.[297] This is true even if the alleged co-signer signed the financial statement

and the purpose of the signature was to affirm the veracity of the information.[298] In general, methods used to establish intent to apply for joint credit must be distinct from methods used simply to affirm the accuracy of information.[299]

An interesting issue is whether a creditor may require both signatures on a refinancing of an account originally signed by two parties. Consider a case in which one party wishes to take out a new loan individually to pay off the old joint loan and meets the creditor's standards for creditworthiness for that new loan, even without the creditor relying on jointly owned property. The applicant in this case should be able to obtain the new loan individually with no co-signer and pay off the old joint obligation. There seems to be no reason to require two signatures for a new loan just because the loan proceeds will go to pay off a loan with two signatories.[300] In fact the official interpretation specifies that for renewals, if a borrower's creditworthiness is reevaluated when credit is renewed, the creditor must determine whether an additional party is still warranted and, if not, release the additional party.[301] If creditors cannot automatically require a co-signer for a renewal, they should not be permitted to do so for a refinancing.

5.6.7 Authorized Users

Credit card and other credit accounts often provide the individual borrower the opportunity to designate another individual as an authorized user. The latter may use the account but is not liable for payment of debts accrued to the account. Although creditors are permitted to decide whether or not to allow authorized users on an account, they may not decide on a prohibited basis as to which individuals are allowed to be authorized users.[302] Thus, if a creditor accepts spouses as authorized users, it may not refuse to accept others as authorized users.[303]

A creditor can restrict the number of authorized users on a card. However, the creditor may not restrict the number of authorized users on a prohibited basis. For example, a creditor may restrict all accounts to one authorized user but may not restrict only the accounts of married women to one authorized user.

Sometimes, the creditor may allow the designation of an authorized user by the account holder on the condition that the authorized user becomes contractually liable for the account. This requirement is permissible as long as the creditor does not

---

indication that such person intended to be jointly responsible for the debt), *aff'd*, 224 Fed. Appx. 415 (5th Cir. 2007).

291 Thus the issue of whether the co-signer signature is voluntary should enable the debtor to withstand a motion for summary judgment. *See, e.g.*, Cadle Co. v. Newhouse, 300 A.D.2d 526, 756 N.Y.S.2d 48 (2002).

292 Farris v. Jefferson Bank, 194 B.R. 931 (Bankr. E.D. Pa. 1996) (when husband and wife held property as tenants by the entirety under state law, wife's signature on mortgage was sufficient to encumber asset and provide secured creditor with right to proceed against property in event of default).

293 Official Interpretations of Reg. B [Official Staff Commentary on Reg. B], 12 C.F.R. pt. 1002 [pt. 202], Supp. I, § 1002.7(d)(1)-3 [§ 202.7(d)(1)-3].

294 *Id.* § 1002.7(d)(1)-3 [§ 202.7(d)(1)-3].

295 Fed. Reserve Bd., Model Form for Credit Application, 12 C.F.R. pt. 202, app. B, *as revised by* 68 Fed. Reg. 13,144, 13,154 (Mar. 18, 2003).

296 Arledge v. BanccorpSouth Bank, 2010 WL 3359539 (S.D. Miss. Aug. 25, 2010) ("Notice of Intent" form constituted "a distinct method to affirm that the plaintiffs intended to apply for joint credit").

297 Regulation B expressly prohibits creditors from presuming that the submission of joint financial information is an application for joint credit. Reg. B, 12 C.F.R. § 1002.7(d)(1) [§ 202.7(d)(1)].

298 Official Interpretations of Reg. B [Official Staff Commentary on Reg. B], 12 C.F.R. pt. 1002 [pt. 202], Supp. I, § 1002.7(d)(1)-3 [§ 202.7(d)(1)-3].

299 *Id.* § 1002.7(d)(1)-3. [§ 202.7(d)(1)-3.]

300 *But see* Sutliff v. County Sav. & Loan Co., 533 F. Supp. 1307 (N.D. Ohio 1982) (no unlawful discrimination when husband and wife were obligors on 1967 demand note and creditor required both spouses to be obligors on 1980 refinancing).

301 Official Interpretations of Reg. B [Official Staff Commentary on Reg. B], 12 C.F.R. pt. 1002 [pt. 202], Supp. I, § 1002.7(d)(5)-3 [§ 202.7(d)(5)-3].

302 *Id.* § 1002.7(a)-1 [§ 202.7(a)-1].

303 *Id.* § 1002.7(a)-2 [§ 202.7(a)-2].

differentiate on any prohibited basis in imposing this requirement.[304] Thus, creditors can require that all authorized users sign the credit agreement but may not require that only authorized users who are spouses sign the agreement. If a checking or NOW account includes an overdraft line of credit, the creditor may require that all persons authorized to draw on the transaction account assume liability for the overdraft.[305]

5.6.8 Signature of Guarantor's Spouse

The rules limiting a creditor's ability to require the signature of an applicant's spouse apply as well to a creditor's attempt to obtain the signature not only of a guarantor but also a guarantor's spouse.[306] For example, if a creditor requires one parent's signature on a credit application in addition to the applicant's, it may not require that the father sign in addition to the mother.

Another example provided by the official interpretations indicate that, when all the officers of a closely held corporation are required to personally guarantee a corporate loan, the creditor may not automatically require that spouses of married officers also sign. However, if an evaluation of an officer's financial circumstances indicates that an additional signature is required, under appropriate circumstances, this extra signatory can be the officer's spouse.[307] Similarly, the ECOA does not prohibit a spouse from signing in a capacity unrelated to marital status, for example, as a guarantor limited partner of a partnership for which the husband is the general partner.[308]

5.7 Designation of Name on Account

The creditor may not prohibit an applicant from opening (or maintaining) an account under any of the following names:[309]

- Birth-given first name (for example, Jane Applicant, rather than Mrs. John Applicant);[310]
- Birth-given surname (for example, Jane Birthname);[311]
- Spouse's surname (for example, Jane Marriedname); or
- Combined surname (for example, Jane Birthname-Marriedname).[312]

A creditor may require, however, that joint applicants on an account designate a single name for purposes of administering the account and that a single name be embossed on any credit cards issued on the account. The creditor may also require that all accounts opened or maintained at the same time be listed in the same way to prevent fraud and to simplify recordkeeping.[313] But the creditor may not require that the name designated on the account or accounts be the husband's name.[314]

There is an exception to these requirements for securities credit, but only to the extent necessary to prevent violation of rules regarding an account in which a broker or dealer has an interest or violation of rules dealing with the aggregation of accounts of spouses.[315]

5.8 Collateral, Security Deposits, Sureties, Other Forms of Creditor Protection

5.8.1 Discriminatory Practices

In addition to the ECOA's co-signature rules, a creditor may not discriminate on a prohibited basis as to the type of protection it demands on a loan, including collateral or security. For example, a creditor cannot require that married women alone put up a home as collateral on a small loan when other applicants need not do so.

Lenders often offer both secured and unsecured loans and may offer lower interest rates for the secured loans. Neverthe-

---

304 *Id.* § 1002.7(a)-1 [§ 202.7(a)-1].

305 *Id.* § 1002.7(a)-3 [§ 202.7(a)-3].

306 *Id.* § 1002.7(d)(6)-1 [§ 202.7(d)(6)-1].

307 *Id.* § 1002.7(d)(6)-1 [§ 202.7(d)(6)-1]; Riggs Nat'l Bank v. Linch, 36 F.3d 370 (4th Cir. 1994) (lender did not violate ECOA by requiring wife to sign as co-guarantor in loan to husband's business after lender discovered that many of the assets listed on husband's personal financial statement were jointly owned by husband and wife and that husband was not independently creditworthy for loan amount requested); Resolution Trust Corp. v. Townsend Assocs. Ltd. P'ship, 840 F. Supp. 1127 (E.D. Mich. 1993) (creditor had legitimate business justification for requiring wife's, as well as husband's, personal guaranty on loans to husband's partnership when creditor determined that husband was not creditworthy because he did not separately own sufficient assets and because assets listed were those jointly held with his wife; guarantors did not come forward with any evidence to show that this determination was purely a pretext to discriminate based upon marital status); *see also* Resolution Trust Corp. v. Forest Grove, Inc., 1993 U.S. Dist. LEXIS 12575 (E.D. Pa. Sept. 7, 1993), *reversed in part on other grounds*, 33 F.3d 284 (3d Cir. 1994); United States v. Lowy, 703 F. Supp. 1040 (E.D.N.Y. 1989) (Small Business Administration's standards of creditworthiness require guarantors for loans to marginal small businesses; proper to require guarantor's wife to sign as well when she had sole title to house, which was collateral, and to prevent fraudulent transfers from her husband to her).

308 *See* Wilmington Trust Co. v. Bethany Group Ltd. P'ship, 1994 Del. Super. LEXIS 146 (Del. Super. Ct. Feb. 1, 1994).

309 Reg. B, 12 C.F.R. § 1002.7(b) [§ 202.7(b)].

310 For an interesting twist on this provision, see Harbaugh v. Cont'l Ill. Nat'l Bank & Trust, 615 F.2d 1169 (7th Cir. 1980) (creditor had no affirmative duty to issue a separate account when plaintiff wife applied for credit using her husband's full name preceded by "Mrs."; offer of credit had been extended to husband only and creditor issued two cards in husband's name that wife was also entitled to use).

311 *In re* Alden's, Inc., 92 F.T.C. 901 (Fed. Trade Comm'n 1978) (creditor was ordered to stop refusing to extend joint accounts to married couples when wife used her birth-given surname or a combined surname rather than her husband's surname).

312 *See also* Reg. B, 12 C.F.R. § 1002.7(a), (b) [§ 202.7(a),(b)].

313 Official Interpretations of Reg. B [Official Staff Commentary on Reg. B], 12 C.F.R. pt. 1002 [pt. 202], Supp. I, § 1002.7(b)-1 [§ 202.7(b)-1].

314 *Id.* at § 1002.7(b)-1 [§ 202.7(b)-1].

315 Reg. B, 12 C.F.R. § 1002.3(b)(2)(iv) [§ 202.3(b)(2)(iv)].

less, if a creditor offers only secured loans to applicants of certain races, even if the interest is lower, this practice is discriminatory if other applicants are given the choice between higher-rate unsecured loans and lower-rate secured loans.

The general rule against discrimination applies not only to collateral but also to co-signers, security deposits, and other forms of protection. For example, under the ECOA, a security deposit or co-signer may not be sought from public assistance recipients if it is not sought from others.[316]

If all a merchant requires as security is a credit card in the consumer's name or a telephone number listed under the consumer's own name, even this requirement may be discriminatory if the creditor does not accept a credit card or telephone number that is in the name of the consumer's spouse.[317] This practice may be viewed as having the effect of discriminating against married, separated, or divorced women who, for historical reasons, never obtained a separate listing under their own name.

The ECOA and Regulation B do not alter or annul any state banking regulations directed only toward ensuring the solvency of financial institutions.[318] These regulations would include those requiring banks to obtain adequate security for loans and adequate documentation of that security.

5.8.2 *Injury Caused by Such Discrimination*

Merely requiring extra security may not seem injurious to a consumer, but such discrimination can often cause the consumer financial damage even if the loan never goes into default, and these damages should be recoverable under the ECOA. If a consumer must put up personal property as collateral, the creditor may require the consumer to purchase property insurance on that collateral. Using a home as security may require various closing costs. These costs are further increased because they are often included in the amount financed, which in turn increases the finance charges and the cost of any credit insurance.

There may be additional damages if the loan goes into default. It might be possible in such a situation, when there is an ECOA violation, to seek not only actual and punitive damages but also the voiding of the co-signer's obligation under the note or other instrument.[319] It should be argued that, were it not for the illegal discrimination, the property would not have been offered as collateral or a co-signer would not have been required to sign the loan.

---

316 *See, e.g.*, Reed v. Northwestern Bell Telephone, Clearinghouse No. 27,524 (D. Minn. 1981).

317 *See* Reg. B, 12 C.F.R. § 1002.6(b)(4) [§ 202.6(b)(4)] (can only require telephone listing at applicant's residence, not in applicant's name); Fed. Trade Comm'n, Informal Staff Opinion, Clearinghouse No. 37,084 (May 26, 1983) (ECOA violation when car rental agency required that a customer without a major credit card have a telephone listing in their own name).

318 Reg. B, 12 C.F.R. § 1002.11(d) [§ 202.11(d)]. Similar federal banking regulations are also unaffected.

319 *See* §§ 11.8.5.3, 11.9.2.2, *infra*.

Chapter 6   Discrimination in Credit Evaluation

6.1 Introduction

This chapter focuses on discrimination in the credit evaluation process. It discusses examples of credit evaluation practices that violate the general rule against discrimination as well as the special ECOA requirements with respect to credit evaluation.

Some of these special ECOA requirements prohibit certain types of credit discrimination even though the discrimination is only indirectly linked to a prohibited basis. Examples are credit decisions based on the applicant's likelihood of childbearing, type of income, telephone listing, and certain aspects of credit history. As discussed in § 6.5, *infra*, these special ECOA rules provide protections for women and, to a lesser extent, for applicants aged sixty-two or over.

Other special ECOA requirements permit creditors in certain situations to take into consideration three of the prohibited bases—the applicant's age, public assistance status, and marital status. These exceptions are set out in §§ 6.6.2, 6.6.3, and 6.6.4, *infra*.

This chapter pays significant attention to the topic of credit scoring—one of the types of credit evaluation systems—because of concerns about whether credit scoring has a disparate impact on protected groups, especially with regard to race and ethnicity.

6.2 Credit Evaluation Practices That Violate the General Rule Against Discrimination

6.2.1 The ECOA and FHA Standards

The ECOA and Regulation B prohibit discrimination in credit evaluation on a prohibited basis. Regulation B specifically states that a creditor shall not take a prohibited basis into account "in any system of evaluating the creditworthiness of applicants."[1] Regulation B also prohibits a creditor from using any information it obtains on an applicant to discriminate on a prohibited basis.[2] These standards essentially apply the general rule against discrimination to credit evaluation.

The Fair Housing Act also generally prohibits any type of discrimination in the evaluation or denial of credit. Department of Housing and Urban Development regulations prohibit using different policies, practices, or procedures in evaluating or determining creditworthiness because of the applicant's race, color, religion, sex, handicap, familial status, or national origin.[3] Furthermore, a lender may not rely on an appraisal that it knows or should have known uses impermissible bases of evaluation.[4]

Thus, both the ECOA and Fair Housing Act standards prohibit virtually any discrimination on a prohibited basis as to credit evaluation.

6.2.2 Examples of Credit Evaluation Practices That Violate the General Rule

6.2.2.1 Applying Different Standards on a Prohibited Basis

The general rule against discrimination prohibits creditors from applying different standards to applicants on a prohibited basis. For example, creditors may not use one set of underwriting standards for white applicants and another, more stringent, set of standards for protected groups.[5]

---

1 Reg. B, 12 C.F.R. § 1002.6(b)(1) [§ 202.6(b)(1)].
2 Reg. B, 12 C.F.R. § 1002.6(a) [§ 202.6(a)].

3 24 C.F.R. § 100.130(b)(1).

    It is critical that the plaintiff link the different treatment of credit applicants with an impermissible basis for such treatment. For example, in Simms v. First Gibraltar Bank, 83 F.3d 1546 (5th Cir. 1996), the plaintiff presented evidence discrediting the lender's articulated reasons for denying credit and showing that the bank's less-than-thorough handling of the plaintiff's mortgage application did not conform generally to customary industry practices. The court nonetheless ruled that this evidence did not support an inference of discrimination because there was no evidence that the bank treated similar, "non-protected" applications differently. Simms v. First Gibraltar Bank, 83 F.3d 1546, 1559 (5th Cir. 1996).

4 24 C.F.R. § 100.135; *see also* 12 C.F.R. § 128.11 (Office of Thrift Supervision nondiscrimination requirements); Steptoe v. Sav. of America, 800 F. Supp. 1542 (N.D. Ohio 1992).

    For more on discrimination in the appraisal process, see § 6.2.2.3, *infra*.

5 The use of different standards for white and minority groups sometimes may not be due to overt racism but to subtle favoritism by the evaluators toward members of the evaluator's racial group. Some researchers have hypothesized that discrimination in credit evaluation may occur not because of discriminatory intent, but due to "cultural affinity" between the evaluator and the credit applicant. *See* Raphael Bostic, *A Test of Cultural Affinity in Home Mortgage Lending* 89, J. of Fin. Serv. Research (Apr. 2003).

    Professor Ian Ayres has identified four distinct types of racial (and gender) animus with varying degrees of discriminatory intent that might motivate disparate treatment in a credit transaction. When motivated by any of these types of animus the seller might

Discrimination can also be present even if an applicant failed to obtain a passing grade on the creditor's test for creditworthiness. The issue is whether other applicants received the same failing grade but were still offered credit. For example, one of the most common standards used in mortgage lending is that a loan must not exceed a certain percentage of the home's value. This loan-to-value ratio is a fairly objective standard; it would not be illegal discrimination to deny credit to all applicants whose ratios were over a certain level.[6] On the other hand, it would be illegal discrimination to almost always deny mortgages to borrowers of color when a loan is above the stated ratio while often making exceptions for white applicants.[7]

Sometimes the differences in credit evaluation are hard to spot and are more easily uncovered by using paired testers.[8] For example, one study found that, when paired testers approached a lender, their expense/income ratios were computed differently, with utility costs being included only for African-American applicants.[9] At other times, African-American testers with the same ratio were told they were just over the limit, but whites were told they qualified.[10]

An example of the difficulty in detecting discrimination in evaluation of creditworthiness can be found in *Cooley v. Sterling Bank*.[11] In *Cooley*, an African-American plaintiff who sought a $100,000 unsecured line of credit attempted to show discrimination in evaluation by retaining an expert to compare his loan application with the files of twenty white applicants. Each of the white applicants had been granted an unsecured line of credit for $100,000 or more, yet the plaintiff's own expert was only able to highlight three of the files that were comparable to the plaintiff's file. Furthermore, the court found that none of these three white borrowers who had been granted credit was "similarly situated" to the plaintiff and, thus, there were no white applicants to whom the plaintiff's application could be compared.[12]

In some cases, using one credit evaluation standard will nevertheless result in differential treatment based on race, even without exceptions being made. For student loans, a student applying for aid will be granted a particular set of loan terms based on the likelihood that other students at that school will default. The concerns about use of such cohort default rates are not about exceptions being made to the standard, but rather about the intentional or disparate impact discrimination which may result from the use of a standard that clearly disadvantages students of color. For example, as discussed in *Rodriguez v. SLM Corp.*,[13] Sallie Mae's underwriting process considers the federal cohort default rate of the applicant's school. Students attending schools with higher loan default rates receive loans with higher interest rates. While Sallie Mae knew that this policy would have a disproportionate impact on students from schools with high populations of students of color, it nevertheless applied this approach across the board. The court allowed claims for intentional and disparate impact discrimination to go forward.

6.2.2.2 Using Different Investigation Procedures on a Prohibited Basis

The general rule against discrimination prohibits creditors from implementing different investigatory procedures on a prohibited basis. Regulation B specifically states that creditors may not discriminate on a prohibited basis as to "investigation procedures."[14] Thus creditors may not order credit reports on the spouses of married women who apply for individual accounts but not on the spouses of married men who apply for individual accounts.[15]

Similarly, creditors may not discriminate as to the information they actually review. When a couple applies for a joint account, it would be discriminatory to solely or primarily consider the husband's credit report without considering the wife's credit report.

6.2.2.3 Appraisal Practices That Violate the General Rule Against Discrimination

In applying for home mortgage loans, the appraisal of the real estate can have a significant impact on whether an applicant qualifies. Differences in appraisal practices on a prohibited basis are specifically prohibited by the Fair Housing Act[16] and should violate the ECOA and sections 1981 and 1982 of the Civil Rights Acts as well.

---

claim that he had no discriminatory intent at all but was acting for "rational" or profit-oriented reasons. However, Professor Ayres argues that even discrimination with a low level of "intent" should be actionable.

6 Thomas v. First Fed. Sav. Bank of Ind., 653 F. Supp. 1330 (N.D. Ind. 1987).

7 *See* §§ 6.4.5.2–6.4.5.4, *infra* (cases involving a similar phenomenon: discriminatory "overrides" with respect to credit score thresholds). *But see* Cooley v. Sterling Bank, 280 F. Supp. 2d 1331 (M.D. Ala. 2003) (bank's denial of unsecured line of credit to African-American applicant on basis of high debt-to-income ratio was not discriminatory, despite the fact that bank had granted unsecured lines of credit to twenty white applicants for all of whom but one the bank had failed to calculate debt-to-income ratios), *aff'd*, 116 Fed. Appx. 242 (11th Cir. 2004).

8 *See* §§ 4.4.4 and 5.3.3.2, *supra* (further discussing of using testers).

9 Cathy Cloud & George Galster, *What Do We Know About Racial Discrimination in Mortgage Markets*, 22 Rev. of Black Pol. Econ. 101 (1993).

10 *Id.*

11 280 F. Supp. 2d 1331 (M.D. Ala. 2003).

12 *Id.*

    The requirement of showing that white borrowers who were granted credit were "similarly situated" is derived from the *Mc-*

Donnell Douglas analysis for disparate treatment, discussed in § 4.2.3.1, *supra*.

13 Rodriguez v. SLM Corp., 2009 WL 598252 (D. Conn. Mar. 6, 2009).

14 Regulation B, 12 C.F.R. § 1002.2(m) [§ 202.2(m)], defines investigation procedures as part of a credit transaction, and Regulation B, 12 C.F.R. § 1002.4 [§ 202.4], prohibits discrimination concerning any aspect of a credit transaction.

15 *In re* Alden's, Inc., 92 F.T.C. 901 (Fed. Trade Comm'n 1978).

16 24 C.F.R. § 100.135; *see also* 12 C.F.R. § 128.11 (Office of Thrift Supervision nondiscrimination requirements).

For example, in one case the plaintiffs, an African-American couple, sued under both the Fair Housing Act and sections 1981 and 1982.[17] The plaintiffs attempted to buy a home that their lender initially appraised at their offer price of $115,000. The bank's chief appraiser disagreed with the valuation, however, and ordered his staff appraiser to redo the numbers. The second appraisal came in at $94,500, and the bank refused to lend the Steptoes the entire sum which they needed to purchase the house. Less than a month later, another buyer bought the house for $115,000. In denying the bank's motion for summary judgment, the court ruled that the Steptoes had made a prima facie case of discrimination in violation of the Fair Housing Act and sections 1981 and 1982.[18]

Discrimination in appraisals can be quite significant. In one disturbing example, an African-American editor for the *Wall Street Journal* reported that he received a surprisingly low appraisal on his home. He had the home reappraised after removing his family pictures from the home and replacing them with pictures of his white secretary and her family. The second appraisal came back significantly higher.[19]

Appraisers may also value property located in communities of color at lower amounts. In some cases, an appraiser may even refuse to issue a valuation for properties in these communities, resulting in automatic denial of a mortgage.[20]

Claims against the creditor for a discriminatory appraisal will need to show some nexus between the creditor and the appraisal firm.[21]

Concerns regarding appraisal practices may have diminished in some instances due to the Home Valuation Code of Conduct, the result of separate agreements made in March 2008 by the Federal Home Loan Mortgage Corporation (Freddie Mac) and Federal National Mortgage Association (Fannie Mae) with the Federal Housing Finance Agency (FHFA) and the New York State attorney general to enhance the independence and accuracy of the appraisal process.[22] However, following the effective date of these rules, one court found that a disparity in appraisals did not create an inference of discrimination against African-American home owners, even when comparable homes had recently sold for much more, another appraiser found a value $70,000 higher, and the insurer had similarly valued the home at the higher amount.[23] While the court of appeals reversed the dismissal of this case and found that the plaintiff had stated a claim for discrimination under the FHA based on the facts alleged, the court also stated that much more information would need to be provided in order to prove the case.[24]

6.2.2.4 Failure to Combine Joint Applicant Income on the Basis of Marital Status

Creditors may not use marital status as grounds for determining whether to grant credit.[25] A creditor who refuses to aggregate the incomes of an unmarried couple applying jointly for a mortgage violates the ECOA by discriminating on the basis of marital status.[26]

6.2.2.5 Requirements for Immediate Payment

One form of discrimination that is not obvious is the refusal to allow a customer to delay payment until some time after the goods or services have been delivered. For example, various tradespeople, doctors, or merchants, while not formally offering credit, will allow certain customers to mail in their payments later while requiring immediate payment up-front from other customers.

Such informal arrangements to defer payment when there is no installment payment schedule or finance charge are generally considered incidental consumer credit under Regulation B.[27] While the ECOA generally applies to incidental consumer credit,[28] Regulation B exempts such credit from many specific ECOA provisions.[29] Nevertheless, incidental consumer credit is not excluded from the general rule against discrimination, so discrimination on a prohibited basis as to when a creditor will defer payment clearly violates the ECOA.[30]

---

17 Steptoe v. Sav. of America, 800 F. Supp. 1542 (N.D. Ohio 1992).

18 *See* § 2.3.2.3.4, *supra*.

19 Joseph Boyce, *L.A. Riots and the "Black Tax,"* Wall St. J., May 12, 1992, at A24.

20 *See, e.g.*, Hood v. Midwest Sav. Bank, 95 Fed. Appx. 768 (6th Cir. 2004) (appraiser's refusal to issue an appraisal did not constitute redlining in violation of the ECOA because she contended there were not "comparable" sales in the neighborhood, which would be necessary for an appraisal).

21 *See* Brown v. Interbay Funding, 2004 WL 2579596 (D. Del. Nov. 8, 2004) (partially granting creditor's motion to dismiss plaintiffs' claim that creditor was liable for appraisal by independent contractor, but denying motion to dismiss claim by plaintiff that creditor relied on discriminatory appraisal in making loan, in violation of 12 C.F.R. § 128.11).

22 *See* Home Valuation Code of Conduct FAQs, *available at* www.efannie mae.com/sf/guides/ssg/relatedsellinginfo/appcode/pdf/hvccfaqs.pdf.

23 Swanson v. Citi, 706 F. Supp. 2d 854 (N.D. Ill. 2009).

24 Swanson v. Citibank, 614 F.3d 400 (7th Cir. 2010).

25 Reg. B, 12 C.F.R. § 1002.2(z) [§ 202.2(z)]; *see* Shuman v. Standard Oil Co., 453 F. Supp. 1150 (N.D. Cal. 1978) (divorced woman's suit withstood motion for partial summary judgment when she alleged that the creditor had discriminated on the basis of sex or marital status as revealed in a credit report).

26 Reg. B, 12 C.F.R. § 1002.6(b)(8) [§ 202.6(b)(8)]; *see* Markham v. Colonial Mortgage Serv. Co., 605 F.2d 566 (D.C. Cir. 1979) (noting that, had the couple been married, the creditor would have been required to consider both of their incomes; however, on remand, deciding that applicants had been denied credit because their combined income was insufficient and not because of their marital status), *aff'd*, Markham v. Colonial Mortgage Serv. Co., Consumer Cred. Guide (CCH) ¶ 97,403 (D.D.C. 1980). *See generally* § 3.4.1, *supra*.

27 *See* § 2.2.6.3, *supra*.

28 *See* § 2.2.6.3, *supra*.

29 Reg. B, 12 C.F.R. § 202.3(c) [§ 1002.3(c)].
   However, incidental business credit is not exempt from these provisions. The Federal Reserve Board had considered exempting incident business credit but decided against it, citing concerns about possible discrimination against minority-owned businesses. 68 Fed. Reg. 13,144, 13,146 (Mar. 18, 2003).

30 Official Interpretations of Reg. B [Official Staff Commentary on Reg. B], 12 C.F.R. pt. 1002 [pt. 202], Supp. I, § 1002.3-1 [§ 202.3-1].

For example, a doctor who does not ordinarily require patients to pay immediately may not demand cash from older patients to avoid a lengthy wait for Medicare payments. Similarly, a grocery store may not run a tab for most customers but refuse to do so for those who pay with Food Stamps.

6.2.2.6 Discrimination in Credit Limits

The amount of credit to be extended is also subject to the general rule against discrimination. Thus, an individual unmarried applicant should be evaluated for and receive the same credit limit as a similarly situated but married applicant.

State law sometimes treats married and unmarried applicants differently with regard to the amount of credit that may be extended. In many states, loan statutes provide for graduated interest rates such that loans up to a certain amount carry one interest rate while any balances above that amount carry a different interest rate. For example, the rate of interest may be 18% on the first $500 of a loan and 12% on the balance above $500. Often, these state statutes also impose ceilings on the loan amount. Prior to the enactment of the ECOA, many statutes contained provisions prohibiting separate extensions of credit to a husband and wife because it might be an attempt to circumvent the ceilings imposed on the amount that could be loaned at the higher interest rates.

The ECOA preempts those state laws which prohibit the separate extension of consumer credit to a husband and wife.[31] State statutes which aggregate or otherwise combine the separate accounts of spouses for the purpose of determining permissible finance charges or loan ceilings are also preempted.[32]

Statutes establishing permissible loan ceilings are to be construed as permitting each spouse to become individually liable to a creditor up to the amount of the loan ceiling, minus the amount for which each is jointly liable. For instance, if a state's permissible loan ceiling is $1000, and a married couple is jointly liable to a creditor for an unpaid debt of $250, each could subsequently become individually liable for $750.[33]

There is potential for creditor abuse in these situations, as an applicant's spouse may be pressured to "voluntarily" apply for an individual account, which would result in higher interest rates for that applicant. When there are two such individual accounts, the attorney should carefully interview the clients to ensure that the creditor was not attempting to use the ECOA to circumvent usury laws.

6.2.2.7 Denial of Credit for Exercise of Rights Under the Consumer Credit Protection Act

One interesting potential use of the ECOA is when a creditor denies credit (or in any other way distinguishes the applicant)

because the applicant does not wish to buy allegedly optional credit insurance. Under the Truth in Lending Act, creditors are required to include charges for mandatory credit insurance in the finance charge calculation but need not do so if the credit insurance is optional[34] An applicant who refuses to purchase "optional" credit insurance and then is denied credit by a creditor may have an ECOA claim for discrimination on the basis of the good faith exercise of rights under the Consumer Credit Protection Act.[35] Although the creditor's actions may also violate other federal and state laws, ECOA punitive damages may be a particularly attractive remedy.

6.3 Understanding Credit Evaluation Systems

6.3.1 Introduction to the Three Types of Credit Evaluation Systems

In order to understand discrimination in the credit evaluation process, it is essential to understand the different systems used for credit evaluation and how these systems operate. There are basically three types of credit evaluation systems used by creditors: credit scoring systems; judgmental systems; or combined systems that share aspects of both of the other two systems.

Each of these systems base their method of evaluating credit applications on the assumption that past credit history is the best predictor of how credit obligations will be handled in the future. Using these systems, some creditors will look only at the credit history and present financial situation of an individual applicant when deciding whether to extend credit to that person. Other creditors will look at both the applicant's history of making payments and at how the applicant compares to an "ideal" credit applicant. Applicants seeking credit from the latter type of creditor may be rejected despite their good credit histories merely because their characteristics as a credit applicant vary too much from those of the ideal applicant.[36]

Theoretically, credit evaluation systems should measure only those characteristics shown by experience to be predictors of a good or bad credit risk. Nevertheless, the legislative history of the ECOA is replete with examples of creditors that rejected whole classes of credit applicants, such as older persons, minorities, or single women, on the unfounded assumption that they were poor credit risks. Many of these assumptions are still built into credit evaluation systems.[37] This type of residual or built-in discrimination is hard to identify because the inner

---

31 15 U.S.C. § 1691d(c); *see also* Reg. B, 12 C.F.R. § 1002.7(a) [§ 202.7(a)].

32 15 U.S.C. § 1691d(d); Reg. B, 12 C.F.R. § 1002.11(c) [§ 202.11(c)].

33 Regulation B, 12 C.F.R. § 202.11(c) n.16, which contained this example, was not included in the 1985 revised Regulation B or the FRB's official staff commentary, but the requirements are unchanged.

34 *See* National Consumer Law Center, Truth in Lending § 3.9.4 (8th ed. 2012).

35 Bryson v. Bank of N.Y., 584 F. Supp. 1306 (S.D.N.Y. 1984).

36 *See, e.g.*, Cherry v. Amoco Oil Co., 490 F. Supp. 1026 (N.D. Ga. 1980) (applicant denied credit because creditor had experienced poor payments on accounts of customers in applicant's zip code area).

37 Assumptions also may be built into the risk-based pricing systems of creditors, resulting in protected classes paying more for credit. *See* § 8.5, *infra*.

workings of credit evaluation systems remain a closely guarded secret within the credit industry.

6.3.2 Credit Scoring Systems

6.3.2.1 Description of Credit Scoring

A credit scoring system is one that numerically weighs or "scores" some or all of the factors considered in the underwriting process. There has been an explosive growth in the use of credit scoring systems over the last two decades, and this growth has been accompanied by some controversy. A detailed analysis of credit scoring and the controversies surrounding it are discussed in another treatise in this series.[38] The relationship between credit scoring and credit discrimination is discussed in § 6.4, *infra*.

Factors used in a credit scoring system may include payment history on past financial obligations, amounts owed, length of credit history, types of credit already held, length of employment, and income level.[39] The number of points received often determines whether the applicant is offered credit and how much credit is granted.

Exactly what is meant by a "credit score" varies depending on the score's creator and the specific industry involved. Basically, there are two types of credit scores: credit history scores and credit application scores.[40]

Consumers have several ways to obtain their credit scores under the Fair Credit Reporting Act (FCRA). They can purchase a credit score, although it will often not be the type of score actually used by lenders.[41] Mortgage lenders must provide credit scores when they are used in conjunction with the extension of credit secured by residential real estate.[42] The Dodd-Frank Wall Street Reform and Consumer Protection Act of 2010 ("Dodd-Frank Act") added a requirement that creditors must disclose the credit scores they used when providing FCRA adverse action and risk-based pricing notices.[43] In July 2011 the Federal Reserve Board revised the model ECOA adverse action notices in order to implement the Dodd-Frank Act's credit score disclosure requirement.[44]

6.3.2.2 Regulation B Definition of Credit Scoring

Regulation B includes a definition of "credit scoring system," which is described under the regulation as "an empirically derived, demonstrably and statistically sound, credit scoring system."[45] However, Regulation B makes limited use of this definition, referring to it only with respect to when creditors are permitted to consider information about age and public assistance status.[46] The Fair Credit Reporting Act contains a definition of "credit score" that is different from that found under Regulation B.[47]

Under Regulation B, an empirically derived, demonstrably and statistically sound, credit scoring system is one which compares, by assignment of points or by other methods, certain key attributes of the applicant or the transaction[48] to the attributes of sample groups or the population of creditworthy and non-creditworthy applicants who have applied to the creditor within a "reasonably preceding" period of time.[49] The total score, taken alone or in conjunction with other information about the applicant, is used to determine whether credit should be granted or denied.[50]

Such a system must satisfy four criteria:[51]

- The data used to develop the system must constitute either the entire applicant file or an appropriate sample of it;[52]
- The system must have the purpose of predicting applicants' creditworthiness with respect to the "legitimate business interests" of the creditor using it—legitimate interests include minimizing operating expenses and bad debts (although no examples of "illegitimate" interests are given in the regulation, one such interest might be the

---

38 National Consumer Law Center, Fair Credit Reporting ch. 14 (7th ed. 2010 and Supp.).

39 *See id.* § 14.5 (describing some of the factors used in some of the most popular credit scoring systems).

40 *Id.* § 14.2.2; *see id.* § 14.4.2 (information on how consumers can obtain a copy of their credit scores from industry giant Fair, Isaac & Co.).

41 15 U.S.C. § 1681g(f)(1). *See generally* National Consumer Law Center, Fair Credit Reporting § 3.3.4 (7th ed. 2010 and Supp.).

42 15 U.S.C. § 1681g(g)(1). *See generally* National Consumer Law Center, Fair Credit Reporting § 8.4.3 (7th ed. 2010 and Supp.).

43 15 U.S.C. § 1681m(a)(2)(A), (h)(5)(E)(ii), *as added by* Pub. L. No. 111-203, tit. X, § 1100F(1), 124 Stat. 1376 (July 21, 2010); *see* § 10.10, *infra. See generally* National Consumer Law Center, Fair Credit Reporting §§ 8.5.2.4, 8.7.3 (7th ed. 2010 and Supp.).

44 76 Fed. Reg. 41590 (July 15, 2011). The model notices are reprinted in Appendix B, *infra*.

45 Reg. B, 12 C.F.R. § 1002.2(t) [§ 202.2(t)].

46 *See* Official Interpretations of Reg. B [Official Staff Commentary on Reg. B], 12 C.F.R. pt. 1002 [pt. 202], Supp. I, § 1002.2(p)-1 [§ 202.2(p)-1] (explaining that the purpose of the definition of credit scoring system is to define when a system may use age as a predictive factor).

47 The Fair Credit Reporting Act defines a credit score as "a numerical value or a categorization derived from a statistical tool or modeling system used by a person who makes or arranges a loan to predict the likelihood or certain credit behaviors, including default (and the numerical value or the categorization derived from such analysis may be referred to as a 'risk predictor' or 'risk score')." 15 U.S.C. § 1681g(f)(1)(A); *see* National Consumer Law Center, Fair Credit Reporting § 14.2.3.1 (7th ed. 2010 and Supp.).

48 Reg. B, 12 C.F.R. § 1002.2(p)(1) [§ 202.2(p)(1)]; *see also* Official Interpretations of Reg. B [Official Staff Commentary on Reg. B], 12 C.F.R. pt. 1002 [pt. 202], Supp. I, § 1002.2(p)-1 [§ 202.2(p)-1].

49 Reg. B, 12 C.F.R. § 1002.2(p)(1) [§ 202.2(p)(1)].
The regulation provides no further guidance on what constitutes a valid "sample group," a "reasonably preceding" period of time, or an "empirical" comparison of applicants or sample groups. *See* David Hsia, *Credit Scoring and the Equal Credit Opportunity Act*, 30 Hastings L.J. 371 (1978) (Federal Reserve Board employee's discussion of the intricacies of credit scoring systems).

50 Reg. B, 12 C.F.R. § 1002.2(p)(1) [§ 202.2(p)(1)]; *see also* Official Interpretations of Reg. B [Official Staff Commentary on Reg. B], 12 C.F.R. pt. 1002 [pt. 202], Supp. I, § 1002.2(p)-1 [§ 202.2(p)-1].

51 Reg. B, 12 C.F.R. § 1002.2(p)(1) [§ 202.2(p)(1)].

52 Reg. B, 12 C.F.R. § 1002.2(p)(1)(i) [§ 202.2(p)(1)(i)].

desire to maintain an all-white clientele in a mortgage market);[53]

- The system must be "developed and validated using accepted statistical principles and methodology";[54] and
- The system should be periodically reviewed and revalidated as to its predictive ability and adjusted accordingly.[55]

Despite the requirement for validating and revalidating a credit scoring system, there are no procedures or standards set forth for these requirements. The lack of revalidation may significantly reduce the predictiveness of scoring models, especially in economic downturns.[56]

Moreover, a creditor suffers few consequences if its system does not meet the Regulation B standards for credit scoring systems. Recall that Regulation B's definition of a credit scoring system is only relevant to the consideration of age and public assistance status in evaluating credit. Furthermore, if a credit scoring system fails to meet Regulation B's definition, then the creditor need merely comply with the requirements of a judgmental system.[57] Practically speaking, the impetus for compliance has come from regulatory agencies that have required creditors to meet the requirements of Regulation B's definition.[58]

6.3.3 Judgmental Systems

A judgmental system is defined by Regulation B as any credit evaluation system other than a "demonstrably and statistically sound, empirically derived credit system"—that is, a system other than a credit scoring system.[59] A judgmental system generally involves a subjective examination of the overall application—often, a general search of the application for characteristics that are "acceptable" to the creditor based on past experience.

At times, a judgmental system operates much like a credit scoring system because the judgmental creditor may favorably assign value to certain characteristics on a credit report, such as a positive payment history. However, unlike the credit scoring system, the judgmental system grants or denies credit based on a general overview of the application rather than on a list of specific factors. The decision to grant or deny credit can be based on a single factor which overshadows the rest of the application. Thus, the outcome is often less predictable under a judgmental system.

There is great potential for judgmental systems to produce discriminatory results because of their subjective nature. At worst, they involve a creditor's judgment, based solely on isolated experiences with supposedly similar applicants, that an applicant is a bad credit risk. In a judgmental system, standards for granting credit can and do vary from one applicant to the next. If the person who takes the application finds the applicant unimpressive, pushy, or difficult to communicate with, credit can be denied merely on that employee's recommendation. When judgmental systems are involved, the leeway given to creditors can also perpetuate past patterns of discrimination because employees are apt to approve applicants most similar to those found suitable in the past.

6.3.4 Combination Systems

Regulation B allows combination systems of credit evaluation, that is, systems that require applicants to pass both a credit scoring and judgmental evaluation. In this fashion, any credit scoring system may be transformed into a combination system whenever an applicant obtains a passing score but is still considered an undesirable applicant by the creditor. Automated underwriting systems for mortgage loans often have cut-offs for automatic approvals and then a middle category for applicants who do not get an automatic approval but for whom an additional, ad hoc analysis is done. Such a combination system would violate the general rule against discrimination if the additional requirements were applied only to protected groups or if they were applied to all applicants but had a disparate impact on protected groups.[60]

6.3.5 Different Requirements for Credit Scoring and Judgmental Systems

Despite the fact that Regulation B goes to some length to define credit scoring systems, judgmental systems, and combination systems, the requirements for the two main types of systems are not significantly different. The only provisions of the regulation that differ depending on whether the creditor uses a credit scoring or a judgmental system are those concerning the consideration of age and public assistance in credit evaluation. These rules are discussed in §§ 6.6.2 and 6.6.3, *infra*.

---

53 Reg. B, 12 C.F.R. § 1002.2(p)(1)(ii) [§ 202.2(p)(1)(ii)].

54 Reg. B, 12 C.F.R.§ 1002.2(p)(1)(iii) [§ 202.2(p)(1)(iii)].

  The services of an expert may be required to establish whether a system satisfies this criterion.

55 Reg. B, 12 C.F.R. § 1002.2(p)(1)(iv) [§ 202.2(p)(1)(iv)].

  No definition of "periodically" is given in the regulation. *See also* Official Interpretations of Reg. B [Official Staff Commentary on Reg. B], 12 C.F.R. pt. 1002 [pt. 202], Supp. I, § 1002.2(p)-2 [§ 202.2(p)-2] (giving some guidance on revalidation procedures).

56 *See* National Consumer Law Center, Fair Credit Reporting § 14.8.4.1 (7th ed. 2010 and Supp.).

57 *See* § 6.6.2.5, *infra* (requirements with respect to age), § 6.6.3.2, *infra* (requirements with respect to public assistance status).

58 For example, the Office of the Comptroller of Currency has required the national banks that it regulates to ensure that the banks' scoring models meet the validation requirements of Regulation B's definition of credit scoring. Office of the Comptroller of the Currency, Credit Scoring Models, OCC Bulletin No. 97-24 (May 20, 1997).

  The National Credit Union Administration has similarly required credit unions to use scoring systems that meet the criteria of Regulation B's definition of credit scoring. Letter from National Credit Union Admin. to credit unions, No. 174 (Aug. 1995).

59 Reg. B, 12 C.F.R. § 1002.2(t) [§ 202.2(t)].

---

60 *See* §§ 6.4.5.2–6.4.5.4, *infra* (example in which requirements were lowered for groups on a prohibited basis, and regarding discriminatory use of credit score "overrides").

6.4 Discrimination Issues Raised by Credit Scoring

6.4.1 Data Indicating That Minority and Other Protected Groups Are Disadvantaged by Credit Scoring

As long as there have been credit scores, there have been concerns that scoring systems contain biases which disproportionately impact protected groups.[61] These concerns are heightened by numerous studies showing that, as a group, certain racial and ethnic groups have lower credit scores than whites. These studies include:

- A 1996 Freddie Mac study which found that African Americans were three times as likely to have FICO scores below 620 as whites. The same study showed that Hispanics are twice as likely as whites to have FICO scores under 620.[62]
- A 1997 analysis by Fair Isaac itself showing that consumers living in minority neighborhoods had lower overall credit scores.[63]
- A study by University of North Carolina researchers of borrowers who received community reinvestment mortgages showing that one-third of African Americans in this pool had credit scores under 620, as compared to only 15% of whites. Furthermore, this same study found that another one-third of African Americans had credit scores between 621 and 660 (as compared to 20% of whites), which means that two-thirds of African Americans in this pool had what is considered marginal or poor credit.[64]
- A 2004 study by Federal Reserve researchers of over 300,000 credit history files, finding that fewer than 40% of consumers who lived in high-minority neighborhoods had credit scores over 701, while nearly 70% of consumers who lived in mostly white neighborhoods had scores over 701.[65]
- A 2004 study published by Harvard's Joint Center for Housing Studies which simulated changes in credit scores based on 200,000 credit files matched with data from the Survey of Consumer Finances. Researchers found that, for the period of 1989 to 2001, the median credit score had increased for whites, from 727 to 738, but the median credit score for African Americans dropped from 693 to 676. The median score dropped even more for Hispanics, from 695 to 670. The percentage of African Americans with credit scores under 660 (the cut-off for "good credit") grew from 27% to 42% and, for Hispanics, it grew from 29% to 49%, while among whites it rose only slightly from 17% to 19%.[66]
- A 2006 study from the Brookings Institution which analyzed 25 million credit reports, finding that counties with high minority populations are more likely to have lower average credit scores than predominately white counties.[67] In the counties with a very low typical score (scores of 560 to 619), Brookings found that about 19% of the population is Hispanic and another 28% is African American. On the other hand, the counties that have higher typical credit scores tend to be essentially all-white counties. In counties where the average credit scores were between 700 and 719, only about 5.1% of the population was Hispanic and just 1.1% was African American. The study's author did caution that his finding was not evidence of bias but "point[ed] to an association, which frankly is not very well understood."[68]
- A 2007 study by the University of Denver, conducted for the National Black Caucus of State Legislators, finding that areas with higher concentrations of African Americans typically had lower credit scores.[69] As the population of African Americans in one city (Charlotte, NC) increased by zip code, the average credit score decreased.[70] As the average credit score by zip code decreased, the number of bank branches similarly decreased while the number of

---

61 Fed. Reserve Bank of Boston, *Perspectives on Credit Scoring and Fair Lending: A Five-Part Article Series: Part 1*, Communities & Banking, Spring 2000, at 2.

62 *See* Fed. Home Loan Mortgage Corp., Automated Underwriting: Making Mortgage Lending Simpler and Fairer for America's Families (Sept. 1996).

63 Fair, Isaac & Co., The Effectiveness of Scoring on Low-to-Moderate Income and High-Minority Area Populations 22 illus. 9 (Aug. 1997).

64 Walter R. Davis, Roberto G. Quercia, Michael A. Stegman, & Eric Stein, *Performance of Community Reinvestment Loans: Implications for Secondary Market Purchases*, *in* Low Income Homeownership: Examining the Unexamined Goal 363 tbl. 12-7 (Nicolas P. Retsinas & Eric S. Belsky eds., 2002) (statistics derived from an analysis of 5549 community reinvestment loans).

   The credit score cut-offs for what is considered to be poor, marginal, and good credit are derived from Freddie Mac's categories used in its Loan Prospector system. Freddie Mac advises lenders that applicants with FICO scores below 620 indicates high risk, between 620 and 660 indicates an uncertain credit profile, and above 660 means they are likely to have acceptable credit reputations. *See* Fed. Home Loan Mortgage Ass'n, Automated Underwriting: Making Mortgage Lending Simpler and Fairer for America's Families (Sept. 1996).

65 Robert B. Avery, Paul S. Calem, & Glenn B. Canner, *Credit Report Accuracy and Access to Credit*, Fed. Reserve Bull. 297 (Summer 2004).

66 Raphael W. Bostic, Paul S. Calem, & Susan M. Wachter, Joint Ctr. for Hous. Studies of Harvard Univ., Hitting the Wall: Credit As an Impediment to Homeownership (Feb. 2004).

67 Matt Fellowes, Brookings Institution, Credit Scores, Reports, and Getting Ahead in America 9–10 (May 2006).

68 *Id.* at 10 (May 2006).

69 Rickie C. Keys, Univ. of Denver Ctr. for African-American Policy, Financial Empowerment for the Unbanked & Underbanked Consumer: "Crossing the Red Line" (Jan. 2007).

   Interestingly, this study was financially supported in part by CompuCredit, an issuer of extremely high-cost, low-credit-limit, subprime credit cards.

70 Rickie C. Keys, Univ. of Denver Ctr. for African-American Policy, Financial Empowerment for the Unbanked & Underbanked Consumer: "Crossing the Red Line" 5 (Jan. 2007).

fringe financial providers increased.[71]

In August 2007, the Federal Reserve Board (FRB) issued a report to Congress on credit scoring and racial disparities, which was mandated by the 2003 amendments to the Fair Credit Reporting Act.[72] This study used the same set of 300,000 credit files as the FRB's earlier study in 2004, matched with Social Security records to provide racial and demographic information.[73] As with the 2004 study, the FRB found significant racial disparities in credit scoring. In one of the two models used by the FRB, the mean score of African Americans was approximately half that of white non-Hispanics (54.0 out of 100 for white non-Hispanics versus 25.6 for African Americans) with Hispanics fairing only slightly better (38.2).[74] Despite these marked racial differences, the FRB concluded that credit scores had likely benefitted consumers by contributing to improved credit availability and affordability, even for minorities.[75]

A 2010 study by the Woodstock Institute found that Illinois residents living in communities of color were far more likely to have lower, non-prime credit scores, while individuals in predominantly white communities were much more likely to have higher, prime credit scores. Statewide, 20.3% of individuals had a credit score of less than 620. However, in zip codes where the population was more than 80% African American, over 54.2% of the individuals had a credit score of less than 620. Conversely, only 16.8% of individuals in predominately white zip codes had a credit score of less than 620, while 67.3% of these residents had a better than a 700 credit score. Only 25% of individuals in predominantly African-American zip codes had credit scores above 700. In zip codes that are majority Latino, 31.4% of individuals had a credit score of less than 620, and only 47.3% had credit scores greater than 700.[76]

A 2012 study by the CFPB examined credit scores for about 200,000 files at the nationwide Credit Reporting Agencies. This study found that the median FICO score for consumers in majority minority ZIP codes was in the thirty-fourth percentile, while it was in the fifty-second percentile for ZIP codes with low minority populations.[77]

In addition to the above studies, there have been several studies examining the relationship between race and insurance credit scores, several of which showed a dramatic difference between the scores of whites and minorities. These studies are discussed in § 6.4.6.2.2, *infra*.

In addition to having lower credit scores, minority consumers are also more likely to lack the credit history necessary to even generate a credit score because they are less likely to have those forms of traditional credit that are reported to credit bureaus. As reported by the Federal Trade Commission, minorities are overrepresented amongst consumers with limited or no credit histories.[78] African Americans constitute 6% of the population with a credit score, but represent 14% of those with no or insufficient credit history to generate a score.[79] Hispanics constitute 8.5% of the population with a credit score, but represent 24.5% of those without a score.[80] Thus, nearly 40% of those consumers without a credit score are African American or Hispanic, but those groups make up only 15% of consumers with a credit score.

Other research confirms this disparity. The University of North Carolina study discussed above found that 22% of Hispanics did not have a sufficient credit history to generate a credit score.[81] A survey of 500 members of the National Association of Hispanic Real Estate Professionals found that nearly one-third said their clients ended up with subprime mortgages because the clients' limited credit histories made them appear high-risk to lenders using traditional FICO scores.[82] Nearly 80% of the Hispanic real estate professionals said that, for every Hispanic household they helped to homeownership, they turned away two prospects because the Hispanic consumers could not qualify using traditional score-based underwriting programs.

In addition to racial disparities, there appears to be a growing credit scoring "gap," in which the divide between "good" and "bad" scorers appears to be growing, reflecting an increasing gulf between the credit haves and have-nots.[83]

---

71 *Id.* at 6.

72 Pub. L. No. 108-159, § 215, 117 Stat. 1952 (2003).

73 Bd. of Governors of the Fed. Reserve System, Report to the Congress on Credit Scoring and Its Effects on the Availability and Affordability of Credit 57–58 (Aug. 2007).

74 *Id.* at 80–81.

75 *Id.* at S-2 (Aug. 2007).

76 Sarah Duda & Geoff Smith, Woodstock Institute, Bridging the Gap: Credit Scores and Economic Opportunity in Illinois Communities of Color 8 (Sept. 2010), *available at* www.woodstockinst.org/publications/download/bridging-the-gap:-Credit-Scores-and-Economic-Opportunity-in-Illinois-Communities-of-Color.

77 Consumer Financial Prot. Bureau, Analysis of Differences Between Consumer- and Creditor-Purchased Credit Scores 18 (Sept. 2012), *available at* http://files.consumerfinance.gov/f/201209_Analysis_Differences_Consumer_Credit.pdf.

78 Fed. Trade Comm'n, Report to Congress Under Sections 318 and 319 of the Fair and Accurate Credit Transactions Act of 2003, at 78 (Dec. 2004).

    This report also noted that a 2003 survey of mortgage lenders found that "no credit score" was the single most important reason why loan applications were not submitted to an automated underwriting system. *Id.* at 79.

79 Fed. Trade Comm'n, Report to Congress Under Sections 318 and 319 of the Fair and Accurate Credit Transactions Act of 2003, at 78 (Dec. 2004).

80 *Id.*

81 Michael Stegman et al., Automated Underwriting: Getting to "Yes" for More Low-Income Applicants, Presentation at the Research Institute for Hous. America Conference (Apr. 2001), *available at* www.housingamerica.org/CH02001-slideshow.html.

    In contrast, an examination of 500,000 consumer credit files found that, for the general population, about one in ten files did not have enough information to generate a score. Consumer Fed'n of America & Nat'l Credit Reporting Ass'n, Credit Score Accuracy and Implications for Consumers 38 (Dec. 17, 2002).

82 Ken Harney, *Giving Credit Where Credit's Due*, Wash. Post, Nov. 11, 2006, at F1.

83 *See* National Consumer Law Center, Fair Credit Reporting § 14.9.2 (7th ed. 2010 and Supp.).

6.4.2 Factors in a Credit Scoring System May Disfavor Minorities and Other Protected Groups

6.4.2.1 Overview

If even a single factor in a credit scoring model correlates to race or other prohibited bases, the results of the model may be discriminatory.[84] The official interpretations appear to concur, noting that an "empirically derived, demonstrably and statistically sound" credit scoring system may be flawed and thus subject to review and challenge under the ECOA.[85] These concerns are intensified by the "black box" nature of credit scoring systems.[86] However, at least one court refused to second-guess an insurance company's use of particular factors in its scoring model.[87] In contrast, plaintiffs have been permitted to proceed with claims that a lender intentionally created credit scoring formulas using hidden factors that discriminated against minority applicants.[88]

6.4.2.2 Discrimination's Legacy

If certain groups have been denied access to credit in the past as a result of discrimination, the use of credit scoring systems may perpetuate that lack of access. Minorities and women probably still lag behind other groups under credit scoring systems because, in terms of credit access, the proverbial playing field is far from level.[89] Indeed, Federal Reserve Board staff observed that the scores "may lack predictive power for the underrepresented segments of the overall population."[90] Federal regulatory examiners have focused on racial disparities in the use of credit scoring.[91]

Credit scoring models often fail to include rent, utility, and other non-standard payment histories that are more typical of lower-income populations. To address these concerns, there have been several initiatives to establish "alternative" credit profiles for populations without a credit history such as immigrants and young consumers.[92] However, some of these credit scoring models are based in part on subprime sources of credit such as payday loans and rent-to-own transactions. The inclusion of these sources has created concerns that such scores will be used to market high-cost credit to consumers who have these alternative scores. Another concern is that alternative scores will not be predictive of a consumer's credit risk, because these forms of credit are structured so differently (and so much more onerously) than traditional forms of credit.[93] Also, some of these "alternative" scores are being used not to expand access to credit for consumers without a traditional credit history, but as a second layer of screening for consumers who already have access to credit.[94]

Another issue is that groups who have historically been discriminated against may rely more heavily on credit obtained from non-traditional sources such as finance companies. Credit scoring models may assign a higher risk rating to such credit sources.[95] Fair Isaac claims that the latest generation of credit

---

84   *See* Office of the Comptroller of the Currency, Credit Scoring Models, OCC Bulletin 97-24 (May 20, 1997) (warning against the use of "models that may include characteristics that may have a disparate impact on a prohibited basis or raise other Equal Credit Opportunity Act (Regulation B) or Fair Housing Act concerns"); Press Release, Office of the Comptroller of the Currency, OCC Alerts Banks to Potential Benefits and Risks of Credit Scoring Models, OCC Bull. No. 97-46 (May 20, 1997), *available at* www.occ.treas.gov (advising national banks "to avoid illegal disparate treatment by insuring that adequate controls exist during the pre-scoring, scoring, and post-scoring states of the credit application process").

85   Official Interpretations of Reg. B [Official Staff Commentary on Reg. B], 12 C.F.R. pt. 1002 [pt. 202], Supp. I, § 1002.2(p)-4 [§ 202.2(p)-4].

86   *See* National Consumer Law Center, Fair Credit Reporting § 14.5.1 (7th ed. 2010 and Supp.).

87   Owens v. Nationwide Mut. Ins. Co., 2005 WL 1837959 (N.D. Tex. Aug. 2, 2005).

88   Rodriguez v. SLM Corp., 2009 WL 598252 (D. Conn. Mar. 6, 2009).

89   *See* Chi Chi Wu & Birny Birnbaum, National Consumer Law Center & Ctr. for Economic Justice, Credit Scoring and Insurance: Costing Consumers Billions and Perpetuating the Economic Racial Divide (June 2007) (positing that use of credit scores perpetuates the "racial wealth divide").

    As one Congressman framed the issue:

> We had 400 years of slavery and 100 years of Jim Crow as distinguished from another group who had property, who owned slaves, who sold slaves, who had discriminatory practices where they could have advantages and they could get credit and they could get loans. They

owned the insurance companies and the banks and the credit bureaus, so they had the wealth. When they lose their job or they have a difficult financial time, they have mama or daddy or grand-daddy's money to fall back on. Their credit scores are good.

> *Use of Credit Information Beyond Lending: Issues and Reform Proposals: Hearing Before the Subcomm. on Financial Institutions and Consumer Credit of the H. Comm. on Fin. Serv. 4*, 111th Cong. (2010) (statement of Congressman Steven Cohen).

    A similar observation has been made by at least one Federal Reserve Board governor. *Governor Lindsey Points to Difficulties with Statistics as Loan-Eligibility Tool*, 63 Banking Rep. (BNA) 280 (Aug. 29, 1994).

90   Credit Risk, Credit Scoring, and the Performance of Home Mortgages, Fed. Res. Bull. 621, 630 (July 1996).

91   *See* Fed. Trade Comm'n, Public Forum on the Consumer and Credit Scoring, Matter No. P994810, at 175 (July 22, 1999) (statement of Bob Cook, Senior Fair Lending Specialist, Federal Reserve Board).

92   *See* National Consumer Law Center, Fair Credit Reporting § 2.7.10 (7th ed. 2010 and Supp.).

93   *Helping Consumers Obtain the Credit They Deserve: Hearings Before the Subcomm. on Fin. Insts. & Consumer Credit of the House Fin. Servs. Comm.*, 109th Cong. 6–7 (May 12, 2005), *available at* www.nclc.org/images/pdf/banking_and_payment_systems/archive/obtain-credit-deserve.pdf (testimony of Margot Saunders, National Consumer Law Center).

94   Jane Kim, *Credit Scorers Find New Ways to Judge You*, Wall St. J., Mar. 11, 2008.

95   According to Experian, the presence of a finance company trade line negatively impacts a credit score because they often carry high interest rates, which hampers the consumer's ability to repay. Experian, Credit Score Basics FAQs, *available at* www.experian.com/consumer/credit_score_faqs.html#17.

scoring models does not penalize consumers for having loans from finance companies. However, Fair Isaac has promoted NextGen as a specialty score for subprime lending,[96] which may offset any benefits to minority consumers. Also, NextGen supposedly gives lower scores to consumers with "thin" files, that is, those with only one or two lines of credit[97]—many of whom will be people of color or low-income consumers. Adoption of NextGEN has been hampered by the prices that the nationwide credit reporting agencies charge for it, which are 500% higher than for classic FICO scores.[98]

6.4.2.3 Underrepresentation in Scoring Model Development

There is a question as to whether people of color and other protected groups are adequately represented in the samples used to calculate credit scores. Because of past discrimination, the pool of past credit recipients may contain a disproportionately low number of members of protected groups. If such is the case, a credit scoring model may underestimate the likelihood of repayment by applicants from these underrepresented groups. For example, Fair, Isaac develops its models using a sample of files from credit reporting agencies that may be as small as 750,000.[99] This is a fraction of 1% of the roughly 210 million files each credit reporting agency maintains.[100] Fair, Isaac has admitted that the databases used to generate their models underrepresent communities of color but claims there is only a slight underrepresentation.[101] VantageScore, which is the credit score created by a joint venture of Equifax, Experian, and TransUnion,[102] uses 15 million credit files from each of these

credit reporting agencies,[103] which produces a somewhat better percentage of 7%.

6.4.2.4 Other Factors That May Disfavor Protected Classes

A potential issue is whether credit scoring systems give more points to home owners. According to Fair, Isaac, one of the categories of factors used to derive FICO scores is the types of credit in use. A good mix may be one that includes a mortgage loan.[104] The question is whether FICO's scoring models explicitly give more points to mortgage holders, which would mean home owners are favored over renters. Racial minorities have lower rates of homeownership than whites.[105]

There is some evidence that low-income and minority households are more prone to "application idiosyncrasies," that is, factors in their credit records that require a subjective interpretation. An example of such a factor would be a period of illness, from which the applicant has since recovered, that caused past delinquencies.[106] Some observers have theorized that there are factors related to loan performance that are impossible to observe—and thus cannot be included in credit scoring systems—but are likely to be correlated with minority status. Omitting minority status means that the scoring models suffer from a lack of these unobservable factors to the detriment of minority applicants.[107] Furthermore, these observers have posited that, while the factors used in scoring models are perfectly appropriate, it is the weighting placed on certain factors that may result in disparate impact.[108]

If a finance company loan is considered negative because of high interest rates, scoring models should logically consider more negative the presence of other even more expensive and potentially abusive loans, such as payday loans, subprime mortgages, and rent-to-own transactions.

96 Nathalie Mainland & Julia Wooding, Fair, Isaac & Co., NextGen FICO Risk Score Conversion FAQ 3 (Apr. 2002); W.A. Lee, *Experian and Fair, Isaac Tweak Subprime Scoring*, Am. Banker, Dec. 28, 2001.

97 Kenneth Harney, *Higher Credit Scores on the Horizon?*, Realty Times, Nov. 12, 2001, at 1; Nathalie Mainland & Julia Wooding, Fair, Isaac & Co., NextGen FICO Risk Score Conversion FAQ 5 (Apr. 2002) ("NextGen does tend to push thicker files upward in the score distribution, while pushing thinner files downward.").

In general, NextGen benefits higher-scoring consumers and thus may exacerbate, not improve, racial disparities in credit scoring. *Id.*

98 *See* Fair Isaac Corp. v. Equifax Inc., 2008 WL 623120 (D. Minn. Mar. 4, 2008).

99 *See* Fed. Trade Comm'n, Credit Scoring (Aug. 1998); *see also* Credit Risk, Credit Scoring, and the Performance of Home Mortgages, Fed. Res. Bull. 621, 628 (July 1996).

100 *See* National Consumer Law Center, Fair Credit Reporting § 1.2.2 (7th ed. 2010 and Supp.).

101 Fair, Isaac & Co., The Effectiveness of Scoring on Low-to-Moderate Income and High-Minority Area Populations 22 (Aug. 1997), *available at* www.fairisaac.com (database used to develop TransUnion's credit scoring system composed of 6.7% residents of minority neighborhoods, compared to 7.8% of the overall U.S. adult population).

102 *See* National Consumer Law Center, Fair Credit Reporting §§ 14.2.2.1,

14.4.1.2 (7th ed. 2010 and Supp.) (more discussion of VantageScore).

103 *See* VantageScore Solutions, L.L.C., VantageScore 2.0: A New Version for a New World (2011).

104 *See* National Consumer Law Center, Fair Credit Reporting §§ 14.5.2.1.1–14.5.2.1.6 (7th ed. 2010 and Supp.); Experian, Credit Score Basics FAQs, *available at* www.experian.com/consumer/credit_score_faqs.html (Experian states that the presence of a mortgage reflects positively and that a credit score will not be "as high as it could be" if the consumer does not have a mortgage).

105 *See* United States Dep't of Hous. & Urban Dev., HUD Statement on Record Homeownership Rates in 2004 (Jan. 27, 2005) (minorities have homeownership rate of 51% compared to the overall homeownership rate of 69%).

At least two studies have noted that home owners have higher credit scores than renters, although this is probably due to a number of factors, including that home owners might start off with the good score and income necessary to obtain a mortgage. Raphael W. Bostic, Paul S. Calem, & Susan M. Wachter, Joint Ctr. for Hous. Studies of Harvard Univ., Hitting the Wall: Credit As an Impediment to Home-ownership (Feb. 2004); David K. Musto & Nicholas Souleles, *A Portfolio View of Consumer Credit* (Fed. Reserve Bank of Philadelphia—Research Dep't, Working Paper No. 05-25, Sept. 2005).

106 Stanley D. Longhofer, Fed. Reserve Bank of Boston, *Mortgage Scoring and the Myth of Overrides, Perspectives on Credit Scoring and Fair Mortgage Lending: Part 5*, Communities & Banking, Fall 2002, at 19.

107 Stanley Longhofer, *The Color of Credit: Mortgage Discrimination, Research, Methodology, and Fair Lending Enforcement* (MIT Press 2002) (book review).

108 *Id.*

Finally, there is a question as to whether credit scoring discriminates against other groups protected by credit discrimination laws.[109] For example, commentators have noted that the "length of credit history" factor may have a disparate impact on women, who on average have shorter credit histories than men.[110]

6.4.2.5 Industry's Response

In response to these concerns, the credit scoring industry and its proponents have consistently maintained that their systems are not discriminatory.[111] Moreover, they claim that credit scoring actually reduces discrimination against protected groups. Credit scoring proponents contend that the human, and potentially discriminatory, element in credit evaluation has been replaced by a system that is blind to race and other prohibited bases. In fact, they point to studies showing that credit scoring systems approve a higher number of borrowers of color than do traditional manual underwriting systems.[112] Some regulators also believe that credit scoring reduces discrimination in credit granting.[113]

6.4.3 The Disparate Impact Analysis for Credit Scoring

If a credit scoring model contains a factor that had a disparate impact on borrowers of color or another protected group, it does not necessarily mean the model violates the ECOA or FHA. Under the disparate impact analysis, a creditor can show a business necessity for using a policy or factor that has a disparate impact.[114] The official interpretations indicate that creditors can show business necessity by showing a "demonstrable relationship" between a policy and creditworthiness.[115] In the case of credit scoring, the OCC has stated that the

business necessity for including a variable in a credit scoring model would be shown if "the variable is statistically related to loan performance, and has an understandable relationship" to creditworthiness.[116] Thus, if a variable or factor in a credit scoring model causes a disparate impact but is "demonstrably" or "understandably" related to creditworthiness, it may be permissible under the ECOA or FHA, unless the plaintiff can show that there is a factor that serves the same purpose and creates a less discriminatory impact.[117]

Note that the business necessity analysis may differ for scoring models used for credit versus insurance. Because credit scores are based on credit histories, there is an explicit and explainable connection to their use to measure creditworthiness. While there might be some correlation between insurance credit scores and loss history, there has been no definitive explanation as to why credit scores are a good measure of "insurance worthiness."[118] Furthermore, one study has found that models using attributes other than credit score yield almost the same correlations with loss ratios as models that use credit scores.[119] Thus, it may be easier to show the existence of a "less discriminatory alternative" for insurance scoring.

With respect to credit scoring in the credit-granting context, there is the potential for less discriminatory alternatives as well. Some commentators have proposed that credit scoring models themselves could be modified so as to reduce racial disparities in credit scores.[120] Such modifications would need to actively take race into account and thus might need to fit into the requirements of a special purpose credit program under Regulation B.[121]

---

109   *See generally* ch. 3, *supra* (discussing which groups are protected under federal and state credit discrimination laws).

110   Cynthia Glassman & Howard Wilkins, *Credit Scoring: Probabilities and Pitfalls*, J. of Retail Banking Serv., Summer 1997, at 56.

111   *Id.*

    Fair, Isaac has maintained that its scoring models do not include prohibited factors, such as race, national origin, or gender. FICO, Understanding Your FICO Score 2 (July 2010), *available at* www.my fico.com/Downloads/Files/myFICO_UYFS_Booklet.pdf.

112   Peter Zorn et al., Inst. of Bus. & Econ. Research, Univ. of California-Berkeley, Automated Underwriting and Lending Outcomes: The Effect of Improved Mortgage Risk Assessment on Under-Served Populations (Aug. 2001) (study showing that manual underwriting approved only 52% of a sample of minority applicants for affordable loans, but Freddie Mac's Loan Prospector system approved 79%).

113   *See* Letter from National Credit Union Admin. to credit unions, No. 174 (Aug. 1995) ("[i]n general, the use of a properly derived credit scoring system reduces the possibility that loan policies may be discriminatory").

    However, the Administration also cautions that a credit scoring system does not provide automatic protection or a "safe harbor" from discrimination challenges.

114   *See* § 4.3.2.5, *supra*.

115   Official Interpretations of Reg. B [Official Staff Commentary on Reg. B], 12 C.F.R. pt. 1002 [pt. 202], Supp. I, § 1002.6(a)-2 [§ 202.6(a)-2].

116   Office of the Comptroller of the Currency, Credit Scoring Models, OCC Bull. No. 97-24, app. at 11 (May 20, 1997).

    While the OCC's pronouncement is only authoritative as to national banks, it may be indicative of how other federal regulators will view this issue.

117   *See* § 4.3.2.6, *supra*.

118   However, one court has held that the supposed ability of credit scores to predict insurance loss ratios represents an adequate "business necessity" to withstand a disparate impact challenge as well as a "legitimate nondiscriminatory reason" to rebut a prima facie showing of disparate treatment under the *McDonnell Douglas* test. Owens v. Nationwide Mut. Ins. Co., 2005 WL 1837959 (N.D. Tex. Aug. 2, 2005).

119   Wayne D. Holdredge & Katharine Barnes, Tillinghast-Towers Perrin, *Good News, Bad News or Both?*, Emphasis 2003/2, Feb. 2003; *see also* James C. Guszcza & Cheng-Sheng Peter Wu, Deloitte & Touche, Does Credit Score Really Explain Insurance Losses: Multivariate Analysis From A Data Mining Point Of View (2003) (paper presented at the Proceedings of the Casualty Actuarial Society) (pricing and underwriting models created without credit variables can be extremely good).

120   Stanley Longhofer, *The Color of Credit: Mortgage Discrimination, Research, Methodology, and Fair Lending Enforcement* (MIT Press 2002) (book review); *see also* Elizabeth Mays, *Credit Scoring and the Fair Lending Issue of Disparate Impact*, in Credit Scoring for Risk Managers: The Handbook for Lenders (2003); Elaine Fortowsky & Michael LaCour-Little, Credit Scoring and Disparate Impact (Dec. 2001), *available at* http://fic.wharton.upenn.edu/fic/lacourpaper.pdf.

121   *See* § 3.9, *supra*.

    Taking race into account to eliminate racial disparities is not a new concept in civil rights law. As Supreme Court Justice Harry

6.4.4 Disparate Impact Litigation Challenging Credit Scoring

A few litigants have brought credit discrimination cases challenging credit scoring.[122] A class action challenged that Fannie Mae's use of credit scores in its Desktop Underwriter automated underwriting system has a disparate impact on African Americans in violation of ECOA and the FHA.[123] The plaintiff's discrimination claims under the FHA and the ECOA survived a motion to dismiss.[124] However, the court did express skepticism about the viability of these claims.[125]

In another case, a court summarily dismissed a *pro se* litigant's lawsuit alleging that credit scoring and use of credit histories creates a disparate impact on African Americans.[126] Interestingly, the court in this case made two questionable assumptions. It assumed that credit scoring and use of credit histories is "race-blind."[127] It also held that Regulation B explicitly permits lenders to use credit scoring, citing 12 C.F.R. § 1002.10(b) [§ 202.10(b)]. However, that section specifically concerns what creditors are required to do when furnishing information to credit bureaus and says nothing about

the use of credit scores or histories in evaluating credit applications.[128]

The disparate impact of credit scores on borrowers of color ironically may make it harder for plaintiffs to prove cases of intentional discrimination. To make out a prima facie case under the circumstantial evidence test for disparate treatment, the plaintiff must show that he or she was qualified for the loan.[129] Without a high enough credit score, the plaintiff will not be able to meet this element.[130]

6.4.5 Discriminatory Uses of Credit Scoring

6.4.5.1 Overview

The prior discussion of credit scoring and potential discrimination focused on the disparate impact created by the scoring systems themselves. However, the potential for discrimination does not stop there. Even assuming a credit scoring system that does not disproportionately affect minorities, credit scoring does not immunize a lender from discrimination. Lenders have found numerous ways to disfavor minority applicants when they are using a scoring model.

6.4.5.2 Discriminatory Score Thresholds

One use of credit scores that clearly puts minority applicants at a disadvantage is the use of different credit score thresholds or "cut-offs" by creditors for white and minority applicants. For example, the Department of Justice (DOJ) filed a lawsuit in 1999 against Associates National Bank (ANB), alleging that ANB implemented different credit score cut-offs for English-language applicants than for Spanish-language applicants.[131] According to the DOJ, ANB segregated its Spanish-language applications into a separate file, then lowered the credit score cut-off for English-language applicants but not for Spanish-language applicants. As a result, the denial rate of credit cards for Spanish-language applicants was higher.[132]

Blackmun noted, "[i]n order to get beyond racism, we must first take account of race. There is no other way. And in order to treat some persons equally, we must treat them differently." Univ. of Cal. Regents v. Bakke, 438 U.S. 265, 98 S. Ct. 2733, 57 L. Ed. 2d 750 (1978).

122 *See, e.g.*, Zamudio v. HSBC North America Holdings Inc., 2008 WL 517138 (N.D. Ill. Feb. 20, 2008) (denying dismissal of disparate impact challenge under Fair Housing Act (FHA) and ECOA to HSBC's automated underwriting system and use of credit scoring); DeHoyos v. Allstate Corp., 240 F.R.D. 269 (W.D. Tex. 2007) (approving settlement in class action brought pursuant to the FHA based on allegedly discriminatory credit scoring system used to compute insurance premiums); Complaint, Rahmaan v. Fed. Nat'l Mortgage Ass'n, 2003 WL 21940044 (D.D.C. May 19, 2003); Stackhaus v. NationsBank Corp., Clearinghouse No. 52,065 (D.D.C. 1996) (No. 96-CV-1077 (NHJ)) (class action brought by Washington Lawyers' Committee for Civil Rights & Urban Affairs alleging, *inter alia*, that defendant's credit scoring system had a racially discriminatory adverse impact on African-American applicants for mortgage loans in the Washington, D.C., area).

123 Rahmaan v. Fed. Nat'l Mortgage Ass'n, 2003 WL 21940044 (D.D.C. May 19, 2003).
      A similar lawsuit was brought against Freddie Mac for use of credit scores in its Loan Prospector automated underwriting system. Beaulialice v. Fed. Home Loan Mortgage Corp., 2007 WL 744646 (M.D. Fla. Mar. 6, 2007).
      That lawsuit was dismissed as time-barred by the ECOA and FHA statute of limitations and by the doctrine of unclean hands. *Id.*

124 Rahmaan v. Fed. Nat'l Mortgage Ass'n, 2003 WL 21940044 (D.D.C. May 19, 2003).

125 *Id.*
      The court noted that the plaintiff had not made out a prima facie claim under a *McDonnell Douglas* analysis. However, the plaintiff appeared to have brought both a disparate impact claim and a disparate treatment claim, and thus it was unclear why the court referred only to the *McDonnell Douglas* analysis. *See* § 4.2.3.1, *supra.*

126 Powell v. American Gen. Finance, 310 F. Supp. 2d 481 (N.D.N.Y. 2004).

127 *Id.*

128 *See* §§ 9.4.1.3, 9.4.1.4, *infra.*
      The court did not consider Regulation B, 12 C.F.R. § 1002.2(p) [§ 202.2(p)], which defines a credit scoring system under Regulation B. *See* § 6.3.2.2, *supra.*
      It also did not consider the caution in the official interpretations that a credit scoring system which relies upon neutral factors can nonetheless be challenged for having a disparate impact. Official Interpretations of Reg. B [Official Staff Commentary on Reg. B], 12 C.F.R. pt. 1002 [pt. 202], Supp. I, § 1002.2(p)-4 [§ 202.2(p)-4].

129 *See* § 4.2.3.1, *infra.*

130 *See, e.g.*, Sutton v. Piper, 344 Fed. Appx. 101 (6th Cir. 2009) (disabled plaintiff failed to show that low credit score was a result of disability, and thus was not entitled to an accommodation of relaxing the minimum credit score criteria for his rental application); Curley v. JP Morgan Chase Bank, 2007 WL 1343793 (W.D. La. May 7, 2007) (plaintiffs failed to make out a prima facie case of discrimination because their credit scores were lower than the 620 minimum required for a loan), *aff'd*, 261 Fed. Appx. 781 (5th Cir. 2008).

131 United States v. Assocs. Nat'l Bank, No. 99-196 (D. Del. Mar. 29, 1999), *available on the companion website to this treatise.*

132 *Id.*

6.4.5.3 Overrides

Another concern, raised by the Office of Comptroller of the Currency (OCC) in 1997, is that, because the credit scores of a large percentage of applicants fall in a gray area, lenders will continue to use subjective or "human" underwriting to review these applications. The OCC expressed concern that decisions to override the credit scores in these situations may undermine the objectivity and/or integrity of credit scoring and lead to discriminatory results.[133]

One instance of discriminatory overrides was challenged by the DOJ in their lawsuit against Deposit Guaranty National Bank (DGNB) that focused on actions taken by DGNB's loan officers in a home improvement loan program. The DOJ alleged that DGNB allowed its loan officers broad discretion to override decisions pertaining to credit-scored loan applications. Many of these decisions were inconsistent with the credit scores of individual applicants.[134] The purpose and effect, according to the DOJ, was to grant credit less frequently to African-American loan applicants in violation of the FHA and ECOA.[135]

In another example, the OCC evaluated the ECOA compliance of Associates National Bank (ANB), a credit card bank, and found what it believed to be a pattern of discrimination based on national origin. The OCC determined that ANB subjected applicants and card holders that had submitted Spanish-language applications for credit cards to stricter underwriting standards and less favorable terms than those submitting English-language applications.[136]

6.4.5.4 "Coaching"

The potential for discrimination in the supposedly objective process of generating credit scores also arises when loan officers engage in selective "coaching" of applicants.[137] If a loan officer provides more information and assistance to white applicants in filling out their applications, those applications may be more likely to generate higher credit application scores and to qualify under automated underwriting systems.[138]

6.4.5.5 Credit Tier Markups

Most lenders now use credit scores to determine not only whether a consumer will be approved for credit but at what price the credit will be provided—so-called "risk-based pricing."

Essentially, the higher the credit score, the lower the price for credit. In addition to questions as to the justifiability of risk-based pricing,[139] many loan brokers and loan officers have "marked up" the price of credit by selling the borrower a higher rate than what the borrower's credit score qualifies him or her for.

Borrowers of color are more often targeted for credit markups, and the mark-ups charged them tend to be higher.[140] A number of cases have challenged these discriminatory mark-ups in the auto lending industry.[141] In the mortgage context, there is evidence that some minorities who receive subprime loans actually had credit scores that qualified them for prime loans.[142] While the Dodd-Frank Wall Street Reform and Consumer Protection Act of 2010 ("Dodd-Frank Act") rules on loan originator compensation and the related regulations issued by the Consumer Financial Protection Bureau substantially restrict mark-up practices, loopholes remain.[143]

6.4.5.6 Use of Different Systems or Scoring Models for Different Populations

The use of a scoring model in one context but not in another could lead to a disparate impact on protected classes. For example, the OCC warned a bank about the potential ECOA implications of the bank's proposal to use a scoring model for loans made over the Internet but a judgmental system for loans made at the branch or by mail or telephone.[144] The OCC noted that, if similarly situated borrowers were treated differently because of the use of credit scoring in one context and a judgmental system in another (or conceivably different scoring systems in different contexts), it could raise a question as to whether the lender is violating Regulation B.[145]

6.4.5.7 Setting Up Credit Scoring Models Differently and Manipulating Data

Auto loan borrowers have also alleged that companies may manipulate a supposedly "color blind" credit scoring system by setting systems up differently for different dealerships. In one case, plaintiffs alleged that dealerships in communities of color may even be required to submit all credit applications to creditors for manual review. In this case, plaintiffs suggested that this type of individualized assessment demonstrates both the potential for and sanctioning of "redlining" loan applications that come from dealerships located in these areas.[146]

---

133 *See* Office of the Comptroller of the Currency, OCC Alerts Banks to Potential Benefits and Risks of Credit Scoring Models (May 20, 1997), *available at* www.occ.treas.gov.

134 *See* United States v. Deposit Guar. Nat'l Bank, No. 3:99CV67OLN (S.D. Miss. 1999), *available on the companion website to this treatise.*

135 *Id.*

136 Complaint, United States v. Assocs. Nat'l Bank, No. 99-196 (D. Del. Mar. 29, 1999), *available on the companion website to this treatise.*

137 *See* § 5.4.3, *supra.*

138 James Carr, *Risk-Based Pricing: Are There Fair Lending Implications?*, Hous. Facts & Findings, Issue 2, Summer 1999.

139 *See* § 8.5.3, *infra; see also* National Consumer Law Center, STOP Predatory Lending § 2.3.3 (2d ed. 2007) (in-depth analysis of various creditor arguments regarding risk).

140 *See* § 8.6.5, *infra.*

141 *See* § 8.6.2, *infra.*

142 *See* § 8.5.3, *infra.*

143 *See* National Consumer Law Center, Truth in Lending § 9.3.2 (8th ed. 2012).

144 Office of the Comptroller of the Currency, OCC Interpretive Letter No. 759, 1999 WL 768185 (May 1, 1996).

145 *Id.*

146 Coburn v. DaimlerChrysler Servs. North America, L.L.C., 2005 WL 736657 (N.D. Ill. Mar. 31, 2005).

6.4.6 Discriminatory Impact of Other Uses of Credit Scores

6.4.6.1 General

The use of credit scores for non-credit related purposes has grown dramatically. Credit scores are being used to determine eligibility and rates for automobile and home owner's insurance.[147] Businesses use them for employment purposes.[148] Utilities use credit scores to determine whether consumers must pay a deposit for utility service.[149] Under the Fair Credit Reporting Act, there are few limits on the use of credit scores for non-credit related consumer transactions.[150]

Each of these uses may give rise to discrimination challenges as well. For example, an employer's use of credit scores can violate federal anti-discrimination laws if an employer intentionally uses them to discriminate or if they disproportionately exclude people in a particular group by race, sex, or another covered basis, unless the employer can justify the test or procedure under the law.[151] The EEOC has brought a case against one employer for its use of credit reports (but not credit scores), alleging that the practice violates Title VII of the Civil Rights Act because it has a disparate impact on African-American applicants.[152]

6.4.6.2 Insurance Credit Scores

6.4.6.2.1 Challenges to insurance credit scores

A particularly controversial issue is the use of credit scores by automobile and home insurers to determine whether to insure a consumer and at what price. The credit scores used by insurers, or "insurance scores," are specially developed for insurers and not the same as generic credit scores, but they nonetheless are based solely on credit history.[153] Several states have passed legislation regulating the practice,[154] based on model legislation written by the National Conference of Insurance Legislators and supported by the insurance industry.[155] State insurance regulators have issued rules reining in insurance credit scoring,[156] including restrictions based upon concerns over disproportionate impact on protected classes.[157] A joint study by the Center for Economic Justice and the National Consumer Law Center estimates that insurance credit scores cost consumers billions of dollars every year, perhaps as much as $67 billion.[158]

The use of insurance scores probably disproportionately burdens racial minorities, given that they have lower credit scores as a group.[159] A number of class actions have been filed challenging the practice, both based on discrimination challenges[160] and

---

147 *See* § 6.4.6.2.2, *infra.*

148 Matt Fellowes, Brookings Institution, Credit Scores, Reports, and Getting Ahead in America, at n.3 (May 2006) (citing 2004 survey of companies by the Society for Human Resource Management as finding that as many as 35% of employers were checking credit reports in 2004, up from 19% in 1996).

149 *See* National Consumer Law Center, Fair Credit Reporting § 14.12 (7th ed. 2010 and Supp.); *see also* National Consumer Law Center, Access to Utility Service § 5.2.4 (5th ed. 2011 and Supp.).

150 15 U.S.C. § 1681(b)(a)(3)(F). *See generally* National Consumer Law Center, Fair Credit Reporting § 7.2.8 (7th ed. 2010 and Supp.).

151 42 U.S.C. § 2000e-2(k); *see* United States Equal Emp't Opportunity Comm'n, EEOC Compliance Manual § 15-V.B (Apr. 2006); United States Equal Emp't Opportunity Comm'n, Employment Tests and Selection Procedures, *available at* www.eeoc.gov/policy/docs/factemployment_procedures.html.

152 Equal Emp't Opportunity Comm'n v. Kaplan Higher Learning Education Corp., 2013 WL 322116 (N.D. Ohio Jan. 28, 2013) (granting summary judgment to employer; EEOC expert's testimony was inadmissible under *Daubert* standard, and without testimony, EEOC failed to set forth a prima facie case of disparate impact).

153 *See* National Consumer Law Center, Fair Credit Reporting § 14.11 (7th ed. 2010 and Supp.).

154 A summary of some of the state insurance laws governing use of credit information is included in National Consumer Law Center, Fair Credit Reporting appx. H (7th ed. 2010 and Supp.).

155 Nat'l Conference of Ins. Legislators, Model Act Regarding Use of Credit Information in Personal Insurance (Nov. 22, 2002); *see* Nat'l Ass'n of Mut. Ins. Cos., NAMIC's State Laws and Legislative Trends State Laws Governing Insurance Scoring Practices (Mar. 7, 2004).

156 *See, e.g.,* State v. Progressive Cas. Ins. Co., 165 P.3d 624 (Alaska 2007) (upholding Alaska Division of Insurance's rejection of insurers' proposal to use "frozen" credit scores for renewals of insurance policy, because proposal would violate Alaska statute's prohibition against using credit scores to reject renewal or to rate renewal of an insurance policy). *But see* Ins. Institute of Mich. v. Comm'r, 785 N.W.2d 67 (Mich. 2010) (finding that insurance commissioner had exceeded her authority in banning, as discriminatory, the use of insurance credit scores for setting premium prices; state supreme court vacated the court of appeals decision and reinstated the trial court decision declaring the rules illegal and unenforceable, and permanently enjoining commissioner from enforcing them).

157 Memorandum, Fla. Office of Ins. Regulation, Use of Credit Reports and Credit Scores by Insurers, Informational Memorandum OIR-06-10M (May 22, 2006) (requires insurers to demonstrate that their use of credit reports and credit scores does not disproportionately affect persons of any race, color, religion, marital status, age, gender, income, national origin, or place of residence).

158 Chi Chi Wu & Birny Birnbaum, National Consumer Law Center & Ctr. for Economic Justice, Credit Scoring and Insurance: Costing Consumers Billions and Perpetuating the Economic Racial Divide (June 2007).

159 *See* § 6.4.6.2.2, *supra.*

    The National Black Caucus of State Legislators passed a resolution urging states to ban insurance credit scoring unless an insurer can demonstrate it does not produce a disparate impact upon minority, low-income, and cash consumers. Nat'l Black Caucus of State Legislators, Resolution 03-81 (Dec. 2002).

160 Melder v. Allstate Corp., 404 F.3d 328 (5th Cir. 2005) (class action alleging that insurer's use of credit scoring violated state insurance law's prohibition on unfair discrimination; Fifth Circuit upheld denial of motion to remand to state court); DeHoyos v. Allstate Corp, 345 F.3d 290 (5th Cir. 2003) (challenge to credit scoring under the Fair Housing Act and federal Civil Rights Acts was not preempted by the McCarran-Ferguson Act); McKenzie v. Southern Farm Bureau Cas. Ins. Co., 2007 WL 2012214 (N.D. Miss. July 6, 2007) (disparate impact challenge under Fair Housing Act to home insurer's use of credit scores is preempted by McCarran-Ferguson Act because Mississippi insurance regulations specifically permit use of insurance credit scores); Owens v. Nationwide Mut. Ins. Co., 2005 WL 1837959 (N.D. Tex. Aug. 2, 2005) (granting summary

---

under the Fair Credit Reporting Act.[161] The leading case, *De-Hoyos v. Allstate Corp.*,[162] resulted in a settlement that required the insurer to implement a new credit scoring algorithm that supposedly results in less disparate impact to borrowers of color and to refund between $50 and $150 to policyholders who file a claim and whose scores rise due to the new formula.[163]

Another court has held on summary judgment that the use of credit scoring in home owner's insurance does not violate section 3604 of the Fair Housing Act or the federal Civil Rights Acts. In *Owens v. Nationwide Mutual Insurance Co.*,[164] the court relied on the supposed ability of credit scores to predict insurance loss ratios to rule that the practice did not discriminate against minorities. The court held that this predictiveness represented both an adequate "business necessity" to withstand a disparate impact challenge as well as a "legitimate nondiscriminatory reason" to rebut a prima facie showing of disparate treatment under the *McDonnell Douglas* test.[165]

Some insurance companies have declined to use credit scoring and instead have adopted evaluation factors that are directly correlated with some protected classes and that clearly disadvantage low- and moderate-income consumers. For example, at least one insurance company has adopted guidelines that directly base insurance rates and eligibility on the factors of education and occupation.[166] State insurance regulators have begun to look into whether the use of education and occupation as factors by insurers discriminates against racial minorities.[167]

6.4.6.2.2 Studies of the disparate impact of insurance credit scores

A number of state insurance commissions have conducted studies on the relationship between insurance scores and certain demographic characteristics, including race, gender, age, and income. A study by the Virginia Bureau of Insurance concluded that credit scoring is an ineffective tool for an insurer to utilize to engage in redlining—that is, disparate treatment—because income and race alone are not reliable predictors of credit score; however, this study did not report findings on disparate impact.[168] A study commissioned by the Washington State Insurance Commissioner showed a correlation between insurance scores and income; however, its findings regarding the racial impact of insurance scoring were inconclusive, primarily because of the small number of minorities sampled from Washington State's relatively homogeneous population.[169]

A Maryland study showed a correlation between race, income and insurance score, finding that the percentage of residents in Baltimore City with high credit scores decreased as the percentage of minorities and lower-income households increased in a neighborhood.[170] However, because the study used data prior to the passage of Maryland's statute regulating insurance scoring, the Maryland Insurance Administration declined to conclude that there was sufficient data to determine whether the use of credit scoring had an adverse impact on low-income or minority populations.[171]

A study conducted by the Missouri Department of Insurance found a stunning correlation between insurance scores and race as well as income, age, marital status, and educational attainment.[172] Using credit score data aggregated at the zip code level collected from the highest volume insurers in Missouri, the study found the following:[173]

- Insurance scores were significantly worse for residents of high-minority zip codes. The average consumer in an "all minority" neighborhood had a credit score that fell into the 18.4th percentile, while the average consumer in a "no minority" neighborhood had a credit score that fell into the 57.3th percentile—a difference of 38.9 percentile points.
- Insurance scores were significantly worse for residents of low-income zip codes. The average consumer in the poorest neighborhood had a credit score 12.8 percentile points lower than residents in the wealthiest communities.

judgment to insurance company on claims alleging that use of credit scores for home owners' insurance violates section 3604 of the Fair Housing Act and the federal Civil Rights Acts); Nat'l Fair Hous. Alliance v. Prudential Ins. Co., 208 F. Supp. 2d 46 (D.D.C. 2002) (class action alleging that the use of credit scores to determine eligibility for home owners' insurance has a disparate impact on minorities in violation of the Fair Housing Act); Ojo v. Farmers Group, Inc., 356 S.W.3d 421 (Tex. 2011) (Texas law permits use of credit scores to set insurance prices, even if it has a racially disparate impact; thus, Fair Housing Act challenge to use of credit scores was reverse-preempted by the McCarran-Ferguson Act); *cf.* Wells v. Shelter Gen. Ins. Co., 217 F. Supp. 2d 744 (S.D. Miss. 2002) (class action challenging use of credit scores under Mississippi insurance law).

161 National Consumer Law Center, Fair Credit Reporting § 14.11 (7th ed. 2010 and Supp.).

162 345 F.3d 290 (5th Cir. 2003).

163 DeHoyos v. Allstate Corp., 240 F.R.D. 269 (W.D. Tex. 2007) (approving class action settlement).
 The settlement also provided for $11 million in attorney fees and expenses. *Id.*

164 2005 WL 1837959 (N.D. Tex. Aug. 2, 2005).

165 *Id.*; *see* §§ 4.2.3, 4.3.2, *supra* (explanation of the disparate impact and disparate treatment tests for proving discrimination).

166 Press Release, Consumer Fed'n of America, GEICO Ties Insurance Rates to Education, Occupation (Mar. 20, 2006); *see also* § 7.3, *infra* (insurance redlining).

167 Matt Brady, *Florida to Probe Race Factor in Carrier Rate Process*, NU Online News Serv., Feb. 7, 2007 (Florida insurance regulator noting that a mechanic with a high school education will pay $4225.36 for auto coverage, but an engineer with a Ph.D. will—controlling for all other factors—pay only $1403.59).

168 Virginia Bureau of Ins., Report on the Use of Credit Reports in Underwriting to the State Commerce & Labor Comm. of the General Assembly (Dec. 1999).

169 Dave Pavelchek & Bruce Brown, Office of Wash. State Ins. Comm'r, Effect of Credit Scoring on Auto Insurance Underwriting and Pricing (Jan. 2003).

170 Maryland Ins. Admin., Report on the Credit Scoring Data of Insurers in Maryland (Feb. 2004).

171 Maryland Ins. Admin., Report on the Credit Scoring Data of Insurers in Maryland (Feb. 2004).

172 Brent Kabler, Missouri Dep't of Ins., Insurance-Based Credit Scores: Impact on Minority and Low Income Populations in Missouri (Jan. 2004).

173 *Id.*

- The correlation between race (high-minority neighbor-hoods) and credit scores remained even after eliminating other variables, such as income, education, marital status, and unemployment. Residency in a minority concentration neighborhood proved to be the single most reliable predictor of credit scores.
- The gap in credit scores was also expressed on a more individualized basis. The average gap between the percentage of minorities with poor scores and non-minorities with poor scores was 28.9%. The gap between lower-income and higher-income households was 29.2%.

The author and researcher of this Missouri study concluded that "the evidence appears to be credible, substantial, and compelling that credit scores have a significant disproportionate impact on minorities and on the poor."[174]

A study conducted by the Texas Department of Insurance resulted in similar findings.[175] Instead of using geographic neighborhood as a proxy for race, the Texas study was able to determine the actual race of policyholders by using motor vehicle records for approximately two million consumers. The Texas study found dramatic disparities by race, finding that African-American and Hispanic consumers constituted over 60% of the consumers having the worst credit scores but less than 10% of the consumers having the best scores.[176] Thus, African Americans and Hispanics were overrepresented in the worse credit score categories and underrepresented in the better credit score categories. The Texas study concluded that there was a consistent pattern of differences in credit scores among the different racial and ethnic groups, with whites and Asians faring better than African Americans and Hispanics.

In July 2007, the Federal Trade Commission (FTC) issued a study on insurance credit scoring and racial disparities, which was mandated by the 2003 amendments to the Fair Credit Reporting Act.[177] The FTC study found substantial racial disparities, with African Americans and Hispanics strongly over-represented in the lowest scoring categories.[178] The FTC study also found that insurance credit scores had a slight effect in serving as a statistical proxy for race and ethnicity. However, the FTC concluded that insurance credit scores also serve as an effective predictor of risk for automobile insurance.[179] Thus, despite the presence of substantial racial disparities, the FTC concluded that insurance credit scores may benefit consumers.[180] Note that in conducting its study, the FTC relied on data supplied by members of the automobile insurance industry.

6.5 Special ECOA Rules Concerning Credit Evaluation

6.5.1 Introduction

The following section discusses the special ECOA prohibitions on certain types of credit discrimination that are indirectly linked to a prohibited basis. Examples are credit decisions based on the applicant's likelihood of childbearing, type of income, telephone listing, and certain aspects of credit history. These special ECOA rules provide protection for women and, to a lesser extent, for applicants aged sixty-two or over.

6.5.2 Income Sources

6.5.2.1 General

The ECOA protects applicants from a creditor's inappropriate consideration of certain sources of the applicant's income. These protected income sources include income derived from part-time employment, alimony, child support, separate maintenance, retirement benefits, or public assistance.[181] These sources of income are related to age, sex, marital status, and public assistance status, and the regulations therefore seek to prevent discrimination based on these sources of income, which could have a disparate impact on a protected group.

6.5.2.2 Appropriate Methods to Evaluate Protected Income

The ECOA protects applicants from inappropriate evaluation of sources of protected income but does not guarantee that every applicant with such income be granted credit. A creditor need not consider income at all in evaluating creditworthiness.[182] If the creditor does consider income, there are several acceptable methods of evaluating income.

A creditor may consider the total amount of income stated by the applicant without taking any steps to evaluate the different sources or components of that income.[183] Alternatively, the creditor may review *every* component of income separately, placing every component in one of two categories—reliable income and unreliable income. The creditor can then disregard *all* the unreliable income or evaluate the applicant based on these two total numbers—reliable and unreliable income.[184] If

---

174 *Id.*
175 Texas Dep't of Ins., Report to the 79th Legislature—Use of Credit Information by Insurers in Texas (Dec. 30, 2004).
176 *Id.*
177 Pub. L. No. 108-159, § 215, 117 Stat. 1952 (2003).
178 Fed. Trade Comm'n, Credit-Based Insurance Scores: Impacts on Consumers of Automobile Insurance 3 (July 2007).
179 *Id.*
180 *Id.* at 23.

181 Official Interpretations of Reg. B [Official Staff Commentary on Reg. B], 12 C.F.R. pt. 1002 [pt. 202], Supp. I, § 1002.6(b)(5)-1 [§ 202.6(b)(5)-1].
     These sources of income were previously called "protected" income. As part of its March 2003 revisions to Regulation B, the Federal Reserve Board removed the phrase "protected income"; however, no substantive change was intended. 68 Fed. Reg. 13,144, 13,156 (Mar. 18, 2003).
182 Official Interpretations of Reg. B [Official Staff Commentary on Reg. B], 12 C.F.R. pt. 1002 [pt. 202], Supp. I, § 1002.6(b)(5)-3 [§ 202.6(b)(5)-3].
183 *Id.*
184 *Id.*

the creditor does not evaluate each component for reliability (for example, it evaluates some components for reliability but not others), then it must automatically treat all protected income as reliable.[185]

6.5.2.3 Individual Evaluation of Protected Income

If the creditor is using the second approach and evaluating every component of the applicant's income for reliability, the creditor may not discount or exclude from consideration the income of an applicant or the spouse of an applicant because of a prohibited basis.[186] In addition, the creditor may not automatically discount or exclude from consideration *any* protected income. The discount or exclusion must be based on the applicant's actual circumstances.[187]

Creditors, therefore, may not use blanket rules which automatically deem a certain type of protected income to be unreliable.[188] The decision must be made on an individual basis and on aggregate statistical relationships such as those underlying credit scoring models.[189]

Creditors may not treat applicants negatively on the basis that their only earned income is derived from a part-time job[190] or that their income is derived from an annuity, pension, or other retirement benefit.[191] The creditor instead may only consider in each individual case the amount and probable continuity of the income.[192] Similarly, alimony, child support, or separate maintenance payments must be considered as income as long as they will be consistently received in the individual applicant's case.[193]

For instance, a creditor may not count only half of the income of a married woman when it would consider all of the income of a married man, or only half of a married woman's income when it would consider the full amount of a single woman's income. Similarly, the creditor may not discount income derived from part-time jobs or from retirement benefits or alimony.

6.5.2.4 Income from Multiple Sources

The previous subsection discussed whether a creditor could treat certain types of protected income as unreliable and thus discount or ignore that income. A separate but related issue is whether creditors may score or treat income differently if it comes from multiple sources rather than from a single source.

This issue is particularly important because women and older applicants are more likely to have multiple sources of income.

The official interpretations state that creditors may not take into account the *number* of sources for protected income (such as alimony, child support, and Social Security). Furthermore, they may not treat negatively the fact that the sole source of *earned* income is from a part-time job.[194]

However, creditors may take into account the fact that the applicant has more than one source of *earned* income, even if one such source is the otherwise protected category of part-time employment. In other words, Regulation B allows consideration of the fact that income is derived from two part-time jobs or from one full-time and one part-time job.[195] The creditor may also treat income earned from an applicant's primary job differently than income from an applicant's second job.[196] These standards apply to both credit scoring and judgmental evaluation systems.

6.5.2.5 Income Sources Associated with Older Applicants

A creditor may not automatically exclude from consideration income of an applicant or applicant's spouse derived from part-time employment, annuities, pensions, or other retirement benefits, or consider only a portion of such income.[197] Evaluation of protected income from sources such as Social Security or retirement benefits must be made on an individual basis and not be based on aggregate statistical relationships such as those underlying credit scoring models. Creditors may not use blanket rules which automatically deem a certain type of protected income to be unreliable and therefore predictive of a higher risk of nonpayment.[198]

Although creditors may not take into account the number of sources of unearned protected income (such as retirement income or Social Security), Regulation B allows consideration of the fact that income is derived from multiple earned income sources (for example, two part-time jobs).[199] But creditors may not treat adversely the fact that an applicant's only source of earned income is from a single part-time job.[200]

---

185 *Id.*

186 Reg. B, 12 C.F.R. § 1002.6(b)(5) [§ 202.6(b)(5)].

187 Official Interpretations of Reg. B [Official Staff Commentary on Reg. B], 12 C.F.R. pt. 1002 [pt. 202], Supp. I, § 1002.6(b)(5)-3 [§ 202.6(b)(5)-3].

188 *Id.* § 1002.6(b)(5)-1, (b)(5)-3 [§ 202.6(b)(5)-1, (b)(5)-3].

189 *Id.* § 1002.6(b)(5)-1 [§ 202.6(b)(5)-1].

190 Reg. B, 12 C.F.R. § 1002.6(b)(5) [§ 202.6(b)(5)]; Official Interpretations of Reg. B [Official Staff Commentary on Reg. B], 12 C.F.R. pt. 1002 [pt. 202], Supp. I, § 1002.6(b)(5)-4 [§ 202.6(b)(5)-4].

191 Reg. B, 12 C.F.R. § 1002.6(b)(5) [§ 202.6(b)(5)].

192 *Id.*

193 *Id.*

194 Official Interpretations of Reg. B [Official Staff Commentary on Reg. B], 12 C.F.R. pt. 1002 [pt. 202], Supp. I, § 1002.6(b)(5)-4 [§ 202.6(b)(5)-4].

195 *Id.*

196 *Id.*

197 Reg. B, 12 C.F.R. § 1002.6(b)(5) [§ 202.6(b)(5)]; *see also* United States v. City Financial Co., Clearinghouse No. 45,752 (N.D. Ga. 1990) (five finance companies agreed to stop refusing to consider income derived from public assistance programs, part-time employment, and retirement benefits); United States v. Gen. Electric Capital Corp., Clearinghouse No. 45,754 (D. Conn. 1989) (lender agreed not to require applicants to be employed full-time and not to exclude income from public assistance, part-time employment, or retirement plans).

198 *See* United States v. Aristar, Inc., Clearinghouse No. 37,083 (S.D. Fla. 1983).

199 *See* § 6.5.2.4, *supra.*

200 Official Interpretations of Reg. B [Official Staff Commentary on

6.5.2.6 Income Sources Historically Associated with Women Applicants

Regulation B prohibits creditors from automatically discounting income from certain sources historically associated with women, such as part-time employment.[201] Other sources of income traditionally available primarily to women, such as alimony, child support, and separate maintenance payments also may not be discounted automatically when an applicant is relying on such income to support the application.[202] A person receiving such income may choose not to include it when submitting a credit application.[203] These sources of income may be evaluated on an individual basis for reliability and probable continuity.[204]

The creditor must consider such payments as income "to the extent that they are likely to be consistently made."[205] Factors that may be used to measure the likelihood of consistent payments include:[206]

- Whether the payments are received pursuant to a written agreement or court decree;
- The length of time that the payments have been received;
- The regularity of receipt of payments;
- The availability of procedures to compel payment; and
- The creditworthiness of the person making the payments to the applicant.

The creditor also may consider the amount and probable continuity of such income.[207]

6.5.2.7 Income Sources Associated with Public Assistance Recipients

Public assistance status as a prohibited basis and treatment of public assistance income as protected income are so closely related that a discussion of one effectively merges into the other. Therefore, discussion of income sources associated with public assistance is detailed in conjunction with the discussion later in this chapter of the ECOA rules concerning public assistance generally.[208]

6.5.3 Spousal Credit History

6.5.3.1 Background

Regulation B attempts to assist two groups of women that historically have had problems with credit histories.[209] First, the ECOA gives special rights to applicants (primarily women—whether married, divorced, or widowed) who have not been able to reap the benefits of their good credit histories because their accounts were recorded in their spouses' (husbands') names. Second, applicants with poor credit histories because their accounts have been recorded in their spouses' (or in both spouses') names may show that this history does not reflect their individual creditworthiness. Additionally, the Consumer Financial Protection Bureau has proposed to make it easier for stay-at-home spouses and others to qualify for credit cards based on household income even if the consumer does not have an independent ability to pay.[210]

Reg. B], 12 C.F.R. pt. 1002 [pt. 202], Supp. I, § 1002.6(b)(5)-4 [§ 202.6(b)(5)-4].

201 Reg. B, 12 C.F.R. § 1002.6(b)(5) [§ 202.6(b)(5)].

202 *Id.*; *see also* United States v. Franklin Acceptance Corp., No. 99-CV-2435 (E.D. Pa. 1999) (consent decree in which creditor agreed not to discount or exclude income from child support or public assistance), *available on the companion website to this treatise*; United States v. City Financial Co., Clearinghouse No. 45,752 (N.D. Ga. 1990) (five finance companies agreed to stop refusing to consider income derived from public assistance programs, part-time employment, retirement benefits, alimony, and child support); United States v. Amoco Oil Co., Clearinghouse No. 33,836 (D.D.C. 1980) (creditor agreed not to use credit scoring system which allegedly discriminated against women by giving income from full-time employment or other sources a greater value than "protected sources" commonly associated with women, such as part-time employment, alimony, and child support payments).

203 *See* Reg. B, 12 C.F.R. § 1002.5(d)(2) [§ 202.5(d)(2)]; Official Interpretations of Reg. B [Official Staff Commentary on Reg. B], 12 C.F.R. pt. 1002 [pt. 202], Supp. I, § 1002.5(d)(2)-1 [§ 202.5(d)(2)-1].

204 Reg. B, 12 C.F.R. § 1002.6(b)(5) [§ 202.6(b)(5)]; Official Interpretations of Reg. B [Official Staff Commentary on Reg. B], 12 C.F.R. pt. 1002 [pt. 202], Supp. I, § 1002.6(b)(5)-1 to (b)(5)-4 [§ 202.6(b)(5)-1 to (b)(5)-4]; *see also* Sallion v. Suntrust Bank, 87 F. Supp. 2d 1323 (N.D. Ga. 2000) (no ECOA violation found when bank required verification of alimony income and plaintiff could not substantiate receipt of payments as required by bank's underwriting guidelines).

205 Reg. B, 12 C.F.R. § 1002.6(b)(5) [§ 202.6(b)(5)]; Official Interpretations of Reg. B [Official Staff Commentary on Reg. B], 12 C.F.R. pt. 1002 [pt. 202], Supp. I, § 1002.6(b)(5)-2 [§ 202.6(b)(5)-2].

206 Official Interpretations of Reg. B [Official Staff Commentary on Reg. B], 12 C.F.R. pt. 1002 [pt. 202], Supp. I, § 1002.6(b)(5)-2 [§ 202.6(b)(5)-2].

207 Reg. B, 12 C.F.R. § 1002.6(b)(5) [§ 202.6(b)(5)].

The Official Interpretations to Regulation B [Official Staff Commentary on Regulation B], 12 C.F.R. pt. 1002 [pt. 202], Supp. I, § 1002.6(b)(5) [§ 202.6(b)(5)], is equally applicable to the treatment of income from sources such as alimony, child support, and separate maintenance payments. *See also* United States v. Security Pac. Financial Systems, Clearinghouse No. 37,095 (S.D. Cal. Dec. 21, 1983) (civil penalty based on allegations that creditors discounted or failed to consider payments from alimony, child support, or separate maintenance); United States v. Amoco Oil Co., Clearinghouse No. 33,836 (D.D.C. 1980) (creditor barred from using credit scoring system which gave income from "protected sources"—such as part-time employment, alimony, and child support payments—less value than full-time employment or other sources); Anchor Sav. & Loan Ass'n v. Equal Opportunities Comm'n, 343 N.W.2d 122 (Wis. Ct. App. 1983) (creditor discriminated against borrower on the basis of marital status in action brought under a city ordinance, *not* the ECOA, when creditor denied a loan to divorced borrower who had support obligations but did not consider similar obligations of married borrowers), *rev'd on other grounds*, 120 Wis. 2d 391 (Wis. 1984).

208 *See* § 6.6.3, *infra*.

209 Reg. B, 12 C.F.R. § 1002.6(b)(6) [§ 202.6(b)(6)].

210 Http://files.consumerfinance.gov/f/201210_cfpb_CARD-Act-proposed-rule.pdf.

6.5.3.2 Supplementing a Minimal Credit History

Regulation B requires creditors who consider the credit history of applicants to consider the credit history, when "available," of accounts designated as accounts that both the applicant and applicant's spouse are permitted to use or for which both are contractually liable.[211] What information is considered available is not defined in Regulation B, but the Federal Reserve Board stated in a letter that creditors are not required to conduct any investigation of whether a spousal account exists given the prohibition against asking about marital status.[212] Essentially, the letter requires that information about a spousal account, including the fact that the primary or joint account holder is a spouse, must be apparent on the face of whatever document or source of information the creditor is evaluating. For example, if the source of information is a credit report, the credit report must show not only that the applicant is an authorized user of a credit account but that the identity of the primary account holder is the applicant's spouse.[213] Thus, the safest course would be for applicants to provide information directly to new creditors about all spousal joint or authorized user accounts.[214]

A creditor who considers the credit history of applicants also must consider, on the applicant's request, the credit history, when available, of any account reported in the name of the applicant's spouse or former spouse whom the applicant can demonstrate accurately reflects the applicant's own creditworthiness.[215] The burden is placed on the applicant to present information on these accounts, without any affirmative duty on the creditor to request the information. The applicant carries the

further burden of demonstrating that these accounts "accurately reflect" the applicant's own creditworthiness.[216]

One method of meeting this burden is to produce checks written on a joint account as payments for accounts listed in the spouse's name. Another is to produce employment records or deposit slips indicating that the applicant actually provided the funds which paid accounts listed in the spouse's name.

A creditor may restrict the types of credit history and credit references that it will consider, provided that the restrictions are applied to all credit applicants without regard to sex, marital status, or any other prohibited basis.[217] The provisions concerning credit history apply only to the extent that the creditor considers credit history in evaluating the creditworthiness of "similarly qualified applicants for a similar type and amount of credit."[218] However, on the applicant's request, a creditor must consider credit information not reported through a credit reporting agency when the information relates to the same types of credit references and history that the creditor would consider if reported through a credit reporting agency.[219]

Note that an inadvertent error by the creditor is not a violation of the above requirements.[220] Inadvertent errors include clerical mistakes, calculation errors, computer malfunctions, and printing errors. An error of legal judgment is not an inadvertent error.[221]

6.5.3.3 Avoiding a Spouse's Bad Credit History

On the applicant's request, the creditor must consider any information that the applicant presents "that tends to indicate" that the credit history being considered by the creditor does not accurately reflect the applicant's creditworthiness.[222] The creditor has no affirmative duty to request this information; the burden is placed on the applicant to explain why the applicant

211 Reg. B, 12 C.F.R. § 1002.6(b)(6)(i) [§ 202.6(b)(6)(i)].
This requirement is in addition to the requirement in Regulation B, 12 C.F.R. § 1002.10 [§ 202.10], that a creditor furnish information to credit reporting agencies regarding the participation of both spouses for any joint or authorized user accounts. *See* §§ 9.4.1.3, 9.4.1.4, *infra*.

212 Letter from Shawn McNulty, Assistant Dir., Div. of Consumer & Cmty. Affairs, Fed. Reserve Bd., to officers and managers in charge of consumer affairs, No. CA 02-6 (Mar. 28, 2002), *available at* www.newyorkfed.org/banking/circulars/11434a.html.

213 Letter from Shawn McNulty, Assistant Dir., Div. of Consumer & Cmty. Affairs, Fed. Reserve Bd., to officers and managers in charge of consumer affairs, No. CA 02-6 (Mar. 28, 2002), *available at* www.newyorkfed.org/banking/circulars/11434a.html.

214 Also, the requirement to consider "available" credit history about spousal joint or authorized user accounts should be read in conjunction with Regulation B, 12 C.F.R. § 1002.10 [§ 202.10], regarding creditors' obligations to report the participation of both spouses on an account when the creditors furnish information to credit reporting agencies. Thus, if the creditors with whom an applicant previously had an account complied with section 202.10 [section 1002.10], the new creditor should have that history "available" to it for purposes of section 202.6(b)(6) [section 1002.6(b)(6)]. If the prior creditors failed to provide such history, consider sending both the prior creditor and the credit reporting agency a written dispute seeking to have such information added. This request will trigger responsibilities under both section 202.10 [section 1002.10], see §§ 9.4.1.3, 9.4.1.4, *infra*, and the Fair Credit Reporting Act, see National Consumer Law Center, Fair Credit Reporting § 4.5 (7th ed. 2010 and Supp.).

215 Reg. B, 12 C.F.R. § 1002.6(b)(6)(iii) [§ 202.6(b)(6)(iii)].

216 *Id.*

217 Official Interpretations of Reg. B [Official Staff Commentary on Reg. B], 12 C.F.R. pt. 1002 [pt. 202], Supp. I, § 1002.6(b)(6)-1 [§ 202.6(b)(6)-1].

218 Reg. B, 12 C.F.R. § 1002.6(b)(6) [§ 202.6(b)(6)].

219 Official Interpretations of Reg. B [Official Staff Commentary on Reg. B], 12 C.F.R. pt. 1002 [pt. 202], Supp. I, § 1002.6(b)(6)-1 [§ 202.6(b)(6)-1].

220 Reg. B, 12 C.F.R. § 1002.16(c) [§ 202.16(c)]; *see also* Sayers v. Gen. Motors Acceptance Corp., 522 F. Supp. 835 (W.D. Mo. 1981) (no ECOA violation when credit denial was based on an inadvertent misinterpretation of the credit history; however, creditor's subsequent willful refusal to comply with notification requirements after being informed of its error did constitute an ECOA violation).

221 Official Interpretations of Reg. B [Official Staff Commentary on Reg. B], 12 C.F.R. pt. 1002 [pt. 202], Supp. I, § 1002.16(c)-1 [§ 202.16(c)-1].

222 Reg. B, 12 C.F.R. § 1002.6(b)(6)(ii) [§ 202.6(b)(6)(ii)].
For instance, an applicant could show that she was unemployed at the time a joint account went into default and had no way to ensure that her then-spouse, who was employed, would make payments. *See* Fed. Trade Comm'n, Informal Staff Opinion, Clearinghouse No. 37,088 (Apr. 5, 1983) (when unmarried cohabitants share use of an account and the account holder's negative credit history is imputed to another cohabitant, the cohabitant may make countervailing information available, and the creditor must consider it).

should not be denied credit because, for example, a poor credit rating is attributable to the conduct of an ex-spouse during the marriage. Also, even though the creditor has an obligation to consider mitigating information presented by an applicant (whether concerning a spouse or ex-spouse), it is not required to ignore the bad history altogether. In addition, at least one court has found that the obligation under the ECOA to consider such information only applies during the initial credit granting process and does not extend to requests for post-denial reconsideration.[223]

In many cases, there is no legitimate reason under the ECOA for a creditor to obtain the credit history of a spouse or ex-spouse if the applicant is seeking an individual account and does not wish to rely on the credit history built up in that other person's name.[224] In that case, the applicant need not be judged on the bad history of the spouse or ex-spouse at all.[225]

Sometimes bad history involving a spouse nevertheless will show up on an applicant's credit history because the applicant was an authorized user of a spouse's account.[226] In that case, it is important for the applicant to affirmatively show why the spouse's negative actions on that account do not accurately reflect the applicant's creditworthiness.

Some creditors have been reporting bankruptcy information regarding a spouse if there is a joint or authorized user spousal account. As a result, the spouse's bankruptcy information appears in the consumer's credit history.[227]

6.5.4 Telephone Listing

A creditor may not consider whether there is a telephone listing in the applicant's name as a factor relevant to creditworthiness; but it may consider the existence of a telephone at the applicant's residence as such a factor.[228] This provision was

primarily designed to protect married women, who may not have had telephone listings in their own names.

6.5.5 Likelihood of Bearing or Rearing Children

In evaluating an applicant's creditworthiness, a creditor may not make assumptions or use aggregate statistics concerning the likelihood that the income of any group of persons will be interrupted or diminished at a future time because those persons will bear or rear children.[229] In addition, creditors are forbidden from denying loans to women who anticipate taking maternity leaves.[230] Read together with the provision of Regulation B[231] which bars creditors from requesting information about an applicant's birth control practices and childbearing or childrearing intentions and capability, this provision prevents creditors from arbitrarily denying credit merely because they assume that a young female applicant will marry, have children, quit her job, and then probably default on her credit obligations.

6.5.6 Availability of Credit Insurance

A creditor may not refuse to extend credit or terminate an account merely because the applicant's age makes him or her ineligible for credit life, health, accident, or disability insurance.[232]

6.6 Allowable Discrimination on a Prohibited Basis

6.6.1 Introduction

In certain special situations, creditors may make credit decisions taking into consideration three of the prohibited bases: the applicant's age, public assistance status, and marital status. These three prohibited bases are not found in other federal discrimination laws, and thus the ECOA limitations on these bases may be determinative.

6.6.2 Age

6.6.2.1 Introduction

Although age is a prohibited basis for discrimination under the ECOA, age is a very different type of prohibited basis than, for

---

223 Jones v. Keycorp Bank, 2008 WL 324126 (E.D. Mich. Feb. 6, 2008) (right to present mitigating information under 12 C.F.R. § 202.6(b)(6)(ii) [§ 1002.6(b)(6)(ii)] does not require creditors to review past denials even when such denials may have been based on faulty information; mitigating information is relevant only to new applications for credit and this right for reconsideration is not limited to a spouse's credit history).

224 *See, e.g.,* United States v. Fid. Fed. Bank, No. 02-CV-03906 (E.D.N.Y. complaint and consent decree filed July 8, 2002) (Department of Justice sued credit card company for, *inter alia,* obtaining credit reports on non-applicant spouses), *available at* www.usdoj.gov (also available on the companion website to this treatise); *In re* Westinghouse Credit Corp., 94 F.T.C. 1280 (Fed. Trade Comm'n 1979) (creditor agreed not to conduct prohibited credit checks on the deceased spouses of applicants); *In re* Alden's, Inc., 92 F.T.C. 901 (Fed. Trade Comm'n 1978) (creditor ordered to stop rejecting married persons' applications for individual accounts on the basis of credit reports obtained on their spouses).

225 *See* § 5.5.2.4, *supra.*

226 As required by 12 C.F.R. § 1002.10 [§ 202.10]. *See* §§ 9.4.1.3, 9.4.1.4, *infra.*

227 *See* §§ 9.4.1.3, 9.4.1.4, *infra* (discussing controversy surrounding issue of whether creditors are legally permitted to do this).

228 Reg. B, 12 C.F.R. § 1002.6(b)(4) [§ 202.6(b)(4)]; *see also* Fed. Trade Comm'n, Informal Staff Opinion, Clearinghouse No. 37,084 (May 26, 1983) (if the customer was permitted to defer payment and

hence would receive "incidental credit," a rental car company would violate the ECOA if it required that a customer without a major credit card have a telephone listing in her own name).

229 Reg. B, 12 C.F.R. § 1002.6(b)(3) [§ 202.6(b)(3)].

230 United States v. Georgia Telco Credit Union, Clearinghouse No. 31,075 (N.D. Ga. 1980); *see also* Williams v. Countrywide Home Loans, 2002 WL 31270283 (Ohio Ct. App. Oct. 11, 2002) (class certification granted in lawsuit alleging lender violated state antidiscrimination law by refusing to consider income of female borrowers that lender believed would be on maternity leave when loan closed).

231 Reg. B, 12 C.F.R. § 1002.5(d)(3) [§ 202.5(d)(3)].

232 Reg. B, 12 C.F.R. § 1002.7(e) [§ 202.7(e)].

example, race or religion. Many types of age discrimination are explicitly authorized under the ECOA, and the ECOA can be seen more as regulating age discrimination than as prohibiting it.

There are detailed rules as to how a creditor may take the age of an applicant into consideration, and some of these rules differ depending on whether a credit scoring or judgmental system is used while others do not. The general rule, which applies no matter what evaluation system is used, is that age may not be taken into consideration at all unless provided for by the regulation.[233] To use age at all in either a credit scoring or judgmental system, the creditor must show that one of the specific exceptions to the general rule applies.

6.6.2.2 General Exceptions to the Prohibition Against Age Discrimination

The first general exception to the rule against age discrimination—which applies to both credit scoring and judgmental systems—is that the creditor can consider the applicant's age to determine if the applicant has the legal capacity to enter into a binding contract.[234] Legal capacity refers primarily to the legal age of majority. That is, if under state law an applicant is too young to enter into a binding contract, the creditor may reject the application on that basis.

The second exception—which also applies whether the creditor is using a credit scoring system or a judgmental system—is that a creditor may consider the age of an applicant sixty-two years old or older in order to give favorable treatment to that applicant[235] or to evaluate a pertinent element of creditworthiness for a reverse mortgage.[236] Thus, assigning the highest point value or bonus points in a credit scoring system to an applicant sixty-two years of age or older would not constitute age discrimination. Nor would it be improper, in a judgmental system, to grant credit to an applicant sixty-two years of age or older who owned no real property, even if younger applicants would not receive a loan without such security.

A creditor may also provide more favorable credit terms to applicants over the age of sixty-two, such as lower interest rates or higher credit limits. More favorable terms may not be offered to those under age sixty-two than those over aged sixty-two except in special purpose credit programs.[237]

6.6.2.3 Relationship to State Laws

State laws addressing credit discrimination are preempted to the extent that they are inconsistent with the ECOA and Regulation B.[238] As described below, Regulation B allows credit

discrimination in favor of older applicants. Regulation B, in order to favor an older applicant, specifically preempts state laws that prohibit creditors from asking or considering an applicant's age.[239]

Somewhat more confusing is a related Regulation B preemption of state laws dealing with age discrimination. As discussed below, Regulation B allows creditors using a credit scoring system to utilize age as a predictive factor but only allows other systems to use age as a "pertinent element of creditworthiness." Regulation B preempts state laws that prohibit *credit scoring systems* from using age as a pertinent element of creditworthiness.[240] In other words, a state statute can prohibit creditors using a judgmental system from considering age at all, except to favor those over the age of sixty-two. The state statute could only limit a credit scoring system's use of age as a pertinent element of creditworthiness.

The ECOA does not preempt state laws that establish an age of majority for various purposes, such as an age below which a person may not enter into an enforceable contract.[241] Nor does it preempt state laws which set a different age of majority for married and unmarried persons.[242]

6.6.2.4 Age Discrimination Rules Applying Only to Credit Scoring Systems

When a creditor uses a credit scoring system, it may use the age of applicants as a predictor of creditworthiness.[243] For example, a forty-year-old applicant may receive five points and a twenty-five-year-old applicant only two points if the creditor's scoring system predicts that forty-year-olds are substantially better risks.

However, creditors may not attach a negative factor or value to applicants who are sixty-two years of age or older.[244] A

---

233 Reg. B, 12 C.F.R. § 1002.6(b)(1) [§ 202.6(b)(1)].

234 Reg. B, 12 C.F.R. § 1002.6(b)(2) [§ 202.6(b)(2)].

235 15 U.S.C. § 1691(b)(4); Reg. B, 12 C.F.R. §§ 1002.2(o), 1002.6(b)(2)(iv) [§§ 202.2(o), 202.6(b)(2)(iv)].

236 Official Interpretations of Reg. B [Official Staff Commentary on Reg. B], 12 C.F.R. pt. 1002 [pt. 202], Supp. I, § 1002.6(b)(2)-4 [§ 202.6(b)(2)-4].

237 *Id.* § 1002.6(b)(2)-1 [§ 202.6(b)(2)-1].

238 15 U.S.C. § 1691d(f); Reg. B, 12 C.F.R. § 1002.11(a) [§ 202.11(a)].

239 Reg. B, 12 C.F.R. § 1002.11(b)(1)(iv) [§ 202.11(b)(1)(iv)].

240 *Id.*

241 Fed. Reserve Bd., Official Board Interpretation § 202.1103, 42 Fed. Reg. 36,810 (July 18, 1977), *as modified by* 42 Fed. Reg. 39,368 (Aug. 4, 1977).

Interpretation section 202.1103 was not included in the official staff commentary because the Federal Reserve Board did not include any interpretations that did not preempt state laws. The reasoning of this interpretation thus apparently is still valid. Moreover, section 202.1103 is an official board interpretation, not a staff interpretation, and thus should not be superseded by a staff commentary.

242 Fed. Reserve Bd., Official Board Interpretation § 202.1103, 42 Fed. Reg. 36,810 (July 18, 1977), *as modified by* 42 Fed. Reg. 39,368 (Aug. 4, 1977).

243 Reg. B, 12 C.F.R. § 1002.6(b)(2)(ii) [§ 202.6(b)(2)(ii)]; *see, e.g.,* Memorandum and Order of Summary Judgment, Saunders v. Citibank S.D., Clearinghouse No. 45,760 (E.D. Md. 1988) (No. JH-87-2930) (creditor did not discriminate against fifty-four-year-old applicant on basis of age, as it had used age permissibly in its empirically derived credit scoring system), *aff'd*, 872 F.2d 419 (4th Cir. 1989) (unpublished).

244 Reg. B, 12 C.F.R. § 1002.6(b)(2)(ii) [§ 202.6(b)(2)(ii)].

Regulation B, 12 C.F.R. § 1002.2(o) [§ 202.2(o)], defines "elderly" as aged sixty-two or older. *See also* Official Interpretations of Reg. B [Official Staff Commentary on Reg. B], 12 C.F.R. pt. 1002 [pt. 202], Supp. I, § 1002.6(b)(2)-2 [§ 202.6(b)(2)-2].

"negative factor or value" is defined by Regulation B as a factor, value, or weight that:

- Is less favorable to older applicants than the creditor's experience warrants; or
- Is less favorable than that assigned to the younger applicants most favored by the creditor in terms of age.[245]

For example, the creditor might assign the following point values to certain age categories:

- Under 25 = 1 point;
- 26–34 = 2 points;
- 36–50 = 3 points;
- 51–61 = 4 points.

Under this system, the creditor could not assign less than four points to an applicant sixty-two or older. However, those aged sixty-two or older may receive a factor higher than any other age group[246] so that, in this example, they could receive five points. Similarly, it is arguably impermissible to weigh favorably the fact that an applicant has young children, because this factor would penalize older applicants.

6.6.2.5 Age Discrimination Rules Applying Only to Judgmental Systems

When a creditor uses a judgmental system,[247] it may consider age only to determine a "pertinent element of creditworthiness."[248] According to Regulation B, a pertinent element of creditworthiness is "any information about applicants that a creditor obtains and considers and that has a demonstrable relationship to a determination of creditworthiness."[249]

Several examples of information displaying this "demonstrable relationship" are listed in the official interpretations of Regulation B.[250] A creditor may not reject an application or terminate an account because the applicant is sixty-two years old. But the creditor that uses a judgmental system may relate the applicant's age to other factors that the creditor considers in measuring creditworthiness. For example, a creditor may consider:

- The applicant's occupation and time remaining before retirement to ascertain whether the applicant's income (including retirement income) would support the extension

of credit until its maturity;[251]
- The adequacy of security offered by the applicant, if the duration of the credit extension would exceed the applicant's life expectancy ("An elderly applicant might not qualify for a 5 percent down, 30-year mortgage loan but might qualify with a larger down payment or a shorter loan maturity.");[252] and
- An applicant's age to assess the significance of the applicant's length of employment or length of residence at current address, for example, a young applicant who has a short work history or an older applicant who has retired recently and moved from a long-time residence.[253]

However, these factors must be evaluated from facts and circumstances relating to the applicant on an individual case-by-case basis, and a creditor cannot "base its decision on age or information related exclusively to age."[254] "Information related exclusively to age" encompasses mortality or life expectancy data.[255] Thus, creditors have been restricted in using age-based mortality statistics to justify a practice of requiring shorter repayment terms for older applicants and prohibited from automatically requiring higher down payments from applicants over the age of sixty-five.[256] Creditors are also prohibited from discriminating against older applicants because their age makes them ineligible for credit life, health, accident, or disability insurance.[257]

If a judgmental system in effect uses the "intuition" of the creditor's employee as a factor weighing against an older applicant, an argument should be made that such consideration is not related to a "pertinent element" of creditworthiness.[258] The burden should then shift to the creditor to prove the

---

245 Reg. B, 12 C.F.R. § 1002.2(v) [§ 202.2(v)].
        Thus older applicants must be given "the *higher* of (1) the score warranted on the basis of the creditors experience with elderly applicants or (2) the score assigned to the class of non-elderly applicants most favored on the basis of age." David Hsia, *Credit Scoring and the Equal Credit Opportunity Act*, 30 Hastings L.J. 371, 411 (1978).
246 Reg. B, 12 C.F.R. § 1002.6(b)(2)(iv) [§ 202.6(b)(2)(iv)]; *see also* 15 U.S.C. § 1691(b)(4).
247 Reg. B, 12 C.F.R. § 1002.6(b)(2)(iii) [§ 202.6(b)(2)(iii)].
248 Reg. B, 12 C.F.R. § 1002.2(y) [§ 202.2(y)].
249 *Id.*
250 Official Interpretations of Reg. B [Official Staff Commentary on Reg. B], 12 C.F.R. pt. 1002 [pt. 202], Supp. I, § 1002.6(b)(2)-3 [§ 202.6(b)(2)-3].

251 *Id.* § 1002.6(b)(2)-3 [§ 202.6(b)(2)-3].
252 *Id.* § 1002.6(b)(2)-3 [§ 202.6(b)(2)-3].
        The creditor's statistics might show that, in this mobile society, a large percentage of mortgages are paid off within five to ten years, so concern about a thirty-year mortgage is arguably a pretext for age discrimination.
253 *Id.* § 1002.6(b)(2)-3 [§ 202.6(b)(2)-3].
254 *Id.*
255 *See* Consent Decree, Fed. Trade Comm'n v. Green Tree Acceptance, Clearinghouse No. 44,437 (N.D. Tex. Dec. 16, 1988).
256 Consent Decree, Fed. Trade Comm'n v. Green Tree Acceptance, Clearinghouse No. 44,327 (N.D. Tex. 1988) (amended complaint alleges creditor violated ECOA by offering or granting loans to older applicants on less favorable terms than equally qualified younger applicants; creditor's policy allegedly was to require down payment higher by 3% of the amount financed than that required of younger applicants for each year the applicant was over sixty-five).
257 Reg. B, 12 C.F.R. § 1002.7(e) [§ 202.7(e)]; *see* § 9.5.1, *infra*.
258 Enforcement actions by federal agencies have made it clear that neither age nor information relating exclusively to age—such as mortality or life expectancy data—is reasonably related to a pertinent element of creditworthiness. *See, e.g.*, Fed. Trade Comm'n v. Green Tree Acceptance, Inc., Clearinghouse No. 44,327 (N.D. Tex. 1988) (agreed motion for leave to amend complaint ¶¶ 9–12; consent order ¶ 5(a)); Consent Order, United States v. Landmark Financial Servs., Inc., No. N-84-3510, Clearinghouse No. 41,275 (D. Md. Dec. 9, 1986) (also prior decision on summary judgment motion).

"demonstrable relationship" of age to a determination of creditworthiness in the applicant's situation.[259]

6.6.2.6 Combination Systems

The official interpretations of Regulation B authorize a credit evaluation process that combines a credit scoring system and a judgmental system.[260] The credit scoring component of the combination system must comply with the special requirements (concerning age and public assistance evaluations) of a credit scoring system. The judgmental component—the component that is not a credit scoring system—must comply with the requirements (concerning age and public assistance evaluations) of a judgmental system.[261] This rule allows the creditor to use age twice, once pursuant to the limitations which apply to credit scoring systems and once pursuant to the different limitations which apply to judgmental systems.

6.6.3 Public Assistance Status

6.6.3.1 General Rule Against Evaluations Based on Public Assistance Status

A creditor may not consider whether an applicant's income is derived from any public assistance program, except as expressly permitted by Regulation B.[262] Credit scoring systems cannot consider the fact that income derives from a public assistance program because Regulation B contains no provision allowing the creditor using a credit scoring system to consider the applicant's public assistance status.[263] Income derived from public assistance programs should not be assigned a negative score in comparison to other forms of income of the same dollar amount.[264]

The DOJ and federal banking regulators have taken the position that the prohibition against discriminatory treatment of public assistance income also requires creditors who consider gross income in credit evaluation to upwardly adjust the amount of public assistance income that is nontaxable to make it comparable to taxable income.[265] However, such "grossing up" of an applicant's income can present other problems, especially with predatory loans, in that it becomes an excuse to make the borrower a loan that is larger than the borrower's real ability to repay the loan. Any "grossing up" should be based on the relevant tax bracket for the applicant's income, rather than the highest bracket available.

6.6.3.2 Exception for Judgmental System

When the creditor uses a judgmental system, it may consider whether the applicant's income is derived from a public assistance program, but only to determine a "pertinent element of creditworthiness."[266] According to Regulation B, a pertinent element of creditworthiness is "any information about applicants that a creditor obtains and considers and that has a demonstrable relationship to a determination of creditworthiness."[267]

Several examples of information displaying this "demonstrable relationship" are listed in the official interpretations:[268]

- The length of time an applicant will likely remain eligible to receive such income;
- Whether the applicant will continue to qualify for benefits based on the status of the applicant's dependents (for instance, the age of the applicant's children may affect future Temporary Assistance to Needy Families payments or Social Security payments to a minor);
- Whether the creditor can attach or garnish the income to ensure payment of the debt in the event of default.

The prohibition against discrimination based on public assistance status provides certain clear-cut limitations on creditor behavior. A creditor absolutely may not maintain a blanket policy of refusing to extend credit to public assistance recipients. It also may not impose stricter loan terms or additional restrictions based upon applicants' receipt of public assistance.[269]

---

259 *See* Reg. B, 12 C.F.R. §§ 1002.2(y), 1002.6(b)(2) [§§ 202.2(y), 202.6(b)(2)]; Official Interpretations of Reg. B [Official Staff Commentary on Reg. B], 12 C.F.R. pt. 1002 [pt. 202], Supp. I, § 1002.6(b)(2)-3 [§ 202.6(b)(2)-3].

260 Official Interpretations of Reg. B [Official Staff Commentary on Reg. B], 12 C.F.R. pt. 1002 [pt. 202], Supp. I, § 1002.6(b)(2)-5 [§ 202.6(b)(2)-5, as renumbered Sept. 30, 1996].

261 Reg. B § 1002.6(b)(2) [§ 202.6(b)(2)].

262 Reg. B § 1002.6(b)(2)(i) [§ 202.6(b)(2)(i)]; Official Interpretations of Reg. B [Official Staff Commentary on Reg. B], 12 C.F.R. pt. 1002 [pt. 202], Supp. I, § 1002.6(b)(2)-6 [§ 202.6(b)(2)-6].

263 *See* United States v. Aristar, Inc., Clearinghouse No. 37,083 (S.D. Fla. Apr. 7, 1983); Reed v. Northwestern Bell Telephone Co., Clearinghouse No. 27,524 (D. Minn. 1981) (credit scoring system unlawfully discriminated against public assistance recipients).

264 *See* Consent Decree, United States v. Franklin Acceptance Corp., No. 99-CV-2435 (E.D. Pa. 1999) (settling allegations that creditor excluded or discounted public assistance income), *available on the companion website to this treatise*; Consent Order, United States v. Household Finance Corp., Clearinghouse No. 38,903 (N.D. Ill. 1984) (based partially on allegations that creditor did not give equal weight to income from public assistance as it did to income from other sources).

265 Complaint and Consent Decree, United States v. Fid. Fed. Bank, No. 02-CV-03906 (E.D.N.Y. July 8, 2002), *available at* www.usdoj.gov *and on the companion website to this treatise*; *see also* Interagency Joint Policy Statement on Discrimination in Lending, 59 Fed. Reg. 18,266 (Apr. 15, 1994) (lender's failure to distinguish taxable and non-taxable gross income has a disparate impact on older and disabled consumers because they are more likely to receive non-taxable income; no business necessity defense because lender has the less discriminatory alternative of "grossing up" income, that is, making it equivalent to gross taxable income by using formulas related to the applicant's tax bracket).

    The Joint Policy Statement is discussed in § 12.2.5, *infra*.

266 Reg. B, 12 C.F.R. § 1002.2(y) [§ 202.2(y)].

267 *Id.*

268 Official Interpretations of Reg. B [Official Staff Commentary on Reg. B], 12 C.F.R. pt. 1002 [pt. 202], Supp. I, § 1002.6(b)(2)-6 [§ 202.6(b)(2)-6].

269 Consent Order, United States v. Money Tree, Inc., No. 6:97-CV-7 (M.D. Ga. Feb. 4, 1997), *available on the companion website to this*

In addition, when the public assistance is based on entitlement and will remain continuous (for example, Social Security benefits), it should be considered comparable to any other form of income. In fact, some states also restrict garnishment of earnings income, thus diminishing further any basis for distinction between public benefits income and earnings income. When an applicant's assistance is based on need rather than entitlement (for example, the Supplemental Nutrition Assistance Program (SNAP)), any creditor that has denied credit should be required to present evidence that it attempted to determine the amount, the expected duration, and the continuity of assistance. Without such evidence, the creditor cannot support the argument that it has considered applications in an individual, nondiscriminatory basis, particularly if termination of needs-based benefits may mean that a new, larger source of income has been established.

Furthermore, a creditor should be required to show that its inquiries about the level of assistance and its continuance bear some relationship to the duration of the credit transaction; an applicant should not be forced to show that benefits will be received indefinitely in order to obtain a one-year loan. If the creditor's inquiries become demeaning, Regulation B arguably can be invoked to prohibit statements that would discourage a reasonable person from making or pursuing a credit application.[270]

6.6.4 Marital Status

A creditor may not consider an applicant's marital status to determine the applicant's creditworthiness, except as otherwise permitted or required by law.[271] In evaluating joint applications, a creditor cannot treat applicants differently based on the existence, absence, or likelihood of a marital relationship between the parties.[272]

The exception "as permitted or required by law" allows a creditor to consider marital status for purposes of ascertaining the rights and remedies applicable to the particular extension of credit.[273] For example, in a secured transaction involving real estate, a creditor may take into account whether state law gives the applicant's spouse an interest in the property being offered as collateral.[274]

This provision must be read along with the provision which sets standards for determining when an applicant's spouse may be required to act as co-signer on a credit instrument[275] and also with the applicable state property law concerning spouses' interest in property and liability for their partners' debts.

In situations in which creditors may request an applicant's marital status, they may categorize the applicant only as unmarried (which includes single, divorced, and widowed persons), married, or separated.[276] The creditor may explain that the category "unmarried" includes single, divorced, and widowed persons, but it is not required to do so.[277]

Some creditors have been reluctant to comply with even this basic requirement. One major creditor was alleged to routinely divide credit applicants into divorced and single categories by circling or otherwise emphasizing information contained in the credit reports obtained on applicants. It agreed to halt this practice after an action was initiated by the Federal Trade Commission.[278]

Soon after the ECOA was enacted, the Comptroller of the Currency decided that national bank creditors were not liable

---

treatise (settling allegations that creditor imposed stricter loan terms on public assistance recipients, required them to make payments earlier than the payments were due, and required them to directly deposit their benefits in repayment of loan). *But see* Brooks v. O'Connor Chevrolet, 2003 WL 22427795 (N.D. Ill. Oct. 23, 2003) (finance company did not discriminate against public assistance recipient by requiring proof of employment for more favorable terms to reinstate defaulted auto loan; finding significant the fact that the borrower had not requested to reinstate the loan but assumed she could not qualify because of the proof of employment requirement).

The court's reasoning in *Brooks* is unusual, requiring that an applicant seek the more favorable term and be denied in order to show discrimination. However, the ECOA has no such requirement to prove discrimination. For example, it should violate the ECOA for a creditor to offer a reduction in interest rates for white borrowers but not for minority borrowers, whether or not any minority borrower actually sought the rate reduction.

270 Reg. B, 12 C.F.R. § 1002.4(b) [§ 202.4(b)]; *see* § 5.4.4, *supra*.
271 Reg. B, 12 C.F.R. § 1002.6(b)(8) [§ 202.6(b)(8)].
272 *Id.*

273 Official Interpretations of Reg. B [Official Staff Commentary on Reg. B], 12 C.F.R. pt. 1002 [pt. 202], Supp. I, § 1002.6(b)(8)-1 [§ 202.6(b)(8)-1].

The federal regulatory agency specifically noted that this exception allows creditors to consider state property laws. 68 Fed. Reg. 13,144, 13,150 (Mar. 18, 2003).

274 68 Fed. Reg. 13,144, 13,150 (Mar. 18, 2003); Segaline v. Bank of America, 2003 WL 21135553 (W.D. Tex. Apr. 18, 2003) (no ECOA violation when creditor denied loan to husband and wife upon learning the couple had divorced; loan was to be secured by the couple's home, and the fact of the divorce affected homestead rights under Texas law).

275 Reg. B, 12 C.F.R. § 1002.7(d) [§ 202.7(d)]; *see, e.g.*, LOL Fin. Co. v. F.J. Faison, Jr., Revocable Trust, 2010 WL 3118630 (D. Minn. July 13, 2010) (requiring wife to sign personal guarantee fit within the 12 C.F.R. § 202.7(d)(2) exception for execution of documents necessary to allow for recovery of assets upon default), *magistrate's report and recommendation adopted*, 2010 WL 3118583 (D. Minn. Aug. 4, 2010); Wilson v. JP Morgan Chase Bank, NA, 2010 WL 2574032 (E.D. Cal. June 25, 2010) (no ECOA violation when creditor required spouse on deed to sign mortgage in order to have enforceable security interest); *In re* Huston, 2010 WL 4607823 (Bankr. E.D. Tenn. Nov. 5, 2010) (same); *see* § 5.6, *supra* (discussing co-signature issues).

276 Reg. B, 12 C.F.R. §§ 1002.2(u), 1002.5(d)(1) [§§ 202.2(u), 202.5(d)(1)].

277 Reg. B, 12 C.F.R. § 1002.5(d)(1) [§ 202.5(d)(1)].

278 *In re* Westinghouse Credit Corp., 94 F.T.C. 1280 (Fed. Trade Comm'n 1979); *see also* Consent Order, United States v. Fireside Thrift, Clearinghouse No. 43,051 (N.D. Cal. Sept. 2, 1986) (creditor agreed not to use terms other than "married" and "separated" on applications); United States v. Capitol Thrift & Loan Ass'n, Clearinghouse No. 43,052 (N.D. Cal. Mar. 20, 1986) (same); Shuman v. Standard Oil, 453 F. Supp. 1150 (N.D. Cal. 1978) (divorced woman alleged that the creditor discriminated against her on the basis of her marital status as revealed in a credit report).

for an ECOA violation found on forms for federally insured loans distributed to them by the Department of Health, Education and Welfare (now the Department of Education and the Department of Health and Human Services) and the Federal Housing Administration. The use of marital status categories other than married, unmarried, and separated on these application forms was considered "a mere technicality . . . beyond the power of the bank to correct."[279] FHA applications now only include the three categories of married, unmarried, and separated. Current federal student loan applications also include the category of divorced or widowed.

A lender's actions to enforce default remedies may also implicate the ECOA's prohibition on discrimination based on marital status.[280] For example, the federal Garn-St. Germain Depository Institutions Act preempts state laws that limit lend-

ers' enforcement of due on sale clauses in mortgages.[281] However, the preemptive reach of the Act excludes transfers of mortgaged property resulting from a decree of divorce or a legal separation agreement "by which the spouse of the borrower becomes an owner of the property."[282] The question then arises, if unmarried co-owners of a home separate and jointly convey their interests to one of co-owners, may the lender accelerate the loan and foreclose solely on the basis of this alleged "default"? It would appear that such action would discriminate against these co-owners based on their marital status. (Note that in some cases separated or divorced homeowners also face challenges enforcing their rights to loss mitigation due to general non-compliance by mortgage servicers with legal requirements.[283])

---

279 Roberta W. Boylan, Office of the Comptroller of Currency, Interpretive Staff Letter, Fed. Banking L. Rep. (CCH) ¶ 85,041 (Oct. 27, 1977).
280 *See* § 9.2.4, *infra*.

281 12 U.S.C. § 1701j-3.
282 12 U.S.C. § 1701j-3(d)(7).
283 For a discussion of the enforceability of due on sale contract provisions, see National Consume Law Center, Foreclosures § 4.6 (4th ed. 2012).

Chapter 7   Redlining

7.1 Introduction and History of Redlining

Redlining refers to the practice of separating out certain neighborhoods for disparate treatment as to mortgage or other types of lending. Redlining began as a result of the policies of the Home Owners' Loan Corporation (HOLC) in the 1930s. The HOLC was created to help families prevent the loss of homes through foreclosure.[1]

The HOLC created a uniform appraisal system. HOLC-trained appraisers then divided cities into different zones and developed a rating system to assess the risks associated with loans made in certain neighborhoods. The rating system consisted of four color-coded categories. The (A) category was considered the least risky and was coded green. The next category, (B), was coded blue. Category (C) was coded yellow and defined as neighborhoods that were in decline. The fourth and lowest category, (D), was coded red.[2]

The HOLC explicitly incorporated ethnic and racial worth into these categories. For example, a 1935 Federal Housing Administration manual for agency underwriters stated that acceptable ratings would depend on neighborhoods being protected against "the occurrence or development of unfavorable influences" such as the "infiltration of inharmonious racial or nationality groups."[3] As a result, many predominantly African-American neighborhoods were rated in category (D) and therefore "redlined." Although evidence suggests that the HOLC made loans even to these red-coded neighborhoods, the system it developed was copied by other lenders, ultimately contributing to the spread of racial redlining.[4]

The Federal Housing Administration, established in 1934, used the HOLC system as a model. The Administration developed an underwriting manual that at least partially attributed stability in neighborhoods to racial homogeneity.[5] It follows that various studies over the years have found patterns of racial redlining in Federal Housing Administration lending.[6]

The Fair Housing Act (FHA) was passed in the 1960s to address this long history of racial redlining in the housing market, expand housing opportunities for members of protected groups, and foster residential integration. Despite progress, studies continued to show the existence of redlining in the provision of home mortgage loans long after passage of the Act.[7] Ongoing government enforcement actions provide evidence of the continued existence of redlining.[8]

7.2 Legal Claims Available to Challenge Redlining

7.2.1 The ECOA, FHA, and Federal Civil Rights Acts

To the extent redlining is based on a desire to avoid making loans to certain ethnic or racial groups or loans in areas where such groups predominate, the practice involves disparate treatment on a prohibited basis in clear violation of credit discrimination statutes.[9] Precedent has developed over the years allowing plaintiffs to use the Fair Housing Act (FHA) to challenge such redlining practices.[10] The ECOA and civil rights statutes

---

1 *See generally* Charles L. Nier, III, Perpetuation of Segregation: Toward a New Historical and Legal Interpretation of Redlining Under the Fair Housing Act, 32 J. Marshall L. Rev. 617 (1999).

2 *Id.*

3 *See* Michael Fitzpatrick, Al Hofeld Jr., & Ira Rheingold, *From Redlining to Reverse Redlining: A History of Obstacles for Minority Homeownership in America*, 34 Clearinghouse Rev. 642 (2001) (quoting John O. Calmore, Spatial Equality and the Kerner Commission Report: A Back to the Future Essay, in Race, Poverty, and American Cities 324 (John Charles Boger & Judith Welch Wegner eds., 1998)).

4 Charles L. Nier, III, *Perpetuation of Segregation: Toward a New Historical and Legal Interpretation of Redlining Under the Fair Housing Act*, 32 J. Marshall L. Rev. 617 (1999) (citing Nancy A. Denton & Douglas A. Massey, American Apartheid: Segregation and the Making of the Underclass 51–52 (1993)).

5 *Id.* (citing Kenneth T. Jackson, Crabgrass Frontier: The Suburbanization of the United States (1985)).

6 *Id.* (citing Melvin L. Oliver & Thomas M. Shapiro, Black Wealth/White Wealth: A New Perspective on Racial Inequality (1995)).

7 *See, e.g.*, Jonathan Brown, Racial Redlining: A Study of Racial Discrimination by Bankers and Mortgage Companies in the United States (1993).

8 *See* § 7.2.2, *infra* (discussing government enforcement cases).

9 *See, e.g.*, Harrison v. Otto G. Heinzeroth Mortgage Co., 430 F. Supp. 893 (N.D. Ohio 1977); Laufman v. Oakley Bldg. & Loan Co., 408 F. Supp. 489 (S.D. Ohio 1976).

10 In general, courts have allowed claims to be brought under both section 3604 and section 3605 of the FHA. *See, e.g.*, Thomas v. First Fed. Sav. Bank of Ind., 653 F. Supp. 1330 (N.D. Ind. 1987) (defining redlining as mortgage credit decisions based on the characteristics of the neighborhood surrounding the would-be borrower's dwelling); Laufman v. Oakley Bldg. & Loan Co., 408 F. Supp. 489 (S.D. Ohio 1976) (plaintiffs also alleged violations of section 3617 of the FHA).

may also be used to challenge redlining.[11]

Proving a redlining violation using these statutes becomes more complicated when the creditor is not motivated by the racial or ethnic composition of a neighborhood but by various legitimate factors relating to creditworthiness that are also correlated to geographic location. Such factors include the average income, default rates, age of housing stock, or housing value in a particular area. The creditor is then using geographic location as a proxy for these other factors.[12]

Because using geographic location to determine creditworthiness often has a disproportionate impact on various racial or ethnic groups, the issue becomes whether alternative credit factors would meet the creditor's needs without causing as much of a disparate impact.[13] For example, could the creditor more directly consider the individual applicant's income and credit history and the age and value of the applicant's residence instead of using geographic area as a proxy for these factors?

Some courts have imposed additional burdens of proof in redlining cases.[14] These courts are often sympathetic to lenders' arguments that their decisions not to lend in particular areas are based on sound business principles, not discrimination.[15]

At least partially in response to this judicial trend, plaintiffs have developed additional theories of relief for lender practices associated with a segregated market. For example, plaintiffs have argued that intentional exploitation of the dual market created by segregation violates the FHA.[16] The elements required to prove such an exploitation theory, as set out by the Seventh Circuit, are: (1) dual housing markets existed as a result of racial segregation, and (2) sellers took advantage of this situation by demanding prices and terms from members of protected groups unreasonably in excess of the prices and terms available to whites for comparable housing.[17]

Another approach is to challenge the type of housing excluded from lending guidelines. For example, in 2009 the National Community Reinvestment Coalition settled FHA claims against NovaStar, alleging discrimination against Native Americans, by prohibiting loans secured by properties located on Indian Reservations; people with disabilities, by prohibiting loans on homes used for adult foster care; and African Americans and Latinos, by prohibiting loans secured by row homes.[18]

7.2.2 Government Enforcement Actions

Government enforcement actions have focused on alleged illegal redlining or discriminatory marketing practices. Most of the government enforcement actions were filed with simultaneous settlement agreements or consent decrees. Although these cases have no direct precedential value, they are important models for public and private fair lending cases.

The first key government lawsuit in the 1990s alleging a pattern or practice of race discrimination under the ECOA and the FHA against a mortgage lender was *United States v. Decatur Federal Savings & Loan Association*.[19] The Department of Justice (DOJ) alleged that Decatur engaged in numerous racially discriminatory practices which denied African Americans in the Atlanta area the same credit opportunities that were given whites.[20] The case resulted in a consent decree with broad affirmative relief that included opening more branches in African-American neighborhoods, establishing greater safeguards on the treatment of applications by African Americans, and close monitoring of compliance with the plan. Decatur also

---

11 Some plaintiffs have combined substantive FHA claims with ECOA procedural claims for lack of proper notice of credit decisions. *See, e.g.*, Cartwright v. American Sav. & Loan Ass'n, 880 F.2d 912 (7th Cir. 1989) (rejecting ECOA substantive and procedural claims because plaintiff's application was properly placed on hold and thus no adverse action taken); Saldana v. Citibank, 1996 U.S. Dist. LEXIS 8327 (N.D. Ill. June 13, 1996) (finding plaintiff did not submit a completed application and therefore rejecting ECOA procedural claims). Note, however, that recovery cannot be had for the same transactions and same violations under both the ECOA and FHA. *See* § 11.6.2, *infra*.

12 Note, however, that as far as the Justice Department is concerned, avoidance of tribal court jurisdiction is not a legitimate business justification for refusing to make secured loans when the collateral is located on a Native American reservation. Complaint and Consent Decree, United States v. Blackpipe State Bank, No. 93-5115 (D.S.D. 1994), *available at* www.justice.gov/crt/about/hce/caselist.php. DOJ enforcement actions, such as *Blackpipe*, are also useful in countering lender arguments that redlining is permissible on reservation property because Native American reservation residents do not generally own their property. *See also* Settlement Agreement, Nat'l Cmty. Reinvestment Coal. v. NovaStar Financial, Inc., No. 1:07-cv-00861 (D.D.C. Oct. 27, 2009) (settling claim, among others, of discrimination when lender prohibited loans secured by properties on tribal lands), *available on the companion website to this treatise*.

13 *See* Old West End Ass'n v. Buckeye Fed. Sav. & Loan, 675 F. Supp. 1100 (N.D. Ohio 1987); Harrison v. Otto G. Heinzeroth Mortgage Co., 430 F. Supp. 893 (N.D. Ohio 1977); Laufman v. Oakley Bldg. & Loan Co., 408 F. Supp. 489 (S.D. Ohio 1976).

14 *See, e.g.*, Cartwright v. American Sav. & Loan Ass'n, 880 F.2d 912 (7th Cir. 1989) (plaintiffs' claims did not fall within section 3604 of the FHA and defendant did not engage in redlining within the definition of section 3605; also denying relief under 42 U.S.C. §§ 1981 and 1982 because plaintiff failed to show intentional discrimination); Saldana v. Citibank, 1996 U.S. Dist. LEXIS 8327 (N.D. Ill. June 13, 1996) (plaintiff failed to show prima facie case of disparate treatment or disparate impact).

15 Cartwright v. American Sav. & Loan Ass'n, 880 F.2d 912 (7th Cir. 1989) (FHA prohibition against denying a loan based on location of the dwelling does not require that a lender disregard its legitimate

---

business interests or make an investment that is not economically sound).

16 *See, e.g.*, Honorable v. The Easy Life Real Estate System, Inc., 100 F. Supp. 2d 885 (N.D. Ill. 2000); *see also* Hobson v. Lincoln Ins. Agency, Inc., 2001 WL 55528 (N.D. Ill. Jan. 22, 2001) (denying defendant's motion to dismiss sections 1981 and 1982 claims in insurance redlining case; noting that dual-market theory not limited to the real estate market).

17 Clark v. Universal Builders, Inc., 706 F.2d 204 (7th Cir. 1983) (*Clark II*); Clark v. Universal Builders, Inc., 501 F.2d 423 (7th Cir. 1974) (*Clark I*).

18 Settlement Agreement, Nat'l Cmty. Reinvestment Coal. v. NovaStar Financial, Inc., No. 1:07-cv-00861 (D.D.C. Oct. 27, 2009), *available on the companion website to this treatise*.

19 Complaint and Consent Decree, United States v. Decatur Fed. Sav. & Loan Ass'n, No. 1:92-CV-2198 (N.D. Ga. 1992), *available at* www.justice.gov/crt/about/hce/caselist.php.

20 *Id.*

agreed to place $1 million in a fund for those aggrieved by its prior actions.[21]

In a case against Chevy Chase Federal Savings Bank, the DOJ alleged that Chevy Chase and its subsidiary, B.F. Saul Mortgage Co., intentionally excluded majority African-American census tracts in their metropolitan District of Columbia service area from access to many of the institution's credit-related services.[22] The complaint also alleged that Chevy Chase engaged in other practices that effectively denied African Americans access to banking services.[23] While Chevy Chase and its subsidiary admitted to no wrongdoing, they agreed to take reasonable actions to obtain a market share of mortgage loans in African-American neighborhoods comparable to their market share in white neighborhoods.

In *United States v. Blackpipe State Bank*,[24] the DOJ alleged that the bank discriminated against Native Americans by refusing to make secured loans when the collateral was located on a reservation, placing credit requirements on Native Americans that it did not require of whites, and charging Native Americans greater interest rates and finance charges than those it charged to whites. Among other things, the bank allegedly had a policy of refusing to make loans secured by collateral subject to tribal court jurisdiction, even though all other lending criteria were met and even though the tribal courts have repossession and collection remedies available.

In *United States v. Albank*[25] the DOJ alleged that Albank refused to fund mortgage loans secured by residential properties located in certain areas in Connecticut and in Westchester County, New York, where significant populations of African Americans and Hispanics lived. Although Albank made exceptions to its policies, the exceptions were made predominately for white borrowers.[26]

In December 2002, a complaint and consent order against Mid America Bank was filed in the Northern District of Illinois.[27] The complaint alleged that, in extending the scope of its business, the bank focused on meeting the lending and credit needs of predominantly white residential areas in Chicago and avoided serving the needs of majority African American and combined African-American/Hispanic neighborhoods.[28] As part of the settlement, the bank agreed to open or acquire two additional branch offices located in designated minority census tracts during the five-year term of the order.[29] In addition, the Bank agreed to invest an average of $2 million each year for the duration of the order to offer residents in the designated minority census tract real estate loan products at more advantageous interest rates and/or terms than would normally be provided.[30]

In a settlement agreement filed in 2004, the DOJ alleged that Old Kent Financial Corporation and Old Kent Bank served the credit needs of the predominantly white neighborhoods of the Detroit metropolitan area to a significantly greater extent than they served the credit needs of predominantly African-American neighborhoods.[31] Under the agreement, the defendants agreed to implement a marketing and outreach program designed to improve their performance in meeting the needs of residents of the majority African-American city of Detroit. In July 2004, First American Bank in Illinois agreed to settle with the Justice Department when faced with similar allegations.[32]

In 2006, the DOJ reached a consent order with Centier Bank of Whiting, Indiana, to resolve allegations that the bank refused to provide lending products and to open branches in predominantly African-American and Hispanic neighborhoods, while making loans and services available in white areas. Under the settlement, the bank agreed to invest more than $4.3 million in new branches, financing, and other programs for minority neighborhoods.[33]

In 2009, the DOJ reached a consent order with First United Security Bank of Thomasville, Alabama, which agreed to invest more than $600,000 and open a new branch in an African-American neighborhood. The complaint alleged that the bank failed to provide its lending products and services on an equal basis to majority African-American areas in west central Alabama (as well as charging residents of those areas more for comparable products).[34]

---

21 *Id.*

22 Consent Decree, United States v. Chevy Chase Fed. Sav. Bank, No. 94-1824-J6 (D.D.C. 1994), *available at* www.justice.gov/crt/about/hce/caselist.php.

23 *Id.*

24 Complaint and Consent Decree, United States v. Blackpipe State Bank, No. 93-5115 (D.S.D. 1994), *available at* www.justice.gov/crt/about/hce/caselist.php.

25 Complaint and Consent Decree, United States v. Albank, No. 97-1296 (N.D.N.Y. Aug. 13, 1997), *available at* www.justice.gov/crt/about/hce/caselist.php.

26 Some commentators have been critical of the DOJ's actions against Chevy Chase and other banks allegedly engaged in discrimination in their marketing. In the view of these commentators, discrimination in marketing is not actionable under the ECOA and the FHA because there is no individual applicant who has been discriminated against. *See* Richard L. Jacobs & Michael B. Mierzewski, *What Hath the Justice Department Wrought*, Banking Pol'y Rep., Feb. 6, 1995, at 8; John Spina, *U.S. v. Albank, FSB: Is 'Justice' Served in the Enforcement of Fair Lending Laws*, 2 N.C. Banking Inst. 207 (1998).

27 Complaint and Consent Order, United States v. Mid America Bank, No. #02C 9458 (N.D. Ill. both filed Dec. 20, 2002), *available at* www.justice.gov/crt/about/hce/caselist.php.

28 *Id.*

29 *Id.*

30 *Id.*

31 *See* Settlement Agreement, United States v. Old Kent Financial Corp., No. 04-71879 (E.D. Mich. 2004), *available at* www.justice.gov/crt/about/hce/caselist.php.

32 Complaint and Consent Order, United States v. First American Bank, No. 04 C 4585 (N.D. Ill. July 13, 2004), *available at* www.justice.gov/crt/about/hce/caselist.php.

33 *See* Consent Order, United States v. Centier Bank, No. 2:06-CV-344 (N.D. Ind. Oct. 13, 2006), *available at* www.justice.gov/crt/about/hce/caselist.php; Press Release, United States Dep't of Justice, Justice Department Reaches Settlement with Centier Bank Regarding Alleged Discrimination in Lending (Oct. 13, 2006), *available at* www.usdoj.gov/opa/pr/2006/October/06_crt_702.html.

34 *See* Agreed Order for Resolution, United States v. First United Security Bank, No. 09-064 (S.D. Ala. Nov. 18, 2009), *available at* www.justice.gov/crt/about/hce/caselist.php.

In 2011, the DOJ settled two similar redlining cases. The settlement with Citizens Republic Bancorp and Citizens Bank of Flint, Michigan, addressed allegations that Citizens Bank, and Republic Bank before it, served the credit needs of the residents of predominantly white neighborhoods in the Detroit metropolitan area to a significantly greater extent than they had served the credit needs of majority African-American neighborhoods. Those neighborhoods are easily recognized because the Detroit metropolitan area has long had highly-segregated residential housing patterns, especially for African-Americans. The banks agreed to invest approximately $3.6 million in Wayne County, Michigan.[35] The DOJ's settlement with Midwest BankCentre followed similar allegations that the bank had served the credit needs of the residents of predominantly white neighborhoods in the Missouri portion of the St. Louis metropolitan area to a significantly greater extent than they have served the credit needs of majority African-American neighborhoods. As with the Detroit case, these areas are also easily recognized because the Missouri portion of the St. Louis metropolitan area has a long history of highly-segregated residential housing patterns, especially for African-Americans. The bank agreed to open a full-service branch in an African-American neighborhood and invest approximately $1.45 million in majority African-American areas of the St. Louis metropolitan area.[36]

7.2.3 Other Federal and State Statutes

The federal credit discrimination statutes and civil rights laws are not the only possible bases for claims in redlining cases. For example, the federal Office of Thrift Supervision (which has since been incorporated into the Office of the Comptroller of the Currency as of July 2011, although the regulations are still in force) promulgated regulations for savings associations' provision of mortgage loans.[37] These regulations list examples of discriminatory lending practices, including requiring fluency in English and the consideration of the average income level of the area where the property is located.[38] The regulation prohibits discrimination based on the age of the dwelling.[39] Instead, the creditor should consider the dwelling's market value and any factors that can be documented that would directly result in a change in that market value.[40] Consideration of age and location may appear to be neutral, but past forms of discrimination may affect the use of such factors and perpetuate old sources of discrimination. For example, use of criteria such as prior history with the same

lender, home ownership, or education may foster past practices that prevented individuals in protected groups from receiving home mortgages, owning homes, or attending higher educational institutions.[41]

State statutes and regulations may also specifically prohibit redlining. For example, a New Jersey statute prohibiting geographic redlining in the granting of home mortgages was not preempted by the ECOA.[42] Several other state statutes prohibit discrimination based on the geographic area of residence.[43]

7.3 Insurance Redlining

7.3.1 Overview

Insurance redlining is the practice of "charging higher rates or declining to write insurance for people who live in particular areas (figuratively, sometimes literally enclosed with a red line on a map)."[44] The definition is usually expanded to include discrimination against individuals on the basis of a factor unrelated to risk in providing residential property and casualty insurance.

Insurance redlining occurs in several forms. Common insurer practices include imposing unnecessary application eligibility criteria, failing to place agents in particular communities, making limited marketing efforts, offering a limited portfolio of insurance products, and offering uncompetitive premiums for homes in certain neighborhoods. The following examples demonstrate how insurance industry activities may discriminate:

Application Eligibility: An agent who claims only to write insurance for dwellings above a certain value or under a certain age is effectively shutting out the poor and minorities in urban areas who proportionally purchase a greater number of older, less expensive homes.

Placement of Agents: Home owners insurance policies are generally sold through insurance agents. Companies without a

35 *See* Settlement Agreement, United States v. Citizens Republic Bancorp., No. 0 2:11-cv-11976 (E.D. Mich. May 5, 2011), *available at* www.justice.gov/crt/about/hce/caselist.php.

36 *See* Agreed Order, United States vs. Midwest BankCentre, No. 4:11-cv-01086 (E.D. Mo. June 16, 2011), *available at* www.justice.gov/crt/about/hce/caselist.php.

37 12 C.F.R. pt. 528 (now part 128 under the OCC).

38 12 C.F.R. § 528.9 (now section 128.9 under the OCC).

39 12 C.F.R. § 528.2 (now section 128.2 under the OCC).

40 12 C.F.R. § 528.9 (now section 128.9 under the OCC).

41 *See* 12 C.F.R. § 528.9 (now section 128.9 under the OCC).

42 Nat'l State Bank v. Long, 630 F.2d 981 (3d Cir. 1980).

43 *See, e.g.*, Cal. Health & Safety Code § 35810 (West); 815 Ill. Comp. Stat. §§ 120/1–120/6; Iowa Code §§ 535A.1 to 535A.9; Md. Code Ann., Com. Law § 12-603 (West); Mich. Comp. Laws §§ 445.1601–445.1614; Minn. Stat. § 363A.09; Mo. Rev. Stat. § 408.575; N.Y. Banking Law § 9-f (McKinney); V.I. Code Ann. tit. 28, § 1031; Wash. Rev. Code §§ 30.04.500–30.04.515; *see* appx. F, *infra* (detailed summary of state credit discrimination laws).

44 *See* Consent Decree, NAACP v. American Family Mut. Ins. Co., 978 F.2d 287, 290 (7th Cir. 1992).

For articles discussing redlining in insurance see, for example, Stephen M. Dane, *The Potential for Racial Discrimination by Homeowners Insurers Through the Use of Geographic Rating Territories*, J. Ins. Regulation, Summer 2006; George Galster, *Do Home Insurance Base Premium Setting Policies Create Disparate Racial Impacts? The Case of Large Insurance Companies in Ohio*, J. Ins. Regulation, Summer 2006; Gregory D. Squires & Charis E. Kubrin, *Racial Profiling, Insurance Style*, J. Ins. Regulation, Summer 2006.

A fuller bibliography of relevant articles is available at the National Association of Insurance Commissioners website at www.naic.org/documents/library_subjects_redlining.pdf.

sufficient number of agents in a given area may be inadvertently discriminating by limiting access to their products and services in that area. Lower-income home owners are disproportionately affected because they do not always have the resources to get to an agency outside their neighborhood. Insurance redlining involves not only decisions about the neighborhoods in which insurance companies will conduct business but also decisions about the agents to whom they will grant contracts.[45]

Marketing: Access to insurance companies can also be limited if the insurer chooses not to list its telephone number in certain telephone books, does not advertise on certain radio stations, omits specific zip codes from its mailing lists, and sends different mail offers to different neighborhoods.

Limited Portfolio of Insurance Offerings: Another practice used by insurers to avoid adequately serving certain areas is offering a subset of their normal product line—for example, limiting the products offered in lower-income areas to either high-priced or low-risk coverage.

Uncompetitive Premiums for Homes: Many insurers charge higher premiums in low-income predominantly minority urban neighborhoods, pricing these consumers out of the marketplace.[46]

Use of Credit Scoring Models: Insurers increasingly use credit scores to determine whether to insure a consumer and at what price.[47] Various studies have begun to document the correlation between insurance scores and race, as well as income, age, marital status, and educational attainment.[48]

Criteria to Establish Eligibility: California voters, for example, passed Proposition 103 which, among other provisions, establishes the factors that must be considered in determining rates and premiums for automobile insurance policies. A major impetus for the bill was to prevent discrimination against drivers who were not previously insured.[49]

Weblining: The widespread use of the Internet to sell products and services raises a new set of questions and concerns regarding insurance redlining.[50] "Weblining" is the use of the World Wide Web to practice any form of redlining.

With respect to insurance, weblining generally occurs either because of unequal access to the Internet or through profiling of potential customers.[51] For example, the practice of offering discounts to consumers who purchase policies on-line may have a disproportionate impact on protected groups to the extent that those groups are less likely to have access to the Internet.[52]

"Digital divide" is the term given to the disparity between high-income and low-income households with respect to access to the Internet. It also refers to the lower numbers of Internet users in communities of color. Some studies show this gap is closing while others show a persistent problem.[53]

Some commentators believe the Internet has the potential to reduce the incidence of discrimination in the insurance industry because on-line shopping allows consumers to avoid face-to-face encounters, during which discrimination often occurs. The Internet may also help improve access to insurance for consumers in neighborhoods where there are no insurance agents. However, these potential benefits can be easily overridden by discriminatory customer profiling. This type of profiling occurs when, for example, Internet users inquiring about special offers are required to provide seemingly innocuous information such as their zip code. Violations may arise if this information is used to deny applications on a discriminatory basis.[54]

7.3.2 The Impact of Insurance Redlining

Insurance redlining seriously undermines the ability of affected individuals to purchase and safeguard their homes. According to one court: "[T]he availability of housing is . . . dependent on the availability of insurance. It is elementary that without insurance, mortgage financing will be unavailable, because a mortgage lender simply will not lend money on the [uninsured] property. Without mortgage financing, homes cannot be purchased."[55] In addition to discouraging the purchase of new homes, redlining puts existing home owners in jeopardy of losing their homes.[56] The Seventh Circuit Court of Appeals

---

45 *See, e.g.*, N.J. Citizen Action, The Citizen Policy & Education Fund, & N.J. Policy Perspective, Insurance Redlining: Is It Happening in Your Neighborhood? (Feb. 2004), *available at* www.njcitizenaction.org/craredlining.html.

46 *See, e.g.*, Barbara Van Kerkhove, The Homeowners Insurance Gap: How Race and Neighborhood Composition Explain Cost and Access Disparities in Rochester and Monroe County, NY (May 2005); N.J. Citizen Action, The Citizen Policy & Education Fund, & N.J. Policy Perspective, Insurance Redlining: Is It Happening in Your Neighborhood? (Feb. 2004), *available at* www.njcitizenaction.org/craredlining.html (finding, among other results, that the price of home owner's insurance was significantly higher for Hispanics than other racial groups).

47 *See generally* §§ 6.4.6.2.1, 6.4.6.2.2, *supra*.

48 §§ 6.4.6.2.1, 6.4.6.2.2, *supra*; *see also* Dehoyos v. Allstate Corp., 345 F.3d 290 (5th Cir. 2003).

49 *See, e.g.*, Found. for Taxpayer & Consumer Rights v. Garamendi, 34 Cal. Rptr. 3d 354 (Cal. Ct. App. 2005).

50 *See generally* Katherine J. Eddy, Gary A. Hernandez, & Joel Muchmore, *Insurance Weblining and Unfair Discrimination in Cyberspace*, 54 SMU L. Rev. 1953 (2001).

51 *See* § 5.3.2.6, *supra*.

52 Offering such discounts may violate insurance ratings laws in some states as well as credit discrimination laws. *See generally* Katherine J. Eddy, Gary A. Hernandez, & Joel Muchmore, *Insurance Weblining and Unfair Discrimination in Cyberspace*, 54 SMU L. Rev. 1953 (2001).

53 *See also* § 3.7.2, *supra*. *See generally* Jim Jansen, Pew Research Ctr., Use of the Internet in Higher-Income Households (2010), *available at* pewinternet.org; Katherine J. Eddy, Gary A. Hernandez, & Joel Muchmore, *Insurance Weblining and Unfair Discrimination in Cyberspace*, 54 SMU L. Rev. 1953 (2001); United States Dep't of Commerce, Nat'l Telecomms. & Info. Admin., A Nation Online: How Americans Are Expanding Their Use of the Internet (Feb. 2002), *available* at www.ntia.doc.gov.

54 *See* Katherine J. Eddy, Gary A. Hernandez, & Joel Muchmore, *Insurance Weblining and Unfair Discrimination in Cyberspace*, 54 SMU L. Rev. 1953 (2001).

55 McDiarmid v. Economy Fire & Cas. Co., 604 F. Supp. 105, 107 (S.D. Ohio 1984).

56 A *Boston Globe* article highlighted a situation in which individuals who owned their homes outright were denied disaster insurance.

provided a concise summary of the problem, stating, "no insurance, no loan; no loan, no house."[57]

Without insurance alternatives, many home owners are forced or pressured into purchasing insurance from an industry-financed high-risk pool. There are numerous problems with this type of insurance. Although the premiums are generally less expensive;

- Deductibles are higher;
- Options are few;
- Personal property coverage is normally not available;
- Overall coverage is usually lower;
- Home inspection and maintenance requirements can be overly rigorous (and too expensive for low-income home owners); and
- This type of insurance gives insurers who do not want to conduct business in a particular neighborhood an excuse not to sell insurance there.

7.3.3 Detecting Insurance Redlining

Insurance redlining, like other forms of discrimination, occurs in overt as well as in subtle ways. Listed below are a few ways to detect unlawful insurance discrimination practices:

Application Criteria: Suspicious signs include applications that require, for example, information on the age or value of a dwelling, prior insurance history (some insurers will not accept customers who have been turned down by other insurance companies), credit rating, or property inspections only in certain neighborhoods.

Insurance Company Training Manuals: Sales and underwriting training, policy, or procedural texts and memos can be very revealing. These documents, in which management communicates their sales and underwriting philosophy, should be checked for overt or subtle bias.

Accessibility of Insurance Company in Certain Areas: The scope of the insurer's marketing efforts, the number of agents, the number of minority and/or bilingual agents, limitations on product offerings, and above-market pricing are all indications that an insurer may be engaged in redlining.

Disclosure Legislation: The insurance industry generally contends that urban pricing patterns are based solely on risk and that pricing disparities between urban and suburban areas and between minority and non-minority neighborhoods are a result of higher incidences and greater severity of losses in urban areas.[58] In the absence of public data on insurance pricing and underwriting, it is difficult to ascertain the accuracy of that pronouncement, and insurance companies are not presently required to share that information.[59] In at least a few states,

advocates have succeeded in their push for expanded disclosure requirements for insurance data.[60] Most of these state laws require zip code disclosure of various types of information. However, the geocoded information that is available varies from state to state.[61]

Testing and Investigation of Insurers: Because information about insurance underwriting and pricing is so difficult to obtain, insurer policies, practices, and pricing that may be discriminatory in intent or effect are not easily uncovered. However, fair housing organizations have successfully used matched-pair testing to determine whether an insurer is unfairly discriminating.[62]

Testing and Investigation of Insurance Cost: For example, a 2002–2003 study in New York focused on differences in the cost of home owner's insurance in Monroe County and the city of Rochester.[63] The study found that home owners in areas with higher proportions of minorities, lower incomes, and lower housing values paid higher annual premiums, including total premiums and premiums adjusted for the value of the proper-

---

Stephen Kurkjian, *Boston's Uninsured Homes*, The Boston Globe, Apr. 25, 1995, at 1, 24.

57 NAACP v. American Family Mut. Ins. Co., 978 F.2d 287, 297 (7th Cir. 1992).

58 *See, e.g.*, Mass. Affordable Hous. Alliance, Opening the Books: The Case for Public Disclosure of Homeowners Insurance Data 4 (1995).

59 For a summary of efforts to obtain insurance policy data by zip

code, see Inner City Press, Insurance Redlining (June 2003), *available at* www.innercitypress.org.

60 In California, for example, regulations require specified insurers to file a "community service statement" annually with the Department of Insurance reporting certain information for each zip code in which the insurer sells insurance or maintains agents. Cal. Code Regs. tit. 10, § 2646.6. The regulation makes those statements available for public inspection. *See* Cal. Code Regs. tit. 10, § 2646.6(c); *see also* Cal. Ins. Code § 1861.07 (West); State Farm Mut. Automobile Ins. Co. v. Garamendi, 12 Cal. Rptr. 3d 343 (Cal. 2004) (statute mandating public disclosure of insurance rates and other factors that might impermissibly affect availability of insurance established absolute rule in favor of public disclosure; information was subject to disclosure even if it contained trade secrets); Farmers Ins. Exch. v. Garamendi, 2004 WL 2165653 (Cal. Ct. App. Sept. 28, 2004) (following *Garamendi*). For disclosure laws in other states, see, for example, 215 Ill. Comp. Stat. § 5/143.25; Mass. Gen. Laws ch. 175, § 4A; Minn. Stat. § 65A.28; Mass. Affordable Hous. Alliance, Insuring Neighborhoods VII (Oct. 30, 2003) (analyzing insurance company's required disclosure data, focusing on market share in underserved neighborhoods).

61 For a study identifying the data that is publicly available and for detailed information about these data sources, see Sally O'Connor, Josh Silver, & Gregory D. Squires, *The Unavailability of Information on Insurance Unavailability: Insurance Redlining and the Absence of Geocoded Disclosure Data*, 12 Hous. Pol'y Debate 347 (2001). The study found that the vast majority of states do not require disclosure by property insurers. Among those that do, a variety of information is collected. At the time the report was published, eight states required some insurers to provide at least some geocoded data to the state insurance commissioner every year. Those states were California, Illinois, Maryland, Massachusetts, Minnesota, Missouri, Texas, and Wisconsin.

62 Cathy Cloud & Shanna L. Smith, *Documenting Discrimination by Homeowners Insurance Companies Through Testing*, in Insurance Redlining 97 (Gregory D. Squires, ed., 1997); *see* § 4.4.4, *supra*.

63 *See* Barbara Van Kerkhove, The Homeowners Insurance Gap: How Race and Neighborhood Composition Explain Cost and Access Disparities in Rochester and Monroe County, NY (May 2005). *See generally* Kirsten E. Keefe, *Insurance Redlining: A New York Study of Homeowners Insurance Disparities*, The Consumer Advocate (Oct.–Dec. 2005).

ties. Home owners in minority and lower-income neighbor-hoods also held policies with less comprehensive coverage. The study found that 67% of white home owners had guaranteed-cost policies and 32% had standard-cost policies. Among mi-nority home owners, the reverse was true, with about 33% holding guarantee policies and 68% with standard replacement policies. Guaranteed replacement provides the most compre-hensive coverage. The report's authors controlled for many of the factors insurers traditionally use in underwriting insurance and found that the two elements that seemed to be driving the cost disparity in premiums were location of the property and the race/ethnicity of the policyholder.

Surveying of Agents: Insurance redlining involves not only decisions about the neighborhoods in which insurance compa-nies will conduct business but also decisions about the agents to whom they will grant contracts.[64]

7.3.4 *Legal Claims Available to Challenge Insurance Redlining*

7.3.4.1 The Equal Credit Opportunity Act

The official interpretations of Regulation B explicitly state that it is *not* a violation of Regulation B for a creditor to obtain and use information about an applicant's age, sex, or marital status for the purpose of determining insurance eligibility and premium rates, although not for the credit decision itself.[65] Still, the ECOA may be applicable when credit has been denied or some other adverse action taken because the applicant refused to purchase insurance. If credit is denied because the applicant refuses to buy optional credit insurance, the applicant may have an ECOA claim for discrimination on the basis of a good faith exercise of rights under the Consumer Credit Protection Act.[66] Borrowers cannot be denied access to credit for merely exer-cising, in good faith, their right not to insure. In addition, if a lender required *only* members of a protected group to purchase credit insurance, these applicants may have an ECOA claim.

7.3.4.2 The Fair Housing Act

7.3.4.2.1 *The FHA applies to insurance*

The federal Fair Housing Act (FHA) is another important option, particularly with respect to the sale of insurance related

to a dwelling, such as home owners' insurance.[67] Throughout the 1980s, there was a split among the circuit courts regarding FHA applicability to insurance.[68] The tide began to turn in 1989 when the Department of Housing and Urban Development (HUD) enacted a regulation prohibiting discriminatory refusals to provide "property or hazard insurance for dwellings" or providing insurance services on a discriminatory basis.[69] Even after the 1989 regulation, the industry continued to argue that the FHA did not apply to insurance, most frequently claiming that the federal claims were preempted by the McCarran-Ferguson Act.[70] In January 1994, President Clinton issued an executive order mandating that HUD promulgate a regulation to clarify the application of the FHA to property insurance.[71] However, in 1995 HUD suspended rulemaking on this issue and has not revisited it.[72]

While HUD went back and forth about whether to clarify the 1989 regulation, courts began to allow FHA claims for insur-ance redlining. The Seventh Circuit Court of Appeals, in *NAACP v. American Family Mutual Insurance Co.*, established the current standard that the provision of property insurance can be reasonably interpreted as the "provision of services or facilities in connection" with the sale or rental of a dwelling and therefore is covered by the FHA.[73]

The rationale for applying the FHA to insurance is that refusing to sell insurance prevents the potential insured from obtaining a mortgage, thereby preventing prospective home owners from purchasing homes.[74] Courts have cited HUD's

---

64 *See, e.g.,* N.J. Citizen Action, The Citizen Policy & Education Fund, & N.J. Policy Perspective, Insurance Redlining: Is It Happening in Your Neighborhood? (Feb. 2004), *available at* www.njcitizenaction.org/craredlining.html.

65 Official Interpretations of Reg. B [Official Staff Commentary of Reg. B], 12 C.F.R. pt. 1002 [pt. 202], Supp. I, § 1002.7(e)-2 [§ 202.7(e)-2].

66 *See, e.g.,* Bryson v. Bank of N.Y., 584 F. Supp. 1306 (S.D.N.Y. 1984) (failing to dismiss ECOA claim when consumer only agreed to credit insurance after being told he could not get loan without it and when bank subsequently denied consumer's loan after he sought clarification of the voluntary nature of the insurance as described in Truth in Lending disclosures).

67 Note, however, that the sale of credit-related insurance, such as mortgage disability insurance, is not a form of "financial assis-tance" for purchasing or maintaining a dwelling and therefore is not covered by the Fair Housing Act. *See* Doukas v. Metro. Life Ins. Co., 882 F. Supp. 1197, 1202 (D.N.H. 1995).

68 *See generally* William E. Murray, *Homeowners Insurance Redlin-ing: The Inadequacy of Federal Remedies and the Future of the Property Insurance War,* 4 Conn. Ins. L.J. 735, 747 (1997–1998).

69 24 C.F.R. § 100.70(d)(4).

70 *See* § 7.3.4.2.2, *infra.*

71 Exec. Order No. 12,892, 59 Fed. Reg. 2939 (Jan. 20, 1994).

72 *See* Gregory D. Squires, *Why an Insurance Regulation to Prohibit Redlining?,* 31 J. Marshall L. Rev. 489, 503 (1998) (arguing that HUD should proceed with rulemaking on property insurance issues under the Fair Housing Act).

73 NAACP v. American Family Mut. Ins. Co., 978 F.2d 287 (7th Cir. 1992); *see also* Nationwide Mut. Ins. Co. v. Cisneros, 52 F.3d 1351 (6th Cir. 1995) (upholding HUD regulations interpreting FHA and prohibiting redlining in property insurance underwriting); United Farm Bureau Mut. Ins. Co. v. Metro. Human Relations Comm'n, 24 F.3d 1008 (7th Cir. 1994) (reaffirming *American Family* holding); Owens v. Nationwide Mut. Ins. Co., 2005 WL 1837959 (N.D. Tex. Aug. 2, 2005) (adopting the Sixth Circuit's conclusions in *Cis-neros*); Burrell v. State Farm & Cas. Co., 226 F. Supp. 2d 427 (S.D.N.Y. 2002); Lindsey v. Allstate Ins. Co., 34 F. Supp. 2d 636 (W.D. Tenn. 1999) (denying defendant's motion to dismiss FHA-based insurance redlining case; plaintiffs alleged discrimination on the basis of race in premiums, claims handling procedures, and policy renewal); Strange v. Nationwide Mut. Ins. Co., 867 F. Supp. 1209 (E.D. Pa. 1994) (FHA bars discrimination in provision of property and hazard insurance).

74 Consent Decree, NAACP v. American Family Mut. Ins. Co., 978 F.2d 287 (7th Cir. 1992); Complaint and Consent Decree, United

enforcement of the FHA in the insurance area to further support this interpretation.[75] The FHA applies not only when redlining involves higher insurance premiums but also to decisions involving renewal of property insurance policies.[76]

NAACP v. American Family Mutual Insurance Co. was the Justice Department's first case brought under the Fair Housing Act to challenge the use of race as a factor in issuing home owners' insurance.[77] The complaint alleged that, since at least 1968, American Family Mutual denied home owners' insurance to or provided inferior insurance for homes in the predominantly African-American areas of metropolitan Milwaukee. In addition to locating its sales offices in white communities, the complaint alleged that American Family also closed sales offices once the racial composition of the community changed from white to black. In the consent decree settling the case, American Family agreed to pay $14.5 million to compensate the victims. The consent decree also required the company to conduct random testing, to recruit qualified prospective customers, and to refrain from excluding homes solely on the basis of sale price of the home or age of the home.

In 1998, the first jury verdict in an insurance redlining case was awarded. The plaintiff was awarded $500,000 in compensatory damages and $100 million in punitive damages.[78] The plaintiff in this case alleged that urban African Americans were specifically excluded from Nationwide Mutual Insurance Co.'s insurance market through discrimination in the underwriting, marketing, advertising, sales, and actuarial practices of the company.

Insurance discrimination should be unlawful under the FHA not only with respect to insurance for the purchase of a home but also for refinancing or otherwise maintaining the property.[79] A 2005 district court decision discusses why the FHA should be equally applicable in cases in which a policy is sought to insure a home already purchased.[80] The court notes that insurance may be necessary to restore a property to its previous condition prior to a loss-inflicting event. Insurance may thus provide a home owner the opportunity to rebuild and sell a home previously damaged. A denial of insurance under these circumstances would restrict the "terms, conditions, or privileges of sale or rental of a dwelling" in violation of section 3604 of the FHA.[81] Denial or cancellation of liability insurance may also be actionable.[82] While the majority of cases allege disparities based on race, insurance discrimination also has been asserted under the FHA's prohibition on discrimination based on disability.[83]

Although most courts agree that the FHA can be used to challenge insurance redlining practices, there is still some disagreement over which section of the FHA is appropriate. The dispute involves the broader section 3604 as opposed to section 3605, which applies specifically to real-estate-related transactions.[84]

Courts have consistently held that sections 3604 and 3605 overlap but are not mutually exclusive.[85] Thus, either or both sections could arguably apply to insurance. The majority trend, set by the Seventh Circuit, is to find that section 3604 applies to insurance.[86] These courts find a direct connection between the availability of property insurance and ability to purchase a home.

The applicability of section 3605 is not as clear. Unlike section 3604, HUD has not promulgated relevant interpretations for section 3605. As a result, the analysis is guided principally by the language of the statute.

The Seventh Circuit quickly dispensed with this argument, finding section 3605 inapplicable to insurance.[87] However, in

---

States v. Nationwide Mut. Ins. Co., No. C2-97-291 (S.D. Ohio Mar. 10, 1997), *available at* www.justice.gov/crt/about/hce/documents/nationsettle.php.

75 *See* Nat'l Fair Hous. Alliance v. Prudential Ins. Co. of America, 208 F. Supp. 2d 46 (D.D.C. 2002).

76 Lindsey v. Allstate Ins. Co., 34 F. Supp. 2d 636 (W.D. Tenn. 1999).

77 *Id.*

78 Housing Opportunities Made Equal, Inc. v. Nationwide Mut. Ins. Co., No. LB-2704 (Va. Cir. Ct. Oct. 26, 1998) (jury verdict).

The Supreme Court of Virginia initially reversed the verdict, finding that the plaintiff lacked standing to file suit. Nationwide Mut. Ins. Co. v. Hous. Opportunities Made Equal, Inc., 523 S.E.2d 217 (Va. 2000).

The same court later vacated that ruling. Nationwide Mut. Ins. Co. v. Hous. Opportunities Made Equal, Inc., 2000 Va. LEXIS 56 (Va. Mar. 3, 2000). The case settled in April 2000.

79 *See, e.g.,* Owens v. Nationwide Mut. Ins. Co., 2005 WL 1837959 (N.D. Tex. Aug. 2, 2005) (limiting the FHA to insurance discrimination affecting a consumer's ability to purchase a home is a limited reading of the case law that is not supported by the redlining cases or by the purpose of the FHA); *see also* Wai v. Allstate Ins. Co., 75 F. Supp. 2d 1 (D.D.C. 1999) (FHA applied to denial of standard landlord's insurance or to providing insurance on less favorable terms to landlords who rented to disabled tenants).

80 Owens v. Nationwide Mut. Ins. Co., 2005 WL 1837959 (N.D. Tex. Aug. 2, 2005).

81 *Id.*

82 Nevels v. Western World Ins. Co., 359 F. Supp. 2d 1110 (W.D. Wash. 2004) (by canceling plaintiff adult family home operators' liability insurance, defendant created a powerful disincentive to provide care for disabled persons).

83 *See* Nevels v. Western World Ins. Co., 359 F. Supp. 2d 1110 (W.D. Wash. 2004) (denying defendant's motion to dismiss because insurer's cancellation of insurance to operators of adult family home based on presence of residents with mental disabilities was actionable under section 3604 of the FHA); Wai v. Allstate Ins. Co., 75 F. Supp. 2d 1 (D.D.C. 1999). *See generally* John F. Stanton, *The Fair Housing Act and Insurance: An Update and the Question of Disability Discrimination,* 31 Hofstra L. Rev. 141 (2002).

84 *See* § 2.3.3.1.3, *supra.* This subsection also reviews the implications of bringing a claim under only section 3604 versus bringing claims under both sections 3604 and 3605.

85 *See, e.g.,* Nationwide Mut. Ins. Co. v. Cisneros, 52 F.3d 1351, 1357 (6th Cir. 1995); NAACP v. American Family Mut. Ins. Co., 978 F.2d 287, 297–301 (7th Cir. 1992). *See generally* § 2.3.3.1.3, *supra.*

86 NAACP v. American Family Mut. Ins. Co., 978 F.2d 287 (7th Cir. 1992); *see also* Nationwide Mut. Ins. Co. v. Cisneros, 52 F.3d 1351, 1357 (6th Cir. 1995).

87 NAACP v. American Family Mut. Ins. Co., 978 F.2d 287 (7th Cir. 1992) (it would strain language past the breaking point to treat property or casualty insurance as "financial assistance"—let alone as assistance for "purchasing . . . a dwelling"); *see also* Home

2002 the district court in the District of Columbia came to the opposite conclusion.[88] This court disagreed with the Seventh Circuit's "narrow" construction of the term "financial assistance" in section 3605. According to the district court, insurance provides the financial assistance necessary to maintain a dwelling and thus it is reasonable to conclude that Congress intended home owners' insurance to fall within the scope of section 3605.[89]

7.3.4.2.2 Preemption and the McCarran-Ferguson Act

Assuming the court agrees with the majority view that the FHA applies, the court must still determine whether the McCarran-Ferguson Act[90] prevents the FHA from applying to the sale of insurance.[91] The McCarran-Ferguson Act prohibits federal statutes from invalidating, superseding, or impairing a state law regulating insurance unless the federal statute specifically relates to the business of insurance. Because the FHA and other federal civil rights laws do not specifically refer to insurance, the cases turn on whether the application of these federal laws would "invalidate, impair or supersede" state laws regulating insurance.

The Seventh Circuit in *NAACP v. American Family Mutual Insurance Co.* avoided the McCarran-Ferguson issue by finding no conflict between the federal Fair Housing Act and Wisconsin's insurance statutes.[92] It upheld the application of the Fair Housing Act to insurance because both federal and state law prohibited racial discrimination in the sale of insurance. According to the court, a federal remedy under the FHA would not frustrate any state policy.[93] Although the FHA provided an

effective private remedy and state law did not, the court found that this distinction did not create a conflict between the two statutes.[94]

An earlier case used a different approach to avoid the McCarran-Ferguson Act issue, holding that the Act does not apply to federal civil rights statutes enacted after the date the McCarran-Ferguson Act was adopted.[95] The Seventh Circuit, while agreeing that the McCarran-Ferguson Act does not preempt a Fair Housing Act claim, harshly criticized the Second Circuit's reasoning.[96]

In later decisions, courts have begun to address this question directly, finding that the FHA is not preempted.[97] For example, in rejecting an insurance company's motion to dismiss based on the McCarran-Ferguson Act, a Texas federal district court noted that courts have consistently rejected this defense in race-based discrimination cases despite comprehensive state regulatory schemes and laws prohibiting discrimination in insurance.[98] In affirming the district court in 2003, the Fifth Circuit noted that every circuit that had considered the question of McCarran-Ferguson Act preemption with respect to the federal civil rights laws or the FHA to date had determined that federal antidiscrimination laws may be applied in an insurance context, even when the state insurance agencies have mechanisms in place to regulate discriminatory practices.[99]

Quest Mortgage L.L.C v. American Family Mut. Ins. Co., 340 F. Supp. 2d 1177 (D. Kan. 2004) (finding, in rejecting section 3605 claim, that insurance is a form of financial protection, not financial assistance); *cf.* Neals v. Mortgage Guar. Ins. Corp., 2011 WL 1897442 (W.D. Pa. Apr. 6, 2011) (citing *Lyons*, discussed below, in determining that private mortgage insurance protects the lender and not homeowner and therefore does not constitute "financial assistance" under section 3605); Lyons v. First American Title Ins. Co, 2009 WL 5195866, at *9–10 (N.D. Cal. Dec. 22, 2009) (declining to hold that title insurance is financial assistance within the scope of section 3605 because it protects lender; emphasizing that this question of the scope of section 3605 was a policy decision best made by an entity with proper rulemaking authority).

88 Nat'l Fair Hous. Alliance, Inc. v. Prudential Ins. Co. of America, 208 F. Supp. 2d 46, 56–58 (D.D.C. 2002) (citing split in authority and concluding that claims of home owners' insurance redlining practices are actionable under either section 3604 or section 3605; *see also* Nevels v. Western World Ins. Co., 359 F. Supp. 2d 1110 (W.D. Wash. 2004) (denying defendant's motion to dismiss plaintiff's section 3605 claim because insurance is essentially necessary for safe maintenance of plaintiffs' adult group homes).

89 Nat'l Fair Hous. Alliance, Inc. v. Prudential Ins. Co. of America, 208 F. Supp. 2d 46, 56–58 (D.D.C. 2002).

90 15 U.S.C. § 1012(b).

91 *See* United States Dep't of the Treasury v. Fabe, 508 U.S. 491, 113 S. Ct. 2202, 124 L. Ed. 23 449 (1993).

92 NAACP v. American Family Mut. Ins. Co., 978 F.2d 287 (7th Cir. 1992).

93 *Id.* at 297 (noting that, if the state wanted to authorize redlining, it need only say so and then an FHA challenge to the practice would

be untenable; however, in this case, federal and state policies determined not to conflict).

94 *Id.*

95 Spirit v. Teachers Ins. & Annuities Ass'n, 691 F.2d 1054 (2d Cir. 1982), *vacated on other grounds*, 463 U.S. 1223 (1983); *accord* Stephens v. Nat'l Distillers & Chem. Corp., 69 F.3d 1226 (2d Cir. 1995).

96 Consent Decree, NAACP v. American Family Mut. Ins. Co., 978 F.2d 287 (7th Cir. 1992).

97 Claims challenging unfair insurance rates through the filed rate doctrine, however, may meet a different fate. In an Eighth Circuit decision regarding race discrimination in insurance pricing issued after the FHA discrimination claims were dismissed, the court found that the remaining claims under the state's filed rate doctrine were preempted by the McCarran-Ferguson Act. *See* Saunders v. Farmers Ins. Exch., 537 F.3d 961 (8th Cir. 2008).

98 Dehoyos v. Allstate Corp., 2002 WL 1491650 (W.D. Tex. Apr. 5, 2002), *aff'd*, 345 F.3d 290 (5th Cir. 2003). The Texas court summarized plaintiffs' case as essentially arguing that Caucasians are in good hands with Allstate but, for non-Caucasians, it is hands off.

99 Dehoyos v. Allstate Corp., 345 F.3d 290 (5th Cir. 2003) (citing Moore v. Liberty Nat'l Life Ins. Co., 267 F.3d 1209 (11th Cir. 2001)); *see also* Nationwide Mut. Ins. Co. v. Cisneros, 52 F.3d 1351 (6th Cir. 1995); Merchants Home Delivery Serv., Inc. v. Frank B. Hall & Co., 50 F.3d 1486 (9th Cir. 1995); NAACP v. American Family Mut. Ins. Co., 978 F.2d (7th Cir. 1992); Mackey v. Nationwide Ins. Cos., 724 F.2d 419 (4th Cir. 1984); Lumpkin v. Farmers Group, Inc., 2007 U.S. Dist. LEXIS 98994 (W.D. Tenn. Apr. 26, 2007); Nevels v. Western World Ins. Co., 359 F. Supp. 2d 1110 (W.D. Wash. 2004). *But see* Saunders v. American Family Mut. Ins. Co., 537 F.3d 961 (8th Cir. 2008) (discrimination claims pursued under state's filed rate doctrine were preempted, reasoning that claim would interfere with state rate-making and penalty regime; noting in dicta however that, while the race discrimination claims were not formally preempted (but rather had been dismissed earlier for other reasons) they were a diversion to the real issue); McKenzie v. Southern Farm Bureau Cas. Ins. Co., 2007 WL 2012214, at *3–4

In a substantial departure from these earlier decisions, the Ninth Circuit, in an en banc decision reversing an earlier Court of Appeals decision finding no reverse preemption, found that a Fair Housing Act challenge to the use of credit scores to underwrite homeowners' insurance could be reverse-preempted by the McCarran-Ferguson Act.[100] While noting that a majority of other circuit courts have found that the McCarran-Ferguson Act applies to civil rights statutes (and citing the fact that four Supreme Court justices had applied it to Title VII claims), the court failed to comment on the fact that most circuit courts—including the Fifth Circuit, which it cited as supporting the application of the McCarran-Ferguson Act to civil rights statutes—have found that federal civil rights laws may be applied in an insurance context. While the Eighth Circuit also has reached a similar conclusion in one case, this matter focused on the more traditional state role under the filed rate doctrine.[101]

7.3.4.3 The Federal Civil Rights Acts

The federal Civil Rights Acts should apply to discrimination in the sale of any form of insurance, because insurance is a contract.[102] While the McCarran-Ferguson Act prevents federal statutes from invalidating state laws that regulate insurance unless the federal statute specifically relates to insurance, preemption of the federal regulation of insurance here is unlikely.[103] Similar to their analysis under the FHA, the courts have almost unanimously found that the Civil Rights Acts are applicable to insurance discrimination and do not violate the McCarran-Ferguson Act.[104] These courts have found that, even

though the Civil Rights Acts do not specifically relate to insurance, they are not preempted because they do not invalidate, supersede, or impair state law.[105]

7.3.4.4 State Laws

In addition to federal laws and regulations, the majority of states have some form of general discrimination laws or unfair insurance practices (UNIP) statute (also known as unfair trade practices acts or UTPA), under which insurance discrimination claims may be brought.

State credit discrimination laws generally provide an excellent vehicle to challenge insurance-related discrimination. For example, New York's highest court allowed a case to proceed in which the plaintiff used the state credit discrimination statute to challenge a credit insurer's exclusion of pregnancy as a covered disability.[106] The court specifically found that the practice involved gender discrimination and that credit insurance terms were terms of the credit offered.[107] The only remaining issue was whether the state insurance code, which also prohibits discrimination, displaces the state credit discrimination statute.[108] The court found that the state credit discrimination statute still applied.[109]

Another approach is to utilize the state UNIP or UTPA statute to challenge insurance discrimination.[110] With wide

---

(N.D. Miss. July 6, 2007) (ruling that McCarran-Ferguson Act barred plaintiff's FHA claim arising from defendant's use of credit information in setting rates, a practice that plaintiff alleged had a disparate impact on minority applicants, when a state insurance regulation permitted the use of such information in setting rates); McClain v. Shelter Gen. Ins. Co., 2007 WL 844769, at *11 (W.D. Mo. Mar. 16, 2007) (discrimination claims pursued under state's filed rate doctrine were preempted, reasoning that claim would interfere with state rate-making and penalty regime; noting in dicta however that, while the race discrimination claims were not formally preempted (but rather had been dismissed earlier for other reasons) they were a diversion to the real issue), *aff'd*, Saunders v. Farmers Ins. Exch., 537 F.3d 961 (8th Cir. 2008).

100 Ojo v. Farmers Group, Inc., 600 F.3d 1205 (9th Cir. 2010) (certification to Texas Supreme Court on whether Texas law permits or prohibits use of factors with racially disparate impact); *see* § 6.4.6.2.1, *supra* (further discussing insurance credit scoring).

101 Saunders v. Farmers Ins. Exch., 537 F.3d 961 (8th Cir. 2008).

102 *See* 42 U.S.C. § 1981.

103 *See* Duane v. Gov't Emps. Ins. Co., 784 F. Supp. 1209 (D. Md. 1992), *aff'd*, 37 F.3d 1036 (4th Cir. 1994).

104 Dehoyos v. Allstate Corp., 345 F.3d 290 (5th Cir. 2003); Moore v. Liberty Nat'l Life Ins. Co., 267 F.3d 1209, 1221 (11th Cir. 2001) (sections 1981 and 1982 do not invalidate, impair, or supersede Alabama's scheme of insurance regulation); Nationwide Mut. Ins. Co. v. Cisneros, 52 F.3d 1351, 1360 (6th Cir. 1995) (the FHA does not specifically mention insurance and thus cannot be construed in such a way as to invalidate, impair, or supersede any state law enacted to regulate the business of insurance); Consent Decree, NAACP v. American Family Mut. Ins. Co., 978 F.2d 287, 295 (7th Cir. 1992) (the FHA is an "Act of Congress" that does not

specifically relate to the business of insurance and, therefore, does not invalidate, impair, or supersede any law enacted by any state for the purpose of regulating the business of insurance); Mackey v. Nationwide Ins. Cos., 724 F.2d 419 (4th Cir. 1984) (disagreeing with conclusion of lower court that McCarran-Ferguson Act bars plaintiff's claims under Fair Housing and Civil Rights Acts); Spirit v. Teachers Ins. & Annuities Ass'n, 691 F.2d 1054 (2d Cir. 1982) (Congress, in enacting a statute primarily intended to deal with the conflict between state regulation of insurers and federal antitrust laws, had no intention of declaring that subsequently enacted civil rights legislation would be inapplicable to any and all of the activities of an insurance company that can be classified as the business of insurance); Owens v. Nationwide Mut. Ins. Co., 2005 WL 1837959 (N.D. Tex. Aug. 2, 2005); Nevels v. Western World Ins. Co., 359 F. Supp. 2d 1110 (W.D. Wash. 2004); Hobson v. Lincoln Ins. Agency, Inc., 2001 WL 55528 (N.D. Ill. Jan. 22, 2001); Wai v. Allstate Ins. Co., 75 F. Supp. 2d 1 (D.D.C. 1999). *But see* Ojo v. Farmers Group, Inc., 600 F.3d 1205 (9th Cir. 2010).

105 *See, e.g.*, Moore v. Liberty Nat'l Life Ins. Co., 267 F.3d 1209, 1221 (11th Cir. 2001) (sections 1981 and 1982 do not invalidate, impair, or supersede Alabama's scheme of insurance regulation).

106 Binghamton GHS Emps. Fed. Credit Union v. New York State Div. of Human Rights, 564 N.E.2d 1051 (N.Y. 1990).

107 *Id.*

108 *See* N.Y. Exec. Law § 296-a(1) (McKinney).

109 Binghamton GHS Emps. Fed. Credit Union v. New York State Div. of Human Rights, 564 N.E.2d 1051 (N.Y. 1990); *cf.* Consent Decree, NAACP v. American Family Mut. Ins. Co., 978 F.2d 287 (7th Cir. 1992) (all parties appear to agree that state's general credit discrimination statute applies to sale of property insurance).

110 The source of most state UNIP statutes is the National Association of Insurance Commissioners' model Unfair Trade Practices Act (UTPA), which attempts to establish minimum standards of insurance practices for consumer protection. *See* Nat'l Ass'n of Ins. Comm'rs, Model Laws, Regulations and Guidelines, 900-1 (NIARS Corp. 1984), *as amended*, 880-1 (Jan. 1993).

variations, state UNIP laws prohibit unfair discrimination in the issuance, renewal, or extent of coverage; rates charged; or other terms or conditions of certain types of insurance.

A number of UNIP statutes prohibit unfair discrimination in the terms or conditions of insurance or prohibit unfair insurance discrimination more generally.[111] Selected UNIP statutes pro-

hibit casualty insurers from discriminating with respect to geographic location of the property to be insured ("redlining")[112] or the age of residential property.[113] At least four UNIP statutes also prohibit casualty insurers from canceling or refusing to issue or renew coverage because of physical or mental disability of the insured.[114]

The majority of UNIP statutes and regulations specifically prohibit, for all types of insurance, discrimination based on certain of the following grounds (the exact grounds varying by statute): race, creed, color, gender, marital status, mental or physical impairments, age, occupation, religion or national origin, domestic abuse.[115]

---

111 Ala. Code § 27-12-11; Alaska Stat. §§ 21.36.090, 21.36.120(c); Ariz. Rev. Stat. Ann. § 20-448; Ark. Code Ann. § 23-66-206(14); Cal. Ins. Code § 679.71 (prohibiting discrimination based on certain characteristics) (West); Cal. Civ. Code § 51(b) (listing characteristics) (West); Cal. Ins. Code § 790.03(f)(1) (West) (prohibiting "unfair discrimination between individuals of the same class and equal expectation of life in the rates charged for any contract of life insurance" or in the terms and conditions of the life insurance contract; Colo. Rev. Stat. § 10-3-1104(1)(f) (prohibition applies to any insurance contract; Conn. Gen. Stat. § 38a-824 (see Conn. Agencies Regs. § 38a-824-3(a)); Del. Code Ann. tit. 18, § 2304(13), (15); Fla. Stat. § 626.9541(1)(g); Ga. Code Ann. § 33-6-4(b)(8)(A); Haw. Rev. Stat. § 431:13-103(a)(7) (prohibition applies to any insurance contract); Idaho Code Ann. § 41-1313; 215 Ill. Comp. Stat. §§ 5/236, 5/364; Ind. Code § 27-4-1-4(7); Iowa Code § 507B.4(3)(g); Kan. Stat. Ann. § 40-2404(7); Ky. Rev. Stat. Ann. § 304.12-080 (West); La. Rev. Stat. Ann. § 22:1964(7); Me. Rev. Stat. tit. 24A, § 2159(1); Md. Code Ann., Ins. §§ 27-208, 27-212(e) (West); Mass. Gen. Laws ch. 176D, § 3(7); Mich. Comp. Laws §§ 500.2019, 500.2020; Minn. Stat. § 72A.20(8), (9); Miss. Code Ann. § 83-5-35(g); Mo. Rev. Stat. § 375.936(11); Mont. Code Ann. § 33-18-206; Neb. Rev. Stat. § 44-1525(7); Nev. Rev. Stat. §§ 686A.100, 686A.130(4); N.H. Rev. Stat. Ann. § 417:4(VIII) (any insurance); N.J. Stat. Ann. § 17B:30-12 (West); N.M. Stat. Ann. § 59A-16-11; N.Y. Ins. Law § 4224(a), (b) (McKinney); N.C. Gen. Stat. § 58-63-15(7); N.D. Cent. Code § 26.1-04-05; Ohio Rev. Code Ann. § 3901.21(F), (M) (West); Okla. Stat. tit. 36, § 1204(7); Or. Rev. Stat. § 746.015; 40 Pa. Stat. Ann. § 1171.5(a)(7) (West); R.I. Gen. Laws § 27-29-4(7); S.C. Code Ann. § 38-57-120; S.D. Codified Laws §§ 58-33-12, 58-33-13, 58-33-26; Tenn. Code Ann. § 56-8-104(7); Utah Code Ann. § 31A-19a-201(1) (West) (rates may not be excessive, inadequate, or unfairly discriminatory), (4)(a) (a rate is unfairly discriminatory if price differentials fail to equitably reflect differences in expected losses and expenses after allowing for practical limitations); Utah Code Ann. § 31A-23a-402(8)(a) (West) (prohibiting unfair or deceptive acts or practices in business of insurance, as defined by commissioner by rule, after a finding that the act or practice is, among other things, unfairly discriminatory); Utah Admin. Code r. 590-83 (prohibiting discrimination based upon sex or marital status), r. 590-129 (prohibiting discrimination based upon blindness and physical or mental impairment); Vt. Stat. Ann. tit. 8, § 4724(7); Va. Code Ann. § 38.2-508; Wash. Rev. Code § 48.18.480; W. Va. Code § 33-11-4(7); Wyo. Stat. Ann. § 26-13-109(a), 26-13-112(c); *see also* Chabner v. United of Omaha Life Ins. Co., 225 F.3d 1042 (9th Cir. 2000) (California

law) (discrimination on the basis of disability); Lans v. Mut. Life Ins. Co. of N.Y., 699 P.2d 1299 (Ariz. Ct. App. 1984) (factual question whether sex discrimination actionable under provision prohibiting discrimination generally); Otero v. Midland Life Ins. Co., 753 So. 2d 579 (Fla. Dist. Ct. App. 1999); Klinginsmith v. Missouri Dep't of Consumer Affairs, 693 S.W.2d 226 (Mo. Ct. App. 1985).

112 Ark. Code Ann. § 23-66-206(14)(C); Colo. Rev. Stat. § 10-3-1104(1)(f)(II), (XIV); Conn. Gen. Stat. § 38a-824 (see Conn. Agencies Regs. § 38a-824-3(a)(1)); Ga. Code Ann. § 33-6-4(b)(8)(A)(iii); Haw. Rev. Stat. § 431:13-103(a)(7)(C); 215 Ill. Comp. Stat. § 5/155.22; Ind. Code § 27-2-17-5(b)(2); Ky. Rev. Stat. Ann. § 304.20-340(3) (West); La. Rev. Stat. Ann. § 22:1964(7)(d); Mich. Comp. Laws § 500.2027(a)(iii); Minn. Stat. § 72A.20(13)(a); Mo. Rev. Stat. § 375.936(11)(c); Mont. Code Ann. § 33-18-210(5); Neb. Rev. Stat. § 44-1525(7)(c); N.C. Gen. Stat. § 58-63-15(7)(c); N.D. Cent. Code §§ 26.1-39-17(3), 26.1-04-03(7)(d); Or. Rev. Stat. § 746.018(2); R.I. Gen. Laws § 27-29-4(7)(iii); Tex. Ins. Code Ann. § 544.002(a)(2) (West); Va. Code Ann. § 38.2-508(4); Wis. Stat. § 628.34 (see Wis. Admin. Code Ins. § 6.68(3)(a)).

113 Ark. Code Ann. § 23-66-206(14)(D); Conn. Gen. Stat. § 38a-824 (see Conn. Agencies Regs. § 38a-824-3(a)(5)); Ga. Code Ann. § 33-6-4(b)(8)(A)(iii); Haw. Rev. Stat. § 431:13-103(a)(7)(D); Ky. Rev. Stat. Ann. § 304.20-340(3) (West); La. Rev. Stat. Ann. § 22:1964(7)(e); Minn. Stat. § 72A.20(13)(b); Mo. Rev. Stat. § 375.936(11)(d); Mont. Code Ann. § 33-18-210(6); Neb. Rev. Stat. § 44-1525(7)(d); N.C. Gen. Stat. § 58-63-15(7)(d); N.D. Cent. Code § 26.1-39-17(3); R.I. Gen. Laws § 27-29-4(7)(iv); Va. Code Ann. § 38.2-508(5); Wis. Stat. § 628.34 (see Wis. Admin. Code Ins. § 6.68(3)(b)).

114 Ga. Code Ann. § 33-6-5(8); Haw. Rev. Stat. § 431:13-103(a)(7)(F); La. Rev. Stat. Ann. § 22:1964(7)(g); Mont. Code Ann. § 33-18-210(8).

115 A discussion of private rights of action under UNIP statutes and of the unfair and deceptive acts and practices implications of UNIP laws may be found in National Consumer Law Center, Unfair and Deceptive Acts and Practices § 10.5.2 (8th ed. 2012).

Chapter 8   Discrimination Law Challenges to Predatory Lending and Unfair Pricing

8.1 Introduction

This chapter examines credit discrimination law's application to predatory lending, unfair credit terms, and even abuses concerning a transaction's cash price. Other consumer law theories can tackle the same practices, as detailed in other NCLC treatises, such as *The Cost of Credit, Truth in Lending*, and *Unfair and Deceptive Acts and Practices*. This chapter demonstrates that the Equal Credit Opportunity Act (ECOA), Fair Housing Act (FHA), federal Civil Rights Acts, and state discrimination statutes may offer a superior or at least alternative approach for those in protected classes to challenge these practices.

Discrimination law not only remedies discriminatory credit denials but, as described in § 8.3, *infra*, also remedies extensions of credit on discriminatory terms. The most obvious case is when a creditor intentionally offers worse financing terms to members of protected classes than to other borrowers.[1] The lender may also discriminate by providing worse credit terms to borrowers who live in areas with a higher percentage of minority residents or may target such communities with abusive loans.[2]

Discrimination in credit terms may also be the result of neutral policies that have a disparate impact[3] on borrowers in protected classes. One example of this is the widespread practice of lenders giving dealers, brokers, and others discretion to add additional finance charges over and above what the lender's objective underwriting criteria require. In the home mortgage context, brokers received additional compensation based on the amount of the upcharge, known as a "yield spread premium."[4] Minorities and other protected classes more often pay upcharges and, when they do, on average they pay higher upcharges than other borrowers. Section 8.6, *infra*, examines discrimination law challenges to this pricing strategy.

Discrimination law can also be used to challenge abusive practices involving the cash price (not just the credit terms) of sales involving homes, cars, and other products. Application of the ECOA, FHA, and federal Civil Rights Acts to unfair cash prices is considered in § 8.7, *infra*.

8.2 Advantages of a Discrimination Law Challenge

Discrimination law challenges to unfair credit terms have many advantages over other consumer law causes of action. State unfair and deceptive acts and practices (UDAP) statutes provide effective remedies for unfair credit terms, but a number of UDAP statutes do not apply to creditors or credit, and a number of UDAP statutes only prohibit deceptive, not unfair, practices.[5] When credit terms are fully disclosed, it may be difficult to demonstrate that they were deceptive.

State usury laws, state anti-predatory lending statutes, and other forms of state credit regulation are clearly applicable to challenge unfair credit terms. But the deregulation movement has repealed or limited many of these laws, and state credit regulation is spotty at best. Even more importantly, federal banking law preempts much state credit regulation,[6] and may even preempt UDAP challenges to credit pricing.[7]

The ECOA, FHA, and federal Civil Rights Acts have none of these shortfalls. These statutes can remedy most forms of unfair lending targeting a protected class. Being federal statutes, they are not preempted by federal banking law and apply in all fifty states.

Federal consumer protection statutes other than the discrimination statutes apply to predatory lending but often have limited utility. The Truth in Lending Act does not regulate the price of credit but only requires disclosure of credit terms. The Home Owners Equity Protection Act (HOEPA) applies to predatory mortgage lending, but most lenders structure their credit terms

---

1 *See, e.g.*, Complaint and Consent Order, United States v. First Nat'l Bank of Gordon, Neb., No. 96-5035 (D.S.D. 1996), *available on the companion website to this treatise* (discrimination in credit terms offered to Native Americans); Complaint and Stipulated Judgment, United States v. Security State Bank of Pecos, No. SA 95CA099 (W.D. Tex. 1995), *available on the companion website to this treatise* (discrimination in credit terms offered Hispanics).

2 *See* § 8.5, *infra* (discussing reverse redlining).

3 *See* § 4.3, *supra*.

4 Most of these types of payments have recently been restricted by regulation. *See* Reg. Z, 12 C.F.R. § 1026.36(d) [§ 226.36(d)]; National Consumer Law Center, Truth in Lending § 9.3.2 (8th ed. 2012).

5 *See* National Consumer Law Center, Unfair and Deceptive Acts and Practices (8th ed. 2012).

6 *See* National Consumer Law Center, Mortgage Lending ch. 5 (2012); National Consumer Law Center, Consumer Credit Regulation ch. 3 (2012).

   The preemption landscape has been changed somewhat by the passage of the Dodd-Frank Wall Street Reform and Consumer Protection Act and related regulations. *See* § 12.4.2.3.6, *infra*.

7 *See* National Consumer Law Center, Unfair and Deceptive Acts and Practices § 2.5.3 (8th ed. 2012).

to avoid the statute's scope. The federal racketeering statute (RICO) is a complex statute requiring enterprise injury and a pattern of mail or wire fraud, or charging more than twice the enforceable interest rate.[8]

Because of the strong federal policy against discrimination, discrimination laws have effective private remedies. Punitive damages are available, while other statutes may provide only actual, minimum, or in some cases treble damages. Furthermore, there is good precedent to obtain sizeable intangible damages in credit discrimination cases.[9]

Common law fraud claims in most states also can lead to punitive damages, but the claims do not allow a successful consumer to recover attorney fees. Moreover, fraud is more difficult to prove than UDAP deception, and the core of a predatory lending case will be unconscionability or unfairness, not fraud or deception.

Because of the strong federal policy against discrimination, courts may also be more receptive to such claims. For example, when predatory terms are part of a written agreement, the court may believe that the consumer agreed to the terms and that therefore there is no unfairness. But even a court that takes a *caveat emptor* approach to claims relating to unconscionability and unfairness may feel differently about conduct that discriminates on the basis of race or membership in another protected class.

Like any other claim, allegations of discrimination will almost certainly be challenged under the heightened pleading standards enunciated in *Ashcroft v. Iqbal*,[10] making it more difficult for cases to survive to discovery.[11]

8.3 Discrimination Laws Reach Discriminatory Credit Terms, Not Just Credit Denials

Lenders sometimes argue that discrimination law applies only to denials of credit, not to the credit terms on which credit is granted. They claim that they cannot be discriminating if they make more loans to minority and other protected communities than they make to others. But such arguments should carry no weight. Offering loans to protected classes on unfavorable terms can be discriminatory.

The ECOA prohibits discrimination against any applicant "with respect to any aspect of a credit transaction."[12] Regulation B defines "credit transaction" to include "terms of credit."[13] Courts have little trouble finding that the ECOA applies to the offering of discriminatory credit terms and not just to denials of credit.[14]

Creditors sometimes point to language in the ECOA defining "adverse action" as being limited only to the denial or revocation of credit or a change in the terms of existing credit.[15] But "adverse action" is just one form of conduct regulated by the ECOA, triggering a creditor's duty to supply a required statement of reasons. Not all conduct regulated by the ECOA involves an "adverse action." The statute's general prohibition against discrimination is not limited to "adverse actions," as defined in the Act, but also to other conduct as well.[16]

The Fair Housing Act prohibits discrimination in the "terms or conditions" of a residential real estate-related transaction. Regulations prohibit "fixing the amount, interest rate, duration or other terms for a loan" based upon membership in a protected class.[17] Courts have therefore held that the FHA applies to discriminatory credit terms and not just to the denial of credit.[18]

---

reverse-redlining or intentional targeting); Palmer v. Homecomings Fin., L.L.C., 677 F. Supp. 2d 233 (D.D.C. 2010); Ng v. HSBC Mortgage Corp., 2010 WL 889256 (E.D.N.Y. Mar. 10, 2010) (allegation of denial of credit not necessary when alleging "reverse-redlining"); Willis v. Countrywide Home Loans Servicing, L.P., 2009 WL 5206475 (D. Md. Dec. 23, 2009) (claim under ECOA or FHA can be made based on discrimination in rejecting request for loan modification); Lomboy v. SCME Mortgage Bankers, 2009 WL 1457738 (N.D. Cal. May 26, 2009); Ware v. Indymac Bank, 534 F. Supp. 2d 835 (N.D. Ill. 2008); Newman v. Apex Fin. Group, Inc., 2008 WL 130924 (N.D. Ill. Jan. 11, 2008); Martinez v. Freedom Mortgage Team, Inc., 527 F. Supp. 2d 827 (N.D. Ill. 2007); Munoz v. Int'l Home Capital Corp., 2004 WL 3086907 (N.D. Cal. May 4, 2004); Gonzalez v. Ameriquest Mortgage Co., 2004 WL 2472249 (N.D. Cal. Mar. 1, 2004); Wilson v. Toussie, 260 F. Supp. 2d 530 (E.D.N.Y. Apr. 25, 2003); Matthews v. New Century Mortgage Corp., 185 F. Supp. 2d 874 (S.D. Ohio 2002); Hargraves v. Capital City Mortgage Corp., 140 F. Supp. 2d 7 (D.D.C. 2000), *on reconsideration*, 147 F. Supp. 2d 1 (D.D.C. 2001); *see also* Rodriguez v. SLM Corp., 2009 WL 598252 (D. Conn. Mar. 6, 2009) (finding that disparate impact claims can be made under ECOA and implicitly recognizing that higher rates are discriminatory); *cf.* JAT Inc. v. Nat'l City Bank of the Midwest, 460 F. Supp. 2d 812 (E.D. Mich. 2006). *But see* Hafiz v. Greenpoint Mortgage Funding, Inc., 652 F. Supp. 2d 1039 (N.D. Cal. 2009) (an ECOA discrimination claim requires, *inter alia*, an allegation that plaintiff was "denied credit" despite being qualified; plaintiff could not show discrimination because she was given a larger loan than she requested); Singh v. Wells Fargo Bank, 2009 WL 2365881 (N.D. Cal. July 30, 2009) (same).

15 15 U.S.C. § 1691(d)(6).

16 Wilson v. Toussie, 260 F. Supp. 2d 530 (E.D.N.Y. 2003).

17 24 C.F.R. § 100.130(b)(2).

18 *See* M & T Mortgage Corp. v. White, 736 F. Supp. 2d 538 (E.D.N.Y. 2010) (allegation of denial of credit not necessary when alleging reverse-redlining or intentional targeting); Ng v. HSBC Mortgage Corp., 2010 WL 889256 (E.D.N.Y. Mar. 10, 2010) (allegation of denial of credit not necessary when alleging reverse-redlining); Davenport v. Litton Loan Servicing, L.P., 725 F. Supp. 2d 862 (N.D. Cal. 2010) (recognizing different prima facie elements for reverse-redlining); Willis v. Countrywide Home Loans Servicing, L.P., 2009 WL 5206475 (D. Md. Dec. 23, 2009) (claim under ECOA or FHA can be made based on discrimination in rejecting request for loan modification); Rodriguez v. Bear Stearns Cos., Inc., 2009 WL 5184702 (D. Conn. Dec. 22, 2009) (implicitly recognizing FHA claim can be made based on discriminatory servicing practices); Newman v. Apex Fin. Group, Inc., 2008 WL 130924 (N.D. Ill. Jan. 11, 2008); Martinez v. Freedom Mortgage Team, Inc., 527 F. Supp.

---

8 *Id.* § 14.2.

9 *See* § 11.8.2.3, *infra*.

10 129 S. Ct. 1937, 173 L. Ed. 2d 868 (2009).

11 *See* § 4.1.2, *supra* (discussing *Iqbal*).

12 15 U.S.C. § 1691(a).

13 Reg. B, 12 C.F.R. § 1002.2(m) [§ 202.2(m)].

14 *See* M & T Mortgage Corp. v. White, 736 F. Supp. 2d 538 (E.D.N.Y. 2010) (allegation of denial of credit not necessary when alleging

The federal Civil Rights Acts have an even broader application. The statute states that all persons shall have the same rights as white citizens to "make and enforce contracts."[19] "Make and enforce contracts" is defined as including "the enjoyment of all benefits, privileges, terms, and conditions of the contractual relationship."[20]

8.4 Class Action Claims

Because of the nature of the claims discussed in this chapter, it will often make sense to bring claims on behalf of a class of borrowers rather than a single individual. Attorneys with limited class action experience should find knowledgeable co-counsel; this is not only prudent but is a prerequisite to class certification, which requires fair and adequate representation.[21]

In a reverse redlining case, class action allegations are appropriate because the very nature of the claim is that the lender is targeting a particular group or neighborhood; all borrowers in the targeted group or neighborhood who receive loans from the lender are subjected to the same unfair or predatory terms. Consumer lenders tend to have standardized credit products. Classwide targeting is a distinct possibility in any case in which the plaintiff is a member of a protected class and has been subjected to predatory lending. If a practitioner looks for such targeting, often it will be found.

In a case challenging discriminatory credit mark-up policies or other facially neutral policies with a disparate impact on a protected class, statistical proof of the disparate impact will almost certainly be required. Both the nature of such statistical claims and the expense of collecting and analyzing the data make class claims appropriate.

Many studies have found that predatory mortgage lenders target minority neighborhoods[22] and that, between 2000 and 2007, subprime lenders had an unusually large share of lending in African American and Hispanic neighborhoods.[23] The De-partment of Housing and Urban Development has found that, in predominantly African American neighborhoods, subprime lending accounted for 51% of home loans, compared with only 9% in predominantly white areas.[24] Strikingly similar results were found in a study of mortgage refinance loans in the Chicago area.[25] Additional studies are cited in § 4.4.5.5, *supra*, discussing disparities that appear in the Home Mortgage Disclosure Act data.

Differences in income between white and minority communities do not fully explain this concentration of predatory lending in minority neighborhoods—the same disparities exist controlling for income and may even increase when comparing higher-income minority and white communities.[26] African

---

2d 827 (N.D. Ill. 2007); Wiltshire v. Dhanraj, 421 F. Supp. 2d 544 (E.D.N.Y. 2005); Gonzalez v. Ameriquest Mortgage Co., 2004 WL 2472249 (N.D. Cal. Mar. 1, 2004); Hargraves v. Capital City Mortgage Corp., 140 F. Supp. 2d 7 (D.D.C. 2000), *on reconsideration*, 147 F. Supp. 2d 1 (D.D.C. 2001); McGlawn v. Pa. Human Relations Comm'n, 891 A.2d 757 (Pa. Commw. Ct. 2006) (state statute based upon the FHA).

19 42 U.S.C. § 1981(a).

20 42 U.S.C. § 1981(b); *see also* Jackson v. Novastar Mortgage, Inc., 2007 WL 4568976 (W.D. Tenn. Dec. 20, 2007).

21 Fed. R. Civ. Pro. 23(a). See the rest of this treatise for a discussion of all aspects of litigating a class action on behalf of consumers.

22 *See generally* Susan Wachter, Elizabeth Renuart, Kathleen C. Engel, & Patricia A. McCoy, *Revisiting a Tale of Three Markets: The Law and Economics of Predatory Lending*, 82 Tex. L. Rev. 413 (2003); Kathleen C. Engel & Patricia A. McCoy, *A Tale of Three Markets: The Law and Economics of Predatory Lending*, 80 Tex. L. Rev. 1255 (2002); Cathy Lesser Mansfield, *The Road to Subprime "HEL" Was Paved with Good Congressional Intentions: Usury Deregulation and the Subprime Home Equity Market*, 51 S.C. L. Rev. 473, 560 (2000).

23 *See, e.g.*, Ass'n of Cmty. Orgs. for Reform Now (ACORN), The High Cost of Credit: Disparities in High-Priced Loans to Minority Home-owners in 125 American Cities (2005), *available at* www.acorn.org; Ass'n of Cmty. Orgs. for Reform Now (ACORN), Separate and Unequal 2004: Predatory Lending in America (2004), *available at* www.acorn.org; Ass'n of Cmty. Orgs. for Reform Now (ACORN), Separate and Unequal 2002: Predatory Lending in America (2002), *available at* www.acorn.org; Ass'n of Cmty. Orgs. for Reform Now (ACORN), The Great Divide: An Analysis of Racial and Economic Disparities in Home Purchase Mortgage Lending Nationally and in Sixty Metropolitan Areas (2001); Cal. Reinvestment Coal., Who Really Gets Higher-Cost Home Loans?: Home Loan Disparities by Income, Race and Ethnicity of Borrowers and Neighborhoods in 12 California Communities in 2004 (Dec. 2005), *available at* www.calreinvest.org; Jim Campen, Changing Patterns XV: Mortgage Lending to Traditionally Underserved Borrowers and Neighborhoods in Boston, Greater Boston and Massachusetts, 2007 (Jan. 2009), *available at* www.mcbc.info/reports/mortgage; Jim Campen, Changing Patterns XIV: Mortgage Lending to Traditionally Underserved Borrowers and Neighborhoods in Boston, Greater Boston and Massachusetts, 2006 (Feb. 2008), *available at* www.mcbc.info/reports/pastreports; Nat'l Council of La Raza, Jeopardizing Hispanic Home-ownership: Predatory Practices in the Homebuying Market (May 2005), *available at* www.nclr.org/content/publications/detail/31596; United States Dep't of Hous. & Urban Dev. (HUD), Unequal Burden: Income and Racial Disparities in Subprime Lending in America (2000), *available at* www.hud.gov; Daniel Immergluck & Marti Wiles, Woodstock Institute, Two Steps Back: The Dual Mortgage Market, Predatory Lending, and the Undoing of Community Development (1999), *available at* www.woodstockinst.org. *See generally* Frank Lopez, *Using the Fair Housing Act to Combat Predatory Lending*, 6 Geo. J. on Poverty L. & Pol'y 73 (1999).

24 United States Dep't of Hous. & Urban Dev., Unequal Burden: Income and Racial Disparities in Subprime Lending in America (2000), *available at* www.hud.gov.

25 Daniel Immergluck & Marti Wiles, Woodstock Institute, Two Steps Back: The Dual Mortgage Market, Predatory Lending, and the Undoing of Community Development (1999), *available at* www.woodstockinst.org (58% in minority communities and 10% in other communities).

26 *See, e.g.*, Ass'n of Cmty. Orgs. for Reform Now (ACORN), Separate and Unequal 2004: Predatory Lending in America (2004), *available at* www.acorn.org; Ass'n of Cmty. Orgs. for Reform Now (ACORN), Separate and Unequal 2002: Predatory Lending in America (2002), *available at* www.acorn.org; Calvin Bradford, Ctr. for Cmty. Change, Risk or Race: Racial Disparities and the Subprime Refinance Market (May 2002) (racial disparities actually increased as borrower income increased), *available at* www.community change.org; Jim Campen, Changing Patterns XV: Mortgage Lending to Traditionally Underserved Borrowers and Neighborhoods in Boston, Greater Boston and Massachusetts, 2007 (Jan. 2009), *available at* www.mcbc.info/reports/mortgage; Jim Campen, Changing

American and Hispanic borrowers are more likely to receive interest-only and payment option mortgages than non-minority borrowers at all levels of income, debt loads, and credit scores.[27] (These loans are among the most risky, often leading to negative amortization, and can easily lead to foreclosure and negative equity when home prices fall.)

Evidence also suggests that subprime mortgage lenders target older home owners.[28] Even after accounting for race, income, and other factors, the likelihood of getting a subprime loan is much higher with older home owners.[29]

It is not only mortgage lenders who target protected classes, but other types of lenders as well.[30] For example, one study showed how lenders offering tax refund anticipation loans target minority neighborhoods.[31]

These studies provide useful support to a discrimination claim, but they are no substitute for careful discovery and development of the facts in each case. While many academics and housing advocates blame reverse redlining for high concentrations of foreclosures in minority neighborhoods and for the resulting harmful effects on the neighborhood and increased burden on public services,[32] some courts have found the chain of causation too attenuated to be the basis for a legal claim.[33]

8.5 Reverse Redlining

8.5.1 General

Redlining is the practice of *denying* credit to particular neighborhoods on a discriminatory basis.[34] The flip side is reverse redlining, the practice of targeting these same communities or protected classes for predatory lending. In some cases, the creditor may not even offer better terms to other borrowers; the key element of reverse redlining is the targeting of protected racial groups, elders, and others for unusually bad credit terms.

Courts increasingly accept reverse redlining as a valid claim under the FHA, ECOA, federal Civil Rights Acts, and state discrimination statutes,[35] and a number of federal enforcement actions have also led to settlements for reverse redlining.[36] The

---

Patterns XIV: Mortgage Lending to Traditionally Underserved Borrowers and Neighborhoods in Boston, Greater Boston and Massachusetts, 2006 (Feb. 2008), *available at* www.mcbc.info/reports/pastreports; Ken Zimmerman, Elvin Wyly, & Hilary Botein, N.J. Institute for Social Justice, Predatory Lending in New Jersey: The Rising Threat to Low-Income Homeowners (2002); Daniel Immergluck & Marti Wiles, Woodstock Institute, Two Steps Back: The Dual Mortgage Market, Predatory Lending, and the Undoing of Community Development (1999), *available at* www.woodstockinst.org.

27 Allen Fishbein & Patrick Woodall, Consumer Fed'n of America, Exotic or Toxic? An Examination of the Non-Traditional Mortgage Market for Consumers and Lenders (May 24, 2006), *available at* www.consumerfed.org/pdfs/Exotic_Toxic_Mortgage_Report0506.pdf.

28 *See, e.g.,* Sharon Hermanson & Neal Walters, America Ass'n of Retired Persons, Subprime Mortgage Lending and Older Borrowers (Mar. 2001), *available at* http://research.aarp.org/consume/dd57_lending.html.

29 Howard Lax, Michael Manti, Paul Raca, & Peter Zorn, *Subprime Lending: An Investigation of Economic Efficiency*, 15 Hous. Pol'y Debate 533, 545, 564 (2004); Kurt Eggert, *Lashed to the Mast and Crying for Help: How Self-Limitation of Autonomy Can Protect Elders from Predatory Lending*, 36 Loy. L.A. L. Rev. 693 (2003); The Nat'l Cmty. Reinvestment Coal., The Broken Credit System: Discrimination and Unequal Access to Affordable Loans by Race and Age (2003); Consumers Union Southwest Reg'l Office, Elderly in the Subprime Market (Oct. 2002); United States Dep't of the Treasury & United States Dep't of Hous. & Urban Dev., Joint Report to Curb Predatory Lending 35–36 (2002), *available at* http://huduser.org/publications/hsgfin/curbing.html; Neal Walters & Sharon Hermanson, AARP Pub. Pol'y Institute, Older Subprime Refinance Mortgage Borrowers (2002), *available at* www.consumersunion.org/pdf/elderly-sub.pdf.

30 Christian Weller, Ctr. for American Progress, Access Denied: Low Income and Minority Families Face More Credit Constraints and Higher Borrowing Costs (Aug. 2007), *available at* www.americanprogress.org.

31 *See* Neighborhood Economic Dev. Advocacy Project, Predatory Tax-Time Loans Strip $324 Million from New York City's Poorest Communities: An Analysis of Tax Refund Anticipation Lending in NYC 2002–2005 (Jan. 2007).

32 *See, e.g.,* John P. Relman, *Foreclosures, Integration, and the Future of the Fair Housing Act*, 41 Ind. L. Rev. 629 (2008); Kathleen C. Engel & Patricia A. McCoy, *From Credit Denial to Predatory Lending: The Challenge of Sustaining Minority Homeownership, in* Segregation: The Rising Costs for America 81 (James H. Carr & Nandinee K. Kutty eds., 2007); Dan Immergluck & Geoff Smith, Woodstock Institute, Risky Business: An Econometric Analysis of the Relationship Between Subprime Lending and Neighborhood Foreclosures (2004), *available at* www.woodstockinst.org/publications/download/risky-business%3a—an-econometric-analysis-of-the-relationship-between-subprime-lending-and-neighborhood-foreclosures.

See also the studies cited above in this subsection.

33 *See* Mayor & City Council of Balt. v. Wells Fargo Bank, 677 F. Supp. 2d 847 (D. Md. 2010); City of Birmingham v. Citigroup, Inc., No. CV-09-BE-467-S (N.D. Ala. Aug. 19, 2009), *available at* www.nclc.org/unreported.

34 *See* ch. 7, *supra.*

35 *See* Barkley v. Olympia Mortgage Co., 2007 WL 2437810 (E.D.N.Y. Aug. 22, 2007); Coelho v. Alliance Mortgage Banking Corp., 2007 WL 1412289 (D.N.J. May 10, 2007); Munoz v. Int'l Home Capital Corp., 2004 WL 3086907 (N.D. Cal. May 4, 2004); Gonzalez v. Ameriquest Mortgage Co., 2004 WL 2472249 (N.D. Cal. Mar. 1, 2004); Wilson v. Toussie, 260 F. Supp. 2d 530, 540 (E.D.N.Y. 2002); Matthews v. New Century Mortgage Corp., 185 F. Supp. 2d 874 (S.D. Ohio 2002); Johnson v. Equicredit Corp. of America, 2002 WL 448991 (N.D. Ill. Mar. 22, 2002); Hargraves v. Capital City Mortgage Corp., 140 F. Supp. 2d 7 (D.D.C. 2000), *on reconsideration,* 147 F. Supp. 2d 1 (D.D.C. 2001); Honorable v. The Easy Life Real Estate System, 100 F. Supp. 2d 885 (N.D. Ill. 2000); Associates Home Equity Servs., Inc. v. Troup, 778 A.2d 529, 537 (N.J. Super. Ct. App. Div. 2001) (based on state discrimination statute); M & T Mortgage Corp. v. Foy, 858 N.Y.S.2d 567 (Sup. Ct. 2008); McGlawn v. Pa. Human Relations Comm'n, 891 A.2d 757 (Pa. Commw. Ct. 2006) (based on state discrimination statute); *see also* Mayor & City Council of Balt. v. Wells Fargo Bank, No. L08CV062 (D. Md. Jan. 8, 2008), *available on the companion website to this treatise* (suit filed alleging FHA violation).

36 *See, e.g.,* United States v. Delta Funding Corp., No. CV 00 1872 (E.D.N.Y. Mar. 30, 2000), *available on the companion website to this treatise;* Consent Judgment, People v. Delta Funding Corp., 99-Civ-4951 (E.D.N.Y. Sept. 17, 1999), *available on the companion website to this treatise;* Fed. Trade Comm'n v. Capital City Mortgage Corp., No. 98-237 (D.D.C. Jan. 29, 1998), *available on the*

basic element of a reverse redlining claim is that members of a protected class have received loans whose terms are unfair or predatory, and the lender either intentionally targeted that protected class or targeted a largely minority neighborhood, with the result that there is a disparate impact on minorities.[37]

Creditors often defend the practice of reverse redlining by claiming they make loans to African Americans or other protected classes on the same terms they make loans to whites—their practices are the same for all their customers. But the law is clear that a discrimination case can be made out even if there is no evidence that similarly qualified applicants are treated more favorably.[38] It is enough to show that a lender targeted a protected class for unfair credit terms.[39] "[T]o hold otherwise would allow predatory lending schemes to continue as long as they are exclusively perpetrated upon one racial group."[40]

8.5.2 Showing That a Lender Targets a Protected Class

A reverse redlining claim requires a showing that the lender targets minorities or other protected classes.[41] This targeting can be proved by detailing how the lender markets its loans. Look for evidence as to where the lender opens storefronts. Opening them in predominantly minority neighborhoods is evidence of targeting.[42] Even more telling is evidence that the lender locates storefronts for its prime lending subsidiaries in white communities but locates its storefronts for its subprime lending in minority communities, particularly when the white and minority neighborhoods have similar income levels.

Lenders also use third parties to market their loans, such as brokers for mortgage loans and car dealers for automobile loans. It is evidence of targeting if a lender solicits brokers or dealers who operate predominantly in minority communities.[43] Evidence of targeting has also been found when lenders pair minority borrowers with minority sales personnel.[44]

Examine advertising for evidence of targeting as well, considering both the nature of the advertisement and where it is placed. Courts have found compelling evidence of targeting when advertising and other displays featured minority consumers or minority celebrities,[45] and was placed in minority media but not in comparable media serving primarily white neighborhoods.[46]

Also question the consumer as to what statements were made by sales personnel. Courts find evidence of targeting when sales personnel indicate to customers that the lender is focusing on minority neighborhoods, or state that the lender's customers typically are minority.[47] Ex-employees may be another important source of evidence. One ex-employee of a finance company testified at a Congressional hearing that, "[i]n fact, my perfect customer would be an uneducated widow who is on a

companion website to this treatise; Settlement Agreement and Order, United States v. Long Beach Mortgage Co., No. CV 96-6159 (C.D. Cal. Sept. 5, 1996), *available on the companion website to this treatise*; Settlement Agreement, *In re* Delta Funding Corp. (N.Y. Banking Dep't Aug. 20, 1999), *available on the companion website to this treatise*.

37 Munoz v. Int'l Home Capital Corp., 2004 WL 3086907 (N.D. Cal. May 4, 2004); Matthews v. New Century Mortgage Corp., 185 F. Supp. 2d 874 (S.D. Ohio 2002); Hargraves v. Capital City Mortgage Corp., 140 F. Supp. 2d 7 (D.D.C. 2000), *on reconsideration*, 147 F. Supp. 2d 1 (D.D.C. 2001); Associates Home Equity Servs., Inc. v. Troup, 778 A.2d 529, 537 (N.J. Super. Ct. App. Div. 2001); McGlawn v. Pa. Human Relations Comm'n, 891 A.2d 757 (Pa. Commw. Ct. 2006); *see* M & T Mortgage Corp. v. White, 736 F. Supp. 2d 538 (E.D.N.Y. 2010) (reciting elements and finding plaintiffs had made sufficient showing of intentional targeting under the FHA and ECOA to preclude summary judgment for defendant); Davenport v. Litton Loan Servicing, L.P., 725 F. Supp. 2d 862 (N.D. Cal. 2010) (reciting elements but finding that plaintiff's allegations were insufficient to establish claim of reverse redlining); Ng v. HSBC Mortgage Corp., 2010 WL 889256 (E.D.N.Y. Mar. 10, 2010) (reciting elements but finding that plaintiff's allegations were insufficient to establish claim of reverse redlining); *see also* Steed v. Everhome Mortgage Co., 308 Fed. Appx. 364 (11th Cir. 2009) (approving of the *Hargraves* analysis); Hafiz v. Greenpoint Mortgage Funding, Inc., 652 F. Supp. 2d 1039 (N.D. Cal. 2009) (reciting elements but finding that plaintiff's allegations were insufficient to establish claim of reverse redlining); Singh v. Wells Fargo Bank, 2009 WL 2365881 (N.D. Cal. July 30, 2009) (same); Williams v. 2000 Homes Inc., 2009 WL 2252528 (E.D.N.Y. July 29, 2009) (reciting elements but finding that plaintiff's allegations were insufficient to establish claim of reverse redlining; plaintiff would need to demonstrate that similarly situated non-minority borrowers received more favorable terms).

38 Coelho v. Alliance Mortgage Banking Corp, 2007 WL 1412289 (D.N.J. May 10, 2007); Hargraves v. Capital City Mortgage Corp., 140 F. Supp. 2d 7 (D.D.C. 2000), *on reconsideration*, 147 F. Supp. 2d 1 (D.D.C. 2001); McGlawn v. Pa. Human Relations Comm'n, 891 A.2d 757 (Pa. Commw. Ct. 2006).

39 Barkley v. Olympia Mortgage Co., 2007 WL 2437810 (E.D.N.Y. Aug. 22, 2007); Hargraves v. Capital City Mortgage Corp., 140 F. Supp. 2d 7 (D.D.C. 2000), *on reconsideration*, 147 F. Supp. 2d 1 (D.D.C. 2001); *see also* Coelho v. Alliance Mortgage Banking Corp, 2007 WL 1412289 (D.N.J. May 10, 2007).

40 Barkley v. Olympia Mortgage Co., 2007 WL 2437810, at *14 (E.D.N.Y. Aug. 22, 2007); *see also* Hargraves v. Capital City Mortgage Corp., 140 F. Supp. 2d 7 (D.D.C. 2000), *on reconsidera-*

tion, 147 F. Supp. 2d 1 (D.D.C. 2001); Contract Buyers League v. F & F Inv., 300 F. Supp. 210 (N.D. Ill. 1969); *see also* M & T Mortgage Corp. v. White, 736 F. Supp. 2d 538 (E.D.N.Y. 2010).

41 *See* § 8.5.1, *supra*.

42 Hargraves v. Capital City Mortgage Corp., 140 F. Supp. 2d 7 (D.D.C. 2000), *on reconsideration*, 147 F. Supp. 2d 1 (D.D.C. 2001).

43 *Id.*; McGlawn v. Pa. Human Relations Comm'n, 891 A.2d 757 (Pa. Commw. Ct. 2006); *see also* Newman v. Apex Financial Group, 2008 WL 130924 (N.D. Ill. Jan. 11, 2008).

44 Barkley v. Olympia Mortgage Co., 2007 WL 2437810 (E.D.N.Y. Aug. 22, 2007).

45 *Id.*; Hargraves v. Capital City Mortgage Corp., 140 F. Supp. 2d 7 (D.D.C. 2000), *on reconsideration*, 147 F. Supp. 2d 1 (D.D.C. 2001); McGlawn v. Pa. Human Relations Comm'n, 891 A.2d 757 (Pa. Commw. Ct. 2006).

46 Barkley v. Olympia Mortgage Co., 2007 WL 2437810 (E.D.N.Y. Aug. 22, 2007); Hargraves v. Capital City Mortgage Corp., 140 F. Supp. 2d 7 (D.D.C. 2000), *on reconsideration*, 147 F. Supp. 2d 1 (D.D.C. 2001); McGlawn v. Pa. Human Relations Comm'n, 891 A.2d 757 (Pa. Commw. Ct. 2006); *cf.* Jackson v. Novastar Mortgage, Inc., 2007 WL 4568976 (W.D. Tenn. Dec. 20, 2007) (advertised on gospel radio).

47 Barkley v. Olympia Mortgage Co., 2007 WL 2437810 (E.D.N.Y. Aug. 22, 2007).

fixed income, hopefully from her deceased husband's pension and Social Security, who has her house paid off, is living off of credit cards, but having a difficult time keeping up with her payments, and who must make a car payment in addition to her credit card payments."[48]

That the lender harbors ill will toward a protected class is *not* a necessary element of targeting. An adequate motivation, for example, can be that the lender has a biased perception that protected classes are especially vulnerable to fraud.[49]

Lenders may argue that they do not target minorities but just happen to do business in minority areas. Of course, targeting a minority community is good evidence that the lender is targeting minorities. Moreover, even if a lender is not targeting minorities, its targeting of a minority community can have a disparate impact on minorities, which would also violate discrimination laws.[50] A disparate impact can be shown by a statistical analysis of the racial composition of a lender's borrowers.[51] A discussion of disparate impact claims can be found in § 4.3, *supra*.

8.5.3 Unfair Credit Terms Sufficient to Show Reverse Redlining

It is not enough to show that a lender targets a protected class. The plaintiff must also show that the lender targets the protected class to offer unfair or predatory loans. Of course, a discrimination claim is also actionable if the lender merely offers less advantageous terms to protected classes than to others.[52] But, if the allegation is that the lender targets protected classes but offers the same terms to others, then the plaintiff must also show that those terms are unfair or predatory.

There are many ways that a loan can be unfair or predatory, but the consumer's proof should always consider a possible lender response that the terms are necessary to match the borrower's risk. As will be shown below, the "borrower risk" defense does not hold water in many contexts.

The borrower risk defense certainly is not valid when the lender does not engage in underwriting and is not concerned about the borrower's ability to repay the loan. The lender is just as happy to foreclose and strip out the equity. Studies find that as many as 80% of predatory loans are second mortgages or mortgage refinancings,[53] meaning that many predatory loans are secured by mortgages in which the consumer has already built up substantial equity in the home. A showing of unfair or predatory terms need not be based on the interest rate compared to the borrower's risk but on the fact that the lender knowingly writes loans the borrower cannot afford. The loan is predatory and unfair because it is written with a high risk of foreclosure, with an eye toward equity stripping.[54] In this case, the fact that the borrower is high risk is not a lender defense, but part of the plaintiff's case.

Also unfair is the practice of flipping lower rate mortgages into higher rate mortgages.[55] Whatever the borrower's risk, the borrower already has a low-rate mortgage, and it is unfair to refinance that mortgage into a high-rate mortgage when the borrower would be better off keeping the low-rate first mortgage and obtaining an additional second mortgage.

Another way to prove a mortgage loan predatory or unfair is to focus on the yield spread premium, broker fees, other fees, prepayment penalties, and other collateral terms.[56] As de-

---

48 *Equity Predators: Stripping, Flipping and Packing Their Way to Profits: Hearing Before the Senate Special Comm. on Aging* 31 (Mar. 16, 1998) (statement of Jim Dough).

49 Barkley v. Olympia Mortgage Co., 2007 WL 2437810 (E.D.N.Y. Aug. 22, 2007).

50 Barrett v. H & R Block, Inc., 652 F. Supp. 2d 104 (D. Mass. 2009); Guerra v. GMAC L.L.C., 2009 WL 449153 (E.D. Pa. Feb. 20, 2009); Hargraves v. Capital City Mortgage Corp., 140 F. Supp. 2d 7 (D.D.C. 2000), *on reconsideration*, 147 F. Supp. 2d 1 (D.D.C. 2001); McGlawn v. Pa. Human Relations Comm'n, 891 A.2d 757 (Pa. Commw. Ct. 2006).

51 McGlawn v. Pa. Human Relations Comm'n, 891 A.2d 757 (Pa. Commw. Ct. 2006).

In an individual case (in which statistical analysis is not possible, or data is available but such data is not cost effective and cannot be done) it may be extremely difficult to show disparate impact or to allege disparate treatment in a way that will survive a motion to dismiss. *See, e.g.*, Hafiz v. Greenpoint Mortgage Funding, Inc., 652 F. Supp. 2d 1039 (N.D. Cal. 2009); Singh v. Wells Fargo Bank, 2009 WL 2365881 (N.D. Cal. July 30, 2009); Williams v. 2000 Homes Inc., 2009 WL 2252528 (E.D.N.Y. July 29, 2009); Joseph v. Northwood Group, L.L.C., 2009 WL 2252336 (S.D.N.Y. July 23, 2009); Akhavein v. Argent Mortgage Co., 2009 WL 2157522 (N.D. Cal. July 18, 2009).

52 Although it is not logically required, some courts, in reciting the elements of a reverse-redlining claim, seem to require that the loan have grossly unfavorable terms, even if there is also a showing that the lender made loans with more favorable terms to other borrowers. *See, e.g.*, Davenport v. Litton Loan Servicing, L.P., 725 F. Supp. 2d 862, 876 (N.D. Cal. 2010) (dismissing claims as outside the

statute of limitations but also discussing reciting requirement that plaintiff allege "that the loan was given on grossly unfavorable terms; and . . . that the lender either intentionally targeted her for unfair loans or currently makes loans on more favorable terms to others"); Matthews v. New Century Mortgage Corp., 185 F. Supp. 2d 874, 886 (S.D. Ohio 2002) ("the plaintiff must show . . . (3) that the loans were given on grossly unfavorable terms; and (4) that the lender continues to provide loans to other applicants with similar qualifications, but on significantly more favorable terms"); Hargraves v. Capital City Mortgage Corp., 140 F. Supp. 2d 7, 20 (D.D.C. 2000) ("In order to show a claim based on reverse redlining, the plaintiffs must show that the defendants' lending practices and loan terms were 'unfair' and 'predatory,' and that the defendants either intentionally targeted on the basis of race, or that there is a disparate impact on the basis of race.").

53 Kenneth Temkin, Jennifer E.H. Johnson, & Diane Levy, Urban Institute, United States Dep't of Hous. & Urban Dev., Office of Pol'y Dev. & Research, Subprime Markets, The Role of GSEs and Risk-Based Pricing (2002).

54 *See* Hargraves v. Capital City Mortgage Corp., 140 F. Supp. 2d 7 (D.D.C. 2000), *on reconsideration*, 147 F. Supp. 2d 1 (D.D.C. 2001); McGlawn v. Pa. Human Relations Comm'n, 891 A.2d 757 (Pa. Commw. Ct. 2006).

55 McGlawn v. Pa. Human Relations Comm'n, 891 A.2d 757 (Pa. Commw. Ct. 2006).

56 *See* Alan M. White, *Risk-Based Mortgage Pricing: Present and Future Research*, 15 Fannie Mae Hous. Pol'y Debate 503 (2004) (discussing these unfair fees).

scribed in § 8.6, *infra*, these fees may not be based upon risk. Thus high fees may be a good indicator of a predatory or unfair loan, and risk cannot be a lender defense.[57] Even high prepayment penalties can be considered unfair, because they prevent the borrower from refinancing into a more reasonable loan.[58]

Of course the interest rate is another key to showing a loan to be predatory or unfair. The consumer should show that the interest rate a lender charges is in excess of what the credit risk indicates.[59] One court has ruled that any mortgage loan over 9% creates a rebuttable presumption that the loan involves reverse redlining.[60] Some courts look at the Home Mortgage Disclosure Act's definitions of a high rate loan (loans with interest rates three percentage points higher than prime mortgage loans carry).[61] But the basic question of fact is whether the interest rate is high compared to the risk involved,[62] or just whether the rates are exorbitant.[63]

One way to show that a loan's price is unfair and not related to risk is to consider the lender's profit margin, as economic theory would suggest that profits would be at a reasonable level if the price were market-based. If higher prices compensate for higher transaction costs and higher risk, subprime lenders' profits would be comparable to the profits earned by those lending to "lower risk" populations. In fact, at least until the subprime market collapse, profits for subprime lenders were often much higher.[64] Moreover, do not just look at the lender's profit, but also look at the profit level for brokers and others originating the loan.

The lender's argument that it requires high prices to match the risk of its borrowers is also countered by evidence that the lender does not perform any significant underwriting, so the lender does not even know whether its customers are high risk or low risk. Studies have shown that many borrowers who end up with high-priced subprime loans have credit histories and credit scores that should qualify them for lower-cost conventional financing.[65] When a lender charges the same high rate to a whole community, it is obvious that pricing is not based on the credit risk of individual borrowers.

8.5.4 Borrowers Should Not Need to Demonstrate Qualification for a Loan

A number of credit discrimination cases dealing with the *denial* of credit enunciate a required element that the consumer "qualify for a loan." While this makes sense in the context of challenging a credit denial, it should not be a necessary element of a reverse redlining claim; as discussed above, one aspect of reverse redlining is that lenders may make very expensive loans to borrowers who are clearly unable to afford them. There is no reason to limit the consumer's rights when the lender knew the consumer could not afford a loan and still offered the loan, either to strip out the consumer's equity in the home or to earn a quick profit.

Nevertheless, in at least one poorly reasoned reverse redlining case, the court rejected the consumer's cause of action because the consumer was given a loan the consumer should not have qualified for but for the lender's predatory practices.[66] Because the consumer was not qualified, the consumer did not "qualify for a loan" and thus had no cause of action, even though the consumer in fact was given a loan.[67]

Other courts have required plaintiffs to show they were qualified for a loan other than the one they received.[68]

8.6 Discriminatory Credit Mark-Up Policies

8.6.1 The Practice Described

In many credit contexts, lenders establish risk-based credit terms for a consumer and then give discretion to dealers, brokers, loan officers, and others to mark up the credit charges based upon subjective factors.

The actual pricing scheme will vary somewhat between automobile financing and mortgage lending, and even from

---

57 Associates Home Equity Servs., Inc. v. Troup, 778 A.2d 529, 537 (N.J. Super. Ct. App. Div. 2001); McGlawn v. Pa. Human Relations Comm'n, 891 A.2d 757 (Pa. Commw. Ct. 2006).

58 McGlawn v. Pa. Human Relations Comm'n, 891 A.2d 757 (Pa. Commw. Ct. 2006); *see also* Debbie Gruenstein Bocian & Richard Zhai, Ctr. for Responsible Lending, Borrowers in Higher Minority Areas More Likely to Receive Prepayment Penalties on Subprime Loans (Jan. 2005), *available at* www.responsiblelending.org/pdfs/rr004-PPP_Minority_Neighborhoods-0105.pdf.

59 M & T Mortgage Corp. v. Foy, 858 N.Y.S.2d 567 (N.Y. Sup. Ct. 2008); McGlawn v. Pa. Human Relations Comm'n, 891 A.2d 757 (Pa. Commw. Ct. 2006).

60 M & T Mortgage Corp. v. Foy, 858 N.Y.S.2d 567 (N.Y. Sup. Ct. 2008).

61 *See* McGlawn v. Pa. Human Relations Comm'n, 891 A.2d 757 (Pa. Commw. Ct. 2006).

62 Associates Home Equity Servs., Inc. v. Troup, 778 A.2d 529, 537 (N.J. Super. Ct. App. Div. 2001); McGlawn v. Pa. Human Relations Comm'n, 891 A.2d 757 (Pa. Commw. Ct. 2006).

63 Hargraves v. Capital City Mortgage Corp., 140 F. Supp. 2d 7 (D.D.C. 2000), *on reconsideration*, 147 F. Supp. 2d 1 (D.D.C. 2001); McGlawn v. Pa. Human Relations Comm'n, 891 A.2d 757 (Pa. Commw. Ct. 2006).

64 *See* Lynn Drysdale & Kathleen E. Keest, *The Two-Tiered Consumer Financial Services Marketplace: The Fringe Banking System and Its Challenge to Current Thinking About the Role of Usury Laws in Today's Society*, 51 S.C. L. Rev. 589 (2000); *see also* Cathy Lesser Mansfield, *The Road to Subprime "HEL" Was Paved with Good Congressional Intentions: Usury Deregulation and the Subprime Home Equity Market*, 51 S.C. L. Rev. 473 (2000).

65 *See generally* Susan Wachter, Elizabeth Renuart, Kathleen C. Engel & Patricia A. McCoy, *Revisiting a Tale of Three Markets: The Law and Economics of Predatory Lending*, 82 Tex. L. Rev. 413 (2003); Kathleen C. Engel & Patricia A. McCoy, *A Tale of Three Markets: The Law and Economics of Predatory Lending*, 80 Tex. L. Rev. 1255 (2002); Cathy Lesser Mansfield, *The Road to Subprime "HEL" Was Paved with Good Congressional Intentions: Usury Deregulation and the Subprime Home Equity Market*, 51 S.C. L. Rev. 473, 560 (2000).

66 Equicredit Corp. of N.Y. v. Turcios, 300 A.D.2d 344 (2002).

67 *Id.*

68 *See* § 4.2.3.3, *supra* (discussing this issue and other elements of a reverse-redlining case).

lender to lender, but there are strong similarities. In automobile financing, the lender establishes what is called a "buy rate," which is the interest rate at which it will purchase the loan from the car dealer. This rate is based upon the lender's objective evaluation of the borrower's credit risk. The dealer is then given discretion to increase that rate up to a cap and keep all or much of the difference. The dealer has little or no exposure to default and thus is basing its mark-up on purely non-risk factors. The existence of the mark-up is not disclosed to the consumer. The result is that borrowers in identical objective risk categories pay different finance rates. Not every consumer is marked up, as that is at the dealer's discretion. Studies show, however, that many loans are marked up, that the mark-up varies from loan to loan, that minorities are much more likely to be marked up, and that the mark-up to minorities will be greater on average than for whites.[69]

In mortgage lending, the lender establishes a "par" rate at which it will either write or purchase a mortgage loan. To the extent to which anyone in the process engages in underwriting and establishing a risk-based price, it is the lender in determining the par rate. Independent loan brokers, the lender's own officers, and correspondent lenders are given discretion to mark up the par rate, up to a cap. The brokers, officers, and correspondent lenders share little or no risk of default, and therefore their mark-up decisions are not based upon risk but upon subjective factors. Furthermore, the brokers often were paid a share of the mark-up, called a "yield spread premium" or "YSP," giving them an incentive to charge borrowers as much as possible. Yield spread premiums are now illegal for most mortgages.[70]

Even before such restrictions went into effect, yield spread premiums, while in and of themselves not illegal, were not insulated from charges of fraud or discrimination.[71] Similarly, the fact that mark-ups in automobile financing are not per se illegal and are a common business practice is no defense to a discrimination claim.[72]

On their face, lenders' pricing policies appear neutral and not to discriminate against protected classes. Overt discrimination is confined to the actions of dealers, brokers, and related lenders. But a number of studies have shown that these pricing policies that give discretion to third parties to mark up financing charges are not neutral. Instead, they have the effect of discriminating based upon membership in a protected class. Minorities and other protected classes have their finance rates marked up more frequently and to a greater extent than whites do.[73] Because of the number of cases that have already litigated this issue,[74] it is also clear that lenders engaging in this pricing policy are aware of its discriminatory impact. Regulators also have long noted the potential for discriminatory pricing inherent in this practice and have warned creditors about it.[75]

8.6.2 Private and Government Litigation of Discretionary Pricing Cases

For over a decade, one of the most active areas of credit discrimination law involved challenges to automobile and home mortgage lenders' discretionary mark-up policies. Unfortunately, the Supreme Court's opinion in *Wal-Mart Stores, Inc. v. Dukes*[76] arguably makes it more difficult to bring a disparate impact claim based on subjectivity in decision making. Although cases challenging discretionary credit mark-ups are distinguishable from *Wal-Mart*, a number of district courts have seized on language in the *Wal-Mart* decision as a reason to deny or revoke class certification in discretionary mark-up cases.[77] Most of the cases discussed in this section date from before the *Wal-Mart* decision, although government enforcement efforts have continued (and arguably become more aggressive) after 2010.

During the early 2000s, successful disparate impact class actions (resulting in significant settlements) were brought against the major automobile lenders: GMAC,[78] Ford Motor

---

69   *See, e.g.*, Report of Howell E. Jackson, *In re* Wells Fargo Lending Practices Litig., No. 3:08-md-01930 (N.D. Cal.), *available on the companion website to this treatise*; Report of Ian Ayres, Barrett v. Option One and H&R Block, No. 1:08-cv-10157 (D. Mass), *available on the companion website to this treatise*; Report of Professor Mark Cohen, Assoc. Professor of Mgmt., Owen Graduate School of Mgmt., Vanderbilt Univ. & Chair, Comm. on L. & Justice, American Statistical Ass'n, Cason v. Nissan Motor Acceptance Corp., No. 3-98-0223 (M.D. Tenn. May 17, 2001), *available on the companion website to this treatise*; Consumer Fed'n of America, The Hidden Markup of Auto Loans: Consumer Costs of Dealer Kickbacks and Inflated Finance Charges (Jan. 2004), *available at* www.consumerfed.org.

70   Reg. Z, 12 C.F.R. § 1026.36(d) [§ 226.36(d)]. *See generally* National Consumer Law Center, Mortgage Lending § 7.3.4.2 (2012).

       The regulations only apply to closed-end credit, leaving compensation paid on home equity lines of credit (HELOCs) open for continued abuse. Regulation Z and the Dodd-Frank Wall Street Reform and Consumer Protection Act also prohibit loan originators from steering consumers to consummate loans in which the loan originator receives greater compensation for the transaction than the originator would have received in other transactions that the originator offered or could have offered to the consumer, except in limited circumstances. *See* National Consumer Law Center, Mortgage Lending § 6.3.6.3 (2012).

71   *See* Martinez v. Freedom Mortgage Team, Inc., 527 F. Supp. 2d 827 (N.D. Ill. 2007).

72   *See* Smith v. Chrysler Financial Co., L.L.C., 2003 WL 328719 (D.N.J. Jan. 15, 2003).

73   *See* § 8.6.5, *infra*.

74   *See* § 8.6.2, *infra*.

75   Letter from E. Philip A. Simpson, Jr., Vice President, Fed. Reserve Bank of Boston, to the Chief Executive Officer of each state member bank and holding company in the First Federal Reserve District, Clearinghouse No. 49,964 (May 26, 1994); Letter from Deval L. Patrick, Assistant Att'y Gen., Civil Rights Div., Dep't of Justice, to lender association representatives concerning department of justice fair lending enforcement program, Clearinghouse No. 52,064 (Feb. 21, 1995) (overages in and of themselves are not unlawful unless a correlation between higher rates and race comes about as a result of unlawful discrimination).

76   131 S. Ct. 2541 (2011).

77   *See* §§ 4.3.2.4.2, *supra*, § 8.6.2, *infra* (discussing identification of specific policy and causation in discretionary mark-up cases).

78   Coleman v. Gen. Motors Acceptance Corp., 196 F.R.D. 315 (M.D. Tenn. 2000) (settlement agreement), *available on the companion website to this treatise* (related cases can be found at 296 F.3d 443 (6th Cir. 2002) and 220 F.R.D. 64 (M.D. Tenn. 2004)).

Credit,[79] Chrysler Finance Co.,[80] Nissan Motor Acceptance Corp.,[81] Toyota Motor Credit,[82] American Honda Finance Corp.,[83] and several others.[84] A large number of cases were also brought against mortgage lenders.[85] The federal government also sued and settled somewhat similar mortgage lending cases in the 1990s and in 2000.[86]

The Federal Trade Commission (FTC) has used its enforcement authority to pursue mortgage companies based on allegations that their discretionary pricing policies are discriminatory. In 2010 the FTC settled an ECOA lawsuit against Golden Empire Mortgage, Inc., et al.[87] The complaint alleged that the defendants violated ECOA, Regulation B, and the FTC Act by charging Hispanic consumers higher prices for mortgage loans than similarly situated non-white consumers.[88] The settlement included injunctive relief and a $1.5 million judgment.[89] In the same year, the FTC modified a prior fair lending settlement with Gateway Funding Diversified Mortgage Services, L.P., and Gateway Funding Inc.[90] The FTC asserted that Gateway violated ECOA and Regulation B by charging African-American and Hispanic consumers higher prices for mortgage loans than non-Hispanic white consumers and failed to develop an effective fair-lending monitoring program that Gateway had previously agreed to do.[91] The modified order provided injunctive relief, including a requirement that Gateway hire a third-party consultant to perform detailed analyses and annual assessments of its lending practices and limits Gateways' exercise over its discretionary pricing policy until the consultant certifies that an adequate monitoring program is in place.[92] The Federal Deposit Insurance Corporation recently settled a similar action against First Mariner Bank Baltimore.[93]

In 2010 the U.S. Attorney General brought an FHA claim along with an ECOA claim against the lender PrimeLending, one of the United States' twenty largest FHA lenders.[94] The complaint alleged that the lender compensated employees for raising a loan's APR and did not supervise the employees' modifications, resulting in higher loan prices for African Ameri-

---

79 Settlement Agreement, Jones v. Ford Motor Credit Co., 2002 WL 88431 (S.D.N.Y. Jan. 22, 2002), *available on the companion website to this treatise* (related cases can be found at 358 F.3d 205 (2d Cir. 2004), 2005 WL 743213 (S.D.N.Y. Mar. 31, 2005), and 2004 WL 1586412 (S.D.N.Y. July 15, 2004)); *see also* Rodriguez v. Ford Motor Credit Co., 2002 WL 655679 (N.D. Ill. Apr. 19, 2002) (denying class certification).

80 Smith v. Chrysler Financial Co., L.L.C., 2005 WL 2739213 (D.N.J. Oct. 24, 2005) (granting final approval of the settlement agreement after a fairness hearing); Smith v. Chrysler Financial Co., L.L.C., 2003 WL 328719 (D.N.J. Jan. 15, 2003) (denying defendant's motion to dismiss).

   See also www.ecoa-settlement.com for a copy of the settlement agreement and other documents.

81 Cason v. Nissan Motor Acceptance Corp., 212 F.R.D. 518 (M.D. Tenn. 2002).

   The June 2003 settlement and the sixth amended complaint are available on the companion website to this treatise.

82 Baltimore v. Toyota Motor Credit Corp., No. CV 01-05564 (C.D. Cal. Jan. 18, 2006) (settlement agreement), *available on the companion website to this treatise*.

83 Settlement Agreement, Willis v. American Honda Finance Corp., No. 3-02-0490 (M.D. Tenn. Jan. 21, 2005), *available on the companion website to this treatise*.

84 *See, e.g.,* Settlement Agreement, Borlay v. Primus Automotive Financial Servs. Inc., No. 02-CV-382 (M.D. Tenn. Nov. 6, 2006), *available on the companion website to this treatise*; Settlement Agreement, Osborne v. Bank of America, No. 3-02-CV-0364 (M.D. Tenn. Jan. 5, 2005), *available on the companion website to this treatise, related case at* 2003 WL 22025077 (M.D. Tenn. July 15, 2003); Settlement Agreement, Russell v. Bank One, No. 02-CV-365 (M.D. Tenn. Dec. 28, 2004), *available on the companion website to this treatise*; Settlement Agreement, Lee v. WFS Financial Inc., No. 02-570 (M.D. Tenn. Aug. 20, 2004), *available on the companion website to this treatise*; Bass v. Wells Fargo Financial Acceptance Inc., No. 02-CV-383 (M.D. Tenn. filed Apr. 16, 2002) (dismissed pursuant to motion to compel arbitration on April 19, 2003).

85 *See* Ramirez v. GreenPoint Mortgage Funding, Inc., 268 F.R.D. 627 (N.D. Cal. 2010); Guerra v. GMAC L.L.C., 2009 WL 449153 (E.D. Pa. Feb. 20, 2009); Taylor v. Accredited Home Lenders, Inc., 580 F. Supp. 2d 1062 (S.D. Cal. 2008); Miller v. Countrywide Bank, 571 F. Supp. 2d 251 (D. Mass. 2008); Ware v. Indymac Bank, 534 F. Supp. 2d 835 (N.D. Ill. 2008); Garcia v. Countrywide Financial Corp., No. 07-1161 (C.D. Cal. Jan. 15, 2008), *available at* www.nclc.org/ unreported; Newman v. Apex Financial Group, 2008 WL 130924 (N.D. Ill. Jan. 11, 2008); Martinez v. Freedom Mortgage Team, 527 F. Supp. 2d 827 (N.D. Ill. 2007); Jackson v. Novastar Mortgage, Inc., 2007 WL 4568976 (W.D. Tenn. Dec. 20, 2007); *see also* appx. G, *infra* (sample complaints); *cf.* Tribett v. BNC Mortgage, 2008 WL 162755 (N.D. Ill. Jan. 17, 2008) (consumer can refile complaint with more specificity).

86 *See* Settlement Agreement and Order, United States v. Delta Funding Corp., No. CV 00 1872 (E.D.N.Y. Mar. 30, 2000), *available on the companion website to this treatise*; Complaint and Settlement Agreement, United States v. Fleet Mortgage Corp., No. CV962279 (E.D.N.Y. 1996), *available on the companion website to this treatise*; Settlement Agreement and Order, United States v. Long Beach Mortgage Co., No. CV 96-6159 (C.D. Cal. Sept. 5, 1996), *available*

on the companion website to this treatise; Complaint and Settlement Agreement, United States v. Huntington Mortgage Co., No. 1:95CV2211 (N.D. Ohio 1995), *available on the companion website to this treatise*.

87 Stipulated Final Judgment and Order, Fed. Trade Comm'n v. Golden Empire Mortgage, Inc., No. CV09-03227 (C.D. Cal. Sept. 24, 2010), *available at* www.ftc.gov/os/caselist/0623061/index.shtm; Letter from Fed. Trade Comm'n to Sandra Braunstein, Director, Div. of Consumers & Cmty. Affairs (Jan. 26, 2011), *available at* www.ftc.gov/os/2011/02/P064808frb.pdf (report to the Federal Reserve Board).

88 Stipulated Final Judgment and Order, Fed. Trade Comm'n v. Golden Empire Mortgage, Inc., No. CV09-03227 (C.D. Cal. Sept. 24, 2010), *available at* www.ftc.gov/os/caselist/0623061/index.shtm.

89 *Id.*

90 Modified Stipulated Final Judgment and Order, Fed. Trade Comm'n v. Gateway Funding Diversified Mortgage Servs., Ltd. P'ship, No. 08-5805 (E.D. Pa. Jan. 22, 2010), *available at* www.ftc.gov/os/caselist/0623063/index.shtm.

91 *Id.*

92 *Id.*

93 *In re* First Mariner Bank Balt., Md., FDIC-07-285b & FDIC-08-358k (Fed. Deposit Ins. Corp. Mar. 22, 2009), *available at* www.fdic.gov/bank/individual/enforcement/2009-04-18.pdf (order to cease and desist, order for restitution, and order to pay).

94 Complaint, United States v. PrimeLending, No. 3:10-cv-02494-P (N.D. Tex. Dec. 8, 2010), *available at* www.justice.gov/crt/about/hce/documents/casesummary.php#pl.

can borrowers when compared with similarly situated white buyers.[95]

In 2010 the Department of Justice simultaneously filed a complaint and proposed consent order alleging that AIG Federal Savings Bank and Wilmington Finance, Inc., charged higher fees to African-American borrowers on wholesale mortgage loans, and discriminated on the basis of race by failing to monitor broker fee pricing decisions by wholesale mortgage brokers.[96] The case was referred by the Office of Thrift Supervision in 2007.[97] The proposed consent order requires the defendants to pay between $6.1 and $7.1 million in damages to aggrieved borrowers and support for credit counseling and financial literacy programs.[98] It also provides for injunctive relief in the event that the defendants reenter the wholesale mortgage business.

In 2011, the Department of Justice filed the largest fair lending lawsuit in its history.[99] The case asserted that Countrywide discriminated against over 200,000 Hispanic and African-American borrowers between 2004 and 2008 by charging those borrowers higher interest rates, fees, and costs for mortgage loans than non-Hispanic white borrowers and steering them into subprime loans, in violation of the ECOA and the Fair Housing Act.[100] The Department of Justice also charged that Countrywide violated the ECOA on the basis of marital status by encouraging non-applicant spouses to give up all their rights and interest in the mortgaged property.[101] The consent order requires Countrywide to pay $335 million into a settlement fund and retain a settlement administrator who will first distribute the funds to the victims of Countrywide's discriminatory practices.[102] Remaining funds, if any, will be distributed to credit and housing counseling organizations in communities

where significant discrimination against African-American and Hispanic borrowers have occurred.[103]

On July 12, 2012, the United States filed a complaint against and simultaneous proposed consent order with Wells Fargo, alleging that it discriminated against more than 34,000 African-American and Hispanic borrowers in its residential mortgage lending operation by giving them subprime, rather than prime, loans and charging them higher fees and costs.[104] The complaint alleged that, between 2004 and 2009, Wells Fargo's policies allowed employees to make decisions about the type of loan product offered and the loan price in a manner disconnected from objective criteria, that these policies set up financial incentives for employees and mortgage brokers to impose unfavorable terms, and that the policies lacked safeguards to prevent and remedy racial and ethnic disparities. In agreeing to the consent order, Wells Fargo did not admit any of the allegations in the complaint but agreed to pay at least $125 million to compensate borrowers who were allegedly aggrieved, to expend $50 million to provide down-payment assistance to low-income borrowers in metro areas hardest hit by the subprime loan foreclosure crisis, and to maintain policies (implemented after the events alleged in the complaint) that disconnect compensation from a loan's terms and conditions.

8.6.3　Elements of the Discrimination Claim: Disparate Impact Versus Disparate Treatment

Dealers, brokers, and others who mark up loans on a subjective basis may discriminate against those belonging to protected classes, setting up a basic disparate treatment claim under the ECOA, the Fair Housing Act (FHA), and the federal Civil Rights statutes. With evidence of disparate treatment, the discrimination case should be a strong one because there is no defense that the higher rate was based upon risk. The risk-based rate has already been established, and the party marking up that rate shares none of the risk of default.[105]

However, most discrimination litigation in this area has been brought against the lender that established the pricing policy, and the legal theory is not disparate treatment but the pricing policy's disparate impact on protected classes.[106]

Section 4.3, *supra*, details the elements of a disparate impact case generally. This section summarizes the elements as applied

---

95　*Id.* The Attorney General filed a proposed consent order along with the complaint that provides that, at the time of the filing, PrimeLending had already revised its pricing policy and, under the order, would agree to continue to implement policies and procedures to ensure that it priced its loans in a nondiscriminatory manner. Proposed Consent Order at 6–7, United States v. PrimeLending, No. 3:10-cv-02494-P (N.D. Tex. Dec. 8, 2010).

96　Complaint, United States v. AIG Fed. Sav. Bank, No. 1:99-mc-09999 (D. Del. Mar. 4, 2010), *available at* www.justice.gov/crt/housing/documents/aigcomp.pdf.

　　In 2010 the Department of Justice established a new unit within its Civil Rights Division to focus exclusively on unfair lending practices. Previously such practices were investigated by the Housing and Civil Enforcement section of the Civil Rights Division.

97　*Id.*

98　Consent Order, United States v. AIG Fed. Savs. Bank, Case No. 1:99-mc-09999 (D. Del. Mar. 4, 2010).

99　Complaint, United States v. Countrywide Financial Corp., Countrywide Home Loans, Inc. & Countrywide Bank, No. cv-11-10540 (C.D. Cal. Dec. 21, 2011), *available at* www.justice.gov/crt/about/hce/caselist.php.

100　*Id.*

101　*Id.*

102　Consent Order, United States v. Countrywide Financial Corp., Countrywide Home Loans, Inc. & Countrywide Bank, No.cv-11-10540 (C.D. Cal. Dec. 21, 2011), *available at* www.justice.gov/crt/about/hce/caselist.php.

103　*Id.*

104　United States v. Wells Fargo Bank, N.A., 891 F. Supp. 2d 143 (D.D.C. 2012).

105　*See, e.g.,* United States v. Pacifico Ford (E.D. Pa. Aug. 21, 2007), *available at* www.usdoj.gov *and on the companion website to this treatise* (settlement involving car dealer's discriminatory mark-ups); United States v. Springfield Ford, Inc. (E.D. Pa. Aug. 21, 2007), *available at* www.usdoj.gov *and on the companion website to this treatise* (same).

106　*See, e.g.,* Garcia v. Countrywide Financial Corp., No. 07-1161 (C.D. Cal. Jan. 15, 2008) (while allowing disparate impact claim to go forward, dismissing disparate treatment claim), *available at* www.nclc.org/unreported.

to a disparate impact claim against a lender for a discretionary mark-up pricing policy. The ECOA and FHA, but probably not the federal Civil Rights Acts, allow claims for disparate impact.[107]

The consumer must identify the specific policy, show the disparate impact of that policy on a protected group, and show a causal link between the policy and the disparate impact.[108] Once the consumer makes a prima facie showing, the defendant bears the burden of rebutting the case by showing a business necessity for its practice.[109] The burden then shifts back to the consumer to show the availability of a less discriminatory alternative.[110] Under the ECOA the lender's intent is irrelevant.[111] Showing lender intent may be useful in a FHA case.[112] Even if proving discriminatory impact does not require proof of either the defendant's intent or knowledge, proof that defendant should have known or at least should have been suspicious of the disparity may help sway the fact finder in plaintiffs' favor.

Issues may arise as to whether an assignee is liable for the credit practices of its assignor. But the ECOA defines a creditor to include a person who participates in the decision to extend credit, clearly applying to assignees who establish a buy or par rate.[113]

8.6.4 Identification of a Specific Policy and Causation

Identification of the specific policy is rarely an issue in discretionary mark-up cases. Courts find sufficient identification when plaintiffs allege a discretionary pricing policy that authorizes the use of subjective criteria to mark up standard interest rates, irrespective of the creditworthiness of the borrower.[114]

A number of lenders have argued that the consumer must identify a specific, objective lender policy that leads to differential rates. It is not enough to point to a lender policy that leaves pricing to the subjective discretion of others. Courts have little trouble rejecting this argument.[115] However, courts may be more skeptical that allowing for discretion constitutes a specific policy in the wake of language used by the Supreme Court in *Wal-Mart v. Dukes*.[116] In *Wal-Mart*, the Supreme Court denied class certification in an employment discrimination case in which plaintiffs alleged that Wal-Mart's policy of giving local supervisors discretion over pay and promotion decisions produced a disparate impact. The Supreme Court found that the proposed class (which included all female employees of Wal-Mart stores nationwide) did not satisfy the commonality requirement of Federal Rule of Civil Procedure 23 because plaintiffs could not identify "a common mode of exercising discretion that pervades the entire company."[117] The Court noted that, even in *Watson*, "merely proving that the discretionary system has produced a racial or sexual disparity *is not enough*" and that "the plaintiff must begin by identifying the specific employment practice that is challenged."[118] The Court also commented that "[o]n its face, [allowing discretion by local supervisors] is just the opposite of a uniform employment practice that would provide the commonality needed for a class action."[119]

The practices complained of in *Wal-Mart* included both pay and promotion decisions that were made based on a number of objective and subjective criteria.[120] Cases challenging discretionary credit mark-ups should be distinguished from *Wal-Mart*

---

107 *See* § 4.3.1, *supra*.

108 *See* § 4.3.2.1, *supra*; *see also* Robinson v. Metro-North Commuter R.R. Co., 267 F.3d 147, 160 (2d Cir. 2001); Ramirez v. GreenPoint Mortgage Funding, Inc., 268 F.R.D. 627 (N.D. Cal. 2010); Guerra v. GMAC L.L.C., 2009 WL 449153 (E.D. Pa. Feb. 20, 2009); Taylor v. Accredited Home Lenders, Inc., 580 F. Supp. 2d 1062 (S.D. Cal. 2008); Miller v. Countrywide Bank, 571 F. Supp. 2d 251 (D. Mass. 2008); Garcia v. Countrywide Financial Corp., No. 07-1161 (C.D. Cal. Jan. 15, 2008), *available at* www.nclc.org/unreported; Smith v. Chrysler Financial Co., L.L.C., 2003 WL 328719 (D.N.J. Jan. 15, 2003); Jones v. Ford Motor Credit Co., 2002 WL 88431 (S.D.N.Y. Jan. 22, 2002); Coleman v. Gen. Motors Acceptance Corp., 196 F.R.D. 315 (M.D. Tenn. 2000).

109 *See* § 4.3.2.5, *supra*; *see also* Smith v. Chrysler Financial Co., L.L.C., 2003 WL 328719 (D.N.J. Jan. 15, 2003); Jones v. Ford Motor Credit Co., 2002 WL 88431 (S.D.N.Y. Jan. 22, 2002).

110 *See* § 4.3.2.6, *supra*; *see also* Smith v. Chrysler Financial Co., L.L.C., 2003 WL 328719 (D.N.J. Jan. 15, 2003); Jones v. Ford Motor Credit Co., 2002 WL 88431 (S.D.N.Y. Jan. 22, 2002).

111 *See* Smith v. Chrysler Financial Co., L.L.C., 2003 WL 328719 (D.N.J. Jan. 15, 2003).

112 *See* § 4.3.2.3, *supra*.

113 15 U.S.C. § 1691a(e); *see also* Miller v. Countrywide Bank, 571 F. Supp. 2d 251 (D. Mass. 2008); Smith v. Chrysler Financial Co., L.L.C., 2003 WL 328719 (D.N.J. Jan. 15, 2003); Jones v. Ford Motor Credit Co., 2002 WL 88431 (S.D.N.Y. Jan. 22, 2002); Coleman v. Gen. Motors Acceptance Corp., 196 F.R.D. 315 (M.D. Tenn. 2000).

114 Barrett v. H & R Block, Inc., 652 F. Supp. 2d 104 (D. Mass. 2009); Guerra v. GMAC L.L.C., 2009 WL 449153 (E.D. Pa. Feb. 20, 2009); Steele v. GE Money Bank, 2009 WL 393860 (N.D. Ill. Feb. 17, 2009); Ramirez v. GreenPoint Mortgage Funding, Inc., 633 F. Supp. 2d 922 (N.D. Cal. 2008); Taylor v. Accredited Home Lenders, Inc., 580 F. Supp. 2d 1062 (S.D. Cal. 2008); Miller v. Countrywide Bank, 571 F. Supp. 2d 251 (D. Mass. 2008); Garcia v. Countrywide Financial Corp., Civ. Action No. 07-1161 (C.D. Cal. Jan. 15, 2008), *available at* www.nclc.org/unreported; Smith v. Chrysler Financial Co., 2003 WL 328719 (D.N.J. Jan. 15, 2003); Jones v. Ford Motor Credit Co., 2002 WL 88431 (S.D.N.Y. Jan. 22, 2002).

115 Watson v. Fort Worth Bank & Trust, 487 U.S. 977, 108 S. Ct. 2777, 101 L. Ed. 2d 827 (1988); Guerra v. GMAC L.L.C., 2009 WL 449153 (E.D. Pa. Feb. 20, 2009); Ramirez v. GreenPoint Mortgage Funding, Inc., 633 F. Supp. 2d 922 (N.D. Cal. 2008); Taylor v. Accredited Home Lenders, Inc., 580 F. Supp. 2d 1062 (S.D. Cal. 2008); Miller v. Countrywide Bank, 571 F. Supp. 2d 251 (D. Mass. 2008); Smith v. Chrysler Financial Co., L.L.C., 2003 WL 328719 (D.N.J. Jan. 15, 2003); Coleman v. Gen. Motors Acceptance Corp., 196 F.R.D. 315 (M.D. Tenn. 2000); Buycks-Robertson v. Citibank Fed. Sav. Bank, 162 F.R.D. 322 (N.D. Ill. 1995).

116 131 S. Ct. 2541 (2011).

117 Wal-Mart Stores, Inc. v. Dukes, 131 S. Ct. 2541, 2554–55 (2011).

118 *Id.* at 2555 (2011) (emphasis in original) (citing Watson v. Fort Worth Bank & Trust, 487 U.S. 977, 994 (1988)).

119 Wal-Mart Stores, Inc. v. Dukes, 131 S. Ct. 2541, 2554 (2011).

120 *Id.* at 2547.

because all the transactions in a credit mark-up case are of the same type and because the factors relevant to each borrower's creditworthiness are objective, measurable, and were in fact used to set the base price before the discretionary mark-up was applied.[121] Nevertheless, a number of district courts have seized on *Wal-Mart* to deny or revoke class certification in cases alleging disparate impact as a result of policies that allow discretionary markups in credit decisions.[122]

Another defense is that the consumer has not identified a policy because there is no policy—the lender is simply permitting parties to negotiate rates, and this is just normal market activity of supply and demand. This defense has been called the "market forces" defense, and it has been soundly rejected by the courts.[123] It would allow companies to avoid discrimination law by keeping the credit pricing decisions subjective. "[S]ubjective criteria, unrelated to creditworthiness, should play *no* part in determining a potential borrower's eligibility for credit."[124]

Lenders may also challenge the consumer's showing of causation, that is, that the identified pricing policy *causes* the disparate impact of higher mark ups for protected classes. Courts have generally not had difficulty seeing the cause and effect relationship between lenders allowing brokers and dealers to use their subjective discretion and the fact that this subjective discretion creates a disparate impact on a protected class.[125]

8.6.5 Statistical Proof of the Discriminatory Impact

The plaintiff has the burden of showing that the identified pricing policy, despite being facially neutral, has a disparate impact on a protected class. To do so requires proof that the protected class pays more in upcharges than other borrowers. The consumer must show "statistical evidence of a kind and degree sufficient to show that the practice in question has caused" the assessment of the higher finance charge mark-up on plaintiffs "because of their membership in a protected group."[126]

In practice, this burden of proof requires the plaintiffs to hire an expert to analyze the lender's files and to produce a detailed report proving the disparate impact statistically by multiple regression analysis.[127] Examples of such reports are found on the companion website to this treatise.[128] For example, in a case against Nissan Motor Acceptance, the plaintiffs' experts found that 71.8% of African-American borrowers were charged a mark-up, compared to only 46.7% of white borrowers. On average, African-American borrowers paid more than twice the amount of discretionary mark-up charged to whites.[129]

While a thorough statistical analysis will be required to prevail on the merits, the consumer can survive a motion to dismiss with far less evidence. Then the consumer can use discovery to obtain information from the lender's files and this data can serve as the basis for the more thorough expert analysis. Courts have allowed cases to survive a motion to dismiss based upon an allegation that the practice has a disparate impact, with supporting allegations of a disparate impact

---

121 *See, e.g.*, Barrett v. H & R Block, Inc., No. 08-10157-RWZ, 2011 WL 1100105 (D. Mass. Mar. 21, 2011) (plaintiffs assert that the discretionary pricing strategy they challenge was executed uniformly, and its adverse effects were felt in the same way by plaintiffs and all class members).

    This decision was issued before *Wal-Mart* but discusses commonality in a way that arguably anticipates and meets the *Wal-Mart* standard. The defendant's motion to decertify the class in light of *Wal-Mart* was pending at the time of this printing.

122 *In re* Countrywide Financial Mortgage Lending Practices Litig., 08-MD-1974, 2011 WL 4862174 (W.D. Ky. Oct. 13, 2011); *In re* Wells Fargo Residential Mortgage Lending Discrimination Litig., 2011 WL 3903117 (N.D. Cal. Sept. 6, 2011); Rodriguez v. Nat'l City Bank, 277 F.R.D. 148 (E.D. Pa. 2011).

123 Miller v. Countrywide Bank, 571 F. Supp. 2d 251 (D. Mass. 2008); *see also* Garcia v. Countrywide Financial Corp., No. 07-1161 (C.D. Cal. Jan. 15, 2008), *available at* www.nclc.org/unreported; Smith v. Chrysler Financial Co., L.L.C., 2003 WL 328719 (D.N.J. Jan. 15, 2003); Jones v. Ford Motor Credit Co., 2002 WL 1334812 (S.D.N.Y. June 17, 2002).

124 Miller v. Countrywide Bank, 571 F. Supp. 2d 251, 258 (D. Mass. 2008).

125 Guerra v. GMAC L.L.C., 2009 WL 449153 (E.D. Pa. Feb. 20, 2009); Steele v. GE Money Bank, 2009 WL 393860 (N.D. Ill. Feb. 17, 2009); Taylor v. Accredited Home Lenders, Inc., 580 F. Supp. 2d 1062 (S.D. Cal. 2008); Miller v. Countrywide Bank, 571 F. Supp. 2d 251 (D. Mass. 2008); Garcia v. Countrywide Financial Corp., Civ. Action No. 07-1161 (C.D. Cal. Jan. 15, 2008), *available at* www.nclc.org/unreported.

126 Watson v. Fort Worth Bank & Trust, 487 U.S. 977, 994, 108 S. Ct. 2777, 101 L. Ed. 2d 827 (1988). *See also* Guerra v. GMAC L.L.C., 2009 WL 449153 (E.D. Pa. Feb. 20, 2009); Steele v. GE Money Bank, 2009 WL 393860 (N.D. Ill. Feb. 17, 2009); *Cf.* Coleman v. Gen. Motors Acceptance Corp., 196 F.R.D. 315 (M.D. Tenn. 2000), *vacated by* 296 F.3d 443 (6th Cir. 2002).

127 *See, e.g.*, Ramirez v. GreenPoint Mortgage Funding, Inc., 268 F.R.D. 627, 641 (N.D. Cal. 2010) ("The relevant evidence, as with most disparate impact cases, will focus on statistical disparities, rather than specific incidents, and on competing explanations for those disparities.") (internal quotations omitted); *In re* Wells Fargo Residential Mortgage Lending Discrimination Litig., 2010 WL 4791687 (N.D. Cal. Nov. 18, 2010) ("[A]ccording to Wells Fargo, the particular loan transactions for each plaintiff must be examined, and each plaintiff must establish that he or she paid more than a similarly situated non-minority borrower. The Court disagrees. Proof of disparate impact is based not on an examination of individual claims, but on a statistical analysis of the class as a whole.") (internal quotations omitted).

128 Report of Howell E. Jackson, in *In re* Wells Fargo Lending Practices Litig., No. 3:08-md-01930 (N.D. Cal.), *available on the companion website to this treatise*; Report of Professor Ian Ayres, Willis v. American Honda Finance Corp., No. 3-02-0490 (M.D. Tenn. June 30, 2004), *available on the companion website to this treatise*; Report of Professor Mark Cohen, Willis v. American Honda Finance Corp., No. 3-02-0490 (M.D. Tenn. June 30, 2004), *available on the companion website to this treatise*; Report of Professor Mark Cohen, Jones v. Ford Motor Credit Co., No. 00 Civ. 8330 (LMM) (S.D.N.Y. Jan. 9, 2004), *available on the companion website to this treatise*; Report of Professor Mark Cohen, Cason v. Nissan Motor Acceptance Corp., No. 3-98-0223 (M.D. Tenn. May 17, 2001), *available on the companion website to this treatise*.

129 Report of Professor Mark Cohen, Cason v. Nissan Motor Acceptance Corp., No. 3-98-0223 (M.D. Tenn. May 17, 2001), *available on the companion website to this treatise*.

found in general studies of groups of lenders, data from a different lender, or Home Mortgage Disclosure Act (HMDA) data or other partial analysis of the particular defendant's customers.[130] In one case, support for the allegation was found in evidence that a lender used brokers in minority areas and its own loan officers in white communities and that yield spread premiums were higher among brokers than loan officers.[131]

8.6.6 Business Necessity and a Less Discriminatory Alternative

When a consumer in a discretionary mark-up case shows that the pricing policy has a disparate impact on a protected class, the lender must present a business necessity for the practice.[132] The fact that the protected class on average includes higher credit risks cannot be a justification because the upcharge is not based upon risk.[133] Lenders may claim a business necessity that they must provide incentives to dealers or brokers so that these third parties will steer business to the lender, not some other lender. But case law indicates that the business necessity should relate to creditworthiness.[134]

In any event, a claim of business necessity can be overcome if the plaintiff shows a less discriminatory alternative. Such an alternative can easily be developed. For example, the lender could instead provide compensation to brokers and dealers in a fixed amount for all customers; the upcharge would not vary due to the broker or dealer's discretion. All borrowers would receive the same rate as all others who are in the same objective rate classification.

8.7 Discrimination in Pricing of Property, Services

8.7.1 Discrimination Laws Apply to Pricing of Property, Services

Although this treatise focuses on credit discrimination, discrimination in the pricing of property and services is a closely related practice that may be challenged under the ECOA, the Fair Housing Act, and the federal Civil Rights Acts. The Fair Housing Act has two major provisions, one dealing with discrimination in financing and the other with discrimination in the sale or rental of a dwelling.[135] As long as a transaction is within the scope of the Fair Housing Act, any form of discrimination concerning purchase price, availability, or leasing terms of a dwelling should be covered under at least one of the two major Fair Housing Act provisions.[136]

Discrimination as to purchase price and other aspects of any sales or lease transaction, whether realty, personalty, or service, is also covered by the federal Civil Rights Acts—as long as the prohibited basis of the discrimination is race or ethnic origin.[137] The Civil Rights Acts' prohibition on price discrimination will apply whether or not credit is involved.[138] On the other hand, case law to date indicates that the Civil Rights Acts allow claims for disparate treatment, but not disparate impact.[139]

Price discrimination also violates the ECOA if the discrimination involves both credit and a creditor. The statute applies to every aspect of the applicant's dealings with a creditor regarding an extension of credit.[140] For example, the ECOA should apply when financing charges are hidden in the cash price and when the cash price is higher for members of a protected class than for other purchasers.

8.7.2 Types of Price Discrimination

One example of illegal price discrimination is when identical goods are sold at different stores owned by the same merchant at different prices, with the higher priced goods being sold in minority neighborhoods. There can also be differences in the goods' quality and the store's policies as to refunds, exchanges, and warranties.[141] The merchant will have to justify this different treatment by increased costs of business in the minority neighborhood. If the ECOA does not apply, the action will have to be brought under the federal Civil Rights Acts, requiring the

---

130   *See* Guerra v. GMAC L.L.C., 2009 WL 449153 (E.D. Pa. Feb. 20, 2009); Steele v. GE Money Bank, 2009 WL 393860 (N.D. Ill. Feb. 17, 2009); Ramirez v. GreenPoint Mortgage Funding, Inc., 633 F. Supp. 2d 922 (N.D. Cal. 2008); Taylor v. Accredited Home Lenders, Inc., 580 F. Supp. 2d 1062 (S.D. Cal. 2008); Miller v. Countrywide Bank, 571 F. Supp. 2d 251 (D. Mass. 2008); Garcia v. Countrywide Financial Corp., No. 07-1161 (C.D. Cal. Jan. 15, 2008), *available at* www.nclc.org/unreported; Newman v. Apex, 2008 WL 130924 (N.D. Ill. Jan. 11, 2008); *see also* Palmer v. Homecomings Financial, L.L.C., 677 F. Supp. 2d 233 (D.D.C. 2010). *But see* U.S. v. Nara Bank, 2010 WL 2766992 (C.D. Cal. May 28, 2010) (finding that no plausible claim for disparate impact was asserted when plaintiff submitted statistics showing that approximately half the borrowers who were members of the protected class paid higher prices but submitted no statistics regarding the prices paid by the other half of borrowers in the protected class).

131   *See* Miller v. Countrywide Bank, 571 F. Supp. 2d 251 (D. Mass. 2008).

132   Ramirez v. GreenPoint Mortgage Funding, Inc., 268 F.R.D. 627, 641 (N.D. Cal. 2010) ("GreenPoint can defend against Plaintiffs' case in two ways: by demonstrating that its discretionary policy had a valid business justification, and by challenging the statistical basis for Plaintiffs' claim . . . In either case, the defense applies across the class."); *see* Smith v. Chrysler Financial Co., L.L.C., 2003 WL 328719 (D.N.J. Jan. 15, 2003).

133   *See* Garcia v. Countrywide Financial Corp., No. 07-1161 (C.D. Cal. Jan. 15, 2008), *available at* www.nclc.org/unreported.

134   *See* § 4.3.2.5, *supra*.

135   42 U.S.C. §§ 3604, 3605; *see also* Subpart B—Discriminatory Housing Practices, 24 C.F.R. pt. 100.

136   *See* § 2.3, *supra*; *see also* Honorable v. Easy Life Real Estate System, 100 F. Supp. 2d 885 (N.D. Ill. 2000).

137   42 U.S.C. §§ 1981, 1982; *see* § 2.4, *supra*.

138   *Cf.* Williams v. Sutherlin, No. 1-96-CV-1215-RCF (N.D. Ga. 1997) (third amended complaint), *available on the companion website to this treatise*.

139   *See* § 4.3.1, *supra*.

140   Reg. B, 12 C.F.R. § 1002.2(m) [§ 202.2(m)]; *see* § 2.2, *supra*.

141   *See generally* David Dante Trott, *Ghettoes Revisited: Antimarkets, Consumption, and Empowerment*, 66 Brook. L. Rev. 1 (2000).

consumer to prove disparate treatment, and not just a disparate impact, based on race.

A similar type of price discrimination occurs in the sale of homes in minority communities, where prices may be higher than whites pay for comparable housing. Several federal Civil Rights and Fair Housing Acts cases have used an exploitation theory to find violations when real estate companies take advantage of a dual housing market to demand prices and terms from members of a protected class unreasonably in excess of those available to whites.[142]

Another form of price discrimination is when prices are reached by negotiation and the result is that protected classes on average pay more than other buyers. Academic studies of car dealership sales, using paired testers with standardized bargaining strategies, show that African Americans are charged more than whites, even when all other differences among the testers were controlled.[143] The studies found significant differences not only in the final price negotiated but even in the initial price offered by the dealership.

The studies' author posited an explanation that dealers were looking for "sucker sales," and that dealers had the biased view such suckers are more likely to be found among minorities.[144] The author has also suggested other grounds for merchant discrimination.[145] One is that merchants wish to discourage minorities from visiting the dealer's place of business, for fear of loss of business among white customers. Another is that the seller simply enjoys disadvantaging a particular group. Sellers might also feel, because of racial discrimination by others, that minorities have fewer marketplace choices than whites, and thus have to pay more.[146]

That negotiated pricing discriminates against minorities is consistent with the discussion in § 8.6, *supra*, as to a disparate impact when a lender's pricing policy gives dealers and brokers discretion to mark up finance charges. The difference is that, in the automobile finance cases, the lender sets a buy rate and the dealer negotiates that rate up. In automobile sales, the manufacturer sets a suggested retail price, and car purchasers attempt to negotiate that price down.

Automobile sales discrimination is further complicated because a vehicle's sale price is only one aspect of a transaction. Part of the price often involves a credit for a trade-in, extra charges for options and, of course, financing charges. A key question is whether the dealer discriminates on the basis of race as to the complete transaction's cost to the consumer. For example, one class action alleged that the defendant automobile dealership chain, on average, made double the profit on its African-American customers as it made on its white customers for vehicle purchases, leases, and related services.[147]

---

142 *See* Clark v. Universal Builders, Inc., 706 F.2d 204 (7th Cir. 1983); Clark v. Universal Builders, 501 F.2d 324 (7th Cir. 1974); Honorable v. Easy Life Real Estate System, 100 F. Supp. 2d 885 (N.D. Ill. 2000).

143 Ian Ayres, *Further Evidence of Discrimination in New Car Negotiations and Estimates of Its Cause*, 94 Mich. L. Rev. 109 (1995); Ian Ayres, *Fair Driving: Gender and Race Discrimination in Retail Car Negotiations*, 104 Harv. L. Rev. 817 (1991).

144 Ian Ayres, *Fair Driving: Gender and Race Discrimination in Retail Car Negotiations*, 104 Harv. L. Rev. 817 (1991).

145 *See* Ian Ayres, Pervasive Prejudice?: Unconventional Evidence of Race and Gender Discrimination (2001); *see* K.G. Jan Pillai & Mark Tulloss, Book Review, *Racial and Gender Discrimination at*

the Cash Counter, 2003 Mich. St. DCL L. Rev 507.

146 *See generally* David Dante Trott, *Ghettoes Revisited: Antimarkets, Consumption, and Empowerment*, 66 Brook. L. Rev. 1 (2000); *see also* Jim Campen, Borrowing Trouble? V: Subprime Mortgage Lending in Greater Boston 2000–2003 (Jan. 2005) (study shows that subprime lenders have greatly disproportionate share of total lending in traditionally underserved neighborhoods).

147 Third Amended Complaint, Williams v. Sutherlin, No. 1-96-CV-1215-RCF (N.D. Ga. 1997), *available on the companion website to this treatise*. However, see the discussion of *Wal-Mart v. Dukes* at § 8.6.4, *supra*; allegations of discrimination in multiple aspects of transactions may have a harder time satisfying the requirement to identify a specific policy leading to the disparate impact.

9.1 Introduction

Federal and state credit discrimination statutes cover a wide range of credit activity. Most of the litigation in this area focuses on the application process and other transactions in which consumers are denied credit on a discriminatory basis. This chapter discusses often overlooked claims that might arise *after* credit is granted.

9.2 Types of Discrimination Subsequent to the Granting of Credit

9.2.1 Loan Servicing

The official interpretations of Regulation B give "administration of accounts" as an example of the types of dealings between creditor and applicant that are covered by the ECOA's general prohibition against discrimination.[1] Thus, a creditor cannot discriminate on a prohibited basis concerning ease of payment, willingness to restructure or postpone payments, or providing information about account balances. Under the Fair Housing Act, such discrimination is likely to violate the prohibition on discrimination concerning the terms and conditions of a loan.[2]

9.2.2 Compliance with Warranties, Other Post-Sale Service

To the extent that a credit discrimination statute covers discrimination concerning the sale price of property or a service, it should also cover discrimination concerning compliance with warranties and other post-sale performance. For example, one court found that a car dealer violated the ECOA when it refused to honor a money-back guarantee because the consumer was Hispanic.[3] Post-sale services may also include creditors' treatment of borrowers who want to negotiate with the creditor to "undo" a bad deal.[4]

In addition, discrimination related to post-sales transactions should be covered by the federal Civil Rights Acts—as long as the prohibited basis is race or ethnic origin. Section 1981, which guarantees to all persons the same right as white citizens to "make and enforce" contracts, defines that phrase to extend to the "making, performance, modification, and termination of contracts" as well as the "enjoyment of all benefits, privileges, terms, and conditions of the contractual relationship."[5] This definition makes clear that section 1981 applies to discrimination that occurs after the formation of the contract. Also, section 1982 provides that all citizens shall have the same right to purchase and hold real and personal property. Differences in performance under a warranty would relate to an individual's right to hold the property.[6]

9.2.3 Changes in Account Status

The ECOA's general rule against discrimination applies not only to the initial granting of credit but to any changes in an account, such as raising the credit limit, changing credit terms, renewing the account, or terminating credit. Regulation B states that the general prohibition applies to "revocation, alteration, or termination of credit."[7]

---

1 Official Interpretations of Reg. B [Official Staff Commentary on Reg. B], 12 C.F.R. § 1002.4-1 [§ 202.4-1].

2 42 U.S.C. § 3604(b); *see* 24 C.F.R. §§ 100.110(b), 100.130(a); *see also* Estate of Davis v. Wells Fargo Bank, 633 F.3d 529 (7th Cir. 2011) (finding that successor mortgagor's offer to modify loan is an "extension of credit" under ECOA and mortgagee is therefore an "applicant" and could bring discrimination claim; finding no evidence of discrimination); Rodriguez v. Bear Stearns Cos., Inc., 2009 WL 5184702 (D. Conn. Dec. 22, 2009) (acknowledging as "a close question" whether plaintiffs sufficiently identified, for purposes of making out a disparate impact claim under the FHA, a facially neutral policy of servicing subprime and prime mortgages differently; ultimately granting summary judgment to defendants). *But see* Neblett v. Chase Bank, 2010 WL 3766762 (S.D.N.Y. Sept. 27, 2010) (allegation of "discrimination, and a deliberate act of malicious intent" to damage credit rating, with nothing more, does not state ECOA claim).

   Prohibited practices may include discriminatory servicing and other actions in response to disaster situations. *See, e.g.*, Ass'n of Cmty. Organizations for Reform Now (ACORN), Another Crisis in the Making! How the Subprime Mortgage Industry Is Sandbagging Katrina-Affected Homeowners (Sept. 22, 2005), *available at* www.consumersunion.org/pdf/ACORN-Katrina.pdf.

3 Luera v. Hilton, Clearinghouse No. 48,549 (Ill. Cir. Ct. Jackson Cnty. 1992).

4 *See* Hamilton v. O'Connor Chevrolet, Inc., 2004 WL 1403711 (N.D. Ill. June 23, 2004) (definition of credit transaction in ECOA could encompass consumer's attempts to alter or terminate her credit arrangement even though her conversations with the creditor occurred weeks after the contract was signed).

5 42 U.S.C. § 1981(b).

6 42 U.S.C. § 1982; *see* § 2.4, *supra* (scope of federal Civil Rights Acts).

7 *See, e.g.*, Powell v. Pentagon Fed. Credit Union, 2010 WL 3732195 (N.D. Ill. Sept. 17, 2010) (denying motion to dismiss; plaintiff whose

The prohibition against discrimination in alteration or termination of credit also extends to discrimination based upon good faith exercise of federal Consumer Credit Protection Act rights. Thus, for example, the ECOA prohibits terminating a credit account as a response to a borrower's exercise of rights under the Fair Credit Billing Act.[8] One interesting question is whether requiring a borrower to either agree to an arbitration provision or have his or her account terminated—a common practice by credit card issuers—may violate the ECOA.[9]

Changes in the terms or conditions of a residential real estate-related transaction also fall under the scope of the Fair Housing Act.[10] Thus, that Act should apply as well to changes in credit limits or terms or termination of accounts.

Section 1981 should also apply to discrimination on the basis of race in changes to a contractual relationship, as it specifically covers any "modification" or "termination" of contracts.[11]

9.2.4 Treatment upon Default

When a consumer is delinquent on an account, a creditor can take various steps to collect the amount due or enforce the credit agreement. Such actions are related to the credit transaction and, under the ECOA, creditors may not treat debtors differently post-default on a prohibited basis. Regulation B specifically mentions collection procedures and termination of credit as covered by the ECOA.[12] The official interpretation states that the general rule against discrimination covers the "treatment of delinquent or slow accounts."[13]

One issue that has arisen in the default context is whether the debtor is an "applicant" within the meaning of the statute. In order to establish a prima facie case, a plaintiff alleging an ECOA violation must meet the definition of an "applicant" who is qualified for assistance.[14] For example, in one case a court refused to rule that a plaintiff whose account had been terminated was not an applicant because he was not applying for new credit or for a renewal of credit. Instead, the court held that the plaintiff, as "a person who has received an extension of credit from a creditor," fell within the definition of "applicant." In addition, the court reasoned, "[a]pplying the term 'applicant' as narrowly as Defendant suggests would preclude a plaintiff with an existing account from bringing a claim for the discriminatory revocation of that account."[15]

With respect to the issue of loan modification, the term "applicant" should extend not only to individuals who apply for such modifications but also to those who do not formally make application yet are offered modification proposals. In *Estate of Davis v. Wells Fargo Bank*,[16] the Seventh Circuit reversed the lower court's determination that a homeowner who had been offered a loan modification proposal did not qualify as an "applicant" under the ECOA because she did not allege that she had applied for an extension, renewal, or a continuation of credit within the two-year statute of limitations for ECOA claims. Construing the statute more expansively than the district court "in light of the broad regulatory definitions," the court on appeal decided it was sufficient that the plaintiff alleged that the defendants offered to modify the terms of her existing loan and that, as the recipient of such offer, the plaintiff "received an extension of credit" and thus qualified as an "applicant" under 12 C.F.R. § 1002.2(e) [§ 202.2(e)]. In addition, the court cited 12 C.F.R. § 1002.2(q) [§ 202.2(q)], which defines the term "extend credit and extension of credit" to include "the refinancing or other renewal of credit." Although remand of this claim was ultimately deemed fruitless, since there was no evidence of discrimination found by the lower court on the parallel FHA claim, this case demonstrates that a

---

account was terminated alleged discrimination based on his railroad disability income and assertion of rights); Brinson v. Citigroup, 2010 WL 1539969 (N.D. Ohio Apr. 16, 2010) (plaintiff who alleged that her credit card limit was decreased due to her gender and marital status stated a claim under the ECOA); Hill v. Chase Bank, 2007 WL 4224073 (N.D. Ind. Nov. 26, 2007) (allowing complaint to be amended to include claim for raising the interest rate on plaintiff's credit card account without providing a valid justification).

    Reg. B, 12 C.F.R. § 1002.2(m) [§ 202.2(m)] defines revocation, alteration, or termination of credit as part of a credit transaction, and Reg. B, 12 C.F.R. § 1002.4 [§ 202.4], prohibits discrimination concerning any aspect of a credit transaction.

8 *See, e.g.*, Hill v. Chase Bank, 2007 WL 4224073 (N.D. Ind. Nov. 26, 2007) (allowing amendment of complaint to include claim that, when plaintiff attempted to exercise rights under the Fair Credit Billing Act by requesting a reason for a credit card interest rate increase, defendant discriminated by failing to respond accurately to the inquiry and disregarding the billing dispute).

9 See §§ 3.4.4.2–3.4.4.4, *supra*, as to why refusal to agree to an arbitration agreement may constitute a good faith exercise of federal Consumer Credit Protection Act rights. *See generally* § 11.5.3, *infra* (discussing ECOA and mandatory arbitration).

10 42 U.S.C. § 3604(b); *see* 24 C.F.R. § 100.110(b).

11 42 U.S.C. § 1981(b). *But see* Alexander v. Wash. Gas Light Co., 481 F. Supp. 2d 16 (D.D.C. 2006) (misapplying decision based on pre-1991 statute), *aff'd*, 2006 WL 3798858 (D.C. Cir. Aug. 24, 2006).

12 Reg. B, 12 C.F.R. § 1002.2(m) [§ 202.2(m)].

13 Official Interpretations of Reg. B [[Official Staff Commentary on Reg. B], 12 C.F.R. pt. 1002 [pt. 202], supp. I § 1002.4-1 [§ 202.4-1].

    Conversely, exercising rights upon default, standing alone, does not violate the ECOA. *See, e.g.*, Marine Midland Bank v. Yoruk,

662 N.Y.S.2d 957, 958 (N.Y. App. Div. 1997) (denial of extension of credit to defaulted mortgagor insufficient to sustain counterclaim for violation of ECOA in action to foreclose).

14 *See, e.g.*, Blair v. Bank of America, N.A., 2012 WL 860411 (D. Or. Mar. 13, 2012) (no ECOA claim when, *inter alia*, plaintiff did not allege that he applied for credit but only that he requested a "temporary extension/modification of loan terms" and did not allege that he was "qualified" for credit or that he was denied credit despite being qualified); Sanders v. United States Dep't of Agric., 2008 WL 2097386 (M.D. Tenn. May 16, 2008) (no evidence that plaintiff actually applied for assistance despite offers of credit assistance and a temporary moratorium on payments); Clark v. Capital One Bank, 2008 WL 508440 (D. Idaho Feb. 19, 2008) (no evidence that plaintiff applied for an extension, renewal, or continuation of credit).

15 Powell v. Pentagon Fed. Credit Union, 2010 WL 3732195 (N.D. Ill. Sept. 17, 2010).

16 633 F.3d 529 (7th Cir. 2011); *see also* Watts v. JP Morgan Chase Bank, N.A., 2012 WL 3638537, at *3 (N.D. Cal. Aug. 22, 2012) ("A modification of an existing loan is an extension of credit for ECOA purposes.").

lender or servicer may be held liable for ECOA violations if a homeowner who is offered a modification proposal is able to provide enough evidence of discrimination to present a genuine issue of fact at the summary judgment stage of proceedings.

The Fair Housing Act also prohibits discrimination concerning treatment of defaults. The statute has been interpreted to bar discrimination in mortgage foreclosures on the basis that this constitutes one of the terms or conditions of a loan.[17]

The Civil Rights Acts could also provide a framework for contesting mortgage foreclosures. Section 1981 applies to discrimination on the basis of race or ethnicity that occurs after the formation of the contractual relationship, including in the terms and conditions of the relationship.[18] One case brought pursuant to section 1982 failed, however, because the plaintiffs did not show that the defendant had foreclosed disproportionately against African-American mortgagors who were in default as compared to white mortgagors in default.[19]

Other examples of post-default issues covered by both the ECOA and Fair Housing Act include how soon a creditor turns an account over for collection or cancels a consumer's line of credit, how soon collateral is seized, how willing a creditor is to reinstate the contract,[20] and how soon a creditor institutes a collection lawsuit. It should violate the statutes if collection procedures begin earlier when the consumer in default is a member of a protected group or if repossessions are more readily instituted in African-American neighborhoods.[21] The use of racial or gender-based epithets in collection efforts is another example of discriminatory behavior that violates credit discrimination statutes.[22]

Also actionable is any discrimination as to the method of charging default penalties. For example, it is discriminatory if one group of borrowers loses all down payments and the product purchased while another group pays a smaller penalty for default, and the disparity is based on consideration of factors such as race, sex, and marital status.[23]

9.3 Collection Against Non-Obligated Spouse Under Necessaries, Family Expense Laws

Many states still have laws on the books dating from the early nineteenth century, when it was widely held that a married woman could not contract in her own name.[24] The courts developed a fiction that the wife was acting as her husband's agent. The husband was presumed to have authorized his wife's purchases, unless the creditor was otherwise notified. Essentially, common law placed a unilateral obligation on the husband to support his wife financially. Although courts generally did not choose to set a minimum level of support that husbands were obligated to provide to their wives, they did hold husbands liable to pay creditors for necessities that their wives

---

17 Harper v. Union Sav. Ass'n, 429 F. Supp. 1254 (N.D. Ohio 1977); Lindsey v. Modern American Mortgage Corp., 383 F. Supp. 293 (N.D. Tex. 1974); Webster Bank v. Oakley, 830 A.2d 139 (Conn. 2003) (citing Harper v. Union Sav. Ass'n and Lindsey v. Modern American Mortgage Corp. with approval); *cf.* Little Earth of United Tribes, Inc. v. United States Dep't of Hous. & Urban Dev., 675 F. Supp. 497 (D. Minn. 1987) (applying Fair Housing Act (FHA) to foreclosure decision by HUD but finding no FHA violation), *aff'd*, 878 F.2d 236 (8th Cir. 1989). *But see* Davis v. Wells Fargo Bank, 685 F. Supp. 2d 838 (N.D. Ill. 2010) (allegations that defendants attempted to foreclose and discriminatorily continued to demand repayment of loan and related fees despite knowledge that initial mortgagee defrauded plaintiff do not state a section 3605 claim), *aff'd*, Estate of Davis v. Wells Fargo Bank, 633 F.3d 529 (7th Cir. 2011); Moore v. Fed. Deposit Ins. Corp., 2009 WL 4405538 (N.D. Ill. Nov. 30, 2009) (allegations involving "post-default action," such as repeatedly ignoring requests for information, workout and documentation, do not state a section 3605 claim as plaintiffs were "not attempting to engage in a residential real estate transaction as the term is defined in the FHA").

18 42 U.S.C. § 1981(b); *see* Small v. Mortgage Electronic Reg. Systems, Inc., 2010 WL 3719314 (E.D. Cal. Sept. 16, 2010) (section 1981 protects plaintiffs, but claim that they were denied privileges to engage in a "mortgage workout" pursuant to TARP (12 U.S.C. § 5201) as a result of discrimination was not supported by factual allegations); § 9.2.2, *supra*.

19 Shipley v. First Fed. Sav. & Loan Ass'n, 703 F. Supp. 1122 (D. Del. 1988), *aff'd*, 877 F.2d 57 (3d Cir. 1989) (table).

   Although the bank had brought a high number of foreclosure actions against African Americans, the evidence did not show that it attempted to foreclose "solely, primarily, or in a disproportionate way against [African American] mortgagors." *Id.*, 703 F. Supp. at 1138.

20 *See* Brooks v. O'Connor Chevrolet, 2003 WL 22427795 (N.D. Ill Oct. 23, 2003) (finance company did not discriminate against public assistance recipient by requiring proof of employment for more favorable terms to reinstate defaulted auto loan; court assumed that ECOA applied to reinstatement of loan but ruled against borrower because she had not requested to reinstate the loan).

21 For example, a survey of replevin court filings in Minnesota by the nation's largest rent-to-own company in the early 1990s showed, among other things, that African-American customers were subject to repossession at a higher rate than white customers and that they were in default prior to repossession for a shorter period on average than white customers, even though both groups had similar income levels. *See* § 2.2.2.2.5, *supra*.

22 *See* Complaint and Consent Decree, United States v. Fid. Fed. Bank, No. 02-CV-03906 (E.D.N.Y. July 8, 2002) (United States Department of Justice sued creditor for allegedly collecting debts from Hispanic credit card holders by making threats related to deportation and immigration-related issues), *available at* www.usdoj.gov *and on the companion website to this treatise*; Sharp v. Chartwell Financial Servs. Ltd., 2000 U.S. Dist. LEXIS 3143 (N.D. Ill. Feb. 28, 2000) (a debt collector's use of racial and gender-based epithets during collection phone calls held actionable).

23 United States v. American Future Systems, Inc., 743 F.2d 169 (3d Cir. 1984).

24 *See, e.g.*, Southern N.H. Medical Ctr. v. Hayes, 992 A.2d 596 (N.H. 2010) (discussing origin of spousal necessities doctrine; remanding for fact-finding on circumstances of spousal separation during time non-debtor spouse received medical treatment); *see* National Consumer Law Center, Collection Actions §§ 5.3.4.3, 9.6 (2d ed. 2011 and Supp.) (discussing these laws in detail); National Consumer Law Center, Fair Debt Collection § 8.8 (7th ed. 2011 and Supp.) (same). *See generally* Marie T. Reilly, *In Good Times and in Debt: The Evolution of Marital Agency and the Meaning of Marriage*, 87 Neb. L. Rev. 373 (2008); Mechele Dickerson, *To Love, Honor & (Oh!) Pay: Should Spouses Be Forced to Pay Each Other's Debts?*, 78 B.U. L. Rev. 961 (1998).

purchased, such as food, clothing, and medical services, under the doctrine of necessaries.[25]

In some circumstances, application of these laws may be preempted by the provision of the ECOA which states that laws prohibiting the separate extension of consumer credit to each party in a marriage shall not apply when each party to the marriage voluntarily applies for separate credit from the same creditor.[26] Thus, when a creditor pursues a non-contractually liable spouse utilizing the necessaries statute, the creditor may be violating the ECOA by discriminating in the collection of debts on the basis of marital status.[27]

However, the ECOA and Regulation B allow a creditor to consider state property laws "directly or indirectly affecting creditworthiness."[28] The issue then becomes whether a family expense or necessaries statute affects an individual spouse's creditworthiness.[29] It might be argued that the amount of outstanding inchoate liability for a spouse's debts under a family necessaries statute affects creditworthiness. However, if such debts cannot be collected without violating the ECOA, they arguably should not even be considered in an evaluation of creditworthiness.[30]

If there is a violation of a credit discrimination statute, attempting to collect a debt based solely on a family expense statute may also violate the Fair Debt Collection Practices Act.[31] Courts have found that, because the ECOA prohibits spousal co-signatures in certain circumstances during the application stage of a transaction, debt collectors cannot later try to go after the non-signing spouse as though she had signed as a financially responsible party.[32]

9.4 Credit Reporting

9.4.1 Credit Reporting Requirements of Regulation B

9.4.1.1 Introduction

Regulation B establishes procedures that creditors must follow when they furnish information about certain accounts to credit reporting agencies.[33] These procedures are designed to ensure that each spouse may build a credit history on the basis of accounts which they both use or for which both are contractually liable even if only one spouse is listed as the primary obligor.

9.4.1.2 Scope and Exemptions

Creditors are not required to furnish credit information on its accounts; these requirements apply only to creditors that choose to furnish credit information to credit bureaus or to other creditors.[34] The requirements do not apply to incidental con-

---

25 *See* Mechele Dickerson, *To Love, Honor & (Oh!) Pay: Should Spouses Be Forced to Pay Each Other's Debts?*, 78 B.U. L. Rev. 961 (1998).

Some states have addressed constitutional equal protection challenges to these statutes by either abolishing them or extending them to women. *See, e.g.,* Account Specialists & Credit Collections, Inc. v. Jackman, 970 P. 2d 202 (Okla. Civ. App. 1998); Medical Ctr. Hosp. of Vt. v. Lorrain, 675 A.2d 1326 (Vt. 1996); *see also* Southern N.H. Medical Ctr. v. Hayes, 992 A.2d 596 (N.H. 2010) (dissent argues for abolition of the necessaries doctrine).

26 15 U.S.C. § 1691d(c); *see also* Reg. B, 12 C.F.R. § 1002.11(b) [§ 202.11(b)].

No court has held that the ECOA preempts the doctrine of necessaries. However, one court stated in *dicta* that it believes the doctrine may be preempted. Edwards v. McCormick, 136 F. Supp. 2d 795, 803 n.9 (S.D. Ohio 2001), *class certification denied*, 196 F.R.D. 487 (S.D. Ohio 2001). Ultimately, the plaintiff in *Edwards* successfully used the ECOA preemption theory to reach a settlement in which the hospital agreed to stop collecting debts from one spouse that were owed by the other spouse, unless both spouses had voluntarily entered into a joint account. Edwards v. Hocking Valley Cmty. Hosp., 87 Fed. Appx. 542 (6th Cir. 2004) (enforcing settlement agreement).

A few other state courts have considered the ECOA in the context of the doctrine of necessaries but have not directly confronted the issue because the cases did not involve credit. *See, e.g.,* Bartrom v. Adjustment Bureau, 618 N.E.2d 1, 7 (Ind. 1993); Medical Ctr. Hosp. of Vt. v. Lorrain, 675 A.2d 1326 (Vt. 1996). These courts cited the ECOA for its policy bases and for the congressional studies leading to its enactment.

27 15 U.S.C. § 1691d(c) specifically provides that, "where such a State law is so preempted, each party to the marriage shall be solely responsible for the debt so contracted." An early interpretation of 15 U.S.C. § 1691d(c), which appears in the explanatory material accompanying the original publication of Regulation B, states: "[I]n states that have laws prohibiting separate extensions of credit for married persons, this section [then Reg. B, 12 C.F.R. § 202.8(a)] . . . will not only pre-empt such laws but also any other provision which would hold one spouse responsible for the debts contracted by the other, for example, a family expense statute." 40 Fed. Reg. 49,298, 49,304 (Oct. 22, 1975) (former 12 C.F.R. § 202.8(a) is now 12 C.F.R. § 202.11(b)(ii) [§ 1002.11(b)(ii)]).

28 15 U.S.C. § 1691d(b); Reg. B, 12 C.F.R. § 1002.6(c) [§ 202.6(c)].

29 "Among the state laws that may be considered by a creditor under this section are laws relating to the doctrines of agency between the spouses' 'necessaries'; and 'family expense statutes.' Also included

are principles of community property management, as those principles affect an applicant's creditworthiness." 40 Fed. Reg. 49,298, 49,304 (Oct. 22, 1975).

30 In addition Regulation B, 12 C.F.R. § 1002.5(c)(1), (c)(2) [§ 202.5(c)(1), (c)(2)], seems to preclude such an inquiry, although subsection (c)(3) arguably would permit it.

31 *See* CMRE Financial Servs., Inc. v. Parton, 109 Cal. Rptr. 3d 139 (Cal. Ct. App. 2010) (remanding for consideration of good faith defense under FDCPA when creditor continued collection actions after non-debtor spouse notified creditor of separation and pending divorce from debtor). *But see* Lester E. Cox Medical Ctrs. v. Huntsman, 2003 WL 22004998 (W.D. Mo. Aug. 5, 2003) (husband was liable for wife's medical bill under necessaries doctrine; not Fair Debt Collection Practices Act violation to dun him for bill).

32 *See, e.g.,* Edwards v. McCormick, 136 F. Supp. 2d 795 (S.D. Ohio 2001), *class cert. denied*, 196 F.R.D. 487 (S.D. Ohio 2001); *see also* § 5.6, *supra* (discussion of when the ECOA prohibits requiring spousal co-signatures).

33 Reg. B, 12 C.F.R. § 1002.10 [§ 202.10]; *see* National Consumer Law Center, Fair Credit Reporting (7th ed. 2010 and Supp.) (information on credit reporting issues in general).

34 Official Interpretations of Reg. B [Official Staff Commentary on Reg. B], 12 C.F.R., pt. 1002 [pt. 202], supp. I § 1002.10-1 [§ 202.10-1].

sumer credit[35] or to securities credit.[36]

The official interpretation provides that the spousal credit reporting requirements also do not apply to business credit.[37] This exemption was initially found in Regulation B but was removed when Regulation B was amended following the Women's Business Ownership Act of 1988.[38] However, it was decided that the exemption in the FRB's official staff commentary (now CFPB's official interpretations) would be retained.[39] The supplementary information accompanying the official interpretations explains the belief that no specific regulatory exemption was necessary as a basis for this exclusion because the reporting rule was designed to protect married women who become divorced or widowed from being left without a credit history of their own. Consequently, it "is not relevant to business applicants such as corporations or partnerships, nor is it intended to apply to individual business applicants such as sole proprietors."[40] The exclusion of business credit ignores the possibility that the same problem of a woman's credit invisibility might occur when the "Pop" in a "Mom-and-Pop" small business dies or the marriage dissolves.

9.4.1.3 Creditors Must Furnish Information About Joint Account Holders and Authorized User Spouses

The spousal credit reporting provisions require a creditor that furnishes credit information to a reporting agency to designate any new account to reflect the participation of both spouses if the applicant's spouse is permitted to use the account or is contractually liable on the account.[41] Spouses who are permitted to use an account but who have not agreed to be liable for the debt are called "authorized users."[42]

The official interpretation states that the creditor need not distinguish between accounts on which the spouse is an authorized user versus accounts for which the spouse is a contractually liable party.[43] However, the Fair Credit Reporting Act requires that this distinction be made.[44] The creditor is not required to designate a new account to reflect that the spouse is a guarantor, surety, endorser, or similar party.[45]

When new parties who are spouses assume a loan, the creditor should change the designation of the account to reflect the new obligors and should subsequently report credit information on the account in the new names.[46] A request to change the manner in which information concerning the account is furnished does not alter the legal liability of either spouse and does not require the creditor to change the name under which the account is maintained.[47]

Regulation B does not require any special system of indexing or recordkeeping, but the creditor must be able to report information in the name of each spouse.[48] If a creditor receives a credit inquiry about the wife, the creditor should be able to locate her credit file without asking for the husband's name.[49] In addition, if the creditor furnishes information about the account to a credit reporting agency, the information should be provided so that the reporting agency can gain access to the information in the name of each spouse.[50]

When reporting credit information in response to an inquiry about one spouse, the creditor must furnish the information only in the name of the spouse mentioned in the inquiry.[51] In response to any other request for credit information, the creditor is required to furnish the information in such a way that the credit reporting agency has access to the information in the name of each spouse.[52]

A failure to comply with these credit reporting requirements is not considered a violation of the ECOA when caused by an inadvertent error, but the creditor must correct the error as soon as possible after discovering it.[53] Inadvertent errors include clerical mistakes, calculation errors, computer malfunctions, and printing errors. An error of legal judgment is not an inadvertent error.[54]

9.4.1.4 Interaction with the Fair Credit Reporting Act

The spousal reporting requirements of Regulation B apply only to accounts held or used by spouses. Nevertheless, the official interpretations permit creditors to designate all joint or authorized user accounts to reflect the participation of both parties even if the parties are not married to each other.[55] The

---

35 Reg. B, 12 C.F.R. § 1002.3(c)(2)(vii) [§ 202.3(c)(2)(vii)]; *see also* § 2.2.6.3, *supra*.

36 Reg. B, 12 C.F.R. § 1002.3(b)(2)(vii) [§ 202.3(b)(2)(vii)]; *see also* § 2.2.6.5, *supra*.

37 Official Interpretations of Reg. B [Official Staff Commentary on Reg. B], 12 C.F.R. pt. 1002 [pt. 202], supp. I § 1002.10-1 [§ 202.10-1].

38 54 Fed. Reg. 50,482, 50,484 (Dec. 7, 1989).

39 *Id.*

40 *Id.*; *see also* 54 Fed. Reg. 29,734, 29,737 (July 14, 1989) (in the supplementary information to the proposed rule, the Federal Reserve Board stated it "believes this provision has no applicability in the context of business credit accounts because any credit history reported about such an account pertains to the business entity and not to the individuals owning the business").

41 Reg. B, 12 C.F.R. § 1002.10(a)(1) [§ 202.10(a)(1)].

42 *See* National Consumer Law Center, Truth in Lending § 7.10.2.1 (8th ed. 2012) (discussing authorized users).

43 Official Interpretations of Reg. B [Official Staff Commentary on Reg. B], 12 C.F.R. pt. 1002 [pt. 202], supp. I § 1002.10-3 [§ 202.10-3].

44 *See* § 9.4.1.4, *infra*.

45 Reg. B, 12 C.F.R. § 1002.10(a)(1) [§ 202.10(a)(1)].

46 Official Interpretations of Reg. B [Official Staff Commentary on Reg. B], 12 C.F.R. pt. 1002 [pt. 202], supp. I § 1002.10(a)-1 [§ 202.10(a)-1].

47 *Id.* § 1002.10(a)-2 [§ 202.10(a)-2].

48 *Id.* § 1002.10(a)-1 [§ 202.10(a)-1].

49 *Id.*

50 Reg. B, 12 C.F.R. § 1002.10(b) [§ 202.10(b)].

51 Reg. B, 12 C.F.R. § 1002.10(c) [§ 202.10(c)].

52 Reg. B, 12 C.F.R. § 1002.10(b) [§ 202.10(b)].

53 Reg. B, 12 C.F.R. § 1002.16(c) [§ 202.16(c)].

54 Official Interpretations of Reg. B [Official Staff Commentary on Reg. B], 12 C.F.R. pt. 1002 [pt. 202], supp. I § 1002.16(c)-1 [§ 202.16(c)-1].

55 *Id.* § 1002.10-2 [§ 202.10-2].

extension of this option to authorized users who are not married has presented problems for consumers when the account holder becomes delinquent or goes into default. The authorized users, who are usually not liable on the account, have their credit records impaired due to the reporting of adverse information attributable to the primary account holder. This provision in the official interpretations may conflict with the accuracy requirements of the Fair Credit Reporting Act (FCRA).[56]

Also conflicting with the FCRA is the provision in the official interpretations stating that creditors need not distinguish between accounts on which the spouse is an authorized user versus accounts for which the spouse is contractually liable.[57] The FCRA's accuracy requirements demand that such a distinction be made.[58] In *Melwani v. First USA Bank*,[59] the Second Circuit held that a creditor was not liable for failing to make a distinction between authorized users and joint account holders. However, the case gives no indication whether the plaintiff sought to hold the creditor liable under the FCRA or fulfilled the FCRA's procedural requirements, which require that a dispute initially be filed with a credit reporting agency.[60]

Subsequently, a federal district court held that Regulation B's provision regarding authorized user reporting does not preempt an FCRA claim for inaccurate credit reporting, noting that regulations promulgated by a federal agency cannot override a different federal statute.[61] The court referred to *Melwani* as having "no precedential value," because it was "an unpublished, three-paragraph summary decision from a different circuit without a recitation of the facts or any meaningful analysis of a case brought by a *pro se* litigant."[62]

Another conflict with the FCRA arises when creditors use Regulation B's spousal reporting requirements to justify reporting bankruptcy information for both spouses when only one spouse has filed for bankruptcy,[63] or for both the primary and joint account holder or authorized user when only one of the parties has filed for bankruptcy.[64] This practice may be misleading in that it can create the mistaken impression that the joint account holder or authorized user has filed for bankruptcy when she has not.[65] The practice has been challenged under the FCRA,[66] and a settlement in one of those cases required the credit reporting agencies to establish procedures to avoid this problem.[67] Note that credit reporting agencies are not liable under the ECOA for this practice because they are not "creditors" and it does not constitute marital status discrimination.[68]

9.4.1.5 "Piggybacking"

The credit scoring algorithms developed by Fair Isaac[69] currently factor into the calculation of a credit score, the information about authorized users that creditors submit pursuant to Regulation B. If the account has a positive payment history, it will raise the score of the authorized user.

The phenomenon has led to the practice of "piggybacking," in which account holders with good credit histories "rent" their positive accounts by adding consumers with poor credit histories as authorized users.[70] As a result of piggybacking, Fair Isaac originally had planned to stop including authorized user accounts in its calculation of credit scores.[71] However, it ap-

---

56 *See generally* National Consumer Law Center, Fair Credit Reporting § 4.2 (7th ed. 2010 and Supp.).

57 Official Interpretations of Reg. B [Official Staff Commentary on Reg. B], 12 C.F.R. pt. 1002 [pt. 202], supp. I § 1002.10-3 [§ 202.10-3].

58 *See* Johnson v. MBNA America Bank, 357 F.3d 426 (4th Cir. 2003) (creditor liable for failing to conduct reasonable investigation after consumer disputed with credit reporting agency that she was liable for a default on the account, because she was an authorized user only). *See generally* National Consumer Law Center, Fair Credit Reporting § 5.6.2 (7th ed. 2010 and Supp.).

59 96 Fed. Appx. 755 (2d Cir. 2004).

60 *See* National Consumer Law Center, Fair Credit Reporting § 6.10 (7th ed. 2010 and Supp.).

61 Abbett v. Bank of America, 2006 WL 581193 (M.D. Ala. Mar. 8, 2006).

62 *Id.* at *6 n.14; *see also* Morris v. Trans Union L.L.C., 420 F. Supp. 2d 733 (S.D. Tex. 2006) (Regulation B does not authorize creditors to designate accounts held by one spouse as joint accounts without some indication that the person reported as a joint account holder intended to be responsible for the debt).

63 For examples of this practice affecting spouses, see Smith v. Ohio Sav. Bank, 2008 WL 2704719 (D. Nev. July 7, 2008); Johnson v. Equifax, Inc., 510 F. Supp. 2d 638 (S.D. Ala. 2007); Spector v. Trans Union, 301 F. Supp. 2d 231 (D. Conn. 2004); Spellman v. Experian Info. Solutions, 2002 WL 799876 (D. Nev. Jan. 20, 2002);

Heupel v. Trans Union, 193 F. Supp. 2d 1234 (N.D. Ala. 2002); Trundle v. Homeside Lending, 162 F. Supp. 2d 396 (D. Md. 2001). *See generally* National Consumer Law Center, Fair Credit Reporting § 4.4.6.10.3 (7th ed. 2010 and Supp.).

64 *See, e.g.*, Dickens v. Trans Union, 18 Fed. Appx. 315 (6th Cir. 2001).

65 Spellman v. Experian Info. Solutions, 2002 WL 799876 (D. Nev. Jan. 20, 2002).
    Among other damaging aspects, this practice dramatically affects the credit score of the spouse who did not file for bankruptcy. *See, e.g.*, Dickens v. Trans Union, 18 Fed. Appx. 315 (6th Cir. 2001).

66 *Compare* Smith v. Ohio Sav. Bank, 2008 WL 2704719 (D. Nev. July 7, 2008) (reasonable jury could conclude that bankruptcy references in plaintiff wife's credit report misled potential creditors into believing that she had filed for bankruptcy), Spector v. Trans Union, 301 F. Supp. 2d 231 (D. Conn. 2004) (genuine issue of fact whether Trans Union violated FCRA by including notation regarding husband's bankruptcy on wife's credit report; summary judgment denied), *and* Spellman v. Experian Info. Solutions, 2002 WL 799876 (D. Nev. Jan. 20, 2002), *with* Johnson v. Equifax, Inc., 510 F. Supp. 2d 638 (S.D. Ala. 2007) ("included in bankruptcy" notation in ex-wife's credit report was accurate and not misleading), Dickens v. Trans Union, 18 Fed. Appx. 315 (6th Cir. 2001), *and* Heupel v. Trans Union, 193 F. Supp. 2d 1234 (N.D. Ala. 2002) ("included in bankruptcy" notation technically accurate and did not violate FCRA). *See generally* National Consumer Law Center, Fair Credit Reporting § 4.4.6.10.3 (7th ed. 2010 and Supp.).

67 Clark v. Experian Info. Solutions, 2004 WL 256433 (D.S.C. Jan. 14, 2004).

68 Spector v. Trans Union, 301 F. Supp. 2d 231 (D. Conn. 2004).

69 *See* § 6.3, *supra*; National Consumer Law Center, Fair Credit Reporting § 14.5 (7th ed. 2010 and Supp.).

70 National Consumer Law Center, Fair Credit Reporting § 14.8.3 (7th ed. 2010 and Supp.).

71 Press Release, Fair Isaac & Co., Fair Isaac Moves to Protect Lenders from Fraudulent Manipulation of Authorized User Credit

pears that doing so might have violated the ECOA, because Fair Isaac has announced that it will instead make adjustments to its scoring models to "support compliance with the Equal Credit Opportunity Act ... while reducing potential impact from tampering."[72] The FTC has also brought enforcement actions against credit repair organizations that offer piggybacking services.[73]

9.4.2 Other Credit Reporting Issues

When a consumer in good faith exercised rights under the Consumer Credit Protection Act (CCPA), creditors may not discriminate in reporting that consumer's credit information to other creditors or to reporting agencies.[74] For example, a creditor may not report a debt as "charged-off,"[75] or give it a similar adverse characterization, when in fact the account was paid or canceled as part of a settlement or judgment in a suit brought by the consumer under CCPA.

The consumer in such a situation might have a cause of action against the creditor under a federal or state fair credit reporting law.[76] In addition, the consumer should have a cause of action under the ECOA for discrimination in the furnishing of credit information on the basis of good faith exercise of CCPA rights.[77] The prohibition concerning discrimination in reporting information should apply even after a creditor has closed an account. Nothing in the ECOA or Fair Housing Act indicates that a credit transaction ceases to be covered once the creditor closes the account.

9.5 Creditor Actions Triggered by Borrower's Increased Age or Change in Name or Marital Status

9.5.1 Rules Limiting Creditor Actions

A creditor may not require reapplication for an open-end account, change the terms of an open-end account, or terminate an open-end account merely because account holders reach a certain age, retire, or change their name or marital status.[78] The creditor may take such actions only if there is evidence of the account holder's inability or unwillingness to repay.

For example, a creditor violates this provision if it has a policy of automatically canceling a wife's supplementary credit card when her husband dies and then automatically renewing her credit after receiving her written consent to become liable for all charges on the new account.[79] Similarly, a creditor may not terminate an account because credit life, health, accident, or disability insurance is unavailable or is no longer available due to the account holder's age.[80]

There are two exceptions to this rule. The creditor may require reapplication from a borrower who is contractually liable on an account on the basis of a change of marital status if (1) the credit was originally granted based on income earned by the borrower's spouse and (2) the creditor has information available indicating that the borrower's income alone may not support the amount of credit currently available.[81] A creditor also may terminate an account when the spouses are jointly liable (even if the action coincides with a change in marital status) and (1) one or both spouses repudiates responsibility for future charges, (2) requests a separate account in his or her own name, or (3) requests that the joint account be closed.[82]

9.5.2 Scope of the Rules Limiting Creditor Actions

9.5.2.1 Rules Apply Only to Open-End Accounts

The rules limiting creditor actions in closing or altering existing accounts apply only to open-end accounts. Open-end credit is defined in Regulation B as "credit extended under a

---

Card Accounts (June 5, 2007); J.W. Elphinstone, *'Piggybacking' Roils Credit Industry*, Associated Press, June 3, 2007.

72 Press Release, Fair Isaac & Co., FICO 08 Score Delivers Predictive Boost Where Lenders Need It Most (Oct. 2008).

73 Fed. Trade Comm'n v. RCA Credit Servs., L.L.C., 2008 WL 5428039 (M.D. Fla. Dec. 31, 2008); *cf.* Brosnan v. Tradeline Solutions, Inc., 2009 WL 1604572 (N.D. Cal. June 5, 2009) (competitor brought Lanham Act lawsuit against credit repair organization that offered piggybacking).

74 *See* § 3.4.4, *supra* (prohibition of discrimination based on exercise of rights under the Consumer Credit Protection Act).

75 A term indicating that the debt was written off as a bad debt.

76 However, creditors reporting their own experience with a consumer are not subject to liability under the federal FCRA. 15 U.S.C. § 1681a(d)(2)(A)(i); *see* National Consumer Law Center, Fair Credit Reporting §§ 2.4.2, 2.5.5, 2.5.6 (7th ed. 2010 and Supp.).

If the credit information is incorrect, however, a creditor may be liable under a state statute or on a theory of deceit or negligent misrepresentation. In addition, the creditor can sometimes be held liable under the FCRA if the consumer challenges incorrect information with a credit reporting agency and the creditor fails to fulfill its obligation to investigate the accuracy of the information. *See* National Consumer Law Center, Fair Credit Reporting (7th ed. 2010 and Supp.).

77 In settlement of many types of disputes, a consumer's attorney should consider requiring, as part of the settlement, that the creditor send a letter to credit reporting agencies correcting any errors in the consumer's credit report. *See* National Consumer Law Center, Fair Credit Reporting ch. 12 (7th ed. 2010 and Supp.) (discussing more completely this issue and sample settlement provisions).

78 Reg. B, 12 C.F.R. § 1002.7(c)(1), (c)(2) [§ 202.7(c)(1), (c)(2)]; Official Interpretations of Reg. B [Official Staff Commentary on Reg. B] to Reg. B, 12 C.F.R. pt. 1002 [pt. 202], Supp. I, § 1002.7(c) (1)-1 [§ 202.7(c)(1)-1].

79 Miller v. American Express Co., 688 F.2d 1235 (9th Cir. 1982) (in challenging American Express' policy of automatically canceling a supplementary card holder's account upon the death of the principal card holder, plaintiff was found to be more than a mere "user" of her husband's account; the ECOA applied because plaintiff was personally liable under the contract creating the supplementary account for all debts charged on her card by any person).

80 Reg. B, 12 C.F.R. § 1002.7(e) [§ 202.7(e)].

81 Reg. B, 12 C.F.R. § 1002.7(c)(2) [§ 202.7(c)(2)].

82 Official Interpretations on Reg. B [Official Staff Commentary on Reg. B] , 12 C.F.R. pt. 1002 [pt. 202], supp. I § 1002.7(c)(1)-1 [§ 202.7(c)(1)-1].

plan under which a creditor may permit an applicant to make purchases or obtain loans from time to time,"[83] as opposed to a one-time closed-end transaction such as a car loan. The classic example of open-end credit is the bank or retail store credit card with which the consumer can make as many or as few purchases or cash advances as desired, usually subject to a dollar limit. The credit may be obtained directly from the creditor or indirectly by use of a credit card, check, or other device.[84]

9.5.2.2 Rules Protect Only Applicants Who Are Contractually Liable

The rules limiting creditor actions in closing or altering existing accounts protect "applicants"[85] who are "contractually liable."[86] Under Regulation B, a person who is contractually liable for a debt is expressly obligated to repay all debts on an account, pursuant to an agreement.[87] Thus, a man who signed an agreement jointly with his wife may have protections against a reapplication requirement upon divorce or the death of his wife, while a man who was merely an authorized user on his wife's account may not.[88]

9.5.3 Status of Account During Reapplication

If a creditor requires a customer to reapply for an existing account, the applicant must be allowed full access to the account under existing terms while the reapplication is pending. The creditor may, however, specify a reasonable time period

within which the account holder must submit the required information.[89]

9.5.4 When Creditor Can Request Updated Information from Account Holders

Creditors are not prohibited from periodically reevaluating the financial status of account holders to determine their ability to repay. For instance, creditors may ask account holders for regular income reports. They may also obtain credit reports on account holders for the purpose of reviewing the account.[90] If such a report indicates that an account holder has retired and as a result has a reduced income, the creditor could use this report as evidence of inability to repay and terminate the account. However, events related to a prohibited basis, such as retirement, reaching a particular age, or change in name or marital status, may not be used to trigger a request for updated information.[91] Similarly, it should violate the ECOA to target only members of protected categories, such as married women, for such updates.

9.6 Continuing Requirement of Co-Signer on Credit Renewal

An earlier chapter details when a creditor may seek a spouse or other party's signature on a loan obligation as a co-signer or other surety.[92] Even when a creditor may obtain this extra signature, the creditor may not automatically seek the second signature on a renewal of the obligation.

Instead, if the borrower's creditworthiness is reevaluated when a credit obligation is renewed, the creditor must determine whether an additional party is still warranted—if not, the creditor must release the additional party.[93] The decision to require an additional party on renewal also may not be made on a prohibited basis.[94]

---

83 Reg. B, 12 C.F.R. § 1002.2(w) [§ 202.2(w)].

84 Reg. B, 12 C.F.R. § 1002.2(w) [§ 202.2(w)].

85 *See* Clark v. Capital One Bank, 2008 WL 508440 (D. Idaho Feb. 19, 2008) (plaintiff claiming marital status discrimination regarding account in hardship category and then sent to collection agency was not an "applicant" under ECOA because she did not apply for an extension, renewal, or continuation of credit).

86 Reg. B, 12 C.F.R. § 1002.7(c) [§ 202.7(c)].

87 Reg. B, 12 C.F.R. § 1002.2(i) [§ 202.2(i)].

88 Reg. B, 12 C.F.R. § 1002.7(c) [§ 202.7(c)]; *see also* Official Interpretations of Reg. B [Official Staff Commentary on Reg. B], 12 C.F.R. pt. 1002 [pt. 202], supp. I § 1002.7(c)(1)-1, (c)(2)-1 [§ 202.7(c)(1)-1, (c)(2)-1]; *cf.* Miller v. American Express Co., 688 F.2d 1235 (9th Cir. 1982) (finding wife's account was in fact a separate account on which she was personally liable even though creditor termed it a "supplementary" account).

Note that the ECOA permits an open-end creditor to condition the designation of an authorized user by the account holder upon the authorized user agreeing to become contractually liable on the account, as long as the condition is not imposed on a discriminatory basis. Official Interpretations of Reg. B [Official Staff Commentary on Reg. B], 12 C.F.R. pt. 1002 [pt. 202], supp. I § 1002.7(a)-1 [§ 202.7(a)-1].

89 Official Interpretations of Reg. B [Official Staff Commentary on Reg. B], 12 C.F.R. pt. 1002 [pt. 202], supp. I § 1002.7(c)(2)-1 [§ 202.7(c)(2)-1].

90 Fair Credit Reporting Act, 15 U.S.C. § 1681b(a)(3)(A).

91 Official Interpretations of Reg. B [Official Staff Commentary on Reg. B], 12 C.F.R. pt. 1002 [pt. 202], supp. I § 1002.7(c)(1)-2 [§ 202.7(c)(1)-2].

92 *See* § 5.6, *supra*.

93 Official Interpretations of Reg. B [Official Staff Commentary on Reg. B], 12 C.F.R. pt. 1002 [pt. 202], supp. I § 1002.7(d)(5)-3 [§ 202.7(d)(5)-3]; *see* Stern v. Espirito Santo Bank, 791 F. Supp. 865 (S.D. Fla. 1992).

94 Stern v. Espirito Santo Bank, 791 F. Supp. 865 (S.D. Fla. 1992).

Chapter 10   ECOA Procedural Requirements

10.1 Introduction

Previous chapters have focused on the ways in which the ECOA and other federal credit discrimination statutes may be used to challenge discriminatory creditor behavior. The ECOA and its implementing Regulation B apply more broadly. Creditors may violate the ECOA and Regulation B not only by engaging in discriminatory actions but also by violating any of a number of procedural requirements intended to ensure compliance.

The ECOA procedural provisions can be powerful tools even in situations in which discrimination cannot be established.[1] In some instances, such claims may be amenable to class actions.[2] Despite the lack of "substantive" discrimination claims, borrowers who prevail on procedural claims may collect punitive damages plus actual damages and attorney fees against creditors who fail to comply.[3]

Although procedural claims may be brought even without evidence of discrimination, there is a strong connection between the procedural and substantive aspects of the ECOA. The ECOA notice provisions require that creditors provide credit applicants with notices stating the reasons for credit denial or for taking other adverse actions on an application. These notices may provide clues to help uncover whether the creditor's decision was discriminatory.

The ECOA notice requirement was designed to fulfill the dual goals of consumer protection and education.[4] The Senate report for the ECOA amendments stated that a strict notice provision was

> [a] strong and necessary adjunct to the antidiscrimination purpose of the legislation, for only if creditors know they must explain their decisions will they effectively be discouraged from discriminatory practices. Yet this requirement fulfills a broader need: rejected credit applicants will now be able to learn where and how their credit status is deficient and this information should have a pervasive and valuable educational benefit. Instead of being told only that they do not meet a particular creditor's standards, consumers particularly should benefit from knowing, for example, that the reason for the denial is their short residence in the area, or their recent change of employment, or their already over-extended financial situation. In those cases in which the creditor may have acted on misinformation or inadequate information, the statement of reasons gives the applicant a chance to rectify the mistake.[5]

Similarly, record retention requirements were enacted to help ensure that consumers would have access to records needed to help prove discrimination claims.

---

1 Jefferson v. Briner, Inc., 2006 WL 1720692 (E.D. Va. June 21, 2006); *see* Jochum v. Pico Credit Corp., 730 F.2d 1041 (5th Cir. 1984); Kivel v. Wealthspring Mortgage Corp., 398 F. Supp. 2d 1049 (D. Minn. 2005); Costa v. Mauro Chevrolet, Inc., 390 F. Supp. 2d 720 (N.D. Ill. 2005); Cannon v. Metro Ford, Inc., 242 F. Supp. 2d 1322 (S.D. Fla. 2002); Polis v. American Liberty Financial, Inc., 237 F. Supp. 2d 681 (S.D. W. Va. 2002); Mungia v. Tony Rizza Oldsmobile, Inc., 2002 WL 554504 (N.D. Ill. Apr. 15, 2002); Treadway v. Gateway Chevrolet, 2002 WL 554513 (N.D. Ill. Apr. 12, 2002), *aff'd*, 362 F.3d 971 (7th Cir. 2004); Rayburn v. Car Credit Ctr. Corp., 2000 U.S. Dist. LEXIS 14944 (N.D. Ill. Oct. 6, 2000) (discrimination is not a prerequisite to an actionable ECOA claim); Williams v. Thomas Pontiac-GMC-Nissan-Hyundai, 1999 U.S. Dist. LEXIS 15045 (N.D. Ill. Sept. 22, 1999); Pinkett v. Payday Today Loans, L.L.C., 1999 WL 592189 (N.D. Ill. Aug. 3, 1999) (failure to provide ECOA rejection notice may be actionable without allegations of discrimination); Titus v. Mortgage Enter., Ltd., 760 N.Y.S.2d 66 (App. Div. 2003).

2 *See, e.g.*, Beard v. Dominion Homes Financial Servs., 2007 WL 2838934 (S.D. Ohio Sept. 26, 2007) (certifying class of borrowers who purchased homes in a particular development from a developer who promised FHA loans and provided other terms; representations regarding FHA loan availability and subsequent failure to provide FHA terms were comparable for all class members).

3 *See, e.g.*, Durdin v. Cheyenne Mountain Bank, 98 P.3d 899 (Colo. App. 2004) ($100,000 actual damages awarded in ECOA notice case); *see also* Moffitt v. Bank of America, N.A., 2009 WL 5217147, at *1–3 (S.D. Ind. Dec. 29, 2010) (plaintiff stated a claim for relief under the ECOA by alleging that plaintiffs are applicants, defendant is a creditor, plaintiffs filed a completed application, defendant took adverse action on the application, and defendant failed to provide notice of adverse action); Errico v. Pac. Capital Bank, N.A., 753 F. Supp. 2d 1034, 2010 WL 4699394, at *6 (N.D. Cal. Nov. 9, 2010) (notice violation may provide a cause of action without regard to

allegations of discrimination under the ECOA); Moreno v. DHI Mortgage Co. GP, Inc., 2010 WL 3430816, at *5 (E.D. Va. Aug. 27, 2010) ($1000 found to be sufficient damages for notice violation when no actual damages, no other applicant affected by violation, and no evidence violation was intentional). *See generally* ch. 11, *infra*.

4 Fischl v. Gen. Motors Acceptance Corp., 708 F.2d 143, 146 (5th Cir. 1983).

5 S. Rep. No. 94-589 (1976), *reprinted in* 1976 U.S.C.A.A.N. 403, 406.

    Pleadings highlighting many of these issues are included on the companion website to this treatise. Selected pleadings are also reprinted in Appendix G, *infra*.

10.2 Overview of ECOA Notice Requirements

Creditor notification requirements vary depending on the situation, and this chapter treats each of these different situations separately: (1) applications approved by the creditor; (2) applications in which the creditor makes a counteroffer as to the terms or amount of credit; (3) adverse actions on applications or on existing accounts; (4) incomplete applications; (5) withdrawn applications; and (6) notices of right to review appraisal reports. This section also covers issues related to the timing, content, and format of notices, including rules allowing electronic disclosures in certain circumstances.

Other federal and state statutes may have notice provisions similar to those found in the ECOA. The Fair Credit Reporting Act notices are discussed in § 10.10, *infra*. Similarly, Department of Housing and Urban Development (HUD) or other government programs may require notice of action taken on an application. These requirements are in addition to, and do not absolve the creditor from complying with, the ECOA notice requirements.[6]

10.3 Notification Requirement for Approved Applications

A creditor must notify an applicant of its decision to approve an application within thirty days after receiving a completed application.[7] This notification may be either express or by implication. For example, implicit notification is given when the applicant receives a credit card, money, property, or other requested services.[8]

10.4 Notification Requirement If Creditor Makes a Counteroffer

10.4.1 Overview

Sometimes the creditor's response to a completed application will be to offer to extend credit, but on substantially different terms or in substantially different amounts than those requested by the applicant. Regulation B requires that a creditor notify an applicant of any counteroffer to the credit requested within thirty days after receiving a completed application.[9]

The counteroffer notice provision is critical in alerting a borrower to differences between the loan presented to her at closing and the loan she had applied for. For example, borrowers often come to a lender with a specific loan amount in mind to pay for home improvements or other uses. The lender may try to inflate that amount, proposing a loan that is significantly different in amount, in terms or in both amount and terms, than what the borrower initially requested. The ECOA notice of counteroffer can provide a warning sign and possibly help convince the borrower to reconsider accepting a bad loan.[10]

Unfortunately, most borrowers seek legal help long after closing and only after they are having trouble paying back the loan. ECOA counteroffer notice violation claims are still important at this point, however, as they can afford a basis for additional remedies to borrowers, including actual and punitive damages.[11]

The critical issue in cases alleging counteroffer notice violations is whether the counteroffer is considered an adverse action. If so, written notice is clearly required. If not, notice of counteroffer is still required but, depending on a court's interpretation, the form and timing of the notice may be different.

10.4.2 Is a Counteroffer an Adverse Action?

The ECOA defines "adverse action" as "a denial or revocation of credit, a change in the terms of an existing credit arrangement, or a refusal to grant credit in substantially the amount or on substantially the terms requested."[12] This definition clearly covers the typical counteroffer situation in which the loan the consumer receives at closing is substantially different than the loan requested.

The problem is that Regulation B includes an "out" for creditors. Regulation B defines an adverse action as a "refusal to grant credit in substantially the amount or on substantially the terms requested in an application unless the creditor makes a counteroffer (to grant credit in a different amount or on other terms) *and* the applicant uses or expressly accepts the credit offered."[13] At least one court explicitly deferred to the regula-

---

6   Official Interpretations of Reg. B [Official Staff Commentary on Reg. B], 12 C.F.R. § 1002.9(b)(2)-9 [§ 202.9(b)(2)-9]; Dep't of Hous. & Urban Dev., Mortgagee Letter 77-17, Consumer Cred. Guide (CCH) ¶ 98,192 (Apr. 22, 1977) (must comply with ECOA and with HUD notification requirement).

7   Reg. B, 12 C.F.R. § 1002.9(a)(1)(i) [§ 202.9(a)(1)(i)]; *see also* § 10.7.2, *infra* (discussion of what constitutes a completed application).

8   Official Interpretations of Reg. B [Official Staff Commentary on Reg. B], 12 C.F.R. pt. 1002 [pt. 202], Supp. I, § 1002.9(a)(1)-2 [§ 202.9(a)(1)-2].

9   Reg. B, 12 C.F.R. § 1002.9(a)(1)(i) [§ 202.9(a)(1)(i)].

10 In 1999, the Federal Reserve Board proposed amending the official staff commentary (renamed under the CFPB as the official interpretations of Regulation B) to clarify that, when a consumer receives a solicitation for a specific amount and the creditor subsequently offers a different amount, the creditor's action constitutes a counteroffer. 64 Fed. Reg. 44,582, 44,588–44,589 (Aug. 16, 1999).

      The Federal Reserve Board decided not to adopt this change, stating instead that this interpretation will be reviewed and reissued for additional public comment. 68 Fed. Reg. 13,144, 13,154 (Mar. 18, 2003).

11 *See generally* ch. 11, *infra*.

12 15 U.S.C. § 1691(d)(6); *see, e.g.,* Torgerson v. Wells Fargo Bank S.D., 2009 WL 255995, at *11 (D.S.D. Feb. 3, 2009).

13 Reg. B, 12 C.F.R. § 1002.2(c)(1)(i) [§ 202.2(c)(1)(i)] (emphasis added).

      One court supported this regulatory exception by stating that the regulatory language does not intend that a borrower will both accept the benefit of the lending and simultaneously pursue an ECOA claim against a lender with whom the borrower has an ongoing

tion despite plaintiff's highlighting of the inconsistency between the statute and regulations.[14]

This regulatory refinement of the statutory definition is critical. Most borrowers who are presented with different loan terms or amounts at closing are not aware of the changes or are induced or coerced into accepting the "new" loan. The regulation seems to provide that there is no adverse action in these circumstances if the borrower accepts or uses the credit offered.[15]

There are a number of issues to look out for with respect to counteroffer notices. First, it is not always clear whether a consumer has actually accepted a counteroffer or whether a previous offer was denied and the creditor made a new offer.[16] For example, in many spot delivery or "yo-yo" cases, the consumer will accept a particular deal and then the dealer will call her back hours or days later to ask the consumer to sign a different contract. The second deal in this situation would not be a counteroffer but instead a termination of the existing account requiring notice. Furthermore, any rider that gives the dealer the right to back out of the contract (which should be analyzed as either a condition-precedent contract, condition-subsequent contract, or an improper combination of both conditions) is not a true counteroffer.[17] However, the Eighth Circuit ruled in 2005 that there was no adverse action in a case in which the dealer failed to obtain credit for a buyer on terms offered in the retail installment contract because the dealer showed that it took significant steps to ensure that the buyer

was extended credit on the terms that she requested and continuously apprised her of the actions being taken.[18]

In addition, there are ambiguities with respect to format and timing of notices. It is clear that written notice is required if the counteroffer is considered to be an adverse action. The creditor must also comply with the other ECOA provisions required for adverse action notices, including providing a statement of reasons.[19] The creditor must notify the applicant of the counteroffer within thirty days after receiving a completed application.[20] The timing and format requirements for counteroffers that are not considered to be adverse actions are discussed in the next section.

Note that, under the FCRA, a creditor is required to provide a "risk-based pricing" notice whenever a consumer is offered credit on less favorable terms based on a credit report or score.[21] These risk-based pricing notices must be provided "under the FCRA where a consumer accepts the offered credit, even where ECOA notices are not required."[22]

10.4.3 Notice Requirements If Counteroffer Is Not an Adverse Action

Separate notice of counteroffer is required even if the counteroffer is not considered an adverse action.[23] Problems arise with respect to whether written notice is required and with respect to the timing of the separate counteroffer notice.

The ECOA and Regulation B do not specify the type of notice required when no adverse action is involved. Both are explicit that written notice is required if there is an adverse action.[24] The official interpretations of Regulation B ("official interpretations") are helpful only with respect to the form of notice for approvals. In this case, the official interpretation states that notification of approval may be express or by implication.[25]

---

contractual relationship. Lopez v. Platinum Home Mortgage Corp., 2006 WL 2269154 (W.D. Mich. Aug. 8, 2006).

14 Diaz v. Paragon Motors of Woodside, Inc., 424 F. Supp. 2d 519 (E.D.N.Y. 2006).

15 *See, e.g.,* Soslau v. PHH Mortgage Corp., 2008 WL 2805606 (E.D. Pa. July 18, 2008) (consumer applied jointly for credit with then spouse, and lender encouraged her to apply individually, saying she was individually qualified; lender then told consumer she only qualified for ARM loan, which she accepted based on lender's promise that she could refinance later; adverse action notice not required because counteroffer accepted); *see also* Kamara v. Columbia Home Loans, L.L.C., 654 F. Supp. 2d 259 (E.D. Pa. 2009) (when defendant offered credit to plaintiff and plaintiff accepted the credit offered, no adverse action occurred); Wenglicki v. Tribeca Lending Corp., 2009 WL 2195221, at *5 (E.D. Pa. July 22, 2009) (borrower who received credit cannot claim to be unaware of action taken on application); Siffel v. NFM, Inc., 2009 WL 1783523, at *2–3 (E.D. Pa. June 23, 2009) (acceptance of different loan terms at closing constitutes acceptance of counteroffer for which no adverse action notice is required), *aff'd,* 386 Fed. Appx.169 (3d Cir. 2010).

16 *See, e.g.,* Crawford v. Franklin Credit Mgmt. Corp., 2011 WL 1118584, at *11–12 (S.D.N.Y. Mar. 23, 2011) (denying summary judgment because of material factual dispute as to whether credit was extended on different terms from those which applicant sought); Willingham v. Novastar Mortgage, Inc., 2006 WL 6676801, at *21–23 (W.D. Tenn. Feb. 7, 2006) (notice of a substantial change in terms is necessary even when the borrower accepts the new loan); Garcia v. Ed Moses Dodge, 2006 WL 2640568 (D. Ariz. Sept. 14, 2006) (unclear whether creditor issued a counteroffer).

17 *See, e.g.,* Miller v. River Oaks Lincoln Mercury, Inc., 2005 WL 2284268 (N.D. Ill. Sept. 19, 2005) (defendant's motion for summary judgment denied when dealer eventually arranged financing but did not provide notice of prior credit denials).

18 Madrigal v. Kline Oldsmobile, Inc., 423 F.3d 819 (8th Cir. 2005).

19 *See* § 10.5, *infra.*

20 Reg. B, 12 C.F.R. § 1002.9(a)(1)(i) [§ 202.9(a)(1)(i)].

21 *See* National Consumer Law Center, Fair Credit Reporting § 8.7 (7th ed. 2010 and Supp.).

22 75 Fed. Reg. 2724 (Jan. 15, 2010).

23 *See, e.g.,* Newton v. United Cos. Financial Corp., 24 F. Supp. 2d 444 (E.D. Pa. 1998) (there are three distinct kinds of action a creditor might take, each triggering a notice requirement: an approval, a counteroffer, and an adverse action); *In re* Armstrong, 288 B.R. 404 (Bankr. E.D. Pa. 2003).

24 15 U.S.C. § 1691(d)(2)(B); Reg. B, 12 C.F.R. § 1002.9(a)(2) [§ 202.9(a)(2)].

25 Official Interpretations of Reg. B [Official Staff Commentary on Reg. B], 12 C.F.R. pt. 1002 [pt. 202], Supp. I, § 1002.9(a)(1)-2 [§ 202.9(a)(1)-2].

At least one court, however, cited the commentary provision § 1002.9 [§ 202.9] comment 3—that oral notification occurs when the creditor communicates the credit decision to the applicant—to show that consideration was given to the fact that some notices may be given orally. *See In re* United Cos. Financial Corp., 277 B.R. 596 (Bankr. D. Del. 2002).

However, another provision in the official interpretations, § 1002.9(c)(3) comment 1 [§ 202.9(c)(3) comment 1], states that, if

Courts have interpreted the statutory and regulatory silence on this issue differently. In *Newton v. United Companies Finance Corp.*, a district court concluded that creditors are required to give borrowers written notice of counteroffer regardless of whether the borrower accepts or rejects the counteroffer.[26] In a later district court case, *Diaz v. Virginia Housing Development Authority*, the court concluded that the counteroffer notice does not have to be in writing if it is not an adverse action.[27]

There are important factual differences between these two leading cases. The *Newton* case included challenges to a wide range of abusive practices. In the *Diaz* case, in contrast, the ECOA procedural notice violation was the only issue remaining on appeal.[28] In *Diaz*, the creditor offered the plaintiffs a different loan product than what they had originally applied for, but this new product was the same kind of credit and in the same amount as the original product.[29] In *Newton*, in contrast, the creditor made significant changes in the terms and type of credit.[30] Furthermore, in the *Diaz* case, the plaintiff had re-

ceived oral notice of counteroffer. The only issue was whether written notice was also required.[31] In *Newton*, the plaintiffs received no written or oral notice of counteroffer.[32]

The issue of whether written or oral notice is required can be crucial. Without a written requirement, lenders can later claim that they orally informed the borrower of a counteroffer. The only evidence that a counteroffer notice was not given may be the borrower's testimony. Judges and juries are often sympathetic to predatory lending victims and thus these cases still may be resolved in the borrower's favor. However, when presented in conjunction with other claims, such as Truth in Lending violations that can be proven with written documentation, the court may be more likely to dismiss the ECOA claims when no written documentation is available.

There are also timing issues to consider. The first is whether notice of counteroffer, either written or oral, must be given prior to closing. The *Newton* court implied such a requirement in the regulation, stating that the lender must notify the borrower of the making of a counteroffer, not just the ultimate approval or denial of the counteroffer.[33] According to the *Newton* court: "The law was designed to give the borrower fair notice that a counteroffer for a larger loan was in the offing within a reasonable time after the lender knew this, which was before the closing."[34]

The same district court revisited this issue in a later case, finding not only that the written notice requirement should not be read into Regulation B but also that neither the ECOA nor Regulation B requires that the notice of counteroffer be given at a time before the loan closing.[35] In this case, the court found that the borrower received notice of the counteroffer when she signed a "borrower's acknowledgment form" at closing.[36]

A related timing issue is the regulatory provision that, after notifying the borrower of a counteroffer that is not an adverse action, the lender has ninety days to notify the applicant of an

---

an applicant fails to provide information in response to an oral request, a creditor must send a written notice to the applicant within the time period specified for notices of approval, counteroffer, or adverse action or for notices of incompleteness. This statement provides some support for the argument that notices of counteroffer should be written.

26 Newton v. United Cos. Financial Corp., 24 F. Supp. 2d 444 (E.D. Pa. 1998); *see also In re* Armstrong, 288 B.R. 404 (Bankr. E.D. Pa. 2003) (written notice must be given if lender makes a counteroffer).

   A later decision in the same district did not overrule *Newton* but rather distinguished it on the grounds that the plaintiffs in *Newton* received no notice at all, whereas the plaintiff in this case allegedly received a form at closing stating the new loan terms. *See* Ricciardi v. Ameriquest Mortgage Co., 2004 WL 739965 (E.D. Pa. Mar. 15, 2004), *adopted by* 2004 WL 1427121 (E.D. Pa. June 24, 2004), *aff'd*, 164 Fed. Appx. 221 (3d Cir. 2006).

27 Diaz v. Va. Hous. Dev. Auth., 117 F. Supp. 2d 500 (E.D. Va. 2000); *see also* Madrigal v. Kline Oldsmobile, Inc., 423 F.3d 819 (8th Cir. 2005) (no adverse action when creditor kept applicant orally informed of status of application, because oral notification is sufficient when action being taken is not adverse); Diaz v. Paragon Motors of Woodside, Inc., 424 F. Supp. 2d 519 (E.D.N.Y. 2006) (requiring written notice of an accepted counteroffer would be contrary to well-established rules of statutory interpretation); Wingert v. Credit Based Asset Servicing & Securitization, 2004 WL 2915306 (W.D. Pa. Aug. 26, 2004); *In re* United Cos. Financial Corp., 277 B.R. 596 (Bankr. D. Del. 2002) (denying class certification in case based on alleged violations of ECOA counteroffer notice requirement and citing *Diaz* with approval that written notice of counteroffer is not required).

28 The substantive claims were dismissed in an earlier decision. Diaz v. Va. Hous. Dev. Auth., 101 F. Supp. 2d 415 (E.D. Va. 2000).

   Plaintiffs had alleged that the housing authority's decision to deny their loan applications because they were not married violated the ECOA. The court found that the creditors' refusal to extend credit was permissible under the exception in the ECOA for special purpose credit programs designed to help economically disadvantaged borrowers. 15 U.S.C. § 1691(c)(1); *see* § 3.8, *supra* (special purpose credit programs).

29 Diaz v. Va. Hous. Dev. Auth., 117 F. Supp. 2d 500 (E.D. Va. 2000).

30 Newton v. United Cos. Financial Corp., 24 F. Supp. 2d 444 (E.D. Pa. 1998).

31 Diaz v. Va. Hous. Dev. Auth., 117 F. Supp. 2d 500 (E.D. Va. 2000) (oral notice sufficient when loan officer called plaintiffs to inform them that their original application had been denied but that they qualified instead for a different loan).

32 This issue was highlighted in a later decision that did not overrule *Newton* but distinguished it on the grounds that the plaintiffs in *Newton* did not receive any notice, whereas the plaintiff in the subsequent case allegedly received notice of the new terms at closing. *See* Ricciardi v. Ameriquest Mortgage Co., 2004 WL 739965 (E.D. Pa. Mar. 15, 2004), *adopted by* 2004 WL 1427121 (E.D. Pa. June 24, 2004), *aff'd*, 164 Fed. Appx. 221 (3d Cir. 2006).

33 Newton v. United Cos. Financial Corp., 24 F. Supp. 2d 444 (E.D. Pa. 1998).

34 *Id.* at 462.

35 Ricciardi v. Ameriquest Mortgage Co., 2004 WL 739965 (E.D. Pa. Mar. 15, 2004), *adopted by* 2004 WL 1427121 (E.D. Pa. June 24, 2004), *aff'd*, 164 Fed. Appx. 221 (3d Cir. 2006); *see also* Miller v. Shore Financial Servs., Inc., 2006 WL 2828584 (E.D. Mich. Sept. 29, 2006) (following *Ricciardi* and finding that documents presented at closing provided sufficiently clear notice of the change in terms).

36 Ricciardi v. Ameriquest Mortgage Co., 2004 WL 739965 (E.D. Pa. Mar. 15, 2004), *adopted by* 2004 WL 1427121 (E.D. Pa. June 24, 2004), *aff'd*, 164 Fed. Appx. 221 (3d Cir. 2006).

approval or denial.[37] This does not, however, require creditors to hold counteroffers open for ninety days or any other particular length of time.[38]

In practice this means that a lender must give notice of counteroffer within thirty days of receiving a completed application.[39] As noted above, there is a split among the courts whether this notice must be written. However, some courts are not even convinced that the counteroffer notice, whether oral or written, must be given within thirty days of application.[40] Assuming this notice is given, the lender then has ninety days to send a notice of its decision on the original application if the applicant does not accept or use the counter-offered credit.[41]

The creditor may also combine a counteroffer with a notice of adverse action.[42] In this instance, the creditor does not need to send a second notice of the action taken if the applicant does not accept the counteroffer, as that information would be contained in the initial notice.[43] A sample of such a combined notice is provided in the federal regulatory agency forms appended to Regulation B.[44]

10.4.4 Written Application Requirement

Another ECOA regulation requires that all home mortgage or refinancing applications must be in writing, as distinct from all other credit applications, which may be made orally.[45] Creditor violation of this written application requirement should entitle a consumer to relief.[46]

This provision is especially important in cases in which a court rules that written notice of adverse action is not required because a borrower accepted or used counter-offered credit. If the counter-offered loan allegedly accepted by the consumer was a refinancing loan, any application for this loan must be in writing. Even if the creditor arguably did not violate the adverse action written notice requirement, it may have violated this written application requirement.

For example, if a borrower initially applies for a home improvement loan, this application may be oral or written pursuant to the ECOA. The creditor may later call the borrower or simply present the borrower at closing with a different loan, in this case a mortgage refinancing loan. Unlike the home improvement loan, Regulation B requires that the application for a mortgage refinancing loan be made in writing.[47] If the lender argues that the borrower "accepted" the refinancing loan at closing, thereby potentially exempting the creditor from the ECOA written adverse action requirements, the creditor will still be in violation of the separate requirement that a refinancing application be in writing. Creditors in that circumstance should not be able to argue that they are not required to comply with either the written application or the written notice provision.[48]

It is important to note that information taken orally and typed up constitutes a written application.[49] In the Federal Trade Commission (FTC) lawsuit against Capital City Mortgage,[50] the FTC alleged that Capital City failed to take written applications for credit primarily for the purchase or refinancing of a dwelling and also failed to provide applicants for credit with written notice of adverse action.[51]

10.5 Notification Requirement for Adverse Actions

10.5.1 Adverse Actions Involving New Credit Accounts

An adverse action is defined as any refusal to grant credit "in substantially the amount or on substantially the terms requested in an application, unless the creditor makes a counteroffer (to grant credit in a different amount or on other terms) and the

---

37 Reg. B, 12 C.F.R. § 1002.9(a)(1)(iv) [§ 202.9(a)(1)(iv)]; *see, e.g.,* Davis v. U.S. Bancorp., 383 F.3d 761 (8th Cir. 2004).

38 Official Interpretations of Reg. B [Official Staff Commentary on Reg. B], 12 C.F.R. pt. 1002 (pt. 202), Supp. I, § 1002.9(a)(1)-5 [§ 202.9(a)(1)-5].

39 *See, e.g.,* Diaz v. Paragon Motors of Woodside, Inc., 424 F. Supp. 2d 519 (E.D.N.Y. 2006) (rejecting creditor's claim that, because counteroffer was accepted, it had no obligation to provide notice to borrower; however, finding that written notice of counteroffer was not required).

40 *See, e.g.,* Lopez v. Platinum Home Mortgage Corp., 2006 WL 2269154 (W.D. Mich. Aug. 8, 2006) (rejecting an ECOA notice claim by borrower who accepted a counteroffer thirty days after applying for a loan).

41 *See* Davis v. U.S. Bancorp., 383 F.3d 761 (8th Cir. 2004) (Regulation B provides that, once a counteroffer has been made, the time limit for sending a notice of adverse action begins anew, and the creditor then has ninety days to send a notice of adverse action to the applicant if she does not accept or use the new credit offered).

42 Official Interpretations of Reg. B [Official Staff Commentary on Reg. B], 12 C.F.R. pt. 1002 [pt. 202], § 1002.9(a)(1)-6 [§ 202.9(a)(1)-6].

43 *Id.*

44 *See* Reg. B, 12 C.F.R. pt. 1002 [pt. 202], Supp. I, app. C, form C-4.

45 Reg. B, 12 C.F.R. §§ 1002.4(c), 1002.13(a) [§§ 202.4(c), 202.13(a)] (a creditor shall take written applications for the dwelling-related types of credit covered by section 1002.13(a) [§ 202.13(a)]).

46 15 U.S.C. § 1691e. *See generally* § 11.8, *infra.*

47 Reg. B, 12 C.F.R. § 1002.4(c)(c) [§ 202.4(c)].

48 Courts are split on whether written notice is required if the counteroffer is not considered to be an adverse action. *See* § 10.4.3, *supra.*

49 *See* § 5.4.2, *supra.*

50 Fed. Trade Comm'n v. Capital City Mortgage Corp., No. 98CV-237 (D.D.C. complaint filed Jan. 30, 1998), *available at* www.ftc.gov/os/caselist/capitalcitymortgage/capitalcitymortgage.htm.
   In February 2005, the FTC, Capital City Mortgage, and other defendants agreed to a stipulated injunction and final order requiring the payment of $750,000 and a $350,000 performance fund, available to the FTC or any borrower if Capital City does not comply with the order. *See* Federal Trade Commission Notice of Filing of Settlement Agreement, Stipulated Injunction, and Final Order, Fed. Trade Comm'n v. Capital City Mortgage, No. 98CV-237 (D.D.C. Feb. 24, 2005), *available at* www.ftc.gov/os/caselist/capitalcity mortgage/capitalcitymortgage.htm.

51 Fed. Trade Comm'n v. Capital City Mortgage Corp., No. 98CV-237 (D.D.C. complaint filed Jan. 30, 1998), *available at* www.ftc.gov/os/caselist/capitalcitymortgage/capitalcitymortgage.htm.

applicant uses or expressly accepts the credit offered."[52]

This definition has been interpreted broadly. For example, one court found that titling the car in the plaintiff's name, refusing to accept payments, attempting to undo the contract, obtaining a subsequent credit report, and then repossessing the vehicle could be construed as sufficient facts to allege denial or termination of credit and to constitute an adverse action.[53] In addition, the Seventh Circuit found that a dealer's decision not to pass on a consumer's credit application was an adverse action.[54] At least one court found that an adverse action occurred when all parties involved in a car finance transaction understood that the consumer had applied for credit at a certain rate and that rate was not offered, even though the credit application did not specify a rate.[55] Instead, the application stated that the consumer sought credit at the "lowest rate available."[56] An adverse action notice was also required to be sent to a consumer when a creditor denied a credit application in the consumer's name but approved it in a co-signer's name.[57] A creditor's request for a larger down payment and a co-signer when none was previously requested constituted an adverse action.[58] Revoking an extension of credit may constitute an adverse action under the ECOA.[59] Regulation B contains a list in subsection 1002.2(c)(1) [subsection 202.2(c)(1)] of actions that are considered adverse actions and, in subsection 1002.2(c)(2) [subsection 202.2(c)(2)], a list of actions that are not adverse. An action that falls within the definitions of both subsection (c)(1) and subsection (c)(2) is governed by (c)(2) and is not an adverse action.[60]

For example, subsection (c)(2) states that an adverse action is not involved when applicable law prohibits the creditor from extending the credit requested.[61] It is not adverse action, for instance, for an automobile dealer to refuse to extend a small loan for a purpose unrelated to the purchase of an automobile, if such loans must be made by a licensed lender under state law. A court also found that a broker's alleged interference with the credit application did not constitute an adverse action.[62]

The refusal to extend credit also is not an adverse action when the creditor does not offer the type of credit or credit plan requested.[63] For example, a creditor does not take adverse action when it rejects an application for a used car loan because its policy is to offer loans only on new cars.[64] Nevertheless, when a creditor does not offer the credit *terms* (such as interest rate or security) requested by the applicant (as opposed to the type of credit), a denial of the application is an adverse action unless the creditor makes a counteroffer that is accepted or used by the applicant.[65]

10.5.2 Adverse Actions Involving Existing Accounts

The issue of when a creditor has taken an adverse action concerning an existing account is somewhat more complex. Termination of an account or an unfavorable change in the terms of an account that does not affect all or a substantial portion of a class of the creditor's accounts is an adverse action.[66] An example of this type of adverse action is the automatic termination of the paid-up account of a recently divorced woman when no other paid-up accounts are terminated.

Similarly, a telephone company's requirement that only certain existing customers pay a $100 deposit would constitute adverse action and entitle the consumers to a statement of specific reasons.[67] In contrast, an increase in the interest rate on

---

52 Reg. B, 12 C.F.R. § 1002.2(c)(1)(i) [§ 202.2(c)(1)(i)].

53 Davis v. Reg'l Acceptance Corp., 300 F. Supp. 2d 377 (E.D. Va. 2002); *see also* Vereen v. Lou Sobh Automotive of Jax, Inc., 2011 WL 1447581, at *3–4 (M.D. Fla. Apr. 14, 2011) (allegation that auto dealer used bailment agreement to evade obligation to provide notice of adverse action survived a motion to dismiss).

54 Treadway v. Gateway Chevrolet Oldsmobile, 362 F.3d 971 (7th Cir. 2004).

55 Bayard v. Behlmann Automotive Servs., 292 F. Supp. 2d 1181 (E.D. Mo. 2003).

56 *See id.* (rejecting defendant's argument that there was no refusal to grant credit on the terms requested).

57 *See* Mungia v. Tony Rizza Oldsmobile Inc., 2002 WL 554504 (N.D. Ill. Apr. 15, 2002) (summary judgment granted to plaintiff when creditor relied on co-signer to inform plaintiff that her credit application had been denied).

58 Love v. O'Connor Chevrolet, Inc., 2006 WL 2460581 (N.D. Ill. Aug. 21, 2006).

59 *See* Meeks v. Murphy Auto Group, Inc., 2009 WL 3669638, at *4 (M.D. Fla. Oct. 30, 2009), *aff'd*, 441 Fed. Appx. 683 (11th Cir. 2011).

60 Reg. B, 12 C.F.R. § 1002.2(c)(3) [§ 202.2(c)(3)]; *see, e.g.*, Southern v. Golden Gate Auto Sales, 487 F. Supp. 2d 951 (N.D. Ill. 2006).

61 Reg. B, 12 C.F.R. § 1002.2(c)(2)(iv) [§ 202.2(c)(2)(iv)]; *see, e.g.*, Rahmaan v. Fed. Nat'l Mortgage Ass'n, 2003 WL 21940044 (D.D.C. May 19, 2003) (motion to dismiss ECOA notice claim against Fannie Mae for its credit scoring model granted because applicable law prohibited Fannie Mae from extending the credit plaintiff requested).

62 Kivel v. Wealthspring Mortgage Corp., 398 F. Supp. 2d 1049 (D. Minn. 2005).

63 Reg. B, 12 C.F.R. § 1002.2(c)(2)(v) [§ 202.2(c)(2)(v)]; *see, e.g.*, Taylor v. Nelson, 2006 WL 266052 (E.D. Pa. Jan. 31, 2006).

64 The acceptance of telephone service conditioned upon payment of a $50 security deposit has also been held not to constitute an adverse credit action. Edwards v. Sprint, Inc., 1998 U.S. App. LEXIS 21040 (9th Cir. Aug. 17, 1998).

65 Official Interpretations of Reg. B [Official Staff Commentary on Reg. B], 12 C.F.R. pt. 1002 [pt. 202], Supp. I, § 1002.2(c)(2)(v)-1 [§ 202.2(c)(2)(v)-1].

66 Reg. B, 12 C.F.R. § 1002.2(c)(1)(ii) [§ 202.2(c)(1)(ii)]; *see, e.g.*, Pierce v. Citibank (S.D.), 843 F. Supp. 646 (D. Or. 1994) (termination of wife's account occurred automatically when husband's delinquent accounts were terminated, even though accounts were unrelated and each was obtained based on establishment of independent creditworthiness).

The court later granted the defendant's motion for summary judgment because, among other reasons, the statute of limitations for bringing the ECOA claims had expired. Pierce v. Citibank (S.D.), 856 F. Supp. 1451 (D. Or. 1994), *aff'd*, 92 F.3d 1193 (9th Cir. 1996) (table) (text available at 1996 U.S. App. LEXIS 18496).

67 *See* O'Dowd v. South Cent. Bell, 729 F.2d 347 (5th Cir. 1984); *see also* Complaint and Settlement, United States v. Sprint Corp., No. 04CU-361 (N.D. Fla. Sept. 9, 2004), *available at* www.ftc.gov/os/caselist/0223160/0223160.shtm (in case brought by the Federal Trade Commission, Sprint agreed to pay $1.125 million in civil

all credit cards issued by the creditor would not be an adverse action.[68]

Refusal to increase the amount of credit available to an applicant who has made an application for an increase is an adverse action.[69] For example, it is an adverse action to reject a consumer's application for an increase of an existing $500 credit limit when the creditor's maximum limit is $1000 and the requirements for requesting an increase were met. It is also an adverse action to lower a previously established credit limit unless the limit was lowered due to account inactivity, default, or delinquency.[70] A refusal to automatically increase a credit line would not be an adverse action if the consumer had overrun the established credit line on a specific credit card purchase without prior authorization.[71]

Termination because the customer moved from the card issuer's service area is still an adverse action unless termination on this ground is explicitly provided for in the credit agreement between the parties.[72] If a creditor decides to terminate all credit accounts with low credit limits (for example, under $400) but keeps other credit accounts, this decision is also an adverse action.[73]

On the other hand, the following would not be adverse actions concerning existing accounts:

- *A change in the terms of an account expressly agreed to by the borrower.*[74]
- *Any action or forbearance relating to an account taken in connection with inactivity, default, or delinquency on that account.*[75] It is not an adverse action, for example, to repossess collateral, accelerate a defaulted loan, or to request the return of a credit card when the consumer has overrun the credit line.[76] It is likewise not adverse action to

notify the borrower erroneously that the account is in default.[77] Similarly, if the applicable contract defined the death of the primary cardholder as a default on the account, then termination on this ground would not be an adverse action.[78] Termination of an account based on a *current* default or delinquency is not an adverse action, but termination based upon a *past* default or delinquency is an adverse action.[79] When a homeowner has moved out of default or delinquency by obtaining a mortgage loan modification, cancellation of such modification when the homeowner was making timely payments under the modification and institution of a foreclosure action may constitute an adverse action.[80]

- *A refusal to extend additional credit under an existing credit arrangement when the additional credit would exceed a previously established credit limit.*[81] This provision has been held to include an application for an extension of a promissory note's maturity date.[82]
- *A refusal or failure to authorize an account transaction at a point of sale or loan,*[83] *except when the refusal is a*

---

penalties for its failure to provide adverse action notices under the ECOA and FCRA to consumers required to pay in advance or pay a deposit before receiving telephone service).

68 *See* Sutliff v. County Sav. & Loan Co., 533 F. Supp. 1307 (N.D. Ohio 1982) (increase in the interest rate on all demand mortgage notes in the same classification as the plaintiffs' note was not adverse action requiring notice to the plaintiffs).

69 Reg. B, 12 C.F.R. § 1002.2(c)(1)(iii) [§ 202.2(c)(1)(iii)].

70 Fed. Trade Comm'n, Unofficial staff letter, Clearinghouse No. 37,089 (Mar. 1983).

71 Official Interpretations of Reg. B [Official Staff Commentary on Reg. B], 12 C.F.R. pt. 1002 [pt. 202], Supp. I, § 1002.2(c)(2)(iii)-2 [§ 202.2(c)(2)(iii)-2].

72 *Id.* § 1002.2(c)(1)(ii)-1 [§ 202.2(c)(1)(ii)-1].

73 *Id.* § 1002.2(c)(1)(ii)-2 [§ 202.2(c)(1)(ii)-2].

74 Reg. B, 12 C.F.R. § 1002.2(c)(2)(i) [§ 202.2(c)(2)(i)].

75 Reg. B, 12 C.F.R. § 1002.2(c)(2)(ii) [§ 202.2(c)(2)(ii)].

There may be an adverse action, however, if the creditor takes action on an account based on a delinquency or default on another account.

76 *See* Haynes v. Bank of Wedowee, 634 F.2d 266 (5th Cir. 1981) (consumer was in default when creditor accelerated the loan, and therefore acceleration did not constitute adverse action under the exception contained in Regulation B, 12 C.F.R. § 202.2(c)(ii); Southern v. Golden Gate Auto Sales, 487 F. Supp. 2d 951 (N.D. Ill. 2006) (repossession and any continued action against the vehicle were taken in connection with delinquency); Baker v. Capital One Bank, 2006 WL 173668 (D. Ariz. Jan. 24, 2006) (reduction in a

consumer's credit limit based on account inactivity is not "adverse action" although creditor withdrew motion for summary judgment on question of whether reinstatement of credit limit to amount lower than borrower requested is an adverse action); *see also* Mchatten v. Chase Home Finance L.L.C., 2010 WL 3882587, at *8 (D. Ariz. Sept. 29, 2010) (ECOA adverse action notice provision does not apply when plaintiff was delinquent in mortgage payments under an existing credit arrangement with defendants); Harara v. ConocoPhillips Co., 377 F. Supp. 2d 779 (N.D. Cal. 2005) (no ECOA notice violation when credit denial was based on plaintiff's default).

77 Schlegel v. Wells Fargo Bank, N.A., 799 F. Supp. 2d 1100, 1106–07 (N.D. Cal. 2011).

78 15 U.S.C. § 1691(d)(6); Reg. B, 12 C.F.R. § 1002.2(c)(2)(ii) [§ 202.2(c)(2)(ii)].

79 Official Interpretations of Reg. B [Official Staff Commentary on Reg. B], 12 C.F.R. pt. 1002 [pt. 202], Supp. I, § 1002.2(c)(2)(ii)-2 [§ 202.2(c)(2)(ii)-2].

In 1999, the Federal Reserve Board proposed revising the official staff commentary to 12 C.F.R. § 202.2(c)(2)(ii) [§ 1002.2(c)(2)(ii)], to clarify that an adverse action does not include another action or a termination of an account due to a current delinquency or default on that account. 64 Fed. Reg. 44,582, 44,619 (Aug. 16, 1999).

The Federal Reserve Board decided not to adopt these proposed changes in final rules published in March 2003, stating instead that the interpretations will be reviewed and reissued for additional public comment. 68 Fed. Reg. 13,144, 13,154 (Mar. 18, 2003).

80 *See* appx. G.8, *infra* (sample complaint alleging breach of ECOA notice requirement when homeowner made modification payment but servicer proceeded to foreclosure).

81 15 U.S.C. § 1691(d)(6); Gillette of Kingston, Inc. v. Bank R.I., 2006 WL 1314259 (R.I. Super. Ct. May 5, 2006) (no notice required when creditor refused to extend additional credit under an existing credit arrangement).

82 Riggs Nat'l Bank v. Webster, 832 F. Supp. 147, 150 (D. Md. 1993) (application for an extension is an application for additional credit beyond a previously established credit limit; denial of said application is not an adverse action).

83 Reg. B, 12 C.F.R. § 1002.2(c)(2)(iii) [§ 202.2(c)(2)(iii)].

For example, a store's refusal to approve a credit card sale over $50 on a weekend, when no credit check can be made by phone, is not an adverse action.

termination or an unfavorable change in the terms of an account that does not affect "all or a substantial portion" of a class of the creditor's accounts or when the refusal is a denial of an application to increase the amount of credit available.[84] The official interpretations of Regulation B give several examples of point-of-sale activity that is not considered adverse action. There is no adverse action when credit is refused because a cardholder attempts to use an expired card or a card that has been reported as stolen or lost or the transaction is over the card's credit limit. Similarly, there is no adverse action when credit is refused because it appears fraud is involved, the card authorization process is not working, or billing statements have been returned for lack of a forwarding address.[85]

- *A mortgagee's acceleration of the mortgage loan following the mortgagor's unauthorized sale of the property.*[86] Notice need not be sent to the mortgagor or to the property purchaser.[87] However, if a mortgagor sells property and the buyer makes an application to the creditor to assume the mortgage loan, then the creditor must notify the buyer of the action taken unless the creditor's policy is not to permit assumptions.[88]

These creditor actions, such as those taken in connection with delinquent accounts, may not constitute adverse actions and thus may not trigger a requirement that creditors notify consumers of the actions taken. Nevertheless, creditors may not discriminate on a prohibited basis in taking such actions because the ECOA's general prohibition on discrimination applies to all aspects of a credit transaction, including revocation, alteration, or termination of credit and collection procedures.[89] Thus, for example, it would violate the ECOA to accelerate loans of public assistance recipients when one payment is in arrears if all other account holders are not treated similarly.

Questions have arisen as to whether adverse action notices are required when a borrower requests a modification of an existing mortgage loan, including a modification offered under the United States Department of Treasury's Making Home Affordable Modification Program (HAMP), and the borrower's request is denied. The Federal Reserve Board (FRB) has issued guidance on this point, and the Treasury Department has issued its own guidelines for loan servicers involved in HAMP. The FRB has determined that: the actions taken by a servicer under a HAMP modification constitute an extension of credit; a borrower's request for a modification constitutes an application; if the HAMP servicer evaluates a borrower's information according to HAMP guidelines, declines the request, and communicates the decision to the borrower, the servicer has taken

adverse action; and thus, unless the borrower is currently delinquent or in default, the servicer must provide an adverse action notice. The FRB has gone further and stated that, even if an adverse action notice is not required under Regulation B, a borrower may find it helpful to receive information as to why the mortgage loan modification request was declined.[90] The Treasury Department directed HAMP servicers to provide written notice to a borrower that has been evaluated for HAMP but is not offered a trial period plan or modification, or is at risk of losing eligibility because the borrower has failed to provide the required financial documentation.[91]

10.5.3 Adverse Actions Involving Counteroffers

The ECOA defines "adverse action" as "a denial or revocation of credit, a change in the terms of an existing credit arrangement, or a refusal to grant credit in substantially the amount or on substantially the terms requested."[92] Regulation B defines an adverse action as a "refusal to grant credit in substantially the amount or on substantially the terms requested in an application unless the creditor makes a counteroffer (to grant credit in a different amount or on other terms) and the applicant uses or expressly accepts the credit offered."[93] At least one court, however, has concluded that a consumer's acceptance of a loan when the terms changed between application and closing is not clearly acceptance of a counteroffer because of the surreptitious nature of the bait and switch.[94]

If a borrower does not use or accept the counteroffer, it is clear that the lender must comply with all ECOA notice pro-

---

84 Reg. B, 12 C.F.R. § 1002.2(c)(2)(iii) [§ 202.2(c)(2)(iii)].

85 Official Interpretations of Reg. B [Official Staff Commentary on Reg. B], 12 C.F.R. pt. 1002 [pt. 202], Supp. I, § 1002.2(c)(2)(iii)-1 [§ 202.2(c)(2)(iii)-1].

86 *Id.* § 1002.2(c)(2)(ii)-1 [§ 202.2(c)(2)(ii)-1].

87 *Id.*

88 *Id.*

89 Reg. B, 12 C.F.R. §§ 1002.2(m), 1002.4 [§§ 202.2(m), 202.4]; *see* ch. 9, *supra*.

90 Fed. Reserve Bd., Div. of Consumer & Regulatory Affairs, Publ'n No. CA 09-13, Mortgage Loan Modifications and Regulation B's Adverse Action Requirement (Dec. 4, 2009).

91 Making Home Affordable Modification Program, Supplemental Directive No. 09-08, at 1 (Nov. 3, 2009), *available at* www.hmp admin.com/portal/docs/hamp_servicer/sd0908.pdf; *see also* Boyd v. U.S. Bank, N.A., 787 F. Supp. 2d 747, 757–58 (N.D. Ill. 2011) (denying motion to dismiss as to claim that creditor failed to provide adverse action notice when denying HAMP modification); Bourdelais v. J.P. Morgan Chase, 2011 WL 1306311, at *8–9 (E.D. Va. Apr. 1, 2011). *But see* Pandit v. Saxon Mortgage Servs., Inc., 2012 WL 4174888, at *7 (E.D.N.Y. Sept. 17, 2012) (denial of a HAMP loan modification did not require adverse action notice because loan was in default); Eichholtz v. Wells Fargo Bank, N.A., 2011 WL 5375375, at *8–9 (E.D. Mich. Nov. 7, 2011); Mashburn v. Wells Fargo Bank, N.A., 2011 WL 2940363, at *6 (W.D. Wash. July 19, 2011) (no adverse action occurred and no notification was required when lender denied loan modification after applicant failed to respond to requests for required information); *In re* Bank of Am, Home Affordable Modification Program (HAMP), 2011 WL 2637222, at *6–7 (D.C. Mass. July 6, 2011); Davis v. CitiMortgage, Inc., 2011 WL 891209, at *2–3 (E.D. Mich. Mar. 11, 2011) (no adverse action occurred and no notification was required when bank after trial period failed to provide permanent HAMP modification).

92 15 U.S.C. § 1691(d)(6).

93 Reg. B, 12 C.F.R. § 1002.2(c)(1)(i) [§ 202.2(c)(1)(i)]; *see* § 10.4.2 *supra* (further discussion of counteroffers).

94 *In re* Ameriquest Mortgage Co. Mortgage Lending Practices Litig., 2007 WL 1202544 (N.D. Ill. Apr. 23, 2007).

visions required for adverse actions.[95]

10.5.4 Content of Adverse Action Notices

10.5.4.1 General

The notification of adverse action must contain the following elements:[96]

- A statement of the action taken (the notice does not have to use the term "adverse action"—the creditor may use any phrase or words that describe the action taken);[97]
- The creditor's name and address;
- The name and address of the federal agency with enforcement authority concerning the transaction;[98] and
- A statement of specific reasons for the action taken or a disclosure of the applicant's right to request a statement of such reasons, with the name, address, and telephone number of the person or office from which the statement of reasons can be obtained.[99]

This notice can be provided at the time the adverse action is taken or at the time of the application if the notification contains the required language disclosing the applicant's right to request a statement.[100]

The notification must also include the following language (or substantially similar language) detailing the applicant's ECOA rights as set out in Regulation B:

> The Federal Equal Credit Opportunity Act prohibits creditors from discriminating against credit applicants on the basis of race, color, religion, national origin, sex, marital status, age (provided the applicant has the capacity to enter into a binding contract); because all or part of the applicant's income derives from any public assistance program; or because the applicant has in good faith exercised any right under the Consumer Credit Protection Act. The federal agency that administers compliance with this law concerning this creditor is (name and address as specified by the appropriate agency listed in appendix A of this regulation).[101]

The exact language used need not be identical to the above quoted language, but it must be substantially similar.[102] For example, a creditor may add a reference to the fact that the ECOA permits age to be considered in certain credit scoring systems, add a reference to a similar state statute or regulation and to a state enforcement agency, or add certain disclosures required under the Fair Credit Reporting Act.[103]

Regulation B includes a series of sample forms for adverse action notices, some of which combine the disclosures required by the ECOA with those required by the Fair Credit Reporting Act.[104] In July 2011, these notices were revised in order to implement the FCRA's requirement, which was added by the Dodd-Frank Wall Street Reform and Consumer Protection Act of 2010,[105] to disclose the credit score used by the creditor in adverse action notices.[106]

10.5.4.2 The Reasons for Adverse Action

10.5.4.2.1 Reasons must be specific

Regulation B includes sample forms listing "specific reasons for adverse action."[107] Several of the sample forms contain lists of reasons, and the creditor is required to check off the appropriate boxes. Examples of the listed reasons include: credit application incomplete, insufficient number of references, unacceptable type of references provided, unable to verify credit references, temporary or irregular employment, unable to verify employment, income insufficient for amount of credit requested, excessive obligations in relation to income, length of residence, limited credit experience, delinquent credit obligations, garnishment, attachment, foreclosure, repossession, or value of collateral not sufficient.

If the creditor uses the Regulation B sample form, it may not rely solely on the listing of reasons on the sample and may not just check the listed reason closest to the creditor's actual reason. The creditor must adapt the form to state the specific reason for the adverse action.[108]

---

95 The notice required for counteroffers that are not adverse actions is discussed in § 10.4.3, *supra.*

96 Reg. B, 12 C.F.R. § 1002.9(a)(2) [§ 202.9(a)(2)].

97 Official Interpretations of Reg. B [Official Staff Commentary on Reg. B], 12 C.F.R. pt. 1002 [pt. 202], Supp. I, § 1002.9-1 [§ 202.9-1].

98 *See* Reg. B, 12 C.F.R. pt. 1002 [pt. 202], app. A (list of agencies to be listed in adverse action notices).

99 Reg. B, 12 C.F.R. § 1002.9(a)(2)(i),(ii) [§ 202.9(a)(2)(i),(ii)].

100 Reg. B, 12 C.F.R. § 1002.9(a)(3)(i)(B) [§ 202.9(a)(3)(i)(B)]; *see also* Curley v. JP Morgan Chase Bank, 2007 WL 1343793 (W.D. La. May 7, 2007) (discussing the provision), *aff'd*, 261 Fed. Appx. 781 (5th Cir. 2008).

101 *See* Reg. B, 12 C.F.R. § 1002.9(b)(1) [§ 202.9(b)(1)].

102 Reg. B, 12 C.F.R. § 1002.9(b)(1) [§ 202.9(b)(1)]; Official Interpretations of Reg. B [Official Staff Commentary on Reg. B], 12 C.F.R.

pt. 1002 [pt. 202], Supp. I, § 1002.9(b)(1)-1 [§ 202.9(b)(1)-1].

103 Official Interpretations of Reg. B [Official Staff Commentary on Reg. B], 12 C.F.R. § 1002.9(b)(1)-1, (2)-9 [§ 202.9(b)(1)-1, (2)-9]; *see* Reg. B, 12 C.F.R. pt. 1002 [pt. 202], Supp. I, app. C, forms C-1 to C-5 (a combination of the ECOA and FCRA disclosures).

104 The model notices are reprinted in Appendix B, *infra.*

105 15 U.S.C. § 1681m(a)(2)(A), *as added by* Pub. L. No. 111-203, tit. X, § 1100F(1), 124 Stat. 2112 (July 21, 2010); *see* § 10.10, *infra. See generally* National Consumer Law Center, Fair Credit Reporting § 8.5.2.4 (7th ed. 2010 and Supp.).

106 76 Fed. Reg. 41,590 (July 15, 2011).

107 *See* Reg. B, 12 C.F.R. pt. 1002 [pt. 202], app. C.

108 Reg. B, 12 C.F.R. pt. 1002 [pt. 202], app. C; *see also* Fischl v. Gen. Motors Acceptance Corp., 708 F.2d 143 (5th Cir. 1983) (creditor's "perfunctory reliance" on the sample form was considered "manifestly inappropriate" because the creditor had indicated that credit had been denied due to insufficient credit references, when the actual reasons were brevity of credit history and excessiveness of the amount to be financed). *But see* Aikens v. Northwestern Dodge, Inc., 2006 WL 59408 (N.D. Ill. Jan. 5, 2006) (in finding that notice met ECOA requirements, distinguishing plaintiff's case from the facts in *Fischl* because the notice in this case did not give rise to more than one interpretation).

A creditor may choose to use some other form, but the reasons stated there must be specific and indicate the principal reason or reasons for the action taken.[109] A creditor may not merely state that the adverse action was based on "internal standards or policies," or that the applicant failed to achieve the qualifying score on a credit scoring system, without indicating specific factors relating to the denial.[110] Moreover, a creditor cannot merely reinstate a terminated account without also specifying why the adverse action was taken.[111] Courts generally agree that long, detailed statements are not required, but some go to the other extreme, requiring mere "transparency."[112] Courts have, for example, approved notices that were ambiguous and required some interpretation by the consumer.[113]

In general, the statement must reasonably indicate the reasons for adverse action but not necessarily the source of the reported reason.[114] However, the source of the reason may be required to be disclosed under the Fair Credit Reporting Act.[115]

The creditor must disclose the reasons for adverse action even if the relationship between the stated reason and predicting creditworthiness may not be clear to the applicant.[116] In providing reasons for adverse action, creditors are not required to describe how or why a factor adversely affected an applicant. For example, the notice may say "length of residence" rather than "too short a period of residence."[117] For example, a telephone company's notice requesting a deposit because of the consumer's "past payment record" was held to be sufficiently specific.[118] In another case, the court upheld reasons stating that the applicant had sufficient balances on revolving credit lines and sufficient credit available considering her income.[119]

Regulation B includes instructions for use of the sample notification forms and gives an example that indicates how specific the creditor must be in providing its reasons for adverse action. For example, it is inadequate to state "insufficient credit references" when the applicant had finance company references but the creditor accepts only bank references. Instead, the notice should indicate "insufficient bank references."[120]

10.5.4.2.2 Reasons must be accurate

The reasons disclosed must relate to and accurately describe those factors actually reviewed, considered, or scored.[121] More-

---

109 Official Interpretations of Reg. B [Official Staff Commentary on Reg. B], 12 C.F.R. pt. 1002 [pt. 202], Supp. I, § 1002.9(b)(2)-1 [§ 202.9(b)(2)-1]; *see* Aikens v. Northwestern Dodge, Inc., 2006 WL 59408 (N.D. Ill. Jan. 5, 2006) (ECOA does not require creditor to utilize the exact language in the sample forms).

110 Reg. B, 12 C.F.R. § 1002.9(b)(2) [§ 202.9(b)(2)]; *see also* United States v. Moore & Mothershead, Clearinghouse No. 45,755 (N.D. Tex. Oct. 20, 1989) (consent decree based on allegations that creditor failed to disclose that a consumer report or other third-party information was used in deciding to deny credit); Fed. Trade Comm'n v. Green Tree Acceptance, Inc., Clearinghouse No. 44,327 (N.D. Tex. 1988) (consent decree requiring $115,000 penalty and injunctive relief for, among other things, failing to give reasons for adverse action or by merely stating that applicants failed to meet the creditor's internal credit underwriting standards); United States v. Winkleman Stores, Clearinghouse No. 40,626 (N.D. Ohio 1985) (consent order based on alleged failure to disclose actual negative factors in credit scoring system); O'Quinn v. Diners Club, Inc., 1978 U.S. Dist. LEXIS 15733 (N.D. Ill. Sept. 1, 1978).

111 Pierce v. Citibank (S.D.), 843 F. Supp. 646 (D. Or. 1994).
      The court later granted the defendant's motion for summary judgment based on, among other grounds, the expiration of the ECOA statute of limitations. Pierce v. Citibank (S.D.), 856 F. Supp. 1451 (D. Or. 1994), *aff'd*, 92 F.3d 1193 (9th Cir. 1996) (table) (text available at 1996 U.S. App. LEXIS 18496).

112 *See, e.g.*, Pettineo v. Harleysville Nat'l Bank & Trust Co., 2006 WL 241243 (E.D. Pa. Jan. 31, 2006) (ECOA notice that included reasons for denial that did apply to plaintiff's situation *and* reasons that did not apply was not in violation of ECOA; ECOA notice provisions require general transparency only).

113 *See, e.g.*, Williams v. MBNA America Bank, 538 F. Supp. 2d 1015, 1020–21 (E.D. Mich. 2008) ("clear and conspicuous" requirement applies to format of notice, not statement of reasons; reasons that plaintiff found incoherent and illogical met the ECOA's requirement); Aikens v. Northwestern Dodge, Inc., 2006 WL 59408 (N.D. Ill. Jan. 5, 2006) (it is irrelevant whether the applicant actually finds the notice educational or helpful); Higgins v. J.C. Penny, Inc., 630 F. Supp. 722 (E.D. Mo. 1986) (notice was sufficient to enable plaintiff to focus her efforts in a particular area and to investigate proprietary of company's decision).

114 *See, e.g.*, Anderson v. Capital One Bank, 224 F.R.D. 444 (W.D. Wis. 2004) (creditor's statement that plaintiff's Social Security number had been reported as assigned to a deceased person considered sufficient reason for denial, and creditor was not required to disclose source of report); *see also* Stoyanovich v. Fine Art Capital, 2007 WL 2363656 (S.D.N.Y. Aug. 17, 2007) (finding creditor violated ECOA notice requirement when creditor noted only that information was obtained from a source "other than consumer reporting agencies" but did not mention the nature of information).

115 *See* National Consumer Law Center, Fair Credit Reporting § 8.5.2 (7th ed. 2010 and Supp.).

116 Official Interpretations of Reg. B [Official Staff Commentary on Reg. B], 12 C.F.R. pt. 1002 [pt. 202], Supp. I, § 1002.9(b)(2)-4 [§ 202.9(b)(2)-4].

117 *Id.* § 1002.9(b)(2)-3 [§ 202.9(b)(2)-3].

118 *See* O'Dowd v. South Cent. Bell, 729 F.2d 347 (5th Cir. 1984).

119 Williams v. MBNA America Bank, 538 F. Supp. 2d 1015 (E.D. Mich. 2008).

120 Reg. B, 12 C.F.R. pt. 1002 [pt. 202], app. C.

121 Official Interpretations of Reg. B [Official Staff Commentary on Reg. B], 12 C.F.R. pt. 1002 [pt. 202], Supp. I, § 1002.9(b)(1)-2 [§ 202.9(b)(2)-2]; *see* Fischl v. Gen. Motors Acceptance Corp., 708 F.2d 143 (5th Cir. 1983) (creditor's "perfunctory reliance" on the sample form was considered "manifestly inappropriate" because the creditor had indicated that credit had been denied due to insufficient credit references, when the actual reasons were brevity of credit history and excessiveness of the amount to be financed); Carroll v. Exxon Co., 434 F. Supp. 557 (E.D. La. 1977). *But see* Pettineo v. Harleysville Nat'l Bank & Trust Co., 2006 WL 241243 (E.D. Pa. Jan. 31, 2006) (ECOA notice that included reasons for denial that did apply to plaintiff's situation *and* reasons that did not apply was not in violation of ECOA; the ECOA notice provisions require general transparency only); Para v. United Carolina Bank, 1998 U.S. Dist. LEXIS 16843 (E.D.N.C. Aug. 25, 1998) (discriminatory animus is clearly not a specific reason a lender might be expected to include in an ECOA notice; notice stating that application was denied because of lack of established earnings record and inadequate capital or assets was considered sufficient even if not the true reasons for denial); Higgins v. J.C. Penney, Inc., 630 F. Supp. 722 (E.D. Mo. 1986) (adverse action notice was adequate that gave "credit bureau report/delinquent history," "type of bank ac-

over, no factor that was a principal reason for the adverse decision may be excluded, even if the relationship of that factor to creditworthiness may not be clear to the applicant.[122]

A creditor may not disclose only "safe" reasons for denying credit, such as the lack of collateral, if the actual reason for denial of credit was a suspicious attribute such as residential zip code or age.[123] A creditor may not give one or two vague reasons for denial of credit when its actual reasons were the applicant's age, type of employment, or residential zip code.[124]

Courts may be more likely to find notices inadequate because a creditor used safe reasons rather than the real reasons if the creditor might actually have listed the real reasons for a denial.[125] Evidence that the creditor's real reason for denying an application was due to discrimination may help prove an ECOA substantive claim but, at least in one court's view, does not violate the provision requiring specific notice of the actual reasons for denial.[126]

It is inadequate to state that no reasons could be provided if the creditor simply failed to locate information on an applicant.[127] It is also inadequate for the creditor's reasons to be based on a credit report the creditor obtained *after* the applicant requested reasons for the denial. On the other hand, if the reasons are based on a credit report or other third-party source, the creditor may not hide this fact.[128]

Listing only one of several reasons is not sufficient. The creditor must disclose the principal reasons, though a specific number of reasons are not mandated, and the official interpretations of Regulation B state that disclosure of more than four reasons is not likely to be helpful to the applicant.[129]

Sometimes a denial is based on an "automatic-denial factor," that is, a negative factor that always results in a denial of credit no matter what other factors are present in the application. Examples might be that the applicant is a minor or is still in default with that creditor. In such situations, the applicable automatic-denial factors must always be disclosed as a reason for denial.[130]

If an application is incomplete and the creditor lacks sufficient data to make a decision, the creditor may either deny the application on that basis or provide a notice of incompleteness.[131] If the creditor denies the application for reasons other than incompleteness, the creditor must provide those reasons.[132]

The reasons given have to be the ones utilized by the creditor, but the reasons do not have to be good ones. For example, if the creditor's reason is based on a credit report containing outdated or unreliable information, there is no ECOA violation. Although the consumer should certainly bring these matters to the creditor's attention and the consumer has important rights to correct information under the Fair Credit Reporting Act,[133] there is no *ECOA* violation for a creditor making a bad credit decision. Under the ECOA, the creditor need not reconsider its denial when the consumer shows that the credit report was wrong.[134] However, Regulation B does require a

---

counts," and "type of credit references" as reasons for denial of credit).

122 Official Interpretations of Reg. B [Official Staff Commentary on Reg. B], 12 C.F.R. § 1002.9(b)(2)-4 [§ 202.9(b)(2)-4].

123 *See* United States v. Fid. Acceptance Corp., Clearinghouse No. 38,923 (D. Minn. 1985) (consent order based in part on alleged failure to disclose to elderly applicants the actual, illegal reasons for denial of credit); United States v. Gen. Motors Acceptance Corp., Clearinghouse No. 38,902 (D.N.M. 1984) (creditor failed to disclose to applicants that rejection or less favorable credit terms were based on their being Native Americans); United States v. Household Finance Corp., Clearinghouse No. 38,903 (N.D. Ill. 1984) (consent order partially based on allegations that creditor failed to provide rejected applicants with accurate and specific reasons, when actual reasons for rejection were based on discriminatory factors).

124 United States v. Montgomery Ward & Co., [1974–1980 Decisions Transfer Binder] Consumer Cred. Guide (CCH) ¶ 97,732 (D.D.C. 1979); United States v. Federated Dep't Stores, Inc., Clearinghouse No. 31,076 (S.D. Ohio 1978); *see also* Carroll v. Exxon Co., 434 F. Supp. 557 (E.D. La. 1977) (ECOA violation when only reason given for adverse action was that credit bureau contacted concerning applicant had been unable to furnish sufficient information about her when, in fact, creditor had denied her credit for four other reasons).

125 For example, in one case, the creditor's statement that "credit references are insufficient" was inadequate when the real reasons were brevity of credit history and excessive loan amount. These real reasons were ones that creditors should not be hesitant to give. Para v. United Carolina Bank, 1998 U.S. Dist. LEXIS 16843 (E.D.N.C. Aug. 25, 1998) (citing Fischl v. Gen. Motors Acceptance Corp., 708 F.2d 143 (5th Cir. 1983)).

126 *See* Para v. United Carolina Bank, 1998 U.S. Dist. LEXIS 16843 (E.D.N.C. Aug. 25, 1998) (discriminatory animus is clearly not a specific reason a lender might be expected to include in an ECOA notice).

127 *In re* Alden's, Inc., 92 F.T.C. 901 (Fed. Trade Comm'n 1978).

128 United States v. Moore & Mothershead, Clearinghouse No. 45,755 (N.D. Tex. Oct. 20, 1989) (consent decree based on allegations that

creditor failed to disclose that a consumer report or other third-party information was used in deciding to deny credit); United States v. Strawbridge & Clothier, Clearinghouse No. 38,925 (E.D. Pa. 1985) (alleged failure to disclose that credit was denied based on information received in credit reports).

129 Official Interpretations of Reg. B [Official Staff Commentary on Reg. B], 12 C.F.R. pt. 1002 [pt. 202], Supp. I, § 1002.9(b)(2)-1 [§ 202.9(b)(2)-1].

130 *Id.* § 1002.9(b)(2)-8 [§ 202.9(b)(2)-8].

131 *See* Schwab v. Kids' Financial, Inc., 2008 WL 349984 (D. Colo. Feb. 7, 2008) (summary judgment denied when factual dispute existed as to whether application was incomplete or lender failed to disclose reasons for adverse action); Reg. B, 12 C.F.R. § 1002.9(c) [§ 202.9(c)] (notice requirement); Official Interpretations of Reg. B [Official Staff Commentary on Reg. B], 12 C.F.R. pt. 1002 [pt. 202], Supp. I, § 1002.9(a)(1)-3 [§ 202.9(a)(1)-3]; § 10.7.3, *infra*.

132 Official Interpretations of Reg. B [Official Staff Commentary on Reg. B], 12 C.F.R. pt. 1002 [pt. 202], Supp. I, § 1002.9(a)(1)-3 [§ 202.9(a)(1)-3].

133 *See* National Consumer Law Center, Fair Credit Reporting (7th ed. 2010 and Supp.).

134 Jones v. KeyCorp Bank, 2008 WL 324126 (E.D. Mich. Feb. 6, 2008) (section 1002.202.6(b)(6)(ii) [section 202.6(b)(6)(ii)] of Regulation B does not require a creditor to revise a past denial of credit based on erroneous credit history information; applicant can provide corrected information with a new application); Grant v. World Class Mortgage Corp., 1990 U.S. Dist. LEXIS 2207 (N.D. Ill. Feb. 20, 1990) ("the statute and regulations do not . . . require that adverse action be based on reliable information, and do not require reconsideration of an application when it turns out that adverse action had been taken upon unreliable information").

creditor to consider at the applicant's request any information provided by the applicant that tends to indicate that the credit history being considered by the creditor does not accurately reflect the applicant's creditworthiness.[135] Interpreting this requirement to mean that the creditor must consider the information only in connection with a new application—rather than in connection with the recently denied application, as some courts have[136]—has the effect of transferring the cost of a mistake by a creditor or credit reporting agency onto the consumer, the person least likely to be able to avoid that cost.

10.5.4.2.3 *Reasons that must be disclosed when a credit scoring system is used*

It is not always obvious what the actual reason for denial of credit is when a creditor uses a credit scoring system, as the system bases the applicant's score on many different variables.[137] Although the credit score is a single number, numerous factors are used to derive that number. The problem is how to isolate the variables that adversely affected an applicant's credit score, causing the denial of the credit application. Analysis is difficult because, to date, credit scoring companies and creditors that use the scores have not been required, for the most part, to disclose information about how these numbers are derived.[138]

The official interpretation indicates that there is no one right system for determining the reasons for a denial based on a credit scoring system, but it does offer suggestions. The creditor could identify the factors on which the applicant's score fell furthest behind the average score for those who were granted credit or the average score for all applicants. Any other method that produces substantially similar results would also be acceptable.[139]

In a judgmental system, that is, any system other than a credit scoring system, the reasons for the denial must relate to those factors in the applicant's record actually reviewed by the person making the decision.[140] If the creditor uses a combined system of credit scoring and judgment, the reasons must relate to the part of the combined system that the applicant failed, that is, either the credit scoring system or the judgmental system.[141] If the application is not approved or denied as a result of the credit scoring but falls into a gray band, and the creditor performs a judgmental assessment and then denies the credit, the reasons disclosed must come from both components of the system.[142]

The same requirement applies when a judgmental assessment is the first component of the combined system.[143]

The Fair Credit Reporting Act (FCRA) requires creditors to disclose credit scores in various situations. Mortgage lenders must provide credit scores when such scores are used in conjunction with the extension of credit secured by residential real estate.[144] The Dodd-Frank Wall Street Reform and Consumer Protection Act of 2010 ("Dodd-Frank Act") added a requirement that creditors must disclose the credit scores they used when providing FCRA adverse action and risk-based pricing notices.[145] In July 2011, the model ECOA adverse action notices was revised in order to implement the Dodd-Frank Act's credit score disclosure requirement.[146]

10.5.4.2.4 *When creditor discloses only the applicant's right to a statement of reasons*

The creditor's notice of adverse action may either state the specific reasons for the action taken or disclose the applicant's right to request a statement of the reasons for the action taken and how that request should be made.[147] When the creditor discloses the right to request a statement of the reasons, the creditor also must disclose the applicant's right to have a creditor's subsequent oral statement of the reasons confirmed in writing.[148]

The applicant has sixty days from being notified of the adverse action to request such reasons.[149] The creditor then must provide the applicant with the reasons for the adverse action taken within thirty days after receiving the request. At this point, the creditor may provide the reasons orally. After receiving the reasons orally, the applicant has the right to request a written confirmation. The creditor must provide the written confirmation within thirty days after receiving such a request.[150]

10.6 General Notice Requirements

10.6.1 *Timing of Notices*

Within thirty days of receiving a completed application, a creditor must notify an applicant of actions taken concerning the creditor's approval of, counteroffer to, or adverse action on the application.[151] The application is considered complete once

---

135 Reg. B, 12 C.F.R. § 1002.6(b)(6)(iii) [§ 202.6(b)(6)(ii)].

136 *See, e.g.,* Jones v. KeyCorp Bank, 2008 WL 324126 (E.D. Mich. Feb. 6, 2008).

137 *See* §§ 6.3.2 (discussion of credit scoring systems), 6.3.2.2 (rules to determine whether a system qualifies as a credit scoring system), *supra.*

138 *See* § 6.3.2, *supra.*

139 Official Interpretations of Reg. B [Official Staff Commentary on Reg. B], 12 C.F.R. pt. 1002 [pt. 202], Supp. I, § 1002.9(b)(2)-5 [§ 202.9(b)(2)-5].

140 *Id.* § 1002.9(b)(2)-6 [§ 202.9(b)(2)-6].

141 *Id.* § 1002.9(b)(2)-7 [§ 202.9(b)(2)-7].

142 *Id.*

143 *Id.*

144 15 U.S.C. § 1681g(g)(1). *See generally* National Consumer Law Center, Fair Credit Reporting § 8.4.3 (7th ed. 2010 and Supp.).

145 15 U.S.C. § 1681m(a)(2)(A), (h)(5)(E)(ii), *as added by* Pub. L. No. 111-203, tit. X, § 1100F(1), 124 Stat. 2112 (July 21, 2010); *see* § 10.10, *infra. See generally* National Consumer Law Center, Fair Credit Reporting §§ 8.5.2.4, 8.7.3 (7th ed. 2010 and Supp.).

146 76 Fed. Reg. 41,590 (July 15, 2011). The model notices are reprinted in Appendix B, *infra.*

147 Reg. B, 12 C.F.R. § 1002.9(a)(2)(ii) [§ 202.9(a)(2)(ii)].

148 Reg. B, 12 C.F.R. § 1002.9(a)(2)(ii) [§ 202.9(a)(2)(ii)].

149 Reg. B, 12 C.F.R. § 1002.9(a)(2)(ii) [§ 202.9(a)(2)(ii)].

The regulation does not indicate whether this sixty-day period begins running when the notification is sent or when the applicant receives it.

150 Reg. B, 12 C.F.R. § 1002.9(a)(2)(ii) [§ 202.9(a)(2)(ii)].

151 Reg. B, 12 C.F.R. § 1002.9(a)(1)(i) [§ 202.9(a)(1)(i)]; *see* Schwab v.

a creditor has obtained all the information it normally considers in making a credit decision.[152] The creditor must send notification of adverse action taken on an incomplete application for credit within thirty days of taking the adverse action.[153]

In addition, the creditor must notify an applicant of action taken within thirty days of taking adverse action on an existing account.[154] With respect to counteroffers that are not adverse actions, the creditor has ninety days after notifying the applicant of the counteroffer to give notice of subsequent action.[155]

These timing requirements can take on special significance when the creditor makes an oral or written promise to supply credit but then goes back on that promise months later. For example, a home improvement contractor violates the ECOA by taking a credit application but denying the loan (or changing the terms or creditor) months later after the work has been completed.[156]

10.6.2 Form of the Notification

10.6.2.1 General

The creditor must give the applicant written notification of an adverse action.[157] Notice of an approval may be explicit or implicit.[158] There is a split among courts that have addressed the issue of whether written notice is required for counteroffers that are not adverse actions.[159] In addition, creditors that have acted on 150 or fewer applications during the preceding calendar year may notify the applicant orally.[160] An oral notification is considered complete when the creditor "communicates" with the applicant.[161]

Notice of adverse action, like other notices required by Regulation B (except notices pertaining to self-testing[162] and information collection for monitoring purposes[163]), must be clear and conspicuous and in a form that the applicant may retain.[164]

The ECOA notification may appear on the front or back or on both sides of a form or letter.[165] The notification can be made in a language other than English, so long as it is available in English upon request.[166]

Regulation B includes a series of sample notices of action taken and statement of reasons.[167] The forms are illustrative and may not be appropriate for all creditors. The forms may require modification for particular applications, but proper use of the forms will satisfy the ECOA's notice requirements.[168]

10.6.2.2 Electronic Notifications

Regulation B provides for electronic delivery of ECOA notifications.[169] The rule was issued in response to passage of the Electronic Signatures in Global and National Commerce Act (E-Sign Act).[170] In accordance with the E-Sign Act, a creditor may provide by electronic communication any disclosure required by Regulation B to be in writing.[171] Disclosures by electronic communication, like disclosures provided in writing, must be provided in a clear and conspicuous manner and in a form the applicant may retain.[172]

For disclosures required to be in writing, the creditor must obtain the applicant's affirmative consent to disclosure by electronic communication, in accordance with the E-Sign Act.[173]

One potential pitfall of electronic disclosure may be attempts by overbearing creditors to entice or coerce consumers into consenting to electronic notifications when the consumers do not actually have Internet access. Creditors might do this by

---

Kids' Financial Inc., 2008 WL 349984 (D. Colo. Feb. 7, 2008) (issue of material fact existed whether application was complete when denial was sent, as defendant had asked for plaintiff's pay stub and alleged that it had not received it when it sent the denial).

152 Official Interpretations of Reg. B [Official Staff Commentary on Reg. B], 12 C.F.R. pt. 1002 [pt. 202], Supp. I, § 1002.9(a)(1)-1 [§ 202.9(a)(1)-1]; *see* § 10.7.2, *infra*.

153 Reg. B, 12 C.F.R. § 1002.9(a)(1)(ii) [§ 202.9(a)(1)(ii)]; *see* § 10.7.3, *infra* (incomplete applications).

154 Reg. B, 12 C.F.R. § 1002.9(a)(1)(iii) [§ 202.9(a)(1)(iii)].

155 Reg. B, 12 C.F.R. § 1002.9(a)(1)(iv) [§ 202.9(a)(1)(iv)].

156 *See* Jochum v. Pico Credit Corp., 730 F.2d 1041 (5th Cir. 1984) (a creditor that failed to notify applicants for a second mortgage home improvement loan that they had been rejected for the loan until after the home improvements had been completed, and then only via the contractor, had no justifiable defense for failing to provide notice of rejection).

157 Reg. B, 12 C.F.R. § 1002.9(a)(2) [§ 202.9(a)(2)].

158 Official Interpretations of Reg. B [Official Staff Commentary on Reg. B], 12 C.F.R. 1002.9(a)(1)-2 [§ 202.9(a)(1)-2].

159 *See* § 10.4.3, *supra*.

160 Reg. B, 12 C.F.R. § 1002.9(d) [§ 202.9(d)]; *see* Taylor v. Nelson, 2006 WL 266052 (E.D. Pa. Jan. 31, 2006). *But see* Palmiotto v. Bank of N.Y., 1989 U.S. Dist. LEXIS 11546 (S.D.N.Y. Sept. 29, 1989) (creditor who did not show that it was eligible to give oral notice could not prevail on its argument that consumer's ECOA claim was time-barred based on date of oral notice).

161 Official Interpretations of Reg. B [Official Staff Commentary on Reg. B], 12 C.F.R. 1002.9-3 [§ 202.9-3]; *see, e.g.*, Curley v. JP Morgan Chase Bank, 2007 WL 1343793 (W.D. La. May 7, 2007)

(oral notice sufficient when defendant orally informed agent of applicant and also said "I'm sorry" when returning application file to applicant), *aff'd*, 261 Fed. Appx. 781 (5th Cir. 2008); Birkett Williams Ford, Inc. v. East Woodworking Co., 456 N.E.2d 1304 (Ohio Ct. App. 1982) (oral notice at time of purchase was sufficient).

162 *See* § 10.14, *infra*.

163 *See* § 10.13, *infra*.

164 Reg. B, 12 C.F.R. § 1002.4(d) [§ 202.4(d)]; *see, e.g.*, Pettineo v. GE Money Bank, 2011 WL 1163308, *4–5 (E.D. Penn. Mar. 30, 2011) (dismissing claim that creditor's notice failed to meet clear and conspicuous standard).

165 Official Interpretations of Reg. B [Official Staff Commentary on Reg. B], 12 C.F.R. pt. 1002 [pt. 202], Supp. I, § 1002.9-4 [§ 202.9-4]; *cf.* Barber v. Rancho Mortgage & Inv. Corp., 32 Cal. Rptr. 2d 906 (Cal. Ct. App. 1994).

166 Reg. B, 12 C.F.R. § 1002.4(e) [§ 202.4(e)].

167 *See* Reg. B, 12 C.F.R. pt. 1002 [pt. 202], app. C.

168 Reg. B, 12 C.F.R. pt. 1002 [pt. 202], app. C.

169 Reg. B, 12 C.F.R. § 1002.4(d)(2) [§ 202.4(d)(2)]; Final Rule, 72 Fed. Reg. 63,445 (Nov. 9, 2007).

170 Pub. L. No. 106-229, 114 Stat. 464 (2000) (codified at 15 U.S.C. §§ 7001–7031).

171 Reg. B, 12 C.F.R. § 1002.4(d)(2) [§ 202.4(d)(2)].

172 Reg. B, 12 C.F.R. § 1002.4(d)(1) [§ 202.4(d)(1)].

173 15 U.S.C. §§ 7001–7031.

penalizing consumers who decline to accept electronic notifications, even if these consumers do not have the ability to access them. However, such practices would likely violate the ECOA's prohibition against discrimination based on good faith exercise of rights under the Consumer Credit Protection Act.[174] Also, because such practices are more likely to affect consumers without computers, they may have a disparate impact on protected classes under the ECOA.[175]

10.6.3 Who Must Receive Notice?

10.6.3.1 Applicants

Creditors are required to notify applicants of action taken. The statute defines an "applicant" as "any person who applies to a creditor directly for an extension, renewal, or continuation of credit or who applies to a creditor indirectly by use of an existing credit plan for an amount exceeding a previously established credit limit."[176]

Regulation B defines an applicant as including "any person who requests or who has received an extension of credit from a creditor," including "any person who is or may become contractually liable regarding an extension of credit."[177] In addition, Regulation B states that, for purposes of section 1002.7(d) [section 202.7(d)], "applicant" includes guarantors, sureties, endorsers, and similar parties.[178]

Regulation B defines "contractually liable" as being expressly obligated to repay all debts on an account pursuant to an agreement.[179] Regulation B defines "extension of credit" as the granting of credit in any form, including but not limited to credit granted in addition to existing credit, open-end credit, refinancings, renewals, and consolidation, or the continuation of existing credit.[180]

Thus a co-signer is an applicant, but an authorized user on someone else's credit account may not be an applicant unless the user is obligated to repay all debts on the account.[181]

A spouse whose signature is improperly required is an applicant. Someone who does not sign the promissory note itself but who is required to sign a mortgage securing that note is contractually liable, because the note can be satisfied from that property.[182] In cases in which a creditor has been requested by a third party to make a specific extension of credit directly or indirectly to an applicant, the notice may be made directly by the creditor or indirectly through the third party, provided that the identity of the creditor is disclosed.[183]

10.6.3.2 Notice to Multiple Applicants

When there is more than one applicant for credit, the required notification need be given to only one applicant—the primary applicant, if one is apparent.[184] There is the possibility of unlawful discrimination in the identification of the primary applicant. A creditor might assume, for instance, that the husband in a married couple is the primary applicant. The Fair Credit Reporting Act (FCRA), in contrast, requires that notice be given to "any consumer" when an adverse action is taken that is based in whole or in part on information contained in a credit report.[185]

For example, in one case, a dealer told a consumer that she needed to find a co-signer in order to finance a car. The dealer told her that, if she met this requirement, the financing would be in her name, not in the name of the co-signer. A court found that the dealer was required to notify the consumer that her application was denied when the creditor ended up approving credit in the co-signer's name only.[186]

---

174 *See* § 3.4.4, *supra.*

175 *See* § 3.7.2, *supra.*

176 15 U.S.C. § 1691a(b).

177 Reg. B, 12 C.F.R. § 1002.2(e) [§ 202.2(e)]; *see, e.g.,* Reynolds v. Reliable Transmissions, Inc., 2010 WL 137573, at *3 (E.D. Va. Apr. 2, 2010) (person in whose name a fraudulent applicant was submitted is an applicant to whom defendant was required to provide notice of adverse action).

178 Reg. B, 12 C.F.R. § 1002.2(e) [§ 202.2(e)].
Section 1002.7(d) [§ 202.7(d)] deals with rules concerning signatures of spouses and others. *See* §§ 2.2.4.2, *supra* (discussing whether guarantors and others are required to comply only with the section 1002.7(d) [§ 202.7(d)] provisions), 5.6, *supra* (discussing spousal signature requirements).

179 Reg. B, 12 C.F.R. § 1002.2(*i*) [§ 202.2(*i*)].

180 Reg. B, 12 C.F.R. § 1002.2(q) [§ 202.2(q)].

181 Reg. B, 12 C.F.R. § 1002.7(c) [§ 202.7(c)]; *see* Miller v. American Express Co., 688 F.2d 1235 (9th Cir. 1982) (in challenging American Express's policy of automatically canceling a supplementary cardholder's account upon the death of the principal cardholder, plaintiff was found to be more than a mere user of her husband's account; the ECOA applied because plaintiff was personally liable under the

contract creating the supplementary account for all debts charged on her card by any person); *see also* Official Interpretations of Reg. B [Official Staff Commentary on Reg. B], 12 C.F.R. pt. 1002 [pt. 202], Supp. I, § 1002.7(c)(1)-1, (2)-1 [§ 202.7(c)(1)-1, (2)-1].
Note that, under the ECOA, a creditor may require that a user become contractually liable on the account in order to be designated an authorized user, as long as the condition is not imposed on a discriminatory basis. Official Interpretations of Reg. B [Official Staff Commentary on Reg. B], 12 C.F.R. § 1002.7(a)-1 [§ 202.7(a)-1].

182 Carter v. Buckeye Rural Electric Coop., 2001 WL 1681104 (S.D. Ohio Sept. 7, 2001) (plaintiff could be "contractually liable" and thus was an "applicant" when electric cooperative added her name to husband's account without her consent); Ford v. Citizens & Southern Nat'l Bank, 700 F. Supp. 1121 (N.D. Ga. 1988) (husband required to put up a mortgage to secure note signed by his wife was contractually liable and therefore was aggrieved party with standing to sue), *aff'd on other grounds*, 928 F.2d 1118 (11th Cir. 1991).

183 15 U.S.C. § 1691(d)(4); Reg. B, 12 C.F.R. § 1002.9(g) [§ 202.9(g)]; *see, e.g.,* Taylor v. Nelson, 2006 WL 266052 (E.D. Pa. Jan. 31, 2006).

184 Reg. B, 12 C.F.R. § 1002.9(f) [§ 202.9(f)]; *see* Mungia v. Tony Rizza Oldsmobile, Inc., 2002 WL 554504 (N.D. Ill. Apr. 15, 2002) (summary judgment granted for plaintiff who applied for credit in her name and was not given notice of denial; creditor instead granted credit in the co-signer's name only and relied on the co-signer to inform plaintiff that her credit application had been denied).

185 *See* National Consumer Law Center, Fair Credit Reporting ch. 8 (7th ed. 2010 and Supp.); § 10.10, *supra.*

186 Mungia v. Tony Rizza Oldsmobile, Inc., 2002 WL 554504 (N.D. Ill. Apr. 15, 2002).

10.6.3.3 Is Actual Receipt Required?

The ECOA obligates the creditor to provide timely notice but does not expressly require actual notice.[187] The written notice may be delivered or mailed to the applicant's last known address.[188] Courts will generally presume that a properly mailed notice is received by the addressee.[189] This presumption can be rebutted.[190]

10.7 Additional Notice Requirements for New Accounts

10.7.1 Application Required

An application is defined in Regulation B as "an oral or written request for an extension of credit that is made in accordance with procedures used by a creditor for the type of credit requested."[191] A creditor has latitude to establish its own application process and to decide the type and amount of information it will require from applicants.[192]

"Procedures used by a creditor" includes not only the creditor's stated procedures but also the actual practices that the creditor follows in making credit decisions.[193] Thus, even if the creditor's stated policy is to require a written application, an oral application is sufficient if the creditor routinely decides to grant or deny credit based on an oral request for credit.[194]

Regulation B permits creditors to take either oral or written applications for credit. However, in no circumstances may a creditor take an oral application for dwelling-related types of credit.[195] When a creditor conducts the application process orally, it still must maintain written records of the process and of its reasons for taking a particular action on the application.[196]

An application, for instance, can consist of a telephone inquiry to a lender, if the lender has a policy or practice of making credit decisions solely on the basis of information received by telephone. When a creditor treats a telephone call as sufficient to take an adverse action, the creditor must request the applicant's name and address in order to provide written notification. If the applicant declines to provide that information, then the creditor has no further notification responsibility.[197]

Even if a creditor does not have a general practice of treating an oral inquiry as an application, if it does so in a particular case, then the inquiry is an application even if it does not meet the creditor's normal standards for an application.[198]

Similarly, pre-qualification and pre-approval programs could trigger the right to notice under certain circumstances.[199] Whether a creditor must provide a notice for a pre-qualification request depends on the creditor's response to the request, not on what the consumer says or asks.[200] If, in giving information to the consumer, the creditor also evaluates information about the consumer, decides to decline the request, and communicates this to the consumer, the creditor has treated the inquiry or pre-qualification request as an application and must then comply with the notice requirements.[201]

However, a creditor may treat a request as an inquiry, not requiring notice, if a creditor evaluates specific information about the consumer and tells the consumer the loan amount, rate, and other terms of credit the consumer could qualify for and explains the application process.[202] If the creditor decides

---

187 *See* Davis v. U.S. Bancorp., 383 F.3d 761 (8th Cir. 2004) (plaintiff did not present evidence to rebut presumption that a properly mailed document is received).

188 Official Interpretations of Reg. B [Official Staff Commentary on Reg. B], 12 C.F.R. pt. 1002 [pt. 202], Supp. I, § 1002.9-3 [§ 202.9-3].

189 *See* Davis v. U.S. Bancorp, 383 F.3d 761 (8th Cir. 2004).

190 Garcia v. Ed Moses Dodge, 2006 WL 2640568 (D. Ariz. Sept. 14, 2006) (denying creditor's motion for summary judgment because of factual dispute regarding delivery); Love v. O'Connor Chevrolet, Inc., 2006 WL 2460581 (N.D. Ill. Aug. 21, 2006) (creditor's production of a notice in response to a subpoena is not enough to raise an evidentiary presumption of delivery); *see, e.g.*, Thele v. Sunrise Chevrolet, Inc., 2004 WL 1194751 (N.D. Ill. May 28, 2004) (finding that plaintiff did not rebut presumption); Jones v. Citibank, 844 F. Supp. 437 (N.D. Ill. 1994) (when plaintiff unequivocally denies receipt of a letter, there is a genuine issue of material fact, and summary judgment is not appropriate).

191 Reg. B, 12 C.F.R. § 1002.2(f) [§ 202.2(f)].
    Application is not defined in the statute. *See also* Lilley v. JPMorgan Chase Bank, 2010 WL 4392561, at *3 (D. Utah Oct. 28, 2010) (ECOA claim dismissed as plaintiffs failed to allege that they made an application for credit in accordance with bank's procedures and, if no application, defendant had no duty to provide notice of adverse action); Official Interpretations of Reg. B [Official Staff Commentary on Reg. B], 12 C.F.R. pt. 1002 [pt. 202], Supp. I, § 1002.2(f)-1 [§ 202.2(f)-1] to -6].

192 Official Interpretations of Reg. B [Official Staff Commentary on Reg. B], 12 C.F.R. pt. 1002 [pt. 202], Supp. I, § 1002.2(f)-1 [§ 202.2(f)-1].

193 *Id.* § 1002.2(f)-2 [§ 202.2(f)-2]; *see* Newton v. United Companies Financial Corp., 24 F. Supp. 2d 444 (E.D. Pa. 1998) (communication with lender found to be de facto application because all information that lender regularly obtained was provided, and the lender regularly treated such communications as applications for credit and made decisions based upon them).

194 Official Interpretations of Reg. B [Official Staff Commentary on Reg. B], 12 C.F.R. pt. 1002 [pt. 202], Supp. I, § 1002.2(f)-2 [§ 202.2(f)-2].

195 Reg. B, 12 C.F.R. § 1002.4(c) [§ 202.4(c)]; *see* § 10.4.4, *supra*.
    "Dwelling-related" types of credit are those covered in section 1002.13(a) [§ 202.13(a)] and include credit primarily for the purchase or refinancing of a dwelling occupied or to be occupied by the applicant as a principal residence and when the extension of credit will be secured by the dwelling.

196 Reg. B, 12 C.F.R. § 1002.12(b) [§ 202.12(b)]; *see also* § 5.4.2, *supra*.

197 Official Interpretations of Reg. B [Official Staff Commentary on Reg. B], 12 C.F.R. pt. 1002 [pt. 202], Supp. I, § 1002.9(A)(1)-7 [§ 202.9(a)(1)-7].

198 *Id.* § 1002.2(f)-2 [§ 202.2(f)-2].

199 *Id.* § 1002.9-5 [§ 202.9-5].

200 *Id.* (referring to Official Interpretations of Reg. B [Official Staff Commentary on Reg. B], 12 C.F.R. pt. 1002 [pt. 202], Supp. I, § 1002.2(f)-3 [§ 202.2(f)-3)]).

201 Official Interpretations of Reg. B [Official Staff Commentary on Reg. B], 12 C.F.R. pt. 1002 [pt. 202], Supp. I, § 1002.2(f)-3 [§ 202.2(f)-3].

202 *Id.* § 1002.9-5 [§ 202.9-5].

that it will not approve the request and communicates that decision to the consumer, there is an application and notice is required.[203] In general, the official interpretations of Regulation B ("the official interpretations") distinguish between inquires and pre-qualification requests on the one hand and certain pre-approval requests on the other for purposes of determining whether an application exists.[204]

10.7.2 Notice Requirements for Completed Applications

The notice requirements for approvals, counteroffers and adverse actions apply only if the applicant submits a completed application.[205] It is critical to plead facts sufficient to show that the consumer has submitted a completed application.[206]

A completed application is defined as an application "in connection with which a creditor has received all the information that the creditor regularly obtains and considers in evaluating applications for the amount and type of credit requested (including but not limited to credit reports, any additional information requested from the applicant, any approvals or reports by governmental agencies or other persons that are necessary to guarantee, insure, or provide security for the credit or collateral)."[207]

The official interpretation provides that, although the regulation gives the creditor latitude to establish its own information requirements, the creditor nevertheless must act with reasonable diligence to collect necessary information.[208] The creditor may violate the ECOA if it deliberately delays obtaining the information necessary to complete an application.[209] The official interpretation suggests the following scenarios: the creditor should promptly request information, such as a credit report,

from third parties after receiving the application; if additional information is needed, such as an address or a telephone number to verify employment, the creditor should contact the applicant promptly.[210] The wide latitude described in the official interpretations should not give a lender leeway—regardless of the substance of its actual practices—to choose in a subjective manner what to call a "completed" application.[211] There is often confusion with respect to whether an application is complete. According to one court, loan documents generally use qualifying language in the earlier stages of the process that is often susceptible to misinterpretation. Examples include noting that a loan application is "conditionally pre-approved" or that the borrower is "conditionally pre-qualified."[212]

In one case, written and oral requests for credit made by home improvement dealers and by the brokers on behalf of the consumers were considered to be completed applications once the lender had received the respective title reports.[213] The court did not accept the lender's argument that the completed loan application was the package sent by the lender's agent to the underwriting department. Instead, the court found that the application process occurs between the prospective borrower and the lender, and the application becomes complete when the lender has enough information to know it cannot extend the requested loan.[214]

10.7.3 Notice Requirements for Incomplete Applications

The creditor must take one of two actions within thirty days of receiving an incomplete application: (1) notify the applicant of the approval of, counteroffer to, or adverse action on the application, or (2) notify the applicant of the incompleteness of the application and that further information is needed.[215]

---

203 *Id.*

204 Official Interpretations of Reg. B [Official Staff Commentary on Reg. B], 12 C.F.R. pt. 1002 [pt. 202], Supp. I, § 1002.2(f)-3 to (f)-5 [§ 202.2(f)-3 to (f)-5]; *see* § 2.2.4.3, *supra.*

205 15 U.S.C. § 1691(d); Reg. B, 12 C.F.R. § 1002.9(a)(1)(i) [§ 202.9(a)(1)(i)].

206 *See, e.g.*, Sanders v. Mountain America Federal Credit Union, 2012 WL 3064741, at *6 (10th Cir. July 30, 2012) (complaint allegation that application was complete survived motion to dismiss).

207 Reg. B, 12 C.F.R. § 1002.2(f) [§ 202.2(f)]; *see, e.g.*, Wright v. Suntrust Bank, 2006 WL 2714717 (N.D. Ga. Sept. 18, 2006) (application not complete when creditor never obtained applicant's credit report, never provided written authorization for credit report, and never paid application fee).

208 Official Interpretations of Reg. B [Official Staff Commentary on Reg. B], 12 C.F.R. § 1002.2(f)-6 [§ 202.2(f)-6]; *see, e.g.*, Errico v. Pac. Capital Bank, N.A., 753 F. Supp. 2d 1034 (N.D. Cal. 2010) (plaintiffs have sufficiently stated a claim for defendants' failure to use reasonable diligence in determining whether plaintiffs had submitted a completed application).

209 *See, e.g.*, Saldana v. Citibank, 1996 U.S. Dist. LEXIS 8327 (N.D. Ill. June 13, 1996) (because Citibank regularly obtains and considers appraisals to complete an application, plaintiff's application was not complete until creditor received appraisal; although not the case here, court stated that there may be an impermissible motive if creditor deliberately delays obtaining the information necessary to complete an application).

210 *Id.; see, e.g.*, Manire v. American Equity Mortgage, Inc., 2005 WL 2173679 (E.D. Mich. Sept. 6, 2005) (application was incomplete when plaintiff allegedly did not return defendant's calls to complete application; court was not persuaded by plaintiff's assertion that he believed that the paperwork he completed constituted a new loan); Kirk v. Kelley Buick of Atlanta, Inc., 336 F. Supp. 2d 1327 (N.D. Ga. 2004) (a lender that sometimes requires verification of an applicant's salary, references, and phone number successfully argued that an application was incomplete without these verifications).

211 Newton v. United Cos. Financial Corp., 24 F. Supp. 2d 444 (E.D. Pa. 1998).

212 Jefferson v. Briner, Inc., 2006 WL 1720692 (E.D. Va. June 21, 2006).

213 *Id.*

214 *Id.* (common sense instructs that an application is something made by the applicant to the lending company, not something that happens between two divisions of the company without any participation on part of the applicant). *But see* Gillette of Kingston, Inc. v. Bank R.I., 2006 WL 1314259 (R.I. Super. Ct. May 5, 2006) (application for credit not complete when process was ongoing and included multiple telephone conversations and requests for interim financial records).

215 Reg. B, 12 C.F.R. § 1002.9(c) [§ 202.9(c)]; *see, e.g.*, Torgerson v. Wells Fargo Bank S.D., 2009 WL 255995, at *12 (D.S.D. Feb. 3, 2009); *see also* Errico v. Pac. Capital Bank, N.A., ___ F. Supp. 2d

If the creditor chooses the first option, the creditor must initially determine that the incompleteness of the application is based on information that the applicant must provide and on the creditor's lack of sufficient data for a credit decision. The creditor may then deny the application, giving as the reason for the denial that the application is incomplete.[216] If the incompleteness does not prevent a credit decision from being made, the creditor may evaluate the application and make a decision. In that situation, the incompleteness is not the reason for the adverse action.[217]

When selecting the second option, the creditor has two additional options. It may send a *written* notice to the applicant specifying the information needed, designating a reasonable period of time to provide the information, and informing the applicant that failure to provide the information requested will result in no further consideration being given to the application.[218] If the applicant does not respond to a written notice within the designated reasonable period of time, the creditor does not need to take further action.[219] If information requested by the creditor is submitted after the time period designated by the creditor, the creditor may require the applicant to make a new application.[220] If the applicant supplies the requested information within the designated time period, the creditor must then take action and notify the applicant of the action taken.[221]

Alternatively, a creditor may inform the applicant orally of the need for additional information.[222] If the application remains incomplete, the creditor must then send written notice of approval, counteroffer, or adverse action or a written notice of incompleteness.[223] If the applicant provides the information, the creditor must notify the applicant of an approval, counteroffer, or adverse action.[224] In addition, creditors that have acted on 150 or fewer applications during the preceding calendar year may satisfy the notice requirement orally.[225]

10.7.4 Withdrawn Applications for Credit

When an applicant expressly withdraws an application for credit, the creditor need not comply with the notification requirements.[226] The creditor must still comply, however, with

___, 2010 WL 4699394, at *7 (N.D. Cal. Nov. 9, 2010) (plaintiffs stated a claim for defendant's failure to notify plaintiffs of incompleteness of application); Official Interpretations of Reg. B [Official Staff Commentary on Reg. B], 12 C.F.R. pt. 1002 [pt. 202], Supp. I, § 1002.9(c)(1)-1 [§ 202.9(c)(1)-1]. *But see* Sanders v. Ethington, 2010 WL 5252843, at *4 (D. Utah Dec. 16, 2010) (dismissing ECOA claim that creditor failed to provide adverse action notice because application was incomplete, but failing to discuss creditor's obligation as to incomplete applications); Lawrence v. Lenders for Cmty. Dev. (LCD), 2010 WL 4922662, at *6 (N.D. Cal. Nov. 29, 2010) (no adverse action occurred when plaintiff conceded that he never provided income tax return requested by defendant to complete loan application).

216 Official Interpretations of Reg. B [Official Staff Commentary on Reg. B], 12 C.F.R. pt. 1002 [pt. 202], Supp. I, § 1002.9(a)(1)-3 [§ 202.9(a)(1)-3]; *see, e.g.,* Wright v. Suntrust Bank, 2006 WL 2714717 (N.D. Ga. Sept. 18, 2006) (genuine issue of fact existed as to whether creditor had an obligation to notify borrower that the application was incomplete because of failure to submit an application fee and written authorization for a credit report).

217 Official Interpretations of Reg. B [Official Staff Commentary on Reg. B], 12 C.F.R. pt. 1002 [pt. 202], Supp. I, § 1002.9(a)(1)-4 [§ 202.9(a)(1)-4].

218 Reg. B, 12 C.F.R. § 1002.9(c)(2) [§ 202.9(c)(2)]; *see* Johnson v. Grossinger Motorcorp., Inc., 753 N.E.2d 431 (Ill. App. Ct. 2001) (holding that written list satisfied ECOA's written notice requirement when car dealer provided consumer with written list of documents required to obtain financing and consumer failed to fully respond).

The requirement that a creditor must provide a notice of incompleteness does not apply to pre-approvals that constitute applications. Official Interpretations of Reg. B [Official Staff Commentary on Reg. B], 12 C.F.R. pt. 1002 [pt. 202], Supp. I, § 1002.9(c)(1)-1 [§ 202.9(c)(1)-1].

219 *See* Reg. B, 12 C.F.R. §§ 1002.2(f), 1002.9(c) [§§ 202.2(f), 202.9(c)]; *see also* Cartwright v. American Sav. & Loan Ass'n, 880 F.2d 912 (7th Cir. 1989) (mortgage lender did not violate ECOA when it placed application on indefinite hold after requesting that applicant herself provide information on comparable housing prices in a largely minority neighborhood; nor was lender required to provide notice of adverse action, because none had occurred).

220 Official Interpretations of Reg. B [Official Staff Commentary on Reg. B], 12 C.F.R. pt. 1002 [pt. 202], Supp. I, § 1002.9(c)(2)-1 [§ 202.9(c)(2)-1].

221 Reg. B, 12 C.F.R. § 1002.9(c)(2) [§ 202.9(c)(2)].

222 Reg. B, 12 C.F.R. § 1002.9(c)(3) [§ 202.9(c)(3)]; *see, e.g.,* Torgerson v. Wells Fargo Bank S.D., 2009 WL 255995, at *13 (D.S.D. Feb. 3, 2009).

223 Reg. B, 12 C.F.R. § 1002.9(c) [§ 202.9(c)]; *see also* Official Interpretations of Reg. B [Official Staff Commentary on Reg. B], 12 C.F.R. pt. 1002 [pt. 202], Supp. I, § 1002.9(c)(3)-1 [§ 202.9(c)(3)-1].

Interestingly, the official interpretation states that, in these circumstances, the creditor must send a written notice to the applicant within the time period specified for notices of approval, counteroffer, or adverse action or for notices of incompleteness. This statement provides some support for the argument that notices of counteroffer should be written. *See* § 10.4.3, *supra*.

224 Payne v. Ken Diepholz Ford Lincoln Mercury, Inc., 2004 WL 40631 (N.D. Ill. Jan. 5, 2004) (summary judgment granted for plaintiff consumer when dealer did not provide a written denial or a written explanation of why application was incomplete); Reg. B, 12 C.F.R. § 1002.9(c)(3) [§ 202.9(c)(3)]; Official Interpretations of Reg. B [Official Staff Commentary on Reg. B], 12 C.F.R. pt. 1002 [pt. 202], Supp. I, § 1002.9(c)(3)-1 [§ 202.9(c)(3)-1].

225 Reg. B, 12 C.F.R. § 1002.9(d) [§ 202.9(d)]; *see* Palmiotto v. Bank of N.Y., 1989 U.S. Dist. LEXIS 11546 (S.D.N.Y. Sept. 29, 1989) (creditor who did not show that it was eligible to give only oral notice could not prevail on its argument that consumer's ECOA claim was time-barred based on date of oral notice).

226 Official Interpretations of Reg. B [Official Staff Commentary on Reg. B], 12 C.F.R. pt. 1002 [pt. 202], Supp. I, § 1002.9-2 [§ 202.9-2]; *see* Thompson v. Galles Chevrolet Co., 807 F.2d 163 (10th Cir. 1986) (when truck purchasers submitted two credit applications to the same finance company through two different dealers and credit was approved on the second application, there was no need for written notification that creditor had stopped considering first application, which was incomplete and arguably withdrawn); Kirk v. Kelley Buick of Atlanta, Inc., 336 F. Supp. 2d 1327 (N.D. Ga. 2004) (creditor admitted that it did not send written notice of incompleteness but argued that applicant withdrew his application; finding genuine factual dispute existed on this issue and thus summary judgment inappropriate); Johnson v. Grossinger Motorcorp., Inc.,

the record retention provisions required by the ECOA.[227]

The regulations provide additional guidance in situations in which the parties contemplate that the applicant will inquire about the application and the creditor approves the application but the applicant does not inquire within thirty days of applying. In these circumstances, the creditor may treat the application as withdrawn.[228]

10.8 Who Must Comply with Notice Requirements?

10.8.1 Creditors, But Not Arrangers of Credit, Are Required to Comply with Notice Provisions

Creditors are required to comply with the ECOA notice requirements.[229] The ECOA identifies three types of creditors who are subject to its requirements:

- Any person who regularly extends, renews, or continues credit;
- Any person who regularly arranges for the extension, renewal, or continuation of credit; or
- Any assignee of an original creditor who participates in the decision to extend, renew, or continue credit.[230]

Regulation B defines "creditor" as a person who, in the ordinary course of business, regularly participates in a credit decision, including setting the terms of the credit.[231]

Arrangers include entities that regularly refer applicants or prospective applicants to creditors, or select or offer to select creditors to whom requests for credit may be made.[232] Arrangers may not provide credit, but their discrimination may prevent applicants from receiving credit. The official interpretation clarifies that this category may include persons such as real estate brokers, automobile dealers, home builders, and home improvement contractors.[233]

There are important differences resulting from categorizing an auto dealer or other entity as a credit arranger as opposed to a creditor. Creditors are subject to liability for violations of all sections of the ECOA, whereas arrangers are liable only for violations of sections 202.4(a) (general rule prohibiting discrimination) and 202.4(b) (general rule against discouraging applications).[234] These limitations mean that arrangers are not responsible for procedural ECOA violations even if they actively participate in, or are the actual cause of, the violation. The most important practical difference is that arrangers are not required to comply with the ECOA notice and record-keeping requirements.

A dealer and other similar entities can fit both the arranger and creditor categories.[235] Many dealers, for example, will argue that, if their activities do not precisely fit within the definition of an arranger in Regulation B and its official interpretations, then they cannot be a creditor. This argument is clearly incorrect. In practice most dealers, home-improvement contractors, and real estate brokers are sufficiently involved in the credit decision-making process to be considered creditors. Yet these entities will offer this argument even in the face of strong evidence that they extended the credit. For example, the dealer may have written a legally binding credit contract but will still try to argue that it is not a creditor or that it is merely an arranger. Courts have begun to recognize that there is a continuum of participation in a credit decision from no involvement, to referring applications to the decision-maker, to final decision-making. At some point, a party becomes a creditor for purposes of the notification requirements of the ECOA.[236]

---

753 N.E.2d 431 (Ill. App. Ct. 2001) (no ECOA notice violation when plaintiff failed to provide creditor with requested documentation prior to repossession and withdrew his application after repossession); Freeman v. Koerner Ford of Scranton, 536 A.2d 340 (Pa. Super. Ct. 1987) (creditor need not give notice of adverse action when plaintiff purchased same vehicle elsewhere three days after application, effectively withdrawing application).

227 Official Interpretations of Reg. B [Official Staff Commentary on Reg. B], 12 C.F.R. pt. 1002 [pt. 202], Supp. I, § 1002.9-2 [§ 202.9-2]; *see* § 10.12, *infra* (record retention requirements).

228 Reg. B, 12 C.F.R. § 1002.9(e) [§ 202.9(e)].

229 *See* § 2.2.5, *supra* (discussing the definition of creditor).

230 15 U.S.C. § 1691a(e).

231 Reg. B, 12 C.F.R. § 1002.2(*l*) [§ 202.2(*l*)].

232 Reg. B, 12 C.F.R. § 1002.2(*l*) [§ 202.2(*l*)].

233 Official Interpretations of Reg. B [Official Staff Commentary on Reg. B], 12 C.F.R. pt. 1002 [pt. 202], Supp. I, § 1002.2(l)-2 [§ 202.2(*l*)-2].

Prior to the 2003 regulatory amendments, the official staff commentary mentioned only real estate brokers in this category. 68 Fed. Reg. 13,144, 13,188 (Mar. 18, 2003).

234 Reg. B, 12 C.F.R. § 1002.2(*l*) [§ 202.2(*l*)]; *see, e.g.*, Williams v. Delamar Car Co., 2011 WL 1811061, at *3 (W.D. Mich. May 12, 2011) (finding that liable dealer who cancelled contract and repossessed car for failure to provide notice of adverse action); Meeks v. Murphy Auto Group, Inc., 2010 WL 5174525, at *4, *10–11 (M.D. Fla. Dec. 15, 2010) (referring dealer did not deny credit, so not required to provide adverse action notice), *aff'd*, 441 Fed. Appx. 683 (11th Cir. 2011); Flowers v. S.W. Motor Sales, Inc., 2008 WL 4614307 (N.D. Ill. Oct. 14, 2008) (plaintiff failed to allege that defendant was a creditor for purposes of the notice requirement); Hunter v. Bev Smith Ford, 2008 WL 1925265 (S.D. Fla. Apr. 29, 2008) (according to contract, dealer did not provide financing, so not a creditor and not required to provide adverse action notice); Conte v. Sonic-Plymouth Cadillac, 2008 WL 783632 (E.D. Mich. Mar. 20, 2008) (plaintiff did not allege that dealer participated in discriminatory practices, so dealer not a creditor and not required to provide adverse action notice, but subject to anti-discrimination provision of ECOA based on referring applicants to creditors); *see also* § 2.2.5.3, *supra*.

It appears that the plaintiffs in these cases failed to allege facts sufficient to require the court to conclude that the dealers participated in the credit transaction and were, therefore, creditors subject to the requirement to provide notice. When possible, facts about the dealer's role in the credit transaction beyond merely referring applicants to creditors should be specifically alleged.

235 *See* § 2.2.5, *supra*.

236 *See* Treadway v. Gateway Chevrolet Oldsmobile, Inc., 362 F.3d 971 (7th Cir. 2004); Drewry v. Starr Motors, 2008 WL 2035607 (E.D. Va. May 12, 2008) (summary judgment denied when disputed material facts exist regarding whether defendant was a creditor

In "spot delivery" or "yo-yo sales" cases, assignees will often argue that they did not participate in the credit decision because the sale was consummated when the contract was initially signed, before the credit information was transmitted to or approved by the assignee.[237] Courts have concluded, to the contrary, that the "true purchase of the car" takes place when financing has been secured, terms have been set, and the final contract has been signed.[238] The assignee in these circumstances should be liable as a creditor regardless of whether it actually extended the credit.[239] The dealer or other entity that initially handled the conditional, unfunded finance contract should also be a creditor and not just an arranger if it was sufficiently involved, as discussed above, in the credit transaction. This should be the case regardless of whether financing is ultimately obtained for the consumer.[240]

10.8.2 Notice By Multiple Creditors

Often, a credit applicant simultaneously submits applications to several creditors to ensure that credit will be obtained from one of them. If the applicant expressly accepts or uses the credit offered by any one creditor in connection with an application to multiple creditors submitted through a third party, no notice of adverse action need be provided by any other creditor that may have rejected the application.[241] If, on the other hand, no credit

is offered by any creditor or the applicant does not expressly accept or use any credit offered, each creditor that took adverse action must comply with Regulation B's adverse action notification requirements either directly or through a third party.[242]

Thus courts have held that either the creditor or the third party, but not both, have to provide the ECOA notice.[243] In general, a third party such as a broker or dealer (or one of the creditors) may provide this notification on behalf of all of the creditors but must identify each creditor that took adverse action.[244] If one notice is provided on behalf of multiple creditors, the notice must contain the name and address of each creditor.[245] The notice must either disclose the applicant's right to a statement of specific reasons within thirty days or give the primary reasons each creditor relied upon in taking the adverse action, clearly indicating which reasons relate to each creditor.[246]

In cases in which the consumer does not receive notice from either party, a creditor is not liable for a third party's failure to give notice if the creditor accurately and in a timely manner provided the third party with the information necessary for the notification *and* maintained reasonable procedures adapted to prevent such violations by the third party.[247] Reasonable procedures might include a contract imposing on the third party

---

required to provide notice of adverse action). *See generally* § 2.2.5.3, *supra*.

237 *See, e.g.*, Aikens v. Northwestern Dodge, Inc., 2004 WL 2967549 (N.D. Ill. Dec. 1, 2004); *see* § 10.4.2, *supra*.

238 Aikens v. Northwestern Dodge, Inc., 2004 WL 2967549 (N.D. Ill. Dec. 1, 2004) (citing Coleman v. Gen. Motors Acceptance Corp., 220 F.R.D. 64 (M.D. Tenn. 2004)).

239 Aikens v. Northwestern Dodge, Inc., 2004 WL 2967549 (N.D. Ill. Dec. 1, 2004) (finance company is in the business of providing financing for automobile purchasers and was a "creditor" even though it did not provide financing in this case).

240 *See, e.g.*, Treadway v. Gateway Chevrolet, Oldsmobile, Inc., 362 F.3d 971 (7th Cir. 2004) (although the dealer failed to get credit for plaintiff, it was still a regular arranger of credit; dealer also far enough along continuum of credit participation to be considered a regular creditor); *see* § 2.2.5.3, *supra* (discussing this issue in detail).

241 Reg. B, 12 C.F.R. § 1002.9(g) [§ 202.9(g)]; *see also* Thompson v. Galles Chevrolet Co., 807 F.2d 163 (10th Cir. 1986) (when truck purchasers submitted two credit applications to same finance company through two different dealers and credit was approved on the second application, there was no need for written notification that the creditor had stopped considering the first application, which was incomplete and arguably withdrawn); Anderson v. Frederick Ford Mercury Inc., 694 F. Supp. 2d 324, 331 (D. Del. 2010) (auto dealer referred applicant to creditors; creditors provided notice of adverse action though dealer did not; notice may be provided by creditor or by third party referring application, so judgment for defendants was granted as a matter of law); Floyd-Keith v. Homecomings Financial, L.L.C., 2010 WL 3927596, at *7 (M.D. Ala. Sept. 17, 2010), *report and recommendation adopted*, Floyd-Keith v. Homecomings Financial, L.L.C., No. 2:09-CV-769-WKW, 2010 WL3943646 (M.D. Ala. Oct. 7, 2010) (defendant sent adverse action notice to plaintiff's broker and asked that notice be sent to plaintiff, so summary judgment for defendant on adverse action notice claim).

242 15 U.S.C. § 1691(d)(4); Reg. B, 12 C.F.R. § 1002.9(g) [§ 202.9(g)].

243 *See, e.g.*, Love v. O'Connor Chevrolet, Inc., 2006 WL 2460581 (N.D. Ill. Aug. 21, 2006); Thele v. Sunrise Chevrolet, 2004 WL 1194751 (N.D. Ill. May 28, 2004); Brand v. Rohr-Ville Motors, Inc., 2003 WL 21078022 (N.D. Ill. May 9, 2003); Najieb v. Chrysler-Plymouth, 2002 WL 31906466 (N.D. Ill. Dec. 31, 2002) (ECOA requires that, when a third party asks a creditor to extend credit to an individual, the notice be made directly by such creditor or indirectly through the third party); Burns v. Elmhurst Auto Mall, Inc., 2001 WL 521840 (N.D. Ill. May 16, 2001); Leguillou v. Lynch Ford, 2000 WL 198796 (N.D. Ill. Feb. 14, 2000).

244 Reg. B, 12 C.F.R. § 1002.99g) [§ 202.9(g)]; Official Interpretations of Reg. B [Official Staff Commentary on Reg. B], 12 C.F.R. pt. 1002 [pt. 202], Supp. I, § 1002.9(g)-1 [§ 202.9(g)-1].

If the creditors are under the jurisdiction of different federal enforcement agencies, the notice need not name each agency; disclosure of just one will suffice. Official Interpretations of Reg. B [Official Staff Commentary on Reg. B], 12 C.F.R. pt. 1002 [pt. 202], Supp. I, § 1002.9(g)-2 [§ 202.9(g)-2].

245 Official Interpretations of Reg. B [Official Staff Commentary on Reg. B], 12 C.F.R. pt. 1002 [pt. 202], Supp. I, § 1002.9(g)-1 [§ 202.9(g)-1]; *see also* High v. McLean Financial Corp., 659 F. Supp. 1561 (D.D.C. 1987) (while neither the law nor regulations provides that a primary lender must inform an applicant that another financial institution is involved in the decision to extend credit, regulations clearly provide that each creditor taking adverse action against applicant must notify applicant of that decision).

246 Official Interpretations of Reg. B [Official Staff Commentary on Reg. B], 12 C.F.R. pt. 1002 [pt. 202], Supp. I, § 1002.9(g)-1 [§ 202.9(g)-1].

247 *Id.* § 1002.9(g)-3 [§ 202.9(g)-3]; *see also* Castro v. Union Nissan, Inc., 2002 WL 1466810 (N.D. Ill. July 8, 2002) (in denying plaintiff's motion for summary judgment, finding that it was unclear whether dealer or finance company was the creditor that took adverse action; if finance company initially attempted to set up financing and subsequently denied credit, then the ECOA notice burden would presumably fall on the finance company).

both an obligation to notify the applicant and a procedure for verifying to the creditor that the notification was given.

There may also be circumstances in which a third party knows, for example, that a dealer falsified the credit application documentation. If the third party denied the application for that reason, it should arguably have sent notice to the applicant explaining that denial was due to the dealer's fraud.

In some cases, the dealer may approve financing but include a condition that allows the dealer to cancel the contract if it cannot assign the loan.[248] To state a cause of action in these circumstances, a plaintiff should plead that she did not receive a notice from either the dealer or the proposed assignee, because either source may give notice.[249]

10.9 Exceptions to Notice Requirements

10.9.1 Incidental Consumer Credit

The ECOA notice requirements do not apply to incidental consumer credit.[250] However, incidental creditors are required to comply with the general prohibition against discrimination, among other ECOA provisions.[251]

Incidental consumer credit is defined as:

- Primarily for personal, family, or household purposes;
- Not made pursuant to the terms of a credit card account;
- Not subject to any finance charge or interest; and
- Not payable by agreement in more than four installments.[252]

Examples of incidental consumer credit may include deferment of payment by doctors, home oil companies, hospitals, and some small retailers (as long as there is no finance charge and no more than four installments).[253]

A state UDAP claim may be a more direct way to challenge the failure to notify the consumer of denial of incidental consumer credit.[254] The creditor's failure to disclose the action taken is an unfair and deceptive act because it is deceptive to fail to disclose an important part of a sales transaction, in this case that the creditor will not defer payment.[255] Nevertheless, it is more difficult to prove a UDAP violation when the creditor has notified the consumer of the denial of credit but has not disclosed the reason for the denial. The reason for the denial of credit may not be a material factor in the purchase of the goods or services.

10.9.2 Business Credit

10.9.2.1 General

The notification requirement applies to applications for business credit but is less strict than for consumer credit applications. There is also one set of rules for relatively small business applicants and another set for larger business applicants. Creditors may, if they choose, comply with the consumer notification requirements for business credit or they may comply with the small business requirements for all businesses.[256]

In deciding whether business or consumer credit is involved, the primary purpose of the application controls.[257] Thus, if a consumer purchases a pick-up truck primarily for consumer use but also for occasional business use, the transaction involves consumer credit. The Truth in Lending Act also uses the primary-purpose test, and cases interpreting that provision may provide useful guidance in this area.[258] Under Truth in Lending, there is little doubt that "primary" is not synonymous with "exclusive." At the very least, though, "primary" must refer to the use of more than half the proceeds of the transaction.[259]

10.9.2.2 Rules for Small Business Applicants

Regulation B contains special notification rules for certain small businesses.[260] These rules apply to businesses with gross revenues of one million dollars or less (except for trade or factoring credit),[261] applications to start a business, and most applications by an individual for business purpose credit (except that, when an applicant applies for credit as a sole proprietor, the revenues of the sole proprietorship govern).[262]

For these small business applicants the creditor has to comply with the same notification requirements as for consumer

248 *See, e.g.*, Brand v. Rohr-Ville Motors, Inc., 2003 WL 21078022 (N.D. Ill. May 9, 2003).

249 *Id.*

250 Reg. B, 12 C.F.R. § 1002.3(c)(20(vi) [§ 202.3(c)(2)(vi)].

251 Official Interpretations of Reg. B [Official Staff Commentary on Reg. B], 12 C.F.R. § 1002.3-1 [§ 202.3-1].

252 Reg. B, 12 C.F.R. § 1002.3(c) [§ 202.3(c)]; *see also* Official Interpretations of Reg. B [Official Staff Commentary on Reg. B], 12 C.F.R. pt. 1002 [pt. 202], Supp. I, § 1002.3(c)-1 [§ 202.3(c)-1]; § 2.2.6.3, *supra.*

253 *See* § 2.2.6.3, *supra.*

254 *See* § 1.8, *supra* (discussing state UDAP statutes).

255 *See* National Consumer Law Center, Unfair and Deceptive Acts and Practices § 4.2.14 (8th ed. 2012).

256 Official Interpretations of Reg. B [Official Staff Commentary on Reg. B], 12 C.F.R. pt. 1002 [pt. 202], Supp. I, § 1002.9(a)(3)-4 [§ 202.9(a)(3)-4].

257 *Id.* § 1002.2(g)-1 [§ 202.2(g)-1, *as amended by* 54 Fed. Reg. 12,471 (Apr. 4, 1990) (formerly section 202.3(d)(1)-1)].

258 *E.g.*, Gallegos v. Stokes, 593 F.2d 372 (10th Cir. 1979); Redhouse v. Quality Ford Sales, Inc., 523 F.2d 1 (10th Cir. 1975) (en banc) (per curiam, superseding 511 F.2d 230 (10th Cir. 1975)); Smith v. Chapman, 436 F. Supp. 58 (W.D. Tex. 1977). *See generally* National Consumer Law Center, Truth in Lending § 2.4.2.1 (8th ed. 2012).

259 *See, e.g.*, Palmer v. Statewide Group, 134 F.3d 378 (9th Cir. 1998) (consumers' use of their home for child care business did not make loan a business loan); Semar v. Platte Valley Fed. Sav. & Loan Ass'n, 791 F.2d 699 (9th Cir. 1986) (loan primarily for personal use if only 10% of proceeds used for business purposes and primary purpose of loan was to pay off a second trust deed loan on the consumer's house); Gombosi v. Carteret Mortgage Corp., 894 F. Supp. 176 (E.D. Pa. 1995) (majority of loan proceeds used for business purpose). *See generally* National Consumer Law Center, Truth in Lending § 2.4.2.1 (8th ed. 2012).

260 Reg. B, 12 C.F.R. § 1002.9(a)93) [§ 202.9(a)(3)].

261 *See* Official Interpretations of Reg. B [Official Staff Commentary on Reg. B], 12 C.F.R. pt. 1002 [pt. 202], Supp. I, § 1002.9(a)(3)-2, (a)(3)-3 [§ 202.9(a)(3)-2, (a)(3)-3] (definitions of trade and factoring credit).

262 *Id.* § 1002.9(a)(3)-1 [§ 202.9(a)(3)-1].

applicants, with the following three exceptions. First, the creditor's notice of any adverse action taken may be made either orally or in writing[263] (for non-business credit only very small creditors may utilize oral notification).

Second, for consumer credit applicants, if a creditor opts not to disclose the reasons for taking an adverse action, the creditor must disclose to the applicant *after the adverse action is taken* that the applicant has a right to a statement of the reasons for the adverse action. For business applicants, the creditor has the option to disclose the applicant's right to a statement of reasons for adverse action in writing *at the time of the application*.[264]

The third exception for small business applicants is that, for telephone applications, a creditor may simply give notice of the action taken or of the right to a statement of reasons over the telephone and is only required to provide written notice if the applicant requests it.[265]

10.9.2.3 Rules for Other Business Applicants

Creditors have the option of complying with an even less restrictive set of notification rules for other business applicants. These different rules apply to businesses with revenues over one million dollars and with respect to applications for trade credit and credit incident to a factoring agreement.[266] The creditor may rely on the applicant's assertion as to the size of the business's revenue.[267]

The creditor may notify the applicant either orally or in writing of action taken within a reasonable time, without any notice of the reasons for the action taken or notice of the right to obtain those reasons.[268] Whether notice is given within a reasonable amount of time is an issue of fact to be submitted to the jury.[269] The creditor only needs to provide a written statement of the reasons for the action taken if the applicant makes a written request for a statement of reasons within sixty days after being notified of the adverse action.[270]

10.9.3 Creditor's Inadvertent Error May Excuse Notice Violations

An inadvertent error by the creditor is not a violation of the notification requirements, provided that the creditor corrects the

error as soon as possible after discovering it.[271] Inadvertent errors include clerical mistakes, calculation errors, computer malfunctions, and printing errors. An error of legal judgment is not an inadvertent error.[272] One case discussing the thirty-day period for responding to requests for specific reasons for adverse action taken has held that a creditor that failed to respond to these requests within the prescribed period could not avail itself of an inadvertent error defense based on the allegation that it employed insufficient staff to respond in a timely fashion.[273]

10.10 Relationship of ECOA Notices to Fair Credit Reporting Act Adverse Action Notices

The Fair Credit Reporting Act (FCRA) requires notice when a credit report forms the basis of a credit denial.[274] Similar to the ECOA, the triggering event for an FCRA notice is "adverse action." The FCRA has a more extensive definition of adverse action however than the ECOA. The first part of the FCRA definition of "adverse action" has the same meaning as in the ECOA definition. The FCRA definition also includes, among other provisions, any determination made or action taken that is done in connection with an application made, or transaction initiated, by any consumer or in connection with a review of an account under the FCRA and adverse to the interests of the consumer.[275] This is often referred to as the "catch all" provision. Courts have found that the FCRA definition is intended to be broader than the ECOA.[276]

This breadth is important, for example, in determining whether the FCRA follows the ECOA in excluding from the adverse action category any counteroffers that are accepted or used.[277] The Federal Trade Commission (FTC) has issued

---

263 Reg. B, 12 C.F.R. § 1002.9(a)(3)(i)(A) [§ 202.9(a)(3)(i)(A)].

264 Reg. B, 12 C.F.R. § 1002.9(a)(3)(i)(B) [§ 202.9(a)(3)(i)(B)].

265 Reg. B, 12 C.F.R. § 1002.9(a)(3)(i)(C) [§ 202.9(a)(3)(i)(C)].

266 Reg. B, 12 C.F.R. § 1002.9(a)(3)(ii) [§ 202.9(a)(3)(ii)].

267 Official Interpretations of Reg. B [Official Staff Commentary on Reg. B], 12 C.F.R. pt. 1002 [pt. 202], Supp. I, § 1002.9(a)(3)-1 [§ 202.9(a)(3)-1].

268 If the notification occurs within the general time frames prescribed in 12 C.F.R. § 1002.9(a)(1) [§ 202.9(a)(1)], that is deemed reasonable. Official Interpretations of Reg. B [Official Staff Commentary on Reg. B], 12 C.F.R. pt. 1002 [pt. 202], Supp. I, § 1002.9(a)(3)-5 [§ 202.9(a)(3)-5].

269 *See, e.g.*, Gillette of Kingston, Inc. v. Bank R.I., 2006 WL 1314259 (R.I. Super. Ct. May 5, 2006).

270 Reg. B, 12 C.F.R. § 1002.9(a)(3)(ii) [§ 202.9(a)(3)(ii)].

271 Reg. B, 12 C.F.R. § 1002.16(c) [§ 202.16(c)]; *see also* Sayers v. Gen. Motors Acceptance Corp., 522 F. Supp. 835 (W.D. Mo. 1981) (no ECOA violation when credit denial was based on an inadvertent misinterpretation of the credit history; however, creditor's subsequent willful refusal to comply with notification requirements after being informed of its error did constitute an ECOA violation).

272 Official Interpretations of Reg. B [Official Staff Commentary on Reg. B], 12 C.F.R. pt. 1002 [pt. 202], Supp. I, § 1002.16(c)-1 [§ 202.16(c)-1].

273 *See* Desselles v. J.C. Penney Co., [1974–1980 Decisions Transfer Binder] Consumer Cred. Guide (CCH) ¶ 97,536 (E.D. La. 1979).

274 15 U.S.C. § 1681m(a); *see also* National Consumer Law Center, Fair Credit Reporting ch. 8 (7th ed. 2010 and Supp.).

275 15 U.S.C. § 1681a(k)(1).

276 *See, e.g.*, Treadway v. Gateway Chevrolet Oldsmobile, Inc., 362 F.3d 971 (7th Cir. 2004) (noting "liberal definition" of the FCRA); Barnes v. Ditech.Com, 2005 WL 913090 (E.D. Pa. Apr. 19, 2005); Thomas v. Cendant Mortgage, 2004 WL 2600772 (E.D. Pa. Nov. 15, 2004); Crane v. American Home Mortgage, Corp., 2004 WL 1529165 (E.D. Pa. July 7, 2004) (Congress intended to define adverse action in the FCRA more broadly than in the ECOA), *clarified by* 2004 WL 2577498 (E.D. Pa. Oct. 21, 2004); Payne v. Ken Diepholz Ford Lincoln Mercury, Inc., 2004 WL 40631 (N.D. Ill. Jan. 5, 2004).

277 This issue is discussed in Baynes v. Alltel Wireless of Ala., Inc., 322 F. Supp. 2d 1307 (M.D. Ala. 2004) (defendant should be required to

contradictory staff opinion letters on this issue.[278] Congress sought to address this problem when it amended the Fair Credit Reporting Act in 2003. The amendments to the FCRA require creditors to provide a "risk-based pricing" notice whenever a consumer is offered credit on less favorable terms based on a credit report or score.[279] These risk-based pricing notices must be provided "under the FCRA where a consumer accepts the offered credit, even where ECOA notices are not required."[280] The FTC and FRB have promulgated regulations, which are discussed in another volume in this series.[281]

There are other important distinctions between the ECOA and FCRA notice requirements. In general, the FCRA requires that notice must be given by a "user" of a consumer report whenever adverse action is based in whole or in part on any information contained in that consumer report.[282] In credit transactions, notice is also required if the adverse action is based on information obtained from a third party other than a consumer reporting agency.[283]

The requirements concerning the content of the FCRA notice are different from the requirements of the ECOA and Regulation B. The FCRA notice must disclose that the consumer has sixty days to request a free copy of the consumer report and that the consumer may dispute the accuracy or completeness of the report with the consumer reporting agency, among other information. The notice is generally intended to help consumers understand that a credit decision was made at least in part based on information contained in a consumer report. The Dodd-Frank Wall Street Reform and Consumer Protection Act of 2010 added a requirement to the FCRA notice that creditors must disclose the credit scores they used in making their decisions.[284] The ECOA notice, in contrast, must state the reasons for denial.[285]

Another important difference is that the ECOA notice must be given within thirty days after a credit application.[286] The FCRA notice should be sent at the same time as the denial, but there is no requirement that the denial meet any time deadlines. Unlike the ECOA adverse action notice, the FCRA notice does not have to be in writing. Oral or electronic notice is also permitted, but the FTC commentary recommends that the notice be in writing.[287]

In some cases, the FCRA provisions may be broader. For example, the ECOA notice need only be given to the primary applicant.[288] The FCRA provision, on the other hand, requires that notice be given to "any consumer" whenever an adverse action is taken that is based in whole or in part on information contained in a credit report.[289] Thus, if a creditor obtains credit reports on an applicant and co-applicant and considers both in deciding to deny credit, the creditor would be required to provide an FCRA notice to both applicants but would have to provide an ECOA notice only to the primary applicant.

Regulation B includes model forms that combine both the FCRA notice and the ECOA notice separately on the same disclosure.[290] Proper use of the model forms will satisfy the ECOA notice requirement.[291] Compliance with just the FCRA notice requirements will ordinarily not comply with the ECOA requirement.[292] In July 2011, these notices were revised in order to implement the FCRA's requirement, which was added by the Dodd-Frank Act,[293] to disclose the credit score used by the creditor in adverse action notices.[294]

There are different remedies for ECOA and FCRA notice violations.[295]

---

assert that plaintiff did not accept a counteroffer as an affirmative defense). *See also* Harper v. Lindsay Chevrolet Oldsmobile, 212 F. Supp. 2d 582 (E.D. Va. 2002) (a denial of credit coupled with a counteroffer that is accepted does not trigger FCRA's notice requirement because there is no adverse action).

After the revision of the FCRA, the Federal Trade Commission (FTC) added language to the official staff commentary for the FCRA that adverse action notice is not required when the creditor makes a counteroffer that is accepted by the consumer. Notice to Users of Consumer Reports: Obligations of Users Under the FCRA, 16 C.F.R. pt. 698, app. H.; 69 Fed. Reg. 69,796 (Nov. 30, 2004).

It appears that this position exceeds the authority Congress granted to the FTC. Due to confusion regarding whether there is a private right of action to enforce these requirements, case law developments may not resolve this question absent a challenge to the FTC under the Administrative Procedures Act or through further revisions by the FTC to the notice. *See generally* National Consumer Law Center, Fair Credit Reporting ch. 8 (7th ed. 2010 and Supp.).

278 *See* Clarke W. Brinkerhoff, Fed. Trade Comm'n, Informal Staff Opinion Letter (May 31, 1996); Letter from Christopher W. Keller, Att'y, Fed. Trade Comm'n, to Judi Vail, Esq., Informal Staff Opinion Letter (June 28, 2003). *See generally* National Consumer Law Center, Fair Credit Reporting ch. 8 (7th ed. 2010 and Supp.).

279 15 U.S.C. § 1681m(h). *See generally* National Consumer Law Center, Fair Credit Reporting § 8.7 (7th ed. 2010 and Supp.).

280 75 Fed. Reg. 2724 (Jan. 15, 2010).

281 *See* National Consumer Law Center, Fair Credit Reporting § 8.7 (7th ed. 2010 and Supp.).

282 15 U.S.C. § 1681m(a).

283 15 U.S.C. § 1681m(b). *See generally* National Consumer Law Center, Fair Credit Reporting ch. 8 (7th ed. 2010 and Supp.).

284 15 U.S.C. § 1681m(a)(2)(A), *as added by* Pub. L. No. 111-203, tit. X, § 1100F(1), 124 Stat. 2112 (July 21, 2010); *see* § 10.10, *infra*. *See generally* National Consumer Law Center, Fair Credit Reporting § 8.5.2.4 (7th ed. 2010 and Supp.).

285 *See* § 10.5.4.2, *supra*.

286 Reg. B, 12 C.F.R. § 1002.9(a)(1)(i) [§ 202.9(a)(1)(i)].

287 15 U.S.C. § 1681m(a); Fed. Trade Comm'n, Official Staff Commentary on the Fair Credit Reporting Act § 615 item 3. *See generally* National Consumer Law Center, Fair Credit Reporting Ch. 8 (7th ed. 2010 and Supp.).

288 Reg. B, 12 C.F.R. § 1002.9(f) [§ 202.9(f)].

289 15 U.S.C. § 1681m(a); *see also* Letter from Christopher W. Keller, Att'y, Fed. Trade Comm'n, to Ryan S. Stinneford, Esq., Informal Staff Opinion Letter (July 14, 2000) (FCRA notice must be given to a co-applicant but not to a guarantor).

290 Reg. B, 12 C.F.R. pt. 1002 [pt. 202], app. C.

291 Reg. B, 12 C.F.R. pt. 1002 [pt. 202], app. C; *see* § 10.6.2, *infra*.

292 Fed. Trade Comm'n, Official Staff Commentary on the Fair Credit Reporting Act § 615 item 1.

293 15 U.S.C. § 1681m(a)(2)(A), *as added by* Pub. L. No. 111-203, tit. X, § 1100F(1), 124 Stat. 2112 (July 21, 2010). *See generally* National Consumer Law Center, Fair Credit Reporting § 8.5.2.4 (7th ed. 2010 and Supp.).

294 76 Fed. Reg. 41590 (July 15, 2011). The model notices are reprinted in Appendix B, *infra*.

295 *See* § 11.8, *infra* (ECOA remedies); National Consumer Law Center, Fair Credit Reporting ch. 11 (7th ed. 2010 and Supp.).

10.11 Right to Receive Appraisal Report

The ECOA was amended (effective July 21, 2011) to require that a creditor furnish an applicant a copy of any and all written appraisals and valuations developed in connection with the applicant's application for a loan that is secured or would have been secured by a first lien on a dwelling promptly upon completion, but in no case later than three days prior to the closing of the loan, whether the creditor grants or denies the applicant's request for credit or the application is incomplete or withdrawn. This change in the law requires that an appraisal be provided as a matter of course rather than only at the applicant's request, as was previously required.

The applicant may be required to pay a reasonable fee to reimburse the creditor for the cost of the appraisal, but a copy shall be provided to the applicant at no additional cost. At the time of the application, the creditor shall notify the applicant in writing of the right to receive a copy of each appraisal and valuation developed in connection with the application.[296] Valuation is defined to include any estimate of the value of a dwelling developed in connection with a creditor's decision to provide credit, including those values developed pursuant to a policy of a government-sponsored enterprise or by an automated valuation model, a broker price opinion, or other methodology or mechanism.[297]

On January 18, 2013, the CFPB issued amendments to Regulation B and the Bureau's official interpretations of the regulation to implement the ECOA amendment concerning appraisals and other valuations.[298] These amendments are effective on January 18, 2014.

Section 1002.14 [section 202.14] of Regulation B is amended, in connection with an application for credit to be secured by a first lien on a dwelling, to:

- Require creditors to notify applicants, within three business days of receiving an application, of the applicant's right to receive a copy of any appraisal developed;
- Require creditors to provide applicants a copy of each appraisal and other written valuation promptly upon their completion or three business days before consummation (for closed-end credit) or account opening (for open-end credit), whichever is earlier;
- Permit applicants to waive the timing requirements for providing these copies; however, applicants who waive the timing requirements must be given a copy of all appraisals and other written valuations at or prior to consummation or account opening or, if the transaction is not consummated or the account is not opened, no later than thirty days after

the creditor determines the transaction will not be consummated or the account will not be opened;

- Prohibit creditors from charging for copies of appraisal or other written valuations but permit creditors to charge an applicant reasonable fees for the cost of the appraisal or other written valuation unless applicable law provides otherwise.

Previously, the ECOA required that creditors provide applicants with notice of their right to receive a copy of any appraisal report on a dwelling that would secure the loan obligation being sought.[299] Violations of the previous requirement, as well as the recently enacted change, entitle a consumer to relief.[300] The statute gave this right concerning any loan that will be secured by a lien on residential real property,[301] whether or not the credit is for a consumer or business purpose.[302] The statute also specifies that the creditor may require reimbursement from the applicant for the cost of the appraisal.[303]

The amendments to Regulation B also redefine appraisals, now called "valuations." Valuations include any report prepared by an appraiser, any document prepared by the creditor's staff that assigns value to the property, a report approved by a government-sponsored enterprise used to describe to the applicant

---

296 15 U.S.C. § 1691(e), *as amended by* Pub. L. No. 111-203, tit. XIV, § 1474, 124 Stat. 2136, 2199 (July 21, 2010).

   This amendment becomes effective on the "designated transfer date" for creation of the new Consumer Financial Protection Bureau, which at this writing was July 21, 2011. *See* 12 U.S.C. § 5582 (definition of "designated transfer date").

297 15 U.S.C. § 1691(e)(6).

298 78 Fed. Reg. 7266 (Jan. 31, 2013).

299 The Federal Deposit Insurance Corporation Improvement Act of 1991, Pub. L. No. 102-242, 105 Stat. 2300, 2306 (adding 15 U.S.C. § 1691(e)).

300 15 U.S.C. § 1691e.

   Claim that creditor failed to provide a copy of the appraisal must be filed within the applicable statute of limitations for ECOA. *See, e.g.*, Moore v. Wells Fargo Bank, N.A., 2011 WL 652844, at *3–4 (E.D. Tenn. Feb. 14, 2011).

   Claim must allege that the borrower requested a copy of the appraisal within a reasonable time. *See, e.g.*, Letvin v. Amera Mortgage Corp., 2011 WL 1603635, at *1213 (D. Haw. Apr. 27, 2011); Kivel v. ABN Amro Mortgage Group, Inc., 2006 WL 1579819 (D. Minn. June 1, 2006) (plaintiff's claim for failure to provide copy of appraisal survived motion to dismiss). *But see* Lowes v. Hill & Co. Real Estate, 2006 WL 463517 (N.D. Cal. Feb. 24, 2006) (citing *Wiltshire* for proposition that it remains unclear whether plaintiffs are able to bring a claim for damages for failure to provide an appraisal); Wiltshire v. Dhanraj, 421 F. Supp. 2d 544 (E.D.N.Y. 2005) (the plain language of section 1691e notwithstanding, plaintiffs have cited no authority and the court's research has revealed none, which indicates that a cause of action exists under the ECOA based on a creditor's failure to furnish an appraisal report; court did not reach a conclusion on the issue, however, because of deficiencies in plaintiff's ECOA claims). *See generally* § 11.8, *infra*.

301 15 U.S.C. § 1691(e).

302 Official Interpretations of Reg. B [Official Staff Commentary on Reg. B], 12 C.F.R. pt. 1002 [pt. 202], Supp. I, § 1002.14(a)-2 [§ 202.14(a)-2].

   This applies to applications for renewal of existing credit secured by a dwelling as well, if the creditor obtains and uses a new appraisal report in evaluating the request. *Id.* § 1002.14(a)-2 [§ 202.14(a)-2]; *see* § 10.11, *supra*.

   Effective January 18, 2014, there will be further amendments to section 1002.14 of Regulation B and its official interpretations. Please refer to appendices B and C, *infra*, for a redlined version of these amendments.

303 15 U.S.C. § 1691(e).

the estimate of the property's value, a report generated by use of an automated valuation model, or a broker price opinion used to estimate the property's value.[304] However, the term does not include other reports such as internal documents that restate the estimated value of the dwelling contained in an appraisal or written valuation being provided to the applicant, government agency statements of appraised value, valuation lists that are publicly available (such as published sales prices or mortgage amounts, tax assessments, and retail price ranges), or valuations such as manufacturer's invoices for manufactured homes.[305]

Prior to the recent amendments, creditors were required to disclose to applicants their right to receive a copy of the appraisal report, unless the creditor automatically provides appraisal reports to all applicants without being requested to do so.[306] The regulation required that notice of this right to an appraisal report be made in writing, must state that the applicant's request for the report must be made in writing, must give the time the applicant has to make a request, and must include the creditor's address.[307] This notice might have been delivered at any time during the application process, but no later than when the creditor provided the requisite notice of action taken.[308] When a transaction involved more than one applicant, notice need only be given to one applicant, but it must be given to the primary applicant if it is readily apparent who that is.[309] Credi-

tors could use the notice of right to request appraisal included in Regulation B or develop their own forms.[310]

The applicant was then required to make the request for the appraisal report within a reasonable period of time after the application.[311] Prior to the amendments, Regulation B stated that the written request must be received by the creditor within ninety days of the creditor's notice of action taken or the applicant's withdrawal of the application.[312]

The statute also required that the creditor "promptly" furnish the appraisal report to the applicant.[313] The regulation stated that, if the applicant timely sent a written request for an appraisal report, the creditor was required to provide the applicant with the report within thirty days of receiving the request, the report, or reimbursement of the cost of the appraisal, whichever occurred last.[314]

10.12 ECOA Record Retention Requirements

10.12.1 *Preservation of Records*

Creditors generally must retain records of credit transactions for approximately as long as the ECOA statute of limitations. A creditor must retain the original or a copy of each of the following documents for twenty-five months following the date it notifies an applicant of the action taken on an application (or of an incomplete application):[315]

- Any application form that the creditor receives;[316]
- Information obtained for monitoring purposes;[317]
- Any other written or recorded information used in evaluating the application and not returned to the applicant upon request;
- Written notification to the applicant of the action taken on the application or notes concerning oral notification;

---

304 Official Interpretations of Reg. B [Official Staff Commentary on Reg. B], 12 C.F.R. pt. 1002 [pt. 202], Supp. I, § 1002.14(b)(3)(1) [§ 202.14(b)(3)(1)]. Effective January 18, 2014, there will be further amendments to section 1002.14 of Regulation B and its official interpretations. Please refer to appendices B and C, *infra*, for a redlined version of these amendments to section 1002.14.

305 *Id.* § 1002.14(c)-2 [§ 202.14(c)-2]. Effective January 18, 2014, there will be further amendments to section 1002.14 of Regulation B and its official interpretations. Please refer to appendices B and C, *infra*, for a redlined version of these amendments.

306 Reg. B, 12 C.F.R. § 1002.14(a) [§ 202.14(a); *see also* Chua v. Barratt American, 2010 WL 987020, at *3 (S.D. Cal. Mar. 17, 2010) (plaintiff alleged that he did not receive notice of right to receive appraisal report but did not allege failure to receive appraisal report itself; defendant's motion to dismiss granted).

Effective January 18, 2014, there will be further amendments to section 1002.14 of Regulation B and its official interpretations. Please refer to appendices B and C, *infra*, for a redlined version of these amendments.

307 Reg. B, 12 C.F.R. § 1002.14(a)(2)(i)-1 [§ 202.14(a)(2)(i)-1]; Lowes v. Hill & Co. Real Estate, 2006 WL 463517 (N.D. Cal. Feb. 24, 2006).

The interim final rule for electronic disclosures would permit notices to be provided solely in electronic form on the application even if the consumer had not consented to receive electronic disclosures. Reg. B, 12 C.F.R. § 1002.16(c) [§ 202.16(c)].

Effective January 18, 2014, there will be further amendments to section 1002.14 of Regulation B and its official interpretations. Please refer to appendices B and C, *infra*, for a redlined version of these amendments.

308 Official Interpretations of Reg. B [Official Staff Commentary on Reg. B], 12 C.F.R. pt. 1002 [pt. 202], Supp. I, § 1002.14(a)(2)(i)-1 [§ 202.14(a)(2)(i)-1]. Effective January 18, 2014, there will be further amendments to section 1002.14 of Regulation B and its official interpretations. Please refer to appendices B and C, *infra*, for a redlined version of these amendments.

309 *Id.*

310 Reg. B, 12 C.F.R. pt. 1002 [pt. 202], app. C, form C-9; *see, e.g.*, Lowes v. Hill & Co. Real Estate, 2006 WL 463517 (N.D. Cal. Feb. 24, 2006) (plaintiff's signature acknowledging receipt of the notice did not constitute a written request for a copy).

311 15 U.S.C. § 1691(e).

312 Reg. B, 12 C.F.R. § 1002.14(a)(2)(ii) [§ 202.14(a)(2)(ii)]. Effective January 18, 2014, there will be further amendments to section 1002.14 of Regulation B and its official interpretations. Please refer to appendices B and C, *infra*, for a redlined version of these amendments.

313 15 U.S.C. § 1691(e).

314 Reg. B, 12 C.F.R. § 1002.14(a)(2)(ii) [§ 202.14(a)(2)(ii)). Effective January 18, 2014, there will be further amendments to section 1002.14 of Regulation B and its official interpretations. Please refer to appendices B and C, *infra*, for a redlined version of these amendments.

315 Reg. B, 12 C.F.R. § 1002.12(b) [§ 202.12(b)].

316 Reg. B, 12 C.F.R. § 1002.12(b)(1)(i) [§ 202.12(b)(1)(i)].

However, the ECOA does not require the creditor to provide the applicant with a copy of the application. *See* Enriquez v. Countrywide Home Loans, F.S.B., 814 F. Supp. 2d 1042, 1062 (D. Haw. 2011); Cootey v. Countrywide Home Loans, Inc., 2011 WL 4853333, at *9 (D. Haw. Oct. 12, 2011).

317 *See* § 4.4.7, *supra*; § 10.13, *infra*.

- Written notification to the applicant of the specific reasons for adverse action taken or notes concerning oral notification; and
- Any written statement submitted by the applicant alleging a violation of the ECOA or Regulation B.

For applications regarding which the creditor is not required to comply with the notice requirements, the creditor need only keep for twenty-five months all written or recorded information in its possession concerning the applicant, including any notation of action taken.[318] This applies, for example, to creditors that are not required to comply with the notice requirements because the transaction involved multiple creditors and only one creditor was required to give notice.[319]

When adverse action has been taken on a credit transaction outside of the application process, such as when the creditor has terminated or changed the terms of an existing account, the creditor also must preserve the following records for twenty-five months after notifying the applicant of the adverse action taken:[320]

- Any written or recorded information concerning the adverse action taken; and
- Any written statement submitted by the applicant alleging a violation of the ECOA or Regulation B.

In addition, for twenty-five months after the date on which an offer of credit is made to potential customers, creditors must keep the text of any pre-screened solicitation, the list of criteria the creditor used to select potential recipients of the solicitation, and any correspondence related to complaints (formal or informal) about the solicitation.[321]

These pre-screened record provisions do not require creditors to establish a separate database or set of files for correspondence relating to complaints about pre-screened solicitations. In addition, creditors are not required to match consumer complaints with specific solicitation programs.[322]

The creditor must also keep information for twenty-five months after a self-test has been completed.[323] The creditor must keep all written or recorded information about the self-test. The information must be retained beyond twenty-five months if the creditor has actual notice that it is under investigation or is subject to an enforcement proceeding for an alleged violation or if it has been served with notice of a civil action. In those cases, the creditor must keep the information until final disposition of the matter, unless an earlier time is allowed by the appropriate agency or court order.[324] It is prudent for plaintiff's counsel to notify the defendant at the time

that the suit is filed of the obligation to preserve records during the pendency of the action. Having received such notice, defendant will be unable to claim that any subsequent record destruction was inadvertent error.

In general, paper copies need not be retained by creditors using a computerized system providing that the information can be regenerated in a timely fashion.[325]

The record retention requirements have been the subject of some government enforcement actions. For example, in 2002, the Comptroller of the Currency took action against a payday lender and its service provider for failing to safeguard loan files in accordance with the ECOA's document retention requirements. According to the OCC, ACE Cash Express, a third-party service provider for payday loans backed by Goleta National Bank, failed to protect 641 loan files, allegedly dumping the files in a dumpster.[326]

10.12.2 Preservation of Records in Case of an Investigation, Enforcement Proceeding, or Civil Action

Any creditor with actual notice that it is under investigation or is subject to an enforcement proceeding for a violation of the ECOA or Regulation B—or has been served with notice that a civil action has been filed—must retain all required records concerning applications in general and those concerning other transactions in which adverse action has been taken. These records must be retained until final disposition of the enforcement proceeding or civil action, unless an earlier time is allowed by order of the agency or court involved.[327]

---

318 Reg. B, 12 C.F.R. § 1002.12(b)(3) [§ 202.12(b)(3)].

319 *See* § 10.8.2, *supra*.

320 Reg. B, 12 C.F.R. § 1002.12(b)(2) [§ 202.12(b)(2)].

321 Reg. B, 12 C.F.R. § 1002.12(b)(7) [§ 202.12(b)(7)].
This requirement was added in final rules published in 2003. 68 Fed. Reg. 13,144, 13,153 (Mar. 18, 2003).

322 68 Fed. Reg. 13,144, 13,153 (Mar. 18, 2003).

323 Reg. B, 12 C.F.R. § 1002.12(b)(6) [§ 202.12(b)(6)]; *see* § 10.14, *infra* (discussion of self tests).

324 Reg. B, 12 C.F.R. § 1002.12(b)(6) [§ 202.12(b)(6)].

325 Official Interpretations of Reg. B [Official Staff Commentary on Reg. B], 12 C.F.R. pt. 1002 [pt. 202], Supp. I, § 1002.12(b)-1 [§ 202.12(b)-1].

326 Consent Order, *In re* ACE Cash Express, Inc., EA No. 2002-92 (Office of the Comptroller of the Currency Oct. 25, 2002), *available at* www.occ.treas.gov/02rellst.htm; Consent Order, *In re* Goleta Nat'l Bank, EA No. 2002-93 (Office of the Comptroller of the Currency Oct. 25, 2002), *available at* www.occ.treas.gov/02rellst.htm; *see also* Maunsell v. Greenspan, 1998 U.S. App. LEXIS 10306 (2d Cir. May 11, 1998) (Federal Reserve Board acted within the scope of its authority in establishing record retention requirement); United States v. City Finance Co., Clearinghouse No. 45,752 (N.D. Ga. 1990) (consent decree partially based on allegations that creditor did not retain written records of applications or statements of adverse action for the required time period); United States v. Fid. Acceptance Corp., Clearinghouse No. 38,923 (D. Minn. 1985) (consent order partially based on creditor's alleged failure to retain records of rejected applications); United States v. Security Pac. Financial Systems, Clearinghouse No. 37,095 (S.D. Cal. 1983) ($140,000 civil penalty partially based on allegations that creditor failed to retain credit applications and related information for twenty-five months following notice of adverse action); United States v. Lender Serv., Inc., Clearinghouse No. 33,788 (N.D. Okla. 1982) (creditor agreed to pay a $10,000 civil penalty partially based on its alleged repeated failure to keep rejected credit applications on file for the required twenty-five months).

327 Reg. B, 12 C.F.R. § 1002.12(b)(4) [§ 202.12(b)(4)].

10.12.3 Retention of Prohibited Information

The ECOA and Regulation B prohibit creditors from requesting certain types of information.[328] However, creditors may retain any information in their files, even if use of it would violate the ECOA or Regulation B, provided that the information was obtained:

- From any source prior to March 23, 1977;
- At any time, from consumer reporting agencies, an applicant, or others without the specific request of the creditor; or
- At any time, if required for federal or state monitoring.[329]

Thus creditors may retain in their files the type of information that formed the basis of much past credit discrimination, provided the information was obtained either voluntarily from the applicant or from a third party, such as a neighbor or a credit reporting agency. Such information would include information on birth control and childbearing; information about marital status even when it is irrelevant to creditworthiness; or references to the race of the applicant or the ethnic makeup of the applicant's neighborhood. However, creditors may not use prohibited information in evaluating credit applications except when expressly permitted to do so.[330]

10.12.4 Transactions Exempt from Record Retention Requirements or Subject to More Limited Requirements

Certain creditors, including public utilities,[331] creditors dealing in securities credit,[332] incidental consumer creditors,[333] and creditors extending credit to governments or governmental subunits and agencies,[334] are exempt from some of Regulation B's record retention requirements.

Creditors providing business credit have different record retention requirements.[335] In the case of relatively small business applicants, the same rules apply as for consumer applicants, except that the twenty-five-month retention period is shortened to twelve months.[336]

In the case of larger business applicants, or with respect to certain specified types of business credit,[337] records need be retained only for sixty days unless, within that time, the applicant makes a written request *either* for a statement of the reasons for an adverse action taken or that the records be retained. In that case, the records are to be retained for twelve months.[338]

In deciding whether an application is for business or consumer credit, the primary purpose of the application controls.[339] Thus, if a consumer purchases a pick-up truck primarily for consumer use but also for occasional business use, the transaction involves consumer credit.

10.12.5 Inadvertent Error

Failure to comply with the ECOA record retention requirements does not constitute a violation when caused by an inadvertent error.[340] Inadvertent errors include clerical mistakes, calculation errors, computer malfunctions, and printing errors. An error of legal judgment is not an inadvertent error.[341] One case discussing the thirty-day period for responding to requests for specific reasons for adverse action taken has held that a creditor, which failed to respond to these requests within the prescribed period, could not avail itself of an inadvertent error defense based on the allegation that it employed insufficient staff to respond in a timely fashion.[342]

When a creditor makes an inadvertent error concerning recordkeeping, the creditor need not correct the past error. The creditor need only correct the error prospectively.[343]

---

328 *See* § 5.5, *supra* (prohibited requests for information).

329 Reg. B, 12 C.F.R. § 1002.12(a) [§ 202.12(a)].

330 Official Interpretations of Reg. B [Official Staff Commentary on Reg. B], 12 C.F.R. pt. 1002 [pt. 202], Supp. I, § 1002.12(a)-2 [§ 202.12(a)-2].

331 Reg. B, 12 C.F.R. § 1002.3(a)(2)(iii) [§ 202.3(a)(2)(iii)]; *see also* § 2.2.6.2, *supra*.

332 Reg. B, 12 C.F.R. § 1002.3(b)(2)(viii) [§ 202.3(b)(2)(viii)]; *see* § 2.2.6.5, *supra*.

333 Reg. B, 12 C.F.R. § 1002.3(c)(2)(viii) [§ 202.3(c)(2)(viii)]; *see* § 2.2.6.3, *supra*.

334 Reg. B, 12 C.F.R. § 1002.3(d)(2) [§ 202.3(d)(2)]; *see also* § 2.2.6.6, *supra*.

335 Reg. B, 12 C.F.R. § 1002.12(b) [§ 202.12(b)].

336 In 1999, the Federal Reserve Board proposed extending the record-retention period for small business applications to twenty-five months. 64 Fed. Reg. 44,582 (Aug. 16, 1999).

The Board did not adopt this change. 68 Fed. Reg. 13,144, 13,152 (Mar. 18, 2003). The Board stated that, although an expanded retention period could assist enforcement agencies, the benefits of

expanding the requirement were outweighed by the compliance burdens. For example, the use of electronic record storage for many business credit records was not as prevalent as the Board believed when it issued the proposal.

337 Reg. B, 12 C.F.R. § 1002.9(a)(3) [§ 202.9(a)(3)]. "Trade credit, credit incident to a factoring agreement, or other similar types of business credit" is defined at Official Interpretations of Reg. B [Official Staff Commentary on Reg. B], 12 C.F.R. pt. 1002 [pt. 202], Supp. I, § 1002.9(a)(3)-2, -3 [§ 202.9(a)(3)-2, -3].

338 Reg. B, 12 C.F.R. § 1002.12(b)(5) [§ 202.12(b)(5)].

339 Official Interpretations of Reg. B [Official Staff Commentary on Reg. B], 12 C.F.R. pt. 1002 [pt. 202], Supp. I, § 1002.2(g)-1 [§ 202.2(g)-1, *as amended by* 54 Fed. Reg. 12,471 (Apr. 4, 1990) (formerly section 202.3(d)(1)-1)].

The Truth in Lending Act also uses the primary-purpose test, and cases interpreting that provision may provide useful guidance. *E.g.*, Gallegos v. Stokes, 593 F.2d 372 (10th Cir. 1979); Redhouse v. Quality Ford Sales, Inc., 523 F.2d 1 (10th Cir. 1975) (en banc) (per curiam), *superseding* 511 F.2d 230 (10th Cir. 1975); Smith v. Chapman, 436 F. Supp. 58 (W.D. Tex. 1977). *See generally* National Consumer Law Center, Truth in Lending § 2.4.2.1 (8th ed. 2012).

340 Reg. B, 12 C.F.R. § 1002.14(c) [§ 202.14(c)]. Effective January 18, 2014, there will be further amendments to section 1002.14 of Regulation B and its official interpretations. Please refer to appendices B and C, *infra*, for a redlined version of these amendments.

341 Official Interpretations of Reg. B [Official Staff Commentary on Reg. B], 12 C.F.R. pt. 1002 [pt. 202], Supp. I, § 1002.16(c)-1 [§ 202.16(c)-1].

342 *See* Desselles v. J.C. Penney Co., [1974–1980 Decisions Transfer Binder] Consumer Cred. Guide (CCH) ¶ 97,536 (E.D. La. 1979).

343 Official Interpretations of Reg. B [Official Staff Commentary on

10.13 Collection of Monitoring Information

Regulation B requires a creditor that receives an application for credit primarily for the purchase or refinance of a dwelling occupied or to be occupied by the applicant as a primary residence, when that dwelling is to serve as the security for the credit sought, to collect information about the race, ethnicity, sex, marital status, and age of the applicant.[344] This information is intended to assist private plaintiffs and government enforcement agencies in determining whether differences in treatment due to a prohibited basis have occurred.

The creditor must ask questions about the race, ethnicity, sex, marital status, and age of the applicant either on the application form or on a separate form that refers to the application. The applicant must be asked, but not required, to provide this information. If the applicant chooses not to provide the information, the creditor must note that fact and must note to the extent possible the ethnicity, race, and sex of the applicant on the basis of visual observation or surname.[345]

The creditor must inform the applicant that the information is being requested by the federal government for the purpose of monitoring compliance with federal statutes prohibiting discrimination. The creditor must also inform the applicant that, if the applicant chooses not to provide this information, the creditor is required to note the ethnicity, race, and sex of the applicant on the basis of visual observation or surname.[346]

The creditor is required to request the following information:

- Ethnicity, using the categories Hispanic or Latino or not Hispanic or Latino;
- Race, using the categories American Indian or Alaska Native, Asian, Black or African American, Native Hawaiian or other Pacific Islander, and White;
- Sex;
- Marital status, using the categories married, unmarried, and separated; and
- Age.[347]

The disclosures to the applicant regarding the collection of monitoring information are not required to be made in any particular format. The "clear and conspicuous" requirement applicable to adverse action notices does not apply to disclosures relating to the collection of monitoring information.[348]

The monitoring information collected must be retained in accordance with the record keeping requirements of Regulation B.[349]

Advocates pursuing a case of discrimination on the basis of race, ethnicity, sex, marital status, and age against a mortgage lender may wish to request the creditor's monitoring information in discovery.

ECOA enforcement actions have included allegations that creditors failed to collect monitoring information as required.[350]

10.14 Self-Testing

The ECOA and Regulation B allow a creditor to investigate its own conduct to determine whether the creditor's practices are in violation of the Act. If such self-tests are conducted in accordance with the ECOA and Regulation B's requirements, and if the creditor corrects any violations identified by the self-test, the information developed in the course of the self-test is privileged.[351]

A self-test is defined as a program, practice, or study that is designed and used specifically to determine the extent or effectiveness of a creditor's compliance with the ECOA and Regulation B.[352] The self-test must create information that is not available from loan files or records relating to the transaction.[353] The privilege applicable to a self-test applies to the

---

Reg. B], 12 C.F.R. pt. 1002 [pt. 202], Supp. I, § 1002.16(c)-2 [§ 202.16(c)-2].

344 Reg. B, 12 C.F.R. § 1002.13(a)(1) [§ 202.13(a)(1)].

345 Reg. B, 12 C.F.R. § 1002.13(b) [§ 202.13(b)].

With respect to the request for monitoring information, note that the official interpretation states that a creditor may treat an application taken through an electronic medium without video capability as if it were received by mail. Official Interpretations of Reg. B [Official Staff Commentary on Reg. B], 12 C.F.R. pt. 1002 [pt. 202], Supp. I, § 1002.13(b)-4(ii) [§ 202.13(b)-4(ii)].

A creditor that accepts an application by telephone or mail must request the monitoring information but need not comply with the requirement to note information based on visual observation if the applicant declines to provide it. Official Interpretations of Reg. B [Official Staff Commentary on Reg. B], 12 C.F.R. pt. 1002 [pt. 202], Supp. I, § 1002.13(b)-3(i) [§ 202.13(b)-3(i)].

346 Reg. B, 12 C.F.R. § 1002.13(c) [§ 202.13(c)].

347 Reg. B, 12 C.F.R. § 1002.13(a)(1) [§ 202.13(a)(1)].

348 Reg. B, 12 C.F.R. § 1002.4(d) [§ 202.4(d)].

In December 2003, the Federal Reserve Board published a proposed rule to define more precisely the standard for providing clear and conspicuous disclosures and to provide a more uniform standard among the Board's regulations. 68 Fed. Reg. 68,786 (Dec. 10, 2003).

The Board noted that the ECOA does not currently address a standard for the form of disclosures, only requiring creditors to disclose information provided in writing in a clear and conspicuous manner. These proposed rules were subsequently formally withdrawn. *See* 69 Fed. Reg. 35,541 (June 25, 2004).

349 *See* § 10.12.1, *supra* (discussing preservation of records).

350 In the Federal Trade Commission (FTC) lawsuit against Capital City Mortgage, the FTC alleged, among other things, that Capital City failed to collect monitoring information as required. Fed. Trade Comm'n v. Capital City Mortgage Corp., No. 98CV-237 (D.D.C. complaint filed Jan. 30, 1998), *available at* www.ftc.gov/os/caselist/capitalcitymortgage/capitalcitymortgage.htm.

351 *See* 12 U.S.C. § 1691c-1; Reg. B, 12 C.F.R. § 1002.15 [§ 202.15].

352 Reg. B, 12 C.F.R. § 1002.15(b)(1) [§ 202.15(b)(1)].

353 A creditor may inquire about the race, color, religion, national origin, or sex of an applicant or other person for the purpose of conducting a self-test. A creditor that makes such an inquiry of an applicant must provide the disclosures required when such information is collected for monitoring purposes. Reg. B, 12 C.F.R. § 1002.5(b)(1) [§ 202.5(b)(1)].

As is the case for disclosures relating to the collection of monitoring information, no particular format is required for the disclosures. Reg. B, 12 C.F.R. § 1002.4(d) [§ 202.4(d)].

results of the self-test, factual information created by the self-test, and analysis, opinions, and conclusions pertaining to the self-test results or report.[354]

In order for the privilege to apply, the creditor must take appropriate corrective action when the self-test shows that it is more likely than not that a violation occurred, even though no violation has been formally adjudicated. The remedial action taken must be reasonably likely to remedy the cause and effect of the likely violation.[355] Among other things, the creditor must provide remedial relief to an applicant identified by the self-test as one whose rights were more likely than not violated. The creditor

is not required to provide relief to testers used in the self-test or for practices that fall outside the statute of limitations.[356]

The results of a privileged self-test may not be used by a government agency or an applicant in any civil action in which a violation of the ECOA or Regulation B is alleged.[357] A creditor loses the privilege by disclosing the privileged information or by failing to retain records of the self-test as required by section 1002.12(b)(6) [§ 202.12(b)(6)] of Regulation B.[358]

An advocate representing an applicant in a case alleging violations of the ECOA should be aware of the existence of the self-testing privilege and of its limitations.

---

354 Reg. B, 12 C.F.R. § 1002.15(b)(2) [§ 202.15(b)(2)].
355 Reg. B, 12 C.F.R. § 1002.15(c)(2) [§ 202.15(c)(2)].

356 Reg. B, 12 C.F.R. § 1002.15(c)(3) [§ 202.15(c)(3)].
357 Reg. B, 12 C.F.R. § 1002.15(d)(1) [§ 202.15(d)(1)].
358 Reg. B, 12 C.F.R. § 1002.15(d)(2) [§ 202.15(d)(2)].

Chapter 11

Litigating a Credit Discrimination Case

11.1 Introduction

This chapter reviews key issues to consider in private credit discrimination litigation. The next chapter focuses on government enforcement actions.

Some plaintiffs may have difficulty establishing standing in credit discrimination cases. These issues are covered in § 11.2, *infra*, including a separate section focusing on standing for testers and non-profit organizations. The next section (§ 11.3, *infra*) discusses possible defendants to sue for credit discrimination.

Section 11.4, *infra*, covers issues related to certifying a class action, focusing on concerns that arise in disparate impact cases. Section 11.5, *infra*, discusses forum selection issues, particularly choices regarding federal versus state court, administrative procedures for FHA claims, and issues related to mandatory arbitration clauses. Section 11.6, *infra*, provides a guide for advocates in selecting causes of action in credit discrimination cases. There is a brief discussion of discovery issues in section 11.7, *infra*, followed by an extensive analysis of private remedies (section 11.8, *infra*). Two key issues are whether plaintiffs may be awarded punitive damages and the types of equitable remedies available in credit discrimination cases.

The final section reviews creditor defenses, including statute of limitations issues (section 11.9, *infra*).

11.2 Does the Plaintiff Have Standing?

11.2.1 General

Under any of the credit discrimination statutes, it is important that the plaintiff be "aggrieved" by the statutory violation. Otherwise, the plaintiff may not have standing under Article III of the United States Constitution. Moreover, both the ECOA and the Fair Housing Act (FHA) explicitly provide private remedies only for "aggrieved" persons.[1]

An aggrieved person is defined in Fair Housing regulations as any person who claims to be injured by a discriminatory housing practice or believes he or she will be injured by a discriminatory housing practice that is about to occur.[2] This requirement that the plaintiff be aggrieved under the Fair Housing Act is to be generously construed to foster "truly integrated and balanced living patterns."[3]

The Supreme Court has held that Congress intended standing under the Fair Housing Act to "extend to the full limits of Article III," thereby eliminating the prudential barriers to standing.[4] There are, however, limits to this broad standard. In particular, federal statutes may not abrogate the minimum requirements of Article III that a plaintiff demonstrate (1) an injury in fact, (2) a causal connection between the injury and the conduct complained of, and (3) the likelihood, as opposed to mere speculation, that the injury will be redressed by a favorable decision.[5] An attenuated causal connection is insufficient for standing; the injuries must be fairly traceable to the actions of the defendants rather than the result of actions of

---

1   15 U.S.C. § 1691e; 42 U.S.C. § 3613; *see, e.g.*, McClain v. American Economy Ins. Co., 424 F.3d 728 (8th Cir. 2005) (home owner, who was falsely told by independent agent that insurer did not write insurance anywhere in the state, did not have Article III standing to sue insurer on basis of its policy of denying home owners' insurance to residents of a particular minority community when home owner's new home was not located within that community). *But see* Whitley v. Taylor Bean & Whitacker Mortgage Corp., 607 F. Supp. 2d 885, 894–95 (N.D. Ill. 2009) (husband who was not co-borrower nevertheless had standing because, as co-owner of the property, he had

signed the mortgage and was in jeopardy of losing his home; daughter living in home did not have standing as she was not party to loan transaction); KB2S, Inc. v. City of San Diego, 2007 WL 173858, at *3 (S.D. Cal. Jan. 17, 2007) ("conjectural" injury from alleged Fair Housing Act violation did not suffice to establish Article III standing), *aff'd*, 325 Fed. Appx. 566 (9th Cir. 2009); Vaughn v. Consumer Home Mortgage Co., 2006 WL 2239324, at *8 (E.D.N.Y. Aug. 6, 2006) (ruling that plaintiffs failed to establish Article III standing in a Fair Housing Act claim brought against the Department of Housing and Urban Development), *aff'd*, 297 Fed. Appx. 23 (2d Cir. 2008); Lee v. Fed. Deposit Ins. Corp., 1997 U.S. Dist. LEXIS 13885 (S.D.N.Y. Sept. 12, 1997); *cf.* Assisted Living Group, Inc. v. Upper Dublin Township, 1997 U.S. Dist. LEXIS 19554 (E.D. Pa. Dec. 2, 1997) (intervention denied in FHA case).

2   24 C.F.R. § 100.20.

Note, however, that the FHA does not cover transactions related to property purchased for investment purposes, even if it is residential property. *See, e.g.*, In re Wells Fargo Residential Mortgage Lending Discrimination Litig., 2010 WL 4791687 (N.D. Cal. Nov. 18, 2010) (finding one named plaintiff lacked standing because he admitted that he purchased mortgaged property solely for investment purposes).

3   Trafficante v. Metro. Life Ins. Co., 409 U.S. 205, 211, 93 S. Ct. 364, 34 L. Ed. 2d 415 (1972).

4   Havens Realty Corp. v. Coleman, 455 U.S. 363, 373–75, 102 S. Ct. 1114, 71 L. Ed. 2d 214 (1982); Gladstone Realtors v. Vill. of Bellwood, 441 U.S. 91, 103, 99 S. Ct. 1601, 60 L. Ed. 2d 66 (1979); Trafficante v. Metro. Life Ins. Co., 409 U.S. 205, 93 S. Ct. 364, 34 L. Ed. 2d 415 (1972).

5   Lujan v. Defenders of Wildlife, 504 U.S. 555, 560–61, 112 S. Ct. 2130, 119 L. Ed. 2d 351 (1992).

independent third parties.[6] Pleadings that describe specific injuries fairly traceable to the defendants conduct will satisfy the causal connection requirement.[7]

The broad FHA standing provisions, for the most part, also apply to the federal Civil Rights Act claims. However, there are a few additional limits to consider when analyzing standing for plaintiffs under these Acts.

For example, if an action is brought under section 1982, the plaintiff must be a United States citizen.[8] The same requirement does not apply for section 1981, the ECOA, or the Fair Housing Act.

Section 1981 protects the right to make and enforce contracts.[9] Thus generally only parties to the contract at issue, and possibly intended third-party beneficiaries, will have standing.[10] However, those who are not parties to contracts may have standing under section 1982, which protects the right to "inherit, purchase, lease, sell, hold and convey real and personal property."

The ECOA has an important standing limitation. Only "applicants" can bring actions. The definition of applicant is broader than the term implies, including not only those who seek credit but those to whom credit has been extended. The term also applies not just to the primary obligor but also to others obligated on the debt.[11]

In general, co-signers are applicants, but an authorized user on someone else's credit account may not be an applicant unless the user is obligated to repay all debts on the account.[12]

A spouse whose signature is improperly required is an applicant. Someone who does not sign the promissory note itself but who is required to sign a mortgage securing that note is contractually liable to at least some extent because the note can be satisfied from that property.[13] There is some question as to whether guarantors are applicants for purposes of all ECOA provisions or only under section 1002.7(d) [section 202.7(d)] (dealing with spouse's signatures).[14]

There are limits to who might be contractually liable and therefore a credit applicant under the ECOA. For example, individual members of a church were not considered applicants for a loan request made on behalf of the non-profit church corporation.[15] In addition, the sole shareholder and officer of a corporation was held not to be an applicant when a loan was sought on behalf of his corporation.[16]

As discussed below, a major practical implication of the applicant standing requirement under the ECOA is that it will

---

6 Mayor of Balt. v. Wells Fargo Bank, 677 F. Supp. 2d 847 (D. Md. 2010) (finding city's allegations of predatory and discriminatory lending practices insufficient when defendant bank was responsible for only a negligible portion of city's vacant housing stock, and there were many factors contributing to the decline in value of its homes).

7 Mayor of Balt. v. Wells Fargo Bank, 2011 WL 1557759 (D. Md. Apr. 22, 2011) (finding the city's allegations of predatory lending and steering of African-American borrowers into subprime loans, when coupled with resultant foreclosures and property vacancies, fairly traceable to defendant's conduct); *see also* City of Memphis v. Wells Fargo Bank, 2011 WL 1706756 (W.D. Tenn. May 4, 2011) (finding standing when plaintiff alleged that defendants' discriminatory lending practices—reverse redlining—resulted in foreclosures and vacancies to fifty specific properties; also noting in the alternative that plaintiff had standing regardless of defendants' factual attacks because when plaintiffs' claims provide a basis of federal jurisdiction that is intertwined with plaintiff's federal cause of action, court should assume jurisdiction over case and decide the case on the merits).

8 *See* § 2.4, *supra.*

9 *See* §§ 1.5, 2.4, *supra.*

10 Domino's Pizza, Inc. v. McDonald, 546 U.S. 470, 126 S. Ct. 1246, 1249 n.3, 163 L. Ed. 2d 1069 (2006) (declining to affirm or exclude the possibility that third-party intended beneficiaries of a contract can bring a claim under section 1981); *see, e.g.,* Hargraves v. Capital City Mortgage Corp., 147 F. Supp. 2d 1, 3 (D.D.C. 2001).

11 *See* Reg. B, 12 C.F.R. § 1002.2(e) [§ 202.2(e)]; § 2.2.4.1, *supra.*

12 Reg. B, 12 C.F.R. § 1002.7(c) [§ 202.7(c)]; *see also* Official Interpretations of Reg. B [Official Staff Commentary on Reg. B], 12 C.F.R. pt. 1002 [pt. 202], Supp. I, §§ 1002.7(c)(1)-1, 1002.7(c)(2)-1 [§§ 202.7(c)(1)-1, 202.7(c)(2)-1]; *cf.* Miller v. American Express Co., 688 F.2d 1235 (9th Cir. 1982) (in challenging American Express's policy of automatically canceling a supplementary card

holder's account upon the death of the principal card holder, plaintiff was found to be more than a mere user of her husband's account; the ECOA applied because plaintiff was personally liable under the contract creating the supplementary account for all debts charged on her card by any person).

Note that, under the ECOA, a creditor may require that a user become contractually liable on the account in order to be designated an authorized user, as long as the condition is not imposed on a discriminatory basis. Official Interpretations of Reg. B [Official Staff Commentary on Reg. B], 12 C.F.R. pt. 1002, Supp. I, § 1002.7(a)-1 [§ 202.7(a)-1].

13 Whitley v. Taylor Bean & Whitacker Mortgage Corp., 607 F. Supp. 2d 885, 894–95 (N.D. Ill. 2009) (husband who was not co-borrower nevertheless had standing because, as co-owner of property, he had signed mortgage and was in jeopardy of losing his home); Carter v. Buckeye Rural Electric Coop., 2001 WL 1681104 (S.D. Ohio Sept. 7, 2001) (plaintiff could be "contractually liable" and thus was an "applicant" when electric cooperative added her name to husband's account without her consent); Ford v. Citizens & Southern Nat'l Bank, 700 F. Supp. 1121 (N.D. Ga. 1988) (husband required to put up a mortgage to secure note signed by his wife was contractually liable and therefore was aggrieved party with standing to sue), *aff'd on other grounds*, 928 F.2d 1118 (11th Cir. 1991).

14 *See* § 2.2.4.2, *supra; see also* Champion Bank v. Reg'l Dev., L.L.C., 2009 WL 1351122 (E.D. Mo. May 13, 2009) (spouse who did not apply for credit but was required to sign as guarantor of husband's business loan was not an "applicant" with standing to bring ECOA claim); Durdin v. Cheyenne Mountain Bank, 98 P. 3d 899 (Colo. App. 2004) (if plaintiff had brought action only as a guarantor, he would not have had standing because claim was not brought under section 1002.7 [section 202.7]; however, plaintiff did have standing as a co-borrower).

15 Hargraves. v. Capital City Mortgage Corp., 147 F. Supp. 2d 1 (D.D.C. 2001) (claims of individual plaintiffs who did not receive or apply for credit as individuals but rather were involved in obtaining a loan for their church were dismissed; the ECOA provides a cause of action for the church, but individuals cannot assert church's legal interest; section 1981 claims also dismissed because the church, not individual plaintiffs, was party to loan contract); Church of Zion Christian Ctr., Inc. v. Southtrust Bank, 1997 U.S. Dist. LEXIS 12425 (S.D. Ala. July 30, 1997) (individual plaintiffs held not to have standing to bring an ECOA action when loan application was made on behalf of a corporation and plaintiffs never entered into any oral or written agreement with defendants).

16 Bentley v. Glickman, 234 B.R. 12 (N.D.N.Y. 1999).

be more difficult for an organization representing applicants to bring an ECOA action than a Fair Housing Act case.[17]

In a class action alleging disparate impact, the defendant may challenge the standing of the named plaintiff in order to show that the named plaintiff's claims are not typical of those of class members. For example, the plaintiff's loan terms may actually have been better than those obtained, on average, by similarly situated whites. However, if the plaintiff has presented viable statistical evidence that his or her terms would probably have been even better yet, absent the allegedly discriminatory practices, then the issue goes to the merits of the case, not typicality.[18]

Additional standing issues when plaintiffs are seeking prospective relief are discussed in § 11.8.5, *infra*.

11.2.2 Do Testers and Non-Profit Organizations Have Standing?

11.2.2.1 General

As noted in the previous section, the ECOA's limiting of actions to those brought on behalf of applicants poses a major barrier for testers and non-profit organizations hoping to bring ECOA claims. Although the definition of applicant may be interpreted broadly, it generally will not apply to organizations acting on behalf of persons alleging discrimination.[19]

Standing for organizations and testers is much more likely to be found in FHA cases. The Department of Housing and Urban Development (HUD) has consistently interpreted the provisions of the fair housing laws to permit the filing of a complaint by any person or organization if an action that occurred or is about to occur would result in an injury to that person or organization.[20] Moreover, a series of United States Supreme Court cases, mainly from the 1970s and early 1980s, found that testers, non-profit housing organizations, and municipalities had standing to bring Fair Housing Act claims. These cases made clear that municipalities can be affected by racial discrimination in housing patterns in various ways, including their tax base, and such injury is sufficient for a municipality to bring a Fair Housing Act case concerning discrimination as to its residents.[21] Similarly, the individual residents of an affected

community have standing by virtue of the loss of the benefits of an integrated community.[22]

The Supreme Court last ruled on this issue in 1982.[23] During this period of Supreme Court silence, the lower courts have split, in many cases eroding the previously generous standing test for testers and organizations.[24]

11.2.2.2 FHA Standing for Testers

Fair housing organizations often employ testers to uncover unlawful housing discrimination. Both the testers and the organizations that employ them may attempt to bring claims of unlawful discrimination. There are distinct issues when considering standing for testers as opposed to standing for organizations.

With respect to testers, courts have come to different conclusions depending on whether the testers can show that they were directly injured by the alleged discriminatory practices. The Supreme Court ruled in *Havens Realty Corp. v. Coleman* that section 3604(d) of the FHA, which entitles any person to truthful information concerning the availability of housing, is a statutorily created right sufficient to confer Article III standing.[25] However, the Court concluded that the white tester in this case did not have standing because he was not provided false information about the availability of housing and therefore was not injured.[26] On the other hand, the African-American tester who was given false information suffered an injury and therefore had standing under the FHA, even if he expected to receive false information and did not intend to rent an apartment.[27] Since the *Havens Realty* ruling, courts have split as to whether tester standing under section 3604(d) is applicable to other provisions of the FHA.[28]

Testers may also show standing through indirect injury. This is most common in cases of racial steering when white residents of a neighborhood, for example, may suffer injury due to the loss of a diverse and integrated neighborhood. In *Havens*

---

17 *See* § 11.2.2–11.2.3, *infra*.

18 Ramirez v. Greenpoint Mortgage Funding, Inc., 268 F.R.D. 627, 638–39 (N.D. Cal. 2010).

19 *See, e.g.*, Evans v. First Fed. Sav. Bank, 669 F. Supp. 915 (N.D. Ind. 1987) (non-profit organization was not an applicant under the ECOA and so lacked standing to bring an ECOA action).

20 Preamble to Final Rule Implementing Fair Housing Act of 1988 § 100.20, 54 Fed. Reg. 3234 (Jan. 23, 1989).

   Note that the preamble was withdrawn from 24 C.F.R. pt. 100 by 61 Fed. Reg. 41,282 (Aug. 7, 1996) as part of the streamlining of regulations. "[T]his rule removes from title 24 the unnecessarily codified preamble to the final rule implementing the Fair Housing Amendments Act of 1988."

21 Havens Realty Corp. v. Coleman, 455 U.S. 363, 102 S. Ct. 1114, 71 L. Ed. 2d 214 (1982); Gladstone Realtors v. Vill. of Bellwood, 441 U.S. 91, 99 S. Ct. 1601, 60 L. Ed. 2d 66 (1979); Vill. of Bellwood v. Dwivedi, 895 F.2d 1521 (7th Cir. 1990).

22 Gladstone Realtors v. Vill. of Bellwood, 441 U.S. 91, 99 S. Ct. 1601, 60 L. Ed. 2d 66 (1979).

23 Havens Realty Corp. v. Coleman, 455 U.S. 363, 102 S. Ct. 1114, 71 L. Ed. 2d 214 (1982).

24 *See generally* Dash T. Douglas, *Standing on Shaky Ground: Standing Under the Fair Housing Act*, 34 Akron L. Rev. 613 (2001).

25 Havens Realty Corp. v. Coleman, 455 U.S. 363, 102 S. Ct. 1114, 71 L. Ed. 2d 214 (1982).

26 *Id.*, 455 U.S. at 375.

27 *Id.*, 455 U.S. at 374.

28 *Compare* Ragin v. Harry Macklowe Real Estate Co., 6 F.3d 898 (2d Cir. 1993) (testers who read allegedly discriminatory housing advertisements but were not necessarily in the market for housing had standing), *with* Wilson v. Glenwood Intermountain Properties, Inc., 98 F.3d 590 (10th Cir. 1996) (reading of a discriminatory advertisement by one who is not in the market for housing is insufficient to confer standing), *and* Ricks v. Beta Dev. Co., 92 F.3d 1193 (9th Cir. 1996) (table) (text available at 1996 WL 436548) (in denying standing to assert a claim under section 3604(f), court limited the *Havens Realty* result to provisions of the Act, such as section 3604(d), explicitly providing protection to "any person"). *See generally* Dash T. Douglas, *Standing on Shaky Ground: Standing Under the Fair Housing Act*, 34 Akron L. Rev. 613 (2001).

Realty, the Court found that the white tester, as noted above, did not suffer a direct injury. In determining whether he had suffered an indirect injury, the key question considered was how wide of a geographic impact racial steering practices could have. The Court found that it was implausible that the discrimination could affect the entire city of Richmond.[29] The Court noted that it had upheld standing in other cases but only within a relatively compact neighborhood. However, the Court found that an injury could possibly still be proven, leaving open the question of how broad an area fits within the definition of a "relatively compact neighborhood."[30]

11.2.2.3 FHA Standing for Organizational Plaintiffs

An organization, such as a non-profit fair housing organization, may have standing to assert its own interests in a Fair Housing Act (FHA) case. A fair housing organization may recover even if unlawful discrimination is found only involving its testers and not involving others.[31] This broad interpretation of standing may also apply to a non-profit corporation seeking to pursue FHA claims on behalf of unnamed third parties.[32]

Although courts agree that organizations may have standing to sue under the FHA, the key issue is what type of damage they must show in order to meet the Article III standing requirement of injury-in-fact. In general, an organization must have suffered a concrete and demonstrable injury to its activities, not merely a setback to the organization's abstract social interests.[33]

As provided in *Havens Realty*,[34] organizations may be sufficiently injured if they can show that the time and resources they spent investigating and pursuing the defendants' discriminatory behavior kept them from providing other services, such as counseling individual clients. In essence, a drain on an organizations' resources caused by an investigation into a defendants' FHA violations can, in a number of circuits, constitute the requisite injury.[35]

The District of Columbia, Third, Fifth, and Ninth Circuits reject this broad interpretation, however, holding that mere diversion of resources for testing or investigative purposes is insufficient to show the requisite injury-in-fact for standing. Rather, in order for an organization to demonstrate the requisite injury, it must show that its activities or mission have been harmed by the defendants' FHA violations separate from its diversion of resources for investigation or litigation.[36] In other

---

29 Havens Realty Corp. v. Coleman, 455 U.S. 377 (1982).

30 *Id.*

31 *See, e.g.*, Cent. Ala. Fair Hous. Ctr., Inc. v. Lowder Realty Co., 236 F.3d 629 (11th Cir. 2000) (even if none of the individual plaintiffs prevail, organization is still entitled to seek damages proximately caused by defendant's unlawful discrimination toward testers; trial court erred by instructing jury that it could find for the organization only if it first found for one of the individual plaintiffs).

32 *See* Oti Kaga, Inc. v. South Dakota Hous. Dev. Auth., 342 F.3d 871 (8th Cir. 2003) (non-profit Native American housing corporation had standing to bring FHA claims in connection with the denial of its applications for low-income housing tax credits based on discrimination against unnamed third parties). *But see* D.B. Indy, L.L.C. v. Talisman Brookdale, 2004 WL 1630976 (D. Minn. July 20, 2004) (no standing in discrimination case based on Civil Rights Acts and state law when plaintiff corporation was not an entity specially created to benefit minority interest nor in the best position to challenge the alleged discrimination).

33 Havens Realty Corp. v. Coleman, 455 U.S. 363, 379, 102 S. Ct. 1114, 71 L. Ed. 2d 214 (1982).

34 *Id.*

35 *See, e.g.*, Fair Hous. Council, Inc. v. Vill. of Olde St. Andrews, Inc., 210 Fed. Appx. 469, 477–79 (6th Cir. 2006) (pre-litigation expenses or lost opportunity costs associated with pre-litigation investigation

are sufficient to create standing under FHA); Hooker v. Weathers, 990 F.2d 913 (6th Cir. 1993) (organization devoted resources to investigate complaints of defendants' discrimination and therefore had standing to sue under the FHA); Ragin v. Harry Macklowe Real Estate Co., 6 F.3d 898 (2d Cir. 1993) (organization had standing to challenge real estate advertisements under the FHA because it had shown that its activities relating to identifying and counteracting defendants' advertising practices diverted staff resources from their regular tasks); Vill. of Bellwood v. Dwivedi, 895 F.2d 1521 (7th Cir. 1990) (organization had standing to bring FHA claim because its investigation into defendants' discrimination deflected time and money from other tasks, and the organization was paid less for its investigative efforts than the costs it incurred); Inclusive Communities Project, Inc. v. Tex. Dep't of Hous. & Comm. Affairs, 749 F. Supp. 2d 486 (N.D. Tex. 2010) (organization had standing to challenge defendants' distribution of low income housing tax credits (LIHTC) under FHA because organization's average cost to secure non-LIHTC housing for its clients was greater than cost to secure LIHTC housing); NAACP v. Ameriquest Mortgage Co., 635 F. Supp. 2d 1096 (C.D. Cal. 2009) (organization had standing under FHA because defendants' discriminatory mortgage lending policies frustrated organization's mission and diverted its resources through investigation, advocacy, and litigation costs); Echeverria v. Krystie Manor, Ltd. P'ship, 2009 WL 857629, at *5 (E.D.N.Y. Mar. 30, 2009) (organization's efforts to educate, counsel, and advocate on behalf of individual plaintiff in response to defendant's housing discrimination was sufficient to show injury for standing under FHA); Equal Rights Ctr. v. Equity Residential, 483 F. Supp. 2d 482, 486–87 (D. Md. 2007) (plaintiff had standing to assert FHA claim because defendants' conduct caused it to divert resources, including those devoted to a two-year investigation of that conduct); *see also* Nev. Fair Hous. Ctr., Inc. v. Clark Cnty., 2007 WL 610640, at *3 (D. Nev. Feb. 23, 2007) (diversion of resources to combat discriminatory practices sufficed to confer standing on organization that had brought an FHA Fair Housing Act claim); Williams v. Poretsky Mgmt., Inc., 955 F. Supp. 490 (D. Md. 1996) (finding standing when organization devoted significant resources to identifying and counteracting defendant's discriminatory practices, and the practices frustrated organization's efforts against discrimination). *But see* Ctr. for Cmty. Justice & Advocacy v. RBS Citizens, N.A., 776 F. Supp. 2d 460 (E.D. Mich. 2011) (nonprofit organization's sole allegation that it had more difficulty negotiating on behalf of one client over another because of defendants' racial discrimination was not a sufficient diversion of resources to show injury for FHA standing under *Havens*).

36 Fair Housing Council of San Fernando Valley v. Roommate.com, L.L.C., 666 F.3d 1216, 1219 (9th Cir. 2012) (though litigation costs alone would be insufficient to show injury, here the organization started new education and outreach campaigns targeting discriminatory advertising and therefore diverted resources independent of litigation costs, thereby frustrating its central mission and showing injury sufficient for FHA standing); Fair Hous. Council v. Montgomery Newspapers, 141 F.3d 71, 79 (3d Cir. 1998) (litigation costs alone are insufficient to show damage for standing purposes, and organization failed to substantiate its claims of non-litigation resource diversion with sufficient evidence, as required at summary judgment phase); Fair Emp't Council v. BMC Mktg. Corp., 28 F.3d

words, "while the diversion of resources to litigation or investigation in anticipation of litigation does not constitute an injury in fact sufficient to support standing, [an] alleged diversion of resources to programs designed to counteract the injury to its interest in promoting fair housing could constitute such an injury."[37]

11.2.3 Associational Standing

The aggrieved individual bringing an ECOA, Fair Housing, or federal Civil Rights Acts suit need not be a member of the protected group being discriminated against, as long as the individual is injured by the discrimination.[38] The "injury in fact" requirement for standing must be a direct injury resulting from the challenged conduct.[39] For example, a white person can bring an action under any of the credit discrimination laws if denied credit because he or she lives in a predominantly African-American neighborhood or associates with African Americans.[40]

Under the Fair Housing Act, the aggrieved individual need not even be the individual turned down for credit but merely someone aggrieved by that action. An individual not seeking credit can bring an action, such as those who would benefit if credit were granted to some other party. For example, consider an owner who rents a two-family home to one white family and one African-American family. If the owner is turned down for a loan to repair the home because an African-American family lives in the house, both the white tenants and the African-American tenants could bring a Fair Housing Act claim.

Neither the ECOA nor the federal Civil Rights Act, however, provides a right for a plaintiff associated with the applicant to challenge the discrimination suffered by the applicant but not by the plaintiff.[41] The ECOA generally only provides remedies to those who apply for credit, not those affiliated with those who apply. For example, the ECOA would only provide a remedy for the landlord and not the African-American tenants if the landlord were denied a loan to fix up the apartment because of the tenants' race. Similarly, section 1981 only protects persons who have (or sought) rights under a contractual relationship, including parties to the contract and, potentially, third-party beneficiaries of the contract. Section 1981 does not provide a remedy to other persons even if they are the target of discrimination and lose benefits as a result of the contract impairment.[42]

Courts may, however, allow an association to bring ECOA claims on behalf of its members as long as Article III standing requirements are met.[43] To make this determination, a court will examine: (a) whether the association's members would otherwise have standing to sue in their own right; (b) whether the interests the association seeks to protect are germane to the organization's purpose; and (c) that neither the claims asserted nor the relief requested requires the participation of the association's individual members in the lawsuit.[44]

1268 (D.C. Cir. 1994) (organization's choice to divert resources to testing was self-inflicted injury and therefore insufficient for standing, though an organization may have standing if it can show that defendants' discrimination was against bona fide employment candidates, not just testers, and therefore impaired organization's programs by increasing the people in need of counseling); Ass'n for Retarded Citizens v. Dallas Cnty. Mental Health & Mental Retardation Ctr. Bd. of Trs., 19 F.3d 241 (5th Cir. 1994) (organization did not have standing because mere redirection of resources to litigation and counseling in response to another party's actions is insufficient to show injury); Spann v. Colonial Vill. Inc., 899 F.2d 24 (D.C. Cir. 1990) (organization spent money reaching out to potential home buyers or renters who were steered away from housing opportunities by defendants' discriminatory advertising, therefore showing sufficient injury to confer standing under the FHA); Nat'l Cmty. Reinvestment Coal. v. Accredited Home Lenders Holding Co., 573 F. Supp. 2d 70, 75 (D.D.C. 2008) (organization engaged in an education and outreach campaign to combat defendants' discriminatory conduct, which was sufficient for standing under FHA, though mere testing would not have been); Isaac v. Norwest Mortgage, 2002 WL 1119854 (N.D. Tex. May 23, 2002) (finding no standing for organizational plaintiff because of lack of distinct and palpable injury to the group or its members), *aff'd*, 58 Fed. Appx. 595 (5th Cir. 2003) (table).

37 Rights Ctr. v. Post Properties, Inc., 633 F.3d 1136, 1140 (D.D.C. 2011) (finding no standing because organization did not prove that its injury was "concrete and particularized" or "actual or imminent").

38 *See* § 3.9, *supra*.

39 *See, e.g.*, McClain v. American Economy Ins. Co., 424 F.3d 728 (8th Cir. 2005) (home owner, who was allegedly told by independent agent that insurer did not write insurance in state, did not have Article III standing to sue insurer on basis of its policy of denying home owners' insurance to residents of minority community when home owner's new home was not located within that community).

40 *See, e.g.*, Official Interpretations of Reg. B [Official Staff Commentary on Reg. B], 12 C.F.R. pt. 1002 [pt. 202], Supp. I, § 1002.2(z)-1 [§ 202.2(z)-1]; Simms v. First Gibraltar Bank, 83 F.3d 1546 (5th Cir. 1996) (white owner of apartment complex in predominantly minority area); Woods-Drake v. Lundy, 667 F.2d 1198 (5th Cir. 1982) (in an eviction case, white plaintiff had minority guests); Cherry v. Amoco Oil Co., 481 F. Supp. 727 (N.D. Ga. 1979); Harrison v. Otto G. Heinzeroth Mortgage Co., 430 F. Supp. 893 (N.D. Ohio 1977) (African-American neighborhood); *see also* § 3.9, *supra*.

41 *See, e.g.*, Hargraves v. Capital City Mortgage Corp., 147 F. Supp. 2d 1 (D.D.C. 2001) (claims of individual plaintiffs who did not receive or apply for credit as individuals but rather were involved in obtaining a loan for their church dismissed; the ECOA provides a cause of action for church, but individuals cannot assert church's legal interest; section 1981 claims also dismissed because church, not individual plaintiffs, was party to loan contract); Church of Zion Christian Ctr., Inc. v. Southtrust Bank, 1997 U.S. Dist. LEXIS 12425 (S.D. Ala. July 30, 1997) (individual plaintiffs held not to have standing to bring an ECOA action when loan application was made on behalf of a corporation and plaintiffs never entered into any oral or written agreement with defendants); *see also* § 11.2.1, *supra*.

42 *See* Domino's Pizza, Inc. v. McDonald, 546 U.S. 470, 126 S. Ct. 1246, 1249 n.3, 163 L. Ed. 2d 1069 (2006) (declining to affirm or exclude the possibility that third-party intended beneficiaries of a contract have rights under section 1981).

43 *See, e.g.*, Rainbow Push Coal. v. Amsouth Bank, 2005 WL 637834 (M.D. Tenn. Mar. 15, 2005) (denying standing because no evidence that provisions of the ECOA at issue were germane to the purpose of Rainbow Push); Ceiba, Inc. v. Ford Motor Credit Co., 2003 WL 22204560 (E.D. Pa. Sept. 22, 2003) (denying standing because plaintiff did not allege that any of its members applied to defendants for credit).

44 Hunt v. Wash. State Apple Adver. Comm'n, 432 U.S. 333, 97 S. Ct. 2434, 53 L. Ed. 2d 383 (1977); *see, e.g.*, NAACP v. Ameriquest

11.3 The Defendant—Who Is Liable?[45]

11.3.1 Direct Creditor Liability

Creditors that directly extend or refuse to extend credit are almost always covered by the credit discrimination laws. There are only a few exceptions. For example, the ECOA and Fair Housing Act do not apply to an individual creditor who only makes one or two isolated loans.[46] The Fair Housing Act is further limited to credit discrimination related to a dwelling. Either the credit must be used in relation to purchasing, fixing, or maintaining a dwelling, or a security interest must be taken on residential real estate.[47] The federal Civil Rights Acts are generally broader in scope, covering creditor discrimination on the basis of race, certain ethnic origins, or citizenship status.

Transactions in which credit is extended by a government or a governmental subdivision, agency, or instrumentality are subject to the provisions of the ECOA and Regulation B, except that no action can be brought against governmental creditors for the recovery of punitive damages.[48] However, if a government agency is operating a special purpose credit program, it is exempted from some of the provisions of the ECOA and Regulation B.[49]

11.3.2 Finding Deep Pockets: Extending Liability Beyond Direct Creditors

11.3.2.1 General

Liability under both the ECOA and the FHA may stretch well beyond the direct creditors who extend or deny credit. This liability is critical because financial players other than the direct creditors often have the deepest pockets. Even if they do not have deep pockets, adding other parties may result in a higher total punitive damages award or higher settlement.[50] The credit arrangers or assignees may also be the most culpable parties, again leading to higher punitive damage awards and also helping the lawsuit to have the most appropriate deterrent effect.

The ECOA covers those who regularly participate in the decision of whether or not to extend credit, including setting the terms of credit. Such entities, whether they are creditors, assignees, transferees, subrogees, or loan purchasers, are directly liable for ECOA violations even if the credit was actually extended by, for example, a car dealer or by another creditor.[51]

Lenders may also be liable for discrimination under traditional agency principles.[52] Arrangers of credit, including brokers and dealers, may be liable under the ECOA for general discrimination violations and violations of the prohibition against discouraging applicants on a prohibited basis.[53]

The Fair Housing Act (FHA) also explicitly extends liability to arrangers, brokers, and others providing financial assistance related to a loan covered by the FHA.[54] In general, section 3605 of the FHA (relating to residential real estate transactions) covers a wide range of actors including makers of loans, purchasers, and those selling, brokering, and appraising real estate.[55] Section 3604, with a few limited exceptions, applies to any seller or renter of property[56] and also to mortgage lending.[57]

Motors Acceptance Corp., 220 F.R.D. 64 (M.D. Tenn. 2004) (based on its alleged role in setting terms and parameters of credit decisions by car dealers, GMAC may be a creditor even as to those customers who obtain their cars through spot deliveries, when dealer signs a retail installment sales contract with car purchaser, who takes title and possession before dealer selects an assignee for the contract and before information about car purchaser is sent to a potential assignee of contract); Smith v. Chrysler Financial Co., 2003 WL 328719, at *4–*5 (D.N.J. Jan. 15, 2003) (designating defendant automobile financing company as an ECOA creditor in its role as assignee of retail installment contracts); Jones v. Ford Motor Credit Co., 2002 WL 88431, at *2–3 (S.D.N.Y. Jan. 22, 2002) (finding defendant to be an ECOA assignee and creditor when it assigned objective credit scores to customers and authorized dealers to subjectively mark them up). *But see* Wright v. Castle Point Mortgage, 2006 WL 1468678, at *4 (D.N.J. May 24, 2006) (no liability under Fair Housing Act when defendant did not originate loan, and plaintiff's claim was based on discriminatory loan terms).

   Knowledge or reasonable notice of the violation is required only for assignees and secondary creditors who did not participate in the credit decision. *See* §§ 2.2.5.4, 2.2.5.5, *supra*.

52 Jackson v. Novastar Mortgage, Inc., 2007 WL 4568976, at *8–9 (W.D. Tenn. Dec. 20, 2007) (refusing to dismiss plaintiff's FHA claim against lender, rejecting defendant's argument that mortgage broker that arranged loan was not lender's agent but rather an independent contractor); Miles v. Century 21 Real Estate L.L.C., 2007 WL 92795, at *13 (E.D. Ark. Jan. 11, 2007) (though plaintiff did not establish actual agency between franchisor and franchisee for purposes of Fair Housing Act liability, plaintiff could establish apparent agency). *But see* Steele v. GE Money Bank, 2009 WL 393860, at *6 (N.D. Ill. Feb. 17, 2009) (allegations that, *inter alia*, lenders provided information, training, and encouragement to brokers to make loans in accordance with their "Discretionary Pricing Policy" were insufficient to "support an inference that the defendant lenders had the ability to control the manner and method in which the brokers carried out their work"; nor was there apparent agency).

53 15 U.S.C. § 1691a(3); Official Interpretations of Reg. B [Official Staff Commentary on Reg. B], 12 C.F.R. pt. 1002 [pt. 202], Supp. I, § 1002.2(l)-2 [§ 202.2(l)-2]; *see* § 2.2.5.3, *supra*.

54 *See* § 2.3, *supra; see also* Coelho v. Alliance Mortgage Banking Corp., 2007 WL 1412289, at *5 (D.N.J. May 10, 2007) (refusing to dismiss FHA claim against mortgage broker, rejecting defendant's argument that "to arrange to make available" a transaction did not fall within scope of to "make available" such a transaction).

55 *See* § 2.3.2.3, *supra*.

56 *See* § 2.3.3.2, *supra*.

57 Nat'l Cmty. Reinvestment Coal. v. Accredited Home Lenders Holding Co., 573 F. Supp. 2d 70, 76 (D.D.C. 2008); Nat'l Cmty. Reinvestment Coal. v. Novastar Financial, Inc., 2008 WL 977351 (D.D.C. Mar. 31, 2008).

Mortgage Co., 635 F. Supp. 2d 1096, 1101–03 (C.D. Cal. 2009) (finding associational standing to bring claims on behalf of plaintiff organization's members for declaratory and injunctive relief regarding discrimination in the terms and conditions of residential mortgage loans).

45 *See generally* § 2.2.5, *supra*.

46 *See* §§ 2.2.5.2, 2.3.2.3.1, 2.3.3.2, *supra*.

47 *See* § 2.3, *supra*.

48 15 U.S.C. § 1691e(b); *see* § 2.2.5.6, *supra*.

49 *See* § 3.8, *supra*.

50 *See* § 11.8.4.3.2, *infra*.

51 Reg. B, 12 C.F.R. § 1002.2(l) [§ 202.2(l)]; *see, e.g.*, Coleman v. Gen.

11.3.2.2 Individual Liability

Individuals may also be liable as long as they meet the threshold requirements for actors covered by the various discrimination laws. For example, in the Federal Trade Commission (FTC) lawsuit against Capital City Mortgage, the court allowed claims to proceed against an individual defendant who was president and sole owner of the defendant company.[58] The court held that a reasonable juror could conclude that this individual was a creditor under the ECOA based on the FTC's allegation that—as the president and sole owner of the company—he directed, controlled, formulated, and participated in the acts and practices of the company and also on the FTC's evidence that he personally requested that certain credit forms be sent to him.[59]

Corporate and non-corporate principals should be liable, based on traditional agency, for the acts of employees and agents who discriminate while acting within the scope of their employment or agency.

In attempting to further extend liability to corporate and non-corporate principals, plaintiffs have argued that the ECOA and FHA impose a non-delegable duty not to discriminate.[60]

However, a United States Supreme Court decision has expressly rejected the non-delegability doctrine, at least when characterized as such.[61] In *Meyer v. Holley*, the Supreme Court found that the FHA imposes liability without fault in accordance with traditional agency principles, imposing vicarious liability upon the corporation, but not on its officers or owners.[62] The Court remanded the case for a decision on whether the broker could be personally liable for the acts of his employees either under state agency law or through piercing of the corporate veil.

The subsequent Ninth Circuit decision on remand highlights the importance of state laws, such as state real estate broker laws, as well as common law theories to hold actors vicariously liable. The Ninth Circuit found that the broker in this case created an agency relationship with the employee who allegedly discriminated against plaintiffs.[63] Among other considerations, the court noted that California state law makes the designated real estate broker of a real estate corporation personally responsible for the supervision of the corporation's salespersons.

The court also found that there was evidence that the broker consented to the employee acting on his behalf and that the employee consented to act on behalf of the broker.[64] The court concluded that the employee acted within the scope of his agency when he committed the act of discrimination that occurred when he was supervising another agent. Such supervision was the broker's duty under state law and therefore was within the scope of the duty he delegated to the employee. The Ninth Circuit reversed and remanded the case to the district court for further proceedings on the issue of the broker's liability as principal for the actions of his agent.[65]

The Supreme Court in *Meyer* did not reach the merits of whether the broker also could be found personally liable through piercing the corporate veil but stated that, on remand, the court

---

58 Fed. Trade Comm'n v. Capital City Mortgage Corp., No. 98-237 (D.D.C. Jan. 29, 1998), *available at* www.ftc.gov *and on the companion website to this treatise.*

The court denied summary judgment on the issue of individual liability with respect to all of these claims. Fed. Trade Comm'n v. Capital City Mortgage Corp., 1998 WL 1469619 (D.D.C. July 13, 1998); *see also* Fed. Trade Comm'n v. Capital City Mortgage Corp., 321 F. Supp. 2d 16 (D.D.C. 2004) (FTC alleged a valid constructive trust claim against defendants, and ECOA civil penalties asserted did not abate with defendant's death). The FTC filed a settlement agreement and stipulated injunction in this case in February 2005. The agreements are available on the FTC website, www.ftc.gov. *See also* Hargraves v. Capital City Mortgage Corp., 140 F. Supp. 2d 7, 27–28 (D.D.C. 2000) (denying, in a case in which plaintiffs sued corporate principal Thomas Nash individually for fraud based upon misrepresentations allegedly made by defendant's agent in the course of arranging loans, Nash's motion for summary judgment due to Nash's ownership and control over Capital City as well as allegations that he signed contract to sell property to home owners, hired agent to list property, received information from agent regarding home owners' financial status, and made decision to make the loan in the form it was offered).

ECOA claims by two plaintiffs who did not receive or apply for credit were ultimately denied in defendant's summary judgment motion. Hargraves v. Capital City Mortgage Corp., 147 F. Supp. 2d 1 (D.D.C. 2001).

59 Fed. Trade Comm'n v. Capital City Mortgage Corp., 1998 WL 1469619 (D.D.C. July 13, 1998); *see also* Nat'l Cmty. Reinvestment Coal. v. NovaStar Financial, Inc., 604 F. Supp. 2d 26, 31 (D.D.C. 2009) (granting leave to amend complaint under FHA to add as a defendant Novastar's president and co-founder; rejecting argument that leave should not be granted because all of his actions were taken in his corporate capacity). *But see* Carter v. Buckeye Rural Electric Coop., 2001 WL 1681104 (S.D. Ohio Sept. 7, 2001) (allegations did not sufficiently demonstrate that individual employees named in lawsuit regularly participated in the decision of whether or not to extend credit).

60 In a 2000 amicus brief, the Department of Justice asserted the position of the United States that the ECOA, like the FHA, imposes

this duty. Brief of the United States as Amicus Curiae, Cason v. Nissan Motor Acceptance Corp., No. 3-98-0223 (M.D. Tenn. July 31, 2000), *available on the companion website to this treatise.*

61 Meyer v. Holley, 537 U.S. 280, 123 S. Ct. 824, 154 L. Ed. 2d 753 (2003) ("we cannot conclude that Congress intended, through silence, to impose this kind of special duty of protection upon individual officers of corporation—who are not principals (or contracting parties) in respect to the corporation's unlawfully acting employee").

62 Meyer v. Holley, 537 U.S. 280, 285 (2003) (it is well established that the FHA provides for vicarious liability); *see also* Simms v. First Mgmt., Inc., 2003 WL 21313928 (D. Kan. May 20, 2003) (following *Meyer* and granting summary judgment to a defendant whose only connection to the case was an ownership interest in another defendant's limited liability company).

63 Holley v. Crank, 400 F.3d 667 (9th Cir. 2005).

64 *Id.*

65 *Id.*; *see also* Connell v. Webb Realty, Inc., 2005 WL 1364641 (W.D. Tenn. June 6, 2005) (discriminatory conduct of a real estate agent is, as a general rule, attributable to owner); McGlawn v. Human Relations Comm'n, 891 A.2d 757 (Pa. Commw. Ct. 2006) (state Human Rights Commission found mortgage broker violated state Human Relations Act by engaging in reverse redlining). *See generally* National Consumer Law Center, Unfair and Deceptive Acts and Practices § 10.2.2 (8th ed. 2012).

was free to consider whether liability could be imputed to the sole owner of the company on that basis. In considering this issue on remand, the Ninth Circuit pointed to evidence that the broker, Meyer, was the sole shareholder at the time of the alleged violation, that he was president and designated officer/broker, and that he failed to treat the corporation as a distinct entity in tax returns.[66] The court found that this evidence supported an inference that Meyer exercised pervasive control over the corporation's affairs. The court also found evidence of thin capitalization and failure to follow corporate formalities. The court held that, at the very least, the allegations in plaintiff's complaint were sufficient to allow the plaintiffs to amend their complaint to specifically allege the argument that the corporate veil should be pierced.[67]

In general, corporations and other entities that are wholly owned by one or a few individuals may be merely a shell to protect the individuals from liability.[68] The individuals may have deep pockets. Informal investigation before the filing of a case and discovery during the litigation can clarify the corporate and/or familial relationships and agency ties that bind the various players together in a fraudulent scheme and assist in piercing the corporate veil.

The most important situations in which there will be no vicarious liability are those involving independent contractors, corporate shareholders, and supervisors, although these parties are still liable for their own wrongful acts.[69]

11.4 Class Actions

Class actions are available under all the credit discrimination statutes, and the same issues arise in such class actions as with any other type of consumer class action.[70] This section focuses on how several of these issues have been decided in the credit discrimination context.

The first issue, naturally, is the decision whether to bring a discrimination suit as an individual or class action. One consideration is that a court may be unwilling to consider pattern and practice evidence in the absence of class certification.[71] The potential for a punitive damages award is another factor to consider. Under the ECOA, punitive damages in class actions

are limited to the lesser of $500,000 or 1% of the creditor's "net worth."[72] Punitive damages are also limited, albeit differently, in individual ECOA actions.[73] In contrast, there are no limits to the size of punitive damages awards under the Fair Housing Act and federal Civil Rights Acts. There may be no need to bring a class action if punitive damages are the major relief sought, as an individual action may produce a large enough punitive damages award to deter future misconduct.

Despite differences in damage amounts and other variations among individual members of a class, it is sometimes possible to certify class actions in discrimination cases. However, there are a number of issues plaintiffs are likely to confront, particularly in disparate impact cases.

As with all class actions, in order to obtain class certification, plaintiffs must meet all four conditions of Federal Rule of Civil Procedure 23(a) and at least one of the subsections of Rule 23(b).[74] The four prongs of Rule 23(a) are commonality, typicality, numerosity, and adequacy of representation.

The commonality prong, which requires that there be questions of law or fact common to the class,[75] may cause difficulties for plaintiffs pursuing disparate impact claims. In *Walmart Stores v. Dukes*, a Title VII case, plaintiffs alleged gender discrimination in hiring and promotion decisions at all of Walmart's stores nationwide.[76] The case was founded upon a disparate impact theory of liability. The Court held that, while commonality does not mandate that all class members make identical claims and arguments, it requires that the "*gravamen* of the [c]omplaint is that defendants discriminated against class members in the same general fashion."[77] The *Wal-Mart* decision therefore counsels that, to satisfy the commonality requirement, there must be "some glue holding the alleged reasons for [the] decisions together, so that the claims of the representative party and the class are capable of resolution by a "common answer."[78]

Several courts have been called on to apply the *Dukes* decision in the context of disparate impact claims alleging discrimination against persons of color in the terms of their mortgages, which occurred under the originator's discretionary pricing policy. In these cases, noting that there are a variety of

---

66 Holley v. Crank, 400 F.3d 667 (9th Cir. 2005).

67 *Id.* (remanding this issue to district court to permit amendment of complaint to advance this theory).

68 *See generally* National Consumer Law Center, The Cost of Credit: Regulation, Preemption, and Industry Abuses chs. 11, 12 (4th ed. 2009 and Supp.).

69 *See, e.g.*, United States v. ERGS, Inc., 2007 WL 174675, at *3 (D. Nev. Jan. 22, 2007) (declining to pierce corporate veil for Fair Housing Act violation when no inequity to plaintiff would arise); Brown v. Interbay Funding, L.L.C., 2004 WL 2579596 (D. Del. Nov. 8, 2004) (real estate company hired to conduct appraisal found to be an independent contractor, and thus creditor not liable for discriminatory appraisal).

70 *See generally* National Consumer Law Center, Consumer Class Actions (8th ed. 2013).

71 *See* Davis v. Coca-Cola Bottling Co. Consol., 516 F.3d 955 (11th Cir. 2008).

72 15 U.S.C. § 1691e(b).

Both the Truth in Lending Act and the Fair Debt Collection Practices Act also refer to the defendants' net worth as a limit on class action damages, albeit statutory damages. Among the key matters that have been litigated concerning the issue of net worth are how to define this term, the point in time to measure it, and the extent of permissible discovery. *See generally* National Consumer Law Center, Truth in Lending § 11.8.3.3 (8th ed. 2012); National Consumer Law Center, Fair Debt Collection § 6.6.3 (7th ed. 2011 and Supp.).

73 *See* § 11.8.4.3.2, *infra.*

74 *See generally* National Consumer Law Center, Consumer Class Actions ch. 10 (8th ed. 2013).

75 Fed. R. Civ. P. 23(a)(2).

76 131 S. Ct. 2541 (2011).

77 Jones v. Ford Motor Credit Co., 2005 WL 743213, at *7 (S.D.N.Y. Mar. 31, 2005) (emphasis added) (citing Open Hous. Ctr., Inc. v. Samson Mgmt. Corp., 152 F.R.D. 472 (S.D.N.Y. 1993)).

78 131 S. Ct. 2541, 2551–52 (2011).

reasons and factors that may influence an individual's discretion to set rates and fees, the courts have held that *Dukes* precludes a finding of commonality absent a showing of a common direction by the lender or a common method of exercising discretion by the loan officers.[79]

Apart from disparate impact cases, commonality is usually a straightforward question that can be addressed with the help of precedent from all manner of consumer claims. However, it should not be taken for granted, as courts may take a constricted view of the test, particularly if the defendant offers evidence of apparent variations among class members.[80]

In addition to meeting all four elements of Rule 23(a), plaintiffs must satisfy the conditions of at least one subsection of Rule 23(b). For example, when Congress passed legislation to permit settlement of claims by black farmers against the USDA, certification under Rule 23(b)(1)(B) was found appropriate because the legislation created a limited fund.[81] A number of courts have granted certification of Rule 23(b)(2) classes,[82] while certification under Rule 23(b)(3) is uncommon.

While plaintiffs in credit discrimination litigation have been more successful in obtaining class certification under Rule 23(b)(2) than under 23(b)(3), the *Dukes* decision has altered the landscape, not just regarding commonality but also for Rule 23(b)(2) certification when some damages are sought. Rule 23(b)(2) allows plaintiffs to seek monetary relief, including disgorgement, in addition to the injunctive or declaratory relief which is at the heart of this subsection, but *Dukes* makes it clear that this is so only if the monetary damages claims are incidental to equitable remedies.[83] The Supreme Court also reiterated the basic requirement that injunctive or declaratory relief be appropriate for the class as a whole, emphasizing "the indivisible nature of the injunctive or declaratory remedy" plaintiffs must be seeking—"the notion that the conduct is such that it can be enjoined or declared unlawful only as to all of the class members or as to none of them."[84] For a court to certify a class under Rule 23(b)(2), plaintiffs will also have to show that they have standing to seek prospective relief, as discussed in § 11.8.5, *infra*.

The procedural protections of notice and opportunity to opt out of class action are unnecessary in Rule 23(b)(2) class action

---

79 *In re* Countrywide Financial Mortgage Lending Practices Litig., __ F.3d __, 2013 WL 149853 (6th Cir. 2013) ("the mere presence of a range within which acts of discretion take place will not suffice to establish commonality"; also noting that plaintiffs had not alleged "companywide policies that contributed to the alleged disparate impact that arose from the delegation of discretion to individual brokers"); Barrett v. Option One Mortgage Corp., 2012 WL 4076465 (D. Mass. Sept. 18, 2012); *In re* Wells Fargo Residential Mortgage Lending Discrimination Litig., 2011 U.S. Dist. LEXIS 99830 (N.D. Cal. Sept. 6, 2011); Rodriguez v. Nat'l City Bank, 2011 WL 5041355 (E.D. Pa. Oct. 24, 2011).

80 In Givens v. Van Devere, Inc., 2012 WL 4092738 (N.D. Ohio Sept. 17, 2012), the court rejected certification of an ECOA class in a suit against a car dealer alleging failure to provide reasons for adverse action when post-delivery financing was denied. The rejection appears to have been based on lack of ascertainability, which in turn impeded a determination of commonality. The court predicated its decision on the defendant's president's affidavit, which stated that there were different contracts signed by different customers and different financing contracts from different banks and that some customers got better terms after their initial denial of credit. The affidavit did not, however, assert that the company had sent an adverse action notice to any of these customers.

81 *In re* Black Farmers Discrimination Litig., 856 F. Supp. 2d 1, 17 (D.D.C. 2011) (noting the inadequacy of fund to pay all claims).

82 *See, e.g.*, Jones v. Ford Motor Credit Co., 2005 WL 743213 (S.D.N.Y. Mar. 31, 2005) (granting certification pursuant to Rules 23(b)(2) and 23(c)(4) for limited purpose of determining whether defendant is liable and, if so, for considering request for declaratory and injunctive relief); Simpson v. Flagstar Bank, 2003 WL 22244789 (S.D. Ind. Aug. 11, 2003) (upholding class certification, in FHA case challenging compensation policy for loan officers, despite defendants' claims that plaintiffs' requests for emotional distress damages requires individual evaluation that would destroy commonality, typicality, and predominance prongs of class certification test); Cason v. Nissan Motor Acceptance Corp., 212 F.R.D. 518 (M.D. Tenn. 2002) (granting class certification under Rule 23(b)(2) for injunctive and declaratory relief only in an ECOA disparate impact case and denying certification under Rule 23(b)(2) for plaintiffs' claim for disgorgement of unjust enrichment as an equitable remedy); Coleman v. Gen. Motors Acceptance Corp., 196 F.R.D. 315 (M.D. Tenn. 2000) (granting class certification in an ECOA disparate impact case under Rule 23(b)(2) and denying

certification under Rule 23(b)(3)), *rev'd*, 296 F.3d 443 (6th Cir. 2002) (grant of Rule 23(b)(2) certification was an abuse of discretion because injunctive relief requested did not predominate over monetary damages), *remanded*, Coleman v. Gen. Motors Acceptance Corp., 220 F.R.D. 64 (M.D. Tenn. 2004) (granting plaintiff's motion for a Rule 23(b)(2) national class for declaratory and injunctive relief only); Buycks-Roberson v. Citibank Fed. Sav. Bank, 162 F.R.D. 322 (N.D. Ill. 1995) (certifying class in disparate impact case only for purposes of determining defendant's liability, if any, and fashioning injunctive relief, at the same time acknowledging that later it would be necessary for individual damage claims to proceed separately). *But see* Thorn v. Jefferson-Pilot Life Ins., 445 F.3d 376 (4th Cir. 2006) (in 42 U.S.C. §§ 1981 and 1982 action, denying class certification under Rule 23(b)(3) because defendant's statute of limitations defenses could not be reviewed on a class basis; also denying class certification under Rule 23(b)(2) because plaintiff's claim for restitution was, first, not a claim for injunctive or declaratory relief as allowed under Rule 23(b)(2) and, second, not an equitable claim); Garcia v. Veneman, 224 F.R.D. 8 (D.D.C. 2004) (denying class certification in discrimination case against United States Department of Agriculture (USDA)), *aff'd sub nom.* Garcia v. Johanns, 444 F.3d 625 (D.C. Cir. 2006); Love v. Veneman, 224 F.R.D. 240 (D.D.C. 2004) (denying class certification in discrimination suit against USDA and stating that the idea of provisional "hybrid" certification is problematical), *aff'd in relevant part, rev'd in part on other grounds sub nom.* Love v. Johanns, 439 F.3d 723 (D.C. Cir. 2006); Rodriguez v. Ford Motor Credit Co., 2002 WL 655679 (N.D. Ill. Apr. 19, 2002) (denying class certification under Rules 23(b)(2) and (b)(3) in automobile financing case due to court concerns that individualized inquiry into reasons for thousands of credit decisions would be required).

83 Prior to the *Dukes* decision, some courts had held that a Rule 23(b)(2) class could be certified for damages as well as injunctive and declaratory relief, so long as the monetary relief did not predominate. These holdings were overruled by Walmart Stores v. Dukes, 131 S. Ct. 2541 (2011) (reversing certification of a (b)(2) class when monetary relief was not merely incidental to equitable relief). *See generally* National Consumer Law Center, Consumer Class Actions § 10.4.3.2 (8th ed. 2013).

84 Walmart Stores v. Dukes, 131 S. Ct. 2541, 2557 (2011).

when only injunctive relief or corresponding declaratory relief is sought because individual claims for damages will not be barred by res judicata.[85] If, however, individualized damages are sought in addition to injunctive or corresponding declaratory relief, then another hurdle to certification of the class under Rule 23(b)(2) may be the due process right to notice and an opportunity to opt out.[86] Different courts have reached a variety of results, with some declining to certify the class and others requiring such notice and rights.[87]

If the requirements of Rule 23(b) can be satisfied, it may also be possible to pursue equitable monetary remedies as a hybrid class (sometimes referred to as bifurcated or divided certification) under Rules 23(b)(2) and 23(b)(3)[88] or by bifurcating the claims and partially certifying a Rule 23(b)(2) class for purposes of liability and injunctive or declaratory relief.[89]

Rule 23(b)(3) requires that issues "common to the members of the class predominate over any questions affecting only individual members, and that a class action is superior to other available methods for the fair and efficient adjudication of the controversy."[90] Rule 23(b)(3) certification may be problematic if there is a need to make individualized causation determinations, as is the case with respect to credit denials or mark-ups.[91] Similar problems may arise in cases in which some claims may be time-barred. Attempting to defeat class certification, defen-

dants may contend that decisions about whether statutes of limitation have expired depend on when class members knew or should have known of the violation and therefore must be made individually.[92] At least in some contexts, this contention can be defeated by arguing that the continuing violation doctrine protects the entire class.[93] If all else fails, the class definition can be limited to those whose transactions are sufficiently recent as to be timely regardless of any tolling doctrines.

As with many other types of consumer claims, plaintiffs should also be prepared for the defendants' attempts to raise counterclaims against class members, particularly if the plaintiffs have defaulted on any loans at issue in the case.[94] In dismissing the defendant's counterclaims in one car financing case, the court noted that allowing the defendant's permissive counterclaims to proceed might undermine the ECOA enforcement scheme by discouraging plaintiffs from bringing ECOA claims.[95] The court also noted that joining the claims and counterclaims would not be in the interest of judicial economy.[96]

11.5 Selecting the Forum

11.5.1 Federal or State Court

11.5.1.1 Reasons to Choose One Forum or the Other

Credit discrimination cases can be brought in either federal or state court.[97] Generally applicable jurisprudential rules may

---

85   Coleman v. Gen. Motors Acceptance Corp., 220 F.R.D. 64 (M.D. Tenn. 2004).

86   *See generally* National Consumer Law Center, Consumer Class Actions (8th ed. 2013).

87   *See, e.g.,* Love v. Veneman, 224 F.R.D. 240 (D.D.C. 2004) (in suit alleging gender discrimination by the United States Department of Agriculture and seeking monetary damages as well as injunctive relief, citing potential due process issues that arise if a non-opt-out Rule 23(b)(2) suit were settled and an absent member of plaintiff class then sought to bring his or her own action for damages), *aff'd in relevant part, rev'd in part on other grounds sub nom.* Love v. Johanns, 439 F.3d 723 (D.C. Cir. 2006). *See generally* National Consumer Law Center, Consumer Class Actions § 10.4.4.2 (8th ed. 2013).

88   *See, e.g.* Johnson v. Meriter Health Servs. Emp. Retirement Plan, 2012 WL 6013457, at *7 (7th Cir. Dec. 4, 2012) (discussing the option for bifurcated certification).

89   Bifurcation is allowed under Fed. R. Civ. P. 23(c)(4), which gives district courts flexibility concerning class certification. *See, e.g.,* Jones v. Ford Motor Credit, 2005 WL 743213 (S.D.N.Y. Mar. 31, 2005) (bifurcating plaintiffs' claims by certifying a class for purposes of determining whether defendant is liable and, if so, whether declaratory and injunctive relief is appropriate, while reserving a decision on certification for purposes of disgorgement). *See generally* National Consumer Law Center, Consumer Class Actions § 10.4.4.5 (8th ed. 2013 and Supp.).

90   *See, e.g.,* Jones v. Ford Motor Credit Co., 2005 WL 743213 (S.D.N.Y. Mar. 31, 2005) (in denying Rule 23(b)(3) certification, finding that plaintiffs never even seriously contended this issue); Smith v. Chrysler Financial Co., 2004 WL 3201002 (D.N.J. Dec. 30, 2004) (Rule 23(b)(3) standard not met; class certification denied).

91   *See also* Walmart Stores v. Dukes, 131 S. Ct. 2541 (2011) (reversing certification of a nationwide class in a case alleging gender discrimination in hiring and promotion decisions at defendant's retail stores). *See generally* National Consumer Law Center, Consumer Class Actions § 10.5.3 (8th ed. 2013).

92   *See, e.g.,* Thorn v. Jefferson-Pilot Life Ins., 445 F.3d 376 (4th Cir. 2006) (in case alleging discriminatory setting of premiums, affirming 2–1 the district court decision that defendant's statute of limitations defense presented individual issues that could not be resolved on a classwide basis because computation depended on when each individual knew or should have known of defendant's dual-rate practice, so that common issues did not predominate under Rule 23(b)(3); also rejecting class certification under Rule 23(b)(2)). *But see In re* Monumental Life Ins. Co., 365 F.3d 408 (5th Cir. 2004) (whether insurance policyholders had constructive notice of their causes of action is an issue that can be decided on a classwide basis).

93   *See generally* § 11.9.2, *infra* (regarding statutes of limitation as a defense).

94   *See generally* National Consumer Law Center, Consumer Class Actions § 7.7 (8th ed. 2013).

95   Jones v. Ford Motor Credit Co., 2002 WL 1334812 (S.D.N.Y. June 17, 2002), *vacated,* 358 F.3d 205 (2d Cir. 2004) (vacating district court judgment that dismissed car company's counterclaims and remanding to district court to rule on class certification and on supplemental jurisdiction over counterclaims; finance company's counterclaims for amounts allegedly due on underlying loans were permissive counterclaims to borrowers' ECOA claims because the latter centered on company's mark-up policy, not plaintiff's nonpayment after contract price was set); *see also* Jones v. Ford Motor Credit Co., 2005 WL 743213 (S.D.N.Y. Mar. 31, 2005) (granting class certification). *See generally* M. Evan Lacke, *The New Breed of Permissive Counterclaim: Supplemental Jurisdiction After 28 U.S.C. § 1367,* 56 S.C. L. Rev. 607 (2005).

96   Jones v. Ford Motor Credit Co., 2002 WL 1334812 (S.D.N.Y. June 17, 2002), *vacated,* 358 F.3d 205 (2d Cir. 2004).

97   15 U.S.C. § 1691e(f); 42 U.S.C. § 3613(a)(1)(A).

affect the viability of such a suit in a particular forum.[98]

The choice of forum should be carefully considered. Relevant factors include:

- Whether a forum's judges are sympathetic to debtors and to civil rights claims;
- Whether state court judges are familiar with the statutes' provisions;
- Whether the client desires or needs a quick determination and the speed of proceedings in each forum;
- Whether there are pendent state law claims, such as deceptive practices, which might be better heard in state court;
- Which court is willing to award truly reasonable fees to attorneys representing low-income consumers;
- The amount of the filing fee, the ability to obtain *in forma pauperis* status, and any bond requirements for injunctive relief;
- Differences in discovery rules; and
- Desirability of available remedies under similar state laws, such as minimum/maximum damages, or restriction to mandatory administrative proceedings.

11.5.1.2 Forum Considerations

11.5.1.2.1 General

If federal court is the preferred forum, then either the requirements for diversity jurisdiction must be met or at least one claim must be made under the federal credit discrimination laws—the ECOA, the Fair Housing Act, or the federal Civil Rights Acts. Care must also be taken in selecting the particular federal court in which the suit is filed as more than one venue may be proper.[99] Under the "local action" doctrine, actions involving land must be litigated in the forum where the land is located.[100]

11.5.1.2.2 Removal and remand

If the plaintiff prefers a state forum, the plaintiff must anticipate that the defendant will prefer a federal forum. If the plaintiff's complaint includes a claim under a federal discrimination law, the defendant may be able to remove a state court case to federal court pursuant to 28 U.S.C. § 1441. This statute provides for removal of any civil action "of which the district courts of the United States have original jurisdiction."[101]

" '[T]he mere presence of a federal issue in a state cause of action does not automatically confer federal-question jurisdiction.' "[102] On the other hand, under the "artful pleading" doctrine, a plaintiff " 'may not avoid federal jurisdiction by omitting from the complaint allegations of federal law that are essential to the establishment of his claim.' "[103] Courts have considered the artful pleading doctrine in both complete preemption and substantial federal question cases. "Subsumed within this second category are those cases where the claim is necessarily federal in character, or where the right to relief depends on the resolution of a substantial, disputed federal question."[104] Application of this doctrine has been rejected, however, and remand granted when the plaintiff's unfair competition claim that referenced violations of the ECOA (as well as RESPA and other federal statutes) could succeed if the plaintiff showed any unlawful, unfair, or fraudulent practice independent of the federal law allegations and the references to federal law would just influence or shape the court's interpretation of his unfair competition claim.[105]

---

98 *See, e.g.*, Emigrant Sav. Bank v. Elan Mgmt. Corp., 688 F.2d 671 (2d Cir. 1982) (removal from state court refused when apartment building management corporation claimed that foreclosure action was racially motivated and was brought in retaliation for its exercise of ECOA rights); Bledsoe v. Fulton Bank, 940 F. Supp. 804 (E.D. Pa. 1996) (plaintiff could not seek declaratory or injunctive relief under ECOA in federal court when she had raised issue defensively in state court).

99 Note that a variety of provisions in 28 U.S.C. § 1391 were amended in 2011, effective for all cases filed on or after January 6, 2012. *See, e.g.*, Mables v. Indymac Bank, 2008 WL 2397681 (N.D. Ill. June 9, 2008) (in putative ECOA and FHA class action denying bank's motion to transfer venue to the California district where its corporate offices were located, even though plaintiffs' counsel previously had filed an almost identical class action case in that district and had then dismissed it the day after the instant case was filed).

100 Prawoto v. Primelending, 720 F. Supp. 2d 1149 (C.D. Cal. May 4, 2010).

101 28 U.S.C. § 1441(a).

102 Fleenor v. Cmty. One Financial, 2010 WL 2889767, at *1 (E.D. Cal. July 21, 2010) (quoting from Lippitt v. Raymond James Fin. Servs., Inc. 340 F.3d 1033, 1041 (9th Cir. 2003)); *accord* Campos v. Deutsche Bank Nat'l Trust Co., 2010 WL 2891544 (C.D. Cal. July 21, 2010).

103 Fleenor v. Cmty. One Fin., 2010 WL 2889767, at *1 (E.D. Cal. July 21, 2010) (quoting Lippitt v. Raymond James Fin. Servs., Inc. 340 F.3d 1033, 1041 (9th Cir. 2003)); Campos v. Deutsche Bank Nat'l Trust Co., 2010 WL 2891544 (C.D. Cal. July 21, 2010).

104 Int'l Union of Operating Eng'rs v. Cnty. of Plumas, 559 F.3d 1041, 1045 (9th Cir. 2009) (" '(a)rising under' federal jurisdiction only arises . . . when the federal law does more than just shape a court's interpretation of state law; the federal law must be at issue"); *see* Waste Control Specialists, L.L.C. v. Envirocare of Tex., Inc., 199 F.3d 781 (5th Cir. 2000); Archer v. Nissan Motor Acceptance Corp., 324 F. Supp. 2d 805 (S.D. Miss. 2004) (for artful pleading doctrine to apply, alleged federal claims must completely preempt state law claims; in this case, no dispute that neither the ECOA nor the Civil Rights Act completely preempts all state law claims, thus removal on this basis is without foundation). *See generally* National Consumer Law Center, The Cost of Credit: Regulation, Preemption, and Industry Abuses § 3.15 (4th ed. 2009 and Supp.) (description of complete preemption doctrine).

105 Campos v. Deutsche Bank Nat'l Trust Co., 2010 WL 2891544 (C.D. Cal. July 21, 2010); Fleenor v. Cmty. One Fin., 2010 WL 2889767, at *2 (E.D. Cal. July 21, 2010) (claims under California Unfair Competition Law); Kononov v. Expedia Home Loans, 2010 WL 2179491 (E.D. Cal. May 27, 2010); Lanin v. Wells Fargo Bank, 2010 WL 2076952 (E.D. Cal. May 24, 2010); Tran v. Metrocities Mortgage, 2010 WL 1924713 (N.D. Cal. May 12, 2010); Cu-Unjieng v. JP Morgan Chase, 2010 WL 1032645 (N.D. Cal. Mar. 19, 2010); Montoya v. Mortgageit, Inc., 2010 WL 546891 (N.D. Cal. Feb. 10, 2010). *But see* Zivanic v. Washington Mut. Bank, 2010 WL 1875732 (N.D. Cal. May 7, 2010) (finding federal jurisdiction under these circumstances when complaint demanded damages unavailable under the state UCL).

Importantly, a state court action in which the only federal claim appears in a counterclaim or defense, and which does not qualify for diversity jurisdiction based on the allegations of the complaint, is outside the ambit of the removal statute.[106] Similarly, under the majority view, a federal claim included in a third-party complaint is not grounds for removal.[107] A minority of courts hold that removal is warranted if the claims are separate and independent from the original action, as opposed to being substantially derived from the same set of facts.[108]

If the case is removed, the plaintiff may wish to try to have the case remanded to state court.[109] When appropriate, the plaintiff should challenge the defendant's claim that the federal court would have had original jurisdiction of the action as filed in state court. The plaintiff may also challenge the removal if it was not timely made.[110] Alternatively, for cases filed prior to January 6, 2012, in which federal claims are asserted along with other claims based on state law but there is no diversity jurisdiction under traditional rules or the Class Action Fairness Act of 2005 (CAFA),[111] the plaintiff could request that the federal court exercise its discretion to remand "all matters in which State law predominates."[112] This principle was generally construed to authorize remand back to state court of either the entire case or individual state law claims when the state law claims predominated over the federal question claims. However, effective January 6, 2012, the controlling statute was amended to provide that, upon removal of an action alleging both federal and state causes of action, "the district court shall sever" the state law claims and "shall remand the severed claims to the State court from which the action was removed."[113]

If the plaintiff is successful in having a removed case remanded to state court based on a lack of subject matter jurisdiction, the plaintiff may be awarded costs and expenses, including reasonable attorney fees.[114]

If the plaintiff wants to stay in state court, the safest course will be to plead an action solely under a state credit discrimination statute or other state law that covers the challenged practice. This alternative is a viable option only when the state claim provides an adequate remedy. If a class action is filed, staying in state court also depends on not including allegations that might justify federal jurisdiction under CAFA.[115]

11.5.1.2.3 Counterclaims and parallel actions

A consumer may also wish to bring a federal credit discrimination law claim as a counterclaim in a creditor's state court collection action. The counterclaim will not provide a basis for either party to remove an action to federal court, because the federal question must appear in the complaint.[116]

When a consumer must assert ECOA, FHA, or other federal claims as compulsory counterclaims in the state collection action to avoid a res judicata bar, and the advocate would prefer to be in federal court, affirmatively filing a parallel action in the federal court should be considered. While the creditor will likely argue that the federal court action should be stayed, strong arguments can be made that the court should exercise federal jurisdiction, retain the case, and allow it to proceed on

---

106 Shamrock Oil & Gas Corp. v. Sheets, 313 U.S. 100, 61 S. Ct. 868, 85 L. Ed. 1214 (1941); *see, e.g.,* Palisades Collections L.L.C. v. Shorts, 552 F.3d 327, 332 (4th Cir. 2008).

107 Courts have noted that third-party defendants are not proper parties for removal because they are not 'defendants' under section 1441(a) and/or because section 1441(c) only applies to claims joined by plaintiffs; that allowing removal by third-party defendants would conflict with other well-established rules regarding removal, including that cases cannot be removed solely on the basis of a defendant's counterclaim; and that the legislative history of the statute indicates the section was not intended to extend the right of removal to third-party defendants. *See, e.g.,* Palisades Collections L.L.C. v. Shorts, 552 F.3d 327, 332 (4th Cir. 2008); First Nat'l Bank of Pulaski v. Curry, 301 F.3d 456, 462–63 (6th Cir. 2002).

108 *See* Bank of N.Y. v. Ukpe, 2009 WL 4895253 (D.N.J. Dec. 9, 2009) (noting minority view, but finding third-party claims of predatory and discriminatory lending in the origination of mortgage loan related to alleged nonpayment to an assignee of the loan, which was the basis for state court foreclosure action, and remanding to state court in which foreclosure action had been brought).

109 *See* 28 U.S.C. § 1441(c).
     A motion to remand on grounds other than lack of subject matter jurisdiction must be filed within thirty days after the filing of the notice of removal. 28 U.S.C. § 1447(c).

110 The notice of removal generally must be filed within thirty days of receipt of the initial pleading or other paper that makes the case removable. *See* 28 U.S.C. § 1446(b).
     Prior to an amendment to this statute, which became effective on January 6, 2012, there was a split in the circuits regarding application of the so-called "later-served" defendant rule. The amendment codified the holding of some courts that each defendant has thirty days from service on it of the initial pleading or other paper that makes the case removable to file for removal, and earlier-served defendants may then elect to join in. 28 U.S.C. § 1446(b)(2)(B) and (C).

111 The Class Action Fairness Act of 2005 added new sections 28 U.S.C. § 1453 and 28 U.S.C. §§ 1711–1715 and amended 28 U.S.C. § 1332, the diversity jurisdiction statute. In general, removal and remands under CAFA present a host of knotty issues, which are discussed in National Consumer Law Center, Consumer Class Actions § 2.4 (8th ed. 2013).

112 *See* 28 U.S.C. § 1441(c); *see also* City of Pittsburgh Comm'n on Human Relations v. Key Bank USA, 163 Fed. Appx. 163, 166 (3d Cir. 2006) (under the language of section 1441(c) at that time, "when a district court has dismissed the claim or claims that gave it original jurisdiction, it should decline to hear pendent state claims, absent *extraordinary circumstances*"; remanding case to state court upon finding creditor's argument that Commission's claims were preempted by federal law insufficient under this test).
     Another option is to seek leave to file an amended complaint deleting all federal claims, hoping that the federal court would then decline to exercise supplemental jurisdiction over the case, which would then allow it to be remanded to state court. *See* Clayton v. Decision One Mortgage Corp., 2009 WL 1544381 (E.D. Mich. June 2, 2009).

113 28 U.S.C. § 1441(c)(2) (eff. Jan. 6, 2012).

114 28 U.S.C. § 1447(c).

115 *See* National Consumer Law Center, Consumer Class Actions § 2.4 (8th ed. 2013).

116 *See* Shamrock Oil & Gas Corp. v. Sheets 313 U.S. 100, 61 S. Ct. 868 (U.S. 1941) (plaintiff and counterclaim defendant were not a "defendant" within statute authorizing removal only by defendant); Gen. Electric Capital Auto Lease, Inc. v. Mires, 788 F. Supp. 948 (E.D. Mich. 1992) (TILA counterclaim).

a normal schedule.[117] Abstention is particularly disfavored when the applicable substantive law is federal.[118] Nevertheless, the district court will have some discretion in the matter.[119] To minimize problems, the consumer should move the federal case along expeditiously and consider filing an early motion for summary judgment in federal court.[120]

11.5.1.2.4 The Rooker-Feldman *doctrine*

There is an additional doctrine to consider if the plaintiff's claims raised in federal court would explicitly or in effect lead to reversal or modification of an adverse state court judgment. The *Rooker-Feldman* doctrine precludes federal court subject matter jurisdiction over claims that in essence seek reversal of a state court judgment because, no matter how erroneous or unconstitutional the state court judgment may be, the Supreme Court of the United States is the only federal court that has jurisdiction to review a state court judgment.[121] The doctrine bars "an action in federal court that alleges an injury 'inextricably intertwined' with a state court decision, such that success in the federal court would require overturning the state court decision,"[122] even if the claim was not directly argued in the state court.[123] These issues are most likely to arise if a plaintiff attempts to raise federal discrimination claims after a foreclosure judgment in state court or other suit based on default on loan obligations.[124]

In a 2005 decision, the Supreme Court noted that lower courts had extended the *Rooker-Feldman* doctrine "far beyond the contours" of the original Supreme Court decisions that gave it its name.[125] The Court explained that lower courts often mistakenly apply the *Rooker-Feldman* doctrine to situations in which the holding actually rests on the affirmative defense of collateral estoppel or res judicata—a decision on the merits— not a finding that the Court lacks subject matter jurisdiction to review or reverse a state court judgment.[126] Federal courts do not lack jurisdiction to consider such affirmative defenses but must apply the preclusion rules of the state in which the prior judgment was entered. These rules will usually include consideration of whether a claim arises out of the same transaction that was the subject of a prior action or was a compulsory counterclaim.[127] A credit discrimination claim is not a compulsory counterclaim in, for example, a foreclosure action because completely different issues and evidence are involved in the breach-of-contract action.[128] However, due to the "inextricably intertwined" test discussed above, whether a counterclaim is compulsory or even permissible has generally been found irrelevant to application of the *Rooker-Feldman* doctrine in federal cases challenging foreclosures on the basis of federal law claims.[129]

---

117 *See generally* National Consumer Law Center, Truth in Lending § 12.6.4 (8th ed. 2012). The Supreme Court has enunciated an "exceptional circumstances test" for surrender of a federal court's obligation to exercise federal jurisdiction. This test applies to cases that do not fall within a specific abstention doctrine. Moses H. Cone Mem'l Hosp. v. Mercury Constr. Corp., 460 U.S. 1, 15, 19, 103 S. Ct. 927, 74 L. Ed. 2d 765 (1983).

118 Vill. of Westfield v. Welch's, 170 F.3d 116 (2d Cir. 1999).

119 Moses H. Cone Mem'l Hosp. v. Mercury Constr. Corp., 460 U.S. 1, 103 S. Ct. 927, 74 L. Ed. 2d 765 (1983); Kent v. Celozzi-Ettleson Chevrolet, Inc., 1999 U.S. Dist. LEXIS 17282 (N.D. Ill. Nov. 1, 1999) (granting stay in favor of state court case raising similar claims).

120 *See* National Consumer Law Center, Truth in Lending § 12.6.4 (8th ed. 2012).

This tactic not only may help prevent a stay but may also help avoid the preclusive effect in federal court of a prior state court adjudication. For information on litigating in bankruptcy court, see National Consumer Law Center, Consumer Bankruptcy Law and Practice ch. 14 (10th ed. 2012).

121 Dist. of Columbia Courts v. Feldman, 460 U.S. 462, 103 S. Ct. 1303, 75 L. Ed. 2d 206 (1983); Rooker v. Fid. Trust Co., 263 U.S. 413, 44 S. Ct. 149, 68 L. Ed. 362 (1923); *see also* Trakansook v. Astoria Fed. Sav. & Loan Ass'n, 2007 WL 1160433 (E.D.N.Y. Apr. 18, 2007), *aff'd*, 2008 WL 4962990 (2d Cir. Nov. 21, 2008).

For further discussion of the *Rooker-Feldman* doctrine, see National Consumer Law Center's Fair Debt Collection § 7.4.4 (7th ed. 2011 and Supp.), Truth in Lending § 11.4.2.4 (8th ed. 2012), and National Consumer Law Center, Foreclosures § 10.6.4 (4th ed. 2012).

122 Epps v. Creditnet, Inc., 320 F.3d 756, 759 (7th Cir. 2003).

123 Ritter v. Ross, 992 F.2d 750, 753 (7th Cir. 1993); *see, e.g.*, Kelley v. Med-1 Solutions, 548 F.3d 600 (7th Cir. 2008) (Fair Debt Collection Practices Act claim relating to collection agency's small claims action in state court barred by *Rooker-Feldman* doctrine).

124 Cases analyzing this issue in the context of foreclosures and TILA

claims are discussed in National Consumer Law Center, Truth in Lending § 11.4.2.4 (8th ed. 2012) and National Consumer Law Center, Foreclosures § 10.6.4 (4th ed. 2012).

125 Exxon Mobil Corp. v. Saudi Basic Industries Corp., 544 U.S. 280, 125 S. Ct. 1517, 161 L. Ed. 2d 454 (2005).

126 *Id.*

127 Res judicata "bars 'repetitious suits involving the same cause of action' once 'a court of competent jurisdiction has entered a final judgment on the merits.' " U.S. v. Tohono O'Odham Nation, 131 S. Ct. 1723, 1730 (2011) (internal citations omitted).

"The now-accepted test in preclusion law for determining whether two suits involve the same claim or cause of action depends on factual overlap, barring 'claims arising from the same transaction.' " *Id.* (transactional test).

If foreclosure is in a court of limited jurisdiction or if it is a summary proceeding that limits the issues that can be raised defensively and/or precludes counterclaims, those claims that were not able to be pursued in the foreclosure action should not be res judicata and may be raised in a new action.

128 *See, e.g.*, Jones v. Ford Motor Credit Co., 358 F.3d 205, 209–10 (2d Cir. 2004) (finance company's counterclaims for amounts allegedly due on underlying loans were permissive counterclaims to borrowers' ECOA claims because the latter centered on company's mark-up policy, not plaintiff's nonpayment after contract price was set); Briggs v. United States, 2008 WL 4667117, at *6 (N.D. Cal. Oct. 22, 2008) ("defendant's counterclaim to collect the unpaid balance on plaintiff's [credit card] debt did not arise from the same 'transaction or occurrence' as plaintiff's illegal-collection claim").

129 These cases are discussed in National Consumer Law Center, Truth in Lending § 11.4.2.4 (8th ed. 2012) and National Consumer Law Center, Foreclosures § 10.6.4 (4th ed. 2012). *See* Stanfield v. Citi-Mortgage, Inc. 2010 WL 3257722, at *1 (D.S.C. Aug. 16, 2010) (when the purpose of plaintiff's *pro se* complaint is to seek relief from the underlying state court foreclosure action, court has no jurisdiction due to *Rooker-Feldman* doctrine; not reaching the question of whether a VA-guaranteed loan is receipt of public assistance protected under the ECOA).

Importantly, lower federal courts may adjudicate claims that are "separable from and collateral to" the merits of the state court judgment.[130]

> [The jurisdictional statute on which *Rooker-Feldman* is based does not] stop a district court from exercising subject-matter jurisdiction simply because a party attempts to litigate in federal court a matter previously litigated in state court. If a federal plaintiff 'present[s] some independent claim, albeit one that denies a legal conclusion that a state court has reached in a case to which he was a party . . ., then there is jurisdiction and state law determines whether the defendant prevails under principles of preclusion.'[131]

For the purposes of *Rooker-Feldman* analysis, a claim is independent if the source of the injury is some action of the defendant other than the state court judgment.[132] The federal plaintiff may not seek to set aside a state judgment but may present an independent claim, even though the claim requires the federal court to deny a legal conclusion that a state court has reached.[133]

There are other limits to the *Rooker-Feldman* doctrine. For example, the doctrine does not apply when a federal action is filed before a state judgment is entered.[134] Also, *Rooker-Feldman* does not apply when the federal defendant was not a party to the state court proceeding,[135] even if the plaintiff was in privity with the state party.[136] Nor does the doctrine apply unless the plaintiff had a reasonable opportunity to present its claim to the state court.[137]

11.5.2 Deciding Whether to Select an Administrative Determination in FHA Cases

11.5.2.1 Administrative Option May Be Pursued Simultaneously with Court Action

There are two ways to make a claim under the Fair Housing Act. The aggrieved party may file an administrative complaint with the Department of Housing and Urban Development (HUD) or commence a private civil action in state or federal court.[138] These two procedures are not mutually exclusive and may be pursued contemporaneously or sequentially. There is no requirement that the administrative remedies be exhausted prior to instituting a private action.[139] The only restriction is that the private action may not be commenced once the actual administrative hearing has begun[140] and an administrative hearing may not go forward if a civil trial has begun.[141]

11.5.2.2 Reasons to Choose Administrative or Judicial Option

The administrative complaint procedure will, in many cases, offer a satisfactory method of redress at a substantially lower cost than a private action. The greatest advantage of the administrative route is this low cost to the complainant, as HUD bears the burden of investigating and determining whether there is reasonable cause to believe discrimination has occurred. Should it make a "cause" finding, one or more government lawyers are assigned to prosecuting the case, either before an administrative law judge or in federal court. In either case, the complainant need not have an attorney or pay any filing fees. The complainant, nevertheless, has the right to intervene in the administrative proceeding, be represented by counsel, and participate in the litigation.[142]

Another advantage to the administrative process is that the HUD conciliation process, discussed below, may help facilitate satisfactory settlements. While in theory the administrative process may be faster than a judicial proceeding, such is not usually the case in practice.

On the other hand, there are drawbacks to the administrative option.[143] The greatest disadvantage is loss of control over the case. Moreover, the administrative complaint may still end up in federal court but will have been delayed getting there during several layers of administrative review.

Remedies are also not as robust in an administrative proceeding. The administrative law judge can award injunctive and equitable relief, actual damages, and attorney fees[144] but may

---

130 *See* National Consumer Law Center, Truth in Lending § 11.4.2.4 (8th ed. 2012); National Consumer Law Center, Foreclosures § 10.6.4 (4th ed. 2012).

131 Exxon Mobil Corp. v. Saudi Basic Industries Corp., 544 U.S. 280, 292, 125 S. Ct. 1517, 161 L. Ed. 2d 454 (2005).

132 *See, e.g.,* McCormick v. Braverman, 451 F.3d 382, 393 (6th Cir. 2006), *cert. denied,* 128 S. Ct. 41 (2007).

133 Brown v. First Nationwide Mortgage Corp., 206 Fed. Appx. 436, 439 (6th Cir. 2006) (per curiam) (citing Exxon Mobil Corp. v. Saudi Basic Industries Corp., 544 U.S. 280, 125 S. Ct. 1517, 161 L. Ed. 2d 454 (2005)).

134 544 U.S. 280, 125 S. Ct. 1517, 161 L. Ed. 2d 454 (2005) (noting also that the *Rooker-Feldman* doctrine is a product of statutory, not constitutional, doctrine).

135 544 U.S. 280, 125 S. Ct. 1517, 161 L. Ed. 2d 454 (2005).

136 Lance v. Dennis, 546 U.S. 459, 126 S. Ct. 1198, 163 L. Ed. 2d 1059 (2006).

137 Long v. Shorebank Dev. Corp., 182 F.3d 548, 558 (7th Cir. 1999).

138 42 U.S.C. §§ 3610–3613.

The statutes of limitations are different for an administrative complaint than for one filed in federal court. An aggrieved person must file a HUD complaint "not later than one year after an alleged discriminatory housing practice has occurred or terminated. . . ." 42 U.S.C. § 3610(a)(1)(A)(i).

An action in state or federal court must be filed "not later than 2 years after the occurrence or termination. . . ." 42 U.S.C. § 3613(a)(1)(A).

139 42 U.S.C. § 3613(a)(2); *see* Gladstone, Realtors v. Vill. of Bellwood, 441 U.S. 91 (1979); Bryant Woods Inn, Inc. v. Howard Cnty., 124 F.3d 597 (4th Cir. 1997); Murphy v. Zoning Comm'n, 148 F. Supp. 2d 173 (D. Conn. 2001).

140 42 U.S.C. § 3613(a)(3).

141 42 U.S.C. § 3612(f).

142 42 U.S.C. § 3612(c).

143 For a discussion of advantages and disadvantages of the administrative process and litigation, see John P. Relman, Housing Discrimination Practice Manual § 3.2(2)(a), (b) (2000 Supp.).

144 While the Fair Housing Act previously required a showing of need

not award punitive damages (although the administrative law judge can assess civil fines that are to be paid to the government, not the complainant). A federal judge, in contrast, is authorized to order all this relief plus punitive damages.[145]

There are also possible conflict-of-interest issues. If the administrative judge does not rule in the aggrieved person's favor or does not grant all of the relief sought, HUD is not required to seek reconsideration on behalf of the complainant or pursue an appeal. In addition, precedent in the employment discrimination area suggests that, once findings of fact and conclusions of law have been issued in the administrative proceeding, the plaintiff may be collaterally estopped from proceeding on the same claims and facts in federal court.[146]

11.5.2.3 How the Administrative Procedure Works

An individual begins the administrative process by filing a complaint with HUD. Although HUD has developed a form to use for housing discrimination complaints, the agency will accept any written statement that contains the allegations of a discriminatory housing practice, provided that the following information is included in the complaint:

- Complainant's name and address;
- Respondent's name and address;
- A description and address of the dwelling which is at issue; and
- A concise statement of the violation including the relevant facts and dates.[147]

HUD is required to refer the complaint to the state or local agency in whose jurisdiction the alleged discrimination occurred if that agency is certified as having a law comparable to the federal Fair Housing Act.[148] The list of certified agencies is updated annually.[149] When a complaint against a federally chartered savings and loan bank is referred to a certified state agency, the bank cannot successfully resist the investigation on the basis of preemption. State anti-discrimination laws at most

only incidentally affect its lending operations.[150] Even if they did so directly, preemption would not apply because the FHA's enforcement scheme trumps OTS regulations.[151]

The state or local agency is given thirty days to commence a proceeding.[152] If the agency fails to do so, the complaint reverts back to HUD.[153] It is important to keep track of these dates and push HUD to begin its investigation if necessary.

After the complaint is filed or reverts back to HUD due to the inaction of a state or local agency, HUD has one-hundred days to conduct an investigation.[154] During the investigatory period, HUD is required to attempt to conciliate the case by negotiating with the aggrieved party and the respondent.[155] If conciliation is successful, both parties must execute an agreement describing the resolution of the complaint or providing for binding arbitration.[156]

If conciliation is not successful and the investigation leads to a finding of reasonable cause, the government must issue a charge on behalf of the aggrieved person.[157] On the other hand, if the government determines that no reasonable cause exists, the complaint will be dismissed.[158]

If the government files a charge, the respondent or the complainant has the right at this stage to elect that the case be removed to federal district court.[159] The purpose of this provision is to ensure that the respondent's constitutional right to a jury trial is not violated. If neither party elects to remove the case, the case is heard by an administrative law judge. The aggrieved party may intervene in the administrative action and is entitled to monetary relief even if he or she does not intervene.[160] The hearing must be held within 120 days after the charge is filed.[161] Thereafter, proceedings for review or enforcement may be brought in federal court.[162]

---

to recover attorney fees, the 1988 amendments eliminated that requirement. 42 U.S.C. § 3612(p).

145 42 U.S.C. § 3613(c).
   A federal judge is also expressly authorized to order affirmative action relief, 42 U.S.C. § 3613(c), while the administrative law judge's mandate is the more vague "equitable relief." 42 U.S.C. § 3612(g)(3).

146 *See, e.g.*, Univ. of Tenn. v. Elliot, 478 U.S. 788, 106 S. Ct. 3220, 92 L. Ed. 2d 635 (1986) (collateral estoppel barred section 1981 claim in federal court when state agency made findings of fact after parties had adequate opportunity to litigate). *See generally* The Chicago Lawyers' Comm. for Civil Rights Under the Law, The Law of Mortgage Lending and Insurance Discrimination, *available at* www.clccrul.org; John P. Relman, Housing Discrimination Practice Manual § 3.2(2) (2000 Supp.); Robert G. Schwemm, Housing Discrimination: Law and Litigation (7th ed. 1997).

147 24 C.F.R. §§ 103.25, 103.30(b).

148 42 U.S.C. § 3610(f); 24 C.F.R. §§ 103.100 to 103.110.

149 For interim updates check the *Federal Register*, the Housing Development Reporter, or on-line at www.hud.gov.

150 USAA Fed. Sav. Bank v. Pa. Human Relations Comm'n, 2011 WL 3715113 (E.D. Pa. Aug. 23, 2011).

151 *Id.* at *6. Note that the Dodd-Frank Wall Street Reform and Consumer Protection Act, Pub. L. No. 111-203, 124 Stat. 1376 (2010), abolished the OTS and replaced its broad preemption regulations with the OCC standard for preemption.

152 42 U.S.C. § 3610(f)(2)(a).

153 24 C.F.R. § 103.110.

154 24 C.F.R. § 103.225.
   In practice, HUD routinely exceeds this 100-day limitation, determining that it is impracticable to conclude the investigation within that time. 42 U.S.C. § 3610(g).

155 24 C.F.R. § 103.300.

156 24 C.F.R. § 103.310; *see* § 11.5.3, *infra* (discussion of problems with binding arbitration).

157 42 U.S.C. § 3610(g); 24 C.F.R. § 103.405.

158 24 C.F.R. § 103.400(a)(1); *see also* United States v. Shanrie Co., 2006 WL 219574 (S.D. Ill. Jan. 26, 2006) (rejecting company's argument that government's alleged failure to adequately conciliate should result in a remand to HUD and further conciliation; the FHA procedural requirements are not intended to function as a barrier to federal district court jurisdiction).

159 42 U.S.C. § 3612(a).

160 42 U.S.C. §§ 3612(c), 3612(g)(3).

161 42 U.S.C. § 3612(g)(1).

162 Ho v. Donovan, 569 F.3d 677 (7th Cir. 2009) (refusal to rent to an African-American prospective tenant in violation of the FHA).

11.5.3 Mandatory Arbitration

11.5.3.1 Introduction

Another NCLC treatise, *Consumer Arbitration Agreements*,[163] examines the enforceability of arbitration agreements in detail. This section introduces the topic and considers issues of special relevance to ECOA and FHA claims.

Arbitration clauses purport to waive the right for a consumer to bring an action in court and instead force consumer disputes against the creditor into binding arbitration. Consumer litigants are almost always better off keeping an action in court. The corporation, not the consumer, selects the arbitration service provider. This provider sets the arbitration rules and establishes the panel of arbitrators. Arbitration is also expensive, far more so than court litigation, because arbitrators are paid by the hour and expect a high rate. Discovery is limited and rulings may be kept secret. The arbitrator need not follow the law nor even reasonably judge the facts. Arbitration clauses will also often limit the consumer's remedies, for example banning classwide relief or certain types of damages.

Consequently, an initial issue in much consumer litigation today is whether the consumer can press claims in court or whether the creditor instead can insist that the consumer take those claims to arbitration. This section examines several theories why an arbitration clause should not be enforced against an ECOA or FHA claim and also considers the availability of classwide arbitration if the case is forced into arbitration. Additional theories to challenge an arbitration requirement and a more comprehensive discussion of the subjects treated here are found in *Consumer Arbitration Agreements*.

11.5.3.2 No Arbitration Requirement Unless Arbitration Agreement Is Produced

It is axiomatic that an arbitration agreement is not binding if there is no agreement with the consumer to submit disputes to arbitration.[164] The defendant in an ECOA, FHA, or other credit discrimination case cannot force arbitration if the defendant cannot produce an agreement between the parties to arbitrate their disputes.

Although mandatory arbitration clauses are pervasive in consumer credit contracts, this is much less the case in mortgage loans. The defendant should always be put to the test of producing the applicable arbitration agreement, and consumers should realize that such agreements are unlikely to be found in certain consumer transactions:

- In 2004, both Fannie Mae and Freddie Mac stopped purchasing mortgage loans containing arbitration clauses.
- A Consumer Financial Protection Bureau regulation (ef-

fective June 1, 2013) prohibits residential mortgage loans or home equity or other open-end loans secured by a consumer's principal dwelling from including terms requiring arbitration of disputes.[165]

- The Consumer Financial Protection Bureau by regulation may prohibit or impose conditions on the use of arbitration clauses involving the sale of a consumer financial product to a consumer.[166] The CFPB must first conduct a study before issuing a rule, and the agency is still conducting the study. Consequently, it is unlikely any such rule limiting arbitration will be issued in the near future, and then the rule will only apply to contracts entered into after the rule's effective date.
- Arbitration requirements are not enforceable when creditors extend consumer credit to active duty military personnel or their dependents.[167] The Department of Defense is allowed to define consumer credit under this statute by regulation[168] and has done so to limit the scope of the statute to payday loans, automobile title loans, and tax refund anticipation loans.[169]

In addition, a number of major banks settled a class action by agreeing not to utilize or enforce arbitration requirements.[170] Settlements have been reached with JPMorganChase, Bank of America, Capital One, and HSBC in which these companies agree not to enforce existing arbitration clauses or insert new arbitration requirements in their contracts for at least three-and-a-half years. Still in the case are Citibank and Discover. These and other creditors (including PNC Bank, TD Bank, and Regions Bank) have announced publicly that they are abandoning mandatory arbitration. Nevertheless, because some creditors abandoned arbitration voluntarily and others have agreed to do so for only three-and-a-half years, such requirements may soon be reinstituted in many credit card agreements.

11.5.3.3 Is an Arbitration Agreement Applicable to the Parties and to the Dispute?

An arbitration agreement is a contract and, like any other contract, is subject to standard contract defenses—for example, that the contract was not consummated, not properly formed,

---

163　National Consumer Law Center, Consumer Arbitration Agreements (6th ed. 2011 and Supp.).

164　*See* Equal Emp't Opportunity Comm'n v. Waffle House, Inc., 534 U.S. 279, 122 S. Ct. 754, 151 L. Ed. 2d 755 (2002); First Options of Chi., Inc. v. Kaplan, 514 U.S. 938, 943, 115 S. Ct. 1920, 1924, 131 L. Ed. 2d 985 (1995).

165　*See* 78 Fed. Reg. 11,279 (Feb. 15, 2013) (adding 12 C.F.R. § 1026.36(h)).

There is an argument that 15 U.S.C. § 1639c, added by Pub. L. No. 111-203, tit. XIV, § 1414, 124 Stat. 1376 (2010)) with a similar statutory prohibition on arbitration in mortgage loans, went into effect instead on July 22, 2010. *See* Pub. L. No. 111-203, § 4, 124 Stat. 1376 (2010).

This effective date issue is discussed in National Consumer Law Center, Truth in Lending § 1.3 (8th ed. 2012).

166　12 U.S.C. § 5518, *added by* Pub. L. No. 111-203, tit. X, § 1028, 124 Stat. 1376 (2010)).

167　10 U.S.C. § 987(e), (f).

168　10 U.S.C. § 987(h).

169　32 C.F.R. pt. 232.

170　*In re* Currency Conversion Fee Antitrust Litig., Robert Ross v. Bank of America, N.A. (USA), No. 368 n.1, M.L. No. 1409 (S.D.N.Y. 2009).

not applicable to the parties, or not enforceable according to its terms. For example, if a creditor's standard form contract includes an arbitration clause, that clause should not apply to an applicant who was denied credit and who never entered into that contract. Even if a credit application states that the applicant agrees to abide by certain provisions if credit is granted, this should not be binding if credit is not granted. The terms have, in effect, been agreed to by the borrower but rejected by the creditor. Because only one side has agreed, there is no binding agreement.

Another common practice is for the creditor, after the credit agreement has been consummated, to send a change of terms that includes an arbitration clause and which indicates that the consumer's continued use of the credit is deemed acceptance of the change in terms. Whether this change in terms is binding on a consumer who borrows new credit after receiving such a notice is discussed in another NCLC treatise.[171] But the change in terms certainly should not apply to a consumer who does not borrow additional funds after the change in terms is announced.

A consumer's claim under a credit discrimination statute may be brought against various entities, including a credit arranger, the originating creditor, or a subsequent assignee. The consumer attorney should determine what parties are explicitly covered by the arbitration agreement and what legal basis a defendant has to claim that it can enforce an arbitration agreement that does not explicitly apply to it.[172] For example, if the language of an arbitration agreement applies to disputes with the creditor, the creditor's agents, and the creditor's assignees, the agreement does not require arbitration of disputes with an independent broker who arranged the loan.

Also note whether the arbitration agreement is found in a document, such as the purchase agreement between the dealer and the consumer, other than the credit agreement. Even if an assignee has grounds to enforce an arbitration agreement found in the loan assigned to it, can it enforce a clause found in a purchase agreement which has not been assigned to it and in which it has no interest? If the arbitration agreement is found in a document signed by the principal consumer obligor, but not in the agreement signed by the co-signer, the arbitration agreement should not be binding on the co-signer, particularly if the co-signer does not benefit from the agreement containing the arbitration clause.[173]

An arbitration agreement may also be unenforceable when the National Arbitration Forum (NAF) is designated as the sole arbitration service provider. The NAF has signed a consent agreement to cease all consumer arbitrations nationwide,[174] so the arbitration agreement cannot be carried out according to its terms. A number of courts—perhaps a majority of courts—now rule that, as a result, the arbitration requirement must be thrown

out.[175] Courts ruling otherwise would have to select the arbitrator if the parties cannot agree on one, because the NAF cannot do so.[176]

11.5.3.4 Who Decides a Challenge to the Arbitration Requirements Enforceability?

As a result of a Supreme Court ruling, the consumer's challenge to an arbitration clause may have to be re-formulated in cases in which the arbitration clause explicitly states that matters of arbitrability are to be left to the arbitrator.[177] The Court upheld such clauses and stated that, even when a court would normally hear a challenge to an arbitration agreement's enforceability, it is left to the arbitrator when there is such a "delegation" clause in the arbitration agreement.

When there is no delegation clause, the court decides "gateway" issues as to whether there is an enforceable arbitration agreement. The court also decides whether the arbitration agreement's delegation to the arbitrator is "clear and unmistakable."[178] If the court does find such a clear and unmistakable delegation clause, then the consumer's court challenge must initially deal with the enforceability of the delegation clause and not with the enforceability of the whole arbitration agreement. Often this will not be difficult but simply requires the consumer to re-phrase the challenge.

For example, if an NAF arbitration agreement has a delegation clause, the consumer does not argue before the court that NAF is integral to enforcement of the arbitration clause. Instead, the consumer argues that NAF is integral to enforcement of the *delegation* clause, so the *delegation* clause is invalid. If the delegation clause is invalid, the consumer can then raise with the court the unenforceability of the whole arbitration agreement, since the delegation clause is no longer enforceable.

11.5.3.5 Classwide Arbitration

Although it is becoming more and more difficult, consumers forced to arbitrate their disputes may still be able to bring the arbitration on a classwide basis. This option, rather than a court-based class action, may in fact be a preferred venue for the consumer.

While creditors typically will try to force litigation into arbitration, they often fear classwide arbitration more than a court-based class action. The arbitration can proceed much faster than a court-based class action, there is virtually no judicial review of a classwide arbitration award, and the arbitrator, being paid by the hour, may not view a complicated case with as much disfavor as a judge with an overwhelmingly large caseload.

171 *See* National Consumer Law Center, Consumer Arbitration Agreements § 5.6.4 (6th ed. 2011 and Supp.).

172 *Id.* § 7.4.

173 *Id.*

174 *See* National Consumer Law Center, Consumer Arbitration Agreements § 5.8.1 (6th ed. 2011 and Supp.).

175 *Id.* § 5.8.2.

176 *Id.*

177 Rent-a-Center, West, Inc. v. Jackson, 130 S. Ct. 2772 (2010).

178 Granite Rock Co. v. Int'l Bhd. of Teamsters, 130 S. Ct. 2847 (2010) (citing First Options of Chicago, Inc. v. Kaplan, 514 U.S. 938 (1995) and AT&T Techs., Inc. v. Communication Workers, 475 U.S. 643 (1986)).

As a result, creditors typically include in their arbitration clauses a ban on classwide relief, and the Supreme Court has made it very difficult to challenge such a contractual ban on class arbitration. In *AT & T Mobility L.L.C. v. Concepcion*,[179] the Court upheld contractual waivers of consumers' right to pursue class arbitration. Nevertheless, *Concepcion* is not the death knell of all credit discrimination class actions. First, the credit agreement must contain a valid arbitration agreement preventing a class action in court. NCLC's *Consumer Arbitration Agreements* (6th ed. 2011 and Supp.) details the fact that not all credit agreements contain arbitration clauses and that there are a number of ways to challenge the enforceability of such clauses, if they do exist. Many of these grounds to challenge an arbitration clause will allow all class members to proceed in court on their credit discrimination claims.

Second, a binding arbitration agreement must also explicitly prohibit class arbitration. Otherwise the arbitrator can interpret an arbitration clause that is silent on the availability of class arbitration as allowing classwide arbitration. Many older arbitration agreements are silent on this issue, and thus there is scope for the arbitrator to allow classwide relief.

This is the case despite a 2010 United States Supreme Court decision in *Stolt-Nielsen S.A. v. AnimalFeeds International Corp.*[180] Key to the *Stolt-Nielsen* decision was the arbitrators' statement that they used policy grounds to allow class arbitration. The Court found that this exceeded the arbitrators' powers and that they could only interpret the arbitration agreement to see if the agreement itself allowed class arbitration. The arbitrators could not make the determination using public policy grounds. The arbitrators must only determine the parties' intent based upon the contract language and surrounding factors.

Since *Stolt-Nielsen*, a number of arbitrators have construed arbitration clauses silent on the issue as allowing class arbitration.[181] There is limited judicial review of an arbitrator's decision construing the contract, and courts have allowed to stand arbitrator decisions that permit classwide relief.[182]

Finally, even if an arbitration agreement explicitly prohibits class arbitration and the arbitration requirement cannot be challenged on other grounds, there is still room after *Concepcion* to attack class arbitration waivers when the consumer seeks to bring a federal discrimination claim. The leading case is *In re American Express Merchants' Litigation*, in which the Second Circuit found a class arbitration waiver to be unenforceable when it would prevent the class from vindicating its federal rights under the antitrust statutes.[183]

The Second Circuit had originally ruled the waiver to be unenforceable. The Supreme Court accepted certiorari and remanded the case to the Second Circuit to reconsider its ruling

in light of the Court's decision in *Stolt-Nielsen*.[184] The Second Circuit, before finalizing its opinion, waited for the Court's ruling in *Concepcion*. Then, after considering the implications of both *Stolt-Nielsen* and *Concepcion,* the Second Circuit reaffirmed its original ruling that the class arbitration ban was unenforceable.

The Second Circuit found that *Concepcion* did not alter its original analysis.[185] Bringing a complex federal antitrust claim on an individual basis would require the individual to incur prohibitive costs for discovery, expert economic studies, and litigation. The arbitration requirement coupled with the class arbitration waiver would in effect immunize the defendant from any private enforcement of their federal statutory rights. The existence of a fee-shifting provision in the federal statute did not change the result because it would leave an individual plaintiff with an unacceptable risk of losing. While this reasoning is certainly persuasive, the Supreme Court has again accepted certiorari in *In re American Express Merchants' Litigation*, and a ruling is expected by June 2013.

The Second Circuit's ruling is directly relevant to federal claims under the ECOA, FHA, and federal civil rights statutes. Key to the consumer's argument will be proof that the cost of expert studies, discovery, and other facets of the litigation make it impossible for an individual to pursue the action on an individual basis and that the individual thus cannot vindicate federal statutory rights under the ECOA, FHA, or federal civil rights statutes.

It may not be enough for the consumer to make conclusory arguments that the cost will be prohibitive. The consumer is best served to introduce evidence of the cost of the litigation, that this cost is prohibitive for the individual, and that federal statutory rights cannot be protected in any other manner.

A series of older Truth in Lending (TIL) cases held that there was not a substantive right to bring a TIL class action in court. On the other hand, unlike TILA, the ECOA also has a very different provision, found in 15 U.S.C. § 1691e(a), that contains an explicit substantive right for class relief: "Any creditor who fails to comply . . . shall be liable . . . for any actual damages sustained by such applicant acting either in an individual capacity or as a member of a class." A ban on classwide arbitration would be directly contrary to a substantive ECOA right.

11.5.3.6 Arbitration Clause Cannot Limit Punitive Damages

The ECOA and FHA explicitly provide a right to punitive damages.[186] An arbitration agreement that prevents a consumer from obtaining relief under a federal statutory claim is unenforceable because it conflicts with the legislature's purpose in enacting the statute. The United States Supreme Court, in

---

179   131 S. Ct. 1740 (2011).

180   130 S. Ct. 1758, 176 L. Ed. 2d 605 (2010).

181   *See* National Consumer Law Center, Consumer Arbitration Agreements § 9.2.2 (6th ed. 2011 and Supp.).

182   *Id.*

183   2012 WL 284518 (2d Cir. Feb. 1, 2012).

184   *See In re* American Express Merchants' Litig., 130 S. Ct. 2401 (2010).

185   *In re* American Express Merchants' Litig., 2012 WL 284518 (2d Cir. Feb. 1, 2012).

186   *See* § 11.8, *infra.*

Mitsubishi Motors Corp. v. Soler Chrysler-Plymouth, Inc., stated that, if an arbitration clause waives the plaintiff's "right to pursue statutory remedies for antitrust violations, we would have little hesitation in condemning the agreement as against public policy."[187] The California Supreme Court summarized the extent of the consensus on this point as: "The principle that an arbitration agreement may not limit statutorily imposed remedies such as punitive damages and attorney fees appears to be undisputed."[188]

Consequently, an arbitration agreement that either explicitly restricts punitive damages or has that practical effect should not be enforced.[189] In a civil rights context, this result is particularly appropriate because the courts have recognized that the threat of punitive damages is crucial to the enforcement of anti-discrimination statutes and that arbitration clauses which bar punitive damages conflict with those statutes.[190] The court should either strip the ban on punitive damages from the arbitration agreement[191] or refuse to enforce the agreement in its entirety.[192]

11.5.3.7 Limits on Recovery of Attorney Fees and Costs; High Arbitration Fees

Essential to the ECOA and FHA regulatory scheme is the authority for courts to award attorney fees to a prevailing consumer but not to a prevailing creditor. This statutory provision, more than any other, makes enforcement of the statute practical. It also deters creditors from improperly contesting meritorious claims. Otherwise, creditors with deep legal pockets could overwhelm any attempt by a consumer to press an action.[193]

Consequently, arbitration agreements that require each party to bear its own attorney fees and costs, regardless of which party prevails, are fundamentally in conflict with the congressional intent underlying the ECOA and the FHA. Such an arbitration provision is unenforceable.[194] This result is particularly appropriate in an FHA claim because the statute reveals its congressional purpose with an unusual provision that, upon application, the court may appoint an attorney for the consumer or authorize an action without the payment of fees, costs, or security.[195] Contrast this congressional purpose with an arbitration proceeding in which arbitration charges can easily exceed $10,000 and in which the consumer may have to front a portion of these fees or even be liable for all of these fees if the consumer does not prevail.

While the Supreme Court places the burden on the consumer to prove that high arbitration fees make pursuing a statutory claim in arbitration impractical,[196] implicit to this holding is the principle that high fees in relation to the consumer's claim can render an arbitration agreement unenforceable. A significant number of courts have in fact examined the consumer's resources and the cost of the arbitration proceeding and determined that the arbitration requirement either conflicts with a statutory purpose or is unconscionable and thus unenforceable.[197] Thus the Third Circuit held in an employment case that a provision requiring the losing party to pay all of the arbitrator's fees would be unenforceable, even though the employee was not guaranteed to be subject to these costs, because the mere prospect of these costs could deter her from vindicating her statutory rights.[198]

Consequently, as a matter of practice, consumers should seek clarification as to their potential liability for arbitration filing fees and the cost of the arbitrator(s). Will the fees be waived because of the consumer's indigency? If so, will just the filing fee be waived or will the much larger hourly fees for the

---

187   473 U.S. 614, 635 n.19, 105 S. Ct. 3346, 87 L. Ed. 2d 444 (1985); *see also* Equal Emp't Opportunity Comm'n v. Waffle House, Inc., 534 U.S. 279, 122 S. Ct. 754, 151 L. Ed. 2d 755 (2002).

188   Armendariz v. Found. Health Psychcare Servs., Inc., 99 Cal. Rptr. 2d 745, 6 P.3d 669 (Cal. 2000); *see also* Booker v. Robert Half Int'l, Inc., 413 F.3d 77 (D.C. Cir. 2005); Walker v. Ryan's Family Steak Houses, Inc., 400 F.3d 370 (6th Cir. 2005); McMullen v. Meijer, Inc., 355 F.3d 485, 491–92 (6th Cir. 2004); Ting v. AT & T, 182 F. Supp. 2d 902, 926 (N.D. Cal. 2002), *aff'd in part, rev'd in part*, 319 F.3d 1126 (9th Cir. 2003). *But see* Febar v. Menard, Inc., 367 F.3d 1048, 1052 (8th Cir. 2004) ("Questions about remedy are also outside our scope of review because they do not affect the validity of the agreement to arbitrate.").

189   National Consumer Law Center, Consumer Arbitration Agreements § 4.4.2.4 (6th ed. 2011 and Supp.). *But see* Anderson v. Va. Coll., L.L.C., 2012 WL 4052198 (S.D. Miss. Sept. 13, 2012).

190   *See* Alexander v. Anthony Int'l, L.L.C., 341 F.3d 256, 267 (3d Cir. 2003); Ingle v. Circuit City Stores, Inc., 328 F.3d 1165, 1178–79 (9th Cir. 2003); Derrickson v. Circuit City Stores, Inc., 1999 U.S. Dist. LEXIS 21100, 81 Fair Empl. Prac. Cas. (BNA) 1533, 1538 (D. Md. Mar. 19, 1999) ("Punitive damages and back pay are powerful deterrents to employers who might otherwise discriminate on the basis of race. The failure of the Circuit City arbitration provision to provide those remedies shields Circuit City from the full force of Section 1981 and prevents Plaintiff from effectively vindicating her rights."), *aff'd sub nom.* Johnson v. Circuit City Stores, Inc., 203 F.3d 821 (4th Cir. 2000) (table); Harper v. Ultimo, 7 Cal. Rptr. 3d 418, 421–22 (Cal. Ct. App. 2003); Romano *ex rel.* Romano v. Manor Care, Inc., 861 So. 2d 59, 63 (Fla. Dist. Ct. App. 2003).

191   Booker v. Robert Half Int'l, Inc., 413 F.3d 77 (D.C. Cir. 2005).

192   Bridge Fund Capital Corp. v. Fastbucks Franchise Corp., 622 F.3d 996 (9th Cir. 2010); Wernett v. Serv. Phoenix, L.L.C., 2009 WL 1955612 (D. Ariz. July 6, 2009); IJL Dominicana S.A. v. It's Just Lunch Int'l, L.L.C., 2009 WL 305187 (C.D. Cal. Feb. 6, 2009); Bencharsky v. Cottman Transmission Systems, L.L.C., 625 F. Supp. 2d 872 (N.D. Cal. 2008); Hialeah Automotive, L.L.C. v. Basulto, 22 So. 3d 586 (Fla. Dist. Ct. App. 2009); *see* National Consumer Law Center, Consumer Arbitration Agreements § 6.7 (6th ed. 2011 and Supp.) (arguments why the complete agreement should be found unenforceable).

193   *See* Graham Oil Co. v. ARCO Products Co., 43 F.3d 1244 (9th Cir. 1994).

194   *See* National Consumer Law Center, Consumer Arbitration Agreements § 4.4.2.2 (6th ed. 2011 and Supp.); *see also id.* § 6.6.4.2 (limit on attorney fees is unconscionable).

195   42 U.S.C. § 3613(b).

196   Green Tree Financial Corp. v. Randolph, 531 U.S. 79, 121 S. Ct. 513, 521, 148 L. Ed. 2d 373 (2000).

197   National Consumer Law Center, Consumer Arbitration Agreements §§ 4.5, 6.6.2 (6th ed. 2011 and Supp.).

198   Parilla v. IAP Worldwide Serv., VI, Inc., 368 F.3d 269, 284–85 (3d Cir. 2004); *see also* National Consumer Law Center, Consumer Arbitration Agreements §§ 4.4.2.3, 6.6.9 (6th ed. 2011 and Supp.).

arbitrator also be waived? Will fees be assessed to the losing party only? What retainer must the consumer pay up front? The key to any arbitration fee challenge is a thorough presentation to the court of admissible evidence establishing the actual fees and charges the arbitration is likely to involve and whether the consumer will in fact be liable for those charges. A detailed analysis of how to challenge excessive arbitration costs as inconsistent with an arbitration requirement is found in NCLC's *Consumer Arbitration Agreements.*[199]

Because of a 2010 Supreme Court decision,[200] the nature of the consumer's challenge as to the cost of arbitration is different if the arbitration agreement also specifies that the arbitrator determines all questions of arbitrability. An arbitration agreement with such a "delegation" clause seeks to require the arbitrator to decide among other issues whether the arbitration's cost is unconscionable. The Supreme Court has stated that, if the consumer wishes to challenge the arbitration requirement in court, the consumer must first ask the court to invalidate the delegation clause.[201]

This does not stop a challenge to arbitration's cost but only changes the nature of that consumer's argument. The consumer will need to show that the delegation clause is unenforceable. The Supreme Court opined that it will be more difficult to show that the delegation clause is substantively unconscionable than the arbitration clause as a whole, since the cost of arbitrating whether the arbitration clause is unenforceable will be less than the cost of an arbitration hearing on the merits. The Court, though, did not comment on one telling infirmity of a delegation provision—that it forces a challenge to be brought before an arbitrator that the arbitration on the merits is too expensive for the consumer. The consumer is forced to argue before the arbitrator that his or her rates are too high. The arbitrator in effect is ruling on his or her own compensation.

11.6 Selecting Causes of Action

11.6.1 Advantages of Various Claims

11.6.1.1 General

Plaintiffs in credit discrimination cases can choose from claims under the ECOA, the Fair Housing Act, certain civil rights statutes (42 U.S.C. § 1981 and 42 U.S.C. § 1982), state credit discrimination statutes, and state statutes that prohibit unfair or deceptive practices (UDAP statutes). With certain important exceptions detailed below, the best strategy is often to plead as many causes of action as are viable.

Each statute has special characteristics that make it appropriate for only certain types of cases. Although these characteristics are detailed throughout this treatise, this subsection will provide a brief overview of some differences among them.

The first question to ask is whether the challenged practice generally involves discrimination on a prohibited basis or whether it only involves a violation of one of the ECOA procedural requirements.[202] For example, a creditor who requires applicants to state their religion violates a specific ECOA procedural prohibition.

The ECOA procedural provisions are powerful tools even in situations in which discrimination is not at issue. Courts have agreed that violations of the ECOA notice requirements, in particular, may arise with or without additional discrimination claims.[203] There is also a possibility that a state equal credit opportunity statute will prohibit the same practice.[204] In these circumstances, the state claim might be considered as an alternative to the federal one.[205]

If a challenged practice involves discrimination, the next step is to determine whether there is an illegal basis for the discrimination. Credit discrimination statutes do not prohibit discrimination generally but only prohibit discrimination based on certain itemized bases.[206]

If the basis for discrimination is not included in one of the credit discrimination statutes, the plaintiff should check whether another state statute prohibits this type of discrimination or whether that basis for discrimination violates a general prohibition of unfair or deceptive acts or practices in the state's UDAP statute. Finally, even if a practice is discriminatory, but only on a non-prohibited basis, it may violate the ECOA, the FHA, and state laws if it also has the effect of discriminating on a prohibited basis.[207]

Sample pleadings and discovery can be found in Appendices G and H, *infra*, and on the companion website to this treatise.

11.6.1.2 Remedies, Forum, and Defenses

The federal discrimination and civil rights laws all have similar remedies, in that they provide for actual and punitive damages, attorney fees, and equitable relief.[208] Private remedy issues are discussed in detail in § 11.8, *infra*. Forum issues are covered in § 11.5, *supra*. Consideration should also be given to the applicable limitations period for each claim. Section 11.9.2, *infra*, covers statute of limitations issues in detail, including the continuing violation and tolling doctrines, and whether claims may be brought defensively beyond the relevant period for

---

199 National Consumer Law Center, Consumer Arbitration Agreements § 6.6.2 (6th ed. 2011 and Supp.).

200 Rent-a-Center, West, Inc. v. Jackson, 130 S. Ct. 2772 (2010).

201 *See* § 11.5.3.4, *supra*.

202 *See generally* § 5.6, ch. 10, *supra* (co-signature requirements).

203 *See* Jochum v. Pico Credit Corp., 730 F.2d 1041 (5th Cir. 1984); Rayburn v. Car Credit Ctr. Corp., 2000 U.S. Dist. LEXIS 14944 (N.D. Ill. Oct. 6, 2000) (discrimination is not a prerequisite to an actionable ECOA claim); Williams v. Thomas Pontiac-GMC-Nissan-Hyundai, 1999 U.S. Dist. LEXIS 15045 (N.D. Ill. Sept. 22, 1999) (denial of motion to dismiss); Pinkett v. Payday Today Loans, L.L.C., 1999 U.S. Dist. LEXIS 12098 (N.D. Ill. July 22, 1999) (failure to provide ECOA rejection notice without allegations of discrimination may be actionable); § 10.1, *supra*.

204 *See* appx. F, *infra*.

205 *See* § 2.5, *supra*.

206 *See generally* ch. 3, *supra*.

207 *See* § 4.3, *supra*.

208 *See* § 11.8, *infra*.

affirmative claims. If claims under these federal statutes are problematic, the applicable state limitations period should be examined. A state credit discrimination statute may, but is not likely to, have a longer limitations period.

11.6.1.3 State Laws Generally Not Preempted

The ECOA preempts only those state laws that are inconsistent with the Act and with Regulation B and then only to the extent of the inconsistency.[209] A state law which is more protective of a credit applicant is not considered inconsistent with the ECOA and Regulation B and is therefore unaffected by them.[210]

An equally or more protective state law dealing explicitly with credit discrimination also may be granted an exemption from the requirements of the ECOA by the federal regulatory agency.[211] Inconsistency may be determined by the federal regulatory agency in response to a request from a "creditor, state or other interested party" for a formal agency determination.[212] It may therefore be difficult to argue that a state law is inconsistent with the ECOA without the support of a previous federal regulatory agency finding, although in clear cases the lack of an agency ruling should not be fatal.

Regulation B lists several types of state laws that are inconsistent with the ECOA and therefore are preempted by it. These laws include:

- Those requiring or permitting a practice or act prohibited by the ECOA and Regulation B;[213]
- Those prohibiting the individual extension of consumer credit to both parties in a marriage if each spouse individually and voluntarily applies for such credit;[214]
- Those prohibiting inquiries or collection of data required to comply with the ECOA or Regulation B;[215]
- Those prohibiting asking or considering age in an empirically derived, demonstrably, and statistically sound credit

scoring system to determine a pertinent element of creditworthiness or to favor an older applicant;[216] or

- Those prohibiting inquiries necessary to establish or administer a special purpose credit program.[217]

Just like the ECOA, the Fair Housing Act and federal Civil Rights Acts should not preempt state laws that afford similar or greater rights to consumers. For example, a 2006 determination by the Pennsylvania Human Relations Commission is notable in that it found reverse redlining to be actionable under the state Human Relations Act and because it held brokers liable for the violations.[218]

Prior to the abolition of the Office of Thrift Supervision (OTS) by the Dodd-Frank Wall Street Reform and Consumer Protection Act,[219] and the replacement of its broad preemption regulations with the OCC standard for preemption, state credit discrimination claims brought against a federal savings association were preempted by the OTS regulations that prohibited discrimination in lending activities.[220] In at least one instance, these regulations were held to supersede the more general anti-discrimination provisions of the ECOA.[221] Under the Dodd-Frank Wall Street Reform and Consumer Protection Act ("Dodd-Frank Act"), contracts entered into prior to July 21, 2010, are still subject to the old preemption rules.[222]

The OCC has not issued regulations preempting fair lending claims against banks. Moreover, in *Cuomo v. Clearing House Association, L.L.C.*,[223] the Supreme Court held that an OCC regulation restricting visitorial powers could not prohibit a state attorney general from bringing a judicial enforcement action against a national bank to enforce state fair lending laws.[224]

---

209 15 U.S.C. § 1691d(f); Reg. B, 12 C.F.R. § 1002.11(a) [§ 202.11(a)].
    Regulation B, 12 C.F.R. § 1002.2(aa) [§ 202.2(aa)] defines "state" as all states, the District of Columbia, the Commonwealth of Puerto Rico, or any territory or possession of the United States.

210 15 U.S.C. § 1691d(f); Reg. B, 12 C.F.R. § 1002.11(a) [§ 202.11(a)]; *see also* Nat'l State Bank v. Long, 630 F.2d 981 (3d Cir. 1980) (the ECOA does not preempt a New Jersey statute prohibiting geographic redlining in the granting of home mortgages, as applied to national banks).

211 *See* 15 U.S.C. § 1691d(g); Reg. B, 12 C.F.R. § 1002.11(e) [§ 202.11(e)]. A state might seek such an exemption to strengthen state enforcement of anti-discrimination statutes.

212 Reg. B, 12 C.F.R. § 1002.11(b)(2) [§ 202.11(b)(2)].
    Regulation B also sets out the procedural steps required of states when seeking a federal regulatory agency determination. Reg. B, 12 C.F.R. § 1002.11(e) [§ 202.11(e)].

213 Reg. B, 12 C.F.R. § 1002.11(b)(1)(i) [§ 202.11(b)(1)(i)].

214 Reg. B, 12 C.F.R. § 1002.11(b)(1)(ii) [§ 202.11(b)(1)(ii)]; *see* § 5.6.1, *supra*.

215 Reg. B, 12 C.F.R. § 1002.11(b)(1)(iii) [§ 202.11(b)(1)(iii)].
    The data collection requirement referred to in the regulation is the monitoring information provision. Reg. B, 12 C.F.R. § 1002.13 [§ 202.13].

216 Reg. B, 12 C.F.R. § 1002.11(b)(1)(iv) [§ 202.11(b)(1)(iv)]; *see* § 6.6.2.3, *supra*.

217 Reg. B, 12 C.F.R. § 1002.11(b)(1)(v) [§ 202.11(b)(1)(v)].
    Special purpose credit programs address the credit needs of economically disadvantaged groups and may request and consider information on race, sex, and other protected categories in ways forbidden to other forms of credit. *See* § 3.8, *supra*.

218 *See* McGlawn v. Human Relations Comm'n, 891 A.2d 757 (Pa. Commw. Ct. 2006) (state Human Rights Commission found mortgage broker violated state Human Relations Act by engaging in reverse redlining; the commission accepted testimony that the brokers were significantly involved in making the loans); § 11.3.2.2, *supra* (further discussing broker liability).

219 Pub. L. No. 111-203, 124 Stat. 1376 (2010).

220 12 U.S.C. § 1464(a); 12 C.F.R. §§ 528.2, 528.9 (rescinded).

221 Thompson v. WFS Financial Inc., 2003 WL 22924458 (Cal. Super. Ct. Nov. 6, 2003) (state law claims preempted by OTS regulations; noting that it was incongruous for Congress expressly to state that the ECOA does not preempt state laws providing greater protection to consumers while, pursuant to the Home Owners Loan Act (HOLA), OTS had issued regulations preempting all state law discrimination claims against federal savings associations); *see also* § 12.4, *infra* (state and local enforcement). *See generally* National Consumer Law Center, The Cost of Credit: Regulation, Preemption, and Industry Abuses ch. 3 (4th ed. 2009 and Supp.).

222 12 U.S.C. § 5553.

223 557 U.S. 519, 536, 129 S. Ct. 2710, 2722, 174 L. Ed. 2d 464 (U.S. 2009).

224 However, the Court also held that the attorney general's letters to banks requesting information about these practices violated the

11.6.2 What Causes of Action May Be Brought in the Same Lawsuit?

The ECOA, federal Fair Housing Act, federal Civil Rights Acts, and state anti-discrimination laws all provide remedies for illegal discrimination. Aggrieved individuals can recover their actual damages only once, but issues sometimes arise as to whether an individual can seek punitive damages under different statutes or minimum or multiple damages under a state statute and punitive damages under a federal one.

The ECOA also establishes rules about joining causes of action. When a particular act or omission by a creditor would constitute a violation of both state law and the ECOA, an action may be brought to recover money damages under only one of them, either the ECOA or state law.[225] No such election is required when the court action is for relief other than money damages (for example, injunctive or declaratory relief) or in an administrative action.[226]

The election provision governing an ECOA action and a state law action indicates that an "action may be brought" under either the ECOA or state law, but not both. It is thus safest to elect one theory or the other before bringing a complaint. Some state credit discrimination laws may have similar provisions, requiring plaintiffs to choose whether to bring an action under the state law or another act.[227]

In addition, the ECOA provides that no person aggrieved by an ECOA violation and, in the same transaction, by a violation of the Fair Housing Act's prohibitions against discrimination concerning residential real estate-related transactions, shall recover under both statutes.[228] This language seems to indicate that the litigant can bring an action under both statutes but must elect one remedy or the other before a final order is issued.[229]

The ECOA does not require an election of causes of action or remedies between an ECOA action and a federal Civil Rights Act claim. Moreover, nothing prevents simultaneous recovery on a Fair Housing Act claim, a federal Civil Rights Act claim, and a state credit discrimination or UDAP claim.[230] However, as with any litigation, only one actual damages recovery can be had for the same injury.

11.7 Discovery Issues

A defendant in a disparate impact case may attempt to shift the focus to the individual transactions made by the named plaintiffs. In furtherance of this effort, it may seek financial information related to their creditworthiness and financial acumen. This information is not relevant to the claim that the defendant discriminated against the plaintiffs by assessing discretionary, subjectively determined fees after the plaintiffs had already objectively qualified for the loans.[231] Courts will recognize when the real purpose of the defendant's discovery is to search for information bearing on the veracity of the representations made by the plaintiffs during the application process, a subject that is irrelevant to a disparate impact claim and that implicates sensitive confidential information.[232]

11.8 Private Remedies

11.8.1 Overview

The various federal statutes that prohibit credit discrimination provide similar remedial schemes.[233] They all provide for actual and punitive damages, equitable relief, and attorney fees for successful claims. None of the federal statutes provide statutory damages.

Some state statutes provide better or different remedies than those available under the federal statutes. Several state credit discrimination statutes provide for minimum statutory damages that are not available under the federal statutes. In addition, some state UDAP statutes provide for treble or minimum statutory damages.[234]

National Bank Act, as they were not issued in the exercise of law enforcement powers "vested in the courts of justice."

225 15 U.S.C. § 1691d(e); *see, e.g.,* Ware v. Indymac Bank, 534 F. Supp. 2d 835 (N.D. Ill. 2008); *see also* Fernandez v. Hull Coop. Bank, 1979 U.S. Dist. LEXIS 8657 (D. Mass. Nov. 8, 1979).

226 15 U.S.C. § 1691d(e).

227 *See, e.g.,* Saldana v. Citibank, 1996 WL 332451 (N.D. Ill. June 13, 1996); Milton v. Bancplus Mortgage Corp., 1996 WL 197532 (N.D. Ill. Apr. 19, 1996).

228 15 U.S.C. § 1691e(i).
   The literal language of the statute is outdated, but its intent is clear. It provides that there cannot be recovery under both the ECOA and 42 U.S.C. § 3612 of the Fair Housing Act. Section 3612 previously authorized a private right of action for damages and injunctive relief. The private relief section, however, has been moved to section 3613, and section 3612 now deals with administrative enforcement of the Fair Housing Act. The notes to section 1691e now clarify this change, referring to 42 U.S.C. § 3613 as the relevant statute.

229 Cooley v. Sterling Bank, 280 F. Supp. 2d 1331 (M.D. Ala. 2003); Walton v. Centrust Mortgage Corp., Fair Housing–Fair Lending Rep.(P-H) ¶ 15,719 (N.D. Ohio Sept. 25, 1991); *see, e.g.,* Barrett v. H & R Block, Inc., 652 F. Supp. 2d 104 (D. Mass. 2009) (rejecting argument that plaintiff may not proceed under both ECOA and FHA causes of action; requiring only that plaintiff later decide under which one to recover); NAACP v. Ameriquest Mortgage Co., 635 F.

Supp. 2d 1096, 1105 (C.D. Cal. 2009) (same); Ware v. Indymac Bank, 534 F. Supp. 2d 835, 840 (N.D. Ill. 2008) (same).

230 For this reason, if suit is brought under one of these statutes but not others, res judicata may bar later claims under the other statutes. *See, e.g.,* Elkadrawy v. Vanguard Group, Inc., 584 F.3d 169 (3d Cir. 2009) (earlier dismissal of Title VII action as untimely bars employee's subsequent section 1981 claim arising from same set of facts).

231 *In re* Wells Fargo Residential Mortgage Lending Discrimination Litig., 2009 WL 1771368, at *5–6 (N.D. Cal. June 19, 2009) (citing cases).

232 *Id.* at *5.

233 The interplay of the ECOA, federal Fair Housing Act, federal Civil Rights Acts, and state anti-discrimination laws is discussed in § 11.6.2, *supra.*

234 *See* §§ 2.5, 2.6, *supra,* 11.8.3, *infra. See generally* National Consumer Law Center, Unfair and Deceptive Acts and Practices ch. 13 (8th ed. 2012).

Except for the absence of a provision for statutory damages, the remedies under federal credit discrimination statutes have much in common with other titles found within the Consumer Credit Protection Act.[235] For example, the ECOA's private remedies are similar to those provided in the Truth in Lending Act (TILA),[236] the Fair Debt Collection Practices Act (FDCPA),[237] and the Fair Credit Reporting Act (FCRA).[238] In many situations, it is possible to use case law under these statutes to support an ECOA claim, particularly if case law on point under the ECOA is limited.[239] All of these statutes have the same purpose of providing remedies for consumers treated unlawfully in credit transactions, all were drafted within a several-year time span, and all use similar language. Nevertheless, there are some important differences between the ECOA's remedial scheme and that found in the other consumer protection statutes. For example, the ECOA provides for punitive damages[240] while the TILA does not, but the TILA provides for minimum statutory damages.[241]

As discussed in the previous section, because a discrimination case may be brought under more than one discrimination statute it is important to know when remedies are cumulative and when the plaintiff must elect one remedy or another.[242]

11.8.2 Actual Damages

11.8.2.1 General

It should not be necessary for a plaintiff to establish actual damages in order to take advantage of other possible statutory remedies, such as punitive damages, equitable and declaratory relief, and attorney fees.[243] There are, however, other sound reasons for establishing the existence of actual damages. The ECOA, for example, explicitly provides that an award of actual damages is one factor to be considered in measuring any award of punitive damages.[244] Also, although the ECOA places a strict limit on the amount of punitive damages that may be awarded, no such limit is placed on actual damages. The interplay of actual and punitive damages in credit discrimination cases in general is considered in § 11.8.4.2, *infra*.

It is also important to recognize that compensable damages are often difficult to prove and are frequently undercompen-

sated. For this reason, plaintiffs should always consider seeking punitive damages as well.[245]

11.8.2.2 Tangible Injury

Actual, out-of-pocket expenses and other tangible injuries are recoverable as actual damages under the ECOA, the federal Fair Housing Act, the federal Civil Rights Acts, and state credit discrimination statutes. These damages can arise in a number of ways. The following should be explored with the consumer:

- Did the consumer obtain credit at a higher interest rate than others similarly situated?
- Did the consumer, after being denied credit, obtain a loan from another creditor at a higher interest rate or purchase the same or similar item at a higher price than that charged by the creditor who originally denied the consumer's application?
- Did the consumer's inability to purchase an item or services because of the denial of credit result in additional costs, such as for extra trips to the creditor's office or store to discuss the denial or for alternative lodging?
- Was the consumer compelled to take time from work to travel to the creditor's office or store to discuss the denial of credit and, if so, was there a resulting loss of pay?
- Was the consumer, whose spouse was the actual credit applicant, required to co-sign the credit contract even though he or she had no separate property or income? If so, it can be argued that the consumer suffered actual damages, potentially amounting to the total liability on the contract or, at a minimum, a diminution of available credit, as a result of the creditor's unlawful requirement.
- Did the consumer incur expense in getting a copy of his or her credit report to investigate whether the reasons for credit denial were legitimate or discriminatory, or to add or delete a spouse's accounts to improve the credit record?
- Did a creditor's failure to give notice of adverse action damage a credit applicant by, for example, preventing him or her from seeking other ways to pay off outstanding debts and avoid serious consequences such as foreclosure?[246]

11.8.2.3 Intangible Damages

Courts under all of the federal discrimination statutes have allowed actual damages for intangible losses, such as emotional distress, pain and suffering, humiliation, or damage to credit rating. One reason for allowing such damages is the strong public policy against discrimination, a public policy opposed not only to the economic injury caused by discrimination but to the damage that discrimination causes to individuals' sense of worth and civil rights and to the very fabric of our society.[247] In

---

235 15 U.S.C. §§ 1601–1693r.

236 15 U.S.C. § 1640(a).

237 15 U.S.C. § 1692k(a), (b).

238 15 U.S.C. § 1681n.

239 *See* Brothers v. First Leasing, 724 F.2d 789 (9th Cir. 1984) (considering truth in lending title of Consumer Credit Protection Act in interpreting equal credit title).

240 15 U.S.C. § 1691e(b).

241 15 U.S.C. § 1640(a); *see* National Consumer Law Center, Truth in Lending § 11.6.3 (8th ed. 2012).

242 *See* § 11.6.2, *supra*.

243 *See, e.g.*, Coburn v. DaimlerChrysler Servs. North America, L.L.C., 2005 WL 736657 (N.D. Ill. Mar. 31, 2005) (the ECOA by its plain terms does not appear to require that a plaintiff suffer actual damages in order potentially to prevail under that statute).

244 15 U.S.C. § 1691e(b); *see* § 11.8.4.3.3.2, *infra*.

245 *See* § 11.8.4, *infra*.

246 *See, e.g.*, Durdin v. Cheyenne Mtn. Bank, 98 P. 3d 899 (Colo. App. 2004) ($100,000 actual damages awarded in ECOA notice case).

247 *See generally* Timothy J. Moran, *Punitive Damages in Fair Hous-*

addition, the explicit provision for punitive damages in both the ECOA and the Fair Housing Act indicates a congressional intent that recovery not be limited to out-of-pocket expenses.

Courts award actual damages for intangible injuries caused by loss of a credit card's convenience, loss of increased purchasing power, and loss of protection in case of emergency;[248] injury from embarrassment, humiliation, and mental distress;[249] injury caused by inconvenience;[250] injury from the deprivation of constitutional rights;[251] and harm to the applicant's actual or reputation for creditworthiness.[252] Significant amounts have been awarded in appropriate cases. For example, in a case brought pursuant to California civil rights law, the jury assessed $150,000 in damages against a mortgage broker who discriminated against African-American loan applicants. The court which upheld the verdict noted that "damages for emotional distress may easily support the entire amount of the verdict."[253]

Actual damages for intangible injury are not in lieu of, or a form of, punitive damages. Thus, the Fifth Circuit affirmed an $1000 award for the "private, momentary and personal affront" caused by a flawed denial of credit even though it held that punitive damages were not available under the facts of the case.[254]

As noted earlier, intangible injuries may be difficult to prove. Awards for emotional distress often undervalue the actual harm. Among other reasons, this low valuation can be due to judges or juries underestimating the emotional harm that discrimination causes to those who experience it.[255] Practitioners should look to other types of consumer claims, such as those under the FDCPA, for guidance in recognizing and proving intangible injury when actual damages are small or nonexistent.[256]

11.8.3 Statutory Damages Under State Statutes

None of the federal discrimination statutes provide for statutory damages. Nevertheless, some relevant state statutes do authorize such damages.

There are two types of such statutes. A number of states' general discrimination statutes provide for minimum statutory damages in the $50 to $1000 range, with $100 or $200 being the most common amount.[257] In addition, many state statutes of general application prohibiting unfair or deceptive acts or practices (UDAP statutes) provide treble or minimum damages.[258] It may be that a violation of a federal or state credit discrimination statute is a per se state UDAP violation, thus triggering UDAP remedies.[259]

Minimum statutory damages are useful when actual damages are small or nonexistent and when defendant's conduct is not willful or sufficiently egregious that a court is likely to award punitive damages. The court will have to award the amount specified by statute if the court finds a statutory violation, no matter the amount of actual damages suffered.[260] Minimum damages are particularly attractive in class actions when the damages suffered by each class member may be small or difficult to prove.[261]

---

ing Litigation: Ending Unwise Restrictions on a Necessary Remedy, 36 Harv. C.R.-C.L. L. Rev. 279 (2001); Larry Heinrich, *The Mental Anguish and Humiliation Suffered by Victims of Housing Discrimination,* 26 J. Marshall L. Rev. 39 (1992).

According to one court, there is little in-depth research on the personal costs of discrimination and racial exclusion. *See* Broome v. Biondi, 17 F. Supp. 2d 211, 225 n.9 (S.D.N.Y. 1997). The court cited some of the research that is available, including Joe R. Feagin & Melvin P. Sikes, Living With Racism: The Black Middle Class Experience 23 (1994) and Ellis Cose, The Rage of a Privileged Class: Why Are Middle Class Blacks Angry? Why Should America Care? (1993).

248 Shuman v. Standard Oil Co., 453 F. Supp. 1150 (N.D. Cal. 1978).

249 *See* Fischl v. Gen. Motors Acceptance Corp., 708 F.2d 143 (5th Cir. 1983) (ECOA actual damages may include mental anguish, humiliation, or embarrassment); Woods-Drake v. Lundy, 667 F.2d 1198 (5th Cir. 1982) (Fair Housing and Civil Rights Act claims); Anderson v. United Finance Co., 666 F.2d 1274 (9th Cir. 1982); Smith v. Anchor Bldg. Corp., 536 F.2d 231 (8th Cir. 1976) (Fair Housing Act (FHA) claim); Williams v. Matthews Co., 499 F.2d 819 (8th Cir. 1974) (FHA claim); Jeanty v. McKey & Poague, Inc., 496 F.2d 1119 (7th Cir. 1974) (FHA claim); Steele v. Title Realty Co., 478 F.2d 380 (10th Cir. 1973) (FHA claim); Sayers v. Gen. Motors Acceptance Corp., 522 F. Supp. 835 (W.D. Mo. 1981) (ECOA claim); Owens v. Magee Finance Serv., 476 F. Supp. 758 (E.D. La. 1979) (ECOA claim); Shuman v. Standard Oil Co., 453 F. Supp. 1150 (N.D. Cal. 1978) (ECOA claim); Morehead v. Lewis, 432 F. Supp. 674 (N.D. Ill. 1977) (FHA claim), *aff'd,* 594 F.2d 867 (7th Cir. 1979).

250 Morehead v. Lewis, 432 F. Supp. 674 (N.D. Ill. 1977).

251 *Id.*

252 *See* Fischl v. Gen. Motors Acceptance Corp., 708 F.2d 143 (5th Cir. 1983) (actual damages under ECOA may include injury to credit reputation); Anderson v. United Finance Co., 666 F.2d 1274 (9th Cir. 1982) (same); Ford v. Citizens & Southern Nat'l Bank, 700 F. Supp. 1121 (N.D. Ga. 1988) (ECOA damages from being required to sign a mortgage could be difficulty in obtaining credit due to that encumbrance); Shuman v. Standard Oil Co., 453 F. Supp. 1150 (N.D. Cal. 1978) (ECOA case).

253 Green v. Rancho Santa Margarita Mortgage Co., 33 Cal. Rptr. 2d 706 (Cal. Ct. App. 1994).

254 Bhandari v. First Nat'l Bank of Commerce, 808 F.2d 1082 (5th Cir. 1987), *rev'd in part on other grounds,* 829 F.2d 1343 (5th Cir. 1987) (en banc), *vacated and remanded,* 492 U.S. 901 (1989), *reinstated by* 887 F.2d 609 (5th Cir. 1989).

255 *See* Timothy J. Moran, *Punitive Damages in Fair Housing Litigation: Ending Unwise Restrictions on a Necessary Remedy,* 36 Harv. C.R.-C.L. L. Rev. 279, 290 (2001) (commenting that predominantly white juries, for example, may not understand the effect of discrimination on a non-white plaintiff).

256 National Consumer Law Center, Fair Debt Collection § 6.3.2 (7th ed. 2011 and Supp.).

257 *See* appx. F, *infra.*

258 National Consumer Law Center, Unfair and Deceptive Acts and Practices (8th ed. 2012).

259 *Id.*

260 In other statutory contexts, the defense contention that statutory damages may not be awarded in the absence of actual damages has been roundly rejected. Cases under the FDCPA are collected at National Consumer Law Center, Fair Debt Collection § 6.4.3.2 (7th ed. 2011 and Supp.). Cases under the FCRA are collected at National Consumer Law Center, Fair Credit Reporting § 11.3.3.3 (7th ed. 2010 and Supp.).

261 National Consumer Law Center, Consumer Class Actions § 10.5.2.1 (7th ed. 2010 and Supp.).

Multiple damage awards (typically treble damages), on the other hand, are particularly useful when actual damages are significant. In a few states, a UDAP violation may permit or even mandate a treble damages award.

When multiple statutory damages are assessed, consumer attorneys may encounter due process challenges similar to those the Supreme Court has upheld regarding the award of large punitive damages. The Supreme Court's decisions in such cases as *BMW of North America, Inc. v. Gore*,[262] *State Farm Mutual Automobile Insurance Co. v. Campbell*,[263] and *Phillip Morris USA v. Williams*[264] require courts to evaluate a punitive damages award using three guideposts: reprehensibility; the ratio between punitive and compensatory damages; and a comparison to the penalties authorized or imposed in comparable cases.[265] These standards for reviewing a jury award, however, are *not* appropriate for even large statutory or treble damage awards, as these are the result of a legislative determination. For this reason, many courts have upheld such awards, finding that they are not subject to the *Gore/State Farm* standards.[266]

In considering these state law remedies it is important to remember that a plaintiff may have to elect, before filing a complaint, whether to pursue a federal ECOA claim or a state law claim.[267]

11.8.4 Punitive Damages

11.8.4.1 General

Punitive damages are available under the ECOA, the Fair Housing Act, and the federal Civil Rights Acts. While some courts are reluctant to award such damages, others are not. A plaintiff's settlement posture and trial prospects are both enhanced if punitive damages may be warranted.

Despite the availability and importance of punitive damages, there are a number of potential barriers plaintiffs face when seeking these awards. Judicial decisions in recent years have limited the availability and amount of punitive damages, as discussed in the following subsections.[268] In addition, the ECOA sets limits on the amount of punitive damages that may be awarded in both individual and class action cases.[269]

11.8.4.2 Punitive Damages in FHA and Federal Civil Rights Cases

Although they are discretionary, punitive damages are often awarded under the Fair Housing Act (FHA). However, if a consumer opts for an administrative hearing under the FHA, the administrative law judge is not empowered to award punitive damages. Punitive damages under the Act are only available if an action is brought before a court.[270]

There are no statutory limits to the size of punitive damages awards in individual cases or class actions under the federal Civil Rights Acts or under the Fair Housing Act.[271] At one time, the Fair Housing Act had a $1000 limit on punitive damages, but Congress repealed this limit in 1988.[272] Since the removal of the cap, punitive damages awards in FHA cases have increased substantially, with frequent awards of $100,000 and more.[273] Nevertheless, some lower courts have improperly limited the awarding of punitive damages in FHA cases. These courts have refused to allow juries to consider the issue of punitive damages, even in cases in which there is sufficient evidence of intentional discrimination. These cases are often appealed and reversed, but they have had a strong chilling

---

262 517 U.S. 559 (1996); *see* National Consumer Law Center, Automobile Fraud § 8.11 (4th ed. 2011 and Supp.) (discussing in detail constitutional limitations on punitive damages).

263 538 U.S. 408 (2003).

264 549 U.S. 346 (2007).

265 BMW of North America, Inc. v. Gore, 517 U.S. 575 (1996).

266 Appellate cases that have so held include Capitol Records, Inc. v. Thomas-Rasset, 692 F.3d 899 (8th Cir. 2012) and Matamoros v. Starbucks Corp., 699 F.3d 129 (1st Cir. 2012). *See generally* National Consumer Law Center, Automobile Fraud § 11.8 (4th ed. 2011 and Supp.).

267 *See* §§ 11.6.1.3, 11.6.2, *supra*.

268 *See also* Exxon Shipping Co. v. Baker, 128 S. Ct. 2605, 171 L. Ed. 2d 570 (2008).

269 15 U.S.C. § 1691e(b); *see* § 11.8.4.3.2, *infra*.

270 *See* § 11.5.2, *supra* (discussion of the administrative alternative to pursue a Fair Housing Act claim).

271 *See* Stokes v. Cetner, 2000 U.S. Dist. LEXIS 2162 (E.D. Mich. Jan. 28, 2000); Broome v. Biondi, 17 F. Supp. 2d 211 (S.D.N.Y. 1997).

272 Pub. L. No. 100-430, 102 Stat. 1633 (1988) (adding 42 U.S.C. § 3613(c)).

The House Judiciary Committee specifically identified "disadvantageous limitations on punitive damages" as one of the weaknesses in the existing fair housing law. H.R. Rep. No. 100-711, at 16 (1988).

273 *See, e.g.*, United States v. Big D Enters., Inc., 184 F.3d 924, 932 (8th Cir. 1999) (upholding punitive damages awards totaling $100,000 to three victims); Little Field v. McGuffey, 954 F.2d 1337, 1348–50 (7th Cir. 1992) (upholding punitive damages award of $100,000 to single plaintiff); Parris v. Pappas, 844 F. Supp. 2d 271 (D. Conn. 2012) (default judgment awarding $150,000 in punitive damages to plaintiff for failure to accommodate); Matarese v. Archstone Pentagon City, 795 F. Supp. 2d 402 (E.D. Va. 2011) (awarding $100,000 in punitive damages to married couple for housing discrimination), *aff'd in part, vacated in part on other grounds*, 468 Fed. Appx. 283 (4th Cir. 2012); Davis v. Lane Mgmt., 524 F. Supp. 2d 1375 (S.D. Fla. 2007) (default judgment award of $420,000 in punitive damages to plaintiff); Campos v. Barney G. Inc., 2007 WL 1341442 (D. Neb. Apr. 3, 2007) (default judgment award including $250,000 in punitive damages to plaintiff); Edwards v. Flagstar Bank, 109 F. Supp. 2d 691, 698 (E.D. Mich. 2000) (awarding $325,000 in punitive damages to single victim of mortgage lending discrimination), *aff'd in part, rev'd in part sub nom.* Paschal v. Flagstar Bank, 295 F.3d 565 (6th Cir. 2002) (punitive damages appeal mooted due to court's holding that claim was barred by statute of limitations); Broome v. Biondi, 17 F. Supp. 2d 211 (S.D.N.Y. 1997) (affirming awards of $410,000 to couple and $47,000 to single individual); Nationwide Mut. Ins. Co. v. Hous. Opportunities Made Equal, Inc., 523 S.E.2d 217 (Va. 2000) (discussing jury's $100 million punitive damages award for fair housing organization in insurance discrimination case; the same court later vacated that ruling, 2000 Va. LEXIS 56 (Va. Mar. 3, 2000), and the case was settled in April 2000).

effect because many other plaintiffs cannot or will not appeal this type of ruling.[274]

As Justice Souter noted in *Exxon Shipping Co. v. Baker*,[275] punitive damages serve to punish wrongdoers and deter similar harmful conduct. Although the outcome in *Exxon Shipping* was unfavorable to plaintiffs in that an original award of $4.5 billion that had already been reduced by the court of appeal to $2.5 billion was further reduced to $507.5 million by the Supreme Court, some parts of the analysis may help plaintiffs in credit discrimination cases. The Court noted that the degree of blame-worthiness of the conduct is an important factor to be weighed in determining not just the propriety of awarding punitive damages but also the appropriate amount of the award.[276] Intentional, malicious, willful, and reckless behavior can all support punitive damages, and "[a]ction taken or omitted in order to augment profit represents an enhanced degree of punishable culpability."[277] Moreover, "egardless of culpability, however, heavier punitive awards have been thought to be justifiable when wrongdoing is hard to detect . . . or when the value of injury and the corresponding compensatory award are small."[278]

The standard for punitive damages focuses on the defendant's state of mind and does not require objective proof that the defendant's behavior was outrageous or egregious.[279] How-

ever, the latter qualities also will support an award of punitive damages.[280]

When, as is often the case, the request for punitive damages is based on the defendant's state of mind rather than objective evidence of egregious conduct, defendants may be allowed to present a "good faith defense" to the claim for punitive damages. Defendants may assert that they did not know their conduct violated the law or that they did not even know that there was a law prohibiting their conduct. The "good faith defense" to punitive damages was most recently discussed by the United States Supreme Court in a Title VII employment discrimination case, *Kolstad v. American Dental Association*.[281] There, the Court held that employers are not subject to punitive damages for discriminatory conduct by their managerial employees if they can show that they maintained and enforced good faith anti-discrimination policies.

Arguably, the good faith defense should not apply to FHA cases because the FHA specifically permits the award of punitive damages in all cases in which liability is found. However, case law to date has been to the contrary.[282] Ignorance of the law should fail as a defense because the deterrent effect of punitive damages is undermined if they are barred simply because a statute is ambiguous.[283] A similar argument was rejected by the Supreme Court in a Fair Debt Collection suit when the Court held that the Act's express bona fide error defense does not apply to mistakes of law. The Court observed:

---

274 *See, e.g.*, Fair Hous. Council v. Penasquitos Casablanca Owner's Ass'n, 381 Fed. Appx. 674 (9th Cir. 2010) (trial court erred in granting judgment as a matter of law against plaintiffs when reasonable jury could find that owners acted with reckless indifference); United States v. Space Hunters, Inc., 429 F.3d 416 (2d Cir. 2005) (in case involving alleged illegal steering of prospective renters based on race and disability, district court's refusal to submit issue of FHA punitive damages to jury was error because the court overlooked ample evidence that defendants acted with malice and reckless indifference); Badami v. Flood, 214 F.3d 994, 997 (8th Cir. 2000) (reversing district court determination that evidence of landlord's refusal to rent home to a family with eight children because of family size did not warrant punitive damage instruction); United States v. Ballistrieri, 981 F.2d 916, 936 (7th Cir. 1992) (reversing district court's decision to enter a directed verdict on punitive damages despite evidence that landlord systematically misrepresented availability of apartments to African-American home seekers); *cf.* U.S. v. Collier, 2010 WL 3881381 (W.D. La. Sept. 28, 2010) (holding without discussion that punitive damages were not warranted despite finding that defendants' actions and statements were disingenuous scheme or device to exclude blacks and evidenced a pattern or practice of racial discrimination). *See generally* Timothy J. Moran, *Punitive Damages in Fair Housing Litigation: Ending Unwise Restrictions on a Necessary Remedy*, 36 Harv. C.R.-C.L. L. Rev. 279 (2001).

275 128 S. Ct. 2605, 2621, 171 L. Ed. 2d 570 (2008).

276 128 S. Ct. 2605, 2621–22 (2008).

277 128 S. Ct. 2605, 2622 (2008); *see also* Smith v. Wade, 461 U.S. 30, 56, 103 S. Ct. 1625, 75 L. Ed. 2d 632 (1983) (section 1983 action; reckless or callous indifference to the federally protected rights of others).

278 Exxon Shipping Co. v. Baker, 128 S. Ct. 2605, 2622 (2008).
   In the case before it, the compensatory award was $507.5 million, which weighed heavily in favor of the court's establishing a baseline ratio of 1:1 for punitive to actual damages.

279 Kolstad v. American Dental Ass'n, 527 U.S. 526, 119 S. Ct. 2118, 144 L. Ed. 2d 494 (1999) (in Title VII employment case, expressly

rejecting the need to show egregious conduct); Preferred Properties v. Indian River Estates, Inc., 276 F.3d 790, 799 (6th Cir. 2002) (citing Smith v. Wade, 461 U.S. 30, 56, 103 S. Ct. 1625, 75 L. Ed. 2d 632 (1983)); Alexander v. Riga, 208 F.3d 419 (3d Cir. 2000); Williams v. Homestead Mgmt., 2005 WL 1118118 (W.D. Mich. May 11, 2005) (citing *Kolstad* and *Preferred Properties* and finding that punitive damages standard was met; illegality of defendant's policy against renting a one-bedroom apartment to an adult and minor should have been apparent); *see also* Snyder v. Bazargani, 241 Fed. Appx. 20, 23 (3d Cir. 2007) (affirming award of punitive damages on FHA and state human relations act claims, ruling that plaintiff did not need to demonstrate "wanton and reckless" misconduct in addition to demonstrating that the conduct was intentional).

280 Exxon Shipping Co. v. Baker, 128 S. Ct. 2605, 171 L. Ed. 2d 570 (2008).

281 527 U.S. 526, 119 S. Ct. 2118, 144 L. Ed. 2d 494 (1999).

282 42 U.S.C. § 3613.
   Courts have concluded that the *Kolstad* reasoning applies in FHA cases. *See* Preferred Properties Inc. v. Indian River Estates, Inc., 276 F.3d 790 (6th Cir. 2002) (allowing good faith defense but finding that defendant did not meet standard; upholding punitive damages award because jury could reasonably have inferred that defendant knew or perceived the risk that his actions violated federal law); Badami v. Flood, 214 F.3d 994, 997 (8th Cir. 2000); Alexander v. Riga, 208 F.3d 419, 430–32 (3d Cir. 2000); *see also* Lincoln v. Case, 340 F.3d 283 (5th Cir. 2003); United States v. Gumbaytay, 757 F. Supp. 2d 1142, 1152 (M.D. Ala. 2010) (good faith defense available); Walker v. Todd Vill., L.L.C., 419 F. Supp. 2d 743, 750 n.7 (D. Md. 2006) (noting that good faith defense is available to punitive damages).

283 *See generally* Timothy J. Moran, *Punitive Damages in Fair Housing Litigation: Ending Unwise Restrictions on a Necessary Remedy*, 36 Harv. C.R.-C.L. L. Rev. 279 (2001).

"debt collectors might have an affirmative incentive not to seek an advisory opinion to resolve ambiguity in the law, as receipt of such advice would prevent them from claiming good-faith immunity for violations and would potentially trigger civil penalties for knowing violations under the FTC Act."[284]

Another critical issue is whether punitive damages can be awarded if the plaintiff fails to prove any compensable harm. There is a split in the circuits on this issue in FHA cases. For example, the Third Circuit has held that compensatory damages are not a prerequisite to punitive damages,[285] while the Fourth and Fifth Circuits have held that they are.[286] Another challenge confronting plaintiffs is that some appellate courts reduce the size of the punitive damages awards made by lower courts.[287]

In contrast, when the plaintiff has experienced a constitutional violation under the federal Civil Rights Acts, courts have consistently upheld awards of punitive damages even in the absence of compensable damages.[288] Also, as discussed in the next subsection, plaintiffs in ECOA cases clearly should be able to receive punitive damages whether or not actual damages have been established.[289]

11.8.4.3 ECOA and Punitive Damages

11.8.4.3.1 Generally

The ECOA contains language that appears to mandate an award of punitive damages. A non-complying creditor "shall be liable . . . for punitive damages in an amount not greater than $10,000 in addition to any actual damages" awarded.[290] The one statutory exception is that no punitive damages are available in actions brought against a creditor that is a government or a governmental subdivision, agency, or instrumentality.[291]

In enacting the ECOA, Congress specifically refused to require that a creditor's violation of the ECOA be "willful" in order to warrant a punitive damages award,[292] despite intensive lobbying for such a clause by credit industry representatives.[293] Instead, Congress adopted the present punitive damages provision, in which the creditor's intent is merely one of several factors to be weighed by the court.

Nevertheless, the clear weight of authority holds that punitive damages are appropriate only if the defendant's conduct was wanton, malicious, or oppressive or if the defendant acted in reckless disregard of the law.[294] Apparently, because even

---

284 Jerman v. Carlisle, McNellie, Rini, Kramer & Ulrich L.P.A., 559 U.S. 573, 1615, 130 S. Ct. 1605, 1615 (2010).

285 Alexander v. Riga, 208 F.3d 419, 430 (3d Cir. 2000).

    The Seventh and Ninth Circuits have also found that punitive damages may be awarded in housing discrimination cases in the absence of compensatory damages, but their statements are arguably dicta. *See* Fountila v. Carter, 571 F.2d 487, 492 (9th Cir. 1978); Rogers v. Loether, 467 F.2d 1110, 1112–13 (7th Cir. 1972), *aff'd sub nom.* Curtis v. Loether, 415 U.S. 189 (1974).

286 La. ACORN Fair Hous. v. LeBlanc, 211 F.3d 298, 303 (5th Cir. 2000) (vacating $10,000 punitive damages award to victims of racial discrimination when jury did not award compensatory damages); People Helpers Found., Inc. v. City of Richmond, 12 F.3d 1321, 1327 (4th Cir. 1993) (acknowledging that language of the FHA did not require an award of actual damages in order to award punitive damages but still found that, when plaintiff had not demonstrated actual harm, punitive damages should also be barred).

    For a discussion of the ramifications of the Louisiana ACORN decision and flaws in the court's reasoning, see Johanna M. Lundgren, *A Weakened Enforcement Power: The Fifth Circuit Limits Punitive Damages Under the Fair Housing Act in Louisiana ACORN Fair Hous. v. LeBlanc*, 46 Loy. L. Rev. 1325 (2000). *See also* Abner v. Kan. City Southern R.R. Co., 513 F.3d 154 (5th Cir. 2008) (upholding jury award of punitive damages without award of compensatory damages in Title VII and section 1981 case; although the court distinguished the FHA and its *Leblanc* decision, many of the same policy arguments it used would apply in Title VII context too).

287 *See, e.g.*, Lincoln v. Case, 340 F.3d 283 (5th Cir. 2003) (court of appeals remitted jury award of $100,000 to $55,000); Allahar v. Zahora, 59 F.3d 693 (7th Cir. 1995) (when white seller initially refused to sell his home to an Indian man, jury awarded $10,000 in compensatory damages and $7500 in punitive damages; the district court set aside the punitive damages award entirely and the Seventh Circuit affirmed, noting that the $20,000 in attorney fees awarded together with compensatory damages would provide adequate compensation); Szwast v. Carlton Apartments, 102 F. Supp. 2d 777 (E.D. Mich. 2000) (reducing a punitive damages award of $400,000 to $30,000 in a case of intentional familial status discrimination in which jury awarded only $3000 in compensatory damages); Darby v. Heather Ridge, 827 F. Supp. 1296, 1300–01 (E.D. Mich. 1993) (reducing jury's punitive damages award of $250,000 to $50,000 to match compensatory damages award). *But see* Quigley v. Winter, 598 F.3d 938 (8th Cir. 2010) (district court reduced jury award of punitive damages from $250,000 to $20,527.50; court of appeals reviewed de novo and increased amount to $54,750); United States v. Big D Enters., Inc., 184 F.3d 924 (8th Cir. 1999) (affirming a punitive damages award of $100,000 to three victims even though jury awarded only $1000 in compensatory damages).

288 *See, e.g.*, La. ACORN Fair Hous. v. LeBlanc, 211 F.3d 298, 303 (5th Cir. 2000) (punitive damages may be awarded in the absence of compensatory damages for section 1982 claims when there is a constitutional violation, but not for FHA claims); Campos-Orrego v. Rivera, 175 F.3d 89, 98 (1st Cir. 1999) (noting that, when the court finds a constitutional violation, an award of actual damages is not required to uphold an award of punitive damages); King v. Macri, 993 F.2d 294, 298 (2d Cir. 1993); Fischl v. Gen. Motors Acceptance Corp. 708 F.2d 143 (5th Cir. 1983) (punitive damages may be awarded under Equal Credit Opportunity Act to unsuccessful credit applicant, regardless of proof of actual damages); Basista v. Weir, 340 F.2d 74, 85–88 (3d Cir. 1965) (no actual damages were required to uphold an award of punitive damages in a section 1983 action).

289 *See* § 11.8.4.3.3.2, *infra*.

290 15 U.S.C. § 1691e(b); *see* Barber v. Rancho Mortgage & Inv. Corp., 32 Cal. Rptr. 2d 906 (Cal. Ct. App. 1994).

291 15 U.S.C. § 1691e(b).

292 The "willfulness" amendment was proposed in the House, H.R. 210, 94th Cong., at 9 (1975), but was later dropped by the House-Senate Conference Committee. In her separate comments appended to the original House bill, Congresswoman Leonor Sullivan explained that the "willfulness" language should be omitted because it connoted a standard used in criminal rather than civil statutes. H.R. 210, 94th Cong., at 9, 18 (1975).

293 *See Proposed Amendments to the Equal Credit Opportunity Act: Hearings on H.R. 14856 and H.R. 14908 Before the Subcomm. on Consumer Affairs of the House Comm. on Banking & Currency*, 93d Cong. 430 (1974) (statement of National Retail Merchants Association representative Kerr); *id.* at 483 (statement of Interbank Card Association counsel Morgan).

294 *See, e.g.*, Anderson v. United Finance Co., 666 F.2d 1274, 1278 (9th Cir. 1982) (section 1691e (b) "does not require an award of punitive

unintentional discrimination can provide the basis for an ECOA action, courts are troubled by the award of punitive damages in every case. Plaintiffs may attempt to counter such reluctance by pointing out that ECOA punitive damages cannot exceed $10,000 in an individual case and can be as low as appropriate based on the standards set out in the statute.[295] Examples of ECOA cases in which punitive damages were awarded or found appropriate based upon a creditor's wanton, malicious, oppressive, or reckless action will also help.[296]

Proof of actual damage is not a prerequisite to a finding of punitive damages under the ECOA.[297] Instead, the size of actual damages is one factor among several in determining the size of the award. If there are no actual damages, other factors may still argue for a substantial punitive damages award.[298] The ECOA instructs courts to consider, "among other relevant factors, the amount of any actual damages awarded, the frequency and persistence of failures of compliance by the creditor, the resources of the creditor, the number of persons adversely affected, and the extent to which the creditor's failure of compliance was intentional."[299]

Moreover, many of the same courts that refuse to make an award of punitive damages mandatory have been generous in awarding plaintiffs damages for such intangible injuries as humiliation, affront, and damage to credit reputation.[300] The clear implication is that the plaintiff should attempt to show

both the creditor's wantonness or recklessness (to establish a right to punitive damages) and also the impact of the practice on the applicant (to establish actual damages for both tangible and intangible injuries).

11.8.4.3.2 Limits on the size of ECOA punitive damage awards

The ECOA limits the size of punitive damages awards. For an individual action, the maximum punitive damages award is $10,000 in addition to any actual damages that are awarded.[301] However, it appears that the $10,000 limit applies to each creditor, applicant, and violation involved in a case, so the total punitive damages in an ECOA individual case can be significantly more than $10,000.[302] The statute says that "any" creditor is liable for $10,000 for failing to comply with "any" requirement relating to the aggrieved "applicant." Thus, if there is more than one creditor, more than one ECOA requirement that is violated, or more than one aggrieved applicant, there can be multiple punitive damages awards. For example, in one case $10,000 in punitive damages was awarded against one creditor for discrimination based on national origin and another $10,000 in punitive damages was awarded against a different but related creditor for failure to notify the applicant of an adverse action.[303]

For a class action, the limit on punitive damages for the entire action is the lesser of $500,000 or 1% of the creditor's net worth.[304] (This means that when a creditor's net worth is less than one million dollars, higher total punitive damages are actually available in an individual action or in one brought by a group of individuals).

These limits only apply to punitive damages, and there is no limit to the size of actual damages that may be recoverable in an individual or class action. Thus, when the maximum punitive damages in a class action is relatively small, proof of actual damages becomes critical.

11.8.4.3.3 Factors in determining the size of ECOA punitive damages awards

11.8.4.3.3.1 General

As noted, the ECOA provides a list of relevant factors to be considered by a court when determining the amount of punitive damages to be awarded. These factors are:

---

damages for every violation of the Act"); Coulibaly v. J.P. Morgan Chase Bank, N.A., 2012 WL 3985285, at *7 (D. Md. Sept. 7, 2012); Reynolds v. Reliable Transmissions, Inc., No. 09–238, 2010 WL 2640065, at *4 (E.D. Va. June 29, 2010); Bayard v. Behlmann Automotive Servs., Inc., 292 F. Supp. 2d 1181, 1187 (E.D. Mo. 2003) ("The concept of damages as 'punitive' implies some degree of blame beyond a technical violation of the [ECOA]."); Newton v. United Cos. Financial Corp., 24 F. Supp. 2d 444 (E.D. Pa. 1998) (punitive damages not awarded because case was one of first impression).

295 *See* §§ 11.8.4.3.2, 11.8.4.3.3.1, *infra.*

296 *See* Fischl v. Gen. Motors Acceptance Corp., 708 F.2d 143 (5th Cir. 1983); Anderson v. United Finance Co., 666 F.2d 1274 (9th Cir. 1982); Schwab v. Kids' Financial Inc., 2009 WL 2486929 (D. Colo. Aug. 12, 2009); Bayard v. Behlmann Automotive Servs., Inc., 292 F. Supp. 2d 1181 (E.D. Mo. 2003); Ricci v. Key Bancshares, 662 F. Supp. 1132 (D. Me. 1987); Sayers v. Gen. Motors Acceptance Corp., 522 F. Supp. 835 (W.D. Mo. 1981); Vander Missen v. Kellogg-Citizens Nat'l Bank, 481 F. Supp. 742 (E.D. Wis. 1979); Shuman v. Standard Oil Co., 453 F. Supp. 1150 (N.D. Cal. 1978); *see also* Fernandez v. Hull Coop. Bank, 1979 U.S. Dist. LEXIS 8657 (D. Mass. Nov. 8, 1979) (following Shuman).

297 Fischl v. Gen. Motors Acceptance Corp., 708 F.2d 143 (5th Cir. 1983); Anderson v. United Finance Co., 666 F.2d 1274 (9th Cir. 1982); Coburn v. Daimler Chrysler Servs. North America, L.L.C., 2005 WL 736657 (N.D. Ill. Mar. 31, 2005); Ricci v. Key Bancshares, 662 F. Supp. 1132 (D. Me. 1987); Cherry v. Amoco Oil Co., 490 F. Supp. 1026 (N.D. Ga. 1980); Smith v. Lakeside Foods Inc., 449 F. Supp. 171 (N.D. Ill. 1978).

298 *See* § 11.8.4.3.3.2, *infra.*

299 15 U.S.C. § 1691e(b).

300 *See* Bhandari v. First Nat'l Bank of Commerce, 808 F.2d 1082 (5th Cir. 1987), *rev'd in part on other grounds*, 829 F.2d 1343 (5th Cir. 1987) (en banc); Fischl v. Gen. Motors Acceptance Corp., 708 F.2d 143 (5th Cir. 1983); Shuman v. Standard Oil Co., 453 F. Supp. 1150 (N.D. Cal. 1978).

301 15 U.S.C. § 1691e(b).

302 *See* Ricci v. Key Bancshares, 662 F. Supp. 1132 (D. Me. 1987).

303 *Id.*

304 *Id.* Both the Truth in Lending Act and the Fair Debt Collection Practices Act also refer to the defendants' net worth as a limit on class action damages, albeit statutory damages. Among the key matters that have been litigated concerning the issue of net worth are how to define this term, the point in time to measure it, and the extent of permissible discovery. *See generally* National Consumer Law Center, Truth in Lending § 11.8.3.3 (8th ed. 2012); National Consumer Law Center, Fair Debt Collection § 6.6.3 (7th ed. 2011 and Supp.).

- The amount of actual damages awarded;
- The frequency and persistence of non-compliance;
- The creditor's resources;
- The number of persons adversely affected;
- The extent to which non-compliance was intentional; and
- Other relevant factors.[305]

These factors are discussed in the following subsections. Not surprisingly, there is no established formula regarding the respective weight to be given to each of the various factors when they are considered together.[306]

11.8.4.3.3.2 Amount of actual damages awarded

The statute provides that, to determine the amount of punitive damages to award, "the court shall consider, among other relevant factors, the amount of any actual damages awarded."[307] Thus while, as noted above, actual damages are not a prerequisite to the award of punitive damages under the ECOA, a large actual damages award is one factor favoring a large punitive damages award.

11.8.4.3.3.3 Frequency and persistence of creditor's non-compliance

Another factor used to determine the amount of punitive damages is the frequency and persistence of the creditor's failure to comply.[308] This factor can be interpreted in two different ways.

First, it can refer to repeated discriminatory acts committed against the consumer within the same or successive transactions, particularly if the defendant has been confronted with evidence of its unlawful actions.

A second interpretation of this provision could be that "frequency and persistence of failures of compliance" by the creditor refers to violations committed against persons other than that particular claimant. To establish these other failures of compliance, the following sources should be investigated:

- State and federal agency compliance reports;
- Court records, which may reveal other suits brought against the creditor;
- Complaints and enforcement proceedings brought against the creditor before state commissions enforcing state equal credit or other civil rights laws;
- The creditor's forms, which may contain facial violations of ECOA prohibitions—such as prohibited inquiries—or may provide no space for a co-signer to sign a security agreement without also becoming liable for the debt;

- The creditor's internal operations guidelines or training manuals as to credit-granting procedures or collection procedures; and
- The creditor's other contracts, which may suggest discriminatory practices; for example, a review may reveal a significant percentage of spousal signatures or a geographic analysis may suggest redlining.

11.8.4.3.3.4 Creditor's resources

Another factor in determining the amount of punitive damages is the resources of the creditor.[309] The statute does not define resources, which could refer to the creditor's net worth, assets, income stream, profits, or some other measure of resources.[310] Congress probably intended resources to mean something other than the net worth of the creditor, as this standard—not "resources"—is used in the very same statute to set the upper limit on awards of punitive damages in class actions.[311]

In order to maximize the value and extent of the creditor's resources being considered when seeking an award of punitive damages in an ECOA case, "creditor" should be defined as broadly as possible in the complaint. For example, the plaintiffs could plead that the creditor is the parent of the finance company that denied credit to the client as well as the local finance company. Plaintiffs should also bring assignees and any others who participated in the credit decision into the case as defendants.

11.8.4.3.3.5 Number of persons adversely affected

In calculating punitive damages, another factor to consider is the number of persons adversely affected.[312] The meaning of this provision is relatively clear when applied to an ECOA class action. In a class action, in which there is a limit on punitive damages, a court would most likely award less than the maximum amount when the class affected is small.[313] Accordingly, to enhance the likelihood of the largest permissible punitive damages award to the class, it may be advantageous to define the class of ECOA plaintiffs as broadly as possible.

In an individual ECOA action, establishing the "number of persons adversely affected" may be more problematic. It is important to conduct discovery to show, if possible, that the creditor has discriminated against persons other than the individual claimant.

---

305 15 U.S.C. § 1691e(b).
306 *See, e.g.,* Moreno v. DHI Mortgage Co. GP, Inc., 2010 WL 3430816, at *5 (E.D. Va. Aug. 27, 2010) (finding an award of $1000 punitive damages sufficient to punish and deter defendant when there were no actual damages, defendant had "rich resources," failure of compliance was persistent as to plaintiff but there was no evidence of other similar violations or that defendant had acted intentionally).
307 15 U.S.C. § 1691e(b).
308 15 U.S.C. § 1691e(b).

309 15 U.S.C. § 1691e(b).
310 *See* Moreno v. DHI Mortgage Co. GP, Inc., 2010 WL 3430816, at *5 (E.D. Va. Aug. 27, 2010) (finding defendant had "rich resources" based on the boast on its website that its parent company was nation's leading homebuilder and that it had forty-three offices nationwide, but not further defining the term and, upon evaluating all relevant factors, awarding only $1000 in punitive damages.
311 15 U.S.C. § 1691e(b). Punitive damages in class actions may not exceed "the lesser of $500,000 or 1 per centum of the net worth of the creditor."
312 15 U.S.C. § 1691e(b).
313 15 U.S.C. § 1691e(b).

11.8.4.3.3.6 Extent to which creditor's non-compliance was intentional

Another relevant factor in determining the amount of punitive damages is "the extent to which the creditor's failure of compliance was intentional."[314] In some circumstances, this factor may overlap with the "frequency and persistence of non-compliance" factor.[315]

11.8.4.3.3.7 Other relevant factors

The ECOA provides that a court shall also consider "other relevant factors," along with the specific factors discussed above,[316] in determining the amount of punitive damages.[317] Nothing in the statute, the legislative history, or case law under the ECOA indicates what might constitute other relevant factors, but factors that could be developed for particular situations might include the parties' relative bargaining power; the sophistication of the parties, particularly if the client's primary language is not English; the unavailability of other sources of credit; and the urgency of the client's need for credit. In addition, reference may be made to factors which courts have considered when making or reviewing awards of punitive damages in other contexts, both under statutory and common law.[318]

11.8.5 Equitable and Declaratory Relief

11.8.5.1 Prospective Relief

Equitable relief can be an effective way to quickly stop a creditor's practice not just on an individual basis but also on behalf of all other potential applicants. Equitable and declaratory relief are available under all of the federal credit discrimination statutes and the federal Civil Rights Acts. The Fair Housing Act specifically states that the court "may grant as relief, as the court deems appropriate, any permanent or temporary injunction, temporary restraining order, or other order."[319] Similarly, the ECOA states that an aggrieved credit applicant may obtain "such equitable and declaratory relief as is necessary to enforce the requirements" of the ECOA.[320]

Equitable relief is particularly important when the creditor involved is a government agency. The ECOA explicitly exempts governmental bodies, subdivisions, and agencies from liability for punitive damages under the ECOA.[321] Also, monetary relief against the head of a state agency, including an order requiring the expenditure of funds administered by a state agency, may be barred due to sovereign immunity. Under the

Supreme Court's decision in *Ex Parte Young*,[322] however, prospective relief against governmental actors is an exception to the bar on imposing liability on states.[323]

When a plaintiff seeks an injunction to stop a creditor's practice, the issue may arise as to whether the plaintiff is likely to be injured in the future and thus has a stake in the injunctive relief. Standing should not be an issue, though, when debtors continue to have a relationship with a creditor and wish to change the creditor's practices. For example, injunctive relief would be appropriate to prevent a creditor from improperly requiring a spouse's signature when credit is renewed.[324]

Standing may be contested in other cases. In general, to show standing to seek prospective relief, the plaintiff must be suffering a continuing injury or be under a real and immediate threat of being injured in the future.[325] Past wrongs are evidence bearing on whether there is a real and immediate threat of repeated injury. The threatened injury must be likely as opposed to merely speculative.[326]

For example, in automobile financing mark-up cases, courts have found that plaintiffs meet standing requirements in part because they suffer ongoing harm by paying higher amounts in car payments each month due to the discriminatory mark-ups.[327] Further, even if plaintiffs could not show that the discrimination was ongoing, they may show a likelihood of future discrimination.[328] In finding that this standard was met in one case, the court cited several plaintiffs' stated intentions to finance future vehicle purchase with the creditor. The court

---

314 15 U.S.C. § 1691e(b).

315 *See* § 11.8.4.3.3.3, *supra*.

316 *See* §§ 11.7.4.3.3.2–11.7.4.3.3.6, *supra*.

317 15 U.S.C. § 1691e(b).

318 *See, e.g.*, National Consumer Law Center, Fair Debt Collection § 2.6 (7th ed. 2011 and Supp.).

319 42 U.S.C. § 3613(c).

320 15 U.S.C. § 1691e(c).

321 15 U.S.C. § 1691e(b).

322 209 U.S. 123, 28 S. Ct. 441 (1908).

323 Greater New Orleans Fair Hous. Action Ctr. v. HUD, 723 F. Supp. 2d 14, 21 (D.D.C. 2010) (allowing fair housing claims seeking injunctive relief that would prohibit certain conduct in the future to proceed, while rejecting plaintiffs' request for retroactive relief as barred by Eleventh Amendment); *see also* Greater New Orleans Fair Hous. Action Ctr. v. HUD, 723 F. Supp. 2d 1 (D.D.C. 2010).

324 Chestnut Hill Gulf, Inc. v. Cumberland Farms, Inc., 788 F. Supp. 616 (D. Mass. 1992) (franchisees were granted preliminary injunction stopping Cumberland Farms' practice of requiring spouses to sign a guarantee as a condition to renewing franchises).

325 City of Los Angeles v. Lyons, 461 U.S. 95, 103 S. Ct. 1660, 75 L. Ed 2d 675 (1983); Tandy v. City of Wichita, 380 F.3d 1277 (10th Cir. 2004); *see also* Ueno v. Napolitano, 2007 WL 1395517, at *4 (E.D.N.Y. May 11, 2007) (mag.) (recommending that court grant an injunction on FHA claim).

326 *See, e.g.*, Tandy v. City of Wichita, 380 F.3d 1277 (10th Cir. 2004) (standing to seek prospective relief found in case based on Rehabilitation Act and Title II of Americans with Disabilities Act when plaintiff had used bus service for many years and averred an intent to use the system in the future; plaintiff experienced lift malfunctions in the past, and court found there was a good chance she would again).

327 *See, e.g.*, Jones v. Ford Motor Credit Co., 2005 WL 743213 (S.D.N.Y. Mar. 31, 2005). *But see* Smith v. Chrysler Financial Co., 2004 WL 3201002 (D.N.J. Dec. 30, 2004) (plaintiffs challenging a mark-up policy failed to establish a real and immediate threat that they would suffer an injury if they purchased another vehicle from the defendant).

    The *Smith* case later settled. *See* Smith v. DaimlerChrysler Servs. North America, 2005 WL 2739213 (D.N.J. Oct. 24, 2005).

328 Jones v. Ford Motor Credit Co., 2005 WL 743213 (S.D.N.Y. Mar. 31, 2005).

found that this helped show that it was reasonable to assume that at least one of the named plaintiffs would purchase a new or used car from a dealer in the future and that it was entirely possible, even likely, that the defendant creditor would end up purchasing that contract.[329]

11.8.5.2 Restitution and Disgorgement

Absent a clear command by Congress that a statute providing for equitable relief excludes certain forms of relief, a court should presume that it has the full scope of equitable powers available for the proper and complete vindication of the statutory purpose.[330] Congress, cognizant of the scope of equity, knows what it is doing when it provides for general equitable relief in a regulatory statute and can, if it chooses, clearly and explicitly limit the scope of a court's equitable powers under any particular regulatory structure in which such an authorization lies.[331]

Neither the Fair Housing Act nor the ECOA, nor their respective legislative histories, even mentions limiting the equitable authority of enforcing courts. Therefore, pursuant to the mandates set forth in both statutes, reviewing courts may explore and utilize the full range of historically available equitable remedies to provide complete relief.[332]

Restitution and disgorgement of profits are part of a court's traditional equitable authority.[333] Even though both may produce a monetary recovery, they are distinct types of equitable remedies and are different from the legal remedy of compensatory damages.[334] Restitution allows a victim to be monetarily compensated for losses resulting from a defendant's acts by returning to the victim some or all of the payments that had been made to the defendant. Disgorgement forces a defendant to give up the amount by which the defendant was unjustly enriched without inquiring whether, or to what extent, identifiable private parties have been damaged.[335] They are poten-tially powerful tools under the Fair Housing Act and the ECOA.[336]

Restitution and disgorgement also may be considered as equitable adjuncts to an injunction decree, which seeks to prevent the commission of new acts that violate the law.[337]

This type of relief has been awarded in Fair Housing Act cases in order to prevent defendants from being allowed to retain funds that were obtained as a result of illegal and unconstitutional conduct.[338] Results in ECOA class action cases have been mixed.[339]

11.8.5.3 Voiding an Individual's Obligation Under a Note or Security Agreement

When creditors require co-signers or guarantors to sign a note or security agreement in violation of the ECOA, it is often

---

329   *Id.*

330   *See* Porter v. Warner Holding Co., 328 U.S. 395, 398, 66 S. Ct. 1086, 90 L. Ed. 1332 (1946) ("[u]nless otherwise provided by statute, all the inherent equitable powers of the District Court are available for the proper and complete exercise of that jurisdiction"); Still v. Cunningham, 94 P.3d 1104 (Alaska 2004).

331   *See* Mitchell v. Robert DeMario Jewelry, Inc., 361 U.S. 288, 292, 80 S. Ct. 332, 4 L. Ed. 2d 323 (1960).

332   Indeed, it has been observed that both the ECOA and the FHA "appear to sanction the pursuit of both legal and equitable remedies, and do not contain any language limiting the types of equitable remedies that are available." Steele v. GE Money Bank, 2009 WL 393860, at *11 (N.D. Ill. Feb. 17, 2009).

333   *See* Mertens v. Hewitt Assocs., 508 U.S. 248, 255, 113 S. Ct. 2063, 124 L. Ed. 2d 161 (1993).

334   *See* Herman v. S.C. Nat'l Bank, 140 F.3d 1413, 1422 (11th Cir. 1998) (ERISA case). *But see* Great-West Life & Annuity Ins. Co. v. Knudson, 534 U.S. 204, 122 S. Ct. 708, 151 L. Ed. 2d 635 (2002) (not all relief falling under rubric of restitution is available in equity); Thorn v. Jefferson-Pilot Life Ins., 445 F.3d 311 (4th Cir. 2006) (claim for restitution was not an equitable claim).

335   *See* Securities & Exch. Comm'n v. Blavin, 760 F.2d 706, 713 (6th Cir. 1985).

336   *See* Silverman v. Eastrich, 51 F.3d 28, 33 (3d Cir. 1995) (citing with approval Integra Bank v. Freeman, 839 F. Supp. 326 (E.D. Pa. 1993)).
      "Congress—in enacting the ECOA—intended that creditors not affirmatively benefit from proscribed acts of credit discrimination. To permit creditors—especially sophisticated credit institutions—to affirmatively benefit by disregarding the requirements of the ECOA would seriously undermine the Congressional intent to eradicate . . . discrimination. This interpretation of the statute best forwards its purposes, particularly in light of a broad remedial provision, Section 1691e(c), in the ECOA." *Id.*

337   *See* Porter v. Warner Holding Co., 328 U.S. 395, 399, 66 S. Ct. 1086, 90 L. Ed. 1332 (1946).

338   *See* Zuch v. Hussey, 394 F. Supp. 1028, 1055 n.13 (E.D. Mich. 1975) (proof of actual profits obtained from sales that are found to be in violation of the Fair Housing Act may, as an appropriate remedy, result in a court order that the defendants forfeit the profits and disgorge them in order to implement the goals of the Act), *aff'd*, 547 F.2d 1168 (6th Cir. 1977) (table); *see also* United States v. J.C. Long, 537 F.2d 1151, 1155 (4th Cir. 1975) (action brought by the Attorney General of the United States for preventive relief, including restitution, for violations of the fair housing provisions of the Civil Rights Act of 1968, the predecessor to the Fair Housing Act); United States v. The Inc. Vill. of Island Park, 888 F. Supp. 419 (E.D.N.Y 1995) (home owners in Fair Housing Act case required to disgorge unjust enrichment obtained through erroneous payment of mortgage subsidies even without proof of wrongdoing).

339   *See, e.g.,* Jones v. Ford Motor Credit Co., 2005 WL 743213 (S.D.N.Y. Mar. 31, 2005) (reserving decision on certification of a class for plaintiffs' claim for disgorgement); Smith v. Chrysler Financial Co., L.L.C., 2004 WL 3201002 (D.N.J. Dec. 30, 2004) (treating all claims as seeking money damages); Cason v. Nissan Motor Acceptance Corp., 212 F.R.D. 518 (M.D. Tenn. 2002) (not determining whether disgorgement is an appropriate remedy or is different from compensatory damages; however, noting that disgorgement, even if measured in the aggregate and based upon wrongdoer's gain, is a request for money that will require individual determinations in order for any such award to be distributed to class members).
      The *Smith* case settled in 2005. *See* Smith v. DaimlerChrysler Servs. North America, 2005 WL 2739213 (D.N.J. Oct. 24, 2005).
      The case against Nissan Motor Acceptance Corp. settled in 2003. *See* Cason v. Nissan Motor Acceptance Corp. (settlement), *available at* www.nclc.org/initiatives/cocounseling/content/settlement_agreement.pdf.
      A memorandum on the issue of unjust enrichment under the ECOA can be found on the companion website to this treatise.

desirable to seek to void the co-signer or guarantor's liability. The most common instance in which the situation arises is when a creditor, in violation of the ECOA, requires a husband to obtain his wife's signature for a loan even though the husband was creditworthy on his own.[340]

In such cases, when the creditor sues to collect on the debt, borrowers may seek to have their ECOA claim treated as an affirmative defense because the presence of any factual issues relating to it will likely prevent the entry of summary judgment for the creditor on its claim.[341] The ECOA claim would then present a factual issue to be addressed at trial. In contrast, lenders seek to have the ECOA claim treated as a counterclaim, which allows the lender to pursue a motion for summary judgment on the debt, separate from the ECOA claim. Also, if the lenders' view prevails, ECOA claims cannot later be used to void the underlying obligation.[342]

There is a split among federal courts on whether the ECOA claim should be treated as a defense or a counterclaim.[343] State courts are also divided.[344]

---

340 The general rule against discrimination prevents a creditor from requiring a spouse or other person to co-sign or guaranty a loan on a prohibited basis. The ECOA also sets out other limitations as to when a creditor may require a guarantor or co-signer. Reg. B, 12 C.F.R. § 1002.7(d)(1) [§ 202.7(d)(1)]; *see* § 5.6, *supra.*

341 *But see* Jones v. Ford Motor Credit Co., 358 F.3d 205, 209–10 (2d Cir. 2004) (finance company's claims for amounts allegedly due on underlying loans were distinct from borrowers' ECOA claims because the latter centered on company's mark-up policy, not plaintiff's nonpayment after contract price was set).

342 *See generally* Ami diLorenzo, *Regulation B: How Lenders Can Fight Back Against the Affirmative Use of Regulation B*, 8 U. Miami Bus. L. Rev. 215 (2000); Andrea Michele Farley, Note, *The Spousal Defense—A Ploy to Escape Payment or Simple Application of the Equal Credit Opportunity Act?*, 49 Vand. L. Rev. 1287 (1996).

343 *Cases allowing the affirmative defense: See, e.g.,* Silverman v. Eastrich Multiple Investor Fund, Ltd. P'ship, 51 F.3d 28 (3d Cir. 1995), *rev'g* 857 F. Supp. 447 (E.D. Pa. 1994); Bolduc v. Beal Bank, 994 F. Supp. 82 (D.N.H. 1998), *preliminary injunction vacated by* 167 F.3d 667 (1st Cir. 1999); Fed. Deposit Ins. Corp. v. Medmark, 897 F. Supp. 511 (D. Kan. 1995); Sharp Electronics Corp. v. Yoggev, 1995 U.S. Dist. LEXIS 5751 (E.D. Pa. Apr. 28, 1995); Integra Bank/Pittsburgh v. Freeman, 839 F. Supp. 326 (E.D. Pa. 1993); American Security Bank v. York, 1992 U.S. Dist. LEXIS 14309 (D.D.C. Sept. 1, 1992).

 Cases refusing to allow the affirmative defense: Matsco v. Clermont Ctr. for Comprehensive Dentistry, 2010 WL 746709 (M.D. Fla. Mar. 2, 2010); Fed. Deposit Ins. Corp. v. 32 Edwardsville, Inc., 873 F. Supp. 1474 (D. Kan. 1995); CMF Va. Land, Ltd. P'ship v. Brinson, 806 F. Supp. 90 (E.D. Va. 1992); Diamond v. Union Bank & Trust, 776 F. Supp. 542 (N.D. Okla. 1991).

 However, those cases refusing to allow the affirmative defense fail to discern the difference between releasing only the liability of the illegally obtained co-signer versus voiding the underlying obligation entirely. *See* Andrea Michele Farley, Note, *The Spousal Defense—A Ploy to Escape Payment or Simple Application of the Equal Credit Opportunity Act?*, 49 Vand. L. Rev. 1287 (1996).

344 *Cases allowing the affirmative defense: See, e.g.,* Douglas Cnty. Nat'l Bank v. Pfeiff, 809 P.2d 1100 (Colo. App. 1991); Banco Popular North America v. Estate of Smith, 2004 WL 1664236 (Conn. Super. Ct. June 29, 2004); Nat'l Collectors & Liquidators, Ltd. P'ship v. Millco of Danbury, Inc., 2001 Conn. Super. LEXIS 2254 (Conn. Super. Ct. July 31, 2001); Eure v. Jefferson Nat'l Bank,

---

Most courts that allow the obligation to be voided will do so only with respect to the impermissibly obligated party (the wife in the above scenario). This party, in these courts' view, should be relieved of her obligation because, but for the ECOA violation, she would not otherwise have incurred the obligation.[345] The wife is relieved from her obligation but the underlying debt is not necessarily void. The husband remains liable. The husband can still make a claim for damages, which can be raised affirmatively within the statute of limitations or by way of recoupment in jurisdictions which allow it.[346]

11.8.5.4 Outcome-Based Injunctive Relief

In some kinds of credit discrimination cases—especially reverse redlining cases—the most visible, provable harm from the discrimination is repossession, foreclosure, or some other consequence that occurs when the harsh terms of the transaction cause the consumer to default. One approach to prospective relief for a class of consumers is to focus not on the terms of the transaction but on these outcomes. Then, the injunctive relief, whether stipulated or entered by the court without the defendant's consent, would bind the defendant to reducing the percentage of customers who end up in, for example, repossession if the case involved car financing. The defendant would then have to change its business model in whatever ways were necessary to reach this goal.

11.8.6 Attorney Fees and Costs

11.8.6.1 General Standards

All of the federal discrimination and civil rights laws provide for attorney fees for prevailing plaintiffs. Although the language of the various statutes' attorney fee provisions differ

---

448 S.E.2d 417 (Va. 1994); Transamerica Commercial Finance Corp. v. Naef, 842 P.2d 539 (Wyo. 1992).

 Cases refusing to allow the affirmative defense: St. Paul Fire & Marine Ins. Co. v. Barge, 483 S.E.2d 883 (Ga. Ct. App. 1997); Spottiswoode v. Levine, 730 A.2d 166 (Me. 1999), *vacated and remanded on other grounds*, 769 A.2d 849 (Me. 2001); Stewart Title Guar. Co. v. WKC Restaurants Venture Co., 961 S.W.2d 874 (Mo. Ct. App. 1998).

345 *See* Silverman v. Eastrich Multiple Investor Fund, Ltd. P'ship, 51 F.3d 28 (3d Cir. 1995); Integra Bank/Pittsburgh v. Freeman, 839 F. Supp. 326, 329 (E.D. Pa. 1993) (while an ECOA violation should not void underlying credit transaction, an offending creditor should not be permitted to look for payment to parties who, but for the ECOA violation, would not have incurred personal liability on underlying debt in the first instance—the creditor is in no worse position than if it had followed the law when credit transaction occurred; but the purpose of the ECOA is not furthered by allowing the permissibly obligated guarantor to assert an ECOA violation as a defense to liability); Still v. Cunningham, 94 P. 3d 1104 (Alaska 2004).

346 Integra Bank/Pittsburgh, 839 F. Supp. 329–30 (E.D. Pa. Nov. 29, 1993) (injury may occur when, for example, an objectively qualified loan applicant or guarantor is nonetheless impermissibly required to secure a spouse's or other party's signature); *see* §§ 5.6, *supra*, 11.9.2.2, *infra.*

somewhat in that some refer to prevailing plaintiffs and some to plaintiffs in a successful action, all apply the same set of standards for determining awards of reasonable attorney fees and costs to plaintiffs. Some also allow awards to successful defendants, but under a much stricter standard, and some do not even authorize such awards.

The ECOA states that the costs of the action together with a reasonable attorney fee, as determined by the court, shall be awarded to a plaintiff in any successful action[347] but makes no provision for an award of fees to a prevailing creditor.[348] The Fair Housing Act and the federal Civil Rights Acts state that the court, in its discretion, may allow the prevailing *party* a reasonable attorney fee and costs.[349]

While the term "party" technically encompasses defendants too, different standards apply to prevailing plaintiffs as opposed to prevailing defendants. A unanimous United States Supreme Court in *Christiansburg Garment Co. v. Equal Employment Opportunity Commission*[350] held that prevailing plaintiffs in a Civil Rights Act case should recover "in all but special circumstances."[351] In contrast, prevailing defendants should only recover fees when the plaintiff's claim was frivolous, unreasonable, or without foundation.[352]

The Supreme Court has indicated that its rulings on various issues concerning Civil Rights Act attorney fee awards—such as those addressing partial success, use of a lodestar, and the like—are in general equally applicable to other federal laws (such as the ECOA) providing attorney fees for prevailing plaintiffs.[353] As a result, for all practical purposes, the various attorney fee provisions found in discrimination laws and con-sumer protection statutes can be treated as interchangeable, and the substantial case law on federal fee-shifting statutes generally should apply to the ECOA, Fair Housing Act, and the federal Civil Rights Acts.

Because of the extensive treatment of federal fee-shifting statutes in other treatises in the National Consumer Law Center's *Consumer Credit and Sales Legal Practice Series* and elsewhere, this section will only provide a brief overview of key Supreme Court cases and the case law specific to the ECOA, FHA and sections 1981 and 1982. Practitioners are urged to supplement this description by consulting other treatises and case law that discuss attorney fee principles under the federal consumer credit and other fee-shifting statutes.[354]

11.8.6.2 When Is an Action Successful?

Like several titles of the Consumer Credit Protection Act, the ECOA awards fees in a "successful action," while the Civil Rights Act standard is that fees are awarded when the aggrieved party "prevails." This is a distinction without a difference.[355]

The extent of a plaintiff's success is a crucial factor in determining the proper amount of attorney fees.[356] When the plaintiff prevails only in the technical sense of receiving nominal damages when large actual damages were sought and fails to obtain any of the other relief requested, attorney fees may be denied.[357]

A question that may arise is whether a consumer is entitled to an award of fees when successful on only one of a number of related claims. As a general rule, prevailing on only one central claim is sufficient for an award of fees on all the related

---

347 15 U.S.C. § 1691e(d).

The ECOA standard for attorney fees is virtually identical to that found in the Truth in Lending Act. *See* National Consumer Law Center, Truth in Lending § 11.9 (8th ed. 2012).

348 Courts in at least two cases in dicta have stated or implied that a prevailing defendant may not rely on the ECOA for an award of attorney fees. *See* Integra Bank/Pittsburgh v. Freeman, 839 F. Supp. 326 (E.D. Pa. 1995); Durdin v. Cheyenne Mountain Bank, 98 P. 3d 899 (Colo. App. 2004).

349 42 U.S.C. §§ 1988(b), 3613(c)(2); *see* Hunter v. Trenton Hous. Auth., 698 A.2d 25, 27 n.4 (N.J. Super. Ct. App. Div. 1997) (common law under federal civil rights litigation that prevailing party should ordinarily recover attorney fees absent special circumstances is equally applicable to FHA).

350 Christiansburg Garment Co. v. Equal Emp't Opportunity Comm'n, 434 U.S. 412, 98 S. Ct. 694, 54 L. Ed. 2d 648 (1978).

351 434 U.S. 417, 98 S. Ct. 694, 54 L. Ed. 2d 648 (1978). While the Court was interpreting Title VII of the Civil Rights Act, 42 U.S.C. § 2000e-5(k), the result should be the same under the Fair Housing Act and 42 U.S.C. § 1988.

352 Christiansburg Garment Co. v. Equal Emp't Opportunity Comm'n 434 U.S. 412, 421, 98 S. Ct. 694, 54 L. Ed. 2d 648 (1978); *see, e.g.*, Taylor v. Harbour Pointe Homeowners Ass'n, 690 F.3d 44, 50 (2d Cir. 2012) (FHA); Bryant Woods Inn, Inc. v. Howard Cnty., 124 F.3d 597 (4th Cir. 1997); *see also* Deadwyler v. Volkswagen of Am., Inc., 748 F. Supp. 1146 (W.D.N.C. 1990), *aff'd*, 1992 U.S. App. LEXIS 14891 (4th Cir. June 25, 1992) (per curiam) ("may" award defendant attorney fees interpreted as requiring fees only when action was frivolous).

353 Hensley v. Eckerhart, 461 U.S. 424, 103 S. Ct. 1933, 76 L. Ed. 2d 40 (1983) (Civil Rights Acts case).

354 In particular, see National Consumer Law Center, Truth in Lending § 11.9 (8th ed. 2012), dealing with attorney fees under the Truth in Lending Act, and National Consumer Law Center, Consumer Class Actions ch. 19 (8th ed. 2013).

355 Buckhannon Bd. & Care Home v. W. Va. Dep't of Health & Human Res., 532 U.S. 598, 603, 121 S. Ct. 1835, 149 L. Ed. 2d 855 (2001); *see, e.g.*, Crabill v. Trans Union, L.L.C., 259 F.3d 662 (7th Cir. 2001) (applying *Buckhannon* to the FCRA and concluding that attorney fees are not available unless plaintiff wins "formal judicial relief").

356 *See* Hensley v. Eckerhart, 461 U.S. 424, 103 S. Ct. 1933, 76 L. Ed. 2d 40 (1983); Tenafly Eruv Ass'n, Inc. v. Borough of Tenafly, 195 Fed. Appx. 93, 98 (3d Cir. 2006) (when unsuccessful Fair Housing Act claim arose from same core facts as successful Free Exercise Clause claim, fees could be awarded based on both claims); Postow v. OBA Fed. Sav. & Loan Ass'n, 627 F.2d 1370 (D.C. Cir. 1980) (Truth in Lending case); *cf*. Smith v. Northwest Financial Acceptance, Inc., 129 F.3d 1408, 1418–19 (10th Cir. 1997); Pigford v. Vilsack, 613 F. Supp. 2d 78 (D.D.C. 2009) (denying fees for work on farmer's unsuccessful ECOA claims that were not related to successful claims); Johnson v. Liberty Mortgage Corp. Northwest, 1997 U.S. Dist. LEXIS 15985 (N.D. Ill. Sept. 30, 1997) (no requirement that fees be proportional to damages), *aff'd*, 192 F.3d 656 (7th Cir. 1999).

357 *See* Farrar v. Hobby, 506 U.S. 103, 113 S. Ct. 566, 121 L. Ed. 2d 494 (1992) (one dollar nominal recovery when twelve million dollars sought). *But see* Buckhannon Bd. & Care Home v. West Va. Dep't of Health & Human Resources, 532 U.S. 598, 604, 121 S. Ct. 1835, 149 L. Ed. 2d 855 (2001) (award of nominal damages may be sufficient basis for award of attorney fees).

claims, but not for work done on claims that are both unrelated and unsuccessful.[358] This general rule applies even when the plaintiff does not prevail against all the defendants,[359] although of course the successful defendants will not be required to contribute to the payment of fees.

If the consumer prevails on an ECOA counterclaim to a creditor's collection action, fees should be awarded for work on the ECOA issues even if the action results in a net recovery for the creditor. If an action is by way of recoupment (after the statute of limitations has run on the discrimination claim), such that the discrimination claim can at most offset the creditor's collection action, an attorney fees award is not thereby limited to the amount at issue in the collection action. A successful defense is a successful action meriting an attorney fees award even if this award exceeds the amount sought by the creditor.[360]

An award of fees need not be predicated on litigating a claim to a final judgment. A consent decree,[361] injunctive relief,[362] or a settlement[363] also may be considered successful actions warranting fee awards. However, a settlement, even a highly favorable settlement, may not suffice as a basis for an award of attorney fees if it is not incorporated into a court order.[364]

Prior to the Supreme Court's decision in *Buckhannon Board and Care Home v. West Virginia Department of Health and Human Resources*, it was widely accepted that a voluntary change in practices or policies in response to a suit could qualify as a successful action. This "catalyst theory" held that a plaintiff prevails and is therefore entitled to a recovery under a federal statutory fee provision when the lawsuit is the cause of the defendant's change of conduct that results in the termination of the litigation.

In *Buckhannon*, the Court rejected the awarding of fees to plaintiffs as prevailing parties under the catalyst theory.[365] Because the plaintiffs in that case had not obtained an enforceable judgment on the merits or a court-ordered consent decree or anything akin thereto, they were not entitled to an award of fees.

The *Buckhannon* case construed the fee-shifting provisions of federal fair housing laws, including the Fair Housing Act and the Americans with Disabilities Act, but the Supreme Court made it clear that it was announcing a general rule that applied to most, if not all, federal fee-shifting statutes.[366] Courts have since applied the ruling to federal fee-shifting statutes which, like the statutes construed in *Buckhannon*, use the term "prevailing party," and also to those using the "successful action" formulation.[367]

Buckhannon states that an enforceable judgment on the merits or a "court-ordered consent decree" is sufficient,[368] and most courts have treated these as examples rather than an exclusive list. On the other hand, in a footnote, the Court contrasted these means of resolving a case with "private settlements" which "do not entail the judicial approval and oversight involved in consent decrees."[369] Although the Court stopped short of an explicit holding that a "private settlement" does not make a plaintiff a prevailing party, most courts have concluded that a private settlement which does not involve some judicial imprimatur or sanction cannot be a basis for a fee award in the absence of an explicit acknowledgment in the agreement that plaintiff's counsel is entitled to an award of reasonable attorney fees.[370] If, however, such an explicit acknowledgment is included in the settlement agreement, then generally neither the courts nor defendants question the right to an award of fees but only the reasonableness and amount thereof.[371]

---

358 Hensley v. Eckerhart, 461 U.S. 424, 103 S. Ct. 1933, 76 L. Ed. 2d 40 (1983).

359 *See generally* National Consumer Law Center, Truth in Lending § 11.9.8 (8th ed. 2012).

360 Carr v. Blazer Financial Servs., Inc., 598 F.2d 1368 (5th Cir. 1979) (Truth in Lending Act (TILA) case); Plant v. Blazer Fin. Servs., Inc., 598 F.2d 1357 (5th Cir. 1979) (TILA case); Bostic v. American Gen. Finance, Inc., 87 F. Supp. 2d 611 (S.D. W. Va. 2000); Burley v. Bastrop Loan Co., 407 F. Supp. 773 (W.D. La. 1975) (TILA case), *rev'd on other grounds*, 590 F.2d 160 (5th Cir. 1979); In re McCausland, 63 B.R. 665 (Bankr. E.D. Pa. 1986) (TILA case); In re DiCianno, 58 B.R. 810 (Bankr. E.D. Pa. 1986) (TILA case).

361 Balark v. City of Chi., 81 F.3d 658 (7th Cir. 1996) (section 1988 case); LaRouche v. Keezer, 20 F.3d 68 (2d Cir. 1994) (section 1988 case).

362 LeBlanc-Sternberg v. Vill. of Airmont, 143 F.3d 765 (2d Cir. 1998) (section 1988 case); Riley v. City of Jackson, 99 F.3d 757 (5th Cir. 1996) (section 1988 case); *cf.* Bisciglia v. Kenosha Unif. School Dist. No. 1, 45 F.3d 223 (7th Cir. 1995) (section 1988 case) (temporary restraining order which merely preserves status quo and does not result in relief on the merits is insufficient).

363 Sablan v. Dep't of Finance, 856 F.2d 1317 (9th Cir. 1988) (section 1988 case); Gram v. Bank of La., 691 F.2d 728 (5th Cir. 1982) (TILA case); Folsom v. Heartland Bank, 2000 U.S. Dist. LEXIS 7890 (D. Kan. May 18, 2000) (TILA case). *See generally* National Consumer Law Center, Truth in Lending § 11.9.2.1 (8th ed. 2012).

364 Buckhannon Bd. & Care Home v. West Va. Dep't of Health & Human Resources, 532 U.S. 598, 121 S. Ct. 1835, 149 L. Ed. 2d 855 (2001).

365 *Id.*, 532 U.S. at 600.

366 *Id.*, 532 U.S. at 600; *see, e.g.,* Hutchinson *ex rel.* Julien v. Patrick, 683 F. Supp. 2d 121, 124 n.1 (D. Mass. 2010) (stating that *Buckhannon* holding was "broadly applicable" and that courts have applied Supreme Court's "prevailing party" jurisprudence to all fee-shifting statutes using that terminology), *aff'd*, 636 F.3d 1 (1st Cir. 2011).

367 *See, e.g.,* Crabill v. Trans Union, 259 F.3d 662 (7th Cir. 2001) (applying *Buckhannon* to the Fair Credit Reporting Act and concluding that attorney fees are not available unless plaintiff wins "formal judicial relief").

368 Buckhannon Bd. & Care Home v. West Va. Dep't of Health & Human Resources, 532 U.S. 598, 121 S. Ct. 1835, 149 L. Ed. 2d 855 (2001).

369 *Id.*, 532 U.S. at 604 n.7.

370 Christina A. v. Bloomberg, 315 F.3d 990, 993 (8th Cir. 2003) (holding that plaintiffs were not prevailing parties by virtue of a court-approved settlement because it was not entered as a judgment on the merits or a consent decree and therefore was not enforceable by the court except by a new action for breach of contract); *see also* T.D. v. LaGrange School Dist. No. 102, 349 F.3d 469 (7th Cir. 2003); John T. v. Del. Cnty. Intermediate Unit, 318 F.3d 545, 558 (3d Cir. 2003).

371 *See, e.g.,* Jenkins v. Gen. Collection, Co., 2009 WL 3631014, at *2 (D. Neb. Oct. 26, 2009) (defendants agreed not to challenge plaintiffs' status as "prevailing parties" for the purpose of attorney fee motion or on appeal of court's award of attorney fees and costs).

What is a court-ordered consent decree and what is a private settlement? The key distinction is likely to be that a consumer has prevailed and is entitled to fees when a final order is entered in the case which permits the court, under the standards set forth in *Kokkonen v. Guardian Life Insurance Co.*[372] to retain jurisdiction for enforcement purposes.[373] An order need not include an admission of liability by the defendant to qualify as a consent decree.[374] If an order meets these standards, it need not be titled "Consent Decree," and it is immaterial whether it repeats the terms of the parties' agreement or incorporates them by referring to a separate document.[375] Thus, an order that cites or incorporates a stipulation that sets forth steps that the defendant agrees to take, thereby subjecting the parties' agreement to judicial oversight and enforcement, qualifies as a court-ordered consent decree.[376]

Even an order of dismissal can meet these standards, at least if the court retains jurisdiction to enforce compliance with the parties' agreement. In some circumstances a remand to an administrative agency also may meet *Buckhannon*'s requirements.[377] A preliminary injunction may be sufficient as a basis for fees, but not if it is reversed, dissolved, or otherwise undone by the final decision in the same case.[378]

Because the court must approve and enter judgment on the settlement of a certified class action,[379] the *Buckhannon* ruling should not affect the award of attorney fees in such actions. In addition, the following ways of settling a case are likely to preserve entitlement to fees:

- Negotiate the payment of fees in an acceptable amount as part of the settlement on the merits.[380]
- Obtain an agreed judgment for money, as long as it is clear that fees have not been waived. A money judgment is a "material alteration of the legal relationship of the parties,"[381] as it creates an obligation of one party to the other that is enforceable by judicial process. The ability to enforce a money judgment by judicial process should be considered the functional equivalent of the judicial oversight that was the hallmark of a court-ordered consent decree for the *Buckhannon* court.[382]
- Obtain an agreed order that specifies steps, sought by the plaintiff in the case, that the defendant will take, as long as the court retains jurisdiction to enforce these specific steps.[383] It is clearer that the plaintiff is the prevailing party if the order the court signs actually recites the steps the defendant will take rather than referring to a separate document, although courts have held that the latter format is also sufficient.

372 511 U.S. 375, 114 S. Ct. 1673, 128 L. Ed. 2d 391 (1994).

373 Richard S. v. Cal. Dep't of Developmental Servs., 317 F.3d 1080 (9th Cir. 2003); Truesdell v. Phila. Hous. Auth., 290 F.3d 159 (3d Cir. 2002) (district court's order incorporating plaintiff's settlement in mandatory terms is sufficient); American Disability Ass'n v. Chmielarz, 289 F.3d 1315 (11th Cir. 2002); Smyth v. Rivero, 282 F.3d 268 (4th Cir. 2002) (consent decree on which fees can be based is one that is enforceable as a judicial decree by the court that entered it); Rolland v. Romney, 292 F. Supp. 2d 268 (D. Mass. 2003) (fees are available under settlement that was judicially enforceable even though it precluded direct enforcement by contempt or breach of contract claim); Vasquez v. Cnty. of Lake, 2002 WL 31256166 (N.D. Ill. Oct. 7, 2002); Melton v. Frigidaire, 805 N.E.2d 322 (Ill. App. Ct. 2004).

374 Buckhannon Bd. & Care Home v. West Va. Dep't of Health & Human Resources, 532 U.S. 598, 121 S. Ct. 1835, 149 L. Ed. 2d 855 (2001); Smalbein v. City of Daytona Beach, 353 F.3d 901 (11th Cir. 2003).

375 T.D. v. LaGrange School Dist. No. 102, 349 F.3d 469 (7th Cir. 2003) (need not be labeled "consent decree"); American Disability Ass'n v. Chmielarz, 289 F.3d 1315 (11th Cir. 2002); Smyth v. Rivero, 282 F.3d 268 (4th Cir. 2002); Nat'l Coal. for Students with Disabilities v. Bush, 173 F. Supp. 2d 1272 (N.D. Fla. 2001) ("the appropriateness of an award of fees surely ought not turn on whether the court does or does not retype the provisions of a settlement agreement as part of an order compelling compliance").

376 Labotest, Inc. v. Bonta, 297 F.3d 892 (9th Cir. 2002) (order incorporating stipulation about steps defendant would take to resolve two claims made plaintiff a prevailing party even though the stipulation stated that it was not a determination of "the issue of plaintiff's entitlement to attorney fees"); Johnny's Icehouse, Inc. v. Amateur Hockey Ass'n, 2001 U.S. Dist. LEXIS 11671 (N.D. Ill. Aug. 7, 2001); *see* American Disability Ass'n v. Chmielarz, 289 F.3d 1315 (11th Cir. 2002) (order of dismissal that approved, adopted, and ratified settlement and retained jurisdiction to enforce it was consent decree and plaintiff was prevailing party). *But cf.* Smyth v. Rivero, 282 F.3d 268 (4th Cir. 2002) (entry dismissing case as moot because of defendant's change of policy was not a consent decree even though it referred to the parties' agreement on one of the issues).

377 *Compare* Former Emps. of Motorola Ceramic Products v. United States, 336 F.3d 1360 (Fed. Cir. 2003) (plaintiffs who obtained remand to agency were prevailing parties), *with* Vaughn v. Principi,

336 F.3d 1351 (Fed. Cir. 2003) (claimant who obtained remand was not prevailing party).

378 Sole v. Wyner, 551 U.S. 74, 127 S. Ct. 2188, 167 L. Ed. 2d 1069 (2007).

379 Fed. R. Civ. P. 23(e).

380 *See* Evans v. Jeff D., 475 U.S. 717, 106 S. Ct. 1531 (1986) (indicating simultaneous fee and merits discussions are acceptable during settlement negotiations if statutory fee is involved). *But see* Albe Conte & Herbert Newberg, Newberg on Class Actions § 1531 (4th ed. 2002) ("Within the context of negotiating for a common fund settlement on behalf of a class, class counsel would have a direct conflict with the class in negotiating for or accepting the defendant's offer for a specific fee award to be paid by the settling defendant, simultaneously with negotiating for a sum for a common recovery for the class").

381 Buckhannon Bd. & Care Home v. West Va. Dep't of Health & Human Resources, 532 U.S. 598, 121 S. Ct. 1835, 1840, 149 L. Ed. 2d 855 (2001).

382 *Id.* at 603 (defining "prevailing party" as one in whose favor a judgment is rendered); Util. Automation 2000, Inc. v. Choctawhatchee Electric Coop., Inc., 298 F.3d 1238 (11th Cir. 2002) (entry of Rule 68 judgment is basis for attorney fees if Marek v. Chesney, 473 U.S. 1, 105 S. Ct. 3012, 87 L. Ed. 2d 1 (1985), does not bar them); Dennis v. Columbia Collection Medical Ctr., Inc., 290 F.3d 639 (4th Cir. 2002) (party who obtains a judgment prevails); Pitchford v. Oakwood Mobile Homes, Inc., 212 F. Supp. 2d 613 (W.D. Va. 2002) (implying that settlement would have been basis for fees if it had been incorporated into court order); *see also* Walker v. City of Mesquite, 313 F.3d 246 (5th Cir. 2002).

383 *See* Perez v. Westchester Cnty. Dep't of Corrections, 587 F.3d 143 (2d Cir. 2009); American Disability Ass'n v. Chmielarz, 289 F.3d 1315 (11th Cir. 2002) (dismissal order that approved, adopted, and ratified settlement, and retained jurisdiction to enforce it, was consent decree and plaintiff was prevailing party).

- Obtain an agreed order of any sort that includes a finding or stipulation that the plaintiff is the prevailing party or is entitled to fees in an amount to be determined by the court.[384] Even a stipulation between the parties, not signed by the court, that the plaintiff is the prevailing party is probably sufficient. While *Buckhannon* does not explicitly endorse this method of preserving the right to attorney fees, the Supreme Court never indicated that winning an enforceable judgment or a court-ordered consent decree is a jurisdictional requirement that cannot be satisfied by a stipulation. Merely reserving the issue of attorney fees for the court, without stipulation that the plaintiff is the prevailing party, may be insufficient, however.[385]
- Negotiate a settlement agreement that provides monetary or other relief to the plaintiff, stipulates that plaintiff has prevailed or has been successful in the action, states that plaintiff is entitled to an award of reasonable attorney fees or at least that defendant does not contest plaintiff's right to such fees, and that the matter of the reasonableness of the fees will be resolved by motion to be heard by the court.

The following settlement methods are less likely to preserve the right to fees:

- A stipulation resolving the merits of the case that is not signed by the court and also does not state that the plaintiff is the prevailing party, even if filed with the court.[386]
- An entry of dismissal, even if the case is dismissed pursuant to an agreement signed by the parties under which the defendant agrees to the relief the plaintiff sought, unless the order embodies or at least refers to the settlement agreement, preferably while retaining jurisdiction to enforce it.

- A favorable monetary settlement with no judicial imprimatur whatsoever.[387]

Cases that seek primarily declaratory or injunctive relief rather than damages are more vulnerable to being rendered moot by unilateral action on the part of the defendant. However, voluntary cessation of a practice does not render a case moot "unless it is absolutely clear that the allegedly wrongful behavior could not reasonably be expected to recur."[388] While a government agency's agreement to change its regulations or a legislature's revision of a statute may make it unlikely that the challenged conduct will recur, a company's unilateral cessation of a practice provides little or no such assurance. Furthermore, even if the declaratory and injunctive claims become moot, that will not prevent consumers from proceeding with damage claims and recovering attorney fees if successful in that regard.[389]

Buckhannon only controls as to federal law. Courts interpreting state fee-shifting statutes may find *Buckhannon* persuasive[390] but are free to adopt their own views about the catalyst theory and the formal requirements of settlements. For example, "California law continues to recognize the catalyst theory and does not require 'a judicially recognized change in the legal relationship between the parties' as a prerequisite for obtaining attorney's fees."[391] Instead, the plaintiff need only establish that the lawsuit was a catalyst motivating the defendants to provide the primary relief sought, that the lawsuit had merit and achieved its catalytic effect by threat of victory and not by threat of its being a nuisance suit, and that the plaintiffs reasonably tried to settle the case before filing the lawsuit.[392] Absent an express state court decision to the contrary, however, it is prudent to assume that state courts will follow *Buckhannon* and to draft settlement documents accordingly.

384　*See* Gomes v. Trustees & President of Univ. of Me., 2003 WL 22004092 (D. Me. Aug. 23, 2003) ("Of course, there is an even more fundamental obstacle that prevents the defendants from qualifying as the prevailing party in this litigation: they never obtained an order from this Court that served to materially alter their legal relationship with the plaintiffs."); Pitchford v. Oakwood Mobile Homes, Inc., 212 F. Supp. 2d 613 (W.D. Va. 2002) (settlement that merely reserved fee issue for court insufficient; court says that it would have sufficed if parties had stipulated that plaintiff was entitled to fees and that court would decide amount).

385　Dorfsman v. Law School Admission Council, 2001 WL 1754726 (E.D. Pa. Nov. 28, 2001); *see also* Oil, Chem. & Atomic Workers Int'l Union v. Dep't of Energy, 288 F.3d 452 (D.C. Cir. 2002) (no fees despite stipulation that dismissal is "without prejudice to the right of plaintiff to obtain . . . an award of attorney's fees"; not discussing whether this provision amounted to a stipulation that plaintiff was prevailing party); Pitchford v. Oakwood Mobile Homes, Inc., 212 F. Supp. 2d 613 (W.D. Va. 2002) (settlement that merely reserved fee issue for court insufficient; stating that it would have sufficed if parties had stipulated that plaintiff was entitled to fees and that court would decide amount). *But cf.* Richard S. v. Cal. Dep't of Developmental Servs., 317 F.3d 1080 (9th Cir. 2003) (stipulation that court retained jurisdiction to resolve attorney fee issues was sufficient when settlement agreement was binding and enforceable by court order).

386　*See, e.g.*, P.N. v. Seattle School Dist., 474 F.3d 1165 (9th Cir. 2007).

387　*See, e.g.*, Petersen v. Gibson, 372 F.3d 862 (7th Cir. 2004).

388　Buckhannon Bd. & Care Home v. West Va. Dep't of Health & Human Resources, 532 U.S. 598, 609, 121 S. Ct. 1835, 149 L. Ed. 2d 855 (2001).

389　*Id.*

390　*See, e.g.*, Wallerstein v. Stew Leonard's Dairy, 780 A.2d 916 (Conn. 2001) (judgment entered under Connecticut equivalent of Rule 68 made plaintiff the prevailing party).

391　Tipton-Whittingham v. City of Los Angeles, 21 Cal. Rptr. 3d 371 (Cal. 2004); *see also* Hugee v. Kimso Apartments, L.L.C. 852 F. Supp. 2d 281, 295 (E.D.N.Y. 2012) (in this fair housing claim by a disabled tenant, noting that New York City's Human Rights Law expressly recognizes the catalyst theory as a basis for prevailing party status); Graham v. Daimler Chrysler Corp., 21 Cal. Rptr. 3d 331 (Cal. 2004); Humphries v. Powder Mill Shopping Plaza, 2011 WL 6127 (N.J. Super. Ct. App. Div. Nov. 4, 2010) (catalyst test is appropriate for determining whether a party is a prevailing one under state law; a settlement that confers relief may still entitle plaintiff to attorney fees in fee-shifting matters), *cert. granted*, 16 A.3d 385 (N.J. 2011), *aff'd in part, rev'd in part on other grounds, and remanded*, Walker v. Giuffre, 35 A.3d 1177 (N.J. 2012); *cf.* Upper Gwynedd Towamencin Mun. Auth. v. Dep't of Envtl. Prot., 9 A.3d 255 (Pa. Commw. Ct. 2010) (catalyst rule may be applied under certain circumstances).

392　Tipton-Whittingham v. City of Los Angeles, 21 Cal. Rptr. 3d 371 (Cal. 2004).

11.8.6.3 Fees for Legal Services, Pro Bono, and *Pro Se* Attorneys

Attorney fees should be awarded to legal services attorneys or other pro bono attorneys, even though the client is not obligated to pay the attorney or even though a fee is not actually charged.[393] Legal services attorneys are generally entitled to market rates in fee-shifting cases.[394] Most circuits, though, refuse to provide attorney fees to *pro se* litigants, irrespective of whether that litigant is an attorney.[395]

11.8.6.4 Calculating the Award

The different circuit courts have adopted somewhat different approaches to calculating attorney fee awards, and some Supreme Court decisions have further complicated the issue. This subsection will only briefly sketch the general approach used by the federal courts, known as the "lodestar" method. The lodestar is the number of allowable hours times a reasonable hourly rate. Allowable hours must be actually documented and reasonably expended.[396] Duplicative or excessive time will not be compensated.

The exact amount of a fee award is in the court's discretion, and an appellate court will only review the amount for an abuse of discretion.[397] But the circuit courts have adopted standards for calculating these awards. Failure to follow these standards, or even failure to show clearly that these standards were followed, may result in reversal.[398]

The allowable hours are those hours claimed and documented by the attorneys that were reasonably expended in reaching a favorable result.[399] The reasonableness of positions taken by plaintiff in settlement negotiations may effect a court's view of the reasonableness of the hours requested.[400] If there is a common core of facts or if the legal theories are related, the attorney should be compensated not only for time spent on claims that succeeded but for all reasonable work on the case, even on counts that failed and for claims that do not provide for attorney fees.[401] Attorney fees should compensate not only attorney time spent but also time spent by paralegals and law clerks who work on a case.[402]

The number of hours reasonably spent is then multiplied by a reasonable hourly rate for the attorney (or paralegal or law clerk). The hourly rate is based on the prevailing rate in the community for an individual with that level of legal skill and experience.[403] Evidence of the prevailing market rate includes affidavits from similarly qualified attorneys, information about fees awarded in analogous cases, and evidence of the fee applicant's rates during the relevant time.[404] Legal aid attorneys and other pro bono attorneys should receive the same hourly rate as attorneys of comparable skill and experience in private practice.[405] While the attorney's customary hourly rate, the rate billed to the consumer or other clients, or the cost of the attorney's time may all be considered as evidence of market rate, none of these is dispositive.[406]

The product of the number of allowable hours times the allowable hourly rate is called the lodestar figure. Once this number is calculated, courts may increase or decrease that number based on various factors.[407] Enhancement of the lodestar, however, is permissible only in "rare and exceptional circumstances."[408]

---

393 Blanchard v. Bergeron, 489 U.S. 87, 109 S. Ct. 939, 103 L. Ed. 2d 67 (1989) (lawyer taking case without compensation does not bar attorney fees award). *See generally* National Consumer Law Center, Truth in Lending § 11.9.3.2 (8th ed. 2012).

394 Blum v. Stenson, 465 U.S. 886, 104 S. Ct. 1541, 79 L. Ed. 2d 891 (1984) (42 U.S.C. § 1988); *see, e.g.,* Rosie D. *ex rel.* John D. v. Patrick, 593 F. Supp. 2d 325 (D. Mass. 2009).

395 Kay v. Ehrler, 499 U.S. 432, 111 S. Ct. 1435, 113 L. Ed. 2d 486 (1991) (civil rights claim). *See generally* National Consumer Law Center, Truth in Lending § 11.9.3.3 (8th ed. 2012).

396 Hensley v. Eckerhart, 461 U.S. 424, 103 S. Ct. 1933, 76 L. Ed. 2d 40 (1983).

397 *See, e.g., id.;* Preferred Properties, Inc. v. Indian River Estates, Inc., 214 Fed. Appx. 538 (6th Cir. 2007) (affirming award under Fair Housing Act, finding no abuse of discretion).

398 *See, e.g.,* Hensley v. Eckerhart, 461 U.S. 424, 103 S. Ct. 1933, 76 L. Ed. 2d. 40 (1983). *See generally* National Consumer Law Center, Truth in Lending § 11.9.4.1 (8th ed. 2012).

399 Hensley v. Eckerhart, 461 U.S. 424, 103 S. Ct. 1933, 76 L. Ed. 2d 40 (1983); *see also* Ingram v. Oroudjian, 647 F.3d 925, 928 (9th Cir. 2011) (finding that district court in this FHA action against a landlord did not abuse its discretion in disallowing time it viewed as having been spent unnecessarily on certain issues).

400 Ingram v. Oroudjian, 647 F.3d 925, 928 (9th Cir. 2011).

401 *Id.* (noting that separating out the hours would be very difficult); *see* Hensley v. Eckerhart, 461 U.S. 424, 440, 103 S. Ct. 1933, 1943 (1983) ("Where a lawsuit consists of related claims, a plaintiff who has won substantial relief should not have his attorney's fee reduced simply because the district court did not adopt each contention raised.").

402 *Cf.* Blanchard v. Bergeron, 489 U.S. 87, 109 S. Ct. 939, 103 L. Ed. 2d 67 (1989) (reserving for another day the issue of fees for legal assistants). However, scores of lower courts have approved substantial awards for paralegal and law clerk time.

403 Blum v. Stenson, 465 U.S. 886, 104 S. Ct. 1541, 79 L. Ed. 2d 891 (1984).

404 *See* Ingram v. Oroudjian, 647 F.3d 925, 928 (9th Cir. 2011) (noting the failure to submit such affidavits as a factor in upholding the district court's reliance on its own knowledge of local market rates and reasonable fees).

405 *Id.; see* § 11.8.6.3, *supra.*

406 Blanchard v. Bergeron, 489 U.S. 87, 97, 109 S. Ct. 939, 103 L. Ed. 2d 67 (1989); Keenan v. City of Phila., 983 F.2d 459, 475 (3d Cir. 1992); Covington v. Dist. of Columbia, 839 F. Supp. 894 (D.D.C. 1993); *cf.* People Who Care v. Rockford Bd. of Education, 90 F.3d 1307 (7th Cir. 1996) (section 1988 case) (attorney's actual billing rate for comparable work is presumptively appropriate to use as the market rate).

407 Hensley v. Eckerhart, 461 U.S. 424, 103 S. Ct. 1933, 76 L. Ed. 2d 240 (1983).

408 Perdue v. Kenny A. *ex rel.* Winn, 130 S. Ct. 1662 (2010) (giving as examples of such exceptional circumstances: when method used to determine hourly rate does not adequately measure attorney's true market value; when attorney's performance includes an extraordinary outlay of expenses and the litigation is exceptionally protracted; and when there is exceptional delay in payment of fees, particularly when delay is unjustifiably caused by the defense).

11.8.6.5 Fee Applications

The Federal Rules of Civil Procedure require motions for attorney fees and expenses to be filed and served no later than fourteen days after judgment.[409] However, all that is required in this time period is notice to the court and to the opposite side that fees will be sought and a fair estimate of the total fees and expenses claimed. A detailed record of hours and rates, affidavits, time records, fee surveys, and other supporting evidence and briefs may be submitted "in due course" following the motion for fees.[410]

The burden of justifying the amount of an attorney fee award falls on the consumer's attorney, who should justify in detail the number of hours claimed, the hourly rates, and any factors claimed to adjust the lodestar upward.[411] Insufficient documentation will be used to reduce the award.[412] While the Supreme Court has not described the standards for record keeping in detail, contemporaneous time records are the preferred practice.[413] Furthermore, counsel "should maintain time records in a manner which will enable a reviewing court to identify distinct claims."[414] So-called "block billing" may cause a court to question the reasonableness of the hours claimed.[415]

11.8.6.6 Costs and Witness Fees

A successful plaintiff should recover costs under an ECOA, Fair Housing Act, or federal Civil Rights Act claim.[416] Costs generally include filing fees, transcripts, deposition costs for at least some depositions, certain expert fees and, other court and litigation expenses not otherwise claimed as attorney fees.[417] In addition, for actions under 42 U.S.C. § 1981, Congress has explicitly granted courts discretion to award expert witness fees

in conjunction with an attorney fees award.[418]

11.8.6.7 Attorney Fees for Litigation of the Fee Award

Attorney fees must be awarded for time reasonably spent recovering fees through a fee application and related proceedings.[419]

11.8.6.8 Appeals of Attorney Fees Awards

If the action is successful but the attorney fees award is inadequate, this issue alone may be appealed.[420] Even if the client does not wish to pursue the appeal, the attorney has standing to do so.[421] If the appeal is successful, fees for time spent on it are likewise recoverable.[422] If the appeal is unsuccessful but the consumer ultimately prevails on remand or thereafter, hours spent on the unsuccessful appeal may be compensable.[423]

11.8.6.9 Interim Fees

In protracted litigation, creditors may slowly deplete the resources of the consumer's attorney by requiring the expenditure of numerous hours that may not be compensated, if at all, until after the termination of the litigation. In some cases interim fees may be awarded, which may support the litigation or place additional pressure upon the lender to settle. In order to qualify for an interim award of fees, the applicant must have prevailed at least to some degree on the merits of his or her claim.[424]

11.8.6.10 Apportionment of Award Among Defendants

Courts may apportion the fee award among several unsuccessful defendants to ensure that a single defendant is not liable for fees greater than those incurred to litigate the case against that defendant. If some but not all the defendants settle, the total

409 Fed. R. Civ. P. 54(d)(2)(B).

410 *See also* Fed. R. Civ. P. 54 advisory committee's note (1993); Matthew Diller, *The Impact of the 1993 Amendments to the Federal Rules of Civil Procedure on Legal Services Practice in the Federal Courts*, 28 Clearinghouse Rev. 134, 140 (June 1994).

 Some local rules may include specific procedures for fee petitions, including deadlines, required supporting documents to be filed by plaintiffs, and identification by defendants of fees they do not contest.

411 Hensley v. Eckerhart, 461 U.S. 424, 103 S. Ct. 1933, 76 L. Ed. 2d 40 (1983). *See generally* National Consumer Law Center, Consumer Class Actions § 19.3.6 (8th ed. 2013); National Consumer Law Center, Truth in Lending § 11.9.4 (8th ed. 2012).

412 Hensley v. Eckerhart, 461 U.S. 424, 103 S. Ct. 1933, 76 L. Ed. 2d 40 (1983).

413 Keenan v. City of Phila., 983 F.2d 459, 472 (3d Cir. 1992) (citing Webb v. Bd. of Education, 471 U.S. 234, 238 n.6 (1985)).

414 Hensley v. Eckerhart, 461 U.S. 424, 437, 103 S. Ct. 1933, 76 L. Ed. 2d 40 (1983).

415 Block billing refers to listing, in a single block, various activities together with the total time spent on all of them. *See, e.g.,* Dixon-Rollins v. Experian Info. Solutions, Inc., 2010 WL 3734547, at *3–4 (E.D. Pa. Sept. 23, 2010) (reducing number of hours).

416 15 U.S.C. § 1691e(d); 42 U.S.C. §§ 1988(b), 3613(c)(2).

417 National Consumer Law Center, Truth in Lending § 11.9.4.5 (8th ed. 2012).

418 42 U.S.C. § 1988(c).

419 Comm'r, Immigration & Naturalization Serv. v. Jean, 496 U.S. 154, 110 S. Ct. 2316, 110 L. Ed. 2d 134 (1990); *see* National Consumer Law Center, Truth in Lending § 11.9.2.3 (8th ed. 2012).

420 Price v. Franklin Inv. Co., 574 F.2d 594 (D.C. Cir. 1978).

 The judgment on the merits and the attorney fees award are separate appealable orders. Budinich v. Becton Dickinson & Co., 486 U.S. 196, 108 S. Ct. 1717, 100 L. Ed. 2d 178 (1988).

421 *See* National Consumer Law Center, Truth in Lending § 11.9.2.4 (8th ed. 2012).

422 Comm'r, Immigration & Naturalization Serv. v. Jean, 496 U.S. 154, 110 S. Ct. 2316, 110 L. Ed. 2d 134 (1990). *See generally* National Consumer Law Center, Truth in Lending § 11.9.2.4 (8th ed. 2012).

423 *See generally* National Consumer Law Center, Truth in Lending § 11.9.2.4 (8th ed. 2012).

424 Hanrahan v. Hampton, 446 U.S. 754, 757, 100 S. Ct. 1987, 64 L. Ed. 2d 670 (1980) (applying 42 U.S.C. § 1988). *See generally* National Consumer Law Center, Truth in Lending § 11.9.7 (8th ed. 2012).

award may be reduced by the amount allocated to attorney fees by any settlement.[425]

11.9 Creditor Defenses

11.9.1 General

This section focuses on the most common creditor defense, the alleged expiration of the statute of limitations, and on additional defenses unique to FHA and ECOA claims. Another frequent defense argument is that false statements in the plaintiff's loan application constitute unclean hands that bar recovery. While a few courts have agreed,[426] the better-reasoned view is that the defense does not apply "where Congress authorizes broad equitable relief to serve important national policies,"[427] as it has done in both the ECOA and FHA.[428]

Creditors may also raise common law defenses in credit discrimination cases.[429] For example, at least one court agreed with the defendants that the plaintiff waived the right to raise the ECOA as a defense by signing a general release of liability. Inasmuch as these defenses are state-specific, they will not be discussed here.

11.9.2 Statute of Limitations

11.9.2.1 Affirmative Actions

11.9.2.1.1 ECOA and FHA claims

11.9.2.1.1.1 General rules: two- or five-year statute of limitations

Until recently, the ECOA and FHA statutes of limitations overlapped. The ECOA limitations period was two years, as is still the case with the FHA period. The ECOA limitations period, though, has been increased to five years by the Dodd-Frank Wall Street Reform and Consumer Protection Act,[430] effective as of July 21, 2011.[431] The ECOA and FHA are often

governed by similar rules, for example regarding tolling, while in other circumstances there are significant disparities.

The longer ECOA statute of limitations should be applicable to claims that had not yet expired under the two-year statute of limitations as of the effective date of July 21, 2011, even if the claims had not yet been filed on that date.[432] The longer limitations period may not apply to claims that by July 20, 2011, were outside the two-year limitations period.[433] In other words, the five-year limitations period most clearly applies to claims accruing on or after July 21, 2009.[434]

In general, the statute of limitations runs from the date the violation occurs.[435] Depending on the circumstances, however, grounds may exist for extending the time period for bringing an ECOA or FHA claim. These include: (1) the discovery rule; (2) the continuing violation doctrine; and (3) equitable tolling, including fraudulent concealment. Each of these doctrines will be discussed in turn in the subsections below.

In addition, tolling may occur during the pendency of an appropriate federal agency proceeding[436] or a United States

---

425 Corder v. Brown, 25 F.3d 833 (9th Cir. 1994).

426 Beaulialice v. Fed. Home Loan Mortgage Corp., 2007 WL 744646, at *8 (M.D. Fla. Mar. 6, 2007); Riggs Nat'l Bank v. Linch, 829 F. Supp. 163, 169 n.7 (E.D. Va. 1993), *aff'd on other grounds*, Riggs Nat'l Bank v. Linch, 36 F.3d 370 (4th Cir. 1994).

427 McKennon v. Nashville Banner Publ'g Co., 513 U.S. 352, 356–57 (1995) (holding that equitable defense of employee misconduct could not preclude employer liability for violating the ADEA).

428 Ramirez v. Greenpoint, 268 F.R.D. 627, 637–38 (N.D. Cal. 2010) (in a case alleging disparate impact in mortgage lending, deciding issue of the effect of misrepresentations in loan application in the context of whether named plaintiffs were typical of the class due to alleged unique defenses against them).

429 Zollman v. Geneva Leasing Assocs., Inc., 780 N.E.2d 387 (Ill. App. Ct. 2002) (plaintiff barred from raising ECOA as an affirmative defense to enforcement of guaranty).

430 15 U.S.C. § 1691e(f), *as amended by* Pub. L. No. 111-203, tit. X, § 1085 (July 21, 2010); 2010 U.S.C.C.A.N. (124 Stat. 1376) 2085.

431 This amendment is found in the Act's Title X (§§ 1001–1100H), Pub. L. No. 111-203, § 1085. Pub. Law 111-203, § 1100G, specifies an effective date for Title X provisions as of the "designated

transfer date." 75 Fed. Reg. 57,252 (Sept. 20, 2010) sets the designated transfer date as July 21, 2011.

432 Several cases have applied an amended, longer statute of limitations to claims not yet barred when the new statute of limitations became effective. *See* Thistlethwaite v. Dowty Woodville Polymer, Ltd., 6 F. Supp. 2d 263 (S.D.N.Y. 1998) (False Claims Act); *see also* Papenthein v. Papenthien, 120 F.3d 1025 (9th Cir. 1995) (retroactively applying state law statute of limitations); Lamke v. Sunstate Equip. Co., 387 F. Supp. 2d 1044 (N.D. Cal. 2004) (same); Thompson v. City of Shasta Lake, 314 F. Supp. 2d 1017 (E.D. Cal. 2004) (same); Motley v. Motley, 60 F. Supp. 2d 380 (D.N.J. 1999) (same); Reeves v. State, 288 S.W.3d 577 (Ark. 2008) (same); Mohica v. 4311 Wilshire, L.L.C., 141 Cal. App. 4th 1069 (Cal. Ct. App. 2005) (same); Roe v. Doe, 20 A.3d 787 (Md. 2011) (same).

 Two decisions issued shortly after the Dodd-Frank Act's passage may be cited concerning the retroactive application of limitations periods extended by it, but neither contradicts the cited line of cases. In Riddle v. Dyncorp., Int'l, 2010 WL 3304245 (N.D. Tex. Aug. 19, 2010), the question was whether the new, longer period under the False Claims Act applies to a claim *which was otherwise already barred at the time the Dodd-Frank Act passed*, since the Act did not explicitly state that the new statute of limitations should be applied retroactively. Additionally, the statement regarding the retroactive application of ECOA in Citgo Petroleum Corp. v. Bulk Petroleum Corp., 2010 WL 3212751 (N.D. Okla. Aug. 12, 2010), was just dicta, since the claim was raised defensively and therefore, as the court held, not barred in any event by the old, shorter limitations period. Neither case contained any discussion or analysis of retroactivity jurisprudence.

433 Citgo Petroleum Corp. v. Bulk Petroleum Corp., 2010 WL 3212751 (N.D. Okla. Aug. 12, 2010) (observing in dicta that a defendant has a property interest once a statute of limitations has run).

434 *But see* Haug v. PNC Financial Servs. Group, Inc., 2013 WL 980440, at *5 (N.D. Ohio Mar. 12, 2013) (in a case filed in 2012 regarding claims arising in 2006, stating in dicta that "any ECOA claim accruing before July 21, 2010, is subject to a two-year limitations period, not the subsequently enacted five-year period").

435 For example, if the claim is in connection with loan servicing, treatment after default, or account administration, the claim runs from occurrence of the alleged discriminatory treatment.

436 *See* 15 U.S.C. § 1691c(a); Reg. B, 12 C.F.R. pt. 1002 [pt. 202] app. A (complete list of federal agencies with ECOA enforcement

Attorney General ECOA civil action[437] that is commenced within the applicable statutory period (now five years) from the date of the occurrence of the violation.[438] In these situations, a victim of the discrimination at issue in the proceeding may bring a private action up to one year after the *commencement* of that proceeding or civil action.[439]

A separate issue is the possible waiver of the usual ECOA statute of limitations when the government is the creditor. In one extraordinary case, Congress in 1999 briefly waived the ECOA statute of limitations for a very narrow class of claimants: African-American farmers who had filed an administrative complaint of non-employment-related discrimination by the United States Department of Agriculture in its agricultural credit programs.[440] The extension of time applied to African-American farmers who had filed their administrative complaint between 1981 and July 1, 1997, provided they filed suit by October 21, 2000.[441]

The statute of limitations for a private cause of action arising under the Fair Housing Act is two years after the occurrence or termination of the discriminatory practice.[442] In contrast, an administrative complaint only may be filed within one year after the occurrence.[443] However, the two-year period is then tolled while any such administrative action is proceeding.[444]

11.9.2.1.1.2 When the statute begins to run

In most cases, the plaintiff discovers the injury on the same date as the violation,[445] and courts will have no difficulty in finding that the statute began to run on that date. Sometimes, however, the plaintiff does not discover the violation until sometime later. In these circumstances, a minority of courts have followed the federal discovery rule and found that the statute does not begin to run until the plaintiff discovered, or in the exercise of reasonable diligence should have discovered, the injury.[446]

For example, in a credit discrimination claim brought under the ECOA, the creditor argued that the alleged violation, if any, occurred on the date the plaintiff entered into the contract. The plaintiff countered, and the court agreed, that the statute did not begin to run until the plaintiff knew or should have known that she was being discriminated against, in this case when she met with attorneys to discuss the case.[447] In a case arising from a

---

powers and the creditors subject to each agency's jurisdiction); § 12.2, *infra*.

437 15 U.S.C. § 1691e(f)(2).

438 15 U.S.C. § 1691e(f)(1).

439 15 U.S.C. § 1691e(f).

It is also worth noting that as there is no statute of limitations in 15 U.S.C. § 1691c, dealing with administrative enforcement, an enforcing agency may use the general five-year statute of limitations, 28 U.S.C. § 2462. United States v. Blake, 751 F. Supp. 951 (W.D. Okla. 1990); Fed. Trade Comm'n v. Green Tree Acceptance, Inc., 1987 U.S. Dist. LEXIS 16750, Consumer Cred. Guide (CCH) ¶ 95,905 (N.D. Tex. Sept. 30, 1987).

440 *See* Agricultural, Rural Dev., Food and Drug Administration, and Related Agencies Appropriation Act, 1999, Pub. L. No. 105-277, § 741, 112 Stat. 2681 (interim rule codified at 7 U.S.C. § 2297). *See generally* § 2.2.5.6, *supra*.

441 *See, e.g.*, Stovall v. Veneman, 394 F. Supp. 2d 21 (D.D.C. 2005) (rejecting plaintiff African-American farmer's claim to extend ECOA statute of limitations because he did not file complaint until 2004 and his claims were based on events that occurred between 1999 and 2001).

442 42 U.S.C. § 3613(a)(1)(A).

443 42 U.S.C. § 3610.

444 42 U.S.C. § 3613(a)(1)(B); *see, e.g.*, Boykin v. Keycorp, 521 F.3d 202 (2d Cir. 2008); *see also* § 11.5.2, *supra* (administrative proceedings).

445 *See, e.g.*, Stonecrest Partners, L.L.C. v. Bank of Hampton Roads, 2010 WL 3732100 (E.D.N.C. Sept. 8, 2010) (holding that wives required to guarantee husbands' loans were deemed to know the legal effect of the documents they signed when they signed them).

446 *See, e.g.*, Estate of Wilson v. Union Acceptance Corp., 2002 WL 31730920 (S.D. Ind. Nov. 19, 2002) (applying discovery rule to ECOA claim); Jones v. Ford Motor Credit Co., 2002 WL 1334812 (S.D.N.Y. June 17, 2002), *vacated*, 358 F.3d 205 (2d Cir. N.Y. 2004) (vacating district court judgment, which dismissed car company's counterclaims and remanding to district court to rule on class certification and on supplemental jurisdiction over counterclaims); Jones v. Citibank, 844 F. Supp. 437, 440–41 (N.D. Ill. 1994) (applying discovery rule to FHA claim). *But see* Archer v. Nissan Motor Acceptance Corp., 550 F.3d 506 (5th Cir. 2008) (discovery rule did not apply because the limitations period in the ECOA is triggered by occurrence of the violation, not its discovery; state's applicable discovery rule did not toll state law limitations period because injury was not a latent one); Garcia v. Brockway, 526 F.3d 456 (9th Cir. 2008) (discovery rule did not apply to FHA design and construction claim); Mays v. Buckeye Rural Electric Coop., Inc., 277 F.3d 873 (6th Cir. 2002); Haug v. PNC Financial Servs. Group, Inc., 2013 WL 980440, at *5 (N.D. Ohio Mar. 12, 2013) (the ECOA limitations period begins to run at the time the violation occurs, not "at the time when the consequences of the action become painful," (quoting Mays v. Buckeye Rural Electric Coop., Inc.)); Thiel v. Veneman, 859 F. Supp. 2d 1182, 1187 (D. Mont. 2012) (discovery rule does not apply to ECOA claims); King v. Ameriquest Mortgage Co., 2009 WL 3681688 (D. Md. Oct. 30, 2009) (period begins with awareness of conduct, not the legal basis for claims); Ruggiero v. K Bank, 2009 WL 1708076 (E.D. Pa. June 17, 2009) (ECOA period begins to run on date wives' guarantees of their husbands' loans was required, not the later discovery of alleged violation); Claybrooks v. Primus Automotive Financial Servs., Inc., 363 F. Supp. 2d 969 (M.D. Tenn. 2005) ("the language of the statute and the apparent intent of Congress in amending 15 U.S.C. § 1691e(f) preclude application of a general discovery rule" to ECOA claim); Mills v. Equicredit Corp., 294 F. Supp. 2d 903 (E.D. Mich. 2003) (statute not tolled because any terms of the loan that could be deemed to be unfair or unaffordable were disclosed in loan agreement and in documents signed by plaintiff); Lewis v. Glickman, 104 F. Supp. 2d 1311, 1319, 1320 (D. Kan. 2000) (following the "general rule in the discrimination context" that the cause of action accrues when the individual first receives notice of adverse action against him and not when effects of that action are felt), *aff'd*, 2002 WL 1435904 (10th Cir. July 3, 2002); Stern v. Espirito Santo Bank, 791 F. Supp. 865 (S.D. Fla. 1992).

Several recent decisions in putative mortgage discrimination class actions have declined to reach the issue. *See, e.g.*, Miller v. Countrywide Bank, 571 F. Supp. 2d 251, 262 (D. Mass. 2008) (motion to dismiss rejected based on tolling under the continuing violation doctrine rather than resolving whether discovery rule applied).

447 Jones v. Ford Motor Credit Co., 2002 U.S. Dist. LEXIS 1098 (S.D.N.Y. Jan. 18, 2002). *But see* Stonecrest Partners, L.L.C. v. Bank of Hampton Roads, 2010 WL 3732100 (E.D.N.C. Sept. 8,

mortgage loan transaction conducted entirely in Spanish, the loan documents had been provided only in English, which the plaintiff was unable to read. The ECOA and FHA claims were found timely because plaintiff did not discover the amount of the allegedly inflated mortgage payments until he made his first payment on the loan, which was less than two years prior to the filing of the action.[448]

If the statute begins to run at the time of violation (or if a court applying the discovery rule determines that the plaintiff discovered or should have discovered the injury at the time of the violation), there still may be some question as to the actual violation date. The date will vary depending on what the violation involves—application procedures, notice of adverse action, post-default collection procedures, and so forth. The violation date may be before or significantly after the application and loan dates. For example, if the violation occurs when a loan is renewed, the two-year period starts from that renewal date, not the date of the original loan.[449]

Courts using the discovery rule will generally apply it only to violations that are either not immediately evident or not readily discernible.[450] Most courts find that the discovery rule actually determines when a claim accrues and is not a tolling doctrine.[451] A minority of courts treat the discovery rule as tolling a statute of limitations that had already begun to run at the time of the violation.[452]

Courts applying the discovery rule generally agree that what matters is a plaintiff's discovery of certain facts, not the plaintiff's understanding of the legal significance of these facts or his or her conclusion that a valid claim exists.[453] When the issue arises in the context of a plaintiff with diminished capacity, however, the key question should be whether the plaintiff had the ability to comprehend the injury. Thus, a borrower who suffered from advanced Alzheimer's disease when the loan was consummated was held to lack this ability.[454]

Another issue arises for violations related to collection procedures. In a transaction in which an alleged violation occurred in the initial contract, the question is whether subsequent collection procedures initiated during the life of the loan represent a new violation for the purpose of measuring whether the statute has run on bringing an affirmative damage claim. At least one court ruled in an ECOA case that the use of collection procedures did not represent a new violation.[455] The same court affirmed this ruling in another case, finding that the institution of a collection action by a lender's successor in interest without ensuring that the original transaction complied with the ECOA did not constitute a new ECOA violation for purposes of the running of the statute of limitations.[456]

In the second of these two cases, the court noted its holding might not apply when the collection action itself is the first discriminatory action.[457] The court distinguished such a situation from the case before the court, in which the alleged ECOA violation related to the initial contract and not necessarily to the collection process per se.[458] The court in these cases also limited its rulings to affirmative ECOA claims, agreeing that ECOA violations may still be raised defensively after the applicable statute has run.[459]

Another area that has been the subject of some litigation is whether an illegal requirement that an individual co-sign a note occurs when the individual signs the note or when the creditor

2010) (holding that wives required to guarantee husbands' loans were deemed to know the legal effect of documents they signed when they signed them).

448 Hernandez v. Sutter West Capital, 2010 WL 539133, at *7 (N.D. Cal. Feb. 8, 2010).

449 *See* Silverman v. Eastrich Multiple Investor Fund, Ltd. P'ship, 51 F.3d 28 (3d Cir. 1995) (because claims by way of recoupment are never barred by statutes of limitations so long as the main action is timely, court did not address creditor's assertion that time in which wife-guarantor could raise a claim under ECOA for impermissibly being required to sign husband's guaranty expired two years after date she signed guaranty nor whether approval of creditor's bankruptcy reorganization plan, which provided for deferral of payment on debt, constituted "renewal" of debt permitting resurrection of claim beyond initial statute of limitations), *rev'g* 857 F. Supp. 447 (E.D. Pa. 1994); Stern v. Espirito Santo Bank, 791 F. Supp. 865 (S.D. Fla. 1992).

450 *See, e.g.,* Cambridge Plating Co. v. NAPCO, Inc., 991 F.2d 21, 26–28 n.6 (1st Cir. 1993); Armstrong v. Trico Marine, Inc., 923 F.2d 55, 58 (5th Cir. 1991); Wilson v. Johns-Manville Sales Corp., 684 F.2d 111, 116 (D.C. Cir. 1982); Stoleson v. United States, 629 F.2d 1265, 1269 (7th Cir. 1980); Phillips v. Better Home Depot, Inc., 2003 WL 25867736, at *25 (E.D.N.Y. Nov. 12, 2003) (finding doctrine applicable to toll ECOA limitations period because, "in a case of discrimination, a victim may not know he or she has been the target of discrimination until meeting other victims or learning more about lending practices in minority communities").

451 *See, e.g.,* Oshiver v. Levin, Fishbein, Sedran & Berman, 38 F.3d 1380, 1386 n.5 (3d Cir. 1994); Alexander v. Beech Aircraft Corp., 952 F.2d 1215, 1226 n.13 (10th Cir. 1991); Resolution Trust Corp. v. Farmer, 865 F. Supp. 1143, 1154 (E.D. Pa. 1994) (stating that the rule "delays" accrual of a claim).

452 *See generally* James R. MacAyeal, *The Discovery Rule and the Continuing Violation Doctrine as Exceptions to the Statute of*

Limitations for Civil Environmental Penalty Claims, 15 Va. Envtl. L.J. 589 (1996).

453 Arriaga v. Wells Fargo Bank, 2012 WL 4498117 (N.D. Ill. Sept. 27, 2012) (*pro se* plaintiffs' ECOA claim was time barred when they "would have known that their cause of action accrued when no appraisal arrived after they had submitted their request," notwithstanding their unawareness of the applicable regulations).

In a different context not involving alleged discrimination, see United States v. Kubrick, 444 U.S. 111, 120, 100 S. Ct. 352, 62 L. Ed. 2d 259 (1979).

454 Estate of Henderson v. Meritage Mortgage Corp., 293 F. Supp. 2d 830 (N.D. Ill. 2003) (analysis applied to RESPA, TILA, HOEPA, FHA, ECOA, and section 1981 claims).

455 Roseman v. Premier Financial Services-East, Ltd. P'ship, 1997 U.S. Dist. LEXIS 13836 (E.D. Pa. Sept. 3, 1997), *further proceedings at* 1998 U.S. Dist. LEXIS 15679 (E.D. Pa. Sept. 29, 1998) (denying motion for summary judgment).

456 Stornawaye Properties, Inc. v. Moses, 76 F. Supp. 2d 607 (E.D. Pa. 1999).

457 Roseman v. Premier Financial Services-East, Ltd. P'ship, 1997 U.S. Dist. LEXIS 13836 (E.D. Pa. Sept. 3, 1997).

458 *Id.*

459 *Id.; see* § 11.9.2.2, *infra.*

first requests that the note be co-signed.[460] There is also uncertainty as to the violation date when a notice of adverse action is not properly given. One court has ruled that the violation date is not the date of oral notification, because the notice must be in writing.[461] On the other hand, if proper written notice is never received, is the date of violation when the consumer somehow becomes aware of the adverse action or is it the latest date the creditor should have mailed a proper written notice? At least one court has stated that the date of the violation is the date by which the creditor was required to provide notice of its adverse action, a harsh result for an innocent applicant.[462]

11.9.2.1.1.3 Extending the time period—continuing violation

The continuing violation doctrine allows plaintiffs to recover for incidents outside of the statutory time limit if at least one instance of the alleged practice occurred within the period and the earlier acts are part of a continuing pattern of discrimination.[463] Lingering effects of the past discrimination are not sufficient.[464] Instead, plaintiffs must show that defendants con-

tinued to commit violations during the statutory period.[465] The theory is applied when the type of violation is one that could not reasonably have been expected to be made the subject of a lawsuit when it first occurred because its character as a violation did not become clear until it was repeated during the limitations period.[466] In reverse redlining cases, for example, plaintiffs may argue that the violation occurs throughout the life of the loan, not merely at closing, especially when there are specific allegations of predatory acts in the creditor's servicing and foreclosure practices.[467]

The United States Supreme Court in *Havens v. Coleman*, an FHA case, held that a pattern or practice may revive otherwise stale acts if these acts are part of a "continuing violation" of the FHA.[468] The FHA explicitly allows the United States Attorney General to commence civil actions when "any person or group of persons is engaged in a pattern or practice" of violating the rights granted under the FHA.[469] Courts have held that private pattern and practice suits are also available and that acts which occurred prior to the limitations period are actionable as long as they are part of the alleged pattern.[470]

The ECOA also states that pattern or practice cases may be brought by the United States Attorney General.[471] A number of courts have thus held that the pattern or practice language supports a private cause of action as to which the limitations period may be tolled while the pattern or practice continues.[472]

---

460 *Compare* Farrell v. Bank of N.H., 929 F.2d 871 (1st Cir. 1991) (violation occurred on date bank sent commitment letter requiring spouse to co-sign, not on later date of actual signature), *and* Fed. Deposit Ins. Corp. v. Skotzke, 881 F. Supp. 364 (S.D. Ind. 1994), *with* Riggs Nat'l Bank v. Webster, 832 F. Supp. 147, 150 (D. Md. 1993) (statute of limitations runs from date that spouse signed the note).

461 Palmiotto v. Bank of N.Y., 1989 U.S. Dist. LEXIS 11546 (N.D.N.Y. Sept. 29, 1989).

462 Para v. United Carolina Bank, 1998 U.S. Dist. LEXIS 16843 (E.D.N.C. Aug. 25, 1998).

463 Bojorquez v. Gutierrez, 2010 WL 2925154, at *4 (N.D. Cal. July 26, 2010) (applying the doctrine to claims of an individual plaintiff challenging, as violative of the FHA, an unlawful conspiracy to sell subprime mortgage-loan products with only English documentation to people of Hispanic nationalities with limited or no ability to speak English that allegedly continued into the limitations period); Cherry v. D.B. Zwirn Special Opportunities Fund, 2010 WL 415313, at *5 (M.D. Fla. Jan. 27, 2010) (finding allegations of a continuing violation sufficient, but dismissing ECOA claim on other procedural grounds), *aff'd*, 433 Fed. Appx. 870 (11th Cir. 2011); *see* Havens Realty Corp. v. Coleman, 455 U.S. 363, 102 S. Ct. 1114, 1125, 71 L. Ed. 2d 214 (1982) (when a plaintiff, pursuant to the FHA, challenges not just one incident of conduct violative of the Act but an unlawful practice that continues into the limitation period, the complaint is timely when it is filed within the statute of limitations for the last asserted occurrence of that practice); Spann v. Colonial Vill., Inc., 899 F.2d 24, 34–35 (D.C. Cir. 1990) (affirming finding of continuing violation when last of "long stream" of advertisements with white models occurred within statutory period); Hargraves v. Capital City Mortgage Corp., 140 F. Supp. 2d 7 (D.D.C. 2000); *see also* Lewis v. City of Chi., 130 S. Ct. 2191 (2010) (even though city's initial decision regarding use of examinations for firefighter jobs that had disparate impact occurred prior to limitations period, a new violation occurred and a timely new claim could arise when city later implemented that decision in selecting classes of firefighters).

464 Ledbetter v. Goodyear Tire & Rubber Co., 550 U.S. 618, 127 S. Ct. 2162, 167 L. Ed. 2d 982 (2007) (later-occurring effects of a discriminatory practice do not extend the limitations period).

The decision in *Ledbetter* was statutorily overruled as to wage

discrimination claims by the Lilly Ledbetter Fair Pay Act of 2009. Pub. L. No. 111-2, 123 Stat. 5 (2009).

However, the Act does not by its terms explicitly apply to ECOA or FHA claims. *See* Garcia v. Brockway, 526 F.3d 456, 462 (9th Cir. 2008) (noting that, under the FHA, a continuing violation "is occasioned by continual unlawful acts," not just "continual ill effects from an original violation").

465 *See* Hargraves v. Capital City Mortgage Corp., 140 F. Supp. 2d 7 (D.D.C. 2000) (allowing plaintiffs to proceed on the theory that continuing violations might include continued charging of exorbitant interest rates for loans plaintiff took out before statutory period, continued collecting of other predatory fees, and any discriminatory actions used to enforce the loans). *But see* Federer v. Midland Mortgage Co., 2012 WL 5880916 (N.D. Ga. Nov. 21, 2012) (insufficient allegations of conduct occurring after the discriminatory loan was issued).

466 *See* Hargraves v. Capital City Mortgage Corp., 140 F. Supp. 2d 7 (D.D.C. 2000) (citing Taylor v. Fed. Deposit Ins. Corp., 132 F.3d 753, 765 (D.C. Cir. 1997)).

467 Hargraves v. Capital City Mortgage Corp., 140 F. Supp. 2d 7 (D.D.C.).

468 Havens Realty Corp. v. Coleman, 455 U.S. 363, 381 n.23, 102 S. Ct. 1114, 71 L. Ed. 2d 214 (1982).

469 42 U.S.C. § 3614(a).

470 Havens Realty Corp. v. Coleman, 455 U.S. 363, 102 S. Ct. 1114, 71 L. Ed 2d 214 (1982); Wallace v. Chi. Hous. Auth., 321 F. Supp. 2d 968 (N.D. Ill. 2004) (rule applies when plaintiff properly alleges a pattern of conduct that violates the FHA).

471 15 U.S.C. § 1691e(h).

472 Garcia v. Veneman, 224 F.R.D. 8 (D.D.C. 2004) (citing Hargraves v. Capital City Mortgage Corp., 140 F. Supp. 2d 7 (D.D.C. 2000)), *aff'd sub nom.* Garcia v. Johanns, 444 F.3d 625 (D.C. Cir. 2006) (also holding that, in order to establish a pattern-and-practice claim, a plaintiff must show that the discrimination was creditor's standard operating procedure—the regular rather than the unusual practice);

These issues have been rendered more complicated by the Supreme Court's analysis of the limitations issue in a Title VII case, *National Railroad Passenger Corp. v. Morgan*,[473] in which the Supreme Court expressed views that significantly narrow the scope of the continuing violation theory. The Court drew a distinction between discrete discriminatory acts, such as termination or failure to promote or hire, and acts contributing to a hostile work environment. The former, according to the Court, are not actionable if beyond the statute of limitations even if they relate to acts alleged in timely filed claims.[474] The plaintiff's hostile workplace claim, however, was not time-barred because it was qualitatively different from related discrete acts. A hostile workplace claim is, by its very nature, indicative of repetitive conduct "that cannot be said to occur on any particular day" and "may not be actionable on its own."[475]

Since that decision, some courts have questioned the scope and applicability of the continuing violation theory in other types of discrimination cases as well.[476] However, there is still vitality to the theory. In particular, the Supreme Court expressly refrained from deciding when, if ever, the theory applies to the type of pattern or practice claims that are frequently made in discrimination cases and, if so, how it applies.[477]

To extend the time period under a pattern and practice claim, plaintiffs cannot merely show a series of discrete occurrences of discrimination.[478] It is also critical that plaintiffs show that the character of the defendant's actions was not apparent when they were committed but became so when viewed in light of later

acts.[479] A district court confronting this issue in a credit discrimination case in 2005 noted the difficulty in comparing credit discrimination cases to employment discrimination cases.[480] In this case, plaintiffs challenged automobile finance mark-up policies that they alleged constituted an overarching pattern of discrimination that persisted to that day. The court found that the *Havens* ruling could save otherwise time-barred claims, provided they are found to be part of the overarching illegal policy.[481] Although the court noted that it also had to consider the more recent discussion in *Morgan*, it found that the plaintiff's claims in this case were more analogous to the hostile work environment claims than discrete discriminatory acts.

> [In both situations, t]he ongoing discrimination plaintiffs allege could only manifest itself after a critical mass of similarly situated people experience it, so as to bring an overarching pattern to light.... Cumulation is necessary to demonstrate an otherwise concealed policy, and plaintiffs allege that GMAC and the dealers acted pursuant to a specific, racially discriminatory policy.[482]

The court further observed that this view conforms to the general principle that limitations periods serve to avoid stale claims. The court also addressed and distinguished its holding from a 2005 Tennessee district court decision granting summary judgment against four individual plaintiffs and holding that the alleged continuing violation did not save their ECOA claims under the facts as presented.[483] Relying on Sixth Circuit authority, the Tennessee court had held that plaintiffs needed to show not only a longstanding, overarching policy of discrimination but also a specific, allegedly discriminatory act during the relevant limitations period that caused injury to the named plaintiffs.[484]

More recently, several courts have endorsed the continuing violation doctrine in putative class actions alleging reverse redlining in violation of the ECOA and the FHA. In denying motions to dismiss on statute of limitations grounds, they have observed that the doctrine eliminates the prospect of repetitive

Rodriguez v. Ford Motor Credit Co., 2002 WL 655679 (N.D. Ill. Apr. 19, 2002); Sallion v. SunTrust Bank, Atlanta, 87 F. Supp. 2d 1323 (N.D. Ga. 2000).

473 536 U.S. 101, 122 S. Ct. 2061, 153 L. Ed. 2d 106 (2002).

474 *Id.*

475 *Id.*, 536 U.S. at 115.

476 Phillips v. Better Home Depot, Inc., 2003 WL 25867736 (E.D.N.Y. Nov. 12, 2003) (rejecting continuing violation theory, but finding equitable tolling applicable); *see, e.g.*, Wallace v. Chi. Hous. Auth., 298 F. Supp. 2d 710 (N.D. Ill. 2003) (*Morgan* decision controls inquiry in FHA case), *on reconsideration in part*, 321 F. Supp. 2d 968 (N.D. Ill. 2004); Haynie v. Veneman, 272 F. Supp. 2d 10 (D.D.C. 2003) (in ECOA case, continuing violation theory cannot be employed to preserve untimely claims founded on discrete acts of discrimination even if they are substantially related to timely claims based on similar discrete acts; the Supreme Court left open the possibility that the continuing violation theory might apply to a pattern and practice discrimination claim).

477 Nat'l R.R. Passenger Corp. v. Morgan, 536 U.S. 101, 115 n.9, 122 S. Ct. 2061, 153 L. Ed. 2d 106 (2002); *see* Thiel v. Veneman, 859 F. Supp. 2d 1182, 1186 (D. Mont. 2012) (rejecting application of continuing violation doctrine in this ECOA claim because, "at all times, Plaintiff alleges different individual acts that when viewed together, do not constitute a discriminatory pattern").

478 *Id.*; Wallace v. Chi. Hous. Auth., 321 F. Supp. 2d 968 (N.D. Ill. 2004) (allowing plaintiffs to proceed but noting concerns that alleged pattern or practice may be characterized more accurately as a series of discrete happenings); *see also* Int'l Bhd. Of Teamsters v. United States, 431 U.S. 324, 336, 97 S. Ct. 1843, 52 L. Ed. 2d 396 (1977) (pattern and practice claims cannot be based on sporadic discriminatory acts but rather on discriminatory conduct that is widespread or routine and regular).

479 Wallace v. Chi. Hous. Auth., 321 F. Supp. 2d 968 (N.D. Ill. 2004) (citing Moskowitz v. Trustees of Purdue Univ., 5 F.3d 279 (7th Cir. 1993)); *see also* Tillery v. Darby-Rogers Co., 2006 WL 2735162, at *4 (M.D. Fla. Sept. 25, 2006) (tolling limitations period for Fair Housing Act claim when plaintiffs could not have learned of violation within statutory period).

480 *See* Davis v. Gen. Motors Acceptance Corp., 406 F. Supp. 2d 698 (N.D. Miss. 2005).

481 *Id.*

482 *Id.* at 706.

483 Claybrooks v. Primus Automotive Financial Servs., Inc., 363 F. Supp. 2d 969 (M.D. Tenn. 2005).

484 *Id.* at 983 (noting that, in *Claybrooks*, plaintiffs' only claims of injury flowed from their own transactions, which preceded the relevant limitations period); *see also* Lewis v. Glickman, 104 F. Supp. 2d 1311 (D. Kan. 2000), *aff'd*, 2002 WL 1435904 (10th Cir. July 3, 2002) (application of continuing violation doctrine not warranted because plaintiffs failed to show that at least one instance of the practice occurred within relevant time frame).

lawsuits directed at the same unlawful conduct,[485] that "each mortgage statement that seeks inflated payments for the loan based upon discriminatory terms is another violation visited upon Plaintiff,"[486] and that the concern for staleness disappears when a continuing practice is alleged.[487]

11.9.2.1.1.4 Extending the time period—equitable tolling

Equitable tolling of the violation is an independent ground for extending the limitations period. It is hornbook law that limitations periods are "customarily subject to 'equitable tolling.' "[488] The Supreme Court has permitted equitable tolling in situations "where the claimant has actively pursued his judicial remedies by filing a defective pleading during the statutory period, or where the complainant has been induced or tricked by his adversary's misconduct into allowing the filing deadline to pass."[489]

The most frequent basis for equitable tolling of an ECOA or FHA violation is fraudulent concealment. Fraudulent concealment is a more difficult standard to meet than the criteria applicable to the discovery rule, discussed above, since it

requires that the creditor actively concealed the violation.[490] Fraudulent concealment mingles elements from both the doctrines of equitable tolling and equitable estoppel.

Courts in different circuits have articulated differing views on the level of improper conduct required to demonstrate fraudulent concealment, often borrowing from case law under other federal or state statutes.[491] The courts generally hold that the statute of limitations can be tolled for fraudulent concealment when the plaintiff demonstrates that (1) the defendant took affirmative steps to conceal the plaintiff's cause of action and (2) the plaintiff could not have discovered the cause of action despite exercising due diligence.[492] The pleading of fraudulent concealment is held to the strict standards of Federal Rule of Civil Procedure 9(b).[493]

---

485 Barrett v. H & R Block, Inc., 652 F. Supp. 2d 104 (D. Mass. 2009) (following *Havens* and citing with approval, *inter alia*, Miller v. Countrywide Bank, on application of the continuing violations doctrine to both FHA and ECOA claims); Miller v. Countrywide Bank, 571 F. Supp. 2d 251, 262 (D. Mass. 2008); *see also* Kyle Graham, *The Continuing Violations Doctrine*, 43 Gonz. L. Rev. 271, 325–26 (2008).

486 Taylor v. Accredited Home Lenders, Inc., 580 F. Supp. 2d 1062, 1066 (S.D. Cal. 2008); *accord* Akhavein v. Argent Mortgage Co., 2009 WL 2157522, at *7 (N.D. Cal. July 18, 2009) (individual ECOA claim; dismissing complaint but granting leave to amend to properly allege discrimination); Lomboy v. SCME Mortgage Bankers, 2009 WL 1457738, at *8 (N.D. Cal. May 26, 2009) (individual claim). *But see* Ledbetter v. Goodyear Tire & Rubber Co., 550 U.S. 618, 127 S. Ct. 2162, 167 L. Ed. 2d 982 (2007) (if a plaintiff does not timely file charges for discrete acts of discrimination, subsequent nondiscriminatory acts that give present effect to past discriminatory acts do no result in new violations. 550 U.S. at 628, 127 S. Ct. 2162).

487 Ramirez v. GreenPoint Mortgage Funding, Inc., 633 F. Supp. 2d 922 (N.D. Cal. 2008).

488 Young v. United States, 535 U.S. 43, 49, 122 S. Ct. 1036, 1040–41 (2002); *see* Irwin v. Dep't of Veterans Affairs, 498 U.S. 89, 96 n.3, 111 S. Ct. 453, 458 (1990) (citing American Pipe & Constr. Co. v. Utah, 414 U.S. 538, 94 S. Ct. 756, 38 L. Ed. 2d 713 (1974) (plaintiff's timely filing of a defective class action tolled the limitations period as to the individual claims of purported class members), Burnett v. N.Y. Cent. R. Co., 380 U.S. 424, 85 S. Ct. 1050, 13 L. Ed. 2d 941 (1965) (plaintiff timely filed complaint in wrong court), and Herb v. Pitcairn, 325 U.S. 77, 65 S. Ct. 954, 89 L. Ed. 1483 (1945) (same)).

489 Young v. United States, 535 U.S. 43, 50, 122 S. Ct. 1036, 1041; *see also* Stovall v. Vilsak, 2012 WL 5426679 (N.D. Ala. Nov. 6, 2012) (finding circumstances insufficient to warrant equitable tolling of ECOA claim against the USDA).

Equitable tolling does not apply when plaintiff elects to try to resolve his claims in a private, non-judicial forum provided by the defendant rather than to initiate action under the ECOA in the courts. Haug v. PNC Financial Servs. Group, Inc. 2013 WL 980440, at *6 (N.D. Ohio Mar. 12, 2013).

490 Thorn v. Jefferson-Pilot Life Ins., 445 F.3d 311 (4th Cir. 2006) (federal equitable tolling principles require proof of unawareness); *see* Matthews v. New Century Mortgage Corp., 185 F. Supp. 2d 874 (S.D. Ohio 2002) (finding fraudulent concealment and therefore tolling statute under the FHA and the ECOA). *But see* Thiel v. Veneman, 859 F. Supp. 2d 1182 (D. Mont. 2012) (if a plaintiff asserts fraudulent concealment against the government, there must be affirmative misconduct, not mere negligence, and a serious injustice outweighing damage to the public interest of estopping the government); Miller v. Countrywide Bank, 571 F. Supp. 2d 251, 262 (D. Mass. 2008) (applying requirements of Fed. R. Civ. P. 9(b) and finding allegations of complaint insufficient, but denying dismissal based on continuing violation doctrine).

Case law under other consumer statutes has effectively argued for the existence of a fraudulent concealment exception to statute of limitations defenses. *See* National Consumer Law Center, Truth in Lending § 12.2.2 (8th ed. 2012) (discussing cases); National Consumer Law Center, Automobile Fraud § 6.4 (4th ed. 2011 and Supp.) (same); *see also* National Consumer Law Center, Fair Debt Collection § 6.10 (7th ed. 2011 and Supp.).

491 *See, e.g.*, Rakes v. United States, 442 F.3d 7, 24 (1st Cir. 2006); Foster v. Equicredit Corp., 2001 U.S. Dist. LEXIS 1881 (E.D. Pa. Jan. 25, 2001).

492 *See* Salois v. Dime Sav. Bank, 128 F.3d 20, 25–26 (1st Cir. 1997); Cada v. Baxter Healthcare Corp. 920 F.2d 446, 450–51 (7th Cir. 1990); Conmar Corp. v. Mitsui & Co., 858 F.2d 499, 502 (9th Cir. 1988) (also holding that silence or passive concealment will suffice when the defendant has a duty to disclose to the plaintiff); Matthews v. New Century Mortgage Corp., 185 F. Supp. 2d 874 (S.D. Ohio 2002) (finding that equitable tolling prevented the FHA and ECOA statutes of limitations from running until the date the borrowers learned of the terms of the loans and the fraud committed upon plaintiff); Greer v. Bank One, 2002 WL 1732366 (N.D. Ill. July 25, 2002) (noting that there appears to be no authority that ECOA's limitations period is subject to equitable tolling, court analyzed claim as though tolling theory was available; plaintiff did not meet standard for equitable tolling, which requires deliberate efforts by defendant to prevent plaintiff from suing within the applicable statute of limitation and required due diligence by plaintiff in discovering the cause of action prior to expiration of the statute), *aff'd sub nom.* Greer v. Cnty. of Cook, 54 Fed. Appx. 232 (7th Cir. 2002); *see also* Phillips v. Better Home Depot, Inc., 2003 WL 25867736, at *25 (E.D.N.Y. Nov. 12, 2003) (finding doctrine applicable to toll ECOA limitations period without prerequisite of active concealment by the defendant because, "in a case of discrimination, a victim may not know he or she has been the target of discrimination until meeting other victims or learning more about lending practices in minority communities").

493 *See, e.g.*, J. Geils Band Emp. Benefit Plan v. Smith Barney Shear-

However, several courts have held that, because the applicability of equitable tolling depends on matters outside the pleadings, it is rarely appropriate for the court to grant a Rule 12(b)(6) motion to dismiss with prejudice when the plaintiff asserts fraudulent concealment in response to a statute of limitations defense.[494]

11.9.2.1.2 Federal Civil Rights Acts claims

The limitations period for the federal Civil Rights Acts are somewhat complicated. The limitations period for a cause of action that could be brought under provisions of the Acts that existed prior to the 1991 amendments to the Acts is determined by state law, so the period may be longer or shorter than the Fair Housing Act and the ECOA's limitations periods. To the extent, however, that a cause of action is made possible by the provisions added by the 1991 amendments, they are subject to the four-year "catch-all" federal statute of limitations of 28 U.S.C. § 1658(a).[495] In either case, federal law determines when the clock begins to run against that period.[496] However, the doctrines that permit extending the limitations period discussed above should also apply to federal Civil Rights Acts claims, at least if they do not conflict with relevant state doctrines.[497] This is because statute of limitations periods for federal Civil Rights Acts claims generally are borrowed from state law.

11.9.2.1.3 State law claims

State credit discrimination acts often have short limitations periods, typically one year but sometimes two or three years.[498] Just as commonly, the statute will not specify a limitations period. In these circumstances, states take varying approaches toward selecting an appropriate limitations period, some using the limitations period for statutory actions, some using those for tort actions, or some using those for specialty actions. These other limitations periods may be as short as one year but may be as long as four years or more.

Many state credit discrimination statutes provide an administrative procedure. Typically, complaints under this administrative procedure must be brought within six months or even sooner.[499]

Another approach is to use a state unfair or deceptive acts or practices (UDAP) statute to challenge discrimination. If a UDAP statute has a longer limitations period (UDAP limitations periods vary significantly, from one year to four or more years[500]), this advantage may be a reason to include a UDAP claim in a discrimination case, even though another discrimination statute also applies.

11.9.2.2 Using Set-Off and Recoupment After Expiration of the Statute of Limitations

In many situations, a client does not seek legal assistance until sued on a debt. Frequently, the statutes of limitations for various credit discrimination claims have run by that time. For example, a client who was coerced years ago to co-sign a loan with a spouse prior to their divorce may be sued now because the ex-spouse cannot be located. Even though the statute of limitations may have run for bringing an affirmative credit discrimination claim or counterclaim against the creditor, such claims usually can be brought by way of set-off or recoupment (in other words, as a defense) to the creditor's collection action.

Although the consumer cannot recover an amount in actual and punitive damages in excess of the debt on which the creditor is seeking collection,[501] generally the limitations period will not apply to an ECOA recoupment claim.[502] Courts

---

son, Inc., 76 F.3d 1245, 1255 (1st Cir. 1996); Steele v. GE Money Bank, 2009 WL 393860, at *10 (N.D. Ill. Feb. 17, 2009) (fraudulent concealment allegations in disparate impact in mortgage lending case failed to satisfy heightened pleading standard of Rule 9(b)); Miller v. Countrywide Bank, 571 F. Supp. 2d 251 (D. Mass. 2008) (same).

494 Huynh v. Chase Manhattan Bank, 465 F.3d 992, 1003–04 (9th Cir. 2006); Reiser v. Residential Funding Corp., 380 F.3d 1027, 1030 (7th Cir. 2004); *see also In re* Cmty. Bank of N. Va., 622 F.3d 275, 302 (3d Cir. 2010) (ruling on objections to class action settlement). *But see* Federer v. Midland Mortgage Co., 2012 WL 5880916 (N.D. Ga. Nov. 21, 2012) (finding equitable tolling inapplicable due to plaintiff's failure to plead any facts showing affirmative concealment of alleged discrimination).

495 Jones v. R.R. Donnelley & Sons Co., 541 U.S. 369, 124 S. Ct. 1836, 158 L. Ed. 2d 645 (2004); *see* § 1.5, *supra*.

496 Thorn v. Jefferson-Pilot Life Ins. Co., 445 F.3d 311 (4th Cir. 2006).

497 *See* Nat'l R.R. Passenger Corp. v. Morgan, 536 U.S. 101, 122 S. Ct. 2061, 153 L. Ed. 2d 106 (2002) (the continuing violation doctrine can apply to section 1981 claims).

498 *See* appx. F, *infra*.

499 *See* appx. F, *infra*.

500 *See* National Consumer Law Center, Unfair and Deceptive Acts and Practices § 11.2 (8th ed. 2012).

501 Stewart Title Guar. Co. v. WKC Restaurants Venture Co., 961 S.W.2d 874 (Mo. Ct. App. 1998) (a recoupment action can mitigate or extinguish debtor's damages but cannot result in an affirmative judgment for debtor).

502 Citgo Petroleum Corp. v. Bulk Petroleum Corp., 2010 WL 3212751 (N.D. Okla. Aug. 12, 2010); *see* Mayes v. Chrysler Credit Corp., 167 F.3d 675 (1st Cir. 1999); Bolduc v. Beal Bank, 167 F.3d 667 (1st Cir. 1999); Silverman v. Eastrich Multiple Investor Fund, Ltd. P'ship, 51 F.3d 28 (3d Cir. 1995) (because claims by way of recoupment are never barred by statute of limitations so long as main action is timely, court did not address creditor's assertion that time in which wife-guarantor could raise a claim under ECOA for impermissibly being required to sign husband's guaranty expired two years after date she signed guaranty nor whether approval of creditor's bankruptcy reorganization plan, which provided for deferral of payment on debt, constituted "renewal" of debt permitting resurrection of claim beyond initial statute of limitations), *rev'g* 857 F. Supp. 447 (E.D. Pa. 1994); Crittenden Trust Co. v. Cabot, 2004 WL 2287763 (D. Me. Oct. 12, 2004); Sovereign Bank v. Catterton, 2004 WL 834721 (E.D. Pa. Apr. 15, 2004); Nowicki v. Green, 1999 U.S. Dist. LEXIS 7058 (E.D. Pa. May 12, 1999); Fed. Deposit Ins. Corp. v. Medmark, Inc., 897 F. Supp. 511 (D. Kan. 1995); Sharp Electronics Corp. v. Yoggev, 1995 U.S. Dist. LEXIS 5751 (E.D. Pa. May 1, 1995); Integra Bank/Pittsburgh v. Freeman, 839 F. Supp. 326 (E.D. Pa. 1993); Machias Sav. Bank v. Ramsdell, 689 A.2d 595 (Me. 1997); Mundaca Inv. Corp. v. Emery, 674 A.2d 923 (Me. 1996); Fed. Deposit Ins. Corp. v. Notis, 602 A.2d 1164 (Me. 1992); Norwest Bank Minn. v. Midwestern Machinery Co., 481 N.W.2d

have also allowed recoupment based on FHA claims.[503] A majority of cases brought under the Truth in Lending Act (TILA) and other consumer protection statutes likewise have concluded that a consumer may utilize otherwise time-barred violations by way of recoupment or set-off if the creditor has filed an action based on the same credit transaction.[504] While most courts agree that the ECOA may be employed to defend against nonpayment of a promissory note, courts disagree as to whether the set-off or recoupment claim should be asserted as a counterclaim for damages or as a special defense of illegality.[505]

Recoupment or set-off is available for otherwise time-barred claims even when asserted in a nominally separate action filed in federal court, for example for declaratory relief.[506] However,

failure to raise a defensive counterclaim may bar a party from doing so in a subsequent action on the grounds of res judicata.[507]

11.9.3 Business Justification Defense

In most credit discrimination cases, the creditor will offer a purportedly legitimate business justification for its actions. Whether a business justification may be raised as a defense depends on the type of action being brought. For example, a business justification is not a defense to a creditor's violation of a specific ECOA requirement, such as failing to send notice of an adverse action or seeking information not permitted to be inquired about.

The business justification defense is only relevant when the plaintiff alleges a violation of the general rule against discrimination, based either on disparate treatment or disparate impact. Furthermore, the nature of the business justification defense varies depending on whether a case involves disparate treatment or impact.

In a disparate treatment case, the role of a legitimate business reason depends on the plaintiff's evidence of disparate treatment on a prohibited basis. If there is direct evidence of discrimination, business justification is likely to be irrelevant.[508] If, on the other hand, circumstantial evidence is being used and is sufficient to establish a prima facie case, then the burden shifts to the defendant to articulate a legitimate nondiscriminatory basis for the adverse action.[509] If the defendant does so, then the burden returns to the plaintiff to show the basis was merely pretextual. This issue is analyzed in greater depth in Chapter 4, *supra*.

In contrast, the issue in disparate impact cases is not whether there is a business justification—there almost always is—or whether this justification was the real reason for the creditor's action. The plaintiff might not even challenge these assertions. Instead, the plaintiff will allege that use of this business justification has a disparate impact on a prohibited basis and that the effect of using this legitimate business factor is to disproportionately deny credit to minorities or other protected groups. The issue then will be how significant the business justification is and whether the same need may be satisfied using alternative criteria that have less disparate impact on minorities. This topic is discussed in detail in Chapter 4, *supra*.

---

875 (Minn. Ct. App. 1992); Boone Nat'l Sav. & Loan Ass'n v. Crouch, 47 S.W.3d 371 (Mo. 2001) (en banc); *see also* Roseman v. Premier Financial Services-East, Ltd. P'ship, 1997 U.S. Dist. LEXIS 13836 (E.D. Pa. Sept. 3, 1997), *further proceedings at* 1998 U.S. Dist. LEXIS 15679 (E.D. Pa. Sept. 29, 1998) (claim for monetary relief barred but defensive claim seeking declaration that obligation is void is not barred by statute of limitations); Marine American State Bank v. Lincoln, 433 N.W.2d 709 (Iowa 1988) ($5000 attorney fees and $5000 punitive damages awarded on ECOA recoupment claim). *But see* Riggs Nat'l Bank v. Linch, 36 F.3d 370 (4th Cir. 1994); Household Bank v. Carlton, 7 F.3d 223 (4th Cir. 1993) (table) (text available at 1993 U.S. App. LEXIS 25139); Fed. Deposit Ins. Corp. v. 32 Edwardsville, Inc., 873 F. Supp. 1474 (D. Kan. 1995); CMF Va. Land, Ltd. P'ship v. Brinson, 806 F. Supp. 90 (E.D. Va. 1992); American Security Bank v. York, 1992 U.S. Dist. LEXIS 14309 (D.D.C. Sept. 1, 1992); Diamond v. Union Bank & Trust, 776 F. Supp. 542 (N.D. Okla. 1991); *In re* Fox, 162 B.R. 729, 732 (Bankr. E.D. Va. 1993) (common law recoupment is not available on a sealed instrument in Virginia); Ford City Bank v. Goldman, 424 N.E.2d 761 (Ill. App. Ct. 1981).

503 *See, e.g.,* Assocs. Home Equity Servs., Inc. v. Troup, 778 A.2d 529, 539 (N.J. Super. Ct. App. Div. 2001) (in allowing recoupment in FHA case, court disagreed with defendant's argument that recoupment was inappropriate because defendant's complaint was in foreclosure, not a collection action).

504 National Consumer Law Center, Truth in Lending § 12.2.5 (8th ed. 2012).

Louisiana, however, has an unusual rule that bars an ECOA, but not an FHA, claim in recoupment: "A prescribed cause of action arising under The Federal Consumer Credit Protection Act may not be used as a defense even if it is incidental to, or connected with, the obligation sought to be enforced by the plaintiff." La. Code Civ. Proc. art. 424.

In the past, Truth in Lending Act rescission claims were also permitted after the three-year period had run when raised by recoupment. The United States Supreme Court foreclosed this possibility as a matter of federal law in Beach v. Ocwen Fed. Bank, 523 U.S. 410, 118 S. Ct. 1408, 140 L. Ed. 2d 566 (1998). However, there may be arguments permitting rescission by way of recoupment under state law. *See* National Consumer Law Center, Truth in Lending § 10.9.6 (8th ed. 2012).

505 *See* § 11.8.5.3, *supra*.

506 Roseman v. Premier Financial Services-East, Ltd. P'ship, 1997 U.S. Dist. LEXIS 13836 (E.D. Pa. Sept. 3, 1997). *But see* Bledsoe v. Fulton Bank, 940 F. Supp. 804 (E.D. Pa. 1996) (plaintiff could not seek declaratory or injunctive relief under ECOA in federal court when she had raised issue defensively in state court).

---

507 *See* Olague v. Vill. of Bensenville, 1997 U.S. Dist. LEXIS 8539 (N.D. Ill. June 11, 1997); *see also* U.S. Fid. & Guar. Co. v. Feibus, 1998 U.S. Dist. LEXIS 20837 (M.D. Pa. Apr. 2, 1998) (denying defendant leave to amend answer to include ECOA counterclaim because excessive time had passed since close of discovery, defendant offered no explanation for the delay, and new discovery would have been required).

508 *See* § 4.2.2, *supra*.

509 *See* § 4.2.3, *supra*.

11.9.4 Special ECOA Defenses

11.9.4.1 Good Faith Compliance

The ECOA states that a creditor is not liable for any act done or omitted "in good faith in conformity" with Regulation B or with the official interpretations, even if the regulation or official interpretations are amended or determined to be invalid.[510] The conduct must not only conform to the regulation but must have been in good-faith conformity. Regulation B defines good faith as actions based on "honesty in fact" in the conduct or transaction.[511]

The issue would arise if, in defending against a claim, a defendant cites to Regulation B or its official interpretations, and the consumer in response challenges the regulation or official interpretations as unreasonably interpreting the statute. Even if the consumer prevails in that challenge, the creditor is still protected as to its past conduct conforming with the regulation or interpretation that was subsequently found to be in error. Similarly, an amendment to the regulation or its official interpretations cannot be applied retroactively to a creditor that complied in good faith with the prior version.

11.9.4.2 The Inadvertent Error Defense

Regulation B establishes an inadvertent error defense in ECOA actions.[512] This defense is limited in scope. First, the inadvertent error defense excuses the creditor only from liability for violations of five specified provisions of Regulation B—those dealing with review of credit history of a spouse's account, notification of action taken on an application, furnishing of credit information to reporting agencies on joint accounts, record retention requirements, and information requested for monitoring purposes.[513] The defense does not apply to actions based on the general rule against discrimination, co-signer requirements, application procedures, credit evaluation systems, or many other specific ECOA provisions.

Even when the five specified provisions are at issue, the creditor must show its actions fall within the Regulation's definition of inadvertent error. An inadvertent error is defined by Regulation B as a mechanical, electronic, or clerical error that a creditor demonstrates was not intentional and occurred

notwithstanding the maintenance of procedures reasonably adapted to avoid such errors.[514]

To make use of this defense the creditor thus has to overcome a number of burdens. It must show that an error was mechanical, electronic, or clerical.[515] An error of law, such as failing altogether to provide appropriate adverse action notices to rejected applicants, should not fall in this category.[516]

The creditor also has the burden of demonstrating that the error was not intentional and that it occurred despite the maintenance of procedures "reasonably adapted" to avoid such errors.[517] For instance, if a creditor routinely fails to furnish information to credit reporting agencies as to both participating spouses when it reports its account experience, the inadvertent error defense will fail against a claim of sex discrimination, because this practice could be shown to be either intentional or preventable under a system with reasonable procedures for checking validity. At a minimum, there should be a showing of some standard verification procedure which is used for all applications. The inadvertent error defense closely corresponds to the "bona fide error" defense under the Truth in Lending Act and the Fair Debt Collection Practices Act, and cases discussing the defense under these statutes should be applicable.[518]

Moreover, upon discovery of an error dealing with record retention or federal monitoring requirements, the creditor must correct the error prospectively.[519] Thus, the defense should not be available if the creditor knows of the inadvertent error before the applicant brings the ECOA claim but has not corrected it.

It should be noted that Regulation B's inadvertent error defense has no counterpart in the ECOA itself. In contrast, as noted, the Truth in Lending Act does statutorily provide for a

---

510 15 U.S.C. § 1691e(e); *see also* Official Interpretations of Reg. B [Official Staff Commentary on Reg. B], 12 C.F.R. pt. 1002 [pt. 202], Introduction-1.

511 Reg. B, 12 C.F.R. § 1002.2(r) [§ 202.2(r)]; *see also* Unif. Commercial Code § 1-201(19) (good faith).

512 Reg. B, 12 C.F.R. § 1002.16(c) [§ 202.16(c) (renumbered from § 202.17(c))].

513 12 C.F.R. § 1002.16(c) [§ 202.16(c) (renumbered from § 202.17(c))] (inadvertent error defense for violations of §§ 1002.6(b)(6) [202.6(b)(6) (consideration of credit history), 1002.9 [202.9] (notification requirements), 1002.10 [202.10] (credit history reporting on joint accounts), 1002.12 [202.12] (record retention requirements), or 1002.3 [202.13] (federal monitoring requirements)); *see also* Official Interpretations of Reg. B [Official Staff Commentary on Reg. B], 12 C.F.R. pt. 1002 [pt. 202], Supp. I, § 1002.16(c) [§ 202.16(c) (renumbered from § 202.17(c))].

514 Reg. B, 12 C.F.R. § 1002.2(s) [§ 202.2(s)].

515 *See* Harbaugh v. Cont'l Ill. Nat'l Bank & Trust Co., 615 F.2d 1169, 1174 (7th Cir. 1980) (apparently condoning "good faith computer programming deficiencies").

516 Official Interpretations of Reg. B [Official Staff Commentary on Reg. B], 12 C.F.R. pt. 1002 [pt. 202], Supp. I, § 1002.16(c)-1 [§ 202.16(c)-1 (renumbered from § 202.17(c)-1)]; *see* Jerman v. Carlisle, McNellie, Rini, Kramer & Ulrich L.P.A., __ U.S. __, 130 S. Ct. 1605, 1615 (2010) (FDCPA bona fide error defense does not apply to an erroneous reading of the law); National Consumer Law Center, Truth in Lending § 12.4.4 (8th ed. 2012) (discussing this issue in the Truth in Lending Act context).

517 *See* Sayers v. Gen. Motors Acceptance Corp., 522 F. Supp. 835 (W.D. Mo. 1981) (an adverse action notice, stating that denial of credit was based on unfavorable information in consumer's credit history, did not give rise to an ECOA violation when it was based on an inadvertent misinterpretation of the credit history; however, creditor's willful refusal to comply with notification requirements after being informed of its error did constitute an ECOA violation); *see also* Gallegos v. Stokes, 593 F.2d 372 (10th Cir. 1979) (Truth in Lending Act (TILA) case); Hinkle v. Rock Springs Nat'l Bank, 538 F.2d 295 (10th Cir. 1976) (TILA case); National Consumer Law Center, Truth in Lending § 12.4.4 (8th ed. 2012).

518 *See* National Consumer Law Center, Truth in Lending § 12.4.4.5 (8th ed. 2012); National Consumer Law Center, Fair Debt Collection §§ 7.2.2, 7.2.3 (7th ed. 2011 and Supp.).

519 Official Interpretations of Reg. B [Official Staff Commentary on Reg. B], 12 C.F.R. pt. 1002 [pt. 202], Supp. I, § 1002.16(c)-2 [§ 202.16(c)-2 (renumbered from § 202.17(c)-2)].

similar creditor defense,[520] as does the Fair Debt Collection Practices Act,[521] suggesting that the omission in the ECOA was purposeful. Thus it might be argued that the Equal Credit Opportunity Act is clearly and unambiguously a strict liability statute[522] and therefore this provision of Regulation B, which is in conflict with such a reading, cannot stand.[523]

11.9.4.3 Creditor's Lack of Reasonable Notice of Violation

When a transaction involves more than one creditor, and one creditor violates the ECOA, the other creditors in a transaction are not liable for the violation to the extent that they lacked "reasonable notice" of the violation before becoming involved in the transaction.[524]

For example, a car dealer may make a preliminary credit determination and require the signature of a spouse before submitting the proposed transaction to a finance company. If this practice violates the ECOA, the finance company might then claim ignorance of the dealer's action and that it is not liable for the dealer's ECOA violations. This argument is only viable if the finance company is not directly liable as a creditor under the ECOA.[525]

11.9.4.4 Special Defenses by FDIC and RTC

When a governmental agency such as the Federal Deposit Insurance Corporation (FDIC) or the Resolution Trust Corpo-ration (RTC) takes over a bank, the ECOA still applies to the bank's pre-takeover transactions. An ECOA violation is normally apparent on the face of the bank's records (for example, requirement of a spouse's signature when the credit application shows the applicant is creditworthy). Thus, courts agree that an ECOA violation may be raised against the RTC or the FDIC either as a special defense of illegality or as a counterclaim for damages.[526] However, when prescribed administrative claims procedures have not been followed, courts lack jurisdiction to entertain affirmative defenses and counterclaims to suits brought by the government receiver.[527]

In addition, a debtor who has broadly released the RTC from any claims and defenses may not use the ECOA against a co-guarantor in a suit for contribution.[528]

11.9.5 Defenses to Fair Housing Act and Civil Rights Acts Claims

The Fair Housing Act and the Civil Rights Acts do not provide for any special defenses. The Fair Housing Act regulations provide a defense when an entity purchases loans. Such an entity may consider factors justified by business necessity, such as considerations employed in normal and prudent transactions.[529] As noted earlier, business justification is an issue in any disparate treatment or disparate impact case as well.[530]

520　15 U.S.C. § 1640(c); *see* National Consumer Law Center, Truth in Lending § 12.4.4.1 (8th ed. 2012).

521　15 U.S.C. § 1692k(c); *see* National Consumer Law Center, Fair Debt Collection § 7.2.5 (7th ed. 2011 and Supp.).

522　A rationale for such a distinction between the ECOA and the other titles of the Consumer Credit Protection Act is that the ECOA was intended to be a civil rights statute rather than simply a consumer protection statute. *See, e.g.,* 50 Fed. Reg. 48,019 (Nov. 20, 1985).

523　"Even for an agency able to claim all the authority possible under *Chevron*, deference to its statutory interpretation is called for only when the devices of judicial construction have been tried and found to yield no clear sense of congressional intent." Gen. Dynamics Land Systems, Inc. v. Cline, 540 U.S. 581, 600, 124 S. Ct. 1236, 157 L. Ed. 2d 1094 (2004).

　　　If the statute is silent or ambiguous with respect to the specific issue, however, "the question for the court is whether the agency's answer is based on a permissible construction of the statute." Chevron, U.S.A. Inc. v. Natural Resources Defense Council, Inc., 467 U.S. 837, 843, 104 S. Ct. 2778, 81 L. Ed. 2d 694 (1984).

524　Reg. B, 12 C.F.R. § 1002.2(l) [§ 202.2(l)]; *see* § 2.2.5.5, *supra.*

525　*See* §§ 2.2.5.4, 2.2.5.5, *supra.*

526　Bolduc v. Beal Bank, SSB, 167 F.3d 667 (1st Cir. 1999) (mutual mistake defense was based on alleged unenforceability of notes as to one debtor under ECOA); CMF Va. Land, Ltd. P'ship v. Brinson, 806 F. Supp. 90 (E.D. Va. 1992); Diamond v. Union Bank & Trust, 776 F. Supp. 542 (N.D. Okla. 1991); Fed. Deposit Ins. Corp. v. Notis, 602 A.2d 1164 (Me. 1992).

　　　These rulings are not inconsistent with the doctrine of D'Oench Duhme & Co. v. Fed. Deposit Ins. Corp., 315 U.S. 447, 62 S. Ct. 676, 86 L. Ed. 956 (1942), *as partially codified in* 12 U.S.C. § 1823(e), that defenses based on unrecorded side agreements are not available. *See generally* National Consumer Law Center, The Cost of Credit: Regulation, Preemption, and Industry Abuses § 10.7.6 (4th ed. 2009 and Supp.).

527　Fed. Deposit Ins. Corp. v. Parkway Executive Office Ctr., 1997 U.S. Dist. LEXIS 12318 (E.D. Pa. Aug. 15, 1997) (defendants did not raise their claims in an administrative proceeding within sixty days under 12 U.S.C. § 1821(d)(6)); Resolution Trust Corp. v. A.W. Assocs., Inc., 869 F. Supp. 1503 (D. Kan. 1994); Resolution Trust Corp. v. Laskin, 843 F. Supp. 1008 (D. Md. 1994) (defendants failed to file a claim with the receiver prior to published claim bar date).

528　Wetzler v. Cantor, 202 B.R. 573 (D. Md. 1996).

529　24 C.F.R. § 100.125(c).

530　*See* § 4.3.2.5, *supra.*

Chapter 12   Government Enforcement

12.1 Introduction

Several federal and state agencies are responsible for ensuring compliance with the various laws prohibiting credit discrimination. This chapter identifies those agencies and their respective enforcement roles and responsibilities under each of the applicable statutes. These agencies have brought some important cases that have explored significant discrimination claims. The substance of these cases is discussed in various other chapters, according to the underlying subject matter of the claims and the federal statute sought to be enforced.

12.2 Federal Agencies Responsible for ECOA Enforcement

12.2.1 The United States Attorney General

The United States Attorney General, as head of the Department of Justice, may bring a civil action against a creditor for violations of the ECOA when (a) a federal agency with ECOA enforcement authority refers a case to the Attorney General for prosecution or (b) the Attorney General has reason to believe that a creditor is engaging in a pattern or practice of ECOA violations.[1] Relief available in such actions includes actual and punitive damages and injunctive relief.[2]

Every year the Attorney General must report to Congress on enforcement efforts under the ECOA.[3] The Attorney General also participates in an interagency task force on fair lending.[4]

The Department of Justice received 109 referrals of alleged ECOA violations from other federal agencies between 2009 and 2011.[5] The majority of the referrals were from the Federal Deposit Insurance Corporation, which referred sixty-eight cases. Of these, fifty-five involved discrimination based on race or national origin.[6]

12.2.2 Consumer Financial Protection Bureau

The Consumer Financial Protection Bureau (CFPB), created by the Dodd-Frank Wall Street Reform and Consumer Protection Act ("Dodd-Frank Act"),[7] now has been given rule-writing authority for all the major consumer financial protection statutes—called the "enumerated statutes"—including the ECOA.[8] The CFPB has rule-writing authority over virtually every type of entity in the financial services area, including banks, credit unions, mortgage lenders, credit bureaus, automobile finance companies, debt collectors, student lenders, and payday lenders. Automobile dealers themselves are generally exempt from CFPB authority. The CFPB also has full enforcement authority over banks and credit unions with $10 billion or more in assets (and all of their subsidiaries). Banking regulators, listed below, have enforcement power over institutions with less than $10 billion in assets.[9]

In addition to enforcement authority, the CFPB also has taken over regulatory supervision and examinations for banks and credit unions with $10 billion or more in assets.[10] For other banks and credit unions, federal bank regulators retain supervision responsibility, but the CFPB can participate in examinations and seek information on a sampling basis.[11] The CFPB has supervision authority over the same non-banks under its enforcement authority: the mortgage industry, private education and payday lenders, the larger participants in other markets, and those shown to pose risks to consumers.[12]

Notably, this change of authority did not change jurisdiction regarding enforcement of the Fair Housing Act (FHA), which is enforced by the Department of Justice, the Department of Housing and Urban Development, and the federal banking regulators. Thus, for institutions with $10 billion or more in assets (as well as smaller institutions), the banking regulatory agencies, not the CFPB, retain authority to enforce the FHA.

---

1 15 U.S.C. § 1691e(h).
2 15 U.S.C. § 1691e(h).
3 15 U.S.C. § 1691(f).
   The reports are available on the Department of Justice website, www.usdoj.gov.
4 15 U.S.C. § 1691(f).
5 *See* United States Dep't of Justice, The Attorney General's 2012 Annual Report to Congress Pursuant to the Equal Credit Opportunity Act Amendments of 1976, at 11 (Apr. 5, 2011).
6 *Id.*

7 Pub. L. No. 111-203, 124 Stat. 1376 (July 21, 2010).
8 12 U.S.C. §§ 5481(12), 5512, *amended by* Pub. L. No. 111-203, §§ 1002(12), 1022, 124 Stat. 1955, 1980 (July 21, 2010).
   The FTC retains FCRA rule-writing and enforcement over the Red Flag Rules for identity theft prevention and the Disposal of Consumer Information Rule.
9 12 U.S.C. § 5516, *amended by* Pub. L. No. 111-203, § 1026, 124 Stat. 1993 (July 21, 2010).
10 12 U.S.C. § 5515.
11 12 U.S.C. § 5516.
12 12 U.S.C. § 5514.

This arrangement requires coordination among the various banking and enforcement agencies.

12.2.3 Federal Trade Commission

As a result of the Dodd-Frank Act,[13] the Federal Trade Commission's (FTC) primary jurisdiction for enforcing the ECOA, among many other consumer statutes, was moved to the newly formed Consumer Financial Protection Bureau. Most dealers of automobiles, motorcycles, boats, recreational vehicles, and motor homes are exempt and stay under FTC authority.[14] While the FTC no longer has ECOA authority over many lenders, it retains authority to enforce the FTC Act against those entities.

12.2.4 The Federal Reserve Board

Until passage of the Dodd-Frank Act,[15] the Federal Reserve Board (FRB) played the most important role in setting ECOA standards by promulgating regulations and staff interpretations of the rule. The Consumer Financial Protection Bureau now also has that role, although the FRB retains jurisdiction over smaller banks previously under its jurisdiction, and the FRB version of Regulation B is still in place.[16]

In fiscal year 2011, the Federal Reserve Board referred to the Justice Department five cases of lending discrimination involving discrimination on the basis of marital status, age, sex, and national origin.[17]

12.2.5 Other Federal Agencies

The ECOA delegates specific enforcement authority to nine different federal agencies, each having jurisdiction over a particular type of credit institution.[18]

Following is a list of banking regulators other than the CFPB and their areas of responsibility (subject to the foregoing discussion on the shift of authority to the CFPB):

1. The Comptroller of the Currency for national banks and federal branches of foreign banks;
2. The Federal Reserve Board (FRB) for member banks of the Federal Reserve System (other than national banks)

and foreign bank branches (other than foreign bank federal and insured state branches);
3. The Federal Deposit Insurance Corp. (FDIC) for banks insured by the FDIC (other than member banks of the Federal Reserve System) and insured state branches of foreign banks;
4. The National Credit Union Administration for federal credit unions;
5. The Secretary of Transportation for carriers regulated by the Surface Transportation Board and for regulated air carriers;
6. The Secretary of Agriculture for activities related to the Packers and Stockyards Act;
7. The Farm Credit Administration for federal land banks and associations, federal intermediate credit banks, and production credit associations;
8. The Securities and Exchange Commission for brokers and dealers; and
9. The Small Business Administration for small business investment companies.[19]

In general, ECOA violations may be enforced with the same remedies and powers that these agencies possess for other matters.[20] For example, violations of credit discrimination laws may result in a lower rating or corrective action following a bank examination.[21] If the agency cannot obtain the violator's compliance, the agency may refer the matter to the Department of Justice for appropriate civil action.[22]

In addition, the Comptroller of the Currency, the FRB, the FDIC, the Consumer Financial Protection Bureau, and the National Credit Union Administration are *required* to refer a matter to the Department of Justice whenever the agency has reason to believe that one or more creditor(s) has engaged in a pattern or practice of denying credit applications on a prohibited basis. They are *permitted* to make such a referral even in the absence of a pattern or practice.[23]

For the 2011 reporting period, the FRB reported that 89% of the institutions examined by the Federal Financial Institutions Examination Council (made up of the FRB, FDIC, the National Credit Union Administration, the Office of the Comptroller of the Currency, the Consumer Financial Protection Bureau, and the State Liaison Committee[24]) were in compliance with Regulation B, up from 82% in 2010.[25] However, in 2009, the figure

---

13 Pub. L. No. 111-203, 124 Stat. 1376 (July 21, 2010).
14 *Id.* § 1029.
    The exemption for motor vehicle dealers does not extend to dealers that retain financing or sell or assign financing to a related entity, such as many "buy here, pay here" dealers. *See id.* § 1029(b)(2).
    Rulewriting regarding motor vehicle dealers remains with the Federal Reserve Board. *See id.* § 1085 (amending 15 U.S.C. § 1691b).
15 Pub. L. No. 111-203, 124 Stat. 1376 (July 21, 2010).
16 The Board retains rule-writing authority over motor vehicle dealers, which are exempt from CFPB jurisdiction. *See* Pub. L. No. 111-203, § 1085, 124 Stat. 1376 (July 21, 2010) (amending 15 U.S.C. § 1691b).
17 Bd. of Governors of the Federal Reserve System, 98th Annual Report 2009, at 120 (May 2012), *available at* www.federalreserve.gov/board docs/rptcongress/annual12/pdf/AR12.pdf.
18 *See* 15 U.S.C. § 1691c; Reg. B, 12 C.F.R. § 1002.1(a) [§ 202.1(a)]; 12 C.F.R. pt. 1002 [pt. 202], app. A.

19 *See* 15 U.S.C. § 1691c; Reg. B, 12 C.F.R. § 1002.1 [§ 202.1]; 12 C.F.R. pt. 1002 [pt. 202], app. A.
20 15 U.S.C. § 1691c(b).
21 *See* J. Adler, *Marital Discrimination Charge*, Am. Banker, July 9, 2007 (describing rare "needs to improve" rating given by the FDIC to a North Carolina bank following a Community Reinvestment Act examination that found that the bank discriminated against borrowers based on their marital status).
22 15 U.S.C. § 1691e(g).
23 15 U.S.C. § 1691e(g).
24 *See generally* www.ffiec.gov (Council's website).
25 Bd. of Governors of the Fed. Reserve System, 98th Annual Report 2011, at 123 (May 2012), *available at* www.federalreserve.gov/ publications/annual-report/files/2011-annual-report.pdf

had dropped to 81%.[26] In 2011, the most frequently cited violations involved failure to: provide a timely and/or accurate notice of approval, counteroffer, or adverse action within thirty days after receiving a completed credit application; include the required information in the credit action notification letter, including ECOA prohibited bases, the name of the federal agency responsible for overseeing compliance with the regulation, and the specific reasons for any adverse action; collect information about applicants seeking credit primarily for the purchase or refinancing of a principal residence—including applicant race, ethnicity, sex, marital status, and age—for government monitoring purposes.[27]

The FDIC developed and began using new screening tools in 2006 to identify those FDIC-supervised institutions with mortgage lending disparities, based upon "higher rate" pricing information supplied by these institutions under the Home Mortgage Disclosure Act (HMDA). These tools also help the agency to assess whether the disparities in loan pricing and denial rates resulted from discriminatory lending or reflected other factors, such as creditworthiness, underwriting, or other nondiscriminatory criteria.

In 2009, the Government Accountability Office (GAO) reported on a study it had conducted of the three enforcement agencies and the five depository institution regulators that share responsibility for overseeing compliance with the FHA and the ECOA.[28] The GAO concluded that the fragmented nature of this oversight contributes to inconsistency and ineffectiveness in enforcing these two acts.[29] In addition, the GAO specifically noted that the HMDA data fails to include information about potentially critical variables, such as credit scores, that might explain differences in treatment of different borrowers and that this failure impaired the effectiveness of the data.[30] The GAO also emphasized that relatively few fair lending cases have been settled but noted that the agencies identified the complexity of fair lending cases, difficulties in recruiting and retaining staff, and the constraints of the ECOA's two-year statute of limitations as challenges that impeded enforcement.[31]

When a creditor's ECOA violation may also constitute a violation of the Fair Housing Act, the appropriate enforcing agency must notify the Department of Housing and Urban Development (HUD) if it does not notify the Department of Justice.[32] The enforcing agency must also notify the applicant or alleged victim of discrimination that the complaint was

referred to HUD and that the Fair Housing Act may provide a remedy for the discriminatory conduct.[33]

12.2.6 Agency Enforcement Policies and Statements

The CFPB's authority to issue regulations under the ECOA does not impair the authority of the FTC or the other enforcing agencies to make rules respecting their own procedures in enforcing compliance with ECOA requirements.[34]

For example, in 1981, the Federal Financial Institutions Examination Council, a formal interagency group that prescribes examination standards for financial institutions, proposed a policy statement calling for vigorous ECOA enforcement by the federal agencies which make up the Council.[35] The policy statement was subsequently adopted by the FRB, the Office of the Comptroller of the Currency, the FDIC, and the National Credit Union Administration.[36]

The Council also proposed a supervisory enforcement policy to implement the policy statement.[37] This enforcement policy was subsequently adopted by three of the five council members: the National Credit Union Administration, the Office of the Comptroller of the Currency, and the FRB. It sets out specific guidelines designed to correct serious violations of ECOA.

In 1993, the Comptroller of the Currency issued new procedures for all national bank examiners to use to identify discrimination in home mortgage loans made by national banks.[38] Yet another enforcement policy was issued in 1994 following the heightened scrutiny of credit availability which inspired a new, more informed look at racial patterns in lending and which startled both the industry and government regulators out of their complacency about fair lending compliance.[39] Ten agencies adopted the 1994 Joint Policy Statement on Discrimination in Lending.[40] The agencies issued this statement in part to respond

---

26 Bd. of Governors of the Fed. Reserve System, 96th Annual Report 2009, at 144–45 (May 2010), *available at* www.federalreserve.gov/boarddocs/rptcongress/annual09/pdf/AR09.pdf.

27 Bd. of Governors of the Fed. Reserve System, 98th Annual Report 2011, at 123 (May 2012), *available at* www.federalreserve.gov/publications/annual-report/files/2011-annual-report.pdf.

28 United States Gov't Accountability Office, Fair Lending: Data Limitations and the Fragmented U.S. Financial Regulatory Structure Challenge Federal Oversight and Enforcement Efforts (July 2009), *available at* www.gao.gov/new.items/d09704.pdf.

29 *Id.* at 61–64.

30 *Id.* at 14.

31 *Id.* at 53–61.

32 15 U.S.C. § 1681e(k).

33 15 U.S.C. § 1681e(k); *see also* Memorandum of Understanding Between Department of Housing and Urban Development and the Federal Financial Institutions Examination Council (FFIEC) Member Agencies, Clearinghouse No. 49,127 (Nov. 1991).

34 15 U.S.C. § 1691c(d).

35 Fed. Financial Institutions Examination Council, Interagency Policy Statement Regarding Enforcement of the Equal Credit Opportunity and Fair Housing Acts, Clearinghouse No. 49,137 (1981).

36 *See* 46 Fed. Reg. 56,500 (Nov. 17, 1981).

37 *See* ECOA Supervisory Enforcement Policy, *available on the companion website to this treatise.*

38 *See* Office of the Comptroller of the Currency, Examining Bulletin on Examining for Residential Lending Discrimination, Clearinghouse No. 49,130 (Apr. 30, 1993).

39 In 1992, after increased public scrutiny of credit availability in Boston and Atlanta, the Federal Reserve Bank of Boston issued a landmark study showing that race played a role in mortgage credit denials. Alicia Munnell, Geoffrey M.B. Tootell, Lynn Z. Browne, & James McEneaney, *Mortgage Lending in Boston: Interpreting HMDA Data*, 86 Am. Econ. Rev. 25 (1996), *available at* www.bos.frb.org/economic/wp/wp1992/wp92_7.pdf.

40 59 Fed. Reg. 18,266 (Apr. 15, 1994).
   The agencies are the Department of Housing and Urban Development, Office of Federal Housing Enterprise Oversight, Depart-

to industry complaints regarding the compliance burdens imposed upon banks by the application of different examination standards by each agency but also in part to recognize the regulatory efficiency of applying uniform standards.

The statement informs lenders of the information that the agencies consider in determining whether lending discrimination exists, how the agencies will respond to lending discrimination, and what steps lenders can take to prevent discriminatory lending practices. In addition, the statement answers thirteen questions often asked by financial institutions and the public. While it specifically states that it does not create any enforceable rights, it provides concrete examples of the three categories of evidence of discrimination that are useful to borrowers, as well as lenders, in understanding the rights conferred by the ECOA and the FHA.[41]

Lenders responded to the joint policy statement with questions and concerns about particular aspects of the statement, including self-testing, minority-only second review programs, employee compensation systems and overages, and disparate impact analysis. To clarify the Justice Department's position with regard to the Joint Policy Statement, on February 21, 1995, the assistant attorney general for civil rights wrote a letter to various lender association representatives.[42] The letter restates the Department's commitment to enforcing fair lending laws and offers guidance to lenders on how certain practices will be treated during an investigation and eventual prosecution.

In 1999, the Federal Financial Institutions Examination Council issued *Interagency Procedures on Fair Lending Examination.* This policy established a uniform set of procedures for its member agencies to use in their examinations to determine compliance with the ECOA and the Fair Housing Act (FHA).[43] The procedures include steps for identifying program discrimination risk factors, identifying lending discrimination risk factors, and compliance review and examination recommendations to evaluate compliance with the ECOA and FHA.[44]

12.3 Fair Housing Act Enforcement

12.3.1 HUD Administrative Enforcement

On its own initiative, and without receiving a consumer complaint, the United States Department of Housing and Urban Development (HUD) can investigate discriminatory practices and initiate an administrative proceeding against a creditor alleging credit discrimination.[45]

At all times HUD must attempt to resolve the matter through conciliation.[46] However, HUD can seek preliminary relief in federal court while an administrative conciliation proceeding is pending.[47]

If conciliation fails to resolve a matter, HUD is to refer the matter to a state or local agency that HUD has certified for this purpose.[48] If the certified agency does not act or no appropriate certified agency is available, then, after HUD determines there is reasonable cause to believe that discrimination exists, the case is referred to a HUD administrative law judge.[49] The administrative law judge may order actual damages, equitable relief, and civil penalties of $10,000 (increasing to $25,000 and $50,000 for repeat violators).[50] Decisions of the administrative law judge are reviewable by the Secretary of HUD and by the federal courts.[51]

Either the complainant, the respondent, or an aggrieved party may avoid the administrative process and instead have the complaint adjudicated immediately in federal court in an action brought by the Department of Justice.[52] The aggrieved party can receive the same relief as if a private action were instituted in court. This election must be made in a timely manner.[53]

---

ment of Justice, Office of the Comptroller of the Currency, Office of Thrift Supervision, Federal Reserve Board, Federal Deposit Insurance Corporation, Federal Housing Finance Board, Federal Trade Commission, and National Credit Union Administration.

41 Overt evidence, evidence of disparate treatment, and evidence of disparate impact. It notes that the "precise contours" of the latter are evolving but that disparate impact must be established (not assumed), often by quantitative or statistical methods; then it must be determined whether there is a business necessity for the practice and, if so, whether there is an alternative practice that has less discriminatory impact. 59 Fed. Reg. 18,266, 18,269 (Apr. 15, 1994); *see* § 4.3, *supra.*

42 Letter from Deval L. Patrick, Assistant Att'y Gen., Civil Rights Div., United States Dep't of Justice, to lender association representatives, Clearinghouse No. 52,064 (Feb. 21, 1995) (concerning Department of Justice Fair Lending Enforcement Program).

43 Fed. Financial Institutions Examination Council, Interagency Fair Lending Examination Procedures (Feb. 12, 1999), *available at* www.ffiec.gov/PDF/fairlend.pdf.

44 *Id.*

---

45 42 U.S.C. § 3610(a)(1)(A).

46 42 U.S.C. § 3610(b); *see* United States v. Hillman Hous. Corp., 212 F. Supp. 2d 252 (S.D.N.Y. 2002); United States v. Sea Winds of Marco, Inc., 893 F. Supp. 1051, 1054–55 (M.D. Fla. 1995) (HUD's alleged failure to engage in good faith conciliation is not a jurisdictional issue).

47 42 U.S.C. § 3610(e).

48 42 U.S.C. § 3610(f).

49 42 U.S.C. § 3612(a), (b); *see, e.g.,* Dep't of Hous. & Urban Dev. v. Mercantile-Safe Deposit & Trust Co., HUDALJ 03-91-0235-1 (June 10, 1993) (initial decision), *available at* www.hud.gov/offices/oha/oalj/cases/fha/pdf/mercntle.pdf.

50 42 U.S.C. § 3612(g)(3).

51 42 U.S.C. § 3612(i).

52 42 U.S.C. § 3612(o); *see* United States v. Tierra Apartments Ltd. P'ship, 865 F. Supp. 624 (D. Neb. 1994) (time limit is not jurisdictional and mandatory, therefore United State's failure to file action within thirty days did not divest court of jurisdiction or require dismissal; *see also* United States v. Bank United (W.D.N.Y. 1999), *available at* www.justice.gov/crt/about/hce/caselist; United States v. Weber, 1993 U.S. Dist. LEXIS 20732 (D. Neb. Oct. 19, 1993).

53 42 U.S.C. § 3612(a); *cf.* Green v. Konover Residential Corp., 1997 U.S. Dist. LEXIS 18893 (D. Conn. Nov. 24, 1997) (Fair Housing Act does not require exhaustion of administrative remedies); Ramos v. Dep't of Hous. & Urban Dev., 1997 U.S. Dist. LEXIS 13894, at *8 (S.D.N.Y. Sept. 11, 1997) (plaintiff may bring FHA action in federal court regardless of status of HUD administrative proceeding); *see* § 11.5.2, *supra.*

HUD also has authority, pursuant to the Federal Housing Enterprises Financial Safety and Soundness Act of 1992,[54] to regulate and enforce fair lending laws against two government-sponsored enterprises (GSEs): Fannie Mae and Freddie Mac.[55] Under the Act, HUD must, by regulation, prohibit the GSEs from discriminating in their mortgage purchases on the basis of race, color, religion, sex, handicap, familial status, age, or national origin.[56] The GSEs also may not discriminate based on the location or age of the dwelling or the neighborhood or census tract where the dwelling is located.[57]

The Act also authorizes HUD to require Fannie Mae and Freddie Mac—significant entities in the secondary mortgage industry—to submit data to assist HUD in investigating whether a mortgage lender has failed to comply with either the FHA or the ECOA and to take remedial action against lenders found to have violated the FHA or ECOA.[58] HUD must periodically review and comment on the GSEs' underwriting and appraisal guidelines to ensure that they are consistent with fair lending laws and must obtain and make available to the GSEs information from other regulatory and enforcement agencies of FHA and ECOA violations by lenders. HUD has issued final rules implementing, among other things, these statutory mandates.[59]

12.3.2 Civil Enforcement of the FHA by the United States Attorney General

The United States Attorney General, as head of the Department of Justice, can on his or her own initiative bring an action in federal court for credit discrimination under the FHA.[60] The case must involve a pattern or practice of discrimination, or the discrimination must raise an issue of general public importance.[61]

The Secretary of HUD may also elect not to follow the administrative procedure in a given case and may request instead that the Attorney General bring an action directly in federal court. Thus the Attorney General may bring a discrimination case in federal court either because the Attorney General determines that there is a pattern or practice of discrimination or because HUD requests that the Attorney General bring a

case. In either case, the court may award equitable relief, monetary damages to aggrieved parties, and a civil penalty not to exceed $50,000 for a first violation (or $100,000 for subsequent violations).[62]

12.4 Enforcement Activities at the State and Local Levels

12.4.1 State and Local Enforcement of Federal Credit Discrimination Statutes

12.4.1.1 Introduction

The ECOA and FHA do *not* explicitly authorize investigations or enforcement by state or local agencies (although the FHA allows for certain administrative enforcement by certified state or local agencies). There are four possible approaches for a state or local agency seeking relief for credit discrimination under federal statutes, as described at §§ 12.4.1.2–12.4.1.5, *infra*.

If a state or local agency has difficulty bringing an action under a federal cause of action, another option is to utilize state discrimination statutes that may explicitly authorize such enforcement. Finally, the state—or even a district attorney in some states—should be able to bring an action for credit discrimination under the state deceptive practices (UDAP) statute.[63]

12.4.1.2 Dodd-Frank Act May Authorize State ECOA Enforcement

The Dodd-Frank Wall Street Reform and Consumer Protection Act of 2010 ("Dodd-Frank Act")[64] provides for state attorney general enforcement of "provisions of this title [Dodd-Frank Title X] or regulations issued under this title,"[65] effective July 21, 2011.[66] 12 U.S.C. § 5536(a)(1)(A) provides that violation of a federal consumer financial law is a Title X violation. As a result, the Dodd-Frank Act appears to authorize state attorney general enforcement of federal consumer financial laws.

The definition of federal consumer financial laws includes the ECOA, but not the FHA,[67] so the state attorney general should be able to enforce the ECOA but not the FHA, at least under the Dodd-Frank Act authority. There is an important

---

54 12 U.S.C. §§ 4501–4641 (as amended by the Housing and Economic Recovery Act of 2008, Pub. L. No. 110-289, 122 Stat. 2654).

55 Although the Housing and Economic Recovery Act of 2008 created a new agency, the Federal Housing Finance Agency, that has supervisory powers over Fannie Mae and Freddie Mac, the Act left intact HUD's authority over the enterprises with respect to the FHA and the ECOA. Pub. L. No. 110-289, § 1122(b), 122 Stat. 2654 (2008).

56 12 U.S.C. § 4545(1) (as amended by Pub. L. No. 110-289, § 1122(b), 122 Stat. 2654).

57 12 U.S.C. § 4545(1) (as amended by Pub. L. No. 110-289, § 1122(b), 122 Stat. 2654).

58 12 U.S.C. § 4545(2) (as amended by Pub. L. No. 110-289, § 1122(b), 122 Stat. 2654).

59 24 C.F.R. pt. 81.

60 42 U.S.C. § 3614(a).

61 42 U.S.C. § 3614(a).

62 42 U.S.C. § 3614(d).

63 *See* National Consumer Law Center, Unfair and Deceptive Acts and Practices § 4.3.9 (8th ed. 2012).

64 Pub. L. No. 111-203, 124 Stat. 1376 (July 21, 2010) (hereinafter "Dodd-Frank Act").

65 12 U.S.C. § 5481(a)(1), *as added by* Pub. L. No. 111-203, tit. X, § 1042(a)(1), 124 Stat. 1955 (July 21, 2010).

66 *Id.* Section 1100G specifies an effective date for Title X provisions as of the "designated transfer date." 75 Fed. Reg. 57,252 (Sept. 20, 2010) sets the designated transfer date as July 21, 2011.

67 12 U.S.C. § 5481(14), *as added by* Pub. L. No. 111-203, tit. X, § 1002(14), 124 Stat. 1955 (July 21, 2010).

exception to state enforcement of the ECOA pursuant to the Dodd-Frank Act. When an action is brought against a national bank or federal savings association, the state attorney general can only enforce rules prescribed by the Consumer Financial Protection Bureau "under a provision of this title."[68] It would appear that this includes ECOA and Regulation B.

12.4.1.3 State Enforcement of Credit Discrimination As Unfair, Deceptive, and Abusive

As described in § 12.4.1.2, *supra*, the Dodd-Frank Act provides for state attorney general enforcement of "provisions of this title [Dodd-Frank Title X] or regulations issued under this title."[69] 12 U.S.C. § 5536(a)(1)(B) prohibits under Title X any "unfair, deceptive, or abusive act or practice" (UDAAP). A state attorney general thus can bring an action in state or federal court to challenge unfair, deceptive, or abusive credit discrimination. This provision is effective July 21, 2011.[70]

It should not be difficult to argue that credit discrimination is "unfair, deceptive or abusive."[71] Of course, in most states the attorney general can bring a similar challenge under a state deceptive practices (UDAP) statute. But in some states credit practices are outside the statute's scope, or a statute only prohibits deceptive but not unfair practices, and no state UDAP statute prohibits abusive practices. UDAAP authority also gives the state attorney general the option of bringing the action in federal court.

Nevertheless, state attorney general UDAAP enforcement is limited when an action is brought against a national bank or federal savings association. In that type of action, the state attorney general can only enforce UDAAP rules issued by the Consumer Financial Protection Bureau and cannot base an enforcement action on the general UDAAP standard.[72]

12.4.1.4 *Parens Patriae*

Under a *parens patriae* theory, a state or local agency acts on behalf of a class of residents of that state or locality to seek relief otherwise available to individuals under state or federal law. In effect, the state is bringing the individuals' action for them. There is authority allowing state officials to enforce the FHA under the *parens patriae* doctrine.[73]

A state may also bring an action in its *parens patriae* capacity to enforce state anti-discrimination laws. If the state brings the action in state court to benefit its population as a whole, the action should not be subject to removal to federal court on diversity grounds.[74] Diversity jurisdiction requires the existence of parties to a lawsuit who are "citizens" of different states. A state bringing an action on behalf of its residents is not a "citizen" of any state.[75] Therefore, diversity jurisdiction is precluded when a state is a party to an action. In addition, *parens patriae* actions are not subject to the requirements of Fed. R. Civ. P. 23 or similar state rules governing class actions. For this reason, courts of appeals have rejected the argument that *parens patriae* actions brought in state courts are subject to removal to federal court under the Class Action Fairness Act.[76]

12.4.1.5 Action Based on Damage to the State or Locality

A state or locality should be able to enforce the ECOA and FHA by claiming that the state or locality itself has been injured by the ECOA or FHA violation. The ECOA provides for private remedies for aggrieved applicants, so the state or locality must meet this definition.[77] The FHA has a broader standing standard.[78]

The City of Baltimore brought an FHA action against Wells Fargo Bank alleging that the bank targeted Baltimore's underserved and vulnerable minority Baltimore neighborhoods for subprime loans, which in turn led to a disproportionately high foreclosure rate in those neighborhoods, causing injury to the city.[79]

---

68 *Id.* § 5481(a)(2).

69 *Id.* § 5481.

70 *Id.* Section 1100G of the Dodd-Frank Act specifies an effective date for Title X provisions as of the "designated transfer date." 75 Fed. Reg. 57,252 (Sept. 20, 2010) sets the designated transfer date as July 21, 2011.

71 *See* National Consumer Law Center, Unfair and Deceptive Acts and Practices § 4.3.9 (8th ed. 2012).

72 12 U.S.C. § 5552(a)(2), *as added by* Pub. L. No. 111-203, tit. X, § 1042(a)(2), 124 Stat. 2012 (July 21, 2010).

73 Support Ministries for Persons with AIDS, Inc. v. Vill. of Waterford, N.Y., 799 F. Supp. 272 (N.D.N.Y. 1992); *see also* Clearing House Ass'n, L.L.C. v. Spitzer, 394 F. Supp. 2d 620 (S.D.N.Y. 2005) (implying *parens patriae* standing is available except for questions of National Bank Act preemption), *aff'd in part and vacated in part*

---

sub nom. Clearing House Ass'n, L.L.C. v. Cuomo, 510 F.3d 105 (2d Cir. 2007), *rev'd in part on other grounds*, 129 S. Ct. 2710 (2009); *cf.* Clearing House Ass'n, L.L.C. v. Cuomo, 510 F.3d 105 (2d Cir. 2007) (discussing *parens patriae* standing for an FHA claim, but finding the question not yet ripe), *rev'd in part on other grounds*, 129 S. Ct. 2710 (2009).

74 Colo. Civil Rights Comm'n v. Wells Fargo Bank and Co., 2011 WL 2610205 (D. Colo. July 1, 2011) (remanding to state court Colorado's action seeking redress under state law in the form of injunctive and declaratory relief and penalties for lender's practices of discrimination based on marital status).

75 *Id.* 411 U.S. 693, 717 (1973) (citing *Moor v. County of Alameda*).

76 28 U.S.C. § 1332(d); *see* Nevada v. Bank of America, 672 F.3d 661 (9th Cir. 2012) (*parens patriae* suit alleging bank violated state's UDAP statute and a prior consent decree in its handling of loan modification requests was not class action or "mass action" subject to CAFA removal); LG Display Co., Ltd. v. Madigan, 665 F.3d 768 (7th Cir. 2011); Washington v. Chimei Innolux Corp., 659 F.3d 842 (9th Cir. 2011); West Virginia *ex rel* McGraw v. CVS Pharmacy Inc., 646 F.3d 169 (4th Cir. 2011), *cert. denied*, 132 S. Ct. 761 (2011); West Virginia ex rel McGraw v. JP Morgan Chase & Co., 842 F. Supp. 2d 984 (S.D. W. Va. 2012). *See generally In re* Vioxx Products Liab. Litig., 843 F. Supp. 2d 654, 662 (E.D. La. 2012) (collecting U.S. district court decisions).

77 *See* § 11.2, *supra*.

78 *See* § 11.2, *supra*.

79 Mayor & City Council of Balt. v. Wells Fargo Bank, No. L08CV062 (D. Md. Jan. 8, 2008), *available on the companion website to this treatise*.

Ruling on the City of Baltimore's third amended complaint, a federal court found sufficient standing based upon specific allegations related to the City's maintenance expenses and diminished property tax revenues for 190 vacant properties foreclosed by Wells Fargo and that this injury was caused in part by Wells Fargo's predatory lending practices.[80] Wells Fargo eventually settled the case as part of a larger action brought by the United States Department of Justice.[81]

The City of Memphis and Shelby County, Tennessee, have also filed an FHA action similar to Baltimore's, and a federal court similarly found standing because the City of Memphis adequately alleged injury and causation related to Wells Fargo's reverse-redlining practices.[82] The complaint focused on the costs of increased government services and loss of property tax revenue traceable to foreclosed properties tied to the alleged discriminatory practices. Wells Fargo settled on terms favorable to the City.

12.4.2 National Bank Preemption of State Enforcement of Credit Discrimination Law

12.4.2.1 Introduction

State credit discrimination statutes often explicitly authorize state attorney general or other agency enforcement.[83] Such state enforcement is generally not preempted by the federal discrimination laws, unless there is a direct conflict between the federal and state discrimination laws.[84] For example, in actions challenging lenders' reverse-redlining practices, the courts have often allowed the cases to proceed under state anti-discrimination laws in conjunction with FHA claims.[85]

Nevertheless, an important issue is the extent to which the National Banking Act and other federal banking law preempts state enforcement and investigation of national bank and federal savings and loans for violations of state discrimination law. This presents two separate issues. First, does federal banking law preempt application of the state law to a national bank or federal savings association? Second, if state law is not preempted, can a state agency investigate and enforce violations of the state statute by a national bank or federal savings association, or do the exclusive "visitorial" powers of the federal Office of the Comptroller of the Currency (OCC) preclude state investigation and enforcement?

12.4.2.2 National Bank Act and OCC Preemption of State Credit Discrimination Statutes

It is implicit in a 2009 Supreme Court decision that federal banking laws and OCC regulations do not preempt the application of state credit discrimination statutes to national banks and federal savings associations. In *Cuomo v. Clearing House*,[86] the Court held that states could enforce non-preempted state laws. The Court assumed that state credit discrimination statutes as applied to national banks were valid and not preempted by the National Bank Act. The Second Circuit opinion in the case also assumed that the New York fair lending law at issue was not substantively preempted.[87] Ultimately, the issue was not whether national banks had to comply with these state laws—they did—but whether and by what means *state officials* could investigate and enforce these state laws against the banks. Decisions prior to *Clearing House*[88] and an OCC Interpretive Letter[89] also confirm that state anti-discrimination laws are not preempted.

The Dodd-Frank Act makes it even clearer that federal banking laws do not preempt state anti-discrimination laws. First, it provides that federal banking law does not occupy the field in any area of state law.[90] Prior to the Dodd-Frank Act, the Office of Thrift Supervision, which formerly regulated federal saving associations, had purported to preempt the field, and the OCC's preemption regulation for national banks did so in all but name.[91]

Second, the Dodd-Frank Act tightens the standard for determining whether a state consumer financial law that directly and specifically regulates a financial transaction involving a national bank or federal savings association is preempted by the National Bank Act or the Home Owners Loan Act.[92] The

---

80 Mayor & City Council of Balt. v. Wells Fargo Bank, N.A. et al., 2011 WL 1557759 (D. Md. Apr. 22, 2011).

81 The proposed consent decree filed on July 12, 2012 is available at www.justice.gov/iso/opa/resources/14201271211384881962.pdf.

82 City of Memphis et al. v. Wells Fargo Bank, N.A., 2011 WL 1706756 (W.D. Tenn. May 4, 2011).

83 *See* appx. F, *infra*.

84 *See* § 11.6.1.3, *supra*.

85 *See, e.g.*, Barkley v. Olympia Mortgage Co., 2007 WL 2437810 (E.D.N.Y. Aug. 22, 2007); Matthews v. New Century Mortgage Corp., 185 F. Supp. 2d 874 (S.D. Ohio 2002); Eva v. Midwest Nat'l Mortgage Banc, Inc., 143 F. Supp. 2d 862 (N.D. Ohio 2001); Assocs. Home Equity Servs., Inc. v. Troup, 343 N.J. Super. 254, 778 A.2d 529 (Super. Ct. App. Div. 2001); *cf.* 15 U.S.C. § 1691d(e) (the ECOA, unlike the FHA, requires an election of remedies between ECOA and state law claims for monetary damages arising from the same transaction).

86 Cuomo v. Clearing House Ass'n, L.L.C., 129 S. Ct. 2710 (2009).

87 *See* Clearing House Ass'n, L.L.C. v. Cuomo, 510 F.3d 105 (2d Cir. 2007), *aff'd in part, rev'd in part on other grounds*, 129 S. Ct. 2710 (2009).

88 Kroske v. US Bank Corp., 432 F.3d 976 (9th Cir. 2005) (state law prohibiting age discrimination is not preempted by section 24 (Fifth) of the NBA allowing banks to terminate certain bank officers "at pleasure," at least to the extent that the state act mirrors its federal counterpart), *amended on other grounds*, 2006 WL 319025 (9th Cir. Feb. 13, 2006); Nat'l State Bank, Elizabeth, N.J. v. Long, 630 F.2d 981 (3d Cir. 1980) (state anti-redlining law does not frustrate federal banking system and therefore is not preempted).

89 Office of the Comptroller of the Currency, Interpretive Letter No. 998 (Mar. 9, 2004).

90 12 U.S.C. §§ 25b(b)(4), 1465(b).

91 *See* National Consumer Law Center, Mortgage Lending § 5.3.2 (2012).

92 12 U.S.C. § 25b(a)(2), *as added by* Pub. L. No. 111-203, tit. X, § 1044(a), 124 Stat. 2014 (July 21, 2010) (NBA); *see* 12 U.S.C. § 1465, *as amended by* Pub. L. No. 111-203, tit. X, § 1046(a), 124 Stat. 2017 (July 21, 2010) (HOLA, incorporating NBA standard)).

Dodd-Frank Act calls for application of the preemption standard enunciated by the Supreme Court in the 1996 *Barnett* decision. Such a law is preempted by federal banking laws only if, in accordance with the Supreme Court's *Barnett Bank* decision,[93] it prevents or substantially interferes with the exercise of powers granted banks under federal law or if it discriminates against national banks or federal savings associations.[94]

This preemption standard applies only to state consumer financial laws. General laws such as those that bar discrimination or unfair or deceptive acts or practices should be even less subject to preemption.[95] However, even if the Dodd-Frank Act standard applies to anti-discrimination laws, the powers granted by federal law to national banks or federal savings associations do not include discriminatory lending, so state fair lending laws cannot prevent or substantially interfere with their exercise of those powers.

12.4.2.3 Visitorial Powers Under the National Bank Act and State Agency Investigation and Enforcement

12.4.2.3.1 Introduction

Assuming that the National Bank Act does not preempt the application of state credit discrimination statutes to national banks or federal thrifts, the question still remains whether only the OCC can investigate and enforce those state laws or whether state or local agencies can do so as well. The question is whether state investigation or enforcement constitutes an exercise of "visitorial powers" and thus interferes with the exclusive examination and supervision powers of the OCC.

The question of visitorial powers only affects actions by a state agency, not by consumers. In other words, while a consumer might be able to bring an action under a non-preempted state law with regard to a national bank or federal thrift, the question arises as to whether a state agency can do the same or whether all agency regulation of national banks and federal thrifts is left to the OCC.

12.4.2.3.2 Supreme Court's Clearing House *decision*

In its decision in *Cuomo v. Clearing House Association, L.L.C.*,[96] the United States Supreme Court considered the extent to which states can investigate and enforce state discrimination laws against national banks. The Court held that states can initiate court actions to enforce non-preempted state credit discrimination laws against national banks, but state officials cannot conduct administrative investigations into national banks' lending practices.

The National Bank Act (NBA)[97] contains general language placing primary responsibility for regulating national banks at the federal level and charges the OCC with administering the NBA: "No national bank shall be subject to any visitorial powers except as authorized by Federal Law, vested in the courts, . . . or . . . directed by Congress."

An OCC implementing regulation prohibited state agency visitorial powers such as conducting examinations of national banks and inspecting or requiring the production of their books or records. But the regulation went further and prohibited states from "prosecuting enforcement actions . . . except in limited circumstances authorized by federal law."[98] In *Clearing House* the banks and the OCC contended that the prohibition on state officials "prosecuting enforcement actions" was consistent with the NBA's delegation of visitorial powers over the banks to the OCC. In their view, this barred all state litigation initiatives, including enforcement of the state's non-preempted civil rights laws in court against national banks.

The Supreme Court rejected this interpretation, ruling that the OCC's regulation went too far in defining what constituted "visitorial powers." The Court distinguished a state's ability to conduct general administrative oversight activities over national banks (which is preempted) and state efforts to obtain judicial enforcement of specific laws against the national banks (which was not preempted). Enforcing state laws as a litigant in a judicial proceeding was not an exercise of "visitorial" powers over a bank.[99] The Court thus invalidated the OCC regulation to the extent it purported to block a state from judicial enforcement actions, since the regulation was not based on a reasonable interpretation of "visitorial" activities. The OCC has amended its regulation to recognize the Supreme Court's ruling.[100]

On the other hand, the Supreme Court ruled the state could not issue its own pre-litigation subpoenas for national banks' records in order to conduct an administrative investigation of the banks' lending practices. Issuing subpoenas outside the context of litigation was a standard exercise of visitorial authority by a state official, and Congress intended to reserve this type of oversight for the OCC.[101]

12.4.2.3.3 Dodd-Frank Act codifies Clearing House *and extends it to savings and loans*

The Dodd-Frank Act codifies the Supreme Court's decision in *Clearing House*[102] by expressly amending the National Bank Act to provide that the limitation on the states' exercise of

---

93 Barnett Bank of Marion Cnty., N.A. v. Nelson, Florida Ins. Comm'r et al., 116 S. Ct. 1103, 134 L. Ed. 2d 237, 517 U.S. 25 (1996).

94 12 U.S.C. §§ 25b(b)(B), 1465.

95 *See* National Consumer Law Center, Mortgage Lending § 5.6.3.5.8 (2012).

96 557 U.S. 519, 129 S. Ct. 2710, 174 L. Ed. 2d 464 (2009).

97 12 U.S.C. § 484(a).

98 12 C.F.R. § 7.4000(a)(1).

99 Cuomo v. Clearing House Ass'n, L.L.C., 557 U.S. 519, 536, 129 S. Ct. 2710, 174 L. Ed. 2d 464 (2009).

100 76 C.F.R. § 43549 (July 26, 2011), *codified at* 12 C.F.R. § 7.4000(b).

101 *But see* Mississippi Dep't of Revenue v. Pikco Finance, Inc., 97 So. 3d 1203 (Miss. 2012) (noting that state agencies can exercise visitorial powers over national banks, including issuance of subpoenas, when enforcing state laws not related to lending activities, such as state tax laws).

102 *See* § 12.4.2.3.2, *supra*.

"visitorial powers" over national banks must not be construed to limit the authority of states to bring actions to enforce non-preempted state laws against national banks.[103] State attorneys general and regulators can enforce non-preempted state laws through judicial proceedings against national banks.[104] However, absent an enforcement action, state officials remain precluded from issuing subpoenas and conducting ongoing administrative oversight and control over national banks.

The Dodd-Frank Act also amends the Home Owners Loan Act to clarify that the same visitorial standards that now apply to national banks under the NBA apply to federally chartered thrifts and savings and loans under the Home Owners Loan Act.[105]

12.4.2.3.4 States regain visitorial powers as to national bank subsidiaries and affiliates

In *Watters v. Wachovia Bank*,[106] the Supreme Court affirmed that a national bank's mortgage business was subject to the OCC's exclusive supervision even when conducted through an operating subsidiary. It therefore concluded that Michigan's licensing, registration, and inspection requirements could not be applied to a national bank operating subsidiary. The Court reached this conclusion based on the National Bank Act itself, without relying on the OCC's now-repealed regulation that generally extended preemption to national bank operating subsidiaries.[107]

The Dodd-Frank Act legislatively overrules the holding in *Watters*. It provides that Title 62 of the Revised Statutes and 12 U.S.C. § 371 "do not preempt, annul, or affect the applicability of any State law" to any national bank subsidiary.[108] As the OCC's exclusive visitorial powers are found in Title 62,[109] the Dodd-Frank Act amendment subjects operating subsidiaries to state laws requiring them to submit to state examinations and supervisory visits. On July 21, 2011, the OCC withdrew its rule that had generally preempted the application of state laws to national bank operating subsidiaries.[110] Since the Dodd-Frank Act also transferred authority over federal savings associations to the OCC, the new rules apply to subsidiaries of federal savings associations as well.[111]

As a result of these developments, state agencies and localities are not precluded from enforcement actions or investigations involving subsidiaries and affiliates of national banks and federal thrifts.

12.4.2.3.5 Implications of Clearing House *and Dodd-Frank Act codification*

Clearing House and the Dodd-Frank Act's codification of that ruling now mean that a state cannot launch an investigation of discriminatory lending practices by issuing an administrative subpoena to a national bank or federal savings association, nor can it go to court to enforce the administrative subpoena.[112] However, *after* initiating a formal lawsuit against a national bank or federal savings association, the state can seek the same information with the aid of discovery tools, including subpoenas.

In addition, *Clearing House* and the Dodd-Frank Act do not limit an *individual's* right to bring an action to enforce non-preempted state anti-discrimination laws against national banks and federal savings and loans associations.[113] Nor does *Clearing House* or the Dodd-Frank Act affect the broad concept of standing for organizations to bring actions to enforce the FHA.[114]

Clearing House and the Dodd-Frank Act also do not restrict state investigations against entities other than national banks and federal savings associations.[115] After the Dodd-Frank Act, state authorities can exercise whatever powers are allowed by state law against operating subsidiaries of these institutions or against other entities affiliated with national banks or federal savings associations. The New York Division of Human Rights launched investigations into the practices of companies providing tax refund anticipation loans (RALs). The tax preparers claimed the state's authority to investigate was limited because they were affiliated with national banks in the loan scheme. But the court found that the state was not prevented from conducting an administrative investigation of the tax preparer.[116]

12.4.2.3.6 The OCC's regulations implementing the Dodd-Frank Act and the Clearing House decision

In July 2011, the OCC published final regulations that purport to implement provisions of the Dodd-Frank Act and the

---

103 12 U.S.C. § 25b(b)(i), *as added by* Pub. L. No. 111-203, tit. X, § 1047(a), 124 Stat. 2018 (July 21, 2010).

104 12 U.S.C. §§ 25b, 5552(a)(2), *as added and amended by* Pub. L. No. 111-203, tit. X, §§ 1042, 1047(a), 124 Stat. 2012, 2018 (July 21, 2010).

105 12 U.S.C. § 1465(a), *as added by* Pub. L. No. 111-203, tit. X, § 1046(a), 124 Stat. 2017 (July 21, 2010).

106 Watters v. Wachovia Bank, 550 U.S. 1, 127 S. Ct. 1559, 167 L. Ed. 2d 389 (2007).

107 Former 12 C.F.R. § 7.4006.

108 12 U.S.C. § 25b(b)(2).

109 *See* Historical and Statutory Notes, References in Text, 12 U.S.C. § 25b (noting that Title 62 includes 12 U.S.C. §§ 481–485).

110 76 Fed. Reg. 43,549 (July 21, 2011) (rescinding 12 C.F.R. § 7.4006).

111 *See* National Consumer Law Center, Mortgage Lending § 5.11.1 (2012).

112 Although the Supreme Court's decision in *Clearing House* discussed only investigation of state laws, the same reasoning might apply to a state attempt to investigate potential violations of federal law such as the FHA or ECOA.

113 *See* § 11.6.1.3, *supra*.

114 *See, e.g.*, Nat'l Cmty. Reinvestment Coal. v. Accredited Home Lenders Holding Co., 573 F. Supp. 2d 70, 74–75 (D.D.C. 2008).

115 Capital One Bank (USA) v. McGraw, 563 F. Supp. 2d 613 (S.D. W. Va. 2008) (affiliated entity that issued credit cards and performed other services on behalf of a national bank was neither a national bank itself nor a subsidiary of one and thus not shielded from state attorney general's subpoena power under OCC visitorial preemption).

116 N.Y. State Div. of Human Rights v. H.& R Block Tax Serv., Inc., 897 N.Y.S.2d 75 (N.Y. App. Div. 2010); *cf.* Jackson Hewitt Tax Serv., Inc. v. Kirkland, 735 F. Supp. 2d 91 (S.D.N.Y. 2010), *aff'd*, 455 Fed. Appx. 16 (2d Cir. 2012).

codification of the Supreme Court's *Clearing House* decision.[117] Some changes in the regulations are straightforward. They clarify that the scope of the exercise of a state's visitorial powers does not include the commencement of legal proceedings in courts against national banks.[118] They delete the preemption protection for subsidiaries of national banks.[119] The regulations make it clear that the same OCC regulations that apply to national banks and their subsidiaries now apply to federal savings and loans associations and their subsidiaries.[120]

In other significant areas, the OCC regulations retain or adopt standards that are inconsistent with the Dodd-Frank Act.[121] Notably, the OCC continues to claim authority to declare categories of state laws preempted. As discussed above,[122] the Dodd-Frank Act requires that federal agencies make these determinations on a case-by-case basis. The OCC also ignored the Dodd-Frank Act's directive to adopt the Supreme Court's *Barnett* standard for preemption and to preempt state laws only if they meet that standard (or if they discriminate against federal depositories or conflict with another federal law). The *Barnett* standard requires a showing that a state law prevents or significantly interferes with the exercise of federal banking regulatory powers.[123] In these and other areas, the OCC exceeded its authority under the Dodd-Frank Act, leaving its interpretations subject to future challenge.

12.4.2.3.7 State investigatory authority upon referral from HUD

Another way in which state agencies can investigate discriminatory practices of any lender under their state laws is through a referral from the Department of Housing and Urban Development (HUD). Under certain circumstances, the FHA requires that HUD initially refer discrimination complaints to state agencies for investigation and enforcement. HUD must make such a referral when it has determined that a state anti-discrimination law contains provisions that are substantially similar to the FHA.[124] In these situations, the state agency may investigate and enforce state anti-discrimination laws against national banks and federally regulated savings and loan associations, just as HUD may do. Preemption is not involved here because the state agency acts at the direction of HUD

pursuant to a delegation expressly authorized by federal law (the FHA).[125]

12.4.3 Examples of State and Local Enforcement

In *People of the State of Illinois v. Wells Fargo & Co.*[126] the attorney general alleged that various Wells Fargo affiliates engaged in discriminatory lending practices that targeted and disproportionately affected African American and Hispanic borrowers, in violation of the Illinois Human Rights Act, the state's Fairness in Lending Act, and the state UDAP statute. The lender's compensation structure rewarded employees for placing borrowers in high-cost loans, and the state produced data showing a pattern of directing high-cost subprime loans to African American and Hispanic borrowers who were otherwise eligible for lower-cost prime loans. The case survived a motion to dismiss[127] and was settled as part of the Department of Justice's nationwide consent decree against Wells Fargo. The Illinois attorney general also filed a similar action against Countrywide Financial[128] that was settled as part of the Department of Justice's nationwide settlement with Countrywide.[129]

Some five years earlier, New York State also reached a settlement with Countrywide Home Loans. Under the settlement, Countrywide agreed to compensate certain minority borrowers who were given improperly costly loans and to institute a $3 million consumer education program, among other commitments.[130]

The Pennsylvania Human Relations Commission reached a decision finding reverse-redlining to be actionable under the state Human Relations Act because it held brokers liable for the violations.[131] More recently, the Commission enforced the state's

---

117 76 Fed. Reg. 43,549 (July 26, 2011) (amending OCC regulations on preemption of state laws (12 C.F.R. §§ 7.4007–7.4009, 34.4), regulation of operating subsidiaries (12 C.F.R. §§ 5.34, 7.4006), states' exercise of visitorial powers (12 C.F.R. § 7.4000), and the applicability of OCC preemption standards to federal savings and loans (7 C.F.R. §§ 7.4010, 34.6)).

118 *See* § 12.4.2.3.2, *supra* (new provision at 12 C.F.R. § 7.4000).

119 *See* § 12.4.2.3.4, *supra* (new provision at 12 C.F.R. §§ 5.34, 7.4006).

120 *See* § 12.4.2.3.4, *supra* (new provision at 12 C.F.R. §§ 7.4010, 34.6).

121 *See* National Consumer Law Center, The Cost of Credit, Regulation, Preemption, and Industry Abuses § 3.4.6.3 (4th ed. 2009 and Supp.).

122 § 12.4.2.3, *supra*.

123 *Id.*

124 42 U.S.C. § 3610(f).

125 USAA Fed. Sav. Bank v. Pa. Human Relations Comm'n, 2011 WL 3715113 (E.D. Pa. Aug. 23, 2011) (rejecting lender's action to bar state agency's investigation of claim of national origin discrimination referred to the state agency by HUD).

126 *See* Press Release, Ill. Att'y Gen.'s Office, Madigan Sues Wells Fargo for Discriminatory and Deceptive Mortgage Lending Practices (July 31, 2009), *available at* www.ag.state.il.us/pressroom/2009_07 (July 31, 2009) (listing includes weblinks to press release, complaint, and supporting studies and documentation).

127 Memorandum and Order, People of the State of Ill. v. Wells Fargo & Co. et al., No. 09 CH 26434 (Oct. 25, 2011) (unpublished), *available on the companion website to this treatise.*

128 People of the State of Ill. v. Countrywide Financial Corp., No. 10-CH-27929 (Cir. Ct. of Cook Cnty., Ch. Div., filed June 29, 2010). A copy of the complaint can be found at http://illinoisattorney general.gov/pressroom/2010_06/index.html.

129 United States v. Countrywide Financial Corp. et al, No. 11-cv-10540 (C.D. Cal., consent order approved Dec. 28, 2011).

130 *See* Press Release, Office of the N.Y. State Att'y Gen., Countrywide Agrees to New Measures to Combat Racial & Ethnic Disparities in Mortgage Loan Pricing (Dec. 5, 2006), *available at* www.oag.state.ny.us/press/2006/dec/dec05a_06.html.

131 *See* McGlawn v. Human Relations Comm'n, 891 A.2d 757 (Pa. Commw. Ct. 2006) (state Human Rights Commission found mortgage broker violated state Human Relations Act by engaging in reverse-redlining).

anti-discrimination statute in a case involving reverse redlining in commercial lending.[132] The Philadelphia Commission on Human Relations has also entered consent decrees with four lending institutions involving alleged violations of anti-discrimination provisions of the Philadelphia Code.[133]

The Massachusetts attorney general has settled its lawsuit against Option One, now known as Sand Canyon, a subsidiary of H&R Block, after alleging that the lender targeted African American and Latino borrowers with high-cost and unaffordable loans. In addition, in the wake of the 1996 landmark study by the Federal Reserve Bank of Boston,[134] the Massachusetts attorney general reached a settlement with ten banks and with the bankers' association to try to ensure that minority borrowers and minority neighborhoods have equal access to credit.

In the early 1990s, a subsidiary of Fleet Financial Group agreed to pay $100 million to settle charges by the Georgia attorney general that the lender "preyed on minority borrowers by charging high fees and interest rates"[135] in violation of the state UDAP statute.

The commission accepted testimony that the brokers were significantly involved in making the loans. For more on broker liability, see § 11.3.2.2, *supra*.

132 Girard Finance Co. v. Pa. Human Relations Comm'n, 52 A. 3d 523 (Pa. Commw. 2012) (upholding Commission's cease and desist order and damages award in proceeding that alleged disparate impact in predatory loan terms made to minority-owned businesses in minority neighborhoods).

133 Consent Order and Decree, Phila. Comm'n on Human Relations v. Boulevard Mortgage Co., Clearinghouse No. 49,139A (Philadelphia Comm'n on Human Relations June 29, 1993) (No. 92110885); Consent Order and Decree, Phila. Comm'n on Human Relations v. St. Edmonds Sav. & Loan, Clearinghouse No. 49,140A (Philadelphia Comm'n on Human Relations May 4, 1993) (No. 92120892); Consent Order and Decree, Phila. Comm'n on Human Relations v. Bank & Trust Co. of Old York Rd., Clearinghouse No. 49,141A (Philadelphia Comm'n on Human Relations Apr. 7, 1993) (No. 92110887); Consent Order and Decree, Phila. Comm'n on Human Relations v. People's Mortgage Co., Clearinghouse No. 49,142A

(Philadelphia Comm'n on Human Relations Feb. 3, 1993) (No. 92110886).

134 *See* Lynn Z. Browne, James McEneaney, Alicia Munnell, & Geoffrey M.B. Tootell, *Mortgage Lending in Boston: Interpreting HMDA Data*, 86 Am. Econ. Rev. 25 (1996), *available at* www.bos.frb.org/economic/wp/wp1992/wp92_7.pdf.

135 Kimberly Blanton & Mitchell Zuckoff, *Fleet to Pay $100m Loan Bias Settlement*, Boston Globe, Dec. 16, 1993, at 1.

Federal Credit Discrimination Statutes

This appendix reprints the current version of federal credit discrimination statutes: the Equal Credit Opportunity Act (ECOA), the Fair Housing Act, and Civil Rights Acts, 42 U.S.C. §§ 1981, 1982, 1988. These statutes are also found on the companion website to this treatise.

The Dodd-Frank Wall Street Reform and Consumer Protection Act ("the Dodd-Frank Act"), Pub. L. No. 111-203, § 1474 (July 21, 2010), adds a new ECOA subsection, 15 U.S.C. § 1691(e), concerning copies of appraisals sent to applicants. Subsection 1691(e) is redlined in this appendix. While there is ambiguity concerning the effective date of certain Title XIV provisions in the Dodd-Frank Act, it may be that subsection 1691(e) does not become effective until January 18, 2014—the effective date of Regulation B amendments relating to subsection 1691(e). *See* 78 Fed. Reg. 7248 (Jan. 31, 2013).

A.1 Equal Credit Opportunity Act, 15 U.S.C. §§ 1691–1691f

TITLE 15. COMMERCE AND TRADE

* * *

CHAPTER 41. CONSUMER CREDIT PROTECTION

* * *

SUBCHAPTER IV—EQUAL CREDIT OPPORTUNITY

§ 1691 note.	Short title
§ 1691 note.	Findings and purpose
§ 1691.	Scope of prohibition
§ 1691a.	Definitions; rules of construction
§ 1691b.	Promulgation of regulations by Board; establishment of Consumer Advisory Council by Board; duties, membership, etc., of Council
§ 1691c.	Administrative enforcement
§ 1691c-1.	Incentives for self-testing and self-correction
§ 1691c-2.	Small business loan data collection
§ 1691d.	Applicability of other laws
§ 1691e.	Civil liability
§ 1691f.	Annual reports to Congress; contents

SOURCE: Pub. L. No. 93-495, § 503, 88 Stat. 1521–1524 (1974), unless otherwise noted.

15 U.S.C. § 1691 note. Short title

This title may be cited as the "Equal Credit Opportunity Act."

[Pub. L. No. 93-495, § 501, 88 Stat. 1525 (1974)]

15 U.S.C. § 1691 note. Findings and purpose

The Congress finds that there is a need to insure that the various financial institutions and other firms engaged in the extensions of credit exercise their responsibility to make credit available with fairness, impartiality, and without discrimination on the basis of sex or marital status. Economic stabilization would be enhanced and competition among the various financial institutions and other firms engaged in the extension of credit would be strengthened by an absence of discrimination on the basis of sex or marital status, as well as by the informed use of credit which Congress has heretofore sought to promote. It is the purpose of this Act to require that financial institutions and other firms engaged in the extension of credit make that credit equally available to all creditworthy customers without regard to sex or marital status.

15 U.S.C. § 1691. Scope of prohibition

(a) Activities constituting discrimination

It shall be unlawful for any creditor to discriminate against any applicant, with respect to any aspect of a credit transaction—

(1) on the basis of race, color, religion, national origin, sex or marital status, or age (provided the applicant has the capacity to contract);

(2) because all or part of the applicant's income derives from any public assistance program; or

(3) because the applicant has in good faith exercised any right under this chapter.

(b) Activities not constituting discrimination

It shall not constitute discrimination for purposes of this subchapter for a creditor—

(1) to make an inquiry of marital status if such inquiry is for the purpose of ascertaining the creditor's rights and remedies applicable to the particular extension of credit and not to discriminate in a determination of credit-worthiness;

(2) to make an inquiry of the applicant's age or of whether the applicant's income derives from any public assistance program if such inquiry is for the purpose of determining the amount and

probable continuance of income levels, credit history, or other pertinent element of credit-worthiness as provided in regulations of the Bureau;

(3) to use any empirically derived credit system which considers age if such system is demonstrably and statistically sound in accordance with regulations of the Bureau, except that in the operation of such system the age of an elderly applicant may not be assigned a negative factor or value;

(4) to make an inquiry or to consider the age of an elderly applicant when the age of such applicant is to be used by the creditor in the extension of credit in favor of such applicant; or

(5) to make an inquiry under section 704B [15 U.S.C. 1691c-2], in accordance with the requirements of that section.

(c) Additional activities not constituting discrimination

It is not a violation of this section for a creditor to refuse to extend credit offered pursuant to—

(1) any credit assistance program expressly authorized by law for an economically disadvantaged class of persons;

(2) any credit assistance program administered by a nonprofit organization for its members or an economically disadvantaged class of persons; or

(3) any special purpose credit program offered by a profit-making organization to meet special social needs which meets standards prescribed in regulations by the Bureau; if such refusal is required by or made pursuant to such program.

(d) Reason for adverse action; procedure applicable; "adverse action" defined

(1) Within thirty days (or such longer reasonable time as specified in regulations of the Bureau for any class of credit transaction) after receipt of a completed application for credit, a creditor shall notify the applicant of its action on the application.

(2) Each applicant against whom adverse action is taken shall be entitled to a statement of reasons for such action from the creditor. A creditor satisfies this obligation by—

(A) providing statements of reasons in writing as a matter of course to applicants against whom adverse action is taken; or

(B) giving written notification of adverse action which discloses (i) the applicant's right to a statement of reasons within thirty days after receipt by the creditor of a request made within sixty days after such notification, and (ii) the identity of the person or office from which such statement may be obtained. Such statement may be given orally if the written notification advises the applicant of his right to have the statement of reasons confirmed in writing on written request.

(3) A statement of reasons meets the requirements of this section only if it contains the specific reasons for the adverse action taken.

(4) Where a creditor has been requested by a third party to make a specific extension of credit directly or indirectly to an applicant, the notification and statement of reasons required by this subsection may be made directly by such creditor, or indirectly through the third party, provided in either case that the identity of the creditor is disclosed.

(5) The requirements of paragraph (2), (3), or (4) may be satisfied by verbal statements or notifications in the case of any creditor who did not act on more than one hundred and fifty applications during the calendar year preceding the calendar year in which the adverse action is taken, as determined under regulations of the Bureau.

(6) For purposes of this subsection, the term "adverse action" means a denial or revocation of credit, a change in the terms of an existing credit arrangement, or a refusal to grant credit in substantially the amount or on substantially the terms requested. Such term does not include a refusal to extend additional credit under an existing credit arrangement where the applicant is delinquent or otherwise in default, or where such additional credit would exceed a previously established credit limit.

(e) Copies furnished to applicants

(1) In general

Each creditor shall furnish to an applicant a copy of any and all written appraisals and valuations developed in connection with the applicant's application for a loan that is secured or would have been secured by a first lien on a dwelling promptly upon completion, but in no case later than 3 days prior to the closing of the loan, whether the creditor grants or denies the applicant's request for credit or the application is incomplete or withdrawn.

(2) Waiver

The applicant may waive the 3 day requirement provided for in paragraph (1), except where otherwise required in law.

(3) Reimbursement

The applicant may be required to pay a reasonable fee to reimburse the creditor for the cost of the appraisal, except where otherwise required in law.

(4) Free copy

Notwithstanding paragraph (3), the creditor shall provide a copy of each written appraisal or valuation at no additional cost to the applicant.

(5) Notification to applicants

At the time of application, the creditor shall notify an applicant in writing of the right to receive a copy of each written appraisal and valuation under this subsection.

(6) Valuation defined

For purposes of this subsection, the term "valuation" shall include any estimate of the value of a dwelling developed in connection with a creditor's decision to provide credit, including those values developed pursuant to a policy of a government sponsored enterprise or by an automated valuation model, a broker price opinion, or other methodology or mechanism.

[Pub. L. No. 94-239, § 2, 90 Stat. 251 (1976); Pub. L. No. 102-242, § 223(d), 105 Stat. 2306 (1991); Pub. L. No. 111-203, tit. X, § 1474, 124 Stat. 2199 (July 21, 2010)]

Effective date: The effective date for subsection (e) may be January 18, 2014. *See* 78 Fed. Reg. 7248 (Jan. 31, 2013).

15 U.S.C. § 1691a. Definitions; rules of construction

(a) The definitions and rules of construction set forth in this section are applicable for the purpose of this subchapter.

(b) The term "applicant" means any person who applies to a creditor directly for an extension, renewal, or continuation of credit, or applies to a creditor indirectly by use of an existing credit plan for an amount exceeding a previously established credit limit.

(c) The term "Bureau" means the Bureau of Consumer Financial Protection.

(d) The term "credit" means the right granted by a creditor to a debtor to defer payment of debt or to incur debts and defer its payment or to purchase property or services and defer payment therefor.

(e) The term "creditor" means any person who regularly extends, renews, or continues credit; any person who regularly arranges for the extension, renewal, or continuation of credit; or any assignee of an original creditor who participates in the decision to extend, renew, or continue credit.

(f) The term "person" means a natural person, a corporation, government or governmental subdivision or agency, trust, estate, partnership, cooperative, or association.

(g) Any reference to any requirement imposed under this subchapter or any provision thereof includes reference to the regulations of the Bureau under this subchapter or the provision thereof in question.

[Pub. L. No. 111-203, tit. X, §§ 1085(1), 1100H, 124 Stat. 2083, 2113 (July 21, 2010)]

15 U.S.C. § 1691b. Promulgation of Regulations by the Bureau

(a) The Bureau shall prescribe regulations to carry out the purposes of this subchapter. These regulations may contain but are not limited to such classifications, differentiation, or other provision, and may provide for such adjustments and exceptions for any class of transactions, as in the judgment of the Bureau are necessary or proper to effectuate the purposes of this subchapter, to prevent circumvention or evasion thereof, or to facilitate or substantiate compliance therewith.

(b) Such regulations may exempt from the provisions of this subchapter any class of transactions that are not primarily for personal, family, or household purposes, or business or commercial loans made available by a financial institution, except that a particular type within a class of such transactions may be exempted if the Bureau determines, after making an express finding that the application of this subchapter or of any provision of this subchapter of such transaction would not contribute substantially to effecting the purposes of this subchapter.

(c) An exemption granted pursuant to subsection (b) shall be for no longer than five years and shall be extended only if the Bureau makes a subsequent determination, in the manner described by such paragraph, that such exemption remains appropriate.

(d) Pursuant to Bureau regulations, entities making business or commercial loans shall maintain such records or other data relating to such loans as may be necessary to evidence compliance with this subsection or enforce any action pursuant to the authority of this chapter. In no event shall such records or data be maintained for a period of less than one year. The Bureau shall promulgate regulations to implement this paragraph in the manner prescribed by chapter 5 of Title 5.

(e) The Bureau shall provide in regulations that an applicant for a business or commercial loan shall be provided a written notice of such applicant's right to receive a written statement of the reasons for the denial of such loan.

(f) Board Authority. Notwithstanding subsection (a), the Board shall prescribe regulations to carry out the purposes of this title with respect to a person described in section 1029(a) of the Consumer Financial Protection Act of 2010. These regulations may contain but are not limited to such classifications, differentiation, or other provision, and may provide for such adjustments and exceptions for any class of transactions, as in the judgment of the Board are necessary or proper to effectuate the purposes of this title, to prevent circumvention or evasion thereof, or to facilitate or substantiate compliance therewith.

(g) Deference. Notwithstanding any power granted to any Federal agency under this title, the deference that a court affords to a Federal agency with respect to a determination made by such agency relating to the meaning or interpretation of any provision of this title that is subject to the jurisdiction of such agency shall be applied as if that agency were the only agency authorized to apply, enforce, interpret, or administer the provisions of this title.

[Pub. L. No. 94-239, § 3(a), 90 Stat. 252 (1976); Pub. L. No. 100-533, § 301, 102 Stat. 2692 (1988); Pub. L. No. 111-203, tit. X, §§ 1085(1), (3), 1100H, 124 Stat. 2083, 2113 (July 21, 2010)]

15 U.S.C. § 1691c. Administrative enforcement

(a) Enforcing agencies

Subject to subtitle B of the Consumer Protection Financial Protection Act of 2010 with the requirements imposed under this subchapter shall be enforced under:

(1) Section 8 of the Federal Deposit Insurance Act, by the appropriate Federal banking agency, as defined in section 3(q) of the Federal Deposit Insurance Act (12 U.S.C. 1813(q)), with respect to—

  (A) national banks, Federal savings associations, and Federal branches and Federal agencies of foreign banks;

  (B) member banks of the Federal Reserve System (other than national banks), branches and agencies of foreign banks (other than Federal branches, Federal agencies, and insured State branches of foreign banks), commercial lending companies owned or controlled by foreign banks, and organizations operating under section 25 or 25A of the Federal Reserve Act; and

  (C) banks and State savings associations insured by the Federal Deposit Insurance Corporation (other than members of the Federal Reserve System), and insured State branches of foreign banks;

(2) The Federal Credit Union Act [12 U.S.C. § 1751 et seq.], by the Administrator of the National Credit Union Administration with respect to any Federal Credit Union.

(3) Subtitle IV of Title 49, by the Secretary of Transportation, with respect to all carriers subject to the jurisdiction of the Surface Transportation Board.

(4) Part A of subtitle VII of title 49, by the Secretary of Transportation with respect to any air carrier or foreign air carrier subject to that part.

(5) The Packers and Stockyards Act, 1921 [7 U.S.C. § 181 et seq.] (except as provided in section 406 of that Act [7 U.S.C. §§ 226, 227]), by the Secretary of Agriculture with respect to any activities subject to that Act.

(6) The Farm Credit Act of 1971 [12 U.S.C. § 2001 et seq.], by the Farm Credit Administration with respect to any Federal land bank, Federal land bank association, Federal intermediate credit bank, and production credit association;

(7) The Securities Exchange Act of 1934 [15 U.S.C. § 78a et seq.], by the Securities and Exchange Commission with respect to brokers and dealers;

(8) The Small Business Investment Act of 1958 [15 U.S.C. § 661 et seq.], by the Small Business Administration, with respect to small business investment companies; and

(9) Subtitle E of the Consumer Financial Protection Act of 2010, by the Bureau, with respect to any person subject to this title.

The terms used in paragraph (1) that are not defined in this subchapter or otherwise defined in section 3(s) of the Federal Deposit Insurance Act [12 U.S.C. 1813(s)] shall have the meaning given to them in section 1(b) of the International Banking Act of 1978 [12 U.S.C. 3101].

(b) Violations of subchapter deemed violations of preexisting statutory requirements; additional agency powers

For the purpose of the exercise by any agency referred to in subsection (a) of this section of its powers under any Act referred to in that subsection, a violation of any requirement imposed under this subchapter shall be deemed to be a violation of a requirement imposed under that Act. In addition to its powers under any provision of law specifically referred to in subsection (a) of this section, each of the agencies referred to in that subsection may exercise for the purpose of enforcing compliance with any requirement imposed under this subchapter, any other authority conferred on it by law. The exercise of the authorities of any of the agencies referred to in subsection (a) of this section for the purpose of enforcing compliance with any requirement imposed under this subchapter shall in no way preclude the exercise of such authorities for the purpose of enforcing compliance with any other provision of law not relating to the prohibition of discrimination on the basis of sex or marital status with respect to any aspect of a credit transaction.

(c) Overall enforcement authority of federal trade commission

Except to the extent that enforcement of the requirements imposed under this title is specifically committed to some other Government agency under any of paragraphs (1) through (8) of subsection (a), and subject to subtitle B of the Consumer Financial Protection Act of 2010, the Federal Trade Commission shall be authorized to enforce such requirements. For the purpose of the exercise by the Federal Trade Commission of its functions and powers under the Federal Trade Commission Act (15 U.S.C. 41 *et seq.*), a violation of any requirement imposed under this subchapter shall be deemed a violation of a requirement imposed under that Act. All of the functions and powers of the Federal Trade Commission under the Federal Trade Commission Act are available to the Federal Trade Commission to enforce compliance by any person with the requirements imposed under this title, irrespective of whether that person is engaged in commerce or meets any other jurisdictional tests under the Federal Trade Commission Act, including the power to enforce any rule prescribed by the Bureau under this title in the same manner as if the violation had been a violation of a Federal Trade Commission trade regulation rule.

(d) Rules and regulations by enforcing agencies

The authority of the Bureau to issue regulations under this subchapter does not impair the authority of any other agency designated in this section to make rules respecting its own procedures in enforcing compliance with requirements imposed under this subchapter.

[Pub. L. No. 94-239, § 4, 90 Stat. 253 (1976); Pub. L. No. 95-473, § 3(b), 92 Stat. 1466 (1978); Pub. L. No. 98-443, § 9(n), 98 Stat. 1708 (1984); Pub. L. No. 101-73, § 744(m), 103 Stat. 439 (1989); Pub. L. No. 102-242, § 212(d), 105 Stat. 2300 (1991); Pub. L. No. 102-550, § 1604(a)(7), 106 Stat. 4082 (1992); Pub. L. No. 104-88, § 315, 109 Stat. 948 (1995); Pub. L. No. 111-203, tit. X, §§ 1085(4)(A)–(C), 1100H, 124 Stat. 2084, 2085, 2113 (July 21, 2010)]

15 U.S.C. § 1691c-1. Incentives for self-testing and self-correction

(a) Privileged information

(1) Conditions for privilege

A report or result of a self-test (as that term is defined by regulations of the Bureau) shall be considered to be privileged under paragraph (2) if a creditor—

(A) conducts, or authorizes an independent third party to conduct, a self-test of any aspect of a credit transaction by a creditor, in order to determine the level or effectiveness of compliance with this subchapter by the creditor; and

(B) has identified any possible violation of this subchapter by the creditor and has taken, or is taking, appropriate corrective action to address any such possible violation.

(2) Privileged self-test

If a creditor meets the conditions specified in subparagraphs (A) and (B) of paragraph (1) with respect to a self-test described in that paragraph, any report or results of that self-test—

(A) shall be privileged; and

(B) may not be obtained or used by any applicant, department, or agency in any—

(i) proceeding or civil action in which one or more violations of this subchapter are alleged; or

(ii) examination or investigation relating to compliance with this subchapter.

(b) Results of self-testing

(1) In general

No provision of this section may be construed to prevent an applicant, department, or agency from obtaining or using a report or results of any self-test in any proceeding or civil action in which a violation of this subchapter is alleged, or in any examination or investigation of compliance with this subchapter if—

(A) the creditor or any person with lawful access to the report or results—

(i) voluntarily releases or discloses all, or any part of, the report or results to the applicant, department, or agency, or to the general public; or

(ii) refers to or describes the report or results as a defense to charges of violations of this subchapter against the creditor to whom the self-test relates; or

(B) the report or results are sought in conjunction with an adjudication or admission of a violation of this subchapter for the sole purpose of determining an appropriate penalty or remedy.

(2) Disclosure for determination of penalty or remedy

Any report or results of a self-test that are disclosed for the purpose specified in paragraph (1)(B)—

(A) shall be used only for the particular proceeding in which the adjudication or admission referred to in paragraph (1)(B) is made; and

(B) may not be used in any other action or proceeding.

(c) Adjudication

An applicant, department, or agency that challenges a privilege asserted under this section may seek a determination of the existence and application of that privilege in—

(1) a court of competent jurisdiction; or

(2) an administrative law proceeding with appropriate jurisdiction.

[Pub. L. No. 104-208, div. A, tit. II, § 2302(a)(1), 110 Stat. 3009-420 (1996); Pub. L. No. 111-203, tit. X, §§ 1085(1), 1100H, 124 Stat. 2083, 2113 (July 21, 2010)]

15 U.S.C. § 1691c-2. Small business loan data collection

(a) Purpose

The purpose of this section is to facilitate enforcement of fair lending laws and enable communities, governmental entities, and creditors to identify business and community development needs and opportunities of women-owned, minority-owned, and small businesses.

(b) Information gathering

Subject to the requirements of this section, in the case of any application to a financial institution for credit for women-owned, minority-owned, or small business, the financial institution shall—

    (1) inquire whether the business is a women-owned, minority-owned, or small business, without regard to whether such application is received in person, by mail, by telephone, by electronic mail or other form of electronic transmission, or by any other means, and whether or not such application is in response to a solicitation by the financial institution; and

    (2) maintain a record of the responses to such inquiry, separate from the application and accompanying information.

(c) Right to refuse

Any applicant for credit may refuse to provide any information requested pursuant to subsection (b) in connection with any application for credit.

(d) No access by underwriters

(1) Limitation

Where feasible, no loan underwriter or other officer or employee of a financial institution, or any affiliate of a financial institution, involved in making any determination concerning an application for credit shall have access to any information provided by the applicant pursuant to a request under subsection (b) in connection with such application.

(2) Limited access

If a financial institution determines that a loan underwriter or other officer or employee of a financial institution, or any affiliate of a financial institution, involved in making any determination concerning an application for credit should have access to any information provided by the applicant pursuant to a request under subsection (b), the financial institution shall provide notice to the applicant of the access of the underwriter to such information, along with notice that the financial institution may not discriminate on the basis of such information.

(e) Form and manner of information

(1) In general

Each financial institution shall compile and maintain, in accordance with regulations of the Bureau, a record of the information provided by any loan applicant pursuant to a request under subsection (b).

(2) Itemization

Information compiled and maintained under paragraph (1) shall be itemized in order to clearly and conspicuously disclose—

    (A) the number of the application and the date on which the application was received;

    (B) the type and purpose of the loan or other credit being applied for;

    (C) the amount of the credit or credit limit applied for, and the amount of the credit transaction or the credit limit approved for such applicant;

    (D) the type of action taken with respect to such application, and the date of such action;

    (E) the census tract in which is located the principal place of business of the women-owned, minority-owned, or small business loan applicant;

    (F) the gross annual revenue of the business in the last fiscal year of the women-owned, minority-owned, or small business loan applicant preceding the date of the application;

    (G) the race, sex, and ethnicity of the principal owners of the business; and

    (H) any additional data that the Bureau determines would aid in fulfilling the purposes of this section.

(3) No personally identifiable information

In compiling and maintaining any record of information under this section, a financial institution may not include in such record the name, specific address (other than the census tract required under paragraph (1)(E)), telephone number, electronic mail address, or any other personally identifiable information concerning any individual who is, or is connected with, the women-owned, minority-owned, or small business loan applicant.

(4) Discretion to delete or modify publicly available data

The Bureau may, at its discretion, delete or modify data collected under this section which is or will be available to the public, if the Bureau determines that the deletion or modification of the data would advance a privacy interest.

(f) Availability of information

(1) Submission to Bureau

The data required to be compiled and maintained under this section by any financial institution shall be submitted annually to the Bureau.

(2) Availability of information

Information compiled and maintained under this section shall be—

    (A) retained for not less than 3 years after the date of preparation;

    (B) made available to any member of the public, upon request, in the form required under regulations prescribed by the Bureau;

    (C) annually made available to the public generally by the Bureau, in such form and in such manner as is determined by the Bureau, by regulation.

(3) Compilation of aggregate data

The Bureau may, at its discretion—

    (A) compile and aggregate data collected under this section for its own use; and

    (B) make public such compilations of aggregate data.

(g) Bureau action

(1) In general

The Bureau shall prescribe such rules and issue such guidance as may be necessary to carry out, enforce, and compile data pursuant to this section.

(2) Exceptions

The Bureau, by rule or order, may adopt exceptions to any requirement of this section and may, conditionally or unconditionally, exempt any financial institution or class of financial institutions from the requirements of this section, as the Bureau deems necessary or appropriate to carry out the purposes of this section.

(3) Guidance

The Bureau shall issue guidance designed to facilitate compliance with the requirements of this section, including assisting financial institutions in working with applicants to determine whether the applicants are women-owned, minority-owned, or small businesses for purposes of this section.

(h) Definitions

For purposes of this section, the following definitions shall apply:

(1) Financial institution

The term "financial institution" means any partnership, company, corporation, association (incorporated or unincorporated), trust, estate, cooperative organization, or other entity that engages in any financial activity.

(2) Small business

The term "small business" has the same meaning as the term "small business concern" in section 3 of the Small Business Act (15 U.S.C. 632).

(3) Small business loan

The term "small business loan" means a loan made to a small business.

(4) Minority

The term 'minority' has the same meaning as in section 1204(c)(3) of the Financial Institutions Reform, Recovery, and Enforcement Act of 1989.

(5) Minority-owned business

The term "minority-owned business" means a business—

　(A) more than 50 percent of the ownership or control of which is held by 1 or more minority individuals; and

　(B) more than 50 percent of the net profit or loss of which accrues to 1 or more minority individuals.

(6) Women-owned business

The term "women-owned business" means a business—

　(A) more than 50 percent of the ownership or control of which is held by 1 or more women; and

　(B) more than 50 percent of the net profit or loss of which accrues to 1 or more women.

[Pub. L. No. 90-321, tit. VII, § 704A, *as added* Pub. L. No. 111-203, tit. X, § 1071(a), 124 Stat. 2056 (July 21, 2010)]

15 U.S.C. § 1691d. Applicability of other laws

(a) Requests for signature of husband and wife for creation of valid lien, etc.

A request for the signature of both parties to a marriage for the purpose of creating a valid lien, passing clear title, waiving inchoate rights to property, or assigning earnings, shall not constitute discrimination under this subchapter: *Provided, however,* That this provision shall not be construed to permit a creditor to take sex or marital status into account in connection with the evaluation of creditworthiness of any applicant.

(b) State property laws affecting creditworthiness

Consideration or application of State property laws directly or indirectly affecting creditworthiness shall not constitute discrimination for purposes of this subchapter.

(c) State laws prohibiting separate extension of consumer credit to husband and wife

Any provision of State law which prohibits the separate extension of consumer credit to each party to a marriage shall not apply in any case where each party to a marriage voluntarily applies for separate credit from the same creditor: *Provided,* That in any case where such a State law is so preempted, each party to the marriage shall be solely responsible for the debt so contracted.

(d) Combining credit accounts of husband and wife with same creditor to determine permissible finance charges or loan ceilings under Federal or State laws

When each party to a marriage separately and voluntarily applies for and obtains separate credit accounts with the same creditor, those accounts shall not be aggregated or otherwise combined for purposes of determining permissible finance charges or permissible loan ceilings under the laws of any State or of the United States.

(e) Election of remedies under subchapter or State law; nature of relief determining applicability

Where the same act or omission constitutes a violation of this subchapter and of applicable State law, a person aggrieved by such conduct may bring a legal action to recover monetary damages either under this subchapter or under such State law, but not both. This election of remedies shall not apply to court actions in which the relief sought does not include monetary damages or to administrative actions.

(f) Compliance with inconsistent State laws; determination of inconsistency

This subchapter does not annul, alter, or affect, or exempt any person subject to the provisions of this subchapter from complying with, the laws of any State with respect to credit discrimination, except to the extent that those laws are inconsistent with any provision of this subchapter, and then only to the extent of the inconsistency. The Bureau is authorized to determine whether such inconsistencies exist. The Bureau may not determine that any State law is inconsistent with any provision of this subchapter if the Bureau determines that such law gives greater protection to the applicant.

(g) Exemption by regulation of credit transactions covered by State law; failure to comply with State law

The Bureau shall by regulation exempt from the requirements of sections 1691 and 1691a of this title any class of credit transactions within any State if it determines that under the law of that State that class of transactions is subject to requirements substantially similar to those imposed under this subchapter or that such law gives greater protection to the applicant, and that there is adequate provision for enforcement. Failure to comply with any requirement of such State law in any transaction so exempted shall constitute a violation of this subchapter for the purposes of section 1691e of this title.

[Pub. L. No. 94-239, § 5, 90 Stat. 253 (1976); Pub. L. No. 111-203, tit. X, §§ 1085(1), 1100H, 124 Stat. 2083, 2113 (July 21, 2010)]

15 U.S.C. § 1691e. Civil liability

(a) Individual or class action for actual damages

Any creditor who fails to comply with any requirement imposed under this subchapter shall be liable to the aggrieved applicant for any actual damages sustained by such applicant acting either in an individual capacity or as a member of a class.

(b) Recovery of punitive damages in individual and class actions for actual damages; exemptions; maximum amount of punitive damages in individual actions; limitation on total recovery in class actions; factors determining amount of award

Any creditor, other than a government or governmental subdivision or agency, who fails to comply with any requirement imposed under this subchapter shall be liable to the aggrieved applicant for punitive damages in an amount not greater than $10,000, in addition to any actual damages provided in subsection (a) of this section, except that in the case of a class action the total recovery under this subsection shall not exceed the lesser of $500,000 or 1 per centum of the net worth of the creditor. In determining the amount of such damages in any action, the court shall consider, among other relevant factors, the amount of any actual damages awarded, the frequency and persistence of failures of compliance by the creditor, the resources of the creditor, the number of persons adversely affected, and the extent to which the creditor's failure of compliance was intentional.

(c) Action for equitable and declaratory relief

Upon application by an aggrieved applicant, the appropriate United States district court or any other court of competent jurisdiction may grant such equitable and declaratory relief as is necessary to enforce the requirements imposed under this subchapter.

(d) Recovery of costs and attorney fees

In the case of any successful action under subsection (a), (b), or (c) of this section, the costs of the action, together with a reasonable attorney's fee as determined by the court, shall be added to any damages awarded by the court under such subsection.

(e) Good faith compliance with rule, regulation, or interpretation of Bureau or interpretation or approval by an official or employee of Bureau of Consumer Financial Protection duly authorized by Bureau

No provision of this subchapter imposing liability shall apply to any act done or omitted in good faith in conformity with any official rule, regulation, or interpretation thereof by the Bureau or in conformity with any interpretation or approval by an official or employee of the Bureau of Consumer Financial Protection duly authorized by the Bureau to issue such interpretations or approvals under such procedures as the Bureau may prescribe therefor, notwithstanding that after such act or omission has occurred, such rule, regulation, interpretation, or approval is amended, rescinded, or determined by judicial or other authority to be invalid for any reason.

(f) Jurisdiction of courts; time for maintenance of action; exceptions

Any action under this section may be brought in the appropriate United States district court without regard to the amount in controversy, or in any other court of competent jurisdiction. No such action shall be brought later than 5 years after the date of the occurrence of the violation, except that—

(1) whenever any agency having responsibility for administrative enforcement under section 1691c of this title commences an enforcement proceeding within 5 years after the date of the occurrence of the violation,

(2) whenever the Attorney General commences a civil action under this section within 5 years after the date of the occurrence of the violation,

then any applicant who has been a victim of the discrimination which is the subject of such proceeding or civil action may bring an action under this section not later than one year after the commencement of that proceeding or action.

(g) Request by responsible enforcement agency to Attorney General for civil action

The agencies having responsibility for administrative enforcement under section 1961c of this title, if unable to obtain compliance with section 1691 of this title, are authorized to refer the matter to the Attorney General with a recommendation that an appropriate civil action be instituted. Each agency referred to in paragraphs (1), (2), and (9) of section 1691c(a) of this title shall refer the matter to the Attorney General whenever the agency has reason to believe that 1 or more creditors has engaged in a pattern or practice of discouraging or denying applications for credit in violation of section 1691(a) of this title. Each such agency may refer the matter to the Attorney General whenever the agency has reason to believe that 1 or more creditors has violated section 1691(a) of this title.

(h) Authority for Attorney General to bring civil action; jurisdiction

When a matter is referred to the Attorney General pursuant to subsection (g) of this section, or whenever he has reason to believe that one or more creditors are engaged in a pattern or practice in violation of this subchapter, the Attorney General may bring a civil action in any appropriate United States district court for such relief as may be appropriate, including actual and punitive damages and injunctive relief.

(i) Recovery under both subchapter and fair housing enforcement provisions prohibited for violation based on same transaction

No person aggrieved by a violation of this subchapter and by a violation of section 3605 of Title 42 shall recover under this subchapter and section 3612 of Title 42, if such violation is based on the same transaction.[1]

(j) Discovery of creditor's granting standards

Nothing in this subchapter shall be construed to prohibit the discovery of a creditor's credit granting standards under appropriate discovery procedures in the court or agency in which an action or proceeding is brought.

(k) Notice to HUD of violations

Whenever an agency referred to in paragraph (1), (2), or (3) of section 1691c(a) of this title—

(1) has reason to believe, as a result of receiving a consumer complaint, conducting a consumer compliance examination, or otherwise, that a violation of this subchapter has occurred;

(2) has reason to believe that the alleged violation would be a violation of the Fair Housing Act [42 U.S.C. § 3601 et seq.]; and

(3) does not refer the matter to the Attorney General pursuant to subsection (g) of this section,

the agency shall notify the Secretary of Housing and Urban Development of the violation, and shall notify the applicant that the Secretary of Housing and Urban Development has been notified of the alleged violation and that remedies for the violation may be available under the Fair Housing Act.

[Pub. L. No. 94-239, § 6, 90 Stat. 253 (1976); Pub. L. No. 102-242, § 223(a)–(c), 105 Stat. 2306 (1991); Pub. L. No. 111-203, tit. X, §§ 1085(1), (5)–(7), 1100H, 124 Stat. 2083, 2113 (July 21, 2010)]

---

1 [*Editor's Note*: At the moment, the literal language of the statute is confusing. It provides that there cannot be recovery under both the ECOA and 42 U.S.C. § 3612. Prior to the Fair Housing Amendments Act of 1988 (Pub. L. No. 100-430, 102 Stat. 1619), section 3612 authorized a private right of action for damages and injunctive relief. The 1988 amendments, however, moved the private relief provision to 42 U.S.C. § 3613; section 3612 now deals with administrative enforcement of the Fair Housing Act.]

15 U.S.C. § 1691f. Annual reports to Congress; contents

Each year, the Bureau and the Attorney General shall, respectively, make reports to the Congress concerning the administration of their functions under this subchapter, including such recommendations as the Bureau and the Attorney General, respectively, deem necessary or appropriate. In addition, each report of the Bureau shall include its assessment of the extent to which compliance with the requirements of this subchapter is being achieved, and a summary of the enforcement actions taken by each of the agencies assigned administrative enforcement responsibilities under section 1691c of this title.

[Pub. L. No. 94-239, § 7, 90 Stat. 255 (1976); Pub. L. No. 96-221, § 610(c), 94 Stat. 174 (1980); Pub. L. No. 111-203, tit. X, §§ 1085(1), 1100H, 124 Stat. 2083, 2113 (July 21, 2010)]

A.2 Fair Housing Act, 42 U.S.C. §§ 3601–3631

TITLE 42. THE PUBLIC HEALTH AND WELFARE

* * *

CHAPTER 45. FAIR HOUSING

SUBCHAPTER I—GENERALLY

SUBCHAPTER II—PREVENTION OF INTIMIDATION

SOURCE: Pub. L. No. 90-284, §§ 801–819, 901, 82 Stat. 81–89 (1968), unless otherwise noted.

42 U.S.C. § 3601. Declaration of policy

It is the policy of the United States to provide, within constitutional limitations, for fair housing throughout the United States.

42 U.S.C. § 3602. Definitions

As used in this subchapter—

(a) "Secretary" means the Secretary of Housing and Urban Development.

(b) "Dwelling" means any building, structure, or portion thereof which is occupied as, or designed or intended for occupancy as, a residence by one or more families, and any vacant land which is offered for sale or lease for the construction or location thereon of any such building, structure, or portion thereof.

(c) "Family" includes a single individual.

(d) "Person" includes one or more individuals, corporations, partnerships, associations, labor organizations, legal representatives, mutual companies, joint-stock companies, trusts, unincorporated organizations, trustees, trustees in cases under Title 11, receivers, and fiduciaries.

(e) "To rent" includes to lease, to sublease, to let and otherwise to grant for a consideration the right to occupy premises not owned by the occupant.

(f) "Discriminatory housing practice" means an act that is unlawful under section 3604, 3605, 3606, or 3617 of this title.

(g) "State" means any of the several States, the District of Columbia, the Commonwealth of Puerto Rico, or any of the territories and possessions of the United States.

(h) "Handicap" means, with respect to a person—
  (1) a physical or mental impairment which substantially limits one or more of such person's major life activities,
  (2) a record of having such an impairment, or
  (3) being regarded as having such an impairment, but such term does not include current, illegal use of or addiction to a controlled substance (as defined in section 802 of Title 21).

(i) "Aggrieved person" includes any person who—
  (1) claims to have been injured by a discriminatory housing practice; or
  (2) believes that such person will be injured by a discriminatory housing practice that is about to occur.

(j) "Complainant" means the person (including the Secretary) who files a complaint under section 3610 of this title.

(k) "Familial status" means one or more individuals (who have not attained the age of 18 years) being domiciled with—

(1) a parent or another person having legal custody of such individual or individuals; or

(2) the designee of such parent or other person having such custody, with the written permission of such parent or other person.

The protections afforded against discrimination on the basis of familial status shall apply to any person who is pregnant or is in the process of securing legal custody of any individual who has not attained the age of 18 years.

(l) "Conciliation" means the attempted resolution of issues raised by a complaint, or by the investigation of such complaint, through informal negotiations involving the aggrieved person, the respondent, and the Secretary.

(m) "Conciliation agreement" means a written agreement setting forth the resolution of the issues in conciliation.

(n) "Respondent" means—

(1) the person or other entity accused in a complaint of an unfair housing practice; and

(2) any other person or entity identified in the course of investigation and notified as required with respect to respondents so identified under section 3610(a) of this title.

(o) "Prevailing party" has the same meaning as such term has in section 1988 of this title.

[Pub. L. No. 95-598, § 331, 92 Stat. 2679 (1978); Pub. L. No. 100-430, § 5, 102 Stat. 1619 (1988)]

42 U.S.C. § 3603. Effective dates of certain prohibitions

(a) Application to certain described dwellings

Subject to the provisions of subsection (b) of this section and section 3607 of this title, the prohibitions against discrimination in the sale or rental of housing set forth in section 3604 of this title shall apply:

(1) Upon enactment of this subchapter, to—

(A) dwellings owned or operated by the Federal Government;

(B) dwellings provided in whole or in part with the aid of loans, advances, grants, or contributions made by the Federal Government, under agreements entered into after November 20, 1962, unless payment due thereon has been made in full prior to April 11, 1968;

(C) dwellings provided in whole or in part by loans insured, guaranteed, or otherwise secured by the credit of the Federal Government, under agreements entered into after November 20, 1962, unless payment thereon has been made in full prior to April 11, 1968: *Provided,* That nothing contained in subparagraphs (B) and (C) of this subsection shall be applicable to dwellings solely by virtue of the fact that they are subject to mortgages held by an FDIC or FSLIC institution; and

(D) dwellings provided by the development or the redevelopment of real property purchased, rented, or otherwise obtained from a State or local public agency receiving Federal financial assistance for slum clearance or urban renewal with respect to such real property under loan or grant contracts entered into after November 20, 1962.

(2) After December 31, 1968, to all dwellings covered by paragraph (1) and to all other dwellings except as exempted by subsection (b) of this section.

(b) Exemptions

Nothing in section 3604 of this title (other than subsection (c)) shall apply to—

(1) any single-family house sold or rented by an owner: *Provided,* That such private individual owner does not own more than three such single-family houses at any one time: *Provided further,* That in the case of the sale of any such single-family house by a private individual owner not residing in such house at the time of such sale or who was not the most recent resident of such house prior to such sale, the exemption granted by this subsection shall apply only with respect to one such sale within any twenty-four month period: *Provided further,* That such bona fide private individual owner does not own any interest in, nor is there owned or reserved on his behalf, under any express or voluntary agreement, title to or any right to all or a portion of the proceeds from the sale or rental of, more than three such single-family houses at any one time: *Provided further,* That after December 31, 1969, the sale or rental of any such single-family house shall be excepted from the application of this title only if such house is sold or rented (A) without the use in any manner of the sales or rental facilities or the sales or rental services of any real estate broker, agent, or salesman, or of such facilities or services of any person in the business of selling or renting dwellings, or of any employee or agent of any such broker, agent, salesman, or person and (B) without the publication, posting or mailing, after notice, of any advertisement or written notice in violation of section 3604(c) of this title; but nothing in this proviso shall prohibit the use of attorneys, escrow agents, abstractors, title companies, and other such professional assistance as necessary to perfect or transfer the title, or

(2) rooms or units in dwellings containing living quarters occupied or intended to be occupied by no more than four families living independently of each other, if the owner actually maintains and occupies one of such living quarters as his residence.

(c) Business of selling or renting dwellings defined

For the purposes of subsection (b) of this section, a person shall be deemed to be in the business of selling or renting dwellings if—

(1) he has, within the preceding twelve months, participated as principal in three or more transactions involving the sale or rental of any dwelling or any interest therein, or

(2) he has, within the preceding twelve months, participated as agent, other than in the sale of his own personal residence in providing sales or rental facilities or sales or rental services in two or more transactions involving the sale or rental of any dwelling or any interest therein, or

(3) he is the owner of any dwelling designed or intended for occupancy by, or occupied by, five or more families.

42 U.S.C. § 3604. Discrimination in the sale or rental of housing and other prohibited practices

As made applicable by section 3603 of this title and except as exempted by sections 3603(b) and 3607 of this title, it shall be unlawful—

(a) To refuse to sell or rent after the making of a bona fide offer, or to refuse to negotiate for the sale or rental of, or otherwise make unavailable or deny, a dwelling to any person because of race, color, religion, sex, familial status, or national origin.

(b) To discriminate against any person in the terms, conditions, or privileges of sale or rental of a dwelling, or in the provision of services or facilities in connection therewith, because of race, color, religion, sex, familial status, or national origin.

(c) To make, print, or publish, or cause to be made, printed, or published any notice, statement, or advertisement, with respect to the sale or rental of a dwelling that indicates any preference, limitation, or discrimination based on race, color, religion, sex, handicap, familial status, or national origin, or an intention to make any such preference, limitation, or discrimination.

(d) To represent to any person because of race, color, religion, sex, handicap, familial status, or national origin that any dwelling is not available for inspection, sale, or rental when such dwelling is in fact so available.

(e) For profit, to induce or attempt to induce any person to sell or rent any dwelling by representations regarding the entry or prospective entry into the neighborhood of a person or persons of a particular race, color, religion, sex, handicap, familial status, or national origin.

(f)

(1) To discriminate in the sale or rental, or to otherwise make unavailable or deny, a dwelling to any buyer or renter because of a handicap of—

    (A) that buyer or renter;

    (B) a person residing in or intending to reside in that dwelling after it is so sold, rented, or made available; or

    (C) any person associated with that buyer or renter.

(2) To discriminate against any person in the terms, conditions, or privileges of sale or rental of a dwelling, or in the provision of services or facilities in connection with such dwelling, because of a handicap of—

    (A) that person; or

    (B) a person residing in or intending to reside in that dwelling after it is so sold, rented, or made available; or

    (C) any person associated with that person.

(3) For purposes of this subsection, discrimination includes—

    (A) a refusal to permit, at the expense of the handicapped person, reasonable modifications of existing premises occupied or to be occupied by such person if such modifications may be necessary to afford such person full enjoyment of the premises except that, in the case of a rental, the landlord may where it is reasonable to do so condition permission for a modification on the renter agreeing to restore the interior of the premises to the condition that existed before the modification, reasonable wear and tear excepted;

    (B) a refusal to make reasonable accommodations in rules, policies, practices, or services, when such accommodations may be necessary to afford such person equal opportunity to use and enjoy a dwelling; or

    (C) in connection with the design and construction of covered multifamily dwellings for first occupancy after the date that is 30 months after September 13, 1988, a failure to design and construct those dwellings in such a manner that—

        (i) the public use and common use portions of such dwellings are readily accessible to and usable by handicapped persons;

        (ii) all the doors designed to allow passage into and within all premises within such dwellings are sufficiently wide to allow passage by handicapped persons in wheelchairs; and

        (iii) all premises within such dwellings contain the following features of adaptive design:

            (I) an accessible route into and through the dwelling;

            (II) light switches, electrical outlets, thermostats, and other environmental controls in accessible locations;

            (III) reinforcements in bathroom walls to allow later installation of grab bars; and

            (IV) usable kitchens and bathrooms such that an individual in a wheelchair can maneuver about the space.

(4) Compliance with the appropriate requirements of the American National Standard for buildings and facilities providing accessibility and usability for physically handicapped people (commonly cited as "ANSI A117.1") suffices to satisfy the requirements of paragraph (3)(C)(iii).

(5)

    (A) If a State or unit of general local government has incorporated into its laws the requirements set forth in paragraph (3)(C), compliance with such laws shall be deemed to satisfy the requirements of that paragraph.

    (B) A State or unit of general local government may review and approve newly constructed covered multifamily dwellings for the purpose of making determinations as to whether the design and construction requirements of paragraph (3)(C) are met.

    (C) The Secretary shall encourage, but may not require, States and units of local government to include in their existing procedures for the review and approval of newly constructed covered multifamily dwellings, determinations as to whether the design and construction of such dwellings are consistent with paragraph (3)(C), and shall provide technical assistance to States and units of local government and other persons to implement the requirements of paragraph (3)(C).

    (D) Nothing in this subchapter shall be construed to require the Secretary to review or approve the plans, designs or construction of all covered multifamily dwellings, to determine whether the design and construction of such dwellings are consistent with the requirements of paragraph 3(C).

(6)

    (A) Nothing in paragraph (5) shall be construed to affect the authority and responsibility of the Secretary or a State or local public agency certified pursuant to section 3610(f)(3) of this title to receive and process complaints or otherwise engage in enforcement activities under this subchapter.

    (B) Determinations by a State or a unit of general local government under paragraphs (5)(A) and (B) shall not be conclusive in enforcement proceedings under this subchapter.

(7) As used in this subsection, the term "covered multifamily dwellings" means—

    (A) buildings consisting of 4 or more units if such buildings have one or more elevators; and

(B) ground floor units in other buildings consisting of 4 or more units.

(8) Nothing in this subchapter shall be construed to invalidate or limit any law of a State or political subdivision of a State, or other jurisdiction in which this subchapter shall be effective, that requires dwellings to be designed and constructed in a manner that affords handicapped persons greater access than is required by this subchapter.

(9) Nothing in this subsection requires that a dwelling be made available to an individual whose tenancy would constitute a direct threat to the health or safety of other individuals or whose tenancy would result in substantial physical damage to the property of others.

[Pub. L. No. 93-383, § 808(b)(1), 88 Stat. 729 (1974); Pub. L. No. 100-430, §§ 6(a)–(b)(2), (e), 15, 102 Stat. 1620, 1622, 1623, 1636 (1988)]

42 U.S.C. § 3605. Discrimination in residential real estate-related transactions

(a) In general

It shall be unlawful for any person or other entity whose business includes engaging in residential real estate-related transactions to discriminate against any person in making available such a transaction, or in the terms or conditions of such a transaction, because of race, color, religion, sex, handicap, familial status, or national origin.

(b) "Residential real estate-related transaction" defined

As used in this section, the term "residential real estate-related transaction" means any of the following:

(1) The making or purchasing of loans or providing other financial assistance—

(A) for purchasing, constructing, improving, repairing, or maintaining a dwelling; or

(B) secured by residential real estate.

(2) The selling, brokering, or appraising of residential real property.

(c) Appraisal exemption

Nothing in this subchapter prohibits a person engaged in the business of furnishing appraisals of real property to take into consideration factors other than race, color, religion, national origin, sex, handicap, or familial status.

[Pub. L. No. 93-383, § 808(b)(2), 88 Stat. 729 (1974); Pub. L. No. 100-430, § 6(c), 102 Stat. 1622 (1988)]

42 U.S.C. § 3606. Discrimination in provision of brokerage services

After December 31, 1968, it shall be unlawful to deny any person access to or membership or participation in any multiple-listing service, real estate brokers' organization or other service, organization, or facility relating to the business of selling or renting dwellings, or to discriminate against him in the terms or conditions of such access, membership, or participation, on account of race, color, religion, sex, handicap, familial status, or national origin.

[Pub. L. No. 93-383, § 808(b)(3), 88 Stat. 729 (1974); Pub. L. No. 100-430, § 6(b)(1), 102 Stat. 1622 (1988)]

42 U.S.C. § 3607. Religious organization and private club exemption

(a) Nothing in this subchapter shall prohibit a religious organization, association, or society, or any nonprofit institution or organization operated, supervised or controlled by or in conjunction with a religious organization, association, or society, from limiting the sale, rental or occupancy of dwellings which it owns or operates for other than a commercial purpose to persons of the same religion, or from giving preference to such persons, unless membership in such religion is restricted on account of race, color, or national origin. Nor shall anything in this subchapter prohibit a private club not in fact open to the public, which as an incident to its primary purpose or purposes provides lodgings which it owns or operates for other than a commercial purpose, from limiting the rental or occupancy of such lodgings to its members or from giving preference to its members.

(b)

(1) Nothing in this subchapter limits the applicability of any reasonable local, State, or Federal restrictions regarding the maximum number of occupants permitted to occupy a dwelling. Nor does any provision in this subchapter regarding familial status apply with respect to housing for older persons.

(2) As used in this section, "housing for older persons" means housing—

(A) provided under any State or Federal program that the Secretary determines is specifically designed and operated to assist elderly persons (as defined in the State or Federal program); or

(B) intended for, and solely occupied by, persons 62 years of age or older; or

(C) intended and operated for occupancy by persons 55 years of age or older, and—

(i) at least 80 percent of the occupied units are occupied by at least one person 55 years of age or older;

(ii) the housing facility or community publishes and adheres to policies and procedures that demonstrate the intent required under this subparagraph; and

(iii) the housing facility or community complies with rules issued by the Secretary for verification of occupancy, which shall—

(I) provide for verification by reliable surveys and affidavits; and

(II) include examples of the types of policies and procedures relevant to a determination of compliance with the requirement clause (ii). Such surveys and affidavits shall be admissible in administrative and judicial proceedings for the purposes of such verification.

(3) Housing shall not fail to meet the requirements for housing for older persons by reason of:

(A) persons residing in such housing as of Sept. 13, 1988, who do not meet the age requirements of subsections (2)(B) or (C): Provided, That new occupants of such housing meet the age requirements of subsections (2)(B) or (C); or

(B) unoccupied units: Provided, That such units are reserved for occupancy by persons who meet the age requirements of subsections (2)(B) or (C).

(4) Nothing in this subchapter prohibits conduct against a person because such person has been convicted by any court of competent jurisdiction of the illegal manufacture or distribution of a controlled substance as defined in section 802 of Title 21.

(5)

    (A) A person shall not be held personally liable for monetary damages for a violation of this chapter if such person reasonably relied, in good faith, on the application of the exemption under this subsection relating to housing for older persons.

    (B) For the purposes of this paragraph, a person may only show good faith reliance on the application of the exemption by showing that—

        (i) such person has no actual knowledge that the facility or community is not, or will not be, eligible for such exemption; and

        (ii) the facility or community has stated formally, in writing, that the facility or community complies with the requirements for such exemption.

[Pub. L. No. 100-430, § 6(d), 102 Stat. 1623 (1988); Pub. L. No. 104-76, §§ 2–3, 109 Stat. 787 (1995)]

42 U.S.C. § 3608. Administration

(a) Authority and responsibility

The authority and responsibility for administering this Act shall be in the Secretary of Housing and Urban Development.

(b) Assistant Secretary

The Department of Housing and Urban Development shall be provided an additional Assistant Secretary.

(c) Delegation of authority; appointment of administrative law judges; location of conciliation meetings; administrative review

The Secretary may delegate any of his functions, duties, and powers to employees of the Department of Housing and Urban Development or to boards of such employees, including functions, duties, and powers with respect to investigating, conciliating, hearing, determining, ordering, certifying, reporting, or otherwise acting as to any work, business, or matter under this subchapter. The person to whom such delegations are made with respect to hearing functions, duties, and powers shall be appointed and shall serve in the Department of Housing and Urban Development in compliance with sections 3105, 3344, 5372, and 7521 of Title 5. Insofar as possible, conciliation meetings shall be held in the cities or other localities where the discriminatory housing practices allegedly occurred. The Secretary shall by rule prescribe such rights of appeal from the decisions of his administrative law judges to other administrative law judges or to other officers in the Department, to boards of officers or to himself, as shall be appropriate and in accordance with law.

(d) Cooperation of Secretary and executive departments and agencies in administration of housing and urban development programs and activities to further fair housing purposes

All executive departments and agencies shall administer their programs and activities relating to housing and urban development (including any Federal agency having regulatory or supervisory authority over financial institutions) in a manner affirmatively to further the purposes of this subchapter and shall cooperate with the Secretary to further such purposes.

(e) Functions of Secretary

The Secretary of Housing and Urban Development shall—

    (1) make studies with respect to the nature and extent of discriminatory housing practices in representative communities, urban, suburban, and rural, throughout the United States;

    (2) publish and disseminate reports, recommendations, and information derived from such studies, including an annual report to the Congress—

        (A) specifying the nature and extent of progress made nationally in eliminating discriminatory housing practices and furthering the purposes of this subchapter, obstacles remaining to achieving equal housing opportunity, and recommendations for further legislative or executive action; and

        (B) containing tabulations of the number of instances (and the reasons therefor) in the preceding year in which—

            (i) investigations are not completed as required by section 3610(a)(1)(B) of this title;

            (ii) determinations are not made within the time specified in section 3610(g) of this title; and

            (iii) hearings are not commenced or findings and conclusions are not made as required by section 3612(g) of this title;

    (3) cooperate with and render technical assistance to Federal, State, local, and other public or private agencies, organizations, and institutions which are formulating or carrying on programs to prevent or eliminate discriminatory housing practices;

    (4) cooperate with and render such technical and other assistance to the Community Relations Service as may be appropriate to further its activities in preventing or eliminating discriminatory housing practices;

    (5) administer the programs and activities relating to housing and urban development in a manner affirmatively to further the policies of this subchapter; and

    (6) annually report to the Congress, and make available to the public, data on the race, color, religion, sex, national origin, age, handicap, and family characteristics of persons and households who are applicants for, participants in, or beneficiaries or potential beneficiaries of, programs administered by the Department to the extent such characteristics are within the coverage of the provisions of law and Executive orders referred to in subsection (f) of this section which apply to such programs (and in order to develop the data to be included and made available to the public under this subsection, the Secretary shall, without regard to any other provision of law, collect such information relating to those characteristics as the Secretary determines to be necessary or appropriate).

(f) Provisions of law applicable to Department programs

The provisions of law and Executive orders to which subsection (e)(6) applies are—

    (1) title VI of the Civil Rights Act of 1964 [42 U.S.C. § 2000d et seq.];

    (2) this subchapter;

    (3) section 794 of Title 29;

    (4) the Age Discrimination Act of 1975 [42 U.S.C. § 6101 et seq.];

    (5) the Equal Credit Opportunity Act [15 U.S.C. § 1691 et seq.];

    (6) section 1982 of this title;

    (7) section 637(a) of Title 15;

    (8) section 1735f-5 of Title 12;

    (9) section 5309 of this title;

    (10) section 1701u of Title 12;

(11) Executive orders 11063 [42 U.S.C. § 1982 note], 11246 [42 U.S.C. § 2000e note], 11625 [15 U.S.C. § 631 note], 12250 [42 U.S.C. § 2000d-1 note], 12259 [42 U.S.C. § 3608 note; now revoked by Ex. Ord. No. 12892, 59 Fed. Reg. 2939 (Jan. 17, 1994), also set out under this section], and 12432 [15 U.S.C. § 637 note]; and

(12) any other provision of law which the Secretary specifies by publication in the Federal Register for the purpose of this subsection.

[Pub. L. No. 95-251, § 3, 92 Stat. 184 (1978); Pub. L. No. 95-454, § 801(a)(3)(J), 92 Stat. 1222 (1978); Pub. L. No. 100-430, § 7, 102 Stat. 1623 (1988)]

42 U.S.C. § 3608a. Collection of certain data

(a) In general

To assess the extent of compliance with Federal fair housing requirements (including the requirements established under title VI of Public Law 88-352 [42 U.S.C. § 2000d et seq.] and title VIII of Public Law 90-284 [42 U.S.C. § 3601 et seq.]), the Secretary of Agriculture shall collect, not less than annually, data on the racial and ethnic characteristics of persons eligible for, assisted, or otherwise benefiting under each community development, housing assistance, and mortgage and loan insurance and guarantee program administered by such Secretary. Such data shall be collected on a building by building basis if the Secretary determines such collection to be appropriate.

(b) Reports to Congress

The Secretary of Agriculture shall include in the annual report of such Secretary to the Congress a summary and evaluation of the data collected by such Secretary under subsection (a) of this section during the preceding year.

[Pub. L. No. 100-242, § 562, 101 Stat. 1944 (1988); Pub. L. No. 104-66, § 1071(e), 109 Stat. 720 (1995)]

42 U.S.C. § 3609. Education and conciliation; conferences and consultation; reports

Immediately after April 11, 1968, the Secretary shall commence such educational and conciliatory activities as in his judgment will further the purposes of this subchapter. He shall call conferences of persons in the housing industry and other interested parties to acquaint them with the provisions of this subchapter and his suggested means of implementing it, and shall endeavor with their advice to work out programs of voluntary compliance and of enforcement. He may pay per diem, travel, and transportation expenses for persons attending such conferences as provided in section 5703 of Title 5. He shall consult with State and local officials and other interested parties to learn the extent, if any, to which housing discrimination exists in their State or locality, and whether and how State or local enforcement programs might be utilized to combat such discrimination in connection with or in place of, the Secretary's enforcement of this subchapter. The Secretary shall issue reports on such conferences and consultations as he deems appropriate.

42 U.S.C. § 3610. Administrative enforcement; preliminary matters

(a) Complaints and answers

(1)

(A)

(i) An aggrieved person may, not later than one year after an alleged discriminatory housing practice has occurred or terminated, file a complaint with the Secretary alleging such discriminatory housing practice. The Secretary, on the Secretary's own initiative, may also file such a complaint.

(ii) Such complaints shall be in writing and shall contain such information and be in such form as the Secretary requires.

(iii) The Secretary may also investigate housing practices to determine whether a complaint should be brought under this section.

(B) Upon the filing of such a complaint—

(i) the Secretary shall serve notice upon the aggrieved person acknowledging such filing and advising the aggrieved person of the time limits and choice of forums provided under this subchapter;

(ii) the Secretary shall, not later than 10 days after such filing or the identification of an additional respondent under paragraph (2), serve on the respondent a notice identifying the alleged discriminatory housing practice and advising such respondent of the procedural rights and obligations of respondents under this subchapter, together with a copy of the original complaint;

(iii) each respondent may file, not later than 10 days after receipt of notice from the Secretary, an answer to such complaint; and

(iv) the Secretary shall make an investigation of the alleged discriminatory housing practice and complete such investigation within 100 days after the filing of the complaint (or, when the Secretary takes further action under subsection (f)(2) of this section with respect to a complaint, within 100 days after the commencement of such further action), unless it is impracticable to do so.

(C) If the Secretary is unable to complete the investigation within 100 days after the filing of the complaint (or, when the Secretary takes further action under subsection (f)(2) of this section with respect to a complaint, within 100 days after the commencement of such further action), the Secretary shall notify the complainant and respondent in writing of the reasons for not doing so.

(D) Complaints and answers shall be under oath or affirmation, and may be reasonably and fairly amended at any time.

(2)

(A) A person who is not named as a respondent in a complaint, but who is identified as a respondent in the course of investigation, may be joined as an additional or substitute respondent upon written notice, under paragraph (1), to such person, from the Secretary.

(B) Such notice, in addition to meeting the requirements of paragraph (1), shall explain the basis for the Secretary's belief that the person to whom the notice is addressed is properly joined as a respondent.

(b) Investigative report and conciliation

   (1) During the period beginning with the filing of such complaint and ending with the filing of a charge or a dismissal by the Secretary, the Secretary shall, to the extent feasible, engage in conciliation with respect to such complaint.

   (2) A conciliation agreement arising out of such conciliation shall be an agreement between the respondent and the complainant, and shall be subject to approval by the Secretary.

   (3) A conciliation agreement may provide for binding arbitration of the dispute arising from the complaint. Any such arbitration that results from a conciliation agreement may award appropriate relief, including monetary relief.

   (4) Each conciliation agreement shall be made public unless the complainant and respondent otherwise agree and the Secretary determines that disclosure is not required to further the purposes of this subchapter.

   (5)

     (A) At the end of each investigation under this section, the Secretary shall prepare a final investigative report containing—

       (i) the names and dates of contacts with witnesses;

       (ii) a summary and the dates of correspondence and other contacts with the aggrieved person and the respondent;

       (iii) a summary description of other pertinent records;

       (iv) a summary of witness statements; and

       (v) answers to interrogatories.

     (B) A final report under this paragraph may be amended if additional evidence is later discovered.

(c) Failure to comply with conciliation agreement

Whenever the Secretary has reasonable cause to believe that a respondent has breached a conciliation agreement, the Secretary shall refer the matter to the Attorney General with a recommendation that a civil action be filed under section 3614 of this title for the enforcement of such agreement.

(d) Prohibitions and requirements with respect to disclosure of information

   (1) Nothing said or done in the course of conciliation under this subchapter may be made public or used as evidence in a subsequent proceeding under this subchapter without the written consent of the persons concerned.

   (2) Notwithstanding paragraph (1), the Secretary shall make available to the aggrieved person and the respondent, at any time, upon request following completion of the Secretary's investigation, information derived from an investigation and any final investigative report relating to that investigation.

(e) Prompt judicial action

   (1) If the Secretary concludes at any time following the filing of a complaint that prompt judicial action is necessary to carry out the purposes of this subchapter, the Secretary may authorize a civil action for appropriate temporary or preliminary relief pending final disposition of the complaint under this section. Upon receipt of such an authorization, the Attorney General shall promptly commence and maintain such an action. Any temporary restraining order or other order granting preliminary or temporary relief shall be issued in accordance with the Federal Rules of Civil Procedure. The commencement of a civil action under this subsection does not affect the initiation or continuation of administrative proceedings under this section and section 3612 of this title.

   (2) Whenever the Secretary has reason to believe that a basis may exist for the commencement of proceedings against any respondent under sections 3614(a) and 3614(c) of this title or for proceedings by any governmental licensing or supervisory authorities, the Secretary shall transmit the information upon which such belief is based to the Attorney General, or to such authorities, as the case may be.

(f) Referral for State or local proceedings

   (1) Whenever a complaint alleges a discriminatory housing practice—

     (A) within the jurisdiction of a State or local public agency; and

     (B) as to which such agency has been certified by the Secretary under this subsection;

   the Secretary shall refer such complaint to that certified agency before taking any action with respect to such complaint.

   (2) Except with the consent of such certified agency, the Secretary, after that referral is made, shall take no further action with respect to such complaint unless—

     (A) the certified agency has failed to commence proceedings with respect to the complaint before the end of the 30th day after the date of such referral;

     (B) the certified agency, having so commenced such proceedings, fails to carry forward such proceedings with reasonable promptness; or

     (C) the Secretary determines that the certified agency no longer qualifies for certification under this subsection with respect to the relevant jurisdiction.

   (3)

     (A) The Secretary may certify an agency under this subsection only if the Secretary determines that—

       (i) the substantive rights protected by such agency in the jurisdiction with respect to which certification is to be made;

       (ii) the procedures followed by such agency;

       (iii) the remedies available to such agency; and

       (iv) the availability of judicial review of such agency's action;

     are substantially equivalent to those created by and under this subchapter.

     (B) Before making such certification, the Secretary shall take into account the current practices and past performance, if any, of such agency.

   (4) During the period which begins on September 13, 1988, and ends 40 months after such date, each agency certified (including an agency certified for interim referrals pursuant to 24 CFR 115.11, unless such agency is subsequently denied recognition under 24 CFR 115.7) for the purposes of this subchapter on the day before such date shall for the purposes of this subsection be considered certified under this subsection with respect to those matters for which such agency was certified on that date. If the Secretary determines in an individual case that an agency has not been able to meet the certification requirements within this 40-month period due to exceptional circumstances, such as the infrequency of legislative sessions in that jurisdiction, the Secretary may extend such period by not more than 8 months.

(5) Not less frequently than every 5 years, the Secretary shall determine whether each agency certified under this subsection continues to qualify for certification. The Secretary shall take appropriate action with respect to any agency not so qualifying.

(g) Reasonable cause determination and effect

(1) The Secretary shall, within 100 days after the filing of the complaint (or, when the Secretary takes further action under subsection (f)(2) of this section with respect to a complaint, within 100 days after the commencement of such further action), determine based on the facts whether reasonable cause exists to believe that a discriminatory housing practice has occurred or is about to occur, unless it is impracticable to do so, or unless the Secretary has approved a conciliation agreement with respect to the complaint. If the Secretary is unable to make the determination within 100 days after the filing of the complaint (or, when the Secretary takes further action under subsection (f)(2) of this section with respect to a complaint, within 100 days after the commencement of such further action), the Secretary shall notify the complainant and respondent in writing of the reasons for not doing so.

(2)

    (A) If the Secretary determines that reasonable cause exists to believe that a discriminatory housing practice has occurred or is about to occur, the Secretary shall, except as provided in subparagraph (C), immediately issue a charge on behalf of the aggrieved person, for further proceedings under section 3612 of this title.

    (B) Such charge—

        (i) shall consist of a short and plain statement of the facts upon which the Secretary has found reasonable cause to believe that a discriminatory housing practice has occurred or is about to occur;

        (ii) shall be based on the final investigative report; and

        (iii) need not be limited to the facts or grounds alleged in the complaint filed under subsection (a) of this section.

    (C) If the Secretary determines that the matter involves the legality of any State or local zoning or other land use law or ordinance, the Secretary shall immediately refer the matter to the Attorney General for appropriate action under section 3614 of this title, instead of issuing such charge.

(3) If the Secretary determines that no reasonable cause exists to believe that a discriminatory housing practice has occurred or is about to occur, the Secretary shall promptly dismiss the complaint. The Secretary shall make public disclosure of each such dismissal.

(4) The Secretary may not issue a charge under this section regarding an alleged discriminatory housing practice after the beginning of the trial of a civil action commenced by the aggrieved party under an Act of Congress or a State law, seeking relief with respect to that discriminatory housing practice.

(h) Service of copies of charge

After the Secretary issues a charge under this section, the Secretary shall cause a copy thereof, together with information as to how to make an election under section 3612(a) of this title and the effect of such an election, to be served—

(1) on each respondent named in such charge, together with a notice of opportunity for a hearing at a time and place specified in the notice, unless that election is made; and

(2) on each aggrieved person on whose behalf the complaint was filed.

[Pub. L. No. 100-430, § 8(2), 102 Stat. 1625 (1988)]

42 U.S.C. § 3611. Subpoenas; giving of evidence

(a) In general

The Secretary may, in accordance with this subsection, issue subpoenas and order discovery in aid of investigations and hearings under this subchapter. Such subpoenas and discovery may be ordered to the same extent and subject to the same limitations as would apply if the subpoenas or discovery were ordered or served in aid of a civil action in the United States district court for the district in which the investigation is taking place.

(b) Witness fees

Witnesses summoned by a subpoena under this subchapter shall be entitled to the same witness and mileage fees as witnesses in proceedings in United States district courts. Fees payable to a witness summoned by a subpoena issued at the request of a party shall be paid by that party or, where a party is unable to pay the fees, by the Secretary.

(c) Criminal penalties

(1) Any person who willfully fails or neglects to attend and testify or to answer any lawful inquiry or to produce records, documents, or other evidence, if it is in such person's power to do so, in obedience to the subpoena or other lawful order under subsection (a) of this section, shall be fined not more than $100,000 or imprisoned not more than one year, or both.

(2) Any person who, with intent thereby to mislead another person in any proceeding under this subchapter—

    (A) makes or causes to be made any false entry or statement of fact in any report, account, record, or other document produced pursuant to subpoena or other lawful order under subsection (a) of this section;

    (B) willfully neglects or fails to make or to cause to be made full, true, and correct entries in such reports, accounts, records, or other documents; or

    (C) willfully mutilates, alters, or by any other means falsifies any documentary evidence;

shall be fined not more than $100,000 or imprisoned not more than one year, or both.

[Pub. L. No. 100-430, § 8(2), 102 Stat. 1628 (1988)]

42 U.S.C. § 3612. Enforcement by Secretary

(a) Election of judicial determination

When a charge is filed under section 3610 of this title, a complainant, a respondent, or an aggrieved person on whose behalf the complaint was filed, may elect to have the claims asserted in that charge decided in a civil action under subsection (*o*) of this section in lieu of a hearing under subsection (b) of this section. The election must be made not later than 20 days after the receipt by the electing person of service under section 3610(h) of this title or, in the case of the Secretary, not later than 20 days after such service. The person making such election shall give notice of doing so to the Secretary and to all other complainants and respondents to whom the charge relates.

(b) Administrative law judge hearing in absence of election

If an election is not made under subsection (a) of this section with respect to a charge filed under section 3610 of this title, the Secretary shall provide an opportunity for a hearing on the record with respect to a charge issued under section 3610 of this title. The Secretary shall delegate the conduct of a hearing under this section to an administrative law judge appointed under section 3105 of Title 5. The administrative law judge shall conduct the hearing at a place in the vicinity in which the discriminatory housing practice is alleged to have occurred or to be about to occur.

(c) Rights of parties

At a hearing under this section, each party may appear in person, be represented by counsel, present evidence, cross-examine witnesses, and obtain the issuance of subpoenas under section 3611 of this title. Any aggrieved person may intervene as a party in the proceeding. The Federal Rules of Evidence apply to the presentation of evidence in such hearing as they would in a civil action in a United States district court.

(d) Expedited discovery and hearing

(1) Discovery in administrative proceedings under this section shall be conducted as expeditiously and inexpensively as possible, consistent with the need of all parties to obtain relevant evidence.

(2) A hearing under this section shall be conducted as expeditiously and inexpensively as possible, consistent with the needs and rights of the parties to obtain a fair hearing and a complete record.

(3) The Secretary shall, not later than 180 days after September 13, 1988, issue rules to implement this subsection.

(e) Resolution of charge

Any resolution of a charge before a final order under this section shall require the consent of the aggrieved person on whose behalf the charge is issued.

(f) Effect of trial of civil action on administrative proceedings

An administrative law judge may not continue administrative proceedings under this section regarding any alleged discriminatory housing practice after the beginning of the trial of a civil action commenced by the aggrieved party under an Act of Congress or a State law, seeking relief with respect to that discriminatory housing practice.

(g) Hearings, findings and conclusions, and order

(1) The administrative law judge shall commence the hearing under this section no later than 120 days following the issuance of the charge, unless it is impracticable to do so. If the administrative law judge is unable to commence the hearing within 120 days after the issuance of the charge, the administrative law judge shall notify the Secretary, the aggrieved person on whose behalf the charge was filed, and the respondent, in writing of the reasons for not doing so.

(2) The administrative law judge shall make findings of fact and conclusions of law within 60 days after the end of the hearing under this section, unless it is impracticable to do so. If the administrative law judge is unable to make findings of fact and conclusions of law within such period, or any succeeding 60-day period thereafter, the administrative law judge shall notify the Secretary, the aggrieved person on whose behalf the charge was filed, and the respondent, in writing of the reasons for not doing so.

(3) If the administrative law judge finds that a respondent has engaged or is about to engage in a discriminatory housing practice, such administrative law judge shall promptly issue an order for such relief as may be appropriate, which may include actual damages suffered by the aggrieved person and injunctive or other equitable relief. Such order may, to vindicate the public interest, assess a civil penalty against the respondent—

(A) in an amount not exceeding $10,000 if the respondent has not been adjudged to have committed any prior discriminatory housing practice;

(B) in an amount not exceeding $25,000 if the respondent has been adjudged to have committed one other discriminatory housing practice during the 5-year period ending on the date of the filing of this charge; and

(C) in an amount not exceeding $50,000 if the respondent has been adjudged to have committed 2 or more discriminatory housing practices during the 7-year period ending on the date of the filing of this charge;

except that if the acts constituting the discriminatory housing practice that is the object of the charge are committed by the same natural person who has been previously adjudged to have committed acts constituting a discriminatory housing practice, then the civil penalties set forth in subparagraphs (B) and (C) may be imposed without regard to the period of time within which any subsequent discriminatory housing practice occurred.

(4) No such order shall affect any contract, sale, encumbrance, or lease consummated before the issuance of such order and involving a bona fide purchaser, encumbrancer, or tenant without actual notice of the charge filed under this title.

(5) In the case of an order with respect to a discriminatory housing practice that occurred in the course of a business subject to a licensing or regulation by a governmental agency, the Secretary shall, not later than 30 days after the date of the issuance of such order (or, if such order is judicially reviewed, 30 days after such order is in substance affirmed upon such review)—

(A) send copies of the findings of fact, conclusions of law, and the order, to that governmental agency; and

(B) recommend to that governmental agency appropriate disciplinary action (including, where appropriate, the suspension or revocation of the license of the respondent).

(6) In the case of an order against a respondent against whom another order was issued within the preceding 5 years under this section, the Secretary shall send a copy of each such order to the Attorney General.

(7) If the administrative law judge finds that the respondent has not engaged or is not about to engage in a discriminatory housing practice, as the case may be, such administrative law judge shall enter an order dismissing the charge. The Secretary shall make public disclosure of each such dismissal.

(h) Review by Secretary; service of final order

(1) The Secretary may review any finding, conclusion, or order issued under subsection (g) of this section. Such review shall be completed not later than 30 days after the finding, conclusion, or order is so issued; otherwise the finding, conclusion, or order becomes final.

(2) The Secretary shall cause the findings of fact and conclusions of law made with respect to any final order for relief under this section, together with a copy of such order, to be served on each aggrieved person and each respondent in the proceeding.

(*i*) Judicial review

(1) Any party aggrieved by a final order for relief under this section granting or denying in whole or in part the relief sought may obtain a review of such order under chapter 158 of Title 28.

(2) Notwithstanding such chapter, venue of the proceeding shall be in the judicial circuit in which the discriminatory housing practice is alleged to have occurred, and filing of the petition for review shall be not later than 30 days after the order is entered.

(j) Court enforcement of administrative order upon petition by Secretary

(1) The Secretary may petition any United States court of appeals for the circuit in which the discriminatory housing practice is alleged to have occurred or in which any respondent resides or transacts business for the enforcement of the order of the administrative law judge and for appropriate temporary relief or restraining order, by filing in such court a written petition praying that such order be enforced and for appropriate temporary relief or restraining order.

(2) The Secretary shall file in court with the petition the record in the proceeding. A copy of such petition shall be forthwith transmitted by the clerk of the court to the parties to the proceeding before the administrative law judge.

(k) Relief which may be granted

(1) Upon the filing of a petition under subsection (i) or (j) of this section, the court may—

(A) grant to the petitioner, or any other party, such temporary relief, restraining order, or other order as the court deems just and proper;

(B) affirm, modify, or set aside, in whole or in part, the order, or remand the order for further proceedings; and

(C) enforce such order to the extent that such order is affirmed or modified.

(2) Any party to the proceeding before the administrative law judge may intervene in the court of appeals.

(3) No objection not made before the administrative law judge shall be considered by the court, unless the failure or neglect to urge such objection is excused because of extraordinary circumstances.

(*l*) Enforcement decree in absence of petition for review

If no petition for review is filed under subsection (i) of this section before the expiration of 45 days after the date the administrative law judge's order is entered, the administrative law judge's findings of fact and order shall be conclusive in connection with any petition for enforcement—

(1) which is filed by the Secretary under subsection (j) of this section after the end of such day; or

(2) under subsection (m) of this section.

(m) Court enforcement of administrative order upon petition of any person entitled to relief

If before the expiration of 60 days after the date the administrative law judge's order is entered, no petition for review has been filed under subsection (i) of this section, and the Secretary has not sought enforcement of the order under subsection (j) of this section, any person entitled to relief under the order may petition for a decree enforcing the order in the United States court of appeals for the circuit in which the discriminatory housing practice is alleged to have occurred.

(n) Entry of decree

The clerk of the court of appeals in which a petition for enforcement is filed under subsection (*l*) or (m) of this section shall forthwith enter a decree enforcing the order and shall transmit a copy of such decree to the Secretary, the respondent named in the petition, and to any other parties to the proceeding before the administrative law judge.

(o) Civil action for enforcement when election is made for such civil action

(1) If an election is made under subsection (a) of this section, the Secretary shall authorize, and not later than 30 days after the election is made the Attorney General shall commence and maintain, a civil action on behalf of the aggrieved person in a United States district court seeking relief under this subsection. Venue for such civil action shall be determined under chapter 87 of Title 28.

(2) Any aggrieved person with respect to the issues to be determined in a civil action under this subsection may intervene as of right in that civil action.

(3) In a civil action under this subsection, if the court finds that a discriminatory housing practice has occurred or is about to occur, the court may grant as relief any relief which a court could grant with respect to such discriminatory housing practice in a civil action under section 3613 of this title. Any relief so granted that would accrue to an aggrieved person in a civil action commenced by that aggrieved person under section 3613 of this title shall also accrue to that aggrieved person in a civil action under this subsection. If monetary relief is sought for the benefit of an aggrieved person who does not intervene in the civil action, the court shall not award such relief if that aggrieved person has not complied with discovery orders entered by the court.

(p) Attorney's fees

In any administrative proceeding brought under this section, or any court proceeding arising therefrom, or any civil action under this section, the administrative law judge or the court, as the case may be, in its discretion, may allow the prevailing party, other than the United States, a reasonable attorney's fee and costs. The United States shall be liable for such fees and costs to the extent provided by section 504 of Title 5 or by section 2412 of Title 28.

[Pub. L. No. 100-430, § 8(2), 102 Stat. 1629 (1988)]

42 U.S.C. § 3613. Enforcement by private persons

(a) Civil action

(1)

(A) An aggrieved person may commence a civil action in an appropriate United States district court or State court not later than 2 years after the occurrence or the termination of an alleged discriminatory housing practice, or the breach of a conciliation agreement entered into under this subchapter, whichever occurs last, to obtain appropriate relief with respect to such discriminatory housing practice or breach.

(B) The computation of such 2-year period shall not include any time during which an administrative proceeding under this subchapter was pending with respect to a complaint or charge under this subchapter based upon such discriminatory housing practice. This subparagraph does not apply to actions arising from a breach of a conciliation agreement.

(2) An aggrieved person may commence a civil action under this subsection whether or not a complaint has been filed under section 3610(a) of this title and without regard to the status of any such complaint, but if the Secretary or a State or local agency has obtained a conciliation agreement with the consent of an aggrieved person, no action may be filed under this subsection by such aggrieved person with respect to the alleged discriminatory housing practice which forms the basis for such complaint except for the purpose of enforcing the terms of such an agreement.

(3) An aggrieved person may not commence a civil action under this subsection with respect to an alleged discriminatory housing practice which forms the basis of a charge issued by the Secretary if an administrative law judge has commenced a hearing on the record under this subchapter with respect to such charge.

(b) Appointment of attorney by court

Upon application by a person alleging a discriminatory housing practice or a person against whom such a practice is alleged, the court may—

(1) appoint an attorney for such person; or

(2) authorize the commencement or continuation of a civil action under subsection (a) of this section without the payment of fees, costs, or security, if in the opinion of the court such person is financially unable to bear the costs of such action.

(c) Relief which may be granted

(1) In a civil action under subsection (a) of this section, if the court finds that a discriminatory housing practice has occurred or is about to occur, the court may award to the plaintiff actual and punitive damages, and subject to subsection (d) of this section, may grant as relief, as the court deems appropriate, any permanent or temporary injunction, temporary restraining order, or other order (including an order enjoining the defendant from engaging in such practice or ordering such affirmative action as may be appropriate).

(2) In a civil action under subsection (a) of this section, the court, in its discretion, may allow the prevailing party, other than the United States, a reasonable attorney's fee and costs. The United States shall be liable for such fees and costs to the same extent as a private person.

(d) Effect on certain sales, encumbrances, and rentals

Relief granted under this section shall not affect any contract, sale, encumbrance, or lease consummated before the granting of such relief and involving a bona fide purchaser, encumbrancer, or tenant, without actual notice of the filing of a complaint with the Secretary or civil action under this subchapter.

(e) Intervention by Attorney General

Upon timely application, the Attorney General may intervene in such civil action, if the Attorney General certifies that the case is of general public importance. Upon such intervention the Attorney General may obtain such relief as would be available to the Attorney General under section 3614(e) of this title in a civil action to which such section applies.

[Pub. L. No. 100-430, § 8(2), 102 Stat. 1633 (1988)]

42 U.S.C. § 3614. Enforcement by the Attorney General

(a) Pattern or practice cases

Whenever the Attorney General has reasonable cause to believe that any person or group of persons is engaged in a pattern or practice of resistance to the full enjoyment of any of the rights granted by this subchapter, or that any group of persons has been denied any of the rights granted by this subchapter and such denial raises an issue of general public importance, the Attorney General may commence a civil action in any appropriate United States district court.

(b) On referral of discriminatory housing practice or conciliation agreement for enforcement

(1)

(A) The Attorney General may commence a civil action in any appropriate United States district court for appropriate relief with respect to a discriminatory housing practice referred to the Attorney General by the Secretary under section 3610(g) of this title.

(B) A civil action under this paragraph may be commenced not later than the expiration of 18 months after the date of the occurrence or the termination of the alleged discriminatory housing practice.

(2)

(A) The Attorney General may commence a civil action in any appropriate United States district court for appropriate relief with respect to breach of a conciliation agreement referred to the Attorney General by the Secretary under section 3610(c) of this title.

(B) A civil action may be commenced under this paragraph not later than the expiration of 90 days after the referral of the alleged breach under section 3610(c) of this title.

(c) Enforcement of subpoenas

The Attorney General, on behalf of the Secretary, or other party at whose request a subpoena is issued, under this subchapter, may enforce such subpoena in appropriate proceedings in the United States district court for the district in which the person to whom the subpoena was addressed resides, was served, or transacts business.

(d) Relief which may be granted in civil actions under subsections (a) and (b)

(1) In a civil action under subsection (a) or (b) of this section, the court—

(A) may award such preventive relief, including a permanent or temporary injunction, restraining order, or other order against the person responsible for a violation of this subchapter as is necessary to assure the full enjoyment of the rights granted by this subchapter;

(B) may award such other relief as the court deems appropriate, including monetary damages to persons aggrieved; and

(C) may, to vindicate the public interest, assess a civil penalty against the respondent—

(i) in an amount not exceeding $50,000, for a first violation; and

(ii) in an amount not exceeding $100,000, for any subsequent violation.

(2) In a civil action under this section, the court, in its discretion, may allow the prevailing party, other than the United States, a reasonable attorney's fee and costs. The United States shall be liable for such fees and costs to the extent provided by section 2412 of Title 28.

(e) Intervention in civil actions

Upon timely application, any person may intervene in a civil action commenced by the Attorney General under subsection (a) or (b) of this section which involves an alleged discriminatory housing practice with respect to which such person is an aggrieved person or a conciliation agreement to which such person is a party. The court may grant such appropriate relief to any such intervening party as is authorized to be granted to a plaintiff in a civil action under section 3613 of this title.

[Pub. L. No. 100-430, § 8(2), 102 Stat. 1634 (1988)]

42 U.S.C. § 3614-1. Incentives for self-testing and self-correction

(a) Privileged information

(1) Conditions for privilege

A report or result of a self-test (as that term is defined by regulation of the Secretary) shall be considered to be privileged under paragraph (2) if any person—

(A) conducts, or authorizes an independent third party to conduct, a self-test of any aspect of a residential real estate related lending transaction of that person, or any part of that transaction, in order to determine the level or effectiveness of compliance with this subchapter by that person; and

(B) has identified any possible violation of this subchapter by that person and has taken, or is taking, appropriate corrective action to address any such possible violation.

(2) Privileged self-test

If a person meets the conditions specified in subparagraphs (A) and (B) of paragraph (1) with respect to a self-test described in that paragraph, any report or results of that self-test—

(A) shall be privileged; and

(B) may not be obtained or used by any applicant, department, or agency in any—

(i) proceeding or civil action in which one or more violations of this subchapter are alleged; or

(ii) examination or investigation relating to compliance with this subchapter.

(b) Results of self-testing

(1) In general

No provision of this section may be construed to prevent an aggrieved person, complainant, department, or agency from obtaining or using a report or results of any self-test in any proceeding or civil action in which a violation of this subchapter is alleged, or in any examination or investigation of compliance with this subchapter if—

(A) the person to whom the self-test relates or any person with lawful access to the report or the results—

(i) voluntarily releases or discloses all, or any part of, the report or results to the aggrieved person, complainant, department, or agency, or to the general public; or

(ii) refers to or describes the report or results as a defense to charges of violations of this subchapter against the person to whom the self-test relates; or

(B) the report or results are sought in conjunction with an adjudication or admission of a violation of this subchapter for the sole purpose of determining an appropriate penalty or remedy.

(2) Disclosure for determination of penalty or remedy

Any report or results of a self-test that are disclosed for the purpose specified in paragraph (1)(B)—

(A) shall be used only for the particular proceeding in which the adjudication or admission referred to in paragraph (1)(B) is made; and

(B) may not be used in any other action or proceeding.

(c) Adjudication

An aggrieved person, complainant, department, or agency that challenges a privilege asserted under this section may seek a determination of the existence and application of that privilege in—

(1) a court of competent jurisdiction; or

(2) an administrative law proceeding with appropriate jurisdiction.

[Pub. L. No. 104-208, div. A, tit. II, § 2302(b)(1), 110 Stat. 3009-421 (1996)]

42 U.S.C. § 3614a. Rules to implement subchapter

The Secretary may make rules (including rules for the collection, maintenance, and analysis of appropriate data) to carry out this subchapter. The Secretary shall give public notice and opportunity for comment with respect to all rules made under this section.

[Pub. L. No. 100-430, § 8(2), 102 Stat. 1635 (1988)]

42 U.S.C. § 3615. Effect on State laws

Nothing in this subchapter shall be construed to invalidate or limit any law of a State or political subdivision of a State, or of any other jurisdiction in which this subchapter shall be effective, that grants, guarantees, or protects the same rights as are granted by this subchapter; but any law of a State, a political subdivision, or other such jurisdiction that purports to require or permit any action that would be a discriminatory housing practice under this subchapter shall to that extent be invalid.

[Renumbered by Pub. L. No. 100-430, § 8(1), 102 Stat. 1625 (1988)]

42 U.S.C. § 3616. Cooperation with State and local agencies administering fair housing laws; utilization of services and personnel; reimbursement; written agreements; publication in Federal Register

The Secretary may cooperate with State and local agencies charged with the administration of State and local fair housing laws and, with the consent of such agencies, utilize the services of such agencies and their employees and, notwithstanding any other provision of law, may reimburse such agencies and their employees for services rendered to assist him in carrying out this subchapter. In furtherance of such cooperative efforts, the Secretary may enter into written agreements with such State or local agencies. All agreements and terminations thereof shall be published in the Federal Register.

[Renumbered by Pub. L. No. 100-430, § 8(1), 102 Stat. 1625 (1988)]

42 U.S.C. § 3616a. Fair housing initiatives program

(a) In general

The Secretary of Housing and Urban Development (in this section referred to as the "Secretary") may make grants to, or (to the extent of amounts provided in appropriation Acts) enter into contracts or cooperative agreements with, State or local governments or their agencies, public or private nonprofit organizations or institutions, or other public or private entities that are formulating or carrying out programs to prevent or eliminate discriminatory housing practices, to develop, implement, carry out, or coordinate—

(1) programs or activities designed to obtain enforcement of the rights granted by title VIII of the Act of April 11, 1968 [42 U.S.C. § 3601 et seq.] (commonly referred to as the Civil Rights Act of 1968), or by State or local laws that provide rights and remedies for alleged discriminatory housing practices that are substantially equivalent to the rights and remedies provided in such title VIII, through such appropriate judicial or administrative proceedings (including informal methods of conference, conciliation, and persuasion) as are available therefor; and

(2) education and outreach programs designed to inform the public concerning rights and obligations under the laws referred to in paragraph (1).

(b) Private enforcement initiatives

(1) In general

The Secretary shall use funds made available under this subsection to conduct, through contracts with private nonprofit fair housing enforcement organizations, investigations of violations of the rights granted under title VIII of the Civil Rights Act of 1968 [42 U.S.C. § 3601 et seq.], and such enforcement activities as appropriate to remedy such violations. The Secretary may enter into multiyear contracts and take such other action as is appropriate to enhance the effectiveness of such investigations and enforcement activities.

(2) Activities

The Secretary shall use funds made available under this subsection to conduct, through contracts with private nonprofit fair housing enforcement organizations, a range of investigative and enforcement activities designed to—

(A) carry out testing and other investigative activities in accordance with subsection (b)(1) of this section, including building the capacity for housing investigative activities in unserved or underserved areas;

(B) discover and remedy discrimination in the public and private real estate markets and real estate-related transactions, including, but not limited to, the making or purchasing of loans or the provision of other financial assistance sales and rentals of housing and housing advertising;

(C) carry out special projects, including the development of prototypes to respond to new or sophisticated forms of discrimination against persons protected under title VIII of the Civil Rights Act of 1968 [42 U.S.C. § 3601 et seq.];

(D) provide technical assistance to local fair housing organizations, and assist in the formation and development of new fair housing organization; and

(E) provide funds for the costs and expenses of litigation, including expert witness fees.

(c) Funding of fair housing organizations

(1) In general

The Secretary shall use funds made available under this section to enter into contracts or cooperative agreements with qualified fair housing enforcement organizations, other private nonprofit fair housing enforcement organizations, and nonprofit groups organizing to build their capacity to provide fair housing enforcement, for the purpose of supporting the continued development or implementation of initiatives which enforce the rights granted under title VIII of the Civil Rights Act of 1968 [42 U.S.C. § 3601 et seq.], as amended. Contracts or cooperative agreements may not provide

more than 50 percent of the operating budget of the recipient organization for any one year.

(2) Capacity enhancement

The Secretary shall use funds made available under this section to help establish, organize, and build the capacity of fair housing enforcement organizations, particularly in those areas of the country which are currently underserved by fair housing enforcement organizations as well as those areas where large concentrations of protected classes exist. For purposes of meeting the objectives of this paragraph, the Secretary may enter into contracts or cooperative agreements with qualified fair housing enforcement organizations. The Secretary shall establish annual goals which reflect the national need for private fair housing enforcement organizations.

(d) Education and outreach

(1) In general

The Secretary, through contracts with one or more qualified fair housing enforcement organizations, other fair housing enforcement organizations, and other nonprofit organizations representing groups of persons protected under title VIII of the Civil Rights Act of 1968 [42 U.S.C. § 3601 et seq.], shall establish a national education and outreach program. The national program shall be designed to provide a centralized, coordinated effort for the development and dissemination of fair housing media products, including—

(A) public service announcements, both audio and video;

(B) television, radio and print advertisements;

(C) posters; and

(D) pamphlets and brochures.

The Secretary shall designate a portion of the amounts provided in subsection (g)(4) of this section for a national program specifically for activities related to the annual national fair housing month. The Secretary shall encourage cooperation with real estate industry organizations in the national education and outreach program. The Secretary shall also encourage the dissemination of educational information and technical assistance to support compliance with the housing adaptability and accessibility guidelines contained in the Fair Housing Act Amendments of 1988.

(2) Regional and local programs

The Secretary, through contracts with fair housing enforcement organizations, other nonprofit organizations representing groups of persons protected under title VIII of the Civil Rights Act of 1968 [42 U.S.C. § 3601 et seq.], State and local agencies certified by the Secretary under section 810(f) of the Fair Housing Act [42 U.S.C. § 3610(f)], or other public or private entities that are formulating or carrying out programs to prevent or eliminate discriminatory housing practices, shall establish or support education and outreach programs at the regional and local levels.

(3) Community-based programs

The Secretary shall provide funding to fair housing organizations and other nonprofit organizations representing groups of persons protected under title VIII of the Civil Rights Act of 1968 [42 U.S.C. § 3601 et seq.], or other public or private entities that are formulating or carrying out programs to prevent or eliminate discriminatory housing practices, to support community-based education and outreach activities, including school, church, and community presentations, conferences, and other educational activities.

(e) Program administration

(1) Not less than 30 days before providing a grant or entering into any contract or cooperative agreement to carry out activities authorized by this section, the Secretary shall submit notification of such proposed grant, contract, or cooperative agreement (including a description of the geographical distribution of such contracts) to the Committee on Banking, Housing, and Urban Affairs of the Senate and the Committee on Banking, Finance and Urban Affairs of the House of Representatives.

(2) [Repealed.]

(f) Regulations

(1) The Secretary shall issue such regulations as may be necessary to carry out the provisions of this section.

(2) The Secretary shall, for use during the demonstration authorized in this section, establish guidelines for testing activities funded under the private enforcement initiative of the fair housing initiatives program. The purpose of such guidelines shall be to ensure that investigations in support of fair housing enforcement efforts described in subsection (a)(1) of this section shall develop credible and objective evidence of discriminatory housing practices. Such guidelines shall apply only to activities funded under this section, shall not be construed to limit or otherwise restrict the use of facts secured through testing not funded under this section in any legal proceeding under Federal fair housing laws, and shall not be used to restrict individuals or entities, including those participating in the fair housing initiatives program, from pursuing any right or remedy guaranteed by Federal law. Not later than 6 months after the end of the demonstration period authorized in this section, the Secretary shall submit to Congress the evaluation of the Secretary of the effectiveness of such guidelines in achieving the purposes of this section.

(3) Such regulations shall include provisions governing applications for assistance under this section, and shall require each such application to contain—

(A) a description of the assisted activities proposed to be undertaken by the applicant, together with the estimated costs and schedule for completion of such activities;

(B) a description of the experience of the applicant in formulating or carrying out programs to prevent or eliminate discriminatory housing practices;

(C) available information, including studies made by or available to the applicant, indicating the nature and extent of discriminatory housing practices occurring in the general location where the applicant proposes to conduct its assisted activities, and the relationship of such activities to such practices;

(D) an estimate of such other public or private resources as may be available to assist the proposed activities;

(E) a description of proposed procedures to be used by the applicant for monitoring conduct and evaluating results of the proposed activities; and

(F) any additional information required by the Secretary.

(4) Regulations issued under this subsection shall not become effective prior to the expiration of 90 days after the Secretary transmits such regulations, in the form such regulations are intended to be published, to the Committee on Banking, Housing, and Urban Affairs of the Senate and the Committee on Banking, Finance and Urban Affairs of the House of Representatives.

(5) The Secretary shall not obligate or expend any amount under this section before the effective date of the regulations required under this subsection.

(g) Authorization of appropriations

There are authorized to be appropriated to carry out the provisions of this section, $21,000,000 for fiscal year 1993 and $26,000,000 for fiscal year 1994, of which—

(1) not less than $3,820,000 for fiscal year 1993 and $8,500,000 for fiscal year 1994 shall be for private enforcement initiatives authorized under subsection (b) of this section, divided equally between activities specified under subsection (b)(1) of this section and those specified under subsection (b)(2) of this section;

(2) not less than $2,230,000 for fiscal year 1993 and $8,500,000 for fiscal year 1994 shall be for qualified fair housing enforcement organizations authorized under subsection (c)(1) of this section;

(3) not less than $2,010,000 for fiscal year 1993 and $4,000,000 for fiscal year 1994 shall be for the creation of new fair housing enforcement organizations authorized under subsection (c)(2) of this section; and

(4) not less than $2,540,000 for fiscal year 1993 and $5,000,000 for fiscal year 1994 shall be for education and outreach programs authorized under subsection (d) of this section, to be divided equally between activities specified under subsection (d)(1) of this section and those specified under subsections (d)(2) and (d)(3) of this section.

Any amount appropriated under this section shall remain available until expended.

(h) Qualified fair housing enforcement organization

(1) The term "qualified fair housing enforcement organization" means any organization that—

(A) is organized as a private, tax-exempt, nonprofit, charitable organization;

(B) has at least 2 years experience in complaint intake, complaint investigation, testing for fair housing violations and enforcement of meritorious claims; and

(C) is engaged in all the activities listed in paragraph (1)(B) at the time of application for assistance under this section.

An organization which is not solely engaged in fair housing enforcement activities may qualify as a qualified fair housing enforcement organization, provided that the organization is actively engaged in each of the activities listed in subparagraph (B).

(2) The term "fair housing enforcement organization" means any organization that—

(A) meets the requirements specified in paragraph (1)(A);

(B) is currently engaged in the activities specified in paragraph (1)(B);

(C) upon the receipt of funds under this section will become engaged in all of the activities specified in paragraph (1)(B); and

(D) for purposes of funding under subsection (b) of this section, has at least 1 year of experience in the activities specified in paragraph (1)(B).

(*i*) Prohibition on use of funds

None of the funds authorized under this section may be used by the Secretary for purposes of settling claims, satisfying judgments or fulfilling court orders in any litigation action involving either the Department or housing providers funded by the Department. None of the funds authorized under this section may be used by the Department for administrative costs.

(j) Reporting requirements

Not later than 180 days after the close of each fiscal year in which assistance under this section is furnished, the Secretary shall prepare and submit to the Congress a comprehensive report which shall contain—

(1) a description of the progress made in accomplishing the objectives of this section;

(2) a summary of all the private enforcement activities carried out under this section and the use of such funds during the preceding fiscal year;

(3) a list of all fair housing enforcement organizations funded under this section during the preceding fiscal year, identified on a State-by-State basis;

(4) a summary of all education and outreach activities funded under this section and the use of such funds during the preceding fiscal year; and

(5) any findings, conclusions, or recommendations of the Secretary as a result of the funded activities.

[Pub. L. No. 100-242, § 561, 101 Stat. 1942 (1988); Pub. L. No. 101-625, § 953, 104 Stat. 4419 (1990); Pub. L. No. 102-550, § 905(b), 106 Stat. 3869 (1992); Pub. L. No. 104-66, § 1071(d), 109 Stat. 720 (1995)]

42 U.S.C. § 3617. Interference, coercion, or intimidation

It shall be unlawful to coerce, intimidate, threaten, or interfere with any person in the exercise or enjoyment of, or on account of his having exercised or enjoyed, or on account of his having aided or encouraged any other person in the exercise or enjoyment of, any right granted or protected by section 3603, 3604, 3605, or 3606 of this title.

[Renumbered and amended by Pub. L. No. 100-430, §§ 8(1), 10, 102 Stat. 1625, 1635 (1988)]

42 U.S.C. § 3618. Authorization of appropriations

There are hereby authorized to be appropriated such sums as are necessary to carry out the purposes of this subchapter.

[Renumbered by Pub. L. No. 100-430, § 8(1), 102 Stat. 1625 (1988)]

42 U.S.C. § 3619. Separability of provisions

If any provision of this subchapter or the application thereof to any person or circumstances is held invalid, the remainder of the subchapter and the application of the provision to other persons not similarly situated or to other circumstances shall not be affected thereby.

[Renumbered by Pub. L. No. 100-430, § 8(1), 102 Stat. 1625 (1988)]

42 U.S.C. § 3631. Violations; penalties

Whoever, whether or not acting under color of law, by force or threat of force willfully injures, intimidates or interferes with, or attempts to injure, intimidate or interfere with—

(a) any person because of his race, color, religion, sex, handicap (as such term is defined in section 3602 of this title), familial status (as such term is defined in section 3602 of this title), or national origin and because he is or has been selling, purchasing, renting, financing, occupying, or contracting or negotiating for the sale, purchase, rental, financing or occupation of any dwelling, or applying for or participating in any service, organization, or facility relating to the business of selling or renting dwellings; or

(b) any person because he is or has been, or in order to intimidate such person or any other person or any class of persons from—

(1) participating, without discrimination on account of race, color, religion, sex, handicap (as such term is defined in section 3602 of this title), familial status (as such term is defined in section 3602 of this title), or national origin, in any of the activities, services, organizations or facilities described in subsection (a) of this section; or

(2) affording another person or class of persons opportunity or protection so to participate; or

(c) any citizen because he is or has been, or in order to discourage such citizen or any other citizen from lawfully aiding or encouraging other persons to participate, without discrimination on account of race, color, religion, sex, handicap (as such term is defined in section 3602 of this title), familial status (as such term is defined in section 3602 of this title), or national origin, in any of the activities, services, organizations or facilities described in subsection (a) of this section, or participating lawfully in speech or peaceful assembly opposing any denial of the opportunity to so participate—

shall be fined under Title 18 or imprisoned not more than one year, or both; and if bodily injury results from the acts committed in violation of this section of if such acts include the use, attempted use, or threatened use of a dangerous weapon, explosives or fire shall by fined under Title 18 or imprisoned not more than ten years, or both; and if death results from the acts committed in violation of this section of if such acts include kidnapping or an attempt to kidnap, aggravated sexual abuse or an attempt to commit aggravated sexual abuse or an attempt to kill, shall be fined under Title 18 or imprisoned for any term of years or for life, or both.

[Pub. L. No. 93-383, § 808(b)(4), 88 Stat. 729 (1974); Pub. L. No. 100-430, § 9, 102 Stat. 1635 (1988); Pub. L. No. 103-322, § 320103(e), 108 Stat. 2110 (1994); Pub. L. No. 104-294, § 604(b)(15), (27), 110 Stat. 3507, 3508 (1996)]

A.3 Civil Rights Acts, 42 U.S.C. §§ 1981, 1982, 1988

TITLE 42. THE PUBLIC HEALTH AND WELFARE

* * *

CHAPTER 21. CIVIL RIGHTS

Subchapter I—Generally

§ 1981.   Equal rights under the law

* * *

§ 1982.   Property rights of citizens

* * *

§ 1988.   Proceedings in vindication of civil rights

* * *

42 U.S.C. § 1981. Equal rights under the law

(a) Statement of equal rights

All persons within the jurisdiction of the United States shall have the same right in every State and Territory to make and enforce contracts, to sue, be parties, give evidence, and to the full and equal benefit of all laws and proceedings for the security of persons and property as is enjoyed by white citizens, and shall be subject to like punishment, pains, penalties, taxes, licenses, and exactions of every kind, and to no other.

(b) "Make and enforce contracts" defined

For purposes of this section, the term "make and enforce contracts" includes the making, performance, modification, and termination of contracts, and the enjoyment of all benefits, privileges, terms, and conditions of the contractual relationship.

(c) Protection against impairment

The rights protected by this section are protected against impairment by nongovernmental discrimination and impairment under color of State law.

[R.S. § 1977 (Act of May 31, 1870, c. 114, § 16, 16 Stat. 144); Pub. L. No. 102-166, § 101, 105 Stat. 1071 (1991)]

* * *

42 U.S.C. § 1982. Property rights of citizens

All citizens of the United States shall have the same right, in every State and Territory, as is enjoyed by white citizens thereof to inherit, purchase, lease, sell, hold, and convey real and personal property.

[R.S. § 1978 (Act of Apr. 9, 1866, c. 31, § 1, 14 Stat. 27)]

* * *

42 U.S.C. § 1988. Proceedings in vindication of civil rights

(a) Applicability of statutory and common law

The jurisdiction in civil and criminal matters conferred on the district and circuit courts by the provisions of this Title and of Title "CIVIL RIGHTS," and of Title "CRIMES," for the protection of all persons in the United States in their civil rights, and for their vindication, shall be exercised and enforced in conformity with the laws of the United States, so far as such laws are suitable to carry the same into effect; but in all cases where they are not adapted to the object, or are deficient in the provisions necessary to furnish suitable remedies and punish offenses against law, the common law, as modified and changed by the constitution and statutes of the State wherein the court having jurisdiction of such civil or criminal cause is held, so far as the same is not inconsistent with the Constitution and laws of the United States, shall be extended to and govern the said courts in the trial and disposition of the cause, and, if it is of a criminal nature, in the infliction of punishment on the party found guilty.

(b) Attorney's fees

In any action or proceeding to enforce a provision of sections 1981, 1981a, 1982, 1983, 1985, and 1986 of this title, title IX of Public Law 92-318 [20 U.S.C. § 1681 et seq.], the Religious Freedom Restoration Act of 1993 [42 U.S.C. § 2000bb et seq.], the Religious Land Use and Institutionalized Persons Act of 2000 [42 U.S.C. § 2000cc et seq.], title VI of the Civil Rights Act of 1964 [42 U.S.C. § 2000d et seq.], or section 13981 of this title, the court, in its discretion, may allow the prevailing party, other than the United States, a reasonable attorney's fee as part of the costs, except that in any action brought against a judicial officer for an act or omission taken in such officer's judicial capacity such officer shall not be held liable for any costs, including attorney's fees, unless such action was clearly in excess of such officer's jurisdiction.

(c) Expert fees

In awarding an attorney's fee under subsection (b) of this section in any action or proceeding to enforce a provision of section 1981 or 1981a of this title, the court, in its discretion, may include expert fees as part of the attorney's fee.

[R.S. § 722 (Acts of Apr. 9, 1866, c. 31, § 3, 14 Stat. 27 and of May 31, 1870, c. 114, § 18, 16 Stat. 144); Pub. L. No. 94-559, § 2, 90 Stat. 2641 (1976); Pub. L. No. 96-481, § 205(c), 94 Stat. 2330 (1980); Pub. L. No. 102-166, §§ 103, 113(a), 105 Stat. 1074, 1079 (1991); Pub. L. No. 103-141, § 4(a), 107 Stat. 1489 (1993); Pub. L. No. 103-322, § 40303, 108 Stat. 1942 (1994); Pub. L. No. 104-317, § 309(b), 110 Stat. 3853 (1996); Pub. L. No. 106-274, § 4(d), 114 Stat. 804 (2000)]

Regulation B (Equal Credit Opportunity)

The Consumer Financial Protection Bureau (CFPB) now has authority to issue Regulation B and its commentary. *See* Pub. L. No. 111-203, tit. X, §§ 1085(3), 1100H, 124 Stat. 2083, 2113 (July 21, 2010). On December 21, 2011, the CFPB issued its version of Regulation B and its commentary and further amended it on January 18, 2013, effective July 18, 2014. The Federal Reserve Board (FRB) has not withdrawn its version of Regulation B and its commentary, certain kinds of credit are not within the CFPB's enforcement authority, and the FRB regulation thus may remain relevant.

What follows is a redline version indicating how the CFPB's Regulation B is changed from the FRB Regulation B. CFPB changes not in effect until January 18, 2014, are redlined with an alternative typeface. (Forms found in Appendix B to Regulation B are *not* redlined, and this supplement contains only the CFPB version of these forms.) The FRB version, this redlined version, and the CFPB's version (with supplemental information) are all found on the companion website to this treatise. The companion website facilitates keyword searches and allows relevant provisions to be imported into word-processable documents.

TITLE ~~12. BANKS AND BANKING~~12—BANKS AND BANKING

CHAPTER ~~II. FEDERAL RESERVE SYSTEM~~X—BUREAU OF CONSUMER FINANCIAL PROTECTION

SUBCHAPTER ~~A. BOARD OF GOVERNORS OF THE M~~—FEDERAL RESERVE SYSTEM—HOME LOAN BANK DISCLOSURES

PART ~~202~~1002—EQUAL CREDIT OPPORTUNITY ACT (REGULATION B)

AUTHORITY: 12 U.S.C. 5512, 5581; 15 U.S.C. §§ 1691–1691fb.

SOURCE: ~~68~~76 Fed. Reg. ~~13,161~~79445 (~~Mar. 18, 2003~~Dec. 21, 2011), unless otherwise noted.

§ ~~202.1~~1002.1 Authority, scope and purpose.

(a) **Authority and scope.** This ~~regulation~~part, known as Regulation B, is issued by the ~~Board of Governors of the Federal Reserve System~~Bureau of Consumer Financial Protection (Bureau) pursuant to ~~title~~Title VII (Equal Credit Opportunity Act) of the Consumer Credit Protection Act, as amended (15 U.S.C. 1601 *et seq.*). Except as otherwise provided herein, this ~~regulation~~part applies to all persons who are creditors, as defined in § ~~202.2(l)~~. 1002.2(l), other than a person excluded from coverage of this part by section 1029 of the Consumer Financial Protection Act of 2010, Title X of the Dodd-Frank Wall Street Reform and Consumer Protection Act, Public Law 111–203, 124 Stat. 1376. Information collection requirements contained in this ~~regulation~~part have been approved by the Office of Management and Budget under the provisions of 44 U.S.C. 3501 *et seq.* and have been assigned OMB No. ~~7100-0201.~~3170–0013.

(b) **Purpose.** The purpose of this ~~regulation~~part is to promote the availability of credit to all creditworthy applicants without regard to race, color, religion, national origin, sex, marital status, or age (provided the applicant has the capacity to contract); to the fact that all or part of the applicant's income derives from a public assistance program; or to the fact that the applicant has in good faith exercised any right under the Consumer Credit Protection Act. The regulation prohibits creditor practices that discriminate on the basis of any of these factors. The regulation also requires creditors to notify applicants of action taken on their applications; to report credit history in the names of both spouses on an account; to retain records of credit applications; to collect information about the applicant's race and other personal characteristics in applications for certain dwelling-related loans; and to provide applicants with copies of appraisal reports used in connection with credit transactions.

§ ~~202.2~~1002.2. Definitions.

For the purposes of this ~~regulation~~part, unless the context indicates otherwise, the following definitions apply.

(a) *Account* means an extension of credit. When employed in relation to an account, the word use refers only to open-end credit.

(b) *Act* means the Equal Credit Opportunity Act (~~title~~Title VII of the Consumer Credit Protection Act).

(c) *Adverse action.*

(1) The term means:

(i) A refusal to grant credit in substantially the amount or on substantially the terms requested in an application unless the creditor makes a counteroffer (to grant credit in a different amount or on other terms) and the applicant uses or expressly accepts the credit offered;

(ii) A termination of an account or an unfavorable change in the terms of an account that does not affect all or substantially all of a class of the creditor's accounts; or

(iii) A refusal to increase the amount of credit available to an applicant who has made an application for an increase.

(2) The term does not include:

(i) A change in the terms of an account expressly agreed to by an applicant~~;~~;

(ii) Any action or forbearance relating to an account taken in connection with inactivity, default, or delinquency as to that account;

(iii) A refusal or failure to authorize an account transaction at point of sale or loan, except when the refusal is a termination or an unfavorable change in the terms of an account that does not affect all or substantially all of a class of the creditor's accounts, or when the refusal is a denial of an application for an increase in the amount of credit available under the account;

(iv) A refusal to extend credit because applicable law prohibits the creditor from extending the credit requested; or

(v) A refusal to extend credit because the creditor does not offer the type of credit or credit plan requested.

(3) An action that falls within the definition of both paragraphs (c)(1) and (c)(2) of this section is governed by paragraph (c)(2) of this section.

(d) *Age* refers only to the age of natural persons and means the number of fully elapsed years from the date of an applicant's birth.

(e) *Applicant* means any person who requests or who has received an extension of credit from a creditor, and includes any person who is or may become contractually liable regarding an extension of credit. For purposes of § ~~202.7~~1002.7(d), the term includes guarantors, sureties, endorsers, and similar parties.

(f) *Application* means an oral or written request for an extension of credit that is made in accordance with procedures used by a creditor for the type of credit requested. The term application does not include the use of an account or line of credit to obtain an amount of credit that is within a previously established credit limit. A *completed application* means an application in connection with which a creditor has received all the information that the creditor regularly obtains and considers in evaluating applications for the amount and type of credit requested (including, but not limited to, credit reports, any additional information requested from the applicant, and any approvals or reports by governmental agencies or other persons that are necessary to guarantee, insure, or provide security for the credit or collateral). The creditor shall exercise reasonable diligence in obtaining such information.

(g) *Business credit* refers to extensions of credit primarily for business or commercial (including agricultural) purposes, but excluding extensions of credit of the types described in § ~~202.3~~§§1002.3(a)–(d).

(h) *Consumer credit* means credit extended to a natural person primarily for personal, family, or household purposes.

(i) *Contractually liable* means expressly obligated to repay all debts arising on an account by reason of an agreement to that effect.

(j) *Credit* means the right granted by a creditor to an applicant to defer payment of a debt, incur debt and defer its payment, or purchase property or services and defer payment therefor.

(k) *Credit card* means any card, plate, coupon book, or other single credit device that may be used from time to time to obtain money, property, or services on credit.

(l) *Creditor* means a person who, in the ordinary course of business, regularly participates in a credit decision, including setting the terms of the credit. The term creditor includes a creditor's assignee, transferee, or subrogee who so participates. For purposes of § ~~202.4~~§§1002.4(a) and (b), the term creditor also includes a person who, in the ordinary course of business, regularly refers applicants or prospective applicants to creditors, or selects or offers to select creditors to whom requests for credit may be made. A person is not a creditor regarding any violation of the Act or this ~~regulation~~part committed by another creditor unless the person knew or had reasonable notice of the act, policy, or practice that constituted the violation before becoming involved in the credit transaction. The term does not include a person whose only participation in a credit transaction involves honoring a credit card.

(m) *Credit transaction* means every aspect of an applicant's dealings with a creditor regarding an application for credit or an existing extension of credit (including, but not limited to, information requirements; investigation procedures; standards of creditworthiness; terms of credit; furnishing of

credit information; revocation, alteration, or termination of credit; and collection procedures).

(n) *Discriminate against an applicant* means to treat an applicant less favorably than other applicants.

(o) *Elderly* means age 62 or older.

(p) *Empirically derived and other credit scoring systems.*

(1) A *credit scoring system* is a system that evaluates an applicant's creditworthiness mechanically, based on key attributes of the applicant and aspects of the transaction, and that determines, alone or in conjunction with an evaluation of additional information about the applicant, whether an applicant is deemed creditworthy. To qualify as an *empirically derived, demonstrably and statistically sound, credit scoring system,* the system must be:

(i) Based on data that are derived from an empirical comparison of sample groups or the population of creditworthy and ~~noncreditworthy~~non-creditworthy applicants who applied for credit within a reasonable preceding period of time;

(ii) Developed for the purpose of evaluating the creditworthiness of applicants with respect to the legitimate business interests of the creditor utilizing the system (including, but not limited to, minimizing bad debt losses and operating expenses in accordance with the creditor's business judgment);

(iii) Developed and validated using accepted statistical principles and methodology; and

(iv) Periodically revalidated by the use of appropriate statistical principles and methodology and adjusted as necessary to maintain predictive ability.

(2) A creditor may use an empirically derived, demonstrably and statistically sound, credit scoring system obtained from another person or may obtain credit experience from which to develop such a system. Any such system must satisfy the criteria set forth in paragraph (p)(1)(i) through (iv) of this section; if the creditor is unable during the development process to validate the system based on its own credit experience in accordance with paragraph (p)(1) of this section, the system must be validated when sufficient credit experience becomes available. A system that fails this validity test is no longer an empirically derived, demonstrably and statistically sound, credit scoring system for that creditor.

(q) *Extend credit* and *extension of credit* mean the granting of credit in any form (including, but not limited to, credit granted in addition to any existing credit or credit limit; credit granted pursuant to an open-end credit plan; the refinancing or other renewal of credit, including the issuance of a new credit card in place of an expiring credit card or in substitution for an existing credit card; the consolidation of two or more obligations; or the continuance of existing credit without any special effort to collect at or after maturity).

(r) *Good faith* means honesty in fact in the conduct or transaction.

(s) *Inadvertent error* means a mechanical, electronic, or clerical error that a creditor demonstrates was not intentional and occurred notwithstanding the maintenance of procedures reasonably adapted to avoid such errors.

(t) *Judgmental system of evaluating applicants* means any system for evaluating the creditworthiness of an applicant other than an empirically derived, demonstrably and statistically sound, credit scoring system.

(u) *Marital status* means the state of being unmarried, married, or separated, as defined by applicable state law. The term "unmarried" includes persons who are single, divorced, or widowed.

(v) *Negative factor or value,* in relation to the age of elderly applicants, means utilizing a factor, value, or weight that is less favorable regarding elderly applicants than the creditor's experience warrants or is less favorable than the factor, value, or weight assigned to the class of applicants that are not classified as elderly and are most favored by a creditor on the basis of age.

(w) *Open-end credit* means credit extended under a plan in which a creditor may permit an applicant to make purchases or obtain loans from time to time directly from the creditor or indirectly by use of a credit card, check, or other device.

(x) *Person* means a natural person, corporation, government or governmental subdivision or agency, trust, estate, partnership, cooperative, or association.

(y) *Pertinent element of creditworthiness,* in relation to a judgmental system of evaluating applicants, means any information about applicants that a creditor obtains and considers and that has a demonstrable relationship to a determination of creditworthiness.

(z) *Prohibited basis* means race, color, religion, national origin, sex, marital status, or age (provided that the applicant has the capacity to enter into a binding contract); the fact that all or part of the applicant's income derives from any public assistance program; or the fact that the applicant has in good faith exercised any right under the Consumer Credit Protection Act or any state law upon which an exemption has been granted by the ~~Board~~Bureau.

(aa) *State* means any state, the District of Columbia, the Commonwealth of Puerto Rico, or any territory or possession of the United States.

§ ~~202.3~~1002.3 Limited exceptions for certain classes of transactions.

(a) Public utilities credit.

(1) *Definition.* Public utilities credit refers to extensions of credit that involve public utility services provided through pipe, wire, or other connected facilities, or radio or similar transmission (including extensions of such facilities), if the charges for service, delayed payment, and any discount for prompt payment are filed with or regulated by a government unit.

(2) *Exceptions.* The following provisions of this ~~regulation~~part do not apply to public utilities credit:

(i) Section ~~202.5~~1002.5(d)(1) concerning information about marital status; and

(ii) Section ~~202.12~~1002.12(b) relating to record retention.

(b) Securities credit.

(1) *Definition.* Securities credit refers to extensions of credit subject to regulation under section 7 of the Securities Exchange Act of 1934 or extensions of credit by a broker or dealer subject to regulation as a broker or dealer under the Securities Exchange Act of 1934.

(2) *Exceptions.* The following provisions of this ~~regulation~~part do not apply to securities credit:

(i) Section ~~202.5~~1002.5(b) concerning information about the sex of an applicant;

(ii) Section ~~202.5~~1002.5(c) concerning information about a spouse or former spouse;

(iii) Section ~~202.5~~1002.5(d)(1) concerning information about marital status;

(iv) Section ~~202.7~~1002.7(b) relating to designation of name to the extent necessary to comply with rules regarding an account in which a broker or dealer has an interest, or rules regarding the aggregation of accounts of spouses to determine controlling interests, beneficial interests, beneficial ownership, or purchase limitations and restrictions;

(v) Section ~~202.7~~1002.7(c) relating to action concerning open-end accounts, to the extent the action taken is on the basis of a change of name or marital status;

(vi) Section ~~202.7~~1002.7(d) relating to the signature of a spouse or other person;

(vii) Section ~~202.10~~1002.10 relating to furnishing of credit information; and

(viii) Section ~~202.12~~1002.12(b) relating to record retention.

(c) Incidental credit.

(1) *Definition.* Incidental credit refers to extensions of consumer credit other than the types described in paragraphs (a) and (b) of this section:

(i) That are not made pursuant to the terms of a credit card account;

(ii) That are not subject to a finance charge (as defined in Regulation Z, 12 CFR ~~226.4~~1026.4); and

(iii) That are not payable by agreement in more than four installments.

(2) *Exceptions.* The following provisions of this ~~regulation~~part do not apply to incidental credit:

(i) Section ~~202.5~~1002.5(b) concerning information about the sex of an applicant, but only to the extent necessary for medical records or similar purposes;

(ii) Section ~~202.5~~1002.5(c) concerning information about a spouse or former spouse;

(iii) Section ~~202.5~~1002.5(d)(1) concerning information about marital status;

(iv) Section ~~202.5~~1002.5(d)(2) concerning information about income derived from alimony, child support, or separate maintenance payments;

(v) Section ~~202.7~~1002.7(d) relating to the signature of a spouse or other person;

(vi) Section ~~202.9~~1002.9 relating to notifications;

(vii) Section ~~202.10~~1002.10 relating to furnishing of credit information; and

(viii) Section ~~202.12~~1002.12(b) relating to record retention.

(d) Government credit.

(1) *Definition.* Government credit refers to extensions of credit made to governments or governmental subdivisions, agencies, or instrumentalities.

(2) *Applicability of regulation.* Except for § ~~202.4~~1002.4(a), the general rule against discrimination on a prohibited basis, the requirements of this ~~regulation~~part do not apply to government credit.

§ ~~202.4~~1002.4 General rules.

(a) Discrimination. A creditor shall not discriminate against an applicant on a prohibited basis regarding any aspect of a credit transaction.

(b) Discouragement. A creditor shall not make any oral or written statement, in advertising or otherwise, to applicants or prospective applicants that would discourage on a prohibited basis a reasonable person from making or pursuing an application.

(c) Written applications. A creditor shall take written applications for the dwelling-related types of credit covered by § ~~202.13~~1002.13(a).

(d) Form of disclosures.

(1) *General rule.* A creditor that provides in writing any disclosures or information required by this ~~regulation~~part must provide the disclosures in a clear and conspicuous manner and, except for the disclosures required by §§ ~~202.5~~1002.5 and ~~202.13,~~ 1002.13, in a form the applicant may retain.

(2) *Disclosures in electronic form.* The disclosures required by this part that are required to be given in writing may be provided to the applicant in electronic form, subject to compliance with the consumer consent and other applicable provisions of the Electronic Signatures in Global and National Commerce Act (E-Sign Act) (15 U.S.C. 7001 *et seq.*). Where the disclosures under §§ ~~202.5~~1002.5(b)(1), ~~202.5~~1002.5(b)(2), ~~202.5~~1002.5(d)(1), ~~202.5~~1002.5 (d)(2), ~~202.13,~~1002.13, and ~~202.14~~1002.14(a)(2)~~(i)~~(i) accompany an application accessed by the applicant in electronic form, these disclosures may be provided to the applicant in electronic form on or with the application form, without regard to the consumer consent or other provisions of the E-Sign Act.

(e) Foreign-language disclosures. Disclosures may be made in languages other than English, provided they are available in English upon request.

[78 Fed. Reg. 7248 (Jan. 31, 2013), eff. Jan. 18, 2014]

§ ~~202.5~~1002.5 Rules concerning requests for information.

(a) General rules.

(1) *Requests for information.* Except as provided in paragraphs (b) through (d) of this section, a creditor may request any information in connection with a credit transaction. This paragraph does not limit or abrogate any Federal or state law regarding privacy, privileged information, credit reporting limitations, or similar restrictions on obtainable information.

(2) *Required collection of information.* Notwithstanding paragraphs (b) through (d) of this section, a creditor shall request information for monitoring purposes as required by §~~202.13~~1002.13 for credit secured by the applicant's dwelling. In addition, a creditor may obtain information required by a regulation, order, or agreement issued by, or entered into with, a court or an enforcement agency (including the Attorney General of the United States or a similar state official) to monitor or enforce compliance with the Act, this ~~regulation~~part, or other ~~federal~~Federal or state statutes or regulations.

(3) *Special-purpose credit.* A creditor may obtain information that is otherwise restricted to determine eligibility for a special purpose credit program, as provided in §~~202.8~~§§1002.8(b), (c), and (d).

(b) **Limitation on information about race, color, religion, national origin, or sex.** A creditor shall not inquire about the race, color, religion, national origin, or sex of an applicant or any other person in connection with a credit transaction, except as provided in paragraphs (b)(1) and (b)(2) of this section.

(1) *Self-test.* A creditor may inquire about the race, color, religion, national origin, or sex of an applicant or any other person in connection with a credit transaction for the purpose of conducting a self-test that meets the requirements of §~~202.15.~~ 1002.15. A creditor that makes such an inquiry shall disclose orally or in writing, at the time the information is requested, that:

(i) The applicant will not be required to provide the information;

(ii) The creditor is requesting the information to monitor its compliance with the ~~federal~~Federal Equal Credit Opportunity Act;

(iii) Federal law prohibits the creditor from discriminating on the basis of this information, or on the basis of an applicant's decision not to furnish the information; and

(iv) If applicable, certain information will be collected based on visual observation or surname if not provided by the applicant or other person.

(2) *Sex.* An applicant may be requested to designate a title on an application form (such as Ms., Miss, Mr., or Mrs.) if the form discloses that the designation of a title is optional. An application form shall otherwise use only terms that are neutral as to sex.

(c) **Information about a spouse or former spouse.**

(1) *General rule.* Except as permitted in this paragraph, a creditor may not request any information concerning the spouse or former spouse of an applicant.

(2) *Permissible inquiries.* A creditor may request any information concerning an applicant's spouse (or former spouse under paragraph (c)(2)(v) of this section) that may be requested about the applicant if:

(i) The spouse will be permitted to use the account;

(ii) The spouse will be contractually liable on the account;

(iii) The applicant is relying on the spouse's income as a basis for repayment of the credit requested;

(iv) The applicant resides in a community property state or is relying on property located in such a state as a basis for repayment of the credit requested; or

(v) The applicant is relying on alimony, child support, or separate maintenance payments from a spouse or former spouse as a basis for repayment of the credit requested.

(3) *Other accounts of the applicant.* A creditor may request that an applicant list any account on which the applicant is contractually liable and to provide the name and address of the person in whose name the account is held. A creditor may also ask an applicant to list the names in which the applicant has previously received credit.

(d) **Other limitations on information requests.**

(1) *Marital status.* If an applicant applies for individual unsecured credit, a creditor shall not inquire about the applicant's marital status unless the applicant resides in a community property state or is relying on property located in such a state as a basis for repayment of the credit requested. If an application is for other than individual unsecured credit, a creditor may inquire about the applicant's marital status, but shall use only the terms *married, unmarried,* and *separated.* A creditor may explain that the category unmarried includes single, divorced, and widowed persons.

(2) *Disclosure about income from alimony, child support, or separate maintenance.* A creditor shall not inquire whether income stated in an application is derived from alimony, child support, or separate maintenance payments unless the creditor discloses to the applicant that such income need not be revealed if the applicant does not want the creditor to consider it in determining the applicant's creditworthiness.

(3) *Childbearing, childrearing.* A creditor shall not inquire about birth control practices, intentions concerning the bearing or rearing of children, or capability to bear children. A creditor may inquire about the number and ages of an applicant's dependents or about dependent-related financial obligations or expenditures, provided such information is requested without regard to sex, marital status, or any other prohibited basis.

(e) **Permanent residency and immigration status.** A creditor may inquire about the permanent residency and immigration status of an applicant or any other person in connection with a credit transaction.

§ ~~202.6~~1002.6 Rules concerning evaluation of applications.

(a) **General rule concerning use of information.** Except as otherwise provided in the Act and this ~~regulation~~part, a creditor may consider any information obtained, so long as the information is not used to discriminate against an applicant on a prohibited basis. The legislative history of the Act indicates that the Congress intended an "effects test" concept, as outlined in the employment field by the Supreme Court in the cases of *Griggs* v. *Duke Power Co.,* 401 U.S. 424 (1971), and *Albemarle Paper Co.* v. *Moody,* 422 U.S. 405 (1975), to be applicable to a creditor's determination of creditworthiness.

(b) **Specific rules concerning use of information.**

(1) Except as provided in the Act and this ~~regulation~~part, a creditor shall not take a prohibited basis into account in any system of evaluating the creditworthiness of applicants.

(2) *Age, receipt of public assistance.*

(i) Except as permitted in this paragraph, a creditor shall not take into account an applicant's age (provided that the applicant has the capacity to enter into a binding contract) or whether an applicant's income derives from any public assistance program.

(ii) In an empirically derived, demonstrably and statistically sound, credit scoring system, a creditor may use an applicant's age as a predictive variable, provided that the age of an elderly applicant is not assigned a negative factor or value.

(iii) In a judgmental system of evaluating creditworthiness, a creditor may consider an applicant's age or whether an applicant's income derives from any public assistance program only for the purpose of determining a pertinent element of creditworthiness.

(iv) In any system of evaluating creditworthiness, a creditor may consider the age of an elderly applicant when such age is used to favor the elderly applicant in extending credit.

(3) *Childbearing, childrearing.* In evaluating creditworthiness, a creditor shall not make assumptions or use aggregate statistics relating to the likelihood that any category of persons will bear or rear children or will, for that reason, receive diminished or interrupted income in the future.

(4) *Telephone listing.* A creditor shall not take into account whether there is a telephone listing in the name of an applicant for consumer credit but may take into account whether there is a telephone in the applicant's residence.

(5) *Income.* A creditor shall not discount or exclude from consideration the income of an applicant or the spouse of an applicant because of a prohibited basis or because the income is derived from part-time employment or is an annuity, pension, or other retirement benefit; a creditor may consider the amount and probable continuance of any income in evaluating an applicant's creditworthiness. When an applicant relies on alimony, child support, or separate maintenance payments in applying for credit, the creditor shall consider such payments as income to the extent that they are likely to be consistently made.

(6) *Credit history.* To the extent that a creditor considers credit history in evaluating the creditworthiness of similarly qualified applicants for a simi-

lar type and amount of credit, in evaluating an applicant's creditworthiness a creditor shall consider:

(i) The credit history, when available, of accounts designated as accounts that the applicant and the applicant's spouse are permitted to use or for which both are contractually liable;

(ii) On the applicant's request, any information the applicant may present that tends to indicate the credit history being considered by the creditor does not accurately reflect the applicant's creditworthiness; and

(iii) On the applicant's request, the credit history, when available, of any account reported in the name of the applicant's spouse or former spouse that the applicant can demonstrate accurately reflects the applicant's creditworthiness.

(7) *Immigration status.* A creditor may consider the applicant's immigration status or status as a permanent resident of the United States, and any additional information that may be necessary to ascertain the creditor's rights and remedies regarding repayment.

(8) *Marital status.* Except as otherwise permitted or required by law, a creditor shall evaluate married and unmarried applicants by the same standards; and in evaluating joint applicants, a creditor shall not treat applicants differently based on the existence, absence, or likelihood of a marital relationship between the parties.

(9) *Race, color, religion, national origin, sex.* Except as otherwise permitted or required by law, a creditor shall not consider race, color, religion, national origin, or sex (or an applicant's or other person's decision not to provide the information) in any aspect of a credit transaction.

(c) State property laws. A creditor's consideration or application of state property laws directly or indirectly affecting creditworthiness does not constitute unlawful discrimination for the purposes of the Act or this ~~regulation~~part.

§ ~~202.7~~1002.7 Rules concerning extensions of credit.

(a) Individual accounts. A creditor shall not refuse to grant an individual account to a creditworthy applicant on the basis of sex, marital status, or any other prohibited basis.

(b) Designation of name. A creditor shall not refuse to allow an applicant to open or maintain an account in a birth-given first name and a surname that is the applicant's birth-given surname, the spouse's surname, or a combined surname.

(c) Action concerning existing open-end accounts.

(1) *Limitations.* In the absence of evidence of the applicant's inability or unwillingness to repay, a creditor shall not take any of the following actions regarding an applicant who is contractually liable on an existing open-end account on the basis of the applicant's reaching a certain age or retiring or on the basis of a change in the applicant's name or marital status:

(i) Require a reapplication, except as provided in paragraph (c)(2) of this section;

(ii) Change the terms of the account; or

(iii) Terminate the account.

(2) *Requiring reapplication.* A creditor may require a reapplication for an open-end account on the basis of a change in the marital status of an applicant who is contractually liable if the credit granted was based in whole or in part on income of the applicant's spouse and if information available to the creditor indicates that the applicant's income may not support the amount of credit currently available.

(d) Signature of spouse or other person.

(1) *Rule for qualified applicant.* Except as provided in this paragraph, a creditor shall not require the signature of an applicant's spouse or other person, other than a joint applicant, on any credit instrument if the applicant qualifies under the creditor's standards of creditworthiness for the amount and terms of the credit requested. A creditor shall not deem the submission of a joint financial statement or other evidence of jointly held assets as an application for joint credit.

(2) *Unsecured credit.* If an applicant requests unsecured credit and relies in part upon property that the applicant owns jointly with another person to satisfy the creditor's standards of creditworthiness, the creditor may require the signature of the other person only on the instrument(s) necessary, or reasonably believed by the creditor to be necessary, under the law of the state in which the property is located, to enable the creditor to reach the property being relied upon in the event of the death or default of the applicant.

(3) *Unsecured credit—community property states.* If a married applicant requests unsecured credit and resides in a community property state, or if the applicant is relying on property located in such a state, a creditor may require the signature of the spouse on any instrument necessary, or reasonably believed by the creditor to be necessary, under applicable state law to make the community property available to satisfy the debt in the event of default if:

(i) Applicable state law denies the applicant power to manage or control sufficient community property to qualify for the credit requested under the creditor's standards of creditworthiness; and

(ii) The applicant does not have sufficient separate property to qualify for the credit requested without regard to community property.

(4) *Secured credit.* If an applicant requests secured credit, a creditor may require the signature of the applicant's spouse or other person on any instrument necessary, or reasonably believed by the creditor to be necessary, under applicable state law to make the property being offered as security available to satisfy the debt in the event of default, for example, an instrument to create a valid lien, pass clear title, waive inchoate rights, or assign earnings.

(5) *Additional parties.* If, under a creditor's standards of creditworthiness, the personal liability of an additional party is necessary to support the credit requested, a creditor may request a cosigner, guar-

antor, endorser, or similar party. The applicant's spouse may serve as an additional party, but the creditor shall not require that the spouse be the additional party.

(6) *Rights of additional parties.* A creditor shall not impose requirements upon an additional party that the creditor is prohibited from imposing upon an applicant under this section.

(e) Insurance. A creditor shall not refuse to extend credit and shall not terminate an account because credit life, health, accident, disability, or other credit-related insurance is not available on the basis of the applicant's age.

§ ~~202.8~~1002.8 Special purpose credit programs.

(a) Standards for programs. Subject to the provisions of paragraph (b) of this section, the Act and this ~~regulation~~part permit a creditor to extend special purpose credit to applicants who meet eligibility requirements under the following types of credit programs:

(1) Any credit assistance program expressly authorized by ~~federal~~Federal or state law for the benefit of an economically disadvantaged class of persons;

(2) Any credit assistance program offered by a not-for-profit organization, as defined under section 501(c) of the Internal Revenue Code of 1954, as amended, for the benefit of its members or for the benefit of an economically disadvantaged class of persons; or

(3) Any special purpose credit program offered by a for-profit organization, or in which such an organization participates to meet special social needs, if:

(i) The program is established and administered pursuant to a written plan that identifies the class of persons that the program is designed to benefit and sets forth the procedures and standards for extending credit pursuant to the program; and

(ii) The program is established and administered to extend credit to a class of persons who, under the organization's customary standards of creditworthiness, probably would not receive such credit or would receive it on less favorable terms than are ordinarily available to other applicants applying to the organization for a similar type and amount of credit.

(b) Rules in other sections.

(1) *General applicability.* All the provisions of this ~~regulation~~part apply to each of the special purpose credit programs described in paragraph (a) of this section except as modified by this section.

(2) *Common characteristics.* A program described in paragraph (a)(2) or (a)(3) of this section qualifies as a special purpose credit program only if it was established and is administered so as not to discriminate against an applicant on any prohibited basis; however, all program participants may be required to share one or more common characteristics (for example, race, national origin, or sex) so long as the program was not established and is not administered with the purpose of evading the requirements of the Act or this ~~regulation~~part.

(c) Special rule concerning requests and use of information. If participants in a special purpose credit program described in paragraph (a) of this section are required to possess one or more common characteristics (for example, race, national origin, or sex) and if the program otherwise satisfies the requirements of paragraph (a) of this section, a creditor may request and consider information regarding the common characteristic(s) in determining the applicant's eligibility for the program.

(d) Special rule in the case of financial need. If financial need is one of the criteria under a special purpose credit program described in paragraph (a) of this section, the creditor may request and consider, in determining an applicant's eligibility for the program, information regarding the applicant's marital status; alimony, child support, and separate maintenance income; and the spouse's financial resources. In addition, a creditor may obtain the signature of an applicant's spouse or other person on an application or credit instrument relating to a special purpose credit program if the signature is required by ~~federal~~Federal or state law.

§ ~~202.9~~1002.9 Notifications.

(a) Notification of action taken, ECOA notice, and statement of specific reasons.

(1) *When notification is required.* A creditor shall notify an applicant of action taken within:

(i) 30 days after receiving a completed application concerning the creditor's approval of, counteroffer to, or adverse action on the application;

(ii) 30 days after taking adverse action on an incomplete application, unless notice is provided in accordance with paragraph (c) of this section;

(iii) 30 days after taking adverse action on an existing account; or

(iv) 90 days after notifying the applicant of a counteroffer if the applicant does not expressly accept or use the credit offered.

(2) *Content of notification when adverse action is taken.* A notification given to an applicant when adverse action is taken shall be in writing and shall contain a statement of the action taken; the name and address of the creditor; a statement of the provisions of §section 701(a) of the Act; the name and address of the ~~federal~~Federal agency that administers compliance with respect to the creditor; and either:

(i) A statement of specific reasons for the action taken; or

(ii) A disclosure of the applicant's right to a statement of specific reasons within 30 days, if the statement is requested within 60 days of the creditor's notification. The disclosure shall include the name, address, and telephone number of the person or office from which the statement of reasons can be obtained. If the creditor chooses to provide the reasons orally, the creditor shall also disclose the applicant's right to have them confirmed in writing within 30 days of receiving the applicant's written request for confirmation.

(3) *Notification to business credit applicants.* For business credit, a creditor shall comply with the notification requirements of this section in the following manner:

(i) With regard to a business that had gross revenues of $1 million or less in its preceding fiscal year (other than an extension of trade credit, credit incident to a factoring agreement, or other similar types of business credit), a creditor shall comply with paragraphs (a)(1) and (2) of this section, except that:

(A) The statement of the action taken may be given orally or in writing, when adverse action is taken;

(B) Disclosure of an applicant's right to a statement of reasons may be given at the time of application, instead of when adverse action is taken, provided the disclosure contains the information required by paragraph (a)(2)(ii) of this section and the ECOA notice specified in paragraph (b)(1) of this section;

(C) For an application made entirely by telephone, a creditor satisfies the requirements of paragraph (a)(3)(i) of this section by an oral statement of the action taken and of the applicant's right to a statement of reasons for adverse action.

(ii) With regard to a business that had gross revenues in excess of $1 million in its preceding fiscal year or an extension of trade credit, credit incident to a factoring agreement, or other similar types of business credit, a creditor shall:

(A) Notify the applicant, within a reasonable time, orally or in writing, of the action taken; and

(B) Provide a written statement of the reasons for adverse action and the ECOA notice specified in paragraph (b)(1) of this section if the applicant makes a written request for the reasons within 60 days of the creditor's notification.

(b) Form of ECOA notice and statement of specific reasons.

(1) *ECOA notice.* To satisfy the disclosure requirements of paragraph (a)(2) of this section regarding section 701(a) of the Act, the creditor shall provide a notice that is substantially similar to the following: The ~~federal~~Federal Equal Credit Opportunity Act prohibits creditors from discriminating against credit applicants on the basis of race, color, religion, national origin, sex, marital status, age (provided the applicant has the capacity to enter into a binding contract); because all or part of the applicant's income derives from any public assistance program; or because the applicant has in good faith exercised any right under the Consumer Credit Protection Act. The ~~federal~~Federal agency that administers compliance with this law concerning this creditor is [name and address as specified by the appropriate agency or agencies listed in ~~appendix A of this regulation~~.Appendix A of this part]. Until January 1, 2013, a creditor may comply with this paragraph (b)(1) and paragraph (a)(2) of this section by including in the notice the name and address as specified by the appropriate agency in Appendix A to 12 CFR Part 202, as in effect on October 1, 2011.

(2) *Statement of specific reasons.* The statement of reasons for adverse action required by paragraph

(a)(2)(i) of this section must be specific and indicate the principal reason(s) for the adverse action. Statements that the adverse action was based on the creditor's internal standards or policies or that the applicant, joint applicant, or similar party failed to achieve a qualifying score on the creditor's credit scoring system are insufficient.

(c) Incomplete applications.

(1) *Notice alternatives.* Within 30 days after receiving an application that is incomplete regarding matters that an applicant can complete, the creditor shall notify the applicant either:

(i) Of action taken, in accordance with paragraph (a) of this section; or

(ii) Of the incompleteness, in accordance with paragraph (c)(2) of this section.

(2) *Notice of incompleteness.* If additional information is needed from an applicant, the creditor shall send a written notice to the applicant specifying the information needed, designating a reasonable period of time for the applicant to provide the information, and informing the applicant that failure to provide the information requested will result in no further consideration being given to the application. The creditor shall have no further obligation under this section if the applicant fails to respond within the designated time period. If the applicant supplies the requested information within the designated time period, the creditor shall take action on the application and notify the applicant in accordance with paragraph (a) of this section.

(3) *Oral request for information.* At its option, a creditor may inform the applicant orally of the need for additional information. If the application remains incomplete the creditor shall send a notice in accordance with paragraph (c)(1) of this section.

(d) Oral notifications by small-volume creditors. In the case of a creditor that did not receive more than 150 applications during the preceding calendar year, the requirements of this section (including statements of specific reasons) are satisfied by oral notifications.

(e) Withdrawal of approved application. When an applicant submits an application and the parties contemplate that the applicant will inquire about its status, if the creditor approves the application and the applicant has not inquired within 30 days after applying, the creditor may treat the application as withdrawn and need not comply with paragraph (a)(1) of this section.

(f) Multiple applicants. When an application involves more than one applicant, notification need only be given to one of them but must be given to the primary applicant where one is readily apparent.

(g) Applications submitted through a third party. When an application is made on behalf of an applicant to more than one creditor and the applicant expressly accepts or uses credit offered by one of the creditors, notification of action taken by any of the other creditors is not required. If no credit is offered or if the applicant does not expressly accept or use the credit offered, each creditor taking adverse action must comply with this section, directly or through a third party. A notice given by a third party shall disclose the identity of each creditor on whose behalf the notice is given.

§ ~~202.10~~1002.10 Furnishing of credit information.

(a) Designation of accounts. A creditor that furnishes credit information shall designate:

(1) Any new account to reflect the participation of both spouses if the applicant's spouse is permitted to use or is contractually liable on the account (other than as a guarantor, surety, endorser, or similar party); and

(2) Any existing account to reflect such participation, within 90 days after receiving a written request to do so from one of the spouses.

(b) Routine reports to consumer reporting agency. If a creditor furnishes credit information to a consumer reporting agency concerning an account designated to reflect the participation of both spouses, the creditor shall furnish the information in a manner that will enable the agency to provide access to the information in the name of each spouse.

(c) Reporting in response to inquiry. If a creditor furnishes credit information in response to an inquiry, concerning an account designated to reflect the participation of both spouses, the creditor shall furnish the information in the name of the spouse about whom the information is requested.

§ ~~202.11~~1002.11 Relation to state law.

(a) Inconsistent state laws. Except as otherwise provided in this section, this ~~regulation~~part alters, affects, or preempts only those state laws that are inconsistent with the Act and this ~~regulation~~part and then only to the extent of the inconsistency. A state law is not inconsistent if it is more protective of an applicant.

(b) Preempted provisions of state law.

(1) A state law is deemed to be inconsistent with the requirements of the Act and this ~~regulation~~part and less protective of an applicant within the meaning of section 705(f) of the Act to the extent that the law:

(i) Requires or permits a practice or act prohibited by the Act or this ~~regulation~~part;

(ii) Prohibits the individual extension of consumer credit to both parties to a marriage if each spouse individually and voluntarily applies for such credit;

(iii) Prohibits inquiries or collection of data required to comply with the Act or this ~~regulation~~part;

(iv) Prohibits asking about or considering age in an empirically derived, demonstrably and statistically sound, credit scoring system to determine a pertinent element of creditworthiness, or to favor an elderly applicant; or

(v) Prohibits inquiries necessary to establish or administer a special purpose credit program as defined by § ~~202.8.~~1002.8.

(2) A creditor, state, or other interested party may request that the ~~Board~~Bureau determine whether a state law is inconsistent with the requirements of the Act and this ~~regulation~~part.

(c) Laws on finance charges, loan ceilings. If married applicants voluntarily apply for and obtain individual accounts with the same creditor, the accounts shall not be aggregated or otherwise combined for purposes of determining permissible finance charges or loan ceilings under any ~~federal~~Federal or state law. Permissible loan ceiling laws shall be construed to permit each spouse to become individually liable up to the amount of the loan ceilings, less the amount for which the applicant is jointly liable.

(d) State and ~~federal~~Federal laws not affected. This section does not alter or annul any provision of state property laws, laws relating to the disposition of decedents' estates, or ~~federal~~Federal or state banking regulations directed only toward insuring the solvency of financial institutions.

(e) Exemption for state-regulated transactions.

(1) *Applications.* A state may apply to the ~~Board~~Bureau for an exemption from the requirements of the Act and this ~~regulation~~part for any class of credit transactions within the state. The ~~Board~~Bureau will grant such an exemption if the ~~Board~~Bureau determines that:

(i) The class of credit transactions is subject to state law requirements substantially similar to those of the Act and this ~~regulation~~part or that applicants are afforded greater protection under state law; and

(ii) There is adequate provision for state enforcement.

(2) *Liability and enforcement.*

(i) No exemption will extend to the civil liability provisions of section 706 of the Act or the administrative enforcement provisions of section 704 of the Act.

(ii) After an exemption has been granted, the requirements of the applicable state law (except for additional requirements not imposed by ~~federal~~Federal law) will constitute the requirements of the Act and this ~~regulation~~part.

§ ~~202.12~~1002.12 Record retention.

(a) Retention of prohibited information. A creditor may retain in its files information that is prohibited by the Act or this ~~regulation~~part for use in evaluating applications, without violating the Act or this ~~regulation~~part, if the information was obtained:

(1) From any source prior to March 23, 1977;

(2) From consumer reporting agencies, an applicant, or others without the specific request of the creditor; or

(3) As required to monitor compliance with the Act and this ~~regulation~~part or other ~~federal~~Federal or state statutes or regulations.

(b) Preservation of records.

(1) *Applications.* For 25 months (12 months for business credit, except as provided in paragraph

(b)(5) of this section) after the date that a creditor notifies an applicant of action taken on an application or of incompleteness, the creditor shall retain in original form or a copy thereof:

(i) Any application that it receives, any information required to be obtained concerning characteristics of the applicant to monitor compliance with the Act and this ~~regulation~~part or other similar law, and any other written or recorded information used in evaluating the application and not returned to the applicant at the applicant's request;

(ii) A copy of the following documents if furnished to the applicant in written form (or, if furnished orally, any notation or memorandum made by the creditor):

(A) The notification of action taken; and

(B) The statement of specific reasons for adverse action; and

(iii) Any written statement submitted by the applicant alleging a violation of the Act or this ~~regulation~~part.

(2) *Existing accounts.* For 25 months (12 months for business credit, except as provided in paragraph (b)(5) of this section) after the date that a creditor notifies an applicant of adverse action regarding an existing account, the creditor shall retain as to that account, in original form or a copy thereof:

(i) Any written or recorded information concerning the adverse action; and

(ii) Any written statement submitted by the applicant alleging a violation of the Act or this ~~regulation~~part.

(3) *Other applications.* For 25 months (12 months for business credit, except as provided in paragraph (b)(5) of this section) after the date that a creditor receives an application for which the creditor is not required to comply with the notification requirements of § ~~202.9,~~1002.9, the creditor shall retain all written or recorded information in its possession concerning the applicant, including any notation of action taken.

(4) *Enforcement proceedings and investigations.* A creditor shall retain the information beyond 25 months (12 months for business credit, except as provided in paragraph (b)(5) of this section) if the creditor has actual notice that it is under investigation or is subject to an enforcement proceeding for an alleged violation of the Act or this part, by the Attorney General of the United States or by an enforcement agency charged with monitoring that creditor's compliance with the Act and this ~~regulation~~part, or if it has been served with notice of an action filed pursuant to section 706 of the Act and § ~~202.16~~1002.16 of this part. The creditor shall retain the information until final disposition of the matter, unless an earlier time is allowed by order of the agency or court.[1]

(5) *Special rule for certain business credit applications.* With regard to a business that had gross revenues in excess of $1 million in its preceding fiscal year, or an extension of trade credit, credit incident to a factoring agreement, or other similar types of business credit, the creditor shall retain records for at least 60 days after notifying the applicant of the action taken. If within that time period the applicant requests in writing the reasons for adverse action or that records be retained, the creditor shall retain records for 12 months.

(6) *Self-tests.* For 25 months after a self-test (as defined in §~~202.15~~1002.15) has been completed, the creditor shall retain all written or recorded information about the self-test. A creditor shall retain information beyond 25 months if it has actual notice that it is under investigation or is subject to an enforcement proceeding for an alleged violation, or if it has been served with notice of a civil action. In such cases, the creditor shall retain the information until final disposition of the matter, unless an earlier time is allowed by the appropriate agency or court order.

(7) *Prescreened solicitations.* For 25 months after the date on which an offer of credit is made to potential customers (12 months for business credit, except as provided in paragraph (b)(5) of this section), the creditor shall retain in original form or a copy thereof:

(i) The text of any prescreened solicitation;

(ii) The list of criteria the creditor used to select potential recipients of the solicitation; and

(iii) Any correspondence related to complaints (formal or informal) about the solicitation.

§ ~~202.13~~1002.13 Information for monitoring purposes.

(a) Information to be requested.

(1) A creditor that receives an application for credit primarily for the purchase or refinancing of a dwelling occupied or to be occupied by the applicant as a principal residence, where the extension of credit will be secured by the dwelling, shall request as part of the application the following information regarding the applicant(s):

(i) Ethnicity, using the categories Hispanic or Latino, and not Hispanic or Latino; and race, using the categories American Indian or Alaska Native, Asian, Black or African American, Native Hawaiian or Other Pacific Islander, and White;

(ii) Sex;

(iii) Marital status, using the categories married, unmarried, and separated; and

(iv) Age.

(2) *Dwelling* means a residential structure that contains one to four units, whether or not that structure is attached to real property. The term includes, but is not limited to, an individual condominium or cooperative unit and a mobile or other manufactured home.

(b) Obtaining information. Questions regarding ethnicity, race, sex, marital status, and age may be listed, at the creditor's option, on the application form or on a separate form that refers to the application. The applicant(s) shall be asked but not required to supply the requested information. If the applicant(s) chooses not to provide the information or any part of it, that fact shall be noted on the form. The creditor shall then also note on the form, to the extent possible, the ethnicity, race, and sex of the applicant(s) on the basis of visual observation or surname.

(c) Disclosure to applicant(s). The creditor shall inform the applicant(s) that the information regarding ethnicity, race, sex, marital status, and age is being requested by the ~~federal government~~Federal Government for the purpose of monitoring compliance with ~~federal~~Federal statutes that prohibit creditors from discriminating against applicants on those bases. The creditor shall also inform the applicant(s) that if the applicant(s) chooses not to provide the information, the creditor is required to note the ethnicity, race and sex on the basis of visual observation or surname.

(d) Substitute monitoring program. A monitoring program required by an agency charged with administrative enforcement under section 704 of the Act may be substituted for the requirements contained in paragraphs (a), (b), and (c) of this section.

§ 1002.14 Rules on providing appraisals and other valuations.

(a) Providing appraisals and other valuations.

(1) *In general.* A creditor shall provide an applicant a copy of all appraisals and other written valuations developed in connection with an application for credit that is to be secured by a first lien on a dwelling. A creditor shall provide a copy of each such appraisal or other written valuation promptly upon completion, or three business days prior to consummation of the transaction (for closed-end credit) or account opening (for open-end credit), whichever is earlier. An applicant may waive the timing requirement in this paragraph (a)(1) and agree to receive any copy at or before consummation or account opening, except where otherwise prohibited by law. Any such waiver must be obtained at least three business days prior to consummation or account opening, unless the waiver pertains solely to the applicant's receipt of a copy of an appraisal or other written valuation that contains only clerical changes from a previous version of the appraisal or other written valuation provided to the applicant three or more business days prior to consummation or account opening. If the applicant provides a waiver and the transaction is not consummated or the account is not opened, the creditor must provide these copies no later than 30 days after the creditor determines consummation will not occur or the account will not be opened.

(2) *Disclosure.* For applications subject to paragraph (a)(1) of this section, a creditor shall mail or deliver to an applicant, not later than the third business day after the creditor receives an application for credit that is to be secured by a first lien on a dwelling, a notice in writing of the applicant's right to receive a copy of all written appraisals developed in connection with the application. In the case of an application for credit that is not to be secured by a first lien on a dwelling at the time of application, if the creditor later determines the credit will be secured by a first lien on a dwelling, the creditor shall mail or deliver the same notice in writing not later than the third business day after the creditor determines that the loan is to be secured by a first lien on a dwelling.

(3) *Reimbursement.* A creditor shall not charge an applicant for providing a copy of appraisals and other written valuations as required under this section, but may require applicants to pay a reasonable fee to reimburse the creditor for the cost of the appraisal or other written valuation unless otherwise provided by law.

(4) *Withdrawn, denied, or incomplete applications.* The requirements set forth in paragraph (a)(1) of this section apply whether credit is extended or denied or if the application is incomplete or withdrawn.

(5) *Copies in electronic form.* The copies required by § 1002.14(a)(1) may be provided to the applicant in electronic form, subject to compliance with the consumer consent and other applicable provisions of the Electronic Signatures in Global and National Commerce Act (E-Sign Act) (15 U.S.C. 7001 *et seq.*).

(b) Definitions. For purposes of paragraph (a) of this section:

(1) *Consummation.* The term "consummation" means the time that a consumer becomes contractually obligated on a closed-end credit transaction.

(2) *Dwelling.* The term "dwelling" means a residential structure that contains one to four units whether or not that structure is attached to real property. The term includes, but is not limited to, an individual condominium or cooperative unit, and a mobile or other manufactured home.

(3) *Valuation.* The term "valuation" means any estimate of the value of a dwelling developed in connection with an application for credit.

[78 Fed. Reg. 7248 (Jan. 31, 2013), eff. Jan. 18, 2014]

§ ~~202.15~~1002.15 Incentives for self-testing and self-correction.

(a) General rules.

(1) *Voluntary self-testing and correction.* The report or results of a self-test that a creditor voluntarily conducts (or authorizes) are privileged as provided in this section. Data collection required by law or by any governmental authority is not a voluntary self-test.

(2) *Corrective action required.* The privilege in this section applies only if the creditor has taken or is taking appropriate corrective action.

(3) *Other privileges.* The privilege created by this section does not preclude the assertion of any other privilege that may also apply.

(b) Self-test defined.

(1) *Definition.* A self-test is any program, practice, or study that:

(i) Is designed and used specifically to determine the extent or effectiveness of a creditor's compliance with the Act or this ~~regulation~~part; and

(ii) Creates data or factual information that is not available and cannot be derived from loan or application files or other records related to credit transactions.

(2) *Types of information privileged.* The privilege under this section applies to the report or results of the self-test, data or factual information created by the self-test, and any analysis, opinions, and conclusions pertaining to the self-test report or results. The privilege covers workpapers or draft documents as well as final documents.

(3) *Types of information not privileged.* The privilege under this section does not apply to:

(i) Information about whether a creditor conducted a self-test, the methodology used or the scope of the self-test, the time period covered by the self-test, or the dates it was conducted; or

(ii) Loan and application files or other business records related to credit transactions, and information derived from such files and records, even if the information has been aggregated, summarized, or reorganized to facilitate analysis.

(c) Appropriate corrective action.

(1) *General requirement.* For the privilege in this section to apply, appropriate corrective action is required when the self-test shows that it is more likely than not that a violation occurred, even though no violation has been formally adjudicated.

(2) *Determining the scope of appropriate corrective action.* A creditor must take corrective action that is reasonably likely to remedy the cause and effect of a likely violation by:

(i) Identifying the policies or practices that are the likely cause of the violation; and

(ii) Assessing the extent and scope of any violation.

(3) *Types of relief.* Appropriate corrective action may include both prospective and remedial relief, except that to establish a privilege under this section:

(i) A creditor is not required to provide remedial relief to a tester used in a self-test;

(ii) A creditor is only required to provide remedial relief to an applicant identified by the self-test as one whose rights were more likely than not violated; and

(iii) A creditor is not required to provide remedial relief to a particular applicant if the statute of limitations applicable to the violation expired before the creditor obtained the results of the self-test or the applicant is otherwise ineligible for such relief.

(4) *No admission of violation.* Taking corrective action is not an admission that a violation occurred.

(d) Scope of privilege.

(1) *General rule.* The report or results of a privileged self-test may not be obtained or used:

(i) By a government agency in any examination or investigation relating to compliance with the Act or this ~~regulation~~part; or

(ii) By a government agency or an applicant (including a prospective applicant who alleges a violation of §~~202.4~~1002.4(b)) in any proceeding or civil action in which a violation of the Act or this ~~regulation~~part is alleged.

(2) *Loss of privilege.* The report or results of a self-test are not privileged under paragraph (d)(1) of this section if the creditor or a person with lawful access to the report or results:

(i) Voluntarily discloses any part of the report or results, or any other information privileged under this section, to an applicant or government agency or to the public;

(ii) Discloses any part of the report or results, or any other information privileged under this section, as a defense to charges that the creditor has violated the Act or regulation; or

(iii) Fails or is unable to produce written or recorded information about the self-test that is required to be retained under §~~202.12~~1002.12(b)(6) when the information is needed to determine whether the privilege applies. This paragraph does not limit any other penalty or remedy that may be available for a violation of §~~202.12.~~1002.12.

(3) *Limited use of privileged information.* Notwithstanding paragraph (d)(1) of this section, the self-test report or results and any other information privileged under this section may be obtained and used by an applicant or government agency solely to determine a penalty or remedy after a violation of the Act or this ~~regulation~~part has been adjudicated or admitted. Disclosures for this limited purpose may be used only for the particular proceeding in which the adjudication or admission was made. Information disclosed under this paragraph (d)(3) remains privileged under paragraph (d)(1) of this section.

§ ~~202.16~~1002.16 Enforcement, penalties and liabilities.

(a) Administrative enforcement.

(1) As set forth more fully in section 704 of the Act, administrative enforcement of the Act and this ~~regulation~~part regarding certain creditors is assigned to the Comptroller of the Currency, Board of Governors of the Federal Reserve System, Board of Directors of the Federal Deposit Insurance Corporation, ~~Office of Thrift Supervision,~~ National Credit Union Administration, Surface Transportation Board, Civil Aeronautics Board, Secretary of Agriculture, Farm Credit Administration, Securities and Exchange Commission, Small Business Administration, ~~and~~ Secretary of Transportation, and Bureau of Consumer Financial Protection.

(2) Except to the extent that administrative enforcement is specifically assigned to some government agency other ~~authorities, compliance with~~than the Bureau, and subject to subtitle B of the Consumer Financial Protection Act of 2010, the Federal Trade Commission is authorized to enforce the requirements imposed under the Act and this ~~regulation is enforced by the Federal Trade Commission~~part.

(b) Penalties and liabilities.

(1) Sections 702(g) and 706(a) and (b) of the Act provide that any creditor that fails to comply with a requirement imposed by the Act or this ~~regulation~~part is subject to civil liability for actual and punitive damages in individual or class actions. Pursuant to sections 702(g) and 704(b), (c), and (d) of the Act, violations of the Act or this ~~regulation~~part also constitute violations of other ~~federal~~Federal laws. Liability for punitive damages can apply only to nongovernmental entities and is limited to $10,000 in individual actions and the lesser of $500,000 or 1 percent of the creditor's net worth in class actions. Section 706(c) provides for equitable and declaratory relief and section 706(d) authorizes the awarding of costs and reasonable attorney's fees to an aggrieved applicant in a successful action.

(2) As provided in section 706(f) of the Act, a civil action under the Act or this ~~regulation~~part may be brought in the appropriate United States district court without regard to the amount in controversy or in any other court of competent jurisdiction within ~~two~~five years after the date of the occurrence of the violation, or within one year after the commencement of an administrative enforcement proceeding or of a civil action brought by the Attorney General of the United States within ~~two~~five years after the alleged violation.

(3) If an agency responsible for administrative enforcement is unable to obtain compliance with the Act or this ~~regulation~~part, it may refer the matter to the Attorney General of the United States. If the ~~Board~~Bureau, the Comptroller of the Currency, the Federal Deposit Insurance Corporation, the ~~Office of Thrift Supervision~~Board of Governors of the Federal Reserve System, or the National Credit Union Administration has reason to believe that one or more creditors have engaged in a pattern or practice of discouraging or denying applications in violation of the Act or this ~~regulation~~part, the agency shall refer the matter to the Attorney General. If the agency has reason to believe that one or more creditors violated section 701(a) of the Act, the agency may refer a matter to the Attorney General.

(4) On referral, or whenever the Attorney General has reason to believe that one or more creditors have engaged in a pattern or practice in violation of the Act or this ~~regulation~~part, the Attorney General may bring a civil action for such relief as may be appropriate, including actual and punitive damages and injunctive relief.

(5) If ~~the Board,~~ the Comptroller of the Currency, the Federal Deposit Insurance Corporation, the ~~Office of Thrift Supervision~~Board of Governors of the Federal Reserve System, or the National Credit Union Administration has reason to believe (as a result of a consumer complaint, a consumer compliance examination, or some other basis) that a violation of the Act or this ~~regulation~~part has occurred which is also a violation of the Fair Housing Act, and the matter is not referred to the Attorney General, the agency shall:

(i) Notify the Secretary of Housing and Urban Development; and

(ii) Inform the applicant that the Secretary of Housing and Urban Development has been notified and that remedies may be available under the Fair Housing Act.

(c) Failure of compliance. A creditor's failure to comply with §§ ~~202.6~~1002.6(b)(6), ~~202.9, 202.10, 202.12 or 202.13~~1002.9, 1002.10, 1002.12 or 1002.13 is not a violation if it results from an inadvertent error. On discovering an error under §§ ~~202.9~~1002.9 and ~~202.10,~~1002.10, the creditor shall correct it as soon as possible. If a creditor inadvertently obtains the monitoring information regarding the ethnicity, race, and sex of the applicant in a dwelling-related transaction not covered by § ~~202.13,~~1002.13, the creditor may retain information and act on the application without violating the regulation.

~~§ 202.17 Data collection for credit applications by women-owned, minority-owned, or small businesses.~~

~~No motor vehicle dealer covered by section 1029(a) of the Dodd-Frank Wall Street Reform and Consumer Protection Act, 12 U.S.C. 5519(a), shall be required to comply with the requirements of section 704B of the Equal Credit Opportunity Act, 15 U.S.C. 1691c-2, until the effective date of final rules issued by the Board to implement section 704B of the Act, 15 U.S.C. 1691c-2. This paragraph shall not be construed to affect the effective date of section 704B of the Act for any person other than a motor vehicle dealer covered by section 1029(a) of the Dodd-Frank Wall Street Reform and Consumer Protection Act.~~

Appendix A to Part ~~202~~1002— Federal Enforcement Agencies To Be Listed in Adverse Action Notices

The following list indicates the ~~federal agencies that enforce Regulation B for particular classes of creditors~~Federal agency or agencies that should be listed in notices provided by creditors pursuant to §1002.9(b)(1). Any questions concerning a particular creditor ~~should~~may be directed to ~~its~~such agencies. This list is not intended to describe agencies' enforcement ~~agency~~authority for ECOA and Regulation B. Terms that are not defined in the Federal Deposit Insurance Act (12 U.S.C. 1813(s)) shall have the meaning given to them in the International Banking Act of 1978 (12 U.S.C. 3101).

1. *Banks, savings associations, and credit unions with total assets of over $10 billion and their affiliates:* Bureau of Consumer Financial Protection, 1700 G Street NW., Washington DC 20006. Such affiliates that are not banks, savings associations, or credit unions also should list, in addition to the Bureau: FTC Regional Office for region in which the creditor operates or Federal Trade Commission, Equal Credit Opportunity, Washington, DC 20580.

2. To the extent not included in item 1 above:

   a. *National banks, ~~and federal~~Federal savings associations, and Federal branches and ~~federal~~Federal agencies of foreign banks:* Office of the Comptroller of the Currency, Customer Assistance Group, 1301 McKinney Street, Suite 3450, Houston, TX 77010~~-9050.~~-9050

   b. *State member banks, branches and agencies of foreign banks (other than ~~federal~~Federal branches, ~~federal~~Federal agencies, and insured state branches of foreign banks), commercial lending companies owned or controlled by foreign banks, and organizations operating under section 25 or 25a~~A~~ of the Federal Reserve Act~~:~~* Federal Reserve Consumer Help Center, P.O. Box 1200, Minneapolis, MN 55480.

   c. *Nonmember Insured Banks~~-and~~, Insured State Branches of Foreign Banks, and Insured State Savings Associations*: FDIC Consumer Response Center, 1100 Walnut Street, Box #11, Kansas City, MO 64106.

   ~~Savings institutions under the Savings Association Insurance Fund of the FDIC and federally chartered savings banks insured under the Bank Insurance Fund of the FDIC (but not including state-chartered savings banks insured under the Bank Insurance Fund): Office of Thrift Supervision, Consumer Response Unit, 1700 G Street, NW., Washington, DC 20552.~~

   d. *Federal Credit Unions:* ~~Regional office of the National Credit Union Administration serving the area in which the federal credit union is located.,~~ Office of Consumer Protection (OCP), Division of Consumer Compliance and Outreach (DCCO), 1775 Duke Street, Alexandria, VA 22314.

3. *Air carriers:* Assistant General Counsel for Aviation Enforcement and Proceedings, Department of Transportation, 400 Seventh Street~~,~~ SW., Washington, DC 20590.

4. *Creditors Subject to Surface Transportation Board:* Office of Proceedings, Surface Transportation Board, Department of Transportation, 1925 K Street NW., Washington, DC ~~20423~~20423.

5. *Creditors Subject to Packers and Stockyards Act:* Nearest Packers and Stockyards Administration area supervisor.

6. *Small Business Investment Companies:* Associ-

ate Deputy Administrator for Capital Access, United States Small Business Administration, 409 Third Street~~,~~ SW., 8th Floor, Washington, DC 20416.

7. *Brokers and Dealers:* Securities and Exchange Commission, Washington, DC 20549.

8. *Federal Land Banks, Federal Land Bank Associations, Federal Intermediate Credit Banks, and Production Credit Associations:* Farm Credit Administration, 1501 Farm Credit Drive, McLean, VA 22102-~~5090.~~5090.

9. *Retailers, Finance Companies, and All Other Creditors Not Listed Above:* FTC Regional Office for region in which the creditor operates or Federal Trade Commission, Equal Credit Opportunity, Washington, DC 20580.

Appendix B to Part ~~202~~1002— Model Application Forms

1. This ~~appendix~~Appendix contains five model credit application forms, each designated for use in a particular type of consumer credit transaction as indicated by the bracketed caption on each form. The first sample form is intended for use in open-end, unsecured transactions; the second for closed-end, secured transactions; the third for closed-end transactions, whether unsecured or secured; the fourth in transactions involving community property or occurring in community property states; and the fifth in residential mortgage transactions which contains a model disclosure for use in complying with § ~~202.13~~1002.13 for certain dwelling-related loans. All forms contained in this ~~appendix~~Appendix are models; their use by creditors is optional.

2. The use or modification of these forms is governed by the following instructions. A creditor may change the forms: by asking for additional information not prohibited by § ~~202.5~~1002.5; by deleting any information request; or by rearranging the format without modifying the substance of the inquiries. In any of these three instances, however, the appropriate notices regarding the optional nature of courtesy titles, the option to disclose alimony, child support, or separate maintenance, and the limitation concerning marital status inquiries must be included in the appropriate places if the items to which they relate appear on the creditor's form.

3. If a creditor uses an appropriate Appendix B model form, or modifies a form in accordance with the above instructions, that creditor shall be deemed to be acting in compliance with the provisions of paragraphs (b), (c) and (d) of § ~~202.5~~1002.5 of this ~~regulation~~part.

[Open-end, unsecured credit]

CREDIT APPLICATION
IMPORTANT: Read these Directions before completing this Application.

Check Appropriate Box

☐ If you are applying for an individual account in your own name and are relying on your own income or assets and not the income or assets of another person as the basis for repayment of the credit requested, complete only Sections A and D.

☐ If you are applying for a joint account or an account that you and another person will use, complete all Sections, providing information in B about the joint applicant or user.

We intend to apply for joint credit. _____ _____
                                    Applicant   Co-Applicant

☐ If you are applying for an individual account, but are relying on income from alimony, child support, or separate maintenance or on the income or assets of another person as the basis for repayment of the credit requested, complete all Sections to the extent possible, providing information in B about the person on whose alimony, support, or maintenance payments or income or assets you are relying.

SECTION A—INFORMATION REGARDING APPLICANT

Full Name (Last, First, Middle): _____ Birthdate: / /

Present Street Address: _____ Years there: _____

City: _____ State: _____ Zip: _____ Telephone: _____

Social Security No.: _____ Driver's License No.: _____

Previous Street Address: _____ Years there: _____

City: _____ State: _____ Zip: _____

Present Employer: _____ Years there: _____ Telephone: _____

Position or title: _____ Name of supervisor: _____

Employer's Address: _____

Previous Employer: _____ Years there: _____

Previous Employer's Address: _____

Present net salary or commission: $ _____ per _____ No. Dependents: _____ Ages: _____

Alimony, child support, or separate maintenance income need not be revealed if you do not wish to have it considered as a basis for repaying this obligation.

Alimony, child support, separate maintenance received under: court order ☐ written agreement ☐ oral understanding ☐

Other income: $ _____ per _____ Source(s) of other income: _____

Is any income listed in this Section likely to be reduced in the next two years?
☐ Yes (Explain in detail on a separate sheet.)   No ☐

Have you ever received credit from us? _____ When? _____ Office: _____

Checking Account No.: _____ Institution and Branch: _____

Savings Account No.: _____ Institution and Branch: _____

Name of nearest relative
not living with you: _____ Telephone: _____

Relationship: _____ Address: _____

SECTION B—INFORMATION REGARDING JOINT APPLICANT, USER, OR OTHER PARTY (Use separate sheets if necessary.)

Full Name (Last, First, Middle): _____ Birthdate: / /

Relationship to Applicant (if any): _____

Present Street Address: _____ Years there: _____

City: _____ State: _____ Zip: _____ Telephone: _____

Social Security No.: _____ Driver's License No.: _____

Present Employer: _____ Years there: _____ Telephone: _____

Position or title: _____ Name of supervisor: _____

Employer's Address: _____

Previous Employer: _____ Years there: _____

Previous Employer's Address: _____

Present net salary or commission: $ _____ per _____ No. Dependents: _____ Ages: _____

Alimony, child support, or separate maintenance income need not be revealed if you do not wish to have it considered as a basis for repaying this obligation.

Alimony, child support, separate maintenance received under: court order ☐ written agreement ☐ oral understanding ☐

Other income: $ _____ per _____ Source(s) of other income: _____

Is any income listed in this Section likely to be reduced in the next two years?
☐ Yes (Explain in detail on a separate sheet.)   No ☐

Checking Account No.: _____ Institution and Branch: _____

Savings Account No.: _____ Institution and Branch: _____

Name of nearest relative not living
with Joint Applicant, User, or Other Party: _____ Telephone: _____

Relationship: _____ Address: _____

SECTION C—MARITAL STATUS
(Do not complete if this is an application for an individual account.)

Applicant: ☐ Married   ☐ Separated   ☐ Unmarried (including single, divorced, and widowed)
Other Party: ☐ Married   ☐ Separated   ☐ Unmarried (including single, divorced, and widowed)

[Open-end, unsecured credit]

SECTION D— ASSET AND DEBT INFORMATION (If Section B has been completed, this Section should be completed giving information about both the Applicant and Joint Applicant, User, or Other Person. Please mark Applicant-related information with an "A." If Section B was not completed, only give information about the Applicant in this Section.)

ASSETS OWNED (use separate sheet if necessary.)

Description of Assets	Value	Subject to Debt? Yes/No	Name(s) of Owner(s)
Cash	$		
Automobiles (Make, Model, Year)			
Cash Value of Life Insurance (Issuer, Face Value)			
Real Estate (Location, Date Acquired)			
Marketable Securities (Issuer, Type, No. of Shares)			
Other (List)			
Total Assets	$		

OUTSTANDING DEBTS (Include charge accounts, installment contracts, credit cards, rent, mortgages, etc. Use separate sheet if necessary.)

Creditor	Type of Debt or Acct. No.	Name in Which Acct. Carried	Original Debt	Present Balance	Monthly Payments	Past Due? Yes/No
1. (Landlord or Mortgage Holder)	☐ Rent Payment ☐ Mortgage		$ (Omit rent)	$ (Omit rent)	$	
2.						
3.						
4.						
5.						
6.						
Total Debts			$	$	$	

(Credit References)   Date Paid

1. $

2.

Are you a co-maker, endorser, or guarantor on any loan or contract?	Yes ☐ No ☐	If "yes" for whom?		To whom?

Are there any unsatisfied judgments against you?   Yes ☐ No ☐   Amount $ If "yes" to whom owed?

Have you been declared bankrupt in the last 14 years?   Yes ☐ No ☐   If "yes" where?   Year

Other Obligations—(E.g., liability to pay alimony, child support, separate maintenance. Use separate sheet if necessary.)

Everything that I have stated in this application is correct to the best of my knowledge. I understand that you will retain this application whether or not it is approved. You are authorized to check my credit and employment history and to answer questions about your credit experience with me.

Applicant's Signature   Date   Other Signature   Date
                                                (Where Applicable)

[Closed-end, secured credit]

CREDIT APPLICATION
IMPORTANT: Read these Directions before completing this Application.

Check Appropriate Box

☐ If you are applying for individual credit in your own name and are relying on your own income or assets and not the income or assets of another person as the basis for repayment of the credit requested, complete Sections A, C, D, and E, omitting B and the second part of C.

☐ If this is an application for joint credit with another person, complete all Sections, providing information in B about the joint applicant.

We intend to apply for joint credit. _____ _____
Applicant   Co-Applicant

☐ If you are applying for individual credit, but are relying on income from alimony, child support, or separate maintenance or on the income or assets or another person as the basis for repayment of the credit requested, complete all Sections to the extent possible, providing information in B about the person on whose alimony, support, or maintenance payments or income or assets you are relying.

Amount Requested   Payment Date Desired   Proceeds of Credit To be Used For _____
$ _____   _____

SECTION A—INFORMATION REGARDING APPLICANT

Full Name (Last, First, Middle): _____ Birthdate: / /

Present Street Address: _____ Years there: _____

City: _____ State: _____ Zip: _____ Telephone: _____

Social Security No.: _____ Driver's License No.: _____

Previous Street Address: _____ Years there: _____

City: _____ State: _____ Zip: _____

Present Employer: _____ Years there: _____ Telephone: _____

Position or title: _____ Name of supervisor: _____

Employer's Address: _____

Previous Employer: _____ Years there: _____

Previous Employer's Address: _____

Present net salary or commission: $ _____ per _____ No. Dependents: _____ Ages: _____

Alimony, child support, or separate maintenance income need not be revealed if you do not wish to have it considered as a basis for repaying this obligation.

Alimony, child support, separate maintenance received under: court order ☐ written agreement ☐ oral understanding ☐

Other income: $ _____ per _____ Source(s) of other income: _____

Is any income listed in this Section likely to be reduced before the credit requested is paid off?
☐ Yes (Explain in detail on a separate sheet.) No ☐

Have you ever received credit from us? _____ When? _____ Office: _____

Checking Account No.: _____ Institution and Branch: _____

Savings Account No.: _____ Institution and Branch: _____

Name of nearest relative
not living with you: _____ Telephone: _____

Relationship: _____ Address: _____

SECTION B—INFORMATION REGARDING JOINT APPLICANT, OR OTHER PARTY (Use separate sheets if necessary.)

Full Name (Last, First, Middle): _____ Birthdate: / /

Relationship to Applicant (if any): _____

Present Street Address: _____ Years there: _____

City: _____ State: _____ Zip: _____ Telephone: _____

Social Security No.: _____ Driver's License No.: _____

Present Employer: _____ Years there: _____ Telephone: _____

Position or title: _____ Name of supervisor: _____

Employer's Address: _____

Previous Employer: _____ Years there: _____

Previous Employer's Address: _____

Present net salary or commission: $ _____ per _____ No. Dependents: _____ Ages: _____

Alimony, child support, or separate maintenance income need not be revealed if you do not wish to have it considered as a basis for repaying this obligation.

Alimony, child support, separate maintenance received under: court order ☐ written agreement ☐ oral understanding ☐

Other income: $ _____ per _____ Source(s) of other income: _____

Is any income listed in this Section likely to be reduced before the credit requested is paid off?
☐ Yes (Explain in detail on a separate sheet.) No ☐

Checking Account No.: _____ Institution and Branch: _____

Savings Account No.: _____ Institution and Branch: _____

Name of nearest relative not living with
Joint Applicant or Other Party: _____

Relationship: _____ Address: _____

SECTION C—MARITAL STATUS
(Do not complete if this is an application for an individual account.)

Applicant: ☐ Married   ☐ Separated   ☐ Unmarried (including single, divorced, and widowed)
Other Party: ☐ Married   ☐ Separated   ☐ Unmarried (including single, divorced, and widowed)

[Closed-end, secured credit]

SECTION D— ASSET AND DEBT INFORMATION (If Section B has been completed, this Section should be completed giving information about both the Applicant and Joint Applicant or Other Person. Please mark Applicant-related information with an "A." If Section B was not completed, only give information about the Applicant in this Section.)

ASSETS OWNED (use separate sheet if necessary.)

Description of Assets	Value	Subject to Debt? Yes/No	Name(s) of Owner(s)
Cash	$		
Automobiles (Make, Model, Year)			
Cash Value of Life Insurance (Issuer, Face Value)			
Real Estate (Location, Date Acquired)			
Marketable Securities (Issuer, Type, No. of Shares)			
Other (List)			
Total Assets	$		

OUTSTANDING DEBTS (Include charge accounts, installment contracts, credit cards, rent, mortgages, etc. Use separate sheet if necessary.)

Creditor	Type of Debt or Acct. No.	Name in Which Acct. Carried	Original Debt	Present Balance	Monthly Payments	Past Due? Yes/No
1. (Landlord or Mortgage Holder)	☐ Rent Payment ☐ Mortgage		$ (Omit rent)	$ (Omit rent)	$	
2.						
3.						
Total Debts			$	$	$	

(Credit References) — Date Paid

1. $

2.

| Are you a co-maker, endorser, or guarantor on any loan or contract? | Yes ☐ No ☐ | If "yes" for whom? | | To whom? |

| Are there any unsatisfied judgments against you? | Yes ☐ No ☐ | Amount $ | If "yes" to whom owed? |

| Have you been declared bankrupt in the last 14 years? | Yes ☐ No ☐ | If "yes" where? | Year |

Other Obligations—(E.g., liability to pay alimony, child support, separate maintenance. Use separate sheet if necessary.)

SECTION E—SECURED CREDIT (Briefly describe the property to be given as security.)

and list names and addresses of all co-owners of the property:

Name   Address

If the security is real estate, give the full name of your spouse (if any): _____

Everything that I have stated in this application is correct to the best of my knowledge. I understand that you will retain this application whether or not it is approved. You are authorized to check my credit and employment history and to answer questions about your credit experience with me.

_____ _____ _____ _____
Applicant's Signature   Date   Other Signature   Date
                                     (Where Applicable)

[Closed-end, unsecured/secured credit]

CREDIT APPLICATION
IMPORTANT: Read these Directions before completing this Application.

Check
Appropriate
Box

☐ If you are applying for individual credit in your own name and are relying on your own income or assets and not the income or assets of another person as the basis for repayment of the credit requested, complete only Sections A and D. If the requested credit is to be secured, also complete the first part of Section C and Section E.

☐ If you are applying for joint credit with another person, complete all Sections except E, providing information in B about the joint applicant. If the requested credit is to be secured, then complete Section E.

We intend to apply for joint credit. _____ _____
                                                Applicant   Co-Applicant

☐ If you are applying for individual credit, but are relying on income from alimony, child support, or separate maintenance or on the income or assets of another person as the basis for repayment of the credit requested, complete all Sections except E to the extent possible, providing information in B about the person on whose alimony, support, or maintenance payments or income or assets you are relying. If the requested credit is to be secured, then complete Section E.

Amount Requested   Payment Date Desired   Proceeds of Credit
$ _____   _____   To be Used For _____

SECTION A—INFORMATION REGARDING APPLICANT

Full Name (Last, First, Middle): _____ Birthdate: / /

Present Street Address: _____ _____ Years there: _____

City: _____ State: _____ Zip: _____ Telephone: _____

Social Security No.: _____ Driver's License No.: _____

Previous Street Address: _____ Years there: _____

City: _____ State: _____ Zip: _____

Present Employer: _____ Years there: _____ Telephone: _____

Position or title: _____ Name of supervisor: _____

Employer's Address: _____

Previous Employer: _____ Years there: _____

Previous Employer's Address: _____

Present net salary or commission: $ _____ per _____ No. Dependents: _____ Ages: _____

Alimony, child support, or separate maintenance income need not be revealed if you do not wish to have it considered as a basis for repaying this obligation.

Alimony, child support, separate maintenance received under: court order ☐ written agreement ☐ oral understanding ☐

Other income: $ _____ per _____ Source(s) of other income: _____

Is any income listed in this Section likely to be reduced before the credit requested is paid off?
☐ Yes (Explain in detail on a separate sheet.)   No ☐

Have you ever received credit from us? _____ When? _____ Office _____

Checking Account No.: _____ Institution and Branch: _____

Savings Account No.: _____ Institution and Branch: _____

Name of nearest relative
not living with you: _____ Telephone: _____

Relationship: _____ Address: _____

SECTION B—INFORMATION REGARDING JOINT APPLICANT, OR OTHER PARTY (Use separate sheets if necessary.)

Full Name (Last, First, Middle): _____ Birthdate: / /

Relationship to Applicant (if any): _____

Present Street Address: _____ Years there: _____

City: _____ State: _____ Zip: _____ Telephone: _____

Social Security No.: _____ Driver's License No.: _____

Present Employer: _____ Years there: _____ Telephone: _____

Position or title: _____ Name of supervisor: _____

Employer's Address: _____

Previous Employer: _____ Years there: _____

Previous Employer's Address: _____

Present net salary or commission: $ _____ per _____ No. Dependents: _____ Ages: _____

Alimony, child support, or separate maintenance income need not be revealed if you do not wish to have it considered as a basis for repaying this obligation.

Alimony, child support, separate maintenance received under: court order ☐ written agreement ☐ oral understanding ☐

Other income: $ _____ per _____ Source(s) of other income: _____

Is any income listed in this Section likely to be reduced before the credit requested is paid off?
☐ Yes (Explain in detail on a separate sheet.)   No ☐

Checking Account No.: _____ Institution and Branch: _____

Savings Account No.: _____ Institution and Branch: _____

Name of nearest relative not living with
Joint Applicant or Other Party: _____ Telephone: _____

Relationship: _____ Address: _____

[Closed-end, unsecured/secured credit]

SECTION C—MARITAL STATUS
(Do not complete if this is an application for individual unsecured credit.)

Applicant: ☐ Married ☐ Separated ☐ Unmarried (including single, divorced, and widowed)
Other Party: ☐ Married ☐ Separated ☐ Unmarried (including single, divorced, and widowed)

SECTION D— ASSET AND DEBT INFORMATION (If Section B has been completed, this Section should be completed giving information about both the Applicant and Joint Applicant or Other Person. Please mark Applicant-related information with an "A." If Section B was not completed, only give information about the Applicant in this Section.)

ASSETS OWNED (use separate sheet if necessary.)

Description of Assets	Value	Subject to Debt? Yes/No	Name(s) of Owner(s)
Cash	$		
Automobiles (Make, Model, Year)			
Cash Value of Life Insurance (Issuer, Face Value)			
Real Estate (Location, Date Acquired)			
Marketable Securities (Issuer, Type, No. of Shares)			
Other (List)			
Total Assets	$		

OUTSTANDING DEBTS (Include charge accounts, installment contracts, credit cards, rent, mortgages, etc. Use separate sheet if necessary.)

Creditor	Type of Debt or Acct. No.	Name in Which Acct. Carried	Original Debt	Present Balance	Monthly Payments	Past Due? Yes/No
1. (Landlord or Mortgage Holder)	☐ Rent Payment ☐ Mortgage		$ (Omit rent)	$ (Omit rent)	$	
2.						
3.						
Total Debts			$	$	$	

(Credit References) Date Paid

1. $

2.

Are you a co-maker, endorser, or guarantor on any loan or contract?	Yes ☐ No ☐	If "yes" for whom?	To whom?

Are there any unsatisfied judgments against you? Yes ☐ No ☐ Amount $ If "yes" to whom owed?

Have you been declared bankrupt in the last 14 years? Yes ☐ No ☐ If "yes" where? Year

Other Obligations—(E.g., liability to pay alimony, child support, separate maintenance. Use separate sheet if necessary.)

SECTION E—SECURED CREDIT (Complete only if credit is to be secured.) Briefly describe the property to be given as security.

and list names and addresses of all co-owners of the property:

Name   Address

If the security is real estate, give the full name of your spouse (if any): _____

Everything that I have stated in this application is correct to the best of my knowledge. I understand that you will retain this application whether or not it is approved. You are authorized to check my credit and employment history and to answer questions about your credit experience with me.

Applicant's Signature   Date   Other Signature   Date
                                             (Where Applicable)

[Community property]

CREDIT APPLICATION
IMPORTANT: Read these Directions before completing this Application.

Check
Appropriate
Box

☐ If you are applying for individual credit in your own name, are not married, and are not relying on alimony, child support, or separate maintenance payments or on the income or assets of another person as the basis for repayment of the credit requested, complete only Sections A and D. If the requested credit is to be secured, also complete Section E.

☐ In all other situations, complete all Sections except E, providing information in B about your spouse, a joint applicant or user, or the person on whose alimony, support, or maintenance payments or income or assets you are relying. If the requested credit is to be secured, also complete Section E.

If you intend to apply for joint credit, please initial here. _____ _____
Applicant   Co-Applicant

| Amount Requested | Payment Date Desired | Proceeds of Credit |
| $ _____ | _____ | To be Used For _____ |

SECTION A—INFORMATION REGARDING APPLICANT

Full Name (Last, First, Middle): _____ Birthdate: / /

Present Street Address: _____ Years there: _____

City: _____ State: _____ Zip: _____ Telephone: _____

Social Security No.: _____ Driver's License No.: _____

Previous Street Address: _____ Years there: _____

City: _____ State: _____ Zip: _____

Present Employer: _____ Years there: _____ Telephone: _____

Position or title: _____ Name of supervisor: _____

Employer's Address: _____

Previous Employer: _____ Years there: _____

Previous Employer's Address: _____

Present net salary or commission: $ _____ per _____ No. Dependents: _____ Ages: _____

Alimony, child support, or separate maintenance income need not be revealed if you do not wish to have it considered as a basis for repaying this obligation.

Alimony, child support, separate maintenance received under: court order ☐ written agreement ☐ oral understanding ☐

Other income: $ _____ per _____ Source(s) of other income: _____

Is any income listed in this Section likely to be reduced in the next two years or before the credit requested is paid off?
☐ Yes (Explain in detail on a separate sheet.) No ☐

Have you ever received credit from us? _____ When? _____ Office: _____

Checking Account No.: _____ Institution and Branch: _____

Savings Account No.: _____ Institution and Branch: _____

Name of nearest relative
not living with you: _____ Telephone: _____

Relationship: _____ Address: _____

SECTION B—INFORMATION REGARDING SPOUSE, JOINT APPLICANT, USER, OR OTHER PARTY (Use separate sheets if necessary.)

Full Name (Last, First, Middle): _____ Birthdate: / /

Relationship to Applicant (if any): _____

Present Street Address: _____ Years there: _____

City: _____ State: _____ Zip: _____ Telephone: _____

Social Security No.: _____ Driver's License No.: _____

Present Employer: _____ Years there: _____ Telephone: _____

Position or title: _____ Name of supervisor: _____

Employer's Address: _____

Previous Employer: _____ Years there: _____

Previous Employer's Address: _____

Present net salary or commission: $ _____ per _____ No. Dependents: _____ Ages: _____

Alimony, child support, or separate maintenance income need not be revealed if you do not wish to have it considered as a basis for repaying this obligation.

Alimony, child support, separate maintenance received under: court order ☐ written agreement ☐ oral understanding ☐

Other income: $ _____ per _____ Source(s) of other income: _____

Is any income listed in this Section likely to be reduced in the next two years or before the credit requested is paid off?
☐ Yes (Explain in detail on a separate sheet.) No ☐

Checking Account No.: _____ Institution and Branch: _____

Savings Account No.: _____ Institution and Branch: _____

Name of nearest relative not living with
Spouse, Joint Applicant, User, or Other Party: _____ Telephone: _____

Relationship: _____ Address: _____

[Community property]

SECTION C—MARITAL STATUS

Applicant: ☐ Married   ☐ Separated   ☐ Unmarried (including single, divorced, and widowed)
Other Party: ☐ Married   ☐ Separated   ☐ Unmarried (including single, divorced, and widowed)

SECTION D— ASSET AND DEBT INFORMATION (If Section B has been completed, this Section should be completed giving information about both the Applicant and Spouse, Joint Applicant, User, or Other Person. Please mark Applicant-related information with an "A." If Section B was not completed, only give information about the Applicant in this Section.)

ASSETS OWNED (use separate sheet if necessary.)

Description of Assets	Value	Subject to Debt? Yes/No	Name(s) of Owner(s)
Cash	$		
Automobiles (Make, Model, Year)			
Cash Value of Life Insurance (Issuer, Face Value)			
Real Estate (Location, Date Acquired)			
Marketable Securities (Issuer, Type, No. of Shares)			
Other (List)			
Total Assets	$		

OUTSTANDING DEBTS (Include charge accounts, installment contracts, credit cards, rent, mortgages, etc. Use separate sheet if necessary.)

Creditor	Type of Debt or Acct. No.	Name in Which Acct. Carried	Original Debt	Present Balance	Monthly Payments	Past Due? Yes/No
1. (Landlord or Mortgage Holder)	☐ Rent Payment ☐ Mortgage		$ (Omit rent)	$ (Omit rent)	$	
2.						
3.						
Total Debts			$	$	$	

(Credit References)		Date Paid
1.	$	
2.		

Are you a co-maker, endorser, or guarantor on any loan or contract?	Yes ☐ No ☐	If "yes" for whom?	To whom?
Are there any unsatisfied judgments against you?	Yes ☐ No ☐	Amount $	If "yes" to whom owed?
Have you been declared bankrupt in the last 14 years?	Yes ☐ No ☐	If "yes" where?	Year

Other Obligations—(E.g., liability to pay alimony, child support, separate maintenance. Use separate sheet if necessary.)

SECTION E—SECURED CREDIT (Complete only if credit is to be secured.) **Briefly describe the property to be given as security.**

and list names and addresses of all co-owners of the property:

Name	Address

Everything that I have stated in this application is correct to the best of my knowledge. I understand that you will retain this application whether or not it is approved. You are authorized to check my credit and employment history and to answer questions about your credit experience with me.

Applicant's Signature	Date	Other Signature (Where Applicable)	Date

Uniform Residential Loan Application

This application is designed to be completed by the applicant(s) with the Lender's assistance. Applicants should complete this form as "Borrower" or "Co-Borrower," as applicable. Co-Borrower information must also be provided (and the appropriate box checked) when ❑ the income or assets of a person other than the "Borrower" (including the Borrower's spouse) will be used as a basis for loan qualification or ❑ the income or assets of the Borrower's spouse will not be used as a basis for loan qualification, but his or her liabilities must be considered because the Borrower resides in a community property state, the security property is located in a community property state, or the Borrower is relying on other property located in a community property state as a basis for repayment of the loan.

I. TYPE OF MORTGAGE AND TERMS OF LOAN

Mortgage Applied for:	❑ VA ❑ FHA	❑ Conventional ❑ USDA/Rural Housing Service	❑ Other (explain):	Agency Case Number	Lender Case Number

Amount $	Interest Rate %	No. of Months	Amortization Type:	❑ Fixed Rate ❑ GPM	❑ Other (explain): ❑ ARM (type):

II. PROPERTY INFORMATION AND PURPOSE OF LOAN

Subject Property Address (street, city, state, & ZIP)	No. of Units

Legal Description of Subject Property (attach description if necessary)	Year Built

Purpose of Loan ❑ Purchase ❑ Construction ❑ Other (explain): ❑ Refinance ❑ Construction-Permanent	Property will be: ❑ Primary Residence ❑ Secondary Residence ❑ Investment

Complete this line if construction or construction-permanent loan.

Year Lot Acquired	Original Cost $	Amount Existing Liens $	(a) Present Value of Lot $	(b) Cost of Improvements $	Total (a + b) $

Complete this line if this is a refinance loan.

Year Acquired	Original Cost $	Amount Existing Liens $	Purpose of Refinance	Describe Improvements ❑ made ❑ to be made
				Cost: $

Title will be held in what Name(s)	Manner in which Title will be held	Estate will be held in: ❑ Fee Simple ❑ Leasehold (show expiration date)
Source of Down Payment, Settlement Charges and/or Subordinate Financing (explain)		

III. BORROWER INFORMATION

Borrower	Co-Borrower
Borrower's Name (include Jr. or Sr. if applicable)	Co-Borrower's Name (include Jr. or Sr. if applicable)

Social Security Number	Home Phone (incl. area code)	DOB (MM/DD/YYYY)	Yrs. School	Social Security Number	Home Phone (incl. area code)	DOB (MM/DD/YYYY)	Yrs. School

❑ Married ❑ Unmarried (include single, ❑ Separated divorced, widowed)	Dependents (not listed by Co-Borrower) no. ages	❑ Married ❑ Unmarried (include single, ❑ Separated divorced, widowed)	Dependents (not listed by Borrower) no. ages

Present Address (street, city, state, ZIP) ❑ Own ❑ Rent _____ No. Yrs.	Present Address (street, city, state, ZIP) ❑ Own ❑ Rent _____ No. Yrs.

Mailing Address, if different from Present Address	Mailing Address, if different from Present Address

If residing at present address for less than two years, complete the following:

Former Address (street, city, state, ZIP) ❑ Own ❑ Rent _____ No. Yrs.	Former Address (street, city, state, ZIP) ❑ Own ❑ Rent _____ No. Yrs.

IV. EMPLOYMENT INFORMATION

Borrower	Co-Borrower

Name & Address of Employer	❑ Self Employed	Yrs. on this job	Name & Address of Employer	❑ Self Employed	Yrs. on this job
		Yrs. employed in this line of work/profession			Yrs. employed in this line of work/profession
Position/Title/Type of Business		Business Phone (incl. area code)	Position/Title/Type of Business		Business Phone (incl. area code)

If employed in current position for less than two years or if currently employed in more than one position, complete the following:

Name & Address of Employer	❑ Self Employed	Dates (from – to)	Name & Address of Employer	❑ Self Employed	Dates (from – to)
		Monthly Income $			Monthly Income $
Position/Title/Type of Business		Business Phone (incl. area code)	Position/Title/Type of Business		Business Phone (incl. area code)

Name & Address of Employer	❑ Self Employed	Dates (from – to)	Name & Address of Employer	❑ Self Employed	Dates (from – to)
		Monthly Income $			Monthly Income $
Position/Title/Type of Business		Business Phone (incl. area code)	Position/Title/Type of Business		Business Phone (incl. area code)

V. MONTHLY INCOME AND COMBINED HOUSING EXPENSE INFORMATION

Gross Monthly Income	Borrower	Co-Borrower	Total	Combined Monthly Housing Expense	Present	Proposed
Base Empl. Income*	$	$	$	Rent	$	
Overtime				First Mortgage (P&I)		$
Bonuses				Other Financing (P&I)		
Commissions				Hazard Insurance		
Dividends/Interest				Real Estate Taxes		
Net Rental Income				Mortgage Insurance		
Other (before completing, see the notice in "describe other income," below)				Homeowner Assn. Dues		
				Other:		
Total	$	$	$	Total	$	$

* Self Employed Borrower(s) may be required to provide additional documentation such as tax returns and financial statements.

Describe Other Income *Notice:* Alimony, child support, or separate maintenance income need not be revealed if the Borrower (B) or Co-Borrower (C) does not choose to have it considered for repaying this loan.

B/C		Monthly Amount
		$

VI. ASSETS AND LIABILITIES

This Statement and any applicable supporting schedules may be completed jointly by both married and unmarried Co-Borrowers if their assets and liabilities are sufficiently joined so that the Statement can be meaningfully and fairly presented on a combined basis; otherwise, separate Statements and Schedules are required. If the Co-Borrower section was completed about a spouse, this Statement and supporting schedules must be completed about that spouse also.

Completed ☐ Jointly ☐ Not Jointly

ASSETS — Description	Cash or Market Value	Liabilities and Pledged Assets. List the creditor's name, address and account number for all outstanding debts, including automobile loans, revolving charge accounts, real estate loans, alimony, child support, stock pledges, etc. Use continuation sheet, if necessary. Indicate by (*) those liabilities which will be satisfied upon sale of real estate owned or upon refinancing of the subject property.	Monthly Payment & Months Left to Pay	Unpaid Balance
Cash deposit toward purchase held by:	$	**LIABILITIES**		
List checking and savings accounts below		Name and address of Company	$ Payment/Months	$
Name and address of Bank, S&L, or Credit Union				
		Acct. no.		
Acct. no.	$	Name and address of Company	$ Payment/Months	$
Name and address of Bank, S&L, or Credit Union				
		Acct. no.		
Acct. no.	$	Name and address of Company	$ Payment/Months	$
Name and address of Bank, S&L, or Credit Union				
		Acct. no.		
Acct. no.	$	Name and address of Company	$ Payment/Months	$
Name and address of Bank, S&L, or Credit Union				
		Acct. no.		
Acct. no.	$	Name and address of Company	$ Payment/Months	$
Stocks & Bonds (Company name/number & description)	$			
		Acct. no.		
		Name and address of Company	$ Payment/Months	$
Life insurance net cash value	$			
Face amount: $				
Subtotal Liquid Assets	$	Acct. no.		
Real estate owned (enter market value from schedule of real estate owned)	$	Name and address of Company	$ Payment/Months	$
Vested interest in retirement fund	$			
Net worth of business(es) owned (attach financial statement)	$			
Automobiles owned (make and year)	$	Acct. no.		
		Alimony/Child Support/Separate Maintenance Payments Owed to:	$	
Other Assets (itemize)	$	Job-Related Expense (child care, union dues, etc.)	$	
		Total Monthly Payments	$	
Total Assets a. $		Net Worth (a minus b) ► $	Total Liabilities b.	$

VI. ASSETS AND LIABILITIES (cont.)

Schedule of Real Estate Owned (If additional properties are owned, use continuation sheet.)

Property Address (enter S if sold, PS if pending sale or R if rental being held for income) ➤	Type of Property	Present Market Value	Amount of Mortgages & Liens	Gross Rental Income	Mortgage Payments	Insurance, Maintenance, Taxes & Misc.	Net Rental Income
		$	$	$	$	$	$
	Totals	$	$	$	$	$	$

List any additional names under which credit has previously been received and indicate appropriate creditor name(s) and account number(s):

Alternate Name	Creditor Name	Account Number

VII. DETAILS OF TRANSACTION

a. Purchase price	$
b. Alterations, improvements, repairs	
c. Land (if acquired separately)	
d. Refinance (incl. debts to be paid off)	
e. Estimated prepaid items	
f. Estimated closing costs	
g. PMI, MIP, Funding Fee	
h. Discount (if Borrower will pay)	
i. Total costs (add items a through h)	
j. Subordinate financing	
k. Borrower's closing costs paid by Seller	
l. Other Credits (explain)	
m. Loan amount (exclude PMI, MIP, Funding Fee financed)	
n. PMI, MIP, Funding Fee financed	
o. Loan amount (add m & n)	
p. Cash from/to Borrower (subtract j, k, l & o from i)	

VIII. DECLARATIONS

If you answer "Yes" to any questions a through i, please use continuation sheet for explanation.

	Borrower Yes	Borrower No	Co-Borrower Yes	Co-Borrower No
a. Are there any outstanding judgments against you?	☐	☐	☐	☐
b. Have you been declared bankrupt within the past 7 years?	☐	☐	☐	☐
c. Have you had property foreclosed upon or given title or deed in lieu thereof in the last 7 years?	☐	☐	☐	☐
d. Are you a party to a lawsuit?	☐	☐	☐	☐
e. Have you directly or indirectly been obligated on any loan which resulted in foreclosure, transfer of title in lieu of foreclosure, or judgment? (This would include such loans as home mortgage loans, SBA loans, home improvement loans, educational loans, manufactured (mobile) home loans, any mortgage, financial obligation, bond, or loan guarantee. If "Yes," provide details, including date, name and address of Lender, FHA or VA case number, if any, and reasons for the action.)	☐	☐	☐	☐
f. Are you presently delinquent or in default on any Federal debt or any other loan, mortgage, financial obligation, bond, or loan guarantee? If "Yes," give details as described in the preceding question.	☐	☐	☐	☐
g. Are you obligated to pay alimony, child support, or separate maintenance?	☐	☐	☐	☐
h. Is any part of the down payment borrowed?	☐	☐	☐	☐
i. Are you a co-maker or endorser on a note?	☐	☐	☐	☐
j. Are you a U.S. citizen?	☐	☐	☐	☐
k. Are you a permanent resident alien?	☐	☐	☐	☐
l. Do you intend to occupy the property as your primary residence? If "Yes," complete question m below.	☐	☐	☐	☐
m. Have you had an ownership interest in a property in the last three years?	☐	☐	☐	☐
(1) What type of property did you own—principal residence (PR), second home (SH), or investment property (IP)?				
(2) How did you hold title to the home—solely by yourself (S), jointly with your spouse (SP), or jointly with another person (O)?				

IX. ACKNOWLEDGMENT AND AGREEMENT

Each of the undersigned specifically represents to Lender and to Lender's actual or potential agents, brokers, processors, attorneys, insurers, servicers, successors and assigns and agrees and acknowledges that: (1) the information provided in this application is true and correct as of the date set forth opposite my signature and that any intentional or negligent misrepresentation of this information contained in this application may result in civil liability, including monetary damages, to any person who may suffer any loss due to reliance upon any misrepresentation that I have made on this application, and/or in criminal penalties including, but not limited to, fine or imprisonment or both under the provisions of Title 18, United States Code, Sec. 1001, et seq.; (2) the loan requested pursuant to this application (the "Loan") will be secured by a mortgage or deed of trust on the property described herein; (3) the property will not be used for any illegal or prohibited purpose or use; (4) all statements made in this application are made for the purpose of obtaining a residential mortgage loan; (5) the property will be occupied as indicated herein; (6) any owner or servicer of the Loan may verify or reverify any information contained in the application from any source named in this application, and Lender, its successors or assigns may retain the original and/or an electronic record of this application, even if the Loan is not approved; (7) the Lender and its agents, brokers, insurers, servicers, successors and assigns may continuously rely on the information contained in the application, and I am obligated to amend and/or supplement the information provided in this application if any of the material facts that I have represented herein should change prior to closing of the Loan; (8) in the event that my payments on the Loan become delinquent, the owner or servicer of the Loan may, in addition to any other rights and remedies that it may have relating to such delinquency, report my name and account information to one or more consumer credit reporting agencies; (9) ownership of the Loan and/or administration of the Loan account may be transferred with such notice as may be required by law; (10) neither Lender nor its agents, brokers, insurers, servicers, successors or assigns has made any representation or warranty, express or implied, to me regarding the property or the condition or value of the property; and (11) my transmission of this application as an "electronic record" containing my "electronic signature," as those terms are defined in applicable federal and/or state laws (excluding audio and video recordings), or my facsimile transmission of this application containing a facsimile of my signature, shall be as effective, enforceable and valid as if a paper version of this application were delivered containing my original written signature.

Borrower's Signature	Date	Co-Borrower's Signature	Date
X		X	

X. INFORMATION FOR GOVERNMENT MONITORING PURPOSES

The following information is requested by the Federal Government for certain types of loans related to a dwelling in order to monitor the lender's compliance with equal credit opportunity, fair housing and home mortgage disclosure laws. You are not required to furnish this information, but are encouraged to do so. The law provides that a lender may discriminate neither on the basis of this information, nor on whether you choose to furnish it. If you furnish the information, please provide both ethnicity and race. For race, you may check more than one designation. If you do not furnish ethnicity, race, or sex, under Federal regulations, this lender is required to note the information on the basis of visual observation or surname. If you do not wish to furnish the information, please check the box below. (Lender must review the above material to assure that the disclosures satisfy all requirements to which the lender is subject under applicable state law for the particular type of loan applied for.)

BORROWER ☐ I do not wish to furnish this information.	**CO-BORROWER** ☐ I do not wish to furnish this information.
Ethnicity: ☐ Hispanic or Latino ☐ Not Hispanic or Latino	**Ethnicity:** ☐ Hispanic or Latino ☐ Not Hispanic or Latino
Race: ☐ American Indian or Alaska Native ☐ Asian ☐ Black or African American ☐ Native Hawaiian or Other Pacific Islander ☐ White	**Race:** ☐ American Indian or Alaska Native ☐ Asian ☐ Black or African American ☐ Native Hawaiian or Other Pacific Islander ☐ White
Sex: ☐ Female ☐ Male	**Sex:** ☐ Female ☐ Male

To be Completed by Interviewer This application was taken by: ☐ Face-to-face interview ☐ Mail ☐ Telephone ☐ Internet	Interviewer's Name (print or type)	Name and Address of Interviewer's Employer
	Interviewer's Signature _____ Date	
	Interviewer's Phone Number (incl. area code)	

Continuation Sheet/Residential Loan Application

Use this continuation sheet if you need more space to complete the Residential Loan Application. Mark B for Borrower or C for Co-Borrower.	Borrower:	Agency Case Number:
	Co-Borrower:	Lender Case Number:

I/We fully understand that it is a Federal crime punishable by fine or imprisonment, or both, to knowingly make any false statements concerning any of the above facts as applicable under the provisions of Title 18, United States Code, Section 1001, et seq.

Borrower's Signature	Date	Co-Borrower's Signature	Date
X		X	

Freddie Mac Form 65   01/04   Page 4 of 4   Fannie Mae Form 1003   01/04

Appendix C to Part 2021002— Sample Notification Forms

1. This ~~appendix~~Appendix contains ten sample notification forms. Forms C-1 through C-4 are intended for use in notifying an applicant that adverse action has been taken on an application or account under §§ ~~202.9~~1002.9(a)(1) and (2)(i) of this ~~regulation~~~~part~~part. Form C-5 is a notice of disclosure of the right to request specific reasons for adverse action under §§ ~~202.9~~1002.9(a)(1) and (2)(ii). Form C-6 is designed for use in notifying an applicant, under § ~~202.9~~1002.9(c)(2), that an application is incomplete. Forms C-7 and C-8 are intended for use in connection with applications for business credit under § ~~202.9~~1002.9(a)(3). Form C-9 is designed for use in notifying an applicant of the right to receive a copy of ~~an appraisal~~appraisals under § ~~202.14.~~1002.14. Form C-10 is designed for use in notifying an applicant for nonmortgage credit that the creditor is requesting applicant characteristic information.

2. Form C-1 contains the Fair Credit Reporting Act disclosure as required by sections 615(a) and (b) of that act. Forms C-2 through C-5 contain only the section 615(a) disclosure (that a creditor obtained information from a consumer reporting agency that was considered in the credit decision ~~and, as applicable, a credit score used in taking adverse action along with related information~~). A creditor must provide the section 615(a) disclosure when adverse action is taken against a consumer based on information from a consumer reporting agency. A creditor must provide the section 615(b) disclosure when adverse action is taken based on information from an outside source other than a consumer reporting agency. In addition, a creditor must provide the section 615(b) disclosure if the creditor obtained information from an affiliate other than information in a consumer report or other than information concerning the affiliate's own transactions or experiences with the consumer. Creditors may comply with the disclosure requirements for adverse action based on information in a consumer report obtained from an affiliate by providing either the section 615(a) or section 615(b) disclosure. Optional language in Forms C-1 through C-5 may be used to direct the consumer to the entity that provided the credit score for any questions about the credit score, along with the entity's contact information. Creditors may use or not use this additional language without losing the safe harbor, since the language is optional.

3. The sample forms are illustrative and may not be appropriate for all creditors. They were designed to include some of the factors that creditors most commonly consider. If a creditor chooses to use the checklist of reasons provided in one of the sample forms in this ~~appendix~~Appendix and if reasons commonly used by the creditor are not provided on the form, the creditor should modify the checklist by substituting or adding other reasons. For example, if "inadequate down payment" or "no deposit relationship with us" are common reasons for taking adverse action on an application, the creditor ought to add or substitute such reasons for those presently contained on the sample forms.

4. If the reasons listed on the forms are not the factors actually used, a creditor will not satisfy the notice requirement by simply checking the closest identifiable factor listed. For example, some creditors consider only references from banks or other depository institutions and disregard finance company references altogether; their statement of reasons should disclose "insufficient bank references," not "insufficient credit references." Similarly, a creditor that considers bank references and other credit references as distinct factors should treat the two factors separately and disclose them as appropriate. The creditor should either add such other factors to the form or check "other" and include the appropriate explanation. The creditor need not, however, describe how or why a factor adversely affected the application. For example, the notice may say "length of residence" rather than "too short a period of residence."

5. A creditor may design its own notification forms or use all or a portion of the forms contained in this ~~appendix~~Appendix. Proper use of Forms C-1 through C-4 will satisfy the requirement of § ~~202.9~~1002.9(a)(2)(i). Proper use of Forms C-5 and C-6 constitutes full compliance with §§ ~~202.9~~1002.9(a)(2)(ii) and ~~202.9~~1002.9(c)(2), respectively. Proper use of Forms C-7 and C-8 will satisfy the requirements of § ~~202.9~~§§1002.9(a)(2)(i) and (ii), respectively, for applications for business credit. Proper use of Form C-9 will satisfy the requirements of § ~~202.14~~1002.14 of this part. Proper use of Form C-10 will satisfy the requirements of § ~~202.5~~1002.5(b)(1).

Form C-1—Sample Notice of Action Taken and Statement of Reasons Statement of Credit Denial, Termination or Change

Date: _____

Applicant's Name: _____

Applicant's Address: _____

Description of Account, Transaction, or Requested Credit:

_____

Description of Action Taken:

_____

Part I—Principal Reason(s) for Credit Denial, Termination, or Other Action Taken Concerning Credit

This section must be completed in all instances.

_____ Credit application incomplete

_____ Insufficient number of credit references provided

_____ Unacceptable type of credit references provided

_____ Unable to verify credit references

_____ Temporary or irregular employment

_____ Unable to verify employment

_____ Length of employment

_____ Income insufficient for amount of credit requested

_____ Excessive obligations in relation to income

_____ Unable to verify income

_____ Length of residence

_____ Temporary residence

_____ Unable to verify residence

_____ No credit file

_____ Limited credit experience

_____ Poor credit performance with us

_____ Delinquent past or present credit obligations with others

_____ Collection action or judgment

_____ Garnishment or attachment

_____ Foreclosure or repossession

_____ Bankruptcy

_____ Number of recent inquiries on credit bureau report

_____ Value or type of collateral not sufficient

_____ Other, specify: _____

Part II—Disclosure of Use of Information Obtained From an Outside Source

This section should be completed if the credit decision was based in whole or in part on information that has been obtained from an outside source.

_____ Our credit decision was based in whole or in part on information obtained in a report from the consumer reporting agency listed below. You have a right under the Fair Credit Reporting Act to know the information contained in your credit file at the consumer reporting agency. The reporting agency played no part in our decision and is unable to supply specific reasons why we have denied credit to you. You also have a right to a free copy of your report from the reporting agency, if you request it no later than 60 days after you receive this notice. In addition, if you find that any information contained in the report you receive is inaccurate or incomplete, you have the right to dispute the matter with the reporting agency.

Name: _____

Address: _____

[Toll-free] Telephone number: _____

[We also obtained your credit score from ~~this~~the consumer reporting agency and used it in making our credit decision. Your credit score is a number that reflects the information in your consumer report. Your credit score can change, depending on how the information in your consumer report changes.

Your credit score: _____

Date: _____

Scores range from a low of _____ to a high of _____.

Key factors that adversely affected your credit score:

_____

_____

_____

_____

[Number of recent inquiries on consumer report, as a key factor]

[If you have any questions regarding your credit score, you should contact [entity that provided the credit score] at:

Address: _____

[[Toll-free] Telephone number:_____]]

_____ Our credit decision was based in whole or in part on information obtained from an affiliate or from an outside source other than a consumer reporting agency. Under the Fair Credit Reporting Act, you have the right to make a written request, no later than 60 days after you receive this notice, for disclosure of the nature of this information.

If you have any questions regarding this notice, you should contact:

Creditor's name:_____

Creditor's address:_____

Creditor's telephone number:_____

Notice: The ~~federal~~Federal Equal Credit Opportunity Act prohibits creditors from discriminating against credit applicants on the basis of race, color, religion, national origin, sex, marital status, age (provided the applicant has the capacity to enter into a binding contract); because all or part of the applicant's income derives from any public assistance program; or because the applicant has in good faith exercised any right under the Consumer Credit Protection Act. The ~~federal~~Federal agency that administers compliance with this law concerning this creditor is (name and address as specified by the appropriate agency listed in ~~appendix~~Appendix A).

Form C-2—Sample Notice of Action Taken and Statement of Reasons

Date

Dear Applicant: Thank you for your recent application. Your request for [a loan/a credit card/an increase in your credit limit] was carefully considered, and we regret that we are unable to approve your application at this time, for the following reason(s):

Your Income:

_____ is below our minimum requirement.

_____ is insufficient to sustain payments on the amount of credit requested.

_____ could not be verified.

Your Employment:

_____ is not of sufficient length to qualify.

_____ could not be verified.

Your Credit History:

_____ of making payments on time was not satisfactory.

_____ could not be verified.

Your Application:

_____ lacks a sufficient number of credit references.

_____ lacks acceptable types of credit references.

_____ reveals that current obligations are excessive in relation to income.

Other: _____

The consumer reporting agency contacted that provided information that influenced our decision in whole or in part was [name, address and [toll-free] telephone number of the reporting agency]. The reporting agency played no part in our decision and is unable to supply specific reasons why we have denied credit to you. You have a right under the Fair Credit Reporting Act to know the information contained in your credit file at the consumer reporting agency. You also have a right to a free copy of your report from the reporting agency, if

you request it no later than 60 days after you receive this notice. In addition, if you find that any information contained in the report you receive is inaccurate or incomplete, you have the right to dispute the matter with the reporting agency. Any questions regarding such information should be directed to [consumer reporting agency]. If you have any questions regarding this letter, you should contact us at [creditor's name, address and telephone number].

[We also obtained your credit score from ~~this~~the consumer reporting agency and used it in making our credit decision. Your credit score is a number that reflects the information in your consumer report. Your credit score can change, depending on how the information in your consumer report changes.

Your credit score:_____

Date: _____

Scores range from a low of _____ to a high of _____.

Key factors that adversely affected your credit score:

_____

_____

_____

_____

[Number of recent inquiries on consumer report, as a key factor]

[If you have any questions regarding your credit score, you should contact [entity that provided the credit score] at:

Address: _____

[[Toll-free] Telephone number:_____]

Notice: The ~~federal~~Federal Equal Credit Opportunity Act prohibits creditors from discriminating against credit applicants on the basis of race, color, religion, national origin, sex, marital status, age (provided the applicant has the capacity to enter into a binding contract); because all or part of the applicant's income derives from any public assistance program; or because the applicant has in good faith exercised any right under the Consumer Credit Protection Act. The ~~federal~~Federal agency that administers compliance with this law concerning this creditor is (name and address as specified by the appropriate agency listed in ~~appendix~~Appendix A).

Form C-3—Sample Notice of Action Taken and Statement of Reasons ~~[(Credit Scoring)]~~

Date

Dear Applicant: Thank you for your recent application for _____. We regret that we are unable to approve your request.

[Reasons for Denial of Credit]

Your application was processed by a [credit scoring] system that assigns a numerical value to the various items of information we consider in evaluating an application. These numerical values are based upon the results of analyses of repayment histories of large numbers of customers.

The information you provided in your application did not score a sufficient number of points for approval of the application. The reasons you did not score well compared with other applicants were:

- Insufficient bank references
- Type of occupation

- Insufficient credit experience
- Number of recent inquiries on credit bureau report

[Your Right to Get Your Consumer Report]

In evaluating your application the consumer reporting agency listed below provided us with information that in whole or in part influenced our decision. The consumer reporting agency played no part in our decision and is unable to supply specific reasons why we have denied credit to you. You have a right under the Fair Credit Reporting Act to know the information contained in your credit file at the consumer reporting agency. It can be obtained by contacting: [~~name~~Name, address, and [toll-free] telephone number of the consumer reporting agency]. You also have a right to a free copy of your report from the reporting agency, if you request it no later than 60 days after you receive this notice. In addition, if you find that any information contained in the report you receive is inaccurate or incomplete, you have the right to dispute the matter with the reporting agency.

[Information about Your Credit Score]

We also obtained your credit score from ~~this~~the consumer reporting agency and used it in making our credit decision. Your credit score is a number that reflects the information in your consumer report. Your credit score can change, depending on how the information in your consumer report changes.

Your credit score:_____

Date: _____

Scores range from a low of _____ to a high of _____.

Key factors that adversely affected your credit score:

_____

_____

_____

_____

[Number of recent inquiries on consumer report, as a key factor]

[If you have any questions regarding your credit score, you should contact [entity that provided the credit score] at:

Address: _____

[Toll-free] Telephone number:_____]

If you have any questions regarding this letter, you should contact us at

Creditor's Name:_____

Address: _____

Telephone: _____

Sincerely,

Notice: The ~~federal~~Federal Equal Credit Opportunity Act prohibits creditors from discriminating against credit applicants on the basis of race, color, religion, national origin, sex, marital status, age (with certain limited exceptions); because all or part of the applicant's income derives from any public assistance program; or because the applicant has in good faith exercised any right under the Consumer Credit Protection Act. The ~~federal~~Federal agency that administers compliance with this law concerning this creditor is (name and address as specified by the appropriate agency listed in ~~appendix~~Appendix A).

Form C-4—Sample Notice of Action Taken, Statement of Reasons and Counteroffer

Date

Dear Applicant: Thank you for your application for _____. We are unable to offer you credit on the terms that you requested for the following reason(s):_____.

We can, however, offer you credit on the following terms: _____

If this offer is acceptable to you, please notify us within [amount of time] at the following address: _____.

Our credit decision on your application was based in whole or in part on information obtained in a report from [name, address and [toll-free] telephone number of the consumer reporting agency]. You have a right under the Fair Credit Reporting Act to know the information contained in your credit file at the consumer reporting agency. The reporting agency played no part in our decision and is unable to supply specific reasons why we have denied credit to you. You also have a right to a free copy of your report from the reporting agency, if you request it no later than 60 days after you receive this notice. In addition, if you find that any information contained in the report you receive is inaccurate or incomplete, you have the right to dispute the matter with the reporting agency.

[We also obtained your credit score from this̶the consumer reporting agency and used it in making our credit decision. Your credit score is a number that reflects the information in your consumer report. Your credit score can change, depending on how the information in your consumer report changes.

Your credit score:_____

Date: _____

Scores range from a low of _____ to a high of _____.

Key factors that adversely affected your credit score:

_____

_____

_____

[Number of recent inquiries on consumer report, as a key factor]

[If you have any questions regarding your credit score, you should contact [entity that provided the credit score] at:

Address: _____

[Toll-free] T̶e̶l̶e̶p̶h̶o̶n̶e̶n̶u̶m̶b̶e̶r̶Telephone number: _____]

You should know that the f̶e̶d̶e̶r̶a̶l̶Federal Equal Credit Opportunity Act prohibits creditors, such as ourselves, from discriminating against credit applicants on the basis of their race, color, religion, national origin, sex, marital status, age (provided the applicant has the capacity to enter into a binding contract), because they receive income from a public assistance program, or because they may have exercised their rights under the Consumer Credit Protection Act. If you believe there has been discrimination in handling your application you should contact the [name and address of the appropriate f̶e̶d̶e̶r̶a̶l̶Federal enforcement agency listed in a̶p̶p̶e̶n̶-̶d̶i̶x̶Appendix A].

Sincerely,

Form C-5—Sample Disclosure of Right t̶o̶To Request Specific Reasons for Credit Denial

Date

Dear Applicant: Thank you for applying to us for _____.

After carefully reviewing your application, we are sorry to advise you that we cannot [open an account for you/grant a loan to you/increase your credit limit] at this time. If you would like a statement of specific reasons why your application was denied, please contact [our credit service manager] shown below within 60 days of the date of this letter. We will provide you with the statement of reasons within 30 days after receiving your request.

Creditor's N̶a̶m̶e̶name

Address

Telephone N̶u̶m̶b̶e̶r̶number

If we obtained information from a consumer reporting agency as part of our consideration of your application, its name, address, and [toll-free] telephone number is shown below. The reporting agency played no part in our decision and is unable to supply specific reasons why we have denied credit to you. [You have a right under the Fair Credit Reporting Act to know the information contained in your credit file at the consumer reporting agency.] You have a right to a free copy of your report from the reporting agency, if you request it no later than 60 days after you receive this notice. In addition, if you find that any information contained in the report you received is inaccurate or incomplete, you have the right to dispute the matter with the reporting agency. You can find out about the information contained in your file (if one was used) by contacting:

Consumer reporting agency's name

Address

[Toll-free] Telephone number

[We also obtained your credit score from this̶the consumer reporting agency and used it in making our credit decision. Your credit score is a number that reflects the information in your consumer report. Your credit score can change, depending on how the information in your consumer report changes.

Your credit score:_____

Date: _____

Scores range from a low of _____ to a high of _____.

Key factors that adversely affected your credit score:

_____

_____

_____

[Number of recent inquiries on consumer report, as a key factor]

[If you have any questions regarding your credit score, you should contact [entity that provided the credit score] at:

Address: _____

[Toll-free] Telephone number:_____]]

Sincerely,

Notice: The f̶e̶d̶e̶r̶a̶l̶Federal Equal Credit Opportunity Act prohibits creditors from discriminating against credit applicants on the basis of race, color, religion, national origin, sex, marital status, age

(provided the applicant has the capacity to enter into a binding contract); because all or part of the applicant's income derives from any public assistance program; or because the applicant has in good faith exercised any right under the Consumer Credit Protection Act. The f̶e̶d̶e̶r̶a̶l̶Federal agency that administers compliance with this law concerning this creditor is (name and address as specified by the appropriate agency listed in a̶p̶p̶e̶n̶d̶i̶x̶Appendix A).

Form C-6—Sample Notice of Incomplete Application and Request for Additional Information

Creditor's name

Address

Telephone number

Date

Dear Applicant: Thank you for your application for credit. The following information is needed to make a decision on your application:_____ :

We need to receive this information by _____ (date). If we do not receive it by that date, we will regrettably be unable to give further consideration to your credit request.

Sincerely,

Form C-7—Sample Notice of Action Taken and Statement of Reasons (Business Credit)

Creditor's N̶a̶m̶e̶name

Creditor's address

Date

Dear Applicant: Thank you for applying to us for credit. We have given your request careful consideration, and regret that we are unable to extend credit to you at this time for the following reasons:

[̶(Insert appropriate reason, such as: Value or type of collateral not sufficient; Lack of established earnings record; Slow or past due in trade or loan payments.]̶)

Sincerely,

Notice: The f̶e̶d̶e̶r̶a̶l̶Federal Equal Credit Opportunity Act prohibits creditors from discriminating against credit applicants on the basis of race, color, religion, national origin, sex, marital status, age (provided the applicant has the capacity to enter into a binding contract); because all or part of the applicant's income derives from any public assistance program; or because the applicant has in good faith exercised any right under the Consumer Credit Protection Act. The f̶e̶d̶e̶r̶a̶l̶Federal agency that administers compliance with this law concerning this creditor is [name and address as specified by the appropriate agency listed in a̶p̶p̶e̶n̶d̶i̶x̶Appendix A].

Form C-8—Sample Disclosure of Right t̶o̶To Request Specific Reasons for Credit Denial Given at Time of Application (Business Credit)

Creditor's name

Creditor's address

If your application for business credit is denied, you have the right to a written statement of the specific reasons for the denial. To obtain the statement, please contact [name, address and telephone number of the person or office from which the statement of reasons can be obtained] within 60 days from the date you are notified of our decision. We will send you a written statement of reasons for the denial within 30 days of receiving your request for the statement.

Notice: The ~~federal~~Federal Equal Credit Opportunity Act prohibits creditors from discriminating against credit applicants on the basis of race, color, religion, national origin, sex, marital status, age (provided the applicant has the capacity to enter into a binding contract); because all or part of the applicant's income derives from any public assistance program; or because the applicant has in good faith exercised any right under the Consumer Credit Protection Act. The ~~federal~~Federal agency that administers compliance with this law concerning this creditor is [name and address as specified by the appropriate agency listed in ~~appendix~~Appendix A].

Form C-9—Sample Disclosure of Right to Receive a Copy of ~~an Appraisal~~Appraisals

We may order an appraisal to determine the property's value and charge you for this appraisal. We will promptly give you a copy of any appraisal, even if your loan does not close. You can pay for an additional appraisal for your own use at your own cost.

~~You have the right to a copy of the appraisal report used in connection with your application for credit. If you wish a copy, please write to us at the mailing address we have provided. We must hear from you no later than 90 days after we notify you about the~~ ~~action taken on your credit application or you withdraw your application.~~

[In your letter, give us the following information:]

Form C-10—Sample Disclosure About Voluntary Data Notation

We are requesting the following information to monitor our compliance with the ~~federal~~Federal Equal Credit Opportunity Act, which prohibits unlawful discrimination. You are not required to provide this information. We will not take this information (or your decision not to provide this information) into account in connection with your application or credit transaction. The law provides that a creditor may not discriminate based on this information, or based on whether or not you choose to provide it. [If you choose not to provide the information, we will note it by visual observation or surname.].

[78 Fed. Reg. 7248 (Jan. 31, 2013), eff. Jan. 18, 2014]

Appendix D to Part ~~2020~~1002— Issuance of ~~Staff~~Official Interpretations

1. *Official ~~Staff~~ Interpretations.* ~~Officials in the Board's Division of Consumer and Community~~ ~~Affairs are authorized to issue official staff interpretations of this regulation. These interpretations~~*Interpretations.* Interpretations of this part issued by officials of the Bureau provide the protection afforded under section 706(e) of the Act. Except in unusual circumstances, such interpretations will not be issued separately but will be incorporated in an official commentary to the regulation, which will be amended periodically.

2. *Requests for Issuance of Official ~~Staff~~ Interpretations.* A request for an official ~~staff~~ interpretation should be in writing and addressed to the Assistant Director, Office of Regulations, Division of ~~Consumer and Community Affairs, Board of Governors of the Federal Reserve System, Washington, DC 20551.~~Research, Markets, and Regulations, Bureau of Consumer Financial Protection, 1700 G Street, NW., Washington, DC 20006. The request should contain a complete statement of all relevant facts concerning the issue, including copies of all pertinent documents.

3. *Scope of Interpretations.* No ~~staff~~ interpretations will be issued approving creditors' forms or statements. This restriction does not apply to forms or statements whose use is required or sanctioned by a government agency.

Appendix C

Official Interpretations of Regulation B

The Consumer Financial Protection Bureau (CFPB) now has authority to issue Regulation B and its commentary. *See* Pub. L. No. 111-203, tit. X, §§ 1085(3), 1100H, 124 Stat. 2083, 2113 (July 21, 2010). On December 21, 2011, the CFPB issued its version of Regulation B and its commentary and further amended it on January 18, 2013, effective July 18, 2014. The Federal Reserve Board (FRB) has not withdrawn its version of Regulation B and its commentary, certain kinds of credit are not within the CFPB's enforcement authority, and the FRB regulation thus may remain relevant.

What follows is a redline version indicating how the CFPB's Regulation B commentary is changed from the FRB Regulation B commentary. CFPB changes not in effect until January 18, 2014, are redlined with an alternative typeface. The FRB version, this redlined version, and the CFPB's version (with supplemental information) are all found on the companion website to this treatise. The companion website facilitates keyword searches and allows relevant provisions to be imported into word-processable documents.

AUTHORITY: 12 U.S.C. 5512, 5581; 15 U.S.C. §§ 1691–1691fb.

SOURCE: 6876 Fed. Reg. 13,16179445 (Mar. 18, 2003Dec. 21, 2011), unless otherwise noted.

Supplement I to Part 2021002— Official Staff-Interpretations

Following is an official staff-interpretation of Regulation B (12 CFR part 202Part 1002) issued under authority delegated by the Federal Reserve Board to officials in the Divisionby the Bureau of Consumer and Community Affairs. Financial Protection. References are to sections of the regulation or the Equal Credit Opportunity Act (15 U.S.C. 1601 *et seq.*).

INTRODUCTION

1. *Official status.* Section 706(e) of the Equal Credit Opportunity Act protects a creditor from civil liability for any act done or omitted in good faith in conformity with an interpretation issued by a duly authorized official of the Federal Reserve Board-Bureau. This commentary is the means by which the DivisionBureau of Consumer and Community Affairs of the Federal Reserve BoardFinancial Protection issues official-staff interpretations of Regulation B. Good-faith compliance with this commentary affords a creditor protection under section 706(e) of the Act.

2. *Issuance of interpretations.* Under Appendix D to the regulation, any person may request an official staff interpretation. Interpretations will be issued at the discretion of designated officials and incorporated in this commentary following publication for comment in the Federalthe Federal Register. Except in unusual circumstances, official-staff interpretations will be issued only by means of this commentary.

3. *Status of previous interpretations. Interpretations of Regulation B previously issued by the Federal Reserve Board and its staff have been incorporated into this commentary as appropriate. All other previous Board and staff interpretations, official and unofficial, are superseded by this commentary.*

4. *Footnotes. Footnotes in the regulation have the same legal effect as the text of the regulation, whether they are explanatory or illustrative in nature.*

5. *Comment designations.* The comments are designated with as much specificity as possible according to the particular regulatory provision addressed. Each comment in the commentary is identified by a number and the regulatory section or paragraph that it interprets. For example, comments to § 202.2 1002.2(c) are further divided by subparagraph, such as comment 2(c)(1)(ii)-1 and comment 2(c)(2)(ii)-1.

Section 202.11002.1—Authority, Scope, and Purpose

1(a) Authority and scope.

1. *Scope.* The Equal Credit Opportunity Act and Regulation B apply to all credit—commercial as well as personal—without regard to the nature or type of the credit or the creditor, except for an entity excluded from coverage of this part (but not the Act) by section 1029 of the Consumer Financial Protection Act of 2010 (12 U.S.C. 5519). If a transaction provides for the deferral of the payment of a debt, it is credit covered by Regulation B even though it may not be a credit transaction covered by Regulation Z (Truth in Lending) (12 CFR part 226Part 1026). Further, the definition of creditor is not restricted to the party or person to whom the obligation is initially payable, as is the case under Regulation Z. Moreover, the Act and regulation apply to all methods of credit evaluation, whether performed judgmentally or by use of a credit scoring system.

2. *Foreign applicability.* Regulation B generally does not apply to lending activities that occur outside the United States. The regulation does apply to lending activities that take place within the United States (as well as the Commonwealth of Puerto Rico and any territory or possession of the United States), whether or not the applicant is a citizen.

3. *BoardBureau.* The term *BoardBureau,* as used in this regulationpart, means the Board of Governors of the Federal Reserve SystemBureau of Consumer Financial Protection.

Section 202.21002.2—Definitions

2(c) Adverse action.

Paragraph 2(c)(1)(i).

1. *Application for credit.* If the applicant applied in accordance with the creditor's procedures, a refusal to refinance or extend the term of a business or other loan is adverse action.

Paragraph 2(c)(1)(ii).

1. *Move from service area.* If a credit card issuer terminates the open-end account of a customer because the customer has moved out of the card issuer's service area, the termination is adverse action unless termination on this ground was ex-

plicitly provided for in the credit agreement between the parties. In cases where termination is adverse action, notification is required under § 202.9.1002.9.

2. *Termination based on credit limit.* If a creditor terminates credit accounts that have low credit limits (for example, under $400) but keeps open accounts with higher credit limits, the termination is adverse action and notification is required under § 202.9.1002.9.

Paragraph 2(c)(2)(ii).

1. *Default—exercise of due-on-sale clause.* If a mortgagor sells or transfers mortgaged property without the consent of the mortgagee, and the mortgagee exercises its contractual right to accelerate the mortgage loan, the mortgagee may treat the mortgagor as being in default. An adverse action notice need not be given to the mortgagor or the transferee. (See comment 2(e)-1 for treatment of a purchaser who requests to assume the loan.)

2. *Current delinquency or default.* The term adverse action does not include a creditor's termination of an account when the accountholder is currently in default or delinquent on that account. Notification in accordance with § 202.91002.9 of the regulation generally is required, however, if the creditor's action is based on a past delinquency or default on the account.

Paragraph 2(c)(2)(iii).

1. *Point-of-sale transactions.* Denial of credit at point of sale is not adverse action except under those circumstances specified in the regulation. For example, denial at point of sale is not adverse action in the following situations:

  i. A credit cardholder presents an expired card or a card that has been reported to the card issuer as lost or stolen.

  ii. The amount of a transaction exceeds a cash advance or credit limit.

  iii. The circumstances (such as excessive use of a credit card in a short period of time) suggest that fraud is involved.

  iv. The authorization facilities are not functioning.

  v. Billing statements have been returned to the creditor for lack of a forwarding address.

2. *Application for increase in available credit.* A refusal or failure to authorize an account transaction at the point of sale or loan is not adverse action except when the refusal is a denial of an application, submitted in accordance with the creditor's procedures, for an increase in the amount of credit.

Paragraph 2(c)(2)(v).

1. *Terms of credit versus type of credit offered.* When an applicant applies for credit and the creditor does not offer the credit terms requested by the applicant (for example, the interest rate, length of maturity, collateral, or amount of downpayment), a denial of the application for that reason is adverse action (unless the creditor makes a counteroffer that is accepted by the applicant) and the applicant is entitled to notification under § 202.9.1002.9.

2(e) Applicant.

1. *Request to assume loan.* If a mortgagor sells or transfers the mortgaged property and the buyer makes an application to the creditor to assume the mortgage loan, the mortgagee must treat the buyer as an applicant unless its policy is not to permit assumptions.

2(f) Application.

1. *General.* A creditor has the latitude under the regulation to establish its own application process and to decide the type and amount of information it will require from credit applicants.

2. *Procedures used.* The term "procedures" refers to the actual practices followed by a creditor for making credit decisions as well as its stated application procedures. For example, if a creditor's stated policy is to require all applications to be in writing on the creditor's application form, but the creditor also makes credit decisions based on oral requests, the creditor's procedures are to accept both oral and written applications.

3. *When an inquiry or prequalification request becomes an application.* A creditor is encouraged to provide consumers with information about loan terms. However, if in giving information to the consumer the creditor also evaluates information about the consumer, decides to decline the request, and communicates this to the consumer, the creditor has treated the inquiry or prequalification request as an application and must then comply with the notification requirements under § 202.9.1002.9. Whether the inquiry or prequalification request becomes an application depends on how the creditor responds to the consumer, not on what the consumer says or asks. (See comment 9-5 for further discussion of prequalification requests; see comment 2(f)-5 for a discussion of preapproval requests.)

4. *Examples of inquiries that are not applications.* The following examples illustrate situations in which only an inquiry has taken place:

  i. A consumer calls to ask about loan terms and an employee explains the creditor's basic loan terms, such as interest rates, loan-to-value ratio, and debt-to-income ratio.

  ii. A consumer calls to ask about interest rates for car loans, and, in order to quote the appropriate rate, the loan officer asks for the make and sales price of the car and the amount of the downpayment, then gives the consumer the rate.

  iii. A consumer asks about terms for a loan to purchase a home and tells the loan officer her income and intended downpayment, but the loan officer only explains the creditor's loan-to-value ratio policy and other basic lending policies, without telling the consumer whether she qualifies for the loan.

  iv. A consumer calls to ask about terms for a loan to purchase vacant land and states his income and the sales price of the property to be financed, and asks whether he qualifies

for a loan; the employee responds by describing the general lending policies, explaining that he would need to look at all of the consumer's qualifications before making a decision, and offering to send an application form to the consumer.

5. *Examples of an application.* An application for credit includes the following situations:

  i. A person asks a financial institution to "pre-approve" her for a loan (for example, to finance a house or a vehicle she plans to buy) and the institution reviews the request under a program in which the institution, after a comprehensive analysis of her creditworthiness, issues a written commitment valid for a designated period of time to extend a loan up to a specified amount. The written commitment may not be subject to conditions other than conditions that require the identification of adequate collateral, conditions that require no material change in the applicant's financial condition or creditworthiness prior to funding the loan, and limited conditions that are not related to the financial condition or creditworthiness of the applicant that the lender ordinarily attaches to a traditional application (such as certification of a clear termite inspection for a home purchase loan, or a maximum mileage requirement for a used car loan). But if the creditor's program does not provide for giving written commitments, requests for pre-approvals are treated as prequalification requests for purposes of the regulation.

  ii. Under the same facts as above, the financial institution evaluates the person's creditworthiness and determines that she does not qualify for a preapproval.

6. *Completed application—diligence requirement.* The regulation defines a completed application in terms that give a creditor the latitude to establish its own information requirements. Nevertheless, the creditor must act with reasonable diligence to collect information needed to complete the application. For example, the creditor should request information from third parties, such as a credit report, promptly after receiving the application. If additional information is needed from the applicant, such as an address or a telephone number to verify employment, the creditor should contact the applicant promptly. (But see comment 9(a)(1)-3, which discusses the creditor's option to deny an application on the basis of incompleteness.)

2(g) Business credit.

1. *Definition.* The test for deciding whether a transaction qualifies as business credit is one of primary purpose. For example, an open-end credit account used for both personal and business purposes is not business credit unless the primary purpose of the account is business-related. A creditor may rely on an applicant's statement of the purpose for the credit requested.

2(j) Credit.

1. *General.* Regulation B covers a wider range of credit transactions than Regulation Z (Truth in Lending). Under Regulation B, a transaction is credit if there is a right to defer payment of a debt—regardless of whether the credit is for personal or commercial purposes, the number of installments required for repayment, or whether the transaction is subject to a finance charge.

2(l) Creditor.

1. *Assignees.* The term creditor includes all persons participating in the credit decision. This may include an assignee or a potential purchaser of the obligation who influences the credit decision by indicating whether or not it will purchase the obligation if the transaction is consummated.

2. *Referrals to creditors.* For certain purposes, the term creditor includes persons such as real estate brokers, automobile dealers, home builders, and home-improvement contractors who do not participate in credit decisions but who only accept applications and refer applicants to creditors, or select or offer to select creditors to whom credit requests can be made. These persons must comply with § ~~202.4~~1002.4(a), the general rule prohibiting discrimination, and with § ~~202.4~~1002.4(b), the general rule against discouraging applications.

2(p) Empirically derived and other credit scoring systems.

1. *Purpose of definition.* The definition under § ~~202.2~~§§ 1002.2(p)(1)(i) through (iv) sets the criteria that a credit system must meet in order to use age as a predictive factor. Credit systems that do not meet these criteria are judgmental systems and may consider age only for the purpose of determining a "pertinent element of creditworthiness." (Both types of systems may favor an elderly applicant. See § ~~202.6~~1002.6(b)(2).)

2. *Periodic revalidation.* The regulation does not specify how often credit scoring systems must be revalidated. The credit scoring system must be revalidated frequently enough to ensure that it continues to meet recognized professional statistical standards for statistical soundness. To ensure that predictive ability is being maintained, the creditor must periodically review the performance of the system. This could be done, for example, by analyzing the loan portfolio to determine the delinquency rate for each score interval, or by analyzing population stability over time to detect deviations of recent applications from the application population used to validate the system. If this analysis indicates that the system no longer predicts risk with statistical soundness, the system must be adjusted as necessary to reestablish its predictive ability. A creditor is responsible for ensuring its system is validated and revalidated based on the creditor's own data.

3. *Pooled data scoring systems.* A scoring system or the data from which to develop such a system may be obtained from either a single credit grantor or multiple credit grantors. The resulting system will qualify as an empirically derived, demonstrably and statistically sound, credit scoring system provided the criteria set forth in paragraph (p)(1)(i) through (iv) of this section are met. A creditor is responsible for ensuring its system is validated and revalidated based on the creditor's own data when it becomes available.

4. *Effects test and disparate treatment.* An empirically derived, demonstrably and statistically sound, credit scoring system may include age as a predictive factor (provided that the age of an elderly applicant is not assigned a negative factor or value). Besides age, no other prohibited basis may be used as a variable. Generally, credit scoring systems treat all applicants objectively and thus avoid problems of disparate treatment. In cases where a credit scoring system is used in conjunction with individual discretion, disparate treatment could conceivably occur in the evaluation process. In addition, neutral factors used in credit scoring systems could nonetheless be subject to challenge under the effects test. (See comment 6(a)-2 for a discussion of the effects test).

2(w) Open-end credit.

1. *Open-end real estate mortgages.* The term "open-end credit" does not include negotiated advances under an open-end real estate mortgage or a letter of credit.

2(z) Prohibited basis.

1. *Persons associated with applicant.* As used in this ~~regulation~~part, prohibited basis refers not only to characteristics—the race, color, religion, national origin, sex, marital status, or age—of an applicant (or officers of an applicant in the case of a corporation) but also to the characteristics of individuals with whom an applicant is affiliated or with whom the applicant associates. This means, for example, that under the general rule stated in § ~~202.4~~1002.4(a), a creditor may not discriminate against an applicant because of that person's personal or business dealings with members of a certain religion, because of the national origin of any persons associated with the extension of credit (such as the tenants in the apartment complex being financed), or because of the race of other residents in the neighborhood where the property offered as collateral is located.

2. *National origin.* A creditor may not refuse to grant credit because an applicant comes from a particular country but may take the applicant's immigration status into account. A creditor may also take into account any applicable law, regulation, or executive order restricting dealings with citizens (or the government) of a particular country or imposing limitations regarding credit extended for their use.

3. *Public assistance program.* Any ~~federal~~Federal, state, or local governmental assistance program that provides a continuing, periodic income supplement, whether premised on entitlement or need, is "public assistance" for purposes of the regulation. The term includes (but is not limited to) Temporary Aid to Needy Families, food stamps, rent and mortgage supplement or assistance programs, social security and supplemental security income, and unemployment compensation. Only physicians, hospitals, and others to whom the benefits are payable need consider Medicare and Medicaid as public assistance.

Section ~~202.3~~1002.3—Limited Exceptions for Certain Classes of Transactions

1. *Scope.* Under this section, procedural requirements of the regulation do not apply to certain types of credit. All classes of transactions remain subject to § ~~202.4~~1002.4(a), the general rule barring discrimination on a prohibited basis, and to any other provision not specifically excepted.

3(a) Public-utilities credit.

1. *Definition.* This definition applies only to credit for the purchase of a utility service, such as electricity, gas, or telephone service. Credit provided or offered by a public utility for some other purpose—such as for financing the purchase of a gas dryer, telephone equipment, or other durable goods, or for insulation or other home improvements—is not excepted.

2. *Security deposits.* A utility company is a creditor when it supplies utility service and bills the user after the service has been provided. Thus, any credit term (such as a requirement for a security deposit) is subject to the regulation's bar against discrimination on a prohibited basis.

3. *Telephone companies.* A telephone company's credit transactions qualify for the exceptions provided in § ~~202.3~~1002.3(a)(2) only if the company is regulated by a government unit or files the charges for service, delayed payment, or any discount for prompt payment with a government unit.

3(c) Incidental credit.

1. *Examples.* If a service provider (such as a hospital, doctor, lawyer, or merchant) allows the client or customer to defer the payment of a bill, this deferral of debt is credit for purposes of the regulation, even though there is no finance charge and no agreement for payment in installments. Because of the exceptions provided by this section, however, these particular credit extensions are excepted from compliance with certain procedural requirements as specified in § ~~202.3~~1002.3(c).

3(d) Government credit.

1. *Credit to governments.* The exception relates to credit extended to (not by) governmental entities. For example, credit extended to a local government is covered by this exception, but credit extended to consumers by a ~~federal~~Federal or state housing

agency does not qualify for special treatment under this category.

Section ~~202.4~~1002.4—General Rules

Paragraph 4(a).

1. *Scope of rule.* The general rule stated in § ~~202.4~~1002.4(a) covers all dealings, without exception, between an applicant and a creditor, whether or not addressed by other provisions of the regulation. Other provisions of the regulation identify specific practices that the ~~Board~~Bureau has decided are impermissible because they could result in credit discrimination on a basis prohibited by the Act. The general rule covers, for example, application procedures, criteria used to evaluate creditworthiness, administration of accounts, and treatment of delinquent or slow accounts. Thus, whether or not specifically prohibited elsewhere in the regulation, a credit practice that treats applicants differently on a prohibited basis violates the law because it violates the general rule. Disparate treatment on a prohibited basis is illegal whether or not it results from a conscious intent to discriminate.

2. *Examples.*
   i. Disparate treatment would exist, for example, in the following situations:
      A. A creditor provides information only on "subprime" and similar products to minority applicants who request information about the creditor's mortgage products, but provides information on a wider variety of mortgage products to similarly situated nonminority applicants.
      B. A creditor provides more comprehensive information to men than to similarly situated women.
      C. A creditor requires a minority applicant to provide greater documentation to obtain a loan than a similarly situated nonminority applicant.
      D. A creditor waives or relaxes credit standards for a nonminority applicant but not for a similarly situated minority applicant.
   ii. Treating applicants differently on a prohibited basis is unlawful if the creditor lacks a legitimate nondiscriminatory reason for its action, or if the asserted reason is found to be a pretext for discrimination.

Paragraph 4(b).

1. *Prospective applicants.* Generally, the regulation's protections apply only to persons who have requested or received an extension of credit. In keeping with the purpose of the Act—to promote the availability of credit on a nondiscriminatory basis—§ ~~202.4~~1002.4(b) covers acts or practices directed at prospective applicants that could discourage a reasonable person, on a prohibited basis, from applying for credit. Practices prohibited by this section include:

   i. A statement that the applicant should not bother to apply, after the applicant states that he is retired.
   ii. The use of words, symbols, models or other forms of communication in advertising that express, imply, or suggest a discriminatory preference or a policy of exclusion in violation of the Act.
   iii. The use of interview scripts that discourage applications on a prohibited basis.

2. *Affirmative advertising.* A creditor may affirmatively solicit or encourage members of traditionally disadvantaged groups to apply for credit, especially groups that might not normally seek credit from that creditor.

Paragraph 4(c).

1. *Requirement for written applications.* Model application forms are provided in Appendix B to the regulation, although use of a printed form is not required. A creditor will satisfy the requirement by writing down the information that it normally considers in making a credit decision. The creditor may complete an application on behalf of an applicant and need not require the applicant to sign the application.

2. *Telephone applications.* A creditor that accepts applications by telephone for dwelling-related credit covered by § ~~202.13~~1002.13 can meet the requirement for written applications by writing down pertinent information that is provided by the applicant.

3. *Computerized entry.* Information entered directly into and retained by a computerized system qualifies as a written application under this paragraph. (See the commentary to § ~~202.13~~1002.13(b), *Applications through electronic media and Applications through video.*)

Paragraph 4(d).

1. *Clear and conspicuous.* This standard requires that disclosures be presented in a reasonably understandable format in a way that does not obscure the required information. No minimum type size is mandated, but the disclosures must be legible, whether typewritten, handwritten, or printed by computer.

2. *Form of disclosures.* Whether the disclosures required to be on or with an application must be in electronic form depends upon the following:
   i. If an applicant accesses a credit application electronically (other than as described under ii below), such as online at a home computer, the creditor must provide the disclosures in electronic form (such as with the application form on its ~~website~~Web site) in order to meet the requirement to provide disclosures in a timely manner on or with the application. If the creditor instead mailed paper disclosures to the applicant, this requirement would not be met.
   ii. In contrast, if an applicant is physically present in the creditor's office, and accesses a credit application electronically, such as via a terminal or kiosk (or if the applicant uses a

terminal or kiosk located on the premises of an affiliate or third party that has arranged with the creditor to provide applications to consumers), the creditor may provide disclosures in either electronic or paper form, provided the creditor complies with the timing, delivery, and retainability requirements of the regulation.

Section ~~202.5~~1002.5—Rules Concerning Requests for Information

5(a) General rules.

Paragraph 5(a)(1).

1. *Requests for information.* This section governs the types of information that a creditor may gather. Section ~~202.6~~1002.6 governs how information may be used.

Paragraph 5(a)(2).

1. *Local laws.* Information that a creditor is allowed to collect pursuant to a "state" statute or regulation includes information required by a local statute, regulation, or ordinance.

2. *Information required by Regulation C.* Regulation C generally requires creditors covered by the Home Mortgage Disclosure Act (HMDA) to collect and report information about the race, ethnicity, and sex of applicants for home-improvement loans and home-purchase loans, including some types of loans not covered by § ~~202.13~~1002.13.

3. *Collecting information on behalf of creditors.* Persons such as loan brokers and correspondents do not violate the ECOA or Regulation B if they collect information that they are otherwise prohibited from collecting, where the purpose of collecting the information is to provide it to a creditor that is subject to the Home Mortgage Disclosure Act or another ~~federal~~Federal or state statute or regulation requiring data collection.

5(d) Other limitations on information requests.

Paragraph 5(d)(1).

1. *Indirect disclosure of prohibited information.* The fact that certain credit-related information may indirectly disclose marital status does not bar a creditor from seeking such information. For example, the creditor may ask about:
   i. The applicant's obligation to pay alimony, child support, or separate maintenance income.
   ii. The source of income to be used as the basis for repaying the credit requested, which could disclose that it is the income of a spouse.
   iii. Whether any obligation disclosed by the applicant has a co-obligor, which could disclose that the co-obligor is a spouse or former spouse.

iv. The ownership of assets, which could disclose the interest of a spouse.

Paragraph 5(d)(2).

1. *Disclosure about income.* The sample application forms in ~~appendix~~Appendix B to the regulation illustrate how a creditor may inform an applicant of the right not to disclose alimony, child support, or separate maintenance income.

2. *General inquiry about source of income.* Since a general inquiry about the source of income may lead an applicant to disclose alimony, child support, or separate maintenance income, a creditor making such an inquiry on an application form should preface the request with the disclosure required by this paragraph.

3. *Specific inquiry about sources of income.* A creditor need not give the disclosure if the inquiry about income is specific and worded in a way that is unlikely to lead the applicant to disclose the fact that income is derived from alimony, child support, or separate maintenance payments. For example, an application form that asks about specific types of income such as salary, wages, or investment income need not include the disclosure.

Section ~~202.6~~1002.6—Rules Concerning Evaluation of Applications

6(a) General rule concerning use of information.

1. *General.* When evaluating an application for credit, a creditor generally may consider any information obtained. However, a creditor may not consider in its evaluation of creditworthiness any information that it is barred by § ~~202.5~~1002.5 from obtaining or from using for any purpose other than to conduct a self-test under § ~~202.15.~~1002.15.

2. *Effects test.* The effects test is a judicial doctrine that was developed in a series of employment cases decided by the U.S. Supreme Court under Title VII of the Civil Rights Act of 1964 (42 U.S.C. 2000e *et seq.*), and the burdens of proof for such employment cases were codified by Congress in the Civil Rights Act of 1991 (42 U.S.C. 2000e-2). Congressional intent that this doctrine apply to the credit area is documented in the Senate Report that accompanied H.R. 6516, No. 94-589, pp. 4–5; and in the House Report that accompanied H.R. 6516, No. 94-210, p.5. The Act and regulation may prohibit a creditor practice that is discriminatory in effect because it has a disproportionately negative impact on a prohibited basis, even though the creditor has no intent to discriminate and the practice appears neutral on its face, unless the creditor practice meets a legitimate business need that cannot reasonably be achieved as well by means that are less disparate in their impact. For example, requiring that applicants have income in excess of a certain amount to qualify for an overdraft line of credit could mean that women and minority applicants will be rejected at a higher rate than men and nonminority applicants. If there is a demonstrable relationship between the income requirement and creditworthiness for the level of credit involved, however, use of the income standard would likely be permissible.

6(b) Specific rules concerning use of information.

Paragraph 6(b)(1).

1. *Prohibited basis—special purpose credit.* In a special purpose credit program, a creditor may consider a prohibited basis to determine whether the applicant possesses a characteristic needed for eligibility. (See § ~~202.8.~~1002.8.)

Paragraph 6(b)(2).

1. *Favoring the elderly.* Any system of evaluating creditworthiness may favor a credit applicant who is age 62 or older. A credit program that offers more favorable credit terms to applicants age 62 or older is also permissible; a program that offers more favorable credit terms to applicants at an age lower than 62 is permissible only if it meets the special-purpose credit requirements of § ~~202.8.~~1002.8.

2. *Consideration of age in a credit scoring system.* Age may be taken directly into account in a credit scoring system that is "demonstrably and statistically sound," as defined in § ~~202.2~~1002.2(p), with one limitation: ~~applicants~~Applicants age 62 years or older must be treated at least as favorably as applicants who are under age 62. If age is scored by assigning points to an applicant's age category, elderly applicants must receive the same or a greater number of points as the most favored class of nonelderly applicants.

i. *Age-split scorecards.* Some credit systems segment the population and use different scorecards based on the age of an applicant. In such a system, one card may cover a narrow age range (for example, applicants in their twenties or younger) who are evaluated under attributes predictive for that age group. A second card may cover all other applicants, who are evaluated under the attributes predictive for that broader class. When a system uses a card covering a wide age range that encompasses elderly applicants, the credit scoring system is not deemed to score age. Thus, the system does not raise the issue of assigning a negative factor or value to the age of elderly applicants. But if a system segments the population by age into multiple scorecards, and includes elderly applicants in a narrower age range, the credit scoring system does score age. To comply with the Act and regulation in such a case, the creditor must ensure that the system does not assign a negative factor or value to the age of elderly applicants as a class.

3. *Consideration of age in a judgmental system.* In a judgmental system, defined in § ~~202.2~~1002.2(t), a creditor may not decide whether to extend credit or set the terms and conditions of credit based on age or information related exclusively to age. Age or age-related information may be considered only in evaluating other "pertinent elements of creditworthiness" that are drawn from the particular facts and circumstances concerning the applicant. For example, a creditor may not reject an application or terminate an account because the applicant is 60 years old. But a creditor that uses a judgmental system may relate the applicant's age to other information about the applicant that the creditor considers in evaluating creditworthiness. As the following examples illustrate, the evaluation must be made in an individualized, case-by-case manner:

i. A creditor may consider the applicant's occupation and length of time to retirement to ascertain whether the applicant's income (including retirement income) will support the extension of credit to its maturity.

ii. A creditor may consider the adequacy of any security offered when the term of the credit extension exceeds the life expectancy of the applicant and the cost of realizing on the collateral could exceed the applicant's equity. An elderly applicant might not qualify for a 5 percent down, 30-year mortgage loan but might qualify with a larger downpayment or a shorter loan maturity.

iii. A creditor may consider the applicant's age to assess the significance of length of employment (a young applicant may have just entered the job market) or length of time at an address (an elderly applicant may recently have retired and moved from a long-term residence).

4. *Consideration of age in a reverse mortgage.* A reverse mortgage is a home-secured loan in which the borrower receives payments from the creditor, and does not become obligated to repay these amounts (other than in the case of default) until the borrower dies, moves permanently from the home, or transfers title to the home, or upon a specified maturity date. Disbursements to the borrower under a reverse mortgage typically are determined by considering the value of the borrower's home, the current interest rate, and the borrower's life expectancy. A reverse mortgage program that requires borrowers to be age 62 or older is permissible under § ~~202.6~~1002.6(b)(2)(iv). In addition, under § ~~202.6~~1002.6(b)(2)(iii), a creditor may consider a borrower's age to evaluate a pertinent element of creditworthiness, such as the amount of the credit or monthly payments that the borrower will receive, or the estimated repayment date.

5. *Consideration of age in a combined system.* A creditor using a credit scoring system that qualifies as "empirically derived" under § ~~202.2~~1002.2(p) may consider other factors (such as a credit report or the applicant's cash flow) on a judgmental basis. Doing so will not negate the classification of the credit scoring component of the combined system as "demonstrably and statistically sound." While age could be used in the credit scoring portion, however, in the judgmental portion age may not be considered directly. It may be used only for the purpose of determining a "pertinent element of

creditworthiness." (See comment 6(b)(2)-3.)

6. *Consideration of public assistance.* When considering income derived from a public assistance program, a creditor may take into account, for example:

i.   The length of time an applicant will likely remain eligible to receive such income.

ii. Whether the applicant will continue to qualify for benefits based on the status of the applicant's dependents (as in the case of Temporary Aid to Needy Families, or social security payments to a minor).

iii. Whether the creditor can attach or garnish the income to assure payment of the debt in the event of default.

Paragraph 6(b)(5).

1. *Consideration of an individual applicant.* A creditor must evaluate income derived from part-time employment, alimony, child support, separate maintenance payments, retirement benefits, or public assistance on an individual basis, not on the basis of aggregate statistics; and must assess its reliability or unreliability by analyzing the applicant's actual circumstances, not by analyzing statistical measures derived from a group.

2. *Payments consistently made.* In determining the likelihood of consistent payments of alimony, child support, or separate maintenance, a creditor may consider factors such as whether payments are received pursuant to a written agreement or court decree; the length of time that the payments have been received; whether the payments are regularly received by the applicant; the availability of court or other procedures to compel payment; and the creditworthiness of the payor, including the credit history of the payor when it is available to the creditor.

3. *Consideration of income.*

i.   A creditor need not consider income at all in evaluating creditworthiness. If a creditor does consider income, there are several acceptable methods, whether in a credit scoring or a judgmental system:

    A. A creditor may score or take into account the total sum of all income stated by the applicant without taking steps to evaluate the income for reliability.

    B. A creditor may evaluate each component of the applicant's income, and then score or take into account income determined to be reliable separately from other income; or the creditor may disregard that portion of income that is not reliable when it aggregates reliable income.

    C. A creditor that does not evaluate all income components for reliability must treat as reliable any component of protected income that is not evaluated.

ii. In considering the separate components of an applicant's income, the creditor may not automatically discount or exclude from consideration any protected income. Any discounting or exclusion must be based on the applicant's actual circumstances.

4. *Part-time employment, sources of income.* A creditor may score or take into account the fact that an applicant has more than one source of earned income—a full-time and a part-time job or two part-time jobs. A creditor may also score or treat earned income from a secondary source differently than earned income from a primary source. The creditor may not, however, score or otherwise take into account the number of sources for income such as retirement income, social security, supplemental security income, and alimony. Nor may the creditor treat negatively the fact that an applicant's only earned income is derived from, for example, a part-time job.

Paragraph 6(b)(6).

1. *Types of credit references.* A creditor may restrict the types of credit history and credit references that it will consider, provided that the restrictions are applied to all credit applicants without regard to sex, marital status, or any other prohibited basis. On the applicant's request, however, a creditor must consider credit information not reported through a credit bureau when the information relates to the same types of credit references and history that the creditor would consider if reported through a credit bureau.

Paragraph 6(b)(7).

1. *National origin—immigration status.* The applicant's immigration status and ties to the community (such as employment and continued residence in the area) could have a bearing on a creditor's ability to obtain repayment. Accordingly, the creditor may consider immigration status and differentiate, for example, between a noncitizen who is a long-time resident with permanent resident status and a noncitizen who is temporarily in this country on a student visa.

2. *National origin—citizenship.* A denial of credit on the ground that an applicant is not a United States citizen is not per se discrimination based on national origin.

Paragraph 6(b)(8).

1. *Prohibited basis—marital status.* A creditor may consider the marital status of an applicant or joint applicant for the purpose of ascertaining the creditor's rights and remedies applicable to the particular extension of credit. For example, in a secured transaction involving real property, a creditor could take into account whether state law gives the applicant's spouse an interest in the property being offered as collateral.

Section ~~202.7~~1002.7—Rules Concerning Extensions of Credit

7(a) Individual accounts.

1. *Open-end credit—authorized user.* A creditor may not require a creditworthy applicant seeking an individual credit account to provide additional signatures. But the creditor may condition the designation of an authorized user by the account holder on the authorized user's becoming contractually liable for the account, as long as the creditor does not differentiate on any prohibited basis in imposing this requirement.

2. *Open-end credit—choice of authorized user.* A creditor that permits an account holder to designate an authorized user may not restrict this designation on a prohibited basis. For example, if the creditor allows the designation of spouses as authorized users, the creditor may not refuse to accept a ~~non-spouse~~non-spouse as an authorized user.

3. *Overdraft authority on transaction accounts.* If a transaction account (such as a checking account or NOW account) includes an overdraft line of credit, the creditor may require that all persons authorized to draw on the transaction account assume liability for any overdraft.

7(b) Designation of name.

1. *Single name on account.* A creditor may require that joint applicants on an account designate a single name for purposes of administering the account and that a single name be embossed on any credit cards issued on the account. But the creditor may not require that the name be the husband's name. (See § ~~202.10~~1002.10 for rules governing the furnishing of credit history on accounts held by spouses.)

7(c) Action concerning existing open-end accounts.

Paragraph 7(c)(1).

1. *Termination coincidental with marital status change.* When an account holder's marital status changes, a creditor generally may not terminate the account unless it has evidence that the account holder is now unable or unwilling to repay. But the creditor may terminate an account on which both spouses are jointly liable, even if the action coincides with a change in marital status, when one or both spouses:

i.   Repudiate responsibility for future charges on the joint account.

ii. Request separate accounts in their own names.

iii. Request that the joint account be closed.

2. *Updating information.* A creditor may periodically request updated information from applicants but may not use events related to a prohibited basis—such as an applicant's retirement or reaching a particular age, or a change in name or marital status—to trigger such a request.

Paragraph 7(c)(2).

1. *Procedure pending reapplication.* A creditor may require a reapplication from an account holder, even when there is no evidence of unwillingness or inability to repay, if (1) the credit was based on the qualifications of a person who is no longer available to support the credit and (2) the creditor has information indicating that the account holder's income may be insufficient to support the credit.

While a reapplication is pending, the creditor must allow the account holder full access to the account under the existing contract terms. The creditor may specify a reasonable time period within which the account holder must submit the required information.

7(d) Signature of spouse or other person.

1. *Qualified applicant.* The signature rules ensure that qualified applicants are able to obtain credit in their own names. Thus, when an applicant requests individual credit, a creditor generally may not require the signature of another person unless the creditor has first determined that the applicant alone does not qualify for the credit requested.

2. *Unqualified applicant.* When an applicant requests individual credit but does not meet a creditor's standards, the creditor may require a cosigner, guarantor, endorser, or similar ~~partie~~party—but cannot require that it be the spouse. (See commentary to § ~~202.7~~§§ 1002.7(d)(5) and (6).)

Paragraph 7(d)(1).

1. *Signature of another person.* It is impermissible for a creditor to require an applicant who is individually creditworthy to provide a cosigner—even if the creditor applies the requirement without regard to sex, marital status, or any other prohibited basis. (But see comment 7(d)(6)-1 concerning guarantors of closely held corporations.)

2. *Joint applicant.* The term "joint applicant" refers to someone who applies contemporaneously with the applicant for shared or joint credit. It does not refer to someone whose signature is required by the creditor as a condition for granting the credit requested.

3. *Evidence of joint application.* A person's intent to be a joint applicant must be evidenced at the time of application. Signatures on a promissory note may not be used to show intent to apply for joint credit. On the other hand, signatures or initials on a credit application affirming applicants' intent to apply for joint credit may be used to establish intent to apply for joint credit. (See Appendix B.) The method used to establish intent must be distinct from the means used by individuals to affirm the accuracy of information. For example, signatures on a joint financial statement affirming the veracity of information are not sufficient to establish intent to apply for joint credit.

Paragraph 7(d)(2).

1. *Jointly owned property.* If an applicant requests unsecured credit, does not own sufficient separate property, and relies on joint property to establish creditworthiness, the creditor must value the applicant's interest in the jointly owned property. A creditor may not request that a nonapplicant joint owner sign any instrument as a condition of the credit extension unless the applicant's interest does not support the amount and terms of the credit sought.

i. *Valuation of applicant's interest.* In determining the value of an applicant's interest in jointly owned property, a creditor may consider factors such as the form of ownership and the property's susceptibility to attachment, execution, severance, or partition; the value of the applicant's interest after such action; and the cost associated with the action. This determination must be based on the existing form of ownership, and not on the possibility of a subsequent change. For example, in determining whether a married applicant's interest in jointly owned property is sufficient to satisfy the creditor's standards of creditworthiness for individual credit, a creditor may not consider that the applicant's separate property could be transferred into tenancy by the entirety after consummation. Similarly, a creditor may not consider the possibility that the couple may divorce. Accordingly, a creditor may not require the signature of the ~~nonapplicant~~non-applicant spouse in these or similar circumstances.

ii. *Other options to support credit.* If the applicant's interest in jointly owned property does not support the amount and terms of credit sought, the creditor may offer the applicant other options to qualify for the extension of credit. For example:
A. Providing a co-signer or other party (§ ~~202.7~~1002.7(d)(5));
B. Requesting that the credit be granted on a secured basis (§ ~~202.7~~1002.7(d)(4)); or
C. Providing the signature of the joint owner on an instrument that ensures access to the property in the event of the applicant's death or default, but does not impose personal liability unless necessary under state law (such as a limited guarantee). A creditor may not routinely require, however, that a joint owner sign an instrument (such as a quitclaim deed) that would result in the forfeiture of the joint owner's interest in the property.

2. *Need for signature—reasonable belief.* A creditor's reasonable belief as to what instruments need to be signed by a person other than the applicant should be supported by a thorough review of pertinent statutory and decisional law or an opinion of the state attorney general.

Paragraph 7(d)(3).

1. *Residency.* In assessing the creditworthiness of a person who applies for credit in a community property state, a creditor may assume that the applicant is a resident of the state unless the applicant indicates otherwise.

Paragraph 7(d)(4).

1. *Creation of enforceable lien.* Some state laws require that both spouses join in executing any instrument by which real property is encumbered. If an applicant offers such property as security for credit, a creditor may require the applicant's spouse to sign the instruments necessary to create a valid security interest in the property. The creditor may

not require the spouse to sign the note evidencing the credit obligation if signing only the mortgage or other security agreement is sufficient to make the property available to satisfy the debt in the event of default. However, if under state law both spouses must sign the note to create an enforceable lien, the creditor may require the signatures.

2. *Need for signature—reasonable belief.* Generally, a signature to make the secured property available will only be needed on a security agreement. A creditor's reasonable belief that, to ensure access to the property, the spouse's signature is needed on an instrument that imposes personal liability should be supported by a thorough review of pertinent statutory and decisional law or an opinion of the state attorney general.

3. *Integrated instruments.* When a creditor uses an integrated instrument that combines the note and the security agreement, the spouse cannot be asked to sign the integrated instrument if the signature is only needed to grant a security interest. But the spouse could be asked to sign an integrated instrument that makes clear—for example, by a legend placed next to the spouse's signature—that the spouse's signature is only to grant a security interest and that signing the instrument does not impose personal liability.

Paragraph 7(d)(5).

1. *Qualifications of additional parties.* In establishing guidelines for eligibility of guarantors, cosigners, or similar additional parties, a creditor may restrict the applicant's choice of additional parties but may not discriminate on the basis of sex, marital status, or any other prohibited basis. For example, the creditor could require that the additional party live in the creditor's market area.

2. *Reliance on income of another person—individual credit.* An applicant who requests individual credit relying on the income of another person (including a spouse in a non-community property state) may be required to provide the signature of the other person to make the income available to pay the debt. In community property states, the signature of a spouse may be required if the applicant relies on the spouse's separate income. If the applicant relies on the spouse's future earnings that as a matter of state law cannot be characterized as community property until earned, the creditor may require the spouse's signature, but need not do so—even if it is the creditor's practice to require the signature when an applicant relies on the future earnings of a person other than a spouse. (See § ~~202.6~~1002.6(c) on consideration of state property laws.)

3. *Renewals.* If the borrower's creditworthiness is reevaluated when a credit obligation is renewed, the creditor must determine whether an additional party is still warranted and, if not warranted, release the additional party.

Paragraph 7(d)(6).

1. *Guarantees.* A guarantee on an extension of credit is part of a credit transaction and therefore

subject to the regulation. A creditor may require the personal guarantee of the partners, directors, or officers of a business, and the shareholders of a closely held corporation, even if the business or corporation is creditworthy. The requirement must be based on the guarantor's relationship with the business or corporation, however, and not on a prohibited basis. For example, a creditor may not require guarantees only for women-owned or minority-owned businesses. Similarly, a creditor may not require guarantees only of the married officers of a business or the married shareholders of a closely held corporation.

2. *Spousal guarantees.* The rules in § ~~202.7~~ 1002.7(d) bar a creditor from requiring the signature of a guarantor's spouse just as they bar the creditor from requiring the signature of an applicant's spouse. For example, although a creditor may require all officers of a closely held corporation to personally guarantee a corporate loan, the creditor may not automatically require that spouses of married officers also sign the guarantee. If an evaluation of the financial circumstances of an officer indicates that an additional signature is necessary, however, the creditor may require the signature of another person in appropriate circumstances in accordance with § ~~202.7~~1002.7(d)(2).

7(e) Insurance.

1. *Differences in terms.* Differences in the availability, rates, and other terms on which credit-related casualty insurance or credit life, health, accident, or disability insurance is offered or provided to an applicant does not violate Regulation B.

2. *Insurance information.* A creditor may obtain information about an applicant's age, sex, or marital status for insurance purposes. The information may only be used for determining eligibility and premium rates for insurance, however, and not in making the credit decision.

Section ~~202.8~~1002.8—Special Purpose Credit Programs

8(a) Standards for programs.

1. *Determining qualified programs.* The ~~Board~~Bureau does not determine whether individual programs qualify for special purpose credit status, or whether a particular program benefits an "economically disadvantaged class of persons." The agency or creditor administering or offering the loan program must make these decisions regarding the status of its program.

2. *Compliance with a program authorized by* ~~federal~~*Federal or state law.* A creditor does not violate Regulation B when it complies in good faith with a regulation promulgated by a government agency implementing a special purpose credit program under § ~~202.8~~1002.8(a)(1). It is the agency's responsibility to promulgate a regulation that is consistent with ~~federal~~Federal and state law.

3. *Expressly authorized.* Credit programs authorized by ~~federal~~Federal or state law include programs offered pursuant to ~~federal~~Federal, state, or local statute, regulation or ordinance, or pursuant to judicial or administrative order.

4. *Creditor liability.* A refusal to grant credit to an applicant is not a violation of the Act or regulation if the applicant does not meet the eligibility requirements under a special purpose credit program.

5. *Determining need.* In designing a special purpose credit program under § ~~202.8~~1002.8(a), a for-profit organization must determine that the program will benefit a class of people who would otherwise be denied credit or would receive it on less favorable terms. This determination can be based on a broad analysis using the organization's own research or data from outside sources, including governmental reports and studies. For example, a creditor might design new products to reach consumers who would not meet, or have not met, its traditional standards of creditworthiness due to such factors as credit inexperience or the use of credit sources that may not report to consumer reporting agencies. Or, a bank could review Home Mortgage Disclosure Act data along with demographic data for its assessment area and conclude that there is a need for a special purpose credit program for low-income minority borrowers.

6. *Elements of the program.* The written plan must contain information that supports the need for the particular program. The plan also must either state a specific period of time for which the program will last, or contain a statement regarding when the program will be reevaluated to determine if there is a continuing need for it.

8(b) Rules in other sections.

1. *Applicability of rules.* A creditor that rejects an application because the applicant does not meet the eligibility requirements (common characteristic or financial need, for example) must nevertheless notify the applicant of action taken as required by § ~~202.9~~1002.9.

8(c) Special rule concerning requests and use of information.

1. *Request of prohibited basis information.* This section permits a creditor to request and consider certain information that would otherwise be prohibited by §§ ~~202.5~~1002.5 and ~~202.6~~1002.6 to determine an applicant's eligibility for a particular program.

2. *Examples.* Examples of programs under which the creditor can ask for and consider information about a prohibited basis are:

   i. Energy conservation programs to assist the elderly, for which the creditor must consider the applicant's age.

   ii. Programs under a Minority Enterprise Small Business Investment Corporation, for which a creditor must consider the applicant's minority status.

8(d) Special rule in the case of financial need.

1. *Request of prohibited basis information.* This section permits a creditor to request and consider certain information that would otherwise be prohibited by §§ ~~202.5~~1002.5 and ~~202.6,~~1002.6, and to require signatures that would otherwise be prohibited by § ~~202.7~~1002.7(d).

2. *Examples.* Examples of programs in which financial need is a criterion are:

   i. Subsidized housing programs for low- to moderate-income households, for which a creditor may have to consider the applicant's receipt of alimony or child support, the spouse's or parents' income, etc.

   ii. Student loan programs based on the family's financial need, for which a creditor may have to consider the spouse's or parents' financial resources.

3. *Student loans.* In a guaranteed student loan program, a creditor may obtain the signature of a parent as a guarantor when required by ~~federal~~Federal or state law or agency regulation, or when the student does not meet the creditor's standards of creditworthiness. (See § ~~202.7~~§§ 1002.7(d)(1) and (5).) The creditor may not require an additional signature when a student has a work or credit history that satisfies the creditor's standards.

Section ~~202.9~~1002.9— Notifications

1. *Use of the term adverse action.* The regulation does not require that a creditor use the term adverse action in communicating to an applicant that a request for an extension of credit has not been approved. In notifying an applicant of adverse action as defined by § ~~202.2~~1002.2(c)(1), a creditor may use any words or phrases that describe the action taken on the application.

2. *Expressly withdrawn applications.* When an applicant expressly withdraws a credit application, the creditor is not required to comply with the notification requirements under § ~~202.9~~1002.9. (The creditor must comply, however, with the record retention requirements of the regulation. See § ~~202.12~~1002.12(b)(3).)

3. *When notification occurs.* Notification occurs when a creditor delivers or mails a notice to the applicant's last known address or, in the case of an oral notification, when the creditor communicates the credit decision to the applicant.

4. *Location of notice.* The notifications required under § ~~202.9~~1002.9 may appear on either or both sides of a form or letter.

5. *Prequalification requests.* Whether a creditor must provide a notice of action taken for a prequalification request depends on the creditor's response to the request, as discussed in comment 2(f)-3. For instance, a creditor may treat the request as an inquiry if the creditor evaluates specific information about the consumer and tells the consumer the

loan amount, rate, and other terms of credit the consumer could qualify for under various loan programs, explaining the process the consumer must follow to submit a mortgage application and the information the creditor will analyze in reaching a credit decision. On the other hand, a creditor has treated a request as an application, and is subject to the adverse action notice requirements of § ~~202.9~~ 1002.9 if, after evaluating information, the creditor decides that it will not approve the request and communicates that decision to the consumer. For example, if the creditor tells the consumer that it would not approve an application for a mortgage because of a bankruptcy in the consumer's record, the creditor has denied an application for credit.

9(a) Notification of action taken, ECOA notice, and statement of specific reasons.

Paragraph 9(a)(1).

1. *Timing of notice—when an application is complete.* Once a creditor has obtained all the information it normally considers in making a credit decision, the application is complete and the creditor has 30 days in which to notify the applicant of the credit decision. (See also comment 2(f)-6.)

2. *Notification of approval.* Notification of approval may be express or by implication. For example, the creditor will satisfy the notification requirement when it gives the applicant the credit card, money, property, or services requested.

3. *Incomplete application—denial for incompleteness.* When an application is incomplete regarding information that the applicant can provide and the creditor lacks sufficient data for a credit decision, the creditor may deny the application giving as the reason for denial that the application is incomplete. The creditor has the option, alternatively, of providing a notice of incompleteness under § ~~202.9~~ 1002.9(c).

4. *Incomplete application—denial for reasons other than incompleteness.* When an application is missing information but provides sufficient data for a credit decision, the creditor may evaluate the application, make its credit decision, and notify the applicant accordingly. If credit is denied, the applicant must be given the specific reasons for the credit denial (or notice of the right to receive the reasons); in this instance missing information or "incomplete application" cannot be given as the reason for the denial.

5. *Length of counteroffer.* Section ~~202.9~~1002.9(a) (1)(iv) does not require a creditor to hold a counteroffer open for 90 days or any other particular length of time.

6. *Counteroffer combined with adverse action notice.* A creditor that gives the applicant a combined counteroffer and adverse action notice that complies with § ~~202.9~~1002.9(a)(2) need not send a second adverse action notice if the applicant does not accept the counteroffer. A sample of a com-

bined notice is contained in form C-4 of Appendix C to the regulation.

7. *Denial of a telephone application.* When an application is made by telephone and adverse action is taken, the creditor must request the applicant's name and address in order to provide written notification under this section. If the applicant declines to provide that information, then the creditor has no further notification responsibility.

Paragraph 9(a)(3).

1. *Coverage.* In determining which rules in this paragraph apply to a given business credit application, a creditor may rely on the applicant's assertion about the revenue size of the business. (Applications to start a business are governed by the rules in § ~~202.9~~1002.9(a)(3)(i).) If an applicant applies for credit as a sole proprietor, the revenues of the sole proprietorship will determine which rules govern the application. However, if an applicant applies for business credit as an individual, the rules in § ~~202.9~~1002.9(a)(3)(i) apply unless the application is for trade or similar credit.

2. *Trade credit.* The term trade credit generally is limited to a financing arrangement that involves a buyer and a seller—such as a supplier who finances the sale of equipment, supplies, or inventory; it does not apply to an extension of credit by a bank or other financial institution for the financing of such items.

3. *Factoring.* Factoring refers to a purchase of accounts receivable, and thus is not subject to the Act or regulation. If there is a credit extension incident to the factoring arrangement, the notification rules in § ~~202.9~~1002.9(a)(3)(ii) apply, as do other relevant sections of the Act and regulation.

4. *Manner of compliance.* In complying with the notice provisions of the Act and regulation, creditors offering business credit may follow the rules governing consumer credit. Similarly, creditors may elect to treat all business credit the same (irrespective of revenue size) by providing notice in accordance with § ~~202.9~~1002.9(a)(3)(i).

5. *Timing of notification.* A creditor subject to § ~~202.9~~1002.9(a)(3)(ii)(A) is required to notify a business credit applicant, orally or in writing, of action taken on an application within a reasonable time of receiving a completed application. Notice provided in accordance with the timing requirements of § ~~202.9~~1002.9(a)(1) is deemed reasonable in all instances.

9(b) Form of ECOA notice and statement of specific reasons.

Paragraph 9(b)(1).

1. *Substantially similar notice.* The ECOA notice sent with a notification of a credit denial or other adverse action will comply with the regulation if it is "substantially similar" to the notice contained in § ~~202.9~~1002.9(b)(1). For example, a creditor may add a reference to the fact that the ECOA permits age to be considered in certain credit scoring sys-

tems, or add a reference to a similar state statute or regulation and to a state enforcement agency.

Paragraph 9(b)(2).

1. *Number of specific reasons.* A creditor must disclose the principal reasons for denying an application or taking other adverse action. The regulation does not mandate that a specific number of reasons be disclosed, but disclosure of more than four reasons is not likely to be helpful to the applicant.

2. *Source of specific reasons.* The specific reasons disclosed under §§ ~~202.9~~1002.9(a)(2) and (b)(2) must relate to and accurately describe the factors actually considered or scored by a creditor.

3. *Description of reasons.* A creditor need not describe how or why a factor adversely affected an applicant. For example, the notice may say "length of residence" rather than "too short a period of residence."

4. *Credit scoring system.* If a creditor bases the denial or other adverse action on a credit scoring system, the reasons disclosed must relate only to those factors actually scored in the system. Moreover, no factor that was a principal reason for adverse action may be excluded from disclosure. The creditor must disclose the actual reasons for denial (for example, "age of automobile") even if the relationship of that factor to predicting creditworthiness may not be clear to the applicant.

5. *Credit scoring—method for selecting reasons.* The regulation does not require that any one method be used for selecting reasons for a credit denial or other adverse action that is based on a credit scoring system. Various methods will meet the requirements of the regulation. One method is to identify the factors for which the applicant's score fell furthest below the average score for each of those factors achieved by applicants whose total score was at or slightly above the minimum passing score. Another method is to identify the factors for which the applicant's score fell furthest below the average score for each of those factors achieved by all applicants. These average scores could be calculated during the development or use of the system. Any other method that produces results substantially similar to either of these methods is also acceptable under the regulation.

6. *Judgmental system.* If a creditor uses a judgmental system, the reasons for the denial or other adverse action must relate to those factors in the applicant's record actually reviewed by the person making the decision.

7. *Combined credit scoring and judgmental system.* If a creditor denies an application based on a credit evaluation system that employs both credit scoring and judgmental components, the reasons for the denial must come from the component of the system that the applicant failed. For example, if a creditor initially credit scores an application and denies the credit request as a result of that scoring, the reasons disclosed to the applicant must relate to the factors scored in the system. If the application

passes the credit scoring stage but the creditor then denies the credit request based on a judgmental assessment of the applicant's record, the reasons disclosed must relate to the factors reviewed judgmentally, even if the factors were also considered in the credit scoring component. If the application is not approved or denied as a result of the credit scoring, but falls into a gray band, and the creditor performs a judgmental assessment and denies the credit after that assessment, the reasons disclosed must come from both components of the system. The same result applies where a judgmental assessment is the first component of the combined system. As provided in comment 9(b)(2)-1, disclosure of more than a combined total of four reasons is not likely to be helpful to the applicant.

8. *Automatic denial.* Some credit decision methods contain features that call for automatic denial because of one or more negative factors in the applicant's record (such as the applicant's previous bad credit history with that creditor, the applicant's declaration of bankruptcy, or the fact that the applicant is a minor). When a creditor denies the credit request because of an automatic-denial factor, the creditor must disclose that specific factor.

9. *Combined ECOA-FCRA disclosures.* The ECOA requires disclosure of the principal reasons for denying or taking other adverse action on an application for an extension of credit. The Fair Credit Reporting Act (FCRA) requires a creditor to disclose when it has based its decision in whole or in part on information from a source other than the applicant or its own files. Disclosing that a ~~consumer~~credit report was obtained and used in the denial of the application, as the FCRA requires, does not satisfy the ECOA requirement to disclose specific reasons. For example, if the applicant's credit history reveals delinquent credit obligations and the application is denied for that reason, to satisfy § ~~202.9~~1002.9(b)(2) the creditor must disclose that the application was denied because of the applicant's delinquent credit obligations. The FCRA also requires a creditor to disclose, as applicable, a credit score it used in taking adverse action along with related information, including up to four key factors that adversely affected the consumer's credit score (or up to five factors if the number of inquiries made with respect to that consumer report is a key factor). Disclosing the key factors that adversely affected the consumer's credit score does not satisfy the ECOA requirement to disclose specific reasons for denying or taking other adverse action on an application or extension of credit. Sample forms C-1 through C-5 of Appendix C of the regulation provide for both the ECOA and FCRA disclosures. See also comment 9(~~ab~~)(2)-1.

9(c) Incomplete applications.

Paragraph 9(c)(1).

1. *Exception for preapprovals.* The requirement to provide a notice of incompleteness does not apply to preapprovals that constitute applications under § ~~202.2~~1002.2(f).

Paragraph 9(c)(2).

1. *Reapplication.* If information requested by a creditor is submitted by an applicant after the expiration of the time period designated by the creditor, the creditor may require the applicant to make a new application.

Paragraph 9(c)(3).

1. *Oral inquiries for additional information.* If an applicant fails to provide the information in response to an oral request, a creditor must send a written notice to the applicant within the 30-day period specified in § ~~202.9~~§§ 1002.9(c)(1) and (2). If the applicant provides the information, the creditor must take action on the application and notify the applicant in accordance with § ~~202.9~~1002.9(a).

9(g) Applications submitted through a third party.

1. *Third parties.* The notification of adverse action may be given by one of the creditors to whom an application was submitted, or by a noncreditor third party. If one notification is provided on behalf of multiple creditors, the notice must contain the name and address of each creditor. The notice must either disclose the applicant's right to a statement of specific reasons within 30 days, or give the primary reasons each creditor relied upon in taking the adverse action—clearly indicating which reasons relate to which creditor.

2. *Third party notice—enforcement agency.* If a single adverse action notice is being provided to an applicant on behalf of several creditors and they are under the jurisdiction of different ~~federal~~Federal enforcement agencies, the notice need not name each agency; disclosure of any one of them will suffice.

3. *Third-party notice—liability.* When a notice is to be provided through a third party, a creditor is not liable for an act or omission of the third party that constitutes a violation of the regulation if the creditor accurately and in a timely manner provided the third party with the information necessary for the notification and maintains reasonable procedures adapted to prevent such violations.

Section ~~202.10~~1002.10— Furnishing of Credit Information

1. *Scope.* The requirements of § ~~202.10~~1002.10 for designating and reporting credit information apply only to consumer credit transactions. Moreover, they apply only to creditors that opt to furnish credit information to credit bureaus or to other creditors; there is no requirement that a creditor furnish credit information on its accounts.

2. *Reporting on all accounts.* The requirements of § ~~202.10~~1002.10 apply only to accounts held or used by spouses. However, a creditor has the option to designate all joint accounts (or all accounts with an authorized user) to reflect the participation of both parties, whether or not the accounts are held by persons married to each other.

3. *Designating accounts.* In designating accounts and reporting credit information, a creditor need not distinguish between accounts on which the spouse is an authorized user and accounts on which the spouse is a contractually liable party.

4. *File and index systems.* The regulation does not require the creation or maintenance of separate files in the name of each participant on a joint or user account, or require any other particular system of recordkeeping or indexing. It requires only that a creditor be able to report information in the name of each spouse on accounts covered by § ~~202.10.~~ 1002.10. Thus, if a creditor receives a credit inquiry about the wife, it should be able to locate her credit file without asking the husband's name.

10(a) Designation of accounts.

1. *New parties.* When new parties who are spouses undertake a legal obligation on an account, as in the case of a mortgage loan assumption, the creditor must change the designation on the account to reflect the new parties and must furnish subsequent credit information on the account in the new names.

2. *Request to change designation of account.* A request to change the manner in which information concerning an account is furnished does not alter the legal liability of either spouse on the account and does not require a creditor to change the name in which the account is maintained.

Section ~~202.11~~1002.11—Relation to State Law

11(a) Inconsistent state laws.

1. *Preemption determination—New York.* The ~~Board has~~Bureau recognizes state law preemption determinations made by the Board of Governors of the Federal Reserve System prior to July 21, 2011, until and unless the Bureau makes and publishes any contrary determination. The Board of Governors determined that the following provisions in the state law of New York are preempted by the ~~federal~~Federal law, effective November 11, 1988:

i.   Article 15, section 296a(1)(b)~~—~~. Unlawful discriminatory practices in relation to credit on the basis of race, creed, color, national origin, age, sex, marital status, or disability. This provision is preempted to the extent that it bars taking a prohibited basis into account when establishing eligibility for certain special-purpose credit programs.

ii. Article 15, section 296a(1)(c)~~—~~. Unlawful discriminatory practice to make any record or inquiry based on race, creed, color, national origin, age, sex, marital status, or disability. This provision is preempted to the extent that it bars a creditor from requesting and considering information regarding the particular characteristics (for example, race, national origin, or sex) required for eligibility for special-purpose credit programs.

2. *Preemption determination—Ohio.* The ~~Board has~~ Bureau recognizes state law preemption determinations made by the Board of Governors of the Federal Reserve System prior to July 21, 2011, until and unless the Bureau makes and publishes any contrary determination. The Board of Governors determined that the following provision in the state law of Ohio is preempted by the ~~federal~~Federal law, effective July 23, 1990:

i. Section 4112.021(B)(1)—Unlawful discriminatory practices in credit transactions. This provision is preempted to the extent that it bars asking or favorably considering the age of an elderly applicant; prohibits the consideration of age in a credit scoring system; permits without limitation the consideration of age in real estate transactions; and limits the consideration of age in special-purpose credit programs to certain government-sponsored programs identified in the state law.

Section ~~202.12~~1002.12—Record Retention

12(a) Retention of prohibited information.

1. *Receipt of prohibited information.* Unless the creditor specifically requested such information, a creditor does not violate this section when it receives prohibited information from a consumer reporting agency.

2. *Use of retained information.* Although a creditor may keep in its files prohibited information as provided in § ~~202.12~~1002.12(a), the creditor may use the information in evaluating credit applications only if permitted to do so by § ~~202.6.~~1002.6.

12(b) Preservation of records.

1. *Copies.* Copies of the original record include carbon copies, photocopies, microfilm or microfiche copies, or copies produced by any other accurate retrieval system, such as documents stored and reproduced by computer. A creditor that uses a computerized or mechanized system need not keep a paper copy of a document (for example, of an adverse action notice) if it can regenerate all pertinent information in a timely manner for examination or other purposes.

2. *Computerized decisions.* A creditor that enters information items from a written application into a computerized or mechanized system and makes the credit decision mechanically, based only on the items of information entered into the system, may comply with § ~~202.12~~1002.12(b) by retaining the information actually entered. It is not required to store the complete written application, nor is it required to enter the remaining items of information into the system. If the transaction is subject to § ~~202.13,~~1002.13, however, the creditor is required to enter and retain the data on personal character-

istics in order to comply with the requirements of that section.

Paragraph 12(b)(3).

1. *Withdrawn and brokered applications.* In most cases, the 25-month retention period for applications runs from the date a notification is sent to the applicant granting or denying the credit requested. In certain transactions, a creditor is not obligated to provide a notice of the action taken. (See, for example, comment 9-2.) In such cases, the 25-month requirement runs from the date of application, as when:

i. An application is withdrawn by the applicant.

ii. An application is submitted to more than one creditor on behalf of the applicant, and the application is approved by one of the other creditors.

12(b)(6) Self-tests.

1. The rule requires all written or recorded information about a self-test to be retained for 25 months after a self-test has been completed. For this purpose, a self-test is completed after the creditor has obtained the results and made a determination about what corrective action, if any, is appropriate. Creditors are required to retain information about the scope of the self-test, the methodology used and time period covered by the self-test, the report or results of the self-test including any analysis or conclusions, and any corrective action taken in response to the self-test.

12(b)(7) Preapplication marketing information.

1. *Prescreened credit solicitations.* The rule requires creditors to retain copies of prescreened credit solicitations. For purposes of this ~~regulation~~ ~~part,~~ a prescreened solicitation is an "offer of credit" as described in 15 U.S.C. 1681a(1) of the Fair Credit Reporting Act. A creditor complies with this rule if it retains a copy of each solicitation mailing that contains different terms, such as the amount of credit offered, annual percentage rate, or annual fee.

2. *List of criteria.* A creditor must retain the list of criteria used to select potential recipients. This includes the criteria used by the creditor both to determine the potential recipients of the particular solicitation and to determine who will actually be offered credit.

3. *Correspondence.* A creditor may retain correspondence relating to consumers' complaints about prescreened solicitations in any manner that is reasonably accessible and is understandable to examiners. There is no requirement to establish a separate database or set of files for such correspondence, or to match consumer complaints with specific solicitation programs.

Section ~~202.13~~1002.13— Information for Monitoring Purposes

13(a) Information to be requested.

1. *Natural person.* Section ~~202.13~~1002.13 applies only to applications from natural persons.

2. *Principal residence.* The requirements of § ~~202.13~~1002.13 apply only if an application relates to a dwelling that is or will be occupied by the applicant as the principal residence. A credit application related to a vacation home or a rental unit is not covered. In the case of a two-to four-unit dwelling, the application is covered if the applicant intends to occupy one of the units as a principal residence.

3. *Temporary financing.* An application for temporary financing to construct a dwelling is not subject to § ~~202.13.~~1002.13. But an application for both a temporary loan to finance construction of a dwelling and a permanent mortgage loan to take effect upon the completion of construction is subject to § ~~202.13.~~1002.13.

4. *New principal residence.* A person can have only one principal residence at a time. However, if a person buys or builds a new dwelling that will become that person's principal residence within a year or upon completion of construction, the new dwelling is considered the principal residence for purposes of § ~~202.13.~~1002.13.

5. *Transactions not covered.* The information-collection requirements of this section apply to applications for credit primarily for the purchase or refinancing of a dwelling that is or will become the applicant's principal residence. Therefore, applications for credit secured by the applicant's principal residence but made primarily for a purpose other than the purchase or refinancing of the principal residence (such as loans for home improvement and debt consolidation) are not subject to the information-collection requirements. An application for an open-end home equity line of credit is not subject to this section unless it is readily apparent to the creditor when the application is taken that the primary purpose of the line is for the purchase or refinancing of a principal dwelling.

6. *Refinancings.* A refinancing occurs when an existing obligation is satisfied and replaced by a new obligation undertaken by the same borrower. A creditor that receives an application to refinance an existing extension of credit made by that creditor for the purchase of the applicant's dwelling may request the monitoring information again but is not required to do so if it was obtained in the earlier transaction.

7. *Data collection under Regulation C.* See comment 5(a)(2)-2.

13(b) Obtaining of information.

1. *Forms for collecting data.* A creditor may collect the information specified in § ~~202.13~~1002.13(a) ei-

ther on an application form or on a separate form referring to the application. The applicant must be offered the option to select more than one racial designation.

2. *Written applications.* The regulation requires written applications for the types of credit covered by § ~~202.13.~~1002.13. A creditor can satisfy this requirement by recording on paper or by means of computer the information that the applicant provides orally and that the creditor normally considers in a credit decision.

3. *Telephone, mail applications.*

i. A creditor that accepts an application by telephone or mail must request the monitoring information.

ii. A creditor that accepts an application by mail need not make a special request for the monitoring information if the applicant has failed to provide it on the application form returned to the creditor.

iii. If it is not evident on the face of an application that it was received by mail, telephone, or via an electronic medium, the creditor should indicate on the form or other application record how the application was received.

4. *Video and other electronic-application processes.*

i. If a creditor takes an application through an electronic medium that allows the creditor to see the applicant, the creditor must treat the application as taken in person. The creditor must note the monitoring information on the basis of visual observation or surname, if the applicant chooses not to provide the information.

ii. If an applicant applies through an electronic medium without video capability, the creditor treats the application as if it were received by mail.

5. *Applications through loan-shopping services.* When a creditor receives an application through an unaffiliated loan-shopping service, it does not have to request the monitoring information for purposes of the ECOA or Regulation B. Creditors subject to the Home Mortgage Disclosure Act should be aware, however, that data collection may be called for under Regulation C (12 CFR part ~~203~~1003), which generally requires creditors to report, among other things, the sex and race of an applicant on brokered applications or applications received through a correspondent.

6. *Inadvertent notation.* If a creditor inadvertently obtains the monitoring information in a dwelling-related transaction not covered by § ~~202.13,~~1002.13, the creditor may process and retain the application without violating the regulation.

13(c) Disclosure to applicants.

1. *Procedures for providing disclosures.* The disclosure to an applicant regarding the monitoring information may be provided in writing. Appendix B contains a sample disclosure. A creditor may devise its own disclosure so long as it is substan-

tially similar. The creditor need not orally request the monitoring information if it is requested in writing.

13(d) Substitute monitoring program.

1. *Substitute program.* An enforcement agency may adopt, under its established rulemaking or enforcement procedures, a program requiring creditors under its jurisdiction to collect information in addition to information required by this section.

Section 1002.14—Rules on Providing Appraisals and Valuations

14(a) Providing appraisals and other valuations.

1. *Multiple applicants.* If there is more than one applicant, the written disclosure about written appraisals, and the copies of appraisals and other written valuations, need only be given to one applicant. However, these materials must be given to the primary applicant where one is readily apparent. Similarly, if there is more than one applicant for credit in the transaction, one applicant may provide a waiver under § 1002.14(a)(1), but it must be the primary applicant where one is readily apparent.

14(a)(1) In general.

1. *Coverage.* Section 1002.14 covers applications for credit to be secured by a first lien on a dwelling, as that term is defined in § 1002.14(b)(2), whether the credit is for a business purpose (for example, a loan to start a business) or a consumer purpose (for example, a loan to purchase a home).

2. *Renewals.* Section 1002.14(a)(1) applies when an applicant requests the renewal of an existing extension of credit and the creditor develops a new appraisal or other written valuation. Section 1002.14(a)(1) does not apply to the extent a creditor uses the appraisals and other written valuations that were previously developed in connection with the prior extension of credit to evaluate the renewal request.

3. *Written.* For purposes of § 1002.14, an "appraisal or other written valuation" includes, without limitation, an appraisal or other valuation received or developed by the creditor in paper form (hard copy); electronically, such as CD or email; or by any other similar media. See § 1002.14(a)(5) regarding the provision of copies of appraisals and other written valuations to applicants via electronic means.

4. *Timing.* Section 1002.14(a)(1) requires that the creditor "provide" copies of appraisals and other written valuations to the applicant "promptly upon completion," or no later than three business days before consummation (for

closed-end credit) or account opening (for open-end credit), whichever is earlier.

i. For purposes of this timing requirement, "provide" means "deliver." Delivery occurs three business days after mailing or delivering the copies to the last-known address of the applicant, or when evidence indicates actual receipt by the applicant, whichever is earlier. Delivery to or actual receipt by the applicant by electronic means must comply with the E-Sign Act, as provided for in § 1002.14(a)(5).

ii. The application and meaning of the "promptly upon completion" standard depends upon the facts and circumstances, including but not limited to when the creditor receives the appraisal or other written valuation, and the extent of any review or revision after the creditor receives it.

iii. "Completion" occurs when the last version is received by the creditor, or when the creditor has reviewed and accepted the appraisal or other written valuation to include any changes or corrections required, whichever is later. See also comment 14(a)(1)-7.

iv. In a transaction that is being consummated (for closed-end credit) or in which the account is being opened (for open-end credit), if an appraisal or other written valuation has been developed but is not yet complete, the deadline for providing a copy of three business days before consummation or account opening still applies, unless the applicant waived that deadline as provided under § 1002.14(a)(1), in which case the copy must be provided at or before consummation or account opening.

v. Even if the transaction will not be consummated (for closed-end credit) or the account will not be opened (for open-end credit), the copy must be provided "promptly upon completion" as provided for in § 1002.14(a)(1), unless the applicant has waived that deadline as provided under § 1002.14(a)(1), in which case as provided for in § 1002.14(a)(1) the copy must be provided to the applicant no later than 30 days after the creditor determines the transaction will not be consummated or the account will not be opened.

5. *Promptly upon completion—examples.* Examples in which the "promptly upon completion" standard would be satisfied include, but are not limited to, those in subparagraphs i, ii, and iii below. Examples in which the "promptly upon completion" standard would not be satisfied include, but are not limited to, those in subparagraphs iv and v below.

i. *Sending a copy of an appraisal within a week of completion with sufficient time before consummation (or account open-*

ing for open-end credit). On day 15 after receipt of the application, the creditor's underwriting department reviews an appraisal and determines it is acceptable. One week later, the creditor sends a copy of the appraisal to the applicant. The applicant actually receives the copy more than three business days before the date of consummation (or account opening). The creditor has provided the copy of the appraisal promptly upon completion.

ii. *Sending a copy of a revised appraisal within a week after completion and with sufficient time before consummation (or account opening for open-end credit).* An appraisal is being revised, and the creditor does not receive the revised appraisal until day 45 after the application, when the creditor immediately determines the revised appraisal is acceptable. A week later, the creditor sends a copy of the revised appraisal to the applicant, and does not send a copy of the initial appraisal to the applicant. The applicant actually receives the copy of the revised appraisal three business days before the date of consummation (or account opening). The creditor has provided the appraisal copy promptly upon completion.

iii. *Sending a copy of an AVM report within a week after its receipt and with sufficient time before consummation (or account opening for open-end credit).* The creditor receives an automated valuation model (AVM) report on day 5 after receipt of the application and treats the AVM report as complete when it is received. On day 12 after receipt of the application, the creditor sends the applicant a copy of the valuation. The applicant actually receives the valuation more than three business days before the date of consummation (or account opening). The creditor has provided the copy of the AVM report promptly upon completion.

iv. *Delay in sending an appraisal.* On day 12 after receipt of the application, the creditor's underwriting department reviews an appraisal and determines it is acceptable. Although the creditor has determined the appraisal is complete, the creditor waits to provide a copy to the applicant until day 42, when the creditor schedules the consummation (or account opening) to occur on day 50. The creditor has not provided the copy of the appraisal promptly upon completion.

v. *Delay in sending an AVM report while waiting for completion of a second valuation.* The creditor receives an AVM report on day 5 after application and completes its review of the AVM report the

day it is received. The creditor also has ordered an appraisal, but the initial version of the appraisal received by the creditor is found to be deficient and is sent for review. The creditor waits 30 days to provide a copy of the completed AVM report, until the appraisal is completed on day 35. The creditor then provides the applicant with copies of the AVM report and the revised appraisal. While the appraisal report was provided promptly upon completion, the AVM report was not.

6. *Waiver.* Section 1002.14(a)(1) permits the applicant to waive the timing requirement if the creditor provides the copies at or before consummation or account opening, except where otherwise prohibited by law. Except where otherwise prohibited by law, an applicant's waiver is effective under § 1002.14(a)(1) in either of the following two situations:

i. If, no later than three business days prior to consummation or account opening, the applicant provides the creditor an affirmative oral or written statement waiving the timing requirement under this rule; or

ii. If, within three business days of consummation or account opening, the applicant provides the creditor an affirmative oral or written statement waiving the timing requirement under this rule and the waiver pertains solely to the applicant's receipt of a copy of an appraisal or other written valuation that contains only clerical changes from a previous version of the appraisal or other written valuation provided to the applicant three or more business days prior to consummation or account opening. For purpose of this second type of waiver, revisions will only be considered to be clerical in nature if they have no impact on the estimated value, and have no impact on the calculation or methodology used to derive the estimate. In addition, under § 1002.14(a)(1) the applicant still must receive the copy of the revision at or prior to consummation or account opening.

7. *Multiple versions of appraisals or valuations.* For purposes of § 1002.14(a)(1), the reference to "all" appraisals and other written valuations does not refer to all versions of the same appraisal or other valuation. If a creditor has received multiple versions of an appraisal or other written valuation, the creditor is required to provide only a copy of the latest version received. If, however, a creditor already has provided a copy of one version of an appraisal or other written valuation to an applicant, and the creditor later receives a revision of that appraisal or other written valuation, then the creditor also must provide the applicant with a copy of the revision to comply with § 1002.14(a)(1). If a creditor receives only one

version of an appraisal or other valuation that is developed in connection with the applicant's application, then that version must be provided to the applicant to comply with § 1002.14(a)(1). See also comment 14(a)(1)-4 above.

14(a)(2) Disclosure.

1. *Appraisal independence requirements not affected.* Nothing in the text of the disclosure required by § 1002.14(a)(2) should be construed to affect, modify, limit, or supersede the operation of any legal, regulatory, or other requirements or standards relating to independence in the conduct of appraisers or the use of applicant-ordered appraisals by creditors.

14(a)(3) Reimbursement.

1. *Photocopy, postage, or other costs.* Creditors may not charge for photocopy, postage, or other costs incurred in providing a copy of an appraisal or other written valuation in accordance with section 14(a)(1).

2. *Reasonable fee for reimbursement.* Section 1002.14(a)(3) does not prohibit a creditor from imposing a reasonable fee to reimburse the creditor's costs of the appraisal or other written valuation, so long as the fee is not increased to cover the costs of providing copies of such appraisals or other written valuations under § 1002.14(a)(1). A creditor's cost may include an administration fee charged to the creditor by an appraisal management company as defined in 12 U.S.C. 3350(11). Section 1002.14(a)(3) does not, however, legally obligate the applicant to pay such fees. Further, creditors may not impose fees for reimbursement of the costs of an appraisal or other valuation where otherwise prohibited by law. For instance, a creditor may not charge a consumer a fee for the performance of a second appraisal if the second appraisal is required under 15 U.S.C. 1639h(b)(2) and 12 CFR 1026.35(c).

14(b) Definitions.

14(b)(1) Consummation.

1. *State law governs.* When a contractual obligation on the consumer's part is created is a matter to be determined under applicable law; § 1002.14 does not make this determination. A contractual commitment agreement, for example, that under applicable law binds the consumer to the credit terms would be consummation. Consummation, however, does not occur merely because the consumer has made some financial investment in the transaction (for example, by paying a nonrefundable fee) unless, of course, applicable law holds otherwise.

2. *Credit vs. sale.* Consummation does not occur when the consumer becomes contractually committed to a sale transaction, unless the

consumer also becomes legally obligated to accept a particular credit arrangement.

14(b)(2) Dwelling.

1. *"Motor vehicles" not covered.* The requirements of § 1002.14 do not apply to "motor vehicles" as defined by 12 U.S.C. 5519(f)(1).

14(b)(3) Valuation.

1. *Valuations—examples.* Examples of valuations include but are not limited to:

 i. A report prepared by an appraiser (whether or not licensed or certified) including the appraiser's estimate or opinion of the property's value.

 ii. A document prepared by the creditor's staff that assigns value to the property.

 iii. A report approved by a government-sponsored enterprise for describing to the applicant the estimate of the property's value developed pursuant to the proprietary methodology or mechanism of the government-sponsored enterprise.

 iv. A report generated by use of an automated valuation model to estimate the property's value.

 v. A broker price opinion prepared by a real estate broker, agent, or sales person to estimate the property's value.

2. *Attachments and exhibits.* The term "valuation" includes any attachments and exhibits that are an integrated part of the valuation.

3. *Other documentation.* Not all documents that discuss or restate a valuation of an applicant's property constitute a "valuation" for purposes of § 1002.14(b)(3). Examples of documents that discuss the valuation of the applicant's property or may reflect its value but nonetheless are not "valuations" include but are not limited to:

 i. Internal documents that merely restate the estimated value of the dwelling contained in an appraisal or written valuation being provided to the applicant.

 ii. Governmental agency statements of appraised value that are publically available.

 iii. Publicly-available lists of valuations (such as published sales prices or mortgage amounts, tax assessments, and retail price ranges).

 iv. Manufacturers' invoices for manufactured homes.

 v. Reports reflecting property inspections that do not provide an estimate or opinion of the value of the property and are not used to develop an estimate or opinion of the value of the property.

[78 Fed. Reg. 7248 (Jan. 31, 2013), eff. Jan. 18, 2014]

Section ~~202.15~~1002.15—Incentives for Self-Testing and Self-Correction

15(a) General rules.

15(a)(1) Voluntary self-testing and correction.

1. Activities required by any governmental authority are not voluntary self-tests. A governmental authority includes both administrative and judicial authorities for ~~federal~~Federal, ~~state~~State, and local governments.

15(a)(2) Corrective action required.

1. To qualify for the privilege, appropriate corrective action is required when the results of a self-test show that it is more likely than not that there has been a violation of the ECOA or this ~~regulation~~part. A self-test is also privileged when it identifies no violations.

2. In some cases, the issue of whether certain information is privileged may arise before the self-test is complete or corrective actions are fully under way. This would not necessarily prevent a creditor from asserting the privilege. In situations where the self-test is not complete, for the privilege to apply the lender must satisfy the regulation's requirements within a reasonable period of time. To assert the privilege where the self-test shows a likely violation, the rule requires, at a minimum, that the creditor establish a plan for corrective action and a method to demonstrate progress in implementing the plan. Creditors must take appropriate corrective action on a timely basis after the results of the self-test are known.

3. A creditor's determination about the type of corrective action needed, or a finding that no corrective action is required, is not conclusive in determining whether the requirements of this paragraph have been satisfied. If a creditor's claim of privilege is challenged, an assessment of the need for corrective action or the type of corrective action that is appropriate must be based on a review of the self-testing results, which may require an *in camera* inspection of the privileged documents.

15(a)(3) Other privileges.

1. A creditor may assert the privilege established under this section in addition to asserting any other privilege that may apply, such as the attorney-client privilege or the work-product privilege. Self-testing data may be privileged under this section whether or not the creditor's assertion of another privilege is upheld.

15(b) Self-test defined.

15(b)(1) Definition.

Paragraph 15(b)(1)(i).

1. To qualify for the privilege, a self-test must be sufficient to constitute a determination of the extent

or effectiveness of the creditor's compliance with the Act and Regulation B. Accordingly, a self-test is only privileged if it was designed and used for that purpose. A self-test that is designed or used to determine compliance with other laws or regulations or for other purposes is not privileged under this rule. For example, a self-test designed to evaluate employee efficiency or customers' satisfaction with the level of service provided by the creditor is not privileged even if evidence of discrimination is uncovered incidentally. If a self-test is designed for multiple purposes, only the portion designed to determine compliance with the ECOA is eligible for the privilege.

Paragraph 15(b)(1)(ii).

1. The principal attribute of self-testing is that it constitutes a voluntary undertaking by the creditor to produce new data or factual information that otherwise would not be available and could not be derived from loan or application files or other records related to credit transactions. Self-testing includes, but is not limited to, the practice of using fictitious applicants for credit (testers), either with or without the use of matched pairs. A creditor may elect to test a defined segment of its business, for example, loan applications processed by a specific branch or loan officer, or applications made for a particular type of credit or loan program. A creditor also may use other methods of generating information that is not available in loan and application files, such as surveying mortgage loan applicants. To the extent permitted by law, creditors might also develop new methods that go beyond traditional pre-application testing, such as hiring testers to submit fictitious loan applications for processing.

2. The privilege does not protect a creditor's analysis performed as part of processing or underwriting a credit application. A creditor's evaluation or analysis of its loan files, Home Mortgage Disclosure Act data, or similar types of records (such as broker or loan officer compensation records) does not produce new information about a creditor's compliance and is not a self-test for purposes of this section. Similarly, a statistical analysis of data derived from existing loan files is not privileged.

15(b)(3) Types of information not privileged.

Paragraph 15(b)(3)(i).

1. The information listed in this paragraph is not privileged and may be used to determine whether the prerequisites for the privilege have been satisfied. Accordingly, a creditor might be asked to identify the self-testing method, for example, whether preapplication testers were used or data were compiled by surveying loan applicants. Information about the scope of the self-test (such as the types of credit transactions examined, or the geographic area covered by the test) also is not privileged.

Paragraph 15(b)(3)(ii).

1. Property appraisal reports, minutes of loan com-

mittee meetings or other documents reflecting the basis for a decision to approve or deny an application, loan policies or procedures, underwriting standards, and broker compensation records are examples of the types of records that are not privileged. If a creditor arranges for testers to submit loan applications for processing, the records are not related to actual credit transactions for purposes of this paragraph and may be privileged self-testing records.

15(c) Appropriate corrective action.

1. The rule only addresses the corrective actions required for a creditor to take advantage of the privilege in this section. A creditor may be required to take other actions or provide additional relief if a formal finding of discrimination is made.

15(c)(1) General requirement.

1. Appropriate corrective action is required even though no violation has been formally adjudicated or admitted by the creditor. In determining whether it is more likely than not that a violation occurred, a creditor must treat testers as if they are actual applicants for credit. A creditor may not refuse to take appropriate corrective action under this section because the self-test used fictitious loan applicants. The fact that a tester's agreement with the creditor waives the tester's legal right to assert a violation does not eliminate the requirement for the creditor to take corrective action, although no remedial relief for the tester is required under paragraph 15(c)(3).

15(c)(2) Determining the scope of appropriate corrective action.

1. Whether a creditor has taken or is taking corrective action that is appropriate will be determined on a case-by-case basis. Generally, the scope of the corrective action that is needed to preserve the privilege is governed by the scope of the self-test. For example, a creditor that self-tests mortgage loans and discovers evidence of discrimination may focus its corrective actions on mortgage loans, and is not required to expand its testing to other types of loans.

2. In identifying the policies or practices that are a likely cause of the violation, a creditor might identify inadequate or improper lending policies, failure to implement established policies, employee conduct, or other causes. The extent and scope of a likely violation may be assessed by determining which areas of operations are likely to be affected by those policies and practices, for example, by determining the types of loans and stages of the application process involved and the branches or offices where the violations may have occurred.

3. Depending on the method and scope of the self-test and the results of the test, appropriate corrective action may include one or more of the following:

    i. If the self-test identifies individuals whose applications were inappropriately processed, offering to extend credit if the application was improperly denied and compensating such persons for out-of-pocket costs and other compensatory damages;

    ii. Correcting institutional policies or procedures that may have contributed to the likely violation, and adopting new policies as appropriate;

    iii. Identifying and then training and/or disciplining the employees involved;

    iv. Developing outreach programs, marketing strategies, or loan products to serve more effectively segments of the lender's markets that may have been affected by the likely discrimination; and

    v. Improving audit and oversight systems to avoid a recurrence of the likely violations.

15(c)(3) Types of relief.

Paragraph 15(c)(3)(ii).

1. The use of pre-application testers to identify policies and practices that illegally discriminate does not require creditors to review existing loan files for the purpose of identifying and compensating applicants who might have been adversely affected.

2. If a self-test identifies a specific applicant who was discriminated against on a prohibited basis, to qualify for the privilege in this section the creditor must provide appropriate remedial relief to that applicant; the creditor is not required to identify other applicants who might also have been adversely affected.

Paragraph 15(c)(3)(iii).

1. A creditor is not required to provide remedial relief to an applicant that would not be available by law. An applicant might also be ineligible for certain types of relief due to changed circumstances. For example, a creditor is not required to offer credit to a denied applicant if the applicant no longer qualifies for the credit due to a change in financial circumstances, although some other type of relief might be appropriate.

15(d)(1) Scope of privilege.

1. The privilege applies with respect to any examination, investigation or proceeding by ~~federal~~Federal, ~~state~~State, or local government agencies relating to compliance with the Act or this ~~regulation~~part. Accordingly, in a case brought under the ECOA, the privilege established under this section preempts any inconsistent laws or court rules to the extent they might require disclosure of privileged self-testing data. The privilege does not apply in other cases (such as in litigation filed solely under a ~~state~~State's fair lending statute). In such cases, if a court orders a creditor to disclose self-test results, the disclosure is not a voluntary disclosure or waiver of the privilege for purposes of paragraph 15(d)(2); a creditor may protect the information by seeking a

protective order to limit availability and use of the self-testing data and prevent dissemination beyond what is necessary in that case. Paragraph 15(d)(1) precludes a party who has obtained privileged information from using it in a case brought under the ECOA, provided the creditor has not lost the privilege through voluntary disclosure under paragraph 15(d)(2).

15(d)(2) Loss of privilege.

Paragraph 15(d)(2)(i).

1. A creditor's corrective action, by itself, is not considered a voluntary disclosure of the self-test report or results. For example, a creditor does not disclose the results of a self-test merely by offering to extend credit to a denied applicant or by inviting the applicant to reapply for credit. Voluntary disclosure could occur under this paragraph, however, if the creditor disclosed the self-test results in connection with a new offer of credit.

2. The disclosure of self-testing results to an independent contractor acting as an auditor or consultant for the creditor on compliance matters does not result in loss of the privilege.

Paragraph 15(d)(2)(ii).

1. The privilege is lost if the creditor discloses privileged information, such as the results of the self-test. The privilege is not lost if the creditor merely reveals or refers to the existence of the self-test.

Paragraph 15(d)(2)(iii).

1. A creditor's claim of privilege may be challenged in a court or administrative law proceeding with appropriate jurisdiction. In resolving the issue, the presiding officer may require the creditor to produce privileged information about the self-test.

15(d)(3) Limited use of privileged information.

1. A creditor may be required to produce privileged documents for the purpose of determining a penalty or remedy after a violation of the ECOA or Regulation B has been formally adjudicated or admitted. A creditor's compliance with such a requirement does not evidence the creditor's intent to forfeit the privilege.

Section ~~202.16~~1002.16— Enforcement, Penalties, and Liabilities

16(c) Failure of compliance.

1. *Inadvertent errors.* Inadvertent errors include, but are not limited to, clerical mistake, calculation error, computer malfunction, and printing error. An error of legal judgment is not an inadvertent error under the regulation.

2. *Correction of error.* For inadvertent errors that

occur under §§ 202.12 1002.12 and 202.13, 1002.13, this section requires that they be corrected prospectively.

Appendix B—Model Application Forms

1. *Freddie Mac/Fannie Mae form—residential loan application.* The uniform residential loan application form (Freddie Mac 65/Fannie Mae 1003), including supplemental form (Freddie Mac 65A/Fannie Mae 1003A), prepared by the Federal Home Loan Mortgage Corporation and the Federal National Mortgage Association and dated October 1992 may be used by creditors without violating this regulation part. Creditors that are governed by the monitoring requirements of this regulation part (which limits collection to applications primarily for the purchase or refinancing of the applicant's principal residence) should delete, strike, or modify the data-collection section on the form when using it for transactions not covered by § 202.13 1002.13(a) to ensure that they do not collect the

information. Creditors that are subject to more extensive collection requirements by a substitute monitoring program under § 202.13 1002.13(d) or by the Home Mortgage Disclosure Act (HMDA) may use the form as issued, in compliance with the substitute program or HMDA.

2. *FHLMC/FNMA form—home improvement loan application.* The home-improvement and energy loan application form (FHLMC 703/FNMA 1012), prepared by the Federal Home Loan Mortgage Corporation and the Federal National Mortgage Association and dated October 1986, complies with the requirements of the regulation for some creditors but not others because of the form's section "Information for Government Monitoring Purposes." Creditors that are governed by § 202.13 1002.13(a) of the regulation (which limits collection to applications primarily for the purchase or refinancing of the applicant's principal residence) should delete, strike, or modify the data-collection section on the form when using it for transactions not covered by § 202.13 1002.13(a) to ensure that they do not collect the information. Creditors that are subject to more extensive collection require-

ments by a substitute monitoring program under § 202.13 1002.13(d) may use the form as issued, in compliance with that substitute program.

Appendix C—Sample Notification Forms

1. Form C-9. Creditors If not otherwise provided under other applicable disclosure requirements, creditors may design their own form, add to, or modify the model form to reflect their individual policies and procedures. For example, a creditor may want to add:

i. i. A telephone number that applicants may call to leave their name and the address to which ana copy of the appraisal report or other written valuation should be sent.

ii. ii. A notice of the cost the applicant will be required to pay the creditor for the appraisal or a copy of the report other valuation.

[78 Fed. Reg. 7216 (Jan. 31, 2013), eff. July 18, 2014]

Appendix D Fair Housing Act Regulations

This appendix reprints selected Fair Housing Act regulations from 24 C.F.R. Part 100, promulgated by the Department of Housing and Urban Development. These regulations, subparts A, B, C, D, and F, are current through May 1, 2013. Subpart E, Housing for Older Persons, is not reprinted. These regulations are also available on the companion website to this treatise, which facilitates key word searches and the importation of relevant provisions into word-processable documents.

AUTHORITY: 42 U.S.C. §§ 3535(d), 3600–3620.

SOURCE: 54 Fed. Reg. 3283 (Jan. 23, 1989); 60 Fed. Reg. 43,327 (Aug. 18, 1995); 61 Fed. Reg. 5205 (Feb. 9, 1996), unless otherwise noted.

Subpart A—General

24 C.F.R. § 100.1 Authority.

This regulation is issued under the authority of the Secretary of Housing and Urban Development to administer and enforce title VIII of the Civil Rights Act of 1968, as amended by the Fair Housing Amendments Act of 1988 (the Fair Housing Act).

24 C.F.R. § 100.5 Scope.

(a) It is the policy of the United States to provide, within constitutional limitations, for fair housing throughout the United States. No person shall be subjected to discrimination because of race, color, religion, sex, handicap, familial status, or national origin in the sale, rental, or advertising of dwellings, in the provision of brokerage services, or in the availability of residential real estate-related transactions.

(b) This part provides the Department's interpretation of the coverage of the Fair Housing Act regarding discrimination related to the sale or rental of dwellings, the provision of services in connection therewith, and the availability of residential real estate-related transactions.

(c) Nothing in this part relieves persons participating in a Federal or Federally-assisted program or activity from other requirements applicable to buildings and dwellings.

24 C.F.R. § 100.10 Exemptions.

(a) This part does not:

(1) Prohibit a religious organization, association, or society, or any nonprofit institution or organization operated, supervised or controlled by or in conjunction with a religious organization, association, or society, from limiting the sale, rental or occupancy of dwellings which it owns or operates for other than a commercial purpose to persons of the same religion, or from giving preference to such persons, unless membership in such religion is restricted because of race, color, or national origin;

(2) Prohibit a private club, not in fact open to the public, which, incident to its primary purpose or purposes, provides lodgings which it owns or operates for other than a commercial purpose, from limiting the rental or occupancy of such lodgings to its members or from giving preference to its members;

(3) Limit the applicability of any reasonable local, State or Federal restrictions regarding the maximum number of occupants permitted to occupy a dwelling; or

(4) Prohibit conduct against a person because such person has been convicted by any court of competent jurisdiction of the illegal manufacture or distribution of a controlled substance as defined in Section 102 of the Controlled Substances Act (21 U.S.C. 802).

(b) Nothing in this part regarding discrimination based on familial status applies with respect to housing for older persons as defined in subpart E of this part.

(c) Nothing in this part, other than the prohibitions against discriminatory advertising, applies to:

(1) The sale or rental of any single family house by an owner, provided the following conditions are met:

(i) The owner does not own or have any interest in more than three single family houses at any one time.

(ii) The house is sold or rented without the use of a real estate broker, agent or salesperson or the facilities of any person in the business of selling or renting dwellings. If the owner selling the house does not reside in it at the time of the sale or was not the most recent resident of the house prior to such sale, the exemption in this paragraph (c)(1) of this section applies to only one such sale in any 24-month period.

(2) Rooms or units in dwellings containing living quarters occupied or intended to be occupied by no more than four families living independently of each other, if the owner actually maintains and occupies one of such living quarters as his or her residence.

24 C.F.R. § 100.20 Definitions.

The terms Department, Fair Housing Act, and Secretary are defined in 24 CFR part 5.[1]

Aggrieved person includes any person who—

(a) Claims to have been injured by a discriminatory housing practice; or

(b) Believes that such person will be injured by a discriminatory housing practice that is about to occur.

Broker or *Agent* includes any person authorized to perform an action on behalf of another person regarding any matter related to the sale or rental of dwellings, including offers, solicitations or contracts and the administration of matters regarding such offers, solicitations or contracts or any residential real estate-related transactions.

Discriminatory housing practice means an act that is unlawful under section 804, 805, 806, or 818 of the Fair Housing Act.

Dwelling means any building, structure or portion thereof which is occupied as, or designed or intended for occupancy as, a residence by one or more families, and any vacant land which is offered for sale or lease for the construction or location thereon of any such building, structure or portion thereof.

Familial status means one or more individuals (who have not attained the age of 18 years) being domiciled with—

(a) A parent or another person having legal custody of such individual or individuals; or

(b) The designee of such parent or other person having such custody, with the written permission of such parent or other person.

The protections afforded against discrimination on the basis of familial status shall apply to any person who is pregnant or is in the process of securing legal custody of any individual who has not attained the age of 18 years.

Handicap is defined in § 100.201.

Person includes one or more individuals, corporations, partnerships, associations, labor organizations, legal representatives, mutual companies, joint-stock companies, trusts, unincorporated organizations, trustees, trustees in cases under title 11 U.S.C., receivers, and fiduciaries.

Person in the business of selling or renting dwellings means any person who:

(a) Within the preceding twelve months, has participated as principal in three or more transactions involving the sale or rental of any dwelling or any interest therein;

(b) Within the preceding twelve months, has participated as agent, other than in the sale of his or her own personal residence, in providing sales or rental facilities or sales or rental services in two or

---

1 [*Editor's Note*: "*Department* means the Department of Housing and Urban Development. . . . *Fair Housing Act* means title VIII of the Civil Rights Act of 1968, as amended by the Fair Housing Amendments Act of 1988 (42 U.S.C. 3601 *et seq.*). . . . *Secretary* means the Secretary of Housing and Urban Development." 24 C.F.R. pt. 5, § 5.100.]

more transactions involving the sale or rental of any dwelling or any interest therein; or

(c) Is the owner of any dwelling designed or intended for occupancy by, or occupied by, five or more families.

State means any of the several states, the District of Columbia, the Commonwealth of Puerto Rico, or any of the territories and possessions of the United States.

Subpart B—Discriminatory Housing Practices

24 C.F.R. § 100.50 Real estate practices prohibited.

(a) This subpart provides the Department's interpretation of conduct that is unlawful housing discrimination under section 804 and section 806 of the Fair Housing Act. In general the prohibited actions are set forth under sections of this subpart which are most applicable to the discriminatory conduct described. However, an action illustrated in one section can constitute a violation under sections in the subpart. For example, the conduct described in § 100.60(b)(3) and (4) would constitute a violation of § 100.65(a) as well as § 100.60(a).

(b) It shall be unlawful to:

(1) Refuse to sell or rent a dwelling after a bona fide offer has been made, or to refuse to negotiate for the sale or rental of a dwelling because of race, color, religion, sex, familial status, or national origin, or to discriminate in the sale or rental of a dwelling because of handicap.

(2) Discriminate in the terms, conditions or privileges of sale or rental of a dwelling, or in the provision of services or facilities in connection with sales or rentals, because of race, color, religion, sex, handicap, familial status, or national origin.

(3) Engage in any conduct relating to the provision of housing which otherwise makes unavailable or denies dwellings to persons because of race, color, religion, sex, handicap, familial status, or national origin.

(4) Make, print or publish, or cause to be made, printed or published, any notice, statement or advertisement with respect to the sale or rental of a dwelling that indicates any preference, limitation or discrimination because of race, color, religion, sex, handicap, familial status, or national origin, or an intention to make any such preference, limitation or discrimination.

(5) Represent to any person because of race, color, religion, sex, handicap, familial status, or national origin that a dwelling is not available for sale or rental when such dwelling is in fact available.

(6) Engage in blockbusting practices in connection with the sale or rental of dwellings because of race, color, religion, sex, handicap, familial status, or national origin.

(7) Deny access to or membership or participation in, or to discriminate against any person in his or her access to or membership or participation in, any multiple-listing service, real estate brokers' association, or other service organization or facility relating to the business of selling or renting a dwelling or in the terms or conditions or membership or participation, because of race, color, religion, sex, handicap, familial status, or national origin.

(c) The application of the Fair Housing Act with respect to persons with handicaps is discussed in subpart D of this part.

24 C.F.R. § 100.60 Unlawful refusal to sell or rent or to negotiate for the sale or rental.

(a) It shall be unlawful for a person to refuse to sell or rent a dwelling to a person who has made a bona fide offer, because of race, color, religion, sex, familial status, or national origin or to refuse to negotiate with a person for the sale or rental of a dwelling because of race, color, religion, sex, familial status, or national origin, or to discriminate against any person in the sale or rental of a dwelling because of handicap.

(b) Prohibited actions under this section include, but are not limited to:

(1) Failing to accept or consider a bona fide offer because of race, color, religion, sex, handicap, familial status, or national origin.

(2) Refusing to sell or rent a dwelling to, or to negotiate for the sale or rental of a dwelling with, any person because of race, color, religion, sex, handicap, familial status, or national origin.

(3) Imposing different sales prices or rental charges for the sale or rental of a dwelling upon any person because of race, color, religion, sex, handicap, familial status, or national origin.

(4) Using different qualification criteria or applications, or sale or rental standards or procedures, such as income standards, application requirements, application fees, credit analysis or sale or rental approval procedures or other requirements, because of race, color, religion, sex, handicap, familial status, or national origin.

(5) Evicting tenants because of their race, color, religion, sex, handicap, familial status, or national origin or because of the race, color, religion, sex, handicap, familial status, or national origin of a tenant's guest.

24 C.F.R. § 100.65 Discrimination in terms, conditions and privileges and in services and facilities.

(a) It shall be unlawful, because of race, color, religion, sex, handicap, familial status, or national origin, to impose different terms, conditions or privileges relating to the sale or rental of a dwelling or to deny or limit services or facilities in connection with the sale or rental of a dwelling.

(b) Prohibited actions under this section include, but are not limited to:

(1) Using different provisions in leases or contracts of sale, such as those relating to rental charges,

security deposits and the terms of a lease and those relating to down payment and closing requirements, because of race, color, religion, sex, handicap, familial status, or national origin.

(2) Failing or delaying maintenance or repairs of sale or rental dwellings because of race, color, religion, sex, handicap, familial status, or national origin.

(3) Failing to process an offer for the sale or rental of a dwelling or to communicate an offer accurately because of race, color, religion, sex, handicap, familial status, or national origin.

(4) Limiting the use of privileges, services or facilities associated with a dwelling because of race, color, religion, sex, handicap, familial status, or national origin of an owner, tenant or a person associated with him or her.

(5) Denying or limiting services or facilities in connection with the sale or rental of a dwelling, because a person failed or refused to provide sexual favors.

24 C.F.R. § 100.70 Other prohibited sale and rental conduct.

(a) It shall be unlawful, because of race, color, religion, sex, handicap, familial status, or national origin, to restrict or attempt to restrict the choices of a person by word or conduct in connection with seeking, negotiating for, buying or renting a dwelling so as to perpetuate, or tend to perpetuate, segregated housing patterns, or to discourage or obstruct choices in a community, neighborhood or development.

(b) It shall be unlawful, because of race, color, religion, sex, handicap, familial status, or national origin, to engage in any conduct relating to the provision of housing or of services and facilities in connection therewith that otherwise makes unavailable or denies dwellings to persons.

(c) Prohibited actions under paragraph (a) of this section, which are generally referred to as unlawful steering practices, include, but are not limited to:

(1) Discouraging any person from inspecting, purchasing or renting a dwelling because of race, color, religion, sex, handicap, familial status, or national origin, or because of the race, color, religion, sex, handicap, familial status, or national origin of persons in a community, neighborhood or development.

(2) Discouraging the purchase or rental of a dwelling because of race, color, religion, sex, handicap, familial status, or national origin, by exaggerating drawbacks or failing to inform any person of desirable features of a dwelling or of a community, neighborhood, or development.

(3) Communicating to any prospective purchaser that he or she would not be comfortable or compatible with existing residents of a community, neighborhood or development because of race, color, religion, sex, handicap, familial status, or national origin.

(4) Assigning any person to a particular section of a community, neighborhood or development, or to a particular floor of a building, because of race, color, religion, sex, handicap, familial status, or national origin.

(d) Prohibited activities relating to dwellings under paragraph (b) of this section include, but are not limited to:

(1) Discharging or taking other adverse action against an employee, broker or agent because he or she refused to participate in a discriminatory housing practice.

(2) Employing codes or other devices to segregate or reject applicants, purchasers or renters, refusing to take or to show listings of dwellings in certain areas because of race, color, religion, sex, handicap, familial status, or national origin, or refusing to deal with certain brokers or agents because they or one or more of their clients are of a particular race, color, religion, sex, handicap, familial status, or national origin.

(3) Denying or delaying the processing of an application made by a purchaser or renter or refusing to approve such a person for occupancy in a cooperative or condominium dwelling because of race, color, religion, sex, handicap, familial status, or national origin.

(4) Refusing to provide municipal services or property or hazard insurance for dwellings or providing such services or insurance differently because of race, color, religion, sex, handicap, familial status, or national origin.

24 C.F.R. § 100.75 Discriminatory advertisements, statements and notices.

(a) It shall be unlawful to make, print or publish, or cause to be made, printed or published, any notice, statement or advertisement with respect to the sale or rental of a dwelling which indicates any preference, limitation or discrimination because of race, color, religion, sex, handicap, familial status, or national origin, or an intention to make any such preference, limitation or discrimination.

(b) The prohibitions in this section shall apply to all written or oral notices or statements by a person engaged in the sale or rental of a dwelling. Written notices and statements include any applications, flyers, brochures, deeds, signs, banners, posters, billboards or any documents used with respect to the sale or rental of a dwelling.

(c) Discriminatory notices, statements and advertisements include, but are not limited to:

(1) Using words, phrases, photographs, illustrations, symbols or forms which convey that dwellings are available or not available to a particular group of persons because of race, color, religion, sex, handicap, familial status, or national origin.

(2) Expressing to agents, brokers, employees, prospective sellers or renters or any other persons a preference for or limitation on any purchaser or renter because of race, color, religion, sex, handicap, familial status, or national origin of such persons.

343

(3) Selecting media or locations for advertising the sale or rental of dwellings which deny particular segments of the housing market information about housing opportunities because of race, color, religion, sex, handicap, familial status, or national origin.

(4) Refusing to publish advertising for the sale or rental of dwellings or requiring different charges or terms for such advertising because of race, color, religion, sex, handicap, familial status, or national origin.

(d) 24 CFR Part 109 provides information to assist persons to advertise dwellings in a nondiscriminatory manner and describes the matters the Department will review in evaluating compliance with the Fair Housing Act and in investigating complaints alleging discriminatory housing practices involving advertising.

24 C.F.R. § 100.80 Discriminatory representations on the availability of dwellings.

(a) It shall be unlawful, because of race, color, religion, sex, handicap, familial status, or national origin, to provide inaccurate or untrue information about the availability of dwellings for sale or rental.

(b) Prohibited actions under this section include, but are not limited to:

(1) Indicating through words or conduct that a dwelling which is available for inspection, sale, or rental has been sold or rented, because of race, color, religion, sex, handicap, familial status, or national origin.

(2) Representing that covenants or other deed, trust or lease provisions which purport to restrict the sale or rental of dwellings because of race, color, religion, sex, handicap, familial status, or national origin preclude the sale or rental of a dwelling to a person.

(3) Enforcing covenants or other deed, trust, or lease provisions which preclude the sale or rental of a dwelling to any person because of race, color, religion, sex, handicap, familial status, or national origin.

(4) Limiting information, by word or conduct, regarding suitably priced dwellings available for inspection, sale or rental, because of race, color, religion, sex, handicap, familial status, or national origin.

(5) Providing false or inaccurate information regarding the availability of a dwelling for sale or rental to any person, including testers, regardless of whether such person is actually seeking housing, because of race, color, religion, sex, handicap, familial status, or national origin.

24 C.F.R. § 100.85 Blockbusting.

(a) It shall be unlawful, for profit, to induce or attempt to induce a person to sell or rent a dwelling by representations regarding the entry or prospective entry into the neighborhood of a person or persons of a particular race, color, religion, sex, familial status, or national origin or with a handicap.

(b) In establishing a discriminatory housing practice under this section it is not necessary that there was in fact profit as long as profit was a factor for engaging in the blockbusting activity.

(c) Prohibited actions under this section include, but are not limited to:

(1) Engaging, for profit, in conduct (including uninvited solicitations for listings) which conveys to a person that a neighborhood is undergoing or is about to undergo a change in the race, color, religion, sex, handicap, familial status, or national origin of persons residing in it, in order to encourage the person to offer a dwelling for sale or rental.

(2) Encouraging, for profit, any person to sell or rent a dwelling through assertions that the entry or prospective entry of persons of a particular race, color, religion, sex, familial status, or national origin, or with handicaps, can or will result in undesirable consequences for the project, neighborhood or community, such as a lowering of property values, an increase in criminal or antisocial behavior, or a decline in the quality of schools or other services or facilities.

24 C.F.R. § 100.90 Discrimination in the provision of brokerage services.

(a) It shall be unlawful to deny any person access to or membership or participation in any multiple listing service, real estate brokers' organization or other service, organization, or facility relating to the business of selling or renting dwellings, or to discriminate against any person in the terms or conditions of such access, membership or participation, because of race, color, religion, sex, handicap, familial status, or national origin.

(b) Prohibited actions under this section include, but are not limited to:

(1) Setting different fees for access to or membership in a multiple listing service because of race, color, religion, sex, handicap, familial status, or national origin.

(2) Denying or limiting benefits accruing to members in a real estate brokers' organization because of race, color, religion, sex, handicap, familial status, or national origin.

(3) Imposing different standards or criteria for membership in a real estate sales or rental organization because of race, color, religion, sex, handicap, familial status, or national origin.

(4) Establishing geographic boundaries or office location or residence requirements for access to or membership or participation in any multiple listing service, real estate brokers' organization or other service, organization or facility relating to the business of selling or renting dwellings, because of race, color, religion, sex, handicap, familial status, or national origin.

Subpart C—Discrimination in Residential Real Estate-Related Transactions

24 C.F.R. § 100.110 Discriminatory practices in residential real estate-related transactions.

(a) This subpart provides the Department's interpretation of the conduct that is unlawful housing discrimination under section 805 of the Fair Housing Act.

(b) It shall be unlawful for any person or other entity whose business includes engaging in residential real estate-related transactions to discriminate against any person in making available such a transaction, or in the terms or conditions of such a transaction, because of race, color, religion, sex, handicap, familial status, or national origin.

24 C.F.R. § 100.115 Residential real estate-related transactions.

The term *residential real estate-related transactions* means:

(a) The making or purchasing of loans or providing other financial assistance—

(1) For purchasing, constructing, improving, repairing or maintaining a dwelling; or

(2) Secured by residential real estate; or

(b) The selling, brokering or appraising of residential real property.

24 C.F.R. § 100.120 Discrimination in the making of loans and in the provision of other financial assistance.

(a) It shall be unlawful for any person or entity whose business includes engaging in residential real estate-related transactions to discriminate against any person in making available loans or other financial assistance for a dwelling, or which is or is to be secured by a dwelling, because of race, color, religion, sex, handicap, familial status, or national origin.

(b) Prohibited practices under this section include, but are not limited to, failing or refusing to provide to any person, in connection with a residential real estate-related transaction, information regarding the availability of loans or other financial assistance, application requirements, procedures or standards for the review and approval of loans or financial assistance, or providing information which is inaccurate or different from that provided others, because of race, color, religion, sex, handicap, familial status, or national origin.

24 C.F.R. § 100.125 Discrimination in the purchasing of loans.

(a) It shall be unlawful for any person or entity engaged in the purchasing of loans or other debts or securities which support the purchase, construction, improvement, repair or maintenance of a dwelling, or which are secured by residential real estate, to refuse to purchase such loans, debts, or securities, or to impose different terms or conditions for such purchases, because of race, color, religion, sex, handicap, familial status, or national origin.

(b) Unlawful conduct under this section includes, but is not limited to:

(1) Purchasing loans or other debts or securities which relate to, or which are secured by dwellings in certain communities or neighborhoods but not in others because of the race, color, religion, sex, handicap, familial status, or national origin of persons in such neighborhoods or communities.

(2) Pooling or packaging loans or other debts or securities which relate to, or which are secured by, dwellings differently because of race, color, religion, sex, handicap, familial status, or national origin.

(3) Imposing or using different terms or conditions on the marketing or sale of securities issued on the basis of loans or other debts or securities which relate to, or which are secured by, dwellings because of race, color, religion, sex, handicap, familial status, or national origin.

(c) This section does not prevent consideration, in the purchasing of loans, of factors justified by business necessity, including requirements of Federal law, relating to a transaction's financial security or to protection against default or reduction of the value of the security. Thus, this provision would not preclude considerations employed in normal and prudent transactions, provided that no such factor may in any way relate to race, color, religion, sex, handicap, familial status or national origin.

24 C.F.R. § 100.130 Discrimination in the terms and conditions for making available loans or other financial assistance.

(a) It shall be unlawful for any person or entity engaged in the making of loans or in the provision of other financial assistance relating to the purchase, construction, improvement, repair or maintenance of dwellings or which are secured by residential real estate to impose different terms or conditions for the availability of such loans or other financial assistance because of race, color, religion, sex, handicap, familial status, or national origin.

(b) Unlawful conduct under this section includes, but is not limited to:

(1) Using different policies, practices or procedures in evaluating or in determining creditworthiness of any person in connection with the provision of any loan or other financial assistance for a dwelling or for any loan or other financial assistance which is secured by residential real estate because of race, color, religion, sex, handicap, familial status, or national origin.

(2) Determining the type of loan or other financial assistance to be provided with respect to a dwelling, or fixing the amount, interest rate, duration or other terms for a loan or other financial assistance for a dwelling or which is secured by residential real estate, because of race, color, religion, sex, handicap, familial status, or national origin.

24 C.F.R. § 100.135 Unlawful practices in the selling, brokering, or appraising of residential real property.

(a) It shall be unlawful for any person or other entity whose business includes engaging in the selling, brokering or appraising of residential real property to discriminate against any person in making available such services, or in the performance of such services, because of race, color, religion, sex, handicap, familial status, or national origin.

(b) For the purposes of this section, the term appraisal means an estimate or opinion of the value of a specified residential real property made in a business context in connection with the sale, rental, financing or refinancing of a dwelling or in connection with any activity that otherwise affects the availability of a residential real estate-related transaction, whether the appraisal is oral or written, or transmitted formally or informally. The appraisal includes all written comments and other documents submitted as support for the estimate or opinion of value.

(c) Nothing in this section prohibits a person engaged in the business of making or furnishing appraisals of residential real property from taking into consideration factors other than race, color, religion, sex, handicap, familial status, or national origin.

(d) Practices which are unlawful under this section include, but are not limited to, using an appraisal of residential real property in connection with the sale, rental, or financing of any dwelling where the person knows or reasonably should know that the appraisal improperly takes into consideration race, color, religion, sex, handicap, familial status or national origin.

[58 Fed. Reg. 2988 (Jan. 7, 1993)]

24 C.F.R. § 100.140 General rules.

(a) *Voluntary self-testing and correction.* The report or results of a self-test a lender voluntarily conducts or authorizes are privileged as provided in this subpart if the lender has taken or is taking appropriate corrective action to address likely violations identified by the self-test. Data collection required by law or any governmental authority (federal, state, or local) is not voluntary.

(b) *Other privileges.* This subpart does not abrogate any evidentiary privilege otherwise provided by law.

[62 Fed. Reg. 66,432 (Dec. 18, 1997)]

24 C.F.R. § 100.141 Definitions.

As used in this subpart:

Lender means a person who engages in a residential real estate-related lending transaction.

Residential real estate-related lending transaction means the making of a loan:

(1) For purchasing, constructing, improving, repairing, or maintaining a dwelling; or

(2) Secured by residential real estate.

Self-test means any program, practice or study a lender voluntarily conducts or authorizes which is designed and used specifically to determine the extent or effectiveness of compliance with the Fair Housing Act. The self-test must create data or factual information that is not available and cannot be derived from loan files, application files, or other residential real estate-related lending transaction records. Self-testing includes, but is not limited to, using fictitious credit applicants (testers) or conducting surveys of applicants or customers, nor is it limited to the pre-application stage of loan processing.

[62 Fed. Reg. 66,432 (Dec. 18, 1997)]

24 C.F.R. § 100.142 Types of information.

(a) The privilege under this subpart covers:

(1) The report or results of the self-test;

(2) Data or factual information created by the self-test;

(3) Workpapers, draft documents and final documents;

(4) Analyses, opinions, and conclusions if they directly result from the self-test report or results.

(b) The privilege does not cover:

(1) Information about whether a lender conducted a self-test, the methodology used or scope of the self-test, the time period covered by the self-test or the dates it was conducted;

(2) Loan files and application files, or other residential real estate-related lending transaction records (e.g., property appraisal reports, loan committee meeting minutes or other documents reflecting the basis for a decision to approve or deny a loan application, loan policies or procedures, underwriting standards, compensation records) and information or data derived from such files and records, even if such data has been aggregated, summarized or reorganized to facilitate analysis.

[62 Fed. Reg. 66,432 (Dec. 18, 1997)]

24 C.F.R. § 100.143 Appropriate corrective action.

(a) The report or results of a self-test are privileged as provided in this subpart if the lender has taken or is taking appropriate corrective action to address likely violations identified by the self-test. Appropriate corrective action is required when a self-test shows it is more likely than not that a violation occurred even though no violation was adjudicated formally.

(b) A lender must take action reasonably likely to remedy the cause and effect of the likely violation and must:

(1) Identify the policies or practices that are the likely cause of the violation, such as inadequate or improper lending policies, failure to implement established policies, employee conduct, or other causes; and

(2) Assess the extent and scope of any likely violation, by determining which areas of operation are likely to be affected by those policies and practices, such as stages of the loan application process, types of loans, or the particular branch where the likely violation has occurred. Generally, the scope of the self-test governs the scope of the appropriate corrective action.

(c) Appropriate corrective action may include both prospective and remedial relief, except that to establish a privilege under this subpart:

(1) A lender is not required to provide remedial relief to a tester in a self-test;

(2) A lender is only required to provide remedial relief to an applicant identified by the self-test as one whose rights were more likely than not violated;

(3) A lender is not required to provide remedial relief to a particular applicant if the statute of limitations applicable to the violation expired before the lender obtained the results of the self-test or the applicant is otherwise ineligible for such relief.

(d) Depending on the facts involved, appropriate corrective action may include, but is not limited to, one or more of the following:

(1) If the self-test identifies individuals whose applications were inappropriately processed, offering to extend credit if the applications were improperly denied; compensating such persons for any damages, both out-of-pocket and compensatory;

(2) Correcting any institutional policies or procedures that may have contributed to the likely violation, and adopting new policies as appropriate;

(3) Identifying, and then training and/or disciplining the employees involved;

(4) Developing outreach programs, marketing strategies, or loan products to serve more effectively the segments of the lender's market that may have been affected by the likely violation; and

(5) Improving audit and oversight systems to avoid a recurrence of the likely violations.

(e) Determination of appropriate corrective action is fact-based. Not every corrective measure listed in paragraph (d) of this section need be taken for each likely violation.

(f) Taking appropriate corrective action is not an admission by a lender that a violation occurred.

[62 Fed. Reg. 66,432 (Dec. 18, 1997)]

24 C.F.R. § 100.144 Scope of privilege.

The report or results of a self-test may not be obtained or used by an aggrieved person, complainant, department or agency in any:

(a) Proceeding or civil action in which a violation of the Fair Housing Act is alleged; or

(b) Examination or investigation relating to compliance with the Fair Housing Act.

[62 Fed. Reg. 66,432 (Dec. 18, 1997)]

24 C.F.R. § 100.145 Loss of privilege.

(a) The self-test report or results are not privileged under this subpart if the lender or person with lawful access to the report or results:

(1) Voluntarily discloses any part of the report or results or any other information privileged under this subpart to any aggrieved person, complainant, department, agency, or to the public; or

(2) Discloses the report or results or any other information privileged under this subpart as a defense to charges a lender violated the Fair Housing Act; or

(3) Fails or is unable to produce self-test records or information needed to determine whether the privilege applies.

(b) Disclosures or other actions undertaken to carry out appropriate corrective action do not cause the lender to lose the privilege.

[62 Fed. Reg. 66,432 (Dec. 18, 1997)]

24 C.F.R. § 100.146 Limited use of privileged information.

Notwithstanding § 100.145, the self-test report or results may be obtained and used by an aggrieved person, applicant, department or agency solely to determine a penalty or remedy after the violation of the Fair Housing Act has been adjudicated or admitted. Disclosures for this limited purpose may be used only for the particular proceeding in which the adjudication or admission is made. Information disclosed under this section remains otherwise privileged under this subpart.

[62 Fed. Reg. 66,432 (Dec. 18, 1997)]

24 C.F.R. § 100.147 Adjudication.

An aggrieved person, complainant, department or agency that challenges a privilege asserted under § 100.144 may seek a determination of the existence and application of that privilege in:

(a) A court of competent jurisdiction; or

(b) An administrative law proceeding with appropriate jurisdiction.

[62 Fed. Reg. 66,432 (Dec. 18, 1997)]

24 C.F.R. § 100.148 Effective date.

The privilege under this subpart applies to self-tests conducted both before and after January 30, 1998, except that a self-test conducted before January 30, 1998 is not privileged:

(a) If there was a court action or administrative proceeding before January 30, 1998, including the filing of a complaint alleging a violation of the Fair Housing Act with the Department or a substantially equivalent state or local agency; or

(b) If any part of the report or results were disclosed before January 30, 1998 to any aggrieved person, complainant, department or agency, or to the general public.

[62 Fed. Reg. 66,432 (Dec. 18, 1997)]

Subpart D—Prohibition Against Discrimination Because of Handicap

24 C.F.R. § 100.200 Purpose.

The purpose of this subpart is to effectuate sections 6(a) and (b) and 15 of the Fair Housing Amendments Act of 1988.

24 C.F.R. § 100.201 Definitions.

As used in this subpart:

* * *

Handicap means, with respect to a person, a physical or mental impairment which substantially limits one or more major life activities; a record of such an impairment; or being regarded as having such an impairment. This term does not include current, illegal use of or addiction to a controlled substance. For purposes of this part, an individual shall not be considered to have a handicap solely because that individual is a transvestite. As used in this definition:

(a) *Physical or mental impairment* includes:

(1) Any physiological disorder or condition, cosmetic disfigurement, or anatomical loss affecting one or more of the following body systems: Neurological; musculoskeletal; special sense organs; respiratory, including speech organs; cardiovascular; reproductive; digestive; genito-urinary; hemic and lymphatic; skin; and endocrine; or

(2) Any mental or psychological disorder, such as mental retardation, organic brain syndrome, emotional or mental illness, and specific learning disabilities. The term physical or mental impairment includes, but is not limited to, such diseases and conditions as orthopedic, visual, speech and hearing impairments, cerebral palsy, autism, epilepsy, muscular dystrophy, multiple sclerosis, cancer, heart disease, diabetes, Human Immunodeficiency Virus infection, mental retardation, emotional illness, drug addiction (other than addiction caused by current, illegal use of a controlled substance) and alcoholism.

(b) *Major life activities* means functions such as caring for one's self, performing manual tasks, walking, seeing, hearing, speaking, breathing, learning and working.

(c) *Has a record of such an impairment* means has a history of, or has been misclassified as having, a mental or physical impairment that substantially limits one or more major life activities.

(d) *Is regarded as having an impairment* means:

(1) Has a physical or mental impairment that does not substantially limit one or more major life activities but that is treated by another person as constituting such a limitation;

(2) Has a physical or mental impairment that substantially limits one or more major life activities only as a result of the attitudes of other toward such impairment; or

(3) Has none of the impairments defined in paragraph (a) of this definition but is treated by another person as having such an impairment.

* * *

24 C.F.R. § 100.202 General prohibitions against discrimination because of handicap.

(a) It shall be unlawful to discriminate in the sale or rental, or to otherwise make unavailable or deny, a dwelling to any buyer or renter because of a handicap of—

(1) That buyer or renter;

(2) A person residing in or intending to reside in that dwelling after it is so sold, rented, or made available; or

(3) Any person associated with that person.

(b) It shall be unlawful to discriminate against any person in the terms, conditions, or privileges of the sale or rental of a dwelling, or in the provision of services or facilities in connection with such dwelling, because of a handicap of—

(1) That buyer or renter;

(2) A person residing in or intending to reside in that dwelling after it is so sold, rented, or made available; or

(3) Any person associated with that person.

(c) It shall be unlawful to make an inquiry to determine whether an applicant for a dwelling, a person intending to reside in that dwelling after it is so sold, rented or made available, or any person associated with that person, has a handicap or to make inquiry as to the nature or severity of a handicap of such a person. However, this paragraph does not prohibit the following inquiries, provided these inquiries are made of all applicants, whether or not they have handicaps:

(1) Inquiry into an applicant's ability to meet the requirements of ownership or tenancy;

(2) Inquiry to determine whether an applicant is qualified for a dwelling available only to persons with handicaps or to persons with a particular type of handicap;

(3) Inquiry to determine whether an applicant for a dwelling is qualified for a priority available to persons with handicaps or to persons with a particular type of handicap;

(4) Inquiring whether an applicant for a dwelling is a current illegal abuser or addict of a controlled substance;

(5) Inquiring whether an applicant has been convicted of the illegal manufacture or distribution of a controlled substance.

(d) Nothing in this subpart requires that a dwelling be made available to an individual whose tenancy would constitute a direct threat to the health or safety of other individuals or whose tenancy would result in substantial physical damage to the property of others.

24 C.F.R. § 100.203 Reasonable modifications of existing premises.

(a) It shall be unlawful for any person to refuse to permit, at the expense of a handicapped person, reasonable modifications of existing premises, occupied or to be occupied by a handicapped person, if the proposed modifications may be necessary to afford the handicapped person full enjoyment of the premises of a dwelling. In the case of a rental, the landlord may, where it is reasonable to do so, condition permission for a modification on the renter agreeing to restore the interior of the premises to the condition that existed before the modification, reasonable wear and tear excepted. The landlord may not increase for handicapped persons any customarily required security deposit. However, where it is necessary in order to ensure with reasonable certainty that funds will be available to pay for the restorations at the end of the tenancy, the landlord may negotiate as part of such a restoration agreement a provision requiring that the tenant pay into an interest bearing escrow account, over a reasonable period, a reasonable amount of money not to exceed the cost of the restorations. The interest in any such account shall accrue to the benefit of the tenant.

(b) A landlord may condition permission for a modification on the renter providing a reasonable description of the proposed modifications as well as reasonable assurances that the work will be done in a workmanlike manner and that any required building permits will be obtained.

(c) The application of paragraph (a) of this section may be illustrated by the following examples:

Example (1): A tenant with a handicap asks his or her landlord for permission to install grab bars in the bathroom at his or her own expense. It is necessary to reinforce the walls with blocking between studs in order to affix the grab bars. It is unlawful for the landlord to refuse to permit the tenant, at the tenant's own expense, from making the modifications necessary to add the grab bars. However, the landlord may condition permission for the modification on the tenant agreeing to restore the bathroom to the condition that existed

before the modification, reasonable wear and tear excepted. It would be reasonable for the landlord to require the tenant to remove the grab bars at the end of the tenancy. The landlord may also reasonably require that the wall to which the grab bars are to be attached be repaired and restored to its original condition, reasonable wear and tear excepted. However, it would be unreasonable for the landlord to require the tenant to remove the blocking, since the reinforced walls will not interfere in any way with the landlord's or the next tenant's use and enjoyment of the premises and may be needed by some future tenant.

Example (2): An applicant for rental housing has a child who uses a wheelchair. The bathroom door in the dwelling unit is too narrow to permit the wheelchair to pass. The applicant asks the landlord for permission to widen the doorway at the applicant's own expense. It is unlawful for the landlord to refuse to permit the applicant to make the modification. Further, the landlord may not, in usual circumstances, condition permission for the modification on the applicant paying for the doorway to be narrowed at the end of the lease because a wider doorway will not interfere with the landlord's or the next tenant's use and enjoyment of the premises.

24 C.F.R. § 100.204 Reasonable accommodations.

(a) It shall be unlawful for any person to refuse to make reasonable accommodations in rules, policies, practices, or services, when such accommodations may be necessary to afford a handicapped person equal opportunity to use and enjoy a dwelling unit, including public and common use areas.

(b) The application of this section may be illustrated by the following examples:

Example (1): A blind applicant for rental housing wants live in a dwelling unit with a seeing eye dog. The building has a no pets policy. It is a violation of § 100.204 for the owner or manager of the apartment complex to refuse to permit the applicant to live in the apartment with a seeing eye dog because, without the seeing eye dog, the blind person will not have an equal opportunity to use and enjoy a dwelling.

Example (2): Progress Gardens is a 300 unit apartment complex with 450 parking spaces which are available to tenants and guests of Progress Gardens on a first come first served basis. John applies for housing in Progress Gardens. John is mobility impaired and is unable to walk more than a short distance and therefore requests that a parking space near his unit be reserved for him so he will not have to walk very far to get to his apartment. It is a violation of § 100.204 for the owner or manager of Progress Gardens to refuse to make this accommodation. Without a reserved space, John might be unable to live in Progress Gardens at all or, when he has to park in a space far from his unit, might have great difficulty getting from his car to his apartment unit. The accommodation therefore is necessary to afford John an equal opportunity to use and enjoy a dwelling. The accommodation is reasonable because it is feasible and practical under the circumstances.

24 C.F.R. § 100.205 Design and construction requirements.

(a) Covered multifamily dwellings for first occupancy after March 13, 1991 shall be designed and constructed to have at least one building entrance on an accessible route unless it is impractical to do so because of the terrain or unusual characteristics of the site. For purposes of this section, a covered multifamily dwelling shall be deemed to be designed and constructed for first occupancy on or before March 13, 1991, if the dwelling is occupied by that date, or if the last building permit or renewal thereof for the dwelling is issued by a State, County or local government on or before June 15, 1990. The burden of establishing impracticality because of terrain or unusual site characteristics is on the person or persons who designed or constructed the housing facility.

(b) The application of paragraph (a) of this section may be illustrated by the following examples:

Example (1): A real estate developer plans to construct six covered multifamily dwelling units on a site with a hilly terrain. Because of the terrain, it will be necessary to climb a long and steep stairway in order to enter the dwellings. Since there is no practical way to provide an accessible route to any of the dwellings, one need not be provided.

Example (2): A real estate developer plans to construct a building consisting of 10 units of multifamily housing on a waterfront site that floods frequently. Because of this unusual characteristic of the site, the builder plans to construct the building on stilts. It is customary for housing in the geographic area where the site is located to be built on stilts. The housing may lawfully be constructed on the proposed site on stilts even though this means that there will be no practical way to provide an accessible route to the building entrance.

Example (3): A real estate developer plans to construct a multifamily housing facility on a particular site. The developer would like the facility to be built on the site to contain as many units as possible. Because of the configuration and terrain of the site, it is possible to construct a building with 105 units on the site provided the site does not have an accessible route leading to the building entrance. It is also possible to construct a building on the site with an accessible route leading to the building entrance. However, such a building would have no more than 100 dwelling units. The building to be constructed on the site must have a building entrance on an accessible route because it is not impractical to provide such an entrance because of the terrain or unusual characteristics of the site.

(c) All covered multifamily dwellings for first occupancy after March 13, 1991 with a building entrance on an accessible route shall be designed and constructed in such a manner that—

(1) The public and common use areas are readily accessible to and usable by handicapped persons;

(2) All the doors designed to allow passage into and within all premises are sufficiently wide to allow passage by handicapped persons in wheelchairs; and

(3) All premises within covered multifamily dwelling units contain the following features of adaptable design:

(i) An accessible route into and through the covered dwelling unit;

(ii) Light switches, electrical outlets, thermostats, and other environmental controls in accessible locations;

(iii) Reinforcements in bathroom walls to allow later installation of grab bars around the toilet, tub, shower, stall and shower seat, where such facilities are provided; and

(iv) Usable kitchens and bathrooms such that an individual in a wheelchair can maneuver about the space.

(d) The application of paragraph (c) of this section may be illustrated by the following examples:

Example (1): A developer plans to construct a 100 unit condominium apartment building with one elevator. In accordance with paragraph (a), the building has at least one accessible route leading to an accessible entrance. All 100 units are covered multifamily dwelling units and they all must be designed and constructed so that they comply with the accessibility requirements of paragraph (c) of this section.

Example (2): A developer plans to construct 30 garden apartments in a three story building. The building will not have an elevator. The building will have one accessible entrance which will be on the first floor. Since the building does not have an elevator, only the ground floor units are covered multifamily units. The ground floor is the first floor because that is the floor that has an accessible entrance. All of the dwelling units on the first floor must meet the accessibility requirements of paragraph (c) of this section and must have access to at least one of each type of public or common use area available for residents in the building.

(e)(1) Compliance with the appropriate requirements of ICC/ANSI A117.1-2003 (incorporated by reference at § 100.201a), ICC/ANSI A117.1-1998 (incorporated by reference at § 100.201a), CABO/ANSI A117.1-1992 (incorporated by reference at § 100.201a), or ANSI A117.1-1986 (incorporated by reference at § 100.201a) suffices to satisfy the requirements of paragraph (c)(3) of this section.

(2) The following also qualify as HUD-recognized safe harbors for compliance with the Fair Housing Act design and construction requirements:

(i) Fair Housing Accessibility Guidelines, March 6, 1991, in conjunction with the Supplement to Notice of Fair Housing Accessibility Guidelines: Questions and Answers About the Guidelines, June 28, 1994;

(ii) Fair Housing Act Design Manual, published by HUD in 1996, updated in 1998;

(iii) 2000 ICC Code Requirements for Housing Accessibility (CRHA), published by the International Code Council (ICC), October 2000 (with corrections contained in ICC-issued errata sheet), if adopted without modification and without waiver of any of the provisions;

(iv) 2000 International Building Code (IBC), as amended by the 2001 Supplement to the International Building Code (2001 IBC Supplement), if adopted without modification and without waiver of any of the provisions intended to address the Fair Housing Act's design and construction requirements;

(v) 2003 International Building Code (IBC), if adopted without modification and without waiver of any of the provisions intended to address the Fair Housing Act's design and construction requirements, and conditioned upon the ICC publishing and distributing a statement to jurisdictions and past and future purchasers of the 2003 IBC stating, "ICC interprets Section 1104.1, and specifically, the Exception to Section 1104.1, to be read together with Section 1107.4, and that the Code requires an accessible pedestrian route from site arrival points to accessible building entrances, unless site impracticality applies. Exception 1 to Section 1107.4 is not applicable to site arrival points for any Type B dwelling units because site impracticality is addressed under Section 1107.7."

(vi) 2006 International Building Code; published by ICC, January 2006, with the January 31, 2007, erratum to correct the text missing from Section 1107.7.5, if adopted without modification and without waiver of any of the provisions intended to address the Fair Housing Act's design and construction requirements, and interpreted in accordance with the relevant 2006 IBC Commentary;

(3) Compliance with any other safe harbor recognized by HUD in the future and announced in the Federal Register will also suffice to satisfy the requirements of paragraph (c)(3) of this section.

(f) Compliance with a duly enacted law of a State or unit of general local government that includes the requirements of paragraphs (a) and (c) of this section satisfies the requirements of paragraphs (a) and (c) of this section.

(g)(1) It is the policy of HUD to encourage States and units of general local government to include, in their existing procedures for the review and approval of newly constructed covered multifamily dwellings, determinations as to whether the design and construction of such dwellings are consistent with paragraphs (a) and (c) of this section.

(2) A State or unit of general local government may review and approve newly constructed multifamily dwellings for the purpose of making determinations as to whether the requirements of paragraphs (a) and (c) of this section are met.

(h) Determinations of compliance or noncompliance by a State or a unit of general local government under paragraph (f) or (g) of this section are not conclusive in enforcement proceedings under the Fair Housing Amendments Act.

(i) This subpart does not invalidate or limit any law of a State or political subdivision of a State that requires dwellings to be designed and constructed in a manner that affords handicapped persons greater access than is required by this subpart.

[56 Fed. Reg. 11,665 (Mar. 20, 1991); 73 Fed. Reg. 63,616 (Oct. 24, 2008)]

* * *

Subpart F—Interference, Coercion or Intimidation

24 C.F.R. § 100.400 Prohibited interference, coercion or intimidation.

(a) This subpart provides the Department's interpretation of the conduct that is unlawful under section 818 of the Fair Housing Act.

(b) It shall be unlawful to coerce, intimidate, threaten, or interfere with any person in the exercise or enjoyment of, or on account of that person having exercised or enjoyed, or on account of that person having aided or encouraged any other person in the exercise or enjoyment of, any right granted or protected by this part.

(c) Conduct made unlawful under this section includes, but is not limited to, the following:

(1) Coercing a person, either orally, in writing, or by other means, to deny or limit the benefits provided that person in connection with the sale or rental of a dwelling or in connection with a residential real estate-related transaction because of race, color, religion, sex, handicap, familial status, or national origin.

(2) Threatening, intimidating or interfering with persons in their enjoyment of a dwelling because of the race, color, religion, sex, handicap, familial status, or national origin of such persons, or of visitors or associates of such persons.

(3) Threatening an employee or agent with dismissal or an adverse employment action, or taking such adverse employment action, for any effort to assist a person seeking access to the sale or rental of a dwelling or seeking access to any residential real estate-related transaction, because of the race, color, religion, sex, handicap, familial status, or national origin of that person or of any person associated with that person.

(4) Intimidating or threatening any person because that person is engaging in activities designed to make other persons aware of, or encouraging such other persons to exercise, rights granted or protected by this part.

(5) Retaliating against any person because that person has made a complaint, testified, assisted, or participated in any manner in a proceeding under the Fair Housing Act.

Home Mortgage Disclosure Act and Regulation C

This appendix is also available on the companion website to this treatise. The companion website facilitates keyword searches and allows relevant provisions to be imported as word-processable documents.

E.1 Home Mortgage Disclosure Act—12 U.S.C §§ 2801–2810

This appendix section reprints the Home Mortgage Disclosure Act, as amended by Title X of the Dodd-Frank Wall Street Reform and Consumer Protection Act, Pub. L. No. 111-203, 124 Stat. 1376 (July 21, 2010). This revised act is effective on July 21, 2011. See Pub. L. No. 111-203, § 1100H, 124 Stat. 1376, 2113 (changes effective on the designated transfer date); 75 Fed. Reg. 57,252 (Sept. 20, 2010) (establishing July 21, 2011, as the designated transfer date).

TITLE 12. BANKS AND BANKING

* * *

CHAPTER 29. HOME MORTGAGE DISCLOSURE

§ 2801. Congressional findings and declaration of purpose
§ 2802. Definitions
§ 2803. Maintenance of records and public disclosure
§ 2804. Enforcement
§ 2805. Relation to State laws
§ 2806. Research and improved methods; authorization of appropriations; recommendations to Congressional committees
§ 2807. Report
§ 2808. Effective date
§ 2809. Compilation of aggregate data
§ 2810. Disclosure by Secretary; commencement, scope, etc.

SOURCE: Pub. L. No. 94-200, 89 Stat. 1125 (1975), unless otherwise noted.

12 U.S.C. § 2801. Congressional findings and declaration of purpose

(a) Findings of Congress

The Congress finds that some depository institutions have sometimes contributed to the decline of certain geographic areas by their failure pursuant to their chartering responsibilities to provide adequate home financing to qualified applicants on reasonable terms and conditions.

(b) Purpose of chapter

The purpose of this chapter is to provide the citizens and public officials of the United States with sufficient information to enable them to determine whether depository institutions are filling their obligations to serve the housing needs of the communities and neighborhoods in which they are located and to assist public officials in their determination of the distribution of public sector investments in a manner designed to improve the private investment environment.

(c) Construction of chapter

Nothing in this chapter is intended to, nor shall it be construed to, encourage unsound lending practices or the allocation of credit.

12 U.S.C. § 2802. Definitions

For purposes of this chapter—

(1) the term "Bureau" means the Bureau of Consumer Financial Protection;

(2) the term "mortgage loan" means a loan which is secured by residential real property or a home improvement loan;

(3) the term "depository institution"—

    (A) means—

        (i) any bank (as defined in section 1813(a)(1) of this title);

        (ii) any savings association (as defined in section 1813(b)(1) of this title); and

        (iii) any credit union, which makes federally related mortgage loans as determined by the Board; and

    (B) includes any other lending institution (as defined in paragraph (4)) other than any institution described in subparagraph (A);

(4) the term "completed application" means an application in which the creditor has received the information that is regularly obtained in evaluating applications for the amount and type of credit requested;

(5) the term "other lending institutions" means any person engaged for profit in the business of mortgage lending;

(6) the term "Board" means the Board of Governors of the Federal Reserve System; and

(7) the term "Secretary" means the Secretary of Housing and Urban Development.

[Pub. L. No. 100-242, § 565(a)(1), 101 Stat. 1945 (1988); Pub. L. No. 101-73, § 1211(d), (e), 103 Stat. 525 (1989); Pub. L. No. 111-203, tit. X, §§ 1094(2), 1100H, 124 Stat. 2097, 2113 (July 21, 2010)]

12 U.S.C. § 2803. Maintenance of records and public disclosure

(a) Duty of depository institutions; nature and content of information

(1) Each depository institution which has a home office or branch office located within a primary metropolitan statistical area, metropolitan statistical area, or consolidated metropolitan statistical area that is not comprised of designated primary metropolitan statistical areas, as defined by the Department of Commerce shall compile and make available, in accordance with regulations of the Bureau, to the public for inspection and copying at the home office, and at least one branch office within each primary metropolitan statistical area, metropolitan statistical area, or consolidated metropolitan statistical area that is not comprised of designated primary metropolitan statistical areas in which the depository institution has an office the number and total dollar amount of mortgage loans which were (A) originated (or for which the institution received completed applications), or (B) purchased by that institution during each fiscal year (beginning with the last full fiscal year of that institution which immediately preceded the effective date of this chapter).

(2) The information required to be maintained and made available under paragraph (1) shall also be itemized in order to clearly and conspicuously disclose the following:

(A) The number and dollar amount for each item referred to in paragraph (1), by census tracts for mortgage loans secured by property located within any county with a population of more than 30,000, within that primary metropolitan statistical area, metropolitan statistical area, or consolidated metropolitan statistical area that is not comprised of designated primary metropolitan statistical areas, otherwise, by county, for mortgage loans secured by property located within any other county within that primary metropolitan statistical area, metropolitan statistical area, or consolidated metropolitan statistical area that is not comprised of designated primary metropolitan statistical areas.

(B) The number and dollar amount for each item referred to in paragraph (1) for all such mortgage loans which are secured by property located outside that primary metropolitan statistical area, metropolitan statistical area, or consolidated metropolitan statistical area that is not comprised of designated primary metropolitan statistical areas.

For the purpose of this paragraph, a depository institution which maintains offices in more than one primary metropolitan statistical area, metropolitan statistical area, or consolidated metropolitan statistical area that is not comprised of designated primary metropolitan statistical areas shall be required to make the information required by this paragraph available at any such office only to the extent that such information relates to mortgage loans which were originated or purchased (or for which completed applications were received) by an office of that depository institution located in the primary metropolitan statistical area, metropolitan statistical area, or consolidated metropolitan statistical area that is not comprised of designated primary metropolitan statistical areas in which the office making such information available is located. For purposes of this paragraph, other lending institutions shall be deemed to have a home office or branch office within a primary metropolitan statistical area, metropolitan statistical area, or consolidated metropolitan statistical area that is not comprised of designated primary metropolitan statistical areas if such institutions have originated or purchased or received completed applications for at least 5 mortgage loans in such area in the preceding calendar year.

(b) Itemization of loan data

Any item of information relating to mortgage loans required to be maintained under subsection (a) of this section shall be further itemized in order to disclose for each such item—

(1) the number and dollar amount of mortgage loans which are insured under title II of the National Housing Act (12 U.S.C. § 1707 *et seq.*) or under title V of the Housing Act of 1949 (42 U.S.C. § 1471 *et seq.*) or which are guaranteed under chapter 37 of title 38;

(2) the number and dollar amount of mortgage loans made to mortgagors who did not, at the time of execution of the mortgage, intend to reside in the property securing the mortgage loan;

(3) the number and dollar amount of home improvement loans;

(4) the number and dollar amount of mortgage loans and completed applications involving mortgagors or mortgage applicants grouped according to census tract, income level, racial characteristics, age, and gender; and

(5) the number and dollar amount of mortgage loans grouped according to measurements of—

(A) the total points and fees payable at origination in connection with the mortgage as determined by the Bureau, taking into account 15 U.S.C. 1602(aa)(4);

(B) the difference between the annual percentage rate associated with the loan and a benchmark rate or rates for all loans;

(C) the term in months of any prepayment penalty or other fee or charge payable on repayment of some portion of principal or the entire principal in advance of scheduled payments; and

(D) such other information as the Bureau may require; and

(6) the number and dollar amount of mortgage loans and completed applications grouped according to measurements of—

(A) the value of the real property pledged or proposed to be pledged as collateral;

(B) the actual or proposed term in months of any introductory period after which the rate of interest may change;

(C) the presence of contractual terms or proposed contractual terms that would allow the mortgagor or applicant to make payments other than fully amortizing payments during any portion of the loan term;

(D) the actual or proposed term in months of the mortgage loan;

(E) the channel through which application was made, including retail, broker, and other relevant categories;

(F) as the Bureau may determine to be appropriate, a unique identifier that identifies the loan originator as set forth in section 1503 of the S.A.F.E. Mortgage Licensing Act of 2008;

(G) as the Bureau may determine to be appropriate, a universal loan identifier;

(H) as the Bureau may determine to be appropriate, the parcel number that corresponds to the real property pledged or proposed to be pledged as collateral;

(I) the credit score of mortgage applicants and mortgagors, in such form as the Bureau may prescribe; and

(J) such other information as the Bureau may require.

(c) Period of maintenance

Any information required to be compiled and made available under this section, other than loan application register information under subsection (j) of this section, shall be maintained and made available for a period of five years after the close of the first year during which such information is required to be maintained and made available.

(d) Duration of disclosure requirements

Notwithstanding the provisions of subsection (a)(1) of this section, data required to be disclosed under this section for 1980 and thereafter shall be disclosed for each calendar year. Any depository institution which is required to make disclosures under this section but which has been making disclosures on some basis other than a calendar year basis shall make available a separate disclosure statement containing data for any period prior to calendar year 1980 which is not covered by the last full year report prior to the 1980 calendar year report.

(e) Format for disclosures

Subject to subsection (h) of this section, the Bureau shall prescribe a standard format for the disclosures required under this section.

(f) Data disclosure system; operation, etc.

The Federal Financial Institutions Examination Council, in consultation with the Secretary, shall implement a system to facilitate access to data required to be disclosed under this section. Such system shall include arrangements for a central depository of data in each primary metropolitan statistical area, metropolitan statistical area, or consolidated metropolitan statistical area that is not comprised of designated primary metropolitan statistical areas. Disclosure statements shall be made available to the public for inspection and copying at such central depository of data for all depository institutions which are required to disclose information under this section (or which are exempted pursuant to section 2805(b) of this title) and which have a home office or branch office within such primary metropolitan statistical area, metropolitan statistical area, or consolidated metropolitan statistical area that is not comprised of designated primary metropolitan statistical areas.

(g) Exceptions

The requirements of subsections (a) and (b) of this section shall not apply with respect to mortgage loans that are—

(1) made (or for which completed applications are received) by any mortgage banking subsidiary of a bank holding company or savings and loan holding company or by any savings and loan service corporation that originates or purchases mortgage loans; and

(2) approved (or for which completed applications are received) by the Secretary for insurance under title I or II of the National Housing Act (12 U.S.C. §§ 1702 *et seq.* and 1707 *et seq.*).

(h) Submission to agencies

(1) In general

The data required to be disclosed under subsection (b) shall be submitted to the Bureau or to the appropriate agency for the institution reporting under this title, in accordance with rules prescribed by the Bureau. Notwithstanding the requirement of subsection (a)(2)(A) for disclosure by census tract, the Bureau, in consultation with other appropriate agencies described in

paragraph (2) and, after notice and comment, shall develop regulations that—

(A) prescribe the format for such disclosures, the method for submission of the data to the appropriate agency, and the procedures for disclosing the information to the public;

(B) require the collection of data required to be disclosed under subsection (b) with respect to loans sold by each institution reporting under this title;

(C) require disclosure of the class of the purchaser of such loans;

(D) permit any reporting institution to submit in writing to the Bureau or to the appropriate agency such additional data or explanations as it deems relevant to the decision to originate or purchase mortgage loans; and

(E) modify or require modification of itemized information, for the purpose of protecting the privacy interests of the mortgage applicants or mortgagors, that is or will be available to the public.

(2) Other appropriate agencies

The appropriate agencies described in this paragraph are—

(A) the appropriate Federal banking agencies, as defined in section 3(q) of the Federal Deposit Insurance Act (12 U.S.C. 1813(q)), with respect to the entities that are subject to the jurisdiction of each such agency, respectively;

(B) the Federal Deposit Insurance Corporation for banks insured by the Federal Deposit Insurance Corporation (other than members of the Federal Reserve System), mutual savings banks, insured State branches of foreign banks, and any other depository institution described in section 303(2)(A) which is not otherwise referred to in this paragraph;

(C) the National Credit Union Administration Board with respect to credit unions; and

(D) the Secretary of Housing and Urban Development with respect to other lending institutions not regulated by the agencies referred to in subparagraph (A) or (B).

(3) Rules for modifications under paragraph (1)

(A) Application

A modification under paragraph (1)(E) shall apply to information concerning—

(i) credit score data described in subsection (b)(6)(I), in a manner that is consistent with the purpose described in paragraph (1)(E); and

(ii) age or any other category of data described in paragraph (5) or (6) of subsection (b), as the Bureau determines to be necessary to satisfy the purpose described in paragraph (1)(E), and in a manner consistent with that purpose.

(B) Standards

The Bureau shall prescribe standards for any modification under paragraph (1)(E) to effectuate the purposes of this title, in light of the privacy interests of mortgage applicants or mortgagors. Where necessary to protect the privacy interests of mortgage applicants or mortgagors, the Bureau shall provide for the disclosure of information described in subparagraph (A) in aggregate or other reasonably modified form, in order to effectuate the purposes of this title.

(*i*) Exemption from certain disclosure requirements

The requirements of subsections (b)(4), (b)(5), and (b)(6) of this section shall not apply with respect to any depository institution described in section 2802(2)(A) of this title which has total assets, as of the most recent full fiscal year of such institution, of $30,000,000 or less.

(j) Loan application register information

(1) In general

In addition to the information required to be disclosed under subsections (a) and (b) of this section, any depository institution which is required to make disclosures under this section shall make available to the public, upon request, loan application register information (as defined by the Bureau by regulation) in the form required under regulations prescribed by the Bureau.

(2) Format of disclosure

(A) Unedited format

Subject to subparagraph (B), the loan application register information described in paragraph (1) may be disclosed by a depository institution without editing or compilation and in such formats as the Bureau may require.

(B) Protection of applicant's privacy interest

The Bureau shall require, by regulation, such deletions as the Bureau may determine to be appropriate to protect—

(i) any privacy interest of any applicant, including the deletion of the applicant's name and identification number, the date of the application, and the date of any determination by the institution with respect to such application; and

(ii) a depository institution from liability under any Federal or State privacy law.

(C) Census tract format encouraged

It is the sense of the Congress that a depository institution should provide loan register information under this section in a format based on the census tract in which the property is located.

(3) Change of form not required

A depository institution meets the disclosure requirement of paragraph (1) if the institution provides the information required under such paragraph in such formats as the Bureau may require.

(4) Reasonable charge for information

Any depository institution which provides information under this subsection may impose a reasonable fee for any cost incurred in reproducing such information.

(5) Time of disclosure

The disclosure of the loan application register information described in paragraph (1) for any year pursuant to a request under paragraph (1) shall be made—

(A) in the case of a request made on or before March 1 of the succeeding year, before April 1 of the succeeding year; and

(B) in the case of a request made after March 1 of the succeeding year, before the end of the 30-day period beginning on the date the request is made.

(6) Retention of information

Notwithstanding subsection (c) of this section, the loan application register information described in paragraph (1) for any year shall be maintained and made available, upon request, for 3 years after the close of the 1st year during which such information is required to be maintained and made available.

(7) Minimizing compliance costs

In prescribing regulations under this subsection, the Bureau shall make every effort to minimize the costs incurred by a depository institution in complying with this subsection and such regulations.

(k) Disclosure of statements by depository institutions

(1) In general

In accordance with procedures established by the Bureau pursuant to this section, any depository institution required to make disclosures under this section—

(A) shall make a disclosure statement available, upon request, to the public no later than 3 business days after the institution receives the statement from the Federal Financial Institutions Examination Council; and

(B) may make such statement available on a floppy disc which may be used with a personal computer or in any other media which is not prohibited under regulations prescribed by the Bureau.

(2) Notice that data is subject to correction after final review

Any disclosure statement provided pursuant to paragraph (1) shall be accompanied by a clear and conspicuous notice that the statement is subject to final review and revision, if necessary.

(3) Reasonable charge for information

Any depository institution which provides a disclosure statement pursuant to paragraph (1) may impose a reasonable fee for any cost incurred in providing or reproducing such statement.

(*l*) Prompt disclosures

(1) In general

Any disclosure of information pursuant to this section or section 2809 of this title shall be made as promptly as possible.

(2) Maximum disclosure period

(A) 6- and 9-month maximum periods

Except as provided in subsections (j)(5) and (k)(1) of this section and regulations prescribed by the Bureau and subject to subparagraph (B), any information required to be disclosed for any year beginning after December 31, 1992, under—

(i) this section shall be made available to the public before September 1 of the succeeding year; and

(ii) section 2809 of this title shall be made available to the public before December 1 of the succeeding year.

(B) Shorter periods encouraged after 1994

With respect to disclosures of information under this section or section 2809 of this title for any year beginning after December 31, 1993, every effort shall be made—

(i) to make information disclosed under this section available to the public before July 1 of the succeeding year; and

(ii) to make information required to be disclosed under section 2809 of this title available to the public before September 1 of the succeeding year.

(3) Improved procedure

The Federal Financial Institutions Examination Council shall make such changes in the system established pursuant to subsection (f) of this section as may be necessary to carry out the requirements of this subsection.

(m) Opportunity to reduce compliance burden

(1) In general

(A) Satisfaction of public availability requirements

A depository institution shall be deemed to have satisfied the public availability requirements of subsection (a) of this section if the institution compiles the information required under that subsection at the home office of the institution and provides notice at the branch locations specified in subsection (a) of this section that such information is available from the home office of the institution upon written request.

(B) Provision of information upon request

Not later than 15 days after the receipt of a written request for any information required to be compiled under subsection (a) of this section, the home office of the depository institution receiving the request shall provide the information pertinent to the location of the branch in question to the person requesting the information.

(2) Form of information

In complying with paragraph (1), a depository institution shall provide the person requesting the information with a copy of the information requested in such formats as the Bureau may require.)

(n) Timing of certain disclosures

The data required to be disclosed under subsection (b) shall be submitted to the Bureau or to the appropriate agency for any institution reporting under this title, in accordance with regulations prescribed by the Bureau. Institutions shall not be required to report new data under paragraph (5) or (6) of subsection (b) before the first January 1 that occurs after the end of the 9-month period beginning on the date on which regulations are issued by the Bureau in final form with respect to such disclosures.

[Pub. L. No. 96-399, § 340(a), 94 Stat. 1657 (1980); Pub. L. No. 98-181, § 701(a), 97 Stat. 1266 (1983); Pub. L. No. 100-242, §§ 565(a)(2), 570(h), 101 Stat. 1945, 1950 (1988); Pub. L. No. 101-73, § 1211(a), (b), (c)(1), (2)(A)–(C), (f), (i), (j), 103 Stat. 524–526 (1989); Pub. L. No. 102-242, § 212(a)(1), 105 Stat. 2299 (1991); Pub. L. No. 102-550, § 932(a), (b), 106 Stat. 3889, 3891 (1992); Pub. L. No. 104-208, § 2225(b), 110 Stat. 3009-416 (1996); Pub. L. No. 111-203, tit. X, §§ 1094(1), (3), 1100H, 124 Stat. 2097, 2113 (July 21, 2010)]

12 U.S.C. § 2804. Enforcement

(a) Regulations

The Bureau shall prescribe such regulations as may be necessary to carry out the purposes of this chapter. These regulations may contain such classifications, differentiations, or other provisions, and may provide for such adjustments and exceptions for any class of transactions, as in the judgment of the Bureau are necessary and proper to effectuate the purposes of this chapter, and prevent circumvention or evasion thereof, or to facilitate compliance therewith.

(b) Powers of certain other agencies

(1) In general

Subject to subtitle B of the Consumer Financial Protection Act of 2010, compliance with the requirements of this title shall be enforced—

(A) under section 8 of the Federal Deposit Insurance Act, The appropriate Federal banking agency, as defined in section 3(q) of the Federal Deposit Insurance Act (12 U.S.C. 1813(q)), with respect to—

(i) any national bank or Federal savings association, and any Federal branch or Federal agency of a foreign bank;

(ii) any member bank of the Federal Reserve System (other than a national bank), branch or agency of a foreign bank (other than a Federal branch, Federal agency, and insured State branch of a foreign bank),

commercial lending company owned or controlled by a foreign bank, and any organization operating under section 25 or 25A of the Federal Reserve Act; and

(iii) any bank or State savings association insured by the Federal Deposit Insurance Corporation (other than a member of the Federal Reserve System), any mutual savings bank as, defined in section 3(f) of the Federal Deposit Insurance Act (12 U.S.C. 1813(f)), any insured State branch of a foreign bank, and any other depository institution not referred to in this paragraph or subparagraph (B) or (C);

(B) subtitle E of the Consumer Financial Protection Act of 2010, by the Bureau, with respect to any person subject to this subtitle;

(C) the Federal Credit Union Act, by the Administrator of the National Credit Union Administration with respect to any insured credit union; and

(D) respect to other lending institutions, by the Secretary of Housing and Urban Development.

(2) Incorporated definitions

The terms used in paragraph (1) that are not defined in this title or otherwise defined in section 3(s) of the Federal Deposit Insurance Act (12 U.S.C. 1813(s)) shall have the same meanings as in section 1(b) of the International Banking Act of 1978 (12 U.S.C. 3101).

(c) Violations of this chapter deemed violations of certain other provisions

For the purpose of the exercise by any agency referred to in subsection (b) of this section of its powers under any Act referred to in that subsection, a violation of any requirement imposed under this chapter shall be deemed to be a violation of a requirement imposed under that Act. In addition to its powers under any provision of law specifically referred to in subsection (b) of this section, each of the agencies referred to in that subsection may exercise, for the purpose of enforcing compliance with any requirement imposed under this chapter, any other authority conferred on it by law.

(d) Overall enforcement authority of the bureau of consumer financial protection

Subject to subtitle B of the Consumer Financial Protection Act of 2010, enforcement of the requirements imposed under this title is committed to each of the agencies under subsection (b). To facilitate research, examinations, and enforcement, all data collected pursuant to section 304 shall be available to the entities listed under subsection (b). The Bureau may exercise its authorities under the Consumer Financial Protection Act of 2010 to exercise principal authority to examine and enforce compliance by any person with the requirements of this title.

[Pub. L. No. 101-73, §§ 744(p)(1), 1211(g), Aug. 9, 1989, 103 Stat. 440, 526 (1989); Pub. L. No. 102-242, § 212(a)(2), 105 Stat. 2299 (1991); Pub. L. No. 111-203, tit. X, §§ 1094(1), (4)(A), (4)(B), 1100H, 124 Stat. 2097, 2100, 2113 (July 21, 2010)]

12 U.S.C. § 2805. Relation to State laws

(a) This chapter does not annul, alter, or affect, or exempt any State-chartered depository institution subject to the provisions of this chapter from complying with the laws of any State or subdivision thereof with respect to public disclosure and record keeping by depositor institutions, except to the extent that those laws are inconsistent with any provision of this chapter, and then only to the extent of the inconsistency. The Bureau is authorized to determine whether such inconsistencies exist. The Bureau may not determine that any such law is inconsistent with any provision of this chapter if the Bureau determines that such law requires the maintenance of records with greater geographic or other detail than is required under this chapter, or that such law otherwise provides greater disclosure than is required under this chapter.

(b) Exemption authority

The Bureau may, by regulation, exempt from the requirements of this title any State-chartered depository institution within any State or subdivision thereof, if the agency determines that, under the law of such State or subdivision, that institution is subject to requirements that are substantially similar to those imposed under this title, and that such law contains adequate provisions for enforcement. Notwithstanding any other provision of this subsection, compliance with the requirements imposed under this subsection shall be enforced by the Office of the Comptroller of the Currency under section 8 of the Federal Deposit Insurance Act, in the case of national banks and Federal savings associations, the deposits of which are insured by the Federal Deposit Insurance Corporation.

[Pub. L. No. 100-628, § 1087(b), 102 Stat. 3280 (1988); Pub. L. No. 101-73, § 744(p)(2), 103 Stat. 440 (1989); Pub. L. No. 111-203, tit. X, §§ 1094(1), (5), 1100H, 124 Stat. 2097, 2100, 2113 (July 21, 2010)]

12 U.S.C. § 2806. Compliance Improvement Methods

(a) In general

(1) Consultation required

The Director of the Bureau of Consumer Financial Protection, with the assistance of the Secretary, the Director of the Bureau of the Census, the Board of Governors of the Federal Reserve System, the Federal Deposit Insurance Corporation, and such other persons as the Bureau deems appropriate, shall develop or assist in the improvement of, methods of matching addresses and census tracts to facilitate compliance by depository institutions in as economical a manner as possible with the requirements of this title.

(2) Authorization of appropriations

There are authorized to be appropriated, such sums as may be necessary to carry out this subsection.

(3) Contracting authority

The Director of the Bureau of Consumer Financial Protection is authorized to utilize, contract with, act through, or compensate any person or agency in order to carry out this subsection.

(b) Recommendations to congress

The Director of the Bureau of Consumer Financial Protection shall recommend to the Committee on Banking, Housing, and Urban Affairs of the Senate and the Committee on Financial Services of the House of Representatives, such additional legislation as the Director of the Bureau of Consumer Financial Protection deems appropriate to carry out the purpose of this title.

[Pub. L. No. 100-628, § 1087(c), 102 Stat. 3280 (1988); Pub. L. No. 101-73, § 744(p)(3), 103 Stat. 440 (1989); Pub. L. No. 111-203, tit. X, §§ 1094(6), 1100H, 124 Stat. 2101, 2113 (July 21, 2010)]

12 U.S.C. § 2807. Report

The Bureau, in consultation with the Secretary of Housing and Urban Development, shall report annually to the Congress on the utility of the requirements of section 2803(b)(4) of this title.

[Pub. L. No. 111-203, tit. X, §§ 1094(1), 1100H, 124 Stat. 2097, 2113 (July 21, 2010)]

12 U.S.C. § 2808. Effective date

(a) In general

This chapter shall take effect on the one hundred and eightieth day beginning after December 31, 1975. Any institution specified in section 2802(2)(A) of this title which has total assets as of its last full fiscal year of $10,000,000 or less is exempt from the provisions of this chapter. The Bureau, in consultation with the Secretary, may exempt institutions described in section 2802(2)(B) of this title that are comparable within their respective industries to institutions that are exempt under the preceding sentence (as determined without regard to the adjustment made by subsection (b) of this section).

(b) CPI adjustments

(1) In general

Subject to paragraph (2), the dollar amount applicable with respect to institutions described in section 2802(2)(A) of this title under the 2d sentence of subsection (a) of this section shall be adjusted annually after December 31, 1996, by the annual percentage increase in the Consumer Price Index for Urban Wage Earners and Clerical Workers published by the Bureau of Labor Statistics.

(2) 1-time adjustment for prior inflation

The first adjustment made under paragraph (1) after September 30, 1996, shall be the percentage by which—

(A) the Consumer Price Index described in such paragraph for the calendar year 1996, exceeds

(B) such Consumer Price Index for the calendar year 1975.

(3) Rounding

The dollar amount applicable under paragraph (1) for any calendar year shall be the amount determined in accordance with subparagraphs (A) and (B) of paragraph (2) and rounded to the nearest multiple of $1,000,000.

[Pub. L. No. 102-242, § 224(a), 105 Stat. 2307 (1991); Pub. L. No. 102-550, § 1604(a)(15), 106 Stat. 4083 (1992); Pub. L. No. 104-208, § 2225(a), 110 Stat. 3009-415 (1996); Pub. L. No. 111-203, tit. X, §§ 1094(1), 1100H, 124 Stat. 2097, 2113 (July 21, 2010)]

12 U.S.C. § 2809. Compilation of aggregate data

(a) Commencement; scope of data and tables

Beginning with data for calendar year 1980, the Federal Financial Institutions Examination Council shall compile each year, for each primary metropolitan statistical area, metropolitan statistical area, or consolidated metropolitan statistical area that is not comprised of designated primary metropolitan statistical areas, aggregate data by census tract for all depository institutions which are required to disclose data under section 2803 of this title or which are exempt pursuant to section 2805(b) of this title. The Council shall also produce tables indicating, for each primary metropolitan statistical area, metropolitan statistical area, or consolidated metropolitan statistical area that is not comprised of designated primary metropolitan statistical areas, aggregate lending patterns for various categories of census tracts grouped according to location, age of housing stock, income level, and racial characteristics.

(b) Staff and data processing resources

The Bureau shall provide staff and data processing resources to the Council to enable it to carry out the provisions of subsection (a) of this section.

(c) Availability to public

The data and tables required pursuant to subsection (a) of this section shall be made available to the public by no later than December 31 of the year following the calendar year on which the data is based.

[Pub. L. No. 96-399, § 340(c), 94 Stat. 1658 (1980); Pub. L. No. 98-181, § 701(a), 97 Stat. 1266 (1983); Pub. L. No. 111-203, tit. X, §§ 1094(1), 1100H, 124 Stat. 2097, 2113 (July 21, 2010)]

12 U.S.C. § 2810. Disclosure by Secretary; commencement, scope, etc.

Beginning with data for calendar year 1980, the Secretary shall make publicly available data in the Secretary's possession for each mortgagee which is not otherwise subject to the requirements of this chapter and which is not exempt pursuant to section 2805(b) of this title (and for each mortgagee making mortgage loans exempted under section 2803(g) of this title), with respect to mortgage loans approved (or for which completed applications are received) by the Secretary for insurance under title I or II of the National Housing Act [12 U.S.C. §§ 1702 *et seq.*, 1707 *et seq.*]. Such data to be disclosed shall consist of data comparable to the data which would be disclosed if such mortgagee were subject to the requirements of section 2803 of this title. Disclosure statements containing data for each such mortgagee for a primary metropolitan statistical area, metropolitan statistical area, or consolidated metropolitan statistical area that is not comprised of designated primary metropolitan statistical areas shall, at a minimum, be publicly available at the central depository of data established pursuant to section 2803(f) of this title for such primary metropolitan statistical area, metropolitan statistical area, or consolidated metropolitan statistical area that is not comprised of designated primary metropolitan statistical areas. The Secretary shall also compile and make publicly available aggregate data for such mortgagees by census tract, and tables indicating aggregate lending patterns, in a manner comparable to the information required to be made publicly available in accordance with section 2809 of this title.

[Pub. L. No. 96-399, § 340(c), 94 Stat. 1658 (1980); Pub. L. 98-181, § 701(a), 97 Stat. 1266 (1983); Pub. L. No. 100-242, § 565(a)(3), 101 Stat. 1945 (1988); Pub. L. No. 101-73, § 1211(c)(2)(D), 103 Stat. 525 (1989)]

E.2 Regulation C

The Consumer Financial Protection Bureau (CFPB) now has authority to issue Regulation C and its commentary. *See* Pub. L. No. 111-203, tit. X, §§ 1085(3), 1100H, 124 Stat. 2083, 2113 (July 21, 2010). On December 19, 2011, the CFPB issued its version of Regulation C and its commentary. *See* 76 Fed. Reg. 78468 (Dec. 19, 2011). The major change from the Federal Reserve Board's (FRB) version is that 12 C.F.R. part 203 citations are replaced by citations to 12 C.F.R. part 1003. Other changes are stylistic and not substantive. The FRB version and the CFPB's version (with supplemental information) are both found on the companion website to this treatise.

TITLE 12—BANKS AND BANKING

CHAPTER X—BUREAU OF CONSUMER FINANCIAL PROTECTION

SUBCHAPTER M—FEDERAL HOME LOAN BANK DISCLOSURES

PART 1003—HOME MORTGAGE DISCLOSURE (REGULATION C)

AUTHORITY: 12 U.S.C. §§ 2803, 2804, 2805, 5512, 5581.

SOURCE: 76 Fed. Reg. 44242 (July 22, 2011); 76 Fed. Reg. 78468 (Dec. 19, 2011), unless otherwise noted.

§ 1003.1. Authority, purpose, and scope.

(a) **Authority.** This part, known as Regulation C, is issued by the Bureau of Consumer Financial Protection (Bureau) pursuant to the Home Mortgage Disclosure Act (HMDA) (12 U.S.C. 2801 *et seq.*), as amended. The information-collection requirements have been approved by the U.S. Office of Management and Budget (OMB) under 44 U.S.C. 3501 *et seq.* and have been assigned OMB numbers for institutions reporting data to the Office of the Comptroller of the Currency (1557–0159), the Federal Deposit Insurance Corporation (3064-0046), the Federal Reserve System (7100-0247), the Department of Housing and Urban Development (HUD) (2502-0529), the National Credit Union Administration (3133-0166), and the Bureau of Consumer Financial Protection (3170-0008).

(b) **Purpose.**

(1) This part implements the Home Mortgage Disclosure Act, which is intended to provide the public with loan data that can be used:

(i) To help determine whether financial institutions are serving the housing needs of their communities;

(ii) To assist public officials in distributing public-sector investment so as to attract private investment to areas where it is needed; and

(iii) To assist in identifying possible discriminatory lending patterns and enforcing antidiscrimination statutes.

(2) Neither the act nor this part is intended to encourage unsound lending practices or the allocation of credit.

(c) **Scope.** This part applies to certain financial institutions, including banks, savings associations, credit unions, and other mortgage lending institutions, as defined in § 1003.2. The regulation requires an institution to report data to the appropriate Federal agency about home purchase loans, home improvement loans, and refinancings that it originates or purchases, or for which it receives applications; and to disclose certain data to the public.

§ 1003.2. Definitions.

In this part:

Act means the Home Mortgage Disclosure Act (HMDA) (12 U.S.C. 2801 *et seq.*), as amended.

Application.—

(1) *In general.* Application means an oral or written request for a home purchase loan, a home improvement loan, or a refinancing that is made in accordance with procedures used by a financial institution for the type of credit requested.

(2) *Preapproval programs.* A request for preapproval for a home purchase loan is an application under this section if the request is reviewed under a program in which the financial institution, after a comprehensive analysis of the creditworthiness of the applicant, issues a written commitment to the applicant valid for a designated period of time to extend a home purchase loan up to a specified amount. The written commitment may not be subject to conditions other than:

(i) Conditions that require the identification of a suitable property;

(ii) Conditions that require that no material change has occurred in the applicant's financial condition or creditworthiness prior to closing; and

(iii) Limited conditions that are not related to the financial condition or creditworthiness of the applicant that the lender ordinarily attaches to a traditional home mortgage application (such as certification of a clear termite inspection).

Branch office means:

(1) Any office of a bank, savings association, or credit union that is approved as a branch by a Federal or state supervisory agency, but excludes free-standing electronic terminals such as automated teller machines; and

(2) Any office of a for-profit mortgage-lending institution (other than a bank, savings association, or credit union) that takes applications from the public for home purchase loans, home improvement loans, or refinancings. A for-profit mortgage-lending institution is also deemed to have a branch office in an MSA or in a Metropolitan Division, if, in the preceding calendar year, it received applications for, originated, or purchased five or more home purchase loans, home improvement loans, or refinancings related to property located in that MSA or Metropolitan Division, respectively.

Dwelling means a residential structure (whether or not attached to real property) located in a state of the United States of America, the District of Columbia, or the Commonwealth of Puerto Rico. The term includes an individual condominium unit, co-operative unit, or mobile or manufactured home.

Financial institution means:

(1) A bank, savings association, or credit union that:

(i) On the preceding December 31 had assets in excess of the asset threshold established and published annually by the Bureau for coverage by the act, based on the year-to-year change in the average of the Consumer Price Index for Urban Wage Earners and Clerical Workers, not seasonally adjusted, for each twelve month period ending in November, with rounding to the nearest million;

(ii) On the preceding December 31, had a home or branch office in an MSA;

(iii) In the preceding calendar year, originated at least one home purchase loan (excluding temporary financing such as a construction loan) or refinancing of a home purchase loan, secured by a first lien on a one-to four-family dwelling; and

(iv) Meets one or more of the following three criteria:

(A) The institution is Federally insured or regulated;

(B) The mortgage loan referred to in paragraph (1)(iii) of this definition was insured, guaranteed, or supplemented by a Federal agency; or

(C) The mortgage loan referred to in paragraph (1)(iii) of this definition was intended by the institution for sale to Fannie Mae or Freddie Mac; and

(2) A for-profit mortgage-lending institution (other than a bank, savings association, or credit union) that:

(i) In the preceding calendar year, either:

(A) Originated home purchase loans, including refinancings of home purchase loans, that equaled at least 10 percent of its loan-origination volume, measured in dollars; or

(B) Originated home purchase loans, including refinancings of home purchase loans, that equaled at least $25 million; and

(ii) On the preceding December 31, had a home or branch office in an MSA; and

(iii) Either:

(A) On the preceding December 31, had total assets of more than $10 million, counting the assets of any parent corporation; or

(B) In the preceding calendar year, originated at least 100 home purchase loans, including refinancings of home purchase loans.

Home-equity line of credit means an open-end credit plan secured by a dwelling as defined in Regulation Z (Truth in Lending), 12 CFR part 1026.

Home improvement loan means:

(1) A loan secured by a lien on a dwelling that is for the purpose, in whole or in part, of repairing, rehabilitating, remodeling, or improving a dwelling or the real property on which it is located; and

(2) A non-dwelling secured loan that is for the purpose, in whole or in part, of repairing, rehabilitating, remodeling, or improving a dwelling or the real property on which it is located, and that is classified by the financial institution as a home improvement loan.

Home purchase loan means a loan secured by and made for the purpose of purchasing a dwelling.

Manufactured home means any residential structure as defined under regulations of the Department of Housing and Urban Development establishing manufactured home construction and safety standards (24 CFR 3280.2).

Metropolitan Statistical Area or MSA and Metropolitan Division or MD.

(1) *Metropolitan Statistical Area* or *MSA* means a metropolitan statistical area as defined by the U.S. Office of Management and Budget.

(2) *Metropolitan Division* or *MD* means a metropolitan division of an MSA, as defined by the U.S. Office of Management and Budget.

Refinancing means a new obligation that satisfies and replaces an existing obligation by the same borrower, in which:

(1) For coverage purposes, the existing obligation is a home purchase loan (as determined by the lender, for example, by reference to available documents; or as stated by the applicant), and both the existing obligation and the new obligation are secured by first liens on dwellings; and

(2) For reporting purposes, both the existing obligation and the new obligation are secured by liens on dwellings.

§ 1003.3. Exempt institutions.

(a) Exemption based on state law.

(1) A state-chartered or state-licensed financial institution is exempt from the requirements of this part if the Bureau determines that the institution is subject to a state disclosure law that contains requirements substantially similar to those imposed by this part and that contains adequate provisions for enforcement.

(2) Any state, state-chartered or state-licensed financial institution, or association of such institutions, may apply to the Bureau for an exemption under paragraph (a) of this section.

(3) An institution that is exempt under paragraph (a) of this section shall use the disclosure form required by its state law and shall submit the data required by that law to its state supervisory agency for purposes of aggregation.

(b) Loss of exemption. An institution losing a state-law exemption under paragraph (a) of this section shall comply with this part beginning with the calendar year following the year for which it last reported loan data under the state disclosure law.

§ 1003.4. Compilation of loan data.

(a) Data format and itemization. A financial institution shall collect data regarding applications for, and originations and purchases of, home purchase loans, home improvement loans, and refinancings for each calendar year. An institution is required to collect data regarding requests under a preapproval program (as defined in § 1003.2) only if the preapproval request is denied or results in the origination of a home purchase loan. All reportable transactions shall be recorded, within thirty calendar days after the end of the calendar quarter in which final action is taken (such as origination or purchase of a loan, or denial or withdrawal of an application), on a register in the format prescribed in Appendix A of this part. The data recorded shall include the following items:

(1) An identifying number for the loan or loan application, and the date the application was received.

(2) The type of loan or application.

(3) The purpose of the loan or application.

(4) Whether the application is a request for preapproval and whether it resulted in a denial or in an origination.

(5) The property type to which the loan or application relates.

(6) The owner-occupancy status of the property to which the loan or application relates.

(7) The amount of the loan or the amount applied for.

(8) The type of action taken, and the date.

(9) The location of the property to which the loan or application relates, by MSA or by Metropolitan Division, by state, by county, and by census tract, if the institution has a home or branch office in that MSA or Metropolitan Division.

(10) The ethnicity, race, and sex of the applicant or borrower, and the gross annual income relied on in processing the application.

(11) The type of entity purchasing a loan that the institution originates or purchases and then sells within the same calendar year (this information need not be included in quarterly updates).

(12)

(i) For originated loans subject to Regulation Z, 12 CFR part 1026, the difference between the loan's annual percentage rate (APR) and the average prime offer rate for a comparable transaction as of the date the interest rate is set, if that difference is equal to or greater than 1.5 percentage points for loans secured by a first lien on a dwelling, or equal to or greater than 3.5 percentage points for loans secured by a subordinate lien on a dwelling.

(ii) "Average prime offer rate" means an annual percentage rate that is derived from average interest rates, points, and other loan pricing terms currently offered to consumers by a representative sample of creditors for mortgage loans that have low-risk pricing characteristics. The Bureau publishes average prime offer rates for a broad range of types of transactions in tables updated at least weekly, as well as the methodology the Bureau uses to derive these rates.

(13) Whether the loan is subject to the Home Ownership and Equity Protection Act of 1994, as implemented in Regulation Z (12 CFR 1026.32).

(14) The lien status of the loan or application (first lien, subordinate lien, or not secured by a lien on a dwelling).

(b) Collection of data on ethnicity, race, sex, and income.

(1) A financial institution shall collect data about the ethnicity, race, and sex of the applicant or borrower as prescribed in Appendix B of this part.

(2) Ethnicity, race, sex, and income data may but need not be collected for loans purchased by the financial institution.

(c) Optional data. A financial institution may report:

(1) The reasons it denied a loan application;

(2) Requests for preapproval that are approved by the institution but not accepted by the applicant; and

(3) Home-equity lines of credit made in whole or in part for the purpose of home improvement or home purchase.

(d) Excluded data. A financial institution shall not report:

(1) Loans originated or purchased by the financial institution acting in a fiduciary capacity (such as trustee);

(2) Loans on unimproved land;

(3) Temporary financing (such as bridge or construction loans);

(4) The purchase of an interest in a pool of loans (such as mortgage-participation certificates, mortgage-backed securities, or real estate mortgage investment conduits);

(5) The purchase solely of the right to service loans; or

(6) Loans acquired as part of a merger or acquisition, or as part of the acquisition of all of the assets and liabilities of a branch office as defined in § 1003.2.

(e) Data reporting for banks and savings associations that are required to report data on small business, small farm, and community development lending under CRA. Banks and savings associations that are required to report data on small business, small farm, and community development lending under regulations that implement the Community Reinvestment Act of 1977 (12 U.S.C. 2901 *et seq.*) shall also collect the location of property located outside MSAs and Metropolitan Divisions in which the institution has a home or branch office, or outside any MSA.

§ 1003.5. Disclosure and reporting.

(a) Reporting to agency.

(1) By March 1 following the calendar year for which the loan data are compiled, a financial institution shall send its complete loan/application register to the agency office specified in Appendix A of this part. The institution shall retain a copy for its records for at least three years.

(2) A subsidiary of a bank or savings association shall complete a separate loan/application register. The subsidiary shall submit the register, directly or through its parent, to the same agency as its parent.

(b) Public disclosure of statement.

(1) The Federal Financial Institutions Examination Council (FFIEC) will prepare a disclosure statement from the data each financial institution submits.

(2) An institution shall make its disclosure statement (prepared by the FFIEC) available to the public at the institution's home office no later than three business days after receiving the disclosure statement from the FFIEC.

(3) In addition, an institution shall either:

(i) Make its disclosure statement available to the public, within ten business days of receiving it, in at least one branch office in each other MSA and each other Metropolitan Division where the institution has offices (the disclosure statement need only contain data relating to the MSA or Metropolitan Division where the branch is located); or

(ii) Post the address for sending written requests in the lobby of each branch office in other MSAs and Metropolitan Divisions where the institution has offices; and mail or deliver a copy of the disclosure statement within fifteen calendar days of receiving a written request (the disclosure statement need only contain data relating to the MSA or Metropolitan Division for which the request is made). Including the address in the general notice required under paragraph (e) of this section satisfies this requirement.

(c) Public disclosure of modified loan/application register. A financial institution shall make its loan/application register available to the public after removing the following information regarding each entry: The application or loan number, the date that the application was received, and the date action was taken. An institution shall make its modified register available following the calendar year for which the data are compiled, by March 31 for a request received on or before March 1, and within thirty calendar days for a request received after March 1. The modified register need only contain data relating to the MSA or Metropolitan Division for which the request is made.

(d) Availability of data. A financial institution shall make its modified register available to the public for a period of three years and its disclosure statement available for a period of five years. An institution shall make the data available for inspection and copying during the hours the office is normally open to the public for business. It may impose a reasonable fee for any cost incurred in providing or reproducing the data.

(e) Notice of availability. A financial institution shall post a general notice about the availability of its HMDA data in the lobby of its home office and of each branch office located in an MSA and Metropolitan Division. An institution shall provide promptly upon request the location of the institution's offices where the statement is available for inspection and copying, or it may include the location in the lobby notice.

(f) Loan aggregation and central data depositories. Using the loan data submitted by financial institutions, the FFIEC will produce reports for individual institutions and reports of aggregate data for each MSA and Metropolitan Division, showing lending patterns by property location, age of housing stock, and income level, sex, ethnicity, and race. These reports will be available to the public at central data depositories located in each MSA and Metropolitan Division. A listing of central data depositories can be obtained from the Federal Financial Institutions Examination Council, Washington, DC 20006.

§ 1003.6. Enforcement.

(a) Administrative enforcement. A violation of the Act or this part is subject to administrative sanctions as provided in section 305 of the Act, including the imposition of civil money penalties, where applicable. Compliance is enforced by the agencies listed in section 305 of the Act (12 U.S.C. 2804).

(b) Bona fide errors.

(1) An error in compiling or recording loan data is not a violation of the act or this part if the error was unintentional and occurred despite the maintenance of procedures reasonably adapted to avoid such errors.

(2) An incorrect entry for a census tract number is deemed a bona fide error, and is not a violation of the act or this part, provided that the institution maintains procedures reasonably adapted to avoid such errors.

(3) If an institution makes a good-faith effort to record all data concerning covered transactions fully and accurately within thirty calendar days after the end of each calendar quarter, and some data are nevertheless inaccurate or incomplete, the error or omission is not a violation of the act or this part provided that the institution corrects or completes the information prior to submitting the loan/application register to its regulatory agency.

Appendix A to Part 1003—Form and Instructions for Completion of HMDA Loan/Application Register

Paperwork Reduction Act Notice

This report is required by law (12 U.S.C. 2801–2810 and 12 CFR 1003). An agency may not conduct or sponsor, and an organization is not required to respond to, a collection of information unless it displays a valid Office of Management and Budget (OMB) Control Number. See 12 CFR 1003.1(a) for the valid OMB Control Numbers applicable to this information collection. Send comments regarding this burden estimate or any other aspect of this collection of information, including suggestions for reducing the burden, to the respective agencies and to OMB, Office of Information and Regulatory Affairs, Paperwork Reduction Project, Washington, DC 20503. Be sure to reference the applicable agency and the OMB Control Number, as found in 12 CFR 1003.1(a), when submitting comments to OMB.

I. Instructions for Completion of Loan/Application Register

A. Application or Loan Information

1. Application or Loan Number. Enter an identifying loan number that can be used later to retrieve the loan or application file. It can be any number of your institution's choosing (not exceeding 25 characters). You may use letters, numerals, or a combination of both.

2. Date Application Received. Enter the date the loan application was received by your institution by month, day, and year. If your institution normally records the date shown on the application form you may use that date instead. Enter "NA" for loans purchased by your institution. For paper submissions only, use numerals in the form MM/DD/YYYY (for example, 01/15/2003). For submissions in electronic form, the proper format is YYYYMMDD.

3. Type of Loan or Application. Indicate the type of loan or application by entering the applicable Code from the following:

Code 1—Conventional (any loan other than FHA, VA, FSA, or RHS loans)
Code 2—FHA-insured (Federal Housing Administration)
Code 3—VA-guaranteed (Veterans Administration)
Code 4—FSA/RHS-guaranteed (Farm Service Agency or Rural Housing Service)

4. Property Type. Indicate the property type by entering the applicable Code from the following:

Code 1—One- to four-family dwelling (other than manufactured housing)
Code 2—Manufactured housing
Code 3—Multifamily dwelling

a. Use Code 1, not Code 3, for loans on individual condominium or cooperative units.

b. If you cannot determine (despite reasonable efforts to find out) whether the loan or application relates to a manufactured home, use Code 1.

5. Purpose of Loan or Application. Indicate the purpose of the loan or application by entering the applicable Code from the following:

Code 1—Home purchase
Code 2—Home improvement
Code 3—Refinancing

a. Do not report a refinancing if, under the loan agreement, you were unconditionally obligated to refinance the obligation, or you were obligated to refinance the obligation subject to conditions within the borrower's control.

6. Owner Occupancy. Indicate whether the property to which the loan or loan application relates is to be owner-occupied as a principal residence by entering the applicable Code from the following:

Code 1—Owner-occupied as a principal dwelling
Code 2—Not owner-occupied as a principal dwelling
Code 3—Not applicable

a. For purchased loans, use Code 1 unless the loan documents or application indicate that the property will not be owner-occupied as a principal residence.

b. Use Code 2 for second homes or vacation homes, as well as for rental properties.

c. Use Code 3 if the property to which the loan relates is a multifamily dwelling; is not located in an MSA; or is located in an MSA or an MD in which your institution has neither a home nor a branch office. Alternatively, at your institution's option, you may report the actual occupancy status, using Code 1 or 2 as applicable.

7. Loan Amount. Enter the amount of the loan or application. Do not report loans below $500. Show the amount in thousands, rounding to the nearest thousand (round $500 up to the next $1,000). For

example, a loan for $167,300 should be entered as 167 and one for $15,500 as 16.

a. For a home purchase loan that you originated, enter the principal amount of the loan.

b. For a home purchase loan that you purchased, enter the unpaid principal balance of the loan at the time of purchase.

c. For a home improvement loan, enter the entire amount of the loan—including unpaid finance charges if that is how such loans are recorded on your books—even if only a part of the proceeds is intended for home improvement.

d. If you opt to report home-equity lines of credit, report only the portion of the line intended for home improvement or home purchase.

e. For a refinancing, indicate the total amount of the refinancing, including both the amount outstanding on the original loan and any amount of "new money."

f. For a loan application that was denied or withdrawn, enter the amount for which the applicant applied.

8. Request for Preapproval of a Home Purchase Loan. Indicate whether the application or loan involved a request for preapproval of a home purchase loan by entering the applicable Code from the following:

Code 1—Preapproval requested
Code 2—Preapproval not requested
Code 3—Not applicable

a. Enter Code 2 if your institution has a covered preapproval program but the applicant does not request a preapproval.

b. Enter Code 3 if your institution does not have a preapproval program as defined in § 1003.2.

c. Enter Code 3 for applications or loans for home improvement or refinancing, and for purchased loans.

B. Action Taken

1. Type of Action. Indicate the type of action taken on the application or loan by using one of the following Codes.

Code 1—Loan originated
Code 2—Application approved but not accepted
Code 3—Application denied
Code 4—Application withdrawn
Code 5—File closed for incompleteness
Code 6—Loan purchased by your institution
Code 7—Preapproval request denied
Code 8—Preapproval request approved but not accepted (optional reporting)

a. Use Code 1 for a loan that is originated, including one resulting from a request for preapproval.

b. For a counteroffer (your offer to the applicant to make the loan on different terms or in a different amount from the terms or amount applied for), use Code 1 if the applicant accepts. Use Code 3 if the applicant turns down the counteroffer or does not respond.

c. Use Code 2 when the application is approved but the applicant (or the loan broker or correspondent) fails to respond to your notification of approval or your commitment letter within the specified time. Do not use this Code for a preapproval request.

d. Use Code 4 only when the application is expressly withdrawn by the applicant before a credit decision is made. Do not use Code 4 if a request for preapproval is withdrawn; preapproval requests that are withdrawn are not reported under HMDA.

e. Use Code 5 if you sent a written notice of incompleteness under § 1002.9(c)(2) of Regulation B (Equal Credit Opportunity) and the applicant did not respond to your request for additional information within the period of time specified in your notice. Do not use this Code for requests for preapproval that are incomplete; these preapproval requests are not reported under HMDA.

2. Date of Action. For paper submissions only, enter the date by month, day, and year, using numerals in the form MM/DD/YYYY (for example, 02/22/2003). For submissions in electronic form, the proper format is YYYYMMDD.

a. For loans originated, enter the settlement or closing date.

b. For loans purchased, enter the date of purchase by your institution.

c. For applications and preapprovals denied, applications and preapprovals approved but not accepted by the applicant, and files closed for incompleteness, enter the date that the action was taken by your institution or the date the notice was sent to the applicant.

d. For applications withdrawn, enter the date you received the applicant's express withdrawal, or enter the date shown on the notification from the applicant, in the case of a written withdrawal.

e. For preapprovals that lead to a loan origination, enter the date of the origination.

C. Property Location

Except as otherwise provided, enter in these columns the applicable Codes for the MSA, or the MD if the MSA is divided into MDs, state, county, and census tract to indicate the location of the property to which a loan relates.

1. MSA or Metropolitan Division. For each loan or loan application, enter the MSA, or the MD number if the MSA is divided into MDs. MSA and MD boundaries are defined by OMB; use the boundaries that were in effect on January 1 of the calendar year for which you are reporting. A listing of MSAs and MDs is available from the appropriate Federal agency to which you report data or the FFIEC.

2. State and County. Use the Federal Information Processing Standard (FIPS) two-digit numerical code for the state and the three-digit numerical code for the county. These codes are available from the appropriate Federal agency to which you report data or the FFIEC.

3. Census Tract. Indicate the census tract where the property is located. Notwithstanding paragraph 6, if the property is located in a county with a population of 30,000 or less in the 2000 Census, enter "NA" (even if the population has increased above 30,000 since 2000), or enter the census tract number. County population data can be obtained from the U.S. Census Bureau.

4. Census Tract Number. For the census tract number, consult the resources provided by the U.S. Census Bureau or the FFIEC.

5. Property Located Outside MSAs or Metropolitan Divisions. For loans on property located outside the MSAs and MDs in which an institution has a home or branch office, or for property located outside of any MSA or MD, the institution may choose one of the following two options. Under option one, the institution may enter the MSA or MD, state and county codes and the census tract number; and if the property is not located in any MSA or MD, the institution may enter "NA" in the MSA or MD column. (Codes exist for all states and counties and numbers exist for all census tracts.) Under this first option, the codes and census tract number must accurately identify the property location. Under the second option, which is not available if paragraph 6 applies, an institution may enter "NA" in all four columns, whether or not the codes or numbers exist for the property location.

6. Data Reporting for Banks and Savings Associations Required To Report Data on Small Business, Small Farm, and Community Development Lending Under the CRA Regulations. If your institution is a bank or savings association that is required to report data under the regulations that implement the CRA, you must enter the property location on your HMDA/LAR even if the property is outside the MSAs or MDs in which you have a home or branch office, or is not located in any MSA.

7. Requests for Preapproval. Notwithstanding paragraphs 1 through 6, if the application is a request for preapproval that is denied or that is approved but not accepted by the applicant, you may enter "NA" in all four columns.

D. Applicant Information—Ethnicity, Race, Sex, and Income

Appendix B contains instructions for the collection of data on ethnicity, race, and sex, and also contains a sample form for data collection.

1. Applicability. Report this information for loans that you originate as well as for applications that do not result in an origination.

a. You need not collect or report this information for loans purchased. If you choose not to report this information, use the Codes for "not applicable."

b. If the borrower or applicant is not a natural person (a corporation or partnership, for example), use the Codes for "not applicable."

2. Mail, Internet, or Telephone Applications. All loan applications, including applications taken by mail, internet, or telephone must use a collection form similar to that shown in Appendix B regarding ethnicity, race, and sex. For applications taken by telephone, the information in the collection form must be stated orally by the lender, except for information that pertains uniquely to applications taken in writing. If the applicant does not provide these data in an application taken by mail or tele-phone or on the internet, enter the Code for "information not provided by applicant in mail, internet, or telephone application" specified in paragraphs I.D.3., 4., and 5. of this appendix. (See Appendix B for complete information on the collection of these data in mail, Internet, or telephone applications.)

3. Ethnicity of Borrower or Applicant. Use the following Codes to indicate the ethnicity of the applicant or borrower under column "A" and of any co-applicant or co-borrower under column "CA."

Code 1—Hispanic or Latino
Code 2—Not Hispanic or Latino
Code 3—Information not provided by applicant in mail, internet, or telephone application
Code 4—Not applicable
Code 5—No co-applicant

4. Race of Borrower or Applicant. Use the following Codes to indicate the race of the applicant or borrower under column "A" and of any co-applicant or co-borrower under column "CA."

Code 1—American Indian or Alaska Native
Code 2—Asian
Code 3—Black or African American
Code 4—Native Hawaiian or Other Pacific Islander
Code 5—White
Code 6—Information not provided by applicant in mail, internet, or telephone application
Code 7—Not applicable
Code 8—No co-applicant

a. If an applicant selects more than one racial designation, enter all Codes corresponding to the applicant's selections.

b. Use Code 4 (for ethnicity) and Code 7 (for race) for "not applicable" only when the applicant or co-applicant is not a natural person or when applicant or co-applicant information is unavailable because the loan has been purchased by your institution.

c. If there is more than one co-applicant, provide the required information only for the first co-applicant listed on the application form. If there are no co-applicants or co-borrowers, use Code 5 (for ethnicity) and Code 8 (for race) for "no co-applicant" in the co-applicant column.

5. Sex of Borrower or Applicant. Use the following Codes to indicate the sex of the applicant or borrower under column "A" and of any co-applicant or co-borrower under column "CA."

Code 1—Male
Code 2—Female
Code 3—Information not provided by applicant in mail, internet, or telephone application
Code 4—Not applicable
Code 5—No co-applicant or co-borrower

a. Use Code 4 for "not applicable" only when the applicant or co-applicant is not a natural person or when applicant or co-applicant information is unavailable because the loan has been purchased by your institution.

b. If there is more than one co-applicant, provide the required information only for the first co-applicant listed on the application form. If there are no co-applicants or co-borrowers, use Code 5 for "no co-applicant" in the co-applicant column.

6. Income. Enter the gross annual income that your institution relied on in making the credit decision.

a. Round all dollar amounts to the nearest thousand (round $500 up to the next $1,000), and show in thousands. For example, report $35,500 as 36.

b. For loans on multifamily dwellings, enter "NA."

c. If no income information is asked for or relied on in the credit decision, enter "NA."

d. If the applicant or co-applicant is not a natural person or the applicant or co-applicant information is unavailable because the loan has been purchased by your institution, enter "NA."

E. Type of Purchaser

Enter the applicable Code to indicate whether a loan that your institution originated or purchased was then sold to a secondary market entity within the same calendar year:

Code 0—Loan was not originated or was not sold in calendar year covered by register
Code 1—Fannie Mae
Code 2—Ginnie Mae
Code 3—Freddie Mac
Code 4—Farmer Mac
Code 5—Private securitization
Code 6—Commercial bank, savings bank, or savings association
Code 7—Life insurance company, credit union, mortgage bank, or finance company
Code 8—Affiliate institution
Code 9—Other type of purchaser

a. Use Code 0 for applications that were denied, withdrawn, or approved but not accepted by the applicant; and for files closed for incompleteness.

b. Use Code 0 if you originated or purchased a loan and did not sell it during that same calendar year. If you sell the loan in a succeeding year, you need not report the sale.

c. Use Code 2 if you conditionally assign a loan to Ginnie Mae in connection with a mortgage-backed security transaction.

d. Use Code 8 for loans sold to an institution affiliated with you, such as your subsidiary or a subsidiary of your parent corporation.

F. Reasons for Denial

1. You may report the reason for denial, and you may indicate up to three reasons, using the following Codes. Leave this column blank if the "action taken" on the application is not a denial. For example, do not complete this column if the application was withdrawn or the file was closed for incompleteness.

Code 1—Debt-to-income ratio
Code 2—Employment history
Code 3—Credit history
Code 4—Collateral

Code 5—Insufficient cash (downpayment, closing costs)
Code 6—Unverifiable information
Code 7—Credit application incomplete
Code 8—Mortgage insurance denied
Code 9—Other

2. If your institution uses the model form for adverse action contained in Appendix C to Regulation B (Form C-1, Sample Notification Form), use the foregoing Codes as follows:

a. Code 1 for: Income insufficient for amount of credit requested, and Excessive obligations in relation to income.

b. Code 2 for: Temporary or irregular employment, and Length of employment.

c. Code 3 for: Insufficient number of credit references provided; Unacceptable type of credit references provided; No credit file; Limited credit experience; Poor credit performance with us; Delinquent past or present credit obligations with others; Garnishment, attachment, foreclosure, repossession, collection action, or judgment; and Bankruptcy.

d. Code 4 for: Value or type of collateral not sufficient.

e. Code 6 for: Unable to verify credit references; Unable to verify employment; Unable to verify income; and Unable to verify residence.

f. Code 7 for: Credit application incomplete.

g. Code 9 for: Length of residence; Temporary residence; and Other reasons specified on notice.

G. Pricing-Related Data

1. Rate Spread.

a. For a home-purchase loan, a refinancing, or a dwelling-secured home improvement loan that you originated, report the spread between the annual percentage rate (APR) and the average prime offer rate for a comparable transaction if the spread is equal to or greater than 1.5 percentage points for first-lien loans or 3.5 percentage points for subordinate-lien loans. To determine whether the rate spread meets this threshold, use the average prime offer rate in effect for the type of transaction as of the date the interest rate was set, and use the APR for the loan, as calculated and disclosed to the consumer under §§ 1026.6 or 1026.18, as applicable, of Regulation Z (12 CFR part 1026). Current and historic average prime offer rates are set forth in the tables published on the FFIEC's Web site (http://www.ffiec.gov/hmda) entitled "Average Prime Offer Rates—Fixed" and "Average Prime Offer Rates—Adjustable." Use the most recently available average prime offer rate. "Most recently available" means the average prime offer rate set forth in the applicable table with the most recent effective date as of the date the interest rate was set. Do not use an average prime offer rate before its effective date.

b. If the loan is not subject to Regulation Z, or is a home improvement loan that is not dwelling-secured, or is a loan that you purchased, enter "NA."

c. Enter "NA" in the case of an application that does not result in a loan origination.

d. Enter the rate spread to two decimal places, and use a leading zero. For example, enter 03.29. If the difference between the APR and the average prime offer rate is a figure with more than two decimal places, round the figure or truncate the digits beyond two decimal places.

e. If the difference between the APR and the average prime offer rate is less than 1.5 percentage points for a first-lien loan and less than 3.5 percentage points for a subordinate-lien loan, enter "NA."

2. Date the interest rate was set. The relevant date to use to determine the average prime offer rate for a comparable transaction is the date on which the loan's interest rate was set by the financial institution for the final time before closing. If an interest rate is set pursuant to a "lock-in" agreement between the lender and the borrower, then the date on which the agreement fixes the interest rate is the date the rate was set. If a rate is re-set after a lock-in agreement is executed (for example, because the borrower exercises a float-down option or the agreement expires), then the relevant date is the date the rate is re-set for the final time before closing. If no lock-in agreement is executed, then the relevant date is the date on which the institution sets the rate for the final time before closing.

3. HOEPA Status.

a. For a loan that you originated or purchased that is subject to the Home Ownership and Equity Protection Act of 1994 (HOEPA), as implemented in Regulation Z (12 CFR 1026.32), because the APR or the points and fees on the loan exceed the HOEPA triggers, enter Code 1.

b. Enter Code 2 in all other cases. For example, enter Code 2 for a loan that you originated or purchased that is not subject to the requirements of HOEPA for any reason; also enter Code 2 in the case of an application that does not result in a loan origination.

H. Lien Status

Use the following Codes for loans that you originate and for applications that do not result in an origination:

Code 1—Secured by a first lien.
Code 2—Secured by a subordinate lien.
Code 3—Not secured by a lien.
Code 4—Not applicable (purchased loan).

a. Use Codes 1 through 3 for loans that you originate, as well as for applications that do not result in an origination (applications that are approved but not accepted, denied, withdrawn, or closed for incompleteness).

b. Use Code 4 for loans that you purchase.

II. Appropriate Federal Agencies for HMDA Reporting

A. You are strongly encouraged to submit your loan/application register via email. If you elect to use this method of transmission and the appropriate Federal agency for your institution is the Bureau of Consumer Financial Protection, the Office of the Comptroller of the Currency, the Federal Deposit Insurance Corporation, or the National Credit Union

Administration, then you should submit your institution's files to the email address dedicated to that purpose by the Bureau, which can be found on the Web site of the FFIEC. If one of the foregoing agencies is the appropriate Federal agency for your institution and you elect to submit your data by regular mail, then use the following address:

HMDA, Federal Reserve Board, Attention: HMDA Processing, (insert name of the appropriate Federal agency for your institution), 20th & Constitution Ave NW., MS N502, Washington, DC 20551-0001.

B. If the Federal Reserve System (but not the Bureau of Consumer Financial Protection) is the appropriate Federal agency for your institution, you

should use the email or regular mail address of your district bank indicated on the Web site of the FFIEC. If the Department of Housing and Urban Development is the appropriate Federal agency for your institution, then you should use the email or regular mail address indicated on the Web site of the FFIEC.

Form FR HMDA-LAR
OMB Nos. 1557-0159 (OCC), 3064-0046
(FDIC), 7100-0247 (FRB), 2502-0529 (HUD),
3133-0166 (NCUA), and 3170-0008 (CFPB).

LOAN/APPLICATION REGISTER
TRANSMITTAL SHEET

You must complete this transmittal sheet (please type or print) and attach it to the Loan/Application Register, required by the Home Mortgage Disclosure Act, that you submit to your supervisory agency.

Reporter's Identification Number	Agency Code	Reporter's Tax Identification Number	Total line entries contained in attached Loan/Application Register
└┴┴┴┴┴┴┴┴┴┴┴┘ – └┴┘		└┴┴┘ – └┴┴┴┴┴┴┴┘	_____

The Loan/Application Register that is attached covers activity during the year_____ and contains a total of _____ pages.

Enter the name and address of your institution. The disclosure statement that is produced by the Federal Financial Institutions Examination Council will be mailed to the address you supply below:

_____
Name of Institution

_____
Address

_____
City, State, ZIP

Enter the name and address of any parent company:

_____
Name of Parent Company

_____
Address

_____
City, State, ZIP

Enter the name, telephone number, facsimile number, and e-mail address of a person who may be contacted about questions regarding your register:

_____	( ) _____	( ) _____	_____
Name	Telephone Number	Facsimile Number	E-Mail Address

An officer of your institution must complete the following section.

I certify to the accuracy of the data contained in this register.

_____	_____	_____
Name of Officer	Signature	Date

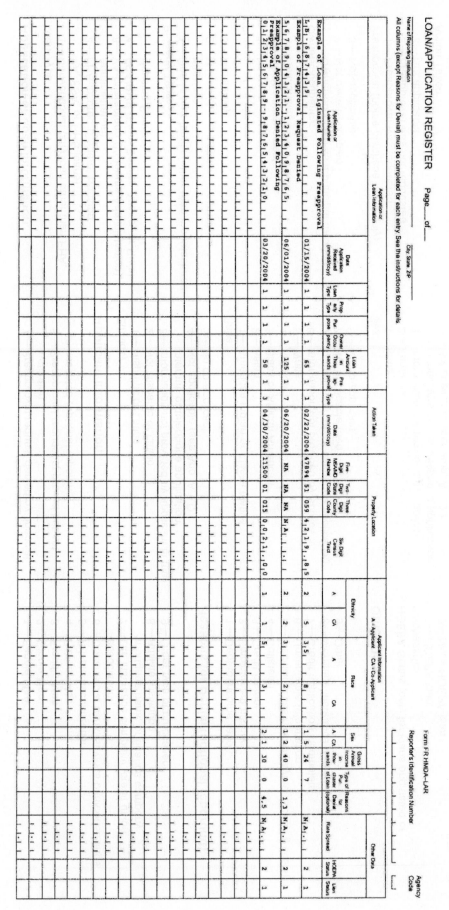

LOAN/APPLICATION REGISTER
CODE SHEET

Use the following codes to complete the Loan/Application Register. The instructions to the HMDA-LAR explain the proper use of each code.

Application or Loan Information

Loan Type:
1— Conventional (any loan other than FHA, VA, FSA, or RHS loans)
2— FHA-insured (Federal Housing Administration)
3— VA-guaranteed (Veterans Administration)
4— FSA/RHS (Farm Service Agency or Rural Housing Service)

Property Type:
1— One to four-family (other than manufactured housing)
2— Manufactured housing
3— Multifamily

Purpose of Loan:
1— Home purchase
2— Home improvement
3— Refinancing

Owner-Occupancy:
1— Owner-occupied as a principal dwelling
2— Not owner-occupied
3— Not applicable

Preapproval (home purchase loans only):
1— Preapproval was requested
2— Preapproval was not requested
3— Not applicable

Action Taken:
1— Loan originated
2— Application approved but not accepted
3— Application denied by financial institution
4— Application withdrawn by applicant
5— File closed for incompleteness
6— Loan purchased by financial institution
7— Preapproval request denied by financial institution
8— Preapproval request approved but not accepted (optional reporting)

Applicant Information

Ethnicity:
1— Hispanic or Latino
2— Not Hispanic or Latino
3— Information not provided by applicant in mail, Internet, or telephone application
4— Not applicable (see App. A, I.D.)
5— No co-applicant

Race:
1— American Indian or Alaska Native
2— Asian
3— Black or African American
4— Native Hawaiian or Other Pacific Islander
5— White
6— Information not provided by applicant in mail, Internet, or telephone application
7— Not applicable (see App. A, I.D.)
8— No co-applicant

Sex:
1— Male
2— Female
3— Information not provided by applicant in mail, Internet, or telephone application
4— Not applicable (see App. A, I.D.)
5— No co-applicant

Type of Purchaser

0— Loan was not originated or was not sold in calendar year covered by register
1— Fannie Mae
2— Ginnie Mae
3— Freddie Mac
4— Farmer Mac
5— Private securitization
6— Commercial bank, savings bank or savings association
7— Life insurance company, credit union, mortgage bank, or finance company
8— Affiliate institution
9— Other type of purchaser

Reasons for Denial (optional reporting)

1— Debt-to-income ratio
2— Employment history
3— Credit history
4— Collateral
5— Insufficient cash (downpayment, closing costs)
6— Unverifiable information
7— Credit application incomplete
8— Mortgage insurance denied
9— Other

Other Data

HOEPA Status (only for loans originated or purchased):
1— HOEPA loan
2— Not a HOEPA loan

Lien Status (only for applications and originations):
1— Secured by a first lien
2— Secured by a subordinate lien
3— Not secured by a lien
4— Not applicable (purchased loans)

Appendix B to Part 203—Form and Instructions for Data Collection on Ethnicity, Race, and Sex

I. Instructions on Collection of Data on Ethnicity, Race, and Sex

You may list questions regarding the ethnicity, race, and sex of the applicant on your loan application form, or on a separate form that refers to the application. (See the sample form below for model language.)

II. Procedures

A. You must ask the applicant for this information (but you cannot require the applicant to provide it) whether the application is taken in person, by mail or telephone, or on the internet. For applications taken by telephone, the information in the collection form must be stated orally by the lender, except for that information which pertains uniquely to applications taken in writing.

B. Inform the applicant that the Federal government requests this information in order to monitor compliance with Federal statutes that prohibit lenders from discriminating against applicants on these bases. Inform the applicant that if the information is not provided where the application is taken in person, you are required to note the data on the basis of visual observation or surname.

C. You must offer the applicant the option of selecting one or more racial designations.

D. If the applicant chooses not to provide the information for an application taken in person, note this fact on the form and then note the applicant's ethnicity, race, and sex on the basis of visual observation and surname, to the extent possible.

E. If the applicant declines to answer these questions or fails to provide the information on an application taken by mail or telephone or on the internet, the data need not be provided. In such a case, indicate that the application was received by mail, telephone, or Internet, if it is not otherwise evident on the face of the application.

SAMPLE DATA-COLLECTION FORM
INFORMATION FOR GOVERNMENT MONITORING PURPOSES

The following information is requested by the federal government for certain types of loans related to a dwelling in order to monitor the lender's compliance with equal credit opportunity, fair housing, and home mortgage disclosure laws. You are not required to furnish this information, but are encouraged to do so. You may select one or more designations for "Race." The law provides that a lender may not dis- criminate on the basis of this information, or on whether you choose to furnish it. However, if you choose not to furnish the information and you have made this application in person, under federal regulations the lender is required to note ethnicity, race, and sex on the basis of visual observation or surname. If you do not wish to furnish the information, please check below.

APPLICANT:

☐ I do not wish to furnish this information

Ethnicity:

☐ Hispanic or Latino
☐ Not Hispanic or Latino

Race:

☐ American Indian or Alaska Native
☐ Asian
☐ Black or African American
☐ Native Hawaiian or Other Pacific Islander
☐ White

Sex:

☐ Female
☐ Male

CO-APPLICANT:

☐ I do not wish to furnish this information

Ethnicity:

☐ Hispanic or Latino
☐ Not Hispanic or Latino

Race:

☐ American Indian or Alaska Native
☐ Asian
☐ Black or African American
☐ Native Hawaiian or Other Pacific Islander
☐ White

Sex:

☐ Female
☐ Male

E.3 Staff Commentary on Regulation C

The Consumer Financial Protection Bureau (CFPB) now has authority to issue Regulation C and its commentary. *See* Pub. L. No. 111-203, tit. X, §§ 1085(3), 1100H, 124 Stat. 2083, 2113 (July 21, 2010). On December 19, 2011, the CFPB issued its version of Regulation C and its commentary. *See* 76 Fed. Reg. 78468 (Dec. 19, 2011). The major change from the Federal Reserve Board's (FRB) version is that 12 C.F.R. part 203 citations are replaced by citations to 12 C.F.R. part 1003. Other changes are stylistic and not substantive. The FRB version and the CFPB's version (with supplemental information) are both found on the companion website to this treatise.

AUTHORITY: 12 U.S.C. §§ 2803, 2804, 2805, 5512, 5581.

SOURCE: 76 Fed. Reg. 44242 (July 22, 2011); 76 Fed. Reg. 78468 (Dec. 19, 2011), unless otherwise noted.

Supplement I to Part 1003—Staff Commentary

Introduction

1. *Status*. The commentary in this supplement is the vehicle by which the Bureau of Consumer Financial Protection issues formal staff interpretations of Regulation C (12 CFR part 1003).

Section 1003.1—Authority, Purpose, and Scope

1(c) Scope.

1. *General*. The comments in this section address issues affecting coverage of institutions and exemptions from coverage.

2. *The broker rule and the meaning of "broker" and "investor."* For the purposes of the guidance given in this commentary, an institution that takes and processes a loan application and arranges for another institution to acquire the loan at or after closing is acting as a "broker," and an institution that acquires a loan from a broker at or after closing is acting as an "investor." (The terms used in this commentary may have different meanings in certain parts of the mortgage lending industry, and other terms may be used in place of these terms, for example in the Federal Housing Administration mortgage insurance programs.) Depending on the facts, a broker may or may not make a credit decision on an application (and thus it may or may not have reporting responsibilities). If the broker makes a credit decision, it reports that decision; if it does not make a credit decision, it does not report. If an investor reviews an application and makes a credit decision prior to closing, the investor reports that decision. If the investor does not review the application prior to closing, it reports only the loans that it purchases; it does not report the loans it does not purchase. An institution that makes a credit decision on an application prior to closing reports that decision regardless of whose name the loan closes in.

3. *Illustrations of the broker rule*. Assume that, prior to closing, four investors receive the same application from a broker; two deny it, one approves it, and one approves it and acquires the loan. In these circumstances, the first two report denials, the third reports the transaction as approved but not accepted, and the fourth reports an origination (whether the loan closes in the name of the broker or the investor). Alternatively, assume that the broker denies a loan before sending it to an investor; in this situation, the broker reports a denial.

4. *Broker's use of investor's underwriting criteria*. If a broker makes a credit decision based on underwriting criteria set by an investor, but without the investor's review prior to closing, the broker has made the credit decision. The broker reports as an origination a loan that it approves and closes, and reports as a denial an application that it turns down (either because the application does not meet the investor's underwriting guidelines or for some other reason). The investor reports as purchases only those loans it purchases.

5. *Insurance and other criteria*. If an institution evaluates an application based on the criteria or actions of a third party other than an investor (such as a government or private insurer or guarantor), the institution must report the action taken on the application (loan originated, approved but not accepted, or denied, for example).

6. *Credit decision of agent is decision of principal*. If an institution approves loans through the actions of an agent, the institution must report the action taken on the application (loan originated, approved but not accepted, or denied, for example). State law determines whether one party is the agent of another.

7. *Affiliate bank underwriting (250.250 review)*. If an institution makes an independent evaluation of the creditworthiness of an applicant (for example, as part of a preclosing review by an affiliate bank under 12 CFR 250.250, a regulation of the Board of Governors of the Federal Reserve System that interprets section 23A of the Federal Reserve Act), the institution is making a credit decision. If the institution then acquires the loan, it reports the loan as an origination whether the loan closes in the name of the institution or its affiliate. An institution that does not acquire the loan but takes some other action reports that action.

8. *Participation loan*. An institution that originates a loan and then sells partial interests to other institutions reports the loan as an origination. An institution that acquires only a partial interest in such a loan does not report the transaction even if it has participated in the underwriting and origination of the loan.

9. *Assumptions*. An assumption occurs when an institution enters into a written agreement accepting a new borrower as the obligor on an existing obligation. An institution reports an assumption (or an application for an assumption) as a home purchase loan in the amount of the outstanding principal. If a transaction does not involve a written agreement between a new borrower and the institution, it is not an assumption for HMDA purposes and is not reported.

Section 1003.2—Definitions

Application.

1. *Consistency With Regulation B*. Bureau interpretations that appear in the official staff commentary to Regulation B (Equal Credit Opportunity, 12 CFR part 1002, Supplement I) are generally applicable to the definition of an application under Regulation C. However, under Regulation C the definition of an application does not include prequalification requests.

2. *Prequalification*. A prequalification request is a request by a prospective loan applicant (other than a request for preapproval) for a preliminary determination on whether the prospective applicant would likely qualify for credit under an institution's standards, or for a determination on the amount of credit for which the prospective applicant would likely qualify. Some institutions evaluate prequalification requests through a procedure that is separate from the institution's normal loan application process; others use the same process. In either case, Regulation C does not require an institution to report prequalification requests on the HMDA/LAR, even though these requests may constitute applications under Regulation B for purposes of adverse action notices.

3. *Requests for preapproval*. To be a covered preapproval program, the written commitment issued under the program must result from a full review of the creditworthiness of the applicant, including such verification of income, resources and other matters as is typically done by the institution as part of its normal credit evaluation program. In addition to conditions involving the identification of a suitable property and verification that no material change has occurred in the applicant's financial condition

or creditworthiness, the written commitment may be subject only to other conditions (unrelated to the financial condition or creditworthiness of the applicant) that the lender ordinarily attaches to a traditional home mortgage application approval. These conditions are limited to conditions such as requiring an acceptable title insurance binder or a certificate indicating clear termite inspection, and, in the case where the applicant plans to use the proceeds from the sale of the applicant's present home to purchase a new home, a settlement statement showing adequate proceeds from the sale of the present home.

Branch office.

1. *Credit union.* For purposes of Regulation C, a "branch" of a credit union is any office where member accounts are established or loans are made, whether or not the office has been approved as a branch by a Federal or state agency. (See 12 U.S.C. 1752.)

2. *Depository institution.* A branch of a depository institution does not include a loan-production office, the office of an affiliate, or the office of a third party such as a loan broker. (But see Appendix A, paragraph I.C.6, which requires certain depository institutions to report property location even for properties located outside those MSAs or Metropolitan Divisions in which the institution has a home or branch office.)

3. *Nondepository institution.* For a nondepository institution, "branch office" does not include the office of an affiliate or other third party such as a loan broker. (But note that certain nondepository institutions must report property location even in MSAs or Metropolitan Divisions where they do not have a physical location.)

Dwelling.

1. *Coverage.* The definition of "dwelling" is not limited to the principal or other residence of the applicant or borrower, and thus includes vacation or second homes and rental properties. A dwelling also includes a multifamily structure such as an apartment building.

2. *Exclusions.* Recreational vehicles such as boats or campers are not dwellings for purposes of HMDA. Also excluded are transitory residences such as hotels, hospitals, and college dormitories, whose occupants have principal residences elsewhere.

Financial institution.

1. *General.* An institution that met the test for coverage under HMDA in year 1, and then ceases to meet the test (for example, because its assets fall below the threshold on December 31 of year 2) stops collecting HMDA data beginning with year 3. Similarly, an institution that did not meet the coverage test for a given year, and then meets the test in the succeeding year, begins collecting HMDA data in the calendar year following the year in which it meets the test for coverage. For example, a for-profit mortgage lending institution (other than a bank, savings association, or credit union) that, in year 1, falls below the thresholds specified in the

definition of Financial institution in § 1003.2, but meets one of them in year 2, need not collect data in year 2, but begins collecting data in year 3.

2. Adjustment of exemption threshold for banks, savings associations, and credit unions. For data collection in 2013, the asset-size exemption threshold is $42 million. Banks, savings associations, and credit unions with assets at or below $42 million as of December 31, 2012, are exempt from collecting data for 2013.

3. *Coverage after a merger.* Several scenarios of data-collection responsibilities for the calendar year of a merger are described below. Under all the scenarios, if the merger results in a covered institution, that institution must begin data collection January 1 of the following calendar year.

  i. Two institutions are not covered by Regulation C because of asset size. The institutions merge. No data collection is required for the year of the merger (even if the merger results in a covered institution).

  ii. A covered institution and an exempt institution merge. The covered institution is the surviving institution. For the year of the merger, data collection is required for the covered institution's transactions. Data collection is optional for transactions handled in offices of the previously exempt institution.

  iii. A covered institution and an exempt institution merge. The exempt institution is the surviving institution, or a new institution is formed. Data collection is required for transactions of the covered institution that take place prior to the merger. Data collection is optional for transactions taking place after the merger date.

  iv. Two covered institutions merge. Data collection is required for the entire year. The surviving or resulting institution files either a consolidated submission or separate submissions for that year.

4. *Originations.* HMDA coverage depends in part on whether an institution has originated home purchase loans. To determine whether activities with respect to a particular loan constitute an origination, institutions should consult, among other parts of the staff commentary, the discussion of the broker rule under §§ 1003.1(c) and 1003.4(a).

5. *Branches of foreign banks—treated as banks.* A Federal branch or a state-licensed insured branch of a foreign bank is a "bank" under section 3(a)(1) of the Federal Deposit Insurance Act (12 U.S.C. 1813(a)), and is covered by HMDA if it meets the tests for a depository institution found in § 1003.2 of Regulation C.

6. *Branches and offices of foreign banks—treated as for-profit mortgage lending institutions.* Federal agencies, state-licensed agencies, state-licensed uninsured branches of foreign banks, commercial lending companies owned or controlled by foreign banks, and entities operating under section 25 or 25A of the Federal Reserve Act, 12 U.S.C. 601 and 611 (Edge Act and agreement corporations) are not "banks" under the Federal Deposit Insurance Act.

These entities are nonetheless covered by HMDA if they meet the tests for a for-profit nondepository mortgage lending institution found in § 1003.2(e)(2) of Regulation C.

Home improvement loan.

1. *Classification requirement for loans not secured by a lien on a dwelling.* An institution has "classified" a loan that is not secured by a lien on a dwelling as a home improvement loan if it has entered the loan on its books as a home improvement loan, or has otherwise coded or identified the loan as a home improvement loan. For example, an institution that has booked a loan or reported it on a "call report" as a home improvement loan has classified it as a home improvement loan. An institution may also classify loans as home improvement loans in other ways (for example, by color-coding loan files).

2. *Improvements to real property.* Home improvements include improvements both to a dwelling and to the real property on which the dwelling is located (for example, installation of a swimming pool, construction of a garage, or landscaping).

3. *Commercial and other loans.* A home improvement loan may include a loan originated outside an institution's residential mortgage lending division (such as a loan to improve an apartment building made through the commercial loan department).

4. *Mixed-use property.* A loan to improve property used for residential and commercial purposes (for example, a building containing apartment units and retail space) is a home improvement loan if the loan proceeds are used primarily to improve the residential portion of the property. If the loan proceeds are used to improve the entire property (for example, to replace the heating system), the loan is a home improvement loan if the property itself is primarily residential. An institution may use any reasonable standard to determine the primary use of the property, such as by square footage or by the income generated. An institution may select the standard to apply on a case-by-case basis. If the loan is unsecured, to report the loan as a home improvement loan the institution must also have classified it as such.

5. *Multiple-category loans.* If a loan is a home improvement loan as well as a refinancing, an institution reports the loan as a home improvement loan.

Home purchase loan.

1. *Multiple properties.* A home purchase loan includes a loan secured by one dwelling and used to purchase another dwelling.

2. *Mixed-use property.* A dwelling-secured loan to purchase property used primarily for residential purposes (for example, an apartment building containing a convenience store) is a home purchase loan. An institution may use any reasonable standard to determine the primary use of the property, such as by square footage or by the income generated. An institution may select the standard to apply on a case-by-case basis.

3. *Farm loan.* A loan to purchase property used primarily for agricultural purposes is not a home purchase loan even if the property includes a dwelling. An institution may use any reasonable standard to determine the primary use of the property, such as by reference to the exemption from Regulation X (Real Estate Settlement Procedures, 12 CFR 1024.5(b)(1)) for a loan on property of 25 acres or more. An institution may select the standard to apply on a case-by-case basis.

4. *Commercial and other loans.* A home purchase loan may include a loan originated outside an institution's residential mortgage lending division (such as a loan for the purchase of an apartment building made through the commercial loan department).

5. *Construction and permanent financing.* A home purchase loan includes both a combined construction/permanent loan and the permanent financing that replaces a construction-only loan. It does not include a construction-only loan, which is considered "temporary financing" under Regulation C and is not reported.

6. *Second mortgages that finance the downpayments on first mortgages.* If an institution making a first mortgage loan to a home purchaser also makes a second mortgage loan to the same purchaser to finance part or all of the home purchaser's downpayment, the institution reports each loan separately as a home purchase loan.

7. *Multiple-category loans.* If a loan is a home purchase loan as well as a home improvement loan, or a refinancing, an institution reports the loan as a home purchase loan.

Manufactured home.

1. *Definition of a manufactured home.* The definition in § 1003.2(i) refers to the Federal building code for factory-built housing established by the Department of Housing and Urban Development (HUD). The HUD code requires generally that housing be essentially ready for occupancy upon leaving the factory and being transported to a building site. Modular homes that meet all of the HUD code standards are included in the definition because they are ready for occupancy upon leaving the factory. Other factory-built homes, such as panelized and pre-cut homes, generally do not meet the HUD code because they require a significant amount of construction on site before they are ready for occupancy. Loans and applications relating to manufactured homes that do not meet the HUD code should not be identified as manufactured housing under HMDA.

Metropolitan Statistical Areas and Metropolitan Divisions.

1. Use of terms "Metropolitan Statistical Area" and "Metropolitan Division." The U.S. Office of Management and Budget defines Metropolitan Statistical Areas and Metropolitan Divisions to provide nationally consistent definitions for collecting, tabulating, and publishing Federal statistics for a set of geographic areas. OMB divides every Metropoli-

tan Statistical Area (MSA) with a population of 2.5 million or more into Metropolitan Divisions (MDs); MSAs with populations under 2.5 million population are not so divided. 67 FR 82228 (December 27, 2000). For all purposes under Regulation C, if an MSA is divided by OMB into MDs, the appropriate geographic unit to be used is the MD; if an MSA is not so divided by OMB into MDs, the appropriate geographic unit to be used is the MSA.

Section 1003.4—Compilation of Loan Data

4(a) Data format and itemization

1. *Reporting requirements.*

  i. An institution reports data on loans that it originated and loans that it purchased during the calendar year described in the report. An institution reports these data even if the loans were subsequently sold by the institution.

  ii. An institution reports the data for loan applications that did not result in originations—for example, applications that the institution denied or that the applicant withdrew during the calendar year covered by the report.

  iii. In the case of brokered loan applications or applications forwarded through a correspondent, the institution reports as originations the loans that it approved and subsequently acquired per a pre-closing arrangement (whether or not they closed in the institution's name). Additionally, the institution reports the data for all applications that did not result in originations—for example, applications that the institution denied or that the applicant withdrew during the calendar year covered by the report (whether or not they would have closed in the institution's name). For all of these loans and applications, the institution reports the required data regarding the borrower's or applicant's ethnicity, race, sex, and income.

  iv. Loan originations are to be reported only once. If the institution is the loan broker or correspondent, it does not report as originations the loans that it forwarded to another lender for approval prior to closing, and that were approved and subsequently acquired by that lender (whether or not they closed in the institution's name).

  v. An institution reports applications that were received in the previous calendar year but were acted upon during the calendar year covered by the current register.

  vi. A financial institution submits all required data to the appropriate Federal agency in one package, with the prescribed transmittal sheet. An officer of the institution certifies to the accuracy of the data.

  vii. The transmittal sheet states the total number of line entries contained in the accompanying data transmission.

2. *Updating—agency requirements.* Certain state or Federal regulations, such as the Federal Deposit Insurance Corporation's regulations, may require an institution to update its data more frequently than is required under Regulation C.

3. *Form of quarterly updating.* An institution may maintain the quarterly updates of the HMDA/LAR in electronic or any other format, provided the institution can make the information available to its regulatory agency in a timely manner upon request.

Paragraph 4(a)(1).

1. *Application date—consistency.* In reporting the date of application, an institution reports the date the application was received or the date shown on the application. Although an institution need not choose the same approach for its entire HMDA submission, it should be generally consistent (such as by routinely using one approach within a particular division of the institution or for a category of loans).

2. *Application date—application forwarded by a broker.* For an application forwarded by a broker, an institution reports the date the application was received by the broker, the date the application was received by the institution, or the date shown on the application. Although an institution need not choose the same approach for its entire HMDA submission, it should be generally consistent (such as by routinely using one approach within a particular division of the institution or for a category of loans).

3. *Application date—reinstated application.* If, within the same calendar year, an applicant asks an institution to reinstate a counteroffer that the applicant previously did not accept (or asks the institution to reconsider an application that was denied, withdrawn, or closed for incompleteness), the institution may treat that request as the continuation of the earlier transaction or as a new transaction. If the institution treats the request for reinstatement or reconsideration as a new transaction, it reports the date of the request as the application date.

4. *Application or loan number.* An institution must ensure that each identifying number is unique within the institution. If an institution's register contains data for branch offices, for example, the institution could use a letter or a numerical code to identify the loans or applications of different branches, or could assign a certain series of numbers to particular branches to avoid duplicate numbers. Institutions are strongly encouraged not to use the applicant's or borrower's name or social security number, for privacy reasons.

5. *Application—year action taken.* An institution must report an application in the calendar year in which the institution takes final action on the application.

Paragraph 4(a)(3).

1. *Purpose—statement of applicant.* An institution may rely on the oral or written statement of an applicant regarding the proposed use of loan proceeds. For example, a lender could use a check-box,

or a purpose line, on a loan application to determine whether or not the applicant intends to use loan proceeds for home improvement purposes.

2. *Purpose—multiple-purpose loan.* If a loan is a home purchase loan as well as a home improvement loan, or a refinancing, an institution reports the loan as a home purchase loan. If a loan is a home improvement loan as well as a refinancing, an institution reports the loan as a home improvement loan.

Paragraph 4(a)(6).

1. *Occupancy—multiple properties.* If a loan relates to multiple properties, the institution reports the owner occupancy status of the property for which property location is being reported. (See the comments to paragraph 4(a)(9).)

Paragraph 4(a)(7).

1. *Loan amount—counteroffer.* If an applicant accepts a counteroffer for an amount different from the amount initially requested, the institution reports the loan amount granted. If an applicant does not accept a counteroffer or fails to respond, the institution reports the loan amount initially requested.

2. *Loan amount—multiple-purpose loan.* Except in the case of a home-equity line of credit, an institution reports the entire amount of the loan, even if only a part of the proceeds is intended for home purchase or home improvement.

3. *Loan amount—home-equity line.* An institution that has chosen to report home-equity lines of credit reports only the part that is intended for home-improvement or home-purchase purposes.

4. *Loan amount—assumption.* An institution that enters into a written agreement accepting a new party as the obligor on a loan reports the amount of the outstanding principal on the assumption as the loan amount.

Paragraph 4(a)(8).

1. *Action taken—counteroffers.* If an institution makes a counteroffer to lend on terms different from the applicant's initial request (for example, for a shorter loan maturity or in a different amount) and the applicant does not accept the counteroffer or fails to respond, the institution reports the action taken as a denial on the original terms requested by the applicant.

2. *Action taken—rescinded transactions.* If a borrower rescinds a transaction after closing, the institution may report the transaction either as an origination or as an application that was approved but not accepted.

3. *Action taken—purchased loans.* An institution reports the loans that it purchased during the calendar year, and does not report the loans that it declined to purchase.

4. *Action taken—conditional approvals.* If an institution issues a loan approval subject to the applicant's meeting underwriting conditions (other than customary loan commitment or loan-closing conditions, such as a clear-title requirement or an acceptable property survey) and the applicant does not meet them, the institution reports the action taken as a denial.

5. *Action taken date—approved but not accepted.* For a loan approved by an institution but not accepted by the applicant, the institution reports any reasonable date, such as the approval date, the deadline for accepting the offer, or the date the file was closed. Although an institution need not choose the same approach for its entire HMDA submission, it should be generally consistent (such as by routinely using one approach within a particular division of the institution or for a category of loans).

6. *Action taken date—originations.* For loan originations, an institution generally reports the settlement or closing date. For loan originations that an institution acquires through a broker, the institution reports either the settlement or closing date, or the date the institution acquired the loan from the broker. If the disbursement of funds takes place on a date later than the settlement or closing date, the institution may use the date of disbursement. For a construction/permanent loan, the institution reports either the settlement or closing date, or the date the loan converts to the permanent financing. Although an institution need not choose the same approach for its entire HMDA submission, it should be generally consistent (such as by routinely using one approach within a particular division of the institution or for a category of loans). Notwithstanding this flexibility regarding the use of the closing date in connection with reporting the date action was taken, the year in which an origination goes to closing is the year in which the institution must report the origination.

7. *Action taken—pending applications.* An institution does not report any loan application still pending at the end of the calendar year; it reports that application on its register for the year in which final action is taken.

Paragraph 4(a)(9).

1. *Property location—multiple properties (home improvement/refinance of home improvement).* For a home improvement loan, an institution reports the property being improved. If more than one property is being improved, the institution reports the location of one of the properties or reports the loan using multiple entries on its HMDA/LAR (with unique identifiers) and allocating the loan amount among the properties.

2. *Property location—multiple properties (home purchase/refinance of home purchase).* For a home purchase loan, an institution reports the property taken as security. If an institution takes more than one property as security, the institution reports the location of the property being purchased if there is just one. If the loan is to purchase multiple properties and is secured by multiple properties, the institution reports the location of one of the properties or reports the loan using multiple entries on its HMDA/LAR (with unique identifiers) and allo-

cating the loan amount among the properties.

3. *Property location—loans purchased from another institution.* The requirement to report the property location by census tract in an MSA or Metropolitan Division where the institution has a home or branch office applies not only to loan applications and originations but also to loans purchased from another institution. This includes loans purchased from an institution that did not have a home or branch office in that MSA or Metropolitan Division and did not collect the property-location information.

4. *Property location—mobile or manufactured home.* If information about the potential site of a mobile or manufactured home is not available, an institution reports using the Code for "not applicable."

Paragraph 4(a)(10).

1. *Applicant data—completion by applicant.* An institution reports the monitoring information as provided by the applicant. For example, if an applicant checks the "Asian" box the institution reports using the "Asian" Code.

2. *Applicant data—completion by lender.* If an applicant fails to provide the requested information for an application taken in person, the institution reports the data on the basis of visual observation or surname.

3. *Applicant data—application completed in person.* When an applicant meets in person with a lender to complete an application that was begun by mail, internet, or telephone, the institution must request the monitoring information. If the meeting occurs after the application process is complete, for example, at closing, the institution is not required to obtain monitoring information.

4. *Applicant data—joint applicant.* A joint applicant may enter the government monitoring information on behalf of an absent joint applicant. If the information is not provided, the institution reports using the Code for "information not provided by applicant in mail, internet, or telephone application."

5. *Applicant data—video and other electronic-application processes.* An institution that accepts applications through electronic media with a video component treats the applications as taken in person and collects the information about the ethnicity, race, and sex of applicants. An institution that accepts applications through electronic media without a video component (for example, the internet or facsimile) treats the applications as accepted by mail.

6. *Income data—income relied on.* An institution reports the gross annual income relied on in evaluating the creditworthiness of applicants. For example, if an institution relies on an applicant's salary to compute a debt-to-income ratio but also relies on the applicant's annual bonus to evaluate creditworthiness, the institution reports the salary and the bonus to the extent relied upon. Similarly, if an institution relies on the income of a cosigner to

evaluate creditworthiness, the institution includes this income to the extent relied upon. But an institution does not include the income of a guarantor who is only secondarily liable.

7. *Income data—co-applicant.* If two persons jointly apply for a loan and both list income on the application, but the institution relies only on the income of one applicant in computing ratios and in evaluating creditworthiness, the institution reports only the income relied on.

8. *Income data—loan to employee.* An institution may report "NA" in the income field for loans to its employees to protect their privacy, even though the institution relied on their income in making its credit decisions.

Paragraph 4(a)(11).

1. *Type of purchaser—loan-participation interests sold to more than one entity.* An institution that originates a loan, and then sells it to more than one entity, reports the "type of purchaser" based on the entity purchasing the greatest interest, if any. If an institution retains a majority interest, it does not report the sale.

2. *Type of purchaser—swapped loans.* Loans "swapped" for mortgage-backed securities are to be treated as sales; the purchaser is the type of entity receiving the loans that are swapped.

Paragraph 4(a)(12)(ii).

1. *Average prime offer rate.* Average prime offer rates are annual percentage rates derived from average interest rates, points, and other loan pricing terms offered to borrowers by a representative sample of lenders for mortgage loans that have low-risk pricing characteristics. Other pricing terms include commonly used indices, margins, and initial fixed-rate periods for variable-rate transactions. Relevant pricing characteristics include a consumer's credit history and transaction characteristics such as the loan-to-value ratio, owner-occupant status, and purpose of the transaction. To obtain average prime offer rates, the Bureau uses a survey of lenders that both meets the criteria of § 1003.4(a)(12)(ii) and provides pricing terms for at least two types of variable-rate transactions and at least two types of non-variable-rate transactions. An example of such a survey is the Freddie Mac Primary Mortgage Market Survey®.

2. *Comparable transaction.* The rate spread reporting requirement applies to a reportable loan with an annual percentage rate that exceeds by the specified margin (or more) the average prime offer rate for a comparable transaction as of the date the interest rate is set. The tables of average prime offer rates published by the Bureau (see comment 4(a)(12)(ii)-3) indicate how to identify the comparable transaction.

3. *Bureau tables.* The Bureau publishes on the FFIEC's Web site (http://www.ffiec.gov/hmda), in table form, average prime offer rates for a wide variety of transaction types. The Bureau calculates an annual percentage rate, consistent with Regulation Z (see 12 CFR 1026.22 and Part 1026, Appendix J), for each transaction type for which pricing terms are available from the survey described in comment 4(a)(12)(ii)-1. The Bureau estimates annual percentage rates for other types of transactions for which direct survey data are not available based on the loan pricing terms available in the survey and other information. The Bureau publishes on the FFIEC's Web site the methodology it uses to arrive at these estimates.

Paragraph 4(a)(14).

1. *Determining lien status for applications and loans originated.*

   i. Lenders are required to report lien status for loans they originate and applications that do not result in originations. Lien status is determined by reference to the best information readily available to the lender at the time final action is taken and to the lender's own procedures. Thus, lenders may rely on the title search they routinely perform as part of their underwriting procedures—for example, for home purchase loans. Regulation C does not require lenders to perform title searches solely to comply with HMDA reporting requirements. Lenders may rely on other information that is readily available to them at the time final action is taken and that they reasonably believe is accurate, such as the applicant's statement on the application or the applicant's credit report. For example, where the applicant indicates on the application that there is a mortgage on the property or where the applicant's credit report shows that the applicant has a mortgage—and that mortgage is not going to be paid off as part of the transaction—the lender may assume that the loan it originates is secured by a subordinate lien. If the same application did not result in an origination—for example, because the application is denied or withdrawn—the lender would report the application as an application for a subordinate-lien loan.

   ii. Lenders may also consider their established procedures when determining lien status for applications that do not result in originations. For example, a consumer applies to a lender to refinance a $100,000 first mortgage; the consumer also has a home equity line of credit for $20,000. If the lender's practice in such a case is to ensure that it will have first-lien position—through a subordination agreement with the holder of the mortgage on the home equity line—then the lender should report the application as an application for a first-lien loan.

Paragraph 4(c)(3).

1. An institution that opts to report home-equity lines reports the disposition of all applications, not just originations.

4(d) Excluded data.

1. *Mergers, purchases in bulk, and branch acquisitions.* If a covered institution acquires loans in bulk from another institution (for example, from the receiver for a failed institution) but no merger or acquisition of the institution, or acquisition of a branch, is involved, the institution reports the loans as purchased loans.

Section 1003.5(a)—Disclosure and Reporting

5(a) Reporting to agency.

1. *Submission of data.* Institutions submit data to the appropriate Federal agencies in an automated, machine-readable form. The format must conform to that of the HMDA/LAR. An institution should contact the appropriate Federal agency for information regarding procedures and technical specifications for automated data submission; in some cases, agencies also make software available for automated data submission. The data are edited before submission, using the edits included in the agency-supplied software or equivalent edits in software available from vendors or developed in-house.

2. *Submission in paper form.* Institutions that report twenty-five or fewer entries on their HMDA/LAR may collect and report the data in paper form. An institution that submits its register in non-automated form sends two copies that are typed or computer printed and must use the format of the HMDA/LAR (but need not use the form itself). Each page must be numbered along with the total number of pages (for example, "Page 1 of 3").

3. *Procedures for entering data.* The required data are entered in the register for each loan origination, each application acted on, and each loan purchased during the calendar year. The institution should decide on the procedure it wants to follow—for example, whether to begin entering the required data, when an application is received, or to wait until final action is taken (such as when a loan goes to closing or an application is denied).

4. *Options for collection.* An institution may collect data on separate registers at different branches, or on separate registers for different loan types (such as for home purchase or home improvement loans, or for loans on multifamily dwellings). Entries need not be grouped on the register by MSA or Metropolitan Division, or chronologically, or by census tract numbers, or in any other particular order.

5. *Change in appropriate Federal agency.* If the appropriate Federal agency for a covered institution changes (as a consequence of a merger or a change in the institution's charter, for example), the institution must report data to the new appropriate Federal agency beginning with the year of the change.

6. *Subsidiaries.* An institution is a subsidiary of a bank or savings association (for purposes of reporting HMDA data to the same agency as the parent) if the bank or savings association holds or controls an ownership interest that is greater than 50 percent of the institution.

7. *Transmittal sheet—additional data submissions.* If an additional data submission becomes necessary

(for example, because the institution discovers that data were omitted from the initial submission, or because revisions are called for), that submission must be accompanied by a transmittal sheet.

8. *Transmittal sheet—revisions or deletions.* If a data submission involves revisions or deletions of previously submitted data, it must state the total of all line entries contained in that submission, including both those representing revisions or deletions of previously submitted entries, and those that are being resubmitted unchanged or are being submitted for the first time. Depository institutions must provide a list of the MSAs or Metropolitan Divisions in which they have home or branch offices.

5(b) Public disclosure of statement.

1. *Business day.* For purposes of § 1003.5, a business day is any calendar day other than a Saturday, Sunday, or legal public holiday.

2. *Format.* An institution may make the disclosure statement available in paper form or, if the person requesting the data agrees, in electronic form.

5(c) Public disclosure of modified loan/application register.

1. *Format.* An institution may make the modified register available in paper or electronic form. Although institutions are not required to make the modified register available in census tract order, they are strongly encouraged to do so in order to enhance its utility to users.

5(e) Notice of availability.

1. *Poster—suggested text.* An institution may use any text that meets the requirements of the regulation. Some of the Federal agencies that receive HMDA data provide HMDA posters that an institution can use to inform the public of the availability of its HMDA data, or the institution may create its own posters. If an institution prints its own, the following language is suggested but is not required:

Home Mortgage Disclosure Act Notice

The HMDA data about our residential mortgage lending are available for review. The data show geographic distribution of loans and applications; ethnicity, race, sex, and income of applicants and borrowers; and information about loan approvals and denials. Inquire at this office regarding the locations where HMDA data may be inspected.

2. *Additional language for institutions making the disclosure statement available on request.* An institution that posts a notice informing the public of the address to which a request should be sent could include the following sentence, for example, in its general notice: "To receive a copy of these data send a written request to [address]."

Section 1003.6—Enforcement

6(b) Bona fide errors.

1. *Bona fide error—information from third parties.* An institution that obtains the property-location information for applications and loans from third parties (such as appraisers or vendors of "geocoding" services) is responsible for ensuring that the information reported on its HMDA/LAR is correct.

[77 Fed. Reg. 8722 (Feb. 15, 2012); 77 Fed. Reg. 76,839 (Dec. 21, 2012)]

State Credit Discrimination Laws

The following is a summary of state statutes prohibiting discrimination in credit. Some statutes are similar to the federal Equal Credit Opportunity Act. Some are part of a state civil rights or human rights act and are at least somewhat general in their application to consumer credit. As part of a general state civil rights code, there may be remedies or administrative procedures available modeled to varying degrees after those provided for in federal civil rights laws. Yet other statutes are based on the federal Fair Housing Act's provisions prohibiting discrimination in residential real estate financing and which therefore apply only to housing financing.

Several states have more than one statute prohibiting discrimination in credit, and the scope of coverage, available remedies, and procedural rules usually vary under each statute. Advocates should therefore review all credit discrimination laws to determine which are applicable to the consumer's situation and, if more than one is applicable, which one is most likely to provide the desired result for the consumer.

Finally, there are two caveats. First, this appendix does not include any administrative regulations that may have been promulgated pursuant to state credit discrimination statutes; practitioners must check for such regulations in their states.

Second, while we have made efforts to ensure that this listing is a complete statutory survey as of this writing, it appears that the process of legislating against credit discrimination was not always done in the most orderly fashion conceivable and at times seems almost haphazard. If readers detect errors or omissions in this appendix, please let us know.

ALABAMA

Fair Housing: Ala. Code §§ 24-8-1 to 24-8-15
Protected Classes: Race, color, religion, sex, familial status, national origin, handicap.
Prohibited Practices: Discriminating in providing financial assistance for the purchase, construction, repair, and maintenance of a dwelling.
Scope of Coverage: Businesses involved in realty-related transactions.
Exclusions: Too numerous to list, see § 24-8-7.
Private Remedies: Permanent or temporary injunction, temporary restraining order, actual damages, punitive damages, court costs, and attorney fees.
Administrative Remedies: Office of ADECA may investigate, conduct hearings and institute court proceedings to seek temporary or preliminary injunctive relief.
Statute of Limitations: Administrative complaint must be filed within 180 days of discriminatory housing practice; civil complaint must be filed within one year.

ALASKA

Civil Rights: Alaska Stat. § 18.80.250 (credit transactions)
Protected Classes: Sex, physical or mental disability, marital status, changes in marital status, pregnancy, parenthood, race, religion, color, or national origin.
Prohibited Practices: Discriminating in transactions involving secured or unsecured credit, housing-related credit, credit for acquisition of unimproved property, credit to a married person or disabled person, credit card in the name of the married person requesting it.

Scope of Coverage: Financial institutions or commercial institutions extending credit.
Exclusions: Doubt about person's legal capacity to contract.
Private Remedies: Individual or class action, injunction, monetary relief. Alaska Stat. § 22.10.020(i).
Administrative Remedies: Commission for Human Rights may investigate, conduct hearings, issue orders, award attorney fees to any private party, subject to judicial review.
Criminal Remedies: Any commercial or financial institution found to have willfully engaged in unlawful credit discrimination is guilty of a misdemeanor (fine of not more than $500; imprisonment for not more than 30 days, or both).
Statute of Limitations: None specified.

Civil Rights: Alaska Stat. §§ 18.80.010 to 18.80.300; Alaska Stat. § 18.80.240 (housing transactions)
Protected Classes: Sex, marital status, change in marital status, pregnancy, race, religion, color or national origin, physical or mental disability.
Prohibited Practices: Discriminating in terms, conditions, or privileges in regard to the sale, lease, or use of realty.
Scope of Coverage: Owners, lessees, managers, or others having the right to sell, lease, or rent real property.
Exclusions: "Singles only" or "married couples only" housing.
Private Remedies: Individual or class action, injunction, monetary relief. Alaska Stat. § 22.10.020(i).
Administrative Remedies: Commission for Human Rights may investigate, conduct hearings, issue orders (including damages) and attorney fees to any private party, subject to judicial review.

Statute of Limitations: None specified.

ARIZONA

Fair Housing: **Ariz. Rev. Stat. Ann. §§ 41-1491 to 41-1491.37**

Protected Classes: Race, color, religion, sex, familial status, disability, or national origin.

Prohibited Practices: Discriminating in providing financial assistance for the purchase, construction, repair, and maintenance of a dwelling. § 41-1491.20.

Scope of Coverage: Businesses involved in realty-related transactions.

Exclusions: Religious organizations or nonprofit entities operated by religious organizations; private club which incidentally provides lodging for its members; a dwelling which rents rooms to one sex only; housing for elderly and non-discriminatory appraisal considerations.

Private Remedies: Actual damages, punitive damages, injunction, costs, attorney fees. § 41-1491.31.

Administrative Remedies: Attorney general or civil rights division may refer to mediation, investigate, file civil action for injunctive relief, actual and punitive damages.

Statute of Limitations: Two years from the termination of the prohibited practice.

ARKANSAS

Civil Rights: **Ark. Code Ann. §§ 16-123-101 to 16-123-108** (credit transactions)

Protected Classes: Race, religion, national origin, gender, or any sensory, mental or physical disability.

Prohibited Practices: Interference with the right to engage in credit and other contractual transactions without discrimination. § 16-123-107(a)(4).

Private Remedies: Civil action for injunction or actual damages or both, costs, and attorney fees permitted. § 16-123-107(b).

Consumer Credit: **Ark. Code Ann. §§ 4-87-101 to 4-87-105**

Protected Classes: Sex and marital status.

Prohibited Practices: Discriminating against equally qualified applicants of protected classes with respect to approval or denial of terms of credit.

Scope of Coverage: Consumer credit sales, consumer loans, any other extension of consumer credit, or issuance, renewal, denial, or terms of any credit card.

Private Remedies: $100 to $500 statutory damages, costs, and reasonable attorney fees.

Administrative Remedies: None specified.

Statute of Limitations: One year from occurrence of violation.

Miscellaneous: Class actions prohibited.

Fair Housing: **Ark. Code Ann. §§ 16-123-201 to 16-123-348**

Protected Classes: Religion, race, color, national origin, sex, disability, or familial status, of applicant or any person residing with applicant.

Prohibited Practices: Discrimination in the granting of financial assistance or financing in connection with a real estate transaction or in connection with the construction, maintenance, or improvement of real property, or to use any application form or keep any record or make any inquiry which indicates directly or indirectly a preference, limitation, specification or discrimination as to any protected class. § 16-123-205.

Scope of Coverage: Persons to whom application is made for financial assistance or financing, for the above purposes.

Exclusions: Application forms prescribed for the use of a lender regulated under the National Housing Act, or by a regulatory board or officer acting under the authority of the state or the United States.

Private Remedies: Civil action for injunction or actual damages or both, and costs and attorney fees permitted. § 16-123-210.

CALIFORNIA

Civil Rights: **Cal. Civ. Code §§ 51 to 52.2 (West)**

Protected Classes: Sex, race, color, religion, ancestry, national origin, disability, age, marital status, sexual orientation, or medical condition.

Prohibited Practices: Discrimination in accommodations, advantages, facilities, privileges, or services of business establishments.

Scope of Coverage: All business establishments.

Exclusions: Qualifying senior citizens housing.

Private Remedies: Not less than $4000, and no more than three times the amount of actual damages; attorney fees.

Public Remedies: The Attorney General, district attorney, city attorney, or any person aggrieved may seek a civil penalty of $25,000, an injunction, restraining order, or other order to prevent a pattern or practice of violation. The Attorney General or any district attorney or city attorney may intervene for the people of the State of California in actions seeking relief from the denial of equal protection of the laws under the Fourteenth Amendment to U.S. Constitution.

Consumer Credit: **Cal. Civ. Code § 1747.80 (West)**

Protected Classes: Race, religious creed, color, national origin, ancestry, or sex.

Prohibited Practices: Refusal to issue credit card on basis of membership in a protected class.

Scope of Coverage: Credit card issuers.

Private Remedies: Actual and punitive damages; injunctive relief.

Consumer Credit: **Cal. Civ. Code §§ 1812.30 to 1812.35 (West)**

Protected Classes: Marital status (single/married).

Prohibited Practices: Offering credit on less favorable terms than to single/married counterparts. § 1812.30.

Scope of Coverage: Credit transactions generally.

Exclusions: None specified.

Private Remedies: Actual and punitive damages; injunction; reasonable attorney fees. No class actions.

Administrative Remedies: Injunction, civil penalty.

Statute of Limitations: Two years from credit denial.

Fair Housing: **Cal. Civ. Code § 53 (West)**

Protected Classes: Race, color, creed, religion, sex, national origin, ancestry, disability.

Prohibited Practices: Provisions in written instruments relating to transfer or use of real property which purport to forbid or restrict conveyance, encumbrance, leasing, or mortgaging of subject real property to member of protected class.

Scope of Coverage: Written instruments relating to real property.

Private Remedies: Declaratory action to void offending restriction or prohibition.

Miscellaneous: **Cal. Gov't Code §§ 12900–12996 (West)** (Department of Fair Employment and Housing)

Protected Classes: Race, color, religion, sex, marital status, national origin, ancestry, familial status, disability, sexual orientation, and source of income, or disability.

Prohibited Practices: Discriminating or harassing in the terms, conditions, or privileges relating to obtaining or using financial assistance for housing accommodations. §§ 12955 to 12989.3.

Scope of Coverage: Covers any person, bank, mortgage company or other financial institution that provides assistance for the purchase, organization, or construction of any housing accommodation.

Exclusions: Discrimination on the basis of familial status does not apply to qualifying housing for older persons; religious organizations.

Private Remedies: Injunction, actual and punitive damages (not more than $10,000), costs, attorney fees.

Administrative Remedies: Order for sale or rental of the housing accommodation or like accommodation, or for provision of denied financial assistance, terms, privileges, or conditions; affirmative or prospective relief, including injunctive relief and actual damages. Civil penalty may be awarded to complainant not to exceed $16,000 for one violation, not to exceed $37,500 if respondent has been adjudged in separate accusation to have committed a prior intentional violation within prior five year period, and between $37,500 and $65,000 if two or more intentional violations within seven year period. § 12987(a)(3).

Statute of Limitations: Administrative complaint must be filed within one year (§ 12980(b)); civil complaint must be filed within the later of two years after the occurrence or termination of the alleged discriminatory practice or breach of administrative conciliation agreement. Civil action may not be commenced if administrative hearing has commenced. § 12989.1.

Miscellaneous: Cal. Health & Safety Code §§ 35800–35833 (West) (redlining)

Protected Classes: Race, color, religion, sex, sexual orientation, marital status, national origin, ancestry, familial status, source of income, or disability (bases defined under Cal. Gov't Code § 12955 (West), incorporated through Cal. Health & Safety Code § 35811 (West)).

Prohibited Practices: Redlining.

COLORADO

Consumer Credit: Colo. Rev. Stat. § 5-3-210

Protected Classes: Race, creed, religion, color, sex, sexual orientation, marital status, national origin, or ancestry.

Prohibited Practices: Denial of credit or making terms or conditions of credit more stringent on basis of membership in a protected class.

Scope of Coverage: Consumer credit sales, consumer leases, consumer loans regulated under Title V of Colorado Consumer Credit Code (C-CCC).

Exclusions: Sellers, lessors, or lenders whose total original unpaid balances arising from consumer credit sales, leases, and loans for previous calendar year are less than $1 million.

Private Remedies: Actual damages but not less than $100 nor more than $1000 for actual exemplary damages; costs and reasonable attorney fees. Colo. Rev. Stat. § 5-5-206.

Administrative Remedies: Administrator of C-CCC may bring administrative cease and desist proceedings or, seek injunction against violations of C-CCC, and a civil penalty for willful violations.

Statute of Limitations: None specified. (Note: The limitations for other specified C-CCC violations are either one year from the last scheduled payment of the agreement, Colo. Rev. Stat. § 5-5-202, or one year after the occurrence of the violation, Colo. Rev. Stat. § 5-5-202(5)).

Fair Housing: Colo. Rev. Stat. §§ 24-34-501 to 24-34-509

Protected Classes: Race, color, creed, religion, sex, sexual orientation, marital status, national origin, ancestry, familial status, disability.

Prohibited Practices: To make or cause to be made any written or oral inquiry regarding membership in a protected class or to discriminate in the terms, conditions, or privileges relating to the use of financial assistance for housing accommodations. § 24-34-502.

Scope of Coverage: Covers any business whose transactions include making loans for residential real estate transactions.

Private Remedies: Injunction, actual and punitive damages, costs, attorney fees.

Statute of Limitations: One year for administrative complaint; two years for private action, excluding time during which administrative proceeding is pending.

CONNECTICUT

Civil Rights: Conn. Gen. Stat. §§ 46a-66, 46a-81f, 46a-98 (credit transactions)

Protected Classes: Sex, gender identity or expression, age, race, color, religious creed, national origin, ancestry, marital status, mental retardation, learning disability, blindness, physical disability, or sexual orientation (if 18 years or older). Provision prohibiting credit discrimination on basis of sexual orientation includes protection for "civil union status." § 46a-81f.

Prohibited Practices: Discriminating against member of protected class (over eighteen years old) in any credit transaction.

Scope of Coverage: Credit transactions (including invitations to apply for credit, applications for credit, extensions of credit, or credit sales), extended by "creditors" (persons who regularly extend credit or arrange for the extension of credit for which payment of a finance charge or interest is required) in connection with loans, sale of property or services or otherwise.

Exclusions: Acts done or omitted in conformity with regulations or rulings of the Banking Commissioner, Federal Reserve Board or other government agencies with jurisdiction under the Equal Credit Opportunity Act will not result in liability.

Private Remedies: Actual damages and punitive damages not exceeding $1,000. In class action, punitive damages are recoverable up to lesser of $5000 or 1% of creditor's net worth. § 46a-98.

Administrative Remedies: Damages resulting from the discriminatory practice. Conn. Gen. Stat. § 46a-86(d).

Statute of Limitations: Administrative complaint must be filed within 180 days after alleged act of discrimination. Conn. Gen. Stat. § 46a-82. Civil action may be filed in lieu of (but not in addition to) administrative action within one year from the date of the alleged violation. § 46a-98.

Miscellaneous: Judicial remedy is in lieu of administrative remedy, not in addition to it.

Civil Rights: Conn. Gen. Stat. §§ 46a-51 to 46a-104 (housing transactions)

Protected Classes: Race, creed, color, national origin, ancestry, sex, marital status, civil union status, age, lawful source of income, familial status, learning disability, physical or mental disability, sexual orientation, gender identity or expression.

Prohibited Practices: Discriminating against member of protected class in (i) the terms, conditions, or privileges of sale or rental of a dwelling, or in providing related services or facilities, (ii) the making or purchasing of loans or providing other financial assistance for the purchase, construction, improvement, repair, or maintenance of a dwelling, or which is secured by residential real estate, or (iii) the brokering, selling, or appraising of residential real property.

Scope of Coverage: Sale or rental of a dwelling; making or purchasing of loans or providing other financial assistance for purchasing, constructing, improving, repairing, or maintaining a dwelling, or which is secured by residential real estate, or selling, brokering, or appraising of residential real estate.

Exclusions: Certain owner-occupied dwellings; housing for older persons; same sex accommodations with shared facilities.

Private Remedies: Injunctive relief, actual damages, attorney fees and costs. § 46a-98a.

Administrative Remedies: Actual damages, attorney fees and costs. § 46a-86(c).

Statute of Limitations: Administrative complaint must be filed within 180 days after alleged act of discrimination (§ 46a-82); civil action must be filed within one year of alleged discriminatory practice (or a breach of a conciliation agreement reached in an administrative proceeding), except that no civil action may be brought after a conciliation agreement is obtained or after commencement of an administrative hearing. § 46a-98a.

DELAWARE

Fair Housing: **Del. Code Ann. tit. 6, §§ 4600–4619**

Protected Classes: Race, color, national origin, religion, creed, sex, marital status, familial status, age (if eighteen or older), or disability, sexual orientation, or disability.

Prohibited Practices: To discriminate against any person in making available a transaction, or in the terms or conditions of any transaction, for the making, brokering, or purchasing of loans, or providing other financial assistance for purchasing, constructing, improving, repairing, or maintaining a dwelling, secured by residential real estate. Tit. 6, § 4604.

Scope of Coverage: All persons who engage in residential real estate transactions, as defined above.

Private Remedies: Civil action in the county in which the discriminatory practice occurred, for actual and punitive damages, or injunction or both, costs, and attorney fees in the discretion of the court. Tit. 6, § 4613. Private person may also intervene in suit brought by Attorney General. Tit. 6, § 4614.

Administrative Remedies: Hearing before the Delaware Human Relations Commission. (Judicial review and enforcement available.) Tit. 6, §§ 4610–4612.

Statute of Limitations: For administrative remedy, one year after occurrence or termination of practice, or of time when practice was or reasonably should have been discovered by aggrieved person, or after breach of conciliation agreement under this chapter—whichever is later. For civil action, two years, as above. Tit. 6, § 4613.

DISTRICT OF COLUMBIA

Civil Rights: **D.C. Code §§ 2-1401.01 to 2-1403.17**

Protected Classes: Actual or perceived race, color, religion, national origin, sex, age, marital status, personal appearance, sexual orientation, gender identity or expression, family responsibilities, disability, matriculation, political affiliation, source of income, genetic information, status as victim of an intrafamily offense, or place of residence or business.

Prohibited Practices: To refuse to lend money, guarantee a loan, accept a deed of trust or mortgage, or otherwise refuse to make funds available for the purchase, acquisition, construction, alteration, rehabilitation, repair, or maintenance of real property; to impose different conditions on such financing, or refuse to provide title or other insurance relating to the ownership or use of any interest in real property, based on the protected classes as above. To discriminate in any financial transaction involving real property on account of the

location of the residence or business ("to red-line"). To make, print, or publish any statement with respect to a transaction in real property, or the financing thereof, which indicates a preference, limitation, or discrimination based on the protected classes. § 2-1402.21.

Private Remedies: Cause of action in any court of competent jurisdiction for damages and other appropriate remedies, including costs and attorney fees. Aggrieved person must elect between administrative and judicial remedy. § 2-1403.16.

Administrative Remedies: Conciliation required. § 2-1403.06. If matter not resolved, hearing before Human Rights Commission. Relief includes administrative order, compensatory damages, costs, and attorney fees. Judicial review and enforcement are available. §§ 2-1403.14 to 2-1403.15.

Statute of Limitations: Administrative complaint must be filed within one year of discriminatory practice or discovery thereof (§ 2-1403.04); civil actions, within two years. Filing administrative complaint precludes civil action unless complaint is dismissed on grounds of administrative convenience or withdrawn; statute tolled while complaint is pending (§ 2-1403.16).

FLORIDA

Consumer Credit: **Fla. Stat. § 725.07**

Protected Classes: Sex, marital status, or race.

Prohibited Practices: No person can discriminate on basis of membership in protected class.

Scope of Coverage: Covers areas of loaning money, granting credit, and providing equal pay for equal services performed.

Exclusions: None specified.

Private Remedies: Compensatory and punitive damages and attorney fees.

Administrative Remedies: None specified.

Statute of Limitations: Same as for claims founded on statutory liability, see Forehand v. Int'l Bus. Machines Corp., 586 F. Supp. 9 (M.D. Fla. 1984), aff'd, 783 F.2d 204 (11th Cir. 1986).

Fair Housing: **Fla. Stat. §§ 760.22 to 760.37**

Protected Classes: Race, color, national origin, sex, handicap (including AIDS, § 760.50), familial status, or religion of applicant, his/her associates or prospective owners, lessees, tenants, or occupants of dwelling in relation to which the financial assistance is given.

Prohibited Practices: Denial of loans or other financial assistance or discrimination in fixing amount, interest rate, duration or other term or condition of financial assistance on a prohibited basis.

Scope of Coverage: Covers housing financing—purchase, construction, improvement, repair, or maintenance of a dwelling—extended by a corporation, association, firm, or enterprise which includes making real estate loans in its business; discriminating against member of protected class in making residential real estate transaction available.

Exclusions: Some specified exemptions provided for some private owners or owner-occupied dwellings; religious organizations using dwelling for other than commercial purposes; private clubs incidentally providing lodging to members; qualifying housing for older persons.

Private Remedies: Actual and punitive damages, costs, and attorney fees to prevailing party. § 760.35.

Administrative Remedies: Aggrieved party may file administrative complaint; commission to seek conciliation or civil penalties.

Statute of Limitations: Administrative complaint must be filed within one year of alleged discriminatory practice. Civil action may be commenced no later than two years after alleged discriminatory practice.

GEORGIA

Consumer Credit: Ga. Code Ann. §§ 7-6-1 to 7-6-2
Protected Classes: Sex, race, religion, national origin, or marital status.
Prohibited Practices: Discriminating or providing requirements which discriminate in the extending of credit or the making of loans.
Scope of Coverage: Banks, lending companies, financial institutions, retail installment seller, or person extending credit.
Private Remedies: Action for damages in court of competent jurisdiction.
Administrative Remedies: None specified.
Statute of Limitations: None specified.
Miscellaneous: Representative party actions (that is class actions) not allowed. Willful violation is misdemeanor with a penalty of a fine no greater than $1,000.

Fair Housing: Ga. Code Ann. §§ 8-3-200 to 8-3-223
Protected Classes: Race, color, religion, sex, disability or handicap, familial status, or national origin of person applying for housing financing or of persons associated with him in connection with such financial assistance, or prospective owners, lessees, tenants, or occupants of the dwelling(s) in relation to which the financial assistance is given.
Prohibited Practices: Denial of loans or other financial assistance or discrimination in fixing amount, interest rate, duration, or other terms or conditions of such credit on a prohibited basis. § 8-3-204.
Scope of Coverage: Covers real estate-related transactions—purchase, construction, improvement, appraisal, repair, or maintenance of a dwelling—extended by a corporation, association, firm, or enterprise which include making real estate loans in its business.
Exclusions: Some specified exemptions provided for some private owners or owner-occupied dwellings; religious organizations using dwelling for other than commercial purposes; private clubs incidentally providing lodging to members; qualifying housing for older persons.
Private Remedies: May enforce § 8-3-204 in court, though court may continue the case if conciliation efforts by administrator may result in satisfactory settlement; injunctive relief, actual damages, punitive damages, court costs, and reasonable attorney fees if a prevailing plaintiff is not financially able to assume such fees.
Administrative Remedies: Aggrieved party may file administrative complaint. Attorney General also may seek injunction against pattern and practice of violation of the statute.
Statute of Limitations: One year for administrative actions and two years for civil actions.

HAWAII

Consumer Credit: Haw. Rev. Stat. §§ 477E-1 to 477E-6
Protected Classes: Marital status.
Prohibited Practices: Discrimination against any applicant with respect to any aspect of a credit transaction; aggregation of loans to determine finance charges or loan ceilings.
Scope of Coverage: Credit transactions by financial institutions, debt adjusters, extenders, or arrangers of credit, assignee who participates in credit decision.
Exclusions: May inquire into marital status to determine creditor's rights and remedies; may request spousal signature to create lien or real property transaction.
Private Remedies: Actual damages, punitive damages up to $10,000 if

not a class action; injunction, attorney fees.
Statute of Limitations: One year from reason to know of the violation.

Fair Housing: Haw. Rev. Stat. §§ 515-1 to 515-20
Protected Classes: Race, sex, including gender identity or expression and sexual orientation, color, religion, ancestry, marital status, familial status, disability, age.
Prohibited Practices: To discriminate on a prohibited basis in financial assistance in connection with a real estate transaction; to use a form of application for financial assistance or retain records or make inquiries in connection with applications for financial assistance which indicate an intent to make limitations, specifications, or discrimination on a prohibited basis. § 515-5.
Scope of Coverage: Credit covered is financial assistance for sale, exchange, rental, or lease of real property or construction, rehabilitation, repair, maintenance, or improvement of real property; creditors covered are "person[s] to whom application is made for [such] financial assistance."
Exclusions: Religious institutions or charitable or educational organization operated by a religious institution to give preference to members of the same religion or one sex in a real property transaction.
Private Remedies: Compensatory and punitive damages, legal and equitable relief, costs, and attorney fees. Haw. Rev. Stat. § 368-17.
Administrative Remedies: Dep't of Commerce & Consumer Affairs may investigate and mediate complaints; issue cease and desist orders, order affirmative relief, actual damages ($500 for each violation unless greater damages are proven); reasonable attorney fees.
Statute of Limitations: Administrative complaint must be filed within 180 days of alleged discriminatory practice; complainant may bring civil action within ninety days of receipt of requested notice of right to sue.

IDAHO

Civil Rights: Idaho Code Ann. §§ 67-5901 to 67-5912 (housing transactions)
Protected Classes: Race, color, religion, sex, national origin, or disability.
Prohibited Practices: Discriminating or using a form that directly or indirectly indicates an intent to make a limitation, specification or discrimination regarding real estate transaction. § 67-5909.
Scope of Coverage: Covers any person to whom an application is made for financial assistance in connection with the sale, construction, rehabilitation, repair, maintenance, or improvement of real property.
Exclusions: Religious organizations.
Private Remedies: Injunction, actual and punitive damages (not more than $1000 per willful violation).
Administrative Remedies: Injunction.
Statute of Limitations: Within one year of administrative complaint.

ILLINOIS

Civil Rights: 775 Ill. Comp. Stat. §§ 5/1-101 to 5/10-104; 775 Ill. Comp. Stat. §§ 5/4-101 to 5/4-104 (credit transactions)
Protected Classes: Race, color, religion, sex, national origin, ancestry, age, sexual orientation, marital status, physical or mental disability, military status, or unfavorable discharge from military service. §§ 5/1-102(A), 5/1-103. Familial status, for real estate transactions. § 5/1-102(D).
Prohibited Practices: Denial or modification of services normally provided by a financial institution, denial, or variation of terms of a

loan; redlining; denial or variation of term of loan without considering all dependable income of each person liable for loan; refuse issuance of credit card on basis of unlawful discrimination; failure to inform credit card applicant, upon request, the reason for rejection of application; utilization of lending standards without economic basis and which constitute unlawful discrimination (that is, discrimination on a prohibited basis).

Scope of Coverage: Loans, including loans for purchase, construction, improvement, repair, or maintenance of housing accommodation, or commercial or industrial purpose loans, by financial institutions; credit cards.

Exclusions: Allows certain practices to determine creditworthiness and allow sound underwriting practices; also permits special purpose credit programs.

Private Remedies: Judicial review of agency action.

Administrative Remedies: Aggrieved party may file administrative complaint with Dep't of Human Rights. Human Rights Commission may order cease and desist, actual damages, attorney fees, extension of goods, services, privileges, or advantages offered by respondent. (Articles 7A and 8A of Human Rights Act.)

Statute of Limitations: Administrative complaint must be filed within 180 days.

Civil Rights: 775 Ill. Comp. Stat. §§ 5/3-101 to 5/3-106 (housing transactions)

Prohibited Classes: Race, color, religion, sex, familial status, national origin, ancestry, age, marital status, disability, or unfavorable discharge from military service.

Prohibited Practices: Refusing to engage in a real estate transaction based on a discrimination or discriminating in making such a transaction available or altering the terms, conditions, or privileges.

Scope of Coverage: Real estate transaction includes brokering, appraising, and making or purchasing loans, or providing other financial assistance.

Exclusions: Certain private sales by owners of single family homes, apartment rentals in five family units in which lessor resides; private rooms; religious organizations limiting sale, rental, or occupancy of dwelling owned or operated for other than a commercial purpose to persons of same religion; restriction of room rentals to single sex, persons convicted under federal law of manufacture or distribution of a controlled substance; and qualifying housing for older persons.

Private Remedies: Actual and punitive damages, injunctive relief, and attorney fees and costs.

Administrative Remedies: Recommended order for appropriate relief. 775 Ill. Comp. Stat. § 5/8A-102.

Statute of Limitations: Administrative complaint must be filed within one year. 775 Ill. Comp. Stat. § 5/7B-102. Civil action must be commenced within two years of termination of alleged violation (tolled while administrative proceeding is pending). 775 Ill. Comp. Stat. § 5/10-102.

Consumer Credit: 815 Ill. Comp. Stat. §§ 140/0.01 to 140/9

Protected Classes: Race, color, religion, national origin, ancestry, age (between forty and seventy), sex, marital status, physical or mental handicap unrelated to the ability to pay or unfavorable discharge from military service.

Prohibited Practices: Denial of credit card on a prohibited basis. § 140/1a. Also prohibits requesting information regarding marital status on a credit card application except for a joint account application or requiring reapplications for credit cards based on change in marital status unless the change causes deterioration in person's financial condition; permits cardholder to use the name he or she regularly uses, to request reasons for denial, and financial status shall be considered individually, if requested, or jointly for a married couple if requested.

Scope of Coverage: Credit card issuers.

Private Remedies: Denial of proper application on a prohibited basis and failure to inform applicant of reason for denial is a civil rights violation. 775 Ill. Comp. Stat. § 5/4-103.

Miscellaneous: Applications conforming to ECOA are deemed to be in compliance with this act.

Consumer Credit: 815 Ill. Comp. Stat. §§ 120/1 to 120/6 (Fairness in Lending Act)

Protected Classes: Geographical location of real estate, applicant's source of income (if regular and dependable), childbearing capacity of applicant or spouse.

Prohibited Practices: Denying loan or varying terms on basis of above, or use other lending standards which have no economic basis or which are discriminatory in effect; also prohibits equity stripping and loan flipping. § 120/3.

Scope of Coverage: Banks, credit unions, insurance companies, mortgage banking companies, savings and loans serving banks, or other residential mortgage lenders, which operate or have a place of business in Illinois.

Exclusions: Act does not preclude use of sound underwriting practices, that is, considering the willingness and ability of borrower to pay back the loan, the market value of the real property, and diversification of the institution's investment portfolio.

Private Remedies: Action in circuit court for compensatory damages. Costs at discretion of the court.

Consumer Credit: 205 Ill. Comp. Stat. § 635/3-8 (financial regulation)

Protected Classes: Race, color, religion, national origin, age, gender, or marital status.

Prohibited Practices: Refusal to grant loan, or varying terms or application procedures because of membership in protected class, or solely because of the geographic location of the proposed security.

Scope of Coverage: Residential mortgage bankers, or any person, partnership, association, corporation, or other entity which engages in the business of brokering, funding, originating, servicing, or purchasing residential mortgage loans.

Administrative Remedies: Commissioner of Savings and Residential Finance may ask Attorney General to sue for injunction. Commissioner may revoke, suspend, or deny license, issue a reprimand, place applicant or licensee on probation and/or impose a fine of up to $10,000. 205 Ill. Comp. Stat. § 635/4-5.

INDIANA

Civil Rights: Ind. Code § 22-9-1-1 to 22-9-1-18 (housing transactions)

Protected Classes: Race, religion, color, sex, disability, national origin, ancestry.

Prohibited Practices: Exclusion of person from equal opportunities relating to acquisition or sale of real estate, extension of credit. § 22-9-1-3.

Scope of Coverage: Individuals, corporations or other organized groups of persons.

Private Remedies: Injunction; actual damages only if lost wages, salary, or commission. § 22-9-1-6(k).

Statute of Limitations: 180 days. § 22-9-1-3(p).

Fair Housing: Ind. Code §§ 22-9.5-1-1 to 22-9.5-11-3

Protected Classes: Race, color, religion, sex, disability, familial status, national origin.

Prohibited Practices: Discriminating in the making or purchasing of loans or providing other financial assistance in connection with the purchase, construction, improvement, repair, or maintenance residential real estate, or which is secured by residential real estate. § 22-9.5-5-1.

Scope of Coverage: Covers any person whose business includes engaging in residential real estate financing to sell, construct, improve, repair, maintain a dwelling.

Exclusions: Persons convicted under state or federal law of illegal manufacture or distribution of a controlled substance; religious organizations and private clubs favoring members; single family units.

Private Remedies: Injunction, actual and punitive damages, costs, attorney fees.

Administrative Remedies: Actual damages, attorney fees, and court costs, and other injunctive or equitable relief.

Statute of Limitations: One year for administrative claim; one year for civil claim (excluding time that an administrative claim is pending).

IOWA

Civil Rights: Iowa Code §§ 216.1 to 216.20; Iowa Code § 216.10 (credit transactions)

Protected Classes: Age, color, creed, national origin, race, religion, marital status, sex, sexual orientation, gender identity, physical disability, familial status.

Prohibited Practices: Refusal to loan or extend consumer credit; imposing finance charges or other terms or conditions more onerous than those regularly extended to persons of similar economic background.

Scope of Coverage: Any creditor extending consumer credit; licensed lenders under Iowa Code Chapters 524, 533, 534, 536 or 536A extending any credit.

Exclusions: Refusal to offer credit life or A & H insurance based on age or disability is not discriminatory if based on bona fide underwriting considerations not prohibited by Iowa Code Chapter 505.

Private Remedies: Administrative complaint must first be sought; judicial relief may be sought after obtaining a 120-day administrative release. District court may order same remedial action which Human Rights Commission could order. § 216.16.

Administrative Remedies: Aggrieved party may file administrative complaint. Civil Rights Commission may order *inter alia* cease and desist, actual damages (including attorney fees), and extension of advantages, facilities, privileges and services denial due to discriminatory practices. § 216.15.

Criminal Penalty: Any person who knowingly engages in a practice which violates the provisions of § 535A.2 or § 535A.9 is guilty of a misdemeanor.

Statute of Limitations: Administrative complaint must be filed within 180 days (§ 216.15); conditions for civil actions (§ 216.16).

Miscellaneous: District court can order respondent's reasonable attorney fees if complainant's action was frivolous. § 216.16.

Civil Rights: Iowa Code § 216.8A (housing transactions)

Protected Classes: Race, color, creed, sex, sexual orientation, gender identity, religion, national origin, disability, familial status.

Prohibited Practices: To discriminate against the making or purchasing of loans or providing other financial assistance in connection with a residential real estate transaction. § 216.8A(4)(b).

Scope of Coverage: Covers any person or entity whose business includes engaging in residential real estate financing for purchase, construction, improvement, repair, or maintenance of residential real estate.

Private Remedies: Administrative complaint must first be sought; judicial relief may be sought after obtaining a 120-day administrative release. District court may order same remedial action which Human Rights Commission could order. Iowa Code § 216.16.

Administrative Remedies: Aggrieved party may file administrative complaint. Civil Rights Commission may order *inter alia* cease and desist, actual damages (including attorney fees), and extension of advantages, facilities, privileges and services denial due to discriminatory practices. Iowa Code § 216.15.

Statute of Limitations: Administrative complaint must be filed within 180 days (Iowa Code § 216.15); conditions for civil actions (Iowa Code § 216.16).

Miscellaneous: District court can order respondent's reasonable attorney fees if complainant's action was frivolous. § 216.16.

Consumer Credit: Iowa Code § 537.3311

Protected Classes: Age, color, creed, national origin, political affiliation, race, religion, sex, marital status, disability, receipt of public assistance, social security benefits, pension benefits, or exercise of rights under Iowa Consumer Credit Code (I-CCC) or other provisions of law.

Prohibited Practices: Refusal to enter into credit transaction or impose terms or conditions more onerous than those regularly extended by that creditor to consumers of similar economic background on prohibited basis.

Scope of Coverage: Consumer credit sales, consumer loans, or consumer leases as defined by I-CCC.

Exclusions: Covers only creditors as defined by I-CCC, that is, regularly engaged in the business of making loans, leases, or selling in credit transactions of same kind. Excludes sales, loans, and leases if amount financed exceeds $25,000, certain sales of interests in land, and first liens on real property securing acquisition or construction debt.

Private Remedies: Actual damages and statutory damages not less than $100 nor more than $1,000, plus costs and attorney fees. Iowa Code § 537.5201.

Administrative Remedies: Code administrator may issue cease and desist order or may seek injunctions, reformation, and actual damages which consumers or a consumer class could get.

Statute of Limitations: Open-end credit, two years after violations; closed-end credit, one year after due date of last scheduled payment. Iowa Code § 537.5201.

Miscellaneous: Statutory damages not available in class actions.

Miscellaneous: Iowa Code §§ 535A.1 to 535A.9 (redlining)

Protected Classes: Income, racial or ethnic characteristics, or the age of structures in a neighborhood.

Prohibited Practices: Redlining. Classifying areas as unsuitable for mortgage loans, denying mortgage loans, or varying the terms of a mortgage loan, that is, requiring a larger down payment, or a shorter amortization period, or a higher interest rate or fees, or unreasonable underappraisal of real estate, because of the above characteristics of the geographic area.

Scope of Coverage: Banks, credit unions, insurance companies, mortgage banking companies, savings and loan associations, industrial loan companies, or any other institution or person who makes mortgage loans and operates or has a place of business in Iowa.

Exclusions: Individuals who make less than five mortgage loans a year. Does not bar the exercise of sound underwriting judgment, concerning the borrower's willingness and ability to repay, the appraised value of the property, and the diversification of the lender's portfolio.

Private Remedies: Civil action for actual damages, costs and attorney fees. § 535A.6. For bad faith noncompliance, civil penalty of up to $1000 in addition to damages. § 535A.8.

Administrative Remedies: Civil enforcement by the superintendents of banking, savings and loan associations, or credit unions, or the commissioner of insurance, depending on the kind of entity involved. Lenders must file disclosure statements regarding their loans with the Iowa Finance Authority.

KANSAS

Civil Rights: **Kan. Stat. Ann. §§ 44-1001 to 44-1044** (housing transactions)

Protected Classes: Race, religion, color, sex, disability, national origin, familial status, or ancestry of applicant, persons associated with applicant, or prospective owners, lessees, tenants, or occupants of real property in relation to which financial assistance is given.

Prohibited Practices: Denial of financial assistance, or making terms or conditions of credit more stringent, or keeping records or forms indicating an intent to make any preference or limitation because of membership in the protected class. § 44-1017.

Scope of Coverage: Covers housing financing—purchase, construction, improvement, repair, or maintenance of real property—extended by financial institutions, persons, or firms or enterprises whose business consists in whole or in part of making real estate loans.

Exclusions: Religious organizations or nonprofit associations operated by a religion may give preference to members of their own organizations; qualifying single-family homeowners; qualifying housing for older persons. § 44-1018.

Private Remedies: De novo review; actual and punitive damages, costs and attorney fees. § 44-1021.

Administrative Remedies: Aggrieved party may file administrative complaint. Civil Rights Commission may *inter alia* issue cease and desist order, order the real estate financing, actual damages. § 44-1019.

Statute of Limitations: Complaint must be filed within one year (§ 44-1019(a)); two years for civil actions (§ 44-1021(d)(1)).

KENTUCKY

Civil Rights: **Ky. Rev. Stat. Ann. §§ 344.010 to 344.990 (West); Ky. Rev. Stat. Ann. § 344.400 (West)** (credit transactions)

Protected Classes: Race, color, religion, national origin and sex.

Prohibited Practices: Deny credit, increase charges, fees, or collateral on any credit, restrict amount or use of credit extended to any person or any related item or service, or attempt to do any of these things on a prohibited basis.

Scope of Coverage: Any credit transaction is covered, which by § 344.010(12) includes loans, retail installment sales transactions, credit cards, for both business and personal purposes, when a finance charge is imposed or repayment is provided in scheduled payments. Creditors covered by § 344.400 are "any person," defined by § 344.010(1) to include individuals, corporations, *et cetera*, but they must extend credit "in the course of the regular trade or commerce," including permitting that payment for purchases may be deferred. § 344.010(12).

Exclusions: The credit history of the individual applicant and the effect of Kentucky law on dower, curtesy, descent and distribution on a particular case may be considered.

Private Remedies: Civil action for injunctive relief, actual damages, costs, and reasonable attorney fees, in addition to other remedies authorized by the chapter. § 344.450.

Administrative Remedies: Aggrieved party may file complaint with human rights commission, which has authority to issue cease and desist orders and, *inter alia*, order that the respondent extend its services, facilities and privileges to all individuals, and payment of actual damages, including compensation for humiliation and embarrassment. §§ 344.200, 344.240.

Statute of Limitations: Administrative complaint must be filed within 180 days of alleged discriminatory practice. § 344.200(1). The limitation provision applicable to an action, commenced in the court under § 344.450, is that of Ky. Rev. Stat. Ann. § 413.120(2) (West), currently five years. *See* Clifton v. Midway College, 702 S.W.2d 835 (Ky. 1986).

Civil Rights: **Ky. Rev. Stat. Ann. § 344.370 (West)** (housing transactions)

Protected Classes: Race, color, religion, national origin, sex, familial status, disability, or age of individual or present or prospective owner, tenant, or occupant of the real property.

Prohibited Practices: Discriminating (a) in granting, denying, or setting terms and conditions of financial assistance or extending services in connection therewith; (b) in using forms or making or keeping records or inquiries which indicate a limitation, specification, or discrimination as to race, color, religion, or national origin or any intent to make such a limitation, specification, or discrimination; (c) by refusing to fully count income and expenses of both spouses, because of sex, when both spouses become or will become joint obligors in real estate transactions.

Scope of Coverage: Financial institutions, defined by Ky. Rev. Stat. Ann. § 344.010(9) (West) as bank, banking organization, mortgage company, or insurance company or other lender to whom application is made for financial assistance for purchase, lease, acquisition, construction, rehabilitation, repair, maintenance, or improvement of real property, or any person or other entity whose business includes engaging in real estate-related transactions.

Remedies: Same as for Ky. Rev. Stat. Ann. § 344.400 (West).

Fair Housing: **Ky. Rev. Stat. Ann. §§ 344.360 to 344.365 (West)** (housing transactions)

Protected Classes: Race, color, religion, sex, familial status, disability, or national origin.

Prohibited Practices: (1) Refusing to sell, exchange, rent, or lease real property; (2) discriminating within the terms, condition, or privileges of the sale, exchange, rental, or lease of real property; (3) refusing to receive a bona fide offer to purchase, rent, or lease real property; (4) refusing to negotiate for the sale, rental, or lease of real property; (5) falsely representing that a property is unavailable; (6) printing or causing to be printed an advertisement that indicates, either directly or indirectly, a limitation, specification, or discrimination; (7) offering, soliciting, accepting, using or retaining a listing of real property for sale, rent, or lease with the understanding that any person may be discriminated against.

Scope of Coverage: Applies to a real estate operator, real estate broker, real estate salesman, or any person employed by or acting on behalf of any of those persons, as defined by Ky. Rev. Stat. Ann. § 344.010(8), (9) (West).

Private Remedies: Same as for Ky. Rev. Stat. Ann. § 344.450 (West).

LOUISIANA

Civil Rights: **La. Rev. Stat. Ann. § 51:2255** (credit transactions)

Protected Classes: Race, creed, color, religion, national origin, disability, or sex.

Prohibited Practices: Deny credit, increase charges, fees, or collateral requirements, restrict amount or use of credit extended or impose different terms or conditions on credit or any item or service related thereto, or to attempt to do any of these things. (The credit history of the individual applicant and the application to the particular case of state law on matrimonial regimes and succession may be considered.)

Scope of Coverage: Applies to "any person," including individuals (La. Rev. Stat. Ann. § 51:2232(9)) in connection with "any credit transaction."

Private Remedies: Civil action for injunctive relief, actual damages, costs, and reasonable attorney fees, in addition to other remedies authorized by the chapter. La. Rev. Stat. Ann. § 51:2264.

Administrative Remedies: Aggrieved party may file complaint with human rights commission, which has authority to issue cease and desist orders and, *inter alia* order that the respondent extend its services, facilities and privileges to all individuals, and payment of actual damages, including compensation for humiliation and embarrassment. La. Rev. Stat. Ann. §§ 51:2257 to 51:2261.

Statute of Limitations: Administrative complaint must be filed within 180 days of alleged discriminatory practice. La. Rev. Stat. Ann. § 51:2257(A). No statute of limitation is specified for the civil action commenced in court.

Civil Rights: **La. Rev. Stat. Ann. §§ 51:2231 to 51:2265; La. Rev. Stat. Ann. § 51:2254** (housing transactions)

Protected Classes: Race, creed, color, religion, national origin, sex, disability, or age of individual or present or prospective owner, tenant, occupant of the immovable property or persons associated with any of these.

Prohibited Practices: Discriminating (a) in granting, denying, or setting terms and conditions of financial assistance or extending services in connection therewith; (b) in using forms or making or keeping records or inquiries which indicate a limitation, specification, or discrimination as to race, creed, color, religion, or national origin or any intent to make such a limitation, specification, or discrimination; (c) by refusing to fully count income and expenses of both spouses, because of sex, when both spouses become or will become joint obligors in real estate transactions.

Scope of Coverage: Appears intended to cover housing financing extended by a financial institution.

Private Remedies: Civil action for injunctive relief, actual damages, costs, and reasonable attorney fees, in addition to other remedies authorized by the chapter. § 51:2264.

Administrative Remedies: Aggrieved party may file complaint with human rights commission, which has authority to issue cease and desist orders and, *inter alia* order that the respondent extend its services, facilities and privileges to all individuals, and payment of actual damages, including compensation for humiliation and embarrassment. §§ 51:2257 to 51:2261.

Statute of Limitations: Administrative complaint must be filed within 180 days of alleged discriminatory practice. § 51:2257(A). No statute of limitation is specified for the civil action commenced in court.

Consumer Credit: **La. Rev. Stat. Ann. §§ 9:3581 to 9:3583**

Protected Classes: Race, color, religion, national origin, sex, or marital status.

Prohibited Practices: To refuse to extend credit on a prohibited basis, to require any applicant of legal age to meet credit qualification standards not required of other similarly situated persons.

Scope of Coverage: Applies to all extensions of credit made in Louisiana between any natural person and any extender of credit.

Private Remedies: None specified. *But see* La. Rev. Stat. Ann. § 51:2255.

Administrative Remedies: None specified. *But see* La. Rev. Stat. Ann. § 51:2255.

Statute of Limitations: None specified. *But see* La. Rev. Stat. Ann. § 51:2255.

Fair Housing: **La. Rev. Stat. Ann. §§ 51:2601 to 51:2614**

Protected Classes: Race, color, religion, sex, handicap, familial status, national origin.

Prohibited Practices: Discriminating in the making or purchasing of loans or other financial assistance in connection with residential real estate. § 51:2607.

Scope of Coverage: Covers any person whose business includes engaging in residential real estate financing for purchasing construction, improving, repairing, or maintaining a dwelling.

Private Remedies: Injunction, actual and punitive damages, costs, attorney fees.

Administrative Remedies: May file complaint with Attorney General who may file a civil action. Relief includes injunction, actual and punitive damages.

Statute of Limitations: One year to file complaint with Attorney General; two years to file private action.

Miscellaneous: **La. Rev. Stat. § 46:2254(G), (I)** (housing financing for handicapped)

Protected Classes: Handicapped persons.

Prohibited Practices: (1) *Inter alia* brokers discriminating in terms, conditions, or privileges of real estate transaction or furnishing services in connection therewith on basis of handicap unrelated to otherwise qualified individual's ability to acquire, rent, or maintain property, (2) financiers discriminating against otherwise qualified applicant on basis of handicap unrelated to individual's ability to acquire, rent, or maintain property, or use forms or make record or inquiry which indicates limitation, specification; or discrimination based on handicap unrelated to ability to acquire, rent, or maintain property.

Scope of Coverage: Financing in connection with real estate transaction or for construction, rehabilitation, repair, maintenance, or improvement of real property.

Private Remedies: Civil action for all legal remedies, including, but not limited to compensatory damages, attorney fees and costs, and any other relief deemed appropriate. If a party filing suit under this chapter loses, the court has discretion to assess reasonable attorney fees and all court costs against him or her.

Statute of Limitations: One year from date of discriminatory act.

Miscellaneous: Complainant must send written notice to prospective defendant at least thirty days prior to filing, detailing discrimination, and both parties must make good faith effort to settle before court action.

MAINE

Civil Rights: **Me. Rev. Stat. Ann. tit. 5, §§ 4595–4598** (credit transactions)

Protected Classes: Age, race, color, sex, marital status, ancestry, religion, national origin, and sexual orientation.

Prohibited Practices: Refuse to extend credit on a prohibited basis.

However, financial institution extending credit to married person may require both husband and wife to sign note and mortgage; may deny credit to a minor; and may consider a person's age in determining terms of credit; complying with terms and conditions of certain bona fide group insurance plans is not discriminatory.

Scope of Coverage: Applies to any extension of credit (defined as the right to defer payment of a debt or to incur debt or purchase property and services and defer payment therefor) by any "creditor" (defined as any person who regularly extends or arranges for the extension of credit for which the payment of a finance charge or interest is required). Also, all financial institutions authorized to do business in the state must comply. Me. Rev. Stat. Ann. tit. 9-B, § 433 (West).

Private Remedies: Civil action for injunctive relief and other appropriate remedies including, but not limited to, *inter alia*, a statutory penalty of $1000 to $3,000, depending on respondent's prior history of discrimination. Attorney fees and costs may, in the court's discretion, be awarded to the prevailing party. Attorney fees and civil penalties may not be awarded unless complaint first filed with human rights commission, which either dismissed complaint or failed to enter into certain conciliation agreement within ninety days of finding reasonable cause. Me. Rev. Stat. Ann. tit. 5, §§ 4613–4622.

Administrative Remedies: Aggrieved party may file complaint with human rights commission, which may attempt conciliation, or may itself file civil action pursuant to Me. Rev. Stat. Ann. tit. 5, § 4613.

Civil Rights: Me. Rev. Stat. Ann. tit. 5, §§ 4551–4632; Me. Rev. Stat. Ann. tit. 5, §§ 4581–4583 (housing transactions)

Protected Classes: Race, color, sex, physical or mental disability, religion, familial status, ancestry, or national origin, and sexual orientation of the applicant or of existing or prospective occupants or tenants.

Prohibited Practices: (1) Make or cause to be made inquiries concerning membership in a protected class of applicant seeking financial assistance or of existing or prospective occupants or tenants of housing accommodations which are the subject of the financing, or (2) discriminating in the granting of financial assistance or in terms, conditions, or privileges relating to obtaining or using the financial assistance on a prohibited basis. Tit. 5, §§ 4582 to 4582-A.

Scope of Coverage: "Any person" to whom application is made for loan or other financial assistance for acquisition, construction, rehabilitation, repair, or maintenance of any housing accommodation (as defined by the act).

Private Remedies: Same as for credit transactions.

Administrative Remedies: Same as for credit transactions.

Statute of Limitations: Administrative complaint must be filed within six months of alleged discriminatory act. Tit. 5, § 4611. Civil action must be brought within two years of alleged discriminatory act. Tit. 5, § 4613.

MARYLAND

Civil Rights: Md. Code Ann., State Gov't §§ 20-101 to 20-1203 (West) (housing transactions)

Protected Classes: Race, color, religion, sex, familial status, national origin, marital status, sexual orientation, or disability.

Prohibited Practices: Refusing to sell or rent after receiving a bona fide offer, or refusing to negotiate for the sale or otherwise make unavailable or deny a dwelling; discriminating in the terms, conditions, or privileges in a sale or rental; printing or causing to have printed advertisements or notices that indicate any preferences, limitations, or discrimination; falsely representing that a dwelling is unavailable; inducing or attempting to induce a sale or rental by misrepresentation. §§ 20-705, 20-706.

Scope of Coverage: Applies to real estate brokers, agents, or salespersons; agents of any real estate broker, agent or sales person; persons in the business of selling or renting dwellings; or agents of a person in the business of selling or renting dwellings. § 20-704.

Exclusions: Religious organizations and private clubs favoring members. § 20-703. Housing for older persons, in the case of provisions concerning familial status. § 20-704.

Private Remedies: Civil actions for injunctions, actual and punitive damages, and attorney fees. § 20-1036.

Administrative Remedies: Aggrieved party may file complaint with Human Relations Commission. The Commission may file a complaint on its own initiative and investigate. The Commission has the authority to issue subpoenas and order discovery. §§ 20-1021, 20-1022.

Statute of Limitations: Administrative complaint must be filed within one year of the alleged discriminatory act. § 20-1021. Civil actions must be filed within two years. § 20-1035.

Miscellaneous: Criminal penalties for bringing malicious, unfounded complaints. § 20-1104.

Consumer Credit: Md. Code Ann., Com. Law §§ 12-701 to 12-708 (West) (Equal Credit Opportunity Act)

Protected Classes: Sex, marital status, race, color, religion, national origin, or age.

Prohibited Practices: Discriminating on a prohibited basis with respect to any aspect of a credit transaction, including seven specifically defined prohibited practices. §§ 12-704, 12-705.

Scope of Coverage: "Creditors," defined as persons who regularly extend, renew, or continue credit (including arrangers) for personal, family, or household purposes, may not discriminate against any "applicant," defined as person applying directly for an extension, renewal, or continuation of credit, or indirectly by use of existing credit plan for an amount greater than previously established limit.

Private Remedies: Civil action for injunctive relief, actual damages, and, in an individual action only, up to $10,000 in punitive damages, costs and attorney fees. In class action, total punitive damage recovery limited to lesser of $100,000 or 1% of creditor's net worth.

Administrative Remedies: Aggrieved party may file complaint with Commissioner of Consumer Credit or State Banking Commissioner, which has authority to issue cease and desist order.

Statute of Limitations: Civil action must be brought within one year of occurrence of violation.

Miscellaneous: Notice of adverse action requirements similar to federal ECOA.

Consumer Credit: Md. Code Ann., Com. Law § 12-113 (West)

Protected Classes: Race, creed, color, age, sex, marital status, handicap, or national origin; geographic area or neighborhood.

Prohibited Practices: Refusing to lend money to any person solely on a prohibited basis.

Scope of Coverage: Lenders operating under subtitle one of Md. Code Ann., Com. Law Title 12 (Credit Regulations) (Md. Code Ann., Com. Law § 12-1019(f) (West)) in lending money to any person.

Exclusions: Certain factors related to geographic area specifically may be the basis for a refusal to lend.

Remedies: None specified.

Consumer Credit: Md. Code Ann., Com. Law § 12-305 (West)

Protected Classes: Race, color, creed, national origin, sex, marital status, or age.

Prohibited Practices: Discriminating against any loan applicant on a prohibited basis. (Denying an application from a minor is not age discrimination.)

Scope of Coverage: Licensees operating under subtitle 3 of Md. Code Ann., Com. Law Title 12 (Md. Code Ann., Com. Law § 12-301(d) (West)) lending to any loan applicant.

Exclusions: If conduct complies with federal ECOA, licensee is not in violation of this law.

Remedies: None specified. Violation is misdemeanor. Md. Code Ann., Com. Law § 12-316 (West).

Consumer Credit: Md. Code Ann., Com. Law § 12-403.1 (West) (secondary mortgages)

Protected Classes: Age.

Prohibited Practices: Discriminating against any applicant solely on basis of age in granting or denying loan application. (Denying application from a person under age eighteen is not age discrimination.)

Scope of Coverage: Secondary mortgage licensees (Md. Code Ann., Com. Law § 12-401(b) & (c) (West)) and lenders expressly exempt from secondary mortgage loan licensing requirements making a secondary mortgage loan (defined by Md. Code Ann., Com. Law § 12-401(i) (West)), in lending to any applicant for a secondary mortgage loan.

Exclusions: "Second mortgage loan" excludes loans to bona fide corporations or commercial loans greater than $75,000.

Private Remedies: If lender violates any provision of subtitle 4 on secondary mortgage loans-credit provisions, it forfeits interest, costs, or other charges with respect to the loan. Md. Code Ann., Com. Law § 12-413 (West).

Consumer Credit: Md. Code Ann., Com. Law § 12-603 (West) (retail installment sales)

Protected Class: Sex, marital status, geographic area of residence, neighborhood of residence, age.

Prohibited Practice: Refusal of credit on basis of being a member of the protected class.

Scope: Sellers or sales finance companies.

Exclusions: Buyer who is under the age of eighteen is not discriminated against solely on the basis of age.

Administrative Remedies: Aggrieved party may file complaint with Commissioner of Consumer Credit, which has the authority to order a cease and desist order. Md. Code Ann., Com. Law § 12-631 (West).

Miscellaneous: Violation is a misdemeanor (fine not exceeding $100 for first offense and not exceeding $500 for any subsequent offense). Md. Code Ann., Com. Law § 12-636 (West).

MASSACHUSETTS

Civil Rights: Mass. Gen. Laws ch. 151B, § 4(10) (credit transactions)

Protected Classes: Recipients of federal, state, or local public assistance, including medical assistance, or tenants receiving federal, state, or local housing subsidies.

Prohibited Practices: Discriminating against any individual solely on basis of receipt of such assistance.

Scope of Coverage: Applies to any person furnishing credit, services, or renting accommodations.

Private Remedies: Persons aggrieved by practices declared unlawful by Ch. 151B, § 4 may bring civil action ninety days after filing administrative complaint with Commission Against Discrimination, or sooner if a commissioner gives written assent, for damages and injunctive relief. (Temporary injunctive relief to prevent injury may be sought at any time.) Attorney fees and costs shall be awarded unless special circumstances would render such award unjust. Ch. 151B, § 9.

Administrative Remedies: Aggrieved party may file complaint with Commission Against Discrimination, which has authority, *inter alia*, to issue cease and desist orders and to take affirmative action to effectuate purposes of chapter.

Miscellaneous: *See generally* 804 Mass. Code Regs. 7.00 (Discrimination in Credit).

Civil Rights: Mass. Gen. Laws ch. 151B, § 4(12) (credit transactions)

Protected Classes: Age sixty-two and over.

Prohibited Practices: Refusing to extend credit or charge account privileges because customer is sixty-two or over.

Scope of Coverage: Covers retail stores that provide credit or charge account privileges.

Private Remedies: Persons aggrieved by practices declared unlawful by Ch. 151B, § 4 may bring civil action ninety days after filing administrative complaint with Commission Against Discrimination, or sooner if a commissioner gives written assent, for damages and injunctive relief. (Temporary injunctive relief to prevent injury may be sought at any time.) Attorney fees and costs shall be awarded unless special circumstances would render such award unjust. Ch. 151B, § 9.

Administrative Remedies: Aggrieved party may file complaint with Commission Against Discrimination, which has authority, *inter alia*, to issue cease and desist orders and to take affirmative action to effectuate purposes of chapter.

Civil Rights: Mass. Gen. Laws ch. 151B, § 4(14) (credit transactions)

Protected Classes: Sex, sexual orientation (excluding persons whose sexual orientation involves minor children as sex object), marital status, or age.

Prohibited Practices: Denying or terminating credit or services or adversely affecting an individual's credit standing on a prohibited basis. (Certain defined conduct relating to consideration of age is specifically authorized.)

Scope of Coverage: Covers any person furnishing credit or services.

Private Remedies: Persons aggrieved by practices declared unlawful by Ch. 151B, § 4 may bring civil action ninety days after filing administrative complaint with Commission Against Discrimination, or sooner if a commissioner gives written assent, for damages and injunctive relief. (Temporary injunctive relief to prevent injury may be sought at any time.) Attorney fees and costs shall be awarded unless special circumstances would render such award unjust. Ch. 151B, § 9.

Administrative Remedies: Aggrieved party may file complaint with Commission Against Discrimination, which has authority, *inter alia*, to issue cease and desist orders and to take affirmative action to effectuate purposes of chapter.

Miscellaneous: *See generally* 804 Mass. Code Regs. 7.00 (Discrimination in Credit).

Civil Rights: Mass. Gen. Laws ch. 151B, §§ 1–10; Mass. Gen. Laws ch. 151B, § 4(3B) (housing transactions)

Protected Classes: Race, color, religion, handicap, national origin, sex, ancestry, children, sexual orientation (excluding persons whose sexual orientation involves minor children as sex object), age, or genetic information.

Prohibited Practices: Discriminating in granting a mortgage loan or in setting terms and conditions. Certain defined conduct is specifically authorized, including, *inter alia*, denying mortgage loan for duration exceeding life expectancy of applicant as determined by reference to the Individual Annuity Mortality Table.

Scope of Coverage: Persons whose business includes making mortgage loans or engaging in residential real estate-related transactions.

Private Remedies: Persons aggrieved by practices declared unlawful by Ch. 151B, § 4 may bring civil action ninety days after filing administrative complaint with Commission Against Discrimination, or sooner if a commissioner gives written assent, for damages and injunctive relief. (Temporary injunctive relief to prevent injury may be sought at any time.) Attorney fees and costs shall be awarded unless special circumstances would render such award unjust. Ch. 151B, § 9.

Administrative Remedies: Aggrieved party may file complaint with Commission Against Discrimination, which has authority, *inter alia*, to issue cease and desist orders and to take affirmative action to effectuate purposes of chapter.

Statute of Limitations: Limitation for civil action is three years after alleged discriminatory act. Administrative complaints must be filed within six months of alleged discriminatory act.

Miscellaneous: *See generally* 804 Mass. Code Regs. 7.00 (Discrimination in Credit).

MICHIGAN

***Civil Rights*: Mich. Comp. Laws. §§ 37.2101 to 37.2901; Mich. Comp. Laws. § 37.2502** (housing transactions)

Protected Classes: Religion, race, color, national origin, age, sex, familial status, or marital status.

Prohibited Practices: Discriminating in the terms, conditions, or privileges of a real estate transaction.

Scope of Coverage: Persons engaging in real estate transactions, or real estate brokerage or sales.

Exclusions: Qualifying multi-family units, owner-occupied accommodations and qualifying housing for senior citizens or persons 50 years of age or older.

Private Remedies: Injunctive relief, damages, attorney fees. §§ 37.2801, 37.2802.

Administrative Remedies: Injunctive relief, attorney fees, civil penalty between $10,000 and $50,000. § 37.2605.

Statute of Limitations: None specified.

***Civil Rights*: Mich. Comp. Laws § 37.2504** (housing transactions)

Protected Classes: Religion, race, color, national origin, age, sex, familial status, marital status.

Prohibited Practices: Discriminating, using a form, or making records or inquiries that indicate a preference or limitation relating to the application for or the purchase of loans for residential real estate transactions.

Scope of Coverage: Covers persons whose business includes engaging in real estate transactions for acquiring, constructing, improving, repairing, or maintaining a dwelling.

Exclusions: Does not apply to applications prescribed for use of a lender regulated as a mortgagee under the national housing act.

Private Remedies: Injunction, damages, attorney fees. Mich. Comp. Laws §§ 37.2801, 37.2802.

Administrative Remedies: Injunction, attorney fees, civil penalty between $10,000 and $50,000. Mich. Comp. Laws § 37.2605.

Statute of Limitations: None specified. *But see* Kresnak v. City of Muskegon Heights, 956 F. Supp. 1327 (W.D. Mich. 1997) (three years); Minor v. Northville Pub. Schools, 605 F. Supp. 1185 (E.D. Mich. 1985).

***Consumer Credit*: Mich. Comp. Laws §§ 493.1 to 493.25**

Protected Classes: Sex or marital status.

Prohibited Practices: Discriminating in the extension of credit on a prohibited basis. § 493.12(4).

Scope of Coverage: Applies to lenders licensed under the Regulatory Loan Act.

Private Remedies: A person making or collecting upon a loan in a prohibited manner is guilty of a misdemeanor and subject to the Credit Reform Act, Mich. Comp. Laws §§ 445.1851–445.1864. § 493.19. Borrower may bring civil action against a regulated lender to (i) seek declaratory judgment that method, act, or practice violates Credit Reform Act, (ii) obtain injunctive relief, (iii) recover $1000 and actual damages if alleged violation involved noncredit car arrangement or $1500 and actual damages relating to any other credit arrangement, and (iv) recover reasonable attorney fees and costs. Mich. Comp. Laws § 445.1861.

***Consumer Credit*: Mich. Comp. Laws § 750.147a**

Protected Classes: Race, color, religion, national origin, sex, marital status, or physical disability.

Prohibited Practices: Discriminating against a member of a protected class in extending credit, granting a loan, or rating a person's creditworthiness.

Scope of Coverage: Covers any person in extending credit, granting a loan, or rating creditworthiness.

Exclusions: Non-profit corporations whose members share the same racial, religious, ethnic, marital or sexual characteristic, or physical handicap and which extend credit or grant loans only to its members.

Private Remedies: Amount of $200 or damages whichever is greater. The prevailing party shall recover court costs and attorney fees.

Administrative Remedies: None specified.

Statute of Limitations: None specified.

Miscellaneous: Class action recovery limited; criminal penalties specified.

***Miscellaneous*: Mich. Comp. Laws § 37.1504** (handicapped/housing rights)

Protected Classes: Disability(housing financing).

Prohibited Practices: Discriminating on the basis of handicap in the making or purchasing of loans for acquiring, improving, repairing, or maintaining real property, or in providing other financial assistance secured by or otherwise related to real property.

Scope of Coverage: Applies to persons to whom application is made for financial assistance in connection with real estate transaction or for repair, construction, rehabilitation, maintenance, or improvement of real property.

Private Remedies: Civil action for damages, injunctive relief, and reasonable attorney fees. Mich. Comp. Laws § 37.1606.

Administrative Remedies: Adopts by reference administrative procedures for unfair employment practices. Mich. Comp. Laws § 37.1605.

***Miscellaneous*: Mich. Comp. Laws §§ 445.1601 to 445.1614** (redlining)

Protected Classes: Race or ethnicity.

Prohibited Practices: Denial of loan application or variation in the terms or conditions of financing residential real estate transactions based on geographic location.

Scope of Coverage: Covers credit granting institutions which include banks, savings and loan associations, unions, state housing authority, or a business entity with an in-state office making or purchasing mortgage loans.

Exclusions: Written policies or criteria uniformly applied to all neighborhoods within a particular metropolitan statistical area.

Private Remedies: $2000 in damages or actual damages plus attorney fees, whichever is greater; no class actions. § 445.1611.

Statute of Limitations: Civil action must be commenced within two years after occurrence giving rise to cause of action. Mich. Comp. Laws § 445.1613.

MINNESOTA

Civil Rights: **Minn. Stat. § 363A.16** (credit transactions)
Protected Classes: Race, color, creed, religion, disability, national origin, sex, sexual orientation, marital status, recipients of public assistance.
Prohibited Practices: Discriminating in extension of credit or in requirements for obtaining credit on a prohibited basis.
Scope of Coverage: Personal or commercial credit.
Private Remedies: Civil action may be filed for injunctive relief; compensatory damages in an amount up to three times actual damages; damages for mental anguish and suffering; punitive damages of up to $8500. The court may, in its discretion, award reasonable attorney fees to the prevailing party. Minn. Stat. §§ 363A.33, 363A.29.
Administrative Remedies: Aggrieved party may file complaint with human rights commission, which has authority to order same relief as courts. Minn. Stat. § 363A.29.
Statute of Limitations: Claim must either be filed as judicial action, or filed administratively with local or state commission within one year of alleged discriminatory practice. One year period is suspended during voluntary dispute resolution process. Minn. Stat. § 363A.28.

Civil Rights: **Minn. Stat. §§ 363A.01 to 363A.41; Minn. Stat. § 363A.09** (housing transactions)
Protected Classes: Race, color, creed, religion, national origin, sex, marital status, sexual orientation, status with regard to public assistance, disability, or familial status of individual or group, or of prospective tenants or occupants of the real property.
Prohibited Practices: (a) Discriminating in real estate financing transaction in granting, withholding, modifying, renewing or setting terms and conditions of financial assistance or services connected therewith, on a prohibited basis; (b) using forms or making inquiries which indicate limitation or discrimination on a prohibited basis; (c) geographic redlining.
Scope of Coverage: Covers persons, financial institutions, lenders to whom application is made for financial assistance for purchase, acquisition, lease, rehabilitation, repair, construction, maintenance of real property.
Private Remedies: Civil action may be filed for injunctive relief; compensatory damages in an amount up to three times actual damages; damages for mental anguish and suffering; punitive damages of up to $8500. The court may, in its discretion, award reasonable attorney fees to the prevailing party. § 363A.33.
Administrative Remedies: Aggrieved party may file complaint with human rights commission, which has authority to order same relief as courts may. § 363A.29.

Consumer Credit: **Minn. Stat. §§ 325G.041 to 325G.042; 363A.16(3)**
Protected Classes: Married women; spouses.
Prohibited Practices: Financial card issuers must issue card in current or former surname, as directed by the woman (may require that a married woman requesting a card in a former surname open a new account). Unequal treatment in evaluating credit history.
Scope of Coverage: Covers issuers of financial transaction cards, which include credit cards, courtesy cards, debit cards, and so forth. § 325G.02.
Exclusions: Telephone company credit cards.
Private Remedies: Violation of § 345G.041 declared an unfair dis-

criminatory practice under Minn. Stat. § 363.03(8). For credit history violations, $1,000. § 325G.042(4).

MISSOURI

Civil Rights: **Mo. Rev. Stat. §§ 213.010 to 213.112** (housing transactions)
Protected Classes: Race, color, religion, national origin, ancestry, familial status, sex, or disability of applicant, person associated with applicant in connection with the loan, or of prospective tenants, owners, lessees, or occupants of the dwelling which is the subject of the loan.
Prohibited Practices: Denying financial assistance or discriminating in setting terms or conditions of financial assistance. § 213.045.
Scope of Coverage: Covers financial institutions, corporation, firm association, etc., whose business consists in whole or in part of making commercial real estate loans, in connection with financial assistance for the purchase, construction, improvement, repair, or maintenance of a dwelling.
Private Remedies: Judicial review of final agency action (§ 213.085); or civil action filed after obtaining a right to sue letter from human rights commission for injunctive relief, actual and punitive damages. Court costs and reasonable attorney fees may be awarded to prevailing party, but will be awarded to respondent only if case was without foundation. § 213.111.
Administrative Remedies: Aggrieved party may file complaint with commission on human rights, which has the authority, *inter alia*, to issue cease and desist orders, order affirmative action to implement purpose of chapter, and actual damages.
Statute of Limitations: Administrative complaint must be filed within 180 days of alleged discriminatory act. § 213.075. Court action must be brought within ninety days of commission's notification letters to the individual, but no later than two years after alleged discriminatory conduct or its reasonable discovery. § 213.011.

Consumer Credit: **Mo. Rev. Stat. §§ 314.100 to 314.115**
Protected Classes: Sex or marital status.
Prohibited Practices: Denying credit solely upon prohibited basis, except that in specified circumstances, creditor can require both spouse's signature.
Scope of Coverage: Covers any creditor and credit without limitation.
Private Remedies: Civil action may be filed for compensatory, and punitive damages not to exceed $1000 for willful violations. § 314.105.
Statute of Limitations: One year from date credit was denied, except that time shall be tolled under certain circumstances. § 314.115.
Miscellaneous: Thirty day demand letter prior to instituting suit is required. § 314.110.

Consumer Credit: **Mo. Rev. Stat. § 408.550**
Protected Classes: Sex, marital status, age, race, religion, or exercise of rights under law.
Prohibited Practices: Denying credit on a prohibited basis, (compliance with ECOA is compliance with this act).
Scope of Coverage: Applies to creditors and transactions covered by Mo. Rev. Stat. §§ 408.015 to 408.562.
Private Remedies: Civil action may be brought for greater of $500 or actual damages, costs and attorney fees. *See also* Mo. Rev. Stat. § 408.562.

Miscellaneous: **Mo. Rev. Stat. § 408.575** (real estate financing)
Protected Classes: Race, color, religion, national origin, handicap, age, marital status, or sex of the applicant or of race, religion, or national

origin of persons living in vicinity of real estate.

Prohibited Practices: Denying real estate loan, or discriminating in any aspect of the loan transaction on a prohibited basis. Prohibition against redlining extends to age of dwelling, or age of structures in immediate neighborhood.

Scope of Coverage: Covers residential real estate loans (defined as loans or refinancing of loan for acquisition, construction, repair, rehabilitation, or remodeling of real estate used or intended to be used as residence by not more than four families) made by financial institutions (defined, *inter alia*, as any association or institution which operates a place of business in Missouri and makes residential real estate loans as part of its business).

Exclusions: Market factors may be considered. Mo. Rev. Stat. § 408.585.

Private Remedies: None specified, but administrative remedies are in addition to remedies "otherwise available" to any individual damaged by violation.

Administrative Remedies: Aggrieved party may file complaint with director of the appropriate regulatory agency, who can attempt conciliation and issue cease and desist order. Mo. Rev. Stat. § 408.600.

Statute of Limitations: None specified.

MONTANA

Civil Rights: Mont. Code Ann. § 49-2-306 (credit transactions)

Protected Classes: Sex, marital status, race, creed, religion, age, physical or mental disability, color, or national origin.

Prohibited Practices: (1) "Financial institutions" cannot discriminate on a prohibited basis in terms or conditions, unless based on reasonable grounds; (2) "creditors" cannot discriminate on a prohibited basis.

Scope of Coverage: Section 49-2-306(1) applies to financial institutions, defined as a commercial bank, savings bank, trust company, finance company, savings and loan association, investment company, or insurance company. Mont. Code Ann. § 49-2-101(13). Section 49-2-306(2) applies to any creditor, defined as a person who regularly or as part of his business arranges for extension of credit for which a financial charge is required, and applies to any credit transaction, including that secured by residential real estate. Mont. Code Ann. § 49-2-101(5)–(7).

Exclusions: Age and mental disability may be a legitimate discriminatory criteria in credit transactions only to the extent it relates to a person's capacity to make or be bound by contract. Mont. Code Ann. § 49-2-403(2).

Private Remedies: Actual and punitive damages; injunctive relief; attorney fees to prevailing party. Mont. Code Ann. § 49-2-510.

Administrative Remedies: Damages, injunctive relief. Mont. Code Ann. §§ 49-2-506, 49-2-510.

Statute of Limitations: Administrative complaint must be filed within 180 days after alleged discriminatory act occurred or was discovered. (May be extended by specified period under certain limited circumstances.) Mont. Code Ann. § 49-2-501(2). Civil action must be filed within two years of violation. Mont. Code Ann. § 49-2-510(5).

Miscellaneous: This chapter provides the exclusive remedy for violations of chapter.

Civil Rights: Mont. Code Ann. §§ 49-2-101 to 49-2-602; Mont. Code Ann. § 49-2-305(7) (housing transactions)

Protected Classes: Sex, marital status, race, creed, religion, age, familial status, physical or mental disability, color, national origin.

Prohibited Practices: Discriminating in the making or purchasing of loans in connection with residential real estate transactions.

Scope of Coverage: Covers person or other entity whose business includes engaging in real estate transactions for purchasing, constructing, improving, repairing, or maintaining housing accommodations.

Private Remedies: Injunction, damages, attorney fees.

Administrative Remedies: Injunction, damages, civil penalty between $10,000 and $25,000. § 49-2-510.

Statute of Limitations: 180 days to file with Human Rights Commission; two years for private action (tolled during administrative proceeding).

NEBRASKA

Fair Housing: Neb. Rev. Stat. §§ 20-301 to 20-344

Protected Classes: Race, color, religion, sex, handicap, familial status, national origin.

Prohibited Practices: Discriminating in the making or purchasing of loans or other financial assistance in connection with residential real estate. § 20-320.

Scope of Coverage: Covers any person whose business includes engaging in residential real estate financing for purchasing, constructing, improving, repairing, or maintaining a dwelling.

Private Remedies: Injunction, actual damages, attorney fees. May file regardless of whether complaint has been filed with Commission unless a conciliation agreement has been reached. § 20-342.

Administrative Remedies: May file complaint with Commissioner who may file a civil action. Relief includes injunction, actual damages, and civil penalty of $10,000 to $50,000. § 20-337.

Statute of Limitations: One year for administrative complaint; two years for private action (tolled during administrative proceeding).

NEVADA

Consumer Credit: Nev. Rev. Stat. §§ 598B.010 to 598B.180 (Equal Opportunity for Credit)

Protected Classes: Sex or marital status.

Prohibited Practices: Discriminating in any aspect of a credit transaction on a prohibited basis. Sets out specific guidelines for considerations in determining creditworthiness, separate accounts, and separate reporting of credit histories.

Scope of Coverage: "Creditors," those who regularly extend, renew, or continue credit or regularly arrange for such, or who participate in the decision to extend, renew, or continue credit as an assignee (credit is the right to incur debt or make purchase and defer payment or defer payment of an existing debt).

Private Remedies: Injured party may file civil action for injunction and damages (must elect between this remedy and ECOA remedies).

Administrative Remedies: Injured party may file complaint with commissioner of financial institutions, which may seek conciliation or issue cease and desist order.

Statute of Limitations: Administrative or civil action must be brought within one year.

Fair Housing: Nev. Rev. Stat. § 207.310

Protected Classes: Race, color, religious creed, national origin, or ancestry of the customer, or person intending to apply for loan, or person associated with the customer in connection with the loan, or prospective owners, lessees, tenants, or occupants of the dwelling which is the subject of the loan, disability, familial status and sex.

Prohibited Practices: Denying or discriminating in terms or conditions of loan or other financial assistance on a prohibited basis.

Scope of Coverage: Banks, savings and loans, insurance company or person whose business consists in whole or in part of making commercial real estate loans, in relation to loans or financial assistance for the purchase, construction, improvement, or repair of a dwelling.

Private Remedies: Injunctive relief, affirmative action as is appropriate, and for actual damages for economic loss, costs, punitive damages, and reasonable attorney fees to prevailing plaintiff. Nev. Rev. Stat. § 118.120.

Statute of Limitations: One year. Nev. Rev. Stat. § 118.120.

Miscellaneous: Violation is a misdemeanor for first and second offenses and a gross misdemeanor for subsequent offenses.

NEW HAMPSHIRE

Civil Rights: **N.H. Rev. Stat. Ann. §§ 354-A:1 to 354-B:6** (housing transactions)

Protected Classes: Age, sex, race, creed, color, marital status, familial status, physical or mental disability, or national origin.

Prohibited Practices: Discrimination against protected classes in making available or varying the terms or conditions of residential real estate related transactions, including the making or purchasing of loans secured by residential real estate, or providing other financial assistance for purchasing, constructing, improving, repairing, or maintaining a dwelling. §§ 354-A:9, 354-A:10.

Scope of Coverage: Any person or other entity whose business includes engaging in residential real estate transactions or the business of selling or renting dwellings or commercial structures.

Administrative Remedies: Complaint before Human Rights Commission, which may attempt conciliation, and conduct adjudicatory hearing, and issue cease and desist orders, award compensatory damages, and impose administrative fines ranging from not more than $10,000 for a first offense to not more than $50,000 for a third or subsequent offense within seven years. Judicial review and enforcement are available. § 354-A:21.

Statute of Limitations: 180 days from date of alleged discriminatory practice.

Miscellaneous: Attorney General may bring civil actions for injunctive relief; individual's right to cause of action not limited by this provision. §§ 354-B:1 to 354-B:3.

NEW JERSEY

Civil Rights: **N.J. Stat. Ann. §§ 10:5-1 to 10:5-42 (West)** (credit transactions)

Protected Classes: Race, creed, color, national origin, ancestry, familial status, marital status, sex, affectional or sexual orientation, handicap (including AIDS), genetic information, domestic partnership status, gender identity or expression, nationality of applicant or, if financing is sought for real property, of its prospective occupants or tenants or source of income used for rental or mortgage payments.

Prohibited Practices: Discriminating in granting, extending, *et cetera*, credit or in setting conditions and terms of credit on a prohibited basis, or using forms or making records or inquiries which suggest limitations or discrimination on a prohibited basis, unless required by law to retain such information. § 10:5-12(i).

Scope of Coverage: Covers banks, banking organizations, mortgage and insurance companies or other financial institutions, lenders, or credit institutions to whom application is made for *any* loan or extension of credit, *including but not limited to* financial assistance for the purchase, construction, repair, rehabilitation, or maintenance of

real property (emphasis added).

Private Remedies: Complainant may file action in court without exhausting administrative remedies. § 10:5-13. Prevailing party may be awarded reasonable attorney fees, though no award shall be made to a respondent unless the charge was brought in bad faith. § 10:5-27.1.

Administrative Remedies: Aggrieved party may file administrative complaint; agency has authority to issue cease and desist orders, and order such affirmative action as will effectuate purpose of chapter. § 10:5-17.

Miscellaneous: **N.J. Stat. Ann. § 17:16F-3 (West)** (redlining)

Protected Classes: Borrowers in specific geographical areas.

Prohibited Practices: Redlining, that is, discriminating in acceptance or discouragement of applications, granting, withholding, extending, modifying, or renewing or the fixing of terms or conditions of mortgage loan on real property located in the municipality of the lending institution simply because of location.

Scope of Coverage: Banking institutions.

Exclusions: Mortgage loans made pursuant to special public or private programs with the goal of increasing mortgages within specified geographic area.

Private Remedies: Actual damages, costs, attorney fees.

Administrative Remedies: Commissioner of banking may issue cease and desist order; if violation continues, may assess penalty of $5000 for each offense.

Statute of Limitations: None specified.

NEW MEXICO

Civil Rights: **N.M. Stat. § 28-1-1 to 28-1-15** (credit transactions)

Protected Classes: Race, religion, color, national origin, ancestry, sex, spousal affiliation, physical or mental handicap, sexual orientation, or gender identity.

Prohibited Practices: (1) Considering membership in a protected class in granting, extending, modifying, renewing credit or in setting terms and conditions thereof or in extending services in connection therewith; (2) using forms or making records or inquiries which suggest limitation or discrimination on a prohibited basis. § 28-1-7(H).

Scope of Coverage: Covers any person to whom application is made for financial assistance for (1) acquisition, construction, rehabilitation, repair, or maintenance of any housing accommodation or real property, or (2) any type of consumer credit, including financing for purchase of consumer good (purchased primarily for personal, family, or household purposes).

Exclusions: Exemptions to general coverage in Human Rights Act identified in § 28-1-9.

Private Remedies: Appeal of adverse administrative action is by trial de novo, including right to jury trial. Court has discretion to award actual damages and reasonable attorney fees to prevailing complaint. § 28-1-13.

Administrative Remedies: Aggrieved party may file complaint with human rights commission, which has authority to order actual damages, reasonable attorney fees if complainant was represented by private counsel, and such affirmative action as it deems necessary. §§ 28-1-10 to 28-1-13.

Statute of Limitations: Administrative complaint must be filed within 180 days after alleged occurrence.

NEW YORK

Civil Rights: **N.Y. Exec. Law § 296-a (McKinney)** (credit transactions)

Protected Classes: Race, creed, color, national origin, age, sex, familial or marital status, military status, sexual orientation, or disability and, in cases of housing financing, of certain persons associated with applicant, or of prospective occupants, or tenants of the real estate in connection with which housing is sought.

Prohibited Practices: Discriminating on a prohibited basis (1) in granting, withholding, extending, renewing, or setting terms and conditions of real property financing (residential and commercial); (2) in granting, withholding, extending, renewing, or setting terms and conditions in connection with any form of credit; (3) using forms or making inquiries or records which suggest limitation or discrimination; (4) making inquiries about childbearing or family planning; (5) refusing to consider, or discount income on a prohibited basis or because of childbearing potential; (6) discriminating against married person on basis of use of surname other than spouse's. Certain additional prohibited and permitted practices are spelled out. Notice of reasons for denial required upon request.

Scope of Coverage: Covers any creditors (person or financial institution which does business in New York and extends or arranges for the extension of credit, N.Y. Exec. Law § 292(22) (McKinney)) in connection with any form of credit (defined as the right to incur debt and defer payment irrespective of whether a finance charge is imposed, N.Y. Exec. Law § 292(20) (McKinney)), including housing financing.

Private Remedies: Judicial review of adverse agency action. N.Y. Exec. Law § 298 (McKinney).

Administrative Remedies: In case of alleged violation by "regulated creditor" (lender licensed or supervised by banking department N.Y. Exec. Law § 292(24) (McKinney)), may either file administrative complaint with superintendent of banking pursuant to N.Y. Exec. Law § 296-a (McKinney) or with human rights division under N.Y. Exec. Law § 297 (McKinney). Complaints concerning other creditors may be filed with the human rights division. Either agency has authority, *inter alia*, to award compensatory damages, issue cease and desist orders, and order the credit be granted.

Statute of Limitations: One year after occurrence of alleged discriminatory act.

Civil Rights: **N.Y. Exec. Law §§ 290–301 (McKinney); N.Y. Exec. Law § 296(5)(a)–(c) (McKinney)** (housing transactions)

Protected Classes: Race, creed, color, national origin, sex, age, disability, marital status, familial status, military status, sexual orientation.

Prohibited Practices: (1) Discriminating in the terms, conditions or privileges of the sale, rental, or lease of a housing accommodation (constructed or to be constructed); (2) discrimination in the terms, conditions, or privileges of the sale, rental, or lease of land or commercial space; (3) refusal to sell, rent, or lease any housing accommodation, land, or commercial space.

Scope of Coverage: (1) Owner, lessee, sub-lessee, assignee, or managing agent of, or other person with right to sell, rent, or lease a housing accommodation or commercial space; (2) owner, lessee, sub-lessee, or managing agent, or other person having right to sell, rent, or lease land or commercial space; (3) real estate brokers or salesmen or employees/agents thereof.

Exclusions: (1) Certain owner-occupied housing and housing exclusively for persons fifty-five years of age or older; (2) & (3) sale, rental, or lease of land or commercial space exclusively to persons fifty-five

years of age or older.

Private Remedies: Damages and other appropriate remedies. § 297(9).

Administrative Remedies: Cease and desist order; extension of accommodation, advantages and privileges; granting the subject credit; compensatory damages; punitive damages (in housing discrimination cases only) not exceeding $10,000. § 297.

Statute of Limitations: Administrative or civil complaint must be filed within one year after alleged discriminatory practice. § 297(5). If the complaint is dismissed prior to an administrative hearing upon plaintiff's request to have election of remedies annulled, right to civil action is subject to statute of limitations from the time of filing of administrative complaint.

Miscellaneous: Civil action is precluded by filing administrative complaint, except when the division dismisses the complaint on grounds of administrative inconvenience, untimeliness, or on the grounds that the election of remedies is annulled, in which case civil action may be brought as if no administrative complaint had been filed.

Miscellaneous: **N.Y. Banking Law § 9-f (McKinney)** (redlining)

Protected Classes: Borrowers in specific geographical areas.

Prohibited Practices: Redlining, that is, refusing to make prudent loan upon security of real property because of its geographic location if the property is located within the geographic district serviced by the banking institution.

Scope of Coverage: Banking institutions equal banks, trust companies, savings banks, savings and loans associations, credit unions, mortgage bankers and foreign banking corporations.

Private Remedies: None specified.

Administrative Remedies: Anyone denied a loan may appeal to the Superintendent of banking for review of the decision.

Statute of Limitations: None specified.

NORTH CAROLINA

Consumer Credit: **N.C. Gen. Stat. §§ 25B-1 to 25B-4**

Protected Classes: Married and unmarried women.

Prohibited Practices: Denying credit in her own name to woman with same creditworthiness as men who would receive credit. Upon written request, credit reporting agencies must give any separate credit histories and history of joint accounts on file.

Scope of Coverage: Covers any credit, defined as obtaining money, labor, or services on a deferred payment basis.

Private Remedies: Civil action may be filed for actual damages and, in the court's discretion, reasonable attorney fees.

Consumer Credit: **N.C. Gen. Stat. §§ 53-164 to 53-191**

Protected Classes: Race, color, religion, national origin, sex, or marital status.

Prohibited Practices: Denying credit or discriminating in setting terms or conditions of credit on a prohibited basis. § 53-180(d).

Scope of Coverage: Covers licensees under North Carolina Consumer Finance Act in connection with any extension of credit.

Exclusions: Certain exclusions to the Act's coverage generally are set out in § 53-191.

Private Remedies: Any loan, the making of which violates *any* provision of the Consumer Finance Act, except in limited circumstances, is void, and the creditor has no right to receive or retain any principal or charges. § 53-166(d).

Miscellaneous: Violation is misdemeanor. § 53-166(c).

Fair Housing: **N.C. Gen. Stat. §§ 41A-1 to 41A-10**

Protected Classes: Race, color, religion, sex, national origin, handicapping condition, or familial status.

Prohibited Practices: Discrimination against protected class, in any residential real estate related transaction, including the making or purchasing of loans or providing financial assistance for purchasing, constructing, improving, repairing, or maintaining a dwelling, or any transaction in which the security is residential real estate. § 41A-4(b1). Discrimination in land use decision or in the permitting of development based on any of the protected classes or that a development or proposed development contains affordable housing. §41A-4(g).

Scope of Coverage: Any person or entity whose business includes engaging in residential real estate related transactions.

Exclusions: Does not forbid lenders to inquire into financial and dependent obligations or basing its action on income and financial abilities of any person, various exemptions described in § 41A-6.

Private Remedies: If conciliation (see immediately below) fails, complainant may request right to sue letter from Commission, and bring civil action for injunctive relief, actual or punitive damages, costs and attorney fees. § 41A-7.

Administrative Remedies: Complaint before Human Relations Commission. Conciliation attempt is mandatory. If conciliation fails, and neither complainant nor Commission chooses to sue, complaint may be pursued in adjudicatory hearing before Commission. Relief "as appropriate" including compensatory damages, and civil penalties. (Not more than $10,000 for first offense, not more than $25,000 for second offense within five years, not more than $50,000 for third or subsequent offense within seven years.) Judicial review of Commission actions is available.

Statute of Limitations: One year to file administrative complaint. Ten days after notice of failure of conciliation (or 130 days of Commission inaction) to request right to sue letter, one year after right to sue letter for civil action.

NORTH DAKOTA

Civil Rights: **N.D. Cent. Code §§ 14-02.4-01 to 14-02.4-23** (credit transactions)

Protected Classes: Race, color, religion, sex, national origin, age, physical or mental disability, marital status, receipt of public assistance.

Prohibited Practices: Denying credit, discriminating in setting terms or conditions on a prohibited basis (may consider credit histories and take actions permitted or required by ECOA). § 14-02.4-17.

Scope of Coverage: Covers any person acting for self or another, in connection with any credit.

Administrative Remedy: Complaint may be filed with state Division of Human Rights.

Private Remedies: May bring civil action for injunctive and equitable relief, and such relief as may be appropriate. Court in its discretion may award prevailing party reasonable attorney fees.

Statute of Limitations: 300 days from alleged discriminatory act or 90 days from conclusion of administrative action's conclusion. § 14-02.4-19.

Fair Housing: **N.D. Cent. Code §§ 14-02.5-01 to 14-02.5-46**

Protected Classes: Race, color, religion, sex, national origin, age, physical or mental disability, marital status, familial status, receipt of public assistance.

Prohibited Practices: Discriminating in providing of services related to sale or rental of dwellings. § 14-02.5-02.

Scope of Coverage: Persons seeking to sell or rent dwellings.

Exclusions: Religious and private organizations favoring members (§§

14-02.5-10, 14-02.5-11); elderly housing; persons convicted of drug-related offenses, persons of the opposite sex seeking to cohabit (§ 14-01.5-02).

Private Remedies: Actual and punitive damages, attorney fees, costs, injunctive relief. § 14-02.5-41.

Administrative Remedies: Civil penalties. § 14-02.5-32.

Statute of Limitations: One year for administrative; two years for civil action.

OHIO

Civil Rights: **Ohio Rev. Code Ann. § 4112.021 (West)** (credit transactions)

Protected Classes: Race, color, religion, age, sex, marital status, national origin, disability, military status, or ancestry.

Prohibited Practices: Lists eleven prohibited practices.

Scope of Coverage: Covers "creditors" (who regularly extend, renew, or continue credit or arrange for such, and assignees who participate in decision to extend, renew, or continue credit) in credit transactions, irrespective of whether a finance charge is imposed. Some provisions specially apply to credit reporting agencies.

Exclusions: Limited exclusions from various subsections are noted as applicable.

Private Remedies: Civil action may be filed for injunctive relief and actual and punitive damages, minimum $100, plus attorney fees. § 4112.021(D).

Administrative Remedies: May file complaint with civil rights commission, which can issue cease and desist orders and order affirmative action to effectuate purposes of act. Actual and punitive damages, attorney fees. Ohio Rev. Code Ann. § 4112.05 (West).

Statute of Limitations: Six months for administrative complaint, Ohio Rev. Code Ann. § 4112.05(B)(1) (West); and 180 days for civil action, § 4112.021(D).

Civil Rights: **Ohio Rev. Code Ann. §§ 4112.01 to 4112.99 (West); Ohio Rev. Code Ann. § 4112.02(H) (West)** (housing transactions)

Protected Classes: Race, color, religion, sex, ancestry, disability, military status, or national origin of present or prospective owner, occupant, or user of such housing.

Prohibited Practices: (1) Refusing to lend money for acquisition, construction, rehabilitation, repair, or maintenance of housing; (2) discriminating in terms or conditions of such a loan; (3) refusing to consider combined income or income of either spouse in connection with mortgage credit. Specifically includes racial composition of neighborhood as an illegitimate reason for refusing credit.

Scope of Coverage: Subsection 4112.02(H)(3), on refusal to lend housing financing money, applies only to persons who lend money as a principal aspect of or incident to their principal business, and not to seller-financed/owner-occupied or casual or occasional lenders. The other subsections 4112.02(H)(5) and (6) do not contain this express limitation on their scope.

Exclusions: *See* Scope of Coverage, *supra*; religious or private organizations favoring members.

Private Remedies: Actual damages, reasonable attorney fees, court costs, expert witness fees, injunctive relief and punitive damages. § 4112.051.

Administrative Remedies: May file complaint with civil rights commission, which can issue cease and desist orders and order affirmative action to effectuate purposes of act. Actual and punitive damages, attorney fees. § 4112.05.

Statute of Limitations: One year for administrative or civil complaint.

OKLAHOMA

Civil Rights: **Okla. Stat. tit. 25, §§ 1451–1453** (housing transactions)
Protected Classes: Race, color, religion, gender, national origin, age, handicap, familial status, receipt of public assistance (as specified). Tit. 25, §§ 1451–1452.
Prohibited Practices: (1) Refusing to consider income of both applicants seeking to buy or lease housing; (2) refusing to consider public assistance or court ordered alimony or child support that is verifiable as valid income; (3) discriminating in terms, conditions, or privilege relating to financial assistance for purchase, repair, maintenance, etc., of housing. Tit. 25, § 1452(A).
Scope of Coverage: Covers any person in connection with housing financing.
Exclusions: Persons convicted for drug-relate offense. Religious organizations, associations, or society or affiliated non-profit entity of sale of housing operated for other than commercial purposes to persons of same religion; private club providing incidental lodging; housing for older persons; owner-occupied single-family housing. Tit. 25, § 1453.
Private Remedies: Actual and punitive damages, reasonable attorney fees, court costs, and injunctive relief. Okla. Stat. tit. 25, § 1506.3.
Administrative Remedies: Aggrieved party may file complaint with human rights commission, which has authority to, *inter alia*, actual damages, reasonable attorney fees, costs, court costs, and injunctive or equitable relief. Okla. Stat. tit. 25, § 1505.
Statute of Limitations: Administrative complaint must be filed within one year of alleged discriminatory act (Okla. Stat. tit. 25, § 1502.2(C)); 180-day limit for complaints stating that a discriminatory practice has been committed specified by Okla. Stat. tit. 25, § 1502(A).
Miscellaneous: Commission order has no effect unless district court issues corresponding order. Okla. Stat. tit. 25, § 1505(E)(7).

Consumer Credit: **Okla. Stat. tit. 14A, § 1-109** (Okla. Consumer Credit Code)
Protected Classes: Sex, marital status.
Prohibited Practices: Limiting or refusing to extend credit solely on a prohibited basis.
Scope of Coverage: Consumer credit sales, consumer leases, consumer loans as defined by Oklahoma Consumer Credit Code.
Private Remedies: None specified.
Administrative Remedies: Enforcement authority delegated to Administrator of Dep't of Consumer Credit.

OREGON

Civil Rights: **Or. Rev. Stat. §§ 659A.001 to 659A.990; Or. Rev. Stat. §§ 659A.420 to 659A.424** (housing transactions)
Protected Classes: Race, color, religion, sex, sexual orientation, disability, marital status, familial status, national origin, source of income.
Prohibited Practices: Discriminating in the making or purchasing of loans or providing other financial assistance in connection with residential real estate. Discrimination may be found even when "facially neutral housing policy" applied. § 659A.421.
Scope of Coverage: Covers any person or entity whose business includes engaging in residential real estate financing for purchasing, constructing, improving, repairing, or maintaining a dwelling.
Private Remedies: Compensatory damages or $200, whichever is greater, punitive damages, costs, attorney fees. § 659A.885(3). May file regardless of whether complaint has been filed with Civil Rights Commission unless a hearing has commenced. Or. Rev. Stat.

§§ 659.121, 659A.870.
Administrative Remedies: Injunction, civil penalty of up to $1000. § 659A.855.
Statute of Limitations: Administrative complaint must be filed within one year of alleged discrimination. § 659A.820(1). Civil action must be filed within two years of occurrence or termination of alleged discriminatory housing practice (tolled during pendency of administrative action), or within two years of breach of settlement agreement. § 659A.875(3).

Consumer Credit: **Or. Rev. Stat. §§ 646A-240 to 646A-244** (financial regulation)
Protected Classes: Persons obligated to pay child support.
Prohibited Practices: Less favorable treatment than any other credit obligation of the same amount, terms, and duration.
Private Remedies: Compensatory damages, injunction, reasonable attorney fees, unless bona fide error or good faith conformity with laws, regulations.

PENNSYLVANIA

Civil Rights: **43 Pa. Cons. Stat. §§ 951–963** (housing transactions)
Protected Classes: Race, color, religious creed, ancestry, national origin, sex, familial status, age, handicap or disability (including use of support animal) of applicant or prospective owner, occupant, or user of real property.
Prohibited Practices: Refusing to finance housing accommodation or commercial property; refusing to lend money or otherwise withhold financing for acquisition, construction and rehabilitation, repair, maintenance of housing accommodation or commercial property, or discriminate in terms or conditions of any such loan; or make inquiries or make or keep records containing question concerning membership in a protected class. § 955(h).
Scope of Coverage: Covers any person in connection with financing commercial real property or housing accommodation.
Exclusions: Religious institutions, charitable or educational organizations; qualifying housing for older persons; bona fide private or fraternal organizations may give preference to members of their own group if calculated to promote the aims of the group.
Private Remedies: If the commission fails to act within specified time period or dismisses the complaint, aggrieved party may bring civil action within two years of notice thereof for injunctive and any other legal and equitable relief as the court deems appropriate. § 962.
Administrative Remedies: Aggrieved party may file complaint with the human relations commission, which may, *inter alia*, order conciliation, cease and desist orders, affirmative action including but not limited to lending money on equal terms and conditions. § 959.
Statute of Limitations: Administrative complaint must be filed within 180 days of illegal discriminatory act. § 959(h).

PUERTO RICO

Fair Housing: **P.R. Laws Ann. tit. 1, § 13(e)**
Protected Classes: Politics, religion, sex, race, or color.
Prohibited Practices: Refusing to grant loan for dwelling construction.
Scope of Coverage: Natural or artificial persons engaged in business of granting loans for dwelling construction.
Private Remedies: Aggrieved party may bring civil action for actual damages, and court may award punitive damages. P.R. Laws Ann. tit. 1, § 14.
Miscellaneous: Violation of civil rights act is also a crime.

RHODE ISLAND

Fair Housing: **R.I. Gen. Laws §§ 34-37-1 to 34-37-9; R.I. Gen. Laws § 34-37-4(b)** (housing transactions)
Protected Classes: Race, color, religion, sex, sexual orientation, marital status, country of ancestral origin, disability, housing status (not having a fixed or regular residence), age, gender identity or expression, or familial status.
Prohibited Practices: Directly or indirectly discriminating in the terms, conditions, or privileges relating to obtaining or using any financial assistance.
Scope of Coverage: Persons to whom application is made for a loan or other form of financial assistance for the acquisition, construction, rehabilitation, repair, or maintenance of any housing accommodation.
Exclusions: Limitation by organizations, association or society, or affiliated non-profit entity, of sale of housing owned or operated for other than commercial purposes to persons of same religion; private clubs providing incidental lodging. § 34-37-4.2. Regarding gender identity, sexual-orientation or-expression discrimination, three-family units in which owner resides. §§ 34-37-4.4, 34-37-4.5.
Private Remedies: Injunction, damages, costs and attorney fees, punitive damages (§ 34-37-5(o)(3)); specifies conditions for private actions.
Administrative Remedies: Injunction, damages, costs, and attorney fees.
Statute of Limitations: Administrative complaint must be filed within one year of occurrence or termination of alleged discriminatory practice. Aggrieved party may seek right to sue in state court within specified period from filing of administrative complaint provided the commission has not secured a settlement or conciliation agreement and a hearing has not commenced. Civil action must then be filed within ninety days from grant of request for right to sue. § 34-37-5.

Fair Housing: **R.I. Gen. Laws § 34-37-4.3** (credit transactions)
Protected Classes: Sex, marital status, race or color, religion, or country of ancestral origin, sexual orientation, familial status, gender identity or expression, disability, age.
Prohibited Practices: Discriminating in granting or extending loan or credit, or in privilege or capacity to obtain credit.
Scope of Coverage: Covers financial organizations governed by R.I. Gen. Laws Title 19 or any other credit-granting commercial institution in conjunction with any form of loan or credit including, but not limited to, credit concerned with housing accommodations.
Exclusions: Limitation by organizations, association or society, or affiliated non-profit entity, of sale of housing owned or operated for other than commercial purposes to persons of same religion; private clubs providing incidental lodging. § 34-37-4.2. Regarding gender identity, sexual orientation, or expression discrimination, three-family units in which owner resides. § 34-37-4.5.
Private Remedies: Injunction, damages, costs and attorney fees, punitive damages. § 34-37-5(o)(3).
Administrative Remedies: Injunction, damages, costs, and attorney fees; amounts specified in § 34-37-5(h)(2).
Statute of Limitations: Administrative complaint must be filed within one year of occurrence or termination of alleged discriminatory practice. Aggrieved party may seek right to sue in state court within specified period from filing of administrative complaint provided the commission has not secured a settlement or conciliation agreement and a hearing has not commenced. Civil action must then be filed within ninety days from grant of request for right to sue. § 34-37-5.

Fair Housing: **R.I. Gen. Laws § 34-37-5.4** (housing transactions)
Protected Classes: Race, color, religion, sex, sexual orientation, marital status, country of ancestral origin, handicap, age, gender identity or expression, familial status.
Prohibited Practices: Discrimination in the making or purchasing of loans or providing other financial assistance for the purchasing, constructing, improving, repairing, or maintenance of residential real estate, in providing such assistance secured by residential real estate, or in the selling, brokering or appraising of residential real estate.
Scope of Coverage: Person or entity whose business includes making or purchasing loans or other financial assistance for purchasing, constructing, repairing, maintaining residential real estate or which is secured by same, or whose business includes selling, brokering, or appraising such property.
Exclusions: Limitation by organizations, association or society, or affiliated non-profit entity, of sale of housing owned or operated for other than commercial purposes to persons of same religion; private clubs providing incidental lodging. R.I. Gen. Laws § 34-37-4.2. Regarding gender identity or expression discrimination, three-family units in which owner resides. R.I. Gen. Laws § 34-37-4.5.
Private Remedies: Injunction, damages, costs and attorney fees, punitive damages. R.I. Gen. Laws § 34-37-5(o)(3).
Administrative Remedies: Injunction, damages, costs and attorney fees, amount specified in R.I. Gen. Laws § 34-37-5(h)(2).
Statute of Limitations: Administrative complaint must be filed within one year of occurrence or termination of alleged discriminatory practice. Aggrieved party may seek right to sue in state court within specified period from filing of administrative complaint provided the commission has not secured a settlement or conciliation agreement and a hearing has not commenced. Civil action must then be filed within ninety days from grant of request for right to sue. R.I. Gen. Laws § 34-37-5.

SOUTH CAROLINA

Fair Housing: **S.C. Code Ann. §§ 31-21-10 to 31-21-150**
Protected Classes: Race, color, religion, sex, familial status, national origin, or handicap.
Prohibited Practices: Refusing to sell or rent or to negotiate for the sale or rental of a dwelling; discriminating against a member of protected class in terms, conditions, or privileges of sale or rental of a dwelling, or in providing related services or facilities.
Scope of Coverage: Person or entity whose business includes making or purchasing of loans or providing other financial assistance in connection with the purchase, improvement, repair, or maintenance of a dwelling or which is secured by residential real estate, or the selling, brokering, or appraising of a dwelling.
Exclusions: Certain single-family homes and owner-occupied four-family units; limitation by religious organizations, associations, or society or affiliated non-profit entity of sale of housing operated for other than commercial purposes and favoring members; private club providing incidental lodging. § 31-21-70.
Private Remedies: Injunction, actual and punitive damages, costs, attorney fees.
Administrative Remedies: Injunction, actual damages, attorney fees, civil penalty.
Statute of Limitations: 180 days for administrative complaint (§ 31-21-120); one year for private action (§ 31-21-140).

Fair Housing: **S.C. Code Ann. § 31-21-60**
Protected Classes: Race, color, religion, sex, handicap, national origin, familial status.
Prohibited Practices: To discriminate in the making or purchasing of

loans or in the terms or conditions of residential real estate transactions.

Scope of Coverage: Covers any person or entity whose business includes engaging in residential real estate financing for purchase, improvement, repair, construction, or maintenance of a dwelling.

Exclusions: Certain single-family homes and owner-occupied four-family units; limitation by religious organizations, associations, or society or affiliated non-profit entity of sale of housing operated for other than commercial purposes and favoring members; private club providing incidental lodging. S.C. Code Ann. § 31-21-70.

Private Remedies: Injunction, actual and punitive damages, costs, attorney fees (for the prevailing party if the court determines the prevailing party cannot financially assume the fees).

Administrative Remedies: Injunction, actual damages, attorney fees, civil penalty.

Statute of Limitations: 180 days for administrative complaint; one year for private action.

SOUTH DAKOTA

Civil Rights: **S.D. Codified Laws §§ 20-13-1 to 20-13-56; S.D. Codified Laws § 20-13-21** (housing transactions/financing)

Protected Classes: Race, color, creed, religion, sex, ancestry, disability, national origin of applicant or prospective occupants or tenants of real property to which transaction relates.

Prohibited Practices: Discrimination against any member of a protected class in the granting, withholding, extending, modifying, renewing or in the rates, terms, conditions, or privileges or the extension of services in any financial assistance relating to the purchase, lease, acquisition, construction, rehabilitation, repair, or maintenance of real property.

Scope of Coverage: Any person, financial institution, lender to whom application is made for purchase, lease, acquisition, construction, rehabilitation, repair, or maintenance of real property.

Private Remedies: Compensatory damages, injunctive relief, attorney fees and costs, and punitive damages.

Administrative Remedies: Cease and desist order, compensatory damages (other than pain and suffering, punitive, or consequential damages) attorney fees and allowable costs.

Statute of Limitations: Administrative complaint must be filed within 180 days of the alleged discriminatory act. § 20-13-31. Plaintiff may elect to have claims asserted in a civil action not later than twenty days after issuance of notice requiring respondent to answer administrative complaint, the action to be filed within one year of such election. § 20-13-35.1.

Miscellaneous: Exhaustion of administrative remedies is not required, but filing of administrative complaint is prerequisite to civil action.

Civil Rights: **S.D. Codified Laws § 20-13-20** (housing transactions)

Protected Classes: Race, color, creed, religion, sex, ancestry, disability, familial status, or national origin.

Prohibited Practices: Discriminating in the terms, conditions, or privileges of the sale, rental, lease, assignment, sublease, or other transfer of real property or housing accommodation or any part, portion, or interest therein.

Scope of Coverage: Any owner of rights to housing or real property or any person acting for an owner, with or without compensation, including persons licensed as a real estate broker or salesman, attorney, auctioneer, agent, or representative by power of attorney or appointment, or any person acting under court order, deed of trust or will.

Exclusions: Certain owner-occupied duplexes; dormitory residences for unmarried students, or sororities or fraternities recognized by a public or private college or university; qualifying residences for older or disabled persons. Discrimination based upon familial status applicable only to housing accommodation. S.D. Codified Laws § 20-13-20.1.

Private Remedies: Compensatory damages, injunctive relief, attorney fees and costs, and punitive damages.

Administrative Remedies: Cease and desist order, compensatory damages (other than pain and suffering, punitive, or consequential damages) attorney fees and allowable costs.

Statute of Limitations: Administrative complaint must be filed within 180 days of the alleged discriminatory act. S.D. Codified Laws § 20-13-31. Plaintiff may elect to have claims asserted in a civil action not later than twenty days after issuance of notice requiring respondent to answer administrative complaint, the action to be filed within one year of such election. S.D. Codified Laws § 20-13-35.1.

TENNESSEE

Civil Rights: **Tenn. Code Ann. §§ 4-21-101 to 4-21-1004; Tenn. Code Ann. § 4-21-601** (housing transactions)

Protected Classes: Race, color, creed, religion, sex, disability, national origin, familial status.

Prohibited Practices: Discrimination in the terms, conditions, or privileges of sale or rental of real property or housing accommodation.

Scope of Coverage: Owner or any person engaging in a real estate transaction, or a broker, salesperson, real estate operator, or other employee or agent of such persons.

Exclusions: Certain owner-occupied duplexes, residences; single-sex dormitories; religious, charitable, or educational institutions. § 4-21-602.

Private Remedies: Injunction, actual and punitive damages, costs, attorney fees. Filing of private action supersedes administrative action. § 4-21-311.

Administrative Remedies: Injunction, actual damages, costs, attorney fees, civil penalty between $10,000 and $50,000. § 4-21-306.

Statute of Limitations: 180 days for administrative complaint; one year for private action.

Miscellaneous: If an administrative action is filed, the human rights commission finds reasonable cause, and no conciliation agreement is reached, then either party must elect to proceed in a civil action within twenty days of receiving notice of permission to do so from the commission. § 4-21-312.

Civil Rights: **Tenn. Code Ann. § 4-21-606** (housing transactions)

Protected Classes: Race, color, creed, religion, sex, disability, national origin, familial status.

Prohibited Practices: To discriminate in the making or purchasing of loans or providing other financial assistance in connection with residential real estate transactions.

Scope of Coverage: Covers any person or entity whose business includes engaging in residential real estate financing for purchase, improvement, repair, or maintenance of a dwelling.

Private Remedies: Injunction, actual and punitive damages, costs, attorney fees. Filing of private action will supersede administrative action. Tenn. Code Ann. § 4-21-311.

Administrative Remedies: Injunction, actual damages, costs, attorney fees, civil penalty between $10,000 and $50,000. Tenn. Code Ann. § 4-21-306.

Statute of Limitations: 180 days for administrative complaint; one year for private action.

Miscellaneous: If an administrative action is filed, the human rights commission finds reasonable cause, and no conciliation agreement is reached, then either party must elect to proceed in a civil action within twenty days of receiving notice of permission to do so from the commission. Tenn. Code Ann. § 4-21-312.

Consumer Credit: Tenn. Code Ann. §§ 47-18-801 to 47-18-805

Protected Classes: Sex, disability, or marital status.

Prohibited Practices: Discriminate between equally qualified people on a prohibited basis with respect to approval, denial, or terms of credit. (Special provision relating to utility service and necessaries doctrine.) §§ 47-18-802, 47-18-805.

Scope of Coverage: Covers creditors extending consumer credit and credit card issuers. (Note: Definition of "consumer" is limited to natural persons, but does not appear to be limited to use of credit for personal, family, or household purposes. § 47-18-103(2)).

Private Remedies: Damages in individual action of $100 minimum to $1000 maximum and attorney fees. Damages in a class action are capped at $10,000, costs, attorney fees. § 47-18-803. No action for UDAP damages. Tenn. Code Ann. § 47-18-109(a)(5).

Statute of Limitations: One year from alleged discriminatory act.

Miscellaneous: Discrimination against the handicapped is also declared to be an unfair or deceptive act, except when committed by creditor or credit card issuer regulated by department of financial institutions, which has authority to investigate and dispose of complaints concerning such creditors. Tenn. Code Ann. § 47-18-104(b)(25).

TEXAS

Consumer Credit: Tex. Fin. Code Ann. § 341.401 (Vernon)

Protected Classes: Sex, race, color, religion, national origin, marital status, age; income from social security or SSI; exercise of rights under the Federal Consumer Credit Protection Act.

Prohibited Practices: Denying an extension of credit, including a loan, or restricting or limiting the credit extended.

Scope of Coverage: Authorized lenders, persons licensed under Tex. Fin. Code Ann. Chapter 342, banks or saving and loan institutions, or other persons involved in open-end credit card transactions (Tex. Fin. Code Ann. § 301.001 (Vernon)) or loans (Tex. Fin. Code Ann. ch. 342 (Vernon)).

Private Remedies: Actual damages, punitive damages (not greater than $10,000) and court costs. Tex. Fin. Code Ann. § 341.402 (Vernon).

Statute of Limitations: Later of two years from occurrence of violation or four years from date of loan or retail installment transaction for closed-end credit; two years from date of occurrence for open-end credit (Tex. Fin. Code Ann. § 341.402 (Vernon)).

Miscellaneous: Claimant must choose to pursue action under this statute or under federal Consumer Credit Protection Act.

Fair Housing: Tex. Prop. Code Ann. §§ 301.001 to 301.171 (Vernon)

Protected Classes: Race, color, religion, sex, disability, national origin, familial status.

Prohibited Practices: To discriminate in the making or purchasing of loans or providing other financial assistance in connection with residential real estate transactions. § 301.026.

Scope of Coverage: Covers any person or entity whose business includes engaging in residential real estate financing for purchase, improvement, repair for maintenance of a dwelling.

Exclusions: Exemptions include religious organizations, private clubs,

elderly housing. §§ 301.041 to 301.044.

Private Remedies: Injunction, actual and punitive damages, costs, attorney fees. § 301.153.

Administrative Remedies: Injunction, actual damages, costs, attorney fees, civil penalty between $10,000 and $50,000. § 301.112.

Statute of Limitations: One year for administrative complaint (§ 301.081); two years for civil action (tolled while administrative proceeding is pending) (§ 301.151).

UTAH

Fair Housing: Utah Code Ann. §§ 57-21-1 to 57-21-14; Utah Code Ann. § 57-21-6

Protected Classes: Race, color, religion, sex, disability, national origin, familial status, source of income, association with member of protected class.

Prohibited Practices: To discriminate in the making or purchasing of loans or providing other financial assistance in connection with residential real estate transactions.

Scope of Coverage: Covers any person or entity whose business includes engaging in residential real estate financing for purchase, improvement, repair for maintenance of a dwelling.

Private Remedies: Injunction, actual and punitive damages, costs, attorney fees. § 57-21-12.

Administrative Remedies: Injunction, actual damages, costs, attorney fees, civil penalty between $10,000 and $50,000. § 57-21-11.

Statute of Limitations: 180 days for administrative complaint (§ 57-21-9); two years for civil action (tolled while administrative proceeding is pending), except that person may not file civil action if a formal adjudicative hearing has commenced (§ 57-21-12).

Miscellaneous: Filing federal court action for relief under federal law based upon act prohibited under §§ 57-21-5, 57-21-6 bars commencement or continuation of any administrative or state court adjudicative proceeding in connection with the same claims. § 57-21-14.

Fair Housing: Utah Code Ann. § 57-21-5

Protected Classes: Race, color, religion, sex, national origin, familial status, source of income, disability, association with member of protected class.

Prohibited Practices: Discrimination against member of protected class in the terms, conditions, or privileges of the sale or rental of any dwelling or in providing related facilities or services.

Scope of Coverage: Any "person," defined as one or more individuals, corporations, limited liability companies, partnerships, associations, labor organizations, legal representatives, mutual companies, joint-stock companies, trusts, unincorporated organizations, trustees, bankruptcy trustees, receivers and fiduciaries.

Private Remedies: Injunction, actual and punitive damages, costs, attorney fees.

Administrative Remedies: Injunction, actual damages, costs, attorney fees, civil penalty between $10,000 and $15,000.

Statute of Limitations: 180 days for administrative complaint; two years for civil action (tolled while administrative proceeding is pending except that person may not file civil action if a formal adjudicatory hearing has commenced (Utah Code Ann. § 57-21-12)).

Miscellaneous: Filing federal court action for relief under federal law based upon act prohibited under Utah Code Ann. §§ 57-21-5, 57-21-6 bars commencement or continuation of any administrative or state court adjudicative proceeding in connection with the same claims. Utah Code Ann. § 57-21-14.

VERMONT

***Consumer Credit*: Vt. Stat. Ann. tit. 8, § 10403**
Protected Classes: Race, color, religion, national origin, age, sexual orientation, gender identity, sex, marital status, handicapping condition.
Prohibited Practices: Discrimination with respect to credit cards and personal, mortgage, and commercial loans.
Scope of Coverage: Financial institutions, licensed lenders.
Private Remedies: Punitive and actual damages; costs and attorney fees permitted.
Administrative Remedies: None specified.

***Fair Housing*: Vt. Stat. Ann. tit. 9, §§ 4500–4507**
Protected Classes: Race, sex, sexual orientation, gender identity, age, marital status, religious creed, color, national origin, handicap, having minor children, receipt of public assistance.
Prohibited Practices: To discriminate in the making or purchasing of loans or providing other financial assistance in connection with residential real estate transactions. Tit. 9, § 4503(a)(6).
Scope of Coverage: Covers any person or entity whose business includes engaging in residential real estate financing for purchase, improvement, repair, or maintenance of a dwelling.
Private Remedies: Injunction, actual and punitive damages, costs, attorney fees. Tit. 9, § 4506.
Administrative Remedies: Injunction, actual damages, costs, attorney fees, civil penalty of no more than $10,000. Vt. Stat. Ann. tit. 9, § 4553.
Statute of Limitations: None specified. If administrative case is not disposed of informally within six months of filing, the commission must either file action in state court or dismiss the proceedings unless all parties consent to extension. Vt. Stat. Ann. tit. 9, § 4554.
Miscellaneous: Initiation or completion of administrative investigation is not a prerequisite to civil action. § 4506(d).

***Miscellaneous*: Vt. Stat. Ann. tit. 9, §§ 2351–2362** (motor vehicle financing)
Protected Classes: Sex, marital status, race, color, religion, national origin, age, sexual orientation, gender identity, or handicapping condition (providing there is legal capacity to contract).
Prohibited Practices: Discriminating against buyer wishing to establish a motor vehicle retail installment contract on a prohibited basis. § 2362.
Scope of Coverage: Covers persons in business of selling motor vehicles in retail installment transactions. § 2351.
Private Remedies: Person not complying with *any* provision of chapter is barred from recovery of any finance charge or late charges, etcetera, and buyer may recoup any such charges paid and attorney fees. In the case of willful violations of any provision of chapter, buyer may recover twice finance and late charges, and attorney fees. § 2361.

***Miscellaneous*: Vt. Stat. Ann. tit. 9, §§ 2401–2410** (retail installment sales)
Protected Classes: Sex, marital status, race, color, religion, national origin, age, sexual orientation, gender identity, or handicapping condition (providing there is legal capacity to contract).
Prohibited Practices: Discriminating against buyer wishing to establish retail installment sales contract or charge agreement. § 2410.
Scope of Coverage: Covers persons regularly and principally in business of selling goods to retail buyers in connection with such transactions. § 2401.
Private Remedies: Same as for violation of motor vehicle retail installment sales act provisions (see above). § 2409.

VIRGIN ISLANDS

***Civil Rights*: V.I. Code Ann. tit. 10, §§ 61–75** (housing transactions)
Protected Classes: Sex, marital status, race, religion, color, or national origin, creed, political affiliation.
Prohibited Practices: Discrimination in provision of services related to obtaining housing accommodations. § 64(8)(a)(ii). Discrimination in extensions, renewals, or terms of financial assistance. § 64(8)(e).
Scope of Coverage: Anyone having right to sell, rent, or lease, or agents thereof. § 64(8)(a). Financial organizations providing financial assistance in matters relating to housing, land, or commercial space. § 64(8)(e).
Exclusions: Owner-occupied two-family units.
Private Remedies: None specified.
Administrative Remedies: Commission for Human Rights may investigate, conduct hearings, and may seek penalties for misdemeanor, or initiate civil actions for injunctions and damages to aggrieved party.
Statute of Limitations: None specified.

***Miscellaneous*: V.I. Code Ann. tit. 28, 1031** (redlining)
Protected Classes: Borrowers seeking loans for property located in a specific neighborhood or geographic area, or in which the loan would be secured by unimproved real estate.
Prohibited Practices: Discriminating on a basis that is arbitrary or unsupported by a reasonable analysis of lending risks in the granting, withholding, extending, modifying or renewing, or in the fixing of rates, terms, conditions or provision of any residential mortgage loan based on geographic location of property or that such loan would be secured by unimproved real estate.
Scope of Coverage: Covers lending institutions when the property to be occupied is within that institution's service area.
Exclusions: Loans made pursuant to a specific private or public program whose purpose is to increase availability of mortgage loans within a specific geographic area.
Private Remedies: Actual damages or punitive damages in the amount of $5000, whichever is greater, but not less than $2500. Court may award court costs and attorney fees.

VIRGINIA

***Consumer Credit*: Va. Code Ann. §§ 59.1-21.19 to 59.1-21.28; §§ 6.2-500 to 6.2-513**
Protected Classes: Race, color, religion, national origin, sex, marital status, or age (provided there is capacity to contract); public welfare recipients.
Prohibited Practices: To discriminate in regard to any aspect of a credit transaction (sets forth several prohibited and permitted practices and requires notice of decision and of right to reasons for adverse action; provisions similar to ECOA).
Scope of Coverage: Covers persons who regularly extend, continue, or renew credit, who regularly arrange for such, and assignees who participate in decision to extend, renew, or continue credit, with respect to credit (defined as the right to incur debt or make purchase and defer payment).
Private Remedies: Actual damages, punitive damages up to $10,000, equitable relief, costs, and attorney fees. § 59.1-21.23; § 6.2-505.
Administrative Remedies: Mediation of complaint of violation. § 59.1-21.26.
Statute of Limitations: Two years from occurrence of alleged violation. § 59.1-21.23(e).
Miscellaneous: Regulations authorized by this chapter should conform

to Federal Reserve Board's ECOA regulations, including exemptions. There is a good faith conformity with FRB regulations defense; and ECOA compliance is compliance with state act. There is an election of remedies provision as to monetary damages.

Fair Housing: **Va. Code Ann. §§ 36-96.1 to 36-96.23**

Protected Classes: Race, color, religion, national origin, sex, elderliness, familial status, handicap.

Prohibited Practices: To discriminate in the making or purchasing of loans or providing other financial assistance in connection with residential real estate transactions.

Scope of Coverage: Covers any person or entity whose business includes engaging in residential real estate financing for purchase, improvement, repair, or maintenance of a dwelling.

Exclusions: Qualifying single-family housing; owner-occupied multi-family units; private membership clubs; religious or related non-profit entities owning dwelling for other than a commercial purpose; single-sex accommodations when matters of personal privacy are involved.

Private Remedies: Injunction, actual, and punitive damages, costs, attorney fees.

Administrative Remedies: Real Estate Board may refer charge to the Attorney General for civil action and court may order injunction, compensatory, and punitive damages, costs, attorney fees, and a civil penalty.

Statute of Limitations: One year for administrative complaint; two years or 180 days after conclusion of administrative process for filing private action, whichever is later.

Fair Housing: **Va. Code Ann. § 36-96.3**

Protected Classes: Race, color, religion, national origin, sex, elderliness, familial status, handicap.

Prohibited Practices: Discrimination against member of protected class in the terms, conditions, or privileges of sale or rental of a dwelling, or in providing related services or facilities.

Scope of Coverage: Any persons, defined as one or more individuals, corporations, partnerships, associations, labor organizations, governmental entities, legal representatives, mutual companies, joint stock companies, trust, unincorporated organizations, trustees, bankruptcy trustees, receivers, and fiduciaries.

Exclusions: Drug-related offenders; qualifying single-family housing; owner-occupied multi-family units; private membership clubs; religious or related non-profit entities owning dwelling for other than a commercial purpose; single-sex accommodations when matters of personal privacy are involved. Va. Code Ann. § 36-96.2.

Private Remedies: Injunction, actual and punitive damages, costs, attorney fees. Va. Code Ann. § 36-96.18.

Administrative Remedies: Real Estate Board may refer charge to the Attorney General for civil action and court may order injunction, compensatory, and punitive damages, costs, attorney fees, and a civil penalty.

Statute of Limitations: One year for administrative complaint (Va. Code Ann. § 36-96.9); civil action must be commenced within later of two years or 180 days after conclusion of administrative process (Va. Code Ann. § 36-96.18).

WASHINGTON

Civil Rights: **Wash. Rev. Code §§ 49.60.010 to 49.60.410; Wash. Rev. Code §§ 49.60.030(1)(d), 49.60.175, 49.60.176** (credit transactions)

Protected Classes: Race, creed, color, national origin, sex, sexual orientation, marital status, family with children, honorably discharged veteran or military status, presence of any sensory, mental, or physical disability, (general declaration of rights in § 49.60.030) or use of trained guide dog or service dog by a disabled person; marital status with respect to credit discrimination (§§ 49.60.175, 49.60.176).

Prohibited Practices: (1) Financial institutions cannot use a prohibited basis to determine creditworthiness (§ 49.60.175); (2) no person can deny or restrict credit, or impose different terms or conditions on credit on a prohibited basis (§ 49.60.176). Effect of community property law may be considered.

Scope of Coverage: Covers financial institutions (in the case of § 49.60.175) or any person (in the case of § 49.60.176) in connection with any credit transaction, defined broadly in § 49.60.040 to include consumer and business credit, when finance charge is imposed or provides for repayment by scheduled payments, extended in regular course of any trade or commerce.

Private Remedies: Any person injured by violation of chapter has right of action for injunctive relief, actual damages, attorney fees, or any other remedy authorized by this chapter or 42 U.S.C. §§ 2000a–2000a-6. § 49.60.030(2).

Administrative Remedies: Aggrieved party may file complaint with human rights commission, which has authority, *inter alia*, to issue cease and desist orders, order affirmative actions to effectuate purposes of chapter, award damages, except that damages for humiliation and mental suffering shall not exceed $10,000. If complaint was frivolous, unreasonable, or groundless, ALJ may award reasonable attorney fees to respondent. § 49.60.250.

Statute of Limitations: Administrative complaint must be filed within six months of alleged act of discrimination. § 49.60.230.

Miscellaneous: UDAP violation, except for those related to real estate transactions, within meaning of Wash. Rev. Code §§ 19.86.020 and 19.86.030, and subject to all provisions thereof, presumably including treble damages provision. § 49.60.030(3).

Civil Rights: **Wash. Rev. Code § 49.60.222(j)** (housing transactions)

Protected Classes: Sex, sexual orientation, marital status, race, creed, color, national origin, honorably discharged veteran or military status, families with children status, sensory, mental or physical disability, including use of a guide dog.

Prohibited Practices: To discriminate in the course of negotiating, executing, or financing a residential real estate transaction.

Scope of Coverage: Covers any person or entity whose business includes engaging in residential real estate financing for purchase, improvement, repair, or maintenance of a dwelling.

Private Remedies: Actual damages, costs, and attorney fees.

Administrative Remedies: May file complaint with Human Rights Commission which may issue injunction and award damages. Wash. Rev. Code § 49.60.225.

Statute of Limitations: One year for administrative action. Complainant may elect to have claims decided in civil action within twenty days of service of reasonable cause finding. Wash. Rev. Code § 49.60.230.

Miscellaneous: **Wash. Rev. Code §§ 30.04.500 to 30.04.515** (Fairness in Lending Act) (redlining)

Protected Classes: Geographic location of real estate offered as security.

Prohibited Practices: Deny or vary the terms of a loan to be secured by a single family residence, by requiring a greater down payment, a shorter amortization period, or a higher interest rate, or by deliberately underappraising the value of the security, because of the geographic location of the property, or utilizing lending standards which have no economic basis.

Scope of Coverage: Banks, trust companies, mutual savings banks, credit unions, mortgage companies, or savings and loan associations which operate or have a place of business in Washington.

Exclusions: Lender may deny on grounds of geographical area if building, remodeling, or continued habitation is prohibited or restricted by local, state, or federal law or regulations. May also follow sound underwriting practices regarding borrower's ability and willingness to repay, the market value of the real estate, and the diversification of the lender's portfolio.

WEST VIRGINIA

Fair Housing: W. Va. Code §§ 5-11A-1 to 5-11A-20

Protected Classes: Sex, race, color, religion, blindness, handicap, familial status, ancestry, national origin.

Prohibited Practices: Discrimination against member of protected class in the terms, conditions, or privileges of sale of rental of a dwelling or in providing related services or facilities.

Scope of Coverage: Sellers and renters of dwellings, excepting single-family residences. W. Va. Code § 5-11-4.

Exclusions: Religious and private organizations favoring members; drug-related offenders; elderly housing in regard to "familial status." W. Va. Code § 5-11-8.

Private Remedies: Injunction, actual and punitive damages, costs, and attorney fees. No action when administrative hearing has begun. W. Va. Code § 5-11-14.

Administrative Remedies: Injunction, actual damages, and other equitable relief, costs, and attorney fees. W. Va. Code § 5-11-13.

Statute of Limitations: One year for administrative complaint (W. Va. Code § 5-11-11); two years for civil action (W. Va. Code § 5-11-14).

Fair Housing: W. Va. Code § 5-11A-6

Protected Classes: Sex, race, color, religion, blindness, handicap, familial status, ancestry, national origin.

Prohibited Practices: To discriminate in (i) making or purchasing of loans or providing other financial assistance which is either secured by residential real estate or used for the purchase, construction, improvement, repair, or maintenance of a dwelling (W. Va. Code § 5-11-6); (ii) selling, brokering, or appraising residential real property (W. Va. Code § 5-11-7).

Scope of Coverage: Covers any person or entity whose business includes engaging in residential real estate financing for purchase, improvement, repair, or maintaining of a dwelling, or the selling, brokering, or appraising of residential real property.

Private Remedies: Injunction, actual and punitive damages, costs, and attorney fees. No action when administrative hearing has begun. W. Va. Code § 5-11-14.

Administrative Remedies: Injunction, actual damages and other equitable relief, costs, and attorney fees. W. Va. Code § 5-11-13.

Statute of Limitations: One year for administrative complaint (W. Va. Code § 5-11-11); two years for private action (W. Va. Code § 5-11-14).

WISCONSIN

Consumer Credit: Wis. Stat. § 138.20

Protected Classes: Physical condition, developmental disability, sex, or marital status (unless there is no legal capacity to contract).

Prohibited Practices: Discriminating in the granting or extension of credit or privilege or capacity to obtain credit. Incorporates violation of Wis. Stat. § 766.56(1) as a violation.

Scope of Coverage: Covers financial organizations, as defined in Wis. Stat. §§ 71.04(8)(a) and 71.25(10)(a) or any other credit-granting commercial institution.

Private Remedies: None specified.

Administrative Remedies: None specified (except that violator may be fined up to $1,000).

Consumer Credit: Wis. Stat. § 224.77 (financial regulation)

Protected Classes: Sex, race, color, handicap, sexual orientation (as defined), religion, national origin, age, ancestry, lawful source of income, sex, marital status, or status as a victim of domestic abuse, sexual assault, or stalking. § 224.77(1)(0).

Prohibited Practices: Unequal treatment, except in relation to housing designed to meet needs of elderly.

Scope of Coverage: Covers mortgage bankers, loan originators, or loan solicitors, as defined.

Private Remedies: May file private action for greater of actual damages (including incidental and consequential damages) or twice amount of loan origination costs but $100 minimum and $25,000 maximum per violation; reasonable costs; and attorney fees. Wis. Stat. § 224.80.

Fair Housing: Wis. Stat. § 106.50

Protected Classes: Sex, race, color, sexual orientation (as defined), disability, religion, national origin, family status, marital status, lawful source of income, age, ancestry, or status as a victim of domestic abuse, sexual assault, or stalking.

Prohibited Practices: Refusing to finance housing or discuss terms thereof, or setting different or more stringent terms or conditions for housing financing (except that terms may differ on the basis of age if reasonably related to individual applicant). § 106.50(2).

Scope of Coverage: Covers "any person."

Exclusions: Qualifying housing for older persons.

Private Remedies: Civil action may be brought for injunctive relief, damages (including punitive), court costs, and attorney fees to a prevailing plaintiff. § 106.50(6m).

Administrative Remedies: Economic and non-economic damages, injunctive relief, attorney fees and costs, but not punitive damages. § 106.50(6)(h),(i).

Statute of Limitations: Administrative complaint must be filed within one year of alleged discrimination. Civil action must be filed within one year of alleged discrimination (tolled while administrative proceeding is pending).

Appendix G Sample Pleadings

The pleadings reprinted in this appendix can also be found on the companion website to this treatise. The companion website also contains a number of additional pleadings that are not reprinted here. All pleadings in the text and on the companion website are for demonstration purposes only and must be adapted by a competent professional to fit the circumstances of a given case and the requirements of local rules and practice.

The companion website also includes expert reports from litigation challenging auto financing mark-up policies. Sample discovery requests for credit discrimination cases can be found in Appendix H, *infra*, and on the companion website. Also available on the companion website are pleadings from selected enforcement actions brought by the Department of Justice.

G.1 Sample Complaint Alleging Denial of Home Mortgage and Discriminatory Appraisal Practices as ECOA, Fair Housing, and Civil Rights Acts Violations

IN THE UNITED STATES DISTRICT COURT
FOR THE NORTHERN DISTRICT OF OHIO

————————————)	
[*Consumers 1 and 2*],)	
Plaintiffs,)	
)	
v.)	
)	
Harrison National Bank, a)	
corporation, Harrison Mortgage)	
Company, a corporation, and)	
Cole & Associates,)	
Defendants.)	
————————————)	

COMPLAINT

For and in support of their complaint against defendants, plaintiffs allege and aver as follows:

1. Plaintiffs [*Consumers 1 and 2*] are black citizens of the United States and of the State of Ohio, residing at [*Consumers' address*].

2. Defendant Harrison National Bank is a corporation registered and doing business in the State of Ohio whose business consists in whole or in part in the making of real estate loans to qualified persons. Defendant Harrison National Bank is a member of the Federal Deposit Insurance Corporation (FDIC) and the Federal Savings & Loan Insurance Corporation (FSLIC).

3. Defendant Harrison Mortgage Company is a corporation registered and doing business in the State of Ohio whose business consists in whole or in part in the making of real estate loans to qualified persons. Defendant Harrison Mortgage Company is a wholly owned subsidiary of defendant Harrison National Bank, and is a member of the Federal Deposit Insurance Company (FDIC) and the Federal Savings & Loan Insurance Corporation (FSLIC).

4. Defendant Cole & Associates is, upon information and belief, a sole proprietorship or partnership with its principal place of business in Ohio, and is engaged in the business of appraising real estate.

5. On November 19, 1993 plaintiffs applied for a real estate mortgage loan from defendants Harrison National Bank and Harrison Mortgage Company for the purchase of certain real estate located at [*Consumers' address*].

6. The terms of the real estate mortgage loan for which application was made were as follows: principal amount—$16,250; term—10 years; interest rate—10%.

7. Plaintiffs met all financial and credit requirements of defendants Harrison National Bank and Harrison Mortgage Company, and were in all respects qualified to receive a real estate mortgage loan in the amount and for the terms for which application was made.

8. Defendants Harrison National Bank and Harrison Mortgage Company received and accepted from plaintiffs $125.00 as a mortgage loan application fee, with actual or constructive knowledge of the location of the real estate located at [*Consumers' address*].

9. As a part of its consideration of plaintiffs' mortgage loan application, defendants Harrison National Bank and Harrison Mortgage Company engaged the services of defendant Cole & Associates to prepare an appraisal of the real estate located at [*Consumers' address*].

10. The appraisal report prepared by defendant Cole & Associates was completed on or about November 28, 1993, and consistently rated the real estate located at [*Consumers' address*] as "average." Average was the second highest possible rating on the scale used in the appraisal report.

11. The appraisal report prepared by defendant Cole & Associates specifically noted that the real estate located at [*Consumers' address*] had no physical inadequacies, needed no repairs, and had no functional obsolescence.

12. Defendant Cole & Associates appraised the property at a value of $24,500.00 using the "cost approach" method of appraisal and at a value of $22,000.00 using the "market data approach" method of appraisal. Thus, the property was appraised at substantially more than the principal amount of the mortgage loan request.

13. The racial population of the neighborhood within which the real estate at [*Consumers' address*] is located is over 90% black.

14. The appraisal report prepared by defendant Cole & Associates made negative comments concerning the age and condition of the neighborhood generally and of other dwellings in the neighborhood, and concluded that the location of the real estate located at [*Consumers' address*] and the condition of the neighborhood within which it was located might have an adverse effect on the marketability of the property.

15. On December 14, 1993 plaintiffs were notified by defendants Harrison National Bank and Harrison Mortgage Company that plaintiffs' application for a real estate mortgage loan had been denied. The stated reason for rejection of the plaintiffs' application was "Ineligible property—property lacks marketability."

16. Plaintiffs subsequently obtained a mortgage loan for the purchase of the real estate located at [*Consumers' address*] from another commercial mortgage lender at less favorable terms.

FIRST CLAIM FOR RELIEF

17. Plaintiffs incorporate herein the allegations contained in paragraphs 1 through 16 above.

18. Defendants Harrison National Bank and Harrison Mortgage Company with racially discriminatory intent denied the mortgage loan for which plaintiffs had applied because of the location of the real estate and/or because of the racial composition of the neighborhood within which it was located.

19. Defendants Harrison National Bank and Harrison Mortgage Company with racially discriminatory intent denied the mortgage loan for which plaintiffs had applied under pretense of using the "unmarketability" of the real estate, when in fact the appraisal report prepared by defendant Cole & Associates on the real estate located at [*Consumers' address*], Toledo, indicated that the real estate was marketable.

20. The appraisal prepared by defendant Cole & Associates was racially discriminatory. It negatively described the location of the Oakwood dwelling, relied upon the physical or economic characteristics of the neighborhood in which the real estate was located, and made negative representations concerning the marketability of the real estate based upon the neighborhood in which it was located.

21. The denial of plaintiffs' mortgage loan application by defendants Harrison National Bank and Harrison Mortgage Company was based in whole or in part on the racially discriminatory appraisal prepared by defendant Cole & Associates.

22. The actions of the defendants Harrison National Bank and Harrison Mortgage Company violated the Fair Housing Act, 42 U.S.C. §§ 3601–3619.

23. As a proximate cause of the denial for racially discriminatory reasons of plaintiffs' mortgage loan application by defendants Harrison National Bank and Harrison Mortgage Company, plaintiffs have suffered compensatory damages in the form of economic loss, humiliation, embarrassment, mental anguish, inconvenience, and the deprivation of civil rights.

24. The actions of defendants Harrison National Bank and Harrison Mortgage Company were intentional and willful and warrant the imposition of punitive damages.

SECOND CLAIM FOR RELIEF

25. Plaintiffs incorporate herein the allegations contained in paragraphs 1 through 24 above.

26. The denial of plaintiffs' mortgage loan application by defendants Harrison National Bank and Harrison Mortgage Company was in violation of 42 U.S.C. § 1981.

27. As a proximate cause of the denial for racially discriminatory reasons for plaintiffs' mortgage loan application by defendants Harrison National Bank and Harrison Mortgage Company, plaintiffs have suffered compensatory damages in the form of economic loss, humiliation, embarrassment, mental anguish, inconvenience, and the deprivation of civil rights.

28. The actions of defendants Harrison National Bank and Harrison Mortgage Company were intentional and willful and warrant the imposition of punitive damages.

THIRD CLAIM FOR RELIEF

29. Plaintiffs incorporate herein the allegations contained in paragraphs 1 through 28 above.

30. The denial of plaintiffs' mortgage loan application by defendants Harrison National Bank and Harrison Mortgage Company was in violation of 42 U.S.C. § 1982.

31. As a proximate cause of the denial for racially discriminatory reasons of plaintiffs' mortgage loan application by defendants Harrison National Bank and Harrison Mortgage Company, plaintiffs have suffered compensatory damages in the form of economic loss, humiliation, embarrassment, mental anguish, inconvenience, and the deprivation of civil rights.

32. The actions of defendants Harrison National Bank and Harrison Mortgage Company were intentional and willful and warrant the imposition of punitive damages.

FOURTH CLAIM FOR RELIEF

33. Plaintiffs incorporate herein the allegations contained in paragraphs 1 through 32 above.

34. The denial of plaintiffs' mortgage loan application by defendants Harrison National Bank and Harrison Mortgage Company constitutes racial discrimination with respect to a credit transaction in violation of the Equal Credit Opportunity Act, 15 U.S.C. §§ 1691–1691f.

35. As a proximate cause of the denial for racially discriminatory reasons of plaintiffs' mortgage loan application by defendants Harrison National Bank and Harrison Mortgage Company, plaintiffs have suffered compensatory damages in the form of economic loss, humiliation, embarrassment, mental anguish, inconvenience, and the deprivation of civil rights.

36. The actions of defendants Harrison National Bank and Harrison Mortgage Company were intentional and willful and warrant the imposition of punitive damages.

FIFTH CLAIM FOR RELIEF

37. Plaintiffs incorporate herein the allegations contained in paragraphs 1 through 36 above.

38. The denial for racially discriminatory reasons of plaintiffs' mortgage loan application by defendants Harrison National Bank and Harrison Mortgage Company deprived plaintiffs of the right and benefits from these defendants' programs for extending home mortgage loans to qualified persons.

39. The conduct of defendants Harrison National Bank and Harrison Mortgage Company thereby excluded plaintiffs from participating in and receiving the benefits of programs or activities receiving federal financial assistance in violation of 42 U.S.C. § 2000d *et seq.*

40. As a proximate cause of the denial for racially discriminatory reasons of plaintiffs' mortgage loan application by defendants Harrison National Bank and Harrison Mortgage Company, plaintiffs have suffered compensatory damages in the form of economic loss, humiliation, embarrassment, mental anguish, inconvenience, and the deprivation of civil rights.

41. The actions of defendants Harrison National Bank and Harrison Mortgage Company were intentional and willful and warrant the imposition of punitive damages.

SIXTH CLAIM FOR RELIEF

42. Plaintiffs incorporate herein the allegations contained in paragraphs 1 through 41 above.

43. The preparation of a racially discriminatory appraisal report by defendant Cole & Associates violated the Fair Housing Act, 42 U.S.C. §§ 3601–3619.

44. As a proximate cause of defendant Cole & Associates' preparation of a racially discriminatory appraisal report in violation of the Fair Housing Act, plaintiffs have suffered compensatory damages in the form of economic loss, humiliation, embarrassment, mental anguish, inconvenience, and the deprivation of civil rights.

45. The actions of defendant Cole & Associates were intentional and willful and warrant the imposition of punitive damages.

SEVENTH CLAIM FOR RELIEF

46. Plaintiffs incorporate herein the allegations contained in paragraphs 1 through 45 above.

47. Defendants Harrison National Bank and Harrison Mortgage Company, and Cole & Associates intentionally conspired among themselves to deprive, either directly or indirectly, plaintiffs of their rights to equal protection of the laws, equal privileges and immunities under the laws, and civil rights generally, all in violation of 42 U.S.C. § 1985(3).

48. As a proximate cause of the defendants' violation of 42 U.S.C. § 1985(3), plaintiffs have suffered compensatory damages in the form of economic loss, humiliation, embarrassment, mental anguish, inconvenience, and the deprivation of civil rights.

49. The actions of defendants Harrison National Bank and Harrison Mortgage Company, and Cole & Associates were intentional and willful and warrant the imposition of punitive damages.

WHEREFORE, plaintiffs pray for the following relief:

(A) A declaratory judgment that the actions of the defendants were intentionally racially discriminatory and in violation of the Fair Housing Act, the Equal Credit Opportunity Act, 42 U.S.C. § 1981, 42 U.S.C. § 1982, 42 U.S.C. § 1985(3), and 42 U.S.C. § 2000d *et seq.*; and

(B) An injunction permanently enjoining the defendants from preparing, using or relying upon racially discriminatory appraisal reports and permanently enjoining the defendants from engaging in the receipt, processing, approval or denial of applications for real estate mortgage loans; and

(C) Compensatory damages in the amount of Fifty Thousand Dollars ($50,000.00) assessed against all defendants jointly and severally; and

(D) Punitive damages in the amount of One Hundred Fifty Thousand Dollars ($150,000.00) assessed against all defendants jointly and severally; and

(E) Attorneys' fees and costs of this action; and

(F) Any other relief to which plaintiffs may be entitled in law or in equity.

JURY DEMAND

Plaintiffs hereby demand a trial by jury on all issues.

G.2 Sample Complaint Alleging Disparate Impact of Discretionary Pricing Policies/Yield Spread Premiums Against Mortgage Lender

UNITED STATES DISTRICT COURT
DISTRICT OF MASSACHUSETTS

————————————)	
[*Consumer 1 to Consumer 12*] on)	
behalf of themselves and all)	
others similarly situated,)	
Plaintiffs,)	
)	
v.)	C.A. NO. ———————
)	*JURY TRIAL DEMANDED*
Option One Mortgage)	
Corporation and H & R Block)	
Mortgage Corp. N/K/A Option)	
One Mortgage Services, Inc.)	
Defendants.)	
————————————)	

SECOND AMENDED CLASS ACTION COMPLAINT

Plaintiffs, [*Consumer 1 to Consumer 12*] (collectively "Plaintiffs"), on behalf of themselves and all others similarly situated, by their undersigned attorneys, allege as follows:

1. This is a class action brought by Plaintiffs, on behalf of themselves and other similarly situated minority homeowners, against Option One Mortgage Corporation and H & R Block Mortgage Corp. (collectively "Defendants"), under the Equal Credit Opportunity Act, 15 U.S.C. § 1691, *et seq.* ("ECOA") and the Fair Housing Act, 42 U.S.C. § 3601 *et seq.* Plaintiffs seek remedies for themselves and the Class (defined in ¶ 126, below) for the discriminatory effects of the Defendants' home financing policies and practices.

2. As described below, the Defendants have established a specific, identifiable and uniform credit pricing system, a component of which, referred to herein as the Discretionary Pricing Policy, authorizes unchecked, subjective surcharge of additional points and fees to an otherwise objective risk-based financing rate. In other words, after a finance rate acceptable to the Defendants is determined by objective criteria (e.g., the individual's credit history, credit score, debt-to-income ratio and loan-to-value ratios), the Defendants' credit pricing policy authorizes additional discretionary finance charges. These subjective, additional finance charges have a widespread discriminatory impact on minority applicants for home mortgage loans, in violation of ECOA and the FHA.

3. The mortgage lending industry has a long history of racial discrimination, offering minorities products and terms that are drastically worse than those given to their similarly-situated white counterparts. Recently, the Federal Reserve Board confirmed that blacks and other minorities are still more likely to pay higher prices for mortgages than whites.

4. In 2003, the National Community Reinvestment Coalition ("NCRC") released a report on credit discrimination titled, "The

Broken System: Discrimination and Unequal Access to Affordable Loans by Race and Age,"[1] that indicated that consumers living in areas with more minority residents are more likely to have mortgages with interest rates higher than the "prevailing and competitive" rates, often because of discrimination in lending.

5. Home Mortgage Disclosure Act ("HMDA") Data for 2006 revealed that black and Hispanic borrowers are more likely to obtain higher-priced loans than are white borrowers.[2] The data indicated that black homeowners who received subprime mortgage loans were much more likely to be issued a higher-rate loan than white borrowers with the same qualifications.

6. In a speech last year, Martin J. Gruenberg, Vice Chairman of the Federal Deposit Insurance Corporation observed that "previous studies have suggested higher-priced, subprime lenders are more active in lower income, urban areas and that minority access to credit is dominated by higher cost lenders."[3]

7. In 2006, the Center for Responsible Lending, a non-profit research organization, uncovered "large and statistically significant" differences between the rates of subprime loans offered to blacks and whites, even when income and credit risk were taken into consideration. Compared to their otherwise similarly-situated white counterparts, blacks were 31–34% more likely to receive higher rate fixed-rate loans and 6–15% more likely to receive adjustable-rate loans.[4]

8. Subprime loans to blacks and other minorities not only impose higher interest rates, they are typically laden with excessive, unreasonable and often improperly disclosed fees as well. *See* n.3.

9. These significant disparities are not mere coincidences. They are the result of a systematic and discriminatory policy of targeting minority borrowers for high-cost loans. Defendants' business practices include implementing and maintaining policies that discriminate against minorities. Plaintiffs bring this lawsuit to seek relief from the harms suffered as a result of Defendants' practices and to enjoin Defendants from continuing its discriminatory practices.

10. The Defendants have established policies for retail and wholesale access to their loan products that subject minority financing applicants to a significantly higher likelihood of exposure to discretionary points and fees. These costs drive up the average cost of a mortgage loan made by one of the defendants to minority homeowners.

11. Plaintiffs seek damages, declaratory and injunctive relief, disgorgement and restitution of monies disparately obtained from minority borrowers.

JURISDICTION AND VENUE

12. Plaintiffs invoke the jurisdiction of this Court pursuant to 28 U.S.C. § 1331, which confers original jurisdiction upon this Court in a civil action arising under federal law.

13. Venue is proper in this Court pursuant to 28 U.S.C. 1391(b) inasmuch as the unlawful discriminatory practices are alleged to have been committed in this District, Defendants regularly conduct business in this District, and some of the named Plaintiffs reside in this District.

---

1 This report is available at http://ncrc.org/policy/cra/documents/ncrcdiscrimstudy.pdf.

2 This report is available at www.ffiec.gov./hmda.

3 *See* "Remarks of Martin J. Gruenberg, Vice Chairman, FDIC; Inter-American Development Bank," October 18, 2006, *available at* http://www.fdic.gov/new/speeches/archives/2006/chairman/spoct1806.html.

4 *See* "Unfair Lending: The Effect of Race and Ethnicity on the Price of Subprime Mortgages," *available at* www.responsiblelending.org.

PARTIES

14. Plaintiffs, [*Consumer 1*] and [*Consumer 2*], ("[*Couple 1*]") are married minority homeowners who reside at [*address*], Massachusetts.

15. Plaintiffs, [*Consumer 3*] and [*Consumer 4*] ("[*Couple 2*]") are married minority homeowners who reside at [*address*], Massachusetts.

16. Plaintiffs, [*Consumer 5*] and [*Consumer 6*] ("[*Couple 3*]") are married minority homeowners who reside at [*address*], Massachusetts.

17. Plaintiff, [*Consumer 7*] is a minority homeowner who resides at [*address*], Massachusetts.

18. Plaintiffs [*Consumer 8*] and [*Consumer 9*] ("[*Couple 4*]") are married minority homeowners who reside at [*address*], Massachusetts.

19. Plaintiff [*Consumer 10*] is a minority homeowner who resides at [*address*],Illinois.

20. Plaintiff [*Consumer 11*] is a minority homeowner who resides at [*address*], Massachusetts.

21. Plaintiff [*Consumer 12*] is a minority homeowner who resides at [*address*], Illinois.

22. Defendant, Option One Mortgage Company ("Option One") is a wholly-owned subsidiary of H & R Block, Inc. Option One was primarily a wholesale mortgage lender and offered its services through its branches and a national network of mortgage brokers until December 2007, when H & R Block, Inc. terminated Option One's loan origination business. Option One maintains a principal place of business at 3 Ada, Irvine, California 92618 and although it is not making new loans, continues its servicing and collection operations.

23. Defendant, H & R Block Mortgage Corp. ("H & R Block Mortgage") is a wholly-owned subsidiary of H & R Block, Inc. H & R Block Mortgage was a retail mortgage lender making direct-to-consumer loans nationwide until H & R Block, Inc. terminated H & R Block Mortgage's loan origination business in 2007. H & R Block Mortgage maintains a principal place of business located at 6561 Irvine Center Drive, Irvine, California 92616.

24. According to the Massachusetts Secretary of State's Office, H & R Block Mortgage Corp. changed its name to Option One Mortgage Services, Inc., on or about July 23, 2007.

A. MORTGAGE LENDING IN THE UNITED STATES HISTORICALLY HAS DISCRIMINATED AGAINST MINORITIES

25. Borrowers who obtain a home loan at an unnecessarily high interest rate will pay hundreds of dollars more each month in mortgage payments, making them more vulnerable to short term economic distress that may result from job loss or medical problems. In consequence, minority homeowners run higher risks of foreclosure, and will accumulate equity in their homes much more slowly than white borrowers. While for some minority borrowers with tarnished credit histories, higher-priced home loans provide the only access to the mortgage market and to homeownership, many other minorities will be paying far more for their mortgages than their credit histories justify.

26. The skyrocketing levels of foreclosures in urban areas, and minority communities in particular, have been tied to the growth of concentrated subprime lending in these areas.[5] Concentrated foreclosures have a devastating impact on cities and neighborhoods. They affect local property values, serve as a magnet for crime, and hurt a city's property tax base.[6]

---

5 Immergluck, Dan and Geoff Smith. March 2004. "Risky Business: An Econometric Analysis of the Relationship Between Subprime Lending and Foreclosures." Woodstock Institute: Chicago, IL.

6 For discussions of the external impacts of foreclosures, *see* Immer-

27. While many institutions specialize in lending to either prime or subprime markets, there is an important set of large lenders that are active in both markets. These lenders utilize diverse lending channels such as branch, broker and correspondent networks that allow them to reach a wide variety of geographic markets. Their size also gives them the capacity to offer an array of products that may be appropriate for customers with different levels of credit quality.

28. According to the Joint Center for Housing Studies at Harvard University's 2005 study called "The Dual Mortgage Market: The Persistence of Discrimination in Mortgage Lending," mortgage lending discrimination today is subtle but pervasive, with minority consumers continuing to have less-than-equal access to loans at the best price and on the best terms that their credit history, income, and other individual financial considerations merit more than three decades after the enactment of national fair lending legislation.

29. The passage of civil rights legislation and fair lending laws in the 1960s and 1970s brought an end to the most virulent forms of overt racial discrimination in the housing markets, but throughout the 1980s and 1990s, mortgage lenders found more subtle ways to discriminate, including maintaining offices only in white neighborhoods and engaging in practices such as redlining (refusing to lend on properties in predominantly minority neighborhoods).

30. After such redlining practices were challenged in the 1990s, mortgage lenders changed tactics once again, making loans to minorities, but charging higher interest rates and loan-related fees than they charged to similarly situated white borrowers. Loan data that mortgage lenders must now compile and disclose under the federal Home Mortgage Disclosure Act ("HMDA") reveals profound loan pricing disparities between minority borrowers and similarly-situated white borrowers.

31. The HMDA requires mortgage lenders to report information about the home loans they process each year. In 2005, lenders reported information on more than 30 million home loan applications pursuant to HMDA. In 1989, Congress required lenders to begin disclosing information about mortgage borrowers' race and ethnicity. In 2004, concerned with potential racial discrimination in loan pricing and recognizing that racial or other types of discrimination can occur when loan officers and mortgage brokers have latitude in setting interest rates, the Federal Reserve Board began requiring lenders to also report information concerning rates, points, and fees, charged to borrowers on high-cost loans.

32. According to the Federal Reserve, both 2004 and 2005 HMDA data revealed that "Blacks and minority borrowers were more likely . . . to have received higher-priced loans than non-Hispanic whites. . . . [which has] increased concern about the fairness of the lending process."[7]

33. HMDA data for 2004 reveals profound loan pricing disparities between minority borrowers and non-Hispanic whites even after controlling for borrowers' gender, income, property location, and loan amount. After accounting for those differences in the 2004 HMDA data, minority borrowers were still almost twice as likely to receive a higher-rate home loan as non-Hispanic whites.[8] In a speech last year, the Vice-Chairman of the Federal Deposit Insurance Corporation, Martin Gruenberg, discussed the 2004 HMDA data and observed that that data "clearly indicated" that minority borrowers are more likely to receive high-cost home loans than are non-Hispanic whites.[9]

34. Likewise, HMDA data for 2005 shows that "for conventional home-purchase loans, the gross mean incidence of higher-priced lending was 54.7 percent for blacks and 17.2 percent for non-Hispanic whites, a difference of 37.5 percentage points." Avery, *supra*, at A159. The situation is similar for refinancing, where there is a difference of 28.3 percentage points between blacks and non-Hispanic whites. *Id.* at A124, A159.

35. The Association of Community Organizations for Reform Now (ACORN) released a report entitled "The High Cost of Credit: Disparities in High-priced Refinanced Loans to Minority Homeowners in 125 American Cities," dated September 27, 2005, that found that "[i]n every metropolitan area where at least 50 refinances were made to African-American homeowners, African-Americans were more likely to receive a high-cost loan than White homeowners."

36. The study found that, nationally, black home purchasers were 2.7 times more likely and Hispanics were 2.3 times more likely than white borrowers to be issued a problematic, subprime loan. Additionally, the ACORN study, available at www.acorn.org, found that nationally, for refinance loans, African Americans were 1.8 times more likely and Hispanics were 1.4 times more likely than white borrowers to be issued a problematic, subprime loan.

37. Differences in economic status are not to blame. These racial disparities were found to persist even among borrowers of the same income level. The ACORN study found that, among upper-income purchasers (defined as persons with incomes 120% or greater than the area median income for their metropolitan area), African Americans were 3.3 times more likely and Hispanics were 3 times more likely than similarly-situated whites to be issued a high-cost, subprime loan. Further, the ACORN study found that, with respect to refinance loans, among upper-income borrowers, African Americans and Hispanics were 1.7 times more likely than similarly-situated whites to be issued a high-cost, subprime loan.

38. While some borrowers in the subprime market are genuine credit risks, minority borrowers have been preyed upon by mortgage lenders and illegally steered into subprime loans. Defendants have engaged in this discriminatory lending by refusing to offer minority borrowers the prime loans offered to similarly-qualified white borrowers.

39. Studies by Freddie Mac and Standard & Poor's have found that 20% to 30% of borrowers who receive subprime mortgages could have qualified for traditional mortgages at the lower rates offered by banks to prime borrowers. This seriously disadvantages the borrower by effectively diluting the equity of the property, placing the borrower in jeopardy of default, and forcing the borrower to spend years paying off additional loan balances without developing any equity in their home.

40. Further, the U.S. Department of Housing and Urban Development found that in neighborhoods where at least 80 percent of the population is African American, borrowers were 2.2 times as likely as borrowers in the nation as a whole to refinance with a subprime lender.

---

gluck, Dan and Geoff Smith. June 2005. *There Goes the Neighborhood: The Effect of Single-Family Mortgage Foreclosures on Property Values.* Woodstock Institute: Chicago, IL; Immergluck, Dan and Geoff Smith. November 2006. "The Impact of Single Family Foreclosures on Neighborhood Crime." *Housing Studies* (21:6); and Apgar, William, Mark Duda, and Rochelle Nawrocki Gorey. February 2005. *The Municipal Costs of Foreclosures: A Chicago Case Study.* Foreclosure Prevention Foundation: Minneapolis, MN.

7 Robert B. Avery, Kenneth P. Brevoort and Glenn B. Canner, "Higher-Priced Home Lending and the 2005 HMDA Data," Federal Reserve Bulletin, A124, A159 (revised Sept. 18, 2006) (http://www.federalreserve.gov/pubs/bulletin/2006/hmda/bull06hmda.pdf).

8 This is available at http://www.responsiblelending.org/pdfs/Testimony-Ernst061306.pdf.

9 This speech is available at http://www.fdic.gov/news/news/speeches/archives/2006/chairman/spoct1806.html.

Higher-income borrowers living in predominately blacks neighborhoods are twice as likely as lower-income white borrowers to have subprime loans.[10]

41. The predatory lending practices of the Defendants and other mortgage lenders lead to dire financial consequences for borrowers. Earlier this year, over eighty consumer groups wrote to federal banking agencies about a particular type of subprime loan, 2/28 the adjustable rate mortgage ("2/28 ARM"). A 2/28 ARM typically contains an average built-in "shock payment" increase of 29%, even if interest rates remain unchanged. Fitch Ratings reports that the actual payment shock may be as high as 48%. The majority of subprime loans made to minorities had these adjustable rates. The Center for Responsible Lending estimates that 2.2 million such subprime loans have ended or will end in foreclosure, a rate of 19%.

42. Each named Plaintiff has a 2/28 ARM.

43. The Center for Responsible Lending published a study in December 2006 on the effects of foreclosure.[11] The report states that the costs of subprime foreclosures fall heavily on African American and Hispanic homeowners, since subprime mortgages are disproportionately made in communities of color. HMDA data shows that over half of loans to black borrowers are higher-cost loans, which, by definition, are a proxy for subprime loans. For Hispanic homeowners, the portion of higher-cost loans is also very high, at four in ten. This data implies that subprime foreclosures will affect eight percent of recent Hispanic borrowers and 10 percent of recent blacks borrowers. By comparison, subprime foreclosures will likely occur among only about four percent of recent white borrowers.

44. The Center for Responsible Lending released an additional study in November, 2007[12] that explains how when a home goes into foreclosure, the negative effects extend beyond individual families losing their homes to surrounding neighbors and the wider community. The 2007 study further reports that a foreclosure on a home lowered the price of other nearby single-family homes, on average, by 0.9 percent. That impact was even higher in lower-income neighborhoods, where each foreclosure dropped home values by an average of 1.44 percent. The study notes that communities of color will be especially harmed, since these communities receive a disproportionate share of subprime home loans.

45. The 2007 study projects that, nationally, foreclosures on subprime home loans originated in 2005 and 2006 will have numerous impacts on the neighborhoods and communities in which they occur. For instance, the study predicts that 44.5 million neighboring homes will experience devaluation because of subprime foreclosures that take place nearby, and the total decline in house values and tax base from nearby foreclosure will be about $223 billion. Homeowners living near foreclosed properties will see their property values decrease $5,000 on average.

46. A growing number of research studies and investigations show that significant racial disparities still exist.[13]

47. Moreover, and importantly, research studies have suggested that borrowers' credit profiles cannot fully explain why some borrowers, and not others, are saddled with higher cost loans. Researchers have raised "doubts that risk can adequately explain racial differences" in high-cost loans.[14] In other words, evidence "suggests that weak borrower credit profiles do not fully explain why some borrowers get stuck with higher-cost home loans."[15]

B. THE DEFENDANTS' DISCRETIONARY PRICING POLICY CONTINUES THE PERVASIVE DISCRIMINATION AGAINST MINORITIES IN MORTGAGE LENDING

48. Option One was one of the largest subprime mortgage-lending companies in the United States. Option One publicly promoted its home financing expertise by means of nationwide advertising campaigns. In its advertisements, Option One solicited persons to apply for financing with Option One either in one of its branch offices or through one of the mortgage brokers whom Option One had authorized to accept applications on its behalf.

49. H & R Block made home-mortgage loans directly to consumers through its subsidiary, H & R Block Mortgage.

50. Option One made home-mortgage loans—the majority of which were subprime loans—that were arranged by its loan officers and/or its network of mortgage brokers. Those loans were made in reliance on Option One's credit-granting policies and with the participation of H & R Block and H & R Block Mortgage Corp.

51. Due to H & R Block's policies as to where to place its offices and how to market its products, minority borrowers were more likely than white borrowers to apply for credit from H & R Block through its sub-prime subsidiary Option One, or from an Option One authorized broker.

52. Even after controlling for differences in credit risk, because of the Discretionary Pricing Policy, loans obtained from Option One or Option One's network of brokers are more expensive, on average, than loans obtained directly from H & R Block or H & R Block Mortgage.

53. H & R Block and H & R Block Mortgage Corp., in the ordinary course of its business, regularly participates in credit decisions made by Option One, including setting the terms of credit available in transactions originated by Option One. H & R Block, H & R Block Mortgage Corp. and Option One jointly established the Discretionary Pricing Policy at issue in this case.

54. H & R Block and H & R Block Mortgage Corp. participated in the decisions to grant credit to the Plaintiffs including, without limitation, by making the Discretionary Pricing Policy applicable to their loans.

55. Based on the latest available Home Mortgage Disclosure Act ("HMDA") data from the Department of Housing and Urban Development, minority homeowners who borrowed from Option One were more likely than whites to have received a high-APR loan.

---

10 *See* "All Other Things Being Equal: A Paired Testing Study of Mortgage Lending Institutions," 2002, available at www.huduser.org.

11 *See* "Losing Ground: Foreclosures in the Subprime Market and Their Cost to Homeowners." December 2006, available at www.responsiblelending.org.

12 "Subprime Spillover: Foreclosures Cost Neighbors $223 Billion; 44.5 Million Homes Lost $5,000 on Average." Center for Responsible Lending, *available at* www.responsiblelending.org.

13 California Reinvestment Coalition, et al., "Paying More for the American Dream: A Multi-State Analysis of Higher Cost Home Purchase Lending" (March 2007) (http://www.nedap.org/pressroom/documents/2007_Report-2005_HMDA.pdf); Ross, "The Continuing Practice and Impact of Discrimination" (Revised July 2006) (Univ. of Connecticut, Working Paper 2005-19R) (http://www.econ.uconn.edu/working/2005-19r.pdf).

14 Bradford, Center for Community Change, "Risk or Race? Racial Disparities and the Subprime Refinance Market" (May 2002) (http://www.knowledgeplex.org/kp/report/report/relfiles/ccc_0729_risk.pdf).

15 California Reinvestment Coalition, et al., "Paying More for the American Dream: A Multi-State Analysis of Higher Cost Home Purchase Lending." (March 2007).

56. A high-APR loan is a loan whose APR is at least three percentage points higher than the interest rate on U.S. Treasury securities of the same maturity, at the time the loan was made.

57. While credit differences may explain some part of the disparities in rate and terms, the Defendants' Discretionary Pricing Policy accounts for a significant portion of the disparity.

58. The Defendants' Discretionary Pricing Policy is unrelated to a borrower's objective credit characteristics such as credit history, credit score, debt-to-income ratio and loan-to-value ratios and results in purely subjective charges that affect the rate otherwise available to borrowers.

59. Option One provided its loan officers and authorized mortgage brokers with substantial information about its loan programs, rates and credit criteria, as well as its policies for compensating its loan officers and mortgage brokers who arranged business for it.

60. Option One authorized certain mortgage brokers to accept applications on its behalf, to quote financing rates and terms (within the limitations set by H & R Block), to inform credit applicants of Option One's financing options and to originate finance transactions using H & R Block's forms, in accordance with its policies.

61. Option One provided its loan officers and brokers with credit applications, loan contracts and other required financing forms, as well as instructions on filling out such documents necessary to complete home mortgage transactions.

62. After a customer provided credit information to one of Option One's loan officers or brokers, Option One computed a financing rate through an objective credit analysis that, in general, discerned the creditworthiness of the customer.

63. These credit analyses considered numerous risk-related variables of creditworthiness, including credit bureau histories, payment amounts, debt ratio, bankruptcies, automobile repossessions, charge-offs, prior foreclosures, payment histories, credit score, debt-to-income ratios, loan-to-value ratios and other risk-related attributes or variables. On information and belief, Option One used these variables to determine a "mortgage score" for each credit applicant.

64. Based on these objective risk-related variables and the resulting mortgage score, Option One derived a risk-based financing rate at which it would provide a home mortgage, often called the "Par Rate." Alternatively, experienced Option One loan officers and brokers estimated the risk-related Par Rate by referring to the applicant's credit bureau determined credit score.

65. Although Option One's initial analysis applied objective criteria to calculate this risk-related Par Rate, Option One then authorized a subjective component in its credit pricing system—the Discretionary Pricing Policy—to impose additional non-risk charges. On information and belief, the applicable Par Rates and authorized discretionary charges were communicated by Option One to its loan officers and brokers via regularly published "rate sheets." On information and belief, such rate sheets were published by Option One via intranet and internet.

66. The discretionary charges are paid by the customer as a component of the total finance charge (the "Contract APR"), without the homeowner knowing that a portion of their contract APR was a non-risk-related charge.

67. Loan officers and brokers had discretion, within the limits set by the Defendants, to impose discretionary mark-ups as additional points in interest—"a rate mark-up," or as points and fees on the loan. When there was a rate mark-up, the Defendants received additional income.

68. The Defendants' Discretionary Pricing Policy, by design, caused persons with identical or similar credit scores to pay different amounts for the cost of credit. As a result of using a subjective pricing component that is designed to charge persons with the same credit profiles different amounts of finance charge, the objective qualities of the initial credit analysis used to calculate the Par Rate are undermined and the potential for race bias became inherent in the transaction.

69. The Discretionary Pricing Policy, although facially neutral (insofar as the Defendants use the same or effectively the same policy for all credit applicants), had a disproportionately adverse effect on minorities compared to similarly situated whites in that minorities paid disparately more discretionary charges (both in frequency and amount) than similarly situated whites. Statistical analysis of discretionary charges imposed on minority and white customers of other mortgage companies that use credit pricing systems structured like that of Option One has revealed that minorities, after controlling for credit risk, are substantially more likely than similarly situated whites to pay such charges.

70. Loan officers and brokers are agents of Option One for the purpose of setting credit price, which always was set based on the Defendants' policy.

71. The disparate impact suffered by minorities is a direct result of the Defendants' Discretionary Pricing Policy in that the Defendants designed, disseminated, controlled, implemented and profited from the Discretionary Pricing Policy creating the disparate impact.

72. The Defendants have a non-delegable duty to ensure that their mortgage financing structure and policies do not have a disparate impact on legally protected classes, such as minorities. Despite having such a non-delegable duty, the Defendants chose to use, a commission-driven, subjective pricing policy that they knew or should have known had a significant and pervasive adverse impact on minority homeowners.

73. The disparities between the terms of the Defendants' transactions involving minority homeowners and the terms involving whites homeowners cannot be a product of chance and cannot be explained by factors unrelated to race, but, instead, are the direct causal result of the use of the discriminatory Discretionary Pricing Policy.

74. There are no legitimate business reasons justifying the Defendants' discriminatory Discretionary Pricing Policy that could not be achieved by a policy that has no discriminatory impact or a greatly reduced discriminatory impact.

C. THE DEFENDANTS' DISCRETIONARY PRICING POLICY DISCRIMINATED AGAINST PLAINTIFFS

Facts Relating To [*Couple 1*]

75. Plaintiffs, [*Couple 1*], reside at [*address*], Massachusetts.

76. On or about January 16, 2004, [*Couple 1*] purchased their home for approximately $277,000.00.

77. On August 19, 2005, [*Couple 1*] refinanced their home loan with Option One.

78. The loan, [*loan number*], was a 30-year, adjustable rate loan with a disclosed APR of 8.653%. The loan amount was $416,000.00. According to the note, the loan had a five-year fixed rate followed by a 25-year variable rate feature and was an interest only loan.

79. According to the HUD-One Settlement Statement, [*Couple 1*] paid $21,641.08 in settlement charges in connection with the loan, including, a $17,500 broker fee to Money-Wise Solutions ("Money-Wise"), an Option One authorized mortgage broker, a $620.00 processing fee to Money-Wise, a $650 underwriting fee to Option One and a $50.00 funding fee to Option One.

80. True and correct copies of Truth-in-Lending disclosure and HUD-One Settlement Statement provided in connection with [*loan number*] are attached hereto and labeled *Exhibit 1* and *Exhibit 2* [*Editor's note: Not reprinted herein*], respectively.

81. On April 6, 2006, [*Couple 1*] refinanced their Option One loan with a second Option One loan.

82. The second loan [*loan number*], which has a loan amount of $500,000, is an adjustable rate loan with a balloon feature, providing for a final payment of $344,113.90. The APR of the second loan was 10.536%.

83. According to the HUD-One Settlement Statement, [*Couple 1*] paid $17,066.32 in settlement charges in connection with the second loan, including, a $3,500 broker fee to Logic Mortgage & Finance ("Logic"), an Option One authorized mortgage broker, a $595.00 processing fee to Logic, an $850 underwriting fee to Option One, a $50.00 funding fee to Option One and a $7,500 loan origination fee to Option One.

84. True and correct copies of the Truth-in-Lending disclosure and HUD-One Settlement Statement provided in connection with [*loan number*] are attached hereto and labeled *Exhibit 3* and *Exhibit 4* [*Editor's note: Not reprinted herein*], respectively.

85. According to credit reports available to Option One, [*Consumer 1*] had an average credit score of 681 and [*Consumer 2*] had an average credit score of 665 as of January 20, 2006.

86. At the time of the transactions, [*Couple 1*] had credit scores that would have qualified with many lenders for a mortgage in the prime-market. Instead, [*Couple 1*] received mortgages at sub-prime rates and on sub-prime terms.

87. H & R Block and H & R Block Mortgage Corp, by various means and through its policies, participated in the decision to grant credit to [*Couple 1*], including the rates and terms on which credit would be granted.

88. On information and belief, unbeknownst to [*Couple 1*], the contract APR on the mortgage loans were actually a combination of an objective, risk-based calculation and a totally subjective, discretionary component added pursuant to the Defendants' Discretionary Pricing Policy.

89. On information and belief, [*Couple 1*] were subject to the Defendants' Discretionary Pricing Policy.

90. On information and belief, [*Couple 1*] were charged a disproportionately greater amount in non-risk-related credit charges than similarly situated white persons.

91. [*Couple 1*] were not offered less expensive loan products that were available to borrowers with their credit characteristics directly from H & R Block or H & R Block Mortgage Corp.

Facts Relating To [*Couple 2*]

92. Plaintiffs, [*Couple 2*], reside at [*address*], Massachusetts with their teenaged son and daughter.

93. On or about April 28, 2006, [*Couple 2*] purchased their home for approximately $390,000 with Option One as the lender.

94. The loan, [*loan number*], is a 30-year adjustable rate loan with a disclosed APR of 10.844%. The loan amount was $360,000. According to the note, the loan had a two-year fixed rate followed by a 28-year variable rate feature.

95. [*Couple 2*] first discovered that the loan had an adjustable rate at the closing, but felt pressured to close because they had sold their previous home on the same day.

96. According to the HUD-One Settlement Statement, [*Couple 2*] paid $13,403.23 in settlement charges in connection with the loan, including, a $6,040.00 broker fee to LEHI Mortgage Services, Inc. ("LEHI"), an Option One authorized mortgage broker, a $570.00 processing fee to LEHI, a $295.00 application fee to LEHI, an $850 underwriting fee to Option One, a $50.00 funding fee to Option One and a $900 loan discount fee to Option One.

97. True and correct copies of the Truth-in-Lending disclosure and HUD-One Settlement Statement provided in connection with [*loan number*] are attached hereto and labeled *Exhibit 5* and *Exhibit 6* [*Editor's note: Not reprinted herein*], respectively.

98. At the time of the transaction, [*Consumer 3*] had a credit score that would have qualified with many lenders for a mortgage in the prime-market. Instead, [*Consumer 3*] received a mortgage at sub-prime rates and on sub-prime terms.

99. H & R Block and H & R Block Mortgage Corp., by various means and through its policies, participated in the decision to grant credit to [*Couple 2*], including the rates and terms on which credit would be granted.

100. On information and belief, unbeknownst to [*Couple 2*], the contract APR on the mortgage loans were actually a combination of an objective, risk-based calculation and a totally subjective, discretionary component added pursuant to the Defendants' Discretionary Pricing Policy.

101. On information and belief, [*Couple 2*] were subject to the Defendants' Discretionary Pricing Policy.

102. On information and belief, [*Couple 2*] were charged a disproportionately greater amount in non-risk-related credit charges than similarly situated white persons.

103. [*Couple 2*] were not offered less expensive loan products that were available to borrowers with their credit characteristics directly from H & R Block or H & R Block Mortgage Corp.

Facts Relating To [*Couple 3*]

104. Plaintiffs, [*Couple 3*] reside at [*address*], Massachusetts with their three children, aged 5 years, 9 years and 11 years.

105. On or about August 4, 2006, [*Couple 3*] refinanced their previous Countrywide Home Loans, Inc. mortgage loan with Option One.

106. Option One split the refinance into two loans, [*loan number*], with a principal amount of $253,600.00 and [*loan number*], with a principal amount of $63,400.00.

107. The larger loan, [*loan number*], is a 30-year adjustable rate loan with a disclosed APR of 10.878%. According to the note, the loan had a two-year fixed rate followed by a 28-year variable rate feature.

108. According to the HUD-One Settlement Statement, [*Couple 3*] paid $11,651.65 in settlement charges in connection with the larger loan, including, a $5,072.00 broker fee to Maritime Mortgage ("Maritime"), an Option One authorized mortgage broker, a $950 underwriting fee to Option One, and a $50.00 funding fee to Option One.

109. True and correct copies of Truth-in-Lending disclosure and HUD-One Settlement Statement provided in connection with [*loan number*] are attached hereto and labeled *Exhibit 7* and *Exhibit 8* [*Editor's note: Not reprinted herein*], respectively.

110. The smaller loan, [*loan number*], is a 30-year fixed rate loan with a disclosed APR of 14.131%.

111. True and correct copies of Truth-in-Lending disclosure and HUD-One Settlement Statement provided in connection with [*loan number*] are attached hereto and labeled *Exhibit 9* and *Exhibit 10* [*Editor's note: Not reprinted herein*], respectively.

112. H & R Block and H & R Block Mortgage Corp., by various means and through its policies, participated in the decision to grant

credit to [*Couple 3*], including the rates and terms on which credit would be granted.

113. On information and belief, unbeknownst to [*Couple 3*], the contract APR on the mortgage loans were actually a combination of an objective, risk-based calculation and a totally subjective, discretionary component added pursuant to the Defendants' Discretionary Pricing Policy.

114. On information and belief, [*Couple 3*] were subject to the Defendants' Discretionary Pricing Policy.

115. On information and belief, [*Couple 3*] were charged a disproportionately greater amount in non-risk-related credit charges than similarly situated white persons.

116. [*Couple 3*] were not offered less expensive loan products that were available to borrowers with their credit characteristics directly from H & R Block or H & R Block Mortgage Corp.

Facts Relating To [*Consumer 7*]

117. Plaintiff, [*Consumer 7*] resides at [*address*], Massachusetts with his wife and their 11 year old daughter.

118. While serving a police detail on [*street name*] in [*town*], [*Consumer 7*] was approached by a mortgage broker from People's Choice Mortgage, Inc. ("People's Choice"), who told [*Consumer 7*] that he could find him a mortgage loan at a lower interest rate.

119. On or about September 29, 2006, [*Consumer 7*] refinanced his previous mortgage loan serviced by AMC Mortgage Services, Inc. with Option One.

120. The loan, [*loan number*], is a 30-year adjustable rate loan with a disclosed APR of 10.829%. According to the note, the loan has a two-year fixed rate followed by a 28-year variable rate feature. The loan note also requires a balloon payment of $340,057.01.

121. According to the HUD-1A Settlement Statement, [*Consumer 7*] paid $12,208.92 in settlement charges in connection with the loan, including, a $4,940.00 broker fee to People's Choice, an Option One authorized mortgage broker, a $500.00 processing fee to People's Choice, a $850.00 underwriting fee to Option One and a $50.00 funding fee to Option One. In addition, Option One paid a $4,940.00 yield spread premium to People's Choice for marking up the interest rate on the loan.

122. True and correct copies of Truth-in-Lending disclosure and HUD-1A Settlement Statement provided in connection with [*loan number*] are attached hereto and labeled *Exhibit 11* and *Exhibit 12* [*Editor's note: Not reprinted herein*], respectively.

123. H & R Block and H & R Block Mortgage Corp., by various means and through its policies, participated in the decision to grant credit to [*Consumer 7*], including the rates and terms on which credit would be granted.

124. On information and belief, unbeknownst to [*Consumer 7*], the contract APR on the mortgage loan was actually a combination of an objective, risk-based calculation and a totally subjective, discretionary component added pursuant to the Defendants' Discretionary Pricing Policy.

125. On information and belief, [*Consumer 7*] was subject to the Defendants' Discretionary Pricing Policy.

126. On information and belief, [*Consumer 7*] was charged a disproportionately greater amount in non-risk-related credit charges than similarly situated white persons.

127. [*Consumer 7*] was not offered less expensive loan products that were available to borrowers with their credit characteristics directly from H & R Block or H & R Block Mortgage Corp.

Facts Relating To [*Couple 4*]

128. Plaintiffs [*Couple 4*] reside at [*address*], Dorchester, Massachusetts 02124.

129. [*Editor's note: Blank in original.*]

130. [*Couple 4*] purchased their home in 1970 for approximately $15,900.00.

131. On August 24, 2007, [*Couple 4*] refinanced their existing home loan with a mortgage loan from Option One.

132. The loan, [*loan number*], was a 30-year, fixed rate loan with a disclosed APR of 10.699%. The loan amount was $321,950.00.

133. According to the HUD-One Settlement Statement, [*Couple 4*] paid $13,370.33 in settlement charges in connection with the loan including a $8,853.63 broker fee to People's Choice Mortgage Inc. ("People's Choice"), an Option One authorized mortgage broker, a $600 processing fee to People's Choice, a $350 application fee to People's Choice, a $850 underwriting fee to Option One and a $50 funding fee to Option One. On [*Couple 4*]'s loan, Option One paid additional broker compensation in the form of a $3,219.50 yield spread premium to People's Choice for marking up the interest rate on the loan.

134. True and correct copies of Truth-in-Lending disclosure and HUD-One Settlement Statement provided in connection with [*loan number*] are attached hereto and labeled *Exhibit 13* and *Exhibit 14* [*Editor's note: Not reprinted herein*], respectively.

135. H & R Block and H & R Block Mortgage, by various means and through their policies, participated in the decision to grant credit to [*Couple 4*], including the rates and terms on which credit would be granted.

136. On information and belief, unbeknownst to [*Couple 4*], the Contract APR on the mortgage loan was actually a combination of an objective, risk-based calculation and a totally subjective, discretionary component added pursuant to Defendants' Discretionary Pricing Policy.

137. On information and belief, [*Couple 4*] were subject to Defendants' Discretionary Pricing Policy.

138. On information and belief, [*Couple 4*] were charged a disproportionately greater amount in non-risk-related credit charges than similarly situated white persons.

139. Defendants did not offer [*Couple 4*] their less expensive loan products that were available to borrowers with their credit characteristics directly under Defendants' policies.

Facts Relating To [*Consumer 10*]

140. Plaintiff [*Consumer 10*] resides at [*address*], Illinois.

141. On or about August 5, 2005, [*Consumer 10*] refinanced her existing home loan with a mortgage loan from Option One.

142. The loan, [*loan number*], is a 30-year adjustable rate loan with a disclosed APR of 10.482%. The loan amount was $182,000.00. According to the note, the loan had a two-year fixed rate followed by a 28-year variable rate feature.

143. According to the HUD-One Settlement Statement, [*Consumer 10*] paid over $7,400 in settlement charges in connection with the loan, including, a $3,640 broker fee to Skyline Title, ("Skyline"), an Option One authorized mortgage broker, a $530 processing fee to Skyline, a $650 underwriting fee to Option One, and a $50 funding fee to Option One.

144. True and correct copies of the Truth-in-Lending disclosure and HUD-One Settlement Statement provided in connection with [*loan number*] are attached hereto and labeled *Exhibit 15* and *Exhibit 16* [*Editor's note: Not reprinted herein*], respectively.

145. H & R Block and H & R Block Mortgage, by various means and through its policies, participated in the decision to grant credit to [*Consumer 10*], including the rates and terms on which credit would be granted.

146. On information and belief, unbeknownst to [*Consumer 10*], the Contract APR on the mortgage loan was actually a combination of an objective, risk-based calculation and a totally subjective, discretionary component added pursuant to Defendants' Discretionary Pricing Policy.

147. On information and belief, [*Consumer 10*] was subject to Defendants' Discretionary Pricing Policy.

148. On information and belief, [*Consumer 10*] was charged a disproportionately greater amount in non-risk-related credit charges than similarly situated white persons.

149. Defendants did not offer [*Consumer 10*] its less expensive loan products that were available to borrowers with her credit characteristics directly under Defendants' policies.

Facts Relating To [*Consumer 11*]

150. Plaintiff [*Consumer 11*] resides at [*address*], Massachusetts.

151. In 2005, [*Consumer 11*] worked part time in H & R Block's call center as a customer service representative arranging appointments for people seeking tax preparation services.

152. During the time [*Consumer 11*] worked for H & R Block, an H & R Block Mortgage loan officer named Gilbert began calling her to suggest that she refinance her then existing home loan with Countrywide Home Loans ("Countrywide") with a loan from H & R Block Mortgage. [*Consumer 11*] does not know how Gilbert obtained her telephone number.

153. Prior to speaking with Gilbert, [*Consumer 11*] had no intention of refinancing her Countrywide loan and explained to Gilbert that she was not interested in refinancing.

154. However, Gilbert continued to call [*Consumer 11*] and eventually convinced her to refinance with H & R Block Mortgage.

155. [*Consumer 11*] refinanced her Countrywide loan with H & R Block Mortgage on May 16, 2005.

156. The loan, [*loan number*], is a 30-year adjustable rate loan with a disclosed APR of 11.759%. According to the note, the loan had a two-year fixed rate followed by a 28-year variable rate feature.

157. According to the HUD-1A Settlement Statement, [*Consumer 11*] paid $9,723.40 in settlement charges in connection with the loan, including, a $6,982.50 loan origination fee to H & R Block Mortgage and a $695 underwriting fee to H & R Block Mortgage.

158. True and correct copies of Truth-in-Lending disclosure and HUD-1A Settlement Statement provided in connection with [*loan number*] are attached hereto and labeled *Exhibit 17* and *Exhibit 18* [*Editor's note: Not reprinted herein*], respectively.

159. H & R Block and Option One by various means and through their policies, participated in the decision to grant credit to [*Consumer 11*], including the rates and terms on which credit would be granted.

160. On information and belief, unbeknownst to [*Consumer 11*], the Contract APR on the mortgage loan was actually a combination of an objective, risk-based calculation and a totally subjective, discretionary component added pursuant to Defendants' Discretionary Pricing Policy.

161. On information and belief, [*Consumer 11*] was subject to Defendants' Discretionary Pricing Policy.

162. On information and belief, [*Consumer 11*] was charged a disproportionately greater amount in non-risk-related credit charges than similarly situated white persons.

163. H & R Block Mortgage did not offer [*Consumer 11*] less expensive loan products that were available to borrowers with her credit characteristics directly under Defendants' policies.

Facts Relating To [*Consumer 12*]

164. Plaintiff [*Consumer 12*] resides at [*address*], Illinois.

165. On or about September 14, 2005, [*Consumer 12*] refinanced her existing home loan with a mortgage loan from Option One. The financing was arranged through Approved Financial, Inc. ("Approved Financial"), an Option One approved mortgage broker.

166. The loan, [*loan number*], is a 30-year adjustable rate loan with a disclosed APR of 9.807%. The loan amount was $130,878.56. This loan was a 2/28 ARM under which the interest rate can rise to 10.1% on the first change date, October 1, 2007, and thereafter can increase by 1% every six months up to a maximum of 13.1%. Option One or its closing agent provided [*Consumer 12*] with only one copy of the Federal Notice of Right To Cancel.

167. According to the HUD-One Settlement Statement, [*Consumer 12*] paid over $6,100.00 in settlement charges in connection with the loan, including, a $2,025.00 "Mortgage Broker Fee" to Approved Financial, a $300 "Application Fee" to Approved Financial, a $300 "processing fee" to Approved Financial, a $650 "underwriting fee" to Option One, and a $50 "funding fee" to Option One.

168. Option One also paid indirect broker compensation in the form of a $1,350.00 yield spread premium to Approved Financial, which imposed a substantial additional cost on [*Consumer 12*].

169. True and correct copies of the Truth-in-Lending disclosure and HUD-One Settlement Statement provided in connection with [*loan number*] are attached hereto and labeled *Exhibit 19* and *Exhibit 20* [*Editor's note: Not reprinted herein*], respectively.

170. H & R Block and H & R Block Mortgage, by various means and through its policies, participated in the decision to grant credit to [*Consumer 12*], including the rates and terms on which credit would be granted.

171. On information and belief, unbeknownst to [*Consumer 12*], the Contract APR on the mortgage loan was actually a combination of an objective, risk-based calculation and a totally subjective, discretionary component added pursuant to Defendants' Discretionary Pricing Policy.

172. On information and belief, [*Consumer 12*] was subject to Defendants' Discretionary Pricing Policy.

173. On information and belief, [*Consumer 12*] was charged a disproportionately greater amount in non-risk-related credit charges than similarly situated white persons.

174. Defendants did not offer [*Consumer 12*] its less expensive loan products that were available to borrowers with her credit characteristics directly under Defendants' policies.

DISCOVERY/FRAUDULENT CONCEALMENT (TOLLING)

175. While long suspected, mortgage lending discrimination has only recently been disclosed and quantified. It has only been in the last few years that mortgage lenders have been required to submit details of their subprime home loans under the Home Mortgage Disclosure Act. The groups that have studied predatory lending and the mortgage market have uncovered incredible racial disparities in the types of mortgages offered.

176. The causes of action alleged herein accrued upon discovery of the discriminatory impact of the Defendants' Discretionary Pricing Policy. Plaintiffs and members of the Class did not discover and could not have discovered through the exercise of reasonable diligence the

factual bases of those claims. Indeed, the data forming the basis of Plaintiffs' claims only recently was released and analyzed in a comprehensive manner. Moreover, because the Defendants knowingly and actively concealed the facts alleged herein, Plaintiffs and the Class have been kept ignorant of vital information essential to the pursuit of these claims, without any fault or lack of diligence on their part.

177. Commission-driven, discretionary pricing systems, such as those used in the mortgage industry and structurally similar to the system utilized by the Defendants, have been found to produce significant discriminatory effects. Knowledge concerning the significant and pervasive discriminatory impact of such commission-driven, discretionary credit pricing systems has been widely circulated within the financing industry for several years, as a result of numerous actions by the United States Department of Justice and federal regulatory agencies. *See*, Facts, section A *supra*. Thus, the Defendants knew or should have known that their credit pricing system causes minority homeowners to pay more for mortgage financing than the amounts paid by white customers with identical or effectively identical credit scores.

178. Despite the fact that the Defendants knew or should have known of the discriminatory effect of their Discretionary Pricing Policy, none of the loan documents inform the customer that its finance rates ultimately are subjective and not based solely on risk-related characteristics.

179. The Defendants were and are under a continuous nondelegable duty to disclose to the Plaintiffs and Class material information regarding their loans. The fact that certain loan terms are subjective and discretionary is information a reasonable borrower would consider important when deciding whether to accept the loan and on what terms. The fact that the subjective and discretionary components result in a disparate impact on minority is also information a reasonable minority borrower would consider important.

180. The Defendants failed to disclose this information, however, and Plaintiffs and Class Members reasonably relied upon the Defendants' representation that terms of their loans would be based on their creditworthiness. The Defendants' financing documents falsely fostered the image that the Defendants offer competitive rates that objectively are set. However, the Defendants never disclosed to its credit applicants the fact that: (a) its credit rates are subjective and can vary significantly among persons with identical credit profiles; and (b) it had authorized and provided a financial incentive to mortgage brokers to subjectively increase the credit rate above the rate otherwise available to the homeowner.

181. Due to the inherent nature of the Defendants' undisclosed Discretionary Pricing Policy and due to the Defendants' deception and concealment, the Defendants' minority customers had no way of knowing or suspecting: (a) the existence of the Defendants' subjective credit pricing policy; (b) that they were charged additional subjective credit charges; (c) that they were charged a disproportionately greater amount for their cost of credit than similarly situated white persons, and or (d) that any part of the loan price was negotiable. Thus, the Defendants are estopped from relying on any statutes of limitation in their defenses of this action.

CLASS ALLEGATIONS

182. Plaintiffs repeat and re-allege every allegation above as if set forth herein in full.

183. Plaintiffs sue on their own behalf and on behalf of a class of persons under Rules 23(a) and (b)(2) and (b)(3) of the Federal Rules of Civil Procedure.

184. This class action is brought pursuant to ECOA and the FHA by the individual named Plaintiffs on behalf of themselves and all minority consumers (the "Class") who obtained an Option One home mortgage loan in the United States between January 1, 2001 and the date of judgment in this action (the "Class Period") and who were subject to the Defendants' Discretionary Pricing Policy pursuant to which they paid discretionary points, fees or interest mark-ups in connection with their loan. The term "minority" refers to blacks and Hispanics as defined by federal law.

185. The phrase "Discretionary Pricing Policy" refers to the Defendants' policy of authorizing its loan officers and brokers to impose subjective, discretionary charges and interest mark-ups that are included in the finance charge loans they originate.

186. Plaintiffs do not know the exact size or identities of the proposed Class, since such information is in the exclusive control of the Defendants. Plaintiffs believe that the Class encompasses many thousands or tens of thousands of individuals who are dispersed geographically throughout the United States. Therefore, the proposed class is so numerous that joinder of all members is impracticable.

187. All members of the Class have been subject to and affected by the same Discretionary Pricing Policy. There are questions of law and fact that are common to the Class, and predominate over any questions affecting only individual members of the Class. These questions include, but are not limited to the following:

a. the nature, scope and operations of Defendants' Discretionary Pricing Policy;

b. whether H & R Block, Inc., H & R Block Bank, Option One, and H & R Block Mortgage are creditors under the ECOA because, for example, in the ordinary course of its business they participate in the decision as to whether or not to extend credit to consumers;

c. whether the Defendants' Discretionary Pricing Policy is a facially neutral credit pricing system that has effected racial discrimination in violation of ECOA;

d. whether there are statistically significant disparities between the amount of the discretionary charges imposed on minority persons and the amount of the discretionary charges imposed on white persons that are unrelated to creditworthiness;

e. whether any legitimate business reason for the Discretionary Pricing Policy can be achieved by a credit pricing system less discriminatory in its impact;

f. whether the Court can enter declaratory and injunctive relief;

g. the proper measure of actual and/or punitive damages and/or restitution; and

h. the proper measure of disgorgement and/or other relief for unjust enrichment.

188. The claims of the individual named Plaintiffs are typical of the claims of the Class and do not conflict with the interests of any other members of the Class in that both the Plaintiffs and the other members of the Class were subject to the same Discretionary Pricing Policy that disproportionately has affected minority homeowners.

189. The individual named Plaintiffs will fairly and adequately represent the interests of the Class. They are committed to the vigorous prosecution of the Class' claims and have retained attorneys who are qualified to pursue this litigation and have experience in class actions—in particular, consumer protection and discrimination actions.

190. A class action is superior to other methods for the fast and efficient adjudication of this controversy. A class action regarding the issues in this case does not create any problems of manageability.

191. In the alternative, Defendants have acted or refused to act on grounds generally applicable to the class, thereby making appropriate final injunctive relief or corresponding declaratory relief with respect to the Class as a whole.

COUNT I

DISCRIMINATION IN VIOLATION OF THE EQUAL CREDIT OPPORTUNITY ACT

192. Plaintiffs repeat and re-allege every allegation above as if set forth herein in full.

193. The Defendants are creditors as defined in ECOA, and in the ordinary course of its business, participated in the decision of whether or not to extend credit to the Plaintiffs, the proposed Class representatives herein, and all prospective Class members.

194. The Defendants designed, disseminated, controlled, implemented and profited from the discriminatory policy and practice alleged herein—the Discretionary Pricing Policy—which has had a disparate economic impact on minorities compared to similarly situated whites.

195. All actions taken by Option One's loan officers and authorized brokers were in accordance with the specific authority granted to them by Option One and were in furtherance of the Defendants' policies and practices.

196. As a result of the Defendants' Discretionary Pricing Policy, the Defendants have collected more in finance charges from minority borrowers than from similarly situated white persons, for reasons unrelated to credit risk.

197. The Defendants' Discretionary Pricing Policy violates the Equal Credit Opportunity Act.

198. Plaintiffs and prospective class members are aggrieved persons as defined in ECOA by virtue of having been subject to the Defendants' discriminatory, Discretionary Pricing Policy.

COUNT II

DISCRIMINATION IN VIOLATION OF THE FAIR HOUSING ACT

199. Plaintiffs repeat and re-allege every allegation above as if set forth herein in full.

200. The Defendants engaged in residential real estate-related transactions with respect to the Plaintiffs, the proposed Class representatives herein, and all prospective Class members.

201. The Defendants' Discretionary Pricing Policy has resulted in discrimination with respect to the Plaintiffs, the proposed Class representatives herein, and all prospective members of the Class.

202. As a result of the Defendants' Discretionary Pricing Policy, the Defendants have collected more in finance charges from minorities than from similarly situated white persons, for reasons unrelated to credit risk.

203. The Defendants' Discretionary Pricing Policy violates the Fair Housing Act and constitutes actionable discrimination on the basis of race.

204. Plaintiffs and the Class are aggrieved persons as defined in FHA by virtue of having been subject to the Defendants' discriminatory, Discretionary Pricing Policy.

PRAYER FOR RELIEF

WHEREFORE, the Plaintiffs respectfully request the following relief:

a. Certify this case as a class action and certify the named Plaintiffs herein to be adequate class representatives and their counsel to be class counsel;

b. Enter a judgment, pursuant to 15 U.S.C. § 1691e(c) and/or 42 U.S.C. § 3613, declaring the acts and practices of Defendants complained of herein to be in violation of ECOA and the FHA;

c. Grant a permanent or final injunction, pursuant to 15 U.S.C. 1691e(c) and/or 42 U.S.C. § 3613(c), enjoining the Defendants, and the Defendants' agents and employees, affiliates and subsidiaries, from continuing to discriminate against Plaintiffs and the members of the Class because of their race through further use of the Discretionary Pricing Policy or any other non-risk-related discretionary pricing policy employed by the Defendants;

d. Order the Defendants, pursuant to 15 U.S.C. § 1691e(c) and/or 42 U.S.C. § 3613(c), to adopt and enforce a policy that requires appropriate training of the Defendants' employees and its brokers and correspondent lenders to prevent discrimination;

e. Order the Defendants, pursuant to 15 U.S.C. § 1691e(c) and/or 42 U.S.C. § 3613(c), to monitor and/or audit the racial pattern of its financings to ensure the cessation of discriminatory effects in its home mortgage transactions;

f. Order disgorgement, pursuant to 15 U.S.C. § 1691e(c), of all disproportionate non-risk charges imposed on minorities by the Defendants' Discretionary Pricing Policy; and order the equitable distribution of such charges to all appropriate class members; together with other relief for unjust enrichment;

g. Order actual and punitive damages and/or restitution to the Plaintiffs and the Class pursuant to 42 U.S.C. § 3613(c);

h. Award Plaintiffs the costs of this action, including the fees and costs of experts, together with reasonable attorneys' fees, pursuant to 15 U.S.C. § 1691e(d) and/or 42 U.S.C. § 3613(c); and

i. Grant Plaintiffs and the Class such other and further relief as this Court finds necessary and proper.

JURY TRIAL DEMANDED

Plaintiffs demand a trial by jury on all issues so triable.

Respectfully submitted,

Attorney for Plaintiffs

G.3 Sample Complaint Alleging Discriminatory Mark-Up Practices Against Automobile Financer

A team of lawyers is responsible for litigating on behalf of consumers in this ECOA auto finance race discrimination class action. The attorneys of record include [*attorneys for consumers*].

IN THE UNITED STATES DISTRICT COURT
FOR THE MIDDLE DISTRICT OF TENNESSEE
AT NASHVILLE

————————————)	
[*Consumer 1*], [*Consumer 2*],)	
[*Consumer 3*], [*Consumer 4*],)	
[*Consumer 5*], [*Consumer 6*],)	
[*Consumer 7*] and [*Consumer 8*])	
on behalf of themselves and all)	
others similarly situated)	
Plaintiffs,)	Civil No. ———————
)	
v.)	
)	
Nissan Motor Acceptance)	
Corporation,)	
Defendant.)	
————————————)	

SIXTH AMENDED CLASS ACTION COMPLAINT

NOW come the Plaintiffs, [*Consumer 1*], [*Consumer 2*], [*Consumer 3*], [*Consumer 4*], [*Consumer 5*], [*Consumer 6*], [*Consumer 7*] and [*Consumer 8*] on behalf of themselves and all others similarly situated, and hereby sue the defendant, stating their cause of action:

I. SHORT AND PLAIN STATEMENT

This is a class action brought by plaintiffs, on behalf of themselves and other similarly situated African-Americans, against Nissan Motor Acceptance Corporation (NMAC) under the Equal Credit Opportunity Act, 15 U.S.C § 1691, *et seq.* (ECOA) to remedy the discriminatory effects of NMAC's policy and practices in providing motor vehicle financing.

NMAC has established a specific, identifiable and uniform credit pricing system, a component of which, referred to herein as the NMAC markup policy, authorizes unchecked, subjective markup of an objective risk-based financing rate. In other words, after a finance rate acceptable to NMAC is determined by objective criteria (i.e., the individual's credit history and deal circumstances), NMAC's credit pricing policy authorizes a subjective markup of that amount. NMAC policy sets the range of markup and determines which loans are subject to markup. The effect of this credit pricing policy is a widespread discriminatory impact on African-American financing applicants, in violation of ECOA. Plaintiffs seek declaratory and injunctive relief, disgorgement and restitution of monies disparately obtained from African-Americans.

II. PARTIES

1. Plaintiffs [*Consumer 1*], [*Consumer 2*], [*Consumer 3*], [*Consumer 4*], [*Consumer 5*], [*Consumer 6*], [*Consumer 7*] and [*Consumer 8*] are African-American adult citizens and residents of Tennessee.

2. Defendant Nissan Motor Acceptance Corporation ("NMAC") is a foreign corporation with its principal place of business at 990 W. 190th Street, Torrance, California. NMAC is a corporation organized, existing, and doing business under the laws of the State of California. NMAC is a subsidiary of Nissan Motor Corporation, USA. NMAC is the American financial arm of Nissan Company, a worldwide Japanese conglomerate.

III. JURISDICTION AND VENUE

3. This Court has jurisdiction over this action and venue is proper. Defendant transacts substantial business in Tennessee, primarily the financing of automobiles, and all or part of defendant's acts alleged in this complaint occurred in the Middle District of Tennessee.

4. This action presents a disparate impact claim based on the Equal Credit Opportunity Act (ECOA), 15 USC § 1691 *et seq.* This Court has original jurisdiction pursuant to 28 USC § 1331 to hear claims based upon the ECOA.

IV. TERMINOLOGY

5. The following terms, as used herein, have the following meanings:

a. **Non-recourse**—"Non-recourse" means that the assignee of a loan agreement cannot require payment by the assignor in the event of the default of the obligor. In a "non-recourse" automobile finance transaction, the finance company (NMAC) bears all the risk of default and the dealer never bears any of the risk of default. After the NMAC finance forms are completed by the customer, the dealer "assigns" the NMAC agreements to NMAC and NMAC then pays the dealer the amount financed as listed on the installment agreement. If the consumer later defaults, the dealer keeps the money it received from NMAC, owes NMAC nothing and has no responsibility regarding the default. The automobile transactions that are included in the proposed class definition are all "non-recourse" transactions.

b. **Tier**—"Tiers" are categories of risk that are assigned after evaluating many factors relative to the person and the proposed purchase. NMAC began using a tier based financing system in approximately 1990. Letter designations are used. "A" tier is the most credit worthy applicant who receives the lowest available rate. "B", "C" and "D" tier customers are progressively less credit worthy and are eligible for progressively higher rates. At different times, NMAC tiers have been referred to by names, numbers and letters. Regardless of the labels given the tiers, the concept is the same, NMAC categorizes its customers by risk and establishes an appropriate risk-related finance charge rate after considering numerous individual and deal attributes. All NMAC customers are assigned a risk tier.

c. **Buy Rate**—"Buy Rate" is the minimum interest rate required by NMAC for a particular transaction. The buy rate for a particular transaction is based on the credit risk tier the customer is assigned by NMAC. Thus, the buy rate is the minimum finance charge for a particular customer after consideration of all risk related variables pertaining to the customer's purchase. The buy rate is always set by NMAC and is never set by the dealer.

d. **Rate Sheets**—"Rate Sheets" or "Dealer Bulletins" refer to the notices that NMAC periodically sends its dealers informing the dealers of the buy rate for the different tiers. In addition to informing the dealer of the buy rate for the different tiers, the rate sheets inform the dealer how much they are allowed to markup the buy rate for each particular tier.

e. **Contract APR**—"Contract APR" (Annual Percentage Rate) is the total finance charge stated as a percentage as shown on the customer's retail installment contract.

f. **Finance Charge Markup**—"Finance Charge Markup" (Markup) is the non-risk finance charge added to the buy rate. Finance charge markup is paid by the customer to NMAC, as a component of the total finance charge (Contract APR), without the customer ever knowing that a portion of their Contract APR was markup. The term "points" is sometimes used to describe markup.

g. **Maximum Markup**—"Maximum Markup" is the maximum number of percentage points that NMAC authorizes a dealer to markup a particular transaction above the risk based buy rate. NMAC sets the dealer markup limit at various amounts depending on the tier and the particular program that the individual is financing under, such as the college graduate program (1% markup limit). In some cases, NMAC does not allow the dealer to markup the buy rate at all and in some cases it allows the dealer to markup the buy rate as much as 5 points.

h. **Dealer Participation**—"Dealer Participation" or "Dealer Commission" is that portion of the markup payable to the dealer by NMAC. During the relevant time period, the dealer has received either 75% or 77% of the markup and NMAC has kept the remainder. None of the NMAC designed forms that the customers are required to sign inform the customers of the markup policy system, or about dealer participation.

i. **NMAC Participation**—"NMAC Participation" is that portion of the markup not included in "Dealer Participation." During the relevant time period, NMAC has kept either 23% or 25% of the markup and the remainder has been paid to the dealer.

V. NMAC'S STRUCTURE

6. NMAC engages in the business of financing vehicles throughout Tennessee and the United States, through dealer/agents who serve as NMAC's credit arrangers/originators. NMAC finances more than 100,000 vehicles annually, all through its dealer arrangers/originators.

7. NMAC promotes and advertises financing expertise, and simple, flexible and convenient vehicle loans which are provided by NMAC at over 1200 Nissan dealerships nationwide.

8. Consumers in Tennessee and throughout the United States are encouraged to visit Nissan dealers to obtain NMAC vehicle financing.

9. In 1991, NMAC consolidated its retail financing operations in its Dallas, Texas processing center. Out of its central processing center, NMAC provides retail financing through approximately twelve hundred (1200) Nissan dealers in the United States.

10. NMAC does not provide automobile financing outside the United States and does not finance anything except vehicles within the United States. NMAC's retail financing system is virtually identical throughout the country.

11. NMAC's buy rates, credit risk tiers, markup limits, credit worthiness requirements, credit approval process, retail installment contract forms, approval notification form, and application forms are the same throughout the United States.

12. The only differences among states involve state usury laws, which would only be applicable to cases in which NMAC's buy rate plus NMAC's maximum markup rate exceed the state usury cap. For instance, most of NMAC's business in Arkansas is Tier A (Preferred) because of the Arkansas usury law.

13. NMAC acknowledges the virtual uniformity of its retail financing system throughout the United States. Without waiving any of the foregoing objections, there are no differences between states in the way that NMAC receives credit applications, reviews and analyzes credit applications and assigns applicants to the appropriate tier, except from time to time NMAC may choose to limit the number of retail contracts it purchases in certain States. Any differences in buy rates would be limited or qualified by any usury limitations imposed by state statute. Any differences in the number of points that can be added to the buy rate for any particular tier would be dictated by usury and other consumer finance laws in any particular state. There are no differences by state in the tier structures, dealers' discretion to charge finance rates greater than NMAC's buy rate, percentage of finance charge paid to dealers or in the way dealers are paid. (NMAC's Response to Plaintiffs' Second Set of Interrogatories, Interrogatory No. 1).

VI. NMAC'S MARKETING

14. NMAC markets its automobile retail financing services to the public under the name "*Signature*FINANCING from NMAC:"

> When you buy or lease with *Signature*FINANCING from Nissan Motor Acceptance Corporation (NMAC), you've made a wise choice. Because with NMAC you get a partner dedicated to one business—providing lease and loan financing for Nissan vehicles. And a company committed to one goal—exceptional customer service. *Signature*FINANCING offers attractive rates and terms, fast response, and financing that is simple, flexible, and convenient. Only for Nissan customers and only from Nissan Motor Acceptance Corporation. (NMAC Web Page, *Signature*FINANCING from NMAC)

15. In its advertising, NMAC gives consumers two options for applying for credit. For consumers who desire to obtain NMAC's *Signature*FINANCING, they are given the option of applying directly through NMAC over the internet or they are directed to apply at NMAC dealers.

16. The customers who choose to apply directly to NMAC over the internet and who are approved, are provided a list of dealerships where they can go to complete the financing process.

17. In addition to referring customers to dealers through consumer advertising, NMAC also sends letters to existing customers with good payment records, informs them that they are pre-approved for additional NMAC financing and provides them documentation of their pre-approval to take to a NMAC dealership to consummate the new finance transaction.

18. Although there are various marketing programs used by NMAC, all of NMAC's marketing programs ultimately direct consumers to NMAC's dealers for consummation of the finance transaction.

VII. NMAC'S DEALER PROGRAM

19. The contractual relationship between NMAC and its non-recourse dealers is outlined in a one page agreement titled "RETAIL PLAN—WITHOUT RECOURSE."

20. The dealer agreement incorporates by reference dealer bulletins (rate sheets) which are used periodically to convey buy rates, markup limits, dealer participation, etc.

21. The dealer bulletins make it clear that NMAC financing must be initiated by a customer completing a NMAC credit application.

22. NMAC provides credit applications, retail Installment contracts, agreements to provide insurance, co-signer agreements, corporate/

partnership resolutions and warranty disclaimers to its dealer arrangers/originators, without charge.

23. NMAC provides training to its dealers through a "dealer hotline" including training related to properly filling out NMAC required forms and, when the design of the forms changes, NMAC sends people to its dealers to reprogram the dealer's computers to work with the new forms.

24. NMAC provides training to dealers, including training regarding "basic selling techniques." One of the job duties of NMAC's sales representatives is to "Assess training needs in assigned dealerships and provide appropriate training in product knowledge and basic selling techniques to dealer personnel."

VIII. STRUCTURE OF NMAC'S CREDIT PRICING SYSTEM

A. The Dealer's Role

25. In NMAC's non-recourse retail financing program, the dealer assumes the role of a credit "arranger" or credit "originator."

26. As an arranger/originator, for customers who are not pre-approved by NMAC, NMAC's non-recourse dealers submit loan applications to NMAC via fax and NMAC faxes back the credit decision to the dealer.

27. NMAC's credit decision is analyzed and communicated back to the dealer anywhere from a nanosecond to thirty (30) minutes.

28. NMAC dealers receive a credit decision on 48% of the applications within a matter of seconds and the remaining 52% average approximately a thirty (30) minute turnaround time.

29. When NMAC is closed, NMAC dealers have the option of using "*Signature*EXPRESS," a NMAC system which grants automatic approval of transactions meeting certain specified criteria.

30. The "*Signature*EXPRESS" program grants automatic approval to credit customers who have a credit bureau credit score that meets a certain criteria and assigns those customers to a credit tier based on the same credit score.

31. Dealers are allowed to add markup to "*Signature*EXPRESS" automatic approvals in the same manner as a pre-approved customer or customers approved through the credit application process.

32. Regardless of the method in which NMAC's credit approval is obtained and the credit tier assigned, the dealer's role is the same. The dealer must comply fully with NMAC's policies and limitations and must complete the NMAC credit forms properly.

33. After obtaining credit approval from NMAC, and after NMAC assigns the credit worthiness tier and the risk-related buy rate, the dealer is then permitted to add the non-risk markup.

34. In setting the markup within the rules and limitations established by NMAC, non-recourse dealers have no reason to consider whether the vehicle is new or used, the number of months being financed, credit worthiness of the customer, occupation of the customer, income of the customer, model of the vehicle being purchased, the trade-in being made or any other risk related variable. Those factors have already been considered by NMAC, who bears the risk.

35. Once an NMAC dealer obtains the customers signature on the NMAC documents, the dealer "pays itself" for the automobile with a NMAC "sight draft" which NMAC provides to the dealer and authorizes the dealer to sign.

36. The NMAC dealer plays no role whatsoever in the process of approving or declining the customer's credit application, establishing the credit risk tier of the customer, or establishing the risk based buy rate component of the contract APR.

37. The dealer's only role in setting the terms of the credit transaction is in the imposition of the non-risk markup, which must be within the parameters authorized by NMAC.

38. The controlling mechanism regarding the imposition of markup is the agreement between the finance company and the dealership. All automobile finance companies, like NMAC, have their own rules and guidelines regarding whether a dealer is allowed to add markup and the limitations thereof.

39. NMAC's "Non-Recourse Dealer Agreement" is the same throughout the United States.

B. NMAC'S Role

40. Unlike the dealer, NMAC bears the full risk of the credit transaction. As the risk-bearer, NMAC employs a sophisticated and highly automated credit analysis process designed to categorize NMAC applicants into credit risk tiers.

41. In determining the appropriate tier, NMAC considers numerous risk related variables including credit bureau histories, payment amount, payment to income ratio, debt ratio, monthly rental obligation, monthly mortgage obligation, bankruptcies, automobile repossessions, charge-offs, foreclosures, payment histories and various other risk related attributes or variables.

42. NMAC's credit evaluation process is a proprietary credit scoring procedure that was developed utilizing a computerized regression analysis after reviewing the credit reports and two years of payment history on two hundred and thirty thousand (230,000) NMAC accounts.

43. NMAC's risk tier assignment process is an objective and automated credit scoring process.

44. NMAC touts its objective and automated tier assignment system as being "unbiased."

45. NMAC is also aware that a purely judgmental system is "more apt to be influenced by bias."

46. Despite recognizing the virtues of an objective based credit pricing system and the corresponding perils of a purely judgmental system, NMAC authorizes, provides incentives for and shares in the profits of the totally subjective markup policy.

47. If a dealer doesn't markup the buy rate, NMAC pays the dealer $100.00 to $150.00 out of the buy rate portion of the finance charge to the dealer as compensation for its role in packaging the finance transaction.

48. By providing the dealer an incentive to markup the buy rate, NMAC not only can keep for itself 23%–25% of the markup, but can keep the entire buy rate portion of the finance charge, undiminished by the dealer's $100.00–$150.00 flat rate compensation.

49. NMAC's credit pricing system empowers NMAC's dealer arrangers/originators to subjectively raise rates at will and rewards the dealer arranger/originators and NMAC for doing so.

50. NMAC, by providing a lucrative enticement to its dealers, obtains benefits from even the dealer participation component of markup which promotes dealer "referrals".

51. The markup policy destroys the objective and non-bias qualities of the automated risk tier system and results in a discriminatory credit pricing system.

52. Although NMAC has a practice of soliciting credit applications direct from the public over the internet, advertising and promoting its "attractive rates and terms" throughout the country, pre-approving existing customers for additional NMAC financing, requiring all customers to apply for credit via a NMAC credit application, and requiring all customers to execute a NMAC retail installment contract, it

stringently enforces a company policy forbidding disclosure of the actual risk based rate to the customers.

53. None of the NMAC documents that finance customers are required to sign disclose the buy rate or the existence of the markup policy.

54. In 1997, [*Consumer 1's and Consumer 2's*] counsel wrote NMAC and inquired as to whether any portion of the 19.49% rate was kicked back or rebated to the dealer. At the time of the inquiry, neither [*Consumer 2*] or [*Consumer 1*] nor any representative of [*Consumers 1 and 2*], knew whether or not [*Consumer 1's and Consumer 2's*] 19.49% rate was equal to or in excess of NMAC's required rate. The letter asked the following questions:

1. How was the finance charge that [*Consumer 1*] and [*Consumer 2*] were required to pay determined?

2. Who made the determination regarding the finance charge rate that [*Consumers 1 and 2*] were required to pay?

3. Is any of the finance charge that [*Consumers 1 and 2*] are paying being "shared" or "rebated" in any manner to any other person or entity?

4. If any of the finance charge that [*Consumers 1 and 2*] are paying is being "kicked back" or "rebated", or will be in the future, to any other person or entity, please inform me what portion of the finance charge is being "kicked back" or "rebated."

55. NMAC's Legal Compliance Office responded, but refused to acknowledge that the markup policy even existed and reported that NMAC's only involvement in [*Consumer 1's and Consumer 2's*] transaction was as a detached after the fact purchaser of the note.

> With regard to your questions concerning finance charges, the interest rate or finance charge is based on a number of factors, including credit-worthiness of the customer. NMAC does not disclose information regarding the contractual and business relationship between NMAC and authorized independent Nissan dealerships. NMAC is a financing entity only, and as such, is not privy to the negotiations between the customer and the dealer. We merely purchase, or are an assignee of, the contract. However, in any event, [*Consumers 1 and 2*] signed the contract agreeing to that interest rate.

56. NMAC's position regarding its involvement in automobile financing, as communicated by its Legal Compliance Office, is starkly different than the image broadcast to the public through brochures, radio, television, newspaper and various other print advertisements. NMAC presents to the world, through its world wide web site, a very involved and active image:

> Three million satisfied NMAC customers are proof positive that we not only provide the funds for their dreams, but that we're also there to answer questions, respond to inquiries, and give unsurpassed customer service. The kind of service that keeps satisfied customers coming back to NMAC again and again.

> At NMAC, we have the financing expertise you expect. We provide Nissan shoppers like you with simple, flexible and convenient loans and leases at more than 1,100 Nissan dealerships nationwide.

> So visit your Nissan dealer soon. Nissan is ready to help you turn a promising test drive into a long and very rewarding journey.

57. NMAC controls and/or influences every aspect of the dealer originated finance program by:

a. Requiring and providing specific NMAC forms to be used and training dealers regarding how to complete the NMAC required finance forms;

b. Evaluating the credit worthiness of each customer and assigning each to a credit risk tier;

c. Establishing the buy rate for each finance transaction based on the risk based tier assignment;

d. Providing a financial incentive for the dealership to add subjective non-risk charges (finance charge markup) to the risk based buy rate which rewards both the dealer and NMAC;

e. Establishing the maximum markup rate for each finance transaction;

f. Determining which loans are subject to markup;

g. Programming dealer's computers to utilize NMAC forms and training its dealers regarding "basic training techniques"; and

h. Establishing the "Dealer Participation" and "NMAC Participation" split for each transaction, which divides the markup between the dealer and NMAC.

IX. NMAC'S ECOA AWARENESS AND FAILURE TO COMPLY

58. The financial industry, including NMAC, has been put on notice for years that commission driven discretionary pricing systems in the real estate mortgage industry, like the system utilized by NMAC, produce significant discriminatory effects.

59. Unlike the real estate mortgage industry, which is required by federal law to collect race information, the automobile financing industry exploits its exemption from gathering race information for ECOA compliance monitoring purposes in order to feign ignorance of the discriminatory impact of its discretionary pricing systems.

60. NMAC has analyzed its data and confirmed the discriminatory effects of its commission driven discretionary pricing system and chosen to ignore and conceal the discriminatory impact.

61. Notice of the discriminatory effect of its commission driven discretionary pricing system, which NMAC has known for years, was distributed throughout the financing and banking industry as a result of legal proceedings by the United States Department of Justice involving similar commission driven discretionary pricing systems in the real estate mortgage industry, including:

a. *United States v. First National Bank of Vicksburg*, No. 5:94 CV 6(B)(N) (S.D. Miss. filed Jan. 21, 1994) (charging African-Americans higher interest rates);

b. *United States v. Blackpipe State Bank*, Civ. Act. No. 93-5115 (D. S.D. filed November 16, 1993) (charging American Indians higher interest rates);

c. *United States v. Huntington Mortgage Co.*, No. 1; 95 CV 2211 (N.D. Ohio filed October 18, 1995) (charging African-Americans higher fees);

d. *United States v. Security State Bank of Pecos*, No. SA 95 CA 0996 (W.D. Tex. filed October 15, 1995) (charging Hispanics higher interest rates);

e. *United States v. First National Bank of Gordon*, No. CIV-96-5035 (W.D.S.D. filed April 15, 1996) (charging American Indians higher interest rates);

f. *United States v. Fleet Mortgage Corp.*, No. 96-2279 (E.D.N.Y. filed May 7, 1996) (charging African-Americans and Hispanics higher interest rates); and

g. *United States v. Long Beach Mortgage Co.*, No. CV-96-6159 (C.D. Cal. filed Sept. 5, 1996) (charging African-Americans, Latinos, women and persons over age 55 higher interest rates).

62. Notice of the discriminatory effect of its commission driven subjective pricing was also distributed throughout the automobile financing and banking industries as a result of a plethora of articles in trade journals following the United States Department of Justice legal proceedings, including:

Two Banks To Pay Damages Following Justice Probes Into Lending Discrimination, Department of Justice Press Release 94-027 (Jan. 21, 1994).

Steve Cocheo, *Justice Department Sues Tiny South Dakota Bank for Loan Bias*, ABA Banking J., Jan. 1994, at 6.

Miles Maguire, *Blackpipe Case; Banker Charged With Bias Called Friend of the Sioux*, Reg. Compliance Watch, Apr. 18, 1994, at 1.

Steve Cocheo, *Can Banks Lend in Indian Country?*, ABA Banking J., May 1994, at 42.

Jaret Seiberg, *Maryland Thrift In Settlement with Justice Department*, Am. Banker, Aug. 23, 1994, at 1.

Holly Boss, *Chevy Chase Federal Reaches $11 Million Pact*, Wall St. J., Aug. 23, 1994, at A2.

Michelle Singletary, *Who's Next After Chevy Chase?*, Wash. Post, Aug. 26, 1994, at B1.

Jaret Seiberg, *Industry Sees Dangerous Extension Of Bias for Discrimination Complaints*, Am. Banker, Aug. 23, 1994, at 4.

Chevy Chase Settlement, Wash. Post, Aug. 23, 1994, at A18.

Chicago Area Lender Agrees with Justice Department to Settle Lending Discrimination Claims, Department of Justice Press Release 95-306 (June 1, 1995).

Justin Fox, *Northern Trust Settles U.S. Suit by Agreeing to Pay Minorities*, Am. Banker, June 2, 1995, at 2.

Ohio Mortgage Company Agrees to Compensate African Americans Charged Higher Prices for Home Mortgages than Whites, Department of Justice Press Release 95-540 (October 18, 1995).

Kenneth R. Harney, *Lender Agrees to Settle Suit on Hidden Fees*, L.A. Times, July 7, 1996, at 1.

Ford Finance Settles in Broker Fee Litigation, Mortgage Marketplace, July 8, 1996, at 4.

Ford Files Settlement in Case Involving Broker Overages, Inside Fair Lending, Sept. 1996, at 9.

Stephen Phillips, *Lenders Likely to Review Policies*, Plain Dealer, Oct. 20, 1995, at 1C.

Edward Hulkosky, *HUD Cracks Down on High-Cost FHA Loans*, Am. Banker, Oct. 20, 1994, at 13.

Jaret Seiberg, *Huntington's Loan Bias Settlement with Justice Department Stirs Debate*, Am. Banker, Oct. 25, 1995, at 1.

Texas Banks to Pay $500,000 for Charging Hispanic Borrowers Higher Interest Rates than Equally Qualified Non-Hispanics, Department of Justice Press Release 95-541 (Oct. 18, 1995).

Justice Department Sues Nebraska Bank for Allegedly Charging Na-

tive Americans Higher Interest Rates, Department of Justice Press Release 96-165 (Apr. 15, 1996).

Nebraska Bank Nailed for Illegal Pricing, Regulatory Compliance Watch, Apr. 22, 1996, at 1.

Fleet Subsidiary To Pay $4 Million to Settle Claims that Blacks and Hispanics Were Charged Higher Loan Prices than Whites, Department of Justice Press Release 96-211 (May 7, 1996).

Kimberly Blanton, *Fleet Mortgage Settles Loan Bias Suit; Will Pay $4M to Minority Customers, End Justice Probe*, Boston Globe, May 8, 1996, at 33.

Long Beach Lender to Pay $3 Million for Allegedly Charging Higher Rates to African Americans, Hispanics, Women and the Elderly, Department of Justice Press Release 96-429 (Sept. 5, 1996).

Jaret Seiberg, *Calif. Lender Paying $4M To Settle U.S. Bias Charges*, Am. Banker, Sept. 6, 1996, at 1.

James S. Granelli, *U.S. Settles with Lender Accused of Overcharging*, L.A. Times, Sept. 6, 1996, at D1.

Kenneth Harney, *Justice Settlement Finds Not all Loan Fees Equal*, Newsday, Sept. 13, 1996, at D2.

63. NMAC does not train its staff regarding ECOA compliance related to credit pricing, does not have anyone assigned to ensure ECOA compliance related to credit pricing, does not engage in ECOA self audits, does not audit its dealer arrangers-originators, does not provide any ECOA training to its dealer arrangers-originators and does not provide any information to its dealer arrangers-originators regarding ECOA credit pricing requirements.

64. Despite clear and unequivocal notice of the unfair and discriminatory impact of a commission driven subjective pricing system, NMAC has continued its discriminatory credit pricing system and has done nothing to monitor or prevent the discriminatory impact of the system.

X. SUMMARY OF NMAC'S RETAIL FINANCE SYSTEM

65. NMAC's retail finance system, one component of which is the finance charge markup policy, can be summarized as follows:

a. Under NMAC's retail finance system, the finance charges that result from the buy rate portion of the contract APR are credit risk based charges that NMAC deems to be appropriate for the particular individual, after analyzing all individual deal and buyer variables.

b. The finance charges that result from the finance charge markup portion of the contract A.P.R. pursuant to NMAC's markup policy are totally subjective non credit risk related charges.

c. Incentives are built into the NMAC finance charge system to encourage imposition of the subjective non risk related charges. NMAC as well as NMAC's dealer's employees, management and owners profit from the imposition of subjective, non risk related charges.

d. NMAC determines the range of allowable markup and which loans are subject to markup.

e. NMAC maintains no monitoring, training or other compliance components to prevent illegal discriminatory impact, despite overwhelming recognition throughout the credit industry of the dangers associated with subjective pricing systems in a commission driven environment.

f. NMAC's finance customers pay all of their contract finance charges, including the portion resulting from the finance charge markup, directly to NMAC.

g. None of the NMAC required finance forms inform the customers that they were charged more than their eligible buy rate and do not inform them their actual contract APR was manipulated by the dealer pursuant to NMAC's markup policy.

XI. [CONSUMER 2] AND [CONSUMER 1]

66. [*Consumers 1 and 2*] are married African-Americans. [*Consumer 2*] is a retired metro bus driver and [*Consumer 1*] provides care for disadvantaged children. In August, 1995, [*Consumer 1*] went to Action Nissan in Nashville, Tennessee for the purpose of buying an automobile.

67. Action Nissan is an authorized Nissan dealer and an agent for NMAC. Action Nissan regularly advertises and sells Nissan products and is an arranger/originator of NMAC financing.

68. On or about August 25, 1995, [*Consumers 1 and 2*] applied for credit with NMAC by completing a NMAC credit application which bore a prominent Nissan Motor Acceptance Corporation logo and which had been provided to Action Nissan by NMAC for purposes of assisting Action in arranging/originating consumer finance transactions on behalf of NMAC. The NMAC application which [*Consumers 1 and 2*] completed was given to them by an Action Nissan employee who provided the NMAC application with the authority and approval of NMAC.

69. On or after August 25, 1995, Action Nissan faxed [*Consumer 1's and Consumer 2's*] NMAC application to NMAC in accordance with the standard business practice of NMAC and its affiliated dealers. NMAC reviewed [*Consumer 1's and Consumer 2's*] application, performed a risk analysis by considering all risk related variables NMAC deemed appropriate, and determined that [*Consumers 1 and 2*] were a "SPL tier" credit risk.

70. After performing its risk evaluation and determining which credit risk tier [*Consumers 1 and 2*] were eligible for, NMAC faxed Action Nissan an authorization indicating that [*Consumers 1 and 2*] were eligible for NMAC financing at "SPL tier."

71. By referring to NMAC's current rate sheet, Action Nissan was able to determine that [*Consumers 1 and 2*] were eligible for NMAC financing at 16.49%. By referring to the same NMAC rate sheet, Action Nissan was also able to determine that NMAC had authorized Action to markup the interest rate to a maximum of 19.49% (3 points).

72. NMAC's arranger/originator, Action Nissan, also presented [*Consumers 1 and 2*] with a retail installment contract which prominently bore the Nissan Motor Acceptance Corporation logo and which had been provided to Action Nissan by NMAC for purposes of assisting Action in arranging/originating NMAC consumer finance transactions.

73. The NMAC retail installment contract which [*Consumers 1 and 2*] signed was given to them by an Action Nissan employee who was acting with the authority and approval of NMAC. [*Consumers 1 and 2*] agreed to a price of $24,292.00, and traded a 1990 Chevrolet Blazer as down payment.

74. [*Consumers 1 and 2*] were presented documents by Action Nissan which indicated they were being financed through NMAC. [*Consumers 1 and 2*] agreed to a six year financing plan, which involved $20,099.06 in finance charges, and a total sales price of $50,388.67.

75. The documents presented to [*Consumers 1 and 2*] represented that the financing documents were prepared by an authorized representative of NMAC, using NMAC documents, at NMAC's rate and under terms set by NMAC. For example,

a. The application that [*Consumers 1 and 2*] completed in order to apply for financing bore a prominent NMAC logo.

b. The retail installment contract had the name "Nissan Motor Acceptance Corporation" and the NMAC logo imprinted in bold at the top of the retail installment contract.

c. The certificate of insurance had the name "Nissan Motor Acceptance Corporation, P.O. Box 660368, Dallas, TX 75266-0368" typed in the block labeled "Creditor."

76. The contract APR (19.49%) on the NMAC retail installment contract was actually a combination of NMAC's required risk based buy rate (16.49%) and a totally subjective finance charge markup (3%), added pursuant to NMAC's credit pricing system.

77. Instead of getting a standard and competitive rate from a large national company based on their credit risk tier, [*Consumers 1 and 2*] received a significantly higher rate as a result of the undisclosed markup. In accordance with the standard method of operation employed to affect the unfair, deceptive, and discriminatory scheme, none of the various documents informed [*Consumers 1 and 2*] that:

a. The rate printed on the contract titled "Nissan Motor Acceptance Corporation" was a negotiable rate, not a required rate based on NMAC's evaluation of their credit risk.

b. The 19.49% rate typed on the contract titled "Nissan Motor Acceptance Corporation" was in fact a subjective rate manipulated by Action Nissan, pursuant to NMAC's credit pricing policies and with the express approval of NMAC;

c. The 19.49% rate was not required by NMAC as a condition of financing.

d. [*Consumers 1 and 2*] were eligible for financing through NMAC at 16.49%, a rate that was 3% points lower than the 19.49% rate on the NMAC contract that was presented to [*Consumers 1 and 2*]. (The difference between 16.49% and 19.49% resulted in $3,504.24 in additional finance charges.)

e. The lower risk based buy rate (16.49%) had been secretly communicated to Action Nissan by NMAC in order to disguise the non-risk related charges imposed by Action Nissan pursuant to NMAC's credit pricing policies.

f. There was an agreement between NMAC and Action Nissan that gave Action Nissan a large financial incentive to present [*Consumers 1 and 2*] with a contract bearing the name of "Nissan Motor Acceptance Corporation" but with a higher rate than actually required by NMAC, or required by credit risk analysis.

78. Pursuant to the undisclosed agreement between NMAC and Action Nissan, NMAC kept 25% of the finance charge markup ($876.06—NMAC Participation) and wrote a $2,628.18 check to Action Nissan for 75% (Dealer Participation).

79. The credit pricing system employed by NMAC caused [*Consumers 1 and 2*], and other African-Americans, to pay higher markup than similarly situated white persons. The additional markup charges imposed on African-Americans were totally unrelated to credit risk factors.

XII. [CONSUMER 3] AND [CONSUMER 4]

80. In August 2000 [*Consumer 3*] and [*Consumer 4*] went to Jim Johnson Nissan in Bowling Green, Kentucky for the purpose of buying an automobile. [*Consumer 3*] and [*Consumer 4*] are married African-Americans. [*Consumer 3*] is an educator and [*Consumer 4*] is employed in medical research.

81. Jim Johnson Nissan is an agent for NMAC and is authorized by NMAC to arrange/originate automobile financing transactions on behalf of NMAC.

82. [*Consumer 3*] and [*Consumer 4*] had previously leased a vehicle from NMAC and had been informed by NMAC that as valued customers they would be approved for financing a vehicle. At Jim Johnson Nissan, [*Consumers 3 and 4*] applied for credit with NMAC.

83. Based on a comprehensive credit risk assessment, NMAC determined that [*Consumers 3 and 4*] were entitled to risk-based credit at 9.75%. NMAC communicated to Jim Johnson Nissan that [*Consumers 3 and 4*] were eligible to purchase the 1997 Nissan pick-up truck at a credit risk-based rate of 9.75%.

84. Pursuant to NMAC's credit pricing policy, NMAC authorized Jim Johnson Nissan to subjectively mark up [*Consumer 3's and Consumer 4's*] buy rate of 9.75% without disclosing either the buy rate or the markup to [*Consumers 3 and 4*]. Acting pursuant to NMAC's credit pricing policy, Jim Johnson Nissan charged [*Consumers 3 and 4*] a contract APR of 12.75%, adding three points of non-disclosed subjective finance charge markup. The undisclosed markup increased [*Consumers 3's and 4's*] cost of credit by approximately 34%. The entire markup was paid by [*Consumers 3 and 4*] to NMAC.

XIII. [CONSUMER 5] and [CONSUMER 6]

85. January 1996, [*Consumer 5*] went to Action Nissan in Nashville, Tennessee for the purpose of buying an automobile.

86. Action Nissan is an agent for NMAC and is authorized by NMAC to arrange/originate automobile financing transactions on behalf of NMAC.

87. While at Action Nissan, [*Consumer 5*] applied for credit with NMAC. [*Consumer 6*], her husband, applied as a co-buyer.

88. Based on a comprehensive credit risk assessment, NMAC determined that [*Consumers 5 and 6*], both African-Americans, were a "Preferred Marquee" credit risk, the highest rating assigned to any NMAC customer.

89. Pursuant to NMAC's credit pricing policy, [*Consumers 5 and 6*] were entitled to a "Preferred Marquee" tier rate (8.99%), subject to the addition of a subjective markup which NMAC authorized Action Nissan to add.

90. Pursuant to NMAC's credit pricing policy, [*Consumers 5 and 6*] were charged a risk-related finance charge of $9560.63 plus a discretionary finance charge mark-up of $2115.36, for a total finance charge of $11,675.99 (10.79% APR).

91. The undisclosed markup increased [*Consumers 5 and 6's*] cost of credit by more than 22% and the entire markup was paid by [*Consumers 5 and 6*] to NMAC.

XIV. [CONSUMER 7] AND [CONSUMER 8]

92. [*Consumer 7*] and [*Consumer 8*] are retired married African-Americans living on fixed incomes in Jackson, Tennessee. In February 2000, two years after this lawsuit was filed, [*Consumers 7 and 8*] agreed to purchase a 1996 Chevrolet Lumina from Carlock Nissan in Jackson, Tennessee.

93. Carlock Nissan is an agent for NMAC and is authorized by NMAC to arrange/originate automobile financing transactions on behalf of NMAC. At Carlock Nissan, [*Consumers 7 and 8*] applied for credit with NMAC. Based on a comprehensive credit risk assessment, NMAC determined that [*Consumers 7 and 8*] were in credit tier BC1 and entitled to a risk based buy rate of 9.75%. NMAC communicated

the 9.75% buy rate to Carlock Nissan after a complete and objective evaluation of [*Consumer 7's and Consumer 8's*] credit worthiness.

94. Pursuant to NMAC's credit pricing policy, Carlock Nissan added three points of undisclosed subjective markup to the buy rate resulting in a contract APR of 12.75%.

95. The undisclosed finance charge markup increased [*Consumers 7 and 8's*] cost of credit by approximately 33% and the entire markup was paid by [*Consumers 7 and 8*] to NMAC.

XV. 1998 ACTION NISSAN STUDY

96. In 1998, a sample of Action Nissan data confirmed the discriminatory impact of NMAC's commission driven credit pricing system. The 1998 statistical sample of data involved only transactions consummated in 1995, the same year [*Consumers 1 and 2*] purchased their automobile from Action Nissan. All sampled transactions were originated in Nashville, Tennessee at Action Nissan, where [*Consumers 1 and 2*] purchased their automobile.

97. The finance charge markups in the sampled transactions were not risk based charges.

98. The sampled transactions indicated that transactions involving white consumers included, on average, an undisclosed finance charge markup of $621.21 per contract.

99. The sampled transactions indicated that transactions involving African Americans included, on average, an undisclosed finance charge markup of $1,004.33 per contract. The additional average non-risk related markup to African-Americans over and above the amount charged to white consumers, was $383.12 per contract and is not a legally justifiable disparity.

100. The sampled transactions indicated that African Americans and other minorities, on average, were charged 63% more in finance charge markup than similarly situated white persons.

XVI. THE 1999 NMAC TENNESSEE STUDY

101. In August, 1999, pursuant to a court order, NMAC produced electronic data containing all finance transactions originated by its thirty-five (35) Tennessee dealer arrangers/originators between January 1, 1995 and December 31, 1998. The court ordered data production was limited to data maintained in NMAC's active database. The data produced consisted of 12,826 finance accounts.

102. A portion of the 12,826 finance accounts were "race coded" in order to perform a statistical analysis of the incidence of finance charge markup and the mean (average) markup by race.

103. Approximately 10,000 of the accounts were "race coded" using information obtained from the Tennessee Department of Safety drivers license files, representing approximately 75% of all accounts.

104. Of the accounts that were "race coded," there were 7,605 with white primary buyers and 1,792 with African-American primary buyers.

105. The 7,605 transactions involving a white consumer as the primary buyer averaged markup of $507.94 per contract.

106. The 1,792 transactions involving an African American consumer as the primary buyer averaged markup of $969.91 per contract. The average markup charged to African Americans exceeded the average to white consumers by $461.97 per contract and is not a legally justifiable disparity.

107. African-Americans, on average, were charged 90.9% more in finance charge markup than white persons.

108. Statistical analysis of the incidence (frequency) of markup indicated African Americans are 268% more likely to experience

finance charge markups than white persons. Further, analysis of this data concluded that the NMAC markup policy results in actual overages fifteen (15) standard deviations greater than the expected incidence of overages.

XVII. THE 2001 NMAC NATIONAL STUDY

109. In 2001 NMAC produced a file containing 1.1 million nationwide records of NMAC financing transactions from March 1993 to September 2000.

110. Of those transactions, 310,718 were race-coded as being black or white by CLC Compliance Technologies, Inc. through driver license data obtained from various state motor vehicles departments in the United States.

111. Plaintiffs' statistical experts analyzed the race-coded data to determine whether or not there is evidence of a disparate impact on black customers of NMAC in that they pay a higher markup than similarly situated whites.

112. The analyses found that 71.8% of black borrowers are charged a markup, as compared to 46.7% of white borrowers.

113. The incidence of a black borrower receiving a positive markup is almost three times greater (2.89) than the white incidence of receiving a markup.

114. In addition, nationally, black borrowers on average pay more than twice the markup paid by whites: $970 versus $462, a difference of $508.

115. Black borrowers whose financing contracts are marked up are charged on average $1351 compared to $989 for whites, a difference of $362.

116. These racial disparities are highly statistically significant as the difference between the "expected" and "actual" chance of an African-American being marked up exceeds the standard deviation by 99.0 times.

117. Accounting for the fact that NMAC's markup policy permits dealers to move customers across different interest rate categories results in even larger racial disparities.

118. These findings are consistent across 33 states where sufficient data exists to draw valid statistical inferences.

119. The national statistical analysis revealed that white NMAC customers are three times more likely than blacks (27.8% v. 9.2%) to borrow at a negative markup.

120. The fact that more than half of white borrowers pay no markup at all is partially attributable to the NMAC credit pricing of special APR programs which restrict or prohibit markup in transactions that disproportionately go to white customers.

XVIII. ONE EXAMPLE

121. An egregious example of the subjective imposition of markup occurred to a young African-American couple, known herein as John and Jane Doe.

122. On July 26, 1995, John and Jane Doe financed an automobile through NMAC. The arranger/originator was a Memphis, Tennessee NMAC dealer operating under the standard non-recourse NMAC plan.

123. NMAC analyzed the credit worthiness of John and Jane Doe, which included consideration of the numerous individual and deal variables, and concluded that the appropriate risk based buy rate for John and Jane Doe was 10.9%.

124. NMAC's arranger/originator, operating within the rules and guidelines of NMAC's markup policy added a finance charge markup of 5.0 percentage points, resulting in a markup of $6,555.32.

125. Of the $6,555.32 in markup, $4,982.04 was paid to NMAC's arranger/originator (dealer participation) and the remaining $1,573.28 was kept by NMAC (NMAC participation).

126. There are thousands of examples within the NMAC data in which the markup exceeds one thousand dollars ($1,000.00).

127. Although egregious examples of markup involve both minorities and non-minorities, the negative impact of the markup policy is borne disproportionately by minorities.

XIX. EQUAL CREDIT OPPORTUNITY ACT

128. Plaintiffs incorporate herein all other allegations contained in the complaint.

129. NMAC is a creditor as defined in Regulation B, Section 202.2(l) of the Equal Credit Opportunity Act.

130. NMAC, in the ordinary course of its business, participated in every decision of whether or not to extend credit to the proposed class representatives and all prospective class members.

131. NMAC, at all times relevant to this complaint, was fully aware of the policy and practice that resulted in the discrimination described herein and, in fact, designed, controlled, implemented and profited from the discriminatory policy and practice, referred to herein as the NMAC markup policy.

132. NMAC is a creditor as defined in Regulation B, Section 202.2(l), in the capacity of a lender, in that all discriminatory actions that were taken by NMAC dealers were in accordance with the specific authority granted to the NMAC dealers by NMAC, all discriminatory actions were implemented using various forms and documents provided by NMAC to the NMAC dealers, all discriminatory actions were taken in furtherance of NMAC's goals and objectives and all discriminatory actions financially benefited NMAC.

133. NMAC delegated to the NMAC dealers the authority to markup finance charges without regard to credit risk factors pursuant to the NMAC markup policy which resulted in unlawful discrimination.

134. All actions taken by NMAC dealers are attributable to NMAC under agency principles based on the doctrines of express authority and apparent authority.

135. NMAC is a creditor as defined in Regulation B, Section 202.2(l), in the capacity of an assignee, since NMAC, in the ordinary course of its business, participated in every decision of whether or not to extend credit to the class representatives and all class members.

136. NMAC dealer arrangers/originators are creditors as defined in Regulation B, Section 202.2(l) in that NMAC dealers, "in the ordinary course of business, regularly refers applicants or prospective applicants to creditors, or selects or offers to select creditors to whom requests for credit may be made."

137. NMAC is liable for any and all ECOA violations committed by NMAC dealers as the assignee of the NMAC dealers. All NMAC retail installment contracts, which were designed and paid for by NMAC, for all dates relevant to this lawsuit, contained the following clause as required by the Federal Trade Commission Holder Rule, 16 CFR Ch. 1, Part 433. (1-1-98) Edition:

> NOTICE: ANY HOLDER OF THIS CONSUMER CREDIT CONTRACT IS SUBJECT TO ALL CLAIMS AND DEFENSES WHICH THE DEBTOR COULD ASSERT AGAINST THE SELLER OF GOODS OR SERVICES OBTAINED PURSUANT HERETO OR WITH THE PROCEEDS HEREOF. RECOVERY HEREUNDER BY THE DEBTOR

SHALL NOT EXCEED AMOUNTS PAID BY THE DEBTOR HEREUNDER.

138. The discriminatory charges that were charged to plaintiffs and the class members arose directly from "credit transactions" as defined in Regulation B, Section 202.2(m).

139. The discretionary charges that resulted from the NMAC markup policy were over and above the finance charge that class representatives and class members were eligible for based on their credit risk rating.

140. The average of the discretionary non-risk related charges imposed class representatives and other African-Americans pursuant to the NMAC markup policy were significantly greater than the average discretionary non-risk related charges imposed on white consumers.

141. The disparities between the terms of the credit transactions involving African Americans and the terms involving white consumers could not have occurred by chance and cannot be explained by factors unrelated to race.

142. NMAC's policies and practices, as described herein, constitute:

a. A pattern or practice of resistance to the full enjoyment of rights secured by the Equal Credit Opportunity Act, 15 U.S.C. §§ 1691-1691f; and

b. Discrimination against applicants with respect to credit transactions, on the basis of race or national origin in violation of the Equal Credit Opportunity Act, 15 U.S.C. § 1691(a)(1) and Regulation B, § 202.4.

143. Plaintiffs and prospective class members are aggrieved persons as defined in the Equal Credit Opportunity Act and have been disadvantaged as a result of NMAC's credit pricing policy.

144. Plaintiffs, on their behalf, and on behalf of all persons similarly situated, sue NMAC pursuant to the ECOA, seeking appropriate class certification, and appropriate equitable and injunctive relief.

XX. ECOA PROOF ANALYSIS—DISPARATE IMPACT

145. Plaintiffs allege that NMAC'S credit pricing policy, although facially neutral, has a disproportionately negative effect on African-Americans and other minorities.

146. Pursuant to a disparate impact analysis, the plaintiffs specifically allege:

a. The specific facially neutral NMAC practice that the plaintiffs are challenging is NMAC's markup policy, a component of NMAC's credit pricing system.

b. The disparity between the frequency and the amount of markup imposed on African Americans and that charged similarly situated white persons indicates a clear causal connection between the markup policy and the discriminatory result.

c. The disparities that exist are consistently evidenced by a statistical review of adequate, competent and relevant data sets.

d. There are no legitimate business reasons to justify NMAC's discriminatory markup policy that could not be achieved by a practice that has a far less discriminatory impact.

XXI. CLASS ACTION ALLEGATIONS

147. Plaintiffs bring this action on behalf of themselves and all other similarly situated persons. Pursuant to Rule 23 of the Federal Rules of Civil Procedure, plaintiffs seek to represent and seek certification of the following class:

Class Definition—All African-American consumers who obtained vehicle financing from NMAC in the United States pursuant to NMAC's "retail plan—without recourse," between January 1, 1990 and the date of judgment.

148. The requirements of Rule 23(a), 23(b)(2) and 23(b)(3) of the Federal Rules of Civil Procedure have been met in that:

a. **Rule 23(a)(1) Numerosity**—Plaintiffs do not know the exact size of the proposed class, since such information is in the exclusive control of defendant. Based on discovery, the nature of the commerce involved, and NMAC publications, plaintiffs believe that the proposed class members exceed 125,000. The members of the proposed class are geographically disbursed throughout the United States so that joinder of all members would be impracticable.

b. **Rule 23(a)(2) Commonality**—All of the legal and factual issues in this class action are common to each proposed class member:

(1) Whether NMAC's credit pricing policy system is a facially neutral system that has effected racial discrimination in violation of the Equal Credit Opportunity Act?

(2) Whether there are disparities between the frequency and the amount of finance charge markup imposed on African Americans and the frequency and amount of the finance charge markup imposed on white persons of equal credit worthiness?

(3) If there is a disparity in finance charge markup, is it statistically significant enough to indicate a causal connection between the NMAC markup policy and the discriminatory result?

(4) If there is a disparity in finance charge markup, is it demonstrated by statistical evidence from an adequate, competent and relevant data set?

(5) If there is a disparity, is there a legitimate business reason to justify NMAC's markup policy that could not be achieved by a practice that has a less disparate impact?

c. **Rule 23(a)(3) Typicality**—Plaintiffs' claims are typical of the proposed class members' claims. Class representatives are (1) African-Americans who obtained vehicle financing from NMAC during the class period; and (2) were and are subject to NMAC's markup policy.

d. **Rule 23(a)(4) Adequacy of Representation**—Plaintiffs can and will fairly and adequately represent and protect the interest of the proposed class, and have no interest that conflicts with or is antagonistic to the interest of the proposed class. Plaintiffs have employed attorneys who are experienced, competent and able to adequately and vigorously pursue this class action claim. No conflict exists between plaintiffs and proposed class members because:

i. the claim of the named plaintiffs are typical of the proposed class members;

ii. all the questions of law and fact regarding the liability of the defendant are common to the proposed class, and overwhelmingly predominate over any individual issues that may exist, such that by prevailing on their own claim, plaintiffs necessarily will establish defendant's liability to all proposed class members;

iii. without the representation provided by plaintiffs, virtually no proposed class member would receive legal redress or representation for their injuries because of the small value of the individual claims and because of the burden of proving a disparate impact claim;

    iv. plaintiffs and their counsel have the necessary legal support, financial and technological resources to adequately and vigorously litigate this class action, and the plaintiffs and counsel are aware of their fiduciary responsibilities to the proposed class members, and are determined to diligently discharge those duties by vigorously seeking the maximum recovery for the proposed class.

149. **Rule 23(b)(2)**—Certification is appropriate under Rule 23 of the Federal Rules of Civil Procedure because defendants have acted on grounds generally applicable to the proposed classes, thereby making appropriate final injunctive relief or corresponding declaratory relief with respect to the class as a whole. Plaintiffs seek to obtain declaratory and injunctive relief requiring NMAC to implement company policies designed to prevent the illegal discrimination described herein. The plaintiffs are requesting injunctive relief restricting or prohibiting subjective markup, requiring ECOA training of NMAC employees; requiring NMAC to provide ECOA training for its dealer arrangers/ originators; and requiring ECOA monitoring to ensure an end to the discriminatory impact of the markup. If NMAC's credit pricing system is declared to be in violation of the ECOA, any restitutionary relief could be calculated by automated and objective means and would be a part of and flow directly from the injunctive or declaratory relief. The injunctive or declaratory relief is clearly predominant.

150. **Rule 23(b)(3)**—A class action is a superior procedural vehicle for the fair and efficient adjudication of the claims asserted herein given that:

    a. Common questions of law and fact overwhelmingly predominate over any individual questions that may arise, such that there would be enormous economies to the courts and the parties in litigating the common issues on a class wide instead of a repetitive individual basis. Since the plaintiffs' proof of discrimination pursuant to the ECOA claim will be based on a disparate impact analysis, the proof is the same for every class member. The proof under a disparate impact analysis is based on proving a facially neutral practice's disproportionately negative impact on minorities as compared to white persons, using relevant data and a competent statistical analysis, not based on what happened to any individual.

    b. The size of a proposed class members individual restitutionary claim is too small to make individual litigation an economically viable alternative, because of the enormity of the opposition and the difficult problems in amassing statistical proof of discrimination, such that few proposed class members would have any interest in individually controlling the prosecution of separate actions;

    c. Class treatment is required for optimal deterrent and compensation and for limiting the court awarded reasonable legal expenses incurred by proposed class members;

    d. Despite the relatively small size of individual claims, their aggregate volume, coupled with the economies of scale inherent in litigating similar claims on a common basis, will enable this case to be litigated as a class action on a cost effective basis, especially when compared with repetitive individual litigation;

    e. No unusual difficulties likely would be encountered in the management of this class in that all questions of law or fact to be litigated at the liability stage are common to the class and all restitutionary relief issues are concomitant with the liability

findings which can be calculated by automated and objective means.

XXII. INJUNCTIVE RELIEF

151. Plaintiffs incorporate all other paragraphs contained in the complaint.

152. Pursuant to the Equal Credit Opportunity Act (15 USC 1691e(c)), and the inherent authority of this Court, appropriate injunctive relief should prohibit further use of the NMAC markup policy, as it presently exists; and/or require NMAC to implement a non-discriminatory dealer compensation system. Plaintiffs suggest that a non-discriminatory system should include all or some of the following:

    a. Prohibition of non-risk related finance charge markup; or

    b. Alternatively, restrictions limiting markup to a fixed amount for all customers;

    c. Alternatively, limitation of markup to a fixed percentage;

    d. Disclosure of markup to the customer;

    e. ECOA training of NMAC employees;

    f. ECOA training for dealer arrangers/originators;

    g. Standards regarding the minimum qualifications of persons engaged in arranging/originating NMAC finance transactions;

    h. Standards requiring NMAC to monitor and/or audit the racial pattern of markup;

    i. Such other injunctive and/or declaratory provisions which eliminate the discriminatory effect of the markup policy and serve the purposes of ECOA.

XXIII. PRAYER FOR RELIEF

WHEREFORE, plaintiffs and the class respectfully request that this Court grant the following relief:

1. Certify this case as a class action and certify the named plaintiffs herein to be adequate class representatives and their counsel to be adequate class counsel;

2. Enter a judgment pursuant to 15 USC 1691e(c) declaring that the acts and practices of defendant complained of herein to be in violation of ECOA;

3. Pursuant to 15 USC 1691e(c), grant a permanent injunction enjoining NMAC from continuing to utilize a credit pricing policy that has a discriminatory impact on African-Americans;

4. Order NMAC, pursuant to 15 USC 1691e(c), to adopt and enforce a credit pricing policy and/or dealer compensation policy without discriminatory effect, and which comply with ECOA;

5. Order disgorgement, pursuant to 15 USC 1691e(c), of all disproportionate non-risk charges imposed on African Americans by NMAC's markup policy; and order the equitable distribution of such charges, as restitutionary relief, to all appropriate class members;

6. Award plaintiffs, pursuant to 15 USC 1691e(d), the costs of this action, including the fees and costs of experts, and reasonable attorneys' fees; and

7. Grant plaintiffs and the Class such other and further relief as this Court finds necessary and proper.

Respectfully Submitted,

[Attorneys for Plaintiffs]

G.4 Sample Individual Complaint Alleging ECOA Co-Signer Violation

IN THE UNITED STATES DISTRICT COURT
FOR THE DISTRICT OF MASSACHUSETTS

————————————)	
[*Consumer*],)	
Plaintiff,)	
)	
v.)	
)	
Friendly Finance Co., a)	
Corporation,)	
Defendant.)	
————————————)	

COMPLAINT

COMES NOW the Plaintiff, [*Consumer*], by her undersigned counsel, in the above-entitled action and alleges as follows:

1. This Complaint is filed and these proceedings are instituted under the "Equal Credit Opportunity" provision of the Federal Consumer Credit Protection Act, 15 U.S.C. § 1691 *et seq.*, and Regulation B, 12 C.F.R. 202.1 *et seq.*, to recover actual and punitive damages, declaratory relief, reasonable attorney's fees and costs of suit by reason of Defendant's violations of that Act. The jurisdiction of this Court is invoked pursuant to 15 U.S.C. § 1691e(f) of the Act.

2. Plaintiff is a natural person and is a resident and a citizen of the Commonwealth of Massachusetts and of the United States.

3. Defendant is a corporation doing business in the Commonwealth of Massachusetts and is subject to the jurisdiction of this Court. At all times relevant herein, Defendant, in the ordinary course of business, regularly extended, offered to extend or arranged for extension of credit to its consumer customers for which a finance charge was imposed.

4. Within two years prior to the filing of this action, Plaintiff entered into a credit transaction with Defendant incident to which Defendant imposed on Plaintiff a finance charge as a part of the transaction. (A copy of the disclosure statement of that transaction is attached hereto as Exhibit "A" and is made a part hereof.)

5. Defendant has violated the Equal Credit Opportunity Act and Regulation B thereunder in that:

  a. Defendant required Plaintiff's husband to obtain the signature of a co-signer on this credit loan contract notwithstanding the fact that:

    i. Plaintiff's husband's application for credit was not a joint application; and

    ii. Plaintiff's husband individually qualified under Defendant's standards for creditworthiness for the amount and terms of the credit requested; and

  b. Defendant required that Plaintiff [*Consumer*] serve as the co-signer on her husband's credit instrument because of her status as his wife.

6. As a result of the aforesaid violations, Defendant is liable to Plaintiff in an amount to be proven at trial, representing Plaintiff's actual damages, punitive damages, costs of Court and reasonable attorney's fees.

WHEREFORE, Plaintiff demands judgment against Defendant as follows:

1. Declare Defendant's actions in the extension of credit to consumers in violation of the Equal Credit Opportunity Act.

2. Award Plaintiff actual damages as will be shown at trial.

3. Award Plaintiff punitive damages in an amount not greater than $10,000.00.

4. Award Plaintiff reasonable attorney's fees as provided by law, costs, and such other relief as the Court may deem just and proper.

DATED: Boston, Massachusetts: ——————

[Attorneys for Plaintiff]

G.5 Sample Class Action Complaint Alleging ECOA Co-Signer Violation

UNITED STATES DISTRICT COURT
WESTERN DISTRICT OF NEW YORK

————————————)		
[*Consumer*], individually and on)		
behalf of all other persons)		
similarly situated,)		
Plaintiff,)		
)	COMPLAINT	
v.)		
)		
ABC Financial Services Co.,)		
Defendant.)		
————————————)		

INTRODUCTION

1. Plaintiff brings this action on behalf of herself and a class of others similarly situated to recover for violations of the Federal Equal Credit Opportunity Act, 15 U.S.C. § 1691 *et seq.* (ECOA) and Regulation B thereunder, 12 C.F.R. § 202.1 *et seq.*

JURISDICTION

2. Jurisdiction is vested in this Court pursuant to 15 U.S.C. § 1691e(f).

PARTIES

3. Plaintiff is a natural person residing in Bison, Erie County, New York, within the Western District of New York.

4. Defendant is, on information and belief, a corporation organized under the laws of the State of New York; it does business in Bison, Erie County, New York, within the Western District of New York. It is a licensed lender subject to Article 9 of the New York Banking Law, and it regularly extends, renews or continues credit; regularly arranges for the extension, renewal or continuation of credit; regularly purchases assignments from original creditors and participates in the decision to extend, renew or continue credit.

CLASS ACTION

5. Plaintiff brings this action on behalf of a class consisting of all other persons who were made by defendant to co-sign loan agreements initiated by their spouses with defendant during the period commencing two years prior to the filing of this action, or who may be made by defendant to co-sign loan agreements initiated by their spouses with defendant in the future.

6. The class is so numerous that joinder of all members is impracticable, including, on information and belief, several hundred persons at least.

7. There are questions of law common to the class, namely whether the procedure followed by defendant of making the spouses of loan applicants co-sign loan agreements violates ECOA and Regulation B, and whether the loan forms used by defendant violate ECOA and Regulation B.

8. The claims of the representative party are typical of the claims of the class and the representative party will fairly and adequately protect the interests of the class. There is no conflict between the representative party and the members of the class and the representative party is represented by counsel employed by a federally funded Legal Services program.

9. A class action may be maintained under Rule 23(b)(2) and 23(b)(3) of the Federal Rules of Civil Procedure, since the party opposing the class has acted or refused to act on grounds generally applicable to the class, thereby making appropriate final injunctive relief or corresponding declaratory relief with respect to the class as a whole, and since the questions of law about the defendant's compliance with ECOA and Regulation B predominate over any questions affecting only individual class members and a class action is superior to other available methods of the fair and efficient adjudication of the controversy.

FACTS

10. On or about December 31, 1993, plaintiff's husband, [*Consumer 2*], and defendant entered into a consumer loan transaction.

11. This transaction was, in part, evidenced by a form entitled Loan Agreement, a true and accurate copy of which is attached hereto, marked plaintiff's Exhibit A, and incorporated herein by reference.

12. The transaction set out in paragraph 10 was also evidenced, in part, by a document purportedly making all disclosures required by the Federal Truth in Lending Act, 15 U.S.C. § 1601 *et seq.*, Regulation Z thereunder 12 C.F.R. § 226.1 *et seq.*, and the New York Banking Law to be made in connection with the particular transaction. A true and accurate copy of this document is attached hereto, marked plaintiff's Exhibit B and incorporated herein by reference.

13. Both plaintiff's Exhibits A and B contain spaces for listing information which are entitled "SPOUSE AGE" and "SPOUSE NAME," in violation of ECOA and Regulation B.

14. Plaintiff was made by defendant to co-sign the loan agreement, plaintiff's Exhibit A, thereby becoming liable to defendant for repayment of the loan.

15. Plaintiff was unemployed at the time of signing the loan agreement.

16. Under New York law, plaintiff's signature on the wage assignment of her husband and the security agreement was sufficient to secure the loan. Plaintiff's signature on the loan agreement was not necessary to secure the transaction.

17. Upon inquiring of defendant as to why she had to sign the loan agreement, plaintiff was informed that requiring a wife to co-sign a loan agreement was routine.

18. Plaintiff was at no time informed by defendant of the effect of her signature should her husband default in payment of the loan.

19. On information and belief, the form of loan agreement and policies of defendant alleged herein have been at all relevant times and still are used by defendant in all of its loan transactions.

STATEMENT OF CLAIM

20. By virtue of the foregoing, defendant has violated and is violating ECOA and Regulation B.

WHEREFORE, Plaintiff demands judgment:

1. Determining that this action is maintainable as a class action under Rule 23 of the Federal Rules of Civil Procedure.

2. Awarding the class $500,000 or one percent of defendant's net worth in punitive damages.

3. Awarding plaintiff $10,000 in punitive damages.

4. Enjoining defendant, its agents, employees and assigns from collecting or attempting to collect by any means from plaintiff any monies outstanding on the said contract of loan with plaintiff and her husband.

5. Enjoining defendant, its agents, employees and assigns from collecting or attempting to collect by any means from the members of the class any monies outstanding on the contracts of loan between defendant and the members of the class and their spouses.

6. Awarding plaintiff reasonable attorney's fees and cost of this action.

7. Awarding plaintiff and the class such other and further relief as seems just and proper.

[*Attorney for Plaintiff*]

G.6 Complaint Alleging Federal ECOA and State ECOA Notice Violations

UNITED STATES DISTRICT COURT
EASTERN DISTRICT OF VIRGINIA
Richmond Division

[*Consumer*],	)
Plaintiff	)
	)
v.	)
	)
SOUTHSIDE BANK	)
SERVE: Joseph Shearin,	)
President, [*address*]	)
Defendant.	)

COMPLAINT

COMES NOW the Plaintiff, [*Consumer*] (hereafter the "Plaintiff") by counsel, and for her complaint against the Defendant, allege as follows:

INTRODUCTION

1. This is a case is brought under the Federal Equal Credit Opportunity Act, 15 U.S.C. § 1691, *et seq.* (ECOA) and the Virginia Equal Credit Opportunity Act, Virginia Code § 59.1-21:1 *et seq.* (VECOA). This law regulates what a person must do when it accepts a consumer's application for credit and acts upon it. It prohibits a creditor from considering a consumer's marital status in an application for credit and requires a creditor who takes an adverse action against a consumer to provide written notice of adverse action with an accurate statement of the reasons for the denial. In this case, the Defendant denied the

Plaintiff's mortgage loan application, at least in part, because she was to be divorced. It also failed to provide an accurate statement of the reason for the denial. The Defendant's conduct in misrepresenting the reason for its adverse action also constitutes the common law tort of fraud.

JURISDICTION

2. Jurisdiction is proper pursuant to the ECOA, 15 U.S.C. 1689e. Supplemental jurisdiction is proper pursuant to 28 U.S.C. § 1367.

PARTIES

3. The Plaintiff is a consumer as defined and governed by the ECOA.

4. Defendant, SOUTHSIDE BANK ("Southside") is a legal entity doing business as a consumer bank and lender. At all times relevant hereto it was a "creditor" as defined and governed by the ECOA and the VECOA.

5. On or about July 2, 2003, the Plaintiff submitted a completed credit application wherein she sought to obtain credit to refinance her automobile loan (the "credit application") (Exhibit "A").

6. Within the credit application, the Defendant required the Plaintiff to disclose her marital status.

7. Within the credit application she submitted to the Defendant, the Plaintiff accurately listed her marital status as "separated."

8. The Defendant considered the Plaintiff's credit application but denied it, taking this adverse action in substantial part because of "the pending separation/divorce" (Exhibit "B").

9. Subsequent to its decision not to approve the credit application for the reasons stated within its own internal e-mail, the Defendant provided the Plaintiff a Notice of Adverse Action which inaccurately stated that the reasons for the denial were "length of residence" and "temporary residence" (Exhibit "C"). These statements were false.

10. The above-alleged conduct of the Defendant was malicious, willful, intentional, grossly negligent and/or with reckless disregard for the rights and interests of the Plaintiff.

11. As a result of the above-alleged conduct of the Defendant, the Plaintiff has suffered substantial actual damages by loss of the credit sought, emotional and mental anguish, and other injury to be established at trial.

COUNT ONE: FEDERAL EQUAL CREDIT OPPORTUNITY ACT

12. Plaintiff reiterates and incorporates the allegations contained in paragraphs 1 through 11 above as if fully set out herein.

13. Defendant violated the Federal ECOA.

(a) by discriminating against the Plaintiff on account of her marital status (15 U.S.C. § 1691(a)).

(b) by failing to provide a notice of adverse action which accurately stated the reasons for the denial (15 U.S.C. § 1691(d)).

14. As a result of the above alleged ECOA violations, Defendants are jointly and severally liable to Plaintiff for his actual damages pursuant to 15 U.S.C. § 1691(e)(a), for punitive damages of $10,000.00 against each Defendant pursuant to 15 U.S.C. § 1691e(b) and for attorneys fees and costs pursuant to 15 U.S.C. § 1691e(d).

15. Plaintiff is entitled to equitable relief against each Defendant requiring delivery of compliant notices in all future instances.

COUNT TWO: VIRGINIA EQUAL CREDIT OPPORTUNITY ACT

16. Plaintiff reiterates and incorporates the allegations contained in paragraphs 1 through 15 above as if fully set out herein.

17. The Defendant violated the Virginia ECOA

(a) by discriminating against the Plaintiff on account of her marital status (Virginia Code § 59.1-21.21:1(a))

(b) by failing to provide a notice of adverse action which accurately stated the reasons for the denial (Virginia Code § 59.1-21.21:1(d)).

18. As a result of the above alleged VECOA violations, Defendants are jointly and severally liable to Plaintiff for his actual damages pursuant to 15 U.S.C. § 1691(e)(a), for punitive damages of $10,000.00 against each Defendant pursuant to 15 U.S.C. § 1691e(b) and for attorneys fees and costs pursuant to 15 U.S.C. § 1691e(d).

19. Plaintiff is entitled to equitable relief against each Defendant requiring delivery of compliant notices in all future instances.

COUNT THREE: FRAUD/MISREPRESENTATION

20. Plaintiff reiterates and incorporates the allegations contained in paragraphs 1 through 19 above as if fully set out herein.

21. The Defendant committed the tort of actual fraud by misrepresenting to the Plaintiff the reasons for its denial of her credit application (the "fraud").

22. The fraud was committed with actual and legal malice. It was deliberate, willful, intentional and with reckless disregard for the rights and interests of the Plaintiff. The Plaintiff is entitled to nominal and punitive damages.

23. The Plaintiff reasonably relied upon the fraud for a period of time until she discovered the real reason for the denial.

24. As a result of the fraud, the Plaintiff suffered substantial actual damages.

WHEREFORE Plaintiff prays for judgment against the Defendant for her actual, liquidated, punitive and statutory damages, for equitable relief; for reasonable attorneys fees and pre-judgment and post-judgment interest; for the costs of litigation; and for such other and further relief as the Court deems just and appropriate.

TRIAL BY JURY IS DEMANDED.

[*Consumer*],

By _____

Of Counsel
[*Attorney for Plaintiff*]

G.7 First Amended Complaint Alleging ECOA Notice and State Fair Housing Violations

UNITED STATES DISTRICT COURT
DISTRICT OF CALIFORNIA
SAN JOSE DIVISION

———————————)	Case No. ———————
[*Consumer 1*] and)	
[*Consumer 2*],)	FIRST AMENDED
Plaintiffs,)	COMPLAINT FOR
)	VIOLATIONS OF THE
v.)	EQUAL CREDIT
)	OPPORTUNITY ACT;
JP Morgan Chase Bank N.A.;)	CALIFORNIA FAIR
Chase Home Finance, LLC;)	EMPLOYMENT AND
U.S. Bank, N.A.; California)	HOUSING ACT; AND
Reconveyance Corporation; and)	CALIFORNIA BUSINESS
DOES 150,)	AND PROFESSIONS CODE
Defendants.)	SECTION 17200
———————————)	DEMAND FOR JURY TRIAL

I. INTRODUCTION

1. With this lawsuit, [*Consumer 1*] and [*Consumer 2*] ("the [*Plaintiff family*]") seek redress for violations of the federal Equal Credit Opportunity Act, California's Fair Employment and Housing Act, and California's Unfair Business Practices Act for failing to (1) properly consider the income the [*Plaintiff family*] received from California State Disability Insurance in evaluating their eligibility for a Home Affordable Modification Program ("HAMP") loan modification; (2) provide the [*Plaintiff family*] with proper written notice regarding the specific reasons they were denied a HAMP modification; and (3) follow the procedural safeguards set forth in California's non-judicial foreclosure statutes.

II. JURISDICTION

2. This Court has subject matter jurisdiction pursuant to 28 U.S.C. §§ 1331 and 1337 based on Plaintiffs' claims under the Equal Credit Opportunity Act, 15 U.S.C. §1691(d).

3. This Court has supplemental jurisdiction pursuant to 28 U.S.C. § 1367 to hear and determine Plaintiffs' state law claims because those claims are related to Plaintiffs' federal law claims and arise out of a common nucleus of related facts. Plaintiffs' state law claims are related to Plaintiffs' federal law claims such that those claims form part of the same case or controversy under Article III of the United States Constitution.

III. INTRADISTRICT ASSIGNMENT

4. Venue is proper in the Northern District of California pursuant to 28 U.S.C. § 1391(b)(2) in that the unlawful conduct that gives rise to these claims occurred within the Northern District of California.

5. Intradistrict assignment in San Jose is proper since Plaintiffs reside in Santa Clara County and the unlawful conduct that gives rise to these claims occurred in Santa Clara County.

IV. THE PARTIES

6. [*Consumer 1*] is a resident of Santa Clara County who has owned and resided in his home located at [*address*].

7. [*Consumer 1*] has Lupus—a chronic autoimmune disorder—and has difficulty walking, requiring the use of a cane. As such, [*Consumer 1*] is a handicapped person within the meaning of California Fair Employment and Housing Act, California Government Code section 12955.3.

8. At the time of the allegations contained herein, [*Consumer 1*] received monthly State Disability Insurance payments in the amount of $2,940.

9. [*Consumer 2*] is Plaintiff [*Consumer 1's*] wife and a resident of Santa Clara County who has owned and resided in her home located at [*address*].

10. The [*Plaintiff family*] is informed and believes, and thereon alleges, that Defendant JP Morgan Chase, N.A. ("Chase") is a corporation organized and existing under the laws of the State of New York. Upon information and belief, Chase regularly conducts business in the State of California and the County of Santa Clara. The [*Plaintiff family*] is informed and believes that Chase's business activity includes mortgage lending, mortgage servicing, and otherwise extending credit to persons in residential real estate matters.

11. The [*Plaintiff family*] is informed and believes that Chase Home Finance LLC, ("Chase Home Finance") is a limited liability company organized and existing under the laws of the State of Ohio. Upon information and belief, Chase Home Finance regularly conducts business in the State of California and the County of Santa Clara. The [*Plaintiff family*] is informed and believes that Chase Home Finance's business activity includes mortgage lending, mortgage servicing and otherwise extending credit to persons in residential real estate matters.

12. The [*Plaintiff family*] is informed and believes, and thereon alleges, that U.S. Bank, N.A. ("U.S. Bank") is a corporation organized and existing under the laws of the State of Delaware. Upon information and belief, U.S. Bank regularly conducts business in the State of California and the County of Santa Clara. The [*Plaintiff family*] is informed and believes that U.S. Bank is the current beneficiary, by assignment, of the promissory note and the Deed of Trust which currently encumbers the [*Plaintiff family*] home.

13. The [*Plaintiff family*] is informed and believes, and thereon alleges, that California Reconveyance Company is a corporation organized and existing under the laws of the state of California. Upon information and belief, California Reconveyance Corporation regularly conducts business in the County of Santa Clara.

14. Plaintiffs are ignorant of the true names and capacities of defendants sued herein as Does 1-50, and therefore sue these defendants by such fictitious names. Plaintiffs will amend this complaint to allege their true names and capacities after they are ascertained. Plaintiffs are informed and believe and thereon allege that the fictitiously named defendants claim some right, title, estate, lien or interest in the property and that defendants' claims constitute a cloud on plaintiffs' interest in the subject property.

15. Plaintiffs are informed and believe that at all relevant times each defendant was the agent or employee of each of the remaining defendants and, in doing the things hereinafter alleged, was acting within the course and scope of such agency and employment.

V. FACTUAL ALLEGATIONS

A. THE MAKING HOME AFFORDABLE PROGRAM

16. The United States Department of the Treasury ("Treasury") established the Home Affordable Modification Program pursuant to the Emergency Economic Stabilization Act of 2008 ("Economic Stabilization Act"). The Economic Stabilization Act directed Treasury to use its authority to protect and preserve homeownership. The Economic Stabilization Act further directed Treasury to implement a plan to maximize assistance to homeowners and encourage mortgage servicers to minimize foreclosures. In furtherance of these goals, Treasury, through Fannie Mae, created HAMP and entered into agreements with loan servicers. *See* Emergency Economic Stabilization Act of 2008, Pub. L. No. 110-343, § 101, 122 Stat, 3765 (October 3, 2008) ("EESA").

17. HAMP's primary purpose is to assist homeowners in default or at imminent risk of default on their home mortgages "by establishing a standardized and streamlined process for servicers to follow in evaluating and conducting modifications of existing mortgages." Financial Stability Oversight Board, Quarterly Report to Congress Pursuant to § 104(g) of the Emergency Economic Stabilization Act of 2008, at 31 (Mar. 31, 2009).

18. To participate in HAMP, servicers enter into a contract ("HAMP Contract") with Fannie Mae, in its capacity as an agent of the United States. *See* Emergency Economic Stabilization Act of 2008 § 101(c)(3). The HAMP Contract incorporates by reference documents issued by Treasury and designated in the HAMP Contract as "Program Documentation." These documents include uniform "Home Affordable Modification Program Guidelines" for modifying loans under HAMP ("Guidelines"), subsequent Supplemental Directives, and "Frequently Asked Questions" ("FAQs") intended to further clarify HAMP program requirements.

19. Once a servicer has elected to participate in HAMP, it must review all mortgage loans in default that it services, under uniform guidelines set out in the HAMP Contract (and additional directives and documentation that the Contract incorporates by reference, HAMP Contract § 1(A) at 2) to determine if the loans can be made affordable. Servicers must perform these analyses whether the loans are held by the servicer itself or if they are merely servicing the mortgage held by another lender or investor.

20. A servicer's obligations under the HAMP Contract are clear. First, it must make a threshold determination of whether the borrower meets minimum eligibility criteria for the program:

- The borrower's mortgage is a first lien originated before January 1, 2009;
- The mortgage has not been previously modified under HAMP;
- The borrower has defaulted (*i.e.,* is 60 days or more delinquent) or default is reasonably foreseeable;
- The mortgage is secured by a one- to four-unit property, one unit of which is the borrower's principal residence, and the property is not vacant or condemned;
- The borrower's monthly payments toward principal, interest, taxes, insurance, and association fees (where applicable) exceed 31 percent of his or her gross monthly income;
- The borrower has experienced financial hardship, and lacks the liquid assets to meet his or her monthly mortgage payments; and
- For single-family residential properties, the unpaid principal balance on the mortgage is less than or equal to $729,750.

21. If the borrower meets these basic eligibility criteria, the servicer is required to conduct a "net present value" ("NPV") test. The test requires the servicer to take a series of steps, such as reducing the interest rate and extending the term of the loan, to adjust the borrower's monthly loan payments to be no more than 31% of the borrower's gross monthly income. The NPV analysis then compares the net present value of cash flow from these modified loan terms to the net present value of the loan without modification—in other words, whether the loan as modified would yield a better financial outcome to the investor than foreclosure.

22. A servicer must send a "Borrower Notice" to every borrower who (1) has been evaluated for HAMP but is not offered a Trial Period Plan, (2) is not offered an official HAMP modification, or (3) is at risk of losing eligibility for HAMP because they have failed to provide required financial documentation. The written notices must comply with all laws, rules and regulations, including the Equal Credit Opportunity Act, when applicable to the transaction. *See* Making Home Affordable Modification Program, Supplemental Directive No. 09-08, at 1 (Nov. 3, 2009).

23. When a borrower is not approved for a HAMP modification because the transaction is NPV negative, the notice must, in addition to an explanation of NPV, include a list of certain input fields that are considered in the NPV decision, and a statement that the borrower may, within 30 calendar days of the date of the notice, request the date the NPV calculation was completed and the values used to populate the NPV input fields. The purpose of providing this information is to allow the borrower the opportunity to correct values that may impact the analysis of the borrower's eligibility.

24. If a borrower is denied a modification because the borrower's income does not meet the 31% monthly mortgage ratio, the servicer can lower the interest rate to as low as 2% and extend the term of the loan to up to 40 years to insure that the borrower can meet the requirement of only paying 31 percent of their gross monthly earnings towards the modified loan. The servicer may also provide for principal forbearance to achieve the target monthly mortgage payment ratio. Making Home Affordable Program; Handbook for Servicers of Non-GSE Mortgages, section 6.3, Version 3.2, June 1, 2011, *available at* www.hmpadmin.com/portal/programs/docs/hamp_servicer/mhahandbook_32.pdf.

25. In 2008, J.P. Morgan Chase accepted $25 billion in funds from the United States Government as part of the Troubled Asset Relief Program ("TARP"), 12 U.S.C. § 5211. On July 31, 2009, Chase entered into a HAMP Contract known as a Servicer Participation Agreement ("SPA") to participate in the HAMP program. The SPA was amended in March 2010. This contract obligates Chase to perform actions to benefit homeowners whose mortgage loans its services, *available at* http://www.treasury.gov/initiatives/financial-stability/housingprograms/mha/Documents_Contracts_Agreements/093010jpmorganchasebanknaSPA.

26. In April 2011, Treasury reported that Chase's performance under HAMP is lacking in terms of homeowner evaluation and assistance. Treasury found that Chase incorrectly evaluated homeowner's eligibility for Making Home Affordable ("MHA") programs, failed to communicate decisions in a timely manner, and failed to accurately execute MHA activities, including correctly evaluating homeowner's monthly income for HAMP eligibility. Because of these failures, Treasury suspended Chase's incentive payments. April 2011 Making Home Affordable Program Report and Servicer Assessments for First Quarter 2010, *available at* http://www.treasury.gov/initiatives/financial-stability/results/MHA-Reports.

B. PLAINTIFFS' HAMP APPLICATIONS AND DEFENDANT CHASE'S CONTRADICTORY AND UNREASONABLY DELAYED RESPONSES

27. [*Consumer 1*] and [*Consumer 2*] purchased the property located at [*address*], on April 12, 2004. It is a single-family home and has been, at all relevant times described in this Complaint, their principal place of residence.

28. On or around March 26, 2004, the [*Plaintiff family*] obtained a loan in the amount of $676,800 from Chase's predecessor in interest Washington Mutual.

29. In 2010, the [*Plaintiff family*] had a total monthly payment of $4470.48 on the home loan. This amount covered principal, interest, and an impound account for property taxes and homeowner's insurance.

30. On or around the beginning of February 2009, [*Consumer 1*] was laid off from his employment. After he was laid off from work, [*Consumer 1's*] disability worsened. [*Consumer 1*] was approved for State Disability Income in November 2009.

31. Because their financial situation had changed, putting them at imminent risk of defaulting on their mortgage obligation, the [*Plaintiff family*] applied for a HAMP modification on or around October 6, 2009.

32. On our around January 27, 2010, [*Consumer 1*] called Chase to check the status of their application. The Chase representative told him that the [*Plaintiffs*] did not qualify for a HAMP modification because they had too many assets to qualify for a modification. The Chase representative further told [*Consumer 1*] that their application was removed from the system on December 16, 2009, because they allegedly had cash reserves sufficient to cover six months of their mortgage-related expenses.

33. However, at the time cited by the Chase representative, the [*Plaintiff family*] actually had cash reserves sufficient to cover only two months of their mortgage-related expenses, which are not excessive reserves for HAMP eligibility purposes. Making Home Affordable Program: Handbook for Servicers of Non-GSE Mortgages, Section 4.1, Version 3.2, June 1, 2011.

34. The [*Plaintiff family*] did not receive a written denial from Chase citing this as a reason for the denial of their application, nor did they receive written notification that their HAMP application was removed from Chase's system.

35. The [*Plaintiff family*] reapplied for a HAMP modification on February 5, 2010. They submitted all of the requested documents to Chase in a timely manner. On February 13, 2010, the [*Plaintiff family*] received a letter from Chase notifying them that their application was under review; the letter also confusingly stated that they should continue to make their trial period payments on time even though the [*Plaintiff family*] had not entered into a Trial Period Payment agreement with Chase. At this time, they were current with their mortgage payments.

36. On May 28, 2010, nearly four months after submitting their second HAMP application, the [*Plaintiff family*] received a letter from Chase dated May 28, 2010, advising them that their application for a HAMP modification was denied because Chase could not verify that the [*Plaintiff family*] lived in the property as their primary residence.

37. In response to the May 28, 2010, letter from Chase, the [*Plaintiff family*] sent Chase a copy of the HUD 1 Settlement Statement showing that they had sold their previous home before purchasing the [*Plaintiffs' property*] in 2004.

38. During a conversation with a Chase representative in June 2010, the [*Plaintiff family*] was told that it was Chase's policy to not consider borrowers for HAMP unless the borrower was in default. They had never missed a mortgage payment before and were applying for a HAMP modification because they were concerned about defaulting on their loan. Their financial situation had changed dramatically and the [*Plaintiff family*] was facing imminent default.

39. In July 2010, while the [*Plaintiff family*] was in the processing of providing Chase with additional information to show that the [*Plaintiffs' property*] was their only residence, they were informed by Chase that their application had been removed from Chase's system and that if the [*Plaintiff family*] remained interested in a modification they would have to reapply.

40. The [*Plaintiff family*] submitted a third HAMP application on or around August 9, 2010. At that time, the [*Plaintiff family*] also included copies of their drivers' licenses and their most recent utility bill because they were worried that they would be denied again based on Chase's inability to verify that the [*Plaintiffs' home*] was their primary residence.

41. During August and September 2010, the [*Plaintiff family*] consistently contacted Chase regarding their HAMP application, submitting updated pay stubs and account information. During a conversation with a Chase representative in September 2010, the [*Plaintiff family*] was told that they could submit [*Consumer 1's*] State Disability Income but that the representative "didn't think that Chase's underwriting is going to include disability payments as income."

42. On October 26, 2010, the [*Plaintiff family*] received a letter from Chase denying them a HAMP modification because Chase was "unable to create an affordable payment equal to 31% of [their] reported monthly gross income without changing the terms of the loan beyond the requirements of the Program."

43. The [*Plaintiff family*] believed the reason for denial to be inaccurate, and on November 13, 2010, sent a letter to Chase asking that Chase reevaluate them for HAMP or, alternatively, that Chase provide them with documentation showing why they were denied the modification. The [*Plaintiff family*] did not receive a response to this letter from Chase.

44. The [*Plaintiff family*] sent another letter to Chase on January 7, 2011, once again requesting to be reevaluated for the HAMP program and, if not, requesting that Chase provide them with a specific reason for the denial.

45. The [*Plaintiff family*] never received a response from Chase regarding their letters dated November 13, 2010, and January 7, 2011.

46. On January 19, 2011, U.S. Bank National Association recorded an Assignment of the Deed of Trust.

47. On January 19, 2011, a Notice of Default was recorded against the [*Plaintiff family's*] property. A Notice of Trustee Sale was recorded on April 20, 2011. The [*Plaintiff family*] is now in jeopardy of losing their family home without ever having been properly evaluated for a HAMP modification due to Defendants' discriminatory acts.

VI. INJURIES

48. The impending foreclosure as a result of Defendants' failure to properly follow ECOA and failure to consider [*Consumer 1's*] State Disability Income in evaluating the [*Plaintiffs*] for a HAMP modification has caused great hardship and distress to Plaintiffs.

49. Defendants have failed to adequately train and supervise their employees, agents, and themselves regarding the federal credit discrimination law and state fair housing law.

50. Defendants, acting individually and in concert with others, directly and through agents, have engaged in a pattern or practice of discrimination based on source of income. Defendants continue to engage in such a pattern or practice of discrimination so as to constitute a continuing violation.

51. By reason of Defendants' unlawful acts and practices, the [*Plaintiff family*] has suffered humiliation, mental anguish, and emotional distress, and the attendant physical injuries and conditions, as well as violation of their civil rights. Accordingly, the [*Plaintiff family*] is entitled to compensatory damages.

52. Defendants acted intentionally, maliciously, wantonly, recklessly, and in bad faith as described herein. Accordingly, the [*Plaintiff family*] is entitled to punitive damages.

53. There now exists an actual controversy between the parties regarding Defendants' duties under the ECOA and FEHA. Accordingly, the [*Plaintiff family*] is entitled to declaratory relief.

54. Unless enjoined, Defendants will continue to engage in the unlawful acts and discrimination described above. The [*Plaintiff family*] has no adequate remedy at law. The [*Plaintiff family*] is now suffering and will continue to suffer irreparable injury from Defendants' acts and their discrimination unless relief is provided by this Court. Accordingly, the [*Plaintiff family*] is entitled to injunctive relief.

VII. CLAIMS

FIRST CAUSE OF ACTION

**Violations of the Federal Equal Credit Opportunity Act—
15 U.S.C. § 1691(d)
(Against Defendants JP Morgan Chase Bank, N.A. and Chase
Home Finance, LLC)**

55. [*Consumer 1*] and [*Consumer 2*] hereby reallege and incorporate by reference the allegations of paragraphs 1 through 54 as though fully set forth herein.

56. The [*Plaintiff family*] are applicants as defined by ECOA, 15 U.S.C. § 1691a(b). The [*Plaintiff family*] applied for HAMP modifications with the Chase Defendants on three separate occasions.

57. At all relevant times herein, the Chase Defendants have been "creditors" as defined by ECOA, 15 U.S.C. § 1691a(e).

58. 15 U.S.C. § 1691(d)(1) provides that "within thirty days . . . after receipt of a completed application for credit, a creditor shall notify an applicant of its actions on the application."

59. 15 U.S.C. § 1691(d)(2) provides that "each applicant against whom a adverse action is taken shall be entitled to a statement of reasons for such action from the creditor."

60. 15 U.S.C. § 1691(d)(6) defines "adverse action" as a "denial or revocation of credit, a change in the terms of an existing credit arrangement or refusal to grant credit in substantially the same amount or on substantially the terms requested."

61. Plaintiffs' applications for HAMP modifications were "applications for credit" as defined by 15 U.S.C. § 1691a(d) and 12 C.F.R. § 202.2(j).

62. Plaintiffs provided the Chase Defendants with completed applications for credit on October 6, 2009, February 5, 2010, and September 27, 2010.

63. The Chase Defendants failed to evaluate and make a determination on Plaintiffs' three separate applications within 30 calendar days as required by HAMP directives and ECOA.

64. When Plaintiffs finally received written denials from the Chase Defendant on May 28, 2010, and again on October 26, 2010, these written notifications were not in compliance with the notification requirements set forth in 15 U.S.C. § 1691(d)(2), as the notifications failed to provide Plaintiffs with specific statements of reasons for the adverse action.

65. The Chase Defendants failed to respond to Plaintiffs' written requests for a statement of reasons for the denial within 30 days of the

Plaintiffs' letters to the Chase Defendants dated November 13, 2010, and January 7, 2011.

66. Plaintiffs never received a written denial from the Chase Defendants in response to their first application for credit in October 2009. Plaintiffs were only notified that this application was denied when they called to check the status of the application in January 2010.

67. The Chase Defendants' failure to (1) notify Plaintiffs of the adverse action taken on their three applications for credit within 30 days from receipt of their completed applications and (2) respond to Plaintiffs' written requests for the statement of reasons for their denial constitutes four separate substantive violations of ECOA.

68. As a result of the above ECOA violations, the Chase Defendants are liable to Plaintiffs for actual damages pursuant to 15 U.S.C. § 1691e(a); punitive damages of $10,000 pursuant to 15 U.S.C. § 1691e(b); and attorneys fees and costs pursuant to 15 U.S.C. § 1691e(d).

69. Plaintiffs are entitled to equitable relief against the Chase Defendants requiring delivery of ECOA-compliant notices in all future instances pursuant to 15 U.S.C. § 1691e(c).

SECOND CAUSE OF ACTION

**Violation of California Fair Employment and Housing Act—
Cal. Gov't Code § 12955 *et seq.*
(Against Defendant JP Morgan Chase Bank, N.A. and Chase
Home Finance, LLC)**

70. [*Consumer 1*] and [*Consumer 2*] hereby reallege and incorporate by reference the allegations of paragraphs 1 through 69 as though fully set forth herein.

71. The Chase Defendants injured Plaintiffs in violation of the California Fair Employment and Housing Act by committing the following discriminatory housing practices:

A. Discriminating because of source of income, in violation of California Government Code §§ 12955(e) and (i);

B. Making statements that indicate a preference, limitation or discrimination based on source of income in the provision of services in connection with a residential real estate related transaction, in violation of California Government Code § 12955(c);

C. Otherwise denying or making unavailable the provision of services in connection with a residential real estate related transaction or in the terms, conditions, or privileges relating to the obtaining or use of that financial assistance because of source of income, in violation of California Government Code § 12955(i); and

D. Imposing policies that have a negative, disproportionate effect on individuals with State Disability Insurance, in violation of California Government Code § 12955.8(b).

72. As a proximate cause of the Chase Defendants' conduct, Plaintiffs were and continue to be damaged, as set forth above, in an amount to be proven at trial.

THIRD CAUSE OF ACTION

**Violations of California Business & Professions Code § 17200
(Against all Defendants)**

73. [*Consumer 1*] and [*Consumer 2*] hereby reallege and incorporate by reference the allegations of paragraphs 1 through 72 as though fully set forth herein.

74. California Business & Professions Code § 17200, *et seq.*, the "Unfair Competition Law" ("the UCL") defines unfair competition to include any unlawful, unfair, or fraudulent business act or practice.

The UCL authorizes this Court to issue whatever orders or judgments may be necessary to prevent unfair or unlawful practices, or to "restore to any person in interest any money or property, real or personal, which may have been acquired by means of such unfair competition." *Id.* § 17203.

75. Defendants' acts and practices alleged herein are unlawful business practices in that they violate federal and state law prohibiting discrimination and wrongful foreclosure, as alleged in this Complaint.

76. Moreover, Defendants' initiation of the foreclosure process without ever genuinely evaluating the [*Plaintiff family*] for a HAMP loan modification violates California law that requires lenders to assess the borrower's financial situation and explore options for avoiding foreclosure before foreclosing on the property, Cal. Civil Code §§ 2923.5 and 2923.6.

77. Defendants' acts and practices challenged alleged herein also constitute unfair business practices. Defendants' refusal to investigate the [*Plaintiff family's*] requests for case escalation, their refusal to postpone foreclosing on the [*Plaintiff family*] pending meaningful determination of their HAMP eligibility, and other acts described in this Complaint offend public policy with regard to the above statutes and regulations. Moreover, Defendants' acts in proceeding with foreclosure before genuinely evaluating the [*Plaintiff family*] for a loan modification offends public policy strongly favoring modification as provided in the federal Home Affordable Modification Program and Cal. Civil Code §§ 2923.5 and 2923.6. All of these acts and practices are substantially injurious to consumers and have no utility that outweighs their substantial harm to consumers.

78. The Court's intervention is necessary to halt and remedy Defendants' unlawful and unfair acts and practices.

79. Pursuant to Business and Professions Code § 17203, the Court should issue an Order preliminary and permanently restraining Defendants and their agents, servants, employees, representatives, and anyone acting on their behalf or direction from engaging in, committing, permitting, or performing, directly or indirectly, any of the unfair, unlawful or deceptive business practices described herein, and awarding restitution; disgorgement of sums wrongfully obtained; and costs of suit.

VII. RELIEF

WHEREFORE, the [*Plaintiff family*] prays for judgment against Defendants as follows:

1. That the Court assume supplemental jurisdiction over all state law claims, pursuant to 28 U.S.C. § 1367;

2. For equitable relief, including an Order compelling Defendants to properly evaluate the [*Plaintiff family*] for a HAMP modification;

3. For injunctive relief against Defendants to prevent future wrongful conduct;

4. For general, compensatory damages, and punitive damages according to proof;

5. For statutory damages according to proof;

6. For an award of attorneys fees, litigation expenses, and costs of suit;

7. For such other and further relief as the Court may deem proper.

[*Date*]

Respectfully submitted,

[*Organization Name*]

_____

[*Attorneys for Plaintiffs*]

JURY DEMAND

Pursuant to Federal Rule of Civil Procedure 38(b), Plaintiffs hereby request a trial by jury as to each and every claim for which they are so entitled.

Dated: _____

Respectfully submitted,

[*Organization Name*]

_____

[*Attorneys for Plaintiffs*]

CERTIFICATION OF INTERESTED ENTITIES OR PERSONS

Pursuant to Local Rule 3-16, the undersigned certifies that as of this date, other than the named parties, there is no such interest to report.

Dated: _____

Respectfully submitted,

[*Organization Name*]

_____

[*Attorneys for Plaintiffs*]

G.8 Complaint Alleging ECOA Notice Violations Against Servicer for Cancellation or Revocation of Final Loan Modification

UNITED STATES DISTRICT COURT
NORTHERN DISTRICT OF CALIFORNIA
SAN FRANCISCO DIVISION

[*Consumer 1*] and [*Consumer 2*], on behalf of themselves and all others similarly situated,))))	
Plaintiff,)	No.
)	CLASS ACTION
v.)	COMPLAINT
)	JURY DEMANDED
Wells Fargo Bank, N.A.,)	
Defendants.)	

COMPLAINT

1. Plaintiffs [*Consumer 1*] and [*Consumer 2*], by their counsel, bring this action on behalf of themselves and all others similarly situated against Wells Fargo Bank, N.A. ("Wells Fargo") to challenge Defendant's failure to comply with the notice provisions of the Equal Credit Opportunity Act when it cancels or revokes final loan modification agreements that it has entered into with its mortgage customers. Plaintiffs also seek relief for breach of contract and unfair and deceptive practices.

THE PARTIES

2. Plaintiffs [*Consumer 1*] and [*Consumer 2*] own a home in Las Cruces, New Mexico. Defendant Wells Fargo Bank, N.A. owned the mortgage on [*Consumers 1 and 2's*] home that was in place in 2009 ("Old Mortgage") and the modified mortgage that became effective on or about June 29, 2010 ("New Mortgage"). Wells Fargo Home Mortgage, a division of Wells Fargo Bank, N.A., services [*Consumers 1 and 2's*] mortgage. Wells Fargo Bank, N.A., owns and controls Wells Fargo Home Mortgage. References to Wells Fargo include Wells Fargo Home Mortgage.

JURISDICTION AND VENUE

3. This Court has subject matter jurisdiction over Count One of this Complaint, which seeks relief under the Equal Credit Opportunity Act (ECOA), pursuant to 28 U.S.C. § 1331 and 15 U.S.C. § 1691e. The Court has jurisdiction over Count Two, which seeks declaratory relief under state law, pursuant to the Class Action Fairness Act ("CAFA"), 28 U.S.C. § 1453, because there is diversity of citizenship and the amount in controversy, on information and belief, exceeds $5,000,000, 28 U.S.C. § 1332(d)(2), and pursuant to supplemental jurisdiction, 28 U.S.C. § 1367. This Court has jurisdiction over Count Three, which seeks injunctive relief under state law, pursuant to supplemental jurisdiction, 28 U.S.C. § 1367.

4. Venue is proper in this Court because Defendant is headquartered in this District and does business here. 28 U.S.C. § 1391(c)

INTRADISTRICT ASSIGNMENT

5. This action could not be said to "arise" in any county in this District as described in Civil L.R. 3-2 but this action is appropriately assigned to the San Francisco Division of the Northern District of California as the defendant has its principal place of business in the City and County of San Francisco and its parent company, Wells Fargo & Co., with whom it has unified operations, is located here.

BACKGROUND

6. The mortgage industry is currently overwhelmed with applications for loan modifications. As a result, the system is malfunctioning in a variety of ways. One of those ways is that mortgage customers are approved for loan modifications and then told they are in default even though they have been complying with the terms of the loan modification agreement. As Iowa Attorney General Tom Miller testified to the Senate Banking Committee on November 16, 2010:

> Perhaps the biggest problem is that loss mitigation and foreclosure exist simultaneously on parallel tracks. This leads to problems when the left hand does not know what the right hand is doing. Thus, we all hear stories of borrowers who thought they were approved for a loan modification receiving a notice of foreclosure sale.

7. On December 1, 2010, John Walsh, Acting Comptroller of the Currency, told the Senate Banking Committee that the dual track system in which banks proceed with foreclosures while evaluating borrowers for loan assistance was "unnecessarily confusing for distressed homeowners" and that he has directed banks, where legally possible, to halt foreclosure proceedings if borrowers are starting loan assistance programs.

8. It appears, however, that banks either do not feel themselves bound by this directive or do not have record keeping systems that recognize that a loan is in the modification process or has been modified.

9. Plaintiffs' situation illustrates the problem. [*Consumers 1 and 2*] are Wells Fargo mortgage customers. Last year, they applied for a loan modification.

10. On or about June 29, 2010, Wells Fargo sent a letter to [*Consumers 1 and 2*] which said: "This letter will confirm our formal approval of a loan modification of your mortgage loan." A copy of the letter is attached hereto as Exhibit A [*Editor's note: Not reprinted herein*]. The letter, and accompanying contract (which [*Consumers 1 and 2*] signed and returned (and which thus became the New Mortgage), said that the modified maturity date of the loan would be July 1, 2050, the new principal and interest payment would be $795.58 and the estimated escrow payment would be $256.99, making the estimated new payment $1,052.57. The New Mortgage was an enforceable contract and replaced the Old Mortgage payment terms.

11. [*Consumers 1 and 2*] made the monthly payments required under the New Mortgage: $1,052.57 on August 1, 2010 ([*Consumers 1 and 2*] had $458.24 in a suspense account, so they were told to send in an additional $594.33 (1,052.57 – 458.24), which they did); $1052.57 on September 1, 2010; $1052.57 on October 1, 2010; and $1052.57 on November 1, 2010.

12. Between the time they received the New Mortgage and November of this year, [*Consumers 1 and 2*] did not receive any notice from Wells Fargo that there was any problem with it or that Wells Fargo considered the Old Mortgage to be still in effect.

13. [*Consumers 1 and 2*] received a letter from a Wells Fargo office in California, dated November 7, 2010, which stated: "Our records show that your mortgage is in default." The delinquency figures in the letter, as well as the fact that the New Mortgage was not in default, make it clear that the letter refers to an alleged delinquency on the Old Mortgage. The November 7 letter, a copy of which is attached hereto as Exhibit B [*Editor's note: Not reprinted herein*], went on to explain that [*Consumers 1 and 2*] had past due payments of $11,256.36, plus a fee of $15.00, and unapplied funds of $5,217.59, leaving a balance of $6,053.77. The letter went on to warn [*Consumers 1 and 2*]:

> To avoid the possibility of acceleration, you must pay this amount plus any additional monthly payments, late charges and other charges that may be due under applicable law after the date of this notice and on or before December 7, 2010, in CERTIFIED funds, to Wells Fargo Home Mortgage, 1200 W 7th Street, Suite L2-200, Los Angeles, CA 90017.
>
> If funds are not received by the above referenced date, we will proceed with acceleration. Once acceleration has occurred, we may take steps to terminate your ownership in the property by a foreclosure proceeding or other action to seize the home or pursue any other remedy permitted under the term of your Mortgage.

Exhibit B [*Editor's note: Not reprinted herein*].

14. [*Consumers 1 and 2*] telephoned Wells Fargo on November 13, the day they received the November 7 letter, to explain that there must be an error as the New Mortgage, not the Old Mortgage, was in effect and was not delinquent. Wells Fargo took the position that there was no New Mortgage in effect. After the telephone conversation, [*Consumers 1 and 2*] received another letter from Wells Fargo (again from

a Wells Fargo office in California)—dated November 14, 2010—telling them again that they were in default, again clearly on the Old Mortgage, but reducing the amount allegedly due and owing to $5,630.26. *See* Exhibit C [*Editor's note: Not reprinted herein*].

15. The November 14 letter said, in pertinent part:

> Our records show that your mortgage is in default.
> * * * The past due payments on this loan are to be made by December 14, 2010, or it will become necessary for us to accelerate the Mortgage Note and pursue the remedies against the property as provided for in the Mortgage or Deed of Trust.

16. The November 7 and 14 letters from Wells Fargo related to the plaintiffs' Old Mortgage. Although the letters refer to the terms of the Old Mortgage, they are evidence that at some time on or before November 7 Wells Fargo had revoked, abrogated or otherwise taken some "adverse action" with respect to the New Mortgage contained in Exhibit A [*Editor's note: Not reprinted herein*]. Under the notice provisions of the Equal Credit Opportunity Act, Wells Fargo had a duty to send [*Consumers 1 and 2*] a written adverse action notice advising them of the adverse action with respect to the New Mortgage. Wells Fargo did not comply with this duty.

17. The November 7 and November 14 letters from Wells Fargo were not adverse action notifications with respect to the New Mortgage, despite the fact that it is possible to deduce from them that an adverse action with respect to the New Mortgage had been taken, because they do not meet the legal requirements of an adverse action notice and clearly were not intended to be adverse action notices as defined in the ECOA. The November 7 and 14 letters were clearly intended to be delinquency notices, which do not have to meet the requirements of an adverse action notice.

18. Wells Fargo was required to provide notice of the adverse action on the New Mortgage within 30 days of taking the action, which was clearly taken at some time on or before November 7. Wells Fargo had until December 7, 2010, at the latest, to give plaintiffs notice of the adverse action taken on their New Mortgage. To date, more than 30 days after December 7, [*Consumers 1 and 2*] have received no adverse action notice.

19. [*Consumers 1 and 2's*] situation reflects a much larger problem, of which the bank's failure to comply with the notice provisions of the Equal Credit Opportunity Act is just one small part: Either Wells Fargo is willfully disregarding its loan modification agreements or the bank has some systemic problem which causes Wells Fargo to ignore its loan modification agreements and court orders modifying mortgages.

20. Thus, for example, in July 2008 in *Wells Fargo Bank, N.A. v. Jones*, 391 B.R. 577 (E.D. La. 2008), a federal court in Louisiana affirmed a bankruptcy court order finding Wells Fargo in violation of the debtor's confirmed plan, and imposing punitive damages, noting:

> The Bankruptcy Court clearly had authority to impose punitive damages against Wells Fargo pursuant to Section 362 because the Bankruptcy Court determined that Wells Fargo's conduct was "egregious."

Id. at 609.

21. In February 2009, a federal bankruptcy court in Florida sanctioned Wells Fargo for violation of a discharge injunction, stating:

> The Court finds that Wells Fargo's actions were both intentional and egregious. Wells Fargo charged improper fees during the life of the Chapter 13 case. Wells Fargo attempted to collect those improper fees

after Plaintiffs received their discharge by making numerous telephone calls and sending numerous ominous letters to Plaintiffs demanding that Plaintiffs become current or face foreclosure. Wells Fargo ignored two letters sent by Plaintiffs' counsel attempting to resolve the matter. Wells Fargo made false entries on Plaintiffs' credit reports. Wells Fargo overcharged Plaintiffs when Plaintiffs' house was sold. Finally, Wells Fargo completely ignored the complaint in this adversary proceeding, opting not to file an answer or to become otherwise involved until after the entry of a default. The Court finds that Wells Fargo's conduct warrants an award of punitive damages in the amount of $15,000.

In re Nibbelink, 403 B.R. 113, 122 (Bkrtcy. M.D. Fla. 2009).

22. In May 2010, in a case filed by Wells Fargo mortgage customers [*Consumers 3 and 4*], Judge Jeff Almquist in Santa Cruz County, California issued a temporary injunction against Wells Fargo based on allegations that Wells Fargo sold [*Consumers 3 and 4's*] home in foreclosure even though the borrowers were complying with a loan modification agreement. www.mercurynews.com\fdcp?1291310674977 (11/30/2010).

23. Also in May 2010, a federal bankruptcy judge in Houston, Texas sanctioned Wells Fargo for repeatedly ignoring an Agreed Judgment modifying a mortgage. In commenting on the testimony of a Wells Fargo witness, a Senior Counsel for the company, the court said:

> The Court finds Grissom's credibility to be lacking in certain respects. First, he gave a Shermanesque statement that Wells Fargo was now in compliance with the Agreed Judgment . . . , but then subsequently had to admit that Wells Fargo's records still contained errors in violation of the Agreed Judgment. . . . Second, he could not explain why there are late charges appearing on Wells Fargo's records. . . . Grissom's failure on these key points, combined with his nonchalance on the stand, reflects a troubling lack of perspective regarding how much is at stake for honest and diligent Chapter 13 debtors, such as the De La Fuentes, who are trying to hold on to their home, and how important it is for Wells Fargo to abide by this Court's orders when dealing with debtors. Grissom appears to be representative of the absence of any sense of urgency within Wells Fargo to maintain accurate records and comply with the law.

In Re De La Fuente, 430 B.R. 764, 783–84 (Bkrtcy. S.D. Texas 2010).

24. In going on to reject Wells Fargo's "mistakes happen" defense, the bankruptcy court noted:

> The Court certainly agrees that "mistakes happen." However, when mistakes happen not once, not twice, but repeatedly, and when actions are not taken to correct these mistakes within a reasonable period of time, the failure to right the wrong—particularly when the basis for the problem is a months-long violation of an agreed judgment—the excuse of "mistakes happen" has no credence. Here, Wells Fargo's failure to take corrective action to comply with the Agreed Judgment does not come within hailing distance of

the realm where "mistakes happen" is a legitimate excuse. Rather, such failure, if not willful refusal to comply with the Agreed Judgment, is at least reckless disregard of the Agreed Judgment.

In Re De La Fuente, 430 B.R. 764, 790–91 (Bkrtcy. S.D. Texas 2010).

25. In November 2010, a judge in Suffolk County, New York, in *Wells Fargo Bank NA v. Meyers*, 34632-09, dismissed a foreclosure action filed by Wells Fargo because Wells Fargo had acted in bad faith by commencing the action one day after the homeowners accepted a loan modification proposal by Wells Fargo.

CLASS ACTION ALLEGATIONS

26. Because plaintiffs believe that they are typical of a much larger pattern of wrongdoing, this action is being brought as a class action pursuant to Fed. R. Civ. P. 23.

27. The acts, practices and conduct of which plaintiffs complain affected a Class consisting of all persons who: (a) have a home mortgage loan owned or serviced by Wells Fargo; (b) were sent a formal approval of a loan modification accompanied by a final loan modification agreement by Wells Fargo with respect to that home mortgage loan; (c) made timely payments as required by the final loan modification agreement; (d) were sent a notice of default from Wells Fargo dated on or after November 13, 2008, after entering into the loan modification agreement; and (e) did not receive, within 30 days of the notice of default, an adverse action notice from Wells Fargo. Plaintiffs reserve the right to amend this proposed class definition based on discovery to ensure that the class members are readily ascertainable based on objective criteria.

28. Upon information and belief, the members of the Class are so numerous that joinder is impractical. Upon information and belief, the Class is comprised of at least hundreds of individuals. Fed. R. Civ. P. 23(a)(1).

29. There are questions of law and fact common to the members of the Class, which questions predominate over any individual issues. Fed. R. Civ. P. 23(a)(2). These common questions include: (a) whether Defendant Wells Fargo had an obligation under the Equal Credit Opportunity Act to provide adverse action notices to customers who were in compliance with their final loan modification agreements when Wells Fargo took adverse action on that new mortgage loan; (b) whether Wells Fargo violated the Equal Credit Opportunity Act when it sent notices of default to customers who were in compliance with their loan modification agreements and did not provide adverse action notices within thirty days thereafter; (c) whether it is a breach of the contractual duty for Wells Fargo to send notices of default to customers who were in compliance with their final loan modification agreements; (d) the appropriate class-wide equitable relief and the appropriate amount of class-wide statutory damages.

30. The claims of plaintiffs are typical of the claims of all members of the Class. Fed. R. Civ. P. 23(a)(3).

31. Plaintiffs will fairly and adequately represent the Class. Plaintiffs are members of the Class. Plaintiffs are willing and able to serve as representatives of the Class and have no knowledge of any possible divergent interests between themselves and any member of the Class. Plaintiffs have retained competent counsel experienced in class actions and complex litigation to provide representation on behalf of themselves and the Class. Fed. R. Civ. P. 23(a)(4).

32. The prosecution of separate actions by individual members of the Class would create a risk of inconsistent or varying adjudications with respect to individual members of the Class, which would estab-

lish incompatible standards of conduct for Defendant. Fed. R. Civ. P. 23(b)(1)(A).

33. The prosecution of separate actions would also create a substantial risk of adjudications with respect to individual members of the Class, which would, as a practical matter, be dispositive of the interests of the other members not parties to the adjudications or substantially impair or impede their ability to protect their interests. Fed. R. Civ. P. 23(b)(1)(B).

34. Wells Fargo has both acted and refused to act on grounds that apply generally to the class, so that final injunctive relief or corresponding declaratory relief is appropriate respecting the class as a whole.

35. Questions of law and fact common to members of the Class predominate over any questions affecting individual members. The determinative facts, laws and legal principles apply universally to plaintiffs and the members of the Class. Fed. R. Civ. P. 23(b)(3).

36. Plaintiffs and the members of the Class all have valid claims against defendant. Each element of each claim is susceptible of common proof.

37. A class action provides a fair and efficient method for the adjudication of this controversy for the following reasons:

(a) The common questions of law and fact predominate over any questions affecting only individual Class members; Fed. R. Civ. P. 23(b)(3).

(b) The Class members are so numerous that joinder is impracticable. However, the Class is not so numerous as to create manageability problems. There are no legal or factual issues which would create manageability problems. Fed. R. Civ. P. 23(b)(3)(D).

(c) Prosecution of separate actions by individual members of the Class would create a risk of inconsistent and varying adjudications against defendant.

(d) Adjudications with respect to individual members of the Class could, as a practical matter, be dispositive of any interest of other members not parties to such adjudication, or substantially impair their ability to protect their interests.

38. The claims of the individual Class members are small in relation to the expenses of litigation, making a class action the only procedure by which Class members can, as a practical matter, redress their grievances. If individual Class members sought relief individually, legal fees would dwarf recoveries for every Class member. However, the total amount of the claims of individual Class members is large enough to justify the expense and effort in maintaining a class action.

COUNT ONE—EQUAL CREDIT OPPORTUNITY ACT

39. Plaintiffs reallege and incorporate paragraphs one through thirty-eight as though fully set forth herein.

40. Federal law contains safeguards that are supposed to prevent what happened to [*Consumers 1 and 2*] from occurring. One safeguard is the notice of adverse action requirement of the Equal Credit Opportunity Act.

41. Originally enacted in 1974 to prohibit discrimination in credit transactions, the Equal Credit Opportunity Act, 15 U.S.C. § 1691, was amended in 1976 to require creditors to furnish written notice of the specific reasons for adverse action taken against an applicant for credit.

42. The ECOA defines "adverse action," stating:

> For purposes of this subsection, the term "adverse action" means a denial or revocation of credit, a

change in the terms of an existing credit arrangement, or a refusal to grant credit in substantially the amount or on substantially the terms requested. Such term does not include a refusal to extend additional credit under an existing credit arrangement where the applicant is delinquent or otherwise in default, or where such additional credit would exceed a previously established credit limit.

15 U.S.C. § 1691(d)(6). Regulations implementing the ECOA are contained in 12 C.F.R. 202. 12 C.F.R. 202.2(c)(1)(ii) defines "adverse action" as including "(ii) A termination of an account or an unfavorable change in the terms of an account."

43. Notice of the adverse action must be provided within 30 days of the adverse action. The ECOA provides:

. . . .

    (d) Reason for adverse action; procedure applicable; "adverse action" defined.

        (1) Within thirty days (or such longer reasonable time as specified in regulations of the Board for any class of credit transaction) after receipt of a completed application for credit, a creditor shall notify the applicant of its action on the application.

15 U.S.C. § 1691(d)

The regulations implementing the ECOA provide at 12 C.F.R. 202.9(a)[:] "A creditor shall notify an applicant of action taken within: (iii) 30 days after taking adverse action on an existing account."

44. 15 U.S.C. § 1691(d) provides:

        (2) Each applicant against whom adverse action is taken shall be entitled to a statement of reasons for such action from the creditor. A creditor satisfies this obligation by—

        (A) providing statements of reasons in writing as a matter of course to applicants against whom adverse action is taken; or

        (B) giving written notification of adverse action which discloses (i) the applicant's right to a statement of reasons within thirty days after receipt by the creditor of a request made within sixty days after such notification, and (ii) the identity of the person or office from which such statement may be obtained. Such statement may be given orally if the written notification advises the applicant of his right to have the statement of reasons confirmed in writing on written request.

        (3) A statement of reasons meets the requirements of this section only if it contains the specific reasons for the adverse action taken.

15 U.S.C. § 1691(d)(3) provides that "A statement of reasons meets the requirements of this section only if it contains the specific reasons for the adverse action taken."

45. The ECOA expressly authorizes private law suits to enforce the statutory requirements. The statute provides: "Any creditor who fails to comply with any requirement imposed under this title shall be liable to the aggrieved applicant for any actual damages sustained by such applicant acting either in an individual capacity or as a member of a class." 15 U.S.C. § 1691e(a). "Any creditor . . . who fails to comply

with any requirement imposed under this title shall be liable to the aggrieved applicant for punitive damages in an amount not greater than $10,000, in addition to any actual damages provided in subsection (a), except that in the case of a class action the total recovery under this subsection shall not exceed the lesser of $500,000 or 1 percent of the net worth of the creditor. In determining the amount of such damages in any action, the court shall consider, among other relevant factors, the amount of any actual damages awarded, the frequency and persistence of failures of compliance by the creditor, the resources of the creditor, the number of persons adversely affected, and the extent to which the creditor's failure of compliance was intentional." 15 U.S.C. § 1691e(b). "Upon application by an aggrieved applicant, the appropriate United States district court . . . may grant such equitable and declaratory relief as is necessary to enforce the requirements imposed under this title." 15 U.S.C. § 1691e(c). "In the case of any successful action under subsection (a), (b), or (c), the costs of the action, together with a reasonable attorney's fee as determined by the court, shall be added to any award of damages awarded by the court under such subsection." 15 U.S.C. § 1691e(d).

46. Wells Fargo violated plaintiffs' rights under the ECOA. [*Consumers 1 and 2*] were applicants for credit within the meaning of the ECOA. Wells Fargo's decision to revoke or abrogate their loan modification agreement, as evidenced by the letter of November 7, 2010, attached hereto as Exhibit B [*Editor's note: Not reprinted herein*], and the letter of November 14, 2010, attached hereto as Exhibit C [*Editor's note: Not reprinted herein*], even though [*Consumers 1 and 2*] were in compliance with their approved final loan modification agreement, evidence that Wells Fargo took adverse action on the New Mortgage within the meaning of the ECOA. Wells Fargo had a duty to send [*Consumers 1 and 2*] a written adverse action notice within thirty days of its adverse action; Wells Fargo did not do so.

47. Wells Fargo violated plaintiffs' rights under the Equal Credit Opportunity Act, and the rights of members of the proposed Class, by taking adverse action—through the revocation or abrogation of a loan modification agreement—and not sending adverse action notices in the form and within the time limits prescribed by the ECOA.

COUNT TWO—BREACH OF CONTRACT INJUNCTION AND DECLARATORY JUDGMENT

48. Plaintiffs reallege and incorporate the above paragraphs one through thirty eight as though fully set forth herein.

49. The terms of the New Mortgage that plaintiffs have with Wells Fargo are set forth in Exhibit A [*Editor's note: Not reprinted herein*]. The other members of the Class also have similar final loan modification agreements with Wells Fargo that are contracts binding Wells Fargo.

50. Plaintiffs and other members of the Class have complied with their loan modification agreements with Wells Fargo. The agreements remain in effect. Nevertheless, Wells Fargo sent notices to plaintiffs and other members of the class stating the borrowers were in default and were obliged to pay Wells Fargo extra money to avoid acceleration of the loan and foreclosure on the mortgage. Wells Fargo thereby violated its contract terms and the inherent duty of good faith and fair dealing.

51. A dispute has arisen between the parties as to whether the final loan modification agreements preclude Wells Fargo from declaring a default, accelerating the loan or foreclosing on the mortgage of borrowers who are in compliance with their loan modification agreements. Plaintiffs and the Class contend that Wells Fargo does not have the right to abrogate the agreements, declare a default, accelerate the loans, send notices of default or foreclose on the mortgages so long as

the borrowers make the required payments under the approved final loan modification agreement and otherwise comply therewith.

52. Without a declaration of the rights of the parties, Wells Fargo will take actions inconsistent with the loan modification agreements. Among other things, without a declaration, there is a real and concrete danger that Wells Fargo will attempt to foreclose on mortgages covered by the loan modification agreements.

53. If Wells Fargo forecloses on mortgages protected by loan modification agreements, plaintiffs and other members of the Class will suffer irreparable injuries.

54. Unless enjoined to honor the loan modification agreements that it has with plaintiffs and the Class, Wells Fargo will continue to send notices of default and take other actions inconsistent with its obligations under the loan modification agreements.

COUNT THREE—UNFAIR AND DECEPTIVE TRADE PRACTICE INJUNCTION

55. Plaintiffs reallege and incorporate the above paragraphs one through thirty eight as though fully set forth herein.

56. Wells Fargo engaged in an unfair and deceptive trade practice, violative of New Mexico law (N.M.S.A. § 57-12-2), when it agreed to modify [*Consumers 1 and 2's*] loan and then told them they were in default, even though [*Consumers 1 and 2*] were complying with the terms of the loan modification agreement. Furthermore, it would be an unfair and deceptive trade practice, as well as an unconscionable trade practice, for Wells Fargo to accelerate [*Consumers 1 and 2's*] loan or foreclose on their mortgage while they are in compliance with the loan modification agreement.

57. Under New Mexico law: "A person likely to be damaged by an unfair or deceptive trade practice or by an unconscionable trade practice of another may be granted an injunction against it under the principles of equity and on terms that the court considers reasonable." N.M.S.A. § 57-12-10 A. Similar laws in other states protect the Class.

58. Absent judicial intervention, plaintiffs are likely to be damaged by Wells Fargo's unfair and deceptive practices. Those potential damages range from emotional distress to loss of their home. Given the balance of equities and the danger of irreparable harm, Wells Fargo should be enjoined from dishonoring the loan modification agreement it entered into with plaintiffs.

PRAYER FOR RELIEF

WHEREFORE, plaintiffs demand judgment including:

1. An order that this action may be maintained as a class action pursuant to Rule 23 of the Federal Rules of Civil Procedure, and appointing plaintiffs as class representatives, and appointing the undersigned as class counsel.

2. An order requiring Wells Fargo to provide plaintiffs and all members of the Class with a written statement of reasons as to why Wells Fargo decided to revoke or abrogate their final loan modification agreements, as a partial remedy for Defendant's violation of the Equal Credit Opportunity Act.

3. An award of $500,000 in statutory punitive damages and all the costs of this suit, including attorney's fees and costs, as a partial remedy for Defendant's violation of the Equal Credit Opportunity Act.

4. A declaration that the loan modification agreements of plaintiffs and other members of the Class are still valid and in effect.

5. An order prohibiting Wells Fargo from abrogating or revoking the loan modification agreements of plaintiffs and other members of the Class as long as the borrower remains in compliance therewith.

6. An order prohibiting Wells Fargo from declaring defaults, accelerating loans or foreclosing on mortgages of plaintiffs and other members of the Class as long as the borrower remains in compliance with the loan modification agreement.

7. Such other and further relief as this Court may deem proper.

Respectfully submitted,

By:_____

[Attorneys for plaintiffs]

G.9 Agreed Pre-Trial Order Including Jury Instructions in ECOA Notice Case

UNITED STATES DISTRICT COURT
EASTERN DISTRICT OF VIRGINIA
Richmond Division

[*Consumer*],	)
Plaintiff	)
	)
v.	) Civil No. _____
	)
Greater MidAtlantic Finance	)
Co., Inc.,	)
Defendant.	)
	)

AGREED PRE-TRIAL ORDER

COMES NOW, the parties, by counsel, and for their proposed Agreed Pre-Trial Order, they state as follows:

AGREED STIPULATIONS OF FACT

1. The parties agree that the following is an accurate timeline of the events in this case:

a. On September 22, 2000 Plaintiff signed a credit application for an automobile loan at Fairfax Hyundai. The application is Exhibit 1.

b. On September 22, 2000, Fairfax Hyundai faxed Plaintiff's credit application and contact sheet to Defendant. The contact sheet is Exhibit 2.

c. On September 22, 2000, Defendant pulled Plaintiff's credit report from Equifax. The credit report which Defendant pulled is Exhibit 3.

d. Defendant pulled the credit report to consider whether to purchase the credit contract between Plaintiff and Fairfax Hyundai.

e. Defendant reviewed the credit information in the credit application to Fairfax Hyundai and the credit report.

f. Defendant and Fairfax Hyundai had previously entered into an agreement regarding such transactions, and that agreement is Exhibit 4.

g. On September 27, 2000, Plaintiff signed the following documents:

Exhibit 6—Buyer's Order
Exhibit 7—Credit Contract as given to Plaintiff
Exhibit 8—Credit Contract as signed by Dealer
Exhibit 9—Deficiency Waiver Addendum

Exhibit 10—Agreement for Insurance

Exhibit 11—Application for Certificate of Title

h. On September 27, 2000, Plaintiff was given possession of the car by Fairfax Hyundai.

i. As part of its decision to consider whether to purchase the credit contract, Defendant required the documents listed on the Funding Check Sheet to be sent to Fairfax Hyundai. The Funding Check Sheet is Exhibit 11.

j. On September 28, 2000, Defendant printed a fax approval notice conditionally approving the purchase of the contract from Fairfax Hyundai. This Fax Approval Notice is Exhibit 12.

k. As part of its decision to consider whether to purchase the credit contract between Plaintiff and Fairfax Hyundai, Defendant called Plaintiff directly to try to verify some of the credit information.

l. By October 12, 2000, Defendant had the documents in its possession that are listed on Exhibit 13.

m. Defendant did not receive verification of the information about consumer's income that it had requested from Fairfax Hyundai.

n. As shown by Exhibit 14, by October 31, 2000, Defendant still had not received the information it had requested.

o. Defendant returned the Credit Contract to Fairfax Hyundai and did not purchase it from Fairfax Hyundai.

p. Defendant never provided any notice to Plaintiff under the Equal Credit Opportunity Act.

q. Defendant made a sufficient number of consumer loans in 2001 to be governed by the Equal Credit Opportunity Act.

r. Fairfax Hyundai did not send any notice of adverse action to Plaintiff because it did not consider itself the lender.

AGREED EXHIBITS

The parties agree that the following documents are true and accurate copies of the originals, that all signatures are authentic, and that these documents are relevant to the issues in this case. Both parties agree that each of these documents is admissible without any further foundation:

Exhibit 1—Credit Application

Exhibit 2—Contact Sheet

Exhibit 3—Equifax Credit report

Exhibit 4—Agreement between Defendant and dealer

Exhibit 5—Dealer's license to sell motor vehicles

Exhibit 6—Buyer's Order

Exhibit 7—Credit Contract as given to Plaintiff

Exhibit 8—Credit Contract as signed by Dealer

Exhibit 9—Deficiency Waiver Addendum

Exhibit 10—Agreement for Insurance

Exhibit 11—Application for Certificate of Title

Exhibit 12—Funding Checklist

Exhibit 13—Defendant's approval sheet printed September 28, 2000

Exhibit 14—Funding Approval Sheet printed October 12, 2000

Exhibit 15—Defendant's memo printed December 6, 2001

AGREED WITNESS LIST

[Consumer]

[Witness 1]

AGREED JURY INSTRUCTIONS

The following jury instructions are agreed without objection by either party:

(Revised P-2)

INSTRUCTION NO. 1

You are the judges of the facts, the credibility of the witnesses, and the weight of the evidence. You may consider the appearance and manner of the witnesses on the stand, their intelligence, their opportunity for knowing the truth and having observed the things about which they testified, their interest in the outcome of the case, their bias, and, if any have been shown, their prior inconsistent statements, or whether they have knowingly testified untruthfully as to any material fact in the case.

You may not arbitrarily disregard believable testimony of a witness. However, after you have considered all the evidence in the case, then you may accept or discard all or part of the testimony of a witness as you think proper.

You are entitled to use your common sense in judging any testimony. From these things and all the other circumstances of the case, you may determine which witnesses are more believable and weigh their testimony accordingly.

Your verdict must be based on the facts as you find them and on the law contained in all of these instructions.

V.M.J.I. No. 2.020 (modified)

(Revised P-3)

INSTRUCTION NO. 2

Any fact that may be proved by direct evidence may be proved by circumstantial evidence; that is, you may draw all reasonable and legitimate inferences and deductions from the evidence.

V.M.J.I. No. 2.100

(Revised P-7)

INSTRUCTION NO. 3

The greater weight of all the evidence is sometimes called the preponderance of the evidence. It is the evidence which you find more persuasive. The testimony of one witness whom you believe can be the greater weight of the evidence.

Each of the claims must be proven by the Plaintiff by the preponderance of the evidence.

V.M.J.I. No. 3.100 (modified)

(Revised P-8)

INSTRUCTION NO. 4

A proximate cause of a loss or damage is a cause which in a natural and continuous sequence produces the loss or damage. It is a cause without which the accident, injury, or damage would not have occurred.

V.M.J.I. No. 5.000

(Revised P-4)

INSTRUCTION NO. 5

The term evidence includes the sworn testimony of the witnesses at this trial, exhibits admitted into the record, all admitted facts, and other evidence that has been presented to you. Remember that the statements, objections and arguments by the lawyers are not evidence in the case.

No evidence may be used to contradict any undisputed fact. Undisputed facts are those facts that are stipulated or found to be true as a matter of law by me. Your role is to use the evidence to determine disputed facts.

(Revised D-7)

INSTRUCTION NO. 6

The burden is on the plaintiff to prove by the greater weight of the evidence each item of damage she claims and to prove that each item was caused by the actions of the defendant. She is not required to prove the exact amount of her damages, but she must show sufficient facts and circumstances to permit you to make a reasonable estimate of each item. If the plaintiff fails to do so, then she cannot recover for that item.

V.M.J.I. 9.010.

(Revised D-3)

INSTRUCTION NO. 7

Within thirty days after receipt of a completed application for credit, a creditor shall notify the applicant of its action on the application.

15 U.S.C. § 1691(d).

(Revised D-4)

INSTRUCTION NO. 8

For purposes of the Equal Credit Opportunity Act the term "adverse action" means a denial or revocation of credit, a change in the terms of an existing credit arrangement, or a refusal to grant credit in substantially the amount or substantially the terms requested.

15 U.S.C. § 1691(d)(6).

(Revised P-17)

INSTRUCTION NO. 9

If the application is incomplete the creditor can provide a notice of incompleteness or provide an adverse action notice to the applicant. Like the adverse action notice, the notice of incompleteness must be in writing and provided within 30 days of receiving the application.

See 12 C.F.R. § 202.9(a)(ii) and 202.9(c).

(Revised D-1)

INSTRUCTION NO. 10

The term "applicant" means any person who applies to a creditor directly for an extension, renewal, or continuation of credit, or applies to a creditor indirectly by use of an existing credit plan for an amount exceeding a previously established credit limit.

15 U.S.C. § 1691a(b).

(Revised D-2)

INSTRUCTION NO. 11

The term "creditor" means any person who regularly extends, renews, or continues credit; any person who regularly arranges for the extension, renewal, or continuation of credit; or any assignee of an original creditor who participates in the decision to extend, renew, or continue credit. A person is not a creditor regarding any violation of the act or this regulation committed by another creditor unless the person knew or had reasonable notice of the act, policy, or practice that constituted the violation before becoming involved in the credit transaction.

15 U.S.C. § 1691a(e); Regulation B, 12 C.F.R. § 202.2(e).

(Revised D-5)

INSTRUCTION NO. 12

The term "credit" means the right granted by a creditor to a debtor to defer payment of debt or to incur debts and defer its payment or to purchase property or services and defer payment therefor.

15 U.S.C. § 1691a(f).

(Revised D-6)

INSTRUCTION NO. 13

"Actual damages" for the violation of the Equal Credit Opportunity Act include recovery for any out-of-pocket expenses and property losses, and also damages for personal humiliation, embarrassment, mental anguish, and emotional distress. There is no fixed standard or measure in the case of intangible items such as humiliation, embarrassment, mental anguish and emotional distress. You must determine a fair and adequate award of these items through the exercise of your judgment and experience in the affairs of the world after considering all the facts and circumstances presented during the trial of this case.

VERDICT FORM

We, the jury, find Defendant's violation of the Equal Credit Opportunity Act caused Plaintiff
$ _____ in damages.
Or, if no amounts awarded at all,
We find that Plaintiff suffered no harm by not receiving proper notice as required by the Equal Credit Opportunity Act.
We, the jury, find that because of Defendant's violation of the Equal Credit Opportunity Act, Defendant should be assessed
$ _____ in punitive damages.

OBJECTED JURY INSTRUCTIONS

The Plaintiff proposes the following jury instruction to which the Defendant objects:

P-1

INSTRUCTION NO. _____

In addition to determining whether the Defendant caused any damages to Plaintiff by violating the Equal Credit Opportunity Act, you are also to determine the amount of punitive damages it should be assessed for any violation. In determining the amount of such damages for this violation, you should consider, among other factors, the amount of any actual damages you find, the frequency and persistence of failures of compliance by the Defendant, the financial resources of the Defendant, and the extent to which the creditor's failure of compliance was intentional.

15 U.S.C. § 1691e(b); *see also Cusman v. Trans Union Corp.*, *115 F. 3d 220, 227* (3d Cir. 1997); *Carroll v. Exxon Co., U.S.A.*, 434 F. Supp. 557, 561 (E.D. La. 1977); *Jones v. Credit Bureau of Huntington, Inc.*, 399 S.E.2d 694, 702, n.8 (W. Va. 1990); *Rutnya v. Collection Accounts Terminal, Inc.*, 478 F. Supp. 980, 982 (N.D. Ill. 1979); *Johnson v. Associates Fin., Inc.*, 369 F. Supp. 1121, 1125 (S.D. Ill, 1974); *Nitti v. Credit Bureau of Rochester, Inc.*, 84 Misc.2d 277, 375 N.Y.S.2d 817, 821.

ENTERED THIS _____ DAY OF FEBRUARY, 2002

_____
[Judge]

WE ASK FOR THIS:

_____
[Attorney for Plaintiff]

_____
[Attorney for Defendant]

G.10 Proposed Jury Instructions in ECOA Notice Case

[Case name]
Plaintiff's Proposed Instruction #_____

The Plaintiff, *[Consumer]*, has brought several Counts against the Defendants, *[Defendant 1]* and *[Defendant 2]*. I will instruct you as to the law governing each Count; however, each Count should be considered separately and independently as if it were the only Count before you. In your deliberations on each Count, you should not consider or be influenced by your decision with respect to other Counts, including decisions regarding damages.

_____Given
_____Given as Modified
_____Refused
_____Withdrawn

Rosario v. Livaditis, 1989 U.S. Dist. LEXIS 13970

In Count I of her Complaint, the Plaintiff, *[Consumer]*, alleges that Defendant, *[Defendant 1]*, violated the Equal Credit Opportunity Act, or ECOA.

_____Given
_____Given as Modified
_____Refused
_____Withdrawn

IPI 21.03 (modified)

In Count III of her Complaint, the Plaintiff, *[Consumer]*, alleges that Defendant, *[Defendant 1]* violated the Truth in Lending Act, or TILA.

_____Given
_____Given as Modified
_____Refused
_____Withdrawn

IPI 21.03 (modified)

In Count IV of her Complaint, the Plaintiff, *[Consumer]*, alleges that Defendant, *[Defendant 2]*, violated the Credit Repair Organiza-

tions Act, or CROA.

_____Given
_____Given as Modified
_____Refused
_____Withdrawn

IPI 21.03 (modified)

In Count V of her Complaint, the Plaintiff, *[Consumer]*, alleges that Defendant, *[Defendant 1]* violated the Illinois Consumer Fraud and Deceptive Business Practices Act.

_____Given
_____Given as Modified
_____Refused
_____Withdrawn

IPI 21.03 (modified)

In Count VI of her Complaint, the Plaintiff, *[Consumer]*, alleges that Defendant, *[Defendant 2]*, violated the Illinois Consumer Fraud and Deceptive Business Practices Act.

_____Given
_____Given as Modified
_____Refused
_____Withdrawn

IPI 21.03 (modified)

When I use the expression "proximate cause," I mean any cause which, in natural or probable sequence, produced the injury complained of.

_____Given
_____Given as Modified
_____Refused
_____Withdrawn

IPI (Civ.) 15.01

When I say that a party has the burden of proof on any proposition, or use the expression "if you find," or "if you decide," I mean you must be persuaded, considering all the evidence in the case, that the proposition on which he has the burden of proof is more probably true than not true.

_____Given
_____Given as Modified
_____Refused
_____Withdrawn

IPI (Civ.) 21.01

The Court has already ruled that Defendant *[Defendant 1]* violated the Equal Credit Opportunity Act. You may award any actual damages sustained by the Plaintiff, and must award punitive damages under the Equal Credit Opportunity Act. The maximum punitive damages that can be awarded are $10,000.

In considering the amount of punitive damages that should be assessed, you should consider the following factors:
— The amount of actual damages awarded;
— The frequency and persistence of noncompliance;
— The Defendant's resources;
— The number of persons adversely affected;
— The extent to which noncompliance was intentional;

_____Given
_____Given as Modified
_____Refused
_____Withdrawn

15 U.S.C. §§ 1691d, 1691e, 1691e(b)

The Court has already ruled that Defendant [*Defendant 1*] violated the Truth in Lending Act. You may award damages under the Truth in Lending Act for:

(A) Any actual damages sustained by Plaintiff as a result of [*Defendant 1's*] violation of the Act;

(B) Statutory damages in an amount up to two times the finance charge Plaintiff was to pay under the finance agreement.

_____Given
_____Given as Modified
_____Refused
_____Withdrawn

15 U.S.C. § 1601 *et seq.*

In Count IV of the Complaint, the Plaintiff [*Consumer*], alleges Defendant [*Defendant 2*] violated the Credit Repair Organizations Act. In order to prove such a claim, the Plaintiff must show that:

The Defendant made any statement, or counseled or advised any consumer to make any statement, which was untrue or misleading (or which, upon the exercise of reasonable care, should be known by the Defendant to be untrue or misleading) with respect to any consumer's credit worthiness, credit standing, or credit capacity to any person to whom the consumer has applied or is applying for an extension of credit.

_____Given
_____Given as Modified
_____Refused
_____Withdrawn

15 U.S.C. § 1679b

If you find [*Defendant 2*] liable under the Credit Repair Organizations Act, you may award damages under the Act for:

(A) Any actual damages sustained by Plaintiff as a result of [*Defendant 2's*] violation of the Act; defined as the greater of—

(1) the amount of any actual damage sustained by such person as a result of such failure;

or

(2) any amount paid by the person to the credit repair organization.

(B) Punitive damages

_____Given
_____Given as Modified
_____Refused
_____Withdrawn

15 U.S.C. §§ 1679b, 1679g

In Counts V and VI of the Complaint, Plaintiff [*Consumer*] alleges Defendants [*Defendant 1*] and [*Defendant 2*] violated the Illinois Consumer Fraud And Deceptive Trade Practices Act.

The Illinois Consumer Fraud Act prohibits any unfair or deceptive act or practice, including but not limited to the use or employment of any deception, fraud, false pretense, false promise, misrepresentation or the concealment, suppression or omission of any material fact with the intent that others rely on the concealment, suppression or omission.

In order to prove such a claim, the Plaintiff must show each of the following:

First, that the Defendant was engaged in trade or commerce in Illinois;

Second, that Defendant engaged in such an unfair or deceptive act or practice within that trade or commerce; and

Third, Plaintiff suffered actual damage as a result of Defendant's conduct.

_____Given
_____Given as Modified
_____Refused
_____Withdrawn

815 ILCS 505/2

If you find either or both Defendants liable under the Illinois Consumer Fraud Act, you may award damages under Act for:

(A) Any actual damages sustained by Plaintiff as a result of the Defendant's violation of the Act;

(B) Punitive damages. I will further explain to you under what circumstances you can award damages for punitive damages.

_____Given
_____Given as Modified
_____Refused
_____Withdrawn

815 ILCS 505/2

An act is deceptive if it creates the likelihood of deception or has the capacity to deceive the persons exposed to the practice in the particular case.

_____Given
_____Given as Modified
_____Refused
_____Withdrawn

Elder v. Coronet, 201 Ill. App. 3d 733, 558 N.E.2d 1312 (1st Dist. 1990).

The Consumer Fraud Act imposes an affirmative duty to disclose material facts pertaining to a transaction: Under the Act, the omission of any material fact is deceptive conduct. Material omissions are actionable even if no duty to disclose the omitted information, other than that imposed by the Consumer Fraud Act itself, existed. A matter is material if it might cause a consumer to act differently. Materiality is objective, to be determined according to the standard of the population to which the Defendant's practices are directed.

_____Given
_____Given as Modified
_____Refused
_____Withdrawn

Crowder v. Bob Oberling Enterprises, Inc., 148 Ill. App. 3d 313, 317, 499 N.E. 2d 115 (1st Dist. 1986); *Celex Group v. Executive Gallery*, 877 F. Supp. 1114 (N.D. Ill. 1995); *Heastie v. Community Bank of Greater Peoria*, 690 F. Supp. 716 (N.D. Ill. 1989); *Kleidon v. Rizza Chevrolet*, 173 Ill. App. 3d 116, 527 N.E.2d 374 (1st Dist. 1988); *Mother Earth Ltd. v. Stawberry Camel, Ltd.*, 72 Ill. App. 3d 37, 52, 390 N.E.2d 393, 406 (1979).

In determining whether a practice is "unfair" you may consider whether the practice offends public policy, is immoral, unethical, oppressive, or unscrupulous, or whether it causes substantial injury to consumers.

_____Given
_____Given as Modified
_____Refused
_____Withdrawn

FTC v. Sperry & Hutchinson Co., 405 U.S. 233, 244 n. 5 (1972); *Scott v. Association for Childbirth at Home*, 88 Ill. 2d 279, 430 N.E.2d 1012 (1981); *Robinson v. Toyota Motor Credit Corporation*, 201 Ill.2d 403, 775 N.E.2d 951 (2002); *Elder v. Coronet*, 201 Ill. App. 3d 733, 558 N.E.2d 1312 (1st Dist. 1990); *People ex rel. Hartigan v. All American Aluminum & Construction Co.*, 171 Ill. App. 3d 27 (1st Dist. 1988).

Actual damage is defined as any wrong or damage done to another, either in his person, rights, reputation or property, or the invasion of a legally protected interest of another. Actual damages include, but are not limited to, emotional distress and mental anguish as well as out of pocket losses.

_____Given
_____Given as Modified
_____Refused
_____Withdrawn

White v. Touch Ross & Co, 163 Ill. App. 3d 94, 516 N.E.2d 509 (1st Dist. 1987); *Village of Bellwood v. Human Rights Commission*, 184 Ill. App. 3d, 339, 354; 541 N.E. 2d 1248, 1258 (1st Dist. 1989); *see also*, *Knierim v. Izzo*, 22 Ill. 2d 73, 1774 N.E. 2d 157; *Lorrillard v. Field Enterprises, Inc.*, 65 Ill. App. 2d 65, 213 N.E. 2d 1; *Shelton v. Barry*, 328 Ill. App. 497, 66 N.E. 2d 697; *ISS International Service System, Inc. v. Illinois Human Rights Commission*, 272 Ill. App. 3d 969, 979 1st Dist. 1995).

If you find for the Plaintiff on any or all of Counts I, V or VI, and that either Defendants' conduct was willful and wanton and proximately caused injury to the Plaintiff, *and*, if you believe that justice and the public good require it, you may, in addition to any damages to which you find the Plaintiff entitled, award an amount which will serve to punish the Defendants and to deter others from the commission of like offenses. Such damages are known as "Punitive Damages."

_____Given
_____Given as Modified
_____Refused
_____Withdrawn

IPI (Civ.) 35.01

G.11 Plaintiffs' Proposed Jury Instructions in Fair Housing and ECOA Notice Case

UNITED STATES DISTRICT COURT
NORTHERN DISTRICT OF CALIFORNIA
(SAN JOSE)

_____)	
[*Consumer 1*] and [*Consumer 2*],)	
Plaintiffs,)	
)	
v.)	Case No. _____
)	PLAINTIFFS' PROPOSED
JP Morgan Chase Bank, N.A,)	SUBSTANTIVE JURY
U.S. Bank National Association,)	INSTRUCTIONS
California Reconveyance)	
Corporation and DOES 150,)	
Defendants.)	
_____)	

PROPOSED JURY INSTRUCTION NO. _____

FAIR HOUSING CLAIMS

PURPOSE OF THE STATUTE

The purpose of California's Fair Employment and Housing Act is to eliminate all traces of discrimination within the housing market. This law is aimed not only at racial discrimination but also discrimination based on source of income, national origin, or disability. This statute prohibits both intentional discrimination (known as "disparate treatment" cases) and instances where, even if no discrimination was intended, the effect of the defendant's practices was discriminatory (known as "disparate impact" cases). I will shortly instruct you on the elements which must be established to prove discrimination under this statute.

Authority: Modern Federal Jury Instructions: 87-32; Cal. Gov't Code § 12920.

PROPOSED JURY INSTRUCTION NO._____

LIABILITY FOR ACTS OF DISCRIMINATION UNDER CALIFORNIA'S FAIR EMPLOYMENT AND HOUSING ACT

Plaintiffs claim that Defendant Chase violated the California Fair Employment and Housing Act by discriminating against Plaintiffs on the basis of source of income. Specifically, Plaintiffs claim that Defendant Chase made statements about [*Consumer 1's*] State Disability Income that indicated a preference or limitation or discrimination based on source of income, or an intention to make that preference, limitation, or discrimination.

Authority: Cal. Gov't Code §§ 12955(c) & (e)(i).

PROPOSED JURY INSTRUCTION NO._____

PROHIBITED CONDUCT UNDER THE FAIR HOUSING LAWS

The fair housing laws make it unlawful to do any of the following things:

1. To make statements that indicate a preference, limitation or discrimination based on source of income in the provision of services in connection with a residential real estate related transaction.

2. To discriminate in the provision of services in connection with residential real estate-related transactions, or in the terms or conditions of such transactions to individuals or groups because of source of income.

Each one of these acts or practices is a separate and independent violation of California's Fair Employment and Housing Act.

Authority: Cal. Gov't Code §§ 12955(c),(i).

PROPOSED JURY INSTRUCTION NO. _____

REAL ESTATE RELATED TRANSACTION—DEFINED

A real estate related transaction is defined as making or purchasing loans or providing other financial assistance that is secured by residential real estate.

Authority: Cal. Gov't Code § 12927(h)(1).

PROPOSED JURY INSTRUCTION NO. _____

SOURCE OF INCOME NEED NOT BE THE SOLE MOTIVATING REASON FOR THE DEFENDANT'S CONDUCT

The Fair Employment and Housing Act is violated if any one of the reasons for the Defendant's actions is unlawful source of income discrimination. Source of income is an impermissible factor to consider in making mortgage loans. The Plaintiffs are not required to prove that source of income was the sole reason for the Defendant's actions, or even that it was the primary reason. The Plaintiffs need only show that source of income was one factor in the conduct that is challenged here.

Authority: Cal. Gov't Code § 12955.8(a); *Hanson v. Veterans Admin.*, 800 F.2d 1381 (5th Cir. 1986); *Robinson v. 12 Lofts Realty, Inc.*, 610 F.2d 1032 (2d Cir. 1979).

PROPOSED JURY INSTRUCTION NO. _____

PROTECTED CLASS—"SOURCE OF INCOME"

"Source of income" is defined to mean any lawful, verifiable income. Source of income discrimination only prohibits consideration of where a person's money is derived. It does not prohibit "economic discrimination" based on the amount of income.

Authority: Cal. Gov't. Code § 12955(e); *Sisemore v. Master Financial, Inc.*, 151 Cal. App. 4th 1386, 1410 (2007).

PROPOSED JURY INSTRUCTION NO. _____

DISCRIMINATORY INTENT NOT NECESSARY

Statements indicating a preference or limitation violate the fair housing laws, even when those statements are made *without* the intent to discriminate or injure. Discriminatory intent on the part of the speaker is not required to establish a discriminatory statement.

Authority: Cal. Gov't Code § 12995 (c); *Housing Rights Ctr. v. Donald Sterling Corp.*, 274 F. Supp. 2d 1129, 1137 (C.D. Cal. 2003); *Ragin (II) v. Harry Macklowe Real Estate,* 6 F.3d 898, 905 (2d Cir. 1993).

FEHA BURDEN OF PROOF—PROHIBITED DISCRIMINATORY STATEMENTS

The second way by which plaintiffs may show a violation of the California Fair Employment and Housing Act by Chase is by proving by a preponderance of the evidence that Chase or its agents made a statement or statements with respect to the application for a HAMP loan modification which expressed a preference, limitation or discrimination based on source of income, or an intention to make any such preference, limitation or discrimination.

Under this method of proof, plaintiffs do not have to prove that Chase or its agents intended to express such a preference, limitation or discrimination, or that source of income was a motivating factor behind the statement. The test to determine whether a statement expresses a preference, limitation or discrimination based upon source of income with respect to the application for a loan modification is whether the statement itself would indicate to an ordinary listener or reader a preference, limitation or discrimination with respect to application for a loan modification based on source of income. Plaintiffs are not required to prove that the message based on source of income was the only message, or even the primary message, communicated by the statement. Plaintiffs need only prove that a message of preference, limitation or discrimination with respect to the application for a loan modification based on source of income was one of the messages communicated by the statement.

Authority: Cal. Gov't Code § 12955(c); *United States v. Hunter*, 459 F.2d 205, 215 (4th Cir.)*, cert. denied*, 409 U.S. 934, 93 S. CT. 235, 34 L.Ed.2d 189 (1972), *Ragin v. New York Times Co.*, 923 F.2d 995, 999-1000 (2d Cir.), *cert. denied*, 502 U.S. 821, 112 S. CT. 81, 116 L.Ed.2d 54 (1991); *Jancik v. HUD*, 44 F.3d 553, 556 (7th Cir.1995) (no discriminatory intent is required); *Fair Housing Congress v. Weber*, 993 F. SUPP. 1286, 1290 (C.D. CAL. 1997) (same).

PROPOSED JURY INSTRUCTION NO. _____

EQUAL CREDIT OPPORTUNITY ACT CLAIMS PURPOSE OF THE STATUTE

The purpose of the federal Equal Credit Opportunity Act's notice provisions is to require creditors to explain their credit decisions, thereby effectively discouraging creditors from discriminatory practices. As Congress and courts have noted, these provisions "are a strong and necessary adjunct to the antidiscrimination purpose of the legislation." The Court has already decided that Defendants are liable for twice violating these notice provisions, and your job is to determine the amount of damages that Defendants should pay Plaintiffs for these violations.

Authority: *Fischl v. General Motors Acceptance Corp.*, 708 F.2d 143, 146-147 (5th Cir. La. 1983); Rep. No. 94-589, 94th Cong., 2d Sess., reprinted in 1976 U.S. Code Cong. & Admin. News, pp. 403, 406. n3; 15 U.S.C. § 1691(d); 12 CFR 202.9(a)(2).

PROPOSED JURY INSTRUCTION NO. _____

COMPENSATORY DAMAGES

It is the duty of the Court to instruct you about the measure of damages. By instructing you on damages, the Court does not mean to suggest for which party your verdict should be rendered.

If you find for the Plaintiffs, you must determine Plaintiffs' damages. Plaintiffs have the burden of proving the extent of their damages by a preponderance of the evidence. If proven, Plaintiffs are entitled to recover an amount which will reasonably compensate Plaintiffs for loss and damage caused by Defendant's discriminatory statements and failure to provide proper notices of adverse action. If you find Defendants violated the law, you may award Plaintiffs reasonable compensation for:

(1) financial losses, including damage to credit reputation.

(2) emotional distress; mental anguish, suffering, or humiliation.

Your award must be based upon the evidence and not upon speculation, guesswork, or conjecture.

Authority: Ninth Circuit Model Civil Jury Instructions 7.1; Cal. Gov't. Code § 12989.2; 15 U.S.C. § 1691e; *Johnson v. Hale*, 13 F.3d 1351, 1352 (9th Cir. 1994); *Anderson v. United Finance Co.*, 666 F.2d 1274, 1277 (9th Cir. 1982).

PROPOSED JURY INSTRUCTION NO. _____

NOMINAL DAMAGES

If you find that Defendant violated the ECOA and the fair housing laws, but that Plaintiffs have failed to prove actual damages, you must return an award of nominal damages not to exceed one dollar.

Authority: Ninth Circuit Model Civil Jury Instructions 7.6, 11.4; *Cabrera v. Jakabovitz*, 24 F.3d 372, 390-391 (2d Cir. 1994).

PROPOSED JURY INSTRUCTION NO. _____

PUNITIVE DAMAGES

Punitive damages may be awarded if you find that the Defendant (1) wantonly, maliciously or oppressively discriminates against an applicant, or (2) the Defendant acts in "reckless disregard of the requirements of the law", even though there was no specific intention to discriminate on unlawful grounds.

Any creditor who fails to comply with any requirement imposed under ECOA shall be liable to the aggrieved applicant for punitive damages in an amount not greater than $ 10,000, in addition to any actual damages.

Authority: Cal. Gov't Code § 12989.2; *Fountila v. Carter*, 571 F.2d 487, 491 (9th Cir. 1978); 15 U.S.C. § 1691e; Reg. B. § 202.16(b)(1); *Shuman v. Standard Oil Co.*, 453 F. Supp. 1150, 1155 (N.D. Cal. 1978); *Anderson v. United Finance Co.*, 666 F.2d 1274, 1278 (9th Cir. Or. 1982) (courts are allowed to award punitive damages under § 1691e(b) even though the creditor's conduct is not wanton, malicious or oppressive, in order to increase the incentive for creditor compliance).

PROPOSED JURY INSTRUCTION NO. _____

CORPORATE DEFENDANT

In this case, Defendant is a corporation. A corporation can only act through its employees, agents, directors, and officers. Therefore, a corporation is responsible for the acts of its employees, agents, directors, and officers performed within the scope of authority.

Authority: Ninth Circuit Model Civil Jury Instructions 6.2.

Dated: _____

[Organization Name]

_____

[Attorneys for Plaintiffs]
Attorneys for Plaintiffs

Sample Discovery

These are sample forms and must be adapted to fit the facts of a particular case and local procedural rules. Note that the Federal Rules of Civil Procedure limit the number of interrogatories to twenty-five, including subparts. This limitation may be avoided only by leave of the court with written stipulation of the parties. The reader should be aware of this limit in cases of federal litigation and in litigation in state courts that similarly limit discovery. If permitted, practitioners should also consider seeking a request for admissions as an alternative or supplement to interrogatories. The consumer's attorney should plan for discovery as soon as he or she receives the case.

These sample discovery forms are also available on the companion website to this treatise. The companion website facilitates keyword searches and allows relevant provisions to be imported into word-processable documents. The companion website includes a number of additional sample discovery requests that are not reprinted here.

H.1 Plaintiff's Interrogatories and Request for Production of Documents in ECOA Notice Case

UNITED STATES DISTRICT COURT
EASTERN DISTRICT OF VIRGINIA
NEWPORT NEWS DIVISION

————————————)
[*Consumer*])
            Plaintiff)
)
v.)
) Civil No. ————————
Greater Mid-Atlantic Finance)
Co., Inc. and Fairfax Hyundai,)
Inc.)
          Defendants.)
————————————)

PLAINTIFF'S FIRST SET OF INTERROGATORIES AND REQUEST FOR PRODUCTION OF DOCUMENTS TO DEFENDANTS

Pursuant to the Federal Rules of Civil Procedure, and the Local Rules for the Eastern District of Virginia, Plaintiff, by counsel, propounds the following Interrogatories and Request for Production of Documents to Defendants, Greater Mid-Atlantic Finance Co., Inc. and Fairfax Hyundai, Inc., to be answered under oath within the time prescribed by the Federal Rules of Civil Procedure and the Local Rules of the United States District Court for the Eastern District of Virginia.

I. DEFINITIONS

As used in these Interrogatories, the words and terms set forth below are defined as follows:

A. "Describe", "specify" and/or "state" shall mean to set forth fully and unambiguously, using technical terms or words of art, if necessary, each and every fact relevant to the answer called for by the Interrogatory of which the defendant or its agents, employees or representatives have knowledge.

B. "Person" shall mean any and all: natural persons; business associates; corporations; partnerships; limited partnerships; joint ventures; estates; trusts; banks savings associations; governmental agencies, departments, commissions, boards or committees.

C. "Agreement" means any common understanding reached by two or more people or entities, whether written or oral, formal or informal.

D. "You" or "your" means the party separately answering these Interrogatories, together with its wholly or partly owned subsidiaries, and its affiliates or parent companies, and each and every other legal entity within its direct or indirect control or in which it holds any equity or other interests, as well as its merged or acquired predecessors in interest (if any), its present and former officers, directors, employees, agents, representatives, and any other persons or corporations acting in a consulting or advisory capacity or acting or purporting to act on behalf of any of the foregoing.

E. Whenever relevant, words in singular shall include the plural thereof. Whenever relevant, use of the words "his", "him" or "he" shall include her, hers and she.

F. "Document" means any written, printed, typed or other graphic material of any kind or nature, and all mechanical, electronic or sound recordings in the defendant's possession or control, or known by it to exist. It shall also mean all drafts nonidentical copies of documents by whatever means made.

G. "Communicate" or "communication" means every manner or means of disclosure or transfer or exchange of information of any kind whether oral or by document or whether face-to-face, by telephone, mail, personal or any other means of delivery.

H.(i) "Identify" or "identity" when used with respect to a natural person means to state his full name, present or last known address, present or last known position or business affiliation, all positions or business affiliations during the time period of these Interrogatories, and a general description of the business in which he is or was engaged in each such position.

(ii) "Identify" or "Identity" when used with respect to any other entity means to state its full name, the address of its principal place of business and the name of its officers.

(iii) "Identify" or "Identity" when used with respect to a document means to state the name and title of the document, the type of document (e.g., letter, memorandum, telegram, chart, etc.), its date, the person who wrote it, the person who signed it, the person to whom it was addressed, the person to whom it was sent, its present location, and its present custodian. If any such document was, but is no longer in the defendant's possession or subject to its control, state what disposition was made of it and explain the circumstances surrounding, and the authorization for, such disposition, and state the date or approximate date thereof. Documents prepared prior to the period covered by these Interrogatories but which relate or refer thereto are to be included.

(iv) "Identify" or "identity" when used with respect to any non-written communication means to state the identity of the natural person making and receiving the communication, their respective principals or employers at the time of the communication, the date, manner and place of the communication, and the substance of the communication.

(v) "Identify" or "identity" when used with respect to a meeting means to state the nature of the meeting (formal gathering, conversation, telephone call, etc.) to identify all persons participating, to provide the date, duration, location(s) and to state the substance of the discussion.

I. The words, "and" and "or" shall each include "and/or".

J. The word "Automobile" when used shall mean the 2000 Dodge Stratus which is the subject of this lawsuit.

K. The word "complaint", unless otherwise noted, means the original and any amended complaint served by the plaintiff in this action.

L. The word "Plaintiff" means [*Consumer*].

II. INSTRUCTIONS

A. The information requested is for all information known to the defendant, its officers, directors, employees and available at the time of answering, including information in the possession of its agents.

B. To the extent any information called for by these Interrogatories is unknown, so state, and set forth such remaining information as is known. If any estimate or general description can reasonably be made in place of unknown information, set forth the best estimate or general description, clearly designating the answer as such, in place of unknown information, and the basis upon which the estimate or general description is made.

To the extent any Interrogatory is objected to, set forth all reasons therefor. If any claim of privilege is asserted as a ground for not answering any Interrogatory, whether in whole or in part, describe the factual basis for such claim in sufficient detail so as to permit the court to adjudicate the validity of the claim.

C. These Interrogatories shall be deemed continuing, so as to require additional answers if further information is obtained between the time answers are served and the time of trial. Such additional answers shall be served from time to time, but not later than thirty (30) days after such additional information is received.

III. INTERROGATORIES

1. For each interrogatory below identify the person or persons supplying the information upon which the particular response is based. Identify all such persons here. (When these interrogatories are answered under oath, by any person, including an attorney, the plaintiff reserve the right to take the oral deposition of such person and to call that person as a witness at trial.)

2. Identify all persons known to you who have knowledge of facts relevant to this case, and state the subject of testimony, giving a brief description thereof, for each person you may call as a witness in this case. If you intend to qualify any of these witness as experts, please so indicate, giving their areas of expertise and their credentials as experts.

3. Identify any exhibits which you intend to offer into evidence in this proceeding.

ANSWER:

4. Identify each document which you may introduce into evidence in this case.

ANSWER:

5. Identify all documents which contain information concerning the transaction, loan and course of dealing at issue, and all documents which contain information concerning each occasion on which you have acquired or sold or obtained a security interest on the automobile. State which, if any, of the documents were furnished to Plaintiff, where and when each such document was furnished to Plaintiff, and all persons who you know or believe could testify that such document(s) was or were furnished to the Plaintiff.

ANSWER:

6. Did the defendant ever receive any written or non-written communication from the plaintiff? If so, specifically list and identify each such communication. For non-written communication, state the content of each such communication. For written communications, document in your answer to *this* interrogatory identify the document and the date of receipt for each document so identified.

ANSWER:

7. Did the defendant ever receive any written or non-written communication from any other person pertaining to the plaintiff? If so, specifically list and identify each such communication. For non-written communication, state the content of each such communication. For written communications, document in your answer to *this* interrogatory identify the document and the date of receipt for each document so identified.

ANSWER:

8. Describe your procedure and policy with respect to the maintenance, preservation and destruction of documents, including whether any documents relating to any information requested in these interrogatories, or related in any way to this lawsuit, have ever been destroyed or are no longer in your custody. For each such document, please state the identity of the document, how, when and why each document was destroyed or otherwise left your control, the identity of any person who participated in any way in the destruction and/or action for destroying the document or to transfer it out of your control or custody; and if the document still exists, identify the person now having control or custody of the document.

ANSWER:

9. State how and when you again obtained possession of the automobile after it had been initially delivered to the Plaintiff.

ANSWER:

10. If you contend that a notice of adverse action was sent to the Plaintiff in compliance with the Equal Credit Opportunity Act (ECOA), identify the notice(s) sent, the party which sent such notice, the date

the notice was sent, the method of delivery of such notice, and all persons with knowledge of when and how such notice was sent, and describe your method of recording or documenting if, when and how such notice was sent to the plaintiff.

ANSWER:

11. State and identify the name and address of every person the defendant intends to call as a witness at trial.

ANSWER:

12. Identify and describe all books, documents, photographs or other tangible things which the defendant will rely on in defense of the claims in the complaint and as to each, state: a) description; b) nature; c) name and address of the person who has custody; d) its location; and e) its condition.

ANSWER:

13. Identify all documents prepared by or on behalf of the defendant used in connection with the training or instruction of any of your employees identified in your responses to these interrogatories.

ANSWER:

14. Does the defendant issue an annual report containing, *inter alia*, gross and net profit and loss, gross sales, assets and liabilities? If the answer is "yes", identify any such annual report issued for either the fiscal or calendar years 1999 up to and including the most recent such report issued.

ANSWER:

15. State your net worth, gross revenue, and net revenue for fiscal and/or calendar years 1999, 2000 and 2001.

ANSWER:

16. State the factual basis of any and all defenses which you have asserted to the Plaintiff's Complaint.

ANSWER:

REQUEST FOR PRODUCTION OF DOCUMENTS

PLEASE TAKE NOTICE, that pursuant to F.R.C.P. 34, the plaintiff, by counsel, requests that you produce in ORIGINAL form for the purposes of inspection, copying and/or testing, the documents described below. Such documents are to be produced at the offices of plaintiff's counsel within the time prescribed by the Federal Rules of Civil Procedure and the Local Rules of the Eastern District of Virginia.

1. The original file(s), including all original documents placed therein, maintained by the defendant, pertaining to the plaintiff.

2. All documents regarding any of defendant's answers to the interrogatories propounded by the plaintiff or identified therein.

3. All documents regarding the plaintiff(s).

4. Your annual report and financial statements for fiscal and/or calendar years 1999 and 2000.

5. All documents you intend to introduce at trial.

[*Consumer*],

By counsel,
[*Attorney for Plaintiff*]

H.2 Interrogatories for ECOA Cosigner Violation

UNITED STATES DISTRICT COURT
SOUTHERN DISTRICT OF FLORIDA

_____)	
[*Consumer*],)	
Plaintiff,)	
)	
v.)	
)	
Fast Finance Corporation,)	
Defendant.)	
_____)	

INTERROGATORIES

Pursuant to Rule 33 of the Federal Rules of Civil Procedure, the following interrogatories are addressed to defendant Fast Finance Corporation by plaintiff, [*Consumer*], to be answered under oath by defendant's representative and returned within thirty (30) days.

1. Please state the name(s) and position(s) of the officer(s) or agent(s) of defendant answering each of the following interrogatories.

2. Prior to answering these interrogatories, have you made a diligent search of all books, records and papers in the custody and control of defendant, with the purpose of providing complete and accurate answers to all questions propounded? If so, please identify each such document.

3. Please describe fully the circumstances leading to the making of loan number 11290-6, including answers to the following, with respect to loan 11290-6:

a. Describe all communications between defendant and the prospective borrower(s) from February 1, 1997 through March 30, 1998 including for each such communication:

(1) the date(s);

(2) the name of each employee of defendant involved;

(3) the name of each prospective borrower involved;

(4) the content;

(5) the name of the person who initiated each such communication.

b. Did the prospective borrower(s) fill out a written application(s) for the extension of credit? If so, please attach a copy(ies).

c. Identify each person on whom credit information was sought. For each such person, please state whether a credit report was obtained. If so, please attach a copy(ies).

d. Did Plaintiff's husband, [*Consumer's spouse*], alone meet defendant's standards of creditworthiness? Please explain fully:

(1) which credit standards he met;

(2) which credit standards he did not meet;

(3) the source and amount of his income relied upon in making the instant extension of credit.

e. Did Plaintiff [*Consumer*], alone, meet defendant's standards of creditworthiness? Please explain fully:

(1) which credit standards she met;

(2) which credit standards she did not meet;

(3) the source and amount of her income relied upon in making the instant extension of credit.

f. Did defendant require that a cosigner or joint applicant be obtained for the loan? If so, please state:

(1) who imposed such a requirement;

(2) why such requirement was imposed;

(3) the name of the particular cosigner or joint applicant required, if any.

   g. Please attach copies of the note and disclosure statement (front and back sides), chattel mortgage agreement, wage assignment, and any other documents executed in conjunction with the loan transaction.

4. Who was present at the signing of loan 11290-6 and the accompanying documents?

5. When were the credit terms of the loan transaction written on the note and accompanying documents? If March 31, 1997, state whether prior to or subsequent to the prospective borrower(s)'s arrival at defendant's office.

6. Please describe the criteria by which defendant determines the creditworthiness of an applicant for credit, including:

(1) copies of any written guidelines;

(2) a description of the credit scoring system used, if any;

(3) copies of any policy manuals or instructions provided by defendant to its employees regarding standards of creditworthiness.

7. If a credit scoring system was used, please state the scores of plaintiff and her former husband.

8. Has defendant distributed to its offices and employees any instructions designed to insure compliance with The Equal Credit Opportunity Act and the regulations promulgated thereunder? If so, please attach copies.

9. From April 1, 1996 to the present for loans transacted in Florida, please state:

   a. The number of loans provided to joint applicants for credit.

   b. Of those loans in subpart (a), for how many loans were the joint applicants spouses?

   c. The number of loans provided to single applicants for credit;

   d. Of those loans in subpart (c), for how many loans was a cosigner required?

   e. Of those loans in subpart (d), for how may loans was the cosigner the spouse of the applicant?

Dated: March 12, 1994.

[Attorneys for Plaintiff]

H.3 Interrogatories for ECOA "Zip Code Redlining"

IN THE UNITED STATES DISTRICT COURT
FOR THE NORTHERN DISTRICT OF MICHIGAN

————————————)	
[*Consumer*],)	
Plaintiff,)	
)	
v.)	
)	
OPEC Oil Company,)	
Defendant.)	
————————————)	

PLAINTIFF'S FIRST SET OF INTERROGATORIES TO DEFENDANT

Comes now, [*Consumer*], plaintiff herein and pursuant to the Federal Rules of Civil Procedure and 15 U.S.C. § 1691e(i) requires the defendant to answer under oath the following interrogatories within the time and in the manner provided by law.

Note A. When used in these interrogatories, the term "Defendant" or any synonym thereof is intended to and shall embrace and include, in addition to said defendant, all employees, agents, servants, attorneys, representatives, private investigators, and others who are in possession of or may have attained information for or on behalf of defendant.

Note B. These interrogatories shall be deemed continuing so as to require supplemental answers if the defendant or the defendant's attorneys obtain further information between the time answers are served and the time of trial.

1. State the names, titles, addresses and telephone numbers of (a) the head of the credit department or division of defendant, (b) the person or persons who reviewed plaintiff's credit application, and (c) the person or persons who made the decision to deny the plaintiff's credit application.

2. In your reply dated August 20, 1998, to the plaintiff denying her credit card application, you listed as one of the principal reasons for your adverse action: "Our credit experience in your immediate geographical area." In connection with this principal reason for your adverse action, state the exact delineation of the plaintiff's "immediate geographical area" by street names, zip code area or census tract. In lieu of this, you may attach a map of the City of Shangrila outlining in red pencil said "immediate geographical area."

3. From within the plaintiff's "immediate geographical area" as delineated in response to Interrogatory 2, state the following:

   (a) the number of credit card applications received by you since March 23, 1998;

   (b) the number of credit card applications received since March 23, 1998, which you approved;

   (c) the number of credit card applications which you denied since March 23, 1998;

   (d) the date that your "credit experience" in plaintiff's "immediate geographical area" was used as a principal reason for denying credit card applications.

4. Are there any other geographical areas within the Shangrila, Michigan, metropolitan area for which your "credit experience" is used by you since March 23, 1998, as a principal reason for denial of

credit card applications? If your answer is affirmative, delineate said areas in the same manner as called for in Interrogatory 2.

5. In connection with your reply to Interrogatory 4, supply the same information as to those geographical areas as provided in response to Interrogatory 3.

6. In connection with your "credit experience" in plaintiff's "immediate geographical area," state in detail what your "credit experience" has been in said area.

7. State the names and titles of the persons who participated in the decision to use plaintiff's "immediate geographical area" as a principal reason for denying credit card applications.

8. Are all credit card applications from within plaintiff's "immediate geographical area" presently denied regardless of other credit factors? If not, state in detail those factors which influence your decision to approve certain applications from within said "geographical area."

9. In your letter of August 20, 1998, denying plaintiff's credit card application, you listed as another principal reason for adverse action the plaintiff's "level of income." In connection therewith, state the following:

(a) the level of income within the plaintiff's "immediate geographical area" which would warrant approval of a credit card application;

(b) the level of income outside of plaintiff's "immediate geographical area" and not within a similar such area, which would warrant approval of a credit card application.

10. State the name and address of any credit reporting agency relied upon by you for credit information about the plaintiff's creditworthiness.

11. State what resources of information you relied on in reaching your decision of adverse action on plaintiff's credit application.

12. In your letter of August 20, 1998 denying plaintiff's credit card application, you listed as a principal reason for adverse action the "type of bank references." State what you mean by the term "type of bank references."

13. Did you verify any credit information on the plaintiff's credit card application by checking with the banks listed thereon? If so, what were the replies and identities of the banks?

14. Do you use any credit evaluation system or weighing system in determining whether to grant or deny credit?

15. If so, state the factors and the weight or points given to each factor in connection with your evaluation of and decision on plaintiff's application.

[Attorney for Plaintiff]

H.4 Plaintiffs' Interrogatories in a Fair Housing Case

UNITED STATES DISTRICT COURT
NORTHERN DISTRICT OF CALIFORNIA
(SAN JOSE)

——————————————)	
[*Consumer 1*] and [*Consumer 2*],)	
Plaintiffs,)	
)	
v.)	Case No. _____
)	
)	PLAINTIFFS' SPECIAL
JP Morgan Chase Bank, N.A.,)	INTERROGATORIES TO JP
U.S. Bank National Association,)	MORGAN CHASE BANK
California Reconveyance)	(SET ONE)
Corporation and DOES 150,)	
Defendants.)	
——————————————)	

Pursuant to Rule 33 of the Federal Rules of Civil Procedure, Plaintiffs [*Consumer 1*] and [*Consumer 2*] (hereinafter "the [*Plaintiffs*]") hereby request that Defendant JP MORGAN CHASE BANK (hereinafter "CHASE") respond in writing to the following interrogatories within thirty (30) days of service of this request.

INSTRUCTIONS and DEFINITIONS

The following instructions and definitions apply to these requests:

1. The words "or" and "and" shall be construed conjunctively or disjunctively to make the request inclusive rather than exclusive.

2. The singular form of any word shall be deemed to include the plural. The plural form of any word shall be deemed to include the singular.

3. The term "DOCUMENTS" shall have the broadest meaning accorded by Fed. R. Civ. P. 34, including, but not limited to, all items defined in Fed. R. Evid. 1001, and all preliminary and final drafts of any such items. The term "document" shall further mean and include all copies of documents on which there appears any marking that does not appear on the originals or other copies thereof, and all drafts or notes made in the preparation of each document. The term "document" shall further mean and include electronic data in whatever form it may exist, including but not limited to all e-mail.

4. "COMMUNICATION" means the transmittal of information in the form of facts, ideas, inquiries or otherwise.

5. "PERSON" means any natural person, company, corporation, partnership, firm, association, government agency or other organization cognizable at law, and the person's agents, attorneys, employees, officers, directors, or others acting on behalf of said person.

6. References to "CHASE," "YOU," or "YOUR" refer to and include JP Morgan Chase Bank, N.A., and Chase Home Finance, LLC and/or (i) all of its affiliates, divisions, units, predecessors-in-interest, successors-in-interest, including, but not limited to, subsidiaries, parent corporations, and assigns; (ii) all of its present and former officers, directors, agents, employees, representatives, accountants, investigators, and attorneys; (iii) any other person acting or purporting to act on its behalf; or (iv) any other person otherwise subject to its control, which controls it, or is under common control with it.

7. "LEGAL COMPLAINT" refers to the complaint filed by [*Consumer 1*] and [*Consumer 2*] in the United States District Court for the Northern District of California, Case No. C11-02780 LHK.

8. "HAMP" means the Home Affordable Modification Program.

9. "PROPERTY" refers to the real property located at [*Plaintiffs' address*].

10. The term "RELATING TO" means pertaining to, referring to, recording, evidencing, containing, setting forth, reflecting, showing, disclosing, describing, explaining, summarizing, supporting, contradicting, refuting, mentioning relating to, or concerning, whether directly or indirectly.

11. The term "IDENTIFY" means to state in detail and with particularity all facts and allegations related thereto.

12. The term "IDENTIFY" when used in connection with a PERSON, shall mean to state the PERSON'S name, business title, residential and business address, and residential and business telephone numbers.

13. The term "DESCRIBE" is a request for a complete description and explanation of facts, circumstances, analysis, opinion, and other information relating to the subject matter of a specific interrogatory.

14. For each and every answer to these Interrogatories:

a. Identify each and every person who participated in supplying information and/or drafting your response or any part thereof;

b. If the answer to any of these Interrogatories was made by referring to or reviewing any documents, identify each document referred to or reviewed and the Interrogatory or Interrogatories in connection with which they were used.

15. The words "or" and "and" shall be construed conjunctively or disjunctively to make the request inclusive rather than exclusive. The singular form of any word shall be deemed to include the plural. The plural form of any word shall be deemed to include the singular.

16. Where an Interrogatory contains a general question or questions, followed by a specific question or questions, the specific question or questions are to be read and interpreted as requesting additional information, not as limiting the general question or questions.

17. With respect to each Interrogatory, identify each document prepared by, or in the possession, custody, or control of you or any of your officers, agents, or employees that relates to or refers to the subject matter of the Interrogatory in question.

18. Whenever information is requested in one of the following Interrogatories or subparts thereof that you previously furnished an answer to in another Interrogatory herein, such information need not be restated. It will be sufficient for you to identify the previous answer containing the information requested.

19. Whenever an Interrogatory calls for information that is not available to you in the form requested, but which is available in another form or can be obtained at least in part from other data in your possession, so state and either (i) supply the information requested in the form in which it is available or (ii) supply the data from which the information requested can be obtained.

20. In answering these Interrogatories every source of information to which you have access should be consulted, regardless of whether the source is within your immediate possession or control. All documents or other information in the possession of experts or consultants should be consulted.

INTERROGATORIES

INTERROGATORY NO. 1: State the name, job title, and business address of each person providing information or helping YOU prepare any response to these discovery requests.

INTERROGATORY NO. 2: IDENTIFY all actions YOU took to analyze the [*Plaintiffs'*] loan for any loss mitigation, including a loan modification under HAMP.

INTERROGATORY NO. 3: For each action listed in response to Interrogatory No. 2, IDENTIFY the dates of any action, the PERSON taking any actions, the job title of each PERSON taking any action, and the employer of each PERSON taking any action.

INTERROGATORY NO. 4: IDENTIFY the dates on which YOU received any DOCUMENTS from the [*Plaintiffs*] related to an application for a loan modification under HAMP or any other form of loss mitigation.

INTERROGATORY NO. 5: IDENTIFY each COMMUNICATION that YOU made or received concerning the [*Plaintiffs'*] applications for loan modification under HAMP.

INTERROGATORY NO. 6: IDENTIFY the values for all inputs used by YOU in any calculation of the Net Present Value "NPV" test under HAMP for the [*Plaintiffs'*] loan modification applications.

INTERROGATORY NO. 7: Describe in detail YOUR written policies and procedures that YOU or YOUR agents followed and utilized to evaluate, qualify or disqualify the [*Plaintiffs*] for any loan modification program, including but not limited to HAMP.

INTERROGATORY NO. 8: Describe in detail and in chronological order all inquiries YOU received from the [*Plaintiffs*] beginning in [*month and year*], regarding loan modification, foreclosure avoidance and loss mitigation programs; including but not limited to, the status of any loan modification application they submitted, correspondence requesting information about how the [*Plaintiffs*] were evaluated for loan modification.

INTERROGATORY NO. 9: DESCRIBE in detail and in chronological order all responses YOU provided to all inquiries by the [*Plaintiffs*] regarding loan modification, foreclosure avoidance and loss mitigation programs; including but not limited to, the status of any loan modification application they submitted, correspondence requesting information about how the [*Plaintiffs*] were evaluated for loan modification.

INTERROGATORY NO. 10: IDENTIFY any PERSON, including any investor or investors, whose approval is necessary to approve a loan modification for the [*Plaintiffs*].

INTERROGATORY NO. 11: IDENTIFY all PERSONS who were and are responsible for making a decision regarding the [*Plaintiffs'*] eligibility for a HAMP modification or any other loan modification.

INTERROGATORY NO. 12: IDENTIFY all reasons the [*Plaintiffs*] were not offered a loan modification under HAMP or any other program.

INTERROGATORY NO. 13: describe in detail any and all telephone conversations or communications between the [*Plaintiffs*] and YOU since [*month and year*].

INTERROGATORY NO. 14: describe your procedures and policies with respect to the maintenance, preservation and destruction of documents.

INTERROGATORY NO. 15: If YOU contend that a notice of adverse action was sent to the [*Plaintiffs*] in compliance with the Equal Credit Opportunity Act (ECOA), IDENTIFY the notices sent, the party who sent such notice, and the date the notices were sent.

INTERROGATORY NO. 16: describe your method of recording or documenting if, when and how such notices of adverse action were sent to the [*Plaintiffs*].

INTERROGATORY NO. 17: IDENTIFY all facts that support YOUR statement that "[w]e are unable to create an affordable payment equal to 31% of the [*Plaintiffs'*] reported monthly gross income without changing the terms of [*Plaintiffs'*] loan beyond the requirements of the program."

INTERROGATORY NO. 18: identify all persons who have knowledge of facts relevant to this LEGAL COMPLAINT.

INTERROGATORY NO. 19: DESCRIBE YOUR policies and procedures with respect to your compliance with the fair housing laws as required by Supplemental Directive 09-02.

INTERROGATORY NO. 20: describe your policies and procedures in regards to disability income when evaluating a borrower for a loan modification under HAMP.

Dated: _____

[*Organization Name*]

_____

[*Attorneys for Plaintiffs*]

H.5 Request for Production of Documents in Fair Housing Case

UNITED STATES DISTRICT COURT
FOR THE NORTHERN DISTRICT OF ILLINOIS
EASTERN DIVISION

_____)	
[*Consumer*], et al.,)	
Plaintiffs,)	
)	
v.)	
) No. _____	
Easy Life Real Estate System,)	
Inc., et al.,)	
Defendants.)	
_____)	

PLAINTIFFS' SECOND REQUEST FOR PRODUCTION OF DOCUMENTS TO DEFENDANTS

Plaintiffs, by and through their undersigned counsel, and pursuant to Fed. R. Civ. P. 34, request that defendants Easy Life Real Estate System, Inc., Ace Realtors, Inc., [*Defendant 1*] and [*Defendant 2*] ("defendants") produce the following documents within 30 days of service hereof.

INSTRUCTIONS AND DEFINITIONS

Plaintiffs incorporate by reference herein the Instructions and Definitions set forth in Plaintiffs' First Set of Interrogatories to Defendants.

DOCUMENTS REQUESTED

1. All log books reflecting "REO" or "real estate owned" properties offered for sale by any of the defendants.

2. Photographs of all "REO" or "real estate owned" properties offered for sale by any of the defendants.

3. Documents reflecting comparable properties to any "REO" or "real estate owned" property offered for sale by any of the defendants.

4. Documents reflecting any estimate of the cost of repairs to make any "REO" or "real estate owned" property sellable.

5. Documents reflecting the estimated selling price of any "REO" or "real estate owned" property offered for sale by any of the defendants.

6. Documents describing the condition of the immediate area surrounding any "REO" or "real estate owned" property offered for sale by any of the defendants.

7. Documents describing your marketing plan for selling "REO" or "real estate owned" properties.

8. All Multiple Listing Service ("MLS") listings for any property offered for sale by any of the defendants.

9. Documents reflecting your policies, procedures, guidelines, rules or practices regarding retention of documents.

10. Documents reflecting your compensation plan for employees.

11. Documents reflecting your compensation plan for agents and/or brokers.

[*Attorneys for Plaintiffs*]

H.6 Plaintiffs' First Request for Production of Documents in Reverse Redlining Case

UNITED STATES DISTRICT COURT
DISTRICT OF MASSACHUSETTS

_____)	
[*Consumer 1 to Consumer 12*] on)	
behalf of themselves and all)	
others similarly situated,)	
Plaintiffs,)	
)	
v.)	
) C.A. NO. _____	
Option One Mortgage Corp. and)	
H & R Block Mortgage Corp.)	
N/K/A Option One Mortgage)	
Services, Inc.,)	
Defendants.)	
_____)	

PLAINTIFFS' FIRST SET OF REQUESTS FOR PRODUCTION OF DOCUMENTS TO DEFENDANT OPTION ONE MORTGAGE CORPORATION

Pursuant to Rules 26 and 34 of the Federal Rules of Civil Procedure, Plaintiffs hereby request that Defendant, Option One Mortgage Corporation ("Option One") produce within thirty (30) days, the documents herein described and permit Plaintiffs and their attorneys to inspect them and copy such of them as they may desire. Plaintiffs request that the documents be made available for this inspection at the offices of their counsel:

[*Attorney for Plaintiffs' name and address*]

All definitions and rules of instructions set forth in Federal Rules of Civil Procedure 26 and 34 shall apply to all document requests herein.

INSTRUCTIONS

1. If any documents requested herein have been lost, discarded or destroyed, each such document shall be identified as completely as possible by stating the following information: the nature of the document, the author and addressee of the document, the date of the document, a brief description of the document, the date of disposal or destruction, the manner of disposal or destruction, the reason for

disposal or destruction, the name of the person authorizing the disposal or destruction or having responsibility for the loss of the document, the name of the person disposing of or destroying the document, and the paragraph number(s) of the request(s) in response to which the document otherwise would have been produced.

2. With respect to any documents that the Defendant declines to produce or communications that the Defendant declines to disclose because of a claim of privilege, including work product, the Defendant should state the nature of the privilege, the legal basis for the privilege and the names of any individuals who have or have had access to the documents for which you claim privilege.

3. You are required to produce documents or things in your possession, custody or control, regardless of whether such documents or materials are possessed directly by you or your directors, officers, agents, employees, representatives, subsidiaries, managing agents, affiliates, investigators, or by your attorneys or their agents, employees, representatives or investigators.

4. Documents are to be produced in full; redacted documents will not constitute compliance with these requests. If any requested document or thing cannot be produced in full, produce it to the extent possible, indicating which document, or portion of the document, is being withheld, and the reason that the document or portion thereof is being withheld.

5. In producing documents, you are requested to produce the original of each document requested, together with all non-identical copies and drafts of that document. If the original of any document cannot be located, a copy shall be provided in lieu thereof, and shall be legible and bound or stapled in the same manner as the original.

6. Documents shall be produced in such fashion as to identify the department, branch or office in whose possession they were located and, where applicable, the natural person in whose possession they were found.

7. Documents attached to each other should not be separated.

8. All requests are deemed continuing requests and you are under a duty to seasonably supplement your production of documents pursuant to the requirements of Federal Rule of Civil Procedure 26(e).

FORM OF PRODUCTION

All Documents, including Electronically Stored Information ("ESI"), produced hereunder shall be copied to a hard drive or other storage media for production to Plaintiffs' counsel in the following disclosure format:

1. **Tagged Image File Format ("TIFF"s).** With the exception of spreadsheets, data compilations and databases as noted below, all Documents shall be produced as single-page Ground IV TIFF images at least 300 dpi.

2. **Optical Character Recognition ("OCR") Text Files.** For each Document, through use of OCR image-processing software, an OCR text file (which shall be searchable or otherwise compatible with keyword search and retrieval software) should be provided along with the TIFF. The text of native files should be extracted directly from the native file. The text files will not contain the redacted portions of the Documents.

3. **Unique IDs.** Each image should have a unique file name, and each page of a produced Document shall have a unique page identifier ("Bates Number") on the face of the image at a location that does not obliterate, conceal or interfere with any information from the source Document. For single-page TIFFs, the unique file name will be the Bates Number of the page. Bates Numbers shall begin with a prefix that can be readily attributable to the producing party. Bates number-

ing should be sequential. If a Bates number or set of Bates numbers is skipped in the production, the producing party will so note.

For Documents originally produced in native format, a unique Document Number shall be included as part of the file name and the original file name and file extension shall be preserved. The following is an example: [Document number—original file name.original extension].

4. **Metadata Fields.** The following Metadata should be provided to the extent they exist: (i) all Metadata set forth in Table 1; and (ii) the parent-child relationships (the association between an attachment and its parent Document) should be indicated in the metadata. The Metadata for Documents which have been deduplicated across custodial files will indicate the names of the custodians in whose files the Documents are located.

5. **Native Format.** Spreadsheets (e.g., Excel, Lotus, etc.) should be produced in native format only. All Metadata should be produced with the native format files. Plaintiffs hereby reserve their right to seek other electronic Documents in their native form.

6. **Database Format.** Spreadsheets, databases and data compilations, such as customer lending databases and contact databases should be produced in "ascii text delimited" format.

7. **Document Production Load Files.** Documents in the production should be provided with an Opticon load file. Every TIFF in each production must be referenced in the production's corresponding load file. The total number of images referenced in a production's load file should match the total number of TIFF files in the production.

8. **File Format.** The **Opticon** load file should be in the following format:

```
MSC000001,MSC001,D:\MSC001\IMAGES\001\MSC000001.TIF,Y,,,3
MSC000002,MSC001,D:\MSC001\IMAGES\001\MSC000002.TIF,,,,
MSC000003,MSC001,D:\MSC001\IMAGES\001\MSC000003.TIF,,,,
MSC000004,MSC001,D:\MSC001\IMAGES\001\MSC000004.TIF,Y,,,2
MSC000005,MSC001,D:\MSC001\IMAGES\001\MSC000005.TIF,,,,
```

9. **Unitizing of Documents.** Distinct Documents should not be merged into a single record, and single Documents should not be split into multiple records (i.e., Documents should be logically unitized).

10. **Parent-Child Relationships.** Parent-child Relationships (the association between an attachment and its parent Document) should be preserved.

11. **Objective Coding Fields.** The following objective coding field should be provided to the extent practicable: (a) beginning Bates number; (b) ending Bates number; (c) beginning attachment Bates number; (d) ending attachment Bates number; (e) number of pages; (f) CD volume; and (g) source/custodian. Additional technical specifications for the Objective Coding and/or Metadata fields are provided in Table 1 attached hereto.

12. **Imaging or Formatting Problems.** Documents that present imaging or formatting problems shall be promptly identified and the parties shall meet and confer to attempt to resolve the problems.

After review and inspection, Plaintiffs retain the right to request that Defendant produce specific Documents in native format.

DEFINITIONS

All definitions and rules of instructions set forth in Fed. Rule Civ. Pro. 30(b)(6) shall apply to all requests for information herein. To the extent a term commonly in use in the mortgage lending business is not defined herein, it shall be understood consistent with the meaning commonly ascribed to that term in the mortgage lending business.

A. "Option One" "Defendant," "You," Or "Your" refers to Option One Mortgage Corporation, n/k/a Sand Canyon Corporation, and any of its divisions, affiliates, officers, directors or managing partners, including without limitation, Option One Mortgage Services, n/k/a Ada Services Corporation.

B. "Correspondence" means any letter, memorandum, e-mail, facsimile or other writing containing a communication from one person to another.

C. "Concerning" means relating to, referring to, describing, discussing, evidencing, explaining and/or constituting.

D. "Document" or "Documents" refers to any and all writings or recordings of any kind and shall include the original and each non-identical copy or draft thereof. The term document shall also include every other means by which information is recorded or transmitted including, but not limited to, electronic mail, Internet postings, tape recordings, video recordings, microfilms, punch cards, computer magnetic tape, computer disks, computer programs, computer databases, storage tapes, printouts, data processing records, and the written information necessary to understand and use such information. A draft or non-identical copy is a separate document within the meaning of this term.

E. "Employee" or "Employees" means any person(s) employed by or acting as an agent of Option One.

F. "Identity" means a person's name, home and business addresses, home and business telephone numbers, home and business email addresses, and present job title and employer.

G. "Loan" or "Loans" means Your mortgage loans, including mobile home mortgage loans, and including purchase money and refinance loans whether originated through retail, wholesale or correspondent lending channels.

H. "Transaction" means the Loan or Loans originated by Option One for any borrower, including loans originated by or through retail, wholesale or correspondent lending channels.

I. "Loan Origination Process" means any and all steps You take *from* the time You identify, communicate with, and/or are approached by a prospective borrower seeking a Loan (including, without limitation, when such contact is made directly by the prospective borrower and/or when it is made by and on behalf of the prospective borrower through a loan broker or correspondent lender) *to* the time funds are advanced in connection with a Loan, including but not limited to the processing of applications, underwriting, rate setting and supervising Loan closings.

J. "Lending Office" means any office of Option One in which applications for Loans to be originated by Option One are taken or processed.

K. "Account Records" means any records of Loans maintained in the ordinary course of business by Option One, including without limitation, electronic records maintained on Loans.

L. "Loan Level Account Data" means loan-by-loan records of loan terms, interest rates, settlement charges and payments made to third parties generated during or following the Loan Origination Process.

M. "Underwriting Data" means records of credit scores, mortgage scores, loan to value ratio, borrower credit characteristics and other individual characteristics that affect whether or not a particular borrower receives a Loan from Option One including, without limitation, loan-by-loan records of a borrowers' credit characteristics.

N. "HMDA Data" means records of any kind made by Option One for the purpose of compliance with the Federal Home Mortgage Disclosure Act including without limitation, loan-by-loan identification of a borrowers' race or minority status.

O. "Minority" or "Minorities" means any non-Caucasians and other minority ethnic or racial groups.

P. "Par Rate" means the lowest interest rate for which a borrower would qualify without mark-up, add-ons, fees or other adjustments to that rate.

Q. "Contract Rate" means the actual rate at which a loan was contracted.

R. "Relevant Time Period" means January 1, 1999 to the present.

REQUESTS FOR PRODUCTION

1. Copies of all of Your Loan Level Account Data, including, without limitation, active account data, financing rate data and data archive tapes regarding Loans originated during the Relevant Time Period. This production should include copies of all documents necessary to fully understand the contents of all electronic data produced, including without limitation, record layouts, data dictionaries and user manuals. This production should also include a full definition and explanation of all electronic codes for all data fields that store information through utilization of codes. Without limiting in any way the electronic data requested, the electronic data produced should include all electronic databases and/or electronic file systems that contain the following information:

   a. the primary borrower's name, address, or other unique identifier;
   b. the co-borrower's name, address, or other unique identifier;
   c. the loan officer, broker or correspondent lender's name and address (or any part thereof, such as state of residence);
   d. the loan application number and loan application type;
   e. the credit score and/or credit tier assigned to the borrower(s), including any exception codes;
   f. the mortgage score assigned to the borrower(s), including any exception codes;
   g. the loan product (including without limitation, whether the loan was a hybrid, an interest-only ARM or an option ARM, or any other type of loan);
   h. the individual terms applicable to the Transaction, both at the start of the contract and during the life of the loan, including without limitation, the term of the Transaction, the interest rate and whether it is fixed or variable, the annual percentage rate, the total amount of the finance charges, the total amount of the prepaid finance charges, the amount financed, the anticipated amount of each monthly payment, the term of the loan (in months), and the date of the first payment;
   i. pre-payment penalty provisions;
   j. whether the loan was conforming;
   k. whether the loan was a jumbo loan;
   l. whether the loan was a no-documentation or low documentation loan;
   m. the Par Rate applicable to the Transaction;
   n. the broker commission amount in dollars and the formula by which the broker commission is determined (e.g., 50% of the markup, or the percentage points of markup above a certain level, etc.);
   o. Your commission or participation amount in dollars, and the formula by which Your commission is determined (e.g., 50% of the markup, or the percentage points of markup above a certain level, etc.);
   p. yield spread premium, broker's points and all other fees and compensation paid to a loan officer, broker, or correspondent lender broken out by amount and category;
   q. the lien status of the loan;

r. Transaction date;

s. funding date;

t. race or ethnicity;

u. the loan applicant's combined debt-to-income ratio;

v. the loan applicant's combined loan-to-value ratio;

w. the loan applicant's total gross monthly income;

x. any other underwriting or pricing factors considered;

y. all data contained on the HUD-1;

2. If any of the information or data specifically listed in Request No. 1 above does not exist in electronic form, a random sample of 5,000 non-electronic loan documents which contain such information for each loan, including but not limited to the loan file, HUD-1's and rate sheets, and the corresponding unique identification numbers.

3. All Documents Concerning policies, practices and procedures for document retention, electronic records and databases, data storage, data back-up, and data archiving.

4. All Documents Concerning Your policies, practices and procedures regarding Account Records, Loan Level Account Data, Underwriting Data and HMDA Data, including but not limited to the policies and procedures for maintaining these records or data, the categories maintained, the form in which these records or data are maintained, the nature of the hardware and software by which these records and data are maintained, any coding used in the process of maintaining these records and data, and the processes by which these records and data can be reviewed, sorted, analyzed and correlated.

5. All Documents that identify any outside contractor(s) and their role(s) in creating, implementing or updating the systems by which Account Records, Loan Level Account Data, Underwriting Data and HMDA Data are stored.

6. All Documents Concerning the Plaintiffs, including but not limited to the following:

a. all Documents that contain any information regarding the Plaintiffs, including information obtained from the Plaintiffs, any representative or reference of the Plaintiffs, or any third party with Plaintiffs' permission, including without limitation, any credit reports;

b. all Documents that were submitted to a broker and/or correspondent lender regarding the Plaintiffs;

c. all Documents that were received from a broker and/or correspondent lender regarding the Plaintiffs;

d. all Documents that indicate, refer or relate to the credit rating or score assigned to the Plaintiffs by a broker and/or correspondent lender and/or Option One;

e. all Documents that indicate, refer or relate to the "tier" or risk category assigned to the Plaintiffs by a broker and/or correspondent lender and/or Option One;

f. all Documents that indicate, refer or relate to how the Plaintiffs were assigned to a "tier" or risk category;

g. all Documents that indicate, refer or relate to the Par Rate at which Option One would have agreed to finance a Loan for Plaintiffs at the time of the Plaintiffs' Transaction(s) with Option One;

h. all Documents indicating the income or potential income a broker and/or correspondent lender and/or Option One or any entity associated or affiliated with a broker and/or correspondent lender and/or Option One has received or may receive in the future that relates in any way to the Plaintiffs' Transaction(s) with Option One and all Documents indicating how such calculations were made;

i. all Documents generated by or for a broker and/or correspondent lender and/or Option One, or used by a broker and/or corre-

spondent lender and/or Option One, that refer or relate in any manner to the Plaintiffs' Transaction(s) and/or loan application, including but not limited to all Documents generated by or for or used by broker and/or correspondent lender and/or Option One;

j. all Documents indicating the commission or other amounts paid to any broker and/or correspondent lender and/or Option One employee in connection with the Plaintiffs' Transaction(s);

k. all Documents concerning Plaintiffs' Transaction(s), including but not limited to applications, good faith estimates, HUD-1's, notices, disclosures, correspondence, internal memoranda, rate sheets, loan agreements, promissory notes, and all other closing and post-closing Documents; and

l. all Documents concerning the broker or correspondent lender for Plaintiffs' loan(s), including but not limited to contracts, applications, guidelines, qualifications, the broker's past history and performance, reports concerning compensation paid to the broker, and reports by MARI, FHA, or VA regarding alleged misconduct by the broker.

7. All Documents Concerning establishing, setting, and/or changing Your rates (whether wholesale or retail) applicable to Your Loans during the Relevant Time Period, including without limitation:

a. Documents indicating, referring or relating to the different Par Rates applicable to different credit tiers, loan amounts, types of loans, or loan terms;

b. authority or discretion of loan officers, brokers and/or correspondent lenders to increase the Par Rate and the maximum amount Option One will permit its loan officers, brokers and/or correspondent lenders to increase the Par Rate;

c. any standards or factors that loan officers, brokers and/or correspondent lenders should, must, may or may not take into account in deciding whether and how much to increase the Par Rate;

d. Your revenue and/or profits associated with upward deviations from Par Rates (or other standard published rates); and

e. audits, studies or publications or articles regarding upward deviations from Par Rates.

8. All Documents setting forth or constituting Your policies, practices and procedures for establishing and creating Your pricing models, including without limitation Documents:

a. Concerning the factors or criteria utilized to price your Loans (such as LTV, FICO, loan size, prepayment penalties, use of piggyback loans or borrower income); and

b. Concerning the policies and procedures for establishing internal prices for Loans directly originated by You.

9. All Documents Concerning Your policies, practices and procedures for setting, changing, tracking, assessing, recording, accounting, evaluating profitability and/or otherwise analyzing the amount of fees, points, brokers' compensation and other charges applicable to Your Loans, including without limitation, yield spread premiums, origination fees, discount points, prepayment penalties, underwriting fees, processing fees, application fees and administration fees.

10. Your rate sheets during the Relevant Time Period together with all documents containing a summary of information and/or codes for information contained in your rate sheets.

11. All Documents Concerning any and all of the Loan types, programs or offerings available to borrowers during the Relevant Time Period, including without limitation:

a. eligibility parameters;

b. underwriting criteria and the appropriate segment of the loan market (such as prime, Alt-A or subprime);

c. any special finance programs offered (for purposes of this request, "special finance program" refers to any program that provides the borrower an additional benefit, such as a lower finance rate or any other more favorable term than that offered to persons who do not qualify for such program).

12. All Documents Concerning Your policies and procedures regarding monitoring and/or ensuring that your borrowers receive the least expensive loan for which they are qualified.

13. For any federal or state investigation conducted during the Relevant Time Period regarding Your Loan financing practices, including but not limited to any investigation by a federal agency or State Attorney General, including but not limited to the Massachusetts' Attorney General, pursuant to the ECOA and/or FHA, all Documents Concerning any such investigation, including without limitation, files, memoranda, correspondence, findings and conclusions, notices of charges, and any electronic data produced by You in response to or as part of any such investigation.

14. All training manuals and other training documents You provided during the Relevant Time Period to loan officers, brokers and/or correspondent lenders, including without limitation, Documents related to:

a. instructions or other information regarding the charging of points, yield spread premiums, closing costs and settlement fees;

b. information regarding maximizing broker and/or correspondent lender profits on Loans by utilizing Your financing products or systems or by selling/assigning financing contracts to You;

c. the requirements of fair lending laws including HMDA, the ECOA and FHA;

15. All Documents Concerning any lawsuits, complaints, charges, allegations, investigations, arbitrations, mediations, or other disputes concerning mortgage lending discrimination and your loan officers, brokers, and/or correspondent lenders in connection with any Loan or Loans.

16. All Documents Concerning Your management and supervision of loan officers, brokers and correspondent lenders, including but not limited to recruitment, retention, incentives, promotion to preferential categories, quality control, fraud oversight or investigation, assessments or evaluations, warnings, counseling, discipline or termination of relationships.

17. All Documents Concerning software of computer systems used to communicate or interface with loan officers, brokers and correspondent lenders, including without limitation, software related to loan boarding, loan registration, underwriting and underwriting guidelines, loan application input, disbursement of loan proceeds, rates, policies and procedures, compliance, profits or compensation.

18. All Documents Concerning audits, reviews or investigations, Board of Director meetings, executive or subcommittee meetings, task force meetings, any other types of assessments, evaluations, meetings or discussions that involved any of the following topics:

a. the collection and/or use of information about race and/or Minority status of Your borrowers and/or potential borrowers;

b. the analysis of disparities in costs and terms of loans that correlate to race and/or Minority status of Your borrowers;

c. HMDA data;

d. fair lending practices;

e. the impact of yield spread premiums, correspondent compensation and/or other fees on Minorities; and/or

f. the impact of policies and procedures for compensation of loan officers, brokers or correspondent lenders on Minorities.

19. All Documents Concerning the collection, evaluation, or use of information concerning the race, race coding process, geographic location, or other demographic information regarding applicants or past, current or potential borrowers, including but not limited to Documents relating to profitability or marketing targets, strategies and materials.

20. All Documents Concerning any efforts by Defendant, without time limitation, to ensure that its Loan Origination Process does not adversely impact Minority borrowers.

21. All Documents Concerning the nature of and process for creating audits of loans to determine whether Minority and non-Minority borrowers received Loans on disparate terms and/or for compliance with fair lending laws.

22. All Documents Concerning audits, analyses, studies, or modeling regarding any of the following topics:

a. disparities for Minority borrowers regarding the pricing of Loans;

b. disparities for Minority borrowers related to the compensation paid to loan officers, brokers or correspondent lenders;

c. disparities for Minority borrowers regarding the availability of Loans;

d. disparities for Minority borrowers regarding the type of Loan product sold;

e. disparities for Minority borrowers regarding the cost of originating Loans;

f. disparities for Minority borrowers regarding the Loan terms;

g. disparities for Minority borrowers regarding prepayments and prepayment rates;

h. disparities for Minority borrowers regarding credit risk and default or delinquency rates; or

i. disparities for Minority borrowers regarding the origination source or channel for Loans (including without limitation, retail broker or correspondent lender).

23. All Documents Concerning Your HMDA compliance and related HMDA Data reporting, including but not limited to databases or any analyses, studies or modeling of HMDA Data.

24. All policy and procedure manuals or other compilations used to administer Your retail and wholesale loan financing programs, including but not limited to any Documents referencing Your credit and/or mortgage scoring system, Your employees' duties, broker's duties, the communication of tier rate, tier rate deviation, broker participation, Your participation or finance rate income, and Your relationship with brokers and/or correspondent lenders.

25. Exemplars of all forms created, utilized, made available, provided or sold by Option One to loan officers, brokers and/or correspondent lenders, including without limitation, all loan application forms.

26. All Documents Concerning Your policies, practices and procedures for establishing and staffing a Lending Office, including without limitation, a listing of the addresses of your Lending Offices and Documents relating to the demographics of the communities where your Lending Offices are located.

27. All Documents relating to compensation of loan officers, brokers or correspondent lenders, including without limitation, Documents Concerning:

a. policies and procedures, including without limitation, any policy, program, or practice by which loan officers, brokers and/or correspondent lenders and Option One will divide between them in any fashion any income realized from the difference between the Par Rate and the contract rate;

b. the formula for division of any revenues generated by payments at rates above the applicable Par Rate in a Transaction between amounts payable to the broker or correspondent lender (e.g., broker and/or correspondent participation) and/or the amount or percentage that is retained by You;

c. contracts;

d. policies and procedures for incentive payments, quotas, bonuses or bonus plans;

e. fee agreements;

f. schedules;

g. studies, analyses, comparisons of compensation or profitability among or between loan officers, brokers or correspondent lenders; and

h. tracking, assessing, recording, accounting, and/or analyzing the aggregate amount of fees paid to individual loan brokers or correspondent lenders with whom You do business.

28. All Documents Concerning Your policies, practices and procedures for establishing, maintaining and competing for business relationships with mortgage brokers and correspondent lenders, including without limitation, incentive programs, turn times, streamlined underwriting and approval and automated underwriting and approval.

29. All Documents Concerning any comparison or categorization of loan officers, brokers or correspondent lenders by any of the following:

a. type of loan products originated;

b. fees;

c. rates;

d. loan terms (including without limitation, prepayment penalties);

e. stated income, stated asset, no-documentation or low-documentation loans;

f. your profitability from loans originated;

g. loan officer, broker or correspondent lender compensation;

h. geographic or demographic or socio-economic information regarding customers;

i. race or ethnicity of borrower;

j. sub-prime, high-cost loans;

k. self-approval of loans;

l. self-verification of loan conditions;

m. streamlined or automated underwriting;

n. piggyback loans;

o. loan origination volume;

p. product incentives; and

q. geographical or socio-demographic marketing strategies.

30. All Documents Concerning all Your processes for monitoring fair lending compliance of any entity with which Option One does business, including without limitation, subsidiaries, parents, sister corporations, loan brokers, correspondent lenders, appraisers, title companies, closing companies, and real estate brokers.

31. All Documents Concerning Your policies, practices and procedures for marketing Loans to, soliciting or targeting potential borrowers, including without limitation, Documents Concerning Your policies, practices and procedures for marketing Loans to, soliciting or targeting potential Minority borrowers.

32. All Documents Concerning the decision of Option One Mortgage to cease its mortgage lending business.

Dated: March 12, 2009.

Attorneys for Plaintiffs

TABLE 1

Field Name	Specification Field Name	Field Type	Length	Introspect Field Name	Introspect Field Type	Introspect Related Comments	Description (E-Mail)	Description (E-Files/ Attachments)
BegDoc	Unique ID	Paragraph	Unlimited	Beg Bates Number	Single Value		The Document ID number associated with the first page of a document.	The Document ID number associated with the first page of a document.
EndDoc	Unique ID	Paragraph	Unlimited	End Bates Number	Single Value		The Document ID number associated with the last page of a document.	The Document ID number associated with the last page of a document.
BegAttach	Unique ID Parent-Child Relationships	Paragraph	Unlimited	Begin Attachment Number	Single Value		The Document ID number associated with the first page of a document.	The Document ID number associated with the first page of a parent document.
	Unique ID Parent-Child Relationships	Paragraph	Unlimited	Page Count	Integer		The number of pages for a document.	The number of pages for a document.
Master-Date		Date	MM/DD/YYYY				The date of a parent document.	The date of a parent document. For attachments to e-mails, this field will be populated with the date sent of the e-mail transmitting the attachment.
SentOn_Time	Time Sent	Paragraph	Unlimited				The Time a document was sent.	

Field Name	Specification Field Name	Field Type	Length	Introspect Field Name	Introspect Field Type	Introspect Related Comments	Description (E-Mail)	Description (E-Files/ Attachments)
Create_Date	Date Created	Date	MM/DD/YYYY					The date a document was created.
Create_Time	Time Created	Paragraph	Unlimited					The time a document was created.
LastMod_Date	Time Last Modified	Paragraph	Unlimited					The time the document was last modified.
Field Name	Specification Field Name	Field Type	Length	Introspect Field Name	Introspect Field Type	Introspect Related Comments	Description (E-Mail)	Description (E-Files/ Attachments)
Received_Time	Date Received	Date	MM/DD/YYYY				The time a document was received.	
Received_Date	Date Received	Date	MM/DD/YYYY				The time a document was received.	
ParentFolder	File Path Folder Name	Paragraph	Unlimited	Folder	Single Value		Denotes the folder information for a document.	Denotes the full path of a document.
Author	Author Display Name (e-mail)	Paragraph	Unlimited	Author	Multivalue	Combine Author and Author_Email field into one Author field.	The display name of the author of a document.	The author of a document from entered metadata.
To	Recipient	Paragraph	Unlimited	Recipient	Multivalue	Combine TO and Recip_Email field into one TO field.	The display name of the recipient(s) of a document.	
CC	CC	Paragraph	Unlimited	CC	Multivalue	Combine CC and CC_Email field into one CC field.	The display name of the copyee(s) of a document.	
BCC	BCC	Paragraph	Unlimited	BCC	Multivalue	Combine BCC and BCC_Email field into one BCC field.	The display name of the blind copyee(s) of a document.	
Subject	Subject (e-mail)	Paragraph	Unlimited	Subject	Multivalue		The subject of a document.	The subject of a document from entered metadata.
OriginalSource	Original Name	Paragraph	Unlimited				The file name of an e-mail store (e.g., Outlook.pst, MyMail.nsf, etc.)	
Custodian	Custodian	Paragraph	Unlimited	Custodian	Multivalue		The custodian of a document (if applicable).	The custodian of a document (if applicable).
NativePath		Paragraph	Unlimited				The full path to a native copy of a document (if applicable).	The full path to a native copy of a document (if applicable).
AttachCount	Numbered Attachments	Paragraph	Unlimited				The number of attachments to a document.	The number of attachments to a document.
FileExt	File Extension	Paragraph	Unlimited				The file extension of a document.	The file extension of a document.
FileName	Original Name	Paragraph	Unlimited					The file name of a document.
FileSize	File Size	Paragraph	Unlimited				The file size of a document (including embedded attachments).	The file size of a document (including embedded attachments).
MD5Hash	MD5 Hash	Paragraph	Unlimited					The MD5 Hash value or "de-duplication key" assigned to a document.
FullText	Text	Paragraph	Unlimited				The full text of the e-mail.	The full text of the e-file/ attachment.

H.7 Plaintiffs' Second Request for Production of Documents in Reverse Redlining Case

UNITED STATES DISTRICT COURT
DISTRICT OF MASSACHUSETTS

----------------------------------)
)
[*Consumer 1 to Consumer 12*],   )
on behalf of themselves and all   )
others similarly situated,   )
               Plaintiffs,   )
)
v.   )
) C.A. No. _____
Option One Mortgage Corp. and   )
H & R Block Mortgage Corp.   )
N/K/A Option One Mortgage   )
Services, Inc.,   )
               Defendants.)
----------------------------------)

SECOND REQUEST FOR PRODUCTION OF DOCUMENTS TO DEFENDANTS SAND CANYON CORPORATION, F/K/A OPTION ONE MORTGAGE CORPORATION AND ADA SERVICES CORPORATION F/K/A H & R BLOCK MORTGAGE CORP. AND OPTION ONE MORTGAGE SERVICES

Pursuant to Rules 26 and 34 of the Federal Rules of Civil Procedure, Plaintiffs hereby request that Defendants produce within thirty (30) days, the documents herein described and permit Plaintiffs and their attorneys to inspect them and copy such of them as they may desire. Plaintiffs request that the documents be made available for this inspection at the offices of their counsel:

[*Attorney for Plaintiffs' name and address*]

All definitions and rules of instructions set forth in Federal Rules of Civil Procedure 26 and 34 shall apply to all document requests herein.

INSTRUCTIONS

1. If any documents requested herein have been lost, discarded or destroyed, each such document shall be identified as completely as possible by stating the following information: the nature of the document, the author and addressee of the document, the date of the document, a brief description of the document, the date of disposal or destruction, the manner of disposal or destruction, the reason for disposal or destruction, the name of the person authorizing the disposal or destruction or having responsibility for the loss of the document, the name of the person disposing of or destroying the document, and the paragraph number(s) of the request(s) in response to which the document otherwise would have been produced.

2. With respect to any documents that the Defendants decline to produce or communications that the Defendants decline to disclose because of a claim of privilege, including work product, the Defendants should state the nature of the privilege, the legal basis for the privilege and the names of any individuals who have or have had access to the documents for which you claim privilege.

3. You are required to produce documents or things in your possession, custody or control, regardless of whether such documents or materials are possessed directly by you or your directors, officers, agents, employees, representatives, subsidiaries, managing agents, affiliates, investigators, or by your attorneys or their agents, employees, representatives or investigators.

4. Documents are to be produced in full; redacted documents will not constitute compliance with these requests. If any requested document or thing cannot be produced in full, produce it to the extent possible, indicating which document, or portion of the document, is being withheld, and the reason that the document or portion thereof is being withheld.

5. In producing documents, you are requested to produce the original of each document requested, together with all non-identical copies and drafts of that document. If the original of any document cannot be located, a copy shall be provided in lieu thereof, and shall be legible and bound or stapled in the same manner as the original.

6. Documents shall be produced in such fashion as to identify the department, branch or office in whose possession they were located and, where applicable, the natural person in whose possession they were found.

7. Documents attached to each other should not be separated.

8. All requests are deemed continuing requests and you are under a duty to seasonably supplement your production of documents pursuant to the requirements of Federal Rule of Civil Procedure 26(e).

FORM OF PRODUCTION

All Documents, including Electronically Stored Information ("ESI"), produced hereunder shall be copied to a hard drive or other storage media for production to Plaintiffs' counsel in the following disclosure format:

1. **Tagged Image File Format ("TIFF"s).** With the exception of spreadsheets, data compilations and databases as noted below, all Documents shall be produced as single-page Ground IV TIFF images at least 300 dpi.

2. **Optical Character Recognition ("OCR") Text Files.** For each Document, through use of OCR image-processing software, an OCR text file (which shall be searchable or otherwise compatible with keyword search and retrieval software) should be provided along with the TIFF. The text of native files should be extracted directly from the native file. The text files will not contain the redacted portions of the Documents.

3. **Unique IDs.** Each image should have a unique file name, and each page of a produced Document shall have a unique page identifier ("Bates Number") on the face of the image at a location that does not obliterate, conceal or interfere with any information from the source Document. For single-page TIFFs, the unique file name will be the Bates Number of the page. Bates Numbers shall begin with a prefix that can be readily attributable to the producing party. Bates numbering should be sequential. If a Bates number or set of Bates numbers is skipped in the production, the producing party will so note.

For Documents originally produced in native format, a unique Document Number shall be included as part of the file name and the original file name and file extension shall be preserved. The following is an example: [Document number—original file name.original extension].

4. **Metadata Fields.** The following Metadata should be provided to the extent they exist: (i) all Metadata set forth in Table 1; and (ii) the parent-child relationships (the association between an attachment and its parent Document) should be indicated in the metadata. The Meta-

data for Documents which have been deduplicated across custodial files will indicate the names of the custodians in whose files the Documents are located.

5. **Native Format.** Spreadsheets (e.g., Excel, Lotus, etc.) should be produced in native format only. All Metadata should be produced with the native format files. Plaintiffs hereby reserve their right to seek other electronic Documents in their native form.

6. **Database Format.** Spreadsheets, databases and data compilations, such as customer lending databases and contact databases should be produced in "ascii text delimited" format.

7. **Document Production Load Files.** Documents in the production should be provided with an Opticon load file. Every TIFF in each production must be referenced in the production's corresponding load file. The total number of images referenced in a production's load file should match the total number of TIFF files in the production.

8. **File Format.** The **Opticon** load file should be in the following format:

MSC000001,MSC001,D:\MSC001\IMAGES\001\MSC000001.TIF,Y,,,3
MSC000002,MSC001,D:\MSC001\IMAGES\001\MSC000002.TIF,,,,
MSC000003,MSC001,D:\MSC001\IMAGES\001\MSC000003.TIF,,,,
MSC000004,MSC001,D:\MSC001\IMAGES\001\MSC000004.TIF,Y,,,2
MSC000005,MSC001,D:\MSC001\IMAGES\001\MSC000005.TIF,,,,

9. **Unitizing of Documents.** Distinct Documents should not be merged into a single record, and single Documents should not be split into multiple records (i.e., Documents should be logically unitized).

10. **Parent-Child Relationships.** Parent-child Relationships (the association between an attachment and its parent Document) should be preserved.

11. **Objective Coding Fields.** The following objective coding field should be provided to the extent practicable: (a) beginning Bates number; (b) ending Bates number; (c) beginning attachment Bates number; (d) ending attachment Bates number; (e) number of pages; (f) CD volume; and (g) source/custodian. Additional technical specifications for the Objective Coding and/or Metadata fields are provided in Table 1 attached hereto.

12. **Imaging or Formatting Problems.** Documents that present imaging or formatting problems shall be promptly identified and the parties shall meet and confer to attempt to resolve the problems.

After review and inspection, Plaintiffs retain the right to request that Defendants produce specific Documents in native format.

DEFINITIONS

All definitions and rules of instructions set forth in Fed. Rule Civ. Pro. 30(b)(6) shall apply to all requests for information herein. To the extent a term commonly in use in the mortgage lending business is not defined herein, it shall be understood consistent with the meaning commonly ascribed to that term in the mortgage lending business.

A. "Sand Canyon" "Defendants," "You," or "Your" refers to Sand Canyon Corporation, f/k/a Option One Mortgage and Ada Services Corporation, f/k/a H&R Block Mortgage Corp. and Option One Mortgage Services and any of its divisions, affiliates, officers, directors, managing partners or agents.

B. "Correspondence" means any letter, memorandum, e-mail, facsimile or other writing containing a communication from one person to another.

C. "Concerning" means relating to, referring to, describing, discussing, evidencing, explaining and/or constituting.

D. "Document" or "Documents" refers to any and all writings or recordings of any kind and shall include the original and each non-

identical copy or draft thereof. The term document shall also include every other means by which information is recorded or transmitted including, but not limited to, electronic mail, Internet postings, tape recordings, video recordings, microfilms, punch cards, computer magnetic tape, computer disks, computer programs, computer databases, storage tapes, printouts, data processing records, and the written information necessary to understand and use such information. A draft or non-identical copy is a separate document within the meaning of this term.

E. "Employee" or "Employees" means any person(s) employed by or acting as an agent of Sand Canyon.

F. "Loan" or "Loans" means Sand Canyon's mortgage loans, including mobile home mortgage loans, and including purchase money and refinance loans whether originated through retail, wholesale or correspondent lending channels.

G. "Loan Origination Process" means any and all steps You take *from* the time You identify, communicate with, and/or are approached by a prospective borrower seeking a Loan (including, without limitation, when such contact is made directly by the prospective borrower and/or when it is made by and on behalf of the prospective borrower through a loan broker or correspondent lender) *to* the time a Loan is placed on Your system, including but not limited to the processing of applications, underwriting, rate setting and supervising Loan closings.

H. "Loan Servicing" means the servicing rights for a Sand Canyon Loan included as part of Your mortgage originations and sales.

I. "Sand Canyon Loan Origination Process" means any and all steps taken by Sand Canyon *from* the time Sand Canyon identified, communicated with, and/or was approached by a prospective borrower seeking a loan (including, without limitation, when such contact was made directly by the prospective borrower and/or when it was made by and on behalf of the prospective borrower through a loan broker or correspondent lender) *to* the time funds were advanced in connection with a loan, including but not limited to the processing of applications, underwriting, rate setting and supervising loan closings.

J. "Sand Canyon Fair Lending Audits" means records of any kind made by Sand Canyon to compare terms of loans made by Sand Canyon to Minority Borrowers with terms of loans made to Sand Canyon to White Borrowers or to review or monitor the terms of loans made to Minority Borrowers.

RELEVANT TIME PERIOD

"Relevant Time Period" means January 1, 2000 to the present.

REQUESTS FOR PRODUCTION

1. All Documents Concerning Your development or modification of Your loan application, pricing, underwriting and approval policies for the Loan types available to borrowers, including without limitation:

   a. Modified and/or streamlined loan application policies and procedures;

   b. Online application processes;

   c. Policies and procedures for Loans requiring less than full documentation;

   d. Streamlined and/or revised procedures for verifying borrowers' information;

   e. Policies and procedures for developing underwriting guidelines and pricing guidelines;

   f. Streamlined and/or automated underwriting policies and criteria, including without limitation, changes with respect to (i) how interest rates were established for borrowers, (ii) what criteria was evaluated to determine a borrower's qualifications for a Sand Canyon loan; and (iii) the verification process;

g. Relaxed eligibility and verification policies and procedures; and

h. Automated loan approval and verification policies and procedures.

2. All Documents Concerning Your policies, practices and procedures regarding measures taken to ascertain or validate borrower documentation, data and information (including but not limited to documentation, data and information related to the borrowers' income, assets and employment), whether or not submitted with the loan application.

3. All audits, reports, analyses, memoranda, email or other Documents Concerning situations, if any, in which borrower documentation, data and information (including but not limited to documentation, data and information related to the borrowers' income, assets and employment), was found to be inaccurate or potentially misrepresented (either prior to funding of the Loan or after the funding of the Loan) in loan applications received during the Relevant Time Period.

4. All Documents constituting the servicing agreements related to Your loans.

5. All Documents Concerning Your policies and procedures regarding Your mortgage Loan Servicing Process, servicing operations and servicing facilities.

6. All Documents Concerning Your ability to modify loans which are serviced by Sand Canyon.

Respectfully submitted,
Attorneys for Plaintiffs

TABLE 1

Field Name	Specification Field Name	Field Type	Length	Introspect Field Name	Introspect Field Type	Introspect Related Comments	Description (E-Mail)	Description (E-Files/ Attachments)
BegDoc	Unique ID	Paragraph	Unlimited	Beg Bates Number	Single Value		The Document ID number associated with the first page of a document.	The Document ID number associated with the first page of a document.
EndDoc	Unique ID	Paragraph	Unlimited	End Bates Number	Single Value		The Document ID number associated with the last page of a document.	The Document ID number associated with the last page of a document.
BegAttach	Unique ID Parent-Child Relationships	Paragraph	Unlimited	Begin Attachment Number	Single Value		The Document ID number associated with the first page of a document.	The Document ID number associated with the first page of a parent document.
	Unique ID Parent-Child Relationships	Paragraph	Unlimited	Page Count	Integer		The number of pages for a document.	The number of pages for a document.
Master-Date		Date	MM/DD/YYYY				The date of a parent document.	The date of a parent document. For attachments to e-mails, this field will be populated with the date sent of the e-mail transmitting the attachment.
SentOn_Time	Time Sent	Paragraph	Unlimited				The Time a document was sent.	
Create_Date	Date Created	Date	MM/DD/YYYY					The date a document was created.
Create_Time	Time Created	Paragraph	Unlimited					The time a document was created.
LastMod_Date	Time Last Modified	Paragraph	Unlimited					The time the document was last modified.
Received_Time	Date Received	Date	MM/DD/YYYY				The time a document was received.	
Received_Date	Date Received	Date	MM/DD/YYYY				The time a document was received.	
ParentFolder	File Path Folder Name	Paragraph	Unlimited	Folder	Single Value		Denotes the folder information for a document.	Denotes the full path of a document.

Field Name	Specification Field Name	Field Type	Length	Introspect Field Name	Introspect Field Type	Introspect Related Comments	Description (E-Mail)	Description (E-Files/ Attachments)
Author	Author Display Name (e-mail)	Paragraph	Unlimited	Author	Multivalue	Combine Author and Author_Email field into one Author field.	The display name of the author of a document.	The author of a document from entered metadata.
To	Recipient	Paragraph	Unlimited	Recipient	Multivalue	Combine TO and Recip_Email field into one TO field.	The display name of the recipient(s) of a document.	
CC	CC	Paragraph	Unlimited	CC	Multivalue	Combine CC and CC_Email field into one CC field.	The display name of the copyee(s) of a document.	
BCC	BCC	Paragraph	Unlimited	BCC	Multivalue	Combine BCC and BCC_Email field into one BCC field.	The display name of the blind copyee(s) of a document.	
Subject	Subject (e-mail)	Paragraph	Unlimited	Subject	Multivalue		The subject of a document.	The subject of a document from entered metadata.
OriginalSource	Original Name	Paragraph	Unlimited			The file name of an e-mail store (e.g., Outlook.pst, MyMail.nsf, etc.)		
Custodian	Custodian	Paragraph	Unlimited	Custodian	Multivalue		The custodian of a document (if applicable).	The custodian of a document (if applicable).
NativePath		Paragraph	Unlimited				The full path to a native copy of a document (if applicable).	The full path to a native copy of a document (if applicable).
AttachCount	Numbered Attachments	Paragraph	Unlimited				The number of attachments to a document.	The number of attachments to a document.
FileExt	File Extension	Paragraph	Unlimited				The file extension of a document.	The file extension of a document.
FileName	Original Name	Paragraph	Unlimited					The file name of a document.
FileSize	File Size	Paragraph	Unlimited				The file size of a document (including embedded attachments).	The file size of a document (including embedded attachments).
MD5Hash	MD5 Hash	Paragraph	Unlimited					The MD5 Hash value or "de-duplication key" assigned to a document.
FullText	Text	Paragraph	Unlimited				The full text of the e-mail.	Full text of the e-file/attachment.

H.8 Request for Production of Documents in HAMP Loan Modification

UNITED STATES DISTRICT COURT
NORTHERN DISTRICT OF CALIFORNIA
(SAN JOSE)

—————————————)
[*Consumer 1*] and [*Consumer 2*],)
                    Plaintiffs,)
) Case No. _____
v.   )
) PLAINTIFFS' REQUESTS
) FOR THE PRODUCTION
JP Morgan Chase Bank, N.A.,   ) FOR DOCUMENTS TO
U.S. Bank National Association,) DEFENDANT JP MORGAN
California Reconveyance   ) CHASE BANK (SET ONE)
Corporation and DOES 150,   )
                    Defendants.)
—————————————)

Pursuant to Rule 34 of the Federal Rules of Civil Procedure, Plaintiffs [*Consumer 1*] and [*Consumer 2*] (hereinafter "the [*Plaintiffs*]") hereby request that Defendant JP MORGAN CHASE BANK (hereinafter "CHASE") produce the following DOCUMENTS and things which are in its possession, custody and/or control. The production and inspection shall take place at [*address*] (or such other place as may be stipulated to by the parties) on or before [*date*], within thirty (30) days of the date of service hereof.

In lieu of production of the originals of the requested DOCUMENTS, Defendant CHASE may serve true, correct and legible copies on the above-named counsel for Plaintiffs on or before the date for production set forth above.

INSTRUCTIONS and DEFINITIONS

The following instructions and definitions apply to these requests:

A. If YOU claim that any document which is required to be produced by YOU in response to any of these document requests is privileged:

1. Identify its title and general subject matter;
2. State its date;
3. Identify its author;
4. Identify the person for whom it was prepared or to whom it was sent;
5. State the nature of the privilege claimed; and
6. State in detail each and every fact upon which YOU base YOUR claim of privilege.

B. If YOU have at any time relinquished possession, custody, or control of, or destroyed, any DOCUMENT that is responsive to these requests, identify each DOCUMENT as specified in part A above and, as to existing DOCUMENTS, identify the person(s) who have possession, custody, or control of such DOCUMENTS.

C. "YOU" "YOUR" or "YOURS" refers to responding party, JP MORGAN CHASE BANK ("CHASE") and its departments, agents, employees, attorneys, consultants, accountants, and any other representative acting for or on their behalf or under their direction.

D. "PLAINTIFFS" means Plaintiffs [*Consumer 1*] and [*Consumer 2*]

E. "COMPLAINT" refers to the complaint filed by [*Consumer 1*] and [*Consumer 2*] in the United States District for the Northern District of California, Case No. _____.

F. The term "PERSON(S)" means all individuals and entities, and as used herein shall be deemed to include, without limitation, natural persons, firms, partnerships, associations, organizations, governmental units, joint ventures, corporations, committees, and any other entities.

G. The term "COMMUNICATION(S)" shall refer to any verbal, written or electronic transfer of information, and includes but is not limited to conversations, conferences, meetings, correspondence, faxes, telegrams, telexes, memoranda, notes and telephone conversations.

H. The term "DOCUMENT" means any writing within the meaning of Fed. R. Civ. P. 34, including, but not limited to, all items defined in Fed. R. Evid. 1001 including, but not limited to, any written recorded or graphic matter, however produced or reproduced, of every kind whether existing in tangible written form, or video or audio tape, or in electronic or computerized form on a computer, computer disk, computer tape, CD-ROM, or otherwise, and regardless of where located, including but not limited to, any summary, schedule, memorandum, note, statement, letter, telegram, interoffice communication, electronic mail, report, diary, desk or pocket calendar or notebook, daybook, appointment book, pamphlet, periodical, worksheet, costsheet, list, graph, chart, index, tape, record, partial or complete report of telephone or oral conversation, compilation, tabulation, study, analysis, transcript, minutes, accounting records, datasheet, data processing card or tape, bill of lading, shipping galley or similar freight documents, and all other memorials of any conversation, meetings and conferences, by telephone or otherwise, and any other writing or recording. The terms "DOCUMENT(S)" shall also include the files in which said DOCUMENTS are maintained.

I. The terms "EVIDENCE", "REFLECT OR RELATE TO," "RELATING TO," and "CONCERNING" shall include anything referring to, supporting, evidencing, reflecting, recording, mentioning, embodying, discussing, recording, summarizing, memorializing, containing, alluding to, responding to, commenting upon, analyzing, setting forth, characterizing, or in any way logically or factually connected to or bearing upon the matter referenced.

J. "IDENTIFY" when used herein shall mean state in detail and with particularity all facts and contentions related thereto.

K. "IDENTIFY" when used in connection with a PERSON shall mean to state the PERSON's name, business title, residential and business addresses, and residential and business telephone numbers.

L. "IDENTIFY" when used in connection with a DOCUMENT shall mean to state the DOCUMENT's date, title, author and general subject matter.

M. "Loss mitigation" refers to any program, plan, proposal, process, or procedure, or any communication, review, or other activity by DEFENDANT relating to curing, bringing current, or otherwise restoring delinquent loans to a current status.

N. "HAMP" refers to the Home Affordable Modification Program.

O. "HAMP APPLICATIONS" refers to PLAINTIFFS' loan modification applications dated October 6, 2009, February 5, 2010, and August 5, 2010.

P. The terms "PROPERTY" shall refer to the real property located at [*property address*].

DOCUMENTS TO BE PRODUCED

REQUEST FOR PRODUCTION NO. 1: All DOCUMENTS that EVIDENCE, REFLECT or RELATE to YOUR knowledge of the PROPERTY from any source.

REQUEST FOR PRODUCTION NO. 2: All DOCUMENTS that RELATE to PLAINTIFFS.

REQUEST FOR PRODUCTION NO. 3: All DOCUMENTS that RELATE to COMMUNICATIONS between YOU and PLAINTIFFS.

REQUEST FOR PRODUCTION NO. 4: All DOCUMENTS REFLECTING any communication between PLAINTIFFS and ANY Defendant.

REQUEST FOR PRODUCTION NO. 5: All DOCUMENTS concerning ANY loan modification application between YOU and PLAINTIFFS.

REQUEST FOR PRODUCTION NO. 6: All DOCUMENTS and COMMUNICATIONS concerning PLAINTIFFS' HAMP loan modification applications, including, but not limited to, notes, emails, and telephone logs.

REQUEST FOR PRODUCTION NO. 7: All DOCUMENTS that RELATE TO the written policies, procedures, directives, or other guidance regarding HAMP that YOU followed or relied on to make a determination on Plaintiffs' HAMP applications dated October 2009, February 2010, and August 2010.

REQUEST FOR PRODUCTION NO. 8: All DOCUMENTS contained in any file that RELATE TO or were used for or were otherwise referenced during any HAMP review conducted on PLAINTIFFS' loan.

REQUEST FOR PRODUCTION NO. 9: All DOCUMENTS that RELATE TO any notices of modification decisions regarding PLAINTIFFS' loan that were actually sent to PLAINTIFFS and any proof of such delivery.

REQUEST FOR PRODUCTION NO. 10: All DOCUMENTS that RELATE TO any servicing guidelines used for the servicing of PLAINTIFFS' mortgage loan that bear on the issue of eligibility for modification.

REQUEST FOR PRODUCTION NO. 11: All documents related in any way to any criteria or system used to determine PLAINTIFFS' eligibility for modification.

REQUEST FOR PRODUCTION NO. 12: All DOCUMENTS reviewed or referenced in order to make the determination underlying YOUR statement that YOU are "unable to create an affordable payment equal to 31% of PLAINTIFFS' reported monthly gross income without changing the terms of the loan beyond the requirements of the Program."

REQUEST FOR PRODUCTION NO. 13: All DOCUMENTS RELATING TO any communication that YOU made to or received from any PERSON acting on behalf of, representing, relaying information for, or otherwise associated with PLAINTIFFS and their mortgage loan.

REQUEST FOR PRODUCTION NO. 14: All DOCUMENTS created, modified, or used by YOU in guiding or prescribing the activities of YOUR agents, employees, officers, or authorized representatives in implementing or carrying out HAMP or its requirements, including, but not limited to, internal training, policies, procedures, and guidance documents.

REQUEST FOR PRODUCTION NO. 15: All DOCUMENTS created, modified, or used by YOU in guiding or prescribing the activities of YOUR agents, employees, officers, or authorized representatives in handling or processing requests for modification or workout of obligations, secured by residential real property, including, but not limited to, internal training, procedures, and guidance documents.

REQUEST FOR PRODUCTION NO. 16: all documents RELATING TO YOUR analysis of PLAINTIFFS' financial situation for a loan modification under HAMP, including the calculations used for the Net Present Value (NPV) test.

REQUEST FOR PRODUCTION NO. 17: Produce an electronic version of each version of the Net Present Value (NPV) model YOU used to analyze PLAINTIFFS' HAMP APPLICATIONS.

REQUEST FOR PRODUCTION NO. 18: all documents regarding the outcome of each evaluation YOU performed of PLAINTIFFS' loan modification requests and the specific rationale underlying your response to these requests.

REQUEST FOR PRODUCTION NO. 19: All DOCUMENTS EVIDENCING YOUR response to PLAINTIFFS' letters dated [*month/day/year*], and [*month/day/year*], to YOU asking that YOU reevaluate them for HAMP or, alternatively, that YOU provide them with documentation showing why they were denied the modification.

REQUEST FOR PRODUCTION NO. 20: All DOCUMENTS REFLECTING the substance of telephone conversations between PLAINTIFFS and YOU, including but not limited to, call logs.

REQUEST FOR PRODUCTION NO. 21: All DOCUMENTS REFLECTING YOUR compliance with Supplemental Directive 09-02, YOUR fair housing obligations under HAMP.

REQUEST FOR PRODUCTION NO. 22. All DOCUMENTS REFLECTING YOUR written policies and procedures to respond to borrower inquiries and complaints in connection with HAMP.

REQUEST FOR PRODUCTION NO. 23: All DOCUMENTS RELATING TO YOUR policies and procedures regarding borrower public benefit income.

Dated: _____

[*Organization Name*]

_____

[*Attorneys for Plaintiffs*]

H.9 Notice of Deposition

UNITED STATES DISTRICT COURT
DISTRICT OF CALIFORNIA
SAN JOSE DIVISION

_____)	
[*Consumer 1*] and [*Consumer 2*],)	
Plaintiffs,)	
)	
v.)	Case No. _____
)	
)	RULE 30(b)(6) NOTICE OF
JP Morgan Chase Bank, N.A.,)	DEPOSITION OF
U.S. Bank National Association,)	DEFENDANT JP MORGAN
California Reconveyance)	CHASE BANK, N.A.
Corporation and DOES 150,)	
Defendants.)	
_____)	

TO DEFENDANT JP MORGAN CHASE BANK, N.A., BY AND THROUGH ITS COUNSEL OF RECORD:

PLEASE TAKE NOTICE that pursuant to Rule 30(b)(6) of the Federal Rules of Civil Procedure, Plaintiffs [*Consumer 1*] and [*Consumer 2*] (hereafter "the [*Plaintiffs*]") shall take the oral deposition of Defendant JP Morgan Chase Bank, N.A. (hereafter "Chase") regarding the [*Plaintiffs'*] eligibility for a Home Affordable Modification Program ("HAMP") loan modification, before a certified shorthand reporter duly commissioned and authorized to administer oaths under Fed. R. Civ. P. 30(c). The deposition shall take place on [*month/day/year*] at the hour of [*time*] and shall continue from day to day, excluding Saturdays, Sundays and holidays, until completed. The deposition will take place at [*address*].

Pursuant to Rule 30(b)(6) of the Federal Rules of Civil Procedure, Chase is obligated to designate one or more of its officers, directors, or managing agents, and/or one or more other persons who consent to testify on its behalf concerning the matters set forth in Attachment A.

Chase is requested to set forth, for each person designated, the matters on which the person will testify.

Dated: _____

[*Organization Name*]

_____

[*Attorneys for Plaintiffs*]

ATTACHMENT A

Definitions

1. The term "DOCUMENT" means the original or copy of handwriting, typewriting, printing, photostatting, photographing, and every other means of recording upon any tangible thing, of any form of communications or representation, including letters, memoranda, notes, transcripts, pleadings, words, pictures, sounds, and symbols, drawings, graphs, charts, photographs, recordings, and other data compilations from which information can be obtained, or any combination of them, or other "writing" of any kind as defined by Rules 26 and 34 of the Federal Rules of Civil Procedure.

2. "PLAINTIFFS" means [*Consumer 1*] and [*Consumer 2*].

3. "CHASE" "DEFENDANT" "YOU" or "YOUR" refers to JP MORGAN CHASE BANK, N.A, and including without limitation past or present officers, directors, agents, attorneys, accountants, contractors, subsidiaries, parents, acquirees, successors, assigns, or predecessors-in-interest, including but not limited to, Chase Home Finance, LLC.

4. The terms "ANY" and "ALL" mean "ANY and ALL."

5. The singular of any term includes the plural, and the plural of any term includes the singular.

6. "RELATING TO" (and any form thereof, including but not limited to "RELATES TO") means pertaining to, in connection with, evidencing, referring to, referencing, noting, describing, embodying, supporting, and/or reflecting.

7. "PERSON" or "PERSONS" means any natural person, firm, entity, corporation, partnership, proprietorship, association, joint venture, other form of business organization or arrangement, and/or government or government agency of any nature of type.

8. "COMMUNICATION" or "COMMUNICATIONS" includes but is not limited to the following: (a) any written letter, memorandum, or other DOCUMENT of any kind transmitted from one PERSON to another PERSON by hand, mail, courier, other delivery service, telecopy, facsimile, telegraph, electronic mail, voicemail, or any other means; (b) any telephone call, whether or not such call was by chance or prearranged, formal or informal; and (c) any conversation or meeting between two or more PERSONS, whether or not such contact was by chance or prearranged, formal or informal.

9. "TRANSACTION" means the HAMP loan modification applications described in Plaintiffs' First Amended Complaint.

TOPICS FOR EXAMINATION

1. Chase's policies and practices RELATING TO the promotion and marketing of the Home Affordable Modification Program.

2. CHASE's guidelines for borrower participation in the Home Affordable Modification Program.

3. CHASE's policies and practices for determining which borrowers are eligible for HAMP modifications.

4. All COMMUNICATIONS between PLAINTIFFS and DEFENDANT.

5. The facts that support YOUR statement in YOUR letter dated October 26, 2010, that "[w]e are unable to create an affordable payment equal to 31% of your reported monthly gross income without changing the terms of PLAINTIFFS' loan beyond the requirements of the program."

6. The facts showing that YOU completed the HAMP modification process specified by the HAMP Guidelines and/or Supplemental Directives before denying PLAINTIFF'S loan modification applications.

7. The specific DOCUMENTS YOU need to determine if a borrower with a HAMP-eligible loan qualifies for a HAMP modification.

8. YOUR process for determining whether to grant or deny a given HAMP modification application.

9. YOUR policies and procedures for retention of detailed records of borrower solicitation and borrower initiated inquiries regarding HAMP.

10. YOUR determination that PLAINTIFFS did not qualify for a HAMP modification.

11. All Net present Value (NPV) calculations and comparisons YOU used in evaluating PLAINTIFFS' eligibility for a HAMP modification.

12. Any investor-based or other prohibitions or limitations YOU contend that restrain YOUR ability to modify PLAINTIFFS' loan and/or investor based or other permissions YOU contend are required from third parties before YOU would be able to modify PLAINTIFFS' loan.

13. YOUR compliance with Supplemental Directive 09-02, YOUR compliance with fair housing obligations under HAMP.

14. YOUR policies and procedures RELATING TO disability benefit income when evaluating a HAMP modification.

15. YOUR policies and procedures RELATING TO borrower inquiries regarding notice of adverse action under the Equal Credit Opportunity Act.

Dated: _____

[*Organization Name*]

_____

[*Attorneys for Plaintiffs*]

Appendix I

Consumer's Guide to Credit Discrimination Laws (Appropriate for Distribution to Clients)

I.1 Introduction

The following information was prepared by federal government regulators to inform consumers about credit discrimination laws. The information can be ordered directly from the relevant agencies. It is also available on-line at:

- Fair housing information can be downloaded from the Department of Housing and Urban Development website, www.hud.gov;
- Equal credit opportunity information can be downloaded from the Federal Trade Commission website, www.ftc.gov;
- Rights to fair lending in home mortgages is available on the Federal Reserve Board website, www.federalreserve.gov.

I.2 Fair Housing—It's Your Right

The following information was prepared by the United States Department of Housing and Urban Development, and may be found on the Department's Homes and Communities website at www.hud.gov/offices/fheo/FHLaws/yourrights.cfm.

Fair Housing Act

HUD has played a lead role in administering the Fair Housing Act since its adoption in 1968. The 1988 amendments, however, have greatly increased the Department's enforcement role. First, the newly protected classes have proven significant sources of new complaints. Second, HUD's expanded enforcement role took the Department beyond investigation and conciliation into the area of mandatory enforcement.

Complaints filed with HUD are investigated by the Office of Fair Housing and Equal Opportunity (FHEO). If the complaint is not successfully conciliated, FHEO determines whether reasonable cause exists to believe that a discriminatory housing practice has occurred. Where reasonable cause is found, the parties to the complaint are notified by HUD's issuance of a Determination, as well as a Charge of Discrimination, and a hearing is scheduled before a HUD administrative law judge. Either party—complainant or respondent—may cause the HUD-scheduled administrative proceeding to be terminated by electing instead to have the matter litigated in Federal court. Whenever a party has so elected, the Department of Justice takes over HUD's role as counsel seeking resolution of the charge on behalf of aggrieved persons, and the matter proceeds as a civil action. Either form of action—the ALJ proceeding or the civil action in Federal court—is subject to review in the U.S. Court of Appeals.

Significant Recent Changes

1. The Housing for Older Persons Act of 1995 (HOPA) makes several changes to the 55 and older exemption. Since the 1988 Amendments, the Fair Housing Act has exempted from its familial status provisions properties that satisfy the Act's 55 and older housing condition.

First, it eliminates the requirement that 55 and older housing have significant facilities and services designed for the elderly. Second, HOPA establishes a "good faith reliance" immunity from damages for persons who in good faith believe that the 55 and older exemption applies to a particular property, if they do not actually know that the property is not eligible for the exemption and if the property has formally stated in writing that it qualifies for the exemption.

HOPA retains the requirement that senior housing must have one person who is 55 years of age or older living in at least 80 percent of its occupied units. It also still requires that senior housing publish and follow policies and procedures that demonstrate an intent to be housing for persons 55 and older.

An exempt property will not violate the Fair Housing Act if it includes families with children, but it does not have to do so. Of course, the property must meet the Act's requirements that at least 80 percent of its occupied units have at least one occupant who is 55 or older, and that it publish and follow policies and procedures that demonstrate an intent to be 55 and older housing.

A Department of Housing and Urban Development rule published in the April 2, 1999, Federal Register implements the Housing for Older Persons Act of 1995 and explains in detail those provisions of the Fair Housing Act that pertain to senior housing.

2. Changes were made to enhance law enforcement, including making amendments to criminal penalties in section 901 of the Civil Rights Act of 1968 for violating the Fair Housing Act.

3. Changes were made to provide incentives for self-testing by lenders for discrimination under the Fair Housing Act and the Equal Credit Opportunity Act. See Title II, subtitle D of the Omnibus Consolidated Appropriations Act, 1997, P.L. 104–208 (9/30/96).

Basic Facts About the Fair Housing Act

What Housing Is Covered?

The Fair Housing Act covers most housing. In some circumstances, the Act exempts owner-occupied buildings with no more than four units, single-family housing sold or rented without the use of a broker, and housing operated by organizations and private clubs that limit occupancy to members.

What Is Prohibited?

In the Sale and Rental of Housing: No one may take any of the following actions based on race, color, national origin, religion, sex, familial status or handicap:

- Refuse to rent or sell housing
- Refuse to negotiate for housing
- Make housing unavailable
- Deny a dwelling
- Set different terms, conditions or privileges for sale or rental of a dwelling
- Provide different housing services or facilities
- Falsely deny that housing is available for inspection, sale, or rental
- For profit, persuade owners to sell or rent (blockbusting) or
- Deny anyone access to or membership in a facility or service (such as a multiple listing service) related to the sale or rental of housing.

In Mortgage Lending: No one may take any of the following actions based on race, color, national origin, religion, sex, familial status or handicap (disability):

- Refuse to make a mortgage loan
- Refuse to provide information regarding loans
- Impose different terms or conditions on a loan, such as different interest rates, points, or fees
- Discriminate in appraising property
- Refuse to purchase a loan or
- Set different terms or conditions for purchasing a loan.

In Addition: It is illegal for anyone to:

- Threaten, coerce, intimidate or interfere with anyone exercising a fair housing right or assisting others who exercise that right
- Advertise or make any statement that indicates a limitation or preference based on race, color, national origin, religion, sex, familial status, or handicap. This prohibition against discriminatory advertising applies to single-family and owner-occupied housing that is otherwise exempt from the Fair Housing Act.

Additional Protection if You Have a Disability

If you or someone associated with you:

- Have a physical or mental disability (including hearing, mobility and visual impairments, chronic alcoholism, chronic mental illness, AIDS, AIDS Related Complex and mental retardation) that substantially limits one or more major life activities
- Have a record of such a disability or
- Are regarded as having such a disability

Your landlord **may not**:

- Refuse to let you make reasonable modifications to your dwelling or common use areas, at your expense, if necessary for the disabled person to use the housing. (Where reasonable, the landlord may permit changes only if you agree to restore the property to its original condition when you move.)
- Refuse to make reasonable accommodations in rules, policies, practices or services if necessary for the disabled person to use the housing.

Example: A building with a "no pets" policy must allow a visually impaired tenant to keep a guide dog.

Example: An apartment complex that offers tenants ample, unassigned parking must honor a request from a mobility-impaired tenant for a reserved space near her apartment if necessary to assure that she can have access to her apartment.

However, housing need not be made available to a person who is a direct threat to the health or safety of others or who currently uses illegal drugs.

Requirements for New Buildings

In buildings that are ready for first occupancy after March 13, 1991, and have an elevator and four or more units:

- Public and common areas must be accessible to persons with disabilities
- Doors and hallways must be wide enough for wheelchairs
- All units must have:
    - —An accessible route into and through the unit
    - —Accessible light switches, electrical outlets, thermostats and other environmental controls
    - —Reinforced bathroom walls to allow later installation of grab bars and
    - —Kitchens and bathrooms that can be used by people in wheelchairs.

If a building with four or more units has no elevator and will be ready for first occupancy after March 13, 1991, these standards apply to ground floor units.

These requirements for new buildings do not replace any more stringent standards in State or local law.

Housing Opportunities for Families

Unless a building or community qualifies as housing for older persons, it may not discriminate based on familial status. That is, it may not discriminate against families in which one or more children under 18 live with:

- A parent
- A person who has legal custody of the child or children or
- The designee of the parent or legal custodian, with the parent or custodian's written permission.

Familial status protection also applies to pregnant women and anyone securing legal custody of a child under 18.

Exemption: Housing for older persons is exempt from the prohibition against familial status discrimination if:

- The HUD Secretary has determined that it is specifically designed for and occupied by elderly persons under a Federal, State or local government program or
- It is occupied solely by persons who are 62 or older or
- It houses at least one person who is 55 or older in at least 80 percent of the occupied units, and adheres to a policy that demonstrates an intent to house persons who are 55 or older.

A transition period permits residents on or before September 13, 1988, to continue living in the housing, regardless of their age, without interfering with the exemption.

If You Think Your Rights Have Been Violated

HUD is ready to help with any problem of housing discrimination. If you think your rights have been violated, the Housing Discrimination Complaint Form is available for you to download, complete and return, or complete online and submit, or you may write HUD a letter, or telephone the HUD Office nearest you. You have one year after an alleged violation to file a complaint with HUD, but you should file it as soon as possible.

What to Tell HUD:

- Your name and address
- The name and address of the person your complaint is against (the respondent)
- The address or other identification to the housing involved
- A short description to the alleged violation (the event that caused you to believe your rights were violated)
- The date(s) to the alleged violation

Where to Write or Call:

Send the Housing Discrimination Complaint Form or a letter to the HUD Office nearest you or you may call that office directly.

If You Are Disabled:

HUD also provides:

- A toll-free TTY phone for the hearing impaired: 1-800-927-9275
- Interpreters
- Tapes and braille materials

- Assistance in reading and completing forms

What Happens when You File a Complaint?

HUD will notify you when it receives your complaint. Normally, HUD also will:

- Notify the alleged violator of your complaint and permit that person to submit an answer
- Investigate your complaint and determine whether there is reasonable cause to believe the Fair Housing Act has been violated
- Notify you if it cannot complete an investigation within 100 days of receiving your complaint

Conciliation

HUD will try to reach an agreement with the person your complaint is against (the respondent). A conciliation agreement must protect both you and the public interest. If an agreement is signed, HUD will take no further action on your complaint. However, if HUD has reasonable cause to believe that a conciliation agreement is breached, HUD will recommend that the Attorney General file suit.

Complaint Referrals

If HUD has determined that your State or local agency has the same fair housing powers as HUD, HUD will refer your complaint to that agency for investigation and notify you of the referral. That agency must begin work on your complaint within 30 days or HUD may take it back.

What if You Need Help Quickly?

If you need immediate help to stop a serious problem that is being caused by a Fair Housing Act violation, HUD may be able to assist you as soon as you file a complaint. HUD may authorize the Attorney General to go to court to seek temporary or preliminary relief, pending the outcome of your complaint, if:

- Irreparable harm is likely to occur without HUD's intervention
- There is substantial evidence that a violation of the Fair Housing Act occurred

Example: A builder agrees to sell a house but, after learning the buyer is black, fails to keep the agreement. The buyer files a complaint with HUD. HUD may authorize the Attorney General to go to court to prevent a sale to any other buyer until HUD investigates the complaint.

What Happens after a Complaint Investigation?

If, after investigating your complaint, HUD finds reasonable cause to believe that discrimination occurred, it will inform you. Your case will be heard in an administrative hearing within

120 days, unless you or the respondent want the case to be heard in Federal district court. Either way, there is no cost to you.

The Administrative Hearing:

If your case goes to an administrative hearing HUD attorneys will litigate the case on your behalf. You may intervene in the case and be represented by your own attorney if you wish. An Administrative Law Judge (ALA) will consider evidence from you and the respondent. If the ALA decides that discrimination occurred, the respondent can be ordered:

- To compensate you for actual damages, including humiliation, pain and suffering.
- To provide injunctive or other equitable relief, for example, to make the housing available to you.
- To pay the Federal Government a civil penalty to vindicate the public interest. The maximum penalties are $16,000 for a first violation and $65,000 for a third violation within seven years.
- To pay reasonable attorney's fees and costs.

Federal District Court

If you or the respondent choose to have your case decided in Federal District Court, the Attorney General will file a suit and litigate it on your behalf. Like the ALA, the District Court can order relief, and award actual damages, attorney's fees and costs. In addition, the court can award punitive damages.

In Addition

You May File Suit: You may file suit, at your expense, in Federal District Court or State Court within two years of an alleged violation. If you cannot afford an attorney, the Court may appoint one for you. You may bring suit even after filing a complaint, if you have not signed a conciliation agreement and an Administrative Law Judge has not started a hearing. A court may award actual and punitive damages and attorney's fees and costs.

Other Tools to Combat Housing Discrimination:

If there is noncompliance with the order of an Administrative Law Judge, HUD may seek temporary relief, enforcement of the order or a restraining order in a United States Court of Appeals.

The Attorney General may file a suit in a Federal District Court if there is reasonable cause to believe a pattern or practice of housing discrimination is occurring.

For Further Information:

The Fair Housing Act and HUD's regulations contain more detail and technical information. If you need a copy of the law or regulations, contact the HUD Office nearest you.

I.3 Equal Credit Opportunity

The following information was prepared by the Federal Trade Commission's Bureau of Consumer Protection, and may be found on the Commission's website at www.ftc.gov/bcp/edu/pubs/consumer/credit/cre15.shtm.

Equal Credit Opportunity: Understanding Your Rights Under the Law

People use credit to pay for education or a house, a remodeling job or a car, or to finance a loan to keep their business operating.

The Federal Trade Commission (FTC), the nation's consumer protection agency, enforces the Equal Credit Opportunity Act (ECOA), which prohibits credit discrimination on the basis of race, color, religion, national origin, sex, marital status, age, or because you get public assistance. Creditors may ask you for most of this information in certain situations, but they may not use it when deciding whether to give you credit or when setting the terms of your credit. Not everyone who applies for credit gets it or gets the same terms: Factors like income, expenses, debts, and credit history are among the considerations lenders use to determine your creditworthiness.

The law provides protections when you deal with any organizations or people who regularly extend credit, including banks, small loan and finance companies, retail and department stores, credit card companies, and credit unions. Everyone who participates in the decision to grant credit or in setting the terms of that credit, including real estate brokers who arrange financing, must comply with the ECOA.

Here's a brief summary of the basic provisions of the ECOA.

I. When You Apply for Credit, Creditors May Not . . .

- Discourage you from applying or reject your application because of your race, color, religion, national origin, sex, marital status, age, or because you receive public assistance.
- Consider your race, sex, or national origin, although you may be asked to disclose this information if you want to. It helps federal agencies enforce anti-discrimination laws. A creditor may consider your immigration status and whether you have the right to stay in the country long enough to repay the debt.
- Impose different terms or conditions, like a higher interest rate or higher fees, on a loan based on your race, color, religion, national origin, sex, marital status, age, or because you receive public assistance.
- Ask if you're widowed or divorced. A creditor may use only the terms: married, unmarried, or separated.
- Ask about your marital status if you're applying for a separate, unsecured account. A creditor may ask you to provide this information if you live in "community property" states: Arizona, California, Idaho, Louisiana, Ne-

vada, New Mexico, Texas, Washington, and Wisconsin. A creditor in any state may ask for this information if you apply for a joint account or one secured by property.

- Ask for information about your spouse, except:
  - if your spouse is applying with you;
  - if your spouse will be allowed to use the account;
  - if you are relying on your spouse's income or on alimony or child support income from a former spouse;
  - if you live in a community property state.
- Ask about your plans for having or raising children, but they can ask questions about expenses related to your dependents.
- Ask if you get alimony, child support, or separate maintenance payments, unless they tell you first that you don't have to provide this information if you aren't relying on these payments to get credit. A creditor may ask if you have to pay alimony, child support, or separate maintenance payments.

II. When Deciding to Grant You Credit or When Setting the Terms of Credit, Creditors May Not . . .

- Consider your race, color, religion, national origin, sex, marital status or whether you get public assistance.
- Consider your age, unless:
  - you're too young to sign contracts, generally under 18;
  - you're at least 62, and the creditor will favor you because of your age;
  - it's used to determine the meaning of other factors important to creditworthiness. For example, a creditor could use your age to determine if your income might drop because you're about to retire;
  - it's used in a valid credit scoring system that favors applicants 62 and older. A credit scoring system assigns points to answers you give on credit applications. For example, your length of employment might be scored differently depending on your age.
- Consider whether you have a telephone account in your name. A creditor may consider whether you have a phone.
- Consider the racial composition of the neighborhood where you want to buy, refinance or improve a house with money you are borrowing.

III. When Evaluating Your Income, Creditors May Not . . .

- Refuse to consider reliable public assistance income the same way as other income.
- Discount income because of your sex or marital status. For example, a creditor cannot count a man's salary at 100 percent and a woman's at 75 percent. A creditor may not assume a woman of childbearing age will stop working to raise children.
- Discount or refuse to consider income because it comes

from part-time employment, Social Security, pensions, or annuities.

- Refuse to consider reliable alimony, child support, or separate maintenance payments. A creditor may ask you for proof that you receive this income consistently.

IV. You Also Have the Right To . . .

- Have credit in your birth name (Mary Smith), your first and your spouse's last name (Mary Jones), or your first name and a combined last name (Mary Smith Jones).
- Get credit without a cosigner, if you meet the creditor's standards.
- Have a cosigner other than your spouse, if one is necessary.
- Keep your own accounts after you change your name, marital status, reach a certain age, or retire, unless the creditor has evidence that you're not willing or able to pay.
- Know whether your application was accepted or rejected within 30 days of filing a complete application.
- Know why your application was rejected. The creditor must tell you the specific reason for the rejection or that you are entitled to learn the reason if you ask within 60 days. An acceptable reason might be: "your income was too low" or "you haven't been employed long enough." An unacceptable reason might be "you didn't meet our minimum standards." That information isn't specific enough.
- Learn the specific reason you were offered less favorable terms than you applied for, but only if you reject these terms. For example, if the lender offers you a smaller loan or a higher interest rate, and you don't accept the offer, you have the right to know why those terms were offered.
- Find out why your account was closed or why the terms of the account were made less favorable, unless the account was inactive or you failed to make payments as agreed.

V. A Special Note to Women

A good credit history—a record of your bill payments—often is necessary to get credit. This can hurt many married, separated, divorced, and widowed women. Typically, there are two reasons women don't have credit histories in their own names: either they lost their credit histories when they married and changed their names, or creditors reported accounts shared by married couples in the husband's name only.

If you're married, separated, divorced, or widowed, contact your local credit reporting companies to make sure all relevant bill payment information is in a file under your own name. Your credit report includes information on where you live, how you pay your bills, and whether you've been sued, arrested or filed for bankruptcy. National credit reporting companies sell the information in your report to creditors, insurers, employers, and other businesses that, in turn, use it to evaluate your applications for credit, insurance, employment, or renting a home.

The Fair Credit Reporting Act (FCRA) requires each of the three nationwide credit reporting companies—Equifax, Experian, and TransUnion—to give you a free copy of your credit report, at your request, once every 12 months. To order your report, visit annualcreditreport.com, call 1-877-322-8228, or complete the Annual Credit Report Request Form and mail it to: Annual Credit Report Request Service, P.O. Box 105281, Atlanta, GA 30348-5281. You can print the form from here.

VI. If You Suspect a Creditor Has Discriminated Against You, Take Action.

- Complain to the creditor. Sometimes you can persuade the creditor to reconsider your application.
- Check with your state Attorney General's office (www.naag.org) to see if the creditor violated state equal credit opportunity laws.
- Consider suing the creditor in federal district court. If you win, you can recover your actual damages and be awarded punitive damages if the court finds that the creditor's conduct was willful. You also may recover reasonable lawyers' fees and court costs. Or you might consider finding others with the same claim, and getting together to file a class action suit. An attorney can advise you on how to proceed.
- Report violations to the appropriate government agency. If you've been denied credit, the creditor must give you the name and address of the agency to contact.

A number of federal agencies share enforcement responsibility for the ECOA. Determining which agency to contact depends on the type of financial institution you dealt with.

For retail and department stores; mortgage, small loan and consumer finance companies; oil companies; public utilities; state credit unions; government lending programs; or travel and expense credit card companies are involved, contact:

Federal Trade Commission
Consumer Response Center
Washington, DC 20580
1-877-FTC-HELP (1-877-382-4357); TDD: 1-866-653-4261
www.ftc.gov
The FTC generally does not intervene in individual disputes, but the information you provide may indicate a pattern of violations that the Commission would investigate.

For nationally-charted banks (National or N.A. will be part of the name):

Comptroller of the Currency
Consumer Assistance Group
1301 McKinney Street
Houston, TX 77010-9050
1-800-613-6743
www.helpwithmybank.gov

For state-chartered banks insured by the Federal Deposit Insurance Corporation, but not members of the Federal Reserve System:

Federal Deposit Insurance Corporation
Consumer Response Center
2345 Grand Boulevard
Suite 100
Kansas City, MO 64108
1-877-ASK-FDIC (1-877-275-3342)
www.fdic.gov

For federally-chartered or federally-insured savings and loans:

Office of Thrift Supervision
Consumer Affairs
1700 G Street NW
Washington, DC 20552
1-800-842-6929; TTY: 800-877-8339
www.ots.treas.gov

For federally-chartered credit unions:

National Credit Union Administration
1775 Duke Street
Suite 4206
Alexandria, VA 22314-3437
1-800-755-1030
www.ncua.gov

For state member banks of the Federal Reserve System:

Federal Reserve Consumer Help Center
P.O. Box 1200
Minneapolis, MN 55480
1-888-851-1920; TDD: 877-766-8533
www.federalreserveconsumerhelp.gov

For discrimination complaints against all kinds of creditors:

Department of Justice
Civil Rights Division
Washington, DC 20530
www.usdoj.gov/crt

Still Not Sure Who to Contact?

If you can't figure out which federal agency has responsibility for the financial institution you dealt with, visit www.federalreserveconsumerhelp.gov or call 1-888-851-1920.

For More Information

The FTC works to prevent fraudulent, deceptive, and unfair business practices in the marketplace and to provide information to help consumers spot, stop, and avoid them. To file a complaint or get free information on consumer issues, visit ftc.gov or call toll-free, 1-877-FTC-HELP (1-877-382-4357); TTY: 1-866-653-4261. Watch a video, *How to File a Complaint*, at ftc.gov/video to learn more. The FTC enters consumer complaints into the Consumer Sentinel Network, a secure online database and investigative tool used by hundreds of civil and criminal law enforcement agencies in the U.S. and abroad.

I.4 Home Mortgages: Understanding Your Rights to Fair Lending

The following information was prepared by the Federal Reserve Board, and may be found on the agency's website at www.federalreserve.gov/pubs/mortgage/MORBRO_3.htm.

Understanding Your Rights to Fair Lending

Federal law protects every homebuyer looking for a mortgage loan against discrimination on the basis of race, color, national origin, religion, sex, marital status, age, receipt of public assistance funds, familial status (having children under the age of 18), handicap, or exercising your rights under other consumer credit protection laws. Lenders may not take any of these factors into account in their dealings with you.

For instance, lenders may not discourage you because of your race or national origin from applying for a mortgage loan. Whatever your color, they must offer you the same credit terms as other applicants with similar loan requests. They may not treat your application differently because of your sex or marital status or familial status. In short, they are barred from taking into account any of the factors listed here in their dealings with applicants or with potential applicants. They should:

- Willingly give you an application and other information you need on how to apply for a loan
- Willingly discuss with you the various mortgage loans they offer and give you an idea whether you can qualify for them
- Diligently act to make a decision—without undue delay—once you provide all the information asked for (including, for example, written evidence of how much you make or how much you have in savings), and once they receive other paperwork required for processing the application (such as a property appraisal)
- Not be influenced by the racial or ethnic composition of the neighborhood where the home you want to buy is located.

If you apply for a mortgage and are turned down, remember that not all institutions have the same lending standards. Shop around for another lender. But if the way you were treated suggests the possibility of unlawful discrimination, you might talk to:

Private fair housing groups

Often these groups can walk you through the mortgage process. They can also help you understand whether your experience suggests that the lender is discriminating unlawfully, and can help you decide whether to file a complaint.

Human rights agencies

These are government agencies set up by a city, county, or state government to deal with discrimination.

Attorneys

They can advise you whether the treatment you received gives you legal grounds for bringing a lawsuit against the lender. They can tell you about monetary damages and other types of relief available to individuals who can prove that illegal discrimination occurred.

Federal or state enforcement agencies

They can check the activities of mortgage lenders to make sure they complied with the laws against lending discrimination. When you write, include your name and address; name and address of the lending institution you are complaining about; address of the house involved; and a short description and the date of the alleged violation.

The Fair Housing Act prohibits discrimination in housing sales or loans on the basis of race, religion, color, national origin, sex, familial status (having children under the age of 18), or handicap.

The Equal Credit Opportunity Act prohibits discrimination in any aspect of a credit transaction on the basis of race, religion, age, color, national origin, receipt of public assistance funds, sex, marital status, or the exercise of any right under the Consumer Credit Protection Act.

Directory of Federal Agencies

The Department of Housing & Urban Development (HUD) has primary responsibility for implementing the Fair Housing Act.

Office of Fair Housing & Equal Opportunity
Dept. of Housing and Urban Development
Washington, DC 20410-2000
1-800-669-9777
http://www.hud.gov/complaints/housediscrim.cfm

Other federal agencies monitor compliance by particular types of lenders.

National Banks, Mortgage Companies Owned by National Banks, and Federal Savings Associations

Office of the Comptroller of the Currency
Customer Assistance Group
1301 McKinney St.
Suite 3450
Houston, TX 77010
(800) 613-6743
www.occ.treas.gov

State Member Banks of the Federal Reserve System

Federal Reserve Consumer Help
PO Box 1200
Minneapolis, MN 55480
888-851-1920 (Phone)
877-888-2520 (Fax)

Email: ConsumerHelp@FederalReserve.gov
www.FederalReserveConsumerHelp.gov

Nonmember Federally Insured State Banks

Federal Deposit Insurance Corporation
Consumer Response Center
1100 Walnut Street, Box 11
Kansas City, MO 64106
(877) ASK-FDIC (877-275-3342)
www.fdic.gov

Savings and Loan Associations

Office of Thrift Supervision
Consumer Programs
1700 G Street, NW, 6th Floor
Washington, DC 20552
(800) 842-6929
www.ots.treas.gov

Federal Credit Unions

National Credit Union Administration

Office of Public and Congressional Affairs
1775 Duke St.
Alexandria, VA 22314
(800) 755-1030
(703) 518-6409 (Fax)
www.ncua.gov

Other Lenders

Federal Trade Commission
Consumer Response Center—240
600 Pennsylvania Avenue, NW
Washington, DC 20580
(877) FTC-HELP (877-382-4357)
www.ftc.gov

Department of Justice

Department of Justice
950 Pennsylvania Avenue, NW
Washington, DC 20530
(202) 514-3301
www.usdoj.gov

Appendix J	Bibliography of Social Science Research on Credit Discrimination Issues

This appendix is also available on the companion website to this treatise. The companion website facilitates keyword searches and allows relevant provisions to be imported as word-processable documents.

ARTICLES AND REPORTS

Robert B. Avery, Kenneth P. Brevoort, & Glenn B. Canner, Board of Governors of the Federal Reserve System, *The 2007 HMDA Data*, Fed. Reserve Bull., Dec. 2008, at A107

Debbie Gruenstein Bocian et al., Center for Responsible Lending, Lost Ground, 2011: Disparities in Mortgage Lending and Foreclosures (Nov. 2011), *available at* www.responsiblelending.org/mortgage-lending/research-analysis/lost-ground-2011.html

Debbie Gruenstein Bocian, Keith S. Ernst, & Wei Li, Center for Responsible Lending, Foreclosures by Race and Ethnicity: The Demographics of a Crisis (June 18, 2010)

Debbie Bocian, Keith Ernst, & Wei Li, Center for Responsible Lending, Unfair Lending: The Effect of Race and Ethnicity on the Price of Subprime Mortgages (May 2006)

Debbie Bocian & Richard Zhai, Center for Responsible Lending, Borrowers in Higher Minority Areas More Likely to Receive Prepayment Penalties on Subprime Loans (Jan. 2005)

Thomas P. Boehm & Alan M. Schlottmann, U.S. Department of Housing & Urban Development, Office of Policy Development & Research, Mortgage Pricing Differentials Across Hispanic, Black and White Households: Evidence from the American Housing Survey (Feb. 2006)

Lynne E. Brown, James McEneaney, Alicia H. Munnell, & Geoffrey Tootell, *Mortgage Lending in Boston: Interpreting HMDA Data*, Am. Econ. Rev., Mar. 1996, at 25

Jim Campen, Massachusetts Community & Banking Council, Changing Patterns XIX: Mortgage Lending to Traditionally Underserved Borrowers & Neighborhoods in Boston, Greater Boston and Massachusetts, 2011 (Dec 2012)

Jim Campen, Massachusetts Community & Banking Council, Changing Patterns XVIII: Mortgage Lending to Traditionally Underserved Borrowers & Neighborhoods in Boston, Greater Boston and Massachusetts, 2010 (Dec. 2011), *available at* www.mcbc.info/files/CP18-DEC11%20Report-web.pdf

California Reinvestment Coalition et al., Paying More for the American Dream IV: The Decline of Prime Mortgage Lending in Communities of Color (May 2010)

California Reinvestment Coalition, From Foreclosure to Re-Redlining: How America's Largest Financial Institutions Devastated California's Communities (Feb. 2010)

California Reinvestment Coalition et al., Paying More for the American Dream: A Multi-State Analysis of Higher Cost Home Purchase Lending (Mar. 2007)

California Reinvestment Coalition, Who Really Gets Higher-Cost Home Loans? (Dec. 2006)

Jim Campen, Massachusetts Community & Banking Council, Borrowing Trouble VII: High-Cost Mortgage Lending in Greater Boston, 2005 (Jan. 2007)

Jim Campen, Massachusetts Community & Banking Council, Changing Patterns XVIII: Mortgage Lending to Traditionally Underserved Borrowers & Neighborhoods in Greater Boston, 1990–2005 (Nov. 2006)

Keith Corbett & Aracely Panameno, Center for Responsible Lending, Wealth-Stripping Payday Loans Trouble Communities of Color (Oct. 2008)

Deyanira Del Rio, Neighborhood Economic Development Advocacy Project, Mortgage Lending and Foreclosures in Immigrant Communities: Expanding Fair Housing and Fair Lending

Opportunity Among Low Income and Undocumented Immigrants (Feb. 2010)

Wendy Edelberg, Board of Governors of the Federal Reserve System, Racial Dispersion in Consumer Credit Interest Rates (May 2007)

Keith Ernst, Center for Responsible Lending, Rural Borrowers More Likely to Be Penalized for Refinancing Subprime Home Loans (Sept. 2004)

Fair Housing Center of Greater Boston, The Gap Persists: A Report on Racial and Ethnic Discrimination in the Greater Boston Home Mortgage Lending Market (May 2006)

John Farley & Gregory D. Squires, *Fences and Neighbors: Segregation in 21st Century America*, 4 Contexts, No. 1, Winter 2005, at 33–39, *reprinted in* The Contexts Reader (Jeff Goodwin and James M. Jasper, eds., W.W. North & Company, 2008)

John Farris & Christopher Richardson, *The Geography of Subprime Mortgage Prepayment Penalty Patterns*, 15 Hous. Pol'y Debate, No. 3, at 687–714 (2004)

Allen Fishbein, Consumer Federation of America, Subprime Locations: Patterns of Geographic Disparity in Subprime Lending (Sept. 2006)

Andrea Freeman, Credit Card Ills: Reducing Racial Disparities in Debt (2011) *available at* http:// works.bepress.com/andrea_freeman/2

Samantha Friedman & Gregory D. Squires, *Does the Community Reinvestment Act Help Minorities Access Traditionally Inaccessible Neighborhoods?*, 52 Social Problems, No. 2, at 209–231 (May 2005)

Ira Goldstein, Harvard Joint Center for Housing Studies, Bringing Subprime Mortgage to Market and the Effects on Lower-Income Borrowers (Feb. 2004)

Ginny Hamilton, Fair Housing Center of Greater Boston, Rooting Out Discrimination in Mortgage Lending: Using HMDA As a Tool for Fair Housing Enforcement (July 2007)

Song Han, Board of Governors of the Federal Reserve System, On the Economics of Discrimination in Credit Markets (Jan. 2002)

Harvard Joint Center for Housing Studies, State of the Nation's Housing 2005 (June 2005)

Daniel Immergluck & Geoff Smith, Woodstock Institute, Risky Business: An Econometric Analysis of the Relationship Between Subprime Lending and Neighborhood Foreclosures (Mar. 2004)

Mark Ireland, Bending Toward Justice: An Empirical Study of Foreclosures in One Neighborhood Three Years After Impact and a Proposed Framework for a Better Community (Oct. 22, 2009), *available at* http://papers.ssrn.com/sol3/papers.cfm?abstract_id=1492777

Andrew Jakabovics & Jeff Chapman, Center for American Progress, Unequal Opportunity Lenders? Analyzing Racial Disparities in Big Banks' Higher Priced Lending (Sept. 2009), *available at* www.americanprogress.org/issues/2009/09/tarp_lending.html

Sunwoong Kim & Gregory Squires, Fannie Mae Foundation, Lender Characteristics and Racial Disparities in Mortgage Lending (Jan. 1995)

Kathy Mitchell & Rob Schneider, Consumers Union, In Over Our Heads: Predatory Lending and Fraud in Manufactured Housing (Feb. 2002)

National Commission on Fair Housing and Equal Opportunity, The Future of Fair Housing (Dec. 9, 2008), *available at* www.civilrights.org/publications/reports/fairhousing

National Community Reinvestment Coalition, Foreclosure in the Nation's Capital: How Unfair and Reckless Lending Undermines Homeownership (2010)

National Community Reinvestment Coalition, Income is No Shield Against Racial Differences in Lending II: A Comparison of High-Cost Lending in America's Metropolitan and Rural Areas (July 2008)

National Community Reinvestment Coalition, Income is No Shield Against Racial Differences in Lending (July 2007)

National Fair Housing Alliance, A Step in the Right Direction: 2010 Fair Housing Trends Report (May 26, 2010)

National Fair Housing Alliance, The Crisis of Housing Segregation: 2007 Fair Housing Trends Report (Apr. 2007)

Raul Hinojosa Ojeda, Albert Jacquez, & Paule Cruz Takash, William C. Velasquez Inst., The End of the American Dream for Blacks and Latinos: How the Home Mortgage Crisis is Destroying Black and Latino Wealth, Jeopardizing America's Future Prosperity and How to Fix It (June 2009), *available at* www.wcvi.org/data/pub/housingwhitepaper061809.htm

Robert G. Quercia, Michael A. Stegman, & Walter R. Davis, Center for Community Capitalism, University of North Carolina at Chapel Hill, The Impact of Predatory Loan Terms on Subprime Foreclosures: The Special Case of Prepayment Penalties and Balloon Payments (Jan. 2005)

Douglas S. Massey & Jacob S. Rugh, *Racial Segregation and the American Foreclosure Crisis*, 75 Am. Sociological Rev., No. 5 (Oct. 2010)

Javier Silva, Demos: A Network for Ideas and Action, A House of Cards: Refinancing the American Dream (Jan. 2005)

Kyle Smith, First Nations Dev. Inst., Predatory Lending in Native American Communities (May 2003), *available at* www.firstnations.org/publications/PredatoryLendinginNACommunities.pdf

Geoff Smith & Sarah Duda, Woodstock Institute, Bridging the Gap II: Examining Trends and Patterns of Personal Bankruptcy in Cook County's Communities of Color (May 2011), *available at* www.woodstockinst.org/research

Gregory D. Squires, *Demobilization of the Individualistic Bias: Housing Market Discrimination As a Contributor to Labor Market and Economic Inequality*, 609 Annals of the Am. Academy of Political & Social Sciences, No. 1, at 200–214 (2007)

Gregory D. Squires, *Uneven Development and Unequal Access to Housing Finance Services*, N.Y. L. Sch. L. Rev. 53 (forthcoming)

Adam Rust, The Community Reinvestment Association of North Carolina, The New Hurdle to Homeownership: How Loan Level Pricing Changes the Cost of and the Access to Mortgage Credit (Aug. 2011)

Margery Austin Turner, Stephen L. Ross, George Galster, & John Yinger, Urban Institute, Discrimination in Metropolitan Housing Markets, National Results from Phase I of HDS2000 (Nov. 2002)

Margery Austin Turner & Felicity Skidmore, Urban Institute & U.S. Department of Housing & Urban Development, Mortgage Lending Discrimination, A Review of Existing Evidence (June 1999)

United States Department of Housing & Urban Development, Unequal Burden: Income and Racial Disparities in Subprime Lending in America (Apr. 2000)

Christian E. Weller, Center for American Progress, Access Denied: Low-Income and Minority Families Face More Credit Constraints and Higher Borrowing Costs (Aug. 2007)

BOOKS

Edward M. Gramlich, Subprime Mortgages: America's Latest Boom and Bust (Urban Inst. Press 2007)

Stephen L. Ross & John Yinger, The Color of Credit: Mortgage Discrimination, Research Methodology and Fair Lending Enforcement (MIT Press 2003)

Gregory D. Squires & Charis E. Kubrin, Privileged Places: Race, Residence, and the Structure of Opportunity (Lynne Rienner Publishers 2006)

John Yinger, The Russell Sage Foundation, Closed Doors, Opportunities Lost: The Continuing Costs of Housing Discrimination (1995)

Appendix K	Useful Credit Discrimination Weblinks

This appendix is also available on the companion website to this treatise. The companion website facilitates keyword searches and allows relevant provisions to be imported as word-processable documents.

I. Government

Board of Governors of the Federal Reserve System, *www.federalreserve.gov*
Comptroller of the Currency, United States Department of Treasury, *www.occ.treas.gov*
Consumer Financial Protection Bureau, *www.consumerfinance.gov*
Federal Deposit Insurance Corporation, *www.fdic.gov*
Federal Trade Commission, *www.ftc.gov*
United States Census Bureau, *www.census.gov*
United States Department of Housing and Urban Development, *www.hud.gov*
United States Department of Justice, *www.usdoj.gov*
United States Equal Employment Opportunity Commission, *www.eeoc.gov*

II. Nonprofit

Affordable Housing Centers of America, *www.ahcoa.org*
American Association of Retired Persons, *www.aarp.org*
California Reinvestment Coalition, *www.calreinvest.org*
Center for Community Change, *www.communitychange.org*
Center for Responsible Lending, *www.responsiblelending.org*
Consumer Action, *www.consumer-action.org*
Consumer Federation of America, *www.consumerfed.org*
Consumers Union, *www.consumersunion.org*
Fairhousinglaw.org (a project of Leadership Conference on Civil Rights (LCCR) and Leadership Conference on Civil Rights Education Fund (LCCREF)), *www.fairhousinglaw.org*
Housing and Economic Rights Advocates, *www.heraca.org*
Inner City Press, *www.innercitypress.org*
Joint Center for Housing Studies, Harvard University, *www.jchs.harvard.edu*
Lambda Legal, *www.lambdalegal.org*
Lawyers' Committee for Civil Rights Under Law, *www.lawyerscommittee.org*
Leadership Conference on Civil Rights, *www.civilrights.org*
National Association for the Advancement of Colored People, *www.naacp.org*
National Community Reinvestment Coalition, *www.ncrc.org*
National Consumer Law Center, *www.consumerlaw.org*
National Council of La Raza, *www.nclr.org*
National Fair Housing Alliance, *www.nationalfairhousing.org*
National Training and Information Center, *www.ntic-us.org*
Neighborhood Economic Development Advocacy Project, *www.nedap.org*
The Sargent Shriver National Center on Poverty Law, *www.povertylaw.org*
Urban Institute, *www.urban.org*
Woodstock Institute, *www.woodstockinst.org*

III. Industry

AnnualCreditReport.com, *www.annualcreditreport.com*

Bankrate.com, *www.bankrate.com*

Choice Trust, *https://personalreports.lexisnexis.com*

Equifax, *www.equifax.com*

Experian, *www.experian.com*

Fair Isaac (FICO), *www.fico.com*

Fannie Mae, *www.fanniemae.com* and *www.efanniemae.com*

Freddie Mac, *www.freddiemac.com*

HUD USER (United States Department of Housing and Urban Development's Policy Development and Research Information Services), *www.huduser.org*

Research Institute for Housing America (Mortgage Bankers Association), *www.housingamerica.org*

TransUnion, *www.transunion.com*

Finding Pleadings and Primary Sources on the Companion Website

L.1 Introduction

Credit Discrimination includes free access to its companion website, which remains free with continued subscription to this title. The companion website includes all appendices found in *Credit Discrimination* plus sample pleadings and dozens of other primary source documents—statutes, regulations, federal and state agency interpretations, and practice aids—all of which are easily located with flexible, powerful search tools. Documents are available in Adobe Acrobat (PDF) format while pleadings are also available in Microsoft Word format.

This appendix describes the documents found on the companion website, how to access and print them, and how to download them to your computer or copy-paste excerpts into a word processing file. Note that the actual site may differ slightly in appearance from the screenshots below.

In addition to this appendix, we highly recommend reading the Help page on the website, found at the top of the left toolbar once you are logged in.

L.2 Pleadings and Primary Sources Found on the Companion Website

The companion website to *Credit Discrimination* contains federal statutes, regulations, commentary, supplemental information, and regulatory history relating to the Equal Credit Opportunity Act, Fair Housing Act, Civil Rights Acts, HMDA, and Community Reinvestment. Pleadings include complaints, interrogatories, document requests, class pleadings, summary judgment motions, expert reports, and jury instructions. The website also includes instructive government enforcement actions, reports, and consumer handouts.

The website does *not* contain the full text of this treatise's chapters. See Appx. L.6, *infra*, for instructions on how to use Internet-based keyword searches to pinpoint page numbers in the treatise where particular topics are discussed.

L.3 How to Access the Website

One-time registration is required to access the companion website. Once registered, a user subsequently logging in will be granted immediate access to all the companion websites he or she is authorized to use. For example, one username and password allows a subscriber to four NCLC titles to access all four related companion websites.

To register for the first time, go to **www.nclc.org/webaccess** and click the "Register as a New User" link. Enter the Companion Website Registration Number found on the packing statement or invoice accompanying this publication, then enter the requested information to create your account. An e-mail address may be used for the username, or a different username may be chosen.

Subscribers do *not* need to register more than once. If subscribers subsequently purchase additional NCLC titles, they will automatically be given access to the corresponding companion websites. Registering a second time with the same registration number overrides a prior username and password. (Note that, if users allow all their subscriptions to lapse and then subsequently purchase a publication, they must register again.)

Once registered, click on the log-in link at www.nclc.org/webaccess, enter the username and password, and select the *Credit Discrimination* website from the list of authorized websites.

An alternative log-in method may be particularly useful for libraries, legal aid offices, or law firms that subscribe to the entire set of NCLC treatises. Simply send an e-mail to publications@nclc.org with a list or range of static IP addresses for which access should be permitted. Users from those addresses can then go to www.nclc.org/ipaccess to be granted access *without* entering a username and password.

Once logged in, users can click the Preferences link located on the top toolbar to change their account information.

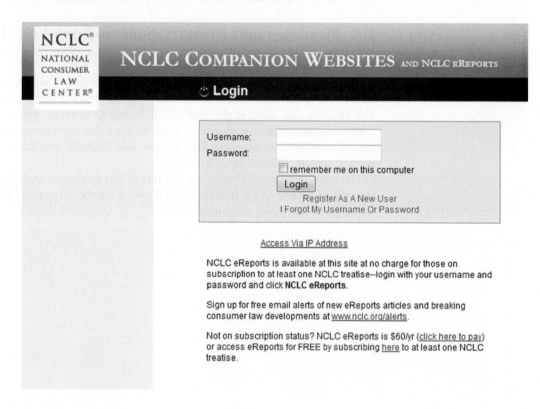

L.4 Locating Documents on the Website

The companion website provides three ways to locate documents:

1. The search page (the home page) uses keyword searches to find documents—full text searches of all documents on the website or searches of just the titles of documents. Enter text in the appropriate field and click the Search button.

- Narrow the search to documents of a certain type (for example, federal regulations or pleadings) by making a selection from the "Document Type" menu, and then perform a full text or document title search.
- To locate a specific appendix section, select the appendix section number (for example, A.2.3) or a partial identifier (for example, A) in the search page's "Appendix" drop-down fields.
- When searching a document's full text, each entry in your search results will include excerpts from the document, showing your search terms highlighted in context.
- Click on the "Search Hints" link for a quick reference to special search operators, wildcards, shortcuts, and complex searches. Read this information closely, as syntax and search operators may be slightly different from those used by other search engines.

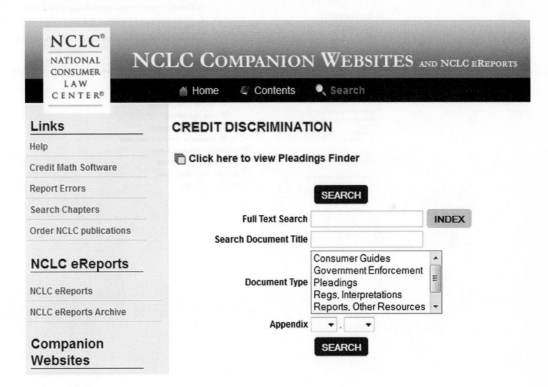

2. The contents page (click the "Contents" tab at the top of the page) is a traditional nested table of contents. Click a branch to expand it into a list of sub-branches or documents. Each document appears once in this contents tree.

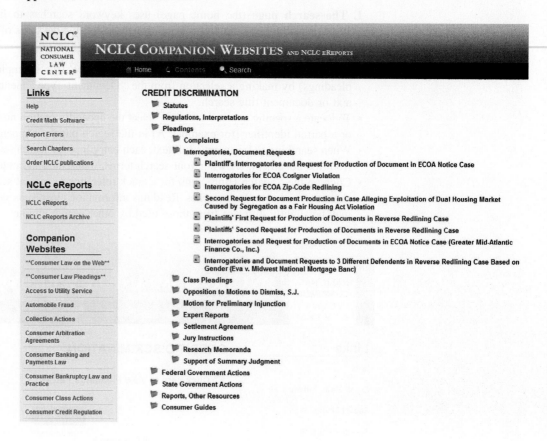

3. The pleading finder page (click the "Pleading Finder" link at the top of the search page) allows pleadings to be located using one or more menus (for example, "Type of Pleading— General" or "Subject"). For many users, this method will be the preferred way to find a pleading. More than one item can be selected from a menu by using the Ctrl key. For example, make one selection from "Type of Pleading—General," one from "Subject," and three from "Legal Claim" to locate all pleadings of that type and subject that contain one or more of the three legal claims selected. If this search produces insufficient results, deselect "Subject" or "Legal Claim" to find pleadings of that type in any subject area or based upon any legal claim.

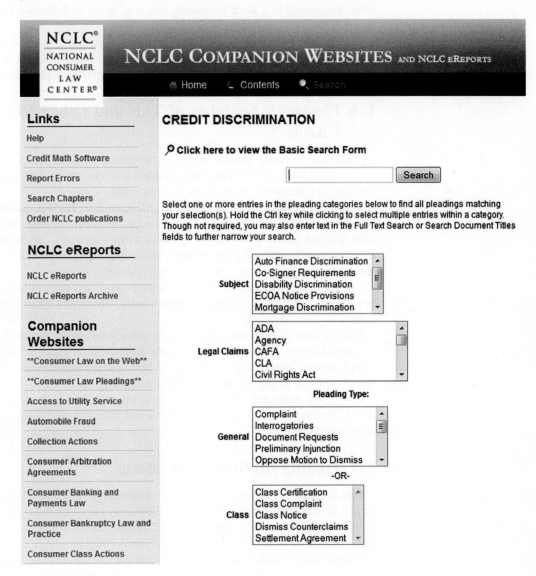

L.5 How to Use the Documents, Find Microsoft Word Versions, and Locate Additional Features

Click a document title in your search results or on the contents page to view the document in your web browser. Text may be copy-pasted directly from the page. or the full document may be downloaded as a Portable Document Format (PDF) file. (You will need a PDF reader to open PDF documents; the free Adobe Reader is available at www.adobe.com.) Additionally, pleadings and certain other documents can be downloaded in Microsoft Word format, enabling the opening of entire documents in a word processing program. Icons to download PDF and Word versions are found at the top of the page.

Links on the left toolbar bring you to credit math software, search tips, other websites, tables of contents and indices of all NCLC treatises, and other practice aids. Links to especially important new developments will be placed toward the bottom of the search page.

L.6 Electronic Searches of This and Other NCLC Titles' Chapters

Completely separate from the treatises' companion websites, NCLC offers a handy online utility to search the full text of this treatise's chapters and appendices. This free search utility is found at www.nclc.org/keyword and requires no registration or log-in.

While the text of the chapters is not available on-line, this web-based search engine will find a word or phrase that can then easily be located in the printed treatise. Select *Credit Discrimination*, enter a search term or combination of search terms—such as a case name, a regulation citation, or other keywords—and the page numbers containing those terms will be listed. Search results are shown in context, enabling selection of the most relevant pages.

The full text of other NCLC treatises, supplements, and other publications can also be searched at www.nclc.org/keyword to locate relevant topics. Just select the desired title or search all NCLC titles.

Current tables of contents, indices, and other information for all twenty titles in the NCLC *Consumer Credit and Sales Legal Practice Series* can be found at www.nclc.org/shop. Click the "For Lawyers" link and scroll down to the book you are interested in. The PDF-format documents found there can be quickly searched for a word or phrase.

The Quick Reference, found at www.nclc.org/qr, is an alphabetical index spanning all twenty NCLC treatises. It lists over 1000 subjects and indicates the book(s) and section(s) where each subject is discussed.

L.7 Finding Additional Pleadings

Pleadings specifically relating to this title are found in Adobe Acrobat (PDF) and Microsoft Word format on the companion website. Over 2000 other pleadings are available in NCLC's *Consumer Law Pleadings* and can be found on the *Consumer Law Pleadings* companion website using the same search techniques discussed above. These 2000 pleadings can also be located using the *Consumer Law Pleadings* index guide, which organizes pleadings by type, subject area, legal claim, title, and other categories identical to those used on the website.

Index and Quick Reference

Quick Reference to the Consumer Law Practice Series

The Quick Reference to the Consumer Law Practice Series pinpoints where to find specific topics analyzed in any of the twenty NCLC treatises. The Quick Reference is now available at www.nclc.org/qr. Placing the Quick Reference on a website ensures that readers have the most up-to-date version, including any revised section numbering.

Another way to locate topics is to go to www.nclc.org/keyword and perform keyword searches within individual treatises or across all NCLC publications. This function allows for compound searches, such as "identity theft (near) punitive damages," and shows results in context, with the appropriate book title and page number where the reference is found.

Pleadings related just to *Credit Discrimination* can be found on the companion website to this title and can be located using different search functions, including the "Pleading Finder." For more information, see page ix, *supra*.

NCLC also has over 2000 additional sample pleadings on websites accompanying our other titles. The best way to locate and access a pleading among this broader group is to use NCLC's *Consumer Law Pleadings Index Guide* or the finding aids on its companion website.

More information on individual treatises in this series is available at What Your Library Should Contain on page v, *supra*, or by going to www.nclc.org/shop.

Index